SHORTER FOURTH EDITION
WITH ESSAYS

LITERATURE
THE HUMAN EXPERIENCE

SHORTER FOURTH EDITION
WITH ESSAYS

LITERATURE
THE HUMAN EXPERIENCE

RICHARD ABCARIAN AND MARVIN KLOTZ, EDITORS

California State University, Northridge

ST. MARTIN'S PRESS

New York

Library of Congress Catalog Number: 87-060571

210
fe
For information, write St. Martin's Press, Inc.,
175 Fifth Avenue, New York, NY 10010
cover design: Darby Downey
cover art: *To Prince Edward Island*, by Alex Colville (National Gallery of Canada, Ottawa)
art research: June Lundborg

ISBN: 0-312-00285-8

Acknowledgments

EDWARD ARNOLD (PUBLISHERS) LTD.: E. M. Forster, "My Wood," from *Abinger Harvest* reprinted by permission of the publisher.
DONALD W. BAKER, "Formal Application," by Donald W. Baker. Reprinted by permission of the author.
ATHENEUM: W. S. Merwin, "For the Anniversary of My Death," from *The Lice*. Copyright © 1967 by W. S. Merwin (N.Y.: Atheneum, 1967). Reprinted with permission of Atheneum Publishers.
   Anthony E. Hecht, "The Dover Bitch," from *The Hard Hours* by Anthony E. Hecht. Copyright © 1954 Anthony E. Hecht; copyright renewed © 1982 Anthony E. Hecht. Reprinted with permission of Atheneum Publishers, Inc.
   Ernest Hemingway, "A Clean Well-Lighted Place," from *Winner Take Nothing* by Ernest Hemingway. Copyright 1933 by Charles Scribner's Sons; copyright renewed © 1961 by Mary Hemingway. Reprinted with permission of Charles Scribner's Sons.
BEACON PRESS: June Jordan, "A Poem about Intelligence for My Brothers and Sisters," from *Passion: New Poems, 1977–1980* by June Jordan. Copyright © 1980 by June Jordan. Reprinted by permission of Beacon Press.
GEORGES BORCHARDT, INC.: Richard Rodriquez, "Going Home Again: The New American Scholarship Boy," reprinted by permission of Georges Borchardt, Inc., on behalf of the author. Copyright © 1975 by Richard Rodriquez. First appeared in *The American Scholar*.
EDWIN BROCK: "Five Ways to Kill a Man" by Edwin Brock. Reprinted by permission of the author.
GWENDOLYN BROOKS, from *The Children of the Poor*, by Gwendolyn Brooks. Reprinted by permission of the author.
JONATHAN CAPE LTD.: Henry Reed, "Naming of Parts," from *A Map of Verona* reprinted with permission of the estate of Henry Reed.
ROBERT CONQUEST: "A Poem About a Poem About a Poem," by Robert Conquest. Reprinted by permission of the author.
CATHERINE DAVIS: "After a Time" by Catherine Davis. Reprinted by permission of the author.
DELACORTE PRESS/SEYMOUR LAWRENCE: Katherine Anne Porter, "The Necessary Enemy," from *The Collected Essays and Occasional Writings of Katherine Anne Porter*. Copyright © 1948 by Katherine Anne Porter. Originally published in *Mademoiselle* as "Love and Hate." Reprinted by permission of Delacorte Press/Seymour Lawrence.
DODD, MEAD, & COMPANY: Arna Bontemps, "A Summer Tragedy," reprinted by permission of Dodd, Mead, & Company from *The Old South* by Arna Bontemps. Copyright © 1973 by Alberta Bontemps, Executrix.
   Paul Laurence Dunbar, "We Wear the Mask". Reprinted by permission of Dodd, Mead & Company, Inc. from *The Complete Poems of Paul Laurence Dunbar*.
DOUBLEDAY: Theodore Roethke, "Elegy for Jane" copyright 1950 by Theodore Roethke and "I Knew A Woman" copyright 1954 by Theodore Roethke from the book *The Collected Poems of Theodore Roethke*. Reprinted by permission of Doubleday & Company, Inc.
FABER AND FABER LIMITED: W. H. Auden, "In Memory of W. B. Yeats," "The Unknown Citizen," and "Musée des Beaux Arts," reprinted by permission of Faber and Faber Ltd from *Collected Poems* by W. H. Auden.
   T. S. Eliot, "The Love Song of J. Alfred Prufrock," reprinted by permission of Faber and Faber Ltd from *Collected Poems 1909–1962* by T. S. Eliot.
   Ted Hughes, "Crow's First Lesson," reprinted by permission of Faber and Faber Ltd from *Crow* by Ted Hughes.
   Philip Larkin, "Aubade," © Philip Larkin 1977. Reprinted by permission of the executors of the Philip Larkin Estate and Faber and Faber Ltd.
FARRAR, STRAUS & GIROUX, INC.: Donald Barthelme, "The Sandman" from *Sadness* by Donald Barthelme. Copyright © 1972 by Donald Barthelme. Reprinted by permission of Farrar, Straus and Giroux, Inc.
   Shirley Jackson, "The Lottery" from *The Lottery* by Shirley Jackson. Copyright © 1948 by Shirley Jackson. Copyright renewed © 1976 by Laurence Hyman, Barry Hyman, Mrs. Sarah Webster and Mrs. Joanne Schnurer. Reprinted by permission of Farrar, Straus & Giroux, Inc.
   Bernard Malamud, "Idiots First" from *Idiots First* by Bernard Malamud. Copyright © 1961, 1963 by Bernard Malamud. Reprinted by permission of Farrar, Straus & Giroux, Inc.

[Acknowledgments and copyrights continue at the back of the book on pages 900–904, which constitute an extension of the copyright page.]

PREFACE

The wide acceptance of the fourth edition of *Literature: The Human Experience* encouraged us to prepare this shorter version for instructors who may prefer a more compact volume. We have retained four plays, twenty-six stories, and one hundred thirty-eight poems from the longer edition. In addition, for the first time we have included essays in the anthology. For the many instructors who teach the essay as a literary form, we hope these eighteen new selections will prove useful.

As in the longer edition, the works in this volume reflect widely diverse cultures and represent literary traditions ranging from 400 B.C. to the present. In choosing the selections, we have been governed by a belief that the first task of an introductory anthology of literature is to engage the reader's interest, to make the experience of literature immediate and intriguing. A corollary of that belief is our conviction that a genuine interest in literary history or the formal analysis of literature arises out of the experience of being engaged by individual works. Thus, we have selected works not primarily because they illustrate critical definitions or lend themselves to a particular approach but because we find them exciting and believe that students will, too.

The arrangement of the works in four thematic groups provides opportunities to explore diverse attitudes toward the same powerful human tendencies and experiences and to contrast formal treatments as well. Each section opens with a short introduction that examines some of the crucial issues embodied in the works that follow. These introductions are deliberately polemical, and, no doubt, readers will sometimes take exception to them. This is all to the good, for we believe that our proper mission as editors is to provide the groundwork for discussion and debate, not to promulgate "truths" for the edification of students. Within each thematic section, the works are grouped by genre—fiction, poetry, drama, essay—and arranged chronologically, according to the author's birthdate. (We also include a date for each individual work. Most of these indicate first appearance in a book, but dates enclosed in parentheses indicate date either of composition or of appearance in a publication other than a book. We have not attempted to date traditional ballads.)

We should perhaps say a word about the questions that we have placed after about half of the stories, most of the poems, all of the plays and essays, and following each thematic section. We believe that too often students are prevented from responding to a work as fully as they might because they are immediately asked questions that require them to confront formal problems. But there are certain kinds of questions, our students have convinced us, that can be helpful by opening individual works that might otherwise prove difficult and by suggesting illuminating thematic connections among various works. The questions in this book are intended to serve this purpose.

We also have provided a number of writing topics following individual selec-tions, and following each of the four thematic sections. In devising the writing topics, we have been guided by two considerations. First, we formulated topics that bear some relationship to the discussion questions that follow a work. Sec-ond, we made the topics specific and concrete, so that even if students do not have the benefit of class discussion, they will understand what they are being called upon to do. There is little virtue in a writing assignment that forces students to spend great energy in understanding the assignment itself.

We have retained from the longer edition several appendices that instructors and students have found useful. The first, a new appendix called "Poems About Poetry," offers some meditations by poets on what poetry is and why it is writ-ten. These nine poems reveal how diverse the motives and aims of poets are as well as the difficulty even poets have in describing exactly what it is they do. Although the emphasis throughout this book is on the value of literature as a means to enjoyment and to a better understanding of our own humanity, the fullest appreciation of literary achievement requires a certain facility in formal matters and some acquaintance with literary history as well. The appendices "Reading Fiction," "Reading Poetry," "Reading Drama," and "Reading Es-says" acquaint readers with some formal concepts and historical considerations basic to the study of the major genres of literary art.

In another appendix, "Three Critical Approaches: Formalist, Sociological, Psychoanalytic," we develop, for one story and one poem, three critical read-ings that emphasize different aspects of the works and reflect the diversity of response that may occur when readers bring different expectations and attitudes to literature. Seeing that a variety of critical approaches may all illuminate a work and complement one another helps to free students, we believe, from a timid acquiescence to some "correct" received view and enables them to re-spond to literature more honestly and openly.

The final appendix, "Writing About Literature," addresses the three major types of student writing: explication, analysis, and comparison and contrast. Each type is defined and discussed and then illustrated with a student essay. In addition, "Writing About Literature" contains extensive discussions—for each type of writing—of poetry, fiction, drama, and the essay. These discussions provide suggested approaches and questions to help students write explication, analysis, and comparison-and-contrast essays for each of the genres.

Sections on the journal and the summary report complement the sections on the formal essay, illustrating other useful purposes student writing can serve. The section on the journal is designed to encourage students to cultivate the habit of writing by keeping a record of their responses to the works they read. The summary report offers a useful way for students to come to terms with the essential elements of a work. It is also worth noting that the section on manu-script mechanics now incorporates the most recent revision of the MLA style sheet.

Finally, we have added to the end of "Writing About Literature" some eighty-five "Suggested Topics for Writing." The topics address all genres and types of writing. In formulating the topics, we have remained mindful that student writing assignments for an introductory literature course will usually range between 500 and 1,000 words. In addition, we have tried to provide enough variety in the questions both to meet the instructor's needs and to engage the student's interest.

The "Glossary of Literary Terms" contains brief excerpts to illustrate the definitions presented there and also makes specific reference to selections in the text.

ACKNOWLEDGMENTS

A great many people have helped us, and among them we should like especially to thank Sabrina Kirby, Virginia Polytechnic Institute and State University; Philip A. Mottola, Adelphi University; Frederick B. Olsen, Alabama State University; E. Suzanne Owens, Ursuline College; and Douglas M. Tedards, University of the Pacific for their careful reviews of the selections that appear in this shorter fourth edition.

We are also grateful to the following colleagues across the country who have sent us numerous helpful reactions and suggestions: Helene Baldwin, Frostburg State College; Michael Baumann, California State University—Chico; Don Blankenship, West Valley College; Colin Bourn, Fitchburg State College; Patrick Broderick, Santa Rosa Junior College; Judith Burnham, Tulsa Junior College; Elizabeth Byers, Virginia Polytechnic Institute and State University; Timothy Bywater, Dixie College; Anthony Canedo, Central Washington University; James Cool, Wilmington College; John Covolo, Lakeland Community College; Michael Crafton, West Georgia College; Susan Day, Illinois State University; Margaret Del Guerico, Montclair State College; Abraham Delson, Westfield State College; Anne DiPardo, Santa Rosa Junior College; Beth Rigel Dougherty, Otterbein College; Marion Dunlap, University of South Carolina—Beaufort; Mildred Durham, Northwest Connecticut Community College; James J. Dyer, Mohawk Valley Community College; David England, Southwest Texas Junior College; Howard Erlichman, Lakeland Community College; Sherwin Fu, University of Wisconsin—Oshkosh; Traci Gardner, Virginia Polytechnic Institute and State University; Robert Gariepy, Eastern Washington University; Linda Geseking, William Paterson College; John Gill, College of San Mateo; Gwendolyn Griswold, Westchester Community College; Stephen Hahn, William Paterson College; Norma Halley, Tulsa Junior College; Mark Halperin, Central Washington University; Barbara Hardy, Harvard University; Patricia Harkin, University of Akron; James Hauser, William Paterson College; Mary Fuller Hayes, Miami University; Morgan Himmelstein, Adelphi University; Jan Hodge, Morningside College; Thomas Howerton, Johnson Technical Institute; Bruce Janoff, University of Pittsburgh; Lisa Jerry, University of Kansas; Dennis Jochims, Lake Sumter Community College; Norman Kelvin, City College—CUNY; Martha Kendall, San Jose City College; William Knepper, Morningside College; Leonard Kriegel, City College—CUNY; Carol Kushner, SUNY—Cortland; Rosemary Lanshe, Broward Community College—Central; Peter LePage, University of Cincinnati; Joyce Lionarons, Ursinus College; Edward Lueders, University of Utah; William H. Malloy, Ursuline College; John D. Maloney, Ohlone College; Edith Milton McCrory, Northwestern Connecticut Community College; Elizabeth McGregor, Boston University; Irene Miranda, Fitchburg State University; Susan Monroe, Keene State College; Kenneth Newell, California State College—Bakersfield; Mickey Pearlman, Iona College; Leonard Pelleteri, Grossmont College; Frank Pike, Glassboro State College; Kay Richard, University of Pennsylvania; Eugene Rister, Maricopa Technical College; Wayne Rittenhouse, Otterbein College; Marion Robinson, San Jose State University; Victoria Sager, Matanuska-Susitna Community College; Joseph Sanders, Lakeland Community College; James A. Scruton, University of Tennessee; Sharon Scruton, Knoxville Business College—Cooper Institute; Nancy Shankle, Texas A & M University; Martha Simonsen, William Rainey Harper College; Roger Smith, Harrisburg Area Community College; Robert H. Stoddard, Holyoke Community College; Marilyn Swanson, William Rainey Harper College; Patricia Swift, Broward Community College—Central; Carlos Tackett, Lakeland Community College; Robert S. Thomson, University of Florida; Gerald Thorson, Saint Olaf College; Vivian Tortorici, Hudson Valley Community College; Ann Trivisonno, Ursuline College; Nancy Veglahn, South Dakota State University; Mason Wang, Saginaw Valley State College; Robert W. Warburton, College of Dupage; Craig H. White, Guilford College; Jane Willingham, Southwest Texas Junior College; Patricia Wilson, Imperial Valley College; Julie Woodruff, Tulsa Junior College—Northeast Campus; and Chris Yopp, Tri-County Technical College.

Finally, we wish to thank the many people at St. Martin's Press for their help in preparing this edition, particularly Nancy Perry, Julie Nord, and Laura Starrett.

Richard Abcarian
Marvin Klotz

CONTENTS

Innocence and Experience   2

DRAMA

ESSAYS

Conformity and Rebellion   176

FICTION

POETRY

DRAMA

ESSAYS

Love and Hate   392

FICTION

POETRY

DRAMA

ESSAYS

The Presence of Death

FICTION

POETRY

DRAMA

ESSAYS

Appendices   782

ALTERNATE TABLE OF CONTENTS

arranged by genre*

FICTION

*Within each genre, authors are listed chronologically by date of birth.

POETRY

ESSAYS

SHORTER FOURTH EDITION
WITH ESSAYS

LITERATURE
THE HUMAN EXPERIENCE

Innocence and Experience

The Peaceable Kingdom, by Edward Hicks

Humans strive to give order and meaning to their lives, to reduce the mystery and unpredictability that constantly threaten them. Life is infinitely more complex and surprising than we imagine, and the categories we establish to give it order and meaning are, for the most part, "momentary stays against confusion." At any time, the equilibrium of our lives, the comfortable image of ourselves and the world around us, may be disrupted suddenly by something new, forcing us into painful reevaluation. These disruptions create pain, anxiety and terror but also wisdom and awareness.

The works in this section deal generally with the movement of a central character from moral simplicities and certainties into a more complex and problematic world. Though these works frequently issue in awareness, even wisdom, their central figures rarely act decisively; the protagonist is more often a passive figure who learns the difference between the ideal world he or she imagines and the injurious real world. If the protagonist survives the ordeal (and he or she doesn't always, emotionally or physically), the protagonist will doubtless be a better human—better able to wrest some satisfaction from a bleak and threatening world. It is no accident that so many of the works here deal with the passage from childhood to adulthood, for childhood is a time of simplicities and certainties that must give way to the complexities and uncertainties of adult life.

Almost universally, innocence is associated with childhood and youth, as experience is with age. We teach the young about an ideal world, without explaining that it has not yet been and may never be achieved. As innocents, they are terribly vulnerable to falsehood, to intrusive sexuality, to the machinations of the wicked who, despite all the moral tales, often do triumph. We know, if we have not already forgotten what the innocence of childhood celebrates, that time and experience will disabuse them.

But the terms *innocence* and *experience* range widely in meaning, and that range is reflected here. Innocence may be defined almost biologically, as illustrated by the sexual innocence of the young boy in James Joyce's "Araby." Or it might be the source of political naiveté, as in George Orwell's "Shooting an Elephant." Innocence may be social—the innocence of the young couple in Joan Didion's "Marrying Absurd" or of Robin in Nathaniel Hawthorne's "My Kinsman, Major Molineux" or the young boy in Frank O'Connor's "My Oedipus Complex." Or innocence may be seen as the child's ignorance of his or her own mortality, as in Gerard Manley Hopkins's "Spring and Fall" and Dylan Thomas's "Fern Hill."

Innocence almost always reflects a foolishness based on ignorance; sometimes, as well, it is the occasion for arrogance. Hulga, in Flannery O'Connor's "Good Country People," looks with disdain on the simple, uneducated folk of her home town. The events of the story prove her to be the victim of her own innocence. In such works as Sophocles's *Oedipus Rex* and Robert Browning's "My Last Duchess," one discovers the tragic and violent consequences of an innocence that is blind.

The contrast between what we thought in our youth and what we have come to know, painfully, as adults stands as an emblem of the passage from innocence to experience. Yet, all of us remain, to one degree or another, innocent throughout life, since we never, except with death, stop learning from experience. Looked at in this way, experience is the ceaseless assault life makes upon our innocence, moving us to a greater wisdom about ourselves and the world.

5

INNOCENCE
AND
EXPERIENCE

The Mistletoe Merchant, 1904 by Pablo Picasso

FICTION

My Kinsman, Major Molineux* 1832

NATHANIEL HAWTHORNE [1804–1864]

After the kings of Great Britain had assumed the right of appointing the colonial governors, the measures of the latter seldom met with the ready and generous approbation which had been paid to those of their predecessors, under the original charters. The people looked with most jealous scrutiny to the exercise of power which did not emanate from themselves, and they usually rewarded their rulers with slender gratitude for the compliances by which, in softening their instructions from beyond the sea, they had incurred the reprehension of those who gave them. The annals of Massachusetts Bay will inform us, that of six governors in the space of about forty years from the surrender of the old charter, under James II., two were imprisoned by a popular insurrection; a third, as Hutchinson inclines to believe, was driven from the province by the whizzing of a musket-ball; a fourth, in the opinion of the same historian, was hastened to his grave by continual bickerings with the House of Representatives; and the remaining two, as well as their successors, till the Revolution, were favored with few and brief intervals of peaceful sway. The inferior members of the court party, in times of high political excitement, led scarcely a more desirable life. These remarks may serve as a preface to the following adventures, which chanced upon a summer night, not far from a hundred years ago. The reader, in order to avoid a long and dry detail of colonial affairs, is requested to dispense with an account of the train of circumstances that had caused much temporary inflammation of the popular mind.

It was near nine o'clock of a moonlight evening, when a boat crossed the ferry with a single passenger, who had obtained his conveyance at that unusual hour by the promise of an extra fare. While he stood on the landing-place, searching in either pocket for the means of fulfilling his agreement, the ferryman lifted a lantern, by the aid of which, and the newly risen moon, he took a very accurate survey of the stranger's figure. He was a youth of barely eighteen years,

---

* This story is considered in detail in the essay "Three Critical Approaches: Formalist, Sociological, Psychoanalytic" at the end of the book.

evidently country-bred, and now, as it should seem, upon his first visit to town. He was clad in a coarse gray coat, well worn, but in excellent repair; his under garments were durably constructed of leather, and fitted tight to a pair of serviceable and well-shaped limbs; his stockings of blue yarn were the incontrovertible work of a mother or a sister; and on his head was a three-cornered hat, which in its better days had perhaps sheltered the graver brow of the lad's father. Under his left arm was a heavy cudgel formed of an oak sapling, and retaining a part of the hardened root; and his equipment was completed by a wallet, not so abundantly stocked as to incommode the vigorous shoulders on which it hung. Brown, curly hair, well-shaped features, and bright, cheerful eyes were nature's gifts, and worth all that art could have done for his adornment.

The youth, one of whose names was Robin, finally drew from his pocket the half of a little province bill of five shillings, which, in the depreciation in that sort of currency, did but satisfy the ferryman's demand, with the surplus of a sexangular piece of parchment, valued at three pence. He then walked forward into the town, with as light a step as if his day's journey had not already exceeded thirty miles, and with as eager an eye as if he were entering London city, instead of the little metropolis of a New England colony. Before Robin had proceeded far, however, it occurred to him that he knew not whither to direct his steps; so he paused, and looked up and down the narrow street, scrutinizing the small and mean wooden buildings that were scattered on either side.

"This low hovel cannot be my kinsman's dwelling," thought he, "nor yonder old house, where the moonlight enters at the broken casement; and truly I see none hereabouts that might be worthy of him. It would have been wise to inquire my way of the ferryman, and doubtless he would have gone with me, and earned a shilling from the Major for his pains. But the next man I meet will do as well."

He resumed his walk, and was glad to perceive that the street now became wider, and the houses more respectable in their appearance. He soon discerned a figure moving on moderately in advance, and hastened his steps to overtake it. As Robin drew nigh, he saw that the passenger was a man in years, with a full periwig of gray hair, a wide-skirted coat of dark cloth, and silk stockings rolled above his knees. He carried a long and polished cane, which he struck down perpendicularly before him at every step; and at regular intervals he uttered two successive hems, of a peculiarly solemn and sepulchral intonation. Having made these observations, Robin laid hold of the skirt of the old man's coat, just when the light from the open door and windows of a barber's shop fell upon both their figures.

"Good evening to you, honored sir," said he, making a low bow, and still retaining his hold of the skirt. "I pray you tell me whereabouts is the dwelling of my kinsman, Major Molineux."

The youth's question was uttered very loudly; and one of the barbers, whose razor was descending on a well-soaped chin, and another who was dressing a Ramillies wig, left their occupations, and came to the door. The citizen, in the mean time, turned a long-favored countenance upon Robin, and answered him in a tone of excessive anger and annoyance. His two sepulchral hems, however, broke into the very centre of his rebuke, with most singular effect, like a thought of the cold grave obtruding among wrathful passions.

"Let go my garment, fellow! I tell you, I know not the man you speak of. What! I have authority, I have—hem, hem—authority; and if this be the respect you show for your betters, your feet shall be brought acquainted with the stocks by daylight, tomorrow morning!"

Robin released the old man's skirt, and hastened away, pursued by an ill-mannered roar of laughter from the barber's shop. He was at first considerably surprised by the result of his question, but, being a shrewd youth, soon thought himself able to account for the mystery.

"This is some country representative," was his conclusion, "who has never seen the inside of my kinsman's door, and lacks the breeding to answer a stranger civilly. The man is old, or verily—I might be tempted to turn back and smite him on the nose. Ah, Robin, Robin! even the barber's boys laugh at you for choosing such a guide! You will be wiser in time, friend Robin."

He now became entangled in a succession of crooked and narrow streets, which crossed each other, and meandered at no great distance from the water-side. The smell of tar was obvious to his nostrils, the masts of vessels pierced the moonlight above the tops of the buildings, and the numerous signs, which Robin paused to read, informed him that he was near the centre of business. But the streets were empty, the shops were closed, and lights were visible only in the second stories of a few dwelling-houses. At length, on the corner of a narrow lane, through which he was passing, he beheld the broad countenance of a British hero swinging before the door of an inn, whence proceeded the voices of many guests. The casement of one of the lower windows was thrown back, and a very thin curtain permitted Robin to distinguish a party at supper, round a well-furnished table. The fragrance of the good cheer steamed forth into the outer air, and the youth could not fail to recollect that the last remnant of his travelling stock of provision had yielded to his morning appetite, and that noon had found and left him dinnerless.

"Oh, that a parchment three-penny might give me a right to sit down at yonder table!" said Robin, with a sigh. "But the Major will make me welcome to the best of his victuals; so I will even step boldly in, and inquire my way to his dwelling."

He entered the tavern, and was guided by the murmur of voices and the fumes of tobacco to the public-room. It was a long and low apartment, with oaken walls, grown dark in the continual smoke, and a floor which was thickly sanded, but of no immaculate purity. A number of persons—the larger part of whom appeared to be mariners, or in some way connected with the sea— occupied the wooden benches, or leather-bottomed chairs, conversing on various matters, and occasionally lending their attention to some topic of general interest. Three or four little groups were draining as many bowls of punch, which the West India trade had long since made a familiar drink in the colony. Others, who had the appearance of men who lived by regular and laborious handicraft, preferred the insulated bliss of an unshared potation, and became more taciturn under its influence. Nearly all, in short, evinced a predilection for the Good Creature in some of its various shapes, for this is a vice to which, as Fast Day sermons of a hundred years ago will testify, we have a long hereditary claim. The only guests to whom Robin's sympathies inclined him were two or three sheepish countrymen, who were using the inn somewhat after the fashion of a Turkish caravansary; they had gotten themselves into the darkest corner of the room, and heedless of the Nicotian atmosphere, were supping on the bread of their own ovens, and the bacon cured in their own chimney-smoke. But though Robin felt a sort of brotherhood with these strangers, his eyes were attracted from them to a person who stood near the door, holding whispered conversation with a group of ill-dressed associates. His features were separately striking almost to grotesqueness, and the whole face left a deep impression on the memory. The forehead bulged out into a double prominence, with a vale between; the nose came boldly forth in an irregular curve, and its bridge was of more than a finger's breadth; the eyebrows were deep and shaggy, and the eyes glowed beneath them like fire in a cave.

While Robin deliberated of whom to inquire respecting his kinsman's dwelling, he was accosted by the innkeeper, a little man in a stained white apron, who had come to pay his professional welcome to the stranger. Being in the second generation from a French Protestant, he seemed to have inherited the courtesy of his parent nation; but no variety of circumstances was ever known to change his voice from the one shrill note in which he now addressed Robin.

"From the country, I presume, sir?" said he, with a profound bow. "Beg leave to congratulate you on your arrival, and trust you intend a long stay with us. Fine town here, sir, beautiful buildings, and much that may interest a stranger. May I hope for the honor of your commands in respect to supper?"

"The man sees a family likeness! the rogue has guessed that I am related to the Major!" thought Robin, who had hitherto experienced little superfluous civility.

All eyes were now turned on the country lad, standing at the door, in his worn three-cornered hat, gray coat, leather breeches, and blue yarn stockings, leaning on an oaken cudgel, and bearing a wallet on his back.

Robin replied to the courteous innkeeper, with such an assumption of confidence as befitted the Major's relative. "My honest friend," he said, "I shall make it a point to patronize your house on some occasion, when"—here he could not help lowering his voice—"when I may have more than a parchment three-pence in my pocket. My present business," continued he, speaking with lofty confidence, "is merely to inquire my way to the dwelling of my kinsman, Major Molineux."

There was a sudden and general movement in the room, which Robin interpreted as expressing the eagerness of each individual to become his guide. But the innkeeper turned his eyes to a written paper on the wall, which he read, or seemed to read, with occasional recurrences to the young man's figure.

"What have we here?" said he, breaking his speech into little dry fragments.

"'Left the house of the subscriber, bounden servant, Hezekiah Mudge,—had on, when he went away, gray coat, leather breeches, master's third-best hat. One pound currency reward to whosoever shall lodge him in any jail of the providence.' Better trudge, boy; better trudge!"

Robin had begun to draw his hand towards the lighter end of the oak cudgel, but a strange hostility in every countenance induced him to relinquish his purpose of breaking the courteous innkeeper's head. As he turned to leave the room, he encountered a sneering glance from the bold-featured personage whom he had before noticed, and no sooner was he beyond the door, than he heard a general laugh, in which the innkeeper's voice might be distinguished, like the dropping of small stones into a kettle.

"Now, is it not strange," thought Robin, with his usual shrewdness,—"is it not strange that the confession of an empty pocket should outweigh the name of my kinsman, Major Molineux? Oh, if I had one of those grinning rascals in the woods, where I and my oak sapling grew up together, I would teach him that my arm is heavy though my purse be light!"

On turning the corner of the narrow lane, Robin found himself in a spacious street, with an unbroken line of lofty houses on each side, and a steepled building at the upper end, whence the ringing of a bell announced the hour of nine. The light of the moon, and the lamps from the numerous shop-windows, discovered people promenading on the pavement, and amongst them Robin had hoped to recognize his hitherto inscrutable relative. The result of his former inquiries made him unwilling to hazard another, in a scene of such publicity, and he determined to walk slowly and silently up the street, thrusting his face close to that of every elderly gentleman, in search of the Major's lineaments. In his progress, Robin encountered many gay and gallant figures. Embroidered garments of showy colors, enormous periwigs, gold-laced hats, and silver-hilted swords glided past him and dazzled his optics. Travelled youths, imitators of the European fine gentlemen of the period, trod jauntily along, half dancing to the fashionable tunes which they hummed, and making poor Robin ashamed of his quiet and natural gait. At length, after many pauses to examine the gorgeous display of goods in the shop-windows, and after suffering some rebukes for the impertinence of his scrutiny into people's faces, the Major's kinsman found himself near the steepled building, still unsuccessful in his search. As yet, however, he had seen only one side of the thronged street; so Robin crossed, and continued the same sort of inquisition down the opposite pavement, with stronger hopes than the philosopher seeking an honest man, but with no better fortune. He had arrived about midway towards the lower end, from which his course began, when he overheard the approach of some one who struck down a cane on the flag-stones at every step, uttering at regular intervals, two sepulchral hems.

"Mercy on us!" quoth Robin, recognizing the sound.

Turning a corner, which chanced to be close at his right hand, he hastened to pursue his researches in some other part of the town. His patience now was wearing low, and he seemed to feel more fatigue from his rambles since he crossed the ferry, than from his journey of several days on the other side. Hunger also pleaded loudly within him, and Robin began to balance the propriety of demanding, violently, and with lifted cudgel, the necessary guidance from the first solitary passenger whom he should meet. While a resolution to this effect was gaining strength, he entered a street of mean appearance, on either side of which a row of ill-built houses was straggling towards the harbor. The moonlight fell upon no passenger along the whole extent, but in the third domicile which Robin passed there was a half-opened door, and his keen glance detected a woman's garment within.

"My luck may be better here," said he to himself.

Accordingly, he approached the door, and beheld it shut closer as he did so; yet an open space remained, sufficing for the fair occupant to observe the stranger, without a corresponding display on her part. All that Robin could discern was a strip of scarlet petticoat, and the occasional sparkle of an eye, as if the moonbeams were trembling on some bright thing.

"Pretty mistress," for I may call her so with a good conscience, thought the shrewd youth, since I know nothing to the contrary,—"my sweet pretty mistress, will you be kind enough to tell me whereabouts I must seek the dwelling of my kinsman, Major Molineux?"

Robin's voice was plaintive and winning, and the female, seeing nothing to be shunned in the handsome country youth, thrust open the door, and came forth into the moonlight. She was a dainty little figure, with a white neck, round arms, and a slender waist, at the extremity of which her scarlet petticoat jutted out over a hoop, as if she were standing in a balloon. Moreover, her face was oval and pretty, her hair dark beneath the little cap, and her bright eyes possessed a sly freedom, which triumphed over those of Robin.

"Major Molineux dwells here," said this fair woman.

Now, her voice was the sweetest Robin had heard that night, yet he could not help doubting whether that sweet voice spoke Gospel truth. He looked up and down the mean street, and then surveyed the house before which they stood. It was a small, dark edifice of two stories, the second of which projected over the lower floor, and the front apartment had the aspect of a shop for petty commodities.

"Now, truly, I am in luck," replied Robin, cunningly, "and so indeed is my kinsman, the Major, in having so pretty a housekeeper. But I prithee trouble him to step to the door; I will deliver him a message from his friends in the country, and then go back to my lodgings at the inn."

"Nay, the Major has been abed this hour or more," said the lady of the scarlet petticoat; "and it would be to little purpose to disturb him to-night, seeing his evening draught was of the strongest. But he is a kind-hearted man, and it would be as much as my life's worth to let a kinsman of his turn away from the door. You are the good old gentleman's very picture, and I could swear that was his rainy-weather hat. Also he has garments very much resembling those leather small-clothes. But come in, I pray, for I bid you hearty welcome in his name."

So saying, the fair and hospitable dame took our hero by the hand; and the touch was light, and the force was gentleness, and though Robin read in her eyes what he did not hear in her words, yet the slender-waisted woman in the scarlet petticoat proved stronger than the athletic country youth. She had drawn his half-willing footsteps nearly to the threshold, when the opening of a door in the neighborhood startled the Major's housekeeper, and, leaving the Major's kinsman, she vanished speedily into her own domicile. A heavy yawn preceded the appearance of a man, who, like the Moonshine of Pyramus and Thisbe,[1] carried a lantern, needlessly aiding his sister luminary in the heavens. As he walked sleepily up the street, he turned his broad, dull face on Robin, and displayed a long staff, spiked at the end.

"Home, vagabond, home!" said the watchman, in accents that seemed to fall asleep as soon as they were uttered. "Home, or we'll set you in the stocks by peep of day!"

"This is the second hint of the kind," thought Robin. "I wish they would end my difficulties, by setting me there to-night."

Nevertheless, the youth felt an instinctive antipathy towards the guardian of midnight order, which at first prevented him from asking his usual question. But just when the man was about to vanish behind the corner, Robin resolved not to lose the opportunity, and shouted lustily after him,—

"I say, friend! will you guide me to the house of my kinsman, Major Molineux?"

The watchman made no reply, but turned the corner and was gone; yet Robin seemed to hear the sound of drowsy laughter stealing along the solitary street. At that moment, also, a pleasant titter saluted him from the open window above his head; he looked up, and caught the sparkle of a saucy eye; a round arm beckoned to him, and next he heard light footsteps descending the staircase within. But Robin, being of the household of a New England clergyman, was a good youth, as well as a shrewd one; so he resisted temptation, and fled away.

He now roamed desperately, and at random, through the town, almost ready to believe that a spell was on him, like that by which a wizard of his country had once kept three pursuers wandering, a whole winter night, within twenty paces of the cottage which they sought. The streets lay before him, strange and desolate, and the lights were extinguished in almost every house. Twice, however, little parties of men, among whom Robin distinguished individuals in outlandish attire, came hurrying along; but, though on both occasions, they paused to address him, such intercourse did not at all enlighten his perplexity. They did but utter a few words in some language of which Robin knew nothing, and perceiving his inability to answer, bestowed a curse upon him in plain English and hastened away. Finally, the lad determined to knock at the door of every mansion that might appear worthy to be occupied by his kinsman, trusting that perseverance would overcome the fatality that had hitherto thwarted him. Firm in this resolve, he was passing beneath the walls of a church, which

---

[1] In Shakespeare's A *Midsummer Night's Dream*, Act V, Scene 1, the moon is represented by a man carrying a lantern in the comic performance of the tragic love story of Pyramus and Thisbe.

formed the corner of two streets, when, as he turned into the shade of its steeple, he encountered a bulky stranger, muffled in a cloak. The man was proceeding with the speed of earnest business, but Robin planted himself full before him, holding the oak cudgel with both hands across his body as a bar to further passage.

"Halt, honest man, and answer me a question," said he, very resolutely. "Tell me, this instant, whereabouts is the dwelling of my kinsman, Major Molineux!"

"Keep your tongue between your teeth, fool, and let me pass!" said a deep, gruff voice, which Robin partly remembered. "Let me pass, or I'll strike you to the earth!"

"No, no, neighbor!" cried Robin, flourishing his cudgel, and then thrusting its larger end close to the man's muffled face. "No, no, I'm not the fool you take me for, nor do you pass till I have an answer to my question. Whereabouts is the dwelling of my kinsman, Major Molineux?"

The stranger, instead of attempting to force his passage, stepped back into the moonlight, unmuffled his face, and stared full into that of Robin.

"Watch here an hour, and Major Molineux will pass by," said he.

Robin gazed with dismay and astonishment on the unprecedented physiognomy of the speaker. The forehead with its double prominence, the broad hooked nose, the shaggy eyebrows, and fiery eyes were those which he had noticed at the inn, but the man's complexion had undergone a singular, or, more properly, a twofold change. One side of the face blazed an intense red, while the other was black as midnight, the division line being in the broad bridge of the nose; and a mouth which seemed to extend from ear to ear was black or red, in contrast to the color of the cheek. The effect was as if two individual devils, a fiend of fire and a fiend of darkness, had united themselves to form this infernal visage. The stranger grinned in Robin's face, muffled his party-colored features, and was out of sight in a moment.

"Strange things we travellers see!" ejaculated Robin.

He seated himself, however, upon the steps of the church-door, resolving to wait the appointed time for his kinsman. A few moments were consumed in philosophical speculations upon the species of man who had just left him; but having settled this point shrewdly, rationally, and satisfactorily, he was compelled to look elsewhere for his amusement. And first he threw his eyes along the street. It was of more respectable appearance than most of those into which he had wandered; and the moon, creating, like the imaginative power, a beautiful strangeness in familiar objects, gave something of romance to a scene that might not have possessed it in the light of day. The irregular and often quaint architecture of the houses, some of whose roofs were broken into numerous little peaks, while others ascended, steep and narrow, into a single point, and others again were square; the pure snow-white of some of their complexions, the aged darkness of others, and the thousand sparklings, reflected from bright substances in the walls of many; these matters engaged Robin's attention for a while, and then began to grow wearisome. Next he endeavored to define the forms of distant objects, starting away, with almost ghostly indistinctness, just as his eye appeared to grasp them; and finally he took a minute survey of an edifice which stood on the opposite side of the street, directly in front of the church door, where he was stationed. It was a large, square mansion, distinguished from its neighbors by a balcony, which rested on tall pillars, and by an elaborate Gothic window, communicating therewith.

"Perhaps this is the very house I have been seeking," thought Robin.

Then he strove to speed away the time, by listening to a murmur which swept continually along the street, yet was scarcely audible, except to an unaccustomed ear like his; it was a low, dull, dreamy sound, compounded of many noises, each of which was at too great a distance to be separately heard. Robin marvelled at this snore of a sleeping town, and marvelled more whenever its continuity was broken by now and then a distant shout, apparently loud where it originated. But altogether it was a sleep-inspiring sound, and, to shake off its drowsy influence, Robin arose, and climbed a window-frame, that he might view the interior of the church. There the moonbeams came trembling in, and fell down upon the deserted pews, and extended along the quiet aisles. A fainter yet more awful radiance was hovering around the pulpit, and one solitary ray had dared to rest upon the open page of the great Bible. Had nature, in that deep hour, become a worshipper in the house which man had builded? Or was that heavenly light the visible sanctity of the place,—visible because no earthly and impure feet were within the walls? The scene made Robin's heart shiver with a sensation of loneliness stronger than he had ever felt in the remotest depths of his native woods; so he turned away and sat down again before the door. There were graves around the church, and now an uneasy thought obtruded into Robin's breast. What if the object of his search, which had been so often and so strangely thwarted, were all the time mouldering in his shroud? What if his kinsman should glide through yonder gate, and nod and smile to him in dimly passing by?

"Oh that any breathing thing were here with me!" said Robin.

Recalling his thoughts from this uncomfortable track, he sent them over forest, hill, and stream, and attempted to imagine how that evening of ambiguity and weariness had been spent by his father's household. He pictured them assembled at the door, beneath the tree, the great old tree, which had been spared for its huge twisted trunk and venerable shade, when a thousand leafy brethren fell. There, at the going down of the summer sun, it was his father's custom to perform domestic worship, that the neighbors might come and join with him like brothers of the family, and that the wayfaring man might pause to drink at that fountain, and keep his heart pure by freshening the memory of home. Robin distinguished the seat of every individual of the little audience; he saw the good man in the midst, holding the Scriptures in the golden light that fell from the western clouds; he beheld him close the book and all rise up to pray. He heard the old thanksgivings for daily mercies, the old supplications for their continuance, to which he had so often listened in weariness, but which were now among his dear remembrances. He perceived the slight inequality of his father's voice when he came to speak of the absent one; he noted how his mother turned her face to the broad and knotted trunk; how his elder brother scorned, because the beard was rough upon his upper lip, to permit his features to be moved; how the younger sister drew down a low hanging branch before her eyes; and how the little one of all, whose sports had hitherto broken the decorum of the scene, understood the prayer for her playmate, and burst into clamorous grief. Then he saw them go in at the door; and when Robin would have entered also, the latch tinkled into its place, and he was excluded from his home.

"Am I here, or there?" cried Robin, starting; for all at once, when his thoughts had become visible and audible in a dream, the long, wide, solitary street shone out before him.

He aroused himself, and endeavored to fix his attention steadily upon the large edifice which he had surveyed before. But still his mind kept vibrating between fancy and reality; by turns, the pillars of the balcony lengthened into the tall, bare stems of pines, dwindled down to human figures, settled again into their true shape and size, and then commenced a new succession of changes. For a single moment, when he deemed himself awake, he could have sworn that a visage—one which he seemed to remember, yet could not absolutely name as his kinsman's—was looking towards him from the Gothic window. A deeper sleep wrestled with and nearly overcame him, but fled at the sound of footsteps along the opposite pavement. Robin rubbed his eyes, discerned a man passing at the foot of the balcony, and addressed him in a loud, peevish, and lamentable cry.

"Hallo, friend! must I wait here all night for my kinsman, Major Molineux?"

The sleeping echoes awoke, and answered the voice; and the passenger, barely able to discern a figure sitting in the oblique shade of the steeple, traversed the street to obtain a nearer view. He was himself a gentleman in his prime, of open, intelligent, cheerful, and altogether prepossessing countenance. Perceiving a country youth, apparently homeless and without friends, he accosted him in a tone of real kindness, which had become strange to Robin's ears.

"Well, my good lad, why are you sitting here?" inquired he. "Can I be of service to you in any way?"

"I am afraid not, sir," replied Robin, despondingly; "yet I shall take it kindly, if you'll answer me a single question. I've been searching, half the night, for one Major Molineux; now, sir, is there really such a person in these parts, or am I dreaming?"

"Major Molineux! The name is not altogether strange to me," said the gentleman, smiling. "Have you any objection to telling me the nature of your business with him?"

Then Robin briefly related that his father was a clergyman, settled on a small salary, at a long distance back in the country, and that he and Major Molineux were brothers' children. The Major, having inherited riches, and acquired civil and military rank, had visited his cousin, in great pomp, a year or two before; had manifested much interest in Robin and an elder brother, and, being childless himself, had thrown out hints respecting the future establishment of one of them in life. The elder brother was destined to succeed to the farm which his father cultivated in the interval of sacred duties; it was therefore determined that Robin should profit by his kinsman's generous intentions, especially as he seemed to be rather the favorite, and was thought to possess other necessary endowments.

"For I have the name of being a shrewd youth," observed Robin, in this part of his story.

"I doubt not you deserve it," replied his new friend, good-naturedly; "but pray proceed."

"Well, sir, being nearly eighteen years old, and well grown, as you see," continued Robin, drawing himself up to his full height, "I thought it high time to begin in the world. So my mother and sister put me in handsome trim, and my father gave me half the remnant of his last year's salary, and five days ago I started for this place, to pay the Major a visit. But, would you believe it, sir! I crossed the ferry a little after dark, and have yet found nobody that would show me the way to his dwelling; only, an hour or two since, I was told to wait here, and Major Molineux would pass by."

"Can you describe the man who told you this?" inquired the gentleman.

"Oh, he was a very ill-favored fellow, sir," replied Robin, "with two great bumps on his forehead, a hook nose, fiery eyes; and, what struck me as the strangest, his face was of two different colors. Do you happen to know such a man, sir?"

"Not intimately," answered the stranger, "but I chanced to meet him a little time previous to your stopping me. I believe you may trust his word, and that the Major will very shortly pass through this street. In the mean time, as I have a singular curiosity to witness your meeting, I will sit down here upon the steps and bear you company."

He seated himself accordingly, and soon engaged his companion in animated discourse. It was but of brief continuance, however, for a noise of shouting, which had long been remotely audible, drew so much nearer that Robin inquired its cause.

"What may be the meaning of this uproar?" asked he. "Truly, if your town be always as noisy, I shall find little sleep while I am an inhabitant."

"Why, indeed, friend Robin, there do appear to be three or four riotous fellows abroad to-night," replied the gentleman. "You must not expect all the stillness of your native woods here in our streets. But the watch will shortly be at the heels of these lads and"—

"Ay, and set them in the stocks by peep of day," interrupted Robin, recollecting his own encounter with the drowsy lantern-bearer. "But, dear sir, if I may trust my ears, an army of watchmen would never make head against such a multitude of rioters. There were at least a thousand voices went up to make that one shout."

"May not a man have several voices, Robin, as well as two complexions?" said his friend.

"Perhaps a man may; but Heaven forbid that a woman should!" responded the shrewd youth, thinking of the seductive tones of the Major's housekeeper.

The sounds of a trumpet in some neighboring street now became so evident and continual, that Robin's curiosity was strongly excited. In addition to the shouts, he heard frequent bursts from many instruments of discord, and a wild and confused laughter filled up the intervals. Robin rose from the steps, and looked wistfully towards a point whither people seemed to be hastening.

"Surely some prodigious merry-making is going on," exclaimed he. "I have laughed very little since I left home, sir, and should be sorry to lose an opportunity. Shall we step round the corner by that darkish house, and take our share of the fun?"

"Sit down again, sit down, good Robin," replied the gentleman, laying his hand on the skirt of the gray coat. "You forget that we must wait here for your kinsman; and there is reason to believe that he will pass by, in the course of a very few moments."

The near approach of the uproar had now disturbed the neighborhood; windows flew open on all sides; and many heads, in the attire of the pillow, and confused by sleep suddenly broken, were protruded to the gaze of whoever had leisure to observe them. Eager voices hailed each other from house to house, all demanding the explanation, which not a soul could give. Half-dressed men hurried towards the unknown commotion, stumbling as they went over the stone steps that thrust themselves into the narrow footwalk. The shouts, the laughter, and the tuneless bray, the antipodes of music, came onwards with increasing din, till scattered individuals, and then denser bodies, began to appear round a corner at the distance of a hundred yards.

"Will you recognize your kinsman, if he passes in this crowd?" inquired the gentleman.

"Indeed, I can't warrant it, sir; but I'll take my stand here, and keep a bright lookout," answered Robin, descending to the outer edge of the pavement.

A mighty stream of people now emptied into the street, and came rolling slowly towards the church. A single horseman wheeled the corner in the midst of them, and close behind him came a band of fearful wind-instruments, sending forth a fresher discord now that no intervening buildings kept it from the ear. Then a redder light disturbed the moonbeams, and a dense multitude of torches shone along the street, concealing, by their glare, whatever object they illuminated. The single horseman, clad in a military dress, and bearing a drawn sword, rode onward as the leader, and, by his fierce and variegated countenance, appeared like war personified; the red of one cheek was an emblem of fire and sword; the blackness of the other betokened the mourning that attends them. In his train were wild figures in the Indian dress, and many fantastic shapes without a model, giving the whole march a visionary air, as if a dream had broken forth from some feverish brain, and were sweeping visibly through the midnight streets. A mass of people, inactive, except as applauding spectators, hemmed the procession in; and several women ran along the sidewalk, piercing the confusion of heavier sounds with their shrill voices of mirth or terror.

"The double-faced fellow has his eye upon me," muttered Robin, with an indefinite but an uncomfortable idea that he was himself to bear a part in the pageantry.

The leader turned himself in the saddle, and fixed his glance full upon the country youth, as the steed went slowly by. When Robin had freed his eyes from those fiery ones, the musicians were passing before him, and the torches were close at hand; but the unsteady brightness of the latter formed a veil which he could not penetrate. The rattling of wheels over the stones sometimes found its way to his ear, and confused traces of a human form appeared at intervals, and then melted into the vivid light. A moment more, and the leader thundered a command to halt: the trumpets vomited a horrid breath, and then held their peace; the shouts and laughter of the people died away, and there remained only a universal hum, allied to silence. Right before Robin's eyes was an un-covered cart. There the torches blazed the brightest, there the moon shone out like day, and there, in tar-and-feathery dignity, sat his kinsman, Major Moli-neux!

He was an elderly man, of large and majestic person, and strong, square features betokening a steady soul; but steady as it was, his enemies had found means to shake it. His face was pale as death, and far more ghastly; the broad forehead was contracted in his agony, so that his eyebrows formed one grizzled line; his eyes were red and wild, and the foam hung white upon his quivering lip. His whole frame was agitated by a quick and continual tremor, which his pride strove to quell, even in those circumstances of overwhelming humiliation. But perhaps the bitterest pang of all was when his eyes met those of Robin; for he evidently knew him on the instant, as the youth stood witnessing the foul disgrace of a head grown gray in honor. They stared at each other in silence, and Robin's knees shook, and his hair bristled, with a mixture of pity and terror. Soon, however, a bewildering excitement began to seize upon his mind; the preceding adventures of the night, the unexpected appearance of the crowd, the torches, the confused din and the hush that followed, the spectre of his kinsman reviled by that great multitude,—all this, and, more than all, a perception of tremendous ridicule in the whole scene, affected him with a sort of mental inebriety. At that moment a voice of sluggish merriment saluted Robin's ears; he turned instinctively, and just behind the corner of the church stood the lantern-bearer, rubbing his eyes, and drowsily enjoying the lad's amazement. Then he heard a peal of laughter like the ringing of silvery bells; a woman twitched his arm, a saucy eye met his, and he saw the lady of the scarlet petticoat. A sharp, dry cachinnation appealed to his memory, and standing on tiptoe in the crowd, with his white apron over his head, he beheld the courteous little innkeeper. And lastly, there sailed over the heads of the multitude a great, broad laugh, broken in the midst by two sepulchral hems; thus, "Haw, haw, haw,—hem, hem,—haw, haw, haw, haw!"

The sound proceeded from the balcony of the opposite edifice, and thither Robin turned his eyes. In front of the Gothic window stood the old citizen, wrapped in a wide gown, his gray periwig exchanged for a nightcap, which was thrust back from his forehead, and his silk stockings hanging about his legs. He supported himself on his polished cane in a fit of convulsive merriment, which manifested itself on his solemn old features like a funny inscription on a tombstone. Then Robin seemed to hear the voices of the barbers, of the guests of the inn, and of all who had made sport of him that night. The contagion was spreading among the multitude, when all at once, it seized upon Robin, and he sent forth a shout of laughter that echoed through the street,—every man shook his sides, every man emptied his lungs, but Robin's shout was the loudest there. The cloud-spirits peeped from their silvery islands, as the congregated mirth went roaring up the sky! The Man in the Moon heard the far bellow. "Oho," quoth he, "the old earth is frolicsome to-night!"

When there was a momentary calm in that tempestuous sea of sound, the leader gave the sign, the procession resumed its march. On they went, like fiends that throng in mockery around some dead potentate, mighty no more, but majestic still in his agony. On they went, in counterfeited pomp, in senseless uproar, in frenzied merriment, trampling all on an old man's heart. On swept the tumult, and left a silent street behind.

"Well, Robin, are you dreaming?" inquired the gentleman, laying his hand on the youth's shoulder.

Robin started, and withdrew his arm from the stone post to which he had instinctively clung, as the living stream rolled by him. His cheek was somewhat pale, and his eye not quite as lively as in the earlier part of the evening.

"Will you be kind enough to show me the way to the ferry?" said he, after a moment's pause.

"You have, then, adopted a new subject of inquiry?" observed his companion, with a smile.

"Why, yes, sir," replied Robin, rather dryly. "Thanks to you, and to my other friends, I have at last met my kinsman, and he will scarce desire to see my face again. I begin to grow weary of a town life, sir. Will you show me the way to the ferry?"

"No, my good friend Robin,—not to-night, at least," said the gentleman. "Some few days hence, if you wish it, I will speed you on your journey. Or, if you prefer to remain with us, perhaps, as you are a shrewd youth, you may rise in the world without the help of your kinsman, Major Molineux."

QUESTIONS

1. Explain the function of the opening paragraph. **2.** Does Robin change as a result of his experiences? **3.** What evidence does the story provide to explain the hostility of the townspeople toward Major Molineux? **4.** A few moments before Robin witnesses the procession that surges forward with his tarred and feathered kinsman, his thoughts turn to his family, and he tries to imagine how they have spent the same night. What function does this daydream serve? **5.** Discuss Hawthorne's use of light and darkness.

The Bride Comes to Yellow Sky

1898

STEPHEN CRANE [1871–1900]

I

The great Pullman was whirling onward with such dignity of motion that a glance from the window seemed simply to prove that the plains of Texas were pouring eastward. Vast flats of green grass, dull-hued space of mesquit and cactus, little groups of frame houses, woods of light and tender trees, all were sweeping into the east, sweeping over the horizon, a precipice.

A newly married pair had boarded this coach at San Antonio. The man's face was reddened from many days in the wind and sun, and a direct result of his new black clothes was that his brick-coloured hands were constantly performing in a most conscious fashion. From time to time he looked down respectfully at his attire. He sat with a hand on each knee, like a man waiting in a barber's shop. The glances he devoted to other passengers were furtive and shy.

The bride was not pretty, nor was she very young. She wore a dress of blue cashmere, with small reservations of velvet here and there, and with steel buttons abounding. She continually twisted her head to regard her puff sleeves, very stiff, straight, and high. They embarrassed her. It was quite apparent that she had cooked, and that she expected to cook, dutifully. The blushes caused by the careless scrutiny of some passengers as she had entered the car were strange to see upon this plain, under-class countenance, which was drawn in placid, almost emotionless lines.

They were evidently very happy. "Ever been in a parlour-car before?" he asked, smiling with delight.

"No," she answered; "I never was. It's fine, ain't it?"

"Great! And then after a while we'll go forward to the diner, and get a big lay-out. Finest meal in the world. Charge a dollar."

"Oh, do they?" cried the bride. "Charge a dollar? Why, that's too much—for us—ain't it, Jack?"

"Not this trip, anyhow," he answered bravely. "We're going to go the whole thing."

Later he explained to her about the trains. "You see, it's a thousand miles from one end of Texas to the other; and this train runs right across it, and never stops but four times." He had the pride of an owner. He pointed out to her the dazzling fittings of the coach; and in truth her eyes opened wider as she contemplated the sea-green figured velvet, the shining brass, silver, and glass, the wood that gleamed as darkly brilliant as the surface of a pool of oil. At one end a bronze figure sturdily held a support for a separated chamber, and at convenient places on the ceiling were frescos in olive and silver.

To the minds of the pair, their surroundings reflected the glory of their marriage that morning in San Antonio; this was the environment of their new estate; and the man's face in particular beamed with an elation that made him appear ridiculous to the negro porter. This individual at times surveyed them from afar with an amused and superior grin. On other occasions he bullied them with skill in ways that did not make it exactly plain to them that they were being bullied. He subtly used all the manners of the most unconquerable kind of snobbery. He oppressed them; but of this oppression they had small knowledge, and they speedily forgot that infrequently a number of travellers covered them with stares of derisive enjoyment. Historically there was supposed to be something infinitely humorous in their situation.

"We are due in Yellow Sky at 3:42," he said, looking tenderly into her eyes.

"Oh, are we?" she said, as if she had not been aware of it. To evince surprise at her husband's statement was part of her wifely amiability. She took from a pocket a little silver watch; and as she held it before her, and stared at it with a frown of attention, the new husband's face shone.

"I bought it in San Anton' from a friend of mine," he told her gleefully.

"It's seventeen minutes past twelve," she said, looking up at him with a kind of shy and clumsy coquetry. A passenger, noting this play, grew excessively sardonic, and winked at himself in one of the numerous mirrors.

At last they went to the dining-car. Two rows of negro waiters, in glowing white suits, surveyed their entrance with the interest, and also the equanimity, of men who had been forewarned. The pair fell to the lot of a waiter who happened to feel pleasure in steering them through their meal. He viewed them with the manner of a fatherly pilot, his countenance radiant with benevolence. The patronage, entwined with the ordinary deference, was not plain to them. And yet, as they returned to their coach, they showed in their faces a sense of escape.

To the left, miles down a long purple slope, was a little ribbon of mist where moved the keening Rio Grande. The train was approaching it at an angle, and the apex was Yellow Sky. Presently it was apparent that, as the distance from Yellow Sky grew shorter, the husband became commensurately restless. His brick-red hands were more insistent in their prominence. Occasionally he was even rather absent-minded and far-away when the bride leaned forward and addressed him.

As a matter of truth, Jack Potter was beginning to find the shadow of a deed weigh upon him like a leaden slab. He, the town marshal of Yellow Sky, a man known, liked, and feared in his corner, a prominent person, had gone to San Antonio to meet a girl he believed he loved, and there, after the usual prayers, had actually induced her to marry him, without consulting Yellow Sky for any part of the transaction. He was now bringing his bride before an innocent and unsuspecting community.

Of course people in Yellow Sky married as it pleased them, in accordance with a general custom; but such was Potter's thought of his duty to his friends, or of their idea of his duty, or of an unspoken form which does not control men in these matters, that he felt he was heinous. He had committed an extraordinary crime. Face to face with this girl in San Antonio, and spurred by his sharp impulse, he had gone headlong over all the social hedges. At San Antonio he was like a man hidden in the dark. A knife to sever any friendly duty, any form, was easy to his hand in that remote city. But the hour of Yellow Sky—the hour of daylight—was approaching.

He knew full well that his marriage was an important thing to his town. It could only be exceeded by the burning of the new hotel. His friends could not forgive him. Frequently he had reflected on the advisability of telling them by telegraph, but a new cowardice had been upon him. He feared to do it. And now the train was hurrying him toward a scene of amazement, glee, and reproach. He glanced out of the window at the line of haze swinging slowly in toward the train.

Yellow Sky had a kind of brass band, which played painfully, to the delight of the populace. He laughed without heart as he thought of it. If the citizens could dream of his prospective arrival with his bride, they would parade the band at the station and escort them, amid cheers and laughing congratulations, to his adobe home.

He resolved that he would use all the devices of speed and plainscraft in making the journey from the station to his house. Once within that safe citadel, he could issue some sort of vocal bulletin, and then not go among the citizens until they had time to wear off a little of their enthusiasm.

The bride looked anxiously at him. "What's worrying you, Jack?"

He laughed again. "I'm not worrying, girl; I'm only thinking of Yellow Sky."

She flushed in comprehension.

A sense of mutual guilt invaded their minds and developed a finer tenderness. They looked at each other with eyes softly aglow. But Potter often laughed the same nervous laugh; the flush upon the bride's face seemed quite permanent.

The traitor to the feelings of Yellow Sky narrowly watched the speeding landscape. "We're nearly there," he said.

Presently the porter came and announced the proximity of Potter's home. He held a brush in his hand, and, with all his airy superiority gone, he brushed Potter's new clothes as the latter slowly turned this way and that way. Potter fumbled out a coin and gave it to the porter, as he had seen others do. It was a heavy and muscle-bound business, as that of a man shoeing his first horse.

The porter took their bag, and as the train began to slow they moved forward to the hooded platform of the car. Presently the two engines and their string of coaches rushed into the station of Yellow Sky.

"They have to take water here," said Potter, from a constricted throat and in mournful cadence, as one announcing death. Before the train stopped his eye had swept the length of the platform, and he was glad and astonished to see there was none upon it but the station-agent, who, with a slightly hurried and anxious air, was walking toward the water-tanks. When the train had halted, the porter alighted first, and placed in position a little temporary step.

"Come on, girl," said Potter, hoarsely. As he helped her down they each laughed on a false note. He took the bag from the negro, and bade his wife cling to his arm. As they slunk rapidly away, his hang-dog glance perceived that they were unloading the two trunks, and also that the station-agent, far ahead near the baggage-car, had turned and was running toward him, making gestures. He laughed, and groaned as he laughed, when he noted the first effect of his marital bliss upon Yellow Sky. He gripped his wife's arm firmly to his side, and they fled. Behind them the porter stood, chuckling fatuously.

II

The California express on the Southern Railway was due at Yellow Sky in twenty-one minutes. There were six men at the bar of the Weary Gentleman saloon. One was a drummer who talked a great deal and rapidly; three were Texans who did not care to talk at that time; and two were Mexican sheep-herders, who did not talk as a general practice in the Weary Gentleman saloon. The barkeeper's dog lay on the board walk that crossed in front of the door. His head was on his paws, and he glanced drowsily here and there with the constant vigilance of a dog that is kicked on occasion. Across the sandy street were some vivid green grass-plots, so wonderful in appearance, amid the sands that burned near them in a blazing sun, that they caused a doubt in the mind. They exactly resembled the grass mats used to represent lawns on the stage. At the cooler end of the railway station, a man without a coat sat in a tilted chair and smoked his pipe. The fresh-cut bank of the Rio Grande circled near the town, and there could be seen beyond it a great plum-coloured plain of mesquit.

Save for the busy drummer and his companions in the saloon, Yellow Sky was dozing. The new-comer leaned gracefully upon the bar, and recited many tales with the confidence of a bard who has come upon a new field.

"—and at the moment that the old man fell downstairs with the bureau in his arms, the old woman was coming up with two scuttles of coal, and of course—"

The drummer's tale was interrupted by a young man who suddenly appeared in the open door. He cried· "Scratchy Wilson's drunk, and has turned loose with both hands." The two Mexicans at once set down their glasses and faded out of the rear entrance of the saloon.

The drummer, innocent and jocular, answered: "All right, old man. S'pose he has? Come in and have a drink, anyhow."

But the information had made such an obvious cleft in every skull in the room that the drummer was obliged to see its importance. All had become instantly solemn. "Say," said he, mystified, "what is this?" His three companions made the introductory gesture of eloquent speech; but the young man at the door forestalled them.

"It means, my friend," he answered, as he came into the saloon, "that for the next two hours this town won't be a health resort."

The barkeeper went to the door, and locked and barred it; reaching out of the window, he pulled in heavy wooden shutters, and barred them. Immediately a solemn chapel-like gloom was upon the place. The drummer was looking from one to another.

"But say," he cried, "what is this, anyhow? You don't mean there is going to be a gun-fight?"

"Don't know whether there'll be a fight or not," answered one man, grimly; "but there'll be some shootin'—some good shootin'."

The young man who had warned them waved his hand. "Oh, there'll be a fight fast enough, if any one wants it. Anybody can get a fight out there in the street. There's a fight just waiting."

The drummer seemed to be swayed between the interest of a foreigner and a perception of personal danger.

"What did you say his name was?" he asked.

"Scratchy Wilson," they answered in chorus.

"And will he kill anybody? What are you going to do? Does this happen often? Does he rampage around like this once a week or so? Can he break in that door?"

"No; he can't break down that door," replied the barkeeper. "He's tried it three times. But when he comes you'd better lay down on the floor, stranger. He's dead sure to shoot at it, and a bullet may come through."

Thereafter the drummer kept a strict eye upon the door. The time had not yet been called for him to hug the floor, but, as a minor precaution, he sidled near to the wall. "Will he kill anybody?" he said again.

The men laughed low and scornfully at the question.

"He's out to shoot, and he's out for trouble. Don't see any good in experimentin' with him."

"But what do you do in a case like this? What do you do?"

A man responded: "Why, he and Jack Potter—"

"But," in chorus the other men interrupted, "Jack Potter's in San Anton'."

"Well, who is he? What's he got to do with it?"

"Oh, he's the town marshal. He goes out and fights Scratchy when he gets on one of these tears."

"Wow!" said the drummer, mopping his brow. "Nice job he's got."

The voices had toned away to mere whisperings. The drummer wished to ask further questions, which were born of an increasing anxiety and bewilderment; but when he attempted them, the men merely looked at him in irritation and motioned him to remain silent. A tense waiting hush was upon them. In the deep shadows of the room their eyes shone as they listened for sounds from the street. One man made three gestures at the barkeeper; and the latter, moving like a ghost, handed him a glass and a bottle. The man poured a full glass of whisky, and set down the bottle noiselessly. He gulped the whisky in a swallow, and turned again toward the door in immovable silence. The drummer saw that the barkeeper, without a sound, had taken a Winchester from beneath the bar. Later he saw this individual beckoning to him, so he tiptoed across the room.

"You better come with me back of the bar."

"No, thanks," said the drummer, perspiring; "I'd rather be where I can make a break for the back door."

Whereupon the man of bottles made a kindly but peremptory gesture. The drummer obeyed it, and, finding himself seated on a box with his head below the level of the bar, balm was laid upon his soul at sight of various zinc and copper fittings that bore a resemblance to armour-plate. The barkeeper took a seat comfortably upon an adjacent box.

"You see," he whispered, "this here Scratchy Wilson is a wonder with a gun—a perfect wonder; and when he goes on the war-trail, we hunt our holes—naturally. He's about the last one of the old gang that used to hang out along the river here. He's a terror when he's drunk. When he's sober he's all right—kind of simple—wouldn't hurt a fly—nicest fellow in town. But when he's drunk—whoo!"

There were periods of stillness. "I wish Jack Potter was back from San Anton'," said the barkeeper. "He shot Wilson up once—in the leg—and he would sail in and pull out the kinks in this thing."

Presently they heard from a distance the sound of a shot, followed by three wild yowls. It instantly removed a bond from the men in the darkened saloon. There was a shuffling of feet. They looked at each other. "Here he comes," they said.

III

A man in a maroon-coloured flannel shirt, which had been purchased for purposes of decoration, and made principally by some Jewish women on the East Side of New York, rounded a corner and walked into the middle of the main street of Yellow Sky. In either hand the man held a long, heavy, blue-black revolver. Often he yelled, and these cries rang through a semblance of a deserted village, shrilly flying over the roofs in a volume that seemed to have no relation to the ordinary vocal strength of a man. It was as if the surrounding stillness formed the arch of a tomb over him. These cries of ferocious challenge rang against walls of silence. And his boots had red tops with gilded imprints, of the kind beloved in winter by little sledding boys on the hillsides of New England.

The man's face flamed in a rage begot of whisky. His eyes, rolling, and yet keen for ambush, hunted the still doorways and windows. He walked with the creeping movement of the midnight cat. As it occurred to him, he roared menacing information. The long revolvers in his hands were as easy as straws; they were moved with an electric swiftness. The little fingers of each hand played sometimes in a musician's way. Plain from the low collar of the shirt, the cords of his neck straightened and sank, straightened and sank, as passion moved him. The only sounds were his terrible invitations. The calm adobes preserved their demeanor at the passing of this small thing in the middle of the street.

There was no offer of fight—no offer of fight. The man called to the sky. There were no attractions. He bellowed and fumed and swayed his revolvers here and everywhere.

The dog of the barkeeper of the Weary Gentleman saloon had not appreciated the advance of events. He yet lay dozing in front of his master's door. At sight of the dog, the man paused and raised his revolver humorously. At sight of the man, the dog sprang up and walked diagonally away, with a sullen head, and growling. The man yelled, and the dog broke into a gallop. As it was about to enter an alley, there was a loud noise, a whistling, and something spat the ground directly before it. The dog screamed, and, wheeling in terror, galloped headlong in a new direction. Again there was a noise, a whistling, and sand was kicked viciously before it. Fear-stricken, the dog turned and flurried like an animal in a pen. The man stood laughing, his weapons at his hips.

Ultimately the man was attracted by the closed door of the Weary Gentleman saloon. He went to it and, hammering with a revolver, demanded drink.

The door remaining imperturbable, he picked a bit of paper from the walk, and nailed it to the framework with a knife. He then turned his back contemptuously upon this popular resort and, walking to the opposite side of the street and spinning there on his heel quickly and lithely, fired at the bit of paper. He missed it by a half-inch. He swore at himself, and went away. Later he comfortably fusilladed the windows of his most intimate friend. The man was playing with this town; it was a toy for him.

But still there was no offer of fight. The name of Jack Potter, his ancient antagonist, entered his mind, and he concluded that it would be a glad thing if he should go to Potter's house and by bombardment induce him to come out and fight. He moved in the direction of his desire, chanting Apache scalp-music.

When he arrived at it, Potter's house presented the same still front as had the other adobes. Taking up a strategic position, the man howled a challenge. But this house regarded him as might a great stone god. It gave no sign. After a decent wait, the man howled further challenges, mingling with them wonderful epithets.

Presently there came the spectacle of a man churning himself into deepest rage over the immobility of a house. He fumed at it as the winter wind attacks a prairie cabin in the North. To the distance there should have gone the sound of a tumult like the fighting of two hundred Mexicans. As necessity bade him, he paused for breath or to reload his revolvers.

IV

Potter and his bride walked sheepishly and with speed. Sometimes they laughed together shamefacedly and low.

"Next corner, dear," he said finally.

They put forth the efforts of a pair walking bowed against a strong wind. Potter was about to raise a finger to point the first appearance of the new home when, as they circled the corner, they came face to face with a man in a maroon-coloured shirt, who was feverishly pushing cartridges into a large revolver. Upon the instant the man dropped his revolver to the ground and, like lightning, whipped another from its holster. The second weapon was aimed at the bridegroom's chest.

There was a silence. Potter's mouth seemed to be merely a grave for his tongue. He exhibited an instinct to at once loosen his arm from the woman's grip, and he dropped the bag to the sand. As for the bride, her face had gone as yellow as old cloth. She was a slave to hideous rites, gazing at the apparitional snake.

The two men faced each other at a distance of three paces. He of the revolver smiled with a new and quiet ferocity.

"Tried to sneak up on me," he said. "Tried to sneak up on me!" His eyes grew more baleful. As Potter made a slight movement, the man thrust his revolver venomously forward. "No; don't you do it, Jack Potter. Don't you move a finger toward a gun just yet. Don't you move an eyelash. The time has come for me to settle with you, and I'm goin' to do it my own way, and loaf along with no interferin'. So if you don't want a gun bent on you, just mind what I tell you."

Potter looked at his enemy. "I ain't got a gun on me, Scratchy," he said. "Honest, I ain't." He was stiffening and steadying, but yet somewhere at the back of his mind a vision of the Pullman floated: the sea-green figured velvet, the shining brass, silver, and glass, the wood that gleamed as darkly brilliant as the surface of a pool of oil—all the glory of the marriage, the environment of the new estate. "You know I fight when it comes to fighting, Scratchy Wilson; but I ain't got a gun on me. You'll have to do all the shootin' yourself."

His enemy's face went livid. He stepped forward, and lashed his weapon to and fro before Potter's chest. "Don't you tell me you ain't got no gun on you, you whelp. Don't tell me no lie like that. There ain't a man in Texas ever seen you without no gun. Don't take me for no kid." His eyes blazed with light, and his throat worked like a pump.

"I ain't takin' you for no kid," answered Potter. His heels had not moved an inch backward. "I'm takin' you for a damn fool. I tell you I ain't got a gun, and I ain't. If you're goin' to shoot me up, you better begin now; you'll never get a chance like this again."

So much enforced reasoning had told on Wilson's rage; he was calmer. "If you ain't got a gun, why ain't you got a gun?" he sneered. "Been to Sunday-school?"

"I ain't got a gun because I've just come from San Anton' with my wife. I'm married," said Potter. "And if I'd thought there was going to be any galoots like you prowling around when I brought my wife home, I'd had a gun, and don't you forget it."

"Married!" said Scratchy, not at all comprehending.

"Yes, married. I'm married," said Potter, distinctly.

"Married?" said Scratchy. Seemingly for the first time, he saw the drooping, drowning woman at the other man's side. "No!" he said. He was like a creature allowed a glimpse of another world. He moved a pace backward, and his arm, with the revolver, dropped to his side. "Is this the lady?" he asked.

"Yes; this is the lady," answered Potter.

There was another period of silence.

"Well," said Wilson at last, slowly, "I s'pose it's all off now."

"It's all off if you say so, Scratchy. You know I didn't make the trouble." Potter lifted his valise.

"Well, I 'low it's off, Jack," said Wilson. He was looking at the ground. "Married!" He was not a student of chivalry; it was merely that in the presence of this foreign condition he was a simple child of the earlier plains. He picked up his starboard revolver, and, placing both weapons in their holsters, he went away. His feet made funnel-shaped tracks in the heavy sand.

QUESTIONS

1. Scratchy is described in the final paragraph as "a simple child of the earlier plains." What does this mean? Was Potter ever a simple child of the earlier plains? **2.** Early in the story we read that ". . . Jack Potter was beginning to find the shadow of a deed weigh upon him like a leaden slab. He, the town marshal of Yellow Sky, a man known, liked, and feared in his corner, a prominent person, had gone to San Antonio to meet a girl he believed he loved, and there, after the usual prayers, had actually induced her to marry him, without consulting Yellow Sky for any part of the transaction. He was now bringing his bride before an innocent and unsuspecting community." Jack Potter, like any man, has a right to marry. How do you account for his feelings as described in this passage? **3.** A "drummer" is a traveling salesman. What effect does his presence have on the "myth of the West"?

WRITING TOPICS

1. How would you characterize Scratchy's behavior? How does it relate to the "myth of the West" preserved in films and western novels? How does the description of Scratchy's shirt at the beginning of part III affect that view of the West? Why is Scratchy disconsolate at the end? **2.** Analyze Crane's metaphors and images. What function do they serve in the story?

Araby*

JAMES JOYCE [1882–1941]

North Richmond Street, being blind, was a quiet street except at the hour when the Christian Brothers' School set the boys free. An uninhabited house of two storeys stood at the blind end, detached from its neighbours in a square ground. The other houses of the street, conscious of decent lives within them, gazed at one another with brown imperturbable faces.

The former tenant of our house, a priest, had died in the back drawing-room. Air, musty from having been long enclosed, hung in all the rooms, and the waste room behind the kitchen was littered with old useless papers. Among these I found a few paper-covered books, the pages of which were curled and damp: *The Abbot*, by Walter Scott, *The Devout Communicant* and *The Memoirs of Vidocq*. I liked the last best because its leaves were yellow. The wild garden behind the house contained a central apple-tree and a few straggling bushes under one of which I found the late tenant's rusty bicycle-pump. He had been a very charitable priest; in his will he had left all his money to institutions and the furniture of his house to his sister.

When the short days of winter came dusk fell before we had well eaten our dinners. When we met in the street the houses had grown sombre. The space of sky above us was the colour of ever-changing violet and towards it the lamps of the street lifted their feeble lanterns. The cold air stung us and we played till our bodies glowed. Our shouts echoed in the silent street. The career of our play brought us through the dark muddy lanes behind the houses where we ran the gauntlet of the rough tribes from the cottages, to the back doors of the dark dripping gardens where odours arose from the ashpits, to the dark odorous stables where a coachman smoothed and combed the horse or shook music from the buckled harness. When we returned to the street light from the kitchen windows had filled the areas. If my uncle was seen turning the corner we hid in the shadow until we had seen him safely housed. Or if Mangan's sister came out on the doorstep to call her brother in to his tea we watched her from our shadow peer up and down the street. We waited to see whether she would remain or go in and, if she remained, we left our shadow and walked up to Mangan's steps resignedly. She was waiting for us, her figure defined by the light from the half-opened door. Her brother always teased her before he obeyed and I stood by the railings looking at her. Her dress swung as she moved her body and the soft rope of her hair tossed from side to side.

Every morning I lay on the floor in the front parlour watching her door. The blind was pulled down to within an inch of the sash so that I could not be seen. When she came out on the doorstep my heart leaped. I ran to the hall, seized

---

* This story is considered in the essay "Reading Fiction" at the end of the book.

my books and followed her. I kept her brown figure always in my eye and, when we came near the point at which our ways diverged, I quickened my pace and passed her. This happened morning after morning. I had never spoken to her, except for a few casual words, and yet her name was like a summons to all my foolish blood.

Her image accompanied me even in places the most hostile to romance. On Saturday evenings when my aunt went marketing I had to go to carry some of the parcels. We walked through the flaring streets, jostled by drunken men and bargaining women, amid the curses of labourers, the shrill litanies of shop-boys who stood on guard by the barrels of pigs' cheeks, the nasal chanting of street-singers, who sang a *come-all-you*[1] about O'Donovan Rossa, or a ballad about the troubles in our native land. These noises converged in a single sensation of life for me: I imagined that I bore my chalice safely through a throng of foes. Her name sprang to my lips at moments in strange prayers and praises which I myself did not understand. My eyes were often full of tears (I could not tell why) and at times a flood from my heart seemed to pour itself out into my bosom. I thought little of the future. I did not know whether I would ever speak to her or not or, if I spoke to her, how I could tell her of my confused adoration. But my body was like a harp and her words and gestures were like fingers running upon the wires.

One evening I went into the back drawing-room in which the priest had died. It was a dark rainy evening and there was no sound in the house. Through one of the broken panes I heard the rain impinge upon the earth, the fine incessant needles of water playing in the sodden beds. Some distant lamp or lighted window gleamed below me. I was thankful that I could see so little. All my senses seemed to desire to veil themselves and, feeling that I was about to slip from them, I pressed the palms of my hands together until they trembled, murmuring: *"O love! O love!"* many times.

At last she spoke to me. When she addressed the first words to me I was so confused that I did not know what to answer. She asked me was I going to *Araby*. I forgot whether I answered yes or no. It would be a splendid bazaar, she said she would love to go.

"And why can't you?" I asked.

While she spoke she turned a silver bracelet round and round her wrist. She could not go, she said, because there would be a retreat that week in her convent. Her brother and two other boys were fighting for their caps and I was alone at the railings. She held one of the spikes, bowing her head towards me. The light from the lamp opposite our door caught the white curve of her neck, lit up her hair that rested there and, falling, lit up the hand upon the railing. It fell over one side of her dress and caught the white border of a petticoat, just visible as she stood at ease.

"It's well for you" she said.

---

[1] A street ballad beginning with these words. This one is about Jeremiah Donovan, a nineteenth-century Irish nationalist popularly known as O'Donovan Rossa.

"If I go," I said, "I will bring you something."

What innumerable follies laid waste my waking and sleeping thoughts after that evening! I wished to annihilate the tedious intervening days. I chafed against the work of school. At night in my bedroom and by day in the classroom her image came between me and the page I strove to read. The syllables of the word *Araby* were called to me through the silence in which my soul luxuriated and cast an Eastern enchantment over me. I asked for leave to go to the bazaar on Saturday night. My aunt was surprised and hoped it was not some Freemason affair. I answered few questions in class. I watched my master's face pass from amiability to sternness; he hoped I was not beginning to idle. I could not call my wandering thoughts together. I had hardly any patience with the serious work of life which, now that it stood between me and my desire, seemed to me child's play, ugly monotonous child's play.

On Saturday morning I reminded my uncle that I wished to go to the bazaar in the evening. He was fussing at the hallstand, looking for the hat-brush, and answered me curtly:

"Yes, boy, I know."

As he was in the hall I could not go into the front parlour and lie at the window. I left the house in bad humour and walked slowly towards the school. The air was pitilessly raw and already my heart misgave me.

When I came home to dinner my uncle had not yet been home. Still it was early. I sat staring at the clock for some time and, when its ticking began to irritate me, I left the room. I mounted the staircase and gained the upper part of the house. The high cold empty gloomy rooms liberated me and I went from room to room singing. From the front window I saw my companions playing below in the street. Their cries reached me weakened and indistinct and, leaning my forehead against the cool glass, I looked over at the dark house where she lived. I may have stood there for an hour, seeing nothing but the brown-clad figure cast by my imagination, touched discreetly by the lamplight at the curved neck, at the hand upon the railings and at the border below the dress.

When I came downstairs again I found Mrs. Mercer sitting at the fire. She was an old garrulous woman, a pawnbroker's widow, who collected used stamps for some pious purpose. I had to endure the gossip of the tea-table. The meal was prolonged beyond an hour and still my uncle did not come. Mrs. Mercer stood up to go: she was sorry she couldn't wait any longer, but it was after eight o'clock and she did not like to be out late, as the night air was bad for her. When she had gone I began to walk up and down the room, clenching my fists. My aunt said:

"I'm afraid you may put off your bazaar for this night of Our Lord."

At nine o'clock I heard my uncle's latchkey in the halldoor. I heard him talking to himself and heard the hallstand rocking when it had received the weight of his overcoat. I could interpret these signs. When he was midway through his dinner I asked him to give me the money to go to the bazaar. He had forgotten.

"The people are in bed and after their first sleep now," he said.

I did not smile. My aunt said to him energetically:

"Can't you give him the money and let him go? You've kept him late enough as it is."

My uncle said he was very sorry he had forgotten. He said he believed in the old saying: "All work and no play makes Jack a dull boy." He asked me where I was going and, when I had told him a second time he asked me did I know *The Arab's Farewell to his Steed*. When I left the kitchen he was about to recite the opening lines of the piece to my aunt.

I held a florin tightly in my hand as I strode down Buckingham Street towards the station. The sight of the streets thronged with buyers and glaring with gas recalled to me the purpose of my journey. I took my seat in a third-class carriage of a deserted train. After an intolerable delay the train moved out of the station slowly. It crept onward among ruinous houses and over the twinkling river. At Westland Row Station a crowd of people pressed to the carriage doors; but the porters moved them back, saying that it was a special train for the bazaar. I remained alone in the bare carriage. In a few minutes the train drew up beside an improvised wooden platform. I passed out on to the road and saw by the lighted dial of a clock that it was ten minutes to ten. In front of me was a large building which displayed the magical name.

I could not find any sixpenny entrance and, fearing that the bazaar would be closed, I passed in quickly through a turnstile, handing a shilling to a weary-looking man. I found myself in a big hall girdled at half its height by a gallery. Nearly all the stalls were closed and the greater part of the hall was in darkness. I recognised a silence like that which pervades a church after a service. I walked into the centre of the bazaar timidly. A few people were gathered about the stalls which were still open. Before a curtain, over which the words *Café Chantant* were written in coloured lamps, two men were counting money on a salver. I listened to the fall of the coins.

Remembering with difficulty why I had come I went over to one of the stalls and examined porcelain vases and flowered tea-sets. At the door of the stall a young lady was talking and laughing with two young gentlemen. I remarked their English accents and listened vaguely to their conversation.

"O, I never said such a thing!"

"O, but you did!"

"O, but I didn't!"

"Didn't she say that?"

"Yes. I heard her."

"O, there's a . . . fib!"

Observing me the young lady came over and asked me did I wish to buy anything. The tone of her voice was not encouraging; she seemed to have spoken to me out of a sense of duty. I looked humbly at the great jars that stood like eastern guards at either side of the dark entrance to the stall and murmured:

"No, thank you."

The young lady changed the position of one of the vases and went back to the two young men. They began to talk of the same subject. Once or twice the young lady glanced at me over her shoulder.

I lingered before her stall, though I knew my stay was useless, to make my interest in her wares seem the more real. Then I turned away slowly and walked down the middle of the bazaar. I allowed the two pennies to fall against the sixpence in my pocket. I heard a voice call from one end of the gallery that the light was out. The upper part of the hall was now completely dark.

Gazing up into the darkness I saw myself as a creature driven and derided by vanity; and my eyes burned with anguish and anger.

A Clean, Well-Lighted Place 1933

ERNEST HEMINGWAY [1898–1961]

It was late and everyone had left the café except an old man who sat in the shadow the leaves of the tree made against the electric light. In the day time the street was dusty, but at night the dew settled the dust and the old man liked to sit late because he was deaf and now at night it was quiet and he felt the difference. The two waiters inside the café knew that the old man was a little drunk, and while he was a good client they knew that if he became too drunk he would leave without paying, so they kept watch on him.

"Last week he tried to commit suicide," one waiter said.

"Why?"

"He was in despair."

"What about?"

"Nothing."

"How do you know it was nothing?"

"He has plenty of money."

They sat together at a table that was close against the wall near the door of the café and looked at the terrace where the tables were all empty except where the old man sat in the shadow of the leaves of the tree that moved slightly in the wind. A girl and a soldier went by in the street. The street light shone on the brass number on his collar. The girl wore no head covering and hurried beside him.

"The guard will pick him up," one waiter said.

"What does it matter if he gets what he's after?"

"He had better get off the street now. The guard will get him. They went by five minutes ago."

The old man sitting in the shadow rapped on his saucer with his glass. The younger waiter went over to him.

"What do you want?"

The old man looked at him. "Another brandy," he said.

"You'll be drunk," the waiter said. The old man looked at him. The waiter went away.

"He'll stay all night," he said to his colleague. "I'm sleepy now. I never get into bed before three o'clock. He should have killed himself last week."

The waiter took the brandy bottle and another saucer from the counter inside the café and marched out to the old man's table. He put down the saucer and poured the glass full of brandy.

"You should have killed yourself last week," he said to the deaf man. The old man motioned with his finger. "A little more," he said. The waiter poured on into the glass so that the brandy slopped over and ran down the stem into the top saucer of the pile. "Thank you," the old man said. The waiter took the bottle back inside the café. He sat down at the table with his colleague again.

"He's drunk now," he said.

"He's drunk every night."

"What did he want to kill himself for?"

"How should I know."

"How did he do it?"

"He hung himself with a rope."

"Who cut him down?"

"His niece."

"Why did they do it?"

"Fear for his soul."

"How much money has he got?"

"He's got plenty."

"He must be eighty years old."

"Anyway I should say he was eighty."

"I wish he would go home. I never get to bed before three o'clock. What kind of hour is that to go to bed?"

"He stays up because he likes it."

"He's lonely. I'm not lonely. I have a wife waiting in bed for me."

"He had a wife once too."

"A wife would be no good to him now."

"You can't tell. He might be better with a wife."

"His niece looks after him. You said she cut him down."

"I know."

"I wouldn't want to be that old. An old man is a nasty thing."

"Not always. This old man is clean. He drinks without spilling. Even now, drunk. Look at him."

"I don't want to look at him. I wish he would go home. He has no regard for those who must work."

The old man looked from his glass across the square, then over at the waiters.

"Another brandy," he said, pointing to his glass. The waiter who was in a hurry came over.

"Finished," he said, speaking with that omission of syntax stupid people employ when talking to drunken people or foreigners. "No more tonight. Close now."

"Another," said the old man.

"No. Finished." The waiter wiped the edge of the table with a towel and shook his head.

The old man stood up, slowly counted the saucers, took a leather coin purse from his pocket and paid for the drinks, leaving half a peseta tip.

The waiter watched him go down the street, a very old man walking unsteadily but with dignity.

"Why didn't you let him stay and drink?" the unhurried waiter asked. They were putting up the shutters. "It is not half-past two."

"I want to go home to bed."

"What is an hour?"

"More to me than to him."

"An hour is the same."

"You talk like an old man yourself. He can buy a bottle and drink at home."

"It's not the same."

"No, it is not," agreed the waiter with a wife. He did not wish to be unjust. He was only in a hurry.

"And you? You have no fear of going home before your usual hour?"

"Are you trying to insult me?"

"No, hombre, only to make a joke."

"No," the waiter who was in a hurry said, rising from pulling down the metal shutters. "I have confidence. I am all confidence."

"You have youth, confidence, and a job," the older waiter said. "You have everything."

"And what do you lack?"

"Everything but work."

"You have everything I have."

"No. I have never had confidence and I am not young."

"Come on. Stop talking nonsense and lock up."

"I am of those who like to stay late at the café," the older waiter said. "With all those who do not want to go to bed. With all those who need a light for the night."

"I want to go home and into bed."

"We are of two different kinds," the older waiter said. He was now dressed to go home. "It is not only a question of youth and confidence although those things are very beautiful. Each night I am reluctant to close up because there may be some one who needs the café."

"Hombre, there are bodegas open all night long."

"You do not understand. This is a clean and pleasant café. It is well lighted. The light is very good and also, now, there are shadows of the leaves."

"Good night," said the younger waiter.

"Good night," the other said. Turning off the electric light he continued the conversation with himself. It is the light of course but it is necessary that the place be clean and pleasant. You do not want music. Certainly you do not want music. Nor can you stand before a bar with dignity although that is all that is provided for these hours. What did he fear? It was not fear or dread. It was a nothing that he knew too well. It was all a nothing and a man was nothing too. It was only that and light was all it needed and a certain cleanness and order. Some lived in it and never felt it but he knew it was nada y pues nada y pues nada.[1] Our nada who art in nada, nada be thy name thy kingdom nada thy will be nada in nada as it is in nada. Give us this nada our daily nada and nada us our nada as we nada our nadas and nada us not into nada but deliver us from nada; pues nada. Hail nothing full of nothing, nothing is with thee. He smiled and stood before a bar with a shining steam pressure coffee machine.

---

[1] Nothing, and then nothing, and then nothing.

"What's yours?" asked the barman.

"Nada."

"Otro loco mas,"[2] said the barman and turned away.

"A little cup," said the waiter.

The barman poured it for him.

"The light is very bright and pleasant but the bar is unpolished," the waiter said.

The barman looked at him but did not answer. It was too late at night for conversation.

"You want another copita?" the barman asked.

"No, thank you," said the waiter and went out. He disliked bars and bodegas. A clean, well-lighted café was a very different thing. Now, without thinking further, he would go home to his room. He would lie in the bed and finally, with daylight, he would go to sleep. After all, he said to himself, it is probably only insomnia. Many must have it.

QUESTION

How do the two waiters differ in their attitudes toward the old man? What bearing does that difference have on the theme of the story?

---

[2] Another crazy one.

My Oedipus Complex   1950

FRANK O'CONNOR   [1903–1966]

Father was in the army all through the war—the first war, I mean—so, up to the age of five, I never saw much of him, and what I saw did not worry me. Sometimes I woke and there was a big figure in khaki peering down at me in the candlelight. Sometimes in the early morning I heard the slamming of the front door and the clatter of nailed boots down the cobbles of the lane. These were Father's entrances and exits. Like Santa Claus he came and went mysteriously.

In fact, I rather liked his visits, though it was an uncomfortable squeeze between Mother and him when I got into the big bed in the early morning. He smoked, which gave him a pleasant musty smell, and shaved, an operation of astounding interest. Each time he left a trail of souvenirs—model tanks and Gurkha knives with handles made of bullet cases, and German helmets and cap badges and button-sticks, and all sorts of military equipment—carefully stowed away in a long box on top of the wardrobe, in case they ever came in handy. There was a bit of the magpie about Father; he expected everything to come in handy. When his back was turned, Mother let me get a chair and rummage through his treasures. She didn't seem to think so highly of them as he did.

The war was the most peaceful period of my life. The window of my attic faced southeast. My mother had curtained it, but that had small effect. I always woke with the first light and, with all the responsibilities of the previous day melted, feeling myself rather like the sun, ready to illumine and rejoice. Life never seemed so simple and clear and full of possibilities as then. I put my feet out from under the clothes—I called them Mrs. Left and Mrs. Right—and invented dramatic situations for them in which they discussed the problems of the day. At least Mrs. Right did; she was very demonstrative, but I hadn't the same control of Mrs. Left, so she mostly contented herself with nodding agreement.

They discussed what Mother and I should do during the day, what Santa Claus should give a fellow for Christmas, and what steps should be taken to brighten the home. There was that little matter of the baby, for instance. Mother and I could never agree about that. Ours was the only house in the terrace without a new baby, and Mother said we couldn't afford one till Father came back from the war because they cost seventeen and six. That showed how simple she was. The Geneys up the road had a baby, and everyone knew they couldn't afford seventeen and six. It was probably a cheap baby, and Mother wanted something really good, but I felt she was too exclusive. The Geneys' baby would have done us fine.

Having settled my plans for the day, I got up, put a chair under the attic window, and lifted the frame high enough to stick out my head. The window overlooked the front gardens of the terrace behind ours, and beyond these it looked over a deep valley to the tall, red-brick houses terraced up the opposite hillside, which were all still in shadow, while those at our side of the valley were all lit up, though with long strange shadows that made them seem unfamiliar; rigid and painted.

After that I went into Mother's room and climbed into the big bed. She woke and I began to tell her of my schemes. By this time, though I never seem to have noticed it, I was petrified in my nightshirt, and I thawed as I talked until, the last frost melted, I fell asleep beside her and woke again only when I heard her below in the kitchen, making the breakfast.

After breakfast we went into town; heard Mass at St. Augustine's and said a prayer for Father, and did the shopping. If the afternoon was fine we either went for a walk in the country or a visit to Mother's great friend in the convent, Mother St. Dominic. Mother had them all praying for Father, and every night, going to bed, I asked God to send him back safe from the war to us. Little, indeed, did I know what I was praying for!

One morning, I got into the big bed, and there, sure enough, was Father in his usual Santa Claus manner, but later, instead of uniform, he put on his best blue suit, and Mother was as pleased as anything. I saw nothing to be pleased about, because, out of uniform, Father was altogether less interesting, but she only beamed, and explained that our prayers had been answered, and off we went to Mass to thank God for having brought Father safely home.

The irony of it! That very day when he came in to dinner he took off his boots and put on his slippers, donned the dirty old cap he wore about the house to save him from colds, crossed his legs, and began to talk gravely to Mother, who looked anxious. Naturally, I disliked her looking anxious, because it destroyed her good looks, so I interrupted him.

"Just a moment, Larry!" she said gently.

This was only what she said when we had boring visitors, so I attached no importance to it and went on talking.

"Do be quiet, Larry!" she said impatiently. "Don't you hear me talking to Daddy?"

This was the first time I had heard those ominous words, "talking to Daddy," and I couldn't help feeling that if this was how God answered prayers, he couldn't listen to them very attentively.

"Why are you talking to Daddy?" I asked with as great a show of indifference as I could muster.

"Because Daddy and I have business to discuss. Now, don't interrupt again!"

In the afternoon, at Mother's request, Father took me for a walk. This time we went into town instead of out to the country, and I thought at first, in my usual optimistic way, that it might be an improvement. It was nothing of the sort. Father and I had quite different notions of a walk in town. He had no proper interest in trams, ships, and horses, and the only thing that seemed to divert him was talking to fellows as old as himself. When I wanted to stop he simply went on, dragging me behind him by the hand; when he wanted to stop I had no alternative but to do the same. I noticed that it seemed to be a sign that he wanted to stop for a long time whenever he leaned against a wall. The second time I saw him do it I got wild. He seemed to be settling himself forever. I pulled him by the coat and trousers, but, unlike Mother who, if you were too persistent, got into a wax and said: "Larry, if you don't behave yourself, I'll give you a good slap," Father had an extraordinary capacity for amiable inattention. I sized him up and wondered would I cry, but he seemed to be too remote to be annoyed even by that. Really, it was like going for a walk with a mountain! He either ignored the wrenching and pummeling entirely, or else glanced down with a grin of amusement from his peak. I had never met anyone so absorbed in himself as he seemed.

At teatime, "talking to Daddy" began again, complicated this time by the fact that he had an evening paper, and every few minutes he put it down and told Mother something new out of it. I felt this was foul play. Man for man, I was prepared to compete with him any time for Mother's attention, but when he had it all made up for him by other people it left me no chance. Several times I tried to change the subject without success.

"You must be quiet while Daddy is reading, Larry," Mother said impatiently.

It was clear that she either genuinely liked talking to Father better than talking to me, or else that he had some terrible hold on her which made her afraid to admit the truth.

"Mummy," I said that night when she was tucking me up, "do you think if I prayed hard God would send Daddy back to the war?"

She seemed to think about that for a moment.

"No, dear," she said with a smile. "I don't think he would."

"Why wouldn't he, Mummy?"

"Because there isn't a war any longer, dear."

"But, Mummy, couldn't God make another war, if he liked?"

"He wouldn't like to, dear. It's not God who makes wars, but bad people."

"Oh!" I said.

I was disappointed about that. I began to think that God wasn't quite what he was cracked up to be.

Next morning I woke at my usual hour, feeling like a bottle of champagne. I put out my feet and invented a long conversation in which Mrs. Right talked of the trouble she had with her own father till she put him in the Home. I didn't quite know what the Home was but it sounded the right place for Father. Then I got my chair and stuck my head out of the attic window. Dawn was just breaking, with a guilty air that made me feel I had caught it in the act. My head bursting with stories and schemes, I stumbled in next door, and in the half-darkness scrambled into the big bed. There was no room at Mother's side so I had to get between her and Father. For the time being I had forgotten about him, and for several minutes I sat bolt upright, racking my brains to know what I could do with him. He was taking up more than his fair share of the bed, and I couldn't get comfortable, so I gave him several kicks that made him grunt and stretch. He made room all right, though. Mother waked and felt for me. I settled back comfortably in the warmth of the bed with my thumb in my mouth.

"Mummy!" I hummed, loudly and contentedly.

"Ssh! dear," she whispered. "Don't wake Daddy!"

This was a new development, which threatened to be even more serious than "talking to Daddy." Life without my early-morning conferences was unthinkable.

"Why?" I asked severely.

"Because poor Daddy is tired."

This seemed to me a quite inadequate reason, and I was sickened by the sentimentality of her "poor Daddy." I never liked that sort of gush; it always struck me as insincere.

"Oh!" I said lightly. Then in my most winning tone: "Do you know where I want to go with you today, Mummy?"

"No, dear," she sighed.

"I want to go down the Glen and fish for thornybacks with my new net, and then I want to go out to the Fox and Hounds, and—"

"Don't-wake-Daddy!" she hissed angrily, clapping her hand across my mouth.

But it was too late. He was awake, or nearly so. He grunted and reached for the matches. Then he stared incredulously at his watch.

"Like a cup of tea, dear?" asked Mother in a meek, hushed voice I had never heard her use before. It sounded almost as though she were afraid.

"Tea?" he exclaimed indignantly. "Do you know what the time is?"

"And after that I want to go up the Rathcooney Road," I said loudly, afraid I'd forget something in all those interruptions.

"Go to sleep at once, Larry!" she said sharply.

I began to snivel. I couldn't concentrate, the way that pair went on, and smothering my early-morning schemes was like burying a family from the cradle.

Father said nothing, but lit his pipe and sucked it, looking out into the shadows without minding Mother or me. I knew he was mad. Every time I made a remark Mother hushed me irritably. I was mortified. I felt it wasn't fair; there was even something sinister in it. Every time I had pointed out to her the waste of making two beds when we could both sleep in one, she had told me it was healthier like that, and now here was this man, this stranger, sleeping with her without the least regard for her health!

He got up early and made tea, but though he brought Mother a cup he brought none for me.

"Mummy," I shouted, "I want a cup of tea, too."

"Yes, dear," she said patiently. "You can drink from Mummy's saucer."

That settled it. Either Father or I would have to leave the house. I didn't want to drink from Mother's saucer; I wanted to be treated as an equal in my own home, so, just to spite her, I drank it all and left none for her. She took that quietly, too.

But that night when she was putting me to bed she said gently: "Larry, I want you to promise me something."

"What is it?" I asked.

"Not to come in and disturb poor Daddy in the morning. Promise?"

"Poor Daddy" again! I was becoming suspicious of everything involving that quite impossible man.

"Why?" I asked.

"Because poor Daddy is worried and tired and he doesn't sleep well."

"Why doesn't he, Mummy?"

"Well, you know, don't you, that while he was at the war Mummy got the pennies from the Post Office?"

"From Miss MacCarthy?"

"That's right. But now, you see, Miss MacCarthy hasn't any more pennies, so Daddy must go out and find us some. You know what would happen if he couldn't?"

"No," I said, "tell us."

"Well, I think we might have to go out and beg for them like the poor old woman on Fridays. We wouldn't like that, would we?"

"No," I agreed. "We wouldn't."

"So you'll promise not to come in and wake him?"

"Promise."

Mind you, I meant that. I knew pennies were a serious matter, and I was all against having to go out and beg like the old woman on Fridays. Mother laid out all my toys in a complete ring round the bed so that, whatever way I got out, I was bound to fall over one of them.

When I woke I remembered my promise all right. I got up and sat on the floor and played—for hours, it seemed to me. Then I got my chair and looked out the attic window for more hours. I wished it was time for Father to wake; I wished someone would make me a cup of tea. I didn't feel in the least like the sun; instead, I was bored and so very, very cold! I simply longed for the warmth and depth of the big featherbed.

At last I could stand it no longer. I went into the next room. As there was still no room at Mother's side I climbed over her and she woke with a start.

"Larry," she whispered, gripping my arm very tightly, "what did you promise?"

"But I did, Mummy," I wailed, caught in the very act. "I was quiet for ever so long."

"Oh, dear, and you're perished!" she said sadly, feeling me all over. "Now, if I let you stay will you promise not to talk?"

"But I want to talk, Mummy," I wailed.

"That has nothing to do with it," she said with a firmness that was new to me. "Daddy wants to sleep. Now, do you understand that?"

I understood it only too well. I wanted to talk, he wanted to sleep—whose house was it, anyway?

"Mummy," I said with equal firmness, "I think it would be healthier for Daddy to sleep in his own bed."

That seemed to stagger her, because she said nothing for a while.

"Now, once for all," she went on, "you're to be perfectly quiet or go back to your own bed. Which is it to be?"

The injustice of it got me down. I had convicted her out of her own mouth of inconsistency and unreasonableness, and she hadn't even attempted to reply. Full of spite, I gave Father a kick, which she didn't notice but which made him grunt and open his eyes in alarm.

"What time is it?" he asked in a panic-stricken voice, not looking at Mother but the door, as if he saw someone there.

"It's early yet," she replied soothingly. "It's only the child. Go to sleep again. . . . Now, Larry," she added, getting out of bed, "you've wakened Daddy and you must go back."

This time, for all her quiet air, I knew she meant it, and knew that my principal rights and privileges were as good as lost unless I asserted them at once. As she lifted me, I gave a screech, enough to wake the dead, not to mind Father. He groaned.

"That damn child! Doesn't he ever sleep?"

"It's only a habit, dear," she said quietly, though I could see she was vexed.

"Well, it's time he got out of it," shouted Father, beginning to heave in the bed. He suddenly gathered all the bedclothes about him, turned to the wall, and then looked back over his shoulder with nothing showing only two small, spiteful, dark eyes. The man looked very wicked.

To open the bedroom door, Mother had to let me down, and I broke free and dashed for the farthest corner, screeching. Father sat bolt upright in bed.

"Shut up, you little puppy!" he said in a choking voice.

I was so astonished that I stopped screeching. Never, never had anyone spoken to me in that tone before. I looked at him incredulously and saw his face convulsed with rage. It was only then that I fully realized how God had codded me, listening to my prayers for the safe return of this monster.

"Shut up, you!" I bawled, beside myself.

"What's that you said?" shouted Father, making a wild leap out of bed.

"Mick, Mick!" cried Mother. "Don't you see the child isn't used to you?"

"I see he's better fed than taught," snarled Father, waving his arms wildly. "He wants his bottom smacked."

All his previous shouting was as nothing to these obscene words referring to my person. They really made my blood boil.

"Smack your own!" I screamed hysterically. "Smack your own! Shut up! Shut up!"

At this he lost his patience and let fly at me. He did it with the lack of conviction you'd expect of a man under Mother's horrified eyes, and it ended up as a mere tap, but the sheer indignity of being struck at all by a stranger, a total stranger who had cajoled his way back from the war into our big bed as a result of my innocent intercession, made me completely dotty. I shrieked and shrieked, and danced in my bare feet, and Father, looking awkward and hairy in nothing but a short grey army shirt, glared down at me like a mountain out for murder. I think it must have been then that I realized he was jealous too. And there stood Mother in her nightdress, looking as if her heart was broken between us. I hoped she felt as she looked. It seemed to me that she deserved it all.

From that morning out my life was a hell. Father and I were enemies, open and avowed. We conducted a series of skirmishes against one another, he trying to steal my time with Mother and I his. When she was sitting on my bed, telling me a story, he took to looking for some pair of old boots which he alleged he had left behind him at the beginning of the war. While he talked to Mother I played loudly with my toys to show my total lack of concern. He created a terrible scene one evening when he came in from work and found me at his box, playing with his regimental badges, Gurkha knives and button-sticks. Mother got up and took the box from me.

"You mustn't play with Daddy's toys unless he lets you, Larry," she said severely. "Daddy doesn't play with yours."

For some reason Father looked at her as if she had struck him and then turned away with a scowl.

"Those are not toys," he growled, taking down the box again to see had I lifted anything. "Some of those curios are very rare and valuable."

But as time went on I saw more and more how he managed to alienate Mother and me. What made it worse was that I couldn't grasp his method or see what attraction he had for Mother. In every possible way he was less winning than I. He had a common accent and made noises at his tea. I thought for a while that it might be the newspapers she was interested in, so I made up bits of news of my own to read to her. Then I thought it might be the smoking, which I personally thought attractive, and took his pipes and went round the house dribbling into them till he caught me. I even made noises at my tea, but Mother only told me I was disgusting. It all seemed to hinge round that unhealthy habit of sleeping together, so I made a point of dropping into their bedroom and nosing round, talking to myself, so that they wouldn't know I was watching them, but they were never up to anything that I could see. In the end it beat me. It seemed to depend on being grownup and giving people rings, and I realized I'd have to wait.

But at the same time I wanted him to see that I was only waiting, not giving up the fight. One evening when he was being particularly obnoxious, chattering away well above my head, I let him have it.

"Mummy," I said, "do you know what I'm going to do when I grow up?"

"No, dear," she replied. "What?"

"I'm going to marry you," I said quietly.

Father gave a great guffaw out of him, but he didn't take me in. I knew it must only be pretense. And Mother, in spite of everything, was pleased. I felt she was probably relieved to know that one day Father's hold on her would be broken.

"Won't that be nice?" she said with a smile.

"It'll be very nice," I said confidently. "Because we're going to have lots and lots of babies."

"That's right, dear," she said placidly. "I think we'll have one soon, and then you'll have plenty of company."

I was no end pleased about that because it showed that in spite of the way she gave in to Father she still considered my wishes. Besides, it would put the Geneys in their place.

It didn't turn out like that, though. To begin with, she was very preoccupied—I supposed about where she would get the seventeen and six—and though Father took to staying out late in the evenings it did me no particular good. She stopped taking me for walks, became as touchy as blazes, and smacked me for nothing at all. Sometimes I wished I'd never mentioned the confounded baby—I seemed to have a genius for bringing calamity on myself.

And calamity it was! Sonny arrived in the most appalling hullabaloo—even that much he couldn't do without a fuss—and from the first moment I disliked him. He was a difficult child—so far as I was concerned he was always difficult—and demanded far too much attention. Mother was simply silly about him, and couldn't see when he was only showing off. As company he was worse than useless. He slept all day, and I had to go round the house on tiptoe to avoid waking him. It wasn't any longer a question of not waking Father. The slogan now was "Don't-wake-Sonny!" I couldn't understand why the child wouldn't sleep at the proper time, so whenever Mother's back was turned I woke him. Sometimes to keep him awake I pinched him as well. Mother caught me at it one day and gave me a most unmerciful flaking.

One evening, when Father was coming from work, I was playing trains in the front garden. I let on not to notice him; instead, I pretended to be talking to myself, and said in a loud voice: "If another bloody baby comes into this house, I'm going out."

Father stopped dead and looked at me over his shoulder.

"What's that you said?" he asked sternly.

"I was only talking to myself," I replied, trying to conceal my panic. "It's private."

He turned and went in without a word. Mind you, I intended it as a solemn warning, but its effect was quite different. Father started being quite nice to me. I could understand that, of course. Mother was quite sickening about Sonny. Even at mealtimes she'd get up and gawk at him in the cradle with an idiotic smile, and tell Father to do the same. He was always polite about it, but he looked so puzzled you could see he didn't know what she was talking about. He complained of the way Sonny cried at night, but she only got cross and said that Sonny never cried except when there was something up with him—which was a flaming lie, because Sonny never had anything up with him, and only cried for attention. It was really painful to see how simple-minded she was. Father wasn't attractive, but he had a fine intelligence. He saw through Sonny, and now he knew that I saw through him as well.

One night I woke with a start. There was someone beside me in the bed. For one wild moment I felt sure it must be Mother, having come to her senses and left Father for good, but then I heard Sonny in convulsions in the next room, and Mother saying: "There! There! There!" and I knew it wasn't she. It was Father. He was lying beside me, wide awake, breathing hard and apparently as mad as hell.

After a while it came to me what he was mad about. It was his turn now. After turning me out of the big bed, he had been turned out himself. Mother had no consideration now for anyone but that poisonous pup, Sonny. I couldn't help feeling sorry for Father. I had been through it all myself, and even at that age I was magnanimous. I began to stroke him down and say: "There! There!" He wasn't exactly responsive.

"Aren't you asleep either?" he snarled.

"Ah, come on and put your arm around us, can't you?" I said, and he did, in a sort of way. Gingerly, I suppose, is how you'd describe it. He was very bony but better than nothing.

At Christmas he went out of his way to buy me a really nice model railway.

QUESTIONS

1. Is the story narrated from the point of view of a young child or a mature man? **2.** Note that the narrator's most ardent wishes—for the return of his father and for a new baby in the house—are granted. What are the consequences for him? **3.** What specific details in the story contribute to the appropriateness of its title? **4.** With whom does the reader sympathize? How does the author control those sympathies?

WRITING TOPIC

Focusing on the ironies embodied in this story, describe the shifting relationships among the main characters.

Good Country People

FLANNERY O'CONNOR   [1925–1964]

Besides the neutral expression that she wore when she was alone, Mrs. Freeman had two others, forward and reverse, that she used for all her human dealings. Her forward expression was steady and driving like the advance of a heavy truck. Her eyes never swerved to left or right but turned as the story turned as if they followed a yellow line down the center of it. She seldom used the other expression because it was not often necessary for her to retract a statement, but when she did, her face came to a complete stop, there was an almost imperceptible movement of her black eyes, during which they seemed to be receding, and then the observer would see that Mrs. Freeman, though she might stand there as real as several grain sacks thrown on top of each other, was no longer there in spirit. As for getting anything across to her when this was the case, Mrs. Hopewell had given it up. She might talk her head off. Mrs. Freeman could never be brought to admit herself wrong on any point. She would stand there and if she could be brought to say anything, it was something like, "Well, I wouldn't of said it was and I wouldn't of said it wasn't," or letting her gaze range over the top kitchen shelf where there was an assortment of dusty bottles, she might remark, "I see you ain't ate many of them figs you put up last summer."

They carried on their most important business in the kitchen at breakfast. Every morning Mrs. Hopewell got up at seven o'clock and lit her gas heater and Joy's. Joy was her daughter, a large blonde girl who had an artificial leg. Mrs. Hopewell thought of her as a child though she was thirty-two years old and highly educated. Joy would get up while her mother was eating and lumber into the bathroom and slam the door, and before long, Mrs. Freeman would arrive at the back door. Joy would hear her mother call, "Come on in," and then they would talk for a while in low voices that were indistinguishable in the bathroom. By the time Joy came in, they had usually finished the weather report and were on one or the other of Mrs. Freeman's daughters, Glynese or Carramae. Joy called them Glycerin and Caramel. Glynese, a redhead, was eighteen and had many admirers; Carramae, a blonde, was only fifteen but already married and pregnant. She could not keep anything on her stomach. Every morning Mrs. Freeman told Mrs. Hopewell how many times she had vomited since the last report.

Mrs. Hopewell liked to tell people that Glynese and Carramae were two of the finest girls she knew and that Mrs. Freeman was a *lady* and that she was never ashamed to take her anywhere or introduce her to anybody they might meet. Then she would tell how she had happened to hire the Freemans in the first place and how they were a godsend to her and how she had had them four years. The reason for her keeping them so long was that they were not trash.

They were good country people. She had telephoned the man whose name they had given as a reference and he had told her that Mr. Freeman was a good farmer but that his wife was the nosiest woman ever to walk the earth. "She's got to be into everything," the man said. "If she don't get there before the dust settles, you can bet she's dead, that's all. She'll want to know all your business. I can stand him real good," he had said, "but me nor my wife neither could have stood that woman one more minute on this place." That had put Mrs. Hopewell off for a few days.

She had hired them in the end because there were no other applicants but she had made up her mind beforehand exactly how she would handle the woman. Since she was the type who had to be into everything, then, Mrs. Hopewell had decided, she would not only let her be into everything, she would *see to it* that she was into everything—she would give her the responsibility of everything, she would put her in charge. Mrs. Hopewell had no bad qualities of her own but she was able to use other people's in such a constructive way that she never felt the lack. She had hired the Freemans and she had kept them four years.

Nothing is perfect. This was one of Mrs. Hopewell's favorite sayings. Another was: that is life! And still another, the most important, was: well, other people have their opinions too. She would make these statements, usually at the table, in a tone of gentle insistence as if no one held them but her, and the large hulking Joy, whose constant outrage had obliterated every expression from her face, would stare just a little to the side of her, her eyes icy blue, with the look of someone who has achieved blindness by an act of will and means to keep it.

When Mrs. Hopewell said to Mrs. Freeman that life was like that, Mrs. Freeman would say, "I always said so myself." Nothing had been arrived at by anyone that had not first been arrived at by her. She was quicker than Mr. Freeman. When Mrs. Hopewell said to her after they had been on the place a while, "You know, you're the wheel behind the wheel," and winked, Mrs. Freeman had said, "I know it. I've always been quick. It's some that are quicker than others."

"Everybody is different," Mrs. Hopewell said.

"Yes, most people is," Mrs. Freeman said.

"It takes all kinds to make the world."

"I always said it did myself."

The girl was used to this kind of dialogue for breakfast and more of it for dinner; sometimes they had it for supper too. When they had no guest they ate in the kitchen because that was easier. Mrs. Freeman always managed to arrive at some point during the meal and to watch them finish it. She would stand in the doorway if it were summer but in the winter she would stand with one elbow on top of the refrigerator and look down on them, or she would stand by the gas heater, lifting the back of her skirt slightly. Occasionally she would stand against the wall and roll her head from side to side. At no time was she in any hurry to leave. All this was very trying on Mrs. Hopewell but she was a woman of great patience. She realized that nothing is perfect and that in the Freemans she had good country people and that if, in this day and age, you get good country people, you had better hang onto them.

She had had plenty of experience with trash. Before the Freemans she had averaged one tenant family a year. The wives of these farmers were not the kind you would want to be around you for very long. Mrs. Hopewell, who had divorced her husband long ago, needed someone to walk over the fields with her; and when Joy had to be impressed for these services, her remarks were usually so ugly and her face so glum that Mrs. Hopewell would say, "If you can't come pleasantly, I don't want you at all," to which the girl, standing square and rigid-shouldered with her neck thrust slightly forward, would reply, "If you want me, here I am—LIKE I AM."

Mrs. Hopewell excused this attitude because of the leg (which had been shot off in a hunting accident when Joy was ten). It was hard for Mrs. Hopewell to realize that her child was thirty-two now and that for more than twenty years she had had only one leg. She thought of her still as a child because it tore her heart to think instead of the poor stout girl in her thirties who had never danced a step or had any *normal* good times. Her name was really Joy but as soon as she was twenty-one and away from home, she had had it legally changed. Mrs. Hopewell was certain that she had thought and thought until she had hit upon the ugliest name in any language. Then she had gone and had the beautiful name, Joy, changed without telling her mother until after she had done it. Her legal name was Hulga.

When Mrs. Hopewell thought the name, Hulga, she thought of the broad blank hull of a battleship. She would not use it. She continued to call her Joy to which the girl responded but in a purely mechanical way.

Hulga had learned to tolerate Mrs. Freeman, who saved her from taking walks with her mother. Even Glynese and Carramae were useful when they occupied attention that might otherwise have been directed at her. At first she had thought she could not stand Mrs. Freeman for she had found that it was not possible to be rude to her. Mrs. Freeman would take on strange resentments and for days together she would be sullen but the source of her displeasure was always obscure; a direct attack, a positive leer, blatant ugliness to her face—these never touched her. And without warning one day, she began calling her Hulga.

She did not call her that in front of Mrs. Hopewell who would have been incensed but when she and the girl happened to be out of the house together, she would say something and add the name Hulga to the end of it, and the big spectacled Joy-Hulga would scowl and redden as if her privacy had been intruded upon. She considered the name her personal affair. She had arrived at it first purely on the basis of its ugly sound and then the full genius of its fitness had struck her. She had a vision of the name working like the ugly sweating Vulcan who stayed in the furnace and to whom, presumably, the goddess had to come when called. She saw it as the name of her highest creative act. One of her major triumphs was that her mother had not been able to turn her dust into

Joy, but the greater one was that she had been able to turn it herself into Hulga. However, Mrs. Freeman's relish for using the name only irritated her. It was as if Mrs. Freeman's beady steel-pointed eyes had penetrated far enough behind her face to reach some secret fact. Something about her seemed to fascinate Mrs. Freeman and then one day Hulga realized that it was the artificial leg. Mrs. Freeman had a special fondness for the details of secret infections, hidden deformities, assaults upon children. Of diseases, she preferred the lingering or incurable. Hulga had heard Mrs. Hopewell give her the details of the hunting accident, how the leg had been literally blasted off, how she had never lost consciousness. Mrs. Freeman could listen to it any time as if it had happened an hour ago.

When Hulga stumped into the kitchen in the morning (she could walk without making the awful noise but she made it—Mrs. Hopewell was certain—because it was ugly-sounding), she glanced at them and did not speak. Mrs. Hopewell would be in her red kimono with her hair tied around her head in rags. She would be sitting at the table, finishing her breakfast and Mrs. Freeman would be hanging by her elbow outward from the refrigerator, looking down at the table. Hulga always put her eggs on the stove to boil and then stood over them with her arms folded, and Mrs. Hopewell would look at her—a kind of indirect gaze divided between her and Mrs. Freeman—and would think that if she would only keep herself up a little, she wouldn't be so bad looking. There was nothing wrong with her face that a pleasant expression wouldn't help. Mrs. Hopewell said that people who looked on the bright side of things would be beautiful even if they were not.

Whenever she looked at Joy this way, she could not help but feel that it would have been better if the child had not taken the Ph.D. It had certainly not brought her out any and now that she had it, there was no more excuse for her to go to school again. Mrs. Hopewell thought it was nice for girls to go to school to have a good time but Joy had "gone through." Anyhow, she would not have been strong enough to go again. The doctors had told Mrs. Hopewell that with the best of care, Joy might see forty-five. She had a weak heart. Joy had made it plain that if it had not been for this condition, she would be far from these red hills and good country people. She would be in a university lecturing to people who knew what she was talking about. And Mrs. Hopewell could very well picture her there, looking like a scarecrow and lecturing to more of the same. Here she went about all day in a six-year-old skirt and a yellow sweat shirt with a faded cowboy on a horse embossed on it. She thought this was funny; Mrs. Hopewell thought it was idiotic and showed simply that she was still a child. She was brilliant but she didn't have a grain of sense. It seemed to Mrs. Hopewell that every year she grew less like other people and more like herself—bloated, rude, and squint-eyed. And she said such strange things! To her own mother she had said—without warning, without excuse, standing up in the middle of a meal with her face purple and her mouth half full—"Woman! do you ever look inside? Do you ever look inside and see what you are *not*?

God!" she had cried sinking down again and staring at her plate, "Malebranche was right: we are not our own light. We are not our own light!" Mrs. Hopewell had no idea to this day what brought that on. She had only made the remark, hoping Joy would take it in, that a smile never hurt anyone.

The girl had taken the Ph.D. in philosophy and this left Mrs. Hopewell at a complete loss. You could say, "My daughter is a nurse," or "My daughter is a school teacher," or even, "My daughter is a chemical engineer." You could not say, "My daughter is a philosopher." That was something that had ended with the Greeks and Romans. All day Joy sat on her neck in a deep chair, reading. Sometimes she went for walks but she didn't like dogs or cats or birds or flowers or nature or nice young men. She looked at nice young men as if she could smell their stupidity.

One day Mrs. Hopewell had picked up one of the books the girl had just put down and opening it at random, she read, "Science, on the other hand, has to assert its soberness and seriousness afresh and declare that it is concerned solely with what-is. Nothing—how can it be for science anything but a horror and a phantasm? If science is right, then one thing stands firm: science wishes to know nothing of nothing. Such is after all the strictly scientific approach to Nothing. We know it by wishing to know nothing of Nothing." These words had been underlined with a blue pencil and they worked on Mrs. Hopewell like some evil incantation in gibberish. She shut the book quickly and went out of the room as if she were having a chill.

This morning when the girl came in, Mrs. Freeman was on Carramae. "She thrown up four times after supper," she said, "and was up twict in the night after three o'clock. Yesterday she didn't do nothing but ramble in the bureau drawer. All she did. Stand up there and see what she could run up on."

"She's got to eat," Mrs. Hopewell muttered, sipping her coffee, while she watched Joy's back at the stove. She was wondering what the child had said to the Bible salesman. She could not imagine what kind of a conversation she could possibly have had with him.

He was a tall gaunt hatless youth who had called yesterday to sell them a Bible. He had appeared at the door, carrying a large black suitcase that weighted him so heavily on one side that he had to brace himself against the door facing. He seemed on the point of collapse but he said in a cheerful voice, "Good morning, Mrs. Cedars!" and set the suitcase down on the mat. He was not a bad-looking young man though he had on a bright blue suit and yellow socks that were not pulled up far enough. He had prominent face bones and a streak of sticky-looking brown hair falling across his forehead.

"I'm Mrs. Hopewell," she said.

"Oh!" he said, pretending to look puzzled but with his eyes sparkling, "I saw it said 'The Cedars,' on the mailbox so I thought you was Mrs. Cedars!" and he burst out in a pleasant laugh. He picked up the satchel and under cover of a pant, he fell forward into her hall. It was rather as if the suitcase had moved first, jerking him after it. "Mrs. Hopewell!" he said and grabbed her hand. "I hope you are well!" and he laughed again and then all at once his face sobered completely. He paused and gave her a straight earnest look and said, "Lady, I've come to speak of serious things."

"Well, come in," she muttered, none too pleased because her dinner was almost ready. He came into the parlor and sat down on the edge of a straight chair and put the suitcase between his feet and glanced around the room as if he were sizing her up by it. Her silver gleamed on the two sideboards; she decided he had never been in a room as elegant as this.

"Mrs. Hopewell," he began, using her name in a way that sounded almost intimate, "I know you believe in Chrustian service."

"Well yes," she murmured.

"I know," he said and paused, looking very wise with his head cocked on one side, "that you're a good woman. Friends have told me."

Mrs. Hopewell never liked to be taken for a fool. "What are you selling?" she asked.

"Bibles," the young man said and his eye raced around the room before he added, "I see you have no family Bible in your parlor, I see that is the one lack you got!"

Mrs. Hopewell could not say, "My daughter is an atheist and won't let me keep the Bible in the parlor." She said, stiffening slightly, "I keep my Bible by my bedside." This was not the truth. It was in the attic somewhere.

"Lady," he said, "the word of God ought to be in the parlor."

"Well, I think that's a matter of taste," she began. "I think . . ."

"Lady," he said, "for a Chrustian, the word of God ought to be in every room in the house besides in his heart. I know you're a Chrustian because I can see it in every line of your face."

She stood up and said, "Well, young man, I don't want to buy a Bible and I smell my dinner burning."

He didn't get up. He began to twist his hands and looking down at them, he said softly, "Well lady, I'll tell you the truth—not many people want to buy one nowadays and besides, I know I'm real simple. I don't know how to say a thing but to say it. I'm just a country boy." He glanced up into her unfriendly face. "People like you don't like to fool with country people like me!"

"Why!" she cried, "good country people are the salt of the earth! Besides, we all have different ways of doing, it takes all kinds to make the world go 'round. That's life!"

"You said a mouthful," he said.

"Why, I think there aren't enough good country people in the world!" she said, stirred. "I think that's what's wrong with it!"

His face had brightened. "I didn't inraduce myself," he said. "I'm Manley Pointer from out in the country around Willohobie, not even from a place, just from near a place."

"You wait a minute," she said. "I have to see about my dinner." She went out to the kitchen and found Joy standing near the door where she had been listening.

"Get rid of the salt of the earth," she said, "and let's eat."

Mrs. Hopewell gave her a pained look and turned the heat down under the vegetables. "*I* can't be rude to anybody," she murmured and went back into the parlor.

He had opened the suitcase and was sitting with a Bible on each knee.

"You might as well put those up," she told him. "I don't want one."

"I appreciate your honesty," he said. "You don't see any more real honest people unless you go way out in the country."

"I know," she said, "real genuine folks!" Through the crack in the door she heard a groan.

"I guess a lot of boys come telling you they're working their way through college," he said, "but I'm not going to tell you that. Somehow," he said, "I don't want to go to college. I want to devote my life to Chrustian service. See," he said, lowering his voice, "I got this heart condition. I may not live long. When you know it's something wrong with you and you may not live long, well then, lady . . ." He paused, with his mouth open, and stared at her.

He and Joy had the same condition! She knew that her eyes were filling with tears but she collected herself quickly and murmured, "Won't you stay for dinner? We'd love to have you!" and was sorry the instant she heard herself say it.

"Yes mam," he said in an abashed voice, "I would sher love to do that!"

Joy had given him one look on being introduced to him and then throughout the meal had not glanced at him again. He had addressed several remarks to her, which she had pretended not to hear. Mrs. Hopewell could not understand deliberate rudeness, although she lived with it, and she felt she had always to overflow with hospitality to make up for Joy's lack of courtesy. She urged him to talk about himself and he did. He said he was the seventh child of twelve and that his father had been crushed under a tree when he himself was eight year old. He had been crushed very badly, in fact, almost cut in two and was practically not recognizable. His mother had got along the best she could by hard working and she had always seen that her children went to Sunday School and that they read the Bible every evening. He was now nineteen year old and he had been selling Bibles for four months. In that time he had sold seventy-seven Bibles and had the promise of two more sales. He wanted to become a missionary because he thought that was the way you could do most for people. "He who losest his life shall find it," he said simply and he was so sincere, so genuine and earnest that Mrs. Hopewell would not for the world have smiled. He prevented his peas from sliding onto the table by blocking them with a piece of bread which he later cleaned his plate with. She could see Joy observing sidewise how he handled his knife and fork and she saw too that every few minutes, the boy would dart a keen appraising glance at the girl as if he were trying to attract her attention.

After dinner Joy cleared the dishes off the table and disappeared and Mrs. Hopewell was left to talk with him. He told her again about his childhood and his father's accident and about various things that had happened to him. Every five minutes or so she would stifle a yawn. He sat for two hours until finally she told him she must go because she had an appointment in town. He packed his Bibles and thanked her and prepared to leave, but in the doorway he stopped and wrung her hand and said that not on any of his trips had he met a lady as nice as her and he asked if he could come again. She had said she would always be happy to see him.

Joy had been standing in the road, apparently looking at something in the distance, when he came down the steps toward her, bent to the side with his heavy valise. He stopped where she was standing and confronted her directly. Mrs. Hopewell could not hear what he said but she trembled to think what Joy would say to him. She could see that after a minute Joy said something and that then the boy began to speak again, making an excited gesture with his free hand. After a minute Joy said something else at which the boy began to speak once more. Then to her amazement, Mrs. Hopewell saw the two of them walk off together, toward the gate. Joy had walked all the way to the gate with him and Mrs. Hopewell could not imagine what they had said to each other, and she had not yet dared to ask.

Mrs. Freeman was insisting upon her attention. She had moved from the refrigerator to the heater so that Mrs. Hopewell had to turn and face her in order to seem to be listening. "Glynese gone out with Harvey Hill again last night," she said. "She had this sty."

"Hill," Mrs. Hopewell said absently, "is that the one who works in the garage?"

"Nome, he's the one that goes to chiropracter school," Mrs. Freeman said. "She had this sty. Been had it two days. So she says when he brought her in the other night he says, 'Lemme get rid of that sty for you,' and she says, 'How?' and he says, 'You just lay yourself down acrost the seat of that car and I'll show you.' So she done it and he popped her neck. Kept on a-popping it several times until she made him quit. This morning," Mrs. Freeman said, "she ain't got no sty. She ain't got no traces of a sty."

"I never heard of that before," Mrs. Hopewell said.

"He ast her to marry him before the Ordinary," Mrs. Freeman went on, "and she told him she wasn't going to be married in no *office*."

"Well, Glynese is a fine girl," Mrs. Hopewell said, "Glynese and Carramae are both fine girls."

"Carramae said when her and Lyman was married Lyman said it sure felt sacred to him. She said he said he wouldn't take five hundred dollars for being married by a preacher."

"How much would he take?" the girl asked from the stove.

"He said he wouldn't take five hundred dollars," Mrs. Freeman repeated.

"Well we all have work to do," Mrs. Hopewell said.

"Lyman said it just felt more sacred to him," Mrs. Freeman said. "The doctor wants Carramae to eat prunes. Says instead of medicine. Says them cramps is coming from pressure. You know where I think it is?"

"She'll be better in a few weeks," Mrs. Hopewell said.

"In the tube," Mrs. Freeman said. "Else she wouldn't be as sick as she is."

Hulga had cracked her two eggs into a saucer and was bringing them to the table along with a cup of coffee that she had filled too full. She sat down carefully and began to eat, meaning to keep Mrs. Freeman there by questions if for any reason she showed an inclination to leave. She could perceive her mother's eye on her. The first roundabout question would be about the Bible salesman and she did not wish to bring it on. "How did he pop her neck?" she asked.

Mrs. Freeman went into a description of how he had popped her neck. She said he owned a '55 Mercury but that Glynese said she would rather marry a man with only a '36 Plymouth who would be married by a preacher. The girl asked what if he had a '32 Plymouth and Mrs. Freeman said what Glynese had said was a '36 Plymouth.

Mrs. Hopewell said there were not many girls with Glynese's common sense. She said what she admired in those girls was their common sense. She said that reminded her that they had a nice visitor yesterday, a young man selling Bibles. "Lord," she said, "he bored me to death but he was so sincere and genuine I couldn't be rude to him. He was just good country people, you know," she said,"—just the salt of the earth."

"I seen him walk up," Mrs. Freeman said, "and then later—I seen him walk off," and Hulga could feel the slight shift in her voice, the slight insinuation, that he had not walked off alone, had he? Her face remained expressionless but the color rose into her neck and she seemed to swallow it down with the next spoonful of egg. Mrs. Freeman was looking at her as if they had a secret together.

"Well, it takes all kinds of people to make the world go 'round," Mrs. Hopewell said. "It's very good we aren't all alike."

"Some people are more alike than others," Mrs. Freeman said.

Hulga got up and stumped, with about twice the noise that was necessary, into her room and locked the door. She was to meet the Bible salesman at ten o'clock at the gate. She had thought about it half the night. She had started thinking of it as a great joke and then she had begun to see profound implications in it. She had lain in bed imagining dialogues for them that were insane on the surface but that reached below to depths that no Bible salesman would be aware of. Their conversation yesterday had been of this kind.

He had stopped in front of her and had simply stood there. His face was bony and sweaty and bright, with a little pointed nose in the center of it, and his look was different from what it had been at the dinner table. He was gazing at her with open curiosity, with fascination, like a child watching a new fantastic animal at the zoo, and he was breathing as if he had run a great distance to reach her. His gaze seemed somehow familiar but she could not think where she had been regarded with it before. For almost a minute he didn't say anything. Then on what seemed an insuck of breath, he whispered, "You ever ate a chicken that was two days old?"

The girl looked at him stonily. He might have just put this question up for consideration at the meeting of a philosophical association. "Yes," she presently replied as if she had considered it from all angles.

"It must have been mighty small!" he said triumphantly and shook all over with little nervous giggles, getting very red in the face, and subsiding finally into his gaze of complete admiration, while the girl's expression remained exactly the same.

"How old are you?" he asked softly.

She waited some time before she answered. Then in a flat voice she said, "Seventeen."

His smiles came in succession like waves breaking on the surface of a little lake. "I see you got a wooden leg," he said. "I think you're real brave. I think you're real sweet."

The girl stood blank and solid and silent.

"Walk to the gate with me," he said. "You're a brave sweet little thing and I liked you the minute I seen you walk in the door."

Hulga began to move forward.

"What's your name?" he asked, smiling down on the top of her head.

"Hulga," she said.

"Hulga," he murmured, "Hulga. Hulga. I never heard of anybody name Hulga before. You're shy, aren't you, Hulga?" he asked.

She nodded, watching his large red hand on the handle of the giant valise.

"I like girls that wear glasses," he said. "I think a lot. I'm not like these people that a serious thought don't ever enter their heads. It's because I may die."

"I may die too," she said suddenly and looked up at him. His eyes were very small and brown, glittering feverishly.

"Listen," he said, "don't you think some people was meant to meet on account of what all they got in common and all? Like they both think serious thoughts and all?" He shifted the valise to his other hand so that the hand nearest her was free. He caught hold of her elbow and shook it a little. "I don't work on Saturday," he said. "I like to walk in the woods and see what Mother Nature is wearing. O'er the hills and far away. Pic-nics and things. Couldn't we go on a pic-nic tomorrow? Say yes, Hulga," he said and gave her a dying look as if he felt his insides about to drop out of him. He had even seemed to sway slightly toward her.

During the night she had imagined that she seduced him. She imagined that the two of them walked on the place until they came to the storage barn beyond the two back fields and there, she imagined, that things came to such a pass that she very easily seduced him and that then, of course, she had to reckon with his remorse. True genius can get an idea across even to an inferior mind. She imagined that she took his remorse in hand and changed it into a deeper understanding of life. She took all his shame away and turned it into something useful.

She set off for the gate at exactly ten o'clock, escaping without drawing Mrs.

Hopewell's attention. She didn't take anything to eat, forgetting that food is usually taken on a picnic. She wore a pair of slacks and a dirty white shirt, and as an afterthought, she had put some Vapex on the collar of it since she did not own any perfume. When she reached the gate no one was there.

She looked up and down the empty highway and had the furious feeling that she had been tricked, that he had only meant to make her walk to the gate after the idea of him. Then suddenly he stood up, very tall, from behind a bush on the opposite embankment. Smiling, he lifted his hat which was new and wide-brimmed. He had not worn it yesterday and she wondered if he had bought it for the occasion. It was toast-colored with a red and white band around it and was slightly too large for him. He stepped from behind the bush still carrying the black valise. He had on the same suit and the same yellow socks sucked down in his shoes from walking. He crossed the highway and said, "I knew you'd come!"

The girl wondered acidly how he had known this. She pointed to the valise and asked, "Why did you bring your Bibles?"

He took her elbow, smiling down on her as if he could not stop. "You can never tell when you'll need the word of God, Hulga," he said. She had a moment in which she doubted that this was actually happening and then they began to climb the embankment. They went down into the pasture toward the woods. The boy walked lightly by her side, bouncing on his toes. The valise did not seem to be heavy today; he even swung it. They crossed half the pasture without saying anything and then, putting his hand easily on the small of her back, he asked softly, "Where does your wooden leg join on?"

She turned an ugly red and glared at him and for an instant the boy looked abashed. "I didn't mean you no harm," he said. "I only meant you're so brave and all. I guess God takes care of you."

"No," she said, looking forward and walking fast, "I don't even believe in God."

At this he stopped and whistled. "No!" he exclaimed as if he were too astonished to say anything else.

She walked on and in a second he was bouncing at her side, fanning with his hat. "That's very unusual for a girl," he remarked, watching her out of the corner of his eye. When they reached the edge of the wood, he put his hand on her back again and drew her against him without a word and kissed her heavily.

The kiss, which had more pressure than feeling behind it, produced that extra surge of adrenalin in the girl that enables one to carry a packed trunk out of a burning house, but in her, the power went at once to the brain. Even before he released her, her mind, clear and detached and ironic anyway, was regarding him from a great distance, with amusement but with pity. She had never been kissed before and she was pleased to discover that it was an unexceptional experience and all a matter of the mind's control. Some people might enjoy drain water if they were told it was vodka. When the boy, looking expectant but uncertain, pushed her gently away, she turned and walked on, saying nothing as if such business, for her, were common enough.

He came along panting at her side, trying to help her when he saw a root that she might trip over. He caught and held back the long swaying blades of thorn vine until she had passed beyond them. She led the way and he came breathing heavily behind her. Then they came out on a sunlit hillside, sloping softly into another one a little smaller. Beyond, they could see the rusted top of the old barn where the extra hay was stored.

The hill was sprinkled with small pink weeds. "Then you ain't saved?" he asked suddenly, stopping.

The girl smiled. It was the first time she had smiled at him at all. "In my economy," she said, "I'm saved and you are damned but I told you I didn't believe in God."

Nothing seemed to destroy the boy's look of admiration. He gazed at her now as if the fantastic animal at the zoo had put its paw through the bars and given him a loving poke. She thought he looked as if he wanted to kiss her again and she walked on before he had the chance.

"Ain't there somewheres we can sit down sometime?" he murmured, his voice softening toward the end of the sentence.

"In that barn," she said.

They made for it rapidly as if it might slide away like a train. It was a large two-story barn, cool and dark inside. The boy pointed up the ladder that led into the loft and said, "It's too bad we can't go up there."

"Why can't we?" she asked.

"Yer leg," he said reverently.

The girl gave him a contemptuous look and putting both hands on the ladder, she climbed it while he stood below, apparently awestruck. She pulled herself expertly through the opening and then looked down at him and said, "Well, come on if you're coming," and he began to climb the ladder, awkwardly bringing the suitcase with him.

"We won't need the Bible," she observed.

"You never can tell," he said, panting. After he had got into the loft, he was a few seconds catching his breath. She had sat down in a pile of straw. A wide sheath of sunlight, filled with dust particles, slanted over her. She lay back against a bale, her face turned away, looking out the front opening of the barn where hay was thrown from a wagon into the loft. The two pink-speckled hillsides lay back against a dark ridge of woods. The sky was cloudless and cold blue. The boy dropped down by her side and put one arm under her and the other over her and began methodically kissing her face, making little noises like a fish. He did not remove his hat but it was pushed far enough back not to interfere. When her glasses got in his way, he took them off of her and slipped them into his pocket.

The girl at first did not return any of the kisses but presently she began to and after she had put several on his cheek, she reached his lips and remained there, kissing him again and again as if she were trying to draw all the breath out of him. His breath was clear and sweet like a child's and the kisses were sticky like a child's. He mumbled about loving her and about knowing when he first seen her that he loved her, but the mumbling was like the sleepy fretting of a child being put to sleep by his mother. Her mind, throughout this, never stopped or lost itself for a second to her feelings. "You ain't said you love me none," he whispered finally, pulling back from her. "You got to say that."

She looked away from him off into the hollow sky and then down at a black ridge and then down farther into what appeared to be two green swelling lakes. She didn't realize he had taken her glasses but this landscape could not seem exceptional to her for she seldom paid any close attention to her surroundings.

"You got to say it," he repeated. "You got to say you love me."

She was always careful how she committed herself. "In a sense," she began, "if you use the word loosely, you might say that. But it's not a word I use. I don't have illusions. I'm one of those people who see *through* to nothing."

The boy was frowning. "You got to say it. I said it and you got to say it," he said.

The girl looked at him almost tenderly. "You poor baby," she murmured. "It's just as well you don't understand," and she pulled him by the neck, face-down, against her. "We are all damned," she said, "but some of us have taken off our blindfolds and see that there's nothing to see. It's a kind of salvation."

The boy's astonished eyes looked blankly through the ends of her hair. "Okay," he almost whined, "but do you love me or don'tcher?"

"Yes," she said and added, "in a sense. But I must tell you something. There mustn't be anything dishonest between us." She lifted his head and looked him in the eye. "I am thirty years old," she said. "I have a number of degrees."

The boy's look was irritated but dogged. "I don't care," he said. "I don't care a thing about what all you done. I just want to know if you love me or don'tcher?" and he caught her to him and wildly planted her face with kisses until she said, "Yes, yes."

"Okay then," he said, letting her go. "Prove it."

She smiled, looking dreamily out on the shifty landscape. She had seduced him without even making up her mind to try. "How?" she asked, feeling that he should be delayed a little.

He leaned over and put his lips to her ear. "Show me where your wooden leg joins on," he whispered.

The girl uttered a sharp little cry and her face instantly drained of color. The obscenity of the suggestion was not what shocked her. As a child she had sometimes been subject to feelings of shame but education had removed the last traces of that as a good surgeon scrapes for cancer; she would no more have felt it over what he was asking than she would have believed in his Bible. But she was as sensitive about the artificial leg as a peacock about his tail. No one ever touched it but her. She took care of it as someone else would his soul, in private and almost with her own eyes turned away. "No," she said.

"I known it," he muttered, sitting up. "You're just playing me for a sucker."

"Oh no no!" she cried. "It joins on at the knee. Only at the knee. Why do you want to see it?"

The boy gave her a long penetrating look. "Because," he said, "it's what makes you different. You ain't like anybody else."

She sat staring at him. There was nothing about her face or her round freezing-blue eyes to indicate that this had moved her; but she felt as if her heart had stopped and left her mind to pump her blood. She decided that for the first time in her life she was face to face with real innocence. This boy, with an instinct that came from beyond wisdom, had touched the truth about her. When after a minute, she said in a hoarse high voice, "All right," it was like surrendering to him completely. It was like losing her own life and finding it again, miraculously, in his.

Very gently he began to roll the slack leg up. The artificial limb, in a white sock and brown flat shoe, was bound in a heavy material like canvas and ended in an ugly jointure where it was attached to the stump. The boy's face and his voice were entirely reverent as he uncovered it and said, "Now show me how to take it off and on."

She took it off for him and put it back on again and then he took it off himself, handling it as tenderly as if it were a real one. "See!" he said with a delighted child's face. "Now I can do it myself!"

"Put it back on," she said. She was thinking that she would run away with him and that every night he would take the leg off and every morning put it back on again. "Put it back on," she said.

"Not yet," he murmured, setting it on its foot out of her reach. "Leave it off for a while. You got me instead."

She gave a little cry of alarm but he pushed her down and began to kiss her again. Without the leg she felt entirely dependent on him. Her brain seemed to have stopped thinking altogether and to be about some other function that it was not very good at. Different expressions raced back and forth over her face. Every now and then the boy, his eyes like two steel spikes, would glance behind him where the leg stood. Finally she pushed him off and said, "Put it back on me now."

"Wait," he said. He leaned the other way and pulled the valise toward him and opened it. It had a pale blue spotted lining and there were only two Bibles in it. He took one of these out and opened the cover of it. It was hollow and contained a pocket flask of whiskey, a pack of cards, and a small blue box with printing on it. He laid these out in front of her one at a time in an evenly spaced row, like one presenting offerings at the shrine of a goddess. He put the blue box in her hand. THIS PRODUCT TO BE USED ONLY FOR THE PREVENTION OF DISEASE, she read, and dropped it. The boy was unscrewing the top of the flask. He stopped and pointed, with a smile, to the deck of cards. It was not an ordinary deck but one with an obscene picture on the back of each card. "Take a swig," he said, offering her the bottle first. He held it in front of her, but like one mesmerized, she did not move.

Her voice when she spoke had an almost pleading sound. "Aren't you," she murmured, "aren't you just good country people?"

The boy cocked his head. He looked as if he were just beginning to understand that she might be trying to insult him. "Yeah," he said, curling his lip slightly, "but it ain't held me back none. I'm as good as you any day in the week."

"Give me my leg," she said.

He pushed it farther away with his foot. "Come on now, let's begin to have us a good time," he said coaxingly. "We ain't got to know one another good yet."

"Give me my leg!" she screamed and tried to lunge for it but he pushed her down easily.

"What's the matter with you all of a sudden?" he asked, frowning as he screwed the top on the flask and put it quickly back inside the Bible. "You just a while ago said you didn't believe in nothing. I thought you was some girl!"

Her face was almost purple. "You're a Christian!" she hissed. "You're a fine Christian! You're just like them all—say one thing and do another. You're a perfect Christian, you're . . ."

The boy's mouth was set angrily. "I hope you don't think," he said in a lofty indignant tone, "that I believe in that crap! I may sell Bibles but I know which end is up and I wasn't born yesterday and I know where I'm going!"

"Give me my leg!" she screeched. He jumped up so quickly that she barely saw him sweep the cards and the blue box back into the Bible and throw the Bible into the valise. She saw him grab the leg and then she saw it for an instant slanted forlornly across the inside of the suitcase with a Bible at either side of its opposite ends. He slammed the lid shut and snatched up the valise and swung it down the hole and then stepped through himself.

When all of him had passed but his head, he turned and regarded her with a look that no longer had any admiration in it. "I've gotten a lot of interesting things," he said. "One time I got a woman's glass eye this way. And you needn't to think you'll catch me because Pointer ain't really my name. I use a different name at every house I call at and don't stay nowhere long. And I'll tell you another thing, Hulga," he said, using the name as if he didn't think much of it, "you ain't so smart. I been believing in nothing ever since I was born!" and then the toast-colored hat disappeared down the hole and the girl was left, sitting on the straw in the dusty sunlight. When she turned her churning face toward the opening, she saw his blue figure struggling successfully over the green speckled lake.

Mrs. Hopewell and Mrs. Freeman, who were in the back pasture, digging up onions, saw him emerge a little later from the woods and head across the meadow toward the highway. "Why, that looks like that nice dull young man that tried to sell me a Bible yesterday," Mrs. Hopewell said, squinting. "He must have been selling them to the Negroes back in there. He was so simple," she said, "but I guess the world would be better off if we were all that simple."

Mrs. Freeman's gaze drove forward and just touched him before he disappeared under the hill. Then she returned her attention to the evil-smelling onion shoot she was lifting from the ground. "Some can't be that simple," she said. "I know I never could."

QUESTIONS

1. Why does Joy feel that changing her name to Hulga is "her highest creative act"? **2.** In what ways do Mrs. Freeman's descriptions of her daughters Glynese and Carramae contribute to the theme of the story? **3.** Is the title ironic? Explain.

WRITING TOPICS

1. Does this story have any admirable characters or heroes in the conventional sense? Explain. **2.** Why does Hulga agree to meet with Manley Pointer? Does Hulga's experience with Manley Pointer confirm her cynical philosophy of "nothing"?

The Lesson

TONI CADE BAMBARA   [b. 1939]

Back in the days when everyone was old and stupid or young and foolish and me and Sugar were the only ones just right, this lady moved on our block with nappy hair and proper speech and no makeup. And quite naturally we laughed at her, laughed the way we did at the junk man who went about his business like he was some big-time president and his sorry-ass horse his secretary. And we kinda hated her too, hated the way we did the winos who cluttered up our parks and pissed on our handball walls and stank up our hallways and stairs so you couldn't halfway play hide-and-seek without a goddamn gas mask. Miss Moore was her name. The only woman on the block with no first name. And she was black as hell, cept for her feet, which were fish-white and spooky. And she was always planning these boring-ass things for us to do, us being my cousin, mostly, who lived on the block cause we all moved North the same time and to the same apartment then spread out gradual to breathe. And our parents would yank our heads into some kinda shape and crisp up our clothes so we'd be presentable for travel with Miss Moore, who always looked like she was going to church, though she never did. Which is just one of the things the grownups talked about when they talked behind her back like a dog. But when she came calling with some sachet she'd sewed up or some gingerbread she'd made or some book, why then they'd all be too embarrassed to turn her down and we'd get handed over all spruced up. She'd been to college and said it was only right that she should take responsibility for the young ones' education, and she not even related by marriage or blood. So they'd go for it. Specially Aunt Gretchen. She was the main gofer in the family. You got some old dumb shit foolishness you want somebody to go for, you send for Aunt Gretchen. She been screwed into the go-along for so long, it's a blood-deep natural thing with her. Which is how she got saddled with me and Sugar and Junior in the first place while our mothers were in a la-de-da apartment up the block having a good ole time.

So this one day Miss Moore rounds us all up at the mailbox and it's puredee hot and she's knockin herself out about arithmetic. And school suppose to let up in summer I heard, but she don't never let up. And the starch in my pinafore scratching the shit outta me and I'm really hating this nappy-head bitch and her goddamn college degree. I'd much rather go to the pool or to the show where it's cool. So me and Sugar leaning on the mailbox being surly, which is a Miss Moore word. And Flyboy checking out what everybody brought for lunch. And Fat Butt already wasting his peanut-butter-and-jelly sandwich like the pig he is. And Junebug punchin on Q.T.'s arm for potato chips. And Rosie Giraffe shifting from one hip to the other waiting for somebody to step on her foot or ask her if she from Georgia so she can kick ass, preferably Mercedes'. And Miss Moore asking us do we know what money is, like we a bunch of retards. I mean real money, she say, like it's only poker chips or monopoly papers we lay on the grocer. So right away I'm tired of this and say so. And would much rather snatch Sugar and go to the Sunset and terrorize the West Indian kids and take their hair ribbons and their money too. And Miss Moore files that remark away for next week's lesson on brotherhood, I can tell. And finally I say we oughta get to the subway cause it's cooler and besides we might meet some cute boys. Sugar done swiped her mama's lipstick, so we ready.

So we heading down the street and she's boring us silly about what things cost and what our parents make and how much goes for rent and how money ain't divided up right in this country. And then she gets to the part about we all poor and live in the slums, which I don't feature. And I'm ready to speak on that, but she steps out in the street and hails two cabs just like that. Then she hustles half the crew in with her and hands me a five-dollar bill and tells me to calculate 10 percent tip for the driver. And we're off. Me and Sugar and Junebug and Flyboy hangin out the window and hollering to everybody, putting lipstick on each other cause Flyboy a faggot anyway, and making farts with our sweaty armpits. But I'm mostly trying to figure how to spend this money. But they all fascinated with the meter ticking and Junebug starts laying bets as to how much it'll read when Flyboy can't hold his breath no more. Then Sugar lays bets as to how much it'll be when we get there. So I'm stuck. Don't nobody want to go for my plan, which is to jump out at the next light and run off to the first bar-b-que we can find. Then the driver tells us to get the hell out cause we there already. And the meter reads eighty-five cents. And I'm stalling to figure out the tip and Sugar say give him a dime. And I decide he don't need it bad as I do, so later for him. But then he tries to take off with Junebug foot still in the door so we talk about his mama something ferocious. Then we check out that we on Fifth Avenue and everybody dressed up in stockings. One lady in a fur coat, hot as it is. White folks crazy.

"This is the place," Miss Moore say, presenting it to us in the voice she uses at the museum. "Let's look in the windows before we go in."

"Can we steal?" Sugar asks very serious like she's getting the ground rules squared away before she plays. "I beg your pardon," say Miss Moore, and we fall out. So she leads us around the windows of the toy store and me and Sugar screamin, "This is mine, that's mine, I gotta have that, that was made for me, I was born for that," till Big Butt drowns us out.

"Hey, I'm goin to buy that there."

"That there? You don't even know what it is, stupid."

"I do so," he say punchin on Rosie Giraffe. "It's a microscope."

"Whatcha gonna do with a microscope, fool?"

"Look at things."

"Like what, Ronald?" ask Miss Moore. And Big Butt ain't got the first notion. So here go Miss Moore gabbing about the thousands of bacteria in a drop of water and the somethinorother in a speck of blood and the million and one living things in the air around us is invisible to the naked eye. And what she say that for? Junebug go to town on that "naked" and we rolling. Then Miss

Moore ask what it cost. So we all jam into the window smudgin it up and the price tag say $300. So then she ask how long'd take for Big Butt and Junebug to save up their allowances. "Too long," I say. "Yeh," adds Sugar, "outgrown it by that time." And Miss Moore say no, you never outgrow learning instruments. "Why, even medical students and interns and," blah, blah, blah. And we ready to choke Big Butt for bringing it up in the first damn place.

"This here costs four hundred eighty dollars," say Rosie Giraffe. So we pile up all over her to see what she pointin out. My eyes tell me it's a chunk of glass cracked with something heavy, and different-color inks dripped into the splits, then the whole thing put into a oven or something. But for $480 it don't make sense.

"That's a paperweight made of semi-precious stones fused together under tremendous pressure," she explains slowly, with her hands doing the mining and all the factory work.

"So what's a paperweight?" asks Rosie Giraffe.

"To weigh paper with, dumbbell," say Flyboy, the wise man from the East.

"Not exactly," say Miss Moore, which is what she say when you warm or way off too. "It's to weigh paper down so it won't scatter and make your desk untidy." So right away me and Sugar curtsy to each other and then to Mercedes who is more the tidy type.

"We don't keep paper on top of the desk in my class," say Junebug, figuring Miss Moore crazy or lyin one.

"At home, then," she say. "Don't you have a calendar and a pencil case and a blotter and a letter-opener on your desk at home where you do your homework?" And she know damn well what our homes look like 'cause she nosys around in them every chance she gets.

"I don't even have a desk," say Junebug. "Do we?"

"No. And I don't get no homework neither," says Big Butt.

"And I don't even have a home," say Flyboy like he do at school to keep the white folks off his back and sorry for him. Send this poor kid to camp posters, is his specialty.

"I do," says Mercedes. "I have a box of stationery on my desk and a picture of my cat. My godmother bought the stationery and the desk. There's a big rose on each sheet and the envelopes smell like roses."

"Who wants to know about your smelly-ass stationery," say Rosie Giraffe fore I can get my two cents in.

"It's important to have a work area all your own so that . . ."

"Will you look at this sailboat, please," say Flyboy, cuttin her off and pointin to the thing like it was his. So once again we tumble all over each other to gaze at this magnificent thing in the toy store which is just big enough to maybe sail two kittens across the pond if you strap them to the posts tight. We all start reciting the price tag like we in assembly. "Handcrafted sailboat of fiberglass at one thousand one hundred ninety-five dollars."

"Unbelievable," I hear myself say and am really stunned. I read it again for myself just in case the group recitation put me in a trance. Same thing. For some reason this pisses me off. We look at Miss Moore and she lookin at us, waiting for I dunno what.

"Who'd pay all that when you can buy a sailboat set for a quarter at Pop's, a tube of glue for a dime, and a ball of string for eight cents? It must have a motor and a whole lot else besides," I say. "My sailboat cost me about fifty cents."

"But will it take water?" say Mercedes with her smart ass.

"Took mine to Alley Pond Park once," say Flyboy. "String broke. Lost it. Pity."

"Sailed mine in Central Park and it keeled over and sank. Had to ask my father for another dollar."

"And you got the strap," laugh Big Butt. "The jerk didn't even have a string on it. My old man wailed on his behind."

Little Q.T. was staring hard at the sailboat and you could see he wanted it bad. But he too little and somebody'd just take it from him. So what the hell. "This boat for kids, Miss Moore?"

"Parents silly to buy something like that just to get all broke up," say Rosie Giraffe.

"That much money it should last forever," I figure.

"My father'd buy it for me if I wanted it."

"Your father, my ass," say Rosie Giraffe getting a chance to finally push Mercedes.

"Must be rich people shop here," say Q.T.

"You are a very bright boy," say Flyboy. "What was your first clue?" And he rap him on the head with the back of his knuckles, since Q.T. the only one he could get away with. Though Q.T. liable to come up behind you years later and get his licks in when you half expect it.

"What I want to know is," I says to Miss Moore though I never talk to her, I wouldn't give the bitch that satisfaction, "is how much a real boat costs? I figure a thousand'd get you a yacht any day."

"Why don't you check that out," she says, "and report back to the group?" Which really pains my ass. If you gonna mess up a perfectly good swim day least you could do is have some answers. "Let's go in," she say like she got something up her sleeve. Only she don't lead the way. So me and Sugar turn the corner to where the entrance is, but when we get there I kinda hang back. Not that I'm scared, what's there to be afraid of, just a toy store. But I feel funny, shame. But what I got to be shamed about? Got as much right to go in as anybody. But somehow I can't seem to get hold of the door, so I step away for Sugar to lead. But she hangs back too. And I look at her and she looks at me and this is ridiculous. I mean, damn, I have never ever been shy about doing nothing or going nowhere. But then Mercedes steps up and then Rosie Giraffe and Big Butt crowd in behind and shove, and next thing we all stuffed into the doorway with only Mercedes squeezing past us, smoothing out her jumper and walking right down the aisle. Then the rest of us tumble in like a glued-together jigsaw done all wrong. And people lookin at us. And it's like the time me and

Sugar crashed into the Catholic church on a dare. But once we got in there and everything so hushed and holy and the candles and the bowin and the handkerchiefs on all the drooping heads, I just couldn't go through with the plan. Which was for me to run up to the altar and do a tap dance while Sugar played the nose flute and messed around in the holy water. And Sugar kept givin me the elbow. Then later teased me so bad I tied her up in the shower and turned it on and locked her in. And she'd be there till this day if Aunt Gretchen hadn't finally figured I was lyin about the boarder takin a shower.

Same thing in the store. We all walkin on tiptoe and hardly touchin the games and puzzles and things. And I watched Miss Moore who is steady watchin us like she waitin for a sign. Like Mama Drewery watches the sky and sniffs the air and takes note of just how much slant is in the bird formation. Then me and Sugar bump smack into each other, so busy gazing at the toys, 'specially the sailboat. But we don't laugh and go into our fat-lady bump-stomach routine. We just stare at that price tag. Then Sugar run a finger over the whole boat. And I'm jealous and want to hit her. Maybe not her, but I sure want to punch somebody in the mouth.

"Watcha bring us here for, Miss Moore?"

"You sound angry, Sylvia. Are you mad about something?" Givin me one of them grins like she tellin a grown-up joke that never turns out to be funny. And she's lookin very closely at me like maybe she plannin to do my portrait from memory. I'm mad, but I won't give her that satisfaction. So I slouch around the store bein very bored and say, "Let's go."

Me and Sugar at the back of the train watchin the tracks whizzin by large then small then gettin gobbled up in the dark. I'm thinkin about this tricky toy I saw in the store. A clown that somersaults on a bar then does chin-ups just cause you yank lightly at his leg. Cost $35. I could see me askin my mother for a $35 birthday clown. "You wanna who that costs what?" she'd say, cocking her head to the side to get a better view of the hole in my head. Thirty-five dollars could buy new bunk beds for Junior and Gretchen's boy. Thirty-five dollars and the whole household could go visit Granddaddy Nelson in the country. Thirty-five dollars would pay for the rent and the piano bill too. Who are these people that spend that much for performing clowns and $1000 for toy sailboats? What kinda work they do and how they live and how come we ain't in on it? Where we are is who we are, Miss Moore always pointin out. But it don't necessarily have to be that way, she always adds then waits for somebody to say that poor people have to wake up and demand their share of the pie and don't none of us know what kind of pie she talkin about in the first damn place. But she ain't so smart cause I still got her four dollars from the taxi and she sure ain't gettin it. Messin up my day with this shit. Sugar nudges me in my pocket and winks.

Miss Moore lines us up in front of the mailbox where we started from, seem like years ago, and I got a headache for thinkin so hard. And we lean all over each other so we can hold up under the draggy-ass lecture she always finishes us off with at the end before we thank her for borin us to tears. But she just looks at us like she readin tea leaves. Finally she say, "Well, what did you think of F. A. O. Schwarz?"

Rosie Giraffe mumbles, "White folks crazy."

"I'd like to go there again when I get my birthday money," says Mercedes, and we shove her out the pack so she has to lean on the mailbox by herself.

"I'd like a shower. Tiring day," say Flyboy.

Then Sugar surprises me by sayin, "You know, Miss Moore, I don't think all of us here put together eat in a year what that sailboat costs." And Miss Moore lights up like somebody goosed her. "And?" she say, urging Sugar on. Only I'm standin on her foot so she don't continue.

"Imagine for a minute what kind of society it is in which some people can spend on a toy what it would cost to feed a family of six or seven. What do you think?"

"I think," say Sugar pushing me off her feet like she never done before, cause I whip her ass in a minute, "that this is not much of a democracy if you ask me. Equal chance to pursue happiness means an equal crack at the dough, don't it?" Miss Moore is besides herself and I am disgusted with Sugar's treachery. So I stand on her foot one more time to see if she'll shove me. She shuts up, and Miss Moore looks at me, sorrowfully I'm thinkin. And somethin weird is goin on, I can feel it in my chest.

"Anybody else learn anything today?" lookin dead at me. I walk away and Sugar has to run to catch up and don't even seem to notice when I shrug her arm off my shoulder.

"Well, we got four dollars anyway," she says.

"Uh hunh."

"We could go to Hascombs and get half a chocolate layer and then go to the Sunset and still have plenty money for potato chips and ice cream sodas."

"Uh hunh."

"Race you to Hascombs," she say.

We start down the block and she gets ahead which is O.K. by me cause I'm goin to the West End and then over to the Drive to think this day through. She can run if she want to and even run faster. But ain't nobody gonna beat me at nuthin.

QUESTIONS

1. Characterize the narrator of this story. **2.** How does the narrator describe her neighborhood? How does she feel when Miss Moore calls the neighborhood a slum? **3.** F. A. O. Schwarz is a famous toy store on Fifth Avenue in New York City, located about three miles south of Harlem where, doubtless, the children live. What lesson does Miss Moore convey by taking them there?

WRITING TOPIC

Is there any evidence at the end of the story that the narrator has been changed by the experience?

INNOCENCE
AND
EXPERIENCE

The Mysterious Rose Garden, by Aubrey Beardsley

POETRY

The Tyger   1794

WILLIAM BLAKE [1757–1827]

Tyger! Tyger! burning bright
In the forests of the night,
What immortal hand or eye
Could frame thy fearful symmetry?

In what distant deeps or skies
Burnt the fire of thine eyes?
On what wings dare he aspire?
What the hand, dare seize the fire?

And what shoulder, & what art,
Could twist the sinews of thy heart?   10
And when thy heart began to beat,
What dread hand? & what dread feet?

What the hammer? what the chain?
In what furnace was thy brain?
What the anvil? what dread grasp
Dare its deadly terrors clasp?

When the stars threw down their spears,
And water'd heaven with their tears,
Did he smile his work to see?
Did he who made the Lamb make thee?   20

Tyger! Tyger! burning bright
In the forests of the night,
What immortal hand or eye
Dare frame thy fearful symmetry?

It Is a Beauteous Evening   1807

WILLIAM WORDSWORTH [1770–1850]

It is a beauteous evening, calm and free,
The holy time is quiet as a Nun
Breathless with adoration; the broad sun
Is sinking down in its tranquility;
The gentleness of heaven broods o'er the Sea:
Listen! the mighty Being is awake,
And doth with his eternal motion make
A sound like thunder—everlastingly.
Dear Child! Dear Girl! that walkest with me here,[1]
If thou appear untouched by solemn thought,   10
Thy nature is not therefore less divine:
Thou liest in Abraham's bosom[2] all the year;
And Worship'st at the Temple's inner shrine,[3]
God being with thee when we know it not.

QUESTION
Why does the poet excuse his "Dear Child's" lack of solemnity?

WRITING TOPIC
Compare this poem with McGinley's "Country Club Sunday."

On First Looking into Chapman's Homer[1]   1816

JOHN KEATS [1795–1821]

Much have I travelled in the realms of gold,
And many goodly states and kingdoms seen:

It Is a Beauteous Evening
  [1] Wordsworth is walking with Caroline, his illegitimate daughter.
  [2] Close to God. See Luke 16:22.
  [3] The Temple's inner shrine is its holiest place. See 1 Kings 8:6.

On First Looking into Chapman's Homer
  [1] George Chapman published translations of *The Iliad* (1611) and *The Odyssey* (1616).

Round many western islands have I been
Which bards in fealty to Apollo[2] hold.
Oft of one wide expanse had I been told
That deep-browed Homer ruled as his demesne;°   realm
Yet did I never breathe its pure serene°   clear air
Till I heard Chapman speak out loud and bold:
Then felt I like some watcher of the skies
When a new planet swims into his ken;   10
Or like stout Cortez[3] when with eagle eyes
He stared at the Pacific—and all his men
Looked at each other with a wild surmise—
    Silent, upon a peak in Darien.

My Last Duchess   1842

ROBERT BROWNING   [1812–1889]

FERRARA

That's my last Duchess painted on the wall,
Looking as if she were alive. I call
That piece a wonder, now: Frà Pandolf's[1] hands
Worked busily a day, and there she stands.
Will't please you sit and look at her? I said
"Frà Pandolf" by design, for never read
Strangers like you that pictured countenance,
The depth and passion of its earnest glance,
But to myself they turned (since none puts by
The curtain I have drawn for you, but I)   10
And seemed as they would ask me, if they durst,
How such a glance came there; so, not the first
Are you to turn and ask thus. Sir, 'twas not
Her husband's presence only, called that spot
Of joy into the Duchess' cheek: perhaps
Frà Pandolf chanced to say "Her mantle laps

---

[2] The god of poetry.
[3] Keats mistakenly attributes the discovery of the Pacific Ocean by Europeans to Hernando Cortez (1485–1547), the Spanish conqueror of Mexico. Vasco Nuñez de Balboa (1475–1517) first saw the Pacific from a mountain located in eastern Panama.

My Last Duchess
[1] Frà Pandolf and Claus of Innsbruck (mentioned in the last line) are fictitious artists.

"Over my lady's wrist too much," or "Paint
"Must never hope to reproduce the faint
"Half-flush that dies along her throat": such stuff
Was courtesy, she thought, and cause enough   20
For calling up that spot of joy. She had
A heart—how shall I say?—too soon made glad,
Too easily impressed; she liked whate'er
She looked on, and her looks went everywhere.
Sir, 'twas all one! My favor at her breast,
The dropping of the daylight in the West,
The bough of cherries some officious fool
Broke in the orchard for her, the white mule
She rode with round the terrace—all and each
Would draw from her alike the approving speech,   30
Or blush, at least. She thanked men—good! but thanked
Somehow—I know not how—as if she ranked
My gift of a nine-hundred-years-old name
With anybody's gift. Who'd stoop to blame
This sort of trifling? Even had you skill
In speech—which I have not—to make your will
Quite clear to such an one, and say, "Just this
"Or that in you disgusts me; here you miss,
"Or there exceed the mark"—and if she let
Herself be lessoned so, nor plainly set
Her wits to yours, forsooth, and made excuse,   40
—E'en then would be some stooping; and I choose
Never to stoop. Oh sir, she smiled, no doubt,
Whene'er I passed her; but who passed without
Much the same smile? This grew; I gave commands;
Then all smiles stopped together. There she stands
As if alive. Will't please you rise? We'll meet
The company below, then. I repeat,
The Count your master's known munificence
Is ample warrant that no just pretense   50
Of mine for dowry will be disallowed;
Though his fair daughter's self, as I avowed
At starting, is my object. Nay, we'll go
Together down, sir. Notice Neptune, though,
Taming a sea-horse, thought a rarity,
Which Claus of Innsbruck cast in bronze for me!

QUESTIONS

1. To whom is the Duke speaking and what is the occasion?   **2.** Contrast the
Duke's moral and aesthetic sensibility.

WRITING TOPIC
How is the reader supposed to respond to the Duke's judgment of his last Duchess? Explain.

Hap   1898

THOMAS HARDY   [1840–1928]

If but some vengeful god would call to me
From up the sky, and laugh: "Thou suffering thing,
Know that thy sorrow is my ecstasy,
That thy love's loss is my hate's profiting!"

Then would I bear it, clench myself, and die,
Steeled by the sense of ire unmerited;
Half-eased in that a Powerfuller than I
Had willed and meted me the tears I shed.

But not so. How arrives it joy lies slain,
And why unblooms the best hope ever sown?   10
—Crass Casualty° obstructs the sun and rain,   chance
And dicing Time for gladness casts a moan. . . .
These purblind Doomsters[1] had as readily strown
Blisses about my pilgrimage as pain.

The Ruined Maid   1902

THOMAS HARDY   [1840–1928]

"O Melia, my dear, this does everything crown!
Who could have supposed I should meet you in Town?
And whence such fair garments, such prosperi-ty?"
"O didn't you know I'd been ruined?" said she.

"You left us in tatters, without shoes or socks,
Tired of digging potatoes, and spudding up docks;°   digging herbs
And now you've gay bracelets and bright feathers three!"
"Yes: that's how we dress when we're ruined," said she.

Hap
   [1] Those who decide one's fate.

"At home in the barton° you said 'thee' and 'thou,'   farmyard
And 'thik onn,' and 'theäs oon,' and 't'other; but now   10
Your talking quite fits 'ee for high compa-ny!"
"Some polish is gained with one's ruin," said she.

"Your hands were like paws then, your face blue and bleak
But now I'm bewitched by your delicate cheek,
And your little gloves fit as on any la-dy!"
"We never do work when we're ruined," said she.

"You used to call home-life a hag-ridden dream,
And you'd sigh, and you'd sock; but at present you seem
To know not of megrims° or melancho-ly!"   sick headaches
"True. One's pretty lively when ruined," said she.   20

"I wish I had feathers, a fine sweeping gown,
And a delicate face, and could strut about Town!"
"My dear—a raw country girl, such as you be,
Cannot quite expect that. You ain't ruined," said she.

Spring and Fall   (1880)

TO A YOUNG CHILD

GERARD MANLEY HOPKINS [1844–1889]

Márgarét, áre you gríeving
Over Goldengrove unleaving?°   losing leaves
Leáves, líke the things of man, you
With your fresh thoughts care for, can you?
Áh! ás the heart grows older
It will come to such sights colder
By and by, nor spare a sigh
Though worlds of wanwood leafmeal[1] lie;
And yet you wíll weep and know why.
Now no matter, child, the name: 10
Sórrow's spríngs are the same.
Nor mouth had, no nor mind, expressed
What heart heard of, ghost° guessed: soul
It ís the blight man was born for,
It is Margaret you mourn for.

Spring and Fall
   [1] Pale woods littered with mouldering leaves.

QUESTIONS
1. In this poem Margaret grieves over the passing of spring and the coming of fall. What does the coming of fall symbolize?   **2.** Why, when Margaret grows older, will she not sigh over the coming of fall?   **3.** What are "Sorrow's springs" (l. 11)?

Terence, This Is Stupid Stuff[1]

1896

A. E. HOUSMAN   [1859–1936]

"Terence, this is stupid stuff:
You eat your victuals fast enough;
There can't be much amiss, 'tis clear,
To see the rate you drink your beer.
But oh, good Lord, the verse you make,
It gives a chap the bellyache.
The cow, the old cow, she is dead;
It sleeps well, the hornéd head:
We poor lads, 'tis our turn now
To hear such tunes as killed the cow.   10
Pretty friendship 'tis to rhyme
Your friends to death before their time
Moping melancholy mad:
Come, pipe a tune to dance to, lad."

Why, if 'tis dancing you would be,
There's brisker pipes than poetry.
Say, for what were hopyards meant,
Or why was Burton built on Trent?[2]
Oh many a peer of England brews
Livelier liquor than the Muse,   20
And malt does more than Milton can
To justify God's ways to man.[3]
Ale, man, ale's the stuff to drink
For fellows whom it hurts to think:

Terence, This Is Stupid Stuff
[1] Housman originally titled the volume in which this poem appeared *The Poems of Terence Hearsay*. Terence was a Roman satiric playwright.
[2] The river Trent provides water for the town's brewing industry.
[3] In the invocation to *Paradise Lost*, Milton declares that his epic will "justify the ways of God to men."

Look into the pewter pot
To see the world as the world's not.
And faith, 'tis pleasant till 'tis past:
The mischief is that 'twill not last.
Oh I have been to Ludlow fair
And left my necktie God knows where,   30
And carried halfway home, or near,
Pints and quarts of Ludlow beer:
Then the world seemed none so bad,
And I myself a sterling lad;
And down in lovely muck I've lain,
Happy till I woke again.
Then I saw the morning sky.
Heigho, the tale was all a lie;
The world, it was the old world yet,
I was I, my things were wet,   40
And nothing now remained to do
But begin the game anew.

    Therefore, since the world has still
Much good, but much less good than ill,
And while the sun and moon endure
Luck's a chance, but trouble's sure,
I'd face it as a wise man would,
And train for ill and not for good.
'Tis true the stuff I bring for sale
Is not so brisk a brew as ale: 50
Out of a stem that scored the hand
I wrung it in a weary land.
But take it: if the smack is sour,
The better for the embittered hour;
It should do good to heart and head
When your soul is in my soul's stead;
And I will friend you, if I may,
In the dark and cloudy day.

    There was a king reigned in the East:
There, when kings will sit to feast,   60
They get their fill before they think
With poisoned meat and poisoned drink.
He gathered all that springs to birth
From the many-venomed earth;
First a little, thence to more,
He sampled all her killing store;
And easy, smiling, seasoned sound,
Sate the king when healths went round.

They put arsenic in his meat
And stared aghast to watch him eat;   70
They poured strychnine in his cup
And shook to see him drink it up:
They shook, they stared as white's their shirt:
Them it was their poison hurt.
—I tell the tale that I heard told.
Mithridates, he died old.[4]

QUESTIONS
1. What does the speaker of the first fourteen lines object to in Terence's poetry? **2.** What is Terence's response to the criticism of his verse? What function of true poetry is implied by his comparison of bad poetry with liquor?

WRITING TOPIC
How does the story of Mithridates (lines 59–76) illustrate the theme of the poem?

Adam's Curse   1902

W. B. YEATS   [1865–1939]

We sat together at one summer's end,
That beautiful mild woman, your close friend,
And you and I, and talked of poetry.
I said, 'A line will take us hours maybe;
Yet if it does not seem a moment's thought,
Our stitching and unstitching has been naught.

Better go down upon your marrow-bones
And scrub a kitchen pavement, or break stones
Like an old pauper, in all kinds of weather;
For to articulate sweet sounds together   10
Is to work harder than all these, and yet
Be thought an idler by the noisy set
Of bankers, schoolmasters, and clergymen
The martyrs call the world.'

                          And thereupon
That beautiful mild woman for whose sake
There's many a one shall find out all heartache

---

[4] Mithridates, the King of Pontus (in Asia Minor), reputedly immunized himself against poisons by administering to himself gradually increasing doses.

On finding that her voice is sweet and low
Replied, 'To be born woman is to know—
Although they do not talk of it at school—   20
That we must labour to be beautiful.'

I said, 'It's certain there is no fine thing
Since Adam's fall but needs much labouring.
There have been lovers who thought love should be
So much compounded of high courtesy
That they would sigh and quote with learned looks
Precedents out of beautiful old books;
Yet now it seems an idle trade enough.'

We sat grown quiet at the name of love;
We saw the last embers of daylight die,
And in the trembling blue-green of the sky   30
A moon, worn as if it had been a shell
Washed by time's waters as they rose and fell
About the stars and broke in days and years.

I had a thought for no one's but your ears:
That you were beautiful, and that I strove
To love you in the old high way of love;
That it had all seemed happy, and yet we'd grown
As weary-hearted as that hollow moon.

Leda and the Swan[1]   1928

WILLIAM BUTLER YEATS   [1865–1939]

A sudden blow: the great wings beating still
Above the staggering girl, her thighs caressed
By the dark webs, her nape caught in his bill;
He holds her helpless breast upon his breast.

How can those terrified vague fingers push
The feathered glory from her loosening thighs?

Leda and the Swan
    [1] In Greek myth, Zeus, in the form of a swan, rapes Leda. As a consequence, Helen and Clytemnestra are born. Each sister marries the king of a city-state; Helen marries Menelaus and Clytemnestra marries Agamemnon. Helen, the most beautiful woman on earth, elopes with Paris, a prince of Troy, an act that precipitates the Trojan War in which Agamemnon commands the combined Greek armies. The war ends with the destruction of Troy. Agamemnon, when he returns to his home, is murdered by his unfaithful wife.

And how can body, laid in that white rush,
But feel the strange heart beating where it lies?

A shudder in the loins engenders there
The broken wall, the burning roof and tower   10
And Agamemnon dead.
                              Being so caught up,
So mastered by the brute blood of the air,
Did she put on his knowledge with his power
Before the indifferent beak could let her drop?

Birches   1916

ROBERT FROST   [1874–1963]

When I see birches bend to left and right
Across the lines of straighter darker trees,
I like to think some boy's been swinging them.
But swinging doesn't bend them down to stay.
Ice-storms do that. Often you must have seen them
Loaded with ice a sunny winter morning
After a rain. They click upon themselves
As the breeze rises, and turn many-colored
As the stir cracks and crazes their enamel.
Soon the sun's warmth makes them shed crystal shells   10
Shattering and avalanching on the snow-crust—
Such heaps of broken glass to sweep away
You'd think the inner dome of heaven had fallen.
They are dragged to the withered bracken by the load,
And they seem not to break; though once they are bowed
So low for long, they never right themselves:
You may see their trunks arching in the woods
Years afterwards, trailing their leaves on the ground
Like girls on hands and knees that throw their hair
Before them over their heads to dry in the sun.   20
But I was going to say when Truth broke in
With all her matter-of-fact about the ice-storm
I should prefer to have some boy bend them
As he went out and in to fetch the cows—
Some boy too far from town to learn baseball,
Whose only play was what he found himself,
Summer or winter, and could play alone.
One by one he subdued his father's trees
By riding them down over and over again

Until he took the stiffness out of them,   30
And not one but hung limp, not one was left
For him to conquer. He learned all there was
To learn about not launching out too soon
And so not carrying the tree away
Clear to the ground. He always kept his poise
To the top branches, climbing carefully
With the same pains you use to fill a cup
Up to the brim, and even above the brim.
Then he flung outward, feet first, with a swish,
Kicking his way down through the air to the ground.   40
So was I once myself a swinger of birches.
And so I dream of going back to be.
It's when I'm weary of considerations,
And life is too much like a pathless wood
Where your face burns and tickles with the cobwebs
Broken across it, and one eye is weeping
From a twig's having lashed across it open.
I'd like to get away from earth awhile
And then come back to it and begin over.
May no fate willfully misunderstand me
And half grant what I wish and snatch me away   50
Not to return. Earth's the right place for love:
I don't know where it's likely to go better.
I'd like to go by climbing a birch tree,
And climb black branches up a snow-white trunk
Toward heaven, till the tree could bear no more,
But dipped its top and set me down again.
That would be good both going and coming back.
One could do worse than be a swinger of birches.

Piano   1918

D. H. LAWRENCE [1885–1930]

Softly, in the dusk, a woman is singing to me;
Taking me back down the vista of years, till I see
A child sitting under the piano, in the boom of the tingling strings
And pressing the small, poised feet of a mother who smiles as she sings.

In spite of myself, the insidious mastery of song
Betrays me back, till the heart of me weeps to belong
To the old Sunday evenings at home, with winter outside
And hymns in the cozy parlour, the tinkling piano our guide.

So now it is vain for the singer to burst into clamour
With the great black piano appassionato. The glamour   10
Of childish days is upon me, my manhood is cast
Down in the flood of remembrance, I weep like a child for the past.

To Carry the Child   1966

STEVIE SMITH [1902–1971]

To carry the child into adult life
Is good? I say it is not,
To carry the child into adult life
Is to be handicapped.

The child in adult life is defenceless
And if he is grown-up, knows it,
And the grown-up looks at the childish part
And despises it.

The child, too, despises the clever grown-up,
The man-of-the-world, the frozen,   10
For the child has the tears alive on his cheek
And the man has none of them.

As the child has colours, and the man sees no
Colours or anything,
Being easy only in things of the mind,
The child is easy in feeling.

Easy in feeling, easily excessive
And in excess powerful,
For instance, if you do not speak to the child
He will make trouble.   20

You would say a man had the upper hand
Of the child, if a child survive,
But I say the child has fingers of strength
To strangle the man alive.

Oh! it is not happy, it is never happy,
To carry the child into adulthood,
Let the children lie down before full growth
And die in their infanthood
And be guilty of no man's blood.

But oh the poor child, the poor child, what can he do,   30
Trapped in a grown-up carapace,
But peer outside of his prison room
With the eye of an anarchist?

Incident   1925

COUNTEE CULLEN   [1903–1946]

Once riding in old Baltimore,
    Heart-filled, head-filled with glee,
I saw a Baltimorean
    Keep looking straight at me.

Now I was eight and very small,
    And he was no whit bigger,
And so I smiled, but he poked out
    His tongue and called me, "Nigger."

I saw the whole of Baltimore
    From May until December: 10
Of all the things that happened there
    That's all that I remember.

Country Club Sunday   1946

PHYLLIS McGINLEY   [1905–1978]

It is a beauteous morning, calm and free.
    The fairways sparkle. Gleam the shaven grasses.
Mirth fills the locker rooms and, hastily,
    Stewards fetch ice, fresh towels, and extra glasses.

On terraces the sandaled women freshen
    Their lipstick; gather to gossip, poised and cool;
And the shrill adolescent takes possession,
    Plunging and splashing, of the swimming pool.

It is a beauteous morn, opinion grants.
    Nothing remains of last night's Summer Formal   10
Save palms and streamers and the wifely glance,

Directed with more watchfulness than normal,
At listless mate who tugs his necktie loose,
Moans, shuns the light, and gulps tomato juice.

QUESTION

1. Compare this poem with Wordsworth's "It Is a Beauteous Evening" (p. 72).
What is the author's purpose in parodying the opening line of the Wordsworth poem?

Tears   1981

JOSEPHINE JACOBSEN   [b. 1908]

Tears leave no mark on the soil
or pavement; certainly not in sand
or in any known rain forest.
Never a mark on stone.
You would think that no one in Persepolis
or Ur ever wept.[1]

You would assume that, like Alice,[2]
we would all be swimming, buffeted
in a tide of tears.
But they disappear. Their heat goes.   10
Yet the globe is salt
With that savor.

The animals want no part in this.
The hare both screams and weeps
at her death, one poet says.
The stag, at death, rolls round drops
down his muzzle; but he is in
Shakespeare's forest.[3]

These cases are mythically rare.
No, it is the human being who persistently   20
weeps; in some countries, openly, in others, not.
Children who, even when frightened, weep most hopefully;

Tears
   [1] Persepolis, the capital city of the Persian kings, was destroyed by Alexander the Great. Ur was a principal city in Babylonia.
   [2] An allusion to Lewis Carroll's *Alice in Wonderland*.
   [3] That is, an imaginary forest.

women, licensed weepers;
men, in secret, or childishly; or nobly.

Could tears not make up a sea of their mass?
It could be salt and wild enough;
it could rouse storms and sink ships,
erode, erode its shores:
tears of rage, of love, of torture,
of loss. Of loss.   30

Must you see the future
in order to weep? Or the past?
Is that why the animals
refuse to shed tears?
But what of the present, the tears of the present?
The awful relief, like breath

after strangling? The generosity
in the verb *to shed?*
They are a classless possession
yet not to be found in the museum   40
of even our greatest city.
Sometimes what was human, turns
into an animal, dry-eyed.

QUESTIONS
1. Why would one think that no one in Persepolis or Ur ever wept? **2.** What distinguishes real animals from mythical animals? What distinguishes human beings from animals? What is the point of the last two lines?

Fern Hill   1946

DYLAN THOMAS [1914–1953]

Now as I was young and easy under the apple boughs
About the lilting house and happy as the grass was green,
    The night above the dingle° starry,   small wooded valley
        Time let me hail and climb
      Golden in the heydays of his eyes,
And honored among wagons I was prince of the apple towns
And once below a time I lordly had the trees and leaves
        Trail with daisies and barley
      Down the rivers of the windfall light.

And I was green and carefree, famous among the barns   10
About the happy yard and singing as the farm was home,
    In the sun that is young once only,
       Time let me play and be
    Golden in the mercy of his means,
And green and golden I was huntsman and herdsman, the calves
Sang to my horn, the foxes on the hills barked clear and cold,
       And the sabbath rang slowly
    In the pebbles of the holy streams.

All the sun long it was running, it was lovely, the hay
Fields high as the house, the tunes from the chimneys, it was air   20
    And playing, lovely and watery
    And fire green as grass.
    And nightly under the simple stars
As I rode to sleep the owls were bearing the farm away,
All the moon long I heard, blessed among stables, the nightjars[1]
    Flying with the ricks, and the horses
      Flashing into the dark.

And then to awake, and the farm, like a wanderer white
With the dew, come back, the cock on his shoulder: it was all
    Shining, it was Adam and maiden,   30
      The sky gathered again
    And the sun grew round that very day.
So it must have been after the birth of the simple light
In the first, spinning place, the spellbound horses walking warm
    Out of the whinnying green stable
      On to the fields of praise.

And honored among foxes and pheasants by the gay house
Under the new made clouds and happy as the heart was long,
    In the sun born over and over,
      I ran my heedless ways,   40
    My wishes raced through the house high hay
And nothing I cared, at my sky blue trades, that time allows
In all his tuneful turning so few and such morning songs
    Before the children green and golden
      Follow him out of grace.

Nothing I cared, in the lamb white days, that time would take me
Up to the swallow thronged loft by the shadow of my hand,

Fern Hill
  [1] Nightjars are harsh-sounding nocturnal birds.

In the moon that is always rising,
    Nor that riding to sleep
I should hear him fly with the high fields   50
And wake to the farm forever fled from the childless land.
Oh as I was young and easy in the mercy of his means,
    Time held me green and dying
Though I sang in my chains like the sea.

QUESTIONS

1. What emotional impact does the color imagery in the poem provide? **2.** Trace the behavior of "time" in the poem. **3.** Fairy tales often begin with the words "once upon a time." Why does Thomas alter that formula in
line 7? **4.** Explain the paradox in line 53.

WRITING TOPICS

1. Lines 17–18, 25, 45–46 incorporate religious language and biblical allusion.
How do those allusions clarify the poet's vision of his childhood? **2.** Compare
this poem with Gerard Manley Hopkins's "Spring and Fall."

Curiosity   1959

ALASTAIR REID [b. 1926]

may have killed the cat; more likely
the cat was just unlucky, or else curious
to see what death was like, having no cause
to go on licking paws, or fathering
litter on litter of kittens, predictably.

    Nevertheless, to be curious
is dangerous enough. To distrust
what is always said, what seems,
to ask odd questions, interfere in dreams,
leave home, smell rats, have hunches   10
does not endear him to those doggy circles
where well-smelt baskets, suitable wives, good lunches
are the order of things, and where prevails
much wagging of incurious heads and tails.

    Face it. Curiosity
will not cause him to die—
only lack of it will.

Never to want to see
the other side of the hill,
or that improbable country   20
where living is an idyll
(although a probable hell)
would kill us all.
Only the curious
have, if they live, a tale
worth telling at all.

    Dogs say he loves too much, is irresponsible,
is changeable, marries too many wives,
deserts his children, chills all dinner tables
with tales of his nine lives.   30
Well, he is lucky. Let him be
nine-lived and contradictory,
curious enough to change, prepared to pay
the cat price, which is to die
and die again and again,
each time with no less pain.
A cat minority of one
is all that can be counted on
to tell the truth. And what he has to tell
on each return from hell   40
is this: that dying is what the living do,
that dying is what the loving do,
and that dead dogs are those who do not know
that hell is where, to live, they have to go.

April Inventory   1959

W. D. SNODGRASS   [b. 1926]

The green catalpa tree has turned
All white; the cherry blooms once more.
In one whole year I haven't learned
A blessed thing they pay you for.
The blossoms snow down in my hair;
The trees and I will soon be bare.

The trees have more than I to spare.
The sleek, expensive girls I teach,
Younger and pinker every year,

Bloom gradually out of reach.   10
The pear tree lets its petals drop
Like dandruff on a tabletop.

The girls have grown so young by now
I have to nudge myself to stare.
This year they smile and mind me how
My teeth are falling with my hair.
In thirty years I may not get
Younger, shrewder, or out of debt.

The tenth time, just a year ago,
I made myself a little list
Of all the things I'd ought to know;   20
Then told my parents, analyst,
And everyone who's trusted me
I'd be substantial, presently.

I haven't read one book about
A book or memorized one plot.
Or found a mind I didn't doubt.
I learned one date. And then forgot.
And one by one the solid scholars
Get the degrees, the jobs, the dollars.   30

And smile above their starchy collars.
I taught my classes Whitehead's notions;
One lovely girl, a song of Mahler's.
Lacking a source-book or promotions,
I showed one child the colors of
A luna moth and how to love.

I taught myself to name my name,
To bark back, loosen love and crying;
To ease my woman so she came,
To ease an old man who was dying.   40
I have not learned how often I
Can win, can love, but choose to die.

I have not learned there is a lie
Love shall be blonder, slimmer, younger;
That my equivocating eye
Loves only by my body's hunger;
That I have poems, true to feel,
Or that the lovely world is real.

While scholars speak authority
And wear their ulcers on their sleeves,   50
My eyes in spectacles shall see
These trees procure and spend their leaves.
There is a value underneath
The gold and silver in my teeth.

Though trees turn bare and girls turn wives,
We shall afford our costly seasons;
There is a gentleness survives
That will outspeak and has its reasons.
There is a loveliness exists,
Preserves us. Not for specialists.   60

QUESTIONS
1. What do the words "I have not learned" (ll. 41, 43) mean in the context of the poem? **2.** In what way does the tone of the first four stanzas differ from the tone of the last two? **3.** What is the meaning of "specialists" in the last line? **4.** What is the speaker's conception of teaching?

WRITING TOPIC
Explicate the final stanza of this poem. Is it an appropriate conclusion? Explain.

Cinderella   1971

ANNE SEXTON   [1928–1974]

You always read about it:
the plumber with twelve children
who wins the Irish Sweepstakes.
From toilets to riches.
That story.

Or the nursemaid,
some luscious sweet from Denmark
who captures the oldest son's heart.
From diapers to Dior.
That story.   10

Or a milkman who serves the wealthy,
eggs, cream, butter, yogurt, milk,
the white truck like an ambulance

who goes into real estate
and makes a pile.
From homogenized to martinis at lunch.

Or the charwoman
who is on the bus when it cracks up
and collects enough from the insurance.
From mops to Bonwit Teller.   20
That story.

Once
the wife of a rich man was on her deathbed
and she said to her daughter Cinderella:
Be devout. Be good. Then I will smile
down from heaven in the seam of a cloud.
The man took another wife who had
two daughters, pretty enough
but with hearts like blackjacks.
Cinderella was their maid.   30
She slept on the sooty hearth each night
and walked around looking like Al Jolson.
Her father brought presents home from town,
jewels and gowns for the other women
but the twig of a tree for Cinderella.
She planted that twig on her mother's grave
and it grew to a tree where a white dove sat.
Whenever she wished for anything the dove
would drop it like an egg upon the ground.
The bird is important, my dears, so heed him.   40

Next came the ball, as you all know.
It was a marriage market.
The prince was looking for a wife.
All but Cinderella were preparing
and gussying up for the big event.
Cinderella begged to go too.
Her stepmother threw a dish of lentils
into the cinders and said: Pick them
up in an hour and you shall go.
The white dove brought all his friends;   50
all the warm wings of the fatherland came,
and picked up the lentils in a jiffy.
No, Cinderella, said the stepmother,
you have no clothes and cannot dance.
That's the way with stepmothers.

Cinderella went to the tree at the grave
and cried forth like a gospel singer:
Mama! Mama! My turtledove,
send me to the prince's ball!
The bird dropped down a golden dress   60
and delicate little gold slippers.
Rather a large package for a simple bird.
So she went. Which is no surprise.
Her stepmother and sisters didn't
recognize her without her cinder face
and the prince took her hand on the spot
and danced with no other the whole day.

As nightfall came she thought she'd better
get home. The prince walked her home
and she disappeared into the pigeon house   70
and although the prince took an axe and broke
it open she was gone. Back to her cinders.
These events repeated themselves for three days.
However on the third day the prince
covered the palace steps with cobbler's wax
and Cinderella's gold shoe stuck upon it.

Now he would find whom the shoe fit
and find his strange dancing girl for keeps.
He went to their house and the two sisters
were delighted because they had lovely feet.   80
The eldest went into a room to try the slipper on
but her big toe got in the way so she simply
sliced it off and put on the slipper.
The prince rode away with her until the white dove
told him to look at the blood pouring forth.
That is the way with amputations.
They don't just heal up like a wish.
The other sister cut off her heel
but the blood told as blood will.
The prince was getting tired.   90
He began to feel like a shoe salesman
but he gave it one last try.
This time Cinderella fit into the shoe
like a love letter into its envelope.

At the wedding ceremony
the two sisters came to curry favor
and the white dove pecked their eyes out.

Two hollow spots were left
like soup spoons.
Cinderella and the prince   100
lived, they say, happily ever after,
like two dolls in a museum case
never bothered by diapers or dust,
never arguing over the timing of an egg,
never telling the same story twice,
never getting a middle-aged spread,
their darling smiles pasted on for eternity.
Regular Bobbsey Twins.[1]
That story.

QUESTIONS

1.   Where does one usually find the first four "stories" mentioned in the poem? Why do such stories interest readers?   2.   The story of Cinderella, of course, is well known. Do you remember your feelings at the success of Cinderella? How are those feelings modified by the last stanza?

WRITING TOPIC

Arguably, the language and formal structure of this poem are rather prosaic. Describe, by examining the image patterns and individual lines, the qualities that make the piece a poem.

First Confession   1961

X. J. KENNEDY   [b. 1929]

Blood thudded in my ears. I scuffed,
    Steps stubborn, to the telltale booth
Beyond whose curtained portal coughed
    The robed repositor of truth.

The slat shot back. The universe
    Bowed down his cratered dome to hear

Cinderella
[1] The ever-cheerful central figures in a series of children's books.

Enumerated my each curse,
    The sip snitched from my old man's beer.

My sloth pride envy lechery,
    The dime held back from Peter's Pence   10
With which I'd bribed my girl to pee
    That I might spy her instruments.

Hovering scale-pans when I'd done
    Settled their balance slow as silt
While in the restless dark I burned
    Bright as a brimstone in my guilt

Until as one feeds birds he doled
    Seven Our Fathers and a Hail
Which I to double-scrub my soul
    Intoned twice at the altar rail   20

Where Sunday in seraphic light
    I knelt, as full of grace as most,
And stuck my tongue out at the priest:
    A fresh roost for the Holy Ghost.

Advice to My Son   1965

PETER MEINKE   [b. 1932]

The trick is, to live your days
as if each one may be your last
(for they go fast, and young men lose their lives
in strange and unimaginable ways)
but at the same time, plan long range
(for they go slow: if you survive
the shattered windshield and the bursting shell
you will arrive
at our approximation here below
of heaven or hell).   10

To be specific, between the peony and the rose
plant squash and spinach, turnips and tomatoes;

beauty is nectar
and nectar, in a desert, saves—
but the stomach craves stronger sustenance
than the honied vine.

Therefore, marry a pretty girl
after seeing her mother;
speak truth to one man,
work with another;   20
and always serve bread with your wine.

But, son,
always serve wine.

QUESTIONS
1. Explain how the advice of lines 17–21 is logically related to the preceding
lines. **2.** What do the final two lines tell the reader about the speaker?

WRITING TOPIC
The advice of the first stanza seems contradictory. In what ways does the second
stanza attempt to resolve the contradiction or explain "The trick" (l. 1)? What do
the various plants and the bread and wine symbolize?

In a Spring Still Not Written Of   1965

ROBERT WALLACE   [b. 1932]

This morning
with a class of girls outdoors, I saw
how frail poems are
in a world burning up with flowers,
in which, overhead,
the great elms
—green, and tall—
stood carrying leaves in their arms.

The girls listened equally
to my drone, reading, and to the bees'   10
ricocheting
among them for the blossom on the bone,
or gazed off at a distant mower's

astronomies of green
and clover, flashing,
threshing in the new, untarnished sunlight.

And all the while, dwindling,
tinier, the voices—Yeats, Marvell, Donne—
sank drowning
in a spring still not written of,   20
as only the sky
clear above the brick bell-tower
—blue, and white—
was shifting toward the hour.

Calm, indifferent, cross-legged
or on elbows half-lying in the grass—
how should the great dead
tell them of dying?
They will come to time for poems at last,
when they have found they are no more   30
the beautiful and young
all poems are for.

QUESTIONS
1. What is the speaker's attitude toward the "class of girls" he is teaching? Toward his job as a teacher? 2. Explain the meaning of the title. 3. Explain the
various meanings of "drone" (l. 10).

WRITING TOPIC
Explain the paradox developed in this poem.

My Mother   1970

ROBERT MEZEY   [b. 1935]

My mother writes from Trenton,
a comedian to the bone
but underneath, serious
and all heart. "Honey," she says,

"be a mensch[1] and Mary too,
its no good to worry, you
are doing the best you can
your Dad and everyone
thinks you turned out very well
as long as you pay your bills   10
nobody can say a word
you can tell them to drop dead
so save a dollar it can't
hurt—remember Frank you went
to highschool with? he still lives
with his wife's mother, his wife
works while he writes his books and
did he ever sell a one
the four kids run around naked
36 and he's never had,   20
you'll forgive my expression
even a pot to piss in
or a window to throw it,
such a smart boy he couldn't
read the footprints on the wall
honey you think you know all
the answers you don't, please try
to put some money away
believe me it wouldn't hurt
artist shmartist life's too short   30
for that kind of, forgive me,
horseshit, I know what you want
better than you, all that counts
is to make a good living
and the best of everything,
as Sholem Aleichem said
he was a great writer did
you ever read his books dear,
you should make what he makes a year
anyway he says some place   40
Poverty is no disgrace
but its no honor either
that's what I say,
                    love,
                          Mother"

My Mother
   [1] Man, in the sense of "human being."

A Poem About Intelligence for My Brothers and Sisters   1980

JUNE JORDAN   [b. 1936]

A few year back and they told me Black
means a hole where other folks
got brain/it was like the cells in the heads
of Black children was out to every hour on the hour naps
Scientists called the phenomenon the Notorious
Jensen Lapse, remember?[1]
Anyway I was thinking
about how to devise
a test for the wise
like a Stanford-Binet   10
for the C. I. A.
you know?
Take Einstein
being the most the unquestionable the outstanding
the maximal mind of the century
right?
And I'm struggling against this lapse leftover
from my Black childhood to fathom why
anybody should say so:
E = mc squared?   20
I try that on this old lady live on my block:
She sweeping away Saturday night from the stoop
and mad as can be because some absolute
jackass have left a kingsize mattress where
she have to sweep around it stains and all she
don't want to know nothing about in the first place
"Mrs. Johnson!" I say, leaning on the gate
between us: "What you think about somebody come up with an *E* equals
    M C 2?"
"How you doin," she answer me, sideways, like she don't   30
want to let on she know I ain
combed my hair yet and here it is
Sunday morning but still I have the nerve

A Poem About Intelligence . . .
  [1] An allusion to Arthur Robert Jensen (b. 1923), an educational psychologist whose long essay entitled "How Much Can We Boost IQ and Scholastic Achievement?" *Harvard Educational Review*, 39 (1969), was perceived by many as an argument that poor educational achievement was a function of inherited intellectual inferiority.

to be bothering serious work with these crazy
questions about
"*E* equals what you say again, dear?"
Then I tell her, "Well
also this same guy? I think
he was undisputed Father of the Atom Bomb!"
"That right." She mumbles or grumbles, not too politely   40
"And dint remember to wear socks when he put on
his shoes!" I add on (getting desperate)
at which point Mrs. Johnson take herself and her broom
a very big step down the stoop away from me
"And never did nothing for nobody in particular
lessen it was a committee
and
used to say, 'What time is it?'
and
you'd say, 'Six o'clock.'   50
and
he'd say, 'Day or night?'
and
and he never made nobody a cup of tea
in his whole brilliant life!"
"and
(my voice rises slightly)
and
he dint never boogie neither: never!"

"Well," say Mrs. Johnson, "Well, honey,   60
I do guess
that's genius for you."

The Last Song on the Jukebox   1983

DAVID KIRBY   [b. 1944]

It was a song about a man, a woman,
another man, and a car. The man
wanted to borrow the other man's car
but he didn't think it right
on account of his going out with
the woman, who was supposed to be the
other man's girlfriend, on the sly.

The woman didn't care. The man
cared, but not so much that he
didn't borrow it anyway. So they   10
went to a roadhouse. They had
several drinks, and the band played
rhythm and blues. Then they went
to a motel. Someone who knew the
other man told, but he got the
room number wrong. The other man
broke into the wrong room and
shot a preacher in the leg,
giving the man and the woman a
chance to escape. What could have   20
been tragic is now seen as comical,
at least with the passage of years.
Today the other man has suspicions
that cannot be verified. He has
sold the car, saying that he cannot
stand the sight of it. The man
no longer sees the woman on the
sly. The woman, who has since married
the other man, still doesn't care.
Neither does the preacher. He was   30
glad he got shot, he'll say from
time to time; he needed the pain.

INNOCENCE
AND
EXPERIENCE

The Red Armchair, 1931 by Pablo Picasso

DRAMA

Oedipus Rex*

SOPHOCLES [496?– 406 B.C.]

(ca. 429 B.C.)

PERSONS REPRESENTED

Oedipus
A Priest
Creon
Teiresias
Iocastê

Messenger
Shepherd of Laïos
Second Messenger
Chorus of Theban Elders

SCENE

Before the palace of Oedipus, King of Thebes. A central door and two lateral doors open onto a platform which runs the length of the facade. On the platform, right and left, are altars; and three steps lead down into the "orchestra," or chorus-ground. At the beginning of the action these steps are crowded by suppliants who have brought branches and chaplets of olive leaves and who lie in various attitudes of despair. Oedipus enters.

Prologue

Oedipus.   My children, generations of the living
In the line of Kadmos,[1] nursed at his ancient hearth:
Why have you strewn yourselves before these altars
In supplication, with your boughs and garlands?
The breath of incense rises from the city
With a sound of prayer and lamentation.

---

* An English version by Dudley Fitts and Robert Fitzgerald.
[1] The legendary founder of Thebes.

Children,

I would not have you speak through messengers,
And therefore I have come myself to hear you—
I, Oedipus, who bear the famous name.
[*To a Priest.*] You, there, since you are eldest in the company,   10
Speak for them all, tell me what preys upon you,
Whether you come in dread, or crave some blessing:
Tell me, and never doubt that I will help you
In every way I can; I should be heartless
Were I not moved to find you suppliant here.
Priest.   Great Oedipus, O powerful King of Thebes!
You see how all the ages of our people
Cling to your altar steps: here are boys
Who can barely stand alone, and here are priests
By weight of age, as I am a priest of God,   20
And young men chosen from those yet unmarried;
As for the others, all that multitude,
They wait with olive chaplets in the squares,
At the two shrines of Pallas,[2] and where Apollo[3]
Speaks in the glowing embers.

Your own eyes

Must tell you: Thebes is in her extremity
And can not lift her head from the surge of death.
A rust consumes the buds and fruits of the earth;
The herds are sick; children die unborn,
And labor is vain. The god of plague and pyre   30
Raids like detestable lightning through the city,
And all the house of Kadmos is laid waste,
All emptied, and all darkened: Death alone
Battens upon the misery of Thebes.

You are not one of the immortal gods, we know;
Yet we have come to you to make our prayer
As to the man of all men best in adversity
And wisest in the ways of God. You saved us
From the Sphinx,[4] that flinty singer, and the tribute
We paid to her so long; yet you were never   40
Better informed than we, nor could we teach you:
It was some god breathed in you to set us free.

---

[2] Athena, goddess of wisdom.
[3] God of sunlight, medicine, and prophecy.
[4] A winged monster, with a woman's head and breasts and a lion's body, that destroyed those who failed to answer her riddle: "What walks on four feet in the morning, two at noon, and three in the evening?" When the young Oedipus correctly answered, "Man" ("three" alluding to a cane in old age), the Sphinx killed herself, and the plague ended.

Therefore, O mighty King, we turn to you:
Find us our safety, find us a remedy,
Whether by counsel of the gods or men.
A king of wisdom tested in the past
Can act in a time of troubles, and act well.
Noblest of men, restore
Life to your city! Think how all men call you
Liberator for your triumph long ago;   50
Ah, when your years of kingship are remembered,
Let them not say *We rose, but later fell*—
Keep the State from going down in the storm!
Once, years ago, with happy augury,
You brought us fortune; be the same again!
No man questions your power to rule the land:
But rule over men, not over a dead city!
Ships are only hulls, citadels are nothing,
When no life moves in the empty passageways.

Oedipus.   Poor children! You may be sure I know   60
All that you longed for in your coming here.
I know that you are deathly sick; and yet,
Sick as you are, not one is as sick as I.
Each of you suffers in himself alone
His anguish, not another's; but my spirit
Groans for the city, for myself, for you.

I was not sleeping, you are not waking me.
No, I have been in tears for a long while
And in my restless thought walked many ways.
In all my search, I found one helpful course,   70
And that I have taken: I have sent Creon,
Son of Menoikeus, brother of the Queen,
To Delphi, Apollo's place of revelation,
To learn there, if he can,
What act or pledge of mine may save the city.
I have counted the days, and now, this very day,
I am troubled, for he has overstayed his time.
What is he doing? He has been gone too long.
Yet whenever he comes back, I should do ill
To scant whatever hint the god may give.   80

Priest.   It is a timely promise. At this instant
They tell me Creon is here.

Oedipus.   O Lord Apollo!
May his news be fair as his face is radiant!

Priest.   It could not be otherwise: he is crowned with bay,
The chaplet is thick with berries.

Oedipus.   We shall soon know;
  He is near enough to hear us now.

[*Enter Creon.*]

                                    O Prince:
  Brother: son of Menoikeus:
  What answer do you bring us from the god?
Creon.   It is favorable. I can tell you, great afflictions
  Will turn out well, if they are taken well.   90
Oedipus.   What was the oracle? These vague words
  Leave me still hanging between hope and fear.
Creon.   Is it your pleasure to hear me with all these
  Gathered around us? I am prepared to speak,
  But should we not go in?
Oedipus.   Let them all hear it.
  It is for them I suffer, more than for myself.
Creon.   Then I will tell you what I heard at Delphi.

  In plain words
  The god commands us to expel from the land of Thebes
  An old defilement that it seems we shelter.   100
  It is a deathly thing, beyond expiation.
  We must not let it feed upon us longer.
Oedipus.   What defilement? How shall we rid ourselves of it?
Creon.   By exile or death, blood for blood. It was
  Murder that brought the plague-wind on the city.
Oedipus.   Murder of whom? Surely the god has named him?
Creon.   My lord: long ago Laïos was our king,
  Before you came to govern us.
Oedipus.   I know;
  I learned of him from others; I never saw him.
Creon.   He was murdered; and Apollo commands us now   110
  To take revenge upon whoever killed him.
Oedipus.   Upon whom? Where are they? Where shall we find a clue
  To solve that crime, after so many years?
Creon.   Here in this land, he said.
                                    If we make enquiry,
  We may touch things that otherwise escape us.
Oedipus.   Tell me: Was Laïos murdered in his house,
  Or in the fields, or in some foreign country?
Creon.   He said he planned to make a pilgrimage.
  He did not come home again.
Oedipus.   And was there no one,
  No witness, no companion, to tell what happened?   120

Creon.   They were all killed but one, and he got away
   So frightened that he could remember one thing only.
Oedipus.   What was that one thing? One may be the key
   To everything, if we resolve to use it.
Creon.   He said that a band of highwaymen attacked them,
   Outnumbered them, and overwhelmed the King.
Oedipus.   Strange, that a highwayman should be so daring—
   Unless some faction here bribed him to do it.
Creon.   We thought of that. But after Laïos' death
   New troubles arose and we had no avenger.   130
Oedipus.   What troubles could prevent your hunting down the killers?
Creon.   The riddling Sphinx's song
   Made us deaf to all mysteries but her own.
Oedipus.   Then once more I must bring what is dark to light.
   It is most fitting that Apollo shows,
   As you do, this compunction for the dead.
   You shall see how I stand by you, as I should,
   To avenge the city and the city's god,
   And not as though it were for some distant friend,
   But for my own sake, to be rid of evil.   140
   Whoever killed King Laïos might—who knows?—
   Decide at any moment to kill me as well.
   By avenging the murdered king I protect myself.
   Come, then, my children: leave the altar steps,
   Lift up your olive boughs!
                One of you go
   And summon the people of Kadmos to gather here.
   I will do all that I can; you may tell them that.

[*Exit a page.*]

   So, with the help of God,
   We shall be saved—or else indeed we are lost.
Priest.   Let us rise, children. It was for this we came,   150
   And now the King has promised it himself.
   Phoibos[5] has sent us an oracle; may he descend
   Himself to save us and drive out the plague.

[*Exeunt Oedipus and Creon into the palace by the central door. The Priest and the suppliants disperse R and L. After a short pause the Chorus enters the orchestra.*]

---

[5] Phoebus Apollo, god of the sun.

Párodos[6]

Chorus.   What is God singing in his profound   [*Strophe 1*]
Delphi of gold and shadow?
What oracle for Thebes, the sunwhipped city?
Fear unjoints me, the roots of my heart tremble.
Now I remember, O Healer, your power, and wonder;
Will you send doom like a sudden cloud, or weave it
Like nightfall of the past?
Speak, speak to us, issue of holy sound:
Dearest to our expectancy: be tender!

Let me pray to Athenê, the immortal daughter of Zeus,   [*Antistrophe 1*]
And to Artemis her sister   11
Who keeps her famous throne in the market ring,
And to Apollo, bowman at the far butts of heaven—

O gods, descend! Like three streams leap against
The fires of our grief, the fires of darkness;
Be swift to bring us rest!

As in the old time from the brilliant house
Of air you stepped to save us, come again!

Now our afflictions have no end,   [*Strophe 2*]
Now all our stricken host lies down   20
And no man fights off death with his mind;

The noble plowland bears no grain,
And groaning mothers can not bear—

See, how our lives like birds take wing,
Like sparks that fly when a fire soars,
To the shore of the god of evening.

The plague burns on, it is pitiless,   [*Antistrophe 2*]
Though pallid children laden with death
Lie unwept in the stony ways,

And old gray women by every path   30
Flock to the strand about the altars

---

[6] The *Párodos* is the ode sung by the Chorus as it entered the theater and moved down the aisles to the playing area. The *strophe*, in Greek tragedy, is the unit of verse the Chorus chanted as it moved to the left in a dance rhythm. The Chorus sang the *antistrophe* as it moved to the right and the *epode* while standing still.

There to strike their breasts and cry
Worship of Phoibos in wailing prayers:
Be kind, God's golden child!

There are no swords in this attack by fire,   [*Strophe* 3]
No shields, but we are ringed with cries.
Send the besieger plunging from our homes
Into the vast sea-room of the Atlantic
Or into the waves that foam eastward of Thrace—
For the day ravages what the night spares—   40

Destroy our enemy, lord of the thunder!
Let him be riven by lightning from heaven!

Phoibus Apollo, stretch the sun's bowstring,   [*Antistrophe* 3]
That golden cord, until it sing for us,
Flashing arrows in heaven!
                    Artemis, Huntress
Race with flaring lights upon our mountains!

O scarlet god, O golden-banded brow,
O Theban Bacchos in a storm of Maenads,[7]

[*Enter Oedipus, C.*]

Whirl upon Death, that all the Undying hate!
Come with blinding cressets, come in joy!   50

Scene 1

Oedipus.   Is this your prayer? It may be answered. Come,
Listen to me, act as the crisis demands,
And you shall have relief from all these evils.

Until now I was a stranger to this tale,
As I had been a stranger to the crime.
Could I track down the murderer without a clue?
But now, friends,
As one who became a citizen after the murder,
I make this proclamation to all Thebans:
If any man knows by whose hand Laïos, son of Labdakos,   10

---

[7] Bacchos is the god of wine and revelry, hence scarlet-faced. The Maenads were Bacchos' female attendants.

Met his death, I direct that man to tell me everything,
No matter what he fears for having so long withheld it.
Let it stand as promised that no further trouble
Will come to him, but he may leave the land in safety.

Moreover: If anyone knows the murderer to be foreign,
Let him not keep silent: he shall have his reward from me.
However, if he does conceal it; if any man
Fearing for his friend or for himself disobeys this edict,
Hear what I propose to do:

I solemnly forbid the people of this country,   20
Where power and throne are mine, ever to receive that man
Or speak to him, no matter who he is, or let him
Join in sacrifice, lustration, or in prayer.
I decree that he be driven from every house,
Being, as he is, corruption itself to us: the Delphic
Voice of Zeus has pronounced this revelation.
Thus I associate myself with the oracle
And take the side of the murdered king.

As for the criminal, I pray to God—
Whether it be a lurking thief, or one of a number—   30
I pray that that man's life be consumed in evil and wretchedness.
And as for me, this curse applies no less
If it should turn out that the culprit is my guest here,
Sharing my hearth.
                        You have heard the penalty.
I lay it on you now to attend to this
For my sake, for Apollo's, for the sick
Sterile city that heaven has abandoned.
Suppose the oracle had given you no command:
Should this defilement go uncleansed for ever?
You should have found the murderer: your king,   40
A noble king, had been destroyed!
                        Now I,
Having the power that he held before me,
Having his bed, begetting children there
Upon his wife, as he would have, had he lived—
Their son would have been my children's brother,
If Laïos had had luck in fatherhood!
(But surely ill luck rushed upon his reign)—
I say I take the son's part, just as though
I were his son, to press the fight for him
And see it won! I'll find the hand that brought   50

Death to Labdakos' and Polydoros' child,
Heir of Kadmos's and Agenor's line.
And as for those who fail me,
May the gods deny them the fruit of the earth,
Fruit of the womb, and may they rot utterly!
Let them be wretched as we are wretched, and worse!

For you, for loyal Thebans, and for all
Who find my actions right, I pray the favor
Of justice, and of all the immortal gods.

Choragos.[8]   Since I am under oath, my lord, I swear   60
I did not do the murder. I can not name
The murderer. Might not the oracle
That has ordained the search tell where to find him?

Oedipus.   An honest question. But no man in the world
Can make the gods do more than the gods will.

Choragos.   There is one last expedient—

Oedipus.   Tell me what it is.
Though it seem slight, you must not hold it back.

Choragos.   A lord clairvoyant to the lord Apollo,
As we all know, is the skilled Teiresias.
One might learn much about this from him, Oedipus.   70

Oedipus.   I am not wasting time:
Creon spoke of this, and I have sent for him—
Twice, in fact; it is strange that he is not here.

Choragos.   The other matter—that old report—seems useless.

Oedipus.   Tell me. I am interested in all reports.

Choragos.   The King was said to have been killed by highwaymen.

Oedipus.   I know. But we have no witnesses to that.

Choragos.   If the killer can feel a particle of dread,
Your curse will bring him out of hiding!

Oedipus.   No.
The man who dared that act will fear no curse.   80

[*Enter the blind seer Teiresias, led by a page.*]

Choragos.   But there is one man who may detect the criminal.
This is Teiresias, this is the holy prophet
In whom, alone of all men, truth was born.

Oedipus.   Teiresias: seer: student of mysteries,
Of all that's taught and all that no man tells,
Secrets of Heaven and secrets of the earth:
Blind though you are, you know the city lies

---

[8] Choragos is the leader of the Chorus.

Sick with plague; and from this plague, my lord,
We find that you alone can guard or save us.

Possibly you did not hear the messengers?   90
Apollo, when we sent to him,
Sent us back word that this great pestilence
Would lift, but only if we established clearly
The identity of those who murdered Laïos.
They must be killed or exiled.
        Can you use
Birdflight or any art of divination
To purify yourself, and Thebes, and me
From this contagion? We are in your hands.
There is no fairer duty
Than that of helping others in distress.   100
Teiresias. How dreadful knowledge of the truth can be
When there's no help in truth! I knew this well,
But did not act on it: else I should not have come.
Oedipus. What is troubling you? Why are your eyes so cold?
Teiresias. Let me go home. Bear your own fate, and I'll
Bear mine. It is better so: trust what I say.
Oedipus. What you say is ungracious and unhelpful
To your native country. Do not refuse to speak.
Teiresias. When it comes to speech, your own is neither temperate
Nor opportune. I wish to be more prudent.   110
Oedipus. In God's name, we all beg you—
Teiresias.   You are all ignorant.
No; I will never tell you what I know.
Now it is my misery; then, it would be yours.
Oedipus. What! You do know something, and will not tell us?
You would betray us all and wreck the State?
Teiresias. I do not intend to torture myself, or you.
Why persist in asking? You will not persuade me.
Oedipus. What a wicked old man you are! You'd try a stone's
Patience! Out with it! Have you no feeling at all?
Teiresias. You call me unfeeling. If you could only see   120
The nature of your own feelings . . .
Oedipus.   Why,
Who would not feel as I do? Who could endure
Your arrogance toward the city?
Teiresias.   What does it matter!
Whether I speak or not, it is bound to come.
Oedipus. Then, if "it" is bound to come, you are bound to tell me.
Teiresias. No, I will not go on. Rage as you please.

Oedipus.   Rage? Why not!
                       And I'll tell you what I think:
You planned it, you had it done, you all but
Killed him with your own hands: if you had eyes,
I'd say the crime was yours, and yours alone.   130
Teiresias.   So? I charge you, then,
Abide by the proclamation you have made:
From this day forth
Never speak again to these men or to me;
You yourself are the pollution of this country.
Oedipus.   You dare say that! Can you possibly think you have
Some way of going free, after such insolence?
Teiresias.   I have gone free. It is the truth sustains me.
Oedipus.   Who taught you shamelessness? It was not your craft.
Teiresias.   You did. You made me speak. I did not want to.   140
Oedipus.   Speak what? Let me hear it again more clearly.
Teiresias.   Was it not clear before? Are you tempting me?
Oedipus.   I did not understand it. Say it again.
Teiresias.   I say that you are the murderer whom you seek.
Oedipus.   Now twice you have spat out infamy! You'll pay for it!
Teiresias.   Would you care for more? Do you wish to be really angry?
Oedipus.   Say what you will. Whatever you say is worthless.
Teiresias.   I say you live in hideous shame with those
Most dear to you. You can not see the evil.
Oedipus.   It seems you can go on mouthing like this for ever.   150
Teiresias.   I can, if there is power in truth.
Oedipus.   There is:
But not for you, not for you,
You sightless, witless, senseless, mad old man!
Teiresias.   You are the madman. There is no one here
Who will not curse you soon, as you curse me.
Oedipus.   You child of endless night! You can not hurt me
Or any other man who sees the sun.
Teiresias.   True: it is not from me your fate will come.
That lies within Apollo's competence,
As it is his concern.
Oedipus.   Tell me: 160
Are you speaking for Creon or for yourself?
Teiresias.   Creon is no threat. You weave your own doom.
Oedipus.   Wealth, power, craft of statesmanship!
Kingly position, everywhere admired!
What savage envy is stored up against these,
If Creon, whom I trusted, Creon my friend,
For this great office which the city once

Put in my hands unsought—if for this power
Creon desires in secret to destroy me!

He has brought this decrepit fortune-teller, this   170
Collector of dirty pennies, this prophet fraud—
Why, he is no more clairvoyant than I am!
                                    Tell us:
Has your mystic mummery ever approached the truth?
When that hellcat the Sphinx was performing here,
What help were you to these people?
Her magic was not for the first man who came along:
It demanded a real exorcist. Your birds—
What good were they? or the gods, for the matter of that?
But I came by,
Oedipus, the simple man, who knows nothing—   180
I thought it out for myself, no birds helped me!
And this is the man you think you can destroy,
That you may be close to Creon when he's king!
Well, you and your friend Creon, it seems to me,
Will suffer most. If you were not an old man,
You would have paid already for your plot.
Choragos.   We can not see that his words or yours
Have been spoken except in anger, Oedipus,
And of anger we have no need. How can God's will
Be accomplished best? That is what most concerns us.   190
Teiresias.   You are a king. But where argument's concerned
I am your man, as much a king as you.
I am not your servant, but Apollo's.
I have no need of Creon to speak for me.

Listen to me. You mock my blindness, do you?
But I say that you, with both your eyes, are blind:
You can not see the wretchedness of your life,
Nor in whose house you live, no, nor with whom.
Who are your father and mother? Can you tell me?
You do not even know the blind wrongs   200
That you have done them, on earth and in the world below.
But the double lash of your parents' curse will whip you
Out of this land some day, with only night
Upon your precious eyes.
Your cries then—where will they not be heard?
What fastness of Kithairon[9] will not echo them?
And that bridal-descant of yours—you'll know it then,

---

[9] A mountain range near Thebes where the infant Oedipus was left to die.

The song they sang when you came here to Thebes
And found your misguided berthing.
All this, and more, that you can not guess at now,   210
Will bring you to yourself among your children.

Be angry, then. Curse Creon. Curse my words.
I tell you, no man that walks upon the earth
Shall be rooted out more horribly than you.
Oedipus.   Am I to bear this from him?—Damnation
Take you! Out of this place! Out of my sight!
Teiresias.   I would not have come at all if you had not asked me.
Oedipus.   Could I have told that you'd talk nonsense, that
You'd come here to make a fool of yourself, and of me?
Teiresias.   A fool? Your parents thought me sane enough.   220
Oedipus.   My parents again!—Wait: who were my parents?
Teiresias.   This day will give you a father, and break your heart.
Oedipus.   Your infantile riddles! Your damned abracadabra!
Teiresias.   You were a great man once at solving riddles.
Oedipus.   Mock me with that if you like; you will find it true.
Teiresias.   It was true enough. It brought about your ruin.
Oedipus.   But if it saved this town?
Teiresias [*to the page*].   Boy, give me your hand.
Oedipus.   Yes, boy; lead him away.

                         —While you are here
We can do nothing. Go; leave us in peace.
Teiresias.   I will go when I have said what I have to say.   230
How can you hurt me? And I tell you again:
The man you have been looking for all this time,
The damned man, the murderer of Laïos,
That man is in Thebes. To your mind he is foreignborn,
But it will soon be shown that he is a Theban,
A revelation that will fail to please.

                         A blind man,
Who has his eyes now; a penniless man, who is rich now;
And he will go tapping the strange earth with his staff;
To the children with whom he lives now he will be
Brother and father—the very same; to her   240
Who bore him, son and husband—the very same
Who came to his father's bed, wet with his father's blood.

Enough. Go think that over.
If later you find error in what I have said,
You may say that I have no skill in prophecy.

[*Exit Teiresias, led by his page. Oedipus goes into the palace.*]

Ode I

Chorus.   The Delphic stone of prophecies   [*Strophe 1*]
 Remembers ancient regicide
 And a still bloody hand.
 That killer's hour of flight has come.
 He must be stronger than riderless
 Coursers of untiring wind,
 For the son of Zeus[10] armed with his father's thunder
 Leaps in lightning after him;
 And the Furies follow him, the sad Furies.[11]

 Holy Parnassos' peak of snow   [*Antistrophe 1*]
 Flashes and blinds that secret man,   11
 That all shall hunt him down:
 Though he may roam the forest shade
 Like a bull gone wild from pasture
 To rage through glooms of stone.
 Doom comes down on him; flight will not avail him;
 For the world's heart calls him desolate,
 And the immortal Furies follow, for ever follow.

 But now a wilder thing is heard   [*Strophe 2*]
 From the old man skilled at hearing Fate in the wingbeat of a bird.   20
 Bewildered as a blown bird, my soul hovers and can not find
 Foothold in this debate, or any reason or rest of mind.
 But no man ever brought—none can bring
 Proof of strife between Thebes' royal house,
 Labdakos' line, and the son of Polybos;[12]
 And never until now has any man brought word
 Of Laïos' dark death staining Oedipus the King.

 Divine Zeus and Apollo hold   [*Antistrophe 2*]
 Perfect intelligence alone of all tales ever told;
 And well though this diviner works, he works in his own night;   30
 No man can judge that rough unknown or trust in second sight,
 For wisdom changes hands among the wise.
 Shall I believe my great lord criminal
 At a raging word that a blind old man let fall?
 I saw him, when the carrion woman faced him of old,
 Prove his heroic mind! These evil words are lies.

---

[10] I.e., Apollo (see note 3).
[11] The goddesses of divine vengeance.
[12] Labdakos was an early king of Thebes and an ancestor of Oedipus. Oedipus is mistakenly referred to as the son of Polybus.

Scene II

Creon.   Men of Thebes:
I am told that heavy accusations
Have been brought against me by King Oedipus.

I am not the kind of man to bear this tamely.

If in these present difficulties
He holds me accountable for any harm to him
Through anything I have said or done—why, then,
I do not value life in this dishonor.
It is not as though this rumor touched upon
Some private indiscretion. The matter is grave.   10
The fact is that I am being called disloyal
To the State, to my fellow citizens, to my friends.
Choragos.   He may have spoken in anger, not from his mind.
Creon.   But did you not hear him say I was the one
Who seduced the old prophet into lying?
Choragos.   The thing was said; I do not know how seriously.
Creon.   But you were watching him! Were his eyes steady?
Did he look like a man in his right mind?
Choragos.   I do not know.
I can not judge the behavior of great men.
But here is the King himself.

[*Enter Oedipus.*]

Oedipus.   So you dared come back.   20
Why? How brazen of you to come to my house,
You murderer!
                        Do you think I do not know
That you plotted to kill me, plotted to steal my throne?
Tell me, in God's name: am I coward, a fool,
That you should dream you could accomplish this?
A fool who could not see your slippery game?
A coward, not to fight back when I saw it?
You are the fool, Creon, are you not? hoping
Without support or friends to get a throne?
Thrones may be won or bought: you could do neither.   30
Creon.   Now listen to me. You have talked; let me talk, too.
You can not judge unless you know the facts.
Oedipus.   You speak well: there is one fact; but I find it hard
To learn from the deadliest enemy I have.
Creon.   That above all I must dispute with you.
Oedipus.   That above all I will not hear you deny.

Creon.   If you think there is anything good in being stubborn
   Against all reason, then I say you are wrong.
Oedipus.   If you think a man can sin against his own kind
   And not be punished for it, I say you are mad.   40
Creon.   I agree. But tell me: what have I done to you?
Oedipus.   You advised me to send for that wizard, did you not?
Creon.   I did. I should do it again.
Oedipus.   Very well. Now tell me:
   How long has it been since Laïos—
Creon.   What of Laïos?
Oedipus.   Since he vanished in that onset by the road?
Creon.   It was long ago, a long time.
Oedipus.   And this prophet,
   Was he practicing here then?
Creon.   He was; and with honor, as now.
Oedipus.   Did he speak of me at that time?
Creon.   He never did;
   At least, not when I was present.
Oedipus.   But . . . the enquiry?
   I suppose you held one?
Creon.   We did, but we learned nothing.   50
Oedipus.   Why did the prophet not speak against me then?
Creon.   I do not know; and I am the kind of man
   Who holds his tongue when he has no facts to go on.
Oedipus.   There's one fact that you know, and you could tell it.
Creon.   What fact is that? If I know it, you shall have it.
Oedipus.   If he were not involved with you, he could not say
   That it was I who murdered Laïos.
Creon.   If he says that, you are the one that knows it!—
   But now it is my turn to question you.
Oedipus.   Put your questions. I am no murderer.   60
Creon.   First then: You married my sister?
Oedipus.   I married your sister.
Creon.   And you rule the kingdom equally with her?
Oedipus.   Everything that she wants she has from me.
Creon.   And I am the third, equal to both of you?
Oedipus.   That is why I call you a bad friend.
Creon.   No. Reason it out, as I have done.
   Think of this first. Would any sane man prefer
   Power, with all a king's anxieties,
   To that same power and the grace of sleep?
   Certainly not I.   70
   I have never longed for the king's power—only his rights.
   Would any wise man differ from me in this?
   As matters stand, I have my way in everything

With your consent, and no responsibilities.
If I were king, I should be a slave to policy.

How could I desire a scepter more
Than what is now mine—untroubled influence?
No, I have not gone mad; I need no honors,
Except those with the perquisites I have now.
I am welcome everywhere; every man salutes me,   80
And those who want your favor seek my ear,
Since I know how to manage what they ask.
Should I exchange this ease for that anxiety?
Besides, no sober mind is treasonable.
I hate anarchy
And never would deal with any man who likes it.

Test what I have said. Go to the priestess
At Delphi, ask if I quoted her correctly.
And as for this other thing: if I am found
Guilty of treason with Teiresias,   90
Then sentence me to death! You have my word
It is a sentence I should cast my vote for—
But not without evidence!
                        You do wrong
When you take good men for bad, bad men for good.
A true friend thrown aside—why, life itself
Is not more precious!
                        In time you will know this well:
For time, and time alone, will show the just man,
Though scoundrels are discovered in a day.
Choragos.   This is well said, and a prudent man would ponder it.
    Judgments too quickly formed are dangerous.   100
Oedipus.   But is he not quick in his duplicity?
    And shall I not be quick to parry him?
    Would you have me stand still, hold my peace, and let
    This man win everything, through my inaction?
Creon.   And you want—what is it, then? To banish me?
Oedipus.   No, not exile. It is your death I want,
    So that all the world may see what treason means.
Creon.   You will persist, then? You will not believe me?
Oedipus.   How can I believe you?
Creon.   Then you are a fool.
Oedipus.   To save myself?
Creon.   In justice, think of me.   110
Oedipus.   You are evil incarnate.
Creon.   But suppose that you are wrong?

Oedipus.   Still I must rule.
Creon.   But not if you rule badly.
Oedipus.   O city, city!
Creon.   It is my city, too!
Choragos.   Now, my lords, be still. I see the Queen,
  Iocastê, coming from her palace chambers;
  And it is time she came, for the sake of you both.
  This dreadful quarrel can be resolved through her.   120

[*Enter Iocastê.*]

Iocastê.   Poor foolish men, what wicked din is this?
  With Thebes sick to death, is it not shameful
  That you should rake some private quarrel up?
  [*To Oedipus.*] Come into the house.
                              —And you, Creon, go now:
  Let us have no more of this tumult over nothing.
Creon.   Nothing? No, sister: what your husband plans for me
  Is one of two great evils: exile or death.
Oedipus.   He is right.
                    Why, woman I have caught him squarely
  Plotting against my life.
Creon.   No! Let me die
  Accurst if ever I have wished you harm!
Iocastê.   Ah, believe it, Oedipus!
  In the name of the gods, respect this oath of his
  For my sake, for the sake of these people here!   130

Choragos.   Open your mind to her my lord. Be ruled by her,   [*Strophe 1*]
  I beg you!
Oedipus.   What would you have me do?
Choragos.   Respect Creon's word. He has never spoken like a fool,
  And now he has sworn an oath.
Oedipus.   You know what you ask?
Choragos   I do.
Oedipus.   Speak on, then.
Choragos.   A friend so sworn should not be baited so,
  In blind malice, and without final proof.
Oedipus.   You are aware, I hope, that what you say
  Means death for me, or exile at the least.

Choragos.   No, I swear by Helios,[13] first in Heaven!   [*Strophe 2*]
  May I die friendless and accurst,   140

---

[13] The sun god.

The worst of deaths, if ever I meant that!
  It is the withering fields
    That hurt my sick heart:
  Must we bear all these ills,
    And now your bad blood as well?

Oedipus.   Then let him go. And let me die, if I must,
Or be driven by him in shame from the land of Thebes.
It is your unhappiness, and not his talk,
That touches me.
               As for him—
Wherever he is, I will hate him as long as I live.   150

Creon.   Ugly in yielding, as you were ugly in rage!
Natures like yours chiefly torment themselves.

Oedipus.   Can you not go? Can you not leave me?

Creon.   I can.
You do not know me; but the city knows me,
And in its eyes I am just, if not in yours.

[*Exit Creon.*]

Choragos.   Lady Iocastê, did you not ask the King to go   [*Antistrophe 1*]
to his chambers?

Iocastê.   First tell me what has happened.

Choragos.   There was suspicion without evidence; yet it rankled
As even false charges will.

Iocastê.   On both sides?

Choragos.   On both.

Iocastê.   But what was said?

Choragos.   Oh let it rest, let it be done with!   160
Have we not suffered enough?

Oedipus.   You see to what your decency has brought you:
You have made difficulties where my heart saw none.

Choragos.   Oedipus, it is not once only I have told you—   [*Antistrophe 2*]
You must know I should count myself unwise
To the point of madness, should I now forsake you—
  You, under whose hand,
    In the storm of another time,
  Our dear land sailed out free.
    But now stand fast at the helm!   170

Iocastê.   In God's name, Oedipus, inform your wife as well:
Why are you so set in this hard anger?

Oedipus.   I will tell you, for none of these men deserves
My confidence as you do. It is Creon's work,
His treachery, his plotting against me.

Iocastê.   Go on, if you can make this clear to me.

Oedipus.   He charges me with the murder of Laïos.

Iocastê.   Has he some knowledge? Or does he speak from hearsay?

Oedipus.   He would not commit himself to such a charge,
But he has brought in that damnable soothsayer   180
To tell his story.

Iocastê.   Set your mind at rest.
If it is a question of soothsayers, I tell you
That you will find no man whose craft gives knowledge
Of the unknowable.

                    Here is my proof:

An oracle was reported to Laïos once
(I will not say from Phoibos himself, but from
His appointed ministers, at any rate)
That his doom would be death at the hands of his own son—
His son, born of his flesh and of mine!

Now, you remember the story: Laïos was killed   190
By marauding strangers where three highways meet;
But his child had not been three days in this world
Before the King had pierced the baby's ankles
And left him to die on a lonely mountainside.

Thus, Apollo never caused that child
To kill his father, and it was not Laïos' fate
To die at the hands of his son, as he had feared.
This is what prophets and prophecies are worth!
Have no dread of them.

                    It is God himself
Who can show us what he wills, in his own way.   200

Oedipus.   How strange a shadowy memory crossed my mind,
Just now while you were speaking; it chilled my heart.

Iocastê.   What do you mean? What memory do you speak of?

Oedipus.   If I understand you, Laïos was killed
At a place where three roads meet.

Iocastê.   So it was said;
We have no later story.

Oedipus.   Where did it happen?

Iocastê.   Phokis, it is called: at a place where the Theban Way
Divides into the roads towards Delphi and Daulia.

Oedipus.   When?

Iocastê.   We had the news not long before you came
And proved the right to your succession here.   210

Oedipus.   Ah, what net has God been weaving for me?

Iocastê.   Oedipus! Why does this trouble you?

Oedipus.   Do not ask me yet.
  First, tell me how Laïos looked, and tell me
  How old he was.

Iocastê.   He was tall, his hair just touched
  With white; his form was not unlike your own.

Oedipus.   I think that I myself may be accurst
  By my own ignorant edict.

Iocastê.   You speak strangely.
  It makes me tremble to look at you, my King.

Oedipus.   I am not sure that the blind man can not see.
  But I should know better if you were to tell me—   220

Iocastê.   Anything—though I dread to hear you ask it.

Oedipus.   Was the King lightly escorted, or did he ride
  With a large company, as a ruler should?

Iocastê.   There were five men with him in all: one was a herald;
  And a single chariot, which he was driving.

Oedipus.   Alas, that makes it plain enough!
                                        But who—
  Who told you how it happened?

Iocastê.   A household servant,
  The only one to escape.

Oedipus.   And is he still
  A servant of ours?

Iocastê.   No; for when he came back at last
  And found you enthroned in the place of the dead king,   230
  He came to me, touched my hand with his, and begged
  That I would send him away to the frontier district
  Where only the shepherds go—
  As far away from the city as I could send him.
  I granted his prayer; for although the man was a slave,
  He had earned more than this favor at my hands.

Oedipus.   Can he be called back quickly?

Iocastê.   Easily.
  But why?

Oedipus.   I have taken too much upon myself
  Without enquiry; therefore I wish to consult him.

Iocastê.   Then he shall come.
                              But am I not one also   240
  To whom you might confide these fears of yours?

Oedipus.   That is your right; it will not be denied you,
  Now least of all; for I have reached a pitch
  Of wild foreboding. Is there anyone
  To whom I should sooner speak?
  Polybos of Corinth is my father.

My mother is a Dorian: Meropê.
I grew up chief among the men of Corinth
Until a strange thing happened—
Not worth my passion, it may be, but strange.   250

At a feast, a drunken man maundering in his cups
Cries out that I am not my father's son!

I contained myself that night, though I felt anger
And a sinking heart. The next day I visited
My father and mother, and questioned them. They stormed,
Calling it all the slanderous rant of a fool;
And this relieved me. Yet the suspicion
Remained always aching in my mind;
I knew there was talk; I could not rest;
And finally, saying nothing to my parents,   260
I went to the shrine at Delphi.
The god dismissed my question without reply;
He spoke of other things.
                          Some were clear,
Full of wretchedness, dreadful, unbearable:
As, that I should lie with my own mother, breed
Children from whom all men would turn their eyes;
And that I should be my father's murderer.

I heard all this, and fled. And from that day
Corinth to me was only in the stars
Descending in that quarter of the sky,   270
As I wandered farther and farther on my way
To a land where I should never see the evil
Sung by the oracle. And I came to this country
Where, so you say, King Laïos was killed.

I will tell you all that happened there, my lady.

There were three highways
Coming together at a place I passed;
And there a herald came towards me, and a chariot
Drawn by horses, with a man such as you describe
Seated in it. The groom leading the horses   280
Forced me off the road at his lord's command;
But as this charioteer lurched over towards me
I struck him in my rage. The old man saw me
And brought his double goad down upon my head
As I came abreast.
                          He was paid back, and more!

Swinging my club in this right hand I knocked him
Out of his car, and he rolled on the ground.

I killed him.

I killed them all.
Now if that stranger and Laïos were—kin,
Where is a man more miserable than I?   290
More hated by the gods? Citizen and alien alike
Must never shelter me or speak to me—
I must be shunned by all.

And I myself

Pronounced this malediction upon myself!

Think of it: I have touched you with these hands,
These hands that killed your husband. What defilement!

Am I all evil, then? It must be so,
Since I must flee from Thebes, yet never again
See my own countrymen, my own country,
For fear of joining my mother in marriage   300
And killing Polybos, my father.

Ah,

If I was created so, born to this fate,
Who could deny the savagery of God?

O holy majesty of heavenly powers!
May I never see that day! Never!
Rather let me vanish from the race of men
Than know the abomination destined me!
Choragos.   We too, my lord, have felt dismay at this.
But there is hope: you have yet to hear the shepherd.
Oedipus.   Indeed, I fear no other hope is left me.   310
Iocastê.   What do you hope from him when he comes?
Oedipus.   This much:
If his account of the murder tallies with yours,
Then I am cleared.
Iocastê.   What was it that I said
Of such importance?
Oedipus.   Why, "marauders," you said,
Killed the King, according to this man's story.
If he maintains that still, if there were several,
Clearly the guilt is not mine: I was alone.
But if he says one man, singlehanded, did it,
Then the evidence all points to me.
Iocastê.   You may be sure that he said there were several;   320
And can he call back that story now? He can not.

The whole city heard it as plainly as I.
But suppose he alters some detail of it:
He can not ever show that Laïos' death
Fulfilled the oracle: for Apollo said
My child was doomed to kill him; and my child—
Poor baby!—it was my child that died first.

No. From now on, where oracles are concerned,
I would not waste a second thought on any.
Oedipus.   You may be right.
                                      But come: let someone go   330
For the shepherd at once. This matter must be settled.
Iocastê.   I will send for him.
I would not wish to cross you in anything.
And surely not in this.— Let us go in.

[*Exeunt into the palace.*]

Ode II

Chorus.   Let me be reverent in the ways of right,   [*Strophe 1*]
Lowly the paths I journey on;
Let all my words and actions keep
The laws of the pure universe
From highest Heaven handed down.
For Heaven is their bright nurse,
Those generations of the realms of light;
Ah, never of mortal kind were they begot,
Nor are they slaves of memory, lost in sleep:
Their Father is greater than Time, and ages not.   10

The tyrant is a child of Pride   [*Antistrophe 1*]
Who drinks from his great sickening cup
Recklessness and vanity,
Until from his high crest headlong
He plummets to the dust of hope.
That strong man is not strong.
But let no fair ambition be denied;
May God protect the wrestler for the State
In government, in comely policy,
Who will fear God, and on His ordinance wait.   20

Haughtiness and the high hand of disdain   [*Strophe 2*]
Tempt and outrage God's holy law;
And any mortal who dares hold

No immortal Power in awe
Will be caught up in a net of pain:
The price for which his levity is sold.
Let each man take due earnings, then,
And keep his hands from holy things,
And from blasphemy stand apart—
Else the crackling blast of heaven   30
Blows on his head, and on his desperate heart;
Though fools will honor impious men,
In their cities no tragic poet sings.

Shall we lose faith in Delphi's obscurities,   [*Antistrophe 2*]
We who have heard the world's core
Discredited, and the sacred wood
Of Zeus at Elis praised no more?
The deeds and the strange prophecies
Must make a pattern yet to be understood.
Źeus, if indeed you are lord of all,   40
Throned in light over night and day,
Mirror this in your endless mind:
Our masters call the oracle
Words on the wind, and the Delphic vision blind!
Their hearts no longer know Apollo,
And reverence for the gods has died away.

Scene III

[*Enter Iocastê.*]

Iocastê.   Princes of Thebes, it has occurred to me
   To visit the altars of the gods, bearing
   These branches as a suppliant, and this incense.
   Our King is not himself: his noble soul
   Is overwrought with fantasies of dread,
   Else he would consider
   The new prophecies in the light of the old.
   He will listen to any voice that speaks disaster,
   And my advice goes for nothing.

[*She approaches the altar, R.*]

                                    To you, then, Apollo,
   Lycean lord, since you are nearest, I turn in prayer.   10
   Receive these offerings, and grant us deliverance
   From defilement. Our hearts are heavy with fear

When we see our leader distracted, as helpless sailors
Are terrified by the confusion of their helmsman.

[*Enter Messenger.*]

Messenger.   Friends, no doubt you can direct me:
  Where shall I find the house of Oedipus,
  Or, better still, where is the King himself?
Choragos.   It is this very place, stranger; he is inside.
  This is his wife and mother of his children.
Messenger.   I wish her happiness in a happy house,   20
  Blest in all the fulfillment of her marriage.
Iocastê.   I wish as much for you: your courtesy
  Deserves a like good fortune. But now, tell me:
  Why have you come? What have you to say to us?
Messenger.   Good news, my lady, for your house and your husband.
Iocastê.   What news? Who sent you here?
Messenger.   I am from Corinth.
  The news I bring ought to mean joy for you,
  Though it may be you will find some grief in it.
Iocastê.   What is it? How can it touch us in both ways?
Messenger.   The people of Corinth, they say,   30
  Intend to call Oedipus to be their king.
Iocastê.   But old Polybos—is he not reigning still?
Messenger.   No. Death holds him in his sepulchre.
Iocastê.   What are you saying? Polybos is dead?
Messenger.   If I am not telling the truth, may I die myself.
Iocastê [*to a maidservant*].   Go in, go quickly; tell this to your master.
  O riddlers of God's will, where are you now!
  This was the man whom Oedipus, long ago,
  Feared so, fled so, in dread of destroying him—
  But it was another fate by which he died.   40

[*Enter Oedipus, C.*]

Oedipus.   Dearest Iocastê, why have you sent for me?
Iocastê.   Listen to what this man says, and then tell me
  What has become of the solemn prophecies.
Oedipus.   Who is this man? What is his news for me?
Iocastê.   He has come from Corinth to announce your father's death!
Oedipus.   Is it true, stranger? Tell me in your own words.
Messenger.   I can not say it more clearly: the King is dead.
Oedipus.   Was it by treason? Or by an attack of illness?
Messenger.   A little thing brings old men to their rest.
Oedipus.   It was sickness, then?
Messenger.   Yes, and his many years.   50

Oedipus.   Ah!
Why should a man respect the Pythian hearth,[14] or
Give heed to the birds that jangle above his head?
They prophesied that I should kill Polybos,
Kill my own father; but he is dead and buried,
And I am here—I never touched him, never,
Unless he died of grief for my departure,
And thus, in a sense, through me. No. Polybos
Has packed the oracles off with him underground.
They are empty words.

Iocastê.   Had I not told you so?   60

Oedipus.   You had; it was my faint heart that betrayed me.

Iocastê.   From now on never think of those things again.

Oedipus.   And yet—must I not fear my mother's bed?

Iocastê.   Why should anyone in this world be afraid,
Since Fate rules us and nothing can be foreseen?
A man should live only for the present day.

Have no more fear of sleeping with your mother:
How many men, in dreams, have lain with their mothers!
No reasonable man is troubled by such things.

Oedipus.   That is true; only—   70
If only my mother were not still alive!
But she is alive. I can not help my dread.

Iocastê.   Yet this news of your father's death is wonderful.

Oedipus.   Wonderful. But I fear the living woman.

Messenger.   Tell me, who is this woman that you fear?

Oedipus.   It is Meropê, man; the wife of King Polybos.

Messenger.   Meropê? Why should you be afraid of her?

Oedipus.   An oracle of the gods, a dreadful saying.

Messenger.   Can you tell me about it or are you sworn to silence?

Oedipus.   I can tell you, and I will.   80
Apollo said through his prophet that I was the man
Who should marry his own mother, shed his father's blood
With his own hands. And so, for all these years
I have kept clear of Corinth, and no harm has come—
Though it would have been sweet to see my parents again.

Messenger.   And is this the fear that drove you out of Corinth?

Oedipus.   Would you have me kill my father?

Messenger.   As for that
You must be reassured by the news I gave you.

Oedipus.   If you could reassure me, I would reward you.

Messenger.   I had that in mind, I will confess: I thought   90
I could count on you when you returned to Corinth.

---

[14] Delphi, where Apollo spoke through an oracle.

Oedipus.   No: I will never go near my parents again.

Messenger.   Ah, son, you still do not know what you are doing—

Oedipus.   What do you mean? In the name of God tell me!

Messenger.   —If these are your reasons for not going home.

Oedipus.   I tell you, I fear the oracle may come true.

Messenger.   And guilt may come upon you through your parents?

Oedipus.   That is the dread that is always in my heart.

Messenger.   Can you not see that all your fears are groundless?

Oedipus.   How can you say that? They are my parents, surely?   100

Messenger.   Polybos was not your father.

Oedipus.   Not my father?

Messenger.   No more your father than the man speaking to you.

Oedipus.   But you are nothing to me!

Messenger.   Neither was he.

Oedipus.   Then why did he call me son?

Messenger.   I will tell you:
  Long ago he had you from my hands, as a gift.

Oedipus.   Then how could he love me so, if I was not his?

Messenger.   He had no children, and his heart turned to you.

Oedipus.   What of you? Did you buy me? Did you find me by chance?

Messenger.   I came upon you in the crooked pass of Kithairon.

Oedipus.   And what were you doing there?

Messenger.   Tending my flocks   110

Oedipus.   A wandering shepherd?

Messenger.   But your savior, son, that day.

Oedipus.   From what did you save me?

Messenger.   Your ankles should tell you that.

Oedipus.   Ah, stranger, why do you speak of that childhood pain?

Messenger.   I cut the bonds that tied your ankles together.

Oedipus.   I have had the mark as long as I can remember.

Messenger.   That was why you were given the name you bear.[15]

Oedipus.   God! Was it my father or my mother who did it?
  Tell me!

Messenger.   I do not know. The man who gave you to me
  Can tell you better than I.   120

Oedipus.   It was not you that found me, but another?

Messenger.   It was another shepherd gave you to me.

Oedipus.   Who was he? Can you tell me who he was?

Messenger.   I think he was said to be one of Laïos' people.

Oedipus.   You mean the Laïos who was king here years ago?

Messenger.   Yes; King Laïos; and the man was one of his herdsmen.

Oedipus.   Is he still alive? Can I see him?

Messenger.   These men here
  Know best about such things.

---

[15] Oedipus literally means "swollen-foot."

Oedipus.   Does anyone here
  Know this shepherd that he is talking about?
  Have you seen him in the fields, or in the town?   130
  If you have, tell me. It is time things were made plain.
Choragos.   I think the man he means is that same shepherd
  You have already asked to see. Iocastê perhaps
  Could tell you something.
Oedipus.   Do you know anything
  About him, Lady? Is he the man we have summoned?
  Is that the man this shepherd means?
Iocastê.   Why think of him?
  Forget this herdsman. Forget it all.
  This talk is a waste of time.
Oedipus.   How can you say that?
  When the clues to my true birth are in my hands?
Iocastê.   For God's love, let us have no more questioning!   140
  Is your life nothing to you?
  My own is pain enough for me to bear.
Oedipus.   You need not worry. Suppose my mother a slave,
  And born of slaves: no baseness can touch you.
Iocastê.   Listen to me, I beg you: do not do this thing!
Oedipus.   I will not listen; the truth must be made known.
Iocastê.   Everything that I say is for your own good!
Oedipus.   My own good
  Snaps my patience, then; I want none of it.
Iocastê.   You are fatally wrong! May you never learn who you are!
Oedipus.   Go, one of you, and bring the shepherd here.   150
  Let us leave this woman to brag of her royal name.
Iocastê.   Ah, miserable!
  That is the only word I have for you now.
  That is the only word I can ever have.

[*Exit into the palace.*]

Choragos.   Why has she left us, Oedipus? Why has she gone
  In such a passion of sorrow? I fear this silence:
  Something dreadful may come of it.
Oedipus.   Let it come!
  However base my birth, I must know about it.
  The Queen, like a woman, is perhaps ashamed
  To think of my low origin. But I   160
  Am a child of Luck; I can not be dishonored.
  Luck is my mother; the passing months, my brothers,
  Have seen me rich and poor.
                          If this is so,

How could I wish that I were someone else?
How could I not be glad to know my birth?

Ode III

Chorus.   If ever the coming time were known   [*Strophe*]
  To my heart's pondering,
  Kithairon, now by Heaven I see the torches
  At the festival of the next full moon,
  And see the dance, and hear the choir sing
  A grace to your gentle shade:
  Mountain where Oedipus was found,
  O mountain guard of a noble race!
  May the god who heals us lend his aid,
  And let that glory come to pass   10
  For our king's cradling-ground.

  Of the nymphs that flower beyond the years,   [*Antistrophe*]
  Who bore you, royal child,
  To Pan of the hills or the timberline Apollo,
  Cold in delight where the upland clears,
  Or Hermês for whom Kyllenê's heights are piled?[16]
  Or flushed as evening cloud,
  Great Dionysos, roamer of mountains,
  He—was it he who found you there,
  And caught you up in his own proud   20
  Arms from the sweet god-ravisher
  Who laughed by the Muses' fountains?

Scene IV

Oedipus.   Sirs: though I do not know the man,
  I think I see him coming, this shepherd we want:
  He is old, like our friend here, and the men
  Bringing him seem to be servants of my house.
  But you can tell, if you have ever seen him.

[*Enter Shepherd escorted by servants.*]

Choragos.   I know him, he was Laïos' man. You can trust him.
Oedipus.   Tell me first, you from Corinth: is this the shepherd
  We were discussing?
Messenger.   This is the very man.

---

[16] Hermês, the herald of the Olympian gods, was born on the mountain of Kyllenê.

Oedipus [*to Shepherd*].   Come here. No, look at me. You must answer
   Everything I ask. You belonged to Laïos?   10
Shepherd.   Yes: born his slave, brought up in his house.
Oedipus.   Tell me what kind of work did you do for him?
Shepherd.   I was a shepherd of his, most of my life.
Oedipus.   Where mainly did you go for pasturage?
Shepherd.   Sometimes Kithairon, sometimes the hills near-by.
Oedipus.   Do you remember ever seeing this man out there?
Shepherd.   What would he be doing there? This man?
Oedipus.   This man standing here. Have you ever seen him before?
Shepherd.   No. At least, not to my recollection.
Messenger.   And that is not strange, my lord. But I'll refresh   20
   His memory: he must remember when we two
   Spent three whole seasons together, March to September,
   On Kithairon or thereabouts. He had two flocks;
   I had one. Each autumn I'd drive mine home
   And he would go back with his to Laïos' sheepfold.—
   Is this not true, just as I have described it?
Shepherd.   True, yes; but it was all so long ago.
Messenger.   Well, then: do you remember, back in those days
   That you gave me a baby boy to bring up as my own?
Shepherd.   What if I did? What are you trying to say?   30
Messenger.   King Oedipus was once that little child.
Shepherd.   Damn you, hold your tongue!
Oedipus.   No more of that!
   It is your tongue needs watching, not this man's.
Shepherd.   My King, my Master, what is it I have done wrong?
Oedipus.   You have not answered his question about the boy.
Shepherd.   He does not know . . . He is only making trouble . . .
Oedipus.   Come, speak plainly, or it will go hard with you.
Shepherd.   In God's name, do not torture an old man!
Oedipus.   Come here, one of you; bind his arms behind him.
Shepherd.   Unhappy king! What more do you wish to learn?   40
Oedipus.   Did you give this man the child he speaks of?
Shepherd.   I did.
   And I would to God I had died that very day.
Oedipus.   You will die now unless you speak the truth.
Shepherd.   Yet if I speak the truth, I am worse than dead.
Oedipus.   Very well; since you insist on delaying—
Shepherd.   No! I have told you already that I gave him the boy.
Oedipus.   Where did you get him? From your house? From somewhere
   else?
Shepherd.   Not from mine, no. A man gave him to me.
Oedipus.   Is that man here? Do you know whose slave he was?
Shepherd.   For God's love, my King, do not ask me any more!   50

Oedipus.   You are a dead man if I have to ask you again.
Shepherd.   Then . . . Then the child was from the palace of Laïos.
Oedipus.   A slave child? or a child of his own line?
Shepherd.   Ah, I am on the brink of dreadful speech!
Oedipus.   And I of dreadful hearing. Yet I must hear.
Shepherd.   If you must be told, then . . .

They said it was Laïos' child,

But it is your wife who can tell you about that.
Oedipus.   My wife!—Did she give it to you?
Shepherd.   My lord, she did.
Oedipus.   Do you know why?
Shepherd.   I was told to get rid of it.
Oedipus.   An unspeakable mother!
Shepherd.   There had been prophecies . . .   60
Oedipus.   Tell me.
Shepherd.   It was said that the boy would kill his own father.
Oedipus.   Then why did you give him over to this old man?
Shepherd.   I pitied the baby, my King,
And I thought that this man would take him far away
To his own country.

He saved him—but for what a fate!

For if you are what this man says you are,
No man living is more wretched than Oedipus.
Oedipus.   Ah God!
It was true!

All the prophecies!

—Now,

O Light, may I look on you for the last time!   70
I, Oedipus,
Oedipus, damned in his birth, in his marriage damned,
Damned in the blood he shed with his own hand!

[He rushes into the palace.]

Ode IV

Chorus.   Alas for the seed of men.   *[Strophe 1]*

What measure shall I give these generations
That breathe on the void and are void
And exist and do not exist?

Who bears more weight of joy
Than mass of sunlight shifting in images,
Or who shall make his thought stay on
That down time drifts away?

Your splendor is all fallen.

O naked brow of wrath and tears,   10
O change of Oedipus!
I who saw your days call no man blest—
Your great days like ghosts gone.

That mind was a strong bow.   [Antistrophe 1]

Deep, how deep you drew it then, hard archer,
At a dim fearful range,
And brought dear glory down!

You overcame the stranger—
The virgin with her hooking lion claws—
And though death sang, stood like a tower   20
To make pale Thebes take heart.

Fortress against our sorrow!

Divine king, giver of laws,
Majestic Oedipus!
No prince in Thebes had ever such renown,
No prince won such grace of power.

And now of all men ever known   [Strophe 2]
Most pitiful is this man's story:
His fortunes are most changed, his state
Fallen to a low slave's   30
Ground under bitter fate.

O Oedipus, most royal one!
The great door that expelled you to the light
Gave at night—ah, gave night to your glory:
As to the father, to the fathering son.

All understood too late.

How could that queen whom Laïos won,
The garden that he harrowed at his height,
Be silent when that act was done?

But all eyes fail before time's eye,   [Antistrophe 2]
All actions come to justice there   41
Though never willed, though far down the deep past,
Your bed, your dread sirings,
Are brought to book at last.

Child by Laïos doomed to die,
Then doomed to lose that fortunate little death,
Would God you never took breath in this air
That with my wailing lips I take to cry:

For I weep the world's outcast.

I was blind, and now I can tell why: 50
Asleep, for you had given ease of breath
To Thebes, while the false years went by.

Exodos

[*Enter, from the palace, Second Messenger.*]

Second Messenger.   Elders of Thebes, most honored in this land,
What horrors are yours to see and hear, what weight
Of sorrow to be endured, if, true to your birth,
You venerate the line of Labdakos!
I think neither Istros nor Phasis, those great rivers,
Could purify this place of the corruption
It shelters now, or soon must bring to light—
Evil not done unconsciously, but willed.

The greatest griefs are those we cause ourselves.
Choragos.   Surely, friend, we have grief enough already;   10
What new sorrow do you mean?
Second Messenger.   The Queen is dead.
Choragos.   Iocastê? Dead? But at whose hand?
Second Messenger.   Her own.
The full horror of what happened you can not know,
For you did not see it; but I, who did, will tell you
As clearly as I can how she met her death.

When she had left us,
In passionate silence, passing through the court,
She ran to her apartment in the house,
Her hair clutched by the fingers of both hands.

She closed the doors behind her; then, by that bed   20
Where long ago the fatal son was conceived—
The son who should bring about his father's death—
We heard her call upon Laïos, dead so many years,
And heard her wail for the double fruit of her marriage,
A husband by her husband, children by her child.

Exactly how she died I do not know:
For Oedipus burst in moaning and would not let us
Keep vigil to the end: it was by him
As he stormed about the room that our eyes were caught.
From one to another of us he went, begging a sword,   30
Cursing the wife who was not his wife, the mother
Whose womb had carried his own children and himself.
I do not know: it was none of us aided him,
But surely one of the gods was in control!
For with a dreadful cry
He hurled his weight, as though wrenched out of himself,
At the twin doors: the bolts gave, and he rushed in.
And there we saw her hanging, her body swaying
From the cruel cord she had noosed about her neck.
A great sob broke from him, heartbreaking to hear,   40
As he loosed the rope and lowered her to the ground.

I would blot out from my mind what happened next!
For the King ripped from her gown the golden brooches
That were her ornament, and raised them, and plunged them down
Straight into his own eyeballs, crying, "No more,
No more shall you look on the misery about me,
The horrors of my own doing! Too long have you known
The faces of those whom I should never have seen,
Too long been blind to those for whom I was searching!
From this hour, go in darkness!" And as he spoke,   50
He struck at his eyes—not once, but many times;
And the blood spattered his beard,
Bursting from his ruined sockets like red hail.

So from the unhappiness of two this evil has sprung,
A curse on the man and woman alike. The old
Happiness of the house of Labdakos
Was happiness enough: where is it today?
It is all wailing and ruin, disgrace, death—all
The misery of mankind that has a name—
And it is wholly and for ever theirs.   60
Choragos.   Is he in agony still? Is there no rest for him?
Second Messenger.   He is calling for someone to lead him to the gates
So that all the children of Kadmos may look upon
His father's murderer, his mother's—no,
I can not say it!
                    And then he will leave Thebes,
Self-exiled, in order that the curse
Which he himself pronounced may depart from the house.
He is weak, and there is none to lead him,

So terrible is his suffering.
                                    But you will see:
Look, the doors are opening; in a moment   70
You will see a thing that would crush a heart of stone.

[*The central door is opened; Oedipus, blinded, is led in.*]

Choragos.   Dreadful indeed for men to see.
    Never have my own eyes
    Looked on a sight so full of fear.

    Oedipus!
    What madness came upon you, what daemon
    Leaped on your life with heavier
    Punishment than a mortal man can bear?
    No: I can not even
    Look at you, poor ruined one.   80
    And I would speak, question, ponder,
    If I were able. No.
    You make me shudder.
Oedipus.   God. God.
    Is there a sorrow greater?
    Where shall I find harbor in this world?
    My voice is hurled far on a dark wind.
    What has God done to me?
Choragos.   Too terrible to think of, or to see.

Oedipus.   O cloud of night,   [*Strophe 1*]
    Never to be turned away: night coming on,   91
    I can not tell how: night like a shroud!

    My fair winds brought me here.
                                    Oh God. Again
    The pain of the spikes where I had sight,
    The flooding pain
    Of memory, never to be gouged out.
Choragos.   This is not strange.
    You suffer it all twice over, remorse in pain,
    Pain in remorse.

Oedipus.   Ah dear friend   [*Antistrophe 1*]
    Are you faithful even yet, you alone?   101
    Are you still standing near me, will you stay here,
    Patient, to care for the blind?
                                    The blind man!

Yet even blind I know who it is attends me,
By the voice's tone—
Though my new darkness hide the comforter.
Choragos.   Oh fearful act!
What god was it drove you to rake black
Night across your eyes?

Oedipus.   Apollo. Apollo. Dear   [*Strophe 2*]
Children, the god was Apollo.   111
He brought my sick, sick fate upon me.
But the blinding hand was my own!
How could I bear to see
When all my sight was horror everywhere?
Choragos.   Everywhere; that is true.
Oedipus.   And now what is left?
Images? Love? A greeting even,
Sweet to the senses? Is there anything?
Ah no, friends: lead me away.   120
Lead me away from Thebes.
                        Lead the great wreck
And hell of Oedipus, whom the gods hate.
Choragos.   Your fate is clear, you are not blind to that.
Would God you had never found it out!

Oedipus.   Death take the man who unbound   [*Antistrophe 2*]
My feet on that hillside
And delivered me from death to life! What life?
If only I had died,
This weight of monstrous doom
Could not have dragged me and my darlings down.   130
Choragos.   I would have wished the same.
Oedipus.   Oh never to have come here
With my father's blood upon me! Never
To have been the man they call his mother's husband!
Oh accurst! Oh child of evil,
To have entered that wretched bed—
                        the selfsame one!
More primal than sin itself, this fell to me.
Choragos.   I do not know how I can answer you.
You were better dead than alive and blind.
Oedipus.   Do not counsel me any more. This punishment   140
That I have laid upon myself is just.
If I had eyes,
I do not know how I could bear the sight
Of my father, when I came to the house of Death,

Or my mother: for I have sinned against them both
So vilely that I could not make my peace
By strangling my own life.
      Or do you think my children,
Born as they were born, would be sweet to my eyes?
Ah never, never! Nor this town with its high walls,
Nor the holy images of the gods.
        For I,   150
Thrice miserable!—Oedipus, noblest of all the line
Of Kadmos, have condemned myself to enjoy
These things no more, by my own malediction
Expelling that man whom the gods declared
To be a defilement in the house of Laïos.
After exposing the rankness of my own guilt,
How could I look men frankly in the eyes?
No, I swear it,
If I could have stifled my hearing at its source,
I would have done it and made all this body   160
A tight cell of misery, blank to light and sound:
So I should have been safe in a dark agony
Beyond all recollection.
       Ah Kithairon!
Why did you shelter me? When I was cast upon you,
Why did I not die? Then I should never
Have shown the world my execrable birth.

Ah Polybos! Corinth, city that I believed
The ancient seat of my ancestors: how fair
I seemed, your child! And all the while this evil
Was cancerous within me!
       For I am sick   170
In my daily life, sick in my origin.

O three roads, dark ravine, woodland and way
Where three roads met: you, drinking my father's blood,
My own blood, spilled by my own hand: can you remember
The unspeakable things I did there, and the things
I went on from there to do?
      O marriage, marriage!
The act that engendered me, and again the act
Performed by the son in the same bed—
        Ah, the net
Of incest, mingling fathers, brothers, sons,
With brides, wives, mothers; the last evil   180
That can be known by men: no tongue can say

How evil!

No. For the love of God, conceal me
Somewhere far from Thebes; or kill me; or hurl me
Into the sea, away from men's eyes for ever.

Come, lead me. You need not fear to touch me.
Of all men, I alone can bear this guilt.

[*Enter Creon.*]

Choragos.   We are not the ones to decide; but Creon here
May fitly judge of what you ask. He only
Is left to protect the city in your place.
Oedipus.   Alas, how can I speak to him? What right have I   190
To beg his courtesy whom I have deeply wronged?
Creon.   I have not come to mock you, Oedipus,
Or to reproach you, either.
[*To attendants.*]   —You, standing there:
If you have lost all respect for man's dignity,
At least respect the flame of Lord Helios:
Do not allow this pollution to show itself
Openly here, an affront to the earth
And Heaven's rain and the light of day. No, take him
Into the house as quickly as you can.
For it is proper   200
That only the close kindred see his grief.
Oedipus.   I pray you in God's name, since your courtesy
Ignores my dark expectation, visiting
With mercy this man of all men most execrable:
Give me what I ask—for your good, not for mine.
Creon.   And what is it that you would have me do?
Oedipus.   Drive me out of this country as quickly as may be
To a place where no human voice can ever greet me.
Creon.   I should have done that before now—only,
God's will had not been wholly revealed to me.   210
Oedipus.   But his command is plain: the parricide
Must be destroyed. I am that evil man.
Creon.   That is the sense of it, yes; but as things are,
We had best discover clearly what is to be done.
Oedipus.   You would learn more about a man like me?
Creon.   You are ready now to listen to the god.
Oedipus.   I will listen. But it is to you
That I must turn for help. I beg you, hear me.

The woman in there—
Give her whatever funeral you think proper: 220

She is your sister.
            —But let me go, Creon!
Let me purge my father's Thebes of the pollution
Of my living here, and go out to the wild hills,
To Kithairon, that has won such fame with me,
The tomb my mother and father appointed for me,
And let me die there, as they willed I should.
And yet I know
Death will not ever come to me through sickness
Or in any natural way: I have been preserved
For some unthinkable fate. But let that be.   230
As for my sons, you need not care for them.
They are men, they will find some way to live.
But my poor daughters, who have shared my table,
Who never before have been parted from their father—
Take care of them, Creon; do this for me.
And will you let me touch them with my hands
A last time, and let us weep together?
Be kind, my lord,
Great prince, be kind!
                Could I but touch them,
They would be mine again, as when I had my eyes.   240

[*Enter Antigone and Ismene, attended.*]

Ah, God!
Is it my dearest children I hear weeping?
Has Creon pitied me and sent my daughters?
Creon.   Yes, Oedipus: I knew that they were dear to you
In the old days, and know you must love them still.
Oedipus.   May God bless you for this—and be a friendlier
Guardian to you than he has been to me!

Children, where are you?
Come quickly to my hands: they are your brother's—
Hands that have brought your father's once clear eyes   250
To this way of seeing—
                Ah dearest ones,
I had neither sight nor knowledge then, your father
By the woman who was the source of his own life!
And I weep for you—having no strength to see you—,
I weep for you when I think of the bitterness
That men will visit upon you all your lives.
What homes, what festivals can you attend
Without being forced to depart again in tears?

And when you come to marriageable age,
Where is the man, my daughters, who would dare   260
Risk the bane that lies on all my children?
Is there any evil wanting? Your father killed
His father; sowed the womb of her who bore him;
Engendered you at the fount of his own existence!
That is what they will say of you.
                             Then whom
Can you ever marry? There are no bridegrooms for you,
And your lives must wither away in sterile dreaming.
O Creon, son of Menoikeus!
You are the only father my daughters have,
Since we, their parents, are both of us gone for ever.   270
They are your own blood: you will not let them
Fall into beggary and loneliness;
You will keep them from the miseries that are mine!
Take pity on them; see, they are only children,
Friendless except for you. Promise me this,
Great Prince, and give me your hand in token of it.

[*Creon clasps his right hand.*]

Children:
I could say much, if you could understand me,
But as it is, I have only this prayer for you:
Live where you can, be as happy as you can—   280
Happier, please God, than God has made your father!
Creon.   Enough. You have wept enough. Now go within.
Oedipus.   I must; but it is hard.
Creon.   Time eases all things.
Oedipus.   But you must promise—
Creon.   Say what you desire.
Oedipus.   Send me from Thebes!
Creon.   God grant that I may!
Oedipus.   But since God hates me . . .
Creon.   No, he will grant your wish.
Oedipus.   You promise?
Creon.   I can not speak beyond my knowledge.
Oedipus.   Then lead me in.
Creon.   Come now, and leave your children.
Oedipus.   No! Do not take them from me!
Creon.   Think no longer
That you are in command here, but rather think   290
How, when you were, you served your own destruction.

[*Exeunt into the house all but the Chorus; the Choragos chants directly to the audience.*]

Choragos.   Men of Thebes: look upon Oedipus.

> This is the king who solved the famous riddle
> And towered up, most powerful of men.
> No mortal eyes but looked on him with envy,
> Yet in the end ruin swept over him.
> Let every man in mankind's frailty
> Consider his last day; and let none
> Presume on his good fortune until he find
> Life, at his death, a memory without pain.   300

QUESTIONS

1.   How does the Prologue establish the mood and theme of the play? What aspects of Oedipus's character are revealed there?   **2.**   Sophocles's audience knew the Oedipus story as you, for instance, know the story of the crucifixion. In the absence of suspense, what literary devices serve to hold the audience's attention?   **3.**   To what extent and in what ways does the chorus contribute to the dramatic development and tension of the play?

WRITING TOPICS

1.   Could Oedipus have avoided the tragic outcome of this drama? What characteristics of Sophocles's world view are suggested by your answer? Is our behavior in the world governed by free will or is our behavior determined? In view of your answers to the preceding questions, of what is Oedipus guilty?   **2.**   The play embodies a pattern of figurative and literal allusions to darkness and light, to vision and blindness. How does that figurative language function, and what relationship does it bear to Oedipus's self-inflicted punishment?

INNOCENCE
AND
EXPERIENCE

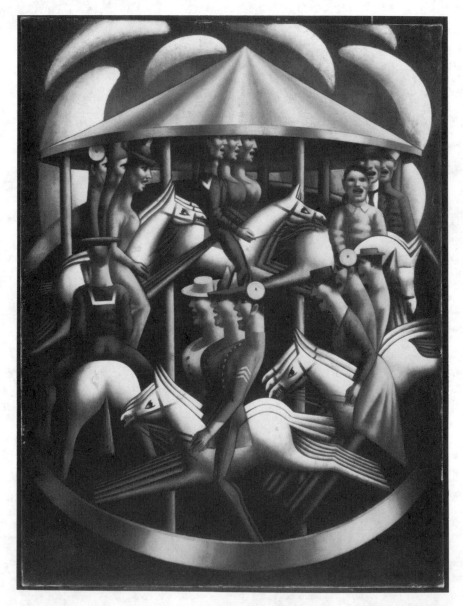

The Merry-Go-Round, 1916 by Mark Gertler.

ESSAYS

Shooting an Elephant (1936)

GEORGE ORWELL [1903–1950]

In Moulmein, in lower Burma, I was hated by large numbers of people—the only time in my life that I have been important enough for this to happen to me. I was sub-divisional police officer of the town, and in an aimless, petty kind of way anti-European feeling was very bitter. No one had the guts to raise a riot, but if a European woman went through the bazaars alone somebody would probably spit betel juice over her dress. As a police officer I was an obvious target and was baited whenever it seemed safe to do so. When a nimble Burman tripped me up on the football field and the referee (another Burman) looked the other way, the crowd yelled with hideous laughter. This happened more than once. In the end the sneering yellow faces of young men that met me everywhere, the insults hooted after me when I was at a safe distance, got badly on my nerves. The young Buddhist priests were the worst of all. There were several thousands of them in the town and none of them seemed to have anything to do except stand on street corners and jeer at Europeans.

All this was perplexing and upsetting. For at that time I had already made up my mind that imperialism was an evil thing and the sooner I chucked up my job and got out of it the better. Theoretically—and secretly, of course—I was all for the Burmese and all against their oppressors, the British. As for the job I was doing, I hated it more bitterly than I can perhaps make clear. In a job like that you see the dirty work of Empire at close quarters. The wretched prisoners huddling in the stinking cages of the lock-ups, the grey, cowed faces of the long-term convicts, the scarred buttocks of the men who had been flogged with bamboos—all these oppressed me with an intolerable sense of guilt. But I could get nothing into perspective. I was young and ill-educated and I had had to think out my problems in the utter silence that is imposed on every Englishman in the East. I did not even know that the British Empire is dying, still less did I know that it is a great deal better than the younger empires that are going to supplant it. All I knew was that I was stuck between my hatred of the empire I served and my rage against the evil-spirited little beasts who tried to make my job impossible. With one part of my mind I thought of the British Raj[1] as an unbreakable tyranny, as something clamped down, *in saecula saeculorum*,[2] upon the will of prostrate peoples; with another part I thought that the greatest joy in the world would be to drive a bayonet into a Buddhist priest's guts. Feelings like these are the normal by-products of imperialism; ask any Anglo-Indian official, if you can catch him off duty.

One day something happened which in a roundabout way was enlightening.   3 It was a tiny incident in itself, but it gave me a better glimpse than I had had before of the real nature of imperialism—the real motive for which despotic governments act. Early one morning the sub-inspector at a police station the other end of the town rang me up on the 'phone and said that an elephant was ravaging the bazaar. Would I please come and do something about it? I did not know what I could do, but I wanted to see what was happening and I got on to a pony and started out. I took my rifle, an old .44 Winchester and much too small to kill an elephant, but I thought the noise might be useful *in terrorem*. Various Burmans stopped me on the way and told me about the elephant's doings. It was not, of course, a wild elephant, but a tame one which had gone "must." It had been chained up, as tame elephants always are when their attack of "must" is due, but on the previous night it had broken its chain and escaped. Its mahout,[3] the only person who could manage it when it was in that state, had set out in pursuit, but had taken the wrong direction and was now twelve hours' journey away, and in the morning the elephant had suddenly reappeared in the town. The Burmese population had no weapons and were quite helpless against it. It had already destroyed somebody's bamboo hut, killed a cow and raided some fruit-stalls and devoured the stock; also it had met the municipal rubbish van and, when the driver jumped out and took to his heels, had turned the van over and inflicted violences upon it.

The Burmese sub-inspector and some Indian constables were waiting for me   4 in the quarter where the elephant had been seen. It was a very poor quarter, a labyrinth of squalid bamboo huts, thatched with palm-leaf, winding all over a steep hillside. I remember that it was a cloudy, stuffy morning at the beginning of the rains. We began questioning the people as to where the elephant had gone and, as usual, failed to get any definite information. That is invariably the case in the East; a story always sounds clear enough at a distance, but the nearer you get to the scene of events the vaguer it becomes. Some of the people said that the elephant had gone in one direction, some said that he had gone in another, some professed not even to have heard of any elephant. I had almost made up my mind that the whole story was a pack of lies, when we heard yells a little distance away. There was a loud, scandalized cry of "Go away, child! Go away this instant!" and an old woman with a switch in her

---

[1] The imperial British government of India and Burma.
[2] For eternity.
[3] The keeper and driver of an elephant.

hand came round the corner of a hut, violently shooing away a crowd of naked children. Some more women followed, clicking their tongues and exclaiming; evidently there was something that the children ought not to have seen. I rounded the hut and saw a man's dead body sprawling in the mud. He was an Indian, a black Dravidian coolie, almost naked, and he could not have been dead many minutes. The people said that the elephant had come suddenly upon him round the corner of the hut, caught him with its trunk, put its foot on his back and ground him into the earth. This was the rainy season and the ground was soft, and his face had scored a trench a foot deep and a couple of yards long. He was lying on his belly with arms crucified and head sharply twisted to one side. His face was coated with mud, the eyes wide open, the teeth bared and grinning with an expression of unendurable agony. (Never tell me, by the way, that the dead look peaceful. Most of the corpses I have seen look devilish.) The friction of the great beast's foot had stripped the skin from his back as neatly as one skins a rabbit. As soon as I saw the dead man I sent an orderly to a friend's house nearby to borrow an elephant rifle. I had already sent back the pony, not wanting it to go mad with fright and throw me if it smelt the elephant.

The orderly came back in a few minutes with a rifle and five cartridges, and   5 meanwhile some Burmans had arrived and told us that the elephant was in the paddy fields below, only a few hundred yards away. As I started forward practically the whole population of the quarter flocked out of the houses and followed me. They had seen the rifle and were all shouting excitedly that I was going to shoot the elephant. They had not shown much interest in the elephant when he was merely ravaging their homes, but it was different now that he was going to be shot. It was a bit of fun to them, as it would be to an English crowd; besides they wanted the meat. It made me vaguely uneasy. I had no intention of shooting the elephant—I had merely sent for the rifle to defend myself if necessary—and it is always unnerving to have a crowd following you. I marched down the hill, looking and feeling a fool, with the rifle over my shoulder and an ever-growing army of people jostling at my heels. At the bottom, when you got a way from the huts, there was a metalled road and beyond that a miry waste of paddy fields a thousand yards across, not yet ploughed but soggy from the first rains and dotted with coarse grass. The elephant was standing eight yards from the road, his left side towards us. He took not the slightest notice of the crowd's approach. He was tearing up branches of grass, beating them against his knees to clean them and stuffing them into his mouth.

I had halted on the road. As soon as I saw the elephant I knew with perfect   6 certainty that I ought not to shoot him. It is a serious matter to shoot a working elephant—it is comparable to destroying a huge and costly piece of machinery—and obviously one ought not to do it if it can possibly be avoided. And at that distance, peacefully eating, the elephant looked no more dangerous than a cow. I thought then and I think now that his attack of "must" was already passing off; in which case he would merely wander harmlessly about until the mahout came back and caught him. Moreover, I did not in the least want to shoot him. I decided that I would watch him for a little while to make sure that he did not turn savage again, and then go home.

But at that moment I glanced round at the crowd that had followed me. It was an immense crowd, two thousand at the least and growing every minute. It blocked the road for a long distance on either side. I looked at the sea of yellow faces above the garish clothes—faces all happy and excited over this bit of fun, all certain that the elephant was going to be shot. They were watching me as they would watch a conjurer about to perform a trick. They did not like me, but with the magical rifle in my hands I was momentarily worth watching. And suddenly I realized that I should have to shoot the elephant after all. The people expected it of me and I had got to do it; I could feel their two thousand wills pressing me forward, irresistibly. And it was at this moment, as I stood there with the rifle in my hands, that I first grasped the hollowness, the futility of the white man's dominion in the East. Here was I, the white man with his gun, standing in front of the unarmed native crowd—seemingly the leading actor of the piece; but in reality I was only an absurd puppet pushed to and fro by the will of those yellow faces behind. I perceived in this moment that when the white man turns tyrant it is his own freedoms that he destroys. He becomes a sort of hollow, posing dummy, the conventionalized figure of a sahib. For it is the condition of his rule that he shall spend his life in trying to impress the "natives," and so in every crisis he has got to do what the "natives" expect of him. He wears a mask, and his face grows to fit it. I had got to shoot the elephant. I had committed myself to doing it when I sent for the rifle. A sahib has got to act like a sahib; he has got to appear resolute, to know his own mind and do definite things. To come all that way, rifle in hand, with two thousand people marching at my heels, and then to trail feebly away, having done nothing—no, that was impossible. The crowd would laugh at me. And my whole life, every white man's life in the East, was one long struggle not to be laughed at.

But I did not want to shoot the elephant. I watched him beating his bunch of grass against his knees, with that preoccupied grandmotherly air that elephants have. It seemed to me that it would be murder to shoot him. At that age I was not squeamish about killing animals, but I had never shot an elephant and never wanted to. (Somehow it always seems worse to kill a *large* animal.) Besides, there was the beast's owner to be considered. Alive, the elephant was worth at least a hundred pounds; dead, he would only be worth the value of his tusks, five pounds, possibly. But I had got to act quickly. I turned to some experienced-looking Burmans who had been there when we arrived, and asked them how the elephant had been behaving. They all said the same thing: he took no notice of you if you left him alone, but he might charge if you went too close to him.

It was perfectly clear to me what I ought to do. I ought to walk up to within, say, twenty-five yards of the elephant and test his behavior. If he charged, I could shoot; if he took no notice of me, it would be safe to leave him until the mahout came back. But also I knew that I was going to do no such thing. I was a poor shot with a rifle and the ground was soft mud into which one would sink at every step. If the elephant charged and I missed him, I should have about as much chance as a toad under a steam-roller. But even then I was not thinking particularly of my own skin, only of the watchful yellow faces behind. For at that moment, with the crowd watching me, I was not afraid in the ordinary sense, as I would have been if I had been alone. A white man mustn't be frightened in front of "natives"; and so, in general, he isn't frightened. The sole thought in my mind was that if anything went wrong those two thousand Burmans would see me pursued, caught, trampled on and reduced to a grinning corpse like that Indian up the hill. And if that happened it was quite probable that some of them would laugh. That would never do. There was only one alternative. I shoved the cartridges into the magazine and lay down on the road to get a better aim.

The crowd grew very still, and a deep, low, happy sigh, as of people who see the theatre curtain go up at last, breathed from innumerable throats. They were going to have their bit of fun after all. The rifle was a beautiful German thing with cross-hair sights. I did not then know that in shooting an elephant one would shoot to cut an imaginary bar running from ear-hole to ear-hole. I ought, therefore, as the elephant was sideways on, to have aimed straight at his ear-hole; actually I aimed several inches in front of this, thinking the brain would be further forward.

When I pulled the trigger I did not hear the bang or feel the kick—one never does when a shot goes home—but I heard the devilish roar of glee that went up from the crowd. In that instant, in too short a time, one would have thought, even for the bullet to get there, a mysterious, terrible change had come over the elephant. He neither stirred nor fell, but every line of his body had altered. He looked suddenly stricken, shrunken, immensely old, as though the frightful impact of the bullet had paralysed him without knocking him down. At last, after what seemed a long time—it might have been five seconds, I dare say—he sagged flabbily to his knees. His mouth slobbered. An enormous senility seemed to have settled upon him. One could have imagined him thousands of years old. I fired again into the same spot. At the second shot he did not collapse but climbed with desperate slowness to his feet and stood weakly upright, with legs sagging and head drooping. I fired a third time. That was the shot that did for him. You could see the agony of it jolt his whole body and knock the last remnant of strength from his legs. But in falling he seemed for a moment to rise, for as his hind legs collapsed beneath him he seemed to tower upward like a huge rock toppling, his trunk reaching skywards like a tree. He trumpeted, for the first and only time. And then down he came, his belly towards me, with a crash that seemed to shake the ground even where I lay.

I got up. The Burmans were already racing past me across the mud. It was obvious that the elephant would never rise again, but he was not dead. He was breathing very rhythmically with long rattling gasps, his great mound of a side painfully rising and falling. His mouth was wide open—I could see far down into caverns of pale pink throat. I waited a long time for him to die, but his breathing did not weaken. Finally I fired my two remaining shots into the spot where I thought his heart must be. The thick blood welled out of him like red velvet, but still he did not die. His body did not even jerk when the shots hit him, the tortured breathing continued without a pause. He was dying, very slowly and in great agony, but in some world remote from me where not even a bullet could damage him further. I felt that I had got to put an end to that dreadful noise. It seemed dreadful to see the great beast lying there, powerless to move and yet powerless to die, and not even to be able to finish him. I sent back for my small rifle and poured shot after shot into his heart and down his throat. They seemed to make no impression. The tortured gasps continued as steadily as the ticking of a clock.

In the end I could not stand it any longer and went away. I heard later that   13
it took him half an hour to die. Burmans were bringing dahs[4] and baskets even before I left, and I was told they had stripped his body almost to the bones by the afternoon.

Afterwards, of course, there were endless discussions about the shooting of   14
the elephant. The owner was furious, but he was only an Indian and could do nothing. Besides, legally I had done the right thing, for a mad elephant has to be killed, like a mad dog, if its owner fails to control it. Among the Europeans opinion was divided. The older men said I was right, the younger men said it was a damn shame to shoot an elephant for killing a coolie, because an elephant was worth more than any damn Coringhee coolie. And afterwards I was very glad that the coolie had been killed; it put me legally in the right and it gave me a sufficient pretext for shooting the elephant. I often wondered whether any of the others grasped that I had done it solely to avoid looking a fool.

QUESTIONS

1. Why does Orwell disclose the significance the event had for him midway through the essay (paragraph 7) rather than saving it for the conclusion? **2.** Examine carefully paragraphs 11 and 12, in which Orwell describes the death of the elephant. Is the reader meant to take the passage literally, or can a case be made that Orwell has imbued the elephant's death with symbolic meaning? **3.** Orwell tells us repeatedly that his sympathies are with the Burmese. Does the language Orwell uses to describe them support his claim? Explain.

WRITING TOPIC

What does Orwell conclude regarding the position of foreign authorities in a hostile country?

---

[4] Knives.

Confessions of a Blue-Chip Black

1982

ROGER WILKINS [b. 1932]

Early in the spring of 1932—six months after Earl's brother, Roy, left Kansas   1
City to go to New York to join the national staff of the National Association
for the Advancement of Colored People, and eight months before Franklin
Roosevelt was elected president for the first time—Earl and Helen Wilkins had
the first and only child to be born of their union. I was born in a little segregated hospital in Kansas City called Phillis Wheatley.[1] The first time my mother
saw me, she cried. My head was too long and my color, she thought, was
blue.

My parents never talked about slavery or my ancestors. Images of Africa were   2
images of backwardness and savagery. Once, when I was a little boy, I said to
my mother after a friend of my parents left the house: "Mr. Bledsoe is black
isn't he, mama."

"Oh," she exclaimed. "Never say anybody is black. That's a terrible thing to   3
say."

Next time Mr. Bledsoe came to the house, I commented, "Mama, Mr.   4
Bledsoe is navy blue."

When I was two years old and my father was in the tuberculosis sanitarium,   5
he wrote me a letter, which I obviously couldn't read, but which tells a lot
about how he planned to raise his Negro son.

Friday, March 22, 1934

Dear Roger—

Let me congratulate you upon having reached your second birthday. Your   6
infancy is now past and it is now that you should begin to turn your thoughts
upon those achievements which are expected of a brilliant young gentleman
well on his way to manhood.

During the next year, you should learn the alphabet; you should learn cer-   7
tain French and English idioms which are a part of every cultivated person's
vocabulary: you should gain complete control of those natural functions which,
uncontrolled, are a source of worry and embarrassment to even the best of
grandmothers: you should learn how to handle table silver so that you will be
able to eat gracefully and conventionally: and you should learn the fundamental rules of social living—politeness, courtesy, consideration for others, and the
rest.

---

[1] Black American poet (1754?–1784).

This should not be difficult for you. You have the best and most patient of mothers in your sterling grandmother and your excellent mother. Great things are expected of you. Never, never forget that. 8

Love,
Your Father

We lived in a neat little stucco house on a hill in a small Negro section called Roundtop. I had no sense of being poor or of any anxiety about money. At our house, not only was there food and furniture and all the rest, there was even a baby grand piano that my mother would play sometimes. And there was a cleaning lady, Mrs. Turner, who came every week. 9

When it was time for me to go to school, the board of education provided us with a big yellow bus, which carried us past four or five perfectly fine schools down to the middle of the large Negro community, to a very old school called Crispus Attucks.[2] I have no memories of those bus rides except for my resentment of the selfishness of the whites who wouldn't let us share those newer-looking schools near to home. 10

My father came home when I was four and died when I was almost nine. He exuded authority. He thought the women hadn't been sufficiently firm with me, so he instituted a spanking program with that same hard hairbrush that my grandmother had used so much to try to insure that I didn't have "nigger-looking" hair. 11

After my father's death, the family moved to New York. Our apartment was in that legendary uptown area called Sugar Hill, where blacks who had it made were said to live the sweet life. I lived with my mother, my grandmother, and my mother's younger sister, Zelma. My Uncle Roy and his wife, Minnie, a New York social worker, lived on the same floor. My Aunt Marvel and her husband, Cecil, lived one floor down. 12

As life in New York settled into a routine, my life came to be dominated by four women: my mother, her sisters, and her mother. Nobody else had any children, so everybody concentrated on me. 13

Sometime early in 1943 my mother's work with the YMCA took her to Grand Rapids, Michigan, where she made a speech and met a forty-four-year-old bachelor doctor who looked like a white man. He had light skin, green eyes, and "good hair"—that is, hair that was as straight and as flat as white people's hair. He looked so like a white person that he could have passed for white. There was much talk about people who had passed. They were generally deemed to be bad people, for they were not simply selfish, but also cruel to those whom they left behind. On the other hand, people who could pass, but did not, were respected. 14

---

[2]American runaway slave killed in 1770 while leading an attack on British troops in Boston.

My mother remarried in October 1943, and soon I was once more on a train   15
with my grandmother, heading toward Grand Rapids and my new home. This
train also took me, at the age of twelve, beyond the last point in my life when
I would feel totally at peace with my blackness.

My new home was in the north end of Grand Rapids, a completely white   16
neighborhood. This would be a place I would henceforth think of as home.
And it would be the place where I would become more Midwestern than Har-
lemite, more American than black, and more complex than was comfortable or necessary for the middle-class conformity that my mother had in mind
for me.

Grand Rapids was pretty single-family houses and green spaces. The houses   17
looked like those in *Look* magazine or in *Life*. You could believe, and I did,
that there was happiness inside. To me, back then, the people seemed to belong to the houses as the houses belonged to the land, and all of it had to do
with being white. They moved and walked and talked as if the place, the country, and the houses were theirs, and I envied them.

I spent the first few weeks exploring Grand Rapids on a new bike my step-   18
father had bought for me. The people I passed would look back at me with
intense and sometimes puzzled looks on their faces as I pedaled by. Nobody
waved or even smiled. They just stopped what they were doing to stand and
look. As soon as I saw them looking, I would look forward and keep on riding.

One day I rode for miles, down and up and down again. I was past Grand   19
Rapids' squatty little downtown, and farther south until I began to see some
Negro people. There were black men and women and some girls, but it was
the boys I was looking for. Then I saw a group: four of them. They were about
my age, and they were dark. Though their clothes were not as sharp as the
boys' in the Harlem Valley, they were old, and I took the look of poverty and
the deep darkness of their faces to mean that they were like the hard boys of
Harlem.

One of them spotted me riding toward them and pointed. "Hey, lookit that   20
bigole skinny bike," he said. Then they all looked at my bike and at me. I
couldn't see expressions on their faces; only the blackness and the coarseness
of their clothes. Before any of the rest of them had a chance to say anything,
I stood up on the pedals and wheeled the bike in a U-turn and headed back
on up toward the north end of town. It took miles for the terror to finally
subside.

Farther on toward home, there was a large athletic field. As I neared the   21
field, I could see some large boys in shorts moving determinedly around a
football. When I got to the top of the hill that overlooked the field, I stopped
and stood, one foot on the ground and one leg hanging over the crossbar,
staring down at them. All the boys were white and big and old—sixteen to
eighteen. I had never seen a football work out before, and I was fascinated. I
completely forgot everything about color, theirs or mine.

Then one of them saw me. He pointed and said, "Look there's the little   22
coon watchin us."

I wanted to be invisible. I was horrified. My heart pounded, and my arms   23
and legs shook, but I managed to get back on my bike and ride home.

The first white friend I made was named Jerry Schild. On the second day of   24
our acquaintance, he took me to his house, above a store run by his parents. I
met his three younger siblings, including a very little one toddling around in
bare feet and a soiled diaper.

While Jerry changed the baby, I looked around the place. It was cheap, all   25
chintz and linoleum. The two soft pieces of furniture, a couch and an over-
stuffed chair, had gaping holes and were hemorrhaging their fillings. And there
were an awful lot of empty brown beer bottles sitting around, both in the
kitchen and out on the back porch. While the place was not dirty, it made me
very sad. Jerry and his family were poor in a way I had never seen people be
poor before, in Kansas city or even in Harlem.

Jerry's father wasn't there that day and Jerry didn't mention him. But later   26
in the week, when I went to call for Jerry, I saw him. I yelled for Jerry from
downstairs in the back and his father came to the railing of the porch on the
second floor. He was a skinny man in overalls with the bib hanging down
crookedly because it was fastened only on the shoulder. His face was narrow
and wrinkled and his eyes were set deep in dark hollows. He had a beer bottle
in his hand and he looked down at me. "Jerry ain't here," he said. He turned
away and went back inside.

One day our front doorbell rang and I could hear my mother's troubled   27
exclamation. "Jerry! What's wrong?" Jerry was crying so hard he could hardly
talk. "My father says I can't play with you anymore because you're not good
enough for us."

Creston High School, which served all the children from the north end of   28
Grand Rapids, was all white and middle-class. Nobody talked to me that first
day, but I was noticed. When I left school at the end of the day I found my
bike leaning up against the fence where I had left it, with a huge glob of slimy
spit on my shaggy saddle cover. People passed by on their way home and
looked at me and spit. I felt a hollowness behind my eyes, but I couldn't cry.
I just got on the bike, stood up on the pedals, and rode it home without sitting
down. And it went that way for about the first two weeks. After the third day,
I got rid of the saddle cover because the plain leather was a lot easier to clean.

But the glacier began to thaw. One day in class, the freckle-faced kid with   29
the crewcut sitting next to me was asking everybody for a pencil. And then he
looked at me and said, "Maybe you can lend me one." Those were the best
words I had heard since I first met Jerry. This kid had included me in the
human race in front of everybody. His name was Jack Waltz.

And after a while when the spitters had subsided and I could ride home   30
sitting down, I began to notice that little kids my size were playing pickup
games in the end zones of the football field. It looked interesting, but I didn't
know anybody and didn't know how they would respond to me. So I just rode
on by for a couple of weeks, slowing down each day, trying to screw up my
courage to go in.

But then one day, I saw Jack Waltz there. I stood around the edges of the 31
group watching. It seemed that they played forever without even noticing me,
but finally someone had to go home and the sides were unbalanced. Somebody
said, "Let's ask him."

As we lined up for our first huddle, I heard somebody on the other side say, 32
"I hope he doesn't have a knife." One of the guys on my side asked me. "Can
you run the ball?" I said yes, so they gave me the ball and I ran three quarters
of the length of the field for a touchdown. And I made other touchdowns and
other long runs before the game was over. When I thought about it later that
night, I became certain that part of my success was due to the imaginary knife
that was running interference for me. But no matter. By the end of the game,
I had a group of friends. Boys named Andy and Don and Bill and Gene and
Rich. We left the field together and some of them waved and yelled, "See ya
tomorra, Rog."

And Don De Young, a pleasant round-faced boy, even lived quite near me. 33
So, after parting from everybody else, he and I went on together down to the
corner of Coit and Knapp. As we parted, he suggested that we meet to go to
school together the next day. I had longed for that but I hadn't suggested it for
fear of a rebuff for overstepping the limits of my race. I had already learned
one of the great tenets of Negro survival in America: to live the reactive life. It
was like the old Negro comedian who once said, "When the man asks how the
weather is, I know nuff to look keerful at his face 'fore even I look out the
window." So, I waited for him to suggest it, and my patience was rewarded. I
was overjoyed and grateful.

I didn't spend all my time in the North End. Soon after I moved to Grand 34
Rapids, Pop introduced me to some patients he had with a son my age. The
boy's name was Lloyd Brown, and his father was a bellman downtown at the
Pantlind Hotel. Lloyd and I often rode bikes and played basketball in his backyard. After a while, my mother asked me why I never had Lloyd come out to
visit me. It was a question I dreaded, but she pressed on. "After all," she said,
"you've had a lot of meals at his house and it's rude not to invite him back." I
knew she was right and I also hated the whole idea of it.

With my friends in the north, race was never mentioned. Ever. I carried my 35
race around with me like an open basket of rotten eggs. I knew I could drop
one at any moment and it would explode with a stench over everything. This
was in the days when the movies either had no blacks at all or featured rank
stereotypes like Stepin Fetchit,[3] and the popular magazines like *Life*, *Look*, the
Saturday Evening Post, and *Colliers* carried no stories about Negroes, had no
ads depicting Negroes, and generally gave the impression that we did not exist
in this society. I knew that my white friends, being well brought up, were just
too polite to mention this disability that I had. And I was grateful to them, but

---

[3] The stage name of Lincoln Perry (1892–1985), a black actor who portrayed lazy, dim-witted
Negroes in many Hollywood films.

terrified, just the same, that maybe someday one of them would have the bad taste to notice what I was.

It seemed to me that my tenuous purchase in this larger white world de- 36 pended on the maintenance between me and my friends in the North End of our unspoken bargain to ignore my difference, my shame, and their embarrassment. If none of us had to deal with it, I thought, we could all handle it. My white friends behaved as if they perceived the bargain exactly as I did. It was a delicate equation, and I was terrified that Lloyd's presence in the North End would rip apart the balance.

I am so ashamed of that shame now that I cringe when I write it. But I 37 understand that boy now as he could not understand himself then. I was an American boy, though I did not fully comprehend that either. I was fully shaped and formed by America, where white people had all the power in sight, and they owned everything in sight except our house. Their beauty was the real beauty; there wasn't any other beauty. A real human being had straight hair, a white face, and thin lips. Other people, who looked different, were lesser beings.

No wonder, then, that most black men desired the forbidden fruit of white 38 loins. No wonder, too, that we thought that the most beautiful and worthy Negro people were those who looked most white. We blacks used to have a saying: "If you're white, you're all right. If you're brown, stick around. If you're black, stand back." I was brown.

It was not that we in my family were direct victims of racism. On the con- 39 trary, my stepfather clearly had a higher income than the parents of most students in my high school. Unlike those of most of my contemporaries, black and white, my parents had college degrees. Within Grand Rapids' tiny Negro community, they were among the elite. The others were the lawyer, the dentist, the undertaker, and the other doctor.

But that is what made race such exquisite agony. I did have a sense that it 40 was unfair for poor Negroes to be relegated to bad jobs—if they had jobs at all—and to bad or miserable housing, but I didn't feel any great sense of identity with them. After all, the poor blacks in New York had also been the hard ones: the ones who tried to take my money, to beat me up, and to keep me perpetually intimidated. Besides, I had heard it intimated around my house that their behavior, sexual or otherwise, left a good deal to be desired.

So I thought that maybe they just weren't ready for this society, but that I 41 was. And it was dreadfully unfair for white people to just look at my face and lips and hair and decide that I was inferior. By being a model student and leader, I thought I was demonstrating how well Negroes could perform if only the handicaps were removed and they were given a chance. But deep down I guess I was also trying to demonstrate that I was not like those other people; that I was different. My message was quite clear: I was *not nigger*. But the world didn't seem quite ready to make such fine distinctions, and it was precisely that fact—though at the time I could scarcely even have admitted it to myself—that was the nub of the race issue for me.

I would sometimes lie on my back and stare up at passing clouds and wonder 42 why God had played a dirty trick by making me a Negro. It all seemed so random. So unfair to me. To *me!* But in school I was gaining more friends, and the teachers respected me. It got so that I could go for days not thinking very much about being Negro, until something made the problem unavoidable.

One day in history class, for instance, the teacher asked each of us to stand   43
and tell in turn where our families had originated. Many of the kids in the class were Dutch with names like Vander Jagt, De Young, and Ripstra. My pal Andy was Scots-Irish. When it came my turn, I stood up and burned with shame and when I would speak, I lied. And then I was even more ashamed because I exposed a deeper shame. "Some of my family was English," I said—Wilkins is an English name—"and the rest of it came from . . . Egypt." Egypt!

One Saturday evening after one of our sandlot games, I went over to Lloyd's.   44
Hearing my stories, Lloyd said mildly that he'd like to come up and play some Saturday. I kept on talking, but all the time my mind was repeating: "Lloyd wants to play. He wants to come up to the North End on Saturday. Next Saturday. Next Saturday." I was trapped.

So, after the final story about the final lunge, when I couldn't put it off any   45
longer, I said. "Sure. Why not?" But, later in the evening, after I had had some time to think, I got Lloyd alone. "Say, look," I said. "Those teams are kinda close, ya know. I mean, we don't switch around. From team to team. Or new guys, ya know?"

Lloyd nodded, but he was getting a funny look on his face . . . part unbe-   46
lieving and part hurt. So I quickly interjected before he could say anything, "Naw, man. Naw. Not like you shouldn't come and play. Just that we gotta have some good reason for you to play on our team, you dig?"

"Yeah," Lloyd said, his face still puzzled, but no longer hurt.   47

"Hey, I know," I said. "I got it. We'll say you're my cousin. If you're my   48
cousin, see, then you gotta play. Nobody can say you can't be on my team, because you're family, right?"

"Oh, right. Okay," Lloyd said, his face brightening. "Sure, we'll say we're   49
cousins. Solid."

I felt relieved as well. I could have a Negro cousin. It wasn't voluntary. It   50
wouldn't be as if I had gone out and made a Negro friend deliberately. A person couldn't help who his cousins were.

There began to be a cultural difference between me and other blacks my age   51
too. Black street language had evolved since my Harlem days, and I had not kept pace. Customs, attitudes, and the other common social currencies of everyday black life had evolved away from me. I didn't know how to talk, to banter, to move my body. If I was tentative and responsive in the North End, where I lived, I was tense, stiff, and awkward when I was with my black contemporaries. One day I was standing outside the church trying, probably at my mother's urging, to make contact. Conversational sallies flew around me while I stood there stiff and mute, unable to participate. Because the language was so foreign to me, I understood little of what was being said, but I did know

that the word used for a white was *paddy*. Then a boy named Nickerson, the one whom my mother particularly wanted me to be friends with, inclined his head slightly toward me and said, to whoops of laughter, "technicolor paddy." My feet felt rooted in stone, and my head was aflame. I never forgot that phrase.

I have rarely felt so alone as I did that day riding home from church. Already   52
partly excluded by my white friends, I was now almost completely alienated from my own people as well. But I felt less uncomfortable and less vulnerable in the white part of town. It was familiar enough to enable me to ward off most unpleasantness.

And then there was the problem of girls. They were everywhere, the girls.   53
They all had budding bosoms, they all smelled pink, they all brushed against the boys in the hall, they were all white, and, in 1947–49, they were all inaccessible.

There were some things you knew without ever knowing how you knew   54
them. You knew that Mississippi was evil and dangerous, that New York was east, and the Pacific ocean was west. And in the same way you knew that white women were the most desirable and dangerous objects in the world. Blacks were lynched in Mississippi and such places sometimes just for looking with the wrong expression at white women. Blacks of a very young age knew that white women of any quality went with the power and style that went with the governance of America—though, God knows, we had so much self-hate that when a white woman went with a Negro man, we promptly decided she was trash, and we also figured that if she would go with him she would go with any Negro.

Nevertheless, as my groin throbbed at fifteen and sixteen and seventeen, *they*   55
were often the only ones there. One of them would be in the hallway opening her locker next to mine. Her blue sweater sleeve would be pushed up to just below the elbow, and as she would reach high on a shelf to stash away a book, I would see the tender dark hair against the white skin of her forearm. And I would ache and want to touch that arm and follow that body hair to its source.

Some of my friends, of course, did touch some of those girls. My friends   56
and I would talk about athletics and school and their loves. But they wouldn't say a word about the dances and the hayrides they went on.

I perceived they liked me and accepted me as long as I moved aside when   57
life's currents took them to where I wasn't supposed to be. I fit into their ways when they talked about girls, even their personal girls. And indeed, I fit into the girls' lives when they were talking about boys, most particularly their own personal boys. Because I was a boy, I had insight. But I was also Negro, and therefore a neuter. So a girl who was alive and sensuous night after night in my fantasies would come to me earnestly in the day and talk about Rich or Gene or Andy. She would ask what he thought about her, whether he liked to dance, whether, if she invited him to her house for a party, he would come. She would tell me her fears and her yearnings, never dreaming for an instant that I had yearnings too and that she was their object.

There may be few more powerful obsessions than a teenage boy's fixation on   58
a love object. In my case it came down to a thin brunette named Marge
McDowell. She was half a grade behind me, and she lived in a small house
on a hill. I found excuses to drive by it all the time. I knew her schedule at
school, so I could manage to be in most of the hallways she had to use going
from class to class. We knew each other, and she had once confided a strong
but fleeting yearning for my friend Rich Kippen. I thought about her constantly.

Finally, late one afternoon after school, I came upon her alone in a hallway.   59
"Marge," I blurted, "can I ask you something?"

She stopped and smiled and said, "Sure, Roger, what?"   60

"Well I was wondering," I said. "I mean. Well, would you go to the hayride   61
next week with me."

Her jaw dropped and her eyes got huge. Then she uttered a small shriek and   62
turned, hugging her books to her bosom the way girls do, and fled. I writhed
with mortification in my bed that night and for many nights after.

In my senior year, I was elected president of the Creston High School stu-   63
dent council. It was a breakthrough of sorts.

QUESTIONS

1. Examine the number and arrangement of the various episodes Wilkins relates
having to do with the cruelty and kindness he experienced with whites. What do
they tell us about the author's views on racism in America?   **2.**   During the explo-
rations of his new home in Michigan, Wilkins accidently biked into the local ghetto;
immediately afterward, he stopped near an athletic field to watch some white youths
playing football. What relevance do these two episodes have to the theme of the
essay, and what significance does their juxtaposition have?   **3.**   Examine the passage in which Wilkins describes his brief friendship with the white boy Jerry Schild.
How does Wilkins manage to make a moral judgment while focusing almost exclusively on objective details?   **4.**   Wilkins makes a distinction (beginning with paragraph 35) between racism in the North and in the South. What is the difference?
Why does he find one less difficult to deal with than the other?   **5.**   Wilkins ends
his essay with an account of his infatuation for Marge McDowell. In what ways is
this an appropriate event on which to conclude?

WRITING TOPIC

In paragraph 38 the author quotes an old black saying: "If you're white, you're all
right. If you're brown, stick around. If you're black, stand back." He then identifies
himself as brown. Show how Wilkins's essay is the account of the life of a person
who was told to "stick around."

Marrying Absurd   1967

JOAN DIDION [b. 1934]

To be married in Las Vegas, Clark County, Nevada, a bride must swear that   1
she is eighteen or has parental permission and a bridegroom that he is twenty-
one or has parental permission. Someone must put up five dollars for the license. (On Sundays and holidays, fifteen dollars. The Clark County Courthouse issues marriage licenses at any time of the day or night except between
noon and one in the afternoon, between eight and nine in the evening, and
between four and five in the morning.) Nothing else is required. The State of
Nevada, alone among these United States, demands neither a premarital blood
test nor a waiting period before or after the issuance of a marriage license.
Driving in across the Mojave from Los Angeles, one sees the signs way out on
the desert, looming up from that moonscape of rattlesnakes and mesquite, even
before the Las Vegas lights appear like a mirage on the horizon: "GETTING
MARRIED? Free License Information First Strip Exit." Perhaps the Las Vegas
wedding industry achieved its peak operational efficiency between 9:00 P.M.
and midnight on August 26, 1965, an otherwise unremarkable Thursday which
happened to be, by Presidential order, the last day on which anyone could
improve his draft status merely by getting married. One hundred and seventy-
one couples were pronounced man and wife in the name of Clark County and
the State of Nevada that night, sixty-seven of them by a single justice of the
peace, Mr. James A. Brennan. Mr. Brennan did one wedding at the Dunes
and the other sixty-six in his office, and charged each couple eight dollars.
One bride lent her veil to six others. "I got it down from five to three minutes,"
Mr. Brennan said later of his feat. "I could've married them *en masse*, but
they're people, not cattle. People expect more when they get married."

What people who get married in Las Vegas actually do expect—what, in the   2
largest sense, their "expectations" are—strikes one as a curious and self-contradictory business. Las Vegas is the most extreme and allegorical of American
settlements, bizarre and beautiful in its venality and in its devotion to immediate gratification, a place the tone of which is set by mobsters and call girls
and ladies' room attendants with amyl nitrite poppers in their uniform pockets.
Almost everyone notes that there is no "time" in Las Vegas, no night and no
day and no past and no future (no Las Vegas casino, however, has taken the
obliteration of the ordinary time sense quite so far as Harold's Club in Reno,
which for a while issued, at odd intervals in the day and night, mimeographed
"bulletins" carrying news from the world outside); neither is there any logical
sense of where one is. One is standing on a highway in the middle of a vast
hostile desert looking at an eighty-foot sign which blinks "STARDUST" or "CAE-
SAR'S PALACE." Yes, but what does that explain? This geographical implausibil-

ity reinforces the sense that what happens there has no connection with "real" life; Nevada cities like Reno and Carson are ranch towns, Western towns, places behind which there is some historical imperative. But Las Vegas seems to exist only in the eye of the beholder. All of which makes it an extraordinarily stimulating and interesting place, but an odd one in which to want to wear a candlelight satin Priscilla of Boston wedding dress with Chantilly lace insets, tapered sleeves and a detachable modified train.

And yet the Las Vegas wedding business seems to appeal to precisely that   3 impulse. "Sincere and Dignified Since 1954," one wedding chapel advertises. There are nineteen such wedding chapels in Las Vegas, intensely competitive, each offering better, faster, and, by implication, more sincere services than the next: Our Photos Best Anywhere, Your Wedding on A Phonograph Record, Candlelight with Your Ceremony, Honeymoon Accommodations, Free Transportation from Your Motel to Courthouse to Chapel and Return to Motel, Religious or Civil Ceremonies, Dressing Rooms, Flowers, Rings, Announcements, Witnesses Available, and Ample Parking. All of these services, like most others in Las Vegas (sauna baths, payroll check cashing, chinchilla coats for sale or rent) are offered twenty-four hours a day, seven days a week, presumably on the premise that marriage, like craps, is a game to be played when the table seems hot.

But what strikes one most about the Strip chapels, with their wishing wells   4 and stained-glass paper windows and their artificial bouvardia, is that so much of their business is by no means a matter of simple convenience, of late-night liaisons between show girls and baby Crosbys. Of course there is some of that. (One night about eleven o'clock in Las Vegas I watched a bride in an orange minidress and masses of flame-colored hair stumble from a Strip chapel on the arm of her bridegroom, who looked the part of the expendable nephew in movies like *Miami Syndicate*. "I gotta get the kids," the bride whimpered. "I gotta pick up the sitter, I gotta get to the midnight show." "What you gotta get," the bridegroom said, opening the door of a Cadillac Coupe de Ville and watching her crumple on the seat, "is sober.") But Las Vegas seems to offer something other than "convenience"; it is merchandising "niceness," the facsimile of proper ritual, to children who do not know how else to find it, how to make the arrangements, how to do it "right." All day and evening long on the Strip, one sees actual wedding parties, waiting under the harsh lights at a crosswalk, standing uneasily in the parking lot of the Frontier while the photographer hired by The Little Church of the West ("Wedding Place of the Stars") certifies the occasion, takes the picture: the bride in a veil and white satin pumps, the bridegroom usually in a white dinner jacket, and even an attendant or two, a sister or a best friend in hot-pink, *peau de soie*, a flirtation veil, a carnation nosegay. "When I Fall in Love It Will Be Forever," the organist plays, and then a few bars of Lohengrin. The mother cries; the stepfather, awkward in his role, invites the chapel hostess to join them for a drink at the Sands. The hostess declines with a professional smile; she has already transferred her interest to the group waiting outside. One bride out, another

in, and again the sign goes up on the chapel door: "One moment please—
Wedding."

I sat next to one such wedding party in a Strip restaurant the last time I was   5
in Las Vegas. The marriage had just taken place; the bride still wore her dress,
the mother her corsage. A bored waiter poured out a few swallows of pink
champagne ("on the house") for everyone but the bride, who was too young to
be served. "You'll need something with more kick than that," the bride's father
said with heavy jocularity to his new son-in-law; the ritual jokes about the
wedding night had a certain Panglossian character, since the bride was clearly
several months pregnant. Another round of pink champagne, this time not on
the house, and the bride began to cry. "It was just as nice," she sobbed, "as I
hoped and dreamed it would be."

QUESTIONS
1. What attitude toward Las Vegas weddings emerges from this essay? What means
(diction, images, descriptive passages, juxtaposition of ideas) does Didion use to
convey that attitude? **2.** Analyze Didion's use of rhythm in this piece. Note how
she uses pairs or triads of elements in her sentences. How do such rhythmic con-
structions act on the reader? **3.** Analyze the last paragraph. What means does
the author use to control the reader's responses to the scene she describes?

WRITING TOPIC
What unstated convictions about marriages are violated by the ceremonies Didion
describes?

Going Home Again: The New American Scholarship Boy   1974

RICHARD RODRIGUEZ   [b. 1944]

At each step, with every graduation from one level of education to the next,   1
the refrain from bystanders was strangely the same: "Your parents must be so
proud of you." I suppose that my parents were proud, although I suspect, too,
that they felt more than pride alone as they watched me advance through my
education. They seemed to know that my education was separating us from
one another, making it difficult to resume familiar intimacies. Mixed with the
instincts of parental pride, a certain hurt also communicated itself—too private
ever to be adequately expressed in words, but real nonetheless.

The autobiographical facts pertinent to this essay are simply stated in two   2
sentences, though they exist in somewhat awkward juxtaposition to each other.
I am the son of Mexican-American parents, who speak a blend of Spanish and
English, but who read neither language easily. I am about to receive a Ph.D.
in English Renaissance literature. What sort of life—what tensions, feelings,
conflicts—connects these two sentences? I look back and remember my life
from the time I was seven or eight years old as one of constant movement away
from a Spanish-speaking folk culture toward the world of the English-language
classroom. As the years passed, I felt myself becoming less like my parents and
less comfortable with the assumption of visiting relatives that I was still the
Spanish-speaking child they remembered. By the time I began college, visits
home became suffused with silent embarrassment: there seemed so little to
share, however strong the ties of our affection. My parents would tell me what
happened in their lives or in the lives of relatives; I would respond with news
of my own. Polite questions would follow. Our conversations came to seem
more like interviews.

A few months ago, my dissertation nearly complete, I came upon my father   3
looking through my bookcase. He quietly fingered the volumes of Milton's
tracts and Augustine's theology with that combination of reverence and distrust
those who are not literate sometimes show for the written word. Silently, I
watched him from the door of the room. However much he would have insisted that he was "proud" of his son for being able to master the texts, I knew,
if pressed further, he would have admitted to complicated feelings about my
success. When he looked across the room and suddenly saw me, his body
tightened slightly with surprise, then we both smiled.

For many years I kept my uneasiness about becoming a success in education   4
to myself. I did so in part because I wanted to avoid vague feelings that, if
considered carefully, I would have no way of dealing with; and in part because

165

I felt that no one else shared my reaction to the opportunity provided by education. When I began to rehearse my story of cultural dislocation publicly, however, I found many listeners willing to admit to similar feelings from their own pasts. Equally impressive was the fact that many among those I spoke with were *not* from nonwhite racial groups, which made me realize that one can grow up to enter the culture of the academy and find it a "foreign" culture for a variety of reasons, ranging from economic status to religious heritage. But why, I next wondered, was it that, though there were so many of us who came from childhood cultures alien to the academy's, we voiced our uneasiness to one another and to ourselves so infrequently? Why did it take *me* so long to acknowledge publicly the culture costs I had paid to earn a Ph.D. in Renaissance English literature? Why, more precisely, am I writing these words only now when my connection to my past barely survives except as nostalgic memory?

Looking back, a person risks losing hold of the present while being confounded by the past. For the child who moves to an academic culture from a culture that dramatically lacks academic traditions, looking back can jeopardize the certainty he has about the desirability of this new academic culture. Richard Hoggart's description, in *The Uses of Literacy*, of the cultural pressures on such a student, whom Hoggart calls the "scholarship boy," helps make the point. The scholarship boy must give nearly unquestioning allegiance to academic culture, Hoggart argues, if he is to succeed at all, so different is the milieu of the classroom from the culture he leaves behind. For a time, the scholarship boy may try to balance his loyalty between his concretely experienced family life and the more abstract mental life of the classroom. In the end, though, he must choose between the two worlds: if he intends to succeed as a student, he must, literally and figuratively, separate himself from his family, with its gregarious life, and find a quiet place to be alone with his thoughts.

After a while, the kind of allegiance the young student might once have given his parents is transferred to the teacher, the new parent. Now without the support of the old ties and certainties of the family, he almost mechanically acquires the assumptions, practices, and style of the classroom milieu. For the loss he might otherwise feel, the scholarship boy substitutes an enormous enthusiasm for nearly everything having to do with school.

How readily I read my own past into the portrait of Hoggart's scholarship boy. Coming from a home in which mostly Spanish was spoken, for example, I had to decide to forget Spanish when I began my education. To succeed in the classroom, I needed psychologically to sever my ties with Spanish. Spanish represented an alternate culture as well as another language—and the basis of my deepest sense of relationship to my family. Although I recently taught myself to read Spanish, the language that I see on the printed page is not quite the language I heard in my youth. That other Spanish, the spoken Spanish of my family, I remember with nostalgia and guilt: guilt because I cannot explain to aunts and uncles why I do not answer their questions any longer in their own idiomatic language. Nor was I able to explain to teachers in graduate school, who regularly expected me to read and speak Spanish with ease, why my very ability to reach graduate school as a student of English literature in the first place required me to loosen my attachments to a language I spoke years earlier. Yet, having lost the ability to speak Spanish, I never forgot it so totally that I could not understand it. Hearing Spanish spoken on the street reminded me of the community I once felt a part of, and still cared deeply about. I never forgot Spanish so thoroughly, in other words, as to move outside the range of its nostalgic pull.

Such moments of guilt and nostalgia were, however, just that—momentary.   8
They punctuated the history of my otherwise successful progress from *barrio*[1] to classroom. Perhaps they even encouraged it. Whenever I felt my determination to succeed wavering, I tightened my hold on the conventions of academic life.

Spanish was one aspect of the problem, my parents another. They could   9
raise deeper, more persistent doubts. They offered encouragement to my brothers and me in our work, but they also spoke, only half jokingly, about the way education was putting "big ideas" into our heads. When we would come home, for example, and challenge assumptions we earlier believed, they would be forced to defend their beliefs (which, given our new verbal skills, they did increasingly less well) or, more frequently, to submit to our logic with the disclaimer. "It's what we were taught in our time to believe. . . ." More important, after we began to leave home for college, they voiced regret about how "changed" we had become, how much further away from one another we had grown. They partly yearned for a return to the time before education assumed their children's primary loyalty. This yearning was renewed each time they saw their nieces and nephews (none of whom continued their education beyond high school, all of whom continued to speak fluent Spanish) living according to the conventions and assumptions of their parents' culture. If I was already troubled by the time I graduated from high school by that refrain of congratulations ("Your parents must be proud. . . ."), I realize now how much more difficult and complicated was my progress into academic life for my parents, as they saw the cultural foundation of their family erode, than it was for me.

Yet my parents were willing to pay the price of alienation and continued to   10
encourage me to become a scholarship boy because they perceived, as others of the lower classes had before them, the relation between education and social mobility. Lacking the former themselves made then acutely aware of its necessity as prerequisite for the latter. They sent their children off to school in the hopes of their acquiring something "better" beyond education. Notice the assumption here that education is something of a tool or license—a means to an end, which has been the traditional way the lower or working classes have viewed the value of education in the past. That education might alter children in more basic ways than providing them with skills, certificates of proficiency,

---

[1]A Hispanic neighborhood.

and even upward mobility, may come as a surprise for some, but the financial cost is usually tolerated.

Complicating my own status as a scholarship boy in the last ten years was the rise, in the mid-1960s, of what was then called "the Third World Student Movement." Racial minority groups, led chiefly by black intellectuals, began to press for greater access to higher education. The assumption behind their criticism, like the assumption of white working-class families, was that educational opportunity was useful for economic and social advancement. The racial minority leaders went one step further, however, and it was this step that was probably most revolutionary. Minority students came to the campus feeling that they were representative of larger groups of people—that, indeed, they were advancing the condition of entire societies by their matriculation. Actually, this assumption was not altogether new to me. Years before, educational success was something my parents urged me to strive for precisely because it would reflect favorably on *all* Mexican-Americans—specifically, my intellectual achievement would help deflate the stereotype of the "dumb Pancho." The early goal was only given greater currency by the rhetoric of the Third World spokesmen. But it was the fact that I felt myself suddenly much more a "public" Mexican-American, a representative of sorts, that was to prove so crucial for me during these years. 11

One college admissions officer assured me one day that he recognized my importance to his school precisely as deriving from the fact that, after graduation, I would surely be "going back to [my] community." More recently, teachers have urged me not to trouble over the fact that I am not "representative" of my culture, assuring me that I can serve as a "model" for those still in the *barrio* working toward academic careers. This is the line that I hear, too, when being interviewed for a faculty position. The interviewer almost invariably assumes that because I am racially a Mexican-American, I can serve as a special counselor to minority students. The expectation is that I still retain the capacity for intimacy with "my people." 12

This new way of thinking about the possible uses of education is what has made the entrance of minority students into higher education so dramatic. When the minority group student was accepted into the academy, he came— in everyone's mind—as part of a "group." When I began college, I barely attracted attention except perhaps as a slightly exotic ("Are you from India?") brown-skinned student; by the time I graduated, my presence was annually noted by, among others, the college public relations office as "one of the fifty-two students with Spanish surnames enrolled this year." By having his presence announced to the campus in this way, the minority group student was unlike any other scholarship boy the campus had seen before. The minority group student now dramatized more publicly, if also in new ways, the issues of cultural dislocation that education forces, issues that are not solely racial in origin. When Richard Rodriguez *became* a Chicano,[2] the dilemmas he earlier had as 13

[2] A Mexican-American.

a scholarship boy were complicated but not decisively altered by the fact that he had assumed a group identity.

The assurance I heard that, somehow, I was being useful to my community   14
by being a student was gratefully believed, because it gave me a way of dealing with the guilt and cynicism that each year came my way along with the scholarships, grants, and, lately, job offers from schools which a few years earlier would have refused me admission as a student. Each year, in fact, it became harder to believe that my success had anything to do with my intellectual performance, and harder to resist the conclusion that it was due to my minority group status. When I drove to the airport, on my way to London as a Fulbright Fellow[3] last year, leaving behind cousins of my age who were already hopelessly burdened by financial insecurity and dead-end jobs, momentary guilt could be relieved by the thought that somehow my trip was beneficial to persons other than myself. But, of course if the thought was a way of dealing with the guilt, it was also the reason for the guilt. Sitting in a university library, I would notice a janitor of my own race and grow uneasy; I was, I knew, in a rough way a beneficiary of his condition. Guilt was accompanied by cynicism. The most dazzlingly talented minority students I know today refuse to believe that their success is wholly based on their own talent, or even that when they speak in a classroom anyone hears them as anything but *the* voice of their minority group. It is scarcely surprising, then, though initially it probably seemed puzzling, that so many of the angriest voices on the campus against the injustices of racism came from those not visibly its primary victims.

It became necessary to believe the rhetoric about the value of one's presence   15
on campus simply as a way of living with one's "success." Among ourselves, however, minority group students often admitted to a shattering sense of loss— the feeling that, somehow, something was happening to us. Especially from students who had not yet become accustomed, as by that time I had, to the campus, I remember hearing confessions of extreme discomfort and isolation. Our close associations, the separate dining-room tables, and the special dormitories helped to relieve some of the pain, but only some of it.

Significant here was the development of the ethnic studies concept—black   16
studies, Chicano studies, et cetera—and the related assumption held by minority group students in a number of departments that they could keep in touch with their old cultures by making these cultures the subject of their study. Here again one notices how different the minority student was from other comparable students: other scholarship boys—poor Jews and the sons of various immigrant cultures—came to the academy singly, much more inclined to accept the courses and material they found. The ethnic studies concept was an indication that, for a multitude of reasons, the new racial minority group students were not willing to give up so easily their ties with their old cultures.

The importance of these new ethnic studies was that they introduced the   17
academy to subject matter that generally deserved to be studied, and at the

---

[3] Under the Fulbright Act (1946), American students are selected to study abroad.

same time offered a staggering critique of the academy's tendency toward parochialism. Most minority group intellectuals never noted this tendency toward academic parochialism. They more often saw the reason for, say, the absence of a course on black literature in an English department as a case of simple racism. That it might instead be an instance of the fact that academic culture can lose track of human societies and whole areas of human experience was rarely raised. Never asking such a question, the minority group students never seemed to wonder either if as teachers their own course might suffer the same cultural limitations other seminars and classes suffered. Consequently, in a peculiar way the new minority group critics of higher education came to justify the academy's assumptions. The possibility that academic culture could encourage one to grow out of touch with cultures beyond its conceptual horizon was never seriously considered.

Too often in the last ten years one heard minority group students repeat the   18
joke, never very funny in the first place, about the racial minority academic who ended up sounding more "white" than white academics. Behind the scorn for such a figure was the belief that the new generation of minority group students would be able to avoid having to make similar kinds of cultural concessions. The pressures that might have led to such conformity went unexamined.

For the last few years my annoyance at hearing such jokes was doubtless   19
related to the fact that I was increasingly beginning to sense that I was the "bleached" academic the minority group students found so laughable. I suppose I had always sensed that my cultural allegiance was undergoing subtle alterations as I was being educated. Only when I finished my course work in graduate school and went off to England for my dissertation year did I grasp how far I had traveled from my cultural origins. My year in England was actually my first opportunity to write and reflect upon the kind of material that I would spend my life producing. It was my first chance, too, to be free simultaneously of the distractions of course-work and of the insecurities of trying to find my niche in academic life. Sitting in the reading room of the British Museum, I no longer doubted that I had joined academic society. Ironically, this feeling of having finally arrived allowed me to look back to the community whence I came. That I was geographically farther away from my home than I had ever been lent a metaphorical resonance to the cultural distance I suddenly felt.

But that feeling was not pleasing. The reward of feeling a part of the world   20
of the British Museum was an odd one. Each morning I would arrive at the reading room and grow increasingly depressed by the silence and what the silence implied—that my life as a scholar would require self-absorption. Who, I wondered, would find my work helpful enough to want to read it? Was not my dissertation—whose title alone would puzzle my relatives—only my grandest exercise thus far in self-enclosure? The sight of the heads around me bent over their texts and papers, many so thoroughly engrossed that they wouldn't look up at the silent clock overhead for hours at a stretch, made me recall the

remarkable noises of life in my family home. The tedious prose I was writing, a prose constantly qualified by footnotes, reminded me of the capacity for passionate statement those of the culture I was born into commanded—and which, could it be, I had now lost.

As I remembered it during those gray English afternoons, the past rushed   21
forward to define more precisely my present condition. Remembering my youth, a time when I was not restricted to a chair but ran barefoot under a summer sun that tightened my skin with its white heat, made the fact that it was only my mind that "moved" each hour in the library painfully obvious.

I did need to figure out where I had lost touch with my past. I started to   22
become alien to my family culture the day I became a scholarship boy. In the British Museum the realization seemed obvious. But later, returning to America, I returned to minority group students who were still speaking of their cultural ties to their past. How was I to tell them what I had learned about myself in England?

A short while ago, a group of enthusiastic Chicano undergraduates came to   23
my office to ask me to teach a course to high school students in the *barrio* on the Chicano novel. This new literature, they assured me, has an important role to play in helping to shape the consciousness of a people currently without adequate representation in literature. Listening to them I was struck immediately with the cultural problems raised by their assumption. I told them that the novel is not capable of dealing with Chicano experience adequately, simply because most Chicanos are not literate, or are at least not yet comfortably so. This is not something Chicanos need to apologize for (though, I suppose, remembering my own childhood ambition to combat stereotypes of the Chicano as mental menial, it is not something easily admitted). Rather the genius and value of those Chicanos who do not read seem to me to be largely that their reliance on voice, the spoken word, has given them the capacity for intimate conversation that I, as someone who now relies heavily on the written word, can only envy. The second problem, I went on, is more in the nature of a technical one: the novel, in my opinion, is not a form capable of being true to the basic sense of communal life that typifies Chicano culture. What the novel as a literary form is best capable of representing is solitary existence set against a large social background. Chicano novelists, not coincidentally, nearly always fail to capture the breathtakingly rich family life of most Chicanos, and instead often describe only the individual Chicano in transit between Mexican and American cultures.

I said all of this to the Chicano students in my office, and could see that   24
little of it made an impression. They seemed only frustrated by what they probably took to be a slick, academic justification for evading social responsibility. After a time, they left me, sitting alone. . . .

There is a danger of being misunderstood here. I am not suggesting that an   25
academic cannot reestablish ties of any kind with his old culture. Indeed, he can have an impact on the culture of his childhood. But as an academic, one

exists by definition in a culture separate from one's nonacademic roots and, therefore, any future ties one has with those who remain "behind" are complicated by one's new cultural perspective.

Paradoxically, the distance separating the academic from his nonacademic   26
past can make his past seem, if not closer, then clearer. It is possible for the academic to understand the culture from which he came "better" than those who still live within it. In my own experience, it has only been as I have come to appraise my past through categories and notions derived from the social sciences that I have been able to think of Chicano life in cultural terms at all. Characteristics I took for granted or noticed only in passing—the spontaneity, the passionate speech, the trust in concrete experience, the willingness to think communally rather than individually—these are all significant phenomena to me now as aspects of a total culture. (My parents have neither the time nor the inclination to think about their culture as a culture.) Able to conceptualize a sense of Chicano culture, I am now also more attracted to that culture than I was before. The temptation now is to try to preserve those traits of my old culture that have not yet, in effect, atrophied.

The racial self-consciousness of minority group students during the last few   27
years, evident in the ethnic costumes, the stylized gestures, and the idiomatic though often evasive devices for insisting on one's continuing membership in the community of the past, are also indications that the minority group student has gained a new appreciation of the culture of his origin precisely because of his earlier alienation from it. As a result, Chicano students sometimes become more Chicano than most Chicanos. I remember, for example, my father's surprise when, walking across my college campus one afternoon, we came upon two Chicano academics wearing serapes. He and my mother were also surprised—indeed offended—when they earlier heard student activists use the word "Chicano." For them the term was a private one, primarily descriptive of persons they knew. It suggested intimacy. Hearing the word shouted into a microphone by a stranger left them bewildered. What they could not understand was that the student activist finds it easier than they to use "Chicano" in a more public way, for his distance from their culture and his membership in academic culture permits a wider and more abstract view.

The Mexican-Americans who begin to call themselves Chicanos in this way   28
are actually forming a new version of what it means to be a Chicano. The culture that didn't see itself as a culture is suddenly prized and identified for being one. The price one pays for this new self-consciousness is the knowledge of just that—it is *new*—and this knowledge is not available to those who remain at home. So it is knowledge that separates as well as unites people. Wanting more desperately than ever to assert his ties with the newly visible culture, the minority group student is tempted to exploit those characteristics of that culture that might yet survive in him. But the self-consciousness never allows one to feel completely at ease with the old culture. Worse, the knowledge of the culture of the past often leaves one feeling strangely solitary. At home, I hear relatives speak and find myself analyzing too much of what they say. It is

embarrassing being a cultural anthropologist in one's own family kitchen. I keep feeling myself little more than a cultural voyeur. I often come away from family gatherings suspecting, in fact, that what conceptions of my culture I carry with me are no more than illusions. Because they were never there before, because no one back home shares them, I grow less and less to trust their reliability: too often they seem no more than mental bubbles floating before an academic's eye.

Many who have taught minority group students in the last decade testify to   29 sensing characteristics of a childhood culture still very much alive in these students. Should the teacher make these students aware of these characteristics? Initially, most of us would probably answer negatively. Better to trust the unconscious survival of the past than the always problematical, sometimes even clownish, re-creations of it. But the cultural past cannot be assured of survival; perhaps many of its characteristics are lost simply because the student is never encouraged to look for them. Even those that do survive do so tenuously. As a teacher, one can only hope that the best qualities in his minority group students' cultural legacy aren't altogether snuffed out by academic education.

More easy to live with and distinguishable from self-conscious awareness of   30 the past are the ways the past unconsciously survives—perhaps even yet survives in me. As it turns out, the issue becomes less acute with time. With each year, the chance that the student is unaware of his cultural legacy is diminished as the habit of academic reflectiveness grows stronger. Although the culture of the academy makes innocence about one's cultural past less likely, this same culture, and the conceptual tools it provides, increases the desire to want to write and speak about the past. The paradox persists.

Awaiting the scholarship boy who finally acknowledges the fact that his per-   31 ceptions of reality have changed is the dilemma of action. The sentimental reaction to this knowledge entails merely a refusal to renew contact with one's nonacademic culture lest one contaminate it. The problem, however, with this sentimental solution is that it overlooks the way academic culture renders one capable of dealing with the transactions of mass society. Academic culture, with its habits of conceptualization and abstraction, allows those of us from other cultures to deal with each other in a mass society. In this sense academic culture does have a profound political impact. Although people intent upon social mobility think of education as a means to an end, education does become an end: its culture allows one to exist more easily in a society increasingly anonymous and impersonal. The truth is, the academic's distance from his own experience brings the capacity for communicating with bureaucracies and understanding one's position in society—a prerequisite for political action.

If the sentimental reaction to nonacademic culture is to fear changing it, the   32 political response, typical especially of working-class and lately minority group leaders, is to see higher education solely in terms of its political and social possibilities. Its cultural consequences, in this view, are disregarded. At this time when we are so keenly aware of social and economic inequality, it might seem beside the point to warn those who are working to bring about equality that education alters culture as well as economic status. And yet, if there is one main criticism that I, as a minority group student, must make of minority group leaders in their past attacks on the "racism" of the academy, it is that they never distinguished between my right to higher education and the desirability of my actually entering the academy—which is another way of saying again that they never recognized that there were things I could lose by becoming a scholarship boy.

Certainly, the academy changes those from alien cultures more than it is   33 changed by them. While minority groups had an impact on higher education, largely because of their advantage in coming as a group, within the last few years students such as myself, who finally ended up certified as academics, also ended up sounding very much like the academics we found when we came to the campus. I do not enjoy making such admissions. But perhaps now the time has come when questions about the cultural costs of education ought to be delayed no longer. Those of us who have been scholarship boys know in our bones that our education has exacted a large price in exchange for the large benefits it has conferred upon us. And what is sadder to consider, after we have paid that price, we go home and casually change the cultures that nurtured us. My parents today understand how they are "Chicanos" in a large and impersonal sense. The gains from such knowledge are clear. But so, too, are the reasons for regret.

QUESTIONS

1. What does Rodriguez finally feel about the education that has alienated him from his family and ethnic culture? **2.** State in your own words the "paradox" Rodriguez defines in paragraph 30.

WRITING TOPIC

Do you think the gulf between the academic and the nonacademic worlds is as wide as Rodriguez claims? What experiences have you had that either prove or disprove the existence of such a gulf?

Innocence and Experience

QUESTIONS AND WRITING TOPICS

1. What support do the works in this section provide for Thomas Gray's well-known observation that "where ignorance is bliss,/ 'Tis folly to be wise"? **Writing Topic:** Use Gray's observation as the basis for an analysis of either Frank O'Connor's "My Oedipus Complex" or Flannery O'Connor's "Good Country People."

2. In such poems as Robert Frost's "Birches" and Stevie Smith's "To Carry the Child," growing up is seen as a growing away from a kind of truth and reality; in other poems, such as Gerard Manley Hopkins's "Spring and Fall," Dylan Thomas's "Fern Hill," and Robert Wallace's "In a Spring Still Not Written of," growing up is seen as growing into truth and reality. Do these two groups of poems embody contradictory and mutually exclusive conceptions of childhood? Explain. **Writing Topic:** Select one poem from each of these two groups and contrast the conception of childhood embodied in each.

3. An eighteenth-century novelist wrote: "Oh Innocence, how glorious and happy a portion art thou to the breast that possesses thee! Thou fearest neither the eyes nor the tongues of men. Truth, the most powerful of all things, is thy strongest friend; and the brighter the light is in which thou art displayed, the more it discovers thy transcendent beauties." Which works in this section support this assessment of innocence? Which works contradict it? How would you characterize the relationship between "truth" and "innocence" in the fiction and the drama presented here? **Writing Topic:** Use this observation as the basis for an analysis of *Oedipus Rex*.

4. A certain arrogance is associated with the innocence of Oedipus in Sophocles's *Oedipus Rex*, Robin in Hawthorne's "My Kinsman, Major Molineux," and Hulga in Flannery O'Connor's "Good Country People." On what is their arrogance based, and how is it modified? **Writing Topic:** Select two of these three works and contrast the nature and the consequences of the central characters' arrogance.

5. James Joyce's "Araby," Frank O'Connor's "My Oedipus Complex," and Flannery O'Connor's "Good Country People" all deal with some aspect of sexuality as a force that moves the protagonist from innocence toward experience. How does the recognition of sexuality function in each of the stories? **Writing Topic:** Choose two of these stories, and discuss the relationship between sexuality and innocence.

6. Which poems in this section depend largely on irony for their force? Can you suggest why irony is a particularly useful device in literature that portrays innocence and experience? **Writing Topic:** Write an analysis of the function of irony in Hardy's "The Ruined Maid" and Sexton's "Cinderella."

7. Is the passage from innocence to experience a loss or a gain or both? Explain. **Writing Topic:** Compare the passage from innocence to experience in Crane's "The Bride Comes to Yellow Sky" and Frank O'Connor's "My Oedipus Complex" or in Roger Wilkins's "Confessions of a Blue-Chip Black" and Richard Rodriguez's "Going Home Again: The New American Scholarship Boy."

Conformity
and
Rebellion

The Uprising, © 1860 by Honoré Daumier

Although the works in this section, like those in "Innocence and Experience," may feature a violation of innocence, the events are usually based on the clash between two well-articulated positions; the rebel, on principle, confronts and struggles with established authority. Central to these works is the sense of tremendous external forces—the state, the church, tradition—which can be obeyed only at the expense of conscience and humanity. Thus Martin Luther King, Jr., rejects "moderation" in "Letter from Birmingham Jail" and Virginia Woolf in "What If Shakespeare Had Had a Sister?" ruefully imagines what would have been the fate of a female Shakespeare. At the most general level, these works confront an ancient dilemma: the very organizations men and women establish to protect and nurture the individual demand—on pain of economic ruin, social ostracism, even death, spiritual or physical—that they violate their most deeply cherished beliefs. When individuals refuse such demands, they translate their awareness of a hostile social order into action against it and precipitate a crisis. And so Yeats celebrates the "terrible beauty" that is born of the abortive rebellion in "Easter 1916," and in A *Doll's House*, Nora Helmer finally realizes that dehumanization is too high a price to pay for security. On a different note, in "Bartleby the Scrivener," Bartleby's "preference" not to conform, his passive resistance, results in a crisis.

Many of the works in this section, particularly the poems, do not treat the theme of conformity and rebellion quite so explicitly and dramatically. Some, like "Women," employ the indirection of irony to expose and attack the costs of conformity; others, like W. H. Auden's "The Unknown Citizen," tell us that the price exacted for total conformity to the industrial superstate is spiritual death. In "Easter 1916," William Butler Yeats meditates upon the awesome meaning of the lives and deaths of political revolutionaries, and in "Harlem," Langston Hughes warns that an inflexible and constricting social order will generate explosion.

Two basic modes, then, inform the literary treatment of conformity and rebellion. While in many of the works, the individual is caught up in a crisis that forces her or him into rebellion, in other works, especially the poems, the focus may be on the individual's failure to move from awareness into action, as in Amy Lowell's "Patterns." Indeed, the portraits of Auden's unknown citizen and of E. E. Cummings's Cambridge ladies affirm the necessity for rebellion by rendering so effectively the hollow life of mindless conformity.

However diverse in treatment and technique, all the works in this section are about individuals trapped by complex sets of external forces that regulate and define their lives. Social beings—men and women—sometimes submit to these forces, but it is always an uneasy submission, for the purpose of these forces is to curb and control people. Individuals may recognize that they must be controlled for some larger good; yet they are aware that established social power is often abusive. The tendency of power, at its best, is to act as a conserving force that brakes the disruptive impulse to abandon and destroy old ways and ideas. At its worst, power is self-serving. The individual must constantly judge which tendency power is enhancing. And since the power of the individual is negligible beside that of frequently abusive social forces, it is not surprising that many artists since the advent of the great nation-states have found a fundamental human dignity in the resistance of the individual to organized society. One of humanity's ancient and profound recognitions, after all, is that the impulse of an abusive governor is always to make unknown citizens of us all.

CONFORMITY
AND
REBELLION

Epoch, 1950 by Ben Shahn.

FICTION

Bartleby the Scrivener   1853
A STORY OF WALL STREET

HERMAN MELVILLE [1819–1891]

I am a rather elderly man. The nature of my avocations, for the last thirty years, has brought me into more than ordinary contact with what would seem an interesting and somewhat singular set of men, of whom, as yet, nothing, that I know of, has ever been written—I mean, the law-copyists, or scriveners. I have known very many of them, professionally and privately, and, if I pleased, could relate divers histories, at which good-natured gentlemen might smile, and sentimental souls might weep. But I waive the biographies of all other scriveners, for a few passages in the life of Bartleby, who was a scrivener, the strangest I ever saw, or heard of. While, of other law-copyists, I might write the complete life, of Bartleby nothing of that sort can be done. I believe that no materials exist for a full and satisfactory biography of this man. It is an irreparable loss to literature. Bartleby was one of those beings of whom nothing is ascertainable, except from the original sources, and, in his case, those are very small. What my own astonished eyes saw of Bartleby, *that* is all I know of him, except, indeed, one vague report, which will appear in the sequel.

Ere introducing the scrivener, as he first appeared to me, it is fit I make some mention of myself, my employees, my business, my chambers, and general surroundings; because some such description is indispensable to an adequate understanding of the chief character about to be presented. Imprimis: I am a man who, from his youth upwards, has been filled with a profound conviction that the easiest way of life is the best. Hence, though I belong to a profession proverbially energetic and nervous, even to turbulence, at times, yet nothing of that sort have I ever suffered to invade my peace. I am one of those unambitious lawyers who never addresses a jury, or in any way draws down public applause; but, in the cool tranquillity of a snug retreat, do a snug business among rich men's bonds, and mortgages, and title-deeds. All who know me, consider me an eminently *safe* man. The late John Jacob Astor,[1] a personage little given to

---

[1] A poor immigrant who rose to become one of the great business tycoons of the nineteenth century.

poetic enthusiasm, had no hesitation in pronouncing my first grand point to be prudence; my next, method. I do not speak it in vanity, but simply record the fact, that I was not unemployed in my profession by the late John Jacob Astor; a name which, I admit, I love to repeat; for it hath a rounded and orbicular sound to it, and rings like unto bullion. I will freely add, that I was not insensible to the late John Jacob Astor's good opinion.

Some time prior to the period at which this little history begins, my avocations had been largely increased. The good old office, now extinct in the State of New York, of a Master in Chancery,[2] had been conferred upon me. It was not a very arduous office, but very pleasantly remunerative. I seldom lose my temper; much more seldom indulge in dangerous indignation at wrongs and outrages; but, I must be permitted to be rash here, and declare that I consider the sudden and violent abrogation of the office of Master in Chancery, by the new Constitution, as a—premature act; inasmuch as I had counted upon a life-lease of the profits, whereas I only received those of a few short years. But this is by the way.

My chambers were up stairs, at No. —— Wall Street. At one end, they looked upon the white wall of the interior of a spacious sky-light shaft, penetrating the building from top to bottom.

This view might have been considered rather tame than otherwise, deficient in what landscape painters call "life." But, if so, the view from the other end of my chambers offered, at least, a contrast, if nothing more. In that direction, my windows commanded an unobstructed view of a lofty brick wall, black by age and everlasting shade; which wall required no spyglass to bring out its lurking beauties, but, for the benefit of all near-sighted spectators, was pushed up to within ten feet of my window panes. Owing to the great height of the surrounding buildings, and my chambers being on the second floor, the interval between this wall and mine not a little resembled a huge square cistern.

At the period just preceding the advent of Bartleby, I had two persons as copyists in my employment, and a promising lad as an office-boy. First, Turkey; second, Nippers; third, Ginger Nut. These may seem names, the like of which are not usually found in the Directory. In truth, they were nicknames, mutually conferred upon each other by my three clerks, and were deemed expressive of their respective persons or characters. Turkey was a short, pursy Englishman, of about my own age—that is, somewhere not far from sixty. In the morning, one might say, his face was of a fine florid hue, but after twelve o'clock, meridian—his dinner hour—it blazed like a grate full of Christmas coals; and continued blazing—but, as it were, with a gradual wane—till six o'clock P.M., or thereabouts; after which, I saw no more of the proprietor of the face, which, gaining its meridian with the sun, seemed to set with it, to rise, culminate, and decline the following day, with the like regularity and undiminished glory. There are many singular coincidences I have known in the course of my life, not the least among which was the fact, that, exactly when Turkey displayed

---

[2] Courts of Chancery often adjudicated business disputes.

his fullest beams from his red and radiant countenance, just then, too, at that critical moment, began the daily period when I considered his business capacities as seriously disturbed for the remainder of the twenty-four hours. Not that he was absolutely idle, or averse to business, then; far from it. The difficulty was, he was apt to be altogether too energetic. There was a strange, inflamed, flurried, flighty recklessness of activity about him. He would be incautious in dipping his pen into his inkstand. All his blots upon my documents were dropped there after twelve o'clock meridian. Indeed, not only would he be reckless, and sadly given to making blots in the afternoon, but, some days, he went further, and was rather noisy. At such times, too, his face flamed with augmented blazonry, as if cannel coal had been heaped on anthracite. He made an unpleasant racket with his chair; spilled his sand-box; in mending his pens, impatiently split them all to pieces, and threw them on the floor in a sudden passion; stood up, and leaned over his table, boxing his papers about in a most indecorous manner, very sad to behold in an elderly man like him. Nevertheless, as he was in many ways a most valuable person to me, and all the time before twelve o'clock meridian, was the quickest, steadiest creature, too, accomplishing a great deal of work in a style not easily to be matched—for these reasons, I was willing to overlook his eccentricities, though, indeed, occasionally, I remonstrated with him. I did this very gently, however, because, though the civilest, nay, the blandest and most reverential of men in the morning, yet, in the afternoon, he was disposed, upon provocation, to be slightly rash with his tongue—in fact, insolent. Now, valuing his morning services as I did, and resolved not to lose them—yet, at the same time, made uncomfortable by his inflamed ways after twelve o'clock—and being a man of peace, unwilling by my admonitions to call forth unseemly retorts from him, I took upon me, one Saturday noon (he was always worse on Saturdays) to hint to him, very kindly, that, perhaps, now that he was growing old, it might be well to abridge his labors; in short, he need not come to my chambers after twelve o'clock, but, dinner over, had best go home to his lodgings, and rest himself till tea-time. But no; he insisted upon his afternoon devotions. His countenance became intolerably fervid, as he oratorically assured me—gesticulating with a long ruler at the other end of the room—that if his services in the morning were useful, how indispensable, then, in the afternoon?

"With submission, sir," said Turkey, on this occasion, "I consider myself your right-hand man. In the morning I but marshal and deploy my columns; but in the afternoon I put myself at their head, and gallantly charge the foe, thus"—and he made a violent thrust with the ruler.

"But the blots, Turkey," intimated I.

"True; but, with submission, sir, behold these hairs! I am getting old. Surely, sir, a blot or two of a warm afternoon is not to be severely urged against gray hairs. Old age—even if it blot the page—is honorable. With submission, sir, we *both* are getting old."

This appeal to my fellow-feeling was hardly to be resisted. At all events, I saw that go he would not. So, I made up my mind to let him stay, resolving, nevertheless, to see to it that, during the afternoon, he had to do with my less important papers.

Nippers, the second on my list, was a whiskered, sallow, and upon the whole, rather piratical-looking young man, of about five and twenty. I always deemed him the victim of two evil powers—ambition and indigestion. The ambition was evinced by a certain impatience of the duties of a mere copyist, an unwarrantable usurpation of strictly professional affairs, such as the original drawing up of legal documents. The indigestion seemed betokened in an occasional nervous testiness and grinning irritability, causing the teeth to audibly grind together over mistakes committed in copying; unnecessary maledictions, hissed, rather than spoken, in the heat of business; and especially by a continual discontent with the height of the table where he worked. Though of a very ingenious, mechanical turn, Nippers could never get this table to suit him. He put chips under it, blocks of various sorts, bits of pasteboard, and at last went so far as to attempt an exquisite adjustment, by final pieces of folded blotting-paper. But no invention would answer. If, for the sake of easing his back, he brought the table lid at a sharp angle well up towards his chin, and wrote there like a man using the steep roof of a Dutch house for his desk, then he declared that it stopped the circulation in his arms. If now he lowered the table to his waistbands, and stooped over it in writing, then there was a sore aching in his back. In short, the truth of the matter was, Nippers knew not what he wanted. Or, if he wanted anything, if was to be rid of a scrivener's table altogether. Among the manifestations of his diseased ambition was a fondness he had for receiving visits from certain ambiguous-looking fellows in seedy coats, whom he called his clients. Indeed, I was aware that not only was he, at times, considerable of a ward-politician, but he occasionally did a little business at the Justices' courts, and was not unknown on the steps of the Tombs.[3] I have good reason to believe, however, that one individual who called upon him at my chambers, and who, with a grand air, he insisted was his client, was no other than a dun, and the alleged title-deed, a bill. But, with all his failings, and the annoyances he caused me, Nippers, like his compatriot Turkey, was a very useful man to me; wrote a neat, swift hand; and, when he chose, was not deficient in a gentlemanly sort of deportment. Added to this, he always dressed in a gentlemanly sort of way; and so, incidentally, reflected credit upon my chambers. Whereas, with respect to Turkey, I had much ado to keep him from being a reproach to me. His clothes were apt to look oily, and smell of eating-houses. He wore his pantaloons very loose and baggy in summer. His coats were execrable; his hat not to be handled. But while the hat was a thing of indifference to me, inasmuch as his natural civility and deference, as a dependent Englishman, always led him to doff it the moment he entered the room, yet his coat was another matter. Concerning his coats, I reasoned with him; but with no effect. The truth was, I suppose, that a man with so small an income could not afford to sport such a lustrous face and a lustrous coat at one and the same time. As Nippers once

---

[3] A prison in New York City.

observed, Turkey's money went chiefly for red ink. One winter day, I presented
Turkey with a highly respectable-looking coat of my own—a padded gray coat,
of a most comfortable warmth, and which buttoned straight up from the knee
to the neck. I thought Turkey would appreciate the favor, and abate his rashness
and obstreperousness of afternoons. But no; I verily believe that buttoning himself up in so downy and blanket-like a coat had a pernicious effect upon him—
upon the same principle that too much oats are bad for horses. In fact, precisely
as a rash, restive horse is said to feel his oats, so Turkey felt his coat. It made
him insolent. He was a man whom prosperity harmed.

Though, concerning the self-indulgent habits of Turkey, I had my own private
surmises, yet, touching Nippers, I was well persuaded that, whatever might be
his faults in other respects, he was, at least, a temperate young man. But,
indeed, nature herself seemed to have been his vintner, and, at his birth, charged
him so thoroughly with an irritable, brandy-like disposition, that all subsequent
potations were needless. When I consider how, amid the stillness of my chambers, Nippers would sometimes impatiently rise from his seat, and stopping over
his table, spread his arms wide apart, seize the whole desk, and move it, and
jerk it, with a grim, grinding motion on the floor, as if the table were a perverse
voluntary agent and vexing him, I plainly perceive that, for Nippers, brandy-
and-water were altogether superfluous.

It was fortunate for me that, owing to its peculiar cause—indigestion—the
irritability and consequent nervousness of Nippers were mainly observable in
the morning, while in the afternoon he was comparatively mild. So that, Turkey's paroxysms only coming on about twelve o'clock, I never had to do with
their eccentricities at one time. Their fits relieved each other, like guards. When
Nippers's was on, Turkey's was off; and *vice versa*. This was a good natural
arrangement, under the circumstances.

Ginger Nut, the third on my list, was a lad, some twelve years old. His father
was a car-man, ambitious of seeing his son on the bench instead of a cart,
before he died. So he sent him to my office, as student at law, errand-boy,
cleaner and sweeper, at the rate of one dollar a week. He had a little desk to
himself; but he did not use it much. Upon inspection, the drawer exhibited a
great array of shells of various sorts of nuts. Indeed, to this quick-witted youth,
the whole noble science of the law was contained in a nutshell. Not the least
among the employments of Ginger Nut, as well as one which he discharged
with the most alacrity, was his duty as cake and apple purveyor for Turkey and
Nippers. Copying law-papers being proverbially a dry, husky sort of business,
my two scriveners were fain to moisten their mouths very often with Spitzen-
bergs, [4] to be had at the numerous stalls nigh the Custom House and Post Office.
Also, they sent Ginger Nut very frequently for that peculiar cake—small, flat,
round, and very spicy—after which he had been named by them. Of a cold
morning, when business was but dull, Turkey would gobble up scores of these
cakes, as if they were mere wafers—indeed, they sell them at the rate of six or

---

[4] A variety of apple.

eight for a penny—the scrape of his pen blending with the crunching of the crisp particles in his mouth. Rashest of all the fiery afternoon blunders and flurried rashnesses of Turkey, was his once moistening a ginger-cake between his lips, and clapping it on to a mortgage, for a seal. I came within an ace of dismissing him then. But he mollified me by making an oriental bow, and saying—

"With submission, sir, it was generous of me to find you in stationery on my own account."

Now my original business—that of a conveyancer and title hunter, and drawer-up of recondite documents of all sorts—was considerably increased by receiving the master's office. There was now great work for scriveners. Not only must I push the clerks already with me, but I must have additional help.

In answer to my advertisement, a motionless young man one morning stood upon my office threshold, the door being open, for it was summer. I can see that figure now—pallidly neat, pitiably respectable, incurably forlorn! It was Bartleby.

After a few words touching his qualifications, I engaged him, glad to have among my corps of copyists a man of so singularly sedate an aspect, which I thought might operate beneficially upon the flighty temper of Turkey, and the fiery one of Nippers.

I should have stated before that ground glass folding-doors divided my premises into two parts, one of which was occupied by my scriveners, the other by myself. According to my humor, I threw open these doors, or closed them. I resolved to assign Bartleby a corner by the folding-doors, but on my side of them, so as to have this quiet man within easy call, in case any trifling thing was to be done. I placed his desk close up to a small side-window in that part of the room, a window which originally had afforded a lateral view of certain grimy backyards and bricks, but which, owing to subsequent erections, commanded at present no view at all, though it gave some light. Within three feet of the panes was a wall, and the light came down from far above, between two lofty buildings, as from a very small opening in a dome. Still further to a satisfactory arrangement, I procured a high green folding screen, which might entirely isolate Bartleby from my sight, though not remove him from my voice. And thus, in a manner, privacy and society were conjoined.

At first, Bartleby did an extraordinary quantity of writing. As if long famishing for something to copy, he seemed to gorge himself on my documents. There was no pause for digestion. He ran a day and night line, copying by sun-light and by candle-light. I should have been quite delighted with his application, had he been cheerfully industrious. But he wrote on silently, palely, mechanically.

It is, of course, an indispensable part of a scrivener's business to verify the accuracy of his copy, word by word. Where there are two or more scriveners in an office, they assist each other in this examination, one reading from the copy, the other holding the original. It is a very dull, wearisome, and lethargic affair. I can readily imagine that, to some sanguine temperaments, it would be altogether intolerable. For example, I cannot credit that the mettlesome poet, Byron, would have contentedly sat down with Bartleby to examine a law document of, say five hundred pages, closely written in a crimpy hand.

Now and then, in the haste of business, it had been my habit to assist in comparing some brief document myself, calling Turkey or Nippers for this purpose. One object I had, in placing Bartleby so handy to me behind the screen, was to avail myself of his services on such trivial occasions. It was on the third day, I think, of his being with me, and before any necessity had arisen for having his own writing examined, that, being much hurried to complete a small affair I had in hand, I abruptly called to Bartleby. In my haste and natural expectancy of instant compliance, I sat with my head bent over the original on my desk, and my right hand sideways, and somewhat nervously extended with the copy, so that, immediately upon emerging from his retreat, Bartleby might snatch it and proceed to business without the least delay.

In this very attitude did I sit when I called to him, rapidly stating what it was I wanted him to do—namely, to examine a small paper with me. Imagine my surprise, nay, my consternation, when, without moving from his privacy, Bartleby, in a singularly mild, firm voice, replied, "I would prefer not to."

I sat awhile in perfect silence, rallying my stunned faculties. Immediately it occurred to me that my ears had deceived me, or Bartleby had entirely misunderstood my meaning. I repeated my request in the clearest tone I could assume; but in quite as clear a one came the previous reply, "I would prefer not to."

"Prefer not to," echoed I, rising in high excitement, and crossing the room with a stride. "What do you mean? Are you moon-struck? I want you to help me compare this sheet here—take it," and I thrust it towards him.

"I would prefer not to," said he.

I looked at him steadfastly. His face was leanly composed; his gray eye dimly calm. Not a wrinkle of agitation rippled him. Had there been the least uneasiness, anger, impatience, or impertinence in his manner; in other words, had there been any thing ordinarily human about him, doubtless I should have violently dismissed him from the premises. But as it was, I should have as soon thought of turning my pale plaster-of-paris bust of Cicero out of doors. I stood gazing at him awhile, as he went on with his own writing, and then reseated myself at my desk. This is very strange, thought I. What had one best do? But my business hurried me. I concluded to forget the matter for the present, reserving it for my future leisure. So calling Nippers from the other room, the paper was speedily examined.

A few days after this, Bartleby concluded four lengthy documents, being quadruplicates of a week's testimony taken before me in my High Court of Chancery. It became necessary to examine them. It was an important suit, and great accuracy was imperative. Having all things arranged, I called Turkey, Nippers, and Ginger Nut from the next room, meaning to place the four copies in the hands of my four clerks, while I should read from the original. Accordingly, Turkey, Nippers, and Ginger Nut had taken their seats in a row, each with his document in his hand, when I called to Bartleby to join this interesting group.

"Bartleby! quick, I am waiting."

I heard a slow scrape of his chair legs on the uncarpeted floor, and soon he appeared standing at the entrance of his hermitage.

"What is wanted?" said he, mildly.

"The copies, the copies," said I, hurriedly. "We are going to examine them. There—" and I held towards him the fourth quadruplicate.

"I would prefer not to," he said, and gently disappeared behind the screen.

For a few moments I was turned into a pillar of salt, standing at the head of my seated column of clerks. Recovering myself, I advanced towards the screen, and demanded the reason for such extraordinary conduct.

"*Why* do you refuse?"

"I would prefer not to."

With any other man I should have flown outright into a dreadful passion, scorned all further words, and thrust him ignominiously from my presence. But there was something about Bartleby that not only strangely disarmed me, but in a wonderful manner, touched and disconcerted me. I began to reason with him.

"These are your own copies we are about to examine. It is labor saving to you, because one examination will answer for your four papers. It is common usage. Every copyist is bound to help examine his copy. Is it not so? Will you not speak? Answer!"

"I prefer not to," he replied in a flutelike tone. It seemed to me that, while I had been addressing him, he carefully revolved every statement that I made; fully comprehended the meaning; could not gainsay the irresistible conclusion; but, at the same time, some paramount consideration prevailed with him to reply as he did.

"You are decided, then, not to comply with my request—a request made according to common usage and common sense?"

He briefly gave me to understand, that on that point my judgment was sound. Yes: his decision was irreversible.

It is not seldom the case that, when a man is browbeaten in some unprecedented and violently unreasonable way, he begins to stagger in his own plainest faith. He begins, as it were, vaguely to surmise that, wonderful as it may be, all the justice and all the reason is on the other side. Accordingly, if any disinterested persons are present, he turns to them for some reinforcement of his own faltering mind.

"Turkey," said I, "what do you think of this? Am I not right?"

"With submission, sir," said Turkey, in his blandest tone, "I think that you are."

"Nippers," said I, "what do *you* think of it?"

"I think I should kick him out of the office."

(The reader, of nice perceptions, will here perceive that, it being morning, Turkey's answer is couched in polite and tranquil terms, but Nippers replies in ill-tempered ones. Or, to repeat a previous sentence, Nippers's ugly mood was on duty, and Turkey's off.)

"Ginger Nut," said I, willing to enlist the smallest suffrage in my behalf, "what do *you* think of it?"

"I think, sir, he's a little *luny*," replied Ginger Nut, with a grin.

"You hear what they say," said I, turning towards the screen, "come forth and do your duty."

But he vouchsafed no reply. I pondered a moment in sore perplexity. But once more business hurried me. I determined again to postpone the consideration of this dilemma to my future leisure. With a little trouble we made out to examine the papers without Bartleby, though at every page or two Turkey deferentially dropped his opinion, that this proceeding was quite out of the common; while Nippers, twitching in his chair with a dyspeptic nervousness, ground out, between his set teeth, occasional hissing maledictions against the stubborn oaf behind the screen. And for his (Nippers's) part, this was the first and the last time he would do another man's business without pay.

Meanwhile Bartleby sat in his hermitage, oblivious to everything but his own peculiar business there.

Some days passed, the scrivener being employed upon another lengthy work. His late remarkable conduct led me to regard his ways narrowly. I observed that he never went to dinner; indeed, that he never went anywhere. As yet I had never, of my personal knowledge, known him to be outside of my office. He was a perpetual sentry in the corner. At about eleven o'clock though, in the morning, I noticed that Ginger Nut would advance toward the opening in Bartleby's screen, as if silently beckoned thither by a gesture invisible to me where I sat. The boy would then leave the office, jingling a few pence, and reappear with a handful of ginger-nuts, which he delivered in the hermitage, receiving two of the cakes for his trouble.

He lives, then, on ginger-nuts, thought I; never eats a dinner, properly speaking; he must be a vegetarian, then; but no; he never eats even vegetables; he eats nothing but ginger-nuts. My mind then ran on in reveries concerning the probable effects upon the human consitution of living entirely on ginger-nuts. Ginger-nuts are so called, because they contain ginger as one of their peculiar constituents, and the final flavoring one. Now, what was ginger? A hot, spicy thing. Was Bartleby hot and spicy? Not at all. Ginger, then, had no effect upon Bartleby. Probably he preferred it should have none.

Nothing so aggravates an earnest person as a passive resistance. If the individual so resisted be of a not inhumane temper, and the resisting one perfectly harmless in his passivity, then, in the better moods of the former, he will endeavor charitably to construe to his imagination what proves impossible to be solved by his judgement. Even so, for the most part, I regarded Bartleby and his ways. Poor fellow! thought I, he means no mischief; it is plain he intends no insolence; his aspect sufficiently evinces that his eccentricities are involuntary. He is useful to me. I can get along with him. If I turn him away, the chances are he will fall in with some less-indulgent employer, and then he will be rudely treated, and perhaps driven forth miserably to starve. Yes. Here I can cheaply purchase a delicious self-approval. To befriend Bartleby; to humor him in his strange willfulness, will cost me little or nothing, while I lay up in my soul what will eventually prove a sweet morsel for my conscience. But this mood was not invariable with me. The passiveness of Bartleby sometimes irritated me. I felt strangely goaded on to encounter him in new opposition—to elicit some angry spark from him answerable to my own. But, indeed, I might as well have essayed to strike fire with my knuckles against a bit of Windsor soap. But one afternoon the evil impulse in me mastered me, and the following little scene ensued:

"Bartleby," said I, "when those papers are all copied, I will compare them with you."

"I would prefer not to."

"How? Surely you do not mean to persist in that mulish vagary?"

No answer.

I threw open the folding-doors near by, and, turning upon Turkey and Nippers, exclaimed:

"Bartleby a second time says, he won't examine his papers. What do you think of it, Turkey?"

It was afternoon, be it remembered. Turkey sat glowing like a brass boiler; his bald head steaming; his hands reeling among his blotted papers.

"Think of it?" roared Turkey; "I think I'll just step behind his screen, and black his eyes for him!"

So saying, Turkey rose to his feet and threw his arms into a pugilistic position. He was hurrying away to make good his promise, when I detained him, alarmed at the effect of incautiously rousing Turkey's combativeness after dinner.

"Sit down, Turkey," said I, "and hear what Nippers has to say. What do you think of it, Nippers? Would I not be justified in immediately dismissing Bartleby?"

"Excuse me, that is for you to decide, sir. I think his conduct quite unusual, and, indeed, unjust, as regards Turkey and myself. But it may only be a passing whim."

"Ah," exclaimed I, "you have strangely changed your mind, then—you speak very gently of him now."

"All beer," cried Turkey; "gentleness is effects of beer—Nippers and I dined together to-day. You see how gentle *I* am, sir. Shall I go and black his eyes?"

"You refer to Bartleby, I suppose. No, not to-day, Turkey," I replied; "pray, put up your fists."

I closed the doors, and again advanced towards Bartleby. I felt additional incentives tempting me to my fate. I burned to be rebelled against again. I remembered that Bartleby never left the office.

"Bartleby," said I, "Ginger Nut is away; just step around to the Post Office, won't you? (it was but a three minutes' walk), and see if there is anything for me."

"I would prefer not to."

"You *will* not?"

"I *prefer* not."

I staggered to my desk, and sat there in a deep study. My blind inveteracy returned. Was there any other thing in which I could procure myself to be ignominiously repulsed by this lean, penniless wight?—my hired clerk? What added thing is there, perfectly reasonable, that he will be sure to refuse to do?

"Bartleby!"

No answer.

"Bartleby," in a louder tone.

No answer.

"Bartleby," I roared.

Like a very ghost, agreeably to the laws of magical invocation, at the third summons, he appeared at the entrance of his hermitage.

"Go to the next room, and tell Nippers to come to me."

"I prefer not to," he respectfully and slowly said and mildly disappeared.

"Very good, Bartleby," said I, in a quiet sort of serenely-severe, self-possessed tone, intimating the unalterable purpose of some terrible retribution very close at hand. At the moment I half intended something of the kind. But upon the whole, as it was drawing towards my dinner-hour, I thought it best to put on my hat and walk home for the day, suffering much from perplexity and distress of mind.

Shall I acknowledge it? The conclusion of this whole business was, that it soon became a fixed fact of my chambers, that a pale young scrivener, by the name of Bartleby, had a desk there; that he copied for me at the usual rate of four cents a folio (one hundred words); but he was permanently exempt from examining the work done by him, that duty being transferred to Turkey and Nippers, out of compliment, doubtless, to their superior acuteness; moreover, said Bartleby was never, on any account, to be dispatched on the most trivial errand of any sort; and that even if entreated to take upon him such a matter, it was generally understood that he would "prefer not to"—in other words, he would refuse point blank.

As days passed on, I became considerably reconciled to Bartleby. His steadiness, his freedom from all dissipation, his incessant industry (except when he chose to throw himself into a standing revery behind his screen), his great stillness, his unalterableness of demeanor under all circumstances, made him a valuable acquisition. One prime thing was this—*he was always there*—first in the morning, continually through the day, and the last at night. I had a singular confidence in his honesty. I felt my most precious papers perfectly safe in his hands. Sometimes, to be sure, I could not, for the very soul of me, avoid falling into sudden spasmodic passions with him. For it was exceeding difficult to bear in mind all the time those strange peculiarities, privileges, and unheard of exemptions, forming the tacit stipulations on Bartleby's part under which he remained in my office. Now and then, in the eagerness of dispatching pressing business, I would inadvertently summon Bartleby, in a short, rapid tone, to put his finger, say, on the incipient tie of a bit of red tape with which I was about compressing some papers. Of course, from behind the screen the usual answer, "I prefer not to," was sure to come; and then, how could a human creature, with the common infirmities of our nature, refrain from bitterly exclaiming upon such perverseness—such unreasonableness. However, every added repulse of this sort which I received only tended to lessen the probability of my repeating the inadvertence.

Here it must be said, that according to the custom of most legal gentlemen occupying chambers in densely-populated law buildings, there were several keys to my door. One was kept by a woman residing in the attic, which person weekly scrubbed and daily swept and dusted my apartments. Another was kept by Turkey for convenience sake. The third I sometimes carried in my own pocket. The fourth I knew not who had.

Now, one Sunday morning I happened to go to Trinity Church, to hear a celebrated preacher, and finding myself rather early on the ground I thought I would walk around to my chambers for a while. Luckily I had my key with me; but upon applying it to the lock, I found it resisted by something inserted from the inside. Quite surprised, I called out; when to my consternation a key was turned from within; and thrusting his lean visage at me, and holding the door ajar, the apparition of Bartleby appeared, in his shirt sleeves, and otherwise in a strangely tattered *déshabillé*, saying quietly that he was sorry, but he was deeply engaged just then, and—preferred not admitting me at present. In a brief word or two, he moreover added, that perhaps I had better walk around the block two or three times, and by that time he would probably have concluded his affairs.

Now, the utterly unsurmised appearance of Bartleby, tenanting my law-chambers of a Sunday morning, with his cadaverously gentlemanly *nonchalance*, yet withal firm and self-possessed, had such a strange effect upon me, that incontinently I slunk away from my own door, and did as desired. But not without sundry twinges of impotent rebellion against the mild effrontery of this unaccountable scrivener. Indeed, it was his wonderful mildness chiefly, which not only disarmed me, but unmanned me as it were. For I consider that one, for the time, is somehow unmanned when he tranquilly permits his hired clerk to dictate to him, and order him away from his own premises. Furthermore, I was full of uneasiness as to what Bartleby could possibly be doing in my office in his shirt sleeves, and in an otherwise dismantled condition of a Sunday morning. Was anything amiss going on? Nay, that was out of the question. It was not to be thought of for a moment that Bartleby was an immoral person. But what could he be doing there?—copying? Nay again, whatever might be his eccentricities, Bartleby was an eminently decorous person. He would be the last man to sit down to his desk in any state approaching to nudity. Besides, it was Sunday; and there was something about Bartleby that forbade the supposition that he would by any secular occupation violate the proprieties of the day.

Nevertheless, my mind was not pacified; and full of a restless curiosity, at last I returned to the door. Without hindrance I inserted my key, opened it, and entered. Bartleby was not to be seen. I looked round anxiously, peeped behind his screen; but it was very plain that he was gone. Upon more closely examining the place, I surmised that for an indefinite period Bartleby must have eaten, dressed, and slept in my office, and that, too, without plate, mirror, or bed. The cushioned seat of a rickety old sofa in one corner bore the faint impress of a lean, reclining form. Rolled away under his desk, I found a blanket; under the empty grate, a blacking box and brush; on a chair, a tin basin, with soap and a ragged towel; in a newspaper a few crumbs of ginger-nuts and a morsel of cheese. Yes, thought I, it is evident enough that Bartleby has been making his home here, keeping bachelor's hall all by himself. Immediately then the thought came sweeping across me, what miserable friendlessness and loneliness are here revealed! His poverty is great; but his solitude, how horrible! Think of it. Of a Sunday, Wall Street is deserted as Petra[5]; and every night of every day it is an emptiness. This building, too, which of week-days hums with industry and life, at nightfall echoes with sheer vacancy, and all through Sunday is forlorn. And here Bartleby makes his home; sole spectator of a solitude which he has seen all populous—a sort of innocent and transformed Marius brooding among the ruins of Carthage![6]

For the first time in my life a feeling of over-powering stinging melancholy seized me. Before, I had never experienced aught but a not unpleasing sadness. The bond of a common humanity now drew me irresistibly to gloom. A fraternal melancholy! for both I and Bartleby were sons of Adam. I remembered the bright silks and sparkling faces I had seen that day, in gala trim, swan-like sailing down the Mississippi of Broadway; and I contrasted them with the pallid copyist, and thought to myself, Ah, happiness courts the light, so we deem the world is gay; but misery hides aloof, so we deem that misery there is none. These sad fancyings—chimeras, doubtless, of a sick and silly brain—led on to other and more special thoughts, concerning the eccentricities of Bartleby. Presentiments of strange discoveries hovered round me. The scrivener's pale form appeared to me laid out, among uncaring strangers, in its shivering winding sheet.

Suddenly I was attracted by Bartleby's closed desk, the key in open sight left in the lock.

I mean no mischief, seek the gratification of no heartless curiosity, thought I; besides, the desk is mine, and its contents, too, so I will make bold to look within. Everything was methodically arranged, the papers smoothly placed. The pigeon holes were deep, and removing the files of documents, I groped into their recesses. Presently I felt something there, and dragged it out. It was an old bandanna handkerchief, heavy and knotted. I opened it, and saw it was a savings bank.

I now recalled all the quiet mysteries which I had noted in the man. I remembered that he never spoke but to answer; that, though at intervals he had

---

[5] A city in Palestine found by explorers in 1812. It had been deserted and lost for centuries.
[6] Caius Marius (155–86 B.C.), a plebeian general who was forced to flee from Rome. Nineteenth-century democratic literature sometimes pictured him old and alone among the ruins of Carthage.

considerable time to himself, yet I had never seen him reading—no, not even a newspaper; that for long periods he would stand looking out, at his pale window behind the screen, upon the dead brick wall; I was quite sure he never visited any refectory or eating house; while his pale face clearly indicated that he never drank beer like Turkey, or tea and coffee even, like other men; that he never went anywhere in particular that I could learn; never went out for a walk, unless, indeed, that was the case at present; that he had declined telling who he was, or whence he came, or whether he had any relatives in the world; that though so thin and pale, he never complained of ill health. And more than all, I remembered a certain unconscious air of pallid—how shall I call it?—of pallid haughtiness, say, or rather an austere reserve about him, which had positively awed me into my tame compliance with his eccentricities, when I had feared to ask him to do the slightest incidental thing for me, even though I might know, from his long-continued motionlessness, that behind his screen he must be standing in one of those dead-wall reveries of his.

Revolving all these things, and coupling them with the recently discovered fact, that he made my office his constant abiding place and home, and not forgetful of his morbid moodiness; revolving all these things, a prudential feeling began to steal over me. My first emotions had been those of pure melancholy and sincerest pity; but just in proportion as the forlornness of Bartleby grew and grew to my imagination, did that same melancholy merge into fear, that pity into repulsion. So true it is, and so terrible, too, that up to a certain point the thought or sight of misery enlists our best affections; but, in certain special cases, beyond that point it does not. They err who would assert that invariably this is owing to the inherent selfishness of the human heart. It rather proceeds from a certain hopelessness of remedying excessive and organic ill. To a sensitive being, pity is not seldom pain. And when at last it is perceived that such pity cannot lead to effectual succor, common sense bids the soul be rid of it. What I saw that morning persuaded me that the scrivener was the victim of innate and incurable disorder. I might give alms to his body; but his body did not pain him; it was his soul that suffered, and his soul I could not reach.

I did not accomplish the purpose of going to Trinity Church that morning. Somehow, the things I had seen disqualified me for the time from churchgoing. I walked homeward, thinking what I would do with Bartleby. Finally, I resolved upon this—I would put certain calm questions to him the next morning, touching his history, etc., and if he declined to answer them openly and unreservedly (and I supposed he would prefer not), then to give him a twenty dollar bill over and above whatever I might owe him, and tell him his services were no longer required; but that if in any other way I could assist him, I would be happy to do so, especially if he desired to return to his native place, wherever that might be, I would willingly help to defray the expenses. Moreover, if, after reaching home, he found himself at any time in want of aid, a letter from him would be sure of a reply.

The next morning came.

"Bartleby," said I, gently calling to him behind his screen.

No reply.

"Bartleby," said I, in a still gentler tone, "come here; I am not going to ask you to do anything you would prefer not to do—I simply wish to speak to you."

Upon this he noiselessly slid into view.

"Will you tell me, Bartleby, where you were born?"

"I would prefer not to."

"Will you tell me *anything* about yourself?"

"I would prefer not to."

"But what reasonable objection can you have to speak to me? I feel friendly towards you."

He did not look at me while I spoke, but kept his glance fixed upon my bust of Cicero, which, as I then sat, was directly behind me, some six inches above my head.

"What is your answer, Bartleby," said I, after waiting a considerable time for a reply, during which his countenance remained immovable, only there was the faintest conceivable tremor of the white attenuated mouth.

"At present I prefer to give no answer," he said, and retired into his hermitage.

It was rather weak in me I confess, but his manner, on this occasion, nettled me. Not only did there seem to lurk in it a certain calm disdain, but his perverseness seemed ungrateful, considering the undeniable good usage and indulgence he had received from me.

Again I sat ruminating what I should do. Mortified as I was at his behavior, and resolved as I had been to dismiss him when I entered my office, nevertheless I strangely felt something superstitious knocking at my heart, and forbidding me to carry out my purpose, and denouncing me for a villain if I dared to breathe one bitter word against this forlornest of mankind. At last, familiarly drawing my chair behind his screen, I sat down and said: "Bartleby, never mind, then, about revealing your history; but let me entreat you, as a friend, to comply as far as may be with the usages of this office. Say now, you will help to examine papers to-morrow or next day: in short, say now, that in a day or two you will begin to be a little reasonable:—say so, Bartleby."

"At present I would prefer not to be a little reasonable," was his mildly cadaverous reply.

Just then the folding-doors opened, and Nippers approached. He seemed suffering from an unusually bad night's rest, induced by severer indigestion than common. He overheard those final words of Bartleby.

"*Prefer not*, eh?" gritted Nippers—"I'd *prefer* him, if I were you, sir," addressing me—"I'd *prefer* him; I'd give him preferences, the stubborn mule! What is it, sir, pray, that he *prefers* not to do now?"

Bartleby moved not a limb.

"Mr. Nippers," said I, "I'd prefer that you would withdraw for the present."

Somehow, of late, I had got into the way of involuntarily using this word "prefer" upon all sorts of not exactly suitable occasions. And I trembled to think that my contact with the scrivener had already and seriously affected me in a mental way. And what further and deeper aberration might it not yet produce? This apprehension had not been without efficacy in determining me to summary measures.

As Nippers, looking very sour and sulky, was departing, Turkey blandly and deferentially approached.

"With submission, sir," said he, "yesterday I was thinking about Bartleby here, and I think that if he would but prefer to take a quart of good ale every day, it would do much towards mending him, and enabling him to assist in examining his papers."

"So you have got the word, too," said I, slightly excited.

"With submission, what word, sir," asked Turkey, respectfully crowding himself into the contracted space behind the screen, and by so doing, making me jostle the scrivener. "What word, sir?"

"I would prefer to be left alone here," said Bartleby, as if offended at being mobbed in his privacy.

"*That's* the word, Turkey," said I—"*that's* it."

"Oh, *prefer?* oh yes—queer word. I never use it myself. But, sir, as I was saying, if he would but prefer—"

"Turkey," interrupted I, "you will please withdraw."

"Oh certainly, sir, if you prefer that I should."

As he opened the folding-door to retire, Nippers at his desk caught a glimpse of me, and asked whether I would prefer to have a certain paper copied on blue paper or white. He did not in the least roguishly accent the word prefer. It was plain that it involuntarily rolled from his tongue. I thought to myself, surely I must get rid of a demented man, who already has in some degree turned the tongues, if not the heads of myself and clerks. But I thought it prudent not to break the dismission at once.

The next day I noticed that Bartleby did nothing but stand at his window in his dead-wall revery. Upon asking him why he did not write, he said that he had decided upon doing no more writing."

"Why, how now? What next?" exclaimed I, "do no more writing?"

"No more."

"And what is the reason?"

"Do you not see the reason for yourself," he indifferently replied.

I looked steadfastly at him, and perceived that his eyes looked dull and glazed. Instantly it occurred to me, that his unexampled diligence in copying by his dim window for the first few weeks of his stay with me might have temporarily impaired his vision.

I was touched. I said something in condolence with him. I hinted that of course he did wisely in abstaining from writing for a while; and urged him to embrace that opportunity of taking wholesome exercise in the open air. This, however, he did not do. A few days after this, my other clerks being absent, and being in a great hurry to dispatch certain letters by the mail, I thought that, having nothing else earthly to do, Bartleby would surely be less inflexible than usual, and carry these letters to the post-office. But he blankly declined. So, much to my inconvenience, I went myself.

Still added days went by. Whether Bartleby's eyes improved or not, I could not say. To all appearance I thought they did. But when I asked him if they did, he vouchsafed no answer. At all events, he would do no copying. At last, in reply to my urgings, he informed me that he had permanently given up copying.

"What!" exclaimed I; "suppose your eyes should get entirely well—better than ever before—would you not copy then?"

"I have given up copying," he answered, and slid aside.

He remained as ever, a fixture in my chamber. Nay—if that were possible— he became still more of a fixture than before. What was to be done? He would do nothing in the office; why should he stay there? In plain fact, he had now become a millstone to me, not only useless as a necklace, but afflictive to bear. Yet I was sorry for him. I speak less than truth when I say that, on his own account, he occasioned me uneasiness. If he would but have named a single relative or friend, I would instantly have written, and urged their taking the poor fellow away to some convenient retreat. But he seemed alone, absolutely alone in the universe. A bit of wreck in the mid Atlantic. At length, necessities connected with my business tyrannized over all other considerations. Decently as I could, I told Bartleby that in six days time he must unconditionally leave the office. I warned him to take measures, in the interval, for procuring some other abode. I offered to assist him in his endeavor, if he himself would but take the first step towards a removal. "And when you finally quit me, Bartleby," added I, "I shall see that you go not away entirely unprovided. Six days from this hour, remember."

At the expiration of that period, I peeped behind the screen, and lo! Bartleby was there.

I buttoned up my coat, balanced myself; advanced slowly towards him, touched his shoulder, and said, "The time has come; you must quit this place; I am sorry for you; here is money; but you must go."

"I would prefer not" he replied, with his back still towards me.

"You *must*."

He remained silent.

Now I had an unbounded confidence in this man's common honesty. He had frequently restored to me sixpences and shillings carelessly dropped upon the floor, for I am apt to be very reckless in such shirt-button affairs. The proceeding, then, which followed will not be deemed extraordinary.

"Bartleby," said I, "I owe you twelve dollars on account; here are thirty-two; the odd twenty are yours—Will you take it?" and I handed the bills towards him.

But he made no motion.

"I will leave them here, then," putting them under a weight on the table. Then taking my hat and cane and going to the door, I tranquilly turned and added—"After you have removed your things from these offices, Bartleby, you will of course lock the door—since every one is now gone for the day but you— and if you please, slip your key underneath the mat, so that I may have it in the morning. I shall not see you again; so good-by to you. If, hereafter, in your new place of abode, I can be of any service to you, do not fail to advise me by letter. Good-by, Bartleby, and fare you well.

But he answered not a word; like the last column of some ruined temple, he remained standing mute and solitary in the middle of the otherwise deserted room.

As I walked home in a pensive mood, my vanity got the better of my pity. I could not but highly plume myself on my masterly management in getting rid of Bartleby. Masterly I call it, and such it must appear to any dispassionate thinker. The beauty of my procedure seemed to consist in its perfect quietness. There was no vulgar bullying, no bravado of any sort, no choleric hectoring, and striding to and fro across the apartment, jerking out vehement commands for Bartleby to bundle himself off with his beggarly traps. Nothing of the kind. Without loudly bidding Bartleby depart—as an inferior genius might have done—I *assumed* the ground that depart he must; and upon that assumption built all I had to say. The more I thought over my procedure, the more I was charmed with it. Nevertheless, next morning, upon awakening, I had my doubts—I had somehow slept off the fumes of vanity. One of the coolest and wisest hours a man has, is just after he awakes in the morning. My procedure seemed as sagacious as ever—but only in theory. How it would prove in practice—there was the rub. It was truly a beautiful thought to have assumed Bartleby's departure; but, after all, that assumption was simply my own, and none of Bartleby's. The great point was, not whether I had assumed that he would quit me, but whether he would prefer so to do. He was more a man of preferences than assumptions.

After breakfast, I walked down town, arguing the probabilities *pro* and *con*. One moment I thought it would prove a miserable failure, and Bartleby would be found all alive at my office as usual; the next moment it seemed certain that I should find his chair empty. And so I kept veering about. At the corner of Broadway and Canal Street, I saw quite an excited group of people standing in earnest conversation.

"I'll take odds he doesn't," said a voice as I passed.

"Doesn't go?—done!" said I; "put up your money."

I was instinctively putting my hand in my pocket to produce my own, when I remembered that this was an election day. The words I had overheard bore no reference to Bartleby, but to the success or non-success of some candidate for the mayoralty. In my intent frame of mind, I had, as it were, imagined that all Broadway shared in my excitement, and were debating the same question with me. I passed on, very thankful that the uproar of the street screened my momentary absent-mindedness.

As I had intended, I was earlier than usual at my office door. I stood listening for a moment. All was still. He must be gone. I tried the knob. The door was locked. Yes, my procedure had worked to a charm; he indeed must be vanished. Yet a certain melancholy mixed with this: I was almost sorry for my brilliant success. I was fumbling under the door mat for the key, which Bartleby was to have left there for me, when accidentally my knee knocked against a panel, producing a summoning sound, and in response a voice came to me from within—"Not yet; I am occupied."

It was Bartleby.

I was thunderstruck. For an instant I stood like the man who, pipe in mouth, was killed one cloudless afternoon long ago in Virginia, by summer lightning; at his own warm open window he was killed, and remained leaning out there upon the dreamy afternoon, till some one touched him, when he fell.

"Not gone!" I murmured at last. But again obeying that wondrous ascendancy which the inscrutable scrivener had over me, and from which ascendancy, for all my chafing, I could not completely escape, I slowly went down stairs and out into the street, and while walking round the block, considered what I should next do in this unheard-of perplexity. Turn the man out by an actual thrusting I could not; to drive him away by calling him hard names would not do; calling in the police was an unpleasant idea; and yet, permit him to enjoy his cadaverous triumph over me—this, too, I could not think of. What was to be done? or, if nothing could be done, was there anything further that I could *assume* in the matter? Yes, as before I had prospectively assumed that Bartleby would depart, so now I might retrospectively assume that departed he was. In the legitimate carrying out of this assumption, I might enter my office in a great hurry, and pretending not to see Bartleby at all, walk straight against him as if he were air. Such a proceeding would in a singular degree have the appearance of a home-thrust. It was hardly possible that Bartleby could withstand such an application of the doctrine of assumptions. But upon second thoughts the success of the plan seemed rather dubious. I resolved to argue the matter over with him again.

"Bartleby," said I, entering the office, with a quietly severe expression, "I am seriously displeased. I am pained, Bartleby. I had thought better of you. I had imagined you of such a gentlemanly organization, that in any delicate dilemma a slight hint would suffice—in short, an assumption. But it appears I am deceived. Why," I added, unaffectedly starting, "you have not even touched that money yet," pointing to it, just where I had left it the evening previous.

He answered nothing.

"Will you, or will you not, quit me?" I now demanded in a sudden passion, advancing close to him.

"I would prefer *not* to quit you," he replied, gently emphasizing the *not*.

"What earthly right have you to stay here? Do you pay any rent? Do you pay my taxes? Or is this property yours?"

He answered nothing.

"Are you ready to go on and write now? Are your eyes recovered? Could you copy a small paper for me this morning? or help examine a few lines? or step round to the post-office? In a word, will you do anything at all, to give a coloring to your refusal to depart the premises?"

He silently retired into his hermitage.

I was now in such a state of nervous resentment that I thought it but prudent to check myself at present from further demonstrations. Bartleby and I were alone. I remembered the tragedy of the unfortunate Adams and the still more unfortunate Colt in the solitary office of the latter; and how poor Colt, being dreadfully incensed by Adams, and imprudently permitting himself to get wildly excited, was at unawares hurried into his fatal act—an act which certainly no man could possibly deplore more than the actor himself.[7] Often it had occurred to me in my ponderings upon the subject, that had that altercation taken place in the public street, or at a private residence, it would not have terminated as it did. It was the circumstance of being alone in a solitary office, up stairs, of a building entirely unhallowed by humanizing domestic associations—an uncarpeted office, doubtless, of a dusty, haggard sort of appearance—this it must have been, which greatly helped to enhance the irritable desperation of the hapless Colt.

But when this old Adam of resentment rose in me and tempted me concerning Bartleby, I grappled him and threw him. How? Why, simply by recalling the divine injunction: "A new commandment give I unto you, that ye love one another." Yes, this it was that saved me. Aside from higher considerations, charity often operates as a vastly wise and prudent principle—a great safeguard to its possessor. Men have committed murder for jealousy's sake, and anger's sake, and hatred's sake, and selfishness' sake, and spiritual pride's sake; but no man that ever I heard of, ever committed a diabolical murder for sweet charity's sake. Mere self-interest, then, if no better motive can be enlisted, should, especially with high-tempered men, prompt all beings to charity and philanthropy. At any rate, upon the occasion in question, I strove to drown my exasperated feelings towards the scrivener by benevolently construing his conduct. Poor fellow, poor fellow! thought I, he don't mean anything; and besides, he has seen hard times, and ought to be indulged.

I endeavored, also, immediately to occupy myself, and at the same time to comfort my despondency. I tried to fancy, that in the course of the morning, at such time as might prove agreeable to him, Bartleby, of his own free accord, would emerge from his hermitage and take up some decided line of march in the direction of the door. But no. Half-past twelve o'clock came; Turkey began to glow in the face, overturn his inkstand, and become generally obstreperous; Nippers abated down into quietude and courtesy; Ginger Nut munched his noon apple; and Bartleby remained standing at his window in one of his profoundest dead-wall reveries. Will it be credited? Ought I to acknowledge it? That afternoon I left the office without saying one further word to him.

Some days now passed, during which, at leisure intervals I looked a little into "Edwards on the Will," and "Priestley on Necessity."[8] Under the circumstances, those books induced a salutary feeling. Gradually I slid into the persuasion that these troubles of mine, touching the scrivener, had been all predestinated from eternity, and Bartleby was billeted upon me for some mysterious purpose of an all-wise Providence, which it was not for a mere mortal like me to fathom. Yes, Bartleby, stay there behind your screen, thought I; I shall persecute you no more; you are harmless and noiseless as any of these old chairs; in short, I never feel so private as when I know you are here. At last I see it, I feel it; I penetrate

---

[7] A sensational homicide case in which Colt murdered Adams in a fit of passion.

[8] Jonathan Edwards (1703–1758), American theologian, and Joseph Priestley (1733–1804), English clergyman and chemist, both held that man's life was predetermined.

to the predestinated purpose of my life. I am content. Others may have loftier parts to enact; but my mission in this world, Bartleby, is to furnish you with office-room for such period as you may see fit to remain.

I believe that this wise and blessed frame of mind would have continued with me, had it not been for the unsolicited and uncharitable remarks obtruded upon me by my professional friends who visited the rooms. But thus it often is, that the constant friction of illiberal minds wears out at last the best resolves of the more generous. Though to be sure, when I reflected upon it, it was not strange that people entering my office should be struck by the peculiar aspect of the unaccountable Bartleby, and so be tempted to throw out some sinister observations concerning him. Sometimes an attorney, having business with me, and calling at my office, and finding no one but the scrivener there, would undertake to obtain some sort of precise information from him touching my whereabouts; but without heeding his idle talk, Bartleby would remain standing immovable in the middle of the room. So after contemplating him in that position for a time, the attorney would depart, no wiser than he came.

Also, when a reference was going on, and the room full of lawyers and witnesses, and business driving fast, some deeply-occupied legal gentleman present, seeing Bartleby wholly unemployed, would request him to run round to his (the legal gentleman's) office and fetch some papers for him. Thereupon, Bartleby would tranquilly decline, and yet remain idle as before. Then the lawyer would give a great stare, and turn to me. And what could I say? At last I was made aware that all through the circle of my professional acquaintance, a whisper of wonder was running round, having reference to the strange creature I kept at my office. This worried me very much. And as the idea came upon me of his possibly turning out a long-lived man, and keep occupying my chambers, and denying my authority; and perplexing my visitors; and scandalizing my professional reputation; and casting a general gloom over the premises; keeping soul and body together to the last upon his savings (for doubtless he spent but half a dime a day), and· in the end perhaps outlive me, and claim possession of my office by right of his perpetual occupancy: as all these dark anticipations crowded upon me more and more, and my friends continually intruded their relentless remarks upon the apparition in my room; a great change was wrought in me. I resolved to gather all my faculties together, and forever rid me of this intolerable incubus.

Ere revolving any complicated project, however, adapted to this end, I first simply suggested to Bartleby the propriety of his permanent departure. In a calm and serious tone, I commended the idea to his careful and mature consideration. But, having taken three days to meditate upon it, he apprised me, that his original determination remained the same; in short, that he still preferred to abide with me.

What shall I do. I now said to myself, buttoning up my coat to the last button. What shall I do? what ought I to do? what does conscience say I *should* do with this man, or, rather, ghost. Rid myself of him, I must; go, he shall. But how? You will not thrust him, the poor, pale, passive mortal—you will not thrust such a helpless creature out of your door? you will not dishonor yourself by such cruelty? No, I will not, I cannot do that. Rather would I let him live and die here, and then mason up his remains in the wall. What, then, will you do? For all your coaxing, he will not budge. Bribes he leaves under your own paper-weight on your table; in short, it is quite plain that he prefers to cling to you.

Then something severe, something unusual must be done. What! surely you will not have him collared by a constable, and commit his innocent pallor to the common jail? And upon what ground could you procure such a thing to be done?—a vagrant, is he? What! he a vagrant, a wanderer, who refuses to budge? It is because he will *not* be a vagrant, then, that you seek to count him *as* a vagrant. This is too absurd. No visible means of support: there I have him. Wrong again: for indubitably he *does* support himself, and that is the only unanswerable proof that any man can show of his possessing the means so to do. No more, then. Since he will not quit me, I must quit him. I will change my offices; I will move elsewhere, and give him fair notice, that if I find him on my new premises I will then proceed against him as a common trespasser.

Acting accordingly, next day I thus addressed him: "I find these chambers too far from the City Hall; the air is unwholesome. In a word, I propose to remove my offices next week, and shall no longer require your services. I tell you this now, in order that you may seek another place."

He made no reply; and nothing more was said.

On the appointed day I engaged carts and men, proceeded to my chambers, and, having but little furniture, everything was removed in a few hours. Throughout, the scrivener remained standing behind the screen, which I directed to be removed the last thing. It was withdrawn; and, being folded up like a huge folio, left him the motionless occupant of a naked room. I stood in the entry watching him a moment, while something from within me upbraided me.

I re-entered, with my hand in my pocket—and—and my heart in my mouth.

"Good-by, Bartleby; I am going—good-by, and God some way bless you; and take that," slipping something in his hand. But it dropped upon the floor, and then—strange to say—I tore myself from him whom I had so longed to be rid of.

Established in my new quarters, for a day or two I kept the door locked, and started at every footfall in the passages. When I returned to my rooms, after any little absence, I would pause at the threshold for an instant, and attentively listen, ere applying my key. But these fears were needless. Bartleby never came nigh me.

I thought all was going well, when a perturbed-looking stranger visited me, inquiring whether I was the person who had recently occupied rooms at No. —— Wall Street.

Full of forebodings, I replied that I was.

"Then, sir," said the stranger, who proved a lawyer, "you are responsible for the man you left there. He refuses to do any copying; he refuses to do anything; he says he prefers not to; and he refuses to quit the premises."

"I am very sorry, sir," said I, with assumed tranquillity, but an inward tremor, "but, really, the man you allude to is nothing to me—he is no relation or apprentice of mine, that you should hold me responsible for him."

"In mercy's name, who is he?"

"I certainly cannot inform you. I know nothing about him. Formerly I employed him as a copyist; but he has done nothing for me now for some time past."

"I shall settle him, then—good morning, sir."

Several days passed, and I heard nothing more; and, though I often felt a charitable prompting to call at the place and see poor Bartleby, yet a certain squeamishness, of I know not what, withheld me.

All is over with him, by this time, thought I, at last, when, through another week, no further intelligence reached me. But, coming to my room the day after, I found several persons waiting at my door in a high state of nervous excitement.

"That's the man—here he comes," cried the foremost one, whom I recognized as the lawyer who had previously called upon me alone.

"You must take him away, sir, at once," cried a portly person among them, advancing upon me, and whom I knew to be the landlord of No. —— Wall Street. "These gentlemen, my tenants, cannot stand it any longer; Mr. B—," pointing to the lawyer, "has turned him out of his room, and he now persists in haunting the building generally, sitting upon the banisters of the stairs by day, and sleeping in the entry by night. Everybody is concerned; clients are leaving the offices; some fears are entertained of a mob; something you must do, and that without delay."

Aghast at this torrent, I fell back before it, and would fain have locked myself in my new quarters. In vain I persisted that Bartleby was nothing to me—no more than to any one else. In vain—I was the last person known to have anything to do with him, and they held me to the terrible account. Fearful, then, of being exposed in the papers (as one person present obscurely threatened), I considered the matter, and, at length, said, that if the lawyer would give me a confidential interview with the scrivener, in his (the lawyer's) own room, I would, that afternoon, strive my best to rid them of the nuisance they complained of.

Going up stairs to my old haunt, there was Bartleby silently sitting upon the banister at the landing.

"What are you doing here, Bartleby?" said I.

"Sitting upon the banister," he mildly replied.

I motioned him into the lawyer's room, who then left us.

"Bartleby," said I, "are you aware that you are the cause of great tribulation to me, by persisting in occupying the entry after being dismissed from the office?"

No answer.

"Now one of two things must take place. Either you must do something, or something must be done to you. Now what sort of business would you like to engage in? Would you like to re-engage in copying for some one?"

"No; I would prefer not to make any change."

"Would you like a clerkship in a dry-goods store?"

"There is too much confinement about that. No, I would not like a clerkship; but I am not particular."

"Too much confinement," I cried, "why you keep yourself confined all the time!"

"I would prefer not to take a clerkship," he rejoined, as if to settle that little item at once.

"How would a bar-tender's business suit you? There is no trying of the eye-sight in that."

"I would not like it at all; though, as I said before, I am not particular."

His unwonted wordiness inspirited me. I returned to the charge.

"Well, then, would you like to travel through the country collecting bills for the merchants? That would improve your health."

"No, I would prefer to be doing something else."

"How, then, would going as a companion to Europe, to entertain some young gentleman with your conversation—how would that suit you?"

"Not at all. It does not strike me that there is anything definite about that. I like to be stationary. But I am not particular."

"Stationary you shall be, then," I cried, now losing all patience, and, for the first time in all my exasperating connection with him, fairly flying into a passion. "If you do not go away from these premises before night, I shall feel bound—indeed, I *am* bound—to—to—to quit the premises myself!" I rather absurdly concluded, knowing not with what possible threat to try to frighten his immo-bility into compliance. Despairing of all further efforts, I was precipitately leav-ing him, when a final thought occurred to me—one which had not been wholly unindulged before.

"Bartleby," said I, in the kindest tone I could assume under such exciting circumstances, "will you go home with me now—not to my office, but my dwelling—and remain there till we can conclude upon some convenient ar-rangement for you at our leisure? Come, let us start now, right away."

"No: at present I would prefer not to make any change at all."

I answered nothing; but, effectually dodging every one by the suddenness and rapidity of my flight, rushed from the building, ran up Wall Street towards Broadway, and, jumping into the first omnibus, was soon removed from pursuit. As soon as tranquillity returned, I distinctly perceived that I had now done all that I possibly could, both in respect to the demands of the landlord and his tenants, and with regard to my own desire and sense of duty, to benefit Bartleby, and shield him from rude persecution. I now strove to be entirely care-free and quiescent; and my conscience justified me in the attempt; though, indeed, it was not so successful as I could have wished. So fearful was I of being again hunted out by the incensed landlord and his exasperated tenants, that, surren-dering my business to Nippers, for a few days, I drove about the upper part of the town and through the suburbs, in my rockaway; crossed over to Jersey City and Hoboken, and paid fugitive visits to Manhattanville and Astoria. In fact, I almost lived in my rockaway for the time.

When again I entered my office, lo, a note from the landlord lay upon the desk. I opened it with trembling hands. It informed me that the writer had sent to the police, and had Bartleby removed to the Tombs as a vagrant. Moreover, since I knew more about him than any one else, he wished me to appear at that place, and make a suitable statement of the facts. These tidings had a conflicting effect upon me. At first I was indignant; but, at last, almost approved. The landlord's energetic, summary disposition, had led him to adopt a procedure which I do not think I would have decided upon myself; and yet, as a last resort, under such peculiar circumstances, it seemed the only plan.

As I afterwards learned, the poor scrivener, when told that he must be conducted to the Tombs, offered not the slightest obstacle, but, in his pale, unmoving way, silently acquiesced.

Some of the compassionate and curious bystanders joined the party; and headed by one of the constables arm in arm with Bartleby, the silent procession filed its way through all the noise, and heat, and joy of the roaring thoroughfares at noon.

The same day I received the note, I went to the Tombs, or, to speak more properly, the Halls of Justice. Seeking the right officer, I stated the purpose of my call, and was informed that the individual I described was, indeed, within. I then assured the functionary that Bartleby was a perfectly honest man, and greatly to be compassionated, however unaccountably eccentric. I narrated all I knew, and closed by suggesting the idea of letting him remain in as indulgent confinement as possible, till something less harsh might be done—though, indeed, I hardly knew what. At all events, if nothing else could be decided upon, the alms-house must receive him. I then begged to have an interview.

Being under no disgraceful charge, and quite serene and harmless in all his ways, they had permitted him freely to wander about the prison, and, especially, in the inclosed grass-platted yards thereof. And so I found him there, standing all alone in the quietest of the yards, his face towards a high wall, while all around, from the narrow slits of the jail windows, I thought I saw peering out upon him the eyes of murderers and thieves.

"Bartleby!"

"I know you," he said, without looking round—"and I want nothing to say to you."

"It was not I that brought you here, Bartleby," said I, keenly pained at his implied suspicion. "And to you, this should not be so vile a place. Nothing reproachful attaches to you by being here. And see, it is not so sad a place as one might think. Look, there is the sky, and here is the grass."

"I know where I am," he replied, but would say nothing more, and so I left him.

As I entered the corridor again, a broad meat-like man, in an apron, accosted me, and, jerking his thumb over his shoulder, said—"Is that your friend?"

"Yes."

"Does he want to starve? If he does, let him live on the prison fare, that's all."

"Who are you?" asked I, not knowing what to make of such an unofficially speaking person in such a place.

"I am the grub-man. Such gentlemen as have friends here, hire me to provide them with something good to eat."

"Is this so?" said I, turning to the turnkey.

He said it was.

"Well, then," said I, slipping some silver into the grub-man's hands (for so they called him), "I want you to give particular attention to my friend there; let him have the best dinner you can get. And you must be as polite to him as possible."

"Introduce me, will you?" said the grub-man, looking at me with an expression which seemed to say he was all impatience for an opportunity to give a specimen of his breeding.

Thinking it would prove of benefit to the scrivener, I acquiesced; and, asking the grub-man his name, went up with him to Bartleby.

"Bartleby, this is a friend; you will find him very useful to you."

"Your sarvant, sir, your sarvant," said the grub-man, making a low salutation behind his apron. "Hope you find it pleasant here, sir; nice grounds—cool apartments—hope you'll stay with us sometime—try to make it agreeable. What will you have for dinner to-day?"

"I prefer not to dine to-day," said Bartleby, turning away. "It would disagree with me; I am unused to dinners." So saying, he slowly moved to the other side of the inclosure, and took up a position fronting the dead-wall.

"How's this?" said the grub-man, addressing me with a stare of astonishment. "He's odd, ain't he?"

"I think he is a little deranged," said I, sadly.

"Deranged? deranged is it? Well, now, upon my word, I thought that friend of yourn was a gentleman forger; they are always pale and genteel-like, them forgers. I can't help pity 'em—can't help it, sir. Did you know Monroe Edwards?" he added, touchingly, and paused. Then, laying his hand piteously on my shoulder, sighed, "he died of consumption at Sing-Sing.[9] So you weren't acquainted with Monroe?"

"No, I was never socially acquainted with any forgers. But I cannot stop longer. Look to my friend yonder. You will not lose by it. I will see you again."

Some few days after this, I again obtained admission to the Tombs, and went through the corridors in quest of Bartleby; but without finding him.

"I saw him coming from his cell not long ago," said a turnkey, "may be he's gone to loiter in the yards."

So I went in that direction.

"Are you looking for the silent man?" said another turnkey, passing me. "Yonder he lies—sleeping in the yard there. 'Tis not twenty minutes since I saw him lie down."

The yard was entirely quiet. It was not accessible to the common prisoners.

---

[9] The state prison near Ossining, New York.

The surrounding walls of amazing thickness, kept off all sounds behind them. The Egyptian character of the masonry weighed upon me with its gloom. But a soft imprisoned turf grew under foot. The heart of the eternal pyramids, it seemed, wherein, by some strange magic, through the clefts, grass-seed, dropped by birds, had sprung.

Strangely huddled at the base of the wall, his knees drawn up, and lying on his side, his head touching the cold stones, I saw the wasted Bartleby. But nothing stirred. I paused; then went close up to him; stooped over, and saw that his dim eyes were open; otherwise he seemed profoundly sleeping. Something prompted me to touch him. I felt his hand, when a tingling shiver ran up my arm and down my spine to my feet.

The round face of the grub-man peered upon me now. "His dinner is ready. Won't he dine to-day, either? Or does he live without dining?"

"Lives without dining," said I, and closed the eyes.

"Eh!—He's asleep, ain't he?"

"With kings and counselors," murmured I.

There would seem little need for proceeding further in this history. Imagination will readily supply the meagre recital of poor Bartleby's interment. But, ere parting with the reader, let me say, that if this little narrative has sufficiently interested him, to awaken curiosity as to who Bartleby was, and what manner of life he led prior to the present narrator's making his acquaintance, I can only reply, that in such curiosity I fully share, but am wholly unable to gratify it. Yet here I hardly know whether I should divulge one little item of rumor, which came to my ear a few months after the scrivener's decease. Upon what basis it rested, I could never ascertain; and hence, how true it is I cannot now tell. But, inasmuch as this vague report has not been without a certain suggestive interest to me, however said, it may prove the same with some others; and so I will briefly mention it. The report was this: that Bartleby had been a subordinate clerk in the Dead Letter Office at Washington, from which he had been suddenly removed by a change in the administration. When I think over this rumor, hardly can I express the emotions which seize me. Dead letters! does it not sound like dead men? Conceive a man by nature and misfortune prone to a pallid hopelessness, can any business seem more fitted to heighten it than that of continually handling these dead letters, and assorting them for the flames? For by the cart-load they are annually burned. Some times from out the folded paper the pale clerk takes a ring—the finger it was meant for, perhaps, moulders in the grave; a bank-note sent in swiftest charity—he whom it would relieve, nor eats nor hungers any more; pardon for those who died despairing; hope for those who died unhoping; good tidings for those who died stifled by unrelieved calamities. On errands of life, these letters speed to death.

Ah, Bartleby! Ah, humanity!

QUESTIONS

1. What is it about Bartleby that so intrigues and fascinates the narrator? Why does the narrator continue to feel a moral obligation to an employee who refuses to work and curtly rejects kindly offers of help? **2.** With his final utterance, "Ah, Bartleby! Ah, humanity!" the narrator apparently penetrates the mystery of Bartleby. The comments seem to suggest that for the narrator Bartleby is a representative of humanity. In what sense might the narrator come to see Bartleby in this light? **3.** What functions do Turkey and Nippers serve? **4.** Would it be fair to describe Bartleby as a rebel without a cause, as a young man who refuses to participate in a comfortable and well-ordered business world but fails to offer any alternative way of life? Justify your answer.

WRITING TOPICS

1. Readers differ as to whether this is the story of Bartleby or the story of the lawyer-narrator. What is your view? **2.** Why does Melville allow the narrator (and the reader) to discover so little about Bartleby and the causes of his behavior? All we learn of Bartleby's past is contained in the next-to-last paragraph. What, if anything, in this paragraph establishes a link between Bartleby and the narrator?

Gladius Dei *

THOMAS MANN [1875–1955]

1902

Munich was radiant. Above the gay squares and white columned temples, the classicistic monuments and the baroque churches, the leaping fountains, the palaces and parks of the Residence there stretched a sky of luminous blue silk. Well-arranged leafy vistas laced with sun and shade lay basking in the sunshine of a beautiful day in early June.

There was a twittering of birds and a blithe holiday spirit in all the little streets. And in the squares and past the rows of villas there swelled, rolled, and hummed the leisurely, entertaining traffic of that easy-going, charming town. Travellers of all nationalities drove about in the slow little droshkies, looking right and left in aimless curiosity at the house-fronts; they mounted and descended museum stairs. Many windows stood open and music was heard from within: practising on piano, cello, or violin—earnest and well-meant amateur efforts; while from the Odeon came the sound of serious work on several grand pianos.

Young people, the kind that can whistle the Nothung motif,[1] who fill the pit of the Schauspielhaus every evening, wandered in and out of the University and Library with literary magazines in their coat pockets. A court carriage stood before the Academy, the home of the plastic arts, which spreads its white wings between the Türkenstrasse and the Siegestor. And colourful groups of models, picturesque old men, women and children in Albanian costume, stood or lounged at the top of the balustrade.

Indolent, unhurried sauntering was the mode in all the long streets of the northern quarter. There life is lived for pleasanter ends than the driving greed of gain. Young artists with little round hats on the backs of their heads, flowing cravats and no canes—carefree bachelors who paid for their lodgings with colour-sketches—were strolling up and down to let the clear blue morning play upon their mood, also to look at the little girls, the pretty, rather plump type, with the brunette bandeaux, the too large feet, and the unobjectionable morals. Every fifth house had studio windows blinking in the sun. Sometimes a fine piece of architecture stood out from a middle-class row, the work of some imaginative young architect; a wide front with shallow bays and decorations in a bizarre style very expressive and full of invention. Or the door to some monotonous façade would be framed in a bold improvisation of flowing lines and sunny colours, with bacchantes, naiads,[2] and rosy-skinned nudes.

---

* Translated by H. T. Lowe-Porter. *Gladius Dei* means "sword of God."

[1] *Nothung* means "sword." The Nothung motif is a musical passage from Richard Wagner's opera *Siegfried. Schauspielhaus* means "theater."

[2] Bacchantes are female followers of Bacchus, the god of wine; naiads are water nymphs.

It was always a joy to linger before the windows of the cabinet-makers and the shops for modern articles *de luxe*. What a sense for luxurious nothings and amusing, significant line was displayed in the shape of everything! Little shops that sold picture frames, sculptures, and antiques there were in endless number; in their windows you might see those busts of Florentine women of the Renaissance, so full of noble poise and poignant charm. And the owners of the smallest and meanest of these shops spoke of Mino da Fiesole[3] and Donatello as though he had received the rights of reproduction from them personally.

But on the Odeonsplatz, in view of the mighty loggia with the spacious mosaic pavement before it, diagonally opposite to the Regent's palace, people were crowding round the large windows and glass show-cases of the big art-shop owned by M. Blüthenzweig. What a glorious display! There were reproductions of the masterpieces of all the galleries in the world, in costly decorated and tinted frames, the good taste of which was precious in its very simplicity. There were copies of modern paintings, works of a joyously sensuous fantasy, in which the antiques seemed born again in humorous and realistic guise; bronze nudes and fragile ornamental glassware; tall, thin earthenware vases with an iridescent glaze produced by a bath in metal steam; *éditions de luxe* which were triumphs of modern binding and presswork, containing the works of the most modish poets, set out with every possible advantage of sumptuous elegance. Cheek by jowl with these, the portraits of artists, musicians, philosophers, actors, writers, displayed to gratify the public taste for personalities.—In the first window, next the book-shop, a large picture stood on an easel, with a crowd of people in front of it, a fine sepia photograph in a wide old-gold frame, a very striking reproduction of the sensation at this year's great international exhibition, to which public attention is always invited by means of effective and artistic posters stuck up everywhere on hoardings among concert programmes and clever advertisements of toilet preparations.

If you looked into the windows of the book-shop your eye met such titles as *Interior Decoration Since the Renaissance, The Renaissance in Modern Decorative Art, The Book as Work of Art, The Decorative Arts, Hunger for Art,* and many more. And you would remember that these thought-provoking pamphlets were sold and read by the thousand and that discussions on these subjects were the preoccupation of all the salons.

You might be lucky enough to meet in person one of the famous fair ones whom less fortunate folk know only through the medium of art; one of those rich and beautiful women whose Titian-blond colouring Nature's most sweet and cunning hand did *not* lay on, but whose diamond parures and beguiling charms had received immortality from the hand of some portrait-painter of genius and whose love-affairs were the talk of the town. These were the queens of the artist balls at carnival-time. They were a little painted, a little made up, full of haughty caprices, worthy of adoration, avid of praise. You might see a

---

[3] Mino da Fiesole and Donatello were fourteenth-century Italian artists.

carriage rolling up the Ludwigstrasse, with such a great painter and his mistress inside. People would be pointing out the sight, standing still to gaze after the pair. Some of them would curtsy. A little more and the very policemen would stand at attention.

Art flourished, art swayed the destinies of the town, art stretched above it her rose-bound sceptre and smiled. On every hand obsequious interest was displayed in her prosperity, on every hand she was served with industry and devotion. There was a downright cult of line, decoration, form, significance, beauty. Munich was radiant.

A youth was coming down the Schellingstrasse. With the bells of cyclists ringing about him he strode across the wooden pavement towards the broad façade of the Ludwigskirche. Looking at him it was as though a shadow passed across the sky, or cast over the spirit some memory of melancholy hours. Did he not love the sun which bathed the lovely city in its festal light? Why did he walk wrapped in his own thoughts, his eyes directed on the ground?

No one in that tolerant and variety-loving town would have taken offence at his wearing no hat; but why need the hood of his ample black cloak have been drawn over his head, shadowing his low, prominent, and peaked forehead, covering his ears and framing his haggard cheeks? What pangs of conscience, what scruples and self-tortures had so availed to hollow out these cheeks? It is frightful, on such a sunny day, to see care sitting in the hollows of the human face. His dark brows thickened at the narrow base of his hooked and prominent nose. His lips were unpleasantly full, his eyes brown and close-lying. When he lifted them, diagonal folds appeared on the peaked brow. His gaze expressed knowledge, limitation, and suffering. Seen in profile his face was strikingly like an old painting preserved at Florence in a narrow cloister cell whence once a frightful and shattering protest issued against life and her triumphs.

Hieronymus walked along the Schellingstrasse with a slow, firm stride, holding his wide cloak together with both hands from inside. Two little girls, two of those pretty, plump little creatures with the bandeaux, the big feet, and the unobjectionable morals, strolled towards him arm in arm, on pleasure bent. They poked each other and laughed, they bent double with laughter, they even broke into a run and ran away still laughing, at his hood and his face. But he paid them no heed. With bent head, looking neither to the right nor to the left, he crossed the Ludwigstrasse and mounted the church steps.

The great wings of the middle portal stood wide open. From somewhere within the consecrated twilight, cool, dank, incense-laden, there came a pale red glow. An old woman with inflamed eyes rose from a prayer-stool and slipped on crutches through the columns. Otherwise the church was empty.

Hieronymus sprinkled brow and breast at the stoup, bent the knee before the high altar, and then paused in the centre nave. Here in the church his stature seemed to have grown. He stood upright and immovable; his head was flung up and his great hooked nose jutted domineeringly above the thick lips. His eyes no longer sought the ground, but looked straight and boldly into the distance, at the crucifix on the high altar. Thus he stood awhile, then retreating he bent the knee again and left the church.

He strode up the Ludwigstrasse, slowly, firmly, with bent head, in the centre of the wide unpaved road, towards the mighty loggia with its statues. But arrived at the Odeonsplatz, he looked up, so that the folds came out on his peaked forehead, and checked his step, his attention being called to the crowd at the windows of the big art-shop of M. Blüthenzweig.

People moved from window to window, pointing out to each other the treasures displayed and exchanging views as they looked over one another's shoulders. Hieronymus mingled among them and did as they did, taking in all these things with his eyes, one by one.

He saw the reproductions of masterpieces from all the galleries in the world, the priceless frames so precious in their simplicity, the Renaissance sculpture, the bronze nudes, the exquisitely bound volumes, the iridescent vases, the portraits of artists, musicians, philosophers, actors, writers; he looked at everything and turned a moment of his scrutiny upon each object. Holding his mantle closely together with both hands from inside, he moved his hood-covered head in short turns from one thing to the next, gazing at each awhile with a dull, inimical, and remotely surprised air, lifting the dark brows which grew so thick at the base of the nose. At length he stood in front of the last window, which contained the startling picture. For a while he looked over the shoulders of people before him and then in his turn reached a position directly in front of the window.

The large red-brown photograph in the choice old-gold frame stood on an easel in the centre. It was a Madonna, but an utterly unconventional one, a work of entirely modern feeling. The figure of the Holy Mother was revealed as enchantingly feminine and beautiful. Her great smouldering eyes were rimmed with darkness, and her delicate and strangely smiling lips were half-parted. Her slender fingers held in a somewhat nervous grasp the hips of a Child, a nude boy of pronounced, almost primitive leanness. He was playing with her breast and glancing aside at the beholder with a wise look in his eyes.

Two other youths stood near Hieronymus, talking about the picture. They were two young men with books under their arms, which they had fetched from the Library or were taking thither. Humanistically educated people, that is, equipped with science and with art.

"The little chap is in luck, devil take me!" said one.

"He seems to be trying to make one envious," replied the other. "A bewildering female!"

"A female to drive a man crazy! Gives you funny ideas about the Immaculate Conception."

"No, she doesn't look exactly immaculate. Have you seen the original?"

"Of course; I was quite bowled over. She makes an even more aphrodisiac impression in colour. Especially the eyes."

"The likeness is pretty plain."

"How so?"

"Don't you know the model? Of course he used his little dressmaker. It is almost a portrait, only with a lot more emphasis on the corruptible. The girl is more innocent."

"I hope so. Life would be altogether too much of a strain if there were many like this *mater amata*."[4]

"The Pinakothek has bought it."

"Really? Well, well! They knew what they were about, anyhow. The treatment of the flesh and the flow of the linen garment are really first-class."

"Yes, an incredibly gifted chap."

"Do you know him?"

"A little. He will have a career, that is certain. He has been invited twice by the Prince Regent."

This last was said as they were taking leave of each other.

"Shall I see you this evening at the theatre?" asked the first. "The Dramatic Club is giving Machiavelli's *Mandragola*."[5]

"Oh, bravo! That will be great, of course. I had meant to go to the Variété, but I shall probably choose our stout Niccolò after all. Good-bye."

They parted, going off to right and left. New people took their places and looked at the famous picture. But Hieronymus stood where he was, motionless, with his head thrust out; his hands clutched convulsively at the mantle as they held it together from inside. His brows were no longer lifted with that cool and unpleasantly surprised expression; they were drawn and darkened; his cheeks, half-shrouded in the black hood, seemed more sunken than ever and his thick lips had gone pale. Slowly his head dropped lower and lower, so that finally his eyes stared upwards at the work of art, while the nostrils of his great nose dilated.

Thus he remained for perhaps a quarter of an hour. The crowd about him melted away, but he did not stir from the spot. At last he turned slowly on the balls of his feet and went hence.

But the picture of the Madonna went with him. Always and ever, whether in his hard and narrow little room or kneeling in the cool church, it stood before his outraged soul, with its smouldering, dark-rimmed eyes, its riddlingly smiling lips—stark and beautiful. And no prayer availed to exorcize it.

But the third night it happened that a command and summons from on high came to Hieronymus, to intercede and lift his voice against the frivolity, blasphemy, and arrogance of beauty. In vain like Moses he protested that he had not the gift of tongues. God's will remained unshaken; in a loud voice He demanded that the faint-hearted Hieronymus go forth to sacrifice amid the jeers of the foe.

---

[4]Beloved mother. The Pinakothek is a municipal art gallery.
[5]Niccolò Machiavelli (1469–1527) was a playwright as well as a political philosopher. His play, *Mandragola*, is a sex comedy.

And since God would have it so, he set forth one morning and wended his way to the great art-shop of M. Blüthenzweig. He wore his hood over his head and held his mantle together in front from inside with both hands as he went.

The air had grown heavy, the sky was livid and thunder threatened. Once more crowds were besieging the show-cases at the art-shop and especially the window where the photograph of the Madonna stood. Hieronymus cast one brief glance thither; then he pushed up the latch of the glass door hung with placards and art magazines. "As God wills," said he, and entered the shop.

A young girl was somewhere at a desk writing in a big book. She was a pretty brunette thing with bandeaux of hair and big feet. She came up to him and asked pleasantly what he would like.

"Thank you," said Hieronymus in a low voice and looked her earnestly in the face, with diagonal wrinkles in his peaked brow. "I would speak not to you but to the owner of this shop, Herr Blüthenzweig."

She hesitated a little, turned away, and took up her work once more. He stood there in the middle of the shop.

Instead of the single specimens in the show-windows there was here a riot and a heaping-up of luxury, a fullness of colour, line, form, style, invention, good taste, and beauty. Hieronymus looked slowly round him, drawing his mantle close with both hands.

There were several people in the shop besides him. At one of the broad tables running across the room sat a man in a yellow suit, with a black goat's-beard, looking at a portfolio of French drawings, over which he now and then emitted a bleating laugh. He was being waited on by an undernourished and vegetarian young man, who kept on dragging up fresh portfolios. Diagonally opposite the bleating man sat an elegant old dame, examining art embroideries with a pattern of fabulous flowers in pale tones standing together on tall perpendicular stalks. An attendant hovered about her too. A leisurely Englishman in a travelling-cap, with his pipe in his mouth, sat at another table. Cold and smooth-shaven, of indefinite age, in his good English clothes, he sat examining bronzes brought to him by M. Blüthenzweig in person. He was holding up by the head the dainty figure of a nude young girl, immature and delicately articulated, her hands crossed in coquettish innocence upon her breast. He studied her thoroughly, turning her slowly about. M. Blüthenzweig, a man with a short, heavy brown beard and bright brown eyes of exactly the same colour, moved in a semicircle round him, rubbing his hands, praising the statuette with all the terms his vocabulary possessed.

"A hundred and fifty marks, sir," he said in English. "Munich art—very charming, in fact. Simply full of charm, you know. Grace itself. Really extremely pretty, good, admirable, in fact." Then he thought of some more and went on: "Highly attractive, fascinating." Then he began again from the beginning.

His nose lay a little flat on his upper lip, so that he breathed constantly with a slight sniff into his moustache. Sometimes he did this as he approached a customer, stooping over as though he were smelling at him. When Hieronymus entered, M. Blüthenzweig had examined him cursorily in this way, then devoted himself again to his Englishman.

The elegant old dame made her selection and left the shop. A man entered. M. Blüthenzweig sniffed briefly at him as though to scent out his capacity to buy and left him to the young bookkeeper. The man purchased a faience bust of young Piero de' Medici, son of Lorenzo, and went out again. The Englishman began to depart. He had acquired the statuette of the young girl and left amid bowings from M. Blüthenzweig. Then the art-dealer turned to Hieronymus and came forward.

"You wanted something?" he said, without any particular courtesy.

Hieronymus held his cloak together with both hands and looked the other in the face almost without winking an eyelash. He parted his big lips slowly and said:

"I have come to you on account of the picture in the window there, the big photograph, the Madonna." His voice was thick and without modulation.

"Yes, quite right," said M. Blüthenzweig briskly and began rubbing his hands. "Seventy marks in the frame. It is unfadable—a first-class reproduction. Highly attractive and full of charm."

Hieronymus was silent. He nodded his head in the hood and shrank a little into himself as the dealer spoke. Then he drew himself up again and said:

"I would remark to you first of all that I am not in the position to purchase anything, nor have I the desire. I am sorry to have to disappoint your expectations. I regret if it upsets you. But in the first place I am poor and in the second I do not love the things you sell. No, I cannot buy anything."

"No? Well, then?" asked M. Blüthenzweig, sniffing a good deal. "Then may I ask—"

"I suppose," Hieronymus went on, "that being what you are you look down on me because I am not in a position to buy."

"Oh—er—not at all," said M. Blüthenzweig. "Not at all. Only—"

"And yet I beg you to hear me and give some consideration to my words."

"Consideration to your words. H'm—may I ask—"

"You may ask," said Hieronymus, "and I will answer you. I have come to beg you to remove that picture, the big photograph, the Madonna, out of your window and never display it again."

M. Blüthenzweig looked awhile dumbly into Hieronymus's face—as though he expected him to be abashed at the words he had just uttered. But as this did not happen he gave a violent sniff and spoke himself:

"Will you be so good as to tell me whether you are here in any official capacity which authorizes you to dictate to me, or what does bring you here?"

"Oh, no," replied Hieronymus, "I have neither office nor dignity from the state. I have no power on my side, sir. What brings me hither is my conscience alone."

M. Blüthenzweig, searching for words, snorted violently into his moustache. At length he said:

"Your conscience . . . . well, you will kindly understand that I take not the faintest interest in your conscience." With which he turned round and moved quickly to his desk at the back of the shop, where he began to write. Both attendants laughed heartily. The pretty Fräulein giggled over her account-book. As for the yellow gentleman with the goat's beard, he was evidently a foreigner, for he gave no sign of comprehension but went on studying the French drawings and emitting from time to time his bleating laugh.

"Just get rid of the man for me," said M. Blüthenzweig shortly over his shoulder to his assistant. He went on writing. The poorly paid young vegetarian approached Hieronymus, smothering his laughter, and the other salesman came up too.

"May we be of service to you in any other way?" the first asked mildly. Hieronymus fixed him with his glazed and suffering eyes.

"No," he said, "you cannot. I beg you to take the Madonna picture out of the window, at once and forever."

"But—why?"

"It is the Holy Mother of God," said Hieronymus in a subdued voice.

"Quite. But you have heard that Herr Blüthenzweig is not inclined to accede to your request."

"We must bear in mind that it is the Holy Mother of God," said Hieronymus again and his head trembled on his neck.

"So we must. But should we not be allowed to exhibit any Madonnas—or paint any?"

"It is not that," said Hieronymus, almost whispering. He drew himself up and shook his head energetically several times. His peaked brow under the hood was entirely furrowed with long, deep cross-folds. "You know very well that it is vice itself that is painted there—naked sensuality. I was standing near two simple young people and overheard with my own ears that it led them astray upon the doctrine of the Immaculate Conception."

"Oh, permit me—that is not the point," said the young salesman, smiling. In his leisure hours he was writing a brochure on the modern movement in art and was well qualified to conduct a cultured conversation. "The picture is a work of art," he went on, "and one must measure it by the appropriate standards as such. It has been very highly praised on all hands. The state has purchased it."

"I know that the state has purchased it," said Hieronymus. "I also know that the artist has twice dined with the Prince Regent. It is common talk—and God knows how people interpret the fact that a man can become famous by such work as this. What does such a fact bear witness to? To the blindness of the world, a blindness inconceivable, if not indeed shamelessly hypocritical. This picture has its origin in sensual lust and is enjoyed in the same—is that true or not? Answer me! And you too answer me, Herr Blüthenzweig!"

A pause ensued. Hieronymus seemed in all seriousness to demand an answer to his question, looking by turns at the staring attendants and the round back M. Blüthenzweig turned upon him, with his own piercing and anguishing brown eyes. Silence reigned. Only the yellow man with the goat's beard, bending over the French drawings, broke it with his bleating laugh.

"It is true," Hieronymus went on in a hoarse voice that shook with his profound indignation. "You do not dare deny it. How then can honour be done to its creator, as though he had endowed mankind with a new ideal possession? How can one stand before it and surrender unthinkingly to the base enjoyment which it purveys, persuading oneself in all seriousness that one is yielding to a noble and elevated sentiment, highly creditable to the human race? Is this reckless ignorance or abandoned ·hypocrisy? My understanding falters, it is completely at a loss when confronted by the absurd fact that a man can achieve renown on this earth by the stupid and shameless exploitation of the animal instincts. Beauty? What is beauty? What forces are they which use beauty as their tool today—and upon what does it work? No· one can fail to know this, Herr Blüthenzweig. But who, understanding it clearly, can fail to feel disgust and pain? It is criminal to play upon the ignorance of the immature, the lewd, the brazen, and the unscrupulous by elevating beauty into an idol to be worshipped, to give it even more power over those who know not affliction and have no knowledge of redemption. You are unknown to me, and you look at me with black looks—yet answer me! Knowledge, I tell you, is the profoundest torture in the world; but it is the purgatory without whose purifying pangs no soul can reach salvation. It is not infantile, blasphemous shallowness that can save us, Herr Blüthenzweig; only knowledge can avail, knowledge in which the passions of our loathsome flesh die away and are quenched."

Silence.—The yellow man with the goat's beard gave a sudden little bleat.

"I think you really must go now," said the underpaid assistant mildly.

But Hieronymus made no move to do so. Drawn up in his hooded cape, he stood with blazing eyes in the centre of the shop and his thick lips poured out condemnation in a voice that was harsh and rusty and clanking.

"Art, you cry; enjoyment, beauty! Enfold the world in beauty and endow all things with the noble grace of style!—Profligate, away! Do you think to wash over with lurid colours the misery of the world? Do you think with the sounds of feasting and music to drown out the voice of the tortured earth? Shameless one, you err! God lets not Himself be mocked, and your impudent deification of the glistering surface of things is an abomination in His eyes. You tell me that I blaspheme art. I say to you that you lie. I do not blaspheme art. Art is no conscienceless delusion, lending itself to reinforce the allurements of the fleshly. Art is the holy torch which turns its light upon all the frightful depths, all the shameful and woeful abysses of life; art is the godly fire laid to the world that, being redeemed by pity, it may flame up and dissolve altogether with its shames and torments.—Take it out, Herr Blüthenzweig, take away the work of that famous painter out of your window—you would do well to burn it with a hot fire and strew its ashes to the four winds—yes, to all the four winds—"

His harsh voice broke off. He had taken a violent backwards step, snatched one arm from his black wrappings, and stretched it passionately forth, gesturing towards the window with a hand that shook as though palsied. And in this commanding attitude he paused. His great hooked nose seemed to jut more than ever, his dark brows were gathered so thick and high that folds crowded upon the peaked forehead shaded by the hood; a hectic flush mantled his hollow cheeks.

But at this point M. Blüthenzweig turned round. Perhaps he was outraged by the idea of burning his seventy-mark reproduction; perhaps Hieronymus's speech had completely exhausted his patience. In any case he was a picture of stern and righteous anger. He pointed with his pen to the door of the shop, gave several short, excited snorts into his moustache, struggled for words, and uttered with the maximum of energy those which he found:

"My fine fellow, if you don't get out at once I will have my packer help you—do you understand?"

"Oh, you cannot intimidate me, you cannot drive me away, you cannot silence my voice!" cried Hieronymus as he clutched his cloak over his chest with his fists and shook his head doughtily. "I know that I am single-handed and powerless, but yet I will not cease until you hear me, Herr Blüthenzweig! Take the picture out of your window and burn it even today! Ah, burn not it alone! Burn all these statues and busts, the sight of which plunges the beholder into sin! Burn these vases and ornaments, these shameless revivals of paganism, these elegantly bound volumes of erotic verse! Burn everything in your shop, Herr Blüthenzweig, for it is a filthiness in God's sight. Burn it, burn it!" he shrieked, beside himself, describing a wild, all-embracing circle with his arm. "The harvest is ripe for the reaper, the measure of the age's shamelessness is full—but I say unto you—"

"Krauthuber!" Herr Blüthenzweig raised his voice and shouted towards a door at the back of the shop. "Come in here at once!"

And in answer to the summons there appeared upon the scene a massive overpowering presence, a vast and awe-inspiring, swollen human bulk, whose limbs merged into each other like links of sausage—a gigantic son of the people, malt-nourished and immoderate, who weighed in, with puffings, bursting with energy, from the packing-room. His appearance in the upper reaches of his form was notable for a fringe of walrus beard; a hide apron fouled with paste covered his body from the waist down, and his yellow shirt-sleeves were rolled back from his heroic arms.

"Will you open the door for this gentleman, Krauthuber?" said M. Blüthenzweig; "and if he should not find the way to it, just help him into the street."

"Huh," said the man, looking from his enraged employer to Hieronymus and back with his little elephant eyes. It was a heavy monosyllable, suggesting reserve force restrained with difficulty. The floor shook with his tread as he went to the door and opened it.

Hieronymus had grown very pale. "Burn—" he shouted once more. He was about to go on when he felt himself turned round by an irresistible power, by a physical preponderance to which no resistance was even thinkable. Slowly and inexorably he was propelled towards the door.

"I am weak," he managed to ejaculate. "My flesh cannot bear the force . . . it cannot hold its ground, no . . . but what does that prove? Burn—"

He stopped. He found himself outside the art-shop. M. Blüthenzweig's giant packer had let him go with one final shove, which set him down on the stone threshold of the shop, supporting himself with one hand. Behind him the door closed with a rattle of glass.

He picked himself up. He stood erect, breathing heavily, and pulled his cloak together with one fist over his breast, letting the other hang down inside. His hollow cheeks had a grey pallor; the nostrils of his great hooked nose opened and closed; his ugly lips were writhen in an expression of hatred and despair and his red-rimmed eyes wandered over the beautiful square like those of a man in a frenzy.

He did not see that people were looking at him with amusement and curiosity. For what he beheld upon the mosaic pavement before the great loggia were all the vanities of this world: the masked costumes of the artist balls, the decorations, vases and art objects, the nude statues, the female busts, the picturesque rebirths of the pagan age, the portraits of famous beauties by the hands of masters, the elegantly bound erotic verse, the art brochures—all these he saw heaped in a pyramid and going up in crackling flames amid loud exultations from the people enthralled by his own frightful words. A yellow background of cloud had drawn up over the Theatinerstrasse, and from it issued wild rumblings; but what he saw was a burning fiery sword, towering in sulphurous light above the joyous city.

"*Gladius Dei super terram* . . ." his thick lips whispered; and drawing himself still higher in his hooded cloak while the hand hanging down inside it twitched convulsively, he murmured, quaking: "*cito et velociter!*"[6]

QUESTIONS

1. How would you characterize Munich as it is described in the first six paragraphs? Does it sound attractive? **2.** What effect does the conversation between the two youths (pp. 419–420) have on the reader? On Hieronymus?

WRITING TOPIC

What finally does the story say about the relationship between art, religion, and morality?

---

[6]*Gladius Dei super terram* means "sword of God over the earth"; *cito et velociter* means "swiftly and quickly."

The Greatest Man in the World   1935

JAMES THURBER   [1894–1961]

Looking back on it now, from the vantage point of 1950, one can only marvel that it hadn't happened long before it did. The United States of America had been, ever since Kitty Hawk, blindly constructing the elaborate petard by which, sooner or later, it must be hoist. It was inevitable that some day there would come roaring out of the skies a national hero of insufficient intelligence, background, and character successfully to endure the mounting orgies of glory prepared for aviators who stayed up a long time or flew a great distance. Both Lindbergh and Byrd, fortunately for national decorum and international amity, had been gentlemen; so had our other famous aviators. They wore their laurels gracefully, withstood the awful weather of publicity, married excellent women, usually of fine family, and quietly retired to private life and the enjoyment of their varying fortunes. No untoward incidents, on a worldwide scale, marred the perfection of their conduct on the perilous heights of fame. The exception to the rule was, however, bound to occur and it did, in July, 1937, when Jack ("Pal") Smurch, erstwhile mechanics' helper in a small garage in Westfield, Iowa, flew a second-hand, single-motored Bresthaven Dragon-Fly III monoplane all the way around the world, without stopping.

Never before in the history of aviation had such a flight as Smurch's ever been dreamed of. No one had even taken seriously the weird floating auxiliary gas tanks, invention of the mad New Hampshire professor of astronomy, Dr. Charles Lewis Gresham, upon which Smurch placed full reliance. When the garage worker, a slightly built, surly, unprepossessing young man of twenty-two appeared at Roosevelt Field in early July, 1937, slowly chewing a great quid of scrap tobacco, and announced "Nobody ain't seen no flyin' yet," the newspapers touched briefly and satirically upon his projected twenty-five-thousand-mile flight. Aeronautical and automotive experts dismissed the idea curtly, implying that it was a hoax, a publicity stunt. The rusty, battered, second-hand plane wouldn't go. The Gresham auxiliary tanks wouldn't work. It was simply a cheap joke.

Smurch, however, after calling on a girl in Brooklyn who worked in the flap-folding department of a large paper-box factory, a girl whom he later described as his "sweet patootie," climbed nonchalantly into his ridiculous plane at dawn of the memorable seventh of July, 1937, spat a curve of tobacco juice into the still air, and took off, carrying with him only a gallon of bootleg gin and six pounds of salami.

When the garage boy thundered out over the ocean the papers were forced to record, in all seriousness, that a mad, unknown young man—his name was variously misspelled—had actually set out upon a preposterous attempt to span the world in a rickety, one-engined contraption, trusting to the long-distance refueling device of a crazy schoolmaster. When, nine days later, without having stopped once, the tiny plane appeared above San Francisco Bay, headed for New York, spluttering and choking, to be sure, but still magnificently and miraculously aloft, the headlines, which long since had crowded everything else off the front page—even the shooting of the Governor of Illinois by the Vileti gang—swelled to unprecedented size, and the news stories began to run to twenty-five and thirty columns. It was noticeable, however, that the accounts of the epoch-making flight touched rather lightly upon the aviator himself. This was not because facts about the hero as a man were too meagre, but because they were too complete.

Reporters, who had been rushed out to Iowa when Smurch's plane was first sighted over the little French coast town of Serly-le-Mar, to dig up the story of the great man's life, had promptly discovered that the story of his life could not be printed. His mother, a sullen short-order cook in a shack restaurant on the edge of a tourists' camping ground near Westfield, met all enquiries as to her son with an angry, "Ah, the hell with him; I hope he drowns." His father appeared to be in jail somewhere for stealing spotlights and laprobes from tourists' automobiles; his younger brother, a weak-minded lad, had but recently escaped from the Preston, Iowa Reformatory and was already wanted in several Western towns for the theft of money-order blanks from post offices. These alarming discoveries were still piling up at the very time that Pal Smurch, the greatest hero of the twentieth century, blear-eyed, dead for sleep, half-starved, was piloting his crazy junk-heap high above the region in which the lamentable story of his private life was being unearthed, headed for New York under greater glory than any man of his time had ever known.

The necessity for printing some account in the papers of the young man's career and personality had led to a remarkable predicament. It was of course impossible to reveal the facts, for a tremendous popular feeling in favor of the young hero had sprung up, like a grass fire, when he was halfway across Europe on his flight around the globe. He was, therefore, described as a modest chap, taciturn, blond, popular with his friends, popular with girls. The only available snapshot of Smurch, taken at the wheel of a phony automobile in a cheap photo studio at an amusement park, was touched up so that the little vulgarian looked quite handsome. His twisted leer was smoothed into a pleasant smile. The truth was, in this way, kept from the youth's ecstatic compatriots; they did not dream that the Smurch family was despised and feared by its neighbors in the obscure Iowa town, nor that the hero himself, because of numerous unsavory exploits, had come to be regarded in Westfield as a nuisance and a menace. He had, the reporters discovered, once knifed the principal of his high school—not mortally, to be sure, but he had knifed him; and on another occasion, surprised in the act of stealing an altar-cloth from a church, he had bashed the sacristan over the head with a pot of Easter lilies; for each of these offences he had served a sentence in the reformatory.

Inwardly, the authorities, both in New York and in Washington, prayed that an understanding Providence might, however awful such a thing seemed, bring disaster to the rusty, battered plane and its illustrious pilot, whose unheard-of flight had aroused the civilized world to hosannas of hysterical praise. The authorities were convinced that the character of the renowned aviator was such that the limelight of adulation was bound to reveal him to all the world, as a congenital hooligan mentally and morally unequipped to cope with his own prodigious fame. "I trust," said the Secretary of State, at one of many secret Cabinet meetings called to consider the national dilemma, "I trust that his mother's prayer will be answered," by which he referred to Mrs. Emma Smurch's wish that her son might be drowned. It was, however, too late for that—Smurch had leaped the Atlantic and then the Pacific as if they were millponds. At three minutes after two o'clock in the afternoon of 17 July, 1937, the garage boy brought his idiotic plane into Roosevelt Field for a perfect three-point landing.

It had, of course, been out of the question to arrange a modest little reception for the greatest flier in the history of the world. He was received at Roosevelt Field with such elaborate and pretentious ceremonies as rocked the world. Fortunately, however, the worn and spent hero promptly swooned, had to be removed bodily from his plane, and was spirited from the field without having opened his mouth once. Thus he did not jeopardize the dignity of this first reception, a reception illumined by the presence of the Secretaries of War and the Navy, Mayor Michael J. Moriarity of New York, the Premier of Canada, Governors Fanniman, Groves, McFeely, and Critchfield, and a brillant array of European diplomats. Smurch did not, in fact, come to in time to take part in the gigantic hullabaloo arranged at City Hall for the next day. He was rushed to a secluded nursing home and confined to bed. It was nine days before he was able to get up, or to be more exact, before he was permitted to get up. Meanwhile the greatest minds in the country, in solemn assembly, had arranged a secret conference of city, state and government officials, which Smurch was to attend for the purpose of being instructed in the ethics and behavior of heroism.

On the day that the little mechanic was finally allowed to get up and dress and, for the first time in two weeks, took a great chew of tobacco, he was permitted to receive the newspapermen—this by way of testing him out. Smurch did not wait for questions. "Youse guys," he said—and the *Times* man winced— "youse guys can tell the cock-eyed world dat I put it over on Lindbergh, see? Yeh—an' made an ass o' them two frogs." The "two frogs" was a reference to a pair of gallant French fliers who, in attempting a flight only halfway round the world, had, two weeks before, unhappily been lost at sea. The *Times* man was bold enough, at this point, to sketch out for Smurch the accepted formula for interviews in cases of this kind; he explained that there should be no arrogant statements belittling the achievements of other heroes, particularly heroes of foreign nations. "Ah, the hell with that," said Smurch. "I did it, see? I did it, an' I'm talkin' about it." And he did talk about it.

None of this extraordinary interview was, of course, printed. On the contrary, the newspapers, already under the disciplined direction of a secret directorate created for the occasion and composed of statesmen and editors, gave out to a panting and restless world that "Jacky," as he had been arbitrarily nicknamed, would consent to say only that he was very happy and that anyone could have done what he did. "My achievement has been, I fear, slightly exaggerated," the *Times* man's article had him protest, with a modest smile. These newspaper stories were kept from the hero, a restriction which did not serve to abate the rising malevolence of his temper. The situation was, indeed, extremely grave, for Pal Smurch was, as he kept insisting, "rarin' to go." He could not much longer be kept from a nation clamorous to lionize him. It was the most desperate crisis the United States of America had faced since the sinking of the *Lusitania*.

On the afternoon of the twenty-seventh of July, Smurch was spirited away to a conference-room in which were gathered mayors, governors, government officials, behaviorist psychologists, and editors. He gave them each a limp, moist paw and a brief unlovely grin. "Hah ya?" he said. When Smurch was seated, the Mayor of New York arose and, with obvious pessimism, attempted to explain what he must say and how he must act when presented to the world, ending his talk with a high tribute to the hero's courage and integrity. The Mayor was followed by Governor Fanniman of New York, who, after a touching declaration of faith, introduced Cameron Spottiswood, Second Secretary of the American Embassy in Paris, the gentlemen selected to coach Smurch in the amenities of public ceremonies. Sitting in a chair, with a soiled yellow tie in his hand and his shirt open at the throat, unshaved, smoking a rolled cigarette, Jack Smurch listened with a leer on his lips. "I get ya, I get ya," he cut in nastily. "Ya want me to ack like a softy, huh? Ya want me to ack like that—baby-faced Lindbergh, huh? Well, nuts to that, see?" Everyone took in his breath sharply; it was a sigh and a hiss. "Mr. Lindbergh," began a United States Senator, purple with rage, "and Mr. Byrd—" Smurch, who was paring his nails with a jackknife, cut in again, "Byrd!" he exclaimed. "Aw fa God's sake, dat big—" Somebody shut off his blasphemies with a sharp word. A newcomer had entered the room. Everyone stood up, except Smurch, who, still busy with his nails, did not even glance up. "Mr. Smurch," said someone sternly, "the President of the United States!" It had been thought that the presence of the Chief Executive might have a chastening effect upon the young hero, and the former had been, thanks to the remarkable co-operation of the press, secretly brought to the obscure conference-room.

A great, painful silence fell. Smurch looked up, waved a hand at the President. "How ya comin'?" he asked, and began rolling a fresh cigarette. The silence deepened. Someone coughed in a strained way. "Geez, it's hot, ain't it?" said Smurch. He loosened two more shirt buttons, revealing a hairy chest and the tattooed word "Sadie" enclosed in a stenciled heart. The great and important men in the room, faced by the most serious crisis in recent American history, exchanged worried frowns. Nobody seemed to know how to proceed. "Come awn, come awn," said Smurch. "Let's get the hell out of here! When do I start cuttin' in on de parties, huh? And what's they goin' to be *in* it?" He rubbed a thumb and a forefinger together meaningly. "Money!" exclaimed a state senator, shocked, pale. "Yeh, money," said Pal, flipping his cigarette out of a window, "an' big money." He began rolling a fresh cigarette. "Big money," he repeated, frowning over the rice paper. He tilted back in his chair, and leered at each gentleman, separately, the leer of an animal that knows its power, the leer of a leopard loose in a bird-and-dog shop. "Aw, fa God's sake, let's get some place where it's cooler," he said. "I been cooped up plenty for three weeks!"

Smurch stood up and walked over to an open window, where he stood staring down into the street, nine floors below. The faint shouting of newsboys floated up to him. He made out his name. "Hot dog!" he cried, grinning, ecstatic. He leaned out over the sill. "You tell 'em, babies!" he shouted down. "Hot diggity dog!" In the tense little knot of men standing behind him, a quick, mad impulse flared up. An unspoken word of appeal, of command, seemed to ring through the room. Yet it was deadly silent. Charles K. L. Brand, secretary to the Mayor of New York City, happened to be standing nearest Smurch; he looked inquiringly at the President of the United States. The President, pale, grim, nodded shortly. Brand, a tall, powerfully built man, once a tackle at Rutgers, stepped forward, seized the greatest man in the world by his left shoulder and the seat of his pants, and pushed him out of the window.

"My God, he's fallen out the window!" cried a quick-witted editor.

"Get me out of here!" cried the President. Several men sprang to his side and he was hurriedly escorted out of a door toward a side-entrance of the building. The editor of the Associated Press took charge, being used to such things. Crisply he ordered certain men to leave, others to stay; quickly he outlined a story which all the papers were to agree on, sent two men to the street to handle that end of the tragedy, commanded a Senator to sob and two Congressmen to go to pieces nervously. In a word, he skillfully set the stage for the gigantic task that was to follow, the task of breaking to a grief-stricken world the sad story of the untimely, accidental death of its most illustrious and spectacular figure.

The funeral was, as you know, the most elaborate, the finest, the solemnest, and the saddest ever held in the United States of America. The monument in Arlington Cemetery, with its clean white shaft of marble and the simple device of a tiny plane carved on its base, is a place for pilgrims, in deep reverence, to visit. The nations of the world paid lofty tributes to little Jacky Smurch, America's greatest hero. At a given hour there were two minutes of silence throughout the nation. Even the inhabitants of the small, bewildered town of Westfield, Iowa, observed this touching ceremony; agents of the Department of Justice saw to that. One of them was especially assigned to stand grimly in the doorway of a little shack restaurant on the edge of the tourists' camping ground just outside the town. There, under his stern scrutiny, Mrs. Emma Smurch bowed her head above two hamburger steaks sizzling on her grill—bowed her head and turned away, so that the Secret Service man could not see the twisted, strangely familiar, leer on her lips.

The Lottery   1948

SHIRLEY JACKSON   [1919–1965]

The morning of June 27th was clear and sunny, with the fresh warmth of a full-summer day; the flowers were blossoming profusely and the grass was richly green. The people of the village began to gather in the square, between the post office and the bank, around ten o'clock; in some towns there were so many people that the lottery took two days and had to be started on June 26th, but in this village, where there were only about three hundred people, the whole lottery took less than two hours, so it could begin at ten o'clock in the morning and still be through in time to allow the villagers to get home for noon dinner.

The children assembled first, of course. School was recently over for the summer, and the feeling of liberty sat uneasily on most of them; they tended to gather together quietly for a while before they broke into boisterous play, and their talk was still of the classroom and the teacher, of books and reprimands. Bobby Martin had already stuffed his pockets full of stones, and the other boys soon followed his example, selecting the smoothest and roundest stones; Bobby and Harry Jones and Dickie Delacroix—the villagers pronounced his name "Dellacroy"—eventually made a great pile of stones in one corner of the square and guarded it against the raids of the other boys. The girls stood aside, talking among themselves, looking over their shoulders at the boys, and the very small children rolled in the dust or clung to the hands of their older brothers or sisters.

Soon the men began to gather, surveying their own children, speaking of planting and rain, tractors and taxes. They stood together, away from the pile of stones in the corner, and their jokes were quiet and they smiled rather than laughed. The women, wearing faded house dresses and sweaters, came shortly after their menfolk. They greeted one another and exchanged bits of gossip as they went to join their husbands. Soon the women, standing by their husbands, began to call to their children, and the children came reluctantly, having to be called four or five times. Bobby Martin ducked under his mother's grasping hand and ran, laughing, back to the pile of stones. His father spoke up sharply, and Bobby came quickly and took his place between his father and his oldest brother.

The lottery was conducted—as were the square dances, the teen-age club, the Halloween program—by Mr. Summers, who had time and energy to devote to civic activities. He was a round-faced, jovial man and he ran the coal business, and people were sorry for him, because he had no children and his wife was a scold. When he arrived in the square, carrying the black wooden box, there was a murmur of conversation among the villagers, and he waved and called, "Little late today, folks." The postmaster, Mr. Graves, followed him, carrying a three-legged stool, and the stool was put in the center of the square and Mr. Summers set the black box down on it. The villagers kept their distance, leaving a space between themselves and the stool, and when Mr. Summers said, "Some of you fellows want to give me a hand?" there was a hesitation before two men, Mr. Martin and his oldest son, Baxter, came forward to hold the box steady on the stool while Mr. Summers stirred up the papers inside it.

The original paraphernalia for the lottery had been lost long ago, and the black box now resting on the stool had been put into use even before Old Man Warner, the oldest man in town, was born. Mr. Summers spoke frequently to the villagers about making a new box, but no one liked to upset even as much tradition as was represented by the black box. There was a story that the present box had been made with some pieces of the box that had preceded it, the one that had been constructed when the first people settled down to make a village here. Every year, after the lottery, Mr. Summers began talking again about a new box, but every year the subject was allowed to fade off without anything's being done. The black box grew shabbier each year; by now it was no longer completely black but splintered badly along one side to show the original wood color, and in some places faded or stained.

Mr. Martin and his oldest son, Baxter, held the black box securely on the stool until Mr. Summers had stirred the papers thoroughly with his hand. Because so much of the ritual had been forgotten or discarded, Mr. Summers had been successful in having slips of paper substituted for the chips of wood that had been used for generations. Chips of wood, Mr. Summers had argued, had been all very well when the village was tiny, but now that the population was more than three hundred and likely to keep on growing, it was necessary to use something that would fit more easily into the black box. The night before the lottery, Mr. Summers and Mr. Graves made up the slips of paper and put them in the box, and it was then taken to the safe of Mr. Summers' coal company and locked up until Mr. Summers was ready to take it to the square next morning. The rest of the year, the box was put away, sometimes one place, sometimes another; it had spent one year in Mr. Graves' barn and another year underfoot in the post office, and sometimes it was set on a shelf in the Martin grocery and left there.

There was a great deal of fussing to be done before Mr. Summers declared the lottery open. There were the lists to make up—of heads of families, heads of households in each family, members of each household in each family. There was the proper swearing-in of Mr. Summers by the postmaster, as the official of the lottery; at one time, some people remembered, there had been a recital of some sort, performed by the official of the lottery, a perfunctory, tuneless chant that had been rattled off duly each year; some people believed that the official of the lottery used to stand just so when he said or sang it, others believed that he was supposed to walk among the people, but years and years ago this part of the ritual had been allowed to lapse. There had been, also, a ritual salute, which the official of the lottery had had to use in addressing each person who came up to draw from the box, but this also had changed with time, until now it was felt necessary only for the official to speak to each person approaching. Mr. Summers was very good at all this; in his clean white shirt and blue jeans, with one hand resting carelessly on the black box, he seemed very proper and important as he talked interminably to Mr. Graves and the Martins.

Just as Mr. Summers finally left off talking and turned to the assembled villagers, Mrs. Hutchinson came hurriedly along the path to the square, her sweater thrown over her shoulders, and slid into place in the back of the crowd. "Clean forgot what day it was," she said to Mrs. Delacroix, who stood next to her, and they both laughed softly. "Thought my old man was out back stacking wood," Mrs. Hutchinson went on, "and then I looked out the window and the kids were gone, and then I remembered it was the twenty-seventh and came a-running." She dried her hands on her apron, and Mrs. Delacroix said, "You're in time, though. They're still talking away up there."

Mrs. Hutchinson craned her neck to see through the crowd and found her husband and children standing near the front. She tapped Mrs. Delacroix on the arm as a farewell and began to make her way through the crowd. The people separated good-humoredly to let her through; two or three people said, in voices just loud enough to be heard across the crowd, "Here comes your Missus, Hutchinson," and "Bill, she made it after all." Mrs. Hutchinson reached her husband, and Mr. Summers, who had been waiting, said cheerfully, "Thought we were going to have to get on without you, Tessie." Mrs. Hutchinson said, grinning, "Wouldn't have me leave m'dishes in the sink, now, would you, Joe?," and soft laughter ran through the crowd as the people stirred back into position after Mrs. Hutchinson's arrival.

"Well, now," Mr. Summers said soberly, "guess we better get started, get this over with, so's we can go back to work. Anybody ain't here?"

"Dunbar," several people said. "Dunbar, Dunbar."

Mr. Summers consulted his list. "Clyde Dunbar," he said. "That's right. He's broke his leg, hasn't he? Who's drawing for him?"

"Me, I guess," a woman said, and Mr. Summers turned to look at her. "Wife draws for her husband," Mr. Summers said. "Don't you have a grown boy to do it for you, Janey?" Although Mr. Summers and everyone else in the village knew the answer perfectly well, it was the business of the official of the lottery to ask such questions formally. Mr. Summers waited with an expression of polite interest while Mrs. Dunbar answered.

"Horace's not but sixteen yet," Mrs. Dunbar said regretfully. "Guess I gotta fill in for the old man this year."

"Right," Mr. Summers said. He made a note on the list he was holding. Then he asked, "Watson boy drawing this year?"

A tall boy in the crowd raised his hand. "Here," he said. "I'm drawing for m'mother and me." He blinked his eyes nervously and ducked his head as several voices in the crowd said things like "Good fellow, Jack," and "Glad to see your mother's got a man to do it."

"Well," Mr. Summers said, "guess that's everyone. Old Man Warner make it?"

"Here," a voice said, and Mr. Summers nodded.

A sudden hush fell on the crowd as Mr. Summers cleared his throat and looked at the list. "All ready?" he called. "Now, I'll read the names—heads of families first—and the men come up and take a paper out of the box. Keep the paper folded in your hand without looking at it until everyone has had a turn. Everything clear?"

The people had done it so many times that they only half listened to the directions; most of them were quiet, wetting their lips, not looking around. Then Mr. Summers raised one hand high and said, "Adams." A man disengaged himself from the crowd and came forward. "Hi, Steve," Mr. Summers said, and Mr. Adams said, "Hi, Joe." They grinned at one another humorlessly and nervously. Then Mr. Adams reached into the black box and took out a folded paper. He held it firmly by one corner as he turned and went hastily back to his place in the crowd, where he stood a little apart from his family, not looking down at his hand.

"Allen." Mr. Summers said. "Anderson. . . . Bentham."

"Seems like there's no time at all between lotteries any more," Mrs. Delacroix said to Mrs. Graves in the back row. "Seems like we got through with the last one only last week."

"Time sure goes fast," Mrs. Graves said.

"Clark. . . . Delacroix."

"There goes my old man," Mrs. Delacroix said. She held her breath while her husband went forward.

"Dunbar," Mr. Summers said, and Mrs. Dunbar went steadily to the box while one of the women said, "Go on, Janey," and another said, "There she goes."

"We're next," Mrs. Graves said. She watched while Mr. Graves came around from the side of the box, greeted Mr. Summers gravely, and selected a slip of paper from the box. By now, all through the crowd there were men holding the small folded papers in their large hands, turning them over and over nervously. Mrs. Dunbar and her two sons stood together, Mrs. Dunbar holding the slip of paper.

"Harburt. . . . Hutchinson."

"Get up there, Bill," Mrs. Hutchinson said, and the people near her laughed.

"Jones."

"They do say," Mr. Adams said to Old Man Warner, who stood next to him, "that over in the north village they're talking of giving up the lottery."

Old Man Warner snorted. "Pack of crazy fools," he said. "Listening to the young folks, nothing's good enough for *them*. Next thing you know, they'll be wanting to go back to living in caves, nobody work any more, live *that* way for a while. Used to be a saying about 'Lottery in June, corn be heavy soon.' First thing you know, we'd all be eating stewed chickweed and acorns. There's *always* been a lottery," he added petulantly. "Bad enough to see young Joe Summers up there joking with everybody."

"Some places have already quit lotteries," Mrs. Adams said.

"Nothing but trouble in *that*," Old Man Warner said stoutly. "Pack of young fools."

"Martin." And Bobby Martin watched his father go forward. "Overdyke. . . . Percy."

"I wish they'd hurry," Mrs. Dunbar said to her older son. "I wish they'd hurry."

"They're almost through," her son said.

"You get ready to run tell Dad," Mrs. Dunbar said.

Mr. Summers called his own name and then stepped forward precisely and selected a slip from the box. Then he called, "Warner."

"Seventy-seventh year I been in the lottery," Old Man Warner said as he went through the crowd. "Seventy-seventh time."

"Watson." The tall boy came awkwardly through the crowd. Someone said, "Don't be nervous, Jack," and Mr. Summers said, "Take your time, son."

"Zanini."

After that, there was a long pause, a breathless pause, until Mr. Summers, holding his slip of paper in the air, said, "All right, fellows." For a minute, no one moved, and then all the slips of paper were opened. Suddenly, all the women began to speak at once, saying, "Who is it," "Who's got it?," "Is it the Dunbars?," "Is it the Watsons?" Then the voices began to say, "It's Hutchinson. It's Bill," "Bill Hutchinson's got it."

"Go tell your father," Mrs. Dunbar said to her older son.

People began to look around to see the Hutchinsons. Bill Hutchinson was standing quiet, staring down at the paper in his hand. Suddenly, Tessie Hutchinson shouted to Mr. Summers, "You didn't give him time enough to take any paper he wanted. I saw you. It wasn't fair!"

"Be a good sport, Tessie," Mrs. Delacroix called, and Mrs. Graves said, "All of us took the same chance."

"Shut up, Tessie," Bill Hutchinson said.

"Well, everyone," Mr. Summers said, "that was done pretty fast, and now we've got to be hurrying a little more to get it done in time." He consulted his next list. "Bill," he said, "you draw for the Hutchinson family. You got any other households in the Hutchinsons?"

"There's Don and Eva," Mrs. Hutchinson yelled. "Make *them* take their chance!"

"Daughters draw with their husbands' families, Tessie," Mr. Summers said gently. "You know that as well as anyone else."

"It wasn't *fair*," Tessie said.

"I guess not, Joe," Bill Hutchinson said regretfully. "My daughter draws with her husband's family, that's only fair. And I've got no other family except the kids."

"Then, as far as drawing for families is concerned, it's you," Mr. Summers said in explanation, "and as far as drawing for households is concerned, that's you, too. Right?"

"Right," Bill Hutchinson said.

"How many kids, Bill?" Mr. Summers asked formally.

"Three," Bill Hutchinson said. "There's Bill, Jr., and Nancy, and little Dave. And Tessie and me."

"All right, then," Mr. Summers said. "Harry, you got their tickets back?"

Mr. Graves nodded and held up the slips of paper. "Put them in the box, then," Mr. Summers directed. "Take Bill's and put it in."

"I think we ought to start over," Mrs. Hutchinson said, as quietly as she could. "I tell you it wasn't *fair*. You didn't give him time enough to choose. *Every*body saw that."

Mr. Graves had selected the five slips and put them in the box, and he dropped all the papers but those onto the ground, where the breeze caught them and lifted them off.

"Listen, everybody," Mrs. Hutchinson was saying to the people around her.

"Ready, Bill?" Mr. Summers asked, and Bill Hutchinson, with one quick glance around at his wife and children, nodded.

"Remember," Mr. Summers said, "take the slips and keep them folded until each person has taken one. Harry, you help little Dave." Mr. Graves took the hand of the little boy, who came willingly with him up to the box. "Take a paper out of the box, Davy," Mr. Summers said. Davy put his hand into the box and laughed. "Take just *one* paper," Mr. Summers said. "Harry, you hold it for him." Mr. Graves took the child's hand and removed the folded paper from the tight fist and held it while little Dave stood next to him and looked up at him wonderingly.

"Nancy next," Mr. Summers said. Nancy was twelve, and her school friends breathed heavily as she went forward, switching her skirt, and took a slip daintily from the box. "Bill, Jr.," Mr. Summers said, and Billy, his face red and his feet over-large, nearly knocked the box over as he got a paper out. "Tessie," Mr. Summers said. She hesitated for a minute, looking around defiantly, and then set her lips and went up to the box. She snatched a paper out and held it behind her.

"Bill," Mr. Summers said, and Bill Hutchinson reached into the box and felt around, bringing his hand out at last with the slip of paper in it.

The crowd was quiet. A girl whispered, "I hope it's not Nancy," and the sound of the whisper reached the edges of the crowd.

"It's not the way it used to be," Old Man Warner said clearly. "People ain't the way they used to be."

"All right," Mr. Summers said. "Open the papers. Harry, you open little Dave's."

Mr. Graves opened the slip of paper and there was a general sigh through the crowd as he held it up and everyone could see that it was blank. Nancy and Bill, Jr., opened theirs at the same time, and both beamed and laughed, turning around to the crowd and holding their slips of paper above their heads.

"Tessie," Mr. Summers said. There was a pause, and then Mr. Summers looked at Bill Hutchinson, and Bill unfolded his paper and showed it. It was blank.

"It's Tessie," Mr. Summers said, and his voice was hushed. "Show us her paper, Bill."

Bill Hutchinson went over to his wife and forced the slip of paper out of her hand. It had a black spot on it, the black spot Mr. Summers had made the night before with the heavy pencil in the coal-company office. Bill Hutchinson held it up, and there was a stir in the crowd.

"All right, folks," Mr. Summers said. "Let's finish quickly."

Although the villagers had forgotten the ritual and lost the original black box, they still remembered to use stones. The pile of stones the boys had made earlier was ready; there were stones on the ground with the blowing scraps of paper that had come out of the box. Mrs. Delacroix selected a stone so large she had to pick it up with both hands and turned to Mrs. Dunbar. "Come on," she said. "Hurry up."

Mrs. Dunbar had small stones in both hands, and she said, gasping for breath, "I can't run at all. You'll have to go ahead and I'll catch up with you."

The children had stones already, and someone gave little Davy Hutchinson a few pebbles.

Tessie Hutchinson was in the center of a cleared space by now, and she held her hands out desperately as the villagers moved in on her. "It isn't fair," she said. A stone hit her on the side of the head.

Old Man Warner was saying, "Come on, come on, everyone." Steve Adams was in the front of the crowd of villagers, with Mrs. Graves beside him.

"It isn't fair, it isn't right," Mrs. Hutchinson screamed, and then they were upon her.

QUESTIONS

1. What evidence in the story suggests that the lottery is a ritualistic ceremony?
2. What set of beliefs underlie the old saying "Lottery in June, corn be heavy soon?" **3.** Might this story be a comment on religious orthodoxy? Explain.

The Ones Who Walk Away from Omelas
1974

URSULA K. LE GUIN   [b. 1929]

With a clamor of bells that set the swallows soaring, the Festival of Summer came to the city Omelas, bright-towered by the sea. The rigging of the boats in harbor sparkled with flags. In the streets between houses with red roofs and painted walls, between old moss-grown gardens and under avenues of trees, past great parks and public buildings, processions moved. Some were decorous: old people in long stiff robes of mauve and grey, grave master workmen, quiet, merry women carrying their babies and chatting as they walked. In other streets the music beat faster, a shimmering of gong and tambourine, and the people went dancing, the procession was a dance. Children dodged in and out, their high calls rising like the swallows' crossing flights over the music and the singing. All the processions wound towards the north side of the city, where on the great water-meadow called the Green Fields boys and girls, naked in the bright air, with mud-stained feet and ankles and long, lithe arms, exercised their restive horses before the race. The horses wore no gear at all but a halter without bit. Their manes were braided with streamers of silver, gold, and green. They flared their nostrils and pranced and boasted to one another; they were vastly excited, the horse being the only animal who has adopted our ceremonies as his own. Far off to the north and west the mountains stood up half encircling Omelas on her bay. The air of morning was so clear that the snow still crowning the Eighteen Peaks burned with white-gold fire across the miles of sunlit air, under the dark blue of the sky. There was just enough wind to make the banners that marked the racecourse snap and flutter now and then. In the silence of the broad green meadows one could hear the music winding through the city streets, farther and nearer and ever approaching, a cheerful faint sweetness of the air that from time to time trembled and gathered together and broke out into the great joyous clanging of the bells.

Joyous! How is one to tell about joy? How describe the citizens of Omelas?

They were not simple folk, you see, though they were happy. But we do not say the words of cheer much any more. All smiles have become archaic. Given a description such as this one tends to make certain assumptions. Given a description such as this one tends to look next for the King, mounted on a splendid stallion and surrounded by his noble knights, or perhaps in a golden litter borne by great-muscled slaves. But there was no king. They did not use swords, or keep slaves. They were not barbarians. I do not know the rules and laws of their society, but I suspect that they were singularly few. As they did without monarchy and slavery, so they also go on without the stock exchange, the advertisement, the secret police, and the bomb. Yet I repeat that these were not simple folk, not dulcet shepherds, noble savages, bland utopians. They were not less complex than us. The trouble is that we have a bad habit, encouraged by pedants and sophisticates, of considering happiness as something rather stupid. Only pain is intellectual, only evil interesting. This is the treason of the artist: a refusal to admit the banality of evil and the terrible boredom of pain. If you can't lick 'em, join 'em. If it hurts, repeat it. But to praise despair is to condemn delight, to embrace violence is to lose hold of everything else. We have almost lost hold; we can no longer describe a happy man, nor make any celebration of joy. How can I tell you about the people of Omelas? They were not naïve and happy children—though their children were, in fact, happy. They were mature, intelligent, passionate adults whose lives were not wretched. O miracle! but I wish I could describe it better. I wish I could convince you. Omelas sounds in my words like a city in a fairy tale, long ago and far away, once upon a time. Perhaps it would be best if you imagined it as your own fancy bids, assuming it will rise to the occasion, for certainly I cannot suit you all. For instance, how about technology? I think that there would be no cars or helicopters in and above the streets; this follows from the fact that the people of Omelas are happy people. Happiness is based on a just discrimination of what is necessary, what is neither necessary nor destructive, and what is destructive. In the middle category, however—that of the unnecessary but undestructive, that of comfort, luxury, exuberance, etc.—they could perfectly well have central heating, subway trains, washing machines, and all kinds of marvelous devices not yet invented here, floating light-sources, fuelless power, a cure for the common cold. Or they could have none of that: it doesn't matter. As you like it. I incline to think that people from towns up and down the coast have been coming in to Omelas during the last days before the Festival on very fast little trains and double-decker trams, and that the train station of Omelas is actually the handsomest building in town, though plainer than the magnificent Farmers' Market. But even granted trains, I fear that Omelas so far strikes some of you as goody-goody. Smiles, bells, parades, horses, bleh. If so, please add an orgy. If an orgy would help, don't hesitate. Let us not, however, have temples from which issue beautiful nude priests and priestesses already half in ecstasy and ready to copulate with any man or woman, lover or stranger, who desires union with the deep godhead of the blood, although that was my first idea. But really it would be better not to have any temples in Omelas—at least, not manned temples. Religion yes, clergy no. Surely the beautiful nudes can just wander about, offering themselves like divine soufflés to the hunger of the needy and the rapture of the flesh. Let them join the processions. Let tambourines be struck above the copulations, and the glory of desire be proclaimed upon the gongs, and (a not unimportant point) let the offspring of these delightful rituals be beloved and looked after by all. One thing I know there is none of in Omelas is guilt. But what else should there be? I thought at first there were no drugs, but that is puritanical. For those who like it, the faint insistent sweetness of *drooz* may perfume the ways of the city, *drooz* which first brings a great lightness and brilliance to the mind and limbs, and then after some hours a dreamy languor, and wonderful visions at last of the very arcana and inmost secrets of the Universe, as well as exciting the pleasure of sex beyond all belief; and it is not habit-forming. For more modest tastes I think there ought to be beer. What else, what else belongs in the joyous city? The sense of victory, surely, the celebration of courage. But as we did without clergy, let us do without soldiers. The joy built upon successful slaughter is not the right kind of joy; it will not do; it is fearful and it is trivial. A boundless and generous contentment, a magnanimous triumph felt not against some outer enemy but in communion with the finest and fairest in the souls of all men everywhere and the splendor of the world's summer: this is what swells the hearts of the people of Omelas, and the victory they celebrate is that of life. I really don't think many of them need to take *drooz*.

Most of the processions have reached the Green Fields by now. A marvelous smell of cooking goes forth from the red and blue tents of the provisioners. The faces of small children are amiably sticky; in the benign grey beard of a man a couple of crumbs of rich pastry are entangled. The youths and girls have mounted their horses and are beginning to group around the starting line of the course. An old woman, small, fat, and laughing, is passing out flowers from a basket, and tall young men wear her flowers in their shining hair. A child of nine or ten sits at the edge of the crowd, alone, playing on a wooden flute. People pause to listen, and they smile, but they do not speak to him, for he never ceases playing and never sees them, his dark eyes wholly rapt in the sweet, thin magic of the tune.

He finishes, and slowly lowers his hands holding the wooden flute.

As if that little private silence were the signal, all at once a trumpet sounds from the pavilion near the starting line: imperious, melancholy, piercing. The horses rear on their slender legs, and some of them neigh in answer. Sober-faced, the young riders stroke the horses' necks and soothe them, whispering, "Quiet, quiet, there my beauty, my hope. . . ." They begin to form in rank along the starting line. The crowds along the racecourse are like a field of grass and flowers in the wind. The Festival of Summer has begun.

Do you believe? Do you accept the festival, the city, the joy? No? Then let me describe one more thing.

In a basement under one of the beautiful public buildings of Omelas, or perhaps in the cellar of one of its spacious private homes, there is a room. It has one locked door, and no window. A little light seeps in dustily between cracks in the boards, secondhand from a cobwebbed window somewhere across the cellar. In one corner of the little room a couple of mops, with stiff, clotted, foul-smelling heads, stand near a rusty bucket. The floor is dirt, a little damp to the touch, as cellar dirt usually is. The room is about three paces long and two wide: a mere broom closet or disused tool room. In the room a child is sitting. It could be a boy or a girl. It looks about six, but actually is nearly ten. It is feeble-minded. Perhaps it was born defective, or perhaps it has become imbecile through fear, malnutrition, and neglect. It picks its nose and occasionally fumbles vaguely with its toes or genitals, as it sits hunched in the corner farthest from the bucket and the two mops. It is afraid of the mops. It finds them horrible. It shuts its eyes, but it knows the mops are still standing there; and the door is locked; and nobody will come. The door is always locked; and nobody ever comes, except that sometimes—the child has no understanding of time or interval—sometimes the door rattles terribly and opens, and a person, or several people, are there. One of them may come in and kick the child to make it stand up. The others never come close, but peer in at it with frightened, disgusted eyes. The food bowl and the water jug are hastily filled, the door is locked, the eyes disappear. The people at the door never say anything, but the child, who has not always lived in the tool room, and can remember sunlight and its mother's voice, sometimes speaks. "I will be good," it says. "Please let me out. I will be good!" They never answer. The child used to scream for help at night, and cry a good deal, but now it only makes a kind of whining, "eh-haa, eh-haa," and it speaks less and less often. It is so thin there are no calves to its legs; its belly protrudes; it lives on a half-bowl of corn meal and grease a day. It is naked. Its buttocks and thighs are a mass of festered sores, as it sits in its own excrement continually.

They all know it is there, all the people of Omelas. Some of them have come to see it, others are content merely to know it is there. They all know that it has to be there. Some of them understand why, and some do not, but all understand that their happiness, the beauty of their city, the tenderness of their friendships, the health of their children, the wisdom of their scholars, the skill of their makers, even the abundance of their harvest and the kindly weathers of their skies, depend wholly on this child's abominable misery.

This is usually explained to children when they are between eight and twelve, whenever they seem capable of understanding; and most of those who come to see the child are young people, though often enough an adult comes, or comes back, to see the child. No matter how well the matter has been explained to them, these young spectators are always shocked and sickened at the sight. They feel disgust, which they had thought themselves superior to. They feel anger, outrage, impotence, despite all the explanations. They would like to do something for the child. But there is nothing they can do. If the child were brought up into the sunlight out of that vile place, if it were cleaned and fed and comforted, that would be a good thing, indeed; but if it were done, in that day and hour all the prosperity and beauty and delight of Omelas would wither and be destroyed. Those are the terms. To exchange all the goodness and grace of every life in Omelas for that single, small improvement: to throw away the happiness of thousands for the chance of the happiness of one: that would be to let guilt within the walls indeed.

The terms are strict and absolute; there may not even be a kind word spoken to the child.

Often the young people go home in tears, or in a tearless rage, when they have seen the child and faced this terrible paradox. They may brood over it for weeks or years. But as time goes on they begin to realize that even if the child could be released, it would not get much good of its freedom: a little vague pleasure of warmth and food, no doubt, but little more. It is too degraded and imbecile to know any real joy. It has been afraid too long ever to be free of fear. Its habits are too uncouth for it to respond to humane treatment. Indeed, after so long it would probably be wretched without walls about it to protect it, and darkness for its eyes, and its own excrement to sit in. Their tears at the bitter injustice dry when they begin to perceive the terrible justice of reality, and to accept it. Yet it is their tears and anger, the trying of their generosity and the acceptance of their helplessness, which are perhaps the true source of the splendor of their lives. Theirs is no vapid, irresponsible happiness. They know that they, like the child, are not free. They know compassion. It is the existence of the child, and their knowledge of its existence, that makes possible the nobility of their architecture, the poignancy of their music, the profundity of their science. It is because of the child that they are so gentle with children. They know that if the wretched one were not there snivelling in the dark, the other one, the flute-player, could make no joyful music as the young riders line up in their beauty for the race in the sunlight of the first morning of summer.

Now do you believe in them? Are they not more credible? But there is one more thing to tell, and this is quite incredible.

At times one of the adolescent girls or boys who go to see the child does not go home to weep or rage, does not, in fact, go home at all. Sometimes also a man or woman much older falls silent for a day or two, and then leaves home. These people go out into the street, and walk down the street alone. They keep walking, and walk straight out of the city of Omelas, through the beautiful gates. They keep walking across the farmlands of Omelas. Each one goes alone, youth or girl, man or woman. Night falls; the traveler must pass down village streets, between the houses with yellow-lit windows, and on out into the darkness of the fields. Each alone, they go west or north, towards the mountains. They go on. They leave Omelas, they walk ahead into the darkness, and they do not come back. The place they go towards is a place even less imaginable to most of us than the city of happiness. I cannot describe it at all. It is possible that it does not exist. But they seem to know where they are going, the ones who walk away from Omelas.

The Sandman

1972

DONALD BARTHELME [b. 1931]

Dear Dr. Hodder, I realize that it is probably wrong to write a letter to one's girl friend's shrink but there are several things going on here that I think ought to be pointed out to you. I thought of making a personal visit but the situation then, as I'm sure you understand, would be completely untenable—I would be *visiting a psychiatrist*. I also understand that in writing to you I am in some sense interfering with the process but you don't have to discuss with Susan what I have said. Please consider this an "eyes only" letter. Please think of it as personal and confidential.

You must be aware, first, that because Susan is my girl friend pretty much everything she discusses with you she also discusses with me. She tells me what she said and what you said. We have been seeing each other for about six months now and I am pretty familiar with her story, or stories. Similarly, with your responses, or at least the general pattern. I know, for example, that my habit of referring to you as "the sandman" annoys you but let me assure you that I mean nothing unpleasant by it. It is simply a nickname. The reference is to the old rhyme: "Sea-sand does the sandman bring/Sleep to end the day/ He dusts the children's eyes with sand/And steals their dreams away." (This is a variant; there are other versions, but this is the one I prefer.) I also understand that you are a little bit shaky because the prestige of analysis is now, as I'm sure you know far better than I, at a nadir. This must tend to make you nervous and who can blame you? One always tends to get a little bit shook when one's methodology is in question. Of course! (By the bye, let me say that I am very pleased that you are one of the ones that talk, instead of just sitting there. I think that's a good thing, an excellent thing, I congratulate you.)

To the point. I fully understand that Susan's wish to terminate with you and buy a piano instead has disturbed you. You have every right to be disturbed and to say that she is not electing the proper course, that what she says conceals something else, that she is evading reality, etc., etc. Go ahead. But there is one possibility here that you might be, just might be, missing. Which is that she means it.

Susan says: "I want to buy a piano."

You think: She wishes to terminate the analysis and escape into the piano.

Or: Yes, it is true that her father wanted her to be a concert pianist and that she studied for twelve years with Goetzmann. But she does not really want to reopen that can of maggots. She wants me to disapprove.

Or: Having failed to achieve a career as a concert pianist, she wishes to fail again. She is now too old to achieve the original objective. The spontaneous organization of defeat!

Or: She is flirting again.

237

Or:

Or:

Or:

Or:

The one thing you cannot consider, by the nature of your training and of the discipline itself, is that she really might want to terminate the analysis and buy a piano. That the piano might be more necessary and valuable to her than the analysis.[1]

What we really have to consider here is the locus of hope. Does hope reside in the analysis or rather in the piano? As a shrink rather than a piano salesman you would naturally tend to opt for the analysis. But there are differences. The piano salesman can stand behind his product; you, unfortunately, cannot. A Steinway is a known quantity, whereas an analysis can succeed or fail. I don't reproach you for this, I simply note it. (An interesting question: Why do laymen feel such a desire to, in plain language, fuck over shrinks? As I am doing here, in a sense? I don't mean hostility in the psychoanalytic encounter, I mean in general. This is an interesting phenomenon and should be investigated by somebody.)

It might be useful if I gave you a little taste of my own experience of analysis. I only went five or six times. Dr. Behring was a tall thin man who never said anything much. If you could get a "What comes to mind?" out of him you were doing splendidly. There was a little incident that is, perhaps, illustrative. I went for my hour one day and told him about something I was worried about. (I was then working for a newspaper down in Texas.) There was a story that four black teenagers had come across a little white boy, about ten, in a vacant lot, sodomized him repeatedly and then put him inside a refrigerator and closed the door (this was before they had that requirement that abandoned refrigerators had to have their doors removed) and he suffocated. I don't know to this day what actually happened, but the cops had picked up *some* black kids and were reportedly beating the shit out of them in an effort to make them confess. I was not on the police run at that time but one of the police reporters told me about it and I told Dr. Behring. A good liberal, he grew white with anger and said what was I doing about it? It was the first time he had talked. So I was shaken— it hadn't occurred to me that I was required to do something about it, he was right—and after I left I called my then sister-in-law, who was at that time secretary to a City Councilman. As you can imagine, such a position is a very powerful one—the councilmen are mostly off making business deals and the executive secretaries run the office—and she got on to the chief of police with an inquiry as to what was going on and if there was any police brutality involved and if so, how much. The case was a very sensational one, you see; *Ebony* had a writer down there trying to cover it but he couldn't get in to see the boys and the cops had roughed him up some, they couldn't understand at that time that

---

[1] For an admirable discussion of this sort of communication failure and many other matters of interest see Percy, "Toward a Triadic Theory of Meaning," *Psychiatry*, Vol. 35 (February 1972), pp. 6–14 *et seq.* [Editors' note: This and all subsequent footnotes to this story are part of the text.]

there could be such a thing as a black reporter. They understood that they had to be a little careful with the white reporters, but a black reporter was beyond them. But my sister-in-law threw her weight (her Councilman's weight) around a bit and suggested to the chief that if there was a serious amount of brutality going on the cops had better stop it, because there was too much outside interest in the case and it would be extremely bad PR if the brutality stuff got out. I also called a guy I knew pretty high up in the sheriff's department and suggested that *he* suggest to his colleagues that they cool it. I hinted at unspeakable political urgencies and he picked it up. The sheriff's department was separate from the police department but they both operated out of the Courthouse Building and they interacted quite a bit, in the normal course. So the long and short of it was that the cops decided to show the four black kids at a press conference to demonstrate that they weren't really beat all to rags, and that took place at four in the afternoon. I went and the kids looked O.K., except for one whose teeth were out and who the cops said had fallen down the stairs. Well, we all know the falling-down-the-stairs story but the point was the *degree* of mishandling and it was clear that the kids had not been half-killed by the cops, as the rumor stated. They were walking and talking naturally, although scared to death, as who would not be? There weren't any TV pictures because the newspaper people always pulled out the plugs of the TV people, at important moments, in those days—it was a standard thing. Now while I admit it sounds callous to be talking about the degree of brutality being minimal, let me tell you that it was no small matter, in that time and place, to force the cops to show the kids to the press at all. It was an achievement, of sorts. So about eight o'clock I called Dr. Behring at home, I hope interrupting his supper, and told him that the kids were O.K., relatively, and he said that was fine, he was glad to hear it. They were later no-billed and I stopped seeing him. That was my experience of analysis and that it may have left me a little sour, I freely grant. Allow for this bias.

To continue. I take exception to your remark that Susan's "openness" is a form of voyeurism. This remark interested me for a while, until I thought about it. Voyeurism I take to be an eroticized expression of curiosity whose chief phenomenological characteristic is the distance maintained between the voyeur and the object. The tension between the desire to draw near the object and the necessity to maintain the distance becomes a libidinous energy nondischarge, which is what the voyeur seeks.[2] The tension. But your remark indicates, in my opinion, a radical misreading of the problem. Susan's "openness"—a willingness of the heart, if you will allow such a term—is not at all comparable to the activities of the voyeur. Susan draws near. Distance is not her thing—not by a long chalk. Frequently, as you know, she gets burned, but she always tries again. What is operating here, I suggest, is an attempt on your part to "stabilize" Susan's behavior in reference to a state-of-affairs that you feel should obtain. Susan gets married and lives happily ever after. Or: There is within Susan a

---

[2] See, for example, Straus, "Shame As a Historiological Problem," in *Phenomenological Psychology.* (New York: Basic Books, 1966), p. 219.

certain amount of creativity which should be liberated and actualized. Susan becomes an artist and lives happily ever after.

But your norms are, I suggest, skewing your view of the problem, and very badly.

Let us take the first case. You reason: If Susan is happy or at least functioning in the present state of affairs (that is, moving from man to man as a silver dollar moves from hand to hand), then why is she seeing a shrink? Something is wrong. New behavior is indicated. Susan is to get married and live happily ever after. May I offer another view? That is, that "seeing a shrink" might be precisely a maneuver in a situation in which Susan *does not want* to get married and live happily ever after? That getting married and living happily ever after might be, for Susan, the worst of fates, and that in order to validate her nonacceptance of this norm she defines herself to herself as shrink-needing? That you are actually certifying the behavior which you seek to change? (When she says to you that she's not shrinkable, you should listen.)

Perhaps, Dr. Hodder, my logic is feeble, perhaps my intuitions are frail. It is, God knows, a complex and difficult question. Your perception that Susan is an artist of some kind *in potentia* is, I think, an acute one. But the proposition "Susan becomes an artist and lives happily ever after" is ridiculous. (I realize that I am couching the proposition in such terms—"happily ever after"—that it is ridiculous on the face of it, but there is ridiculousness piled upon ridiculousness.) Let me point out, if it has escaped your notice, that what an artist does, is fail. Any reading of the literature[3] (I mean the theory of artistic creation), however summary, will persuade you instantly that the paradigmatic artistic experience is that of failure. The actualization fails to meet, equal, the intuition. There is something "out there" which cannot be brought "here." This is standard. I don't mean bad artists, I mean good artists. There is no such thing as a "successful artist" (except, of course, in worldly terms). The proposition should read, "Susan becomes an artist and lives unhappily ever after." This is the case. Don't be deceived.

What I am saying is, that the therapy of choice is not clear. I deeply sympathize. You have a dilemma.

I ask you to note, by the way, that Susan's is not a seeking after instant gratification as dealt out by so-called encounter or sensitivity groups, nude marathons, or dope. None of this is what is going down. "Joy" is not Susan's bag. I praise her for seeking out you rather than getting involved with any of this other idiocy. Her forte, I would suggest, is mind, and if there are games being played they are being conducted with taste, decorum, and some amount of intellectual rigor. Not-bad games. When I take Susan out to dinner she does not order chocolate-covered ants, even if they are on the menu. (Have you, by the way, tried Alfredo's, at the corner of Bank and Hudson streets? It's wonderful.) (Parenthetically, the problem of analysts sleeping with their patients is well known and I understand that Susan has been routinely seducing you—a

---

[3] Especially, perhaps, Ehrenzweig, *The Hidden Order of Art* (University of California Press, 1966), pp. 234–9.

reflex, she can't help it—throughout the analysis. I understand that there is a new splinter group of therapists, behaviorists of some kind, who take this to be some kind of ethic? Is this true? Does this mean that they do it only when they want to, or whether they want to or not? At a dinner party the other evening a lady analyst was saying that three cases of this kind had recently come to her attention and she seemed to think that this was rather a lot. The problem of maintaining mentorship is, as we know, not easy. I think you have done very well in this regard, and God knows it must have been difficult, given those skirts Susan wears that unbutton up to the crotch and which she routinely leaves unbuttoned to the third button.)

Am I wandering too much for you? Bear with me. The world is waiting for the sunrise.

We are left, I submit, with the problem of her depressions. They are, I agree, terrible. Your idea that I am not "supportive" enough is, I think, wrong. I have found, as a practical matter, that the best thing to do is to just do ordinary things, read the newspaper for example, or watch basketball, or wash the dishes. That seems to allow her to come out of it better than any amount of so-called "support." (About the *chasmus hystericus* or hysterical yawning I don't worry any more. It is masking behavior, of course, but after all, you must allow us our tics. The world is waiting for the sunrise.) What do you do with a patient who finds the world unsatisfactory? The world *is* unsatisfactory; only a fool would deny it. I know that your own ongoing psychic structuralization is still going on—you are thirty-seven and I am forty-one—but you must be old enough by now to realize that shit is shit. Susan's perception that America has somehow got hold of the greed ethic and that the greed ethic has turned America into a tidy little hell is not, I think, wrong. What do you do with such a perception? Apply Band-Aids, I suppose. About her depressions, I wouldn't do anything. I'd leave them alone. Put on a record.[4]

Let me tell you a story.

One night we were at her place, about three a.m., and this man called, another lover, quite a well-known musician who is very good, very fast—a good man. He asked Susan "Is he there?," meaning me, and she said "Yes," and he said, "What are you doing?," and she said, "What do you think?," and he said, "When will you be finished?," and she said, "Never." Are you, Doctor dear, in a position to appreciate the beauty of this reply, in this context?

What I am saying is that Susan is wonderful. As *is*. There are not so many things around to which that word can be accurately applied. Therefore I must view your efforts to improve her with, let us say, a certain amount of ambivalence. If this makes me a negative factor in the analysis, so be it. I will be a negative factor until the cows come home, and cheerfully. I can't help it, Doctor, I am voting for the piano.

With best wishes,

---

[4] For example, Harrison, "Wah Wah," Apple Records, STCH 639, Side One, Track 3.

"Repent, Harlequin!" Said the Ticktockman (1965)

HARLAN ELLISON [b. 1934]

There are always those who ask, what is it all about? For those who need to ask, for those who need points sharply made, who need to know "where it's at," this:

> *"The mass of men serve the state thus, not as men mainly, but as machines, with their bodies. They are the standing army, and the militia, jailors, constables, posse comitatus, etc. In most cases there is no free exercise whatever of the judgment or of the moral sense; but they put themselves on a level with wood and earth and stones; and wooden men can perhaps be manufactured that will serve the purpose as well. Such command no more respect than men of straw or a lump of dirt. They have the same sort of worth only as horses and dogs. Yet such as these even are commonly esteemed good citizens. Others—as most legislators, politicians, lawyers, ministers, and office-holders—serve the state chiefly with their heads; and, as they rarely make any moral distinctions, they are as likely to serve the Devil, without intending it, as God. A very few, as heroes, patriots, martyrs, reformers in the great sense, and men, serve the state with their consciences also, and so necessarily resist it for the most part; and they are commonly treated as enemies by it."*
>
> *Henry David Thoreau,*
> CIVIL DISOBEDIENCE

That is the heart of it. Now begin in the middle, and later learn the beginning; the end will take care of itself.

But because it was the very world it was, the very world they had allowed it to *become*, for months his activities did not come to the alarmed attention of The Ones Who Kept The Machine Functioning Smoothly, the ones who poured the very best butter over the cams and mainsprings of the culture. Not until it had become obvious that somehow, someway, he had become a notoriety, a celebrity, perhaps even a hero for (what Officialdom inescapably tagged) "an emotionally disturbed segment of the populace," did they turn it over to the Ticktockman and his legal machinery. But by then, because it was the very world it was, and they had no way to predict he would happen—possibly a strain of disease long-defunct, now, suddenly, reborn in a system where immunity had been forgotten, had lapsed—he had been allowed to become too real. Now he had form and substance.

He had become a *personality*, something they had filtered out of the system many decades before. But there it was, and there *he* was, a very definitely

242

imposing personality. In certain circles—middle-class circles—it was thought disgusting. Vulgar ostentation. Anarchistic. Shameful. In others, there was only sniggering: those strata where thought is subjugated to form and ritual, niceties, proprieties. But down below, ah, down below, where the people always needed their saints and sinners, their bread and circuses, their heroes and villains, he was considered a Bolivar; a Napoleon; a Robin Hood; a Dick Bong (Ace of Aces); a Jesus; a Jomo Kenyatta.

And at the top—where, like socially-attuned Shipwreck Kellys, every tremor and vibration threatens to dislodge the wealthy, powerful and titled from their flagpoles—he was considered a menace; a heretic; a rebel; a disgrace; a peril. He was known down the line, to the very heart-meat core, but the important reactions were high above and far below. At the very top, at the very bottom.

So his file was turned over, along with his time-card and his cardioplate, to the office of the Ticktockman.

The Ticktockman: very much over six feet tall, often silent, a soft purring man when things went timewise. The Ticktockman.

Even in the cubicles of the hierarchy, where fear was generated, seldom suffered, he was called the Ticktockman. But no one called him that to his mask.

You don't call a man a hated name, not when that man, behind his mask, is capable of revoking the minutes, the hours, the days and nights, the years of your life. He was called the Master Timekeeper to his mask. It was safer that way.

"This is *what* he is," said the Ticktockman with genuine softness, "but not *who* he is. This time-card I'm holding in my left hand has a name on it, but it is the name of *what* he is, not *who* he is. The cardioplate here in my right hand is also named, but not *whom* named, merely *what* named. Before I can exercise proper revocation, I have to know *who* this *what* is."

To his staff, all the ferrets, all the loggers, all the finks, all the commex, even the mineez, he said, "Who is this Harlequin?"

He was not purring smoothly. Timewise, it was jangle.

However, it *was* the longest speech they had ever heard him utter at one time, the staff, the ferrets, the loggers, the finks, the commex, but not the mineez, who usually weren't around to know, in any case. But even they scurried to find out.

Who is the Harlequin?

High above the third level of the city, he crouched on the humming aluminum-frame platform of the air-boat (foof! air-boat, indeed! swizzleskid is what it was, with a tow-rack jerry-rigged) and he stared down at the neat Mondrian arrangement of the buildings.

Somewhere nearby, he could hear the metronomic left-right-left of the 2:47 P. M. shift, entering the Timkin roller-bearing plant in their sneakers. A minute later, precisely, he heard the softer right-left-right of the 5:00 A. M. formation, going home.

An elfin grin spread across his tanned features, and his dimples appeared for a moment. Then, scratching at his thatch of auburn hair, he shrugged within his motley, as though girding himself for what came next, and threw the joystick forward, and bent into the wind as the air-boat dropped. He skimmed over a slidewalk, purposely dropping a few feet to crease the tassels of the ladies of fashion, and—inserting thumbs in large ears—he stuck out his tongue, rolled his eyes and went wugga-wugga-wugga. It was a minor diversion. One pedestrian skittered and tumbled, sending parcels everywhichway, another wet herself, a third keeled slantwise and the walk was stopped automatically by the servitors till she could be resuscitated. It was a minor diversion.

Then he swirled away on a vagrant breeze, and was gone. Hi-ho.

As he rounded the cornice of the Time-Motion Study Building, he saw the shift, just boarding the slidewalk. With practiced motion and an absolute conservation of movement, they sidestepped up onto the slow-strip and (in a chorus line reminiscent of a Busby Berkeley film of the antediluvian 1930s) advanced across the strips ostrich-walking till they were lined up on the expresstrip.

Once more, in anticipation, the elfin grin spread, and there was a tooth missing back there on the left side. He dipped, skimmed, and swooped over them; and then, scrunching about on the air-boat, he released the holding pins that fastened shut the ends of the home-made pouring troughs that kept his cargo from dumping prematurely. And as he pulled the trough-pins, the air-boat slid over the factory workers and one hundred and fifty thousand dollars' worth of jelly beans cascaded down on the expresstrip.

Jelly beans! Millions and billions of purples and yellows and greens and licorice and grape and raspberry and mint and round and smooth and crunchy outside and soft-mealy inside and sugary and bouncing jouncing tumbling clittering clattering skittering fell on the heads and shoulders and hardhats and carapaces of the Timkin workers, tinkling on the slidewalk and bouncing away and rolling about underfoot and filling the sky on their way down with all the colors of joy and childhood and holidays, coming down in a steady rain, a solid wash, a torrent of color and sweetness out of the sky from above, and entering a universe of sanity and metronomic order with quite-mad coocoo newness. Jelly beans!

The shift workers howled and laughed and were pelted, and broke ranks, and the jelly beans managed to work their way into the mechanism of the slidewalks after which there was a hideous scraping as the sound of a million fingernails rasped down a quarter of a million blackboards, followed by a coughing and a sputtering, and then the slidewalks all stopped and everyone was dumped this-awayandthataway in a jackstraw tumble, still laughing and popping little jelly bean eggs of childish color into their mouths. It was a holiday, and a jollity, an absolute insanity, a giggle. But . . .

The shift was delayed seven minutes.

They did not get home for seven minutes.

The master schedule was thrown off by seven minutes.

Quotas were delayed by inoperative slidewalks for seven minutes.

He had tapped the first domino in the line, and one after another, like chik chik chik, the others had fallen.

The System had been seven minutes' worth of disrupted. It was a tiny matter, one hardly worthy of note, but in a society where the single driving force was order and unity and equality and promptness and clocklike precision and attention to the clock, reverence of the gods of the passage of time, it was a disaster of major importance.

So he was ordered to appear before the Ticktockman. It was broadcast across every channel of the communications web. He was ordered to be *there* at 7:00 dammit on time. And they waited, and they waited, but he didn't show up till almost ten-thirty, at which time he merely sang a little song about moonlight in a place no one had ever heard of, called Vermont, and vanished again. But they had all been waiting since seven, and it wrecked *hell* with their schedules. So the question remained: Who is the Harlequin?

But the *unasked* question (more important of the two) was: how did we get *into* this position, where a laughing, irresponsible japer of jabberwocky and jive could disrupt our entire economic and cultural life with a hundred and fifty thousand dollars' worth of jelly beans. . . .

Jelly for God's sake *beans*. This is madness! Where did he get the money to buy a hundred and fifty thousand dollars' worth of jelly beans? (They knew it would have cost that much, because they had a team of Situation Analysts pulled off another assignment, and rushed to the slidewalk scene to sweep up and count the candies, and produce findings, which disrupted *their* schedules and threw their entire branch at least a day behind.) Jelly beans! Jelly . . . *beans?* Now wait a second—a second accounted for—no one has manufactured jelly beans for over a hundred years. Where did he get jelly beans?

That's another good question. More than likely it will never be answered to your complete satisfaction. But then, how many questions ever are?

The middle you know. Here is the beginning. How it starts:

A desk pad. Day for day, and turn each day. 9:00—open the mail. 9:45—appointment with planning commission board. 10:30—discuss installation progress charts with J. L. 11:45—pray for rain. 12:00—lunch. *And so it goes.*

"I'm sorry, Miss Grant, but the time for interviews was set at 2:30, and it's almost five now. I'm sorry you're late, but those are the rules. You'll have to wait till next year to submit application for this college again." *And so it goes.*

The 10:10 local stops at Cresthaven, Galesville, Tonawanda Junction, Selby and Farnhurst, but not at Indiana City, Lucasville and Colton, except on Sunday. The 10:35 express stops at Galesville, Selby and Indiana City, except on Sundays & Holidays, at which time it stops at . . . *and so it goes.*

"I couldn't wait, Fred. I had to be at Pierre Cartain's by 3:00, and you said you'd meet me under the clock in the terminal at 2:45, and you weren't there, so I had to go on. You're always late, Fred. If you'd been there, we could have sewed it up together, but as it was, well, I took the order alone . . ." *And so it goes.*

Dear Mr. and Mrs. Atterley: In reference to your son Gerold's constant tardiness, I am afraid we will have to suspend him from school unless some more reliable method can be instituted guaranteeing he will arrive at his classes on time. Granted he is an exemplary student, and his marks are high, his constant flouting of the schedules of this school makes it impractical to maintain him in a system where the other children seem capable of getting where they are supposed to be on time *and so it goes.*

YOU CANNOT VOTE UNLESS YOU APPEAR AT 8:45 A.M.

"I don't care if the script is *good,* I need it Thursday!"

CHECK-OUT TIME IS 2:00 P.M.

"You got here late. The job's taken. Sorry."

YOUR SALARY HAS BEEN DOCKED FOR TWENTY MINUTES TIME LOST.

"God, what time is it, I've gotta run!"

And so it goes. And so it goes. And so it goes. And so it goes goes goes goes goes tick tock tick tock tick tock and one day we no longer let time serve us, we serve time and we are slaves of the schedule, worshippers of the sun's passing; bound into a life predicated on restrictions because the system will not function if we don't keep the schedule tight.

Until it becomes more than a minor inconvenience to be late. It becomes a sin. Then a crime. Then a crime punishable by this:

EFFECTIVE 15 JULY 2389, 12:00:00 midnight, the office of the Master Timekeeper will require all citizens to submit their time-cards and cardioplates for processing. In accordance with Statute 555-7-SGH-999 governing the revocation of time per capita, all cardioplates will be keyed to the individual holder and—

What they had done, was to devise a method of curtailing the amount of life a person could have. If he was ten minutes late, he lost ten minutes of his life. An hour was proportionately worth more revocation. If someone was consistently tardy, he might find himself, on a Sunday night, receiving a communique from the Master Timekeeper that his time had run out, and he would be "turned off" at high noon on Monday, please straighten your affairs, sir, madame or bisex.

And so, by this simple scientific expedient (utilizing a scientific process held dearly secret by the Ticktockman's office) the System was maintained. It was the only expedient thing to do. It was, after all, patriotic. The schedules had to be met. After all, there *was* a war on!

But, wasn't there always?

"Now that is really disgusting," the Harlequin said, when Pretty Alice showed him the wanted poster. "Disgusting and *highly* improbable. After all, this isn't the Day of the Desperado. A *wanted* poster!"

"You know," Pretty Alice noted, "you speak with a great deal of inflection."

"I'm sorry," said the Harlequin, humbly.

"No need to be sorry. You're always saying 'I'm sorry.' You have such massive guilt, Everett, it's really very sad."

"I'm sorry," he said again, then pursed his lips so the dimples appeared momentarily. He hadn't wanted to say that at all. "I have to go out again. I have to *do* something."

Pretty Alice slammed her coffee-bulb down on the counter. "Oh for God's *sake*, Everett, can't you stay home just *one* night! Must you always be out in that ghastly clown suit, running around an*noy*ing people?"

"I'm—" He stopped, and clapped the jester's hat onto his auburn thatch with a tiny tingling of bells. He rose, rinsed out his coffee-bulb at the spray, and put it into the dryer for a moment. "I have to go."

She didn't answer. The faxbox was purring, and she pulled a sheet out, read it, threw it toward him on the counter. "It's about you. Of course. You're ridiculous."

He read it quickly. It said the Ticktockman was trying to locate him. He didn't care, he was going out to be late again. At the door, dredging for an exit line, he hurled back petulantly, "Well, *you* speak with inflection, *too!*"

Pretty Alice rolled her pretty eyes heavenward. "You're ridiculous." The Harlequin stalked out, slamming the door, which sighed shut softly, and locked itself.

There was a gentle knock, and Pretty Alice got up with an exhalation of exasperated breath, and opened the door. He stood there. "I'll be back about ten-thirty, okay?"

She pulled a rueful face. "Why do you tell me that? Why? You *know* you'll be late! You *know* it! You're *always* late, so why do you tell me these dumb things?" She closed the door.

On the other side, the Harlequin nodded to himself. *She's right. She's always right. I'll be late. I'm always late. Why do I tell her these dumb things?*

He shrugged again, and went off to be late once more.

He had fired off the firecracker rockets that said: I will attend the 115th annual International Medical Association Invocation at 8:00 P.M. precisely. I do hope you will all be able to join me.

The words had burned in the sky, and of course the authorities were there, lying in wait for him. They assumed, naturally, that he would be late. He arrived twenty minutes early, while they were setting up the spiderwebs to trap and hold him. Blowing a large bullhorn, he frightened and unnerved them so, their own moisturized encirclement webs sucked closed, and they were hauled up, kicking and shrieking, high above the amphitheater's floor. The Harlequin laughed and laughed, and apologized profusely. The physicians, gathered in solemn conclave, roared with laughter, and accepted the Harlequin's apologies with exaggerated bowing and posturing, and a merry time was had by all, who thought the Harlequin was a regular foofaraw in fancy pants; all, that is, but the authorities, who had been sent out by the office of the Ticktockman; they hung there like so much dockside cargo, hauled up above the floor of the amphitheater in a most unseemly fashion.

(In another part of the same city where the Harlequin carried on his "activities," totally unrelated in every way to what concerns us here, save that it illustrates the Ticktockman's power and import, a man named Marshall Delahanty received his turn-off notice from the Ticktockman's office. His wife received the notification from the gray-suited minee who delivered it, with the traditional "look of sorrow" plastered hideously across his face. She knew what it was, even without unsealing it. It was a billet-doux of immediate recognition to everyone these days. She gasped, and held it as though it were a glass slide tinged with botulism, and prayed it was not for her. Let it be for Marsh, she thought, brutally, realistically, or one of the kids, but not for me, please dear God, not for me. And then she opened it, and it *was* for Marsh, and she was at one and the same time horrified and relieved. The next trooper in the line had caught the bullet. "Marshall," she screamed, "Marshall! Termination, Marshall! OhmiGod, Marshall, whattl we do, whattl we do, Marshall omigod-marshall . . ." and in their home that night was the sound of tearing paper and fear, and the stink of madness went up the flue and there was nothing, absolutely nothing they could do about it.

(But Marshall Delahanty tried to run. And early the next day, when turn-off time came, he was deep in the Canadian forest two hundred miles away, and the office of the Ticktockman blanked his cardioplate, and Marshall Delahanty keeled over, running, and his heart stopped, and the blood dried up on its way to his brain, and he was dead that's all. One light went out on the sector map in the office of the Master Timekeeper, while notification was entered for fax reproduction, and Georgette Delahanty's name was entered on the dole roles till she could remarry. Which is the end of the footnote, and all the point that need be made, except don't laugh, because that is what would happen to the Harlequin if ever the Ticktockman found out his real name. It isn't funny.)

The shopping level of the city was thronged with the Thursday-colors of the buyers. Women in canary yellow chitons and men in pseudo-Tyrolean outfits that were jade and leather and fit very tightly, save for the balloon pants.

When the Harlequin appeared on the still-being-constructed shell of the new Efficiency Shopping Center, his bullhorn to his elfishly-laughing lips, everyone pointed and stared, and he berated them:

"Why let them order you about? Why let them tell you to hurry and scurry like ants or maggots? Take your time! Saunter a while! Enjoy the sunshine, enjoy the breeze, let life carry you at your own pace! Don't be slaves of time, it's a helluva way to die, slowly, by degrees . . . down with the Ticktockman!"

Who's the nut? Most of the shoppers wanted to know. Who's the nut oh wow I'm gonna be late I gotta run . . .

And the construction gang on the Shopping Center received an urgent order from the office of the Master Timekeeper that the dangerous criminal known as the Harlequin was atop their spire, and their aid was urgently needed in apprehending him. The work crew said no, they would lose time on their construction schedule, but the Ticktockman managed to pull the proper threads of governmental webbing, and they were told to cease work and catch that nitwit up there on the spire; up there with the bullhorn. So a dozen and more burly workers began climbing into their construction platforms, releasing the a-grav plates, and rising toward the Harlequin.

After the debacle (in which, through the Harlequin's attention to personal safety, no one was seriously injured), the workers tried to reassemble, and assault him again, but it was too late. He had vanished. It had attracted quite a crowd, however, and the shopping cycle was thrown off by hours, simply hours. The purchasing needs of the system were therefore falling behind, and so measures were taken to accelerate the cycle for the rest of the day, but it got bogged down and speeded up and they sold too many float-valves and not nearly enough wegglers, which meant that the popli ratio was off, which made it necessary to rush cases and cases of spoiling Smash-O to stores that usually needed a case only every three or four hours. The shipments were bollixed, the transshipments were misrouted, and in the end, even the swizzleskid industries felt it.

"Don't come back till you have him!" the Ticktockman said, very quietly, very sincerely, extremely dangerously.

They used dogs. They used probes. They used cardioplate crossoffs. They used teepers. They used bribery. They used stiktytes. They used intimidation. They used torment. They used torture. They used finks. They used cops. They used search&seizure. They used fallaron. They used betterment incentive. They used fingerprints. They used the Bertillon system. They used cunning. They used guile. They used treachery. They used Raoul Mitgong, but he didn't help much. They used applied physics. They used techniques of criminology.

And what the hell: they caught him.

After all, his name was Everett C. Marm, and he wasn't much to begin with, except a man who had no sense of time.

"Repent, Harlequin!" said the Ticktockman.

"Get stuffed!" the Harlequin replied, sneering.

"You've been late a total of sixty-three years, five months, three weeks, two days, twelve hours, forty-one minutes, fifty-nine seconds, point oh three six one one one one microseconds. You've used up everything you can, and more. I'm going to turn you off."

"Scare someone else. I'd rather be dead than live in a dumb world with a bogeyman like you."

"It's my job."

"You're full of it. You're a tyrant. You have no right to order people around and kill them if they show up late."

"You can't adjust. You can't fit in."

"Unstrap me, and I'll fit my fist into your mouth."

"You're a non-conformist."

"That didn't used to be a felony."

"It is now. Live in the world around you."

"I hate it. It's a terrible world."

"Not everyone thinks so. Most people enjoy order."

"I don't, and most of the people I know don't."

"That's not true. How do you think we caught you?"

"I'm not interested."

"A girl named Pretty Alice told us who you were."

"That's a lie."

"It's true. You unnerve her. She wants to belong; she wants to conform; I'm going to turn you off."

"Then do it already, and stop arguing with me."

"I'm not going to turn you off."

"You're an idiot!"

"Repent, Harlequin!" said the Ticktockman.

"Get stuffed."

So they sent him to Coventry. And in Coventry they worked him over. It was just like what they did to Winston Smith in *Nineteen Eighty-Four*, which was a book none of them knew about, but the techniques are really quite ancient, and so they did it to Everett C. Marm; and one day, quite a long time later, the Harlequin appeared on the communications web, appearing elfin and dimpled and bright-eyed, and not at all brainwashed, and he said he had been wrong, that it was a good, a very good thing indeed, to belong, to be right on time hip-ho and away we go, and everyone stared up at him on the public screens that covered an entire city block, and they said to themselves, well, you see, he was just a nut after all, and if that's the way the system is run, then let's do it that way, because it doesn't pay to fight city hall, or in this case, the Ticktockman. So Everett C. Marm was destroyed, which was a loss, because of what Thoreau said earlier, but you can't make an omelet without breaking a few eggs, and in every revolution a few die who shouldn't, but they have to, because that's the way it happens, and if you make only a little change, then it seems to be worthwhile. Or, to make the point lucidly:

"Uh, excuse me, sir, I, uh, don't know how to uh, to uh, tell you this, but you were three minutes late. The schedule is a little, uh, bit off."

He grinned sheepishly.

"That's ridiculous!" murmured the Ticktockman behind his mask. "Check your watch." And then he went into his office, going *mrmee, mrmee, mrmee, mrmee.*

Everyday Use

1973

FOR YOUR GRANDMAMA

ALICE WALKER   [b. 1944]

I will wait for her in the yard that Maggie and I made so clean and wavy yesterday afternoon. A yard like this is more comfortable than most people know. It is not just a yard. It is like an extended living room. When the hard clay is swept clean as a floor and the fine sand around the edges lined with tiny, irregular grooves anyone can come and sit and look up into the elm tree and wait for the breezes that never come inside the house.

Maggie will be nervous until after her sister goes: she will stand hopelessly in corners homely and ashamed of the burn scars down her arms and legs, eyeing her sister with a mixture of envy and awe. She thinks her sister has held life always in the palm of one hand, that "no" is a word the world never learned to say to her.

You've no doubt seen those TV shows where the child who has "made it" is confronted, as a surprise, by her own mother and father, tottering in weakly from backstage. (A pleasant surprise, of course: What would they do if parent and child came on the show only to curse out and insult each other?) On TV mother and child embrace and smile into each other's faces. Sometimes the mother and father weep, the child wraps them in her arms and leans across the table to tell how she would not have made it without their help. I have seen these programs.

Sometimes I dream a dream in which Dee and I are suddenly brought together on a TV program of this sort. Out of a dark and soft-seated limousine I am ushered into a bright room filled with many people. There I meet a smiling, gray, sporty man like Johnny Carson who shakes my hand and tells me what a fine girl I have. Then we are on the stage and Dee is embracing me with tears in her eyes. She pins on my dress a large orchid, even though she has told me once that she thinks orchids are tacky flowers.

In real life I am a large, big-boned woman with rough, man-working hands. In the winter I wear flannel nightgowns to bed and overalls during the day. I can kill and clean a hog as mercilessly as a man. My fat keeps me hot in zero weather. I can work all day, breaking ice to get water for washing. I can eat pork liver cooked over the open fire minutes after it comes steaming from the hog. One winter I knocked a bull calf straight in the brain between the eyes with a sledge hammer and had the meat hung up to chill before nightfall. But of course all this does not show on television. I am the way my daughter would want me to be: a hundred pounds lighter, my skin like an uncooked barley pancake. My hair glistens in the hot bright lights. Johnny Carson has much to do to keep up with my quick and witty tongue.

But that is a mistake. I know even before I wake up. Who ever knew a Johnson with a quick tongue? Who can even imagine me looking a strange white man in the eye? It seems to me I have talked to them always with one foot raised in flight, with my head turned in whichever way is farthest from them. Dee, though. She would always look anyone in the eye. Hesitation was no part of her nature.

"How do I look, Mama?" Maggie says, showing just enough of her thin body enveloped in pink skirt and red blouse for me to know she's there, almost hidden by the door.

"Come out into the yard," I say.

Have you ever seen a lame animal, perhaps a dog run over by some careless person rich enough to own a car, sidle up to someone who is ignorant enough to be kind to him? That is the way my Maggie walks. She has been like this, chin on chest, eyes on ground, feet in shuffle, ever since the fire that burned the other house to the ground.

Dee is lighter than Maggie, with nicer hair and a fuller figure. She's a woman now, though sometimes I forget. How long ago was it that the other house burned? Ten, twelve years? Sometimes I can still hear the flames and feel Maggie's arm sticking to me, her hair smoking and her dress falling off her in little black papery flakes. Her eyes seemed stretched open, blazed open by the flames reflected in them. And Dee. I see her standing off under the sweet gum tree she used to dig gum out of; a look of concentration on her face as she watched the last dingy gray board of the house fall in toward the red-hot brick chimney. Why don't you do a dance around the ashes? I'd wanted to ask her. She had hated the house that much.

I used to think she hated Maggie, too. But that was before we raised the money, the church and me, to send her to Augusta to school. She used to read to us without pity; forcing words, lies, other folks' habits, whole lives upon us two, sitting trapped and ignorant underneath her voice. She washed us in a river of make-believe, burned us with a lot of knowledge we didn't necessarily need to know. Pressed us to her with the serious way she read, to shove us away at just the moment, like dimwits, we seemed about to understand.

Dee wanted nice things. A yellow organdy dress to wear to her graduation from high school; black pumps to match a green suit she'd made from an old suit somebody gave me. She was determined to stare down any disaster in her efforts. Her eyelids would not flicker for minutes at a time. Often I fought off the temptation to shake her. At sixteen she had a style of her own: and knew what style was.

I never had an education myself. After second grade the school was closed down. Don't ask me why: in 1927 colored asked fewer questions than they do now. Sometimes Maggie reads to me. She stumbles along good-naturedly but can't see well. She knows she is not bright. Like good looks and money, quickness passed her by. She will marry John Thomas (who has mossy teeth in an earnest face) and then I'll be free to sit here and I guess just sing church songs to myself. Although I never was a good singer. Never could carry a tune. I was always better at a man's job. I used to love to milk till I was hoofed in the side in '49. Cows are soothing and slow and don't bother you, unless you try to milk them the wrong way.

I have deliberately turned my back on the house. It is three rooms, just like the one that burned, except the roof is tin; they don't make shingle roofs any more. There are no real windows, just some holes cut in the sides, like the portholes in a ship, but not round and not square, with rawhide holding the shutters up on the outside. This house is in a pasture, too, like the other one. No doubt when Dee sees it she will want to tear it down. She wrote me once that no matter where we "choose" to live, she will manage to come see us. But she will never bring her friends. Maggie and I thought about this and Maggie asked me, "Mama, when did Dee ever *have* any friends?"

She had a few. Furtive boys in pink shirts hanging about on washday after school. Nervous girls who never laughed. Impressed with her they worshiped the well-turned phrase, the cute shape, the scalding humor that erupted like bubbles in lye. She read to them.

When she was courting Jimmy T she didn't have much time to pay to us, but turned all her faultfinding power on him. He *flew* to marry a cheap gal from a family of ignorant flashy people. She hardly had time to recompose herself.

When she comes I will meet—but there they are!

Maggie attempts to make a dash for the house, in her shuffling way, but I stay her with my hand. "Come back here," I say. And she stops and tries to dig a well in the sand with her toe.

It is hard to see them clearly through the strong sun. But even the first glimpse of leg out of the car tells me it is Dee. Her feet were always neat-looking, as if God himself had shaped them with a certain style. From the other side of the car comes a short, stocky man. Hair is all over his head a foot long and hanging from his chin like a kinky mule tail. I hear Maggie suck in her breath. "Uhnnnh," is what it sounds like. Like when you see the wriggling end of a snake just in front of your foot on the road. "Uhnnnh."

Dee next. A dress down to the ground, in this hot weather. A dress so loud it hurts my eyes. There are yellows and oranges enough to throw back the light of the sun. I feel my whole face warming from the heat waves it throws out. Earrings, too, gold and hanging down to her shoulders. Bracelets dangling and making noises when she moves her arm up to shake the folds of the dress out of her armpits. The dress is loose and flows, and as she walks closer, I like it. I hear Maggie go "Uhnnnh" again. It is her sister's hair. It stands straight up like the wool on a sheep. It is black as night and around the edges are two long pigtails that rope about like small lizards disappearing behind her ears.

"Wa-su-zo-Tean-o!" she says, coming on in that gliding way the dress makes her move. The short stocky fellow with the hair to his navel is all grinning and he follows up with "Asalamalakim, my mother and sister!" He moves to hug

Maggie but she falls back, right up against the back of my chair. I feel her trembling there and when I look up I see the perspiration falling off her chin.

"Don't get up," says Dee. Since I am stout it takes something of a push. You can see me trying to move a second or two before I make it. She turns, showing white heels through her sandals, and goes back to the car. Out she peeks next with a Polaroid. She stoops down quickly and lines up picture after picture of me sitting there in front of the house with Maggie cowering behind me. She never takes a shot without making sure the house is included. When a cow comes nibbling around the edge of the yard she snaps it and me and Maggie *and* the house. Then she puts the Polaroid in the back seat of the car, and comes up and kisses me on the forehead.

Meanwhile Asalamalakim is going through the motions with Maggie's hand. Maggie's hand is as limp as a fish, and probably as cold, despite the sweat, and she keeps trying to pull it back. It looks like Asalamalakim wants to shake hands but wants to do it fancy. Or maybe he don't know how people shake hands. Anyhow, he soon gives up on Maggie.

"Well," I say. "Dee."

"No, Mama," she says. "Not 'Dee,' Wangero Leewanika Kemanjo!"

"What happened to 'Dee'?" I wanted to know.

"She's dead," Wangero said. "I couldn't bear it any longer being named after the people who oppress me."

"You know as well as me you was named after your aunt Dicie," I said. Dicie is my sister. She named Dee. We called her "Big Dee" after Dee was born.

"But who was *she* named after?" asked Wangero.

"I guess after Grandma Dee," I said.

"And who was she named after?" asked Wangero.

"Her mother," I said, and saw Wangero was getting tired. "That's about as far back as I can trace it," I said. Though, in fact, I probably could have carried it back beyond the Civil War through the branches.

"Well," said Asalamalakim, "there you are."

"Uhnnnh," I heard Maggie say.

"There I was not," I said, "before 'Dicie' cropped up in our family, so why should I try to trace it that far back?"

He just stood there grinning, looking down on me like somebody inspecting a Model A car. Every once in a while he and Wangero sent eye signals over my head.

"How do you pronounce this name?" I asked.

"You don't have to call me by it if you don't want to," said Wangero.

"Why shouln't I?" I asked. "If that's what you want us to call you, we'll call you."

"I know it might sound awkward at first," said Wangero.

"I'll get used to it," I said. "Ream it out again."

Well, soon we got the name out of the way. Asalamalakim had a name twice as long and three times as hard. After I tripped over it two or three times he told me to just call him Hakim-a-barber. I wanted to ask him was he a barber, but I didn't really think he was, so I didn't ask.

"You must belong to those beef-cattle peoples down the road," I said. They said "Asalamalakim" when they met you, too, but they didn't shake hands. Always too busy: feeding the cattle, fixing the fences, putting up salt-lick shelters, throwing down hay. When the white folks poisoned some of the herd the men stayed up all night with rifles in their hands. I walked a mile and a half just to see the sight.

Hakim-a-barber said, "I accept some of their doctrines, but farming and raising cattle is not my style." (They didn't tell me, and I didn't ask, whether Wangero [Dee] had really gone and married him.)

We sat down to eat and right away he said he didn't eat collards and pork was unclean. Wangero, though, went on through the chitlins and corn bread, the greens and everything else. She talked a blue streak over the sweet potatoes. Everything delighted her. Even the fact that we still used the benches her daddy made for the table when we couldn't afford to buy chairs.

"Oh, Mama!" she cried. Then turned to Hakim-a-barber. "I never knew how lovely these benches are. You can feel the rump prints," she said, running her hands underneath her and along the bench. Then she gave a sigh and her hand closed over Grandma Dee's butter dish. "That's it!" she said. "I knew there was something I wanted to ask you if I could have." She jumped up from the table and went over in the corner where the churn stood, the milk in its clabber by now. She looked at the churn and looked at it.

"This churn top is what I need," she said. "Didn't Uncle Buddy whittle it out of a tree you all used to have?"

"Yes," I said.

"Uh huh," she said happily. "And I want the dasher, too."

"Uncle Buddy whittle that, too?" asked the barber.

Dee (Wangero) looked up at me.

"Aunt Dee's first husband whittled the dash," said Maggie so low you almost couldn't hear her. "His name was Henry, but they called him Stash."

"Maggie's brain is like an elephant's," Wangero said, laughing. "I can use the churn top as a centerpiece for the alcove table," she said, sliding a plate over the churn, "and I'll think of something artistic to do with the dasher."

When she finished wrapping the dasher the handle stuck out. I took it for a moment in my hands. You didn't even have to look close to see where hands pushing the dasher up and down to make butter had left a kind of sink in the wood. In fact, there were a lot of small sinks; you could see where thumbs and fingers had sunk into the wood. It was beautiful light yellow wood, from a tree that grew in the yard where Big Dee and Stash had lived.

After dinner Dee (Wangero) went to the trunk at the foot of my bed and started rifling through it. Maggie hung back in the kitchen over the dishpan. Out came Wangero with two quilts. They had been pieced by Grandma Dee and then Big Dee and me had hung them on the quilt frames on the front porch and quilted them. One was in the Lone Star pattern. The other was Walk Around the Mountain. In both of them were scraps of dresses Grandma Dee had worn fifty and more years ago. Bits and pieces of Grandpa Jarrell's Paisley shirts. And one teeny faded blue piece, about the size of a penny matchbox, that was from Great Grandpa Ezra's uniform that he wore in the Civil War.

"Mama," Wangero said sweet as a bird. "Can I have these old quilts?"

I heard something fall in the kitchen, and a minute later the kitchen door slammed.

"Why don't you take one or two of the others?" I asked "These old things was just done by me and Big Dee from some tops your grandma pieced before she died."

"No," said Wangero. "I don't want those. They are stitched around the borders by machine."

"That's make them last better," I said.

"That's not the point," said Wangero. "These are all pieces of dresses Grandma used to wear. She did all this stitching by hand. Imagine!" She held the quilts securely in her arms, stroking them.

"Some of the pieces, like those lavender ones, come from old clothes her mother handed down to her," I said, moving up to touch the quilts. Dee (Wangero) moved back just enough so that I couldn't reach the quilts. They already belonged to her.

"Imagine!" she breathed again, clutching them closely to her bosom.

"The truth is," I said, "I promised to give them quilts to Maggie, for when she marries John Thomas."

She gasped like a bee had stung her.

"Maggie can't appreciate these quilts!" she said. "She'd probably be backward enough to put them to everyday use."

"I reckon she would," I said. "God knows I been saving 'em for long enough with nobody using 'em. I hope she will!" I didn't want to bring up how I had offered Dee (Wangero) a quilt when she went away to college. Then she had told me they were old-fashioned, out of style.

"But they're *priceless*!" she was saying now, furiously; for she has a temper. "Maggie would put them on the bed and in five years they'd be in rags. Less than that!"

"She can always make some more," I said. "Maggie knows how to quilt."

Dee (Wangero) looked at me with hatred. "You just will not understand. The point is these quilts, *these* quilts!"

"Well," I said, stumped. "What would *you* do with them?"

"Hang them," she said. As if that was the only thing you *could* do with quilts.

Maggie by now was standing in the door. I could almost hear the sound her feet made as they scraped over each other.

"She can have them, Mama," she said, like somebody used to never winning anything, or having anything reserved for her. "I can 'member Grandma Dee without the quilts."

I looked at her hard. She had filled her bottom lip with checkerberry snuff and it gave her face a kind of dopey, hangdog look. It was Grandma Dee and Big Dee who taught her how to quilt herself. She stood there with her scarred hands hidden in the folds of her skirt. She looked at her sister with something like fear but she wasn't mad at her. This was Maggie's portion. This was the way she knew God to work.

When I looked at her like that something hit me in the top of my head and ran down to the soles of my feet. Just like when I'm in church and the spirit of God touches me and I get happy and shout. I did something I never had done before: hugged Maggie to me, then dragged her on into the room, snatched the quilts out of Miss Wangero's hands and dumped them into Maggie's lap. Maggie just sat there on my bed with her mouth open.

"Take one or two of the others," I said to Dee.

But she turned without a word and went out to Hakim-a-barber.

"You just don't understand," she said, as Maggie and I came out to the car.

"What don't I understand?" I wanted to know.

"Your heritage," she said. And then she turned to Maggie, kissed her, and said, "You ought to try to make something of yourself, too, Maggie. It's really a new day for us. But from the way you and Mama still live you'd never know it."

She put on some sunglasses that hid everything above the tip of her nose and her chin.

Maggie smiled; maybe at the sunglasses. But a real smile, not scared. After we watched the car dust settle I asked Maggie to bring me a dip of snuff. And then the two of us sat there just enjoying, until it was time to go in the house and go to bed.

CONFORMITY
AND
REBELLION

Au Moulin Rouge. Le Depart du Quadrille, 1892 after a painting by Henri de Toulouse-Lautrec.

POETRY

Sonnet XVII (1655)

JOHN MILTON [1608–1674]

When I consider how my light is spent,[1]
    Ere half my days, in this dark world and wide,
    And that one talent[2] which is death to hide
    Lodged with me useless, though my soul more bent
To serve therewith my maker, and present
    My true account, lest he, returning, chide.
    'Doth God exact day-labour, light denied?'
    I fondly° ask; but Patience, to prevent   foolishly
That murmur, soon replies: 'God doth not need
    Either man's work or his own gifts; who best   10
    Bear his mild yoke, they serve him best; his state
Is kingly—thousands at his bidding speed
    And post o'er land and ocean without rest:
    They also serve who only stand and wait.'

The World Is
Too Much with Us 1807

WILLIAM WORDSWORTH [1770–1850]

The world is too much with us; late and soon,
Getting and spending, we lay waste our powers;
Little we see in Nature that is ours;

Sonnet XVII
    [1] Milton was blind when he wrote this sonnet.
    [2] The parable of the Master who gave his servants "talents" (literally, coins of precious metal) occurs in Matthew 25:14–30.

We have given our hearts away, a sordid boon!
This Sea that bares her bosom to the moon,
The winds that will be howling at all hours,
And are up-gathered now like sleeping flowers,
For this, for everything, we are out of tune;
It moves us not.—Great God! I'd rather be
A Pagan suckled in a creed outworn;   10
So might I, standing on this pleasant lea,
Have glimpses that would make me less forlorn;
Have sight of Proteus rising from the sea;
Or hear Old Triton blow his wreathèd horn.[1]

QUESTIONS
1. What does "world" mean in line 1? **2.** What does Wordsworth complain of
in the first four lines? **3.** In lines 4–8 Wordsworth tells us what we have lost; in
the concluding lines he suggests a remedy. What is that remedy? What do Proteus
and Triton symbolize?

WRITING TOPIC
In what ways does Wordsworth's use of images both define what we have lost
and suggest a remedy for this loss?

Sonnet: To Science   (1829)

EDGAR ALLAN POE   [1809–1849]

Science! true daughter of Old Time thou art!
Who alterest all things with thy peering eyes.
Why preyest thou thus upon the poet's heart,
Vulture, whose wings are dull realities?
How should he love thee? or how deem thee wise,
Who wouldst not leave him in his wandering
To seek for treasure in the jewelled skies,
Albeit he soared with an undaunted wing?
Hast thou not dragged Diana[1] from her car?
And driven the Hamadryad[2] from the wood   10

The World . . .
    [1] Proteus and Triton are both figures from Greek mythology. Proteus had the power to assume
different forms; Triton was often represented as blowing on a conch shell.

Sonnet: To Science
    [1] Diana is a Roman goddess and her car is the moon.
    [2] The Hamadryad and Naiad (line 12) are nymphs associated, in classical mythology, with woods
and fountains.

To seek a shelter in some happier star?
Hast thou not torn the Naiad from her flood,
The Elfin from the green grass, and from me
The summer dream beneath the tamarind tree?

QUESTIONS

1. How does Poe characterize science? How does he characterize the poet?
2. Why does Poe allude to Diana, the Hamadryad, and the Naiad? What impact upon the imagination has scientific inquiry?

Ulysses[1]   (1833)

ALFRED, LORD TENNYSON [1809–1892]

It little profits that an idle king,
By this still hearth, among these barren crags,
Matched with an aged wife, I mete and dole
Unequal laws unto a savage race,
That hoard, and sleep, and feed, and know not me.

I cannot rest from travel; I will drink
Life to the lees. All times I have enjoyed
Greatly, have suffered greatly, both with those
That loved me, and alone; on shore, and when
Through scudding drifts the rainy Hyades[2]   10
Vexed the dim sea. I am become a name;
For always roaming with a hungry heart
Much have I seen and known—cities of men
And manners, climates, councils, governments,
Myself not least, but honored of them all—
And drunk delight of battle with my peers,
Far on the ringing plains of windy Troy.
I am a part of all that I have met;
Yet all experience is an arch wherethrough
Gleams that untraveled world whose margin fades   20
Forever and forever when I move.
How dull it is to pause, to make an end,

Ulysses
  [1] Ulysses, according to Greek legend, was the king of Ithaca and a hero of the Trojan War. Tennyson represents him as eager to resume the life of travel and adventure.
  [2] A group of stars in the constellation Taurus. According to Greek mythology, the rising of these stars with the sun foretold rain.

To rust unburnished, not to shine in use!
As though to breathe were life! Life piled on life
Were all too little, and of one to me
Little remains; but every hour is saved
From that eternal silence, something more,
A bringer of new things; and vile it were
For some three suns to store and hoard myself,
And this gray spirit yearning in desire   30
To follow knowledge like a sinking star,
Beyond the utmost bound of human thought.

    This is my son, mine own Telemachus,
To whom I leave the scepter and the isle—
Well-loved of me, discerning to fulfill
This labor, by slow prudence to make mild
A rugged people, and through soft degrees
Subdue them to the useful and the good.
Most blameless is he, centered in the sphere
Of common duties, decent not to fail   40
In offices of tenderness, and pay
Meet° adoration to my household gods,   proper
When I am gone. He works his work, I mine.

    There lies the port; the vessel puffs her sail;
There gloom the dark, broad seas. My mariners,
Souls that have toiled, and wrought, and thought with me—
That ever with a frolic welcome took
The thunder and the sunshine, and opposed
Free hearts, free foreheads—you and I are old;
Old age hath yet his honor and his toil.   50
Death closes all; but something ere the end,
Some work of noble note, may yet be done,
Not unbecoming men that strove with Gods.
The lights begin to twinkle from the rocks;
The long day wanes; the slow moon climbs; the deep
Moans round with many voices. Come, my friends,
'Tis not too late to seek a newer world.
Push off, and sitting well in order smite
The sounding furrows; for my purpose holds
To sail beyond the sunset, and the baths   60
Of all the western stars, until I die.
It may be that the gulfs will wash us down;
It may be we shall touch the Happy Isles,[3]

---

[3] The Islands of the Blessed (also Elysium), thought to be in the far western oceans, where those favored by the gods, such as Achilles, enjoyed life after death.

And see the great Achilles, whom we knew.
Though much is taken, much abides; and though
We are not now that strength which in old days
Moved earth and heaven, that which we are, we are—
One equal temper of heroic hearts,
Made weak by time and fate, but strong in will
To strive, to seek, to find, and not to yield.   70

QUESTIONS
1. Is Ulysses' desire to abdicate his duties as king irresponsible? Defend your
answer.   **2.**   Contrast Ulysses with his son Telemachus as the latter is described
in lines 33–43. Is Telemachus admirable? Explain.

WRITING TOPIC
At the conclusion of the poem Ulysses is determined not to yield. Yield to what?

Much Madness
Is Divinest Sense   (1862)

EMILY DICKINSON   [1830–1886]

Much Madness is divinest Sense—
To a discerning Eye—
Much Sense—the starkest Madness—
'Tis the Majority
In this, as All, prevail—
Assent—and you are sane—
Demur—you're straightway dangerous—
And handled with a Chain—

What Soft—
Cherubic Creatures   (ca. 1862)

EMILY DICKINSON   [1830–1886]

What Soft—Cherubic Creatures—
These Gentlewomen are—
One would as soon assault a Plush—
Or violate a Star—

Such Dimity Convictions—
A Horror so refined
Of freckled Human Nature—
Of Deity—ashamed—

It's such a common-Glory—
A Fisherman's—Degree—   10
Redemption—Brittle Lady—
Be so—ashamed of Thee—

Easter 1916¹   (1916)

WILLIAM BUTLER YEATS   [1865–1939]

I have met them at close of day
Coming with vivid faces
From counter or desk among grey
Eighteenth-century houses.
I have passed with a nod of the head
Or polite meaningless words,
Or have lingered awhile and said
Polite meaningless words,
And thought before I had done
Of a mocking tale or a gibe   10
To please a companion
Around the fire at the club,
Being certain that they and I
But lived where motley is worn:
All changed, changed utterly:
A terrible beauty is born.

That woman's days were spent
In ignorant good-will,
Her nights in argument
Until her voice grew shrill.   20
What voice more sweet than hers

Easter 1916
  ¹ On Easter Sunday of 1916, a group of Irish nationalists seized key points in Ireland, including
the Dublin Post Office, from which they proclaimed an independent Irish Republic. At first, most
Irishmen were indifferent to the nationalists' futile and heroic gesture, but as the rebellion was
crushed and the leaders executed, they became heroes in their countrymen's eyes. Some of those
leaders are alluded to in the second stanza and are named in lines 75 and 76.

When, young and beautiful,
She rode to harriers?
This man had kept a school
And rode our winged horse;[2]
This other his helper and friend
Was coming into his force;
He might have won fame in the end,
So sensitive his nature seemed,
So daring and sweet his thought.   30
This other man I had dreamed
A drunken, vainglorious lout.
He had done most bitter wrong
To some who are near my heart,
Yet I number him in the song;
He, too, has resigned his part
In the casual comedy;
He, too, has been changed in his turn,
Transformed utterly:
A terrible beauty is born.   40

Hearts with one purpose alone
Through summer and winter seem
Enchanted to a stone
To trouble the living stream.
The horse that comes from the road,
The rider, the birds that range
From cloud to tumbling cloud,
Minute by minute they change;
A shadow of cloud on the stream
Changes minute by minute;   50
A horse-hoof slides on the brim,
And a horse plashes within it;
The long-legged moor-hens dive,
And hens to moor-cocks call;
Minute by minute they live:
The stone's in the midst of all.

Too long a sacrifice
Can make a stone of the heart.
O when may it suffice?
That is Heaven's part, our part   60
To murmur name upon name,
As a mother names her child

---

[2] In Greek mythology, a winged horse is associated with poetic inspiration.

When sleep at last has come
On limbs that had run wild.
What is it but nightfall?
No, no, not night but death;
Was it needless death after all?
For England may keep faith
For all that is done and said.
We know their dream; enough   70
To know they dreamed and are dead;
And what if excess of love
Bewildered them till they died?
I write it out in a verse—
MacDonagh and MacBride
And Connolly and Pearse
Now and in time to be,
Wherever green is worn,
Are changed, changed utterly:
A terrible beauty is born.   80

QUESTIONS
1. What is "changed utterly," and in what sense can beauty be "terrible"? **2.** What does "they" in line 55 refer to? What does the "stone" in lines
43 and 56 symbolize? What is Yeats contrasting? **3.** How does the poet answer
the question he asks in line 67?

WRITING TOPIC
In the first stanza the attitude of the poet toward the people he is describing is
indifferent, even contemptuous. How is that attitude modified in the rest of the
poem?

Miniver Cheevy   1910

EDWIN ARLINGTON ROBINSON   [1869–1935]

Miniver Cheevy, child of scorn,
    Grew lean while he assailed the seasons;
He wept that he was ever born,
    And he had reasons.

Miniver loved the days of old
    When swords were bright and steeds were prancing;
The vision of a warrior bold
    Would set him dancing.

Miniver sighed for what was not,
    And dreamed, and rested from his labors;   10
He dreamed of Thebes and Camelot,
    And Priam's neighbors.[1]

Miniver mourned the ripe renown
    . That made so many a name so fragrant;
He mourned Romance, now on the town,
    And Art, a vagrant.

Miniver loved the Medici,[2]
    Albeit he had never seen one;
He would have sinned incessantly
    Could he have been one.   20

Miniver cursed the commonplace
    And eyed a khaki suit with loathing;
He missed the medieval grace
    Of iron clothing.

Miniver scorned the gold he sought,
    But sore annoyed was he without it;
Miniver thought, and thought, and thought,
    And thought about it.

Miniver Cheevy, born too late,
    Scratched his head and kept on thinking;   30
Miniver coughed, and called it fate,
    And kept on drinking.

We Wear the Mask   1896

PAUL LAURENCE DUNBAR   [1872–1906]

We wear the mask that grins and lies,
It hides our cheeks and shades our eyes—
This debt we pay to human guile;

Miniver Cheevy
  [1] Thebes was an ancient Greek city, famous in history and legend; Camelot was the site of the legendary King Arthur's court; Priam was king of Troy during the Trojan War.
  [2] A family of bankers and statesmen, notorious for their cruelty, who ruled Florence for nearly two centuries during the Italian Renaissance.

With torn and bleeding hearts we smile,
And mouth with myriad subtleties.

Why should the world be over-wise,
In counting all our tears and sighs?
Nay, let them only see us, while
    We wear the mask.

We smile, but, O great Christ, our cries   10
To thee from tortured souls arise.
We sing, but oh the clay is vile
Beneath our feet, and long the mile;
But let the world dream otherwise,
    We wear the mask!

Patterns   1916

AMY LOWELL [1874–1925]

I walk down the garden-paths,
And all the daffodils
Are blowing, and the bright blue squills.
I walk down the patterned garden-paths
In my stiff, brocaded gown.
With my powdered hair and jeweled fan,
I too am a rare
Pattern. As I wander down
The garden-paths.

My dress is richly figured,   10
And the train
Makes a pink and silver stain
On the gravel, and the thrift
Of the borders.
Just a plate of current fashion,
Tripping by in high-heeled, ribboned shoes.
Not a softness anywhere about me,
Only whalebone and brocade.
And I sink on a seat in the shade
Of a lime tree. For my passion   20
Wars against the stiff brocade.
The daffodils and squills

Flutter in the breeze
As they please.
And I weep;
For the lime-tree is in blossom
And one small flower has dropped upon my bosom.

And the plashing of waterdrops
In the marble fountain
Comes down the garden-paths.   30
The dripping never stops.
Underneath my stiffened gown
Is the softness of a woman bathing in a marble basin,
A basin in the midst of hedges grown
So thick, she cannot see her lover hiding,
But she guesses he is near,
And the sliding of the water
Seems the stroking of a dear
Hand upon her.
What is Summer in a fine brocaded gown!   40
I should like to see it lying in a heap upon the ground.
All the pink and silver crumpled up on the ground.

I would be the pink and silver as I ran along the paths,
And he would stumble after,
Bewildered by my laughter.
I should see the sun flashing from his sword-hilt and the buckles on his
    shoes.
I would choose
To lead him in a maze along the patterned paths,
A bright and laughing maze for my heavy-booted lover.
Till he caught me in the shade,   50
And the buttons of his waistcoat bruised my body as he clasped me,
Aching, melting, unafraid.
With the shadows of the leaves and the sundrops,
And the plopping of the waterdrops,
All about us in the open afternoon—
I am very like to swoon
With the weight of this brocade,
For the sun sifts through the shade.

Underneath the fallen blossom
In my bosom   60
Is a letter I have hid.
It was brought to me this morning by a rider from the Duke.
"Madam, we regret to inform you that Lord Hartwell
Died in action Thursday se'nnight."

As I read it in the white, morning sunlight,
The letters squirmed like snakes.
"Any answer, Madam," said my footman.
"No," I told him.
"See that the messenger takes some refreshment.
No, no answer."   70
And I walked into the garden,
Up and down the patterned paths,
In my stiff, correct brocade.
The blue and yellow flowers stood up proudly in the sun,
Each one.
I stood upright too,
Held rigid to the pattern
By the stiffness of my gown;
Up and down I walked,
Up and down.   80

In a month he would have been my husband.
In a month, here, underneath this lime,
We would have broke the pattern;
He for me, and I for him,
He as Colonel, I as Lady,
On this shady seat.
He had a whim
That sunlight carried blessing.
And I answered, "It shall be as you have said."
Now he is dead.   90

In Summer and in Winter I shall walk
Up and down
The patterned garden-paths
In my stiff, brocaded gown.
The squills and daffodils
Will give place to pillared roses, and to asters, and to snow.
I shall go
Up and down
In my gown.
Gorgeously arrayed,   100
Boned and stayed.
And the softness of my body will be guarded from embrace
By each button, hook, and lace.
For the man who should loose me is dead,
Fighting with the Duke in Flanders,
In a pattern called a war.
Christ! What are patterns for?

Departmental   1936

ROBERT FROST   [1874–1963]

An ant on the table cloth
Ran into a dormant moth
Of many times his size.
He showed not the least surprise.
His business wasn't with such.
He gave it scarcely a touch,
And was off on his duty run.
Yet if he encountered one
Of the hive's enquiry squad
Whose work is to find out God   10
And the nature of time and space,
He would put him onto the case.
Ants are a curious race;
One crossing with hurried tread
The body of one of their dead
Isn't given a moment's arrest—
Seems not even impressed.
But he no doubt reports to any
With whom he crosses antennae,
And they no doubt report   20
To the higher up at court.
Then word goes forth in Formic:
"Death's come to Jerry McCormic,
Our selfless forager Jerry.
Will the special Janizary
Whose office it is to bury
The dead of the commissary
Go bring him home to his people.
Lay him in state on a sepal.
Wrap him for shroud in a petal.   30
Embalm him with ichor of nettle.
This is the word of your Queen."
And presently on the scene
Appears a solemn mortician;
And taking formal position
With feelers calmly atwiddle,
Seizes the dead by the middle,
And heaving him high in air,
Carries him out of there.
No one stands round to stare.   40

It is nobody else's affair.
It couldn't be called ungentle.
But how thoroughly departmental.

QUESTIONS
1. What comment does this poem make on human society? Is ant society a good metaphor for human society? Explain. **2.** How do the diction and rhyme help establish the tone?

WRITING TOPIC
How does the diction in this poem convey the speaker's attitude toward the social order he describes?

Sunday Morning   1923

WALLACE STEVENS   [1879–1955]

I

Complacencies of the peignoir, and late
Coffee and oranges in a sunny chair,
And the green freedom of a cockatoo
Upon a rug mingle to dissipate
The holy hush of ancient sacrifice.
She dreams a little, and she feels the dark
Encroachment of that old catastrophe,
As a calm darkens among water-lights.
The pungent oranges and bright, green wings
Seem things in some procession of the dead,   10
Winding across wide water, without sound.
The day is like wide water, without sound,
Stilled for the passing of her dreaming feet
Over the seas, to silent Palestine,
Dominion of the blood and sepulchre.

II

Why should she give her bounty to the dead?
What is divinity if it can come
Only in silent shadows and in dreams?
Shall she not find in comforts of the sun,
In pungent fruit and bright, green wings, or else   20

In any balm or beauty of the earth,
Things to be cherished like the thought of heaven?
Divinity must live within herself:
Passions of rain, or moods in falling snow;
Grievings in loneliness, or unsubdued
Elations when the forest blooms; gusty
Emotions on wet roads on autumn nights;
All pleasures and all pains, remembering
The bough of summer and the winter branch.
These are the measures destined for her soul.   30

III

Jove in the clouds had his inhuman birth.[1]
No mother suckled him, no sweet land gave
Large-mannered motions to his mythy mind
He moved among us, as a muttering king,
Magnificent, would move among his hinds,°   farm servants
Until our blood, commingling, virginal,
With heaven, brought such requital to desire
The very hinds discerned it, in a star.
Shall our blood fail? Or shall it come to be
The blood of paradise? And shall the earth   40
Seem all of paradise that we shall know?
The sky will be much friendlier then than now,
A part of labor and a part of pain,
And next in glory to enduring love,
Not this dividing and indifferent blue.

IV

She says, "I am content when wakened birds,
Before they fly, test the reality
Of misty fields, by their sweet questionings;
But when the birds are gone, and their warm fields
Return no more, where, then, is paradise?"   50
There is not any haunt of prophecy,
Nor any old chimera[2] of the grave,
Neither the golden underground, nor isle
Melodious, where spirits gat them home,
Nor visionary south, nor cloudy palm

Sunday Morning
   [1] Jove is Jupiter, the principal god of the Romans, who, unlike Jesus, had an "inhuman birth."
   [2] A monster with a lion's head, a goat's body, and a serpent's tail. Here an emblem for the belief in other worlds described in the following lines.

Remote on heaven's hill, that has endured
As April's green endures; or will endure
Like her remembrance of awakened birds,
Or her desire for June and evening, tipped
By the consummation of the swallow's wings.   60

V

She says, "But in contentment I still feel
The need of some imperishable bliss."
Death is the mother of beauty; hence from her,
Alone, shall come fulfilment to our dreams
And our desires. Although she strews the leaves
Of sure obliteration on our paths,
The path sick sorrow took, the many paths
Where triumph rang its brassy phrase, or love
Whispered a little out of tenderness,
She makes the willow shiver in the sun   70
For maidens who were wont to sit and gaze
Upon the grass, relinquished to their feet.
She causes boys to pile new plums and pears
On disregarded plate. The maidens taste
And stray impassioned in the littering leaves.

VI

Is there no change of death in paradise?
Does ripe fruit never fall? Or do the boughs
Hang always heavy in that perfect sky,
Unchanging, yet so like our perishing earth,
With rivers like our own that seek for seas   80
They never find, the same receding shores
That never touch with inarticulate pang?
Why set the pear upon those river-banks
Or spice the shores with odors of the plum?
Alas, that they should wear our colors there,
The silken weavings of our afternoons,
And pick the strings of our insipid lutes!
Death is the mother of beauty, mystical,
Within whose burning bosom we devise
Our earthly mothers waiting, sleeplessly.   90

VII

Supple and turbulent, a ring of men
Shall chant in orgy on a summer morn
Their boisterous devotion to the sun,

Not as a god, but as a god might be,
Naked among them, like a savage source.
Their chant shall be a chant of paradise,
Out of their blood, returning to the sky;
And in their chant shall enter, voice by voice,
The windy lake wherein their lord delights,
The trees, like serafin, and echoing hills,   100
That choir among themselves long afterward.
They shall know well the heavenly fellowship
Of men that perish and of summer morn.
And whence they came and whither they shall go
The dew upon their feet shall manifest.

VIII

She hears, upon that water without sound,
A voice that cries, "The tomb in Palestine
Is not the porch of spirits lingering.
It is the grave of Jesus, where he lay."
We live in an old chaos of the sun,   110
Or old dependency of day and night,
Or island solitude, unsponsored, free,
Of that wide water, inescapable.
Deer walk upon our mountains, and the quail
Whistle about us their spontaneous cries;
Sweet berries ripen in the wilderness;
And, in the isolation of the sky,
At evening, casual flocks of pigeons make
Ambiguous undulations as they sink,
Downward to darkness, on extended wings.   120

QUESTIONS

1. In the opening stanza, the woman's enjoyment of a late Sunday morning breakfast in a relaxed and sensuous atmosphere is troubled by thoughts of what Sunday morning should mean to her. What are the thoughts that disturb her complacency? **2.** What does the speaker mean when he says, "Death is the mother of beauty" (ll. 63 and 88)? **3.** In stanza VI, what is the speaker's attitude toward the conventional Christian conception of paradise? **4.** Stanza VII presents the speaker's vision of an alternative religion. How does it differ from the paradise of stanza VI? **5.** In what ways does the cry of the voice in the final stanza (ll. 107–110) state the woman's dilemma? How do the lines about the pigeons at the end of the poem sum up the speaker's belief?

WRITING TOPIC

This poem is, in a sense, a commentary by the speaker on the woman's desire for truth and certainty more enduring than the physical world can provide. Is the speaker sympathetic to her quest? Explain.

If We Must Die

1922

CLAUDE McKAY   [1890–1948]

If we must die, let it not be like hogs
Hunted and penned in an inglorious spot,
While round us bark the mad and hungry dogs,
Making their mock at our accursèd lot.
If we must die, O let us nobly die,
So that our precious blood may not be shed
In vain; then even the monsters we defy
Shall be constrained to honor us though dead!
O kinsmen! we must meet the common foe!
Though far outnumbered let us show us brave,   10
And for their thousand blows deal one deathblow!
What though before us lies the open grave?
Like men we'll face the murderous, cowardly pack,
Pressed to the wall, dying, but fighting back!

the Cambridge ladies who live in furnished souls

1923

E. E. CUMMINGS   [1894–1962]

the Cambridge ladies who live in furnished souls
are unbeautiful and have comfortable minds
(also, with the church's protestant blessings
daughters, unscented shapeless spirited)
they believe in Christ and Longfellow, both dead,
are invariably interested in so many things—
at the present writing one still finds
delighted fingers knitting for the is it Poles?
perhaps. While permanent faces coyly bandy
scandal of Mrs. N and Professor D   10
. . . . the Cambridge ladies do not care, above
Cambridge if sometimes in its box of
sky lavender and cornerless, the
moon rattles like a fragment of angry candy

QUESTIONS

1. What images does the poet use to describe "the Cambridge ladies"? What do the images suggest? **2.** What is the effect of the interruption "is it" in line

8? **3.** In the final lines, the moon seems to protest against the superficiality of these women. What is the effect of comparing the moon to a fragment of candy?

WRITING TOPIC
Compare this poem with Emily Dickinson's "What Soft—Cherubic Creatures."

Harlem   1951

LANGSTON HUGHES [1902–1967]

What happens to a dream deferred?

    Does it dry up
    like a raisin in the sun?
    Or fester like a sore—
    And then run?
    Does it stink like rotten meat?
    Or crust and sugar over—
    like a syrupy sweet?

    Maybe it just sags
    like a heavy load.   10

    Or does it explode?

Same in Blues   1951

LANGSTON HUGHES [1902–1967]

I said to my baby,
Baby take it slow.
I can't, she said, I can't!
I got to go!

    There's a certain
    amount of traveling
    in a dream deferred.

Lulu said to Leonard,
I want a diamond ring.
Leonard said to Lulu,   10
You won't get a goddam thing!

A certain
amount of nothing
in a dream deferred.

Daddy, daddy, daddy,
All I want is you.
You can have me, baby—
but my lovin' days is through.

A certain
amount of impotence   20
in a dream deferred.

Three parties
On my party line—
But that third party,
Lord, ain't mine!

There's liable
to be confusion
in a dream deferred.

From river to river
Uptown and down,   30
There's liable to be confusion
when a dream gets kicked around.

The Unknown Citizen   1940

(To JS/07/M/378 This Marble Monument Is Erected
by the State)

W. H. AUDEN   [1907–1973]

He was found by the Bureau of Statistics to be
One against whom there was no official complaint,
And all the reports on his conduct agree
That, in the modern sense of an old-fashioned word, he was a saint,
For in everything he did he served the Greater Community.
Except for the War till the day he retired
He worked in a factory and never got fired,
But satisfied his employers, Fudge Motors Inc.
Yet he wasn't a scab or odd in his views,

For his Union reports that he paid his dues,   10
(Our report on his Union shows it was sound)
And our Social Psychology workers found
That he was popular with his mates and liked a drink.
The Press are convinced that he bought a paper every day
And that his reactions to advertisements were normal in every way.
Policies taken out in his name prove that he was fully insured,
And his Health-card shows he was once in hospital but left it cured.
Both Producers Research and High-Grade Living declare
He was fully sensible to the advantages of the Installment Plan
And had everything necessary to the Modern Man,   20
A phonograph, a radio, a car and a frigidaire.
Our researchers into Public Opinion are content
That he held the proper opinions for the time of year;
When there was peace, he was for peace; when there was war, he went.
He was married and added five children to the population,
Which our Eugenist says was the right number for a parent of his generation,
And our teachers report that he never interfered with their education.
Was he free? Was he happy? The question is absurd:
Had anything been wrong, we should certainly have heard.

From a Correct Address in a
Suburb of a Major City   1971

HELEN SORRELLS   [b. 1908]

She wears her middle age like a cowled
gown, sleeved in it, folded high
at the breast,

charming, proper at cocktails
but the inner one raging
and how to hide her,

how to keep her leashed, contain
the heat of her, the soaring cry
never yet loosed,

demanding a chance before the years devour her,   10
before the marrow of her fine long legs
congeals and she

settles forever for this street, this house,
her face set to the world
sweet, sweet

above the shocked, astonished
hunger.

Myth   1973

MURIEL RUKEYSER   [1913–1980]

Long afterward, Oedipus, old and blinded, walked the
roads.[1]   He smelled a familiar smell.   It was
the Sphinx.   Oedipus said, "I want to ask one question.
Why didn't I recognize my mother?"   "You gave the
wrong answer," said the Sphinx.   "But that was what
made everything possible," said Oedipus.   "No," she said.
"When I asked, What walks on four legs in the morning,
two at noon, and three in the evening, you answered,
Man.   You didn't say anything about woman."
"When you say Man," said Oedipus, "you include women   10
too. Everyone knows that."   She said, "That's what
you think."

The Conscientious Objector   1947

KARL SHAPIRO   [b. 1913]

The gates clanged and they walked you into jail
More tense than felons but relieved to find
The hostile world shut out, flags that dripped
From every mother's windowpane, obscene
The bloodlust sweating from the public heart,
The dog authority slavering at your throat.
A sense of quiet, of pulling down the blind
Possessed you. Punishment you felt was clean.

Myth

[1]Oedipus became King of Thebes when he solved the riddle of the Sphinx quoted in the poem.
He blinded himself when he discovered that he had married his own mother.

The decks, the catwalks, and the narrow light
Composed a ship. This was a mutinous crew   10
Troubling the captains for plain decencies,
A *Mayflower* brim with pilgrims headed out
To establish new theocracies to west,
A Noah's ark coasting the topmost seas
Ten miles above the sodomites and fish.
These inmates loved the only living doves.

Like all men hunted from the world you made
A good community, voyaging the storm
To no safe Plymouth or green Ararat;
Trouble or calm, the men with Bibles prayed,   20
The gaunt politicals construed our hate.
The opposite of all armies, you were best
Opposing uniformity and yourselves;
Prison and personality were your fate.

You suffered not so physically but knew
Maltreatment, hunger, ennui of the mind.
Well might the soldier kissing the hot beach
Erupting in his face damn all your kind.
Yet you who saved neither yourselves nor us
Are equally with those who shed the blood   30
The heroes of our cause. Your conscience is
What we come back to in the armistice.

QUESTIONS
1. Who is the speaker of this poem, and what are his assumptions about "good citizenship"? **2.** Why does the conscientious objector feel that punishment is clean (l. 8)? **3.** The prison is compared to the Mayflower and Noah's ark. Do you find the allusive comparisons between the prisoners and the occupants of the Mayflower and the ark effective? Explain. **4.** What, finally, are the differences between the man described here and Auden's unknown citizen? Is the conscientious objector "free"? "Happy"? Is he an unknown citizen?

Naming of Parts   1946

HENRY REED [b. 1914]

Today we have naming of parts. Yesterday,
We had daily cleaning. And tomorrow morning

We shall have what to do after firing. But today,
Today we have naming of parts. Japonica
Glistens like coral in all of the neighboring gardens,
        And today we have naming of parts.

This is the lower sling swivel. And this
Is the upper sling swivel, whose use you will see,
When you are given your slings. And this is the piling swivel,
Which in your case you have not got. The branches   10
Hold in the gardens their silent, eloquent gestures,
        Which in our case we have not got.

This is the safety-catch, which is always released
With an easy flick of the thumb. And please do not let me
See anyone using his finger. You can do it quite easy
If you have any strength in your thumb. The blossoms
Are fragile and motionless, never letting anyone see
        Any of them using their finger.

And this you can see is the bolt. The purpose of this
Is to open the breech, as you see. We can slide it   20
Rapidly backwards and forwards: we call this
Easing the spring. And rapidly backwards and forwards
The early bees are assaulting and fumbling the flowers:
        They call it easing the Spring.

They call it easing the Spring: it is perfectly easy
If you have any strength in your thumb: like the bolt,
And the breech, and the cocking-piece, and the point of balance,
Which in our case we have not got; and the almond-blossom
Silent in all of the gardens and the bees going backwards and forwards,
        For today we have naming of parts.   30

QUESTIONS
1. The poem has two speakers. Identify their speeches, and characterize the speakers. 2. The last line of each stanza repeats a phrase from within the stanza. What is the effect of the repetition?

WRITING TOPIC
This poem incorporates a subtle underlying sexuality. Trace the language that generates it. What function does that sexuality serve in the poem?

from

The Children of the Poor   (1949)

GWENDOLYN BROOKS   [b. 1917]

4

First fight. Then fiddle. Ply the slipping string
With feathery sorcery; muzzle the note
With hurting love, the music that they wrote
Bewitch, bewilder. Qualify to sing
Threadwise. Devise no salt, no hempen thing
For the dear instrument to bear. Devote
The bow to silks and honey. Be remote
A while from malice and from murdering.
But first to arms, to armor. Carry hate
In front of you and harmony behind.   10
Be deaf to music and to beauty blind.
Win war. Rise bloody, maybe not too late
For having first to civilize a space
Wherein to play your violin with grace.

11

Life for my child is simple, and is good.
He knows his wish. Yes, but that is not all.
Because I know mine too.
And we both want joy of undeep and unabiding things,
Like kicking over a chair or throwing blocks out of a window
Or tipping over an icebox pan
Or snatching down curtains or fingering an electric outlet
Or a journey or a friend or an illegal kiss.
No. There is more to it than that.
It is that he has never been afraid.   10
Rather, he reaches out and lo the chair falls with a beautiful crash,
And the blocks fall, down on the people's heads,
And the water comes slooshing sloppily out across the floor.
And so forth.
Not that success, for him, is sure, infallible.
But never has he been afraid to reach.
His lesions are legion.
But reaching is his rule.

QUESTIONS

1. In sonnet 4, the poet advises the children: "First fight, Then fiddle." The meaning of "fight" is clear. What does "fiddle" symbolize?   **2.** Why does the poet advocate violence? **3.** Is the child described in poem 11 different from the children addressed in sonnet 4? **4.** Explain the meaning of line 4 in poem 11. **5.** What does "reaching" in the last line mean?

In Goya's Greatest Scenes 1958

LAWRENCE FERLINGHETTI [b. 1919]

In Goya's greatest scenes[1] we seem to see
       the people of the world
  exactly at the moment when
    they first attained the title of
        'suffering humanity'
   They writhe upon the page
      in a veritable rage
        of adversity
   Heaped up
     groaning with babies and bayonets   10
        under cement skies
   in an abstract landscape of blasted trees
    bent statues bats wings and beaks
     slippery gibbets
   cadavers and carnivorous cocks
  and all the final hollering monsters
   of the
     'imagination of disaster'
  they are so bloody real
     it is as if they really still existed   20

  And they do

    Only the landscape is changed

They still are ranged along the roads
  plagued by legionaires
     false windmills and demented roosters

They are the same people
     only further from home
  on freeways fifty lanes wide
    on a concrete continent

In Goya's Greatest Scenes
 [1] Francisco Jose de Goya (1764–1828), famous Spanish artist, celebrated for his representations of "suffering humanity."

spaced with bland billboards   30
illustrating imbecile illusions of happiness

The scene shows fewer tumbrils²
                        but more maimed citizens
                                        in painted cars
            and they have strange license plates
        and engines
                    that devour America

QUESTIONS
1. To whom does the word "they" refer in line 26?   **2.** What is responsible for the "suffering" of modern American "humanity"?

Women   1970

MAY SWENSON   [b. 1919]

Women   Or they
  should be   should be
    pedestals   little horses
      moving   those wooden
        pedestals   sweet
          moving   oldfashioned
            to the   painted
              motions   rocking
                of men   horses

            the gladdest things in the toyroom

          The   feelingly
          pegs   and then
          of their   unfeelingly
          ears   To be
          so familiar   joyfully
          and dear   ridden
          to the trusting   rockingly
        fists   ridden until
    To be chafed   the restored

---

² Carts in which prisoners were conducted to the place of execution.

egos dismount and the legs stride away

immobile	willing
sweetlipped	to be set
sturdy	into motion
and smiling	Women
women	should be
should always	pedestals
be waiting	to men

Poetry of Departures   1955

PHILIP LARKIN   [1922–1985]

Sometimes you hear, fifth-hand,
As epitaph:
He chucked up everything
And just cleared off,
And always the voice will sound
Certain you approve
This audacious, purifying,
Elemental move.

And they are right, I think.
We all hate home   10
And having to be there:
I detest my room,
Its specially-chosen junk,
The good books, the good bed,
And my life, in perfect order:
So to hear it said

He walked out on the whole crowd
Leaves me flushed and stirred,
Like *Then she undid her dress*
Or *Take that you bastard;*   20
Surely I can, if he did?
And that helps me stay
Sober and industrious.
But I'd go today,

Yes, swagger the nut-strewn roads,
Crouch in the fo'c'sle

Stubbly with goodness, if
It weren't so artificial,
Such a deliberate step backwards
To create an object: 30
Books; china; a life
Reprehensibly perfect.

QUESTIONS

1. What motivates the kind of person who "chucked up everything and just cleared off"? Why might such an action be characterized as "purifying" and "elemental"?
2. In what sense is the simile of lines 16–20 appropriate? What function does it serve?   **3.** Why does the poet conclude that departing is "artificial" (l.28) and that perfection is "reprehensible" (l.32)?

Formal Application   (1963)

DONALD W. BAKER   [b. 1923]

"The poets apparently want to rejoin the human race."   TIME

I shall begin by learning to throw
the knife, first at trees, until it sticks
in the trunk and quivers every time;

next from a chair, using only wrist
and fingers, at a thing on the ground,
a fresh ant hill or a fallen leaf;

then at a moving object, perhaps
a pieplate swinging on twine, until
I pot it at least twice in three tries.

Meanwhile, I shall be teaching the birds   10
that the skinny fellow in sneakers
is a source of suet and bread crumbs,

first putting them on a shingle nailed
to a pine tree, next scattering them
on the needles, closer and closer

to my seat, until the proper bird,
a towhee, I think, in black and rust
and gray, takes tossed crumbs six feet away.

Finally, I shall coordinate
conditioned reflex and functional   20
form and qualify as Modern Man.

You see the splash of blood and feathers
and the blade pinning it to the tree?
It's called an "Audubon Crucifix."

The phrase has pleasing (even pious)
connotations, like *Arbeit Macht Frei*,
"Molotov Cocktail," and *Enola Gay*.[1]

QUESTIONS
1. What did *Time* mean by the line Baker uses as an epigraph to this poem? How, for example, are poets not members of the human race? What does the title of the poem mean? **2.** In what sense does "Audubon Crucifix" have "pleasing (even pious) connotations"? What are the pleasing connotations of the expressions in the last two lines? According to this poem, what are the attributes necessary to join the human race?

Hard Rock Returns to Prison from the Hospital for the Criminal Insane   1968

ETHERIDGE KNIGHT {b. 1933}

Hard Rock was "known not to take no shit
From nobody," and he had the scars to prove it:
Split purple lips, lumped ears, welts above
His yellow eyes, and one long scar that cut
Across his temple and plowed through a thick
Canopy of kinky hair.

The WORD was that Hard Rock wasn't a mean nigger
Anymore, that the doctors had bored a hole in his head,
Cut out part of his brain, and shot electricity
Through the rest. When they brought Hard Rock back,   10

Formal Application

[1]*Arbeit Macht Frei*, the motto of the German Nazi party, means "labor liberates." A Molotov cocktail is a homemade hand grenade named after Vyacheslav M. Molotov, the foreign minister of Russia during the reign of Joseph Stalin. *Enola Gay* was the name of the United States plane that dropped the atomic bomb on Hiroshima in 1945.

Handcuffed and chained, he was turned loose,
Like a freshly gelded stallion, to try his new status.
And we all waited and watched, like Indians at a corral,
To see if the WORD was true.

As we waited we wrapped ourselves in the cloak
Of his exploits: "Man, the last time, it took eight
Screws to put him in the Hole." "Yeah, remember when he
Smacked the captain with his dinner tray?" "He set
The record for time in the Hole—67 straight days!"
"Ol Hard Rock! man, that's one crazy nigger."   20
And then the jewel of a myth that Hard Rock had once bit
A screw on the thumb and poisoned him with syphilitic spit.

The testing came, to see if Hard Rock was really tame.
A hillbilly called him a black son of a bitch
And didn't lose his teeth, a screw who knew Hard Rock
From before shook him down and barked in his face.
And Hard Rock did *nothing*. Just grinned and looked silly,
His eyes empty like knot holes in a fence.

And even after we discovered that it took Hard Rock
Exactly 3 minutes to tell you his first name,   30
We told ourselves that he had just wised up,
Was being cool; but we could not fool ourselves for long,
And we turned away, our eyes on the ground. Crushed.

He had been our Destroyer, the doer of things
We dreamed of doing but could not bring ourselves to do,
The fears of years, like a biting whip,
Had cut grooves too deeply across our backs.

Confession to Settle a Curse   1972

ROSMARIE WALDROP   [b. 1935]

You don't
know
who I am
because
you don't know
my mother
she's always been an exemplary mother
told me so herself
there were reasons she

had to lock   10
everything that could be locked
there's much can be
locked
in a good German household crowded
with wardrobes dressers sideboards
bookcases cupboards chests bureaus
desks trunks caskets coffers all with lock
and key
and locked
it was lots of trouble   20
for her
just carry that enormous key ring
be bothered all the time
I wanted scissors stationery
my winter coat and she had to unlock
the drawer get it out and lock
all up again
me she reproached for lacking
confidence not being open
I have a mother I can tell everything   30
she told me so
I've
been bound
made fast
locked
by the key witch
but a small
winner
I'm not
in turn locking   40
a child
in my arms.

Dreams   1968

NIKKI GIOVANNI   [b. 1943]

i used to dream militant
dreams of taking
over america to show
these white folks how it should be
done
i used to dream radical dreams
of blowing everyone away with my perceptive powers

of correct analysis
i even used to think i'd be the one
to stop the riot and negotiate the peace   10
then i awoke and dug
that if i dreamed natural
dreams of being a natural
woman doing what a woman
does when she's natural
i would have a revolution

The Colonel   1981

CAROLYN FORCHÉ   [b. 1950]

What you have heard is true. I was in his house. His wife carried a tray of coffee and sugar. His daughter filed her nails, his son went out for the night. There were daily papers, pet dogs, a pistol on the cushion beside him. The moon swung bare on its black cord over the house. On the television was a cop show. It was in English. Broken bottles were embedded in the walls round the house to scoop the kneecaps from a man's legs or cut his hands to lace. On the windows there were gratings like those in liquor stores. We had dinner, rack of lamb, good wine, a gold bell was on the table for calling the maid. The maid brought green mangoes, salt, a type of bread. I was asked how I enjoyed the country. There was a brief commercial in Spanish. His wife took everything away. There was some talk then of how difficult it had become to govern. The parrot said hello on the terrace. The colonel told it to shut up, and pushed himself from the table. My friend said to me with his eyes: say nothing. The colonel returned with a sack used to bring groceries home. He spilled many human ears on the table. They were like dried peach halves. There is no other way to say this. He took one of them in his hands, shook it in our faces, dropped it into a water glass. It came alive there. I am tired of fooling around he said. As for the rights of anyone, tell your people they can go fuck themselves. He swept the ears to the floor with his arm and held the last of his wine in the air. Something for your poetry, no? he said. Some of the ears on the floor caught this scrap of his voice. Some of the ears on the floor were pressed to the ground.

QUESTIONS
1.   What is the occasion of this poem? Where is it set? How would you characterize the colonel's family?   **2.**   "There was some talk of how difficult it had become to govern." Can you suggest why it had become difficult to govern? How does the colonel respond to these difficulties?   **3.**   What does the last sentence suggest?

WRITING TOPIC
This piece is printed as if it were prose. Does it have any of the formal characteristics of a poem?

CONFORMITY
AND
REBELLION

Self-Portrait, c. 1900, by Gwen John.

DRAMA

A Doll's House*

(1879)

HENRIK IBSEN [1828–1906]

CHARACTERS

Torvald Helmer, a lawyer
Nora, his wife
Dr. Rank
Mrs. Linde
Krogstad

The Helmers' three small children
Anne-Marie, the children's nurse
A Housemaid
A Porter

SCENE. *The Helmers' living room.*

Act I

A pleasant, tastefully but not expensively furnished, living room. A door on the rear wall, right, leads to the front hall, another door, left, to Helmer's study. Between the two doors a piano. A third door in the middle of the left wall; further front a window. Near the window a round table and a small couch. Towards the rear of the right wall a fourth door; further front a tile stove with a rocking chair and a couple of armchairs in front of it. Between the stove and the door a small table. Copperplate etchings on the walls. A whatnot with porcelain figurines and other small objects. A small bookcase with de luxe editions. A rug on the floor; fire in the stove. Winter day.

The doorbell rings, then the sound of the front door opening. Nora, dressed for outdoors, enters, humming cheerfully. She carries several packages, which she puts down on the table, right. She leaves the door to the front hall open; there a Porter is seen holding a Christmas tree and a basket. He gives them to the Maid who has let them in.

Nora. Be sure to hide the Christmas tree, Helene. The children mustn't see it before tonight when we've trimmed it. (*Opens her purse; to the Porter.*) How much?

---

* A new translation by Otto Reinert.

Porter.   Fifty øre.

Nora.   Here's a crown. No, keep the change. *(The Porter thanks her, leaves. Nora closes the door. She keeps laughing quietly to herself as she takes off her coat, etc. She takes a bag of macaroons from her pocket and eats a couple. She walks cautiously over to the door to the study and listens.)* Yes, he's home. *(Resumes her humming, walks over to the table, right.)*

Helmer *(in his study).*   Is that my little lark twittering out there?

Nora *(opening some packages).*   That's right.

Helmer.   My squirrel bustling about?

Nora.   Yes.

Helmer.   When did squirrel come home?

Nora.   Just now. *(Puts the bag of macaroons back in her pocket, wipes her mouth.)* Come out here, Torvald. I want to show you what I've bought.

Helmer.   I'm busy! *(After a little while he opens the door and looks in, pen in hand.)* Bought, eh? All that? So little wastrel has been throwing money around again?

Nora.   Oh but Torvald, this Christmas we can be a little extravagant, can't we? It's the first Christmas we don't have to scrimp.

Helmer.   I don't know about that. We certainly don't have money to waste.

Nora.   Yes, Torvald, we do. A little, anyway. Just a tiny little bit? Now that you're going to get that big salary and make lots and lots of money.

Helmer.   Starting at New Year's, yes. But payday isn't till the end of the quarter.

Nora.   That doesn't matter. We can always borrow.

Helmer.   Nora! *(Goes over to her and playfully pulls her ear.)* There you go being irresponsible again. Suppose I borrowed a thousand crowns today and you spent it all for Christmas and on New Year's Eve a tile hit me in the head and laid me out cold.

Nora *(putting her hand over his mouth).*   I won't have you say such horrid things.

Helmer.   But suppose it happened. Then what?

Nora.   If it did, I wouldn't care whether we owed money or not.

Helmer.   But what about the people I had borrowed from?

Nora.   Who cares about them! They are strangers.

Helmer.   Nora, Nora, you *are* a woman! No, really! You know how I feel about that. No debts! A home in debt isn't a free home, and if it isn't free it isn't beautiful. We've managed nicely so far, you and I, and that's the way we'll go on. It won't be for much longer.

Nora *(walks over toward the stove).*   All right, Torvald. Whatever you say.

Helmer *(follows her).*   Come, come, my little songbird mustn't droop her wings. What's this? Can't have a pouty squirrel in the house, you know. *(Takes out his wallet.)* Nora, what do you think I have here?

Nora *(turns around quickly).*   Money!

Helmer.   Here. *(Gives her some bills.)* Don't you think I know Christmas is expensive?

Nora *(counting)*.   Ten—twenty—thirty—forty. Thank you, thank you, Torvald. This helps a lot.

Helmer.   I certainly hope so.

Nora.   It does, it does. But I want to show you what I got. It was cheap, too. Look. New clothes for Ivar. And a sword. And a horse and trumpet for Bob. And a doll and a little bed for Emmy. It isn't any good, but it wouldn't last, anyway. And here's some dress material and scarves for the maids. I feel bad about old Anne-Marie, though. She really should be getting much more.

Helmer.   And what's in here?

Nora *(cries)*.   Not till tonight!

Helmer.   I see. But now what does my little prodigal have in mind for herself?

Nora.   Oh, nothing. I really don't care.

Helmer.   Of course you do. Tell me what you'd like. Within reason.

Nora.   Oh, I don't know. Really, I don't. The only thing—

Helmer.   Well?

Nora *(fiddling with his buttons, without looking at him)*.   If you really want to give me something, you might—you could—

Helmer.   All right, let's have it.

Nora *(quickly)*.   Some money, Torvald. Just as much as you think you can spare. Then I'll buy myself something one of these days.

Helmer.   No, really Nora—

Nora.   Oh yes, please, Torvald. Please? I'll wrap the money in pretty gold paper and hang it on the tree. Won't that be nice?

Helmer.   What's the name for little birds that are always spending money?

Nora.   Wastrels, I know. But please let's do it my way, Torvald. Then I'll have time to decide what I need most. Now that's sensible, isn't it?

Helmer *(smiling)*.   Oh, very sensible. That is, if you really bought yourself something you could use. But it all disappears in the household expenses or you buy things you don't need. And then you come back to me for more.

Nora.   Oh, but Torvald—

Helmer.   That's the truth, dear little Nora, and you know it. *(Puts his arm around her.)* My wastrel is a little sweetheart, but she *does* go through an awful lot of money awfully fast. You've no idea how expensive it is for a man to keep a wastrel.

Nora.   That's not fair, Torvald. I really save all I can.

Helmer *(laughs)*.   Oh, I believe that. All you can. Meaning, exactly nothing!

Nora *(hums, smiles mysteriously)*.   You don't know all the things we songbirds and squirrels need money for, Torvald.

Helmer.   You know, you're funny. Just like your father. You're always looking for ways to get money, but as soon as you do it runs through your fingers and you can never say what you spent it for. Well, I guess I'll just have to take you the way you are. It's in your blood. Yes, that sort of thing is hereditary, Nora.

Nora.   In that case, I wish I had inherited many of Daddy's qualities.

Helmer.   And I don't want you any different from just what you are—my own sweet little songbird. Hey!—I think I just noticed something. Aren't you looking—what's the word?—a little—sly—?

Nora.   I am?

Helmer.   You definitely are. Look at me.

Nora (*looks at him*).   Well?

Helmer (*wagging a finger*).   Little sweet-tooth hasn't by any chance been on a rampage today, has she?

Nora.   Of course not. Whatever makes you think that?

Helmer.   A little detour by the pastryshop maybe?

Nora.   No, I assure you, Torvald—

Helmer.   Nibbled a little jam?

Nora.   Certainly not!

Helmer.   Munched a macaroon or two?

Nora.   No, really, Torvald, I honestly—

Helmer.   All right. Of course I was only joking.

Nora (*walks toward the table, right*).   You know I wouldn't do anything to displease you.

Helmer.   I know. And I have your promise. (*Over to her.*) All right, keep your little Christmas secrets to yourself, Nora darling. They'll all come out tonight, I suppose, when we light the tree.

Nora.   Did you remember to invite Rank?

Helmer.   No, but there's no need to. He knows he'll have dinner with us. Anyway, I'll see him later this morning. I'll ask him then. I did order some good wine. Oh Nora, you've no idea how much I'm looking forward to tonight!

Nora.   Me, too. And the children Torvald! They'll have such a good time!

Helmer.   You know, it *is* nice to have a good, safe job and a comfortable income. Feels good just thinking about it. Don't you agree?

Nora.   Oh, it's wonderful!

Helmer.   Remember last Christmas? For three whole weeks you shut yourself up every evening till long after midnight making ornaments for the Christmas tree and I don't know what else. Some big surprise for all of us, anyway. I'll be damned if I've ever been so bored in my whole life!

Nora.   I wasn't bored at all!

Helmer (*smiling*).   But you've got to admit you didn't have much to show for it in the end.

Nora.   Oh, don't tease me again about that! Could I help it that the cat got in and tore up everything?

Helmer.   Of course you couldn't, my poor little Nora. You just wanted to please the rest of us, and that's the important thing. But I *am* glad the hard times are behind us. Aren't you?

Nora.   Oh yes. I think it's just wonderful.

Helmer.   This year, I won't be bored and lonely. And you won't have to strain your dear eyes and your delicate little hands—

Nora *(claps her hands)*.   No I won't, will I Torvald? Oh, how wonderful, how lovely, to hear you say that! *(Puts her arm under his.)* Let me tell you how I think we should arrange things, Torvald. Soon as Christmas is over—*(The doorbell rings.)* Someone's at the door. *(Straightens things up a bit.)* A caller, I suppose. Bother!

Helmer.   Remember, I'm not home for visitors.

The Maid *(in the door to the front hall)*.   Ma'am, there's a lady here—

Nora.   All right. Ask her to come in.

The Maid *(to Helmer)*.   And the Doctor just arrived.

Helmer.   Is he in the study?

The Maid.   Yes, sir.

Helmer exits into his study. The Maid shows Mrs. Linde in and closes the door behind her as she leaves. Mrs. Linde is in travel dress.

Mrs. Linde *(timid and a little hesitant)*.   Good morning, Nora.

Nora *(uncertainly)*.   Good morning.

Mrs. Linde.   I don't believe you know who I am.

Nora.   No—I'm not sure—Though I know I should—Of course! Kristine! It's you!

Mrs. Linde.   Yes, it's me.

Nora.   And I didn't even recognize you! I had no idea! *(In a lower voice.)* You've changed, Kristine.

Mrs. Linde.   I'm sure I have. It's been nine or ten long years.

Nora.   Has it really been that long? Yes, you're right. I've been so happy these last eight years. And now you're here. Such a long trip in the middle of winter. How brave!

Mrs. Linde.   I got in on the steamer this morning.

Nora.   To have some fun over the holidays, of course. That's lovely. For we are going to have fun. But take off your coat! You aren't cold, are you? *(Helps her.)* There, now! Let's sit down here by the fire and just relax and talk. No, you sit there. I want the rocking chair. *(Takes her hands.)* And now you've got your old face back. It was just for a minute, right at first—Though you are a little more pale, Kristine. And maybe a little thinner.

Mrs. Linde.   And much, much older, Nora.

Nora.   Maybe a little older. Just a teeny-weeny bit, not much. *(Interrupts herself, serious.)* Oh, but how thoughtless of me, chatting away like this! Sweet, good Kristine, can you forgive me?

Mrs. Linde.   Forgive you what, Nora?

Nora *(in a low voice)*.   You poor dear, you lost your husband, didn't you?

Mrs. Linde.   Three years ago, yes.

Nora.   I know. I saw it in the paper. Oh please believe me, Kristine. I really meant to write you, but I never got around to it. Something was always coming up.

Mrs. Linde.   Of course, Nora. I understand.

Nora. No, that wasn't very nice of me. You poor thing, all you must have been through. And he didn't leave you much, either, did he?

Mrs. Linde. No.

Nora. And no children?

Mrs. Linde. No.

Nora. Nothing at all, in other words?

Mrs. Linde. Not so much as a sense of loss—a grief to live on—

Nora (incredulous). But Kristine, how can that *be*?

Mrs. Linde (with a sad smile, strokes Nora's hair). That's the way it sometimes is, Nora.

Nora. All alone. How awful for you. I have three darling children. You can't see them right now, though; they're out with their nurse. But now you must tell me everything—

Mrs. Linde. No, no; I'd rather listen to you.

Nora. No, you begin. Today I won't be selfish. Today I'll think only of you. Except there's one thing I've just got to tell you first. Something marvelous that's happened to us just these last few days. You haven't heard, have you?

Mrs. Linde. No; tell me.

Nora. Just think. My husband's been made manager of the Mutual Bank.

Mrs. Linde. Your husband—! Oh, I'm so glad!

Nora. Yes, isn't that great? You see, private law practice is so uncertain, especially when you won't have anything to do with cases that aren't—you know—quite nice. And of course Torvald won't do that and I quite agree with him. Oh, you've no idea how delighted we are! He takes over at New Year's, and he'll be getting a big salary and all sorts of extras. From now on we'll be able to live in quite a different way—exactly as we like. Oh, Kristine! I feel so carefree and happy! It's lovely to have lots and lots of money and not have to worry about a thing! Don't you agree?

Mrs. Linde. It would be nice to have enough at any rate.

Nora. No, I don't mean just enough. I mean lots and lots!

Mrs. Linde (smiles). Nora, Nora, when are you going to be sensible? In school you spent a great deal of money.

Nora (quietly laughing). Yes, and Torvald says I still do. (Raises her finger at Mrs. Linde.) But "Nora, Nora" isn't so crazy as you all think. Believe me, we've had nothing to be extravagant with. We've both had to work.

Mrs. Linde. You too?

Nora. Yes. Oh, it's been little things, mostly—sewing, crocheting, embroidery—that sort of thing. (Casually.) And other things too. You know, of course, that Torvald left government service when we got married? There was no chance of promotion in his department, and of course he had to make more money than he had been making. So for the first few years he worked altogether too hard. He had to take jobs on the side and work night and day. It turned out to be too much for him. He became seriously ill. The doctors told him he needed to go south.

Mrs. Linde. That's right; you spent a year in Italy, didn't you?

Nora.   Yes, we did. But you won't believe how hard it was to get away. Ivar had just been born. But of course we had to go. Oh, it was a wonderful trip. And it saved Torvald's life. But it took a lot of money, Kristine.

Mrs. Linde.   I'm sure it did.

Nora.   Twelve hundred specie dollars. Four thousand eight hundred crowns. That's a lot of money.

Mrs. Linde.   Yes. So it's lucky you have it when something like that happens.

Nora.   Well, actually we got the money from Daddy.

Mrs. Linde.   I see. That was about the time your father died, I believe.

Nora.   Yes, just about then. And I couldn't even go and take care of him. I was expecting little Ivar any day. And I had poor Torvald to look after, desperately sick and all. My dear, good Daddy! I never saw him again, Kristine. That's the saddest thing that's happened to me since I got married.

Mrs. Linde.   I know you were very fond of him. But then you went to Italy?

Nora.   Yes, for now we had the money, and the doctors urged us to go. So we left about a month later.

Mrs. Linde.   And when you came back your husband was well again?

Nora.   Healthy as a horse!

Mrs. Linde.   But—the doctor?

Nora.   What do you mean?

Mrs. Linde.   I thought the maid said it was the doctor, that gentleman who came the same time I did.

Nora.   Oh, that's Dr. Rank. He doesn't come as a doctor. He's our closest friend. He looks in at least once every day. No, Torvald hasn't been sick once since then. And the children are strong and healthy, too, and so am I. *(Jumps up and claps her hands.)* Oh God, Kristine! Isn't it wonderful to be alive and happy! Isn't it just lovely!—But now I'm being mean again, talking only about myself and my things. *(Sits down on a footstool close to Mrs. Linde and puts her arms on her lap.)* Please don't be angry with me! Tell me, is it really true that you didn't care for your husband? Then why did you marry him?

Mrs. Linde.   Mother was still alive then, but she was bedridden and helpless. And I had my two younger brothers to look after. I didn't think I had the right to turn him down.

Nora.   No, I suppose not. So he had money then?

Mrs. Linde.   He was quite well off, I think. But it was an uncertain business, Nora. When he died, the whole thing collapsed and there was nothing left.

Nora.   And then—?

Mrs. Linde.   Well, I had to manage as best I could. With a little store and a little school and anything else I could think of. The last three years have been one long work day for me, Nora, without any rest. But now it's over. My poor mother doesn't need me any more. She's passed away. And the boys are on their own too. They've both got jobs and support themselves.

Nora.   What a relief for you—

Mrs. Linde.   No, not relief. Just a great emptiness. Nobody to live for any more. *(Gets up restlessly.)* That's why I couldn't stand it any longer in that little hole. Here in town it has to be easier to find something to keep me busy and occupy my thoughts. With a little luck I should be able to find a permanent job, something in an office—

Nora.   Oh but Kristine, that's exhausting work, and you look worn out already. It would be much better for you to go to a resort.

Mrs. Linde (*walks over to the window*).   I don't have a Daddy who can give me the money, Nora.

Nora (*getting up*).   Oh, don't be angry with me.

Mrs. Linde (*over to her*).   Dear Nora, don't *you* be angry with *me*. That's the worst thing about my kind of situation: you become so bitter. You've nobody to work for, and yet you have to look out for yourself, somehow. You've got to keep on living, and so you become selfish. Do you know—when you told me about your husband's new position I was delighted not so much for your sake as for my own.

Nora.   Why was that? Oh, I see. You think maybe Torvald can give you a job?

Mrs. Linde.   That's what I had in mind.

Nora.   And he will too, Kristine. Just leave it to me. I'll be ever so subtle about it. I'll think of something nice to tell him, something he'll like. Oh I so much want to help you.

Mrs. Linde.   That's very good of you, Nora—making an effort like that for me. Especially since you've known so little trouble and hardship in your own life.

Nora.   I—?—have known so little—?

Mrs. Linde (*smiling*).   Oh well, a little sewing or whatever it was. You're still a child, Nora.

Nora (*with a toss of her head, walks away*).   You shouldn't sound so superior.

Mrs. Linde.   I shouldn't?

Nora.   You're just like all the others. None of you think I'm good for anything really serious.

Mrs. Linde.   Well, now—

Nora.   That I've never been through anything difficult.

Mrs. Linde.   But Nora! You just told me all your troubles!

Nora.   That's nothing! (*Lowers her voice.*) I haven't told you about *it*.

Mrs. Linde.   It? What's that? What do you mean?

Nora.   You patronize me, Kristine, and that's not fair. You're proud that you worked so long and so hard for your mother.

Mrs. Linde.   I don't think I patronize anyone. But it *is* true that I'm both proud and happy that I could make mother's last years comparatively easy.

Nora.   And you're proud of all you did for your brothers.

Mrs. Linde.   I think I have the right to be.

Nora.   And so do I. But now I want to tell you something, Kristine. I have something to be proud and happy about too.

Mrs. Linde.   I don't doubt that for a moment. But what exactly do you mean?

Nora.   Not so loud! Torvald mustn't hear—not for anything in the world. Nobody must know about this, Kristine. Nobody but you.

Mrs. Linde. But what is it?

Nora. Come here. *(Pulls her down on the couch beside her.)* You see, I *do* have something to be proud and happy about. I've saved Torvald's life.

Mrs. Linde. Saved—? How do you mean—"saved"?

Nora. I told you about our trip to Italy. Torvald would have died if he hadn't gone.

Mrs. Linde. I understand that. And so your father gave you the money you needed.

Nora *(smiles).* Yes, that's what Torvald and all the others think. But—

Mrs. Linde. But what?

Nora. Daddy didn't give us a penny. *I* raised that money.

Mrs. Linde. *You* did? That whole big amount?

Nora. Twelve hundred specie dollars. Four thousand eight hundred crowns. *Now* what do you say?

Mrs. Linde. But Nora, how could you? Did you win in the state lottery?

Nora *(contemptuously).* State lottery! *(Snorts.)* What is so great about that?

Mrs. Linde. Where did it come from then?

Nora *(humming and smiling, enjoying her secret).* Hmmm. Tra-la-la-la-la!

Mrs. Linde. You certainly couldn't have borrowed it.

Nora. Oh? And why not?

Mrs. Linde. A wife can't borrow money without her husband's consent.

Nora *(with a toss of her head).* Oh, I don't know—take a wife with a little bit of a head for business—a wife who knows how to manage things—

Mrs. Linde. But Nora, I don't understand at all—

Nora. You don't have to. I didn't say I borrowed the money, did I? I could have gotten it some other way. *(Leans back.)* An admirer may have given it to me. When you're as tolerably goodlooking as I am—

Mrs. Linde. Oh, you're crazy.

Nora. I think you're dying from curiosity, Kristine.

Mrs. Linde. I'm beginning to think you've done something very foolish, Nora.

Nora *(sits up).* Is it foolish to save your husband's life?

Mrs. Linde. I say it's foolish to act behind his back.

Nora. But don't you see: he couldn't be told! You're missing the whole point, Kristine. We couldn't even let him know how seriously ill he was. The doctors came to *me* and told me his life was in danger, that nothing could save him but a stay in the south. Don't you think I tried to work on him? I told him how lovely it would be if I could go abroad like other young wives. I cried and begged. I said he'd better remember what condition I was in, that he had to be nice to me and do what I wanted. I even hinted he could borrow the money. But that almost made him angry with me. He told me I was being irresponsible and that it was his duty as my husband not to give in to my moods and whims—I think that's what he called it. All right, I said to myself, you've got to be saved somehow, and so I found a way—

Mrs. Linde. And your husband never learned from your father that the money didn't come from him?

Nora.   Never. Daddy died that same week. I thought of telling him all about it and ask him not to say anything. But since he was so sick—It turned out I didn't have to—

Mrs. Linde.   And you've never told your husband?

Nora.   Of course not! Good heavens, how could I? He, with his strict principles! Besides, you know how men are. Torvald would find it embarrassing and humiliating to learn that he owed me anything. It would upset our whole relationship. Our happy, beautiful home would no longer be what it is.

Mrs. Linde.   Aren't you ever going to tell him?

Nora *(reflectively, half smiling).*   Yes—one day, maybe. Many, many years from now, when I'm no longer young and pretty. Don't laugh! I mean when Torvald no longer feels about me the way he does now, when he no longer thinks it's fun when I dance for him and put on costumes and recite for him. Then it will be good to have something in reserve—*(Interrupts herself.)* Oh, I'm just being silly! That day will never come.—Well, now, Kristine, what do you think of my great secret? Don't you think I'm good for something too?—By the way, you wouldn't believe all the worry I've had because of it. It's been very hard to meet my obligations on schedule. You see, in business there's something called quarterly interest and something called installments on the principal, and those are terribly hard to come up with. I've had to save a little here and a little there, whenever I could. I couldn't use much of the housekeeping money, for Torvald has to eat well. And I couldn't use what I got for clothes for the children. They have to look nice, and I didn't think it would be right to spend less than I got—the sweet little things!

Mrs. Linde.   Poor Nora! So you had to take it from your own allowance!

Nora.   Yes, of course. After all, it was my affair. Every time Torvald gave me money for a new dress and things like that, I never used more than half of it. I always bought the cheapest, simplest things for myself. Thank God, everything looks good on me, so Torvald never noticed. But it was hard many times, Kristine, for it's fun to have pretty clothes. Don't you think?

Mrs. Linde.   Certainly.

Nora.   Anyway, I had other ways of making money too. Last winter I was lucky enough to get some copying work. So I locked the door and sat up writing every night till quite late. God! I often got so tired—! But it was great fun, too, working and making money. It was almost like being a man.

Mrs. Linde.   But how much have you been able to pay off this way?

Nora.   I couldn't tell you exactly. You see, it's very difficult to keep track of business like that. All I know is I have been paying off as much as I've been able to scrape together. Many times I just didn't know what to do. *(Smiles.)* Then I used to imagine a rich old gentleman had fallen in love with me—

Mrs. Linde.   What! What old gentleman?

Nora.   Phooey! And now he was dead and they were reading his will, and there it said in big letters, "All my money is to be paid in cash immediately to the charming Mrs. Nora Helmer."

Mrs. Linde.   But dearest Nora—who *was* this old gentleman?

Nora.   For heaven's sake, Kristine, don't you see? There *was* no old gentleman.

He was just somebody I made up when I couldn't think of any way to raise the money. But never mind him. The old bore can be anyone he likes to for all I care. I have no use for him or his last will, for now I don't have a single worry in the world. *(Jumps up.)* Dear God, what a lovely thought this is! To be able to play and have fun with the children, to have everything nice and pretty in the house, just the way Torvald likes it! Not a care! And soon spring will be here, and the air will be blue and high. Maybe we can travel again. Maybe I'll see the ocean again! Oh, yes, yes!—it's wonderful to be alive and happy!

The doorbell rings.

Mrs. Linde *(getting up).*   There's the doorbell. Maybe I better be going.
Nora.   No, please stay. I'm sure it's just someone for Torvald—
The Maid *(in the hall door).*   Excuse me, ma'am. There's a gentleman here who'd like to see Mr. Helmer.
Nora.   You mean the bank manager.
The Maid.   Sorry, ma'am; the bank manager. But I didn't know—since the Doctor is with him—
Nora.   Who is the gentleman?
Krogstad *(appearing in the door).*   It's just me, Mrs. Helmer.

Mrs. Linde starts, looks, turns away toward the window.

Nora *(takes a step toward him, tense, in a low voice).*   You? What do you want? What do you want with my husband?
Krogstad.   Bank business—in a way. I have a small job in the Mutual, and I understand your husband is going to be our new boss—
Nora.   So it's just—
Krogstad.   Just routine business, ma'am. Nothing else.
Nora.   All right. In that case, why don't you go through the door to the office.

Dismisses him casually as she closes the door. Walks over to the stove and tends the fire.

Mrs. Linde.   Nora—who was that man?
Nora.   His name's Krogstad. He's a lawyer.
Mrs. Linde.   So it *was* him.
Nora.   Do you know him?
Mrs. Linde.   I used to—many years ago. For a while he clerked in our part of the country.
Nora.   Right. He did.
Mrs. Linde.   He has changed a great deal.
Nora.   I believe he had a very unhappy marriage.
Mrs. Linde.   And now he's a widower, isn't he?
Nora.   With many children. There now; it's burning nicely again. *(Closes the stove and moves the rocking chair a little to the side.)*

Mrs. Linde. They say he's into all sorts of business.

Nora. Really? Maybe so. I wouldn't know. But let's not think about business. It's such a bore.

Dr. Rank *(appears in the door to Helmer's study).* No, I don't want to be in the way. I'd rather talk to your wife a bit. *(Closes the door and notices Mrs. Linde.)* Oh, I beg your pardon. I believe I'm in the way here too.

Nora. No, not at all. *(Introduces them.)* Dr. Rank. Mrs. Linde.

Rank. Aha. A name often heard in this house. I believe I passed you on the stairs coming up.

Mrs. Linde. Yes. I'm afraid I climb stairs very slowly. They aren't good for me.

Rank. I see. A slight case of inner decay, perhaps?

Mrs. Linde. Overwork, rather.

Rank. Oh, is that all? And now you've come to town to relax at all the parties?

Mrs. Linde. I have come to look for a job.

Rank. A proven cure for overwork, I take it?

Mrs. Linde. One has to live, Doctor.

Rank. Yes, that seems to be the common opinion.

Nora. Come on, Dr. Rank—you want to live just as much as the rest of us.

Rank. Of course I do. Miserable as I am, I prefer to go on being tortured as long as possible. All my patients feel the same way. And that's true of the moral invalids too. Helmer is talking with a specimen right this minute.

Mrs. Linde *(in a low voice).* Ah!

Nora. What do you mean?

Rank. Oh, this lawyer, Krogstad. You don't know him. The roots of his character are decayed. But even he began by saying something about having *to live*—as if it were a matter of the highest importance.

Nora. Oh? What did he want with Torvald?

Rank. I don't really know. All I heard was something about the bank.

Nora. I didn't know that Krog—that this Krogstad had anything to do with the Mutual Bank.

Rank. Yes, he seems to have some kind of job there. *(To Mrs. Linde.)* I don't know if you are familiar in your part of the country with the kind of person who is always running around trying to sniff out cases of moral decrepitude and as soon as he finds one puts the individual under observation in some excellent position or other. All the healthy ones are left out in the cold.

Mrs. Linde. I should think it's the sick who need looking after the most.

Rank *(shrugs his shoulders).* There we are. That's the attitude that turns society into a hospital.

Nora, absorbed in her own thoughts, suddenly starts giggling and clapping her hands.

Rank. What's so funny about that? Do you even know what society is?

Nora. What do I care about your stupid society! I laughed at something entirely different—something terribly amusing. Tell me, Dr. Rank—all the employees in the Mutual Bank, from now on they'll all be dependent on Torvald, right?

Rank.   Is that what you find so enormously amusing?

Nora *(smiles and hums).*   That's my business, that's my business! *(Walks around.)* Yes, I do think it's fun that we—that Torvald is going to have so much influence on so many people's lives. *(Brings out the bag of macaroons.)* Have a macaroon, Dr. Rank.

Rank.   Well, well—macaroons. I thought they were banned around here.

Nora.   Yes, but these were some that Kristine gave me.

Mrs. Linde.   What! I?

Nora.   That's all right. Don't look so scared. You couldn't know that Torvald won't let me have them. He's afraid they'll ruin my teeth. But who cares! Just once in a while—! Right, Dr. Rank? Have one! *(Puts a macaroon into his mouth.)* You too, Kristine. And one for me. A very small one. Or at most two. *(Walks around again.)* Yes, I really feel very, very happy. Now there's just one thing I'm dying to do.

Rank.   Oh? And what's that?

Nora.   Something I'm dying to say so Torvald could hear.

Rank.   And why can't you?

Nora.   I don't dare to, for it's not nice.

Mrs. Linde.   Not nice?

Rank.   In that case, I guess you'd better not. But surely to the two of us—? What is it you'd like to say for Helmer to hear?

Nora.   I want to say, "Goddammit!"

Rank.   Are you out of your mind!

Mrs. Linde.   For heaven's sake, Nora!

Rank.   Say it. Here he comes.

Nora *(hiding the macaroons).*   Shhh!

Helmer enters from his study, carrying his hat and overcoat.

Nora *(going to him).*   Well, dear, did you get rid of him?

Helmer.   Yes, he just left.

Nora.   Torvald, I want you to meet Kristine. She's just come to town.

Helmer.   Kristine—? I'm sorry; I don't think—

Nora.   Mrs. Linde, Torvald dear. Mrs. Kristine Linde.

Helmer.   Ah, yes. A childhood friend of my wife's, I suppose.

Mrs. Linde.   Yes, we've known each other for a long time.

Nora.   Just think; she has come all this way just to see you.

Helmer.   I'm not sure I understand—

Mrs. Linde.   Well, not really—

Nora.   You see, Kristine is an absolutely fantastic secretary, and she would so much like to work for a competent executive and learn more than she knows already—

Helmer.   Very sensible, I'm sure, Mrs. Linde.

Nora.   So when she heard about your appointment—there was a wire—she came here as fast as she could. How about it, Torvald? Couldn't you do something for Kristine? For my sake. Please?

Helmer.   Quite possibly. I take it you're a widow, Mrs. Linde?

Mrs. Linde.   Yes.

Helmer.   And you've had offic_ experience?

Mrs. Linde.   Some—yes.

Helmer.   In that case I think it's quite likely that I'll be able to find you a position.

Nora *(claps her hands)*.   I knew it! I knew it!

Helmer.   You've arrived at a most opportune time, Mrs. Linde.

Mrs. Linde.   Oh, how can I ever thank you—

Helmer.   Not at all, not at all. *(Puts his coat on.)* But today you'll have to excuse me—

Rank.   Wait a minute; I'll come with you. *(Gets his fur coat from the front hall, warms it by the stove.)*

Nora.   Don't be long, Torvald.

Helmer.   An hour or so; no more.

Nora.   Are you leaving, too, Kristine?

Mrs. Linde *(putting on her things)*.   Yes, I'd better go and find a place to stay.

Helmer.   Good. Then we'll be going the same way.

Nora *(helping her)*.   I'm sorry this place is so small, but I don't think we very well could—

Mrs. Linde.   Of course! Don't be silly, Nora. Goodbye, and thank you for everything.

Nora.   Goodbye. We'll see you soon. You'll be back this evening, of course. And you too, Dr. Rank; right? If you feel well enough? Of course you will. Just wrap yourself up.

General small talk as all exit into the hall. Children's voices are heard on the stairs.

Nora.   There they are! There they are! *(She runs and opens the door. The nurse Anne-Marie enters with the children.)*

Nora.   Come in! Come in! *(Bends over and kisses them.)* Oh, you sweet, sweet darlings! Look at them, Kristine! Aren't they beautiful?

Rank.   No standing around in the draft!

Helmer.   Come along, Mrs. Linde. This place isn't fit for anyone but mothers right now.

Dr. Rank, Helmer, and Mrs. Linde go down the stairs. The Nurse enters the living room with the children. Nora follows, closing the door behind her.

Nora.   My, how nice you all look! Such red cheeks! Like apples and roses. *(The children all talk at the same time.)* You've had so much fun? I bet you have. Oh, isn't that nice! You pulled both Emmy and Bob on your sleigh? Both at the same time? That's very good, Ivar. Oh, let me hold her for a minute, Anne-Marie. My sweet little doll baby! *(Takes the smallest of the children from the Nurse and dances with her.)* Yes, yes, of course; Mama'll dance with you too, Bob. What? You threw snowballs? Oh, I wish I'd been there! No, no; *I* want to take their clothes off, Anne-Marie. Please let me; I think it's so much fun. You go on in. You look frozen. There's hot coffee on the stove.

The Nurse exits into the room to the left. Nora takes the children's wraps off and throws them all around. They all keep telling her things at the same time.

Nora.   Oh, really? A big dog ran after you? But it didn't bite you. Of course not. Dogs don't bite sweet little doll babies. Don't peek at the packages, Ivar! What's in them? Wouldn't you like to know! No, no; that's something terrible! Play? You want to play? What do you want to play? Okay, let's play hide-and-seek. Bob hides first. You want *me* to? All right. I'll go first.

Laughing and shouting, Nora and the children play in the living room and in the adjacent room, right. Finally, Nora hides herself under the table; the children rush in, look for her, can't find her. They hear her low giggle, run to the table, lift the rug that covers it, see her. General hilarity. She crawls out, pretends to scare them. New delight. In the meantime there has been a knock on the door between the living room and the front hall, but nobody has noticed. Now the door is opened halfway; Krogstad appears. He waits a little. The play goes on.

Krogstad.   Pardon me, Mrs. Helmer—
Nora *(with a muted cry turns around, jumps up).*   Ah! What do you want?
Krogstad.   I'm sorry. The front door was open. Somebody must have forgotten to close it—
Nora *(standing up).*   My husband isn't here, Mr. Krogstad.
Krogstad.   I know.
Nora.   So what do you want?
Krogstad.   I'd like a word with you.
Nora.   With—? *(To the children.)* Go in to Anne-Marie. What? No, the strange man won't do anything bad to Mama. When he's gone we'll play some more.

She takes the children into the room to the left and closes the door.

Nora *(tense, troubled).*   You want to speak with me?
Krogstad.   Yes I do.
Nora.   Today—? It isn't the first of the month yet.
Krogstad.   No, it's Christmas Eve. It's up to you what kind of holiday you'll have.
Nora.   What do you want? I can't possibly—
Krogstad.   Let's not talk about that just yet. There's something else. You do have a few minutes, don't you?

Nora.   Yes. Yes, of course. That is,—

Krogstad.   Good. I was sitting in Olsen's restaurant when I saw your husband go by.

Nora.   Yes—?

Krogstad.   —with a lady.

Nora.   What of it?

Krogstad.   May I be so free as to ask: wasn't that lady Mrs. Linde?

Nora.   Yes.

Krogstad.   Just arrived in town?

Nora.   Yes, today.

Krogstad.   She's a good friend of yours, I understand?

Nora.   Yes, she is. But I fail to see—

Krogstad.   I used to know her myself.

Nora.   I know that.

Krogstad.   So you know about that. I thought as much. In that case, let me ask you a simple question. Is Mrs. Linde going to be employed in the bank?

Nora.   What makes you think you have the right to cross-examine me like this, Mr. Krogstad—you, one of my husband's employees? But since you ask, I'll tell you. Yes, Mrs. Linde is going to be working in the bank. And it was I who recommended her, Mr. Krogstad. Now you know.

Krogstad.   So I was right.

Nora *(walks up and down).*   After all, one does have a little influence, you know. Just because you're a woman, it doesn't mean that—Really, Mr. Krogstad, people in a subordinate position should be careful not to offend someone who—oh well—

Krogstad.   —has influence?

Nora.   Exactly.

Krogstad *(changing his tone).*   Mrs. Helmer, I must ask you to be good enough to use your influence on my behalf.

Nora.   What do you mean?

Krogstad.   I want you to make sure that I am going to keep my subordinate position in the bank.

Nora.   I don't understand. Who is going to take your position away from you?

Krogstad.   There's no point in playing ignorant with me, Mrs. Helmer. I can very well appreciate that your friend would find it unpleasant to run into me. So now I know who I can thank for my dismissal.

Nora.   But I assure you—

Krogstad.   Never mind. Just want to say you still have time. I advise you to use your influence to prevent it.

Nora.   But Mr. Krogstad, I don't have any influence—none at all.

Krogstad.   No? I thought you just said—

Nora.   Of course I didn't mean it that way. I! Whatever makes you think that I have any influence of that kind on my husband?

Krogstad.   I went to law school with your husband. I have no reason to think that the bank manager is less susceptible than other husbands.

Nora.   If you're going to insult my husband, I'll ask you to leave.

Krogstad.   You're brave, Mrs. Helmer.

Nora.   I'm not afraid of you any more. After New Year's I'll be out of this thing with you.

Krogstad (*more controlled*).   Listen, Mrs. Helmer. If necessary I'll fight as for my life to keep my little job in the bank.

Nora.   So it seems.

Krogstad.   It isn't just the money; that's really the smallest part of it. There is something else—Well, I guess I might as well tell you. It's like this. I'm sure you know, like everybody else, that some years ago I committed—an impropriety.

Nora.   I believe I've heard it mentioned.

Krogstad.   The case never came to court, but from that moment all doors were closed to me. So I took up the kind of business you know about. I had to do something, and I think I can say about myself that I have not been among the worst. But now I want to get out of all that. My sons are growing up. For their sake I must get back as much of my good name as I can. This job in the bank was like the first rung on the ladder. And now your husband wants to kick me down and leave me back in the mud again.

Nora.   But I swear to you, Mr. Krogstad; it's not at all in my power to help you.

Krogstad.   That's because you don't want to. But I have the means to force you.

Nora.   You don't mean you're going to tell my husband I owe you money?

Krogstad.   And if I did?

Nora.   That would be a mean thing to do. (*Almost crying.*) That secret, which is my joy and my pride—for him to learn about it in such a coarse and ugly manner—to learn it from *you*—! It would be terribly unpleasant for me.

Krogstad.   Just unpleasant?

Nora (*heatedly*).   But go ahead! Do it! It will be worse for you than for me. When my husband realizes what a bad person you are, you'll be sure to lose your job.

Krogstad.   I asked you if it was just domestic unpleasantness you were afraid of?

Nora.   When my husband finds out, of course he'll pay off the loan, and then we won't have anything more to do with you.

Krogstad (*stepping closer*).   Listen, Mrs. Helmer—either you have a very bad memory, or you don't know much about business. I think I had better straighten you out on a few things.

Nora.   What do you mean?

Krogstad.   When your husband was ill, you came to me to borrow twelve hundred dollars.

Nora.   I knew nobody else.

Krogstad.   I promised to get you the money—

Nora.   And you did.

Krogstad.   I promised to get you the money on certain conditions. At the time you were so anxious about your husband's health and so set on getting him away that I doubt very much that you paid much attention to the details of our transaction. That's why I remind you of them now. Anyway, I promised to get you the money if you would sign an I.O.U., which I drafted.

Nora.   And which I signed.

Krogstad.   Good. But below your signature I added a few lines, making your father security for the loan. Your father was supposed to put his signature to those lines.

Nora.   Supposed to—? He did.

Krogstad.   I had left the date blank. That is, your father was to date his own signature. You recall that, don't you, Mrs. Helmer?

Nora.   I guess so—

Krogstad.   I gave the note to you. You were to mail it to your father. Am I correct?

Nora.   Yes.

Krogstad.   And of course you did so right away, for no more than five or six days later you brought the paper back to me, signed by your father. Then I paid you the money.

Nora.   Well? And haven't I been keeping up with the payments?

Krogstad.   Fairly well, yes. But to get back to what we were talking about— those were difficult days for you, weren't they, Mrs. Helmer?

Nora.   Yes, they were.

Krogstad.   Your father was quite ill, I believe.

Nora.   He was dying.

Krogstad.   And died shortly afterwards?

Nora.   That's right.

Krogstad.   Tell me, Mrs. Helmer; do you happen to remember the date of your father's death? I mean the exact day of the month?

Nora.   Daddy died on September 29.

Krogstad.   Quite correct. I have ascertained that fact. That's why there is something peculiar about this *(takes out a piece of paper)*, which I can't account for.

Nora.   Peculiar? How? I don't understand—

Krogstad.   It seems very peculiar, Mrs. Helmer, that your father signed this promissory note three days after his death.

Nora.   How so? I don't see what—

Krogstad.   Your father died on September 29. Now look. He has dated his signature October 2. Isn't that odd?

Nora remains silent.

Krogstad.   Can you explain it?

Nora is still silent.

Krogstad.   I also find it striking that the date and the month and the year are not in your father's handwriting but in a hand I think I recognize. Well, that might be explained. Your father may have forgotten to date his signature and somebody else may have done it here, guessing at the date before he had learned of your father's death. That's all right. It's only the signature itself that matters. And that is genuine, isn't it, Mrs. Helmer? Your father *did* put his name to this note?

Nora *(after a brief silence tosses her head back and looks defiantly at him).*   No, he didn't. *I* wrote Daddy's name.

Krogstad.   Mrs. Helmer—do you realize what a dangerous admission you just made?

Nora.   Why? You'll get your money soon.

Krogstad.   Let me ask you something. Why didn't you mail this note to your father?

Nora.   Because it was impossible. Daddy was sick—you know that. If I had asked him to sign it, I would have had to tell him what the money was for. But I couldn't tell him, as sick as he was, that my husband's life was in danger. That was impossible. Surely you can see that.

Krogstad.   Then it would have been better for you if you had given up your trip abroad.

Nora.   No, that was impossible! That trip was to save my husband's life. I couldn't give it up.

Krogstad.   But didn't you realize that what you did amounted to fraud against me?

Nora.   I couldn't let that make any difference. I didn't care about you at all. I hated the way you made all those difficulties for me, even though you knew the danger my husband was in. I thought you were cold and unfeeling.

Krogstad.   Mrs. Helmer, obviously you have no clear idea of what you have done. Let me tell you that what I did that time was no more and no worse. And it ruined my name and reputation.

Nora.   You! Are you trying to tell me that you did something brave once in order to save your wife's life?

Krogstad.   The law doesn't ask about motives.

Nora.   Then it's a bad law.

Krogstad.   Bad or not—if I produce this note in court you'll be judged according to the law.

Nora.   I refuse to believe you. A daughter shouldn't have the right to spare her dying old father worry and anxiety? A wife shouldn't have the right to save her husband's life? I don't know the laws very well, but I'm sure that somewhere they make allowance for cases like that. And you, a lawyer, don't know that? I think you must be a bad lawyer, Mr. Krogstad.

Krogstad.   That may be. But business—the kind of business you and I have with one another—don't you think I know something about that? Very well. Do what you like. But let me tell you this: if I'm going to be kicked out again, you'll keep me company. *(He bows and exits through the front hall.)*

Nora *(pauses thoughtfully; then, with a defiant toss of her head).*   Oh, nonsense! Trying to scare me like that! I'm not all that silly. *(Starts picking up* *the children's clothes; soon stops.)* But—? No! That's impossible! I did it for love!

The Children *(in the door to the left).*   Mama, the strange man just left. We saw him.

Nora.   Yes, yes; I know. But don't tell anybody about the strange man. Do you hear? Not even Daddy.

The Children.   We won't. But now you'll play with us again, won't you, Mama?

Nora.   No, not right now.

The Children.   But Mama—you promised.

Nora.   I know, but I can't just now. Go to your own room. I've so much to do. Be nice now, my little darlings. Do as I say. *(She nudges them gently into the other room and closes the door. She sits down on the couch, picks up a piece of embroidery, makes a few stitches, then stops.)* No! *(Throws the embroidery down, goes to the hall door and calls out.)* Helene! Bring the Christmas tree in here, please! *(Goes to the table, left, opens the drawer, halts.)* No—that's impossible!

The Maid *(with the Christmas tree).*   Where do you want it, ma'am?

Nora.   There. The middle of the floor.

The Maid.   You want anything else?

Nora.   No, thanks. I have everything I need. *(The Maid goes out. Nora starts trimming the tree.)* I want candles—and flowers—That awful man! Oh, non-sense! There's nothing wrong. This will be a lovely tree. I'll do everything you want me to, Torvald. I'll sing for you—dance for you—

Helmer, a bundle of papers under his arm, enters from outside.

Nora.   Ah—you're back already?

Helmer.   Yes. Has anybody been here?

Nora.   Here? No.

Helmer.   That's funny. I saw Krogstad leaving just now.

Nora.   Oh? Oh yes, that's right. Krogstad was here for just a moment.

Helmer.   I can tell from your face that he came to ask you to put in a word for him.

Nora.   Yes.

Helmer.   And it was supposed to be your own idea, wasn't it? You were not to tell me he'd been here. He asked you that too, didn't he?

Nora.   Yes, Torvald, but—

Helmer.   Nora, Nora, how could you! Talk to a man like that and make him promises! And lying to me about it afterwards—!

Nora.   Lying—?

Helmer.   Didn't you say nobody had been here? *(Shakes his finger at her.)* My little songbird must never do that again. Songbirds are supposed to have clean beaks to chirp with—no false notes. *(Puts his arm around her waist.)* Isn't that so? Of course it is. *(Lets her go.)* And that's enough about that. *(Sits* *down in front of the fireplace.)* Ah, it's nice and warm in here. *(Begins to leaf through his papers.)*

Nora *(busy with the tree; after a brief pause).*   Torvald.

Helmer.   Yes.

Nora.   I'm looking forward so much to the Stenborgs' costume party day after tomorrow.

Helmer.   And I can't wait to find out what you're going to surprise me with.

Nora.   Oh, that silly idea!

Helmer.   Oh?

Nora.   I can't think of anything. It all seems so foolish and pointless.

Helmer.   Ah, my little Nora admits that?

Nora *(behind his chair, her arms on the back of the chair).*   Are you very busy, Torvald?

Helmer.   Well—

Nora.   What are all those papers?

Helmer.   Bank business.

Nora.   Already?

Helmer.   I've asked the board to give me the authority to make certain changes in organization and personnel. That's what I'll be doing over the holidays. I want it all settled before New Year's.

Nora.   So that's why this poor Krogstad—

Helmer.   Hm.

Nora *(leisurely playing with the hair on his neck).*   If you weren't so busy, Torvald, I'd ask you for a great big favor.

Helmer.   Let's hear it, anyway.

Nora.   I don't know anyone with better taste than you, and I want so much to look nice at the party. Couldn't you sort of take charge of me, Torvald, and decide what I'll wear—Help me with my costume?

Helmer.   Aha! Little Lady Obstinate is looking for someone to rescue her?

Nora.   Yes, Torvald. I won't get anywhere without your help.

Helmer.   All right. I'll think about it. We'll come up with something.

Nora.   Oh, you *are* nice! *(Goes back to the Christmas tree. A pause.)* Those red flowers look so pretty.—Tell me, was it really all that bad what this Krogstad fellow did?

Helmer.   He forged signatures. Do you have any idea what that means?

Nora.   Couldn't it have been because he felt he had to?

Helmer.   Yes, or like so many others he may simply have been thoughtless. I'm not so heartless as to condemn a man absolutely because of a single imprudent act.

Nora.   Of course not, Torvald!

Helmer.   People like him can redeem themselves morally by openly confessing their crime and taking their punishment.

Nora.   Punishment—?

Helmer.   But that was not the way Krogstad chose. He got out of it with tricks and evasions. That's what has corrupted him.

Nora.   So you think that if—?

Helmer.   Can't you imagine how a guilty person like that has to lie and fake and dissemble wherever he goes—putting on a mask before everybody he's close to, even his own wife and children. It's this thing with the children that's the worst part of it, Nora.

Nora.   Why is that?

Helmer.   Because when a man lives inside such a circle of stinking lies he brings infection into his own home and contaminates his whole family. With every breath of air his children inhale the germs of something ugly.

Nora (*moving closer behind him*).   Are you so sure of that? ·

Helmer.   Of course I am. I have seen enough examples of that in my work. Nearly all young criminals have had mothers who lied.

Nora.   Why mothers—particularly?

Helmer.   Most often mothers. But of course fathers tend to have the same influence. Every lawyer knows that. And yet, for years this Krogstad has been poisoning his own children in an atmosphere of lies and deceit. That's why I call him a lost soul morally. (*Reaches out for her hands.*) And that's why my sweet little Nora must promise me never to take his side again. Let's shake on that.—What? What's this? Give me your hand. There! Now that's settled. I assure you, I would find it impossible to work in the same room with that man. I feel literally sick when I'm around people like that.

Nora (*withdraws her hand and goes to the other side of the Christmas tree*).   It's so hot in here. And I have so much to do.

Helmer (*gets up and collects his papers*).   Yes, and I really should try to get some of this reading done before dinner. I must think about your costume too. And maybe just possibly I'll have something to wrap in gilt paper and hang on the Christmas tree. (*Puts his hand on her head.*) Oh my adorable little songbird! (*Enters his study and closes the door.*)

Nora (*after a pause, in a low voice*).   It's all a lot of nonsense. It's not that way at all. It's impossible. It has to be impossible.

The Nurse (*in the door, left*).   The little ones are asking ever so nicely if they can't come in and be with their mama.

Nora.   No, no, no! Don't let them in here! You stay with them, Anne-Marie.

The Nurse.   If you say so, ma'am. (*Closes the door.*)

Nora (*pale with terror*).   Corrupt my little children—! Poison my home—? (*Brief pause; she lifts her head.*) That's not true. Never. Never in a million years.

Act II

The same room. The Christmas tree is in the corner by the piano, stripped shabby-looking, with burnt-down candles. Nora's outside clothes are on the couch. Nora is alone. She walks around restlessly. She stops by the couch and picks up her coat.

Nora *(drops the coat again).*   There's somebody now! *(Goes to the door, listens.)* No. Nobody. Of course not—not on Christmas. And not tomorrow either.[1]—But perhaps—*(Opens the door and looks.)* No, nothing in the mailbox. All empty. *(Comes forward.)* How silly I am! Of course he isn't serious. Nothing like that could happen. After all, I have three small children.

The Nurse enters from the room, left, carrying a big carton.

The Nurse.   Well, at last I found it—the box with your costume.
Nora.   Thanks. Just put it on the table.
Nurse *(does so).*   But it's all a big mess, I'm afraid.
Nora.   Oh, I wish I could tear the whole thing to little pieces!
Nurse.   Heavens! It's not as bad as all that. It can be fixed all right. All it takes is a little patience.
Nora.   I'll go over and get Mrs. Linde to help me.
Nurse.   Going out again? In this awful weather? You'll catch a cold.
Nora.   That might not be such a bad thing. How are the children?
Nurse.   The poor little dears are playing with their presents, but—
Nora.   Do they keep asking for me?
Nurse.   Well, you know, they're used to being with their mamma.
Nora.   I know. But Anne-Marie, from now on I can't be with them as much as before.
Nurse.   Oh well. Little children get used to everything.
Nora.   You think so? Do you think they'll forget their mamma if I were gone altogether?
Nurse.   Goodness me—gone altogether?
Nora.   Listen, Anne-Marie—something I've wondered about. How could you bring yourself to leave your child with strangers?
Nurse.   But I had to, if I were to nurse you.
Nora.   Yes, but how could you *want* to?
Nurse.   When I could get such a nice place? When something like that happens to a poor young girl, she'd better be grateful for whatever she gets. For *he* didn't do a thing for me—the louse!
Nora.   But your daughter has forgotten all about you, hasn't she?
Nurse.   Oh no! Not at all! She wrote to me both when she was confirmed and when she got married.
Nora *(putting her arms around her neck).*   You dear old thing—you were a good mother to me when I was little.
Nurse.   Poor little Nora had no one else, you know.
Nora.   And if my little ones didn't, I know you'd—oh, I'm being silly! *(Opens the carton.)* Go in to them, please. I really should—. Tomorrow you'll see how pretty I'll be.
Nurse.   I know. There won't be anybody at that party half as pretty as you, ma'am. *(Goes out, left.)*

---

[1] In Norway both December 25 and 26 are legal holidays.

Nora *(begins to take clothes out of the carton; in a moment she throws it all down).*   If only I dared to go out. If only I knew nobody would come. That nothing would happen while I was gone.—How silly! Nobody'll come. Just don't think about it. Brush the muff. Beautiful gloves. Beautiful gloves. Forget it. Forget it. One, two, three, four, five, six—*(Cries out.)* There they are! *(Moves toward the door, stops irresolutely.)*

Mrs. Linde enters from the hall. She has already taken off her coat.

Nora.   Oh, it's you, Kristine. There's no one else out there, is there? I'm so glad you're here.

Mrs. Linde.   They told me you'd asked for me.

Nora.   I just happened to walk by. I need your help with something—badly. Let's sit here on the couch. Look. Torvald and I are going to a costume party tomorrow night—at Consul Stenborg's upstairs—and Torvald wants me to go as a Neapolitan fisher girl and dance the tarantella. I learned it when we were on Capri.

Mrs. Linde.   Well, well! So you'll be putting on a whole show?

Nora.   Yes. Torvald thinks I should. Look, here's the costume. Torvald had it made for me while we were there. But it's all so torn and everything. I just don't know—

Mrs. Linde.   Oh, that can be fixed. It's not that much. The trimmings have come loose in a few places. Do you have needle and thread? Ah, here we are. All set.

Nora.   I really appreciate it, Kristine.

Mrs. Linde *(sewing).*   So you'll be in disguise tomorrow night, eh? You know—I may come by for just a moment, just to look at you.—Oh dear. I haven't even thanked you for the nice evening last night.

Nora *(gets up, moves around).*   Oh, I don't know. I don't think last night was as nice as it usually is.—You should have come to town a little earlier, Kristine.—Yes, Torvald knows how to make it nice and pretty around here.

Mrs. Linde.   You too, I should think. After all, you're your father's daughter. By the way, is Dr. Rank always as depressed as he was last night?

Nora.   No, last night was unusual. He's a very sick man, you know—very sick. Poor Rank, his spine is rotting away. Tuberculosis, I think. You see, his father was a nasty old man with mistresses and all that sort of thing. Rank has been sickly ever since he was a little boy.

Mrs. Linde *(dropping her sewing to her lap).*   But dearest Nora, where have you learned about things like that?

Nora *(still walking about).*   Oh, you know—with three children you sometimes get to talk with—other wives. Some of them know quite a bit about medicine. So you pick up a few things.

Mrs. Linde *(resumes her sewing; after a brief pause).*   Does Dr. Rank come here every day?

Nora.   Every single day. He's Torvald's oldest and best friend, after all. And my friend too, for that matter. He's part of the family, almost.

Mrs. Linde.   But tell me, is he quite sincere? I mean, isn't he the kind of man who likes to say nice things to people?

Nora.   No, not at all. Rather the opposite, in fact. What makes you say that?

Mrs. Linde.   When you introduced us yesterday, he told me he'd often heard my name mentioned in this house. But later on it was quite obvious that your husband really had no idea who I was. So how could Dr. Rank—?

Nora.   You're right, Kristine, but I can explain that. You see, Torvald loves me so very much that he wants me all to himself. That's what he says. When we were first married he got almost jealous when I as much as mentioned anybody from back home that I was fond of. So of course I soon stopped doing that. But with Dr. Rank I often talk about home. You see, he likes to listen to me.

Mrs. Linde.   Look here, Nora. In many ways you're still a child. After all, I'm quite a bit older than you and have had more experience. I want to give you a piece of advice. I think you should get out of this thing with Dr. Rank.

Nora.   Get out of what thing?

Mrs. Linde.   Several things in fact, if you want my opinion. Yesterday you said something about a rich admirer who was going to give you money—

Nora.   One who doesn't exist, unfortunately. What of it?

Mrs. Linde.   Does Dr. Rank have money?

Nora.   Yes, he does.

Mrs. Linde.   And no dependents?

Nora.   No. But—?

Mrs. Linde.   And he comes here every day?

Nora.   Yes, I told you that already.

Mrs. Linde.   But how can that sensitive man be so tactless?

Nora.   I haven't the slightest idea what you're talking about.

Mrs. Linde.   Don't play games with me, Nora. Don't you think I know who you borrowed the twelve hundred dollars from?

Nora.   Are you out of your mind! The very idea—! A friend of both of us who sees us every day—! What a dreadfully uncomfortable position that would be!

Mrs. Linde.   So it really isn't Dr. Rank?

Nora.   Most certainly not! I would never have dreamed of asking him—not for a moment. Anyway, he didn't have any money then. He inherited it afterwards.

Mrs. Linde.   Well, I still think it may have been lucky for you, Nora dear.

Nora.   The idea! It would never have occurred to me to ask Dr. Rank—. Though I'm sure that if I *did* ask him—

Mrs. Linde.   But of course you wouldn't.

Nora.   Of course not. I can't imagine that that would ever be necessary. But I am quite sure that if I told Dr. Rank—

Mrs. Linde.   Behind your husband's back?

Nora.   I must get out of—this other thing. That's also behind his back. I *must* get out of it.

Mrs. Linde.   That's what I told you yesterday. But—

Nora *(walking up and down).*   A man manages these things so much better than a woman—

Mrs. Linde.   One's husband, yes.

Nora.   Silly, silly! *(Stops.)* When you've paid off all you owe, you get your I.O.U. back; right?

Mrs. Linde.   Yes, of course.

Nora.   And you can tear it into a hundred thousand little pieces and burn it— that dirty, filthy, paper!

Mrs. Linde *(looks hard at her, puts down her sewing, rises slowly).*   Nora— you're hiding something from me.

Nora.   Can you tell?

Mrs. Linde.   Something's happened to you, Nora, since yesterday morning. What is it?

Nora *(going to her).*   Kristine! *(Listens.)* Shhh. Torvald just came back. Listen. Why don't you go in to the children for a while. Torvald can't stand having sewing around. Get Anne-Marie to help you.

Mrs. Linde *(gathers some of the sewing things together).*   All right, but I'm not leaving here till you and I have talked.

She goes out left, just as Helmer enters from the front hall.

Nora *(towards him).*   I have been waiting and waiting for you, Torvald.

Helmer.   Was that the dressmaker?

Nora.   No, it was Kristine. She's helping me with my costume. Oh Torvald, just wait till you see how nice I'll look!

Helmer.   I told you. Pretty good idea I had, wasn't it?

Nora.   Lovely! And wasn't it nice of me to go along with it?

Helmer *(his hand under her chin).*   Nice? To do what your husband tells you? All right, you little rascal; I know you didn't mean it that way. But don't let me interrupt you. I suppose you want to try it on.

Nora.   And you'll be working?

Helmer.   Yes. *(Shows her a pile of papers.)* Look. I've been down to the bank. *(Is about to enter his study.)*

Nora.   Torvald.

Helmer *(halts).*   Yes?

Nora.   What if your little squirrel asked you ever so nicely—

Helmer.   For what?

Nora.   Would you do it?

Helmer.   Depends on what it is.

Nora.   Squirrel would run around and do all sorts of fun tricks if you'd be nice and agreeable.

Helmer.   All right. What is it?

Nora.   Lark would chirp and twitter in all the rooms, up and down—

Helmer.   So what? Lark does that anyway.

Nora.   I'll be your elfmaid and dance for you in the moonlight, Torvald.

Helmer.   Nora, don't tell me it's the same thing you mentioned this morning?

Nora (*closer to, him*).   Yes, Torvald. I beg you!

Helmer.   You really have the nerve to bring that up again?

Nora.   Yes. You've just got to do as I say. You *must* let Krogstad keep his job.

Helmer.   My dear Nora. It's his job I intend to give to Mrs. Linde.

Nora.   I know. And that's ever so nice of you. But can't you just fire somebody else?

Helmer.   This is incredible! You just don't give up do you? Because you make some foolish promise, *I* am supposed to—!

Nora.   That's not the reason, Torvald. It's for your own sake. That man writes for the worst newspapers. You've said so yourself. There's no telling what he may do to you. I'm scared to death of him.

Helmer.   Ah, I understand. You're afraid because of what happened before.

Nora.   What do you mean?

Helmer.   You're thinking of your father, of course.

Nora.   Yes. Yes, you're right. Remember the awful things they wrote about Daddy in the newspapers. I really think they might have forced him to resign if the ministry hadn't sent you to look into the charges and if you hadn't been so helpful and understanding.

Helmer.   My dear little Nora, there is a world of difference between your father and me. Your father's official conduct was not above reproach. Mine is, and I intend for it to remain that way as long as I hold my position.

Nora.   Oh, but you don't know what vicious people like that may think of. Oh, Torvald! Now all of us could be so happy together here in our own home, peaceful and carefree. Such a good life, Torvald, for you and me and the children! That's why I implore you—

Helmer.   And it's exactly because you plead for him that you make it impossible for me to keep him. It's already common knowledge in the bank that I intend to let Krogstad go. If it gets out that the new manager has changed his mind because of his wife—

Nora.   Yes? What then?

Helmer.   No, of course, that wouldn't matter at all as long as little Mrs. Pig-head here got her way! Do you want me to make myself look ridiculous before my whole staff—make people think I can be swayed by just anybody—by outsiders? Believe me, I would soon enough find out what the consequences would be! Besides, there's another thing that makes it absolutely impossible for Krogstad to stay on in the bank now that I'm in charge.

Nora.   What's that?

Helmer.   I suppose in a pinch I could overlook his moral shortcomings—

Nora.   Yes, you could; couldn't you, Torvald?

Helmer.   And I understand he's quite a good worker, too. But we've known each other for a long time. It's one of those imprudent relationships you get into when you're young that embarrass you for the rest of your life. I guess I might as well be frank with you: he and I are on a first name basis. And that tactless fellow never hides the fact even when other people are around. Rather, he seems to think it entitles him to be familiar with me. Every chance he gets he comes out with his damn "Torvald, Torvald." I'm telling you, I find it most awkward. He would make my position in the bank intolerable.

Nora.   You don't really mean any of this, Torvald.

Helmer.   Oh? I don't? And why not?

Nora.   No, for it's all so petty.

Helmer.   What! Petty? You think I'm being petty!

Nora.   No, I *don't* think you are petty, Torvald dear. That's exactly why I—

Helmer.   Never mind. You think my reasons are petty, so it follows that I must be petty too. Petty! Indeed! By God, I'll put an end to this right now! *(Opens the door to the front hall and calls out.)* Helene!

Nora.   What are you doing?

Helmer *(searching among his papers).*   Making a decision. *(The Maid enters.)* Here. Take this letter. Go out with it right away. Find somebody to deliver it. But quick. The address is on the envelope. Wait. Here's money.

The Maid.   Very good sir. *(She takes the letter and goes out.)*

Helmer *(collecting his papers).*   There now, little Mrs. Obstinate!

Nora *(breathless).*   Torvald—what was that letter?

Helmer.   Krogstad's dismissal.

Nora.   Call it back, Torvald! There's still time! Oh Torvald, please—call it back! For my sake, for your own sake, for the sake of the children! Listen to me, Torvald! Do it! You don't know what you're doing to all of us!

Helmer.   Too late.

Nora.   Yes. Too late.

Helmer.   Dear Nora, I forgive you this fear you're in, although it really is an insult to me. Yes, it is! It's an insult to think that I am scared of a shabby scrivener's revenge. But I forgive you, for it's such a beautiful proof how much you love me. *(Takes her in his arms.)* And that's the way it should be, my sweet darling. Whatever happens, you'll see that when things get really rough I have both strength and courage. You'll find out that I am man enough to shoulder the whole burden.

Nora *(terrified).*   What do you mean by that?

Helmer.   All of it, I tell you—

Nora *(composed).*   You'll never have to do that.

Helmer.   Good. Then we'll share the burden, Nora—like husband and wife, the way it ought to be. *(Caresses her.)* Now are you satisfied? There, there there. Not that look in your eyes—like a frightened dove. It's all your own foolish imagination.—Why don't you practice the tarantella—and your tambourine, too. I'll be in the inner office and close both doors, so I won't hear you. You can make as much noise as you like. *(Turning in the doorway.)* And when Rank comes, tell him where to find me. *(He nods to her, enters his study carrying his papers, and closes the door.)*

Nora *(transfixed by terror, whispers).*   He would do it. He'll do it. He'll do it in spite of the whole world.—No, this mustn't happen. Anything rather than that! There must be a way—! *(The doorbell rings.)* Dr. Rank! Anything rather than that! Anything—anything at all!

She passes her hand over her face, pulls herself together, and opens the door to the hall. Dr. Rank is out there, hanging up his coat. Darkness begins to fall during the following scene.

Nora. Hello there, Dr. Rank. I recognized your ringing. Don't go in to Torvald yet. I think he's busy.

Rank. And you?

Nora (*as he enters and she closes the door behind him*). You know I always have time for you.

Rank. Thanks. I'll make use of that as long as I can.

Nora. What do you mean by that—As long as you can?

Rank. Does that frighten you?

Nora. Well, it's a funny expression. As if something was going to happen.

Rank. Something is going to happen that I've long been expecting. But I admit I hadn't thought it would come quite so soon.

Nora (*seizes his arm*). What is it you've found out? Dr. Rank—tell me!

Rank (*sits down by the stove*). I'm going downhill fast. There's nothing to do about that.

Nora (*with audible relief*). So it's you—

Rank. Who else? No point in lying to myself. I'm in worse shape than any of my other patients, Mrs. Helmer. These last few days I've been making up my inner status. Bankrupt. Chances are that within a month I'll be rotting up in the cemetery.

Nora. Shame on you! Talking that horrid way!

Rank. The thing itself is horrid—damn horrid. The worst of it, though, is all that other horror that comes first. There is only one more test I need to make. After that I'll have a pretty good idea when I'll start coming apart. There is something I want to say to you. Helmer's refined nature can't stand anything hideous. I don't want him in my sick room.

Nora. Oh, but Dr. Rank—

Rank. I don't want him there. Under no circumstance. I'll close my door to him. As soon as I have full certainty that the worst is about to begin I'll give you my card with a black cross on it. Then you'll know the last horror of destruction has started.

Nora. Today you're really quite impossible. And I had hoped you'd be in a particularly good mood.

Rank. With death on my hands? Paying for someone else's sins? Is there justice in that? And yet there isn't a single family that isn't ruled by the same law of ruthless retribution, in one way or another.

Nora (*puts her hands over her ears*). Poppycock! Be fun! Be fun!

Rank. Well, yes. You may just as well laugh at the whole thing. My poor, innocent spine is suffering from my father's frolics as a young lieutenant.

Nora (*over by the table, left*). Right. He was addicted to asparagus and goose liver paté, wasn't he?

Rank. And truffles.

Nora.   Of course. Truffles. And oysters too, I think.

Rank.   And oysters. Obviously.

Nora.   And all the port and champagne that go with it. It's really too bad that goodies like that ruin your backbone.

Rank.   Particularly an unfortunate backbone that never enjoyed any of it.

Nora.   Ah yes, that's the saddest part of it all.

Rank (*looks searchingly at her*).   Hm—

Nora (*after a brief pause*).   Why did you smile just then?

Rank.   No, it was you that laughed.

Nora.   No, it was you that smiled, Dr. Rank!

Rank (*gets up*).   You're more of a mischief-maker than I thought.

Nora.   I feel in the mood for mischief today.

Rank.   So it seems.

Nora (*with both her hands on his shoulders*).   Dear, dear Dr. Rank, don't you go and die and leave Torvald and me.

Rank.   Oh, you won't miss me for very long. Those who go away are soon forgotten.

Nora (*with an anxious look*).   Do you believe that?

Rank.   You'll make new friends, and then—

Nora.   Who'll make new friends?

Rank.   Both you and Helmer, once I'm gone. You yourself seem to have made a good start already. What was this Mrs. Linde doing here last night?

Nora.   Aha—Don't tell me you're jealous of poor Kristine?

Rank.   Yes, I am. She'll be my successor in this house. As soon as I have made my excuses, that woman is likely to—

Nora.   Shh—not so loud. She's in there.

Rank.   Today too? There you are!

Nora.   She's mending my costume. My God, you really *are* unreasonable. (*Sits down on the couch*). Now be nice, Dr. Rank. Tomorrow you'll see how beautifully I'll dance, and then you are to pretend I'm dancing just for you— and for Torvald too, of course. (*Takes several items out of the carton.*) Sit down, Dr. Rank; I want to show you something.

Rank (*sitting down*).   What?

Nora.   Look.

Rank.   Silk stockings.

Nora.   Flesh-colored. Aren't they lovely? Now it's getting dark in here, but tomorrow—No, no. You only get to see the foot. Oh well, you might as well see all of it.

Rank.   Hmm.

Nora.   Why do you look so critical? Don't you think they'll fit?

Rank.   That's something I can't possibly have a reasoned opinion about.

Nora (*looks at him for a moment*).   Shame on you. (*Slaps his ear lightly with the stocking.*) That's what you get. (*Puts the things back in the carton.*)

Rank.   And what other treasures are you going to show me?

Nora.   Nothing at all, because you're naughty. (*She hums a little and rummages in the carton.*)

Rank *(after a brief silence)*.   When I sit here like this, talking confidently with you, I can't imagine—I can't possibly imagine what would have become of me if I hadn't had you and Helmer.

Nora *(smiles)*.   Well, yes—I do believe you like being with us.

Rank *(in a lower voice, lost in thought)*.   And then to have to go away from it all—

Nora.   Nonsense. You are not going anywhere.

Rank *(as before)*.   —and not to leave behind as much as a poor little token of gratitude, hardly a brief memory of someone missed, nothing but a vacant place that anyone can fill.

Nora.   And what if I were to ask you—? No—

Rank.   Ask me what?

Nora.   For a great proof of your friendship—

Rank.   Yes, yes—?

Nora.   No, I mean—for an enormous favor—

Rank.   Would you really for once make me as happy as all that?

Nora.   But you don't even know what it is.

Rank.   Well, then; tell me.

Nora.   Oh, but I can't, Dr. Rank. It's altogether too much to ask—It's advice and help and a favor—

Rank.   So much the better. I can't even begin to guess what it is you have in mind. So for heaven's sake tell me! Don't you trust me?

Nora.   Yes, I trust you more than anyone else I know. You are my best and most faithful friend. I know that. So I will tell you. All right, Dr. Rank. There is something you can help me prevent. You know how much Torvald loves me—beyond all words. Never for a moment would he hesitate to give his life for me.

Rank *(leaning over to her)*.   Nora—do you really think he's the only one—?

Nora *(with a slight start)*.   Who—?

Rank.   —would gladly give his life for you.

Nora *(heavily)*.   I see.

Rank.   I have sworn an oath to myself to tell you before I go. I'll never find a better occasion.—All right, Nora; now you know. And now you also know that you can confide in me more than in anyone else.

Nora *(gets up; in a calm, steady voice)*.   Let me get by.

Rank *(makes room for her but remains seated)*.   Nora—

Nora *(in the door to the front hall)*.   Helene, bring the lamp in here, please. *(Walks over to the stove.)* Oh, dear Dr. Rank. That really wasn't very nice of you.

Rank *(gets up)*.   That I have loved you as much as anybody—was that not nice?

Nora.   No; not that. But that you told me. There was no need for that.

Rank.   What do you mean? Have you known—?

The Maid enters with the lamp, puts it on the table, and goes out.

Rank.   Nora—Mrs. Helmer—I'm asking you: did you know?

Nora.   Oh, how can I tell what I knew and didn't know! I really can't say—But that you could be so awkward, Dr. Rank! Just when everything was so comfortable.

Rank.   Well, anyway, now you know that I'm at your service with my life and soul. And now you must speak.

Nora *(looks at him).*   After what just happened?

Rank.   I beg of you—let me know what it is.

Nora.   There is nothing I can tell you now.

Rank.   Yes, yes. You mustn't punish me this way. Please let me do for you whatever anyone *can* do.

Nora.   Now there is nothing you can do. Besides, I don't think I really need any help, anyway. It's probably just my imagination. Of course that's all it is. I'm sure of it! *(Sits down in the rocking chair, looks at him, smiles.)* Well, well, well, Dr. Rank! What a fine gentleman you turned out to be! Aren't you ashamed of yourself, now that we have light?

Rank.   No, not really. But perhaps I ought to leave—and not come back?

Nora.   Don't be silly; of course not! You'll come here exactly as you have been doing. You know perfectly well that Torvald can't do without you.

Rank.   Yes, but what about you?

Nora.   Oh, I always think it's perfectly delightful when you come.

Rank.   That's the very thing that misled me. You are a riddle to me. It has often seemed to me that you'd just as soon be with me as with Helmer.

Nora.   Well, you see, there are people you love, and then there are other people you'd almost rather be with.

Rank.   Yes, there is something in that.

Nora.   When I lived at home with Daddy, of course I loved him most. But I always thought it was so much fun to sneak off down to the maids' room, for they never gave me good advice and they always talked about such fun things.

Rank.   Aha! So it's *their* place I have taken.

Nora *(jumps up and goes over to him).*   Oh dear, kind Dr. Rank, you know very well I didn't mean it that way. Can't you see that with Torvald it is the way it used to be with Daddy?

The Maid enters from the front hall.

The Maid.   Ma'am! *(Whispers to her and gives her a caller's card.)*

Nora *(glances at the card).*   Ah! *(Puts it in her pocket.)*

Rank.   Anything wrong?

Nora.   No, no; not at all. It's nothing—just my new costume—

Rank.   But your costume is lying right there!

Nora.   Oh yes, that one. But this is another one. I ordered it. Torvald mustn't know—

Rank.   Aha. So that's the great secret.

Nora.   That's it. Why don't you go in to him, please. He's in the inner office. And keep him there for a while—

Rank.   Don't worry. He won't get away. *(Enters Helmer's study.)*

Nora *(to the Maid).*   You say he's waiting in the kitchen?

The Maid.   Yes. He came up the back stairs.

Nora.   But didn't you tell him there was somebody with me?

The Maid.   Yes, but he wouldn't listen.

Nora.   He won't leave?

The Maid.   No, not till he's had a word with you, ma'am.

Nora.   All right. But try not to make any noise. And, Helene—don't tell anyone he's here. It's supposed to be a surprise for my husband.

The Maid.   I understand, ma'am—*(She leaves.)*

Nora.   The terrible is happening. It's happening, after all. No, no, no. It can't happen. It won't happen. *(She bolts the study door.)*

The maid opens the front hall door for Krogstad and closes the door behind him. He wears a fur coat for traveling, boots, and a fur hat.

Nora *(toward him).*   Keep your voice down. My husband's home.

Krogstad.   That's all right.

Nora.   What do you want?

Krogstad.   To find out something.

Nora.   Be quick, then. What is it?

Krogstad.   I expect you know I've been fired.

Nora.   I couldn't prevent it, Mr. Krogstad. I fought for you as long and as hard as I could but it didn't do any good.

Krogstad.   Your husband doesn't love you any more than that? He knows what I can do to you, and yet he runs the risk—

Nora.   Surely you didn't think I'd tell him?

Krogstad.   No, I really didn't. It wouldn't be like Torvald Helmer to show that kind of guts—

Nora.   Mr. Krogstad, I insist that you show respect for my husband.

Krogstad.   By all means. All due respect. But since you're so anxious to keep this a secret, may I assume that you are a little better informed than yesterday about exactly what you have done?

Nora.   Better than *you* could ever teach me.

Krogstad.   Of course. Such a bad lawyer as I am—

Nora.   What do you want of me?

Krogstad.   I just wanted to find out how you are, Mrs. Helmer. I've been thinking about you all day. You see, even a bill collector, a pen pusher, a— anyway, someone like me—even he has a little of what they call a heart.

Nora.   Then show it. Think of my little children.

Krogstad.   Have you and your husband thought of mine? Never mind. All I want to tell you is that you don't need to take this business too seriously. I have no intention of bringing charges right away.

Nora.   Oh no, you wouldn't; would you? I knew you wouldn't.

Krogstad.   The whole thing can be settled quite amiably. Nobody else needs to know anything. It will be between the three of us.

Nora.   My husband must never find out about this.

Krogstad. How are you going to prevent that? Maybe you can pay me the balance on the loan?

Nora. No, not right now.

Krogstad. Or do you have a way of raising the money one of these next few days?

Nora. None I intend to make use of.

Krogstad. It wouldn't do you any good, anyway. Even if you had the cash in your hand right this minute, I wouldn't give you your note back. It wouldn't make any difference *how* much money you offered me.

Nora. Then you'll have to tell me what you plan to use the note *for*.

Krogstad. Just keep it; that's all. Have it on hand, so to speak. I won't say a word to anybody else. So if you've been thinking about doing something desperate—

Nora. I have.

Krogstad. —like leaving house and home—

Nora. I have!

Krogstad. —or even something worse—

Nora. How did you know?

Krogstad. —then: don't.

Nora. How did you know I was thinking of *that*?

Krogstad. Most of us do, right at first. I did, too, but when it came down to it I didn't have the courage—

Nora *(tonelessly)*. Nor do I.

Krogstad *(relieved)*. See what I mean? I thought so. You don't either.

Nora. I don't. I don't.

Krogstad. Besides, it would be very silly of you. Once that first domestic blow-up is behind you—. Here in my pocket is a letter for your husband.

Nora. Telling him everything?

Krogstad. As delicately as possible.

Nora *(quickly)*. He mustn't get that letter. Tear it up. I'll get you the money somehow.

Krogstad. Excuse me, Mrs. Helmer, I thought I just told you—

Nora. I'm not talking about the money I owe you. Just let me know how much money you want from my husband, and I'll get it for you.

Krogstad. I want no money from your husband.

Nora. Then, what *do* you want?

Krogstad. I'll tell you, Mrs. Helmer. I want to rehabilitate myself; I want to get up in the world; and your husband is going to help me. For a year and a half I haven't done anything disreputable. All that time I have been struggling with the most miserable circumstances. I was content to work my way up step by step. Now I've been kicked out, and I'm no longer satisfied just getting my old job back. I want more than that; I want to get to the top. I'm being quite serious. I want the bank to take me back but in a higher position. I want your husband to create a new job for me—

Nora. He'll never do that!

Krogstad. He will. I know him. He won't dare not to. And once I'm back inside and he and I are working together, you'll see! Within a year I'll be the manager's right hand. It will be Nils Krogstad and not Torvald Helmer who'll be running the Mutual Bank!

Nora.   You'll never see that happen!

Krogstad.   Are you thinking of—?

Nora.   Now I *do* have the courage.

Krogstad.   You can't scare me. A fine, spoiled lady like you—

Nora.   You'll see, you'll see!

Krogstad.   Under the ice, perhaps? Down into that cold, black water? Then spring comes, and you float up again—hideous, can't be identified, hair all gone—

Nora.   You don't frighten me.

Krogstad.   Nor you me. One doesn't do that sort of thing, Mrs. Helmer. Besides, what good would it do? He'd still be in my power.

Nora.   Afterwards? When I'm no longer—?

Krogstad.   Aren't you forgetting that your reputation would be in my hands?

Nora stares at him, speechless.

Krogstad.   All right; now I've told you what to expect. So don't do anything foolish. When Helmer gets my letter I expect to hear from him. And don't you forget that it's your husband himself who forces me to use such means again. That I'll never forgive him. Goodbye, Mrs. Helmer. *(Goes out through the hall.)*

Nora *(at the door, opens it a little, listens).*   He's going. And no letter. Of course not! That would be impossible! *(Opens the door more.)* What's he doing? He's still there. Doesn't go down. Having second thoughts—? Will he—?

The sound of a letter dropping into the mailbox. Then Krogstad's steps are heard going down the stairs, gradually dying away.

Nora *(with a muted cry runs forward to the table by the couch; brief pause).*   In the mailbox. *(Tiptoes back to the door to the front hall.)* There it is. Torvald, Torvald—now we're lost!

Mrs. Linde *(enters from the left, carrying Nora's Capri costume).*   There now. I think it's all fixed. Why don't we try it on you—

Nora *(in a low, hoarse voice).*   Kristine, come here.

Mrs. Linde.   What's wrong with you? You look quite beside yourself.

Nora.   Come over here. Do you see that letter? There, look—through the glass in the mailbox.

Mrs. Linde.   Yes, yes; I see it.

Nora.   That letter is from Krogstad.

Mrs. Linde.   Nora—it was Krogstad who lent you the money!

Nora.   Yes, and now Torvald will find out about it.

Mrs. Linde.   Oh believe me, Nora. That's the best thing for both of you.

Nora.   There's more to it than you know. I forged a signature—
Mrs. Linde.   Oh my God—!
Nora.   I just want to tell you this, Kristine, that you must be my witness.
Mrs. Linde.   Witness? How? Witness to what?
Nora.   If I lose my mind—and that could very well happen—
Mrs. Linde.   Nora!
Nora.   —or if something were to happen to me—something that made it impossible for me to be here—
Mrs. Linde.   Nora, Nora! You're not yourself!
Nora.   —and if someone were to take all the blame, assume the whole responsibility—Do you understand—?
Mrs. Linde.   Yes, yes; but how can you think—!
Nora.   Then you are to witness that that's not so, Kristine. I am not beside myself. I am perfectly rational, and what I'm telling you is that nobody else has known about this. I've done it all by myself, the whole thing. Just remember that.
Mrs. Linde.   I will. But I don't understand any of it.
Nora.   Oh, how could you! For it's the wonderful that's about to happen.
Mrs. Linde.   The wonderful?
Nora.   Yes, the wonderful. But it's so terrible, Kristine. It mustn't happen for anything in the whole world!
Mrs. Linde.   I'm going over to talk to Krogstad right now.
Nora.   No, don't. Don't go to him. He'll do something bad to you.
Mrs. Linde.   There was a time when he would have done anything for me.
Nora.   He!
Mrs. Linde.   Where does he live?
Nora.   Oh, I don't know—Yes, wait a minute—(*Reaches into her pocket.*) here's his card.—But the letter, the letter—!
Helmer (*in his study, knocks on the door*).   Nora!
Nora (*cries out in fear*).   Oh, what is it? What do you want?
Helmer.   That's all right. Nothing to be scared about. We're not coming in. For one thing, you've bolted the door, you know. Are you modeling your costume?
Nora.   Yes, yes; I am. I'm going to be so pretty, Torvald.
Mrs. Linde (*having looked at the card*).   He lives just around the corner.
Nora.   Yes, but it's no use. Nothing can save us now. The letter is in the mailbox.
Mrs. Linde.   And your husband has the key?
Nora.   Yes. He always keeps it with him.
Mrs. Linde.   Krogstad must ask for his letter back, unread. He's got to think up some pretext or other—
Nora.   But this is just the time of day when Torvald—
Mrs. Linde.   Delay him. Go in to him. I'll be back as soon as I can. (*She hurries out through the hall door.*)
Nora (*walks over to Helmer's door, opens it, and peeks in*).   Torvald

Helmer *(still offstage).*   Well, well! So now one's allowed in one's own living room again. Come on, Rank. Now we'll see—*(In the doorway.)* But what's this?

Nora.   What, Torvald dear?

Helmer.   Rank prepared me for a splendid metamorphosis.

Rank *(in the doorway).*   That's how I understood it. Evidently I was mistaken.

Nora.   Nobody gets to admire me in my costume before tomorrow.

Helmer.   But, dearest Nora—you look all done in. Have you been practicing too hard?

Nora.   No, I haven't practiced at all.

Helmer.   But you'll have to, you know.

Nora.   I know it, Torvald. I simply must. But I can't do a thing unless you help me. I have forgotten everything.

Helmer.   Oh it will all come back. We'll work on it.

Nora.   Oh yes, please, Torvald. You just have to help me. Promise? I am so nervous. That big party—. You mustn't do anything else tonight. Not a bit of business. Don't even touch a pen. Will you promise, Torvald?

Helmer.   I promise. Tonight I'll be entirely at your service—you helpless little thing.—Just a moment, though. First I want to—*(Goes to the door to the front hall.)*

Nora.   What are you doing out there?

Helmer.   Just looking to see if there's any mail.

Nora.   No, no! Don't, Torvald!

Helmer.   Why not?

Nora.   Torvald, I beg you. There is no mail.

Helmer.   Let me just look, anyway. *(Is about to go out.)*

Nora by the piano, plays the first bars of the tarantella dance.

Helmer *(halts at the door).*   Aha!

Nora.   I won't be able to dance tomorrow if I don't get to practice with you.

Helmer *(goes to her).*   Are you really all that scared, Nora dear?

Nora.   Yes, so terribly scared. Let's try it right now. There's still time before we eat. Oh please, sit down and play for me, Torvald. Teach me, coach me, the way you always do.

Helmer.   Of course I will, my darling, if that's what you want. *(Sits down at the piano.)*

Nora takes the tambourine out of the carton, as well as a long, many-colored shawl. She quickly drapes the shawl around herself, then leaps into the middle of the floor.

Nora.   Play for me! I want to dance!

Helmer plays and Nora dances. Dr. Rank stands by the piano behind Helmer and watches.

Helmer *(playing)*.   Slow down, slow down!
Nora.   Can't!
Helmer.   Not so violent, Nora!
Nora.   It has to be this way.
Helmer *(stops playing)*.   No, no. This won't do at all.
Nora *(laughing, swinging her tambourine)*.   What did I tell you?
Rank.   Why don't you let me play?
Helmer *(getting up)*.   Good idea. Then I can direct her better.

Rank sits down at the piano and starts playing. Nora dances more and more wildly. Helmer stands over by the stove, repeatedly correcting her. She doesn't seem to hear. Her hair comes loose and falls down over her shoulders. She doesn't notice but keeps on dancing. Mrs. Linde enters.

Mrs. Linde *(stops by the door, dumbfounded)*.   Ah—!
Nora *(dancing)*.   We're having such fun, Kristine!
Helmer.   My dearest Nora, you're dancing as if it were a matter of life and death!
Nora.   It is! It is!
Helmer.   Rank, stop. This is sheer madness. Stop, I say!

Rank stops playing; Nora suddenly stops dancing.

Helmer *(goes over to her)*.   If I hadn't seen it I wouldn't have believed it. You've forgotten every single thing I ever taught you.
Nora *(tosses away the tambourine)*.   See? I told you.
Helmer.   Well! You certainly need coaching.
Nora.   Didn't I tell you I did? Now you've seen for yourself. I'll need your help till the very minute we're leaving for the party. Will you promise, Torvald?
Helmer.   You can count on it.
Nora.   You're not to think of anything except me—not tonight and not to-morrow. You're not to read any letters—not to look in the mailbox—
Helmer.   Ah, I see. You're still afraid of that man.
Nora.   Yes—yes, that too.
Helmer.   Nora, I can tell from looking at you. There's a letter from him out there.
Nora.   I don't know. I think so. But you're not to read it now. I don't want anything ugly to come between us before it's all over.
Rank *(to Helmer in a low voice)*.   Better not argue with her.
Helmer *(throws his arm around her)*.   The child shall have her way. But to-morrow night, when you've done your dance—
Nora.   Then you'll be free.
The Maid *(in the door, right)*.   Dinner can be served any time, ma'am.
Nora.   We want champagne, Helene.
The Maid.   Very good, ma'am. *(Goes out.)*

Helmer.   Aha! Having a party, eh?

Nora.   Champagne from now till sunrise! *(Calls out.)* And some macaroons, Helene. Lots!—just this once.

Helmer *(taking her hands).*   There, there—I don't like this wild—frenzy—Be my own sweet little lark again, the way you always are.

Nora.   Oh, I will. But you go on in. You too, Dr. Rank. Kristine, please help me put up my hair.

Rank *(in a low voice to Helmer as they go out).*   You don't think she is—you know—expecting—?

Helmer.   Oh no. Nothing like that. It's just this childish fear I was telling you about. *(They go out, right.)*

Nora.   Well?

Mrs. Linde.   Left town.

Nora.   I saw it in your face.

Mrs. Linde.   He'll be back tomorrow night. I left him a note.

Nora.   You shouldn't have. I don't want you to try to stop anything. You see, it's a kind of ecstasy, too, this waiting for the wonderful.

Mrs. Linde.   But what is it you're waiting *for*?

Nora.   You wouldn't understand. Why don't you go in to the others. I'll be there in a minute.

Mrs. Linde enters the dining room, right.

Nora. *(stands still for a little while, as if collecting herself; she looks at her watch).*   Five o'clock. Seven hours till midnight. Twenty-four more hours till next midnight. Then the tarantella is over. Twenty-four plus seven—thirty-one more hours to live.

Helmer *(in the door, right).*   What's happening to my little lark?

Nora *(to him, with open arms).*   Here's your lark!

Act III

The same room. The table by the couch and the chairs around it have been moved to the middle of the floor. A lighted lamp is on the table. The door to the front hall is open. Dance music is heard from upstairs.

Mrs. Linde is seated by the table, idly leafing through the pages of a book. She tries to read but seems unable to concentrate. Once or twice she turns her head in the direction of the door, anxiously listening.

Mrs. Linde *(looks at her watch).*   Not yet. It's almost too late. If only he hasn't—(Listens again.)* Ah! There he is. *(She goes to the hall and opens the*

front door carefully. Quiet footsteps on the stairs. She whispers.) Come in.
There's nobody here.

Krogstad *(in the door).*   I found your note when I got home. What's this all
about?

Mrs. Linde.   I've got to talk to you.

Krogstad.   Oh? And it has to be here?

Mrs. Linde.   It couldn't be at my place. My room doesn't have a separate
entrance. Come in. We're quite alone. The maid is asleep and the Helmers
are at a party upstairs.

Krogstad *(entering).*   Really? The Helmers are dancing tonight, are they?

Mrs. Linde.   And why not?

Krogstad.   You're right. Why not, indeed.

Mrs. Linde.   All right, Krogstad. Let's talk, you and I.

Krogstad.   I didn't know we had anything to talk about.

Mrs. Linde.   We have much to talk about.

Krogstad.   I didn't think so.

Mrs. Linde.   No, because you've never really understood me.

Krogstad.   What was there to understand? What happened was perfectly commonplace. A heartless woman jilts a man when she gets a more attractive
offer.

Mrs. Linde.   Do you think I'm all that heartless? And do you think it was easy
for me to break with you?

Krogstad.   No?

Mrs. Linde.   You really thought it was?

Krogstad.   If it wasn't, why did you write the way you did that time?

Mrs. Linde.   What else could I do? If I had to make a break, I also had the
duty to destroy whatever feelings you had for me.

Krogstad *(clenching his hands).*   So that's the way it was. And you did—*that*—
just for money!

Mrs. Linde.   Don't forget I had a helpless mother and two small brothers. We
couldn't wait for you, Krogstad. You know yourself how uncertain your prospects were then.

Krogstad.   All right. But you still didn't have the right to throw me over for
somebody else.

Mrs. Linde.   I don't know. I have asked myself that question many times. Did
I have that right?

Krogstad *(in a lower voice).*   When I lost you I lost my footing. Look at me
now. A shipwrecked man on a raft.

Mrs. Linde.   Rescue may be near.

Krogstad.   It *was* near. Then you came between.

Mrs. Linde.   I didn't know that, Krogstad. Only today did I find out it's your
job I'm taking over in the bank.

Krogstad.   I believe you when you say so. But now that you *do* know, aren't
you going to step aside?

Mrs. Linde.   No, for it wouldn't do you any good.

Krogstad.   Whether it would or not—*I* would do it.

Mrs. Linde.   I have learned common sense. Life and hard necessity have taught me that.

Krogstad.   And life has taught me not to believe in pretty speeches.

Mrs. Linde.   Then life has taught you a very sensible thing. But you do believe in actions, don't you?

Krogstad.   How do you mean?

Mrs. Linde.   You referred to yourself just now as a shipwrecked man.

Krogstad.   It seems to me I had every reason to do so.

Mrs. Linde.   And I am a shipwrecked woman. No one to grieve for, no one to care for.

Krogstad.   You made your choice.

Mrs. Linde.   I had no other choice that time.

Krogstad.   Let's say you didn't. What then?

Mrs. Linde.   Krogstad, how would it be if we two shipwrecked people got together?

Krogstad.   What's this!

Mrs. Linde.   Two on one wreck are better off than each on his own.

Krogstad.   Kristine!

Mrs. Linde.   Why do you think I came to town?

Krogstad.   Surely not because of me?

Mrs. Linde.   If I'm going to live at all I must work. All my life, for as long as I can remember, I have worked. That's been my one and only pleasure. But now that I'm all alone in the world I feel nothing but this terrible emptiness and desolation. There is no joy in working just for yourself. Krogstad—give me someone and something to work for.

Krogstad.   I don't believe this. Only hysterical females go in for that kind of high-minded self-sacrifice.

Mrs. Linde.   Did you ever know me to be hysterical?

Krogstad.   You really could do this? Listen—do you know about my past? All of it?

Mrs. Linde.   Yes, I do.

Krogstad.   Do you also know what people think of me around here?

Mrs. Linde.   A little while ago you sounded as if you thought that together with me you might have become a different person.

Krogstad.   I'm sure of it.

Mrs. Linde.   Couldn't that still be?

Krogstad.   Kristine—do you know what you are doing? Yes, I see you do. And you think you have the courage—?

Mrs. Linde.   I need someone to be a mother to, and your children need a mother. You and I need one another. Nils, I believe in you—in the real you. Together with you I dare to do anything.

Krogstad (*seizes her hands*).   Thanks, thanks, Kristine—now I know I'll raise myself in the eyes of others—Ah, but I forget—!

Mrs. Linde (*listening*).   Shh!—There's the tarantella. You must go; hurry!

Krogstad.   Why? What is it?

Mrs. Linde.   Do you hear what they're playing up there? When that dance is over they'll be down.

Krogstad.   All right. I'm leaving. The whole thing is pointless, anyway. Of course you don't know what I'm doing to the Helmers.

Mrs. Linde.   Yes, Krogstad; I do know.

Krogstad.   Still, you're brave enough—?

Mrs. Linde.   I very well understand to what extremes despair can drive a man like you.

Krogstad.   If only it could be undone!

Mrs. Linde.   It could, for your letter is still out there in the mailbox.

Krogstad.   Are you sure?

Mrs. Linde.   Quite sure. But—

Krogstad (*looks searchingly at her*).   Maybe I'm beginning to understand. You want to save your friend at any cost. Be honest with me. That's it, isn't it?

Mrs. Linde.   Krogstad, you may sell yourself once for somebody else's sake, but you don't do it twice.

Krogstad.   I'll demand my letter back.

Mrs. Linde.   No, no.

Krogstad.   Yes, of course. I'll wait here till Helmer comes down. Then I'll ask him for my letter. I'll tell him it's just about my dismissal—that he shouldn't read it.

Mrs. Linde.   No, Krogstad. You are not to ask for that letter back.

Krogstad.   But tell me—wasn't that the real reason you wanted to meet me here?

Mrs. Linde.   At first it was, because I was so frightened. But that was yesterday. Since then I have seen the most incredible things going on in this house. Helmer must learn the whole truth. This miserable secret must come out in the open; those two must come to a full understanding. They simply can't continue with all this concealment and evasion.

Krogstad.   All right; if you want to take that chance. But there is one thing I *can* do, and I'll do that right now.

Mrs. Linde (*listening*).   But hurry! Go! The dance is over. We aren't safe another minute.

Krogstad.   I'll be waiting for you downstairs.

Mrs. Linde.   Yes, do. You must see me home.

Krogstad.   I've never been so happy in my whole life. (*He leaves through the front door. The door between the living room and the front hall remains open.*)

Mrs. Linde (*straightens up the room a little and gets her things ready*).   What a change! Oh yes!—what a change! People to work for—to live for—a home to bring happiness to. I can't wait to get to work—! If only they'd come soon— (*Listens.*) Ah, there they are. Get my coat on—(*Puts on her coat and hat.*)

Helmer's and Nora's voices are heard outside. A key is turned in the lock, and Helmer almost forces Nora into the hall. She is dressed in her Italian costume, with a big black shawl over her shoulders. He is in evening dress under an open black cloak.

Nora *(in the door, still resisting).*   No, no, no! I don't want to! I want to go back upstairs. I don't want to leave so early.

Helmer.   But dearest Nora—

Nora.   Oh please, Torvald—please! I'm asking you as nicely as I can—just another hour!

Helmer.   Not another minute, sweet. You know we agreed. There now. Get inside. You'll catch a cold out here. *(She still resists, but he guides her gently into the room.)*

Mrs. Linde.   Good evening.

Nora.   Kristine!

Helmer.   Ah, Mrs. Linde. Still here?

Mrs. Linde.   I know. I really should apologize, but I so much wanted to see Nora in her costume.

Nora.   You've been waiting up for me?

Mrs. Linde.   Yes, unfortunately I didn't get here in time. You were already upstairs, but I just didn't feel like leaving till I had seen you.

Helmer *(removing Nora's shawl).*   Yes, do take a good look at her, Mrs. Linde. I think I may say she's worth looking at. Isn't she lovely?

Mrs. Linde.   She certainly is—

Helmer.   Isn't she a miracle of loveliness, though? That was the general opinion at the party, too. But dreadfully obstinate—that she is, the sweet little thing. What can we do about that? Will you believe it—I practically had to use force to get her away.

Nora.   Oh Torvald, you're going to be sorry you didn't give me even half an hour more.

Helmer.   See what I mean, Mrs. Linde? She dances the tarantella—she is a tremendous success—quite deservedly so, though perhaps her performance was a little too natural—I mean, more than could be reconciled with the rules of art. But all right! The point is: she's a success, a tremendous success. So should I let her stay after that? Weaken the effect? Of course not. So I take my lovely little Capri girl—I might say, my capricious little Capri girl— under my arm—a quick turn around the room—a graceful bow in all directions, and—as they say in the novels—the beautiful apparition is gone. A finale should always be done for effect, Mrs. Linde, but there doesn't seem to be any way of getting that into Nora's head. Poooh—! It's hot in here. *(Throws his cloak down on a chair and opens the door to his room.)* Why, it's dark in here! Of course. Excuse me—(Goes inside and lights a couple of candles.)

Nora *(in a hurried, breathless whisper).*   Well?

Mrs. Linde *(in a low voice).*   I have talked to him.

Nora.   And—?

Mrs. Linde.   Nora—you've got to tell your husband everything.

Nora *(no expression in her voice)*.   I knew it.

Mrs. Linde.   You have nothing to fear from Krogstad. But you must speak.

Nora.   I'll say nothing.

Mrs. Linde.   Then the letter will.

Nora.   Thank you, Kristine. Now I know what I have to do. Shh!

Helmer *(returning)*.   Well, Mrs. Linde, have you looked your fill?

Mrs. Linde.   Yes. And now I'll say goodnight.

Helmer.   So soon? Is that your knitting?

Mrs. Linde *(takes it)*.   Yes, thank you. I almost forgot.

Helmer.   So you knit, do you?

Mrs. Linde.   Oh yes.

Helmer.   You know—you ought to take up embroidery instead.

Mrs. Linde.   Oh? Why?

Helmer.   Because it's so much more beautiful. Look. You hold the embroidery so—in your left hand. Then with your right you move the needle—like this— in an easy, elongated arc—you see?

Mrs. Linde.   Maybe you're right—

Helmer.   Knitting, on the other hand, can never be anything but ugly. Look here: arms pressed close to the sides—the needles going up and down—there's something Chinese about it somehow—. That really was an excellent champagne they served us tonight.

Mrs. Linde.   Well, goodnight, Nora. And don't be obstinate any more.

Helmer.   Well said, Mrs. Linde!

Mrs. Linde.   Goodnight, sir.

Helmer *(sees her to the front door)*.   Goodnight, goodnight. I hope you'll get home all right? I'd be very glad to—but of course you don't have far to walk, do you? Goodnight, goodnight. *(She leaves. He closes the door behind her and returns to the living room.)* There! At last we got rid of her. She really is an incredible bore, that woman.

Nora.   Aren't you very tired, Torvald?

Helmer.   No, not in the least.

Nora.   Not sleepy either?

Helmer.   Not at all. Quite the opposite. I feel enormously—animated. How about you? Yes, you do look tired and sleepy.

Nora.   Yes, I am very tired. Soon I'll be asleep.

Helmer.   What did I tell you? I was right, wasn't I? Good thing I didn't let you stay any longer.

Nora.   Everything you do is right.

Helmer *(kissing her forehead)*.   Now my little lark is talking like a human being. But did you notice what splended spirits Rank was in tonight?

Nora.   Was he? I didn't notice. I didn't get to talk with him.

Helmer.   Nor did I—hardly. But I haven't seen him in such a good mood for a long time. *(Looks at her, comes closer to her.)* Ah! It does feel good to be back in our own home again, to be quite alone with you—my young, lovely, ravishing woman!

Nora.   Don't look at me like that, Torvald!

Helmer.   Am I not to look at my most precious possession? All that loveliness
that is mine, nobody's but mine, all of it mine.

Nora *(walks to the other side of the table)*.   I won't have you talk to me like
that tonight.

Helmer *(follows her)*.   The tarantella is still in your blood. I can tell. That
only makes you all the more alluring. Listen! The guests are beginning to
leave. *(Softly.)* Nora—soon the whole house will be quiet.

Nora.   Yes, I hope so.

Helmer.   Yes, don't you, my darling? Do you know—when I'm at a party with
you, like tonight—do you know why I hardly ever talk to you, why I keep
away from you, only look at you once in a while—a few stolen glances—do
you know why I do that? It's because I pretend that you are my secret love,
my young, secret bride-to-be, and nobody has the slightest suspicion that
there is anything between us.

Nora.   Yes, I know. All your thoughts are with me.

Helmer.   Then when we're leaving and I lay your shawl around your delicate
young shoulders—around that wonderful curve of your neck—then I imagine
you're my young bride, that we're coming away from the wedding, that I am
taking you to my home for the first time—that I am alone with you for the
first time—quite alone with you, you young, trembling beauty! I have desired
you all evening—there hasn't been a longing in me that hasn't been for you.
When you were dancing the tarantella, chasing, inviting—my blood was on
fire; I couldn't stand it any longer—that's why I brought you down so early—

Nora.   Leave me now, Torvald. Please! I don't want all this.

Helmer.   What do you mean? You're only playing your little teasing bird game
with me; aren't you, Nora? Don't want to? I'm your husband, aren't I?

There is a knock on the front door.

Nora *(with a start)*.   Did you hear that—?

Helmer *(on his way to the hall)*.   Who is it?

Rank *(outside)*.   It's me. May I come in for a moment?

Helmer *(in a low voice, annoyed)*.   Oh, what does he want now? *(Aloud.)* Just
a minute. *(Opens the door.)* Well! How good of you not to pass by our door.

Rank.   I thought I heard your voice, so I felt like saying hello. *(Looks around.)*
Ah yes—this dear, familiar room. What a cozy, comfortable place you have
here, you two.

Helmer.   Looked to me as if you were quite comfortable upstairs too.

Rank.   I certainly was. Why not? Why not enjoy all you can in this world? As
much as you can for as long as you can, anyway. Excellent wine.

Helmer.   The champagne, particularly.

Rank.   You noticed that too? Incredible how much I managed to put away.

Nora.   Torvald drank a lot of champagne tonight, too.

Rank.   Did he?

Nora.   Yes, he did, and then he's always so much fun afterwards.

Rank.   Well, why not have some fun in the evening after a well spent day?

Helmer.   Well spent? I'm afraid I can't claim that.

Rank (*slapping him lightly on the shoulder*).   But you see, I can!

Nora.   Dr. Rank, I believe you must have been conducting a scientific test today.

Rank.   Exactly.

Helmer.   What do you know—little Nora talking about scientific tests!

Nora.   May I congratulate you on the result?

Rank.   You may indeed.

Nora.   It was a good one?

Rank.   The best possible for both doctor and patient—certainty.

Nora (*a quick query*).   Certainty?

Rank.   Absolute certainty. So why shouldn't I have myself an enjoyable evening afterwards?

Nora.   I quite agree with you, Dr. Rank. You should.

Helmer.   And so do I. If only you don't pay for it tomorrow.

Rank.   Oh well—you get nothing for nothing in this world.

Nora.   Dr. Rank—you are fond of costume parties, aren't you?

Rank.   Yes, particularly when there is a reasonable number of amusing disguises.

Nora.   Listen—what are the two of us going to be the next time?

Helmer.   You frivolous little thing! Already thinking about the next party!

Rank.   You and I? That's easy. You'll be Fortune's Child.

Helmer.   Yes, but what is a fitting costume for that?

Rank.   Let your wife appear just the way she always is.

Helmer.   Beautiful. Very good indeed. But how about yourself? Don't you know what you'll go as?

Rank.   Yes, my friend. I know precisely what I'll be.

Helmer.   Yes?

Rank.   At the next masquerade I'll be invisible.

Helmer.   That's a funny idea.

Rank.   There's a certain black hat—you've heard about the hat that makes you invisible, haven't you? You put that on, and nobody can see you.

Helmer (*suppressing a smile*).   I guess that's right.

Rank.   But I'm forgetting what I came for. Helmer, give me a cigar—one of your dark Havanas.

Helmer.   With the greatest pleasure. (*Offers him his case.*)

Rank (*takes one and cuts off the tip*).   Thanks.

Nora (*striking a match*).   Let me give you a light.

Rank.   Thanks. (*She holds the match; he lights his cigar.*) And now goodbye!

Helmer.   Goodbye, goodbye, my friend.

Nora.   Sleep well, Dr. Rank.

Rank.   I thank you.

Nora.   Wish me the same.

Rank.   You? Well, if you really want me to—. Sleep well. And thanks for the light. (*He nods to both of them and goes out.*)

Helmer *(in a low voice).*   He had had quite a bit to drink.
Nora *(absently).*   Maybe so.

Helmer takes out his keys and goes out into the hall.

Nora.   Torvald—what are you doing out there?
Helmer.   Emptying the mailbox. It is quite full. There wouldn't be room for the newspapers in the morning—
Nora.   Are you going to work tonight?
Helmer.   You know very well I won't.—Say! What's this? Somebody's been at the lock.
Nora.   The lock—?
Helmer.   Yes. Why, I wonder. I hate to think that any of the maids—. Here's a broken hairpin. It's one of yours. Nora.
Nora *(quickly).*   Then it must be one of the children.
Helmer.   You better make damn sure they stop that. Hm, hm.—There! I got it open, finally. *(Gathers up the mail, calls out to the kitchen.)* Helene?— Oh Helene—turn out the light here in the hall, will you? *(He comes back into the living room and closes the door.)* Look how it's been piling up. *(Shows her the bundle of letters. Starts leafing through it.)* What's this?
Nora *(by the window).*   The letter! Oh no, no, Torvald!
Helmer.   Two calling cards—from Rank.
Nora.   From Dr. Rank?
Helmer *(looking at them).*   "Doctor medicinae Rank." They were on top. He must have put them there when he left just now.
Nora.   Anything written on them?
Helmer.   A black cross above the name. What a macabre idea. Like announcing his own death.
Nora.   That's what it is.
Helmer.   Hm? You know about this? Has he said anything to you?
Nora.   That card means he has said goodbye to us. He'll lock himself up to die.
Helmer.   My poor friend. I knew of course he wouldn't be with me very long. But so soon—. And hiding himself away like a wounded animal—
Nora.   When it has to be, it's better it happens without words. Don't you think so, Torvald?
Helmer *(walking up and down).*   He'd grown so close to us. I find it hard to think of him as gone. With his suffering and loneliness he was like a clouded background for our happy sunshine. Well, it may be better this way. For him, at any rate. *(Stops.)* And perhaps for us, too, Nora. For now we have nobody but each other. *(Embraces her.)* Oh you—my beloved wife! I feel I just can't hold you close enough. Do you know, Nora—many times I have wished some great danger threatened you, so I could risk my life and blood and everything—everything, for your sake.

Nora *(frees herself and says in a strong and firm voice)*.   I think you should go and read your letters now, Torvald.

Helmer.   No, no—not tonight. I want to be with you, my darling.

Nora.   With the thought of your dying friend—?

Helmer.   You are right. This has shaken both of us. Something not beautiful has come between us. Thoughts of death and dissolution. We must try to get over it—out of it. Till then—we'll each go to our own room.

Nora *(her arms around his neck)*.   Torvald—goodnight! Goodnight!

Helmer *(kisses her forehead)*.   Goodnight, my little songbird. Sleep well, Nora. Now I'll read my letters. *(He goes into his room, carrying the mail. Closes the door.)*

Nora *(her eyes desperate, her hands groping, finds Helmer's black cloak and throws it around her; she whispers, quickly, brokenly, hoarsely)*.   Never see him again. Never. Never. Never. *(Puts her shawl over her head.)* And never see the children again, either. Never; never.—The black, icy water—fathomless—this—! If only it was all over.—Now he has it. Now he's reading it. No, no; not yet. Torvald—goodbye—you—the children—

She is about to hurry through the hall, when Helmer flings open the door to his room and stands there with an open letter in his hand.

Helmer.   Nora!

Nora *(cries out)*.   Ah—!

Helmer.   What is it? You know what's in this letter?

Nora.   Yes, I do! Let me go! Let me out!

Helmer *(holds her back)*.   Where do you think you're going?

Nora *(trying to tear herself loose from him)*.   I won't let you save me, Torvald!

Helmer *(tumbles back)*.   True! Is it true what he writes? Oh my God! No, no—this can't possibly be true.

Nora.   It is true. I have loved you more than anything else in the whole world.

Helmer.   Oh, don't give me any silly excuses.

Nora *(taking a step towards him)*.   Torvald—!

Helmer.   You wretch! What have you done!

Nora.   Let me go. You are not to sacrifice yourself for me. You are not to take the blame.

Helmer.   No more playacting. *(Locks the door to the front hall.)* You'll stay here and answer me. Do you understand what you have done? Answer me! Do you understand?

Nora *(gazes steadily at him with an increasingly frozen expression)*.   Yes. Now I'm beginning to understand.

Helmer *(walking up and down)*.   What a dreadful awakening. All these years—all these eight years—she, my pride and my joy—a hypocrite, a liar—oh worse! worse!—a criminal! Oh, the bottomless ugliness in all this! Damn! Damn! Damn!

Nora, silent, keeps gazing at him.

Helmer *(stops in front of her).*   I ought to have guessed that something like this would happen. I should have expected it. All your father's loose principles—Silence! You have inherited every one of your father's loose principles. No religion, no morals, no sense of duty—. Now I am being punished for my leniency with him. I did it for your sake, and this is how you pay me back.

Nora.   Yes. This is how.

Helmer.   You have ruined all my happiness. My whole future—that's what you have destroyed. Oh, it's terrible to think about. I am at the mercy of an unscrupulous man. He can do with me whatever he likes, demand anything of me, command me and dispose of me just as he pleases—I dare not say a word! To go down so miserably, to be destroyed—all because of an irresponsible woman!

Nora.   When I am gone from the world, you'll be free.

Helmer.   No noble gestures, please. Your father was always full of such phrases too. What good would it do me if you were gone from the world, as you put it? Not the slightest good at all. He could still make the whole thing public, and if he did, people would be likely to think I had been your accomplice. They might even think it was my idea—that it was I who urged you to do it! And for all this I have you to thank—you, whom I've borne on my hands through all the years of our marriage. *Now* do you understand what you've done to me?

Nora *(with cold calm).*   Yes.

Helmer.   I just can't get it into my head that this is happening; it's all so incredible. But we have to come to terms with it somehow. Take your shawl off. Take it off, I say! I have to satisfy him one way or another. The whole affair must be kept quiet at whatever cost.—And as far as you and I are concerned, nothing must seem to have changed. I'm talking about appearances, of course. You'll go on living here; that goes without saying. But I won't let you bring up the children; I dare not trust you with them. —Oh! Having to say this to one I have loved so much, and whom I still—! But all that is past. It's not a question of happiness any more but of hanging on to what can be salvaged—pieces, appearances—*(The doorbell rings.)*

Helmer *(jumps).*   What's that? So late. Is the worst—? Has he—! Hide, Nora! Say you're sick.

Nora doesn't move. Helmer opens the door to the hall.

The Maid *(half dressed, out in the hall).*   A letter for your wife, sir.

Helmer.   Give it to me. *(Takes the letter and closes the door.)* Yes, it's from him. But I won't let you have it. I'll read it myself.

Nora.   Yes—you read it.

Helmer *(by the lamp).*   I hardly dare. Perhaps we're lost, both you and I. No;

I've got to know. *(Tears the letter open, glances through it, looks at an enclosure; a cry of joy.)* Nora!

Nora looks at him with a question in her eyes.

Helmer. Nora!—No, I must read it again.—Yes, yes; it is so! I'm saved! Nora, I'm saved!

Nora. And I?

Helmer. You too, of course; we're both saved, both you and I. Look! He's returning your note. He writes that he's sorry, he regrets, a happy turn in his life—oh, it doesn't matter what he writes. We're saved, Nora! Nobody can do anything to you now. Oh Nora, Nora—. No, I want to get rid of this disgusting thing first. Let me see—*(Looks at the signature.)* No, I don't want to see it. I don't want it to be more than a bad dream, the whole thing. *(Tears up the note and both letters, throws the pieces in the stove, and watches them burn.)* There! Now it's gone.—He wrote that ever since Christmas Eve—. Good God, Nora, these must have been three terrible days for you.

Nora. I have fought a hard fight these last three days.

Helmer. And been in agony and seen no other way out than—. No, we won't think of all that ugliness. We'll just rejoice and tell ourselves it's over, it's all over! Oh, listen to me, Nora. You don't seem to understand. It's over. What *is* it? Why do you look like that—that frozen expression on your face? Oh my poor little Nora, don't you think I know what it is? You can't make yourself believe that I have forgiven you. But I have, Nora; I swear to you, I have forgiven you for everything. Of course I know that what you did was for love of me.

Nora. That is true.

Helmer. You have loved me the way a wife ought to love her husband. You just didn't have the wisdom to judge the means. But do you think I love you any less because you don't know how to act on your own? Of course not. Just lean on me. I'll advise you; I'll guide you. I wouldn't be a man if I didn't find you twice as attractive because of your womanly helplessness. You mustn't pay any attention to the hard words I said to you right at first. It was just that first shock when I thought everything was collapsing all around me. I have forgiven you, Nora. I swear to you—I really have forgiven you.

Nora. I thank you for your forgiveness. *(She goes out through the door, right.)*

Helmer. No, stay—*(Looks into the room she entered.)* What are you doing in there?

Nora *(within).* Getting out of my costume.

Helmer *(by the open door).* Good, good. Try to calm down and compose yourself, my poor little frightened songbird. Rest safely; I have broad wings to cover you with. *(Walks around near the door.)* What a nice and cozy home we have, Nora. Here's shelter for you. Here I'll keep you safe like a hunted dove I have rescued from the hawk's talons. Believe me: I'll know how to quiet your beating heart. It will happen by and by, Nora; you'll see. Why, tomorrow you'll look at all this in quite a different light. And soon everything will be just the way it was before. I won't need to keep reassuring you that I have forgiven you; you'll feel it yourself. Did you really think I could have abandoned you, or even reproached you? Oh, you don't know a real man's heart, Nora. There is something unspeakably sweet and satisfactory for a man to know deep in himself that he has forgiven his wife—forgiven her in all the fullness of his honest heart. You see, that way she becomes his very own all over again—in a double sense, you might say. He has, so to speak, given her a second birth; it is as if she had become his wife and his child, both. From now on that's what you'll be to me, you lost and helpless creature. Don't worry about a thing, Nora. Only be frank with me, and I'll be your will and your conscience.—What's this? You're not in bed? You've changed your dress—!

Nora (*in an everyday dress*).   Yes, Torvald. I have changed my dress.

Helmer.   But why—now—this late—?

Nora.   I'm not going to sleep tonight.

Helmer.   But my dear Nora—

Nora (*looks at her watch*).   It isn't all that late. Sit down here with me, Torvald. You and I have much to talk about. (*Sits down at the table.*)

Helmer.   Nora—what is this all about? That rigid face—

Nora.   Sit down. This will take a while. I have much to say to you.

Helmer (*sits down, facing her across the table*).   You worry me, Nora. I don't understand you.

Nora.   No, that's just it. You don't understand me. And I have never understood you—not till tonight. No, don't interrupt me. Just listen to what I have to say.—This is a settling of accounts, Torvald.

Helmer.   What do you mean by that?

Nora (*after a brief silence*).   Doesn't one thing strike you, now that we are sitting together like this?

Helmer.   What would that be?

Nora.   We have been married for eight years. Doesn't it occur to you that this is the first time that you and I, husband and wife, are having a serious talk?

Helmer.   Well—serious—. What do you mean by that?

Nora.   For eight whole years—longer, in fact—ever since we first met, we have never talked seriously to each other about a single serious thing.

Helmer.   You mean I should forever have been telling you about worries you couldn't have helped me with anyway?

Nora.   I am not talking about worries. I'm saying we have never tried seriously to get to the bottom of anything together.

Helmer.   But dearest Nora, I hardly think that would have been something *you*—

Nora.   That's the whole point. You have never understood me. Great wrong has been done to me, Torvald. First by Daddy and then by you.

Helmer.   What! By us two? We who have loved you more deeply than anyone else?

Nora (*shakes her head*).   You never loved me—neither Daddy nor you. You only thought it was fun to be in love with me.

Helmer   But, Nora—what an expression to use!

Nora.   That's the way it has been, Torvald. When I was home with Daddy, he told me all his opinions, and so they became my opinions too. If I disagreed with him I kept it to myself, for he wouldn't have liked that. He called me his little doll baby, and he played with me the way I played with my dolls. Then I came to your house—

Helmer.   What a way to talk about our marriage!

Nora (*imperturbably*).   I mean that I passed from Daddy's hands into yours. You arranged everything according to your taste, and so I came to share it— or I pretended to; I'm not sure which. I think it was a little of both, now one and now the other. When I look back on it now, it seems to me I've been living here like a pauper—just a hand-to-mouth kind of existence. I have earned my keep by doing tricks for you, Torvald. But that's the way you wanted it. You have great sins against me to answer for, Daddy and you. It's your fault that nothing has become of me.

Helmer.   Nora, you're being both unreasonable and ungrateful. Haven't you been happy here?

Nora.   No, never. I thought I was, but I wasn't.

Helmer.   Not—not happy!

Nora.   No; just having fun. And you have always been very good to me. But our home has never been more than a playroom. I have been your doll wife here, just the way I used to be Daddy's doll child. And the children have been my dolls. I thought it was fun when you played with me, just as they thought it was fun when I played with them. That's been our marriage, Torvald.

Helmer.   There is something in what you are saying—exaggerated and hysterical though it is. But from now on things will be different. Playtime is over; it's time for growing up.

Nora.   Whose growing up—mine or the children's?

Helmer.   Both yours and the children's, Nora darling.

Nora.   Oh Torvald, you're not the man to bring me up to be the right kind of wife for you.

Helmer.   How can you say that?

Nora.   And I—? What qualifications do I have for bringing up the children?

Helmer.   Nora!

Nora.   You said so yourself a minute ago—that you didn't dare to trust me with them.

Helmer.   In the first flush of anger, yes. Surely, you're not going to count that.

Nora.   But you were quite right. I am *not* qualified. Something else has to come first. Somehow I have to grow up myself. And you are not the man to help me do that. That's a job I have to do by myself. And that's why I'm leaving you.

Helmer (*jumps up*).   What did you say!

Nora.   I have to be by myself if I am to find out about myself and about all the other things too. So I can't stay here with you any longer.

Helmer.   Nora, Nora!

Nora.   I'm leaving now. I'm sure Kristine will put me up for tonight.

Helmer.   You're out of your mind! I won't let you! I forbid you!

Nora.   You can't forbid me anything any more; it won't do any good. I'm taking my own things with me. I won't accept anything from you, either now or later.

Helmer.   But this is madness!

Nora.   Tomorrow I'm going home—I mean back to my old home town. It will be easier for me to find some kind of job there.

Helmer.   Oh, you blind, inexperienced creature—!

Nora.   I must see to it that I get experience, Torvald.

Helmer.   Leaving your home, your husband, your children! Not a thought of what people will say!

Nora.   I can't worry about that. All I know is that I have to leave.

Helmer.   Oh, this is shocking! Betraying your most sacred duties like this!

Nora.   And what do you consider my most sacred duties?

Helmer.   Do I need to tell you that? They are your duties to your husband and your children.

Nora.   I have other duties equally sacred.

Helmer.   You do not. What duties would they be?

Nora.   My duties to myself.

Helmer.   You are a wife and a mother before you are anything else.

Nora.   I don't believe that any more. I believe I am first of all a human being, just as much as you—or at any rate that I must try to become one. Oh, I know very well that most people agree with you, Torvald, and that it says something like that in all the books. But what people say and what the books say is no longer enough for me. I have to think about these things myself and see if I can't find the answers.

Helmer.   You mean to tell me you don't know what your proper place in your own home is? Don't you have a reliable guide in such matters? Don't you have religion?

Nora.   Oh but Torvald—I don't really know what religion is.

Helmer.   What are you saying!

Nora.   All I know is what the Reverend Hansen told me when he prepared me for confirmation. He said that religion was *this* and it was *that*. When I get by myself, away from here, I'll have to look into that, too. I have to decide if what the Reverend Hansen said was right, or anyway if it is right for *me*.

Helmer.   Oh, this is unheard of in a young woman! If religion can't guide you, let me appeal to your conscience. For surely you have moral feelings? Or—answer me—maybe you don't?

Nora.   Well, you see, Torvald, I don't really know what to say. I just don't know. I am confused about these things. All I know is that my ideas are quite different from yours. I have just found out that the laws are different from what I thought they were, but in no way can I get it into my head that those laws are right. A woman shouldn't have the right to spare her dying old father or save her husband's life! I just can't believe that.

Helmer.   You speak like a child. You don't understand the society you live in.

Nora.   No, I don't. But I want to find out about it. I have to make up my mind who is right, society or I.

Helmer.   You are sick, Nora; you have a fever. I really don't think you are in your right mind.

Nora.   I have never felt so clearheaded and sure of myself as I do tonight.

Helmer.   And clearheaded and sure of yourself you're leaving your husband and children?

Nora.   Yes.

Helmer.   Then there is only one possible explanation.

Nora.   What?

Helmer.   You don't love me any more.

Nora   No, that's just it.

Helmer.   Nora! Can you say that?

Nora.   I am sorry, Torvald, for you have always been so good to me. But I can't help it. I don't love you any more.

Helmer *(with forced composure).*   And this too is a clear and sure conviction?

Nora.   Completely clear and sure. That's why I don't want to stay here any more.

Helmer.   And are you ready to explain to me how I came to forfeit your love?

Nora.   Certainly I am. It was tonight, when the wonderful didn't happen. That was when I realized you were not the man I thought you were.

Helmer.   You have to explain. I don't understand.

Nora.   I have waited patiently for eight years, for I wasn't such a fool that I thought the wonderful is something that happens any old day. Then this—thing—came crashing in on me, and then there wasn't a doubt in my mind that now—now comes the wonderful. When Krogstad's letter was in that mailbox, never for a moment did it even occur to me that you would submit to his conditions. I was so absolutely certain that you would say to him: make the whole thing public—tell everybody. And when that had happened—

Helmer.   Yes, then what? When I had surrendered my wife to shame and disgrace—!

Nora.   When that had happened, I was absolutely certain that you would stand up and take the blame and say, "I'm the guilty one."

Helmer.   Nora!

Nora.   You mean I never would have accepted such a sacrifice from you? Of course not. But what would my protests have counted against yours? *That* was the wonderful I was hoping for in terror. And to prevent that I was going to kill myself.

Helmer.   I'd gladly work nights and days for you, Nora—endure sorrow and want for your sake. But nobody sacrifices his *honor* for his love.

Nora.   A hundred thousand women have done so.

Helmer.   Oh, you think and talk like a silly child.

Nora.   All right. But you don't think and talk like the man I can live with. When you had gotten over your fright—not because of what threatened *me* but because of the risk to *you*—and the whole danger was past, then you acted as if nothing at all had happened. Once again I was your little songbird, your doll, just as before, only now you had to handle her even more carefully, because she was so frail and weak. *(Rises.)* Torvald—that moment I realized that I had been living here for eight years with a stranger and had borne him three children—Oh, I can't stand thinking about it! I feel like tearing myself to pieces!

Helmer *(heavily)*.   I see it, I see it. An abyss has opened up between us.—Oh but Nora—surely it can be filled?

Nora.   The way I am now I am no wife for you.

Helmer.   I have it in me to change.

Nora.   Perhaps—if your doll is taken from you.

Helmer.   To part—to part from you! No, no, Nora! I can't grasp that thought!

Nora *(goes out, right)*.   All the more reason why it has to be. *(She returns with her outdoor clothes and a small bag, which she sets down on the chair by the table.)*

Helmer.   Nora, Nora! Not now! Wait till tomorrow.

Nora *(putting on her coat)*.   I can't spend the night in a stranger's rooms.

Helmer.   But couldn't we live here together like brother and sister—?

Nora *(tying on her hat)*.   You know very well that wouldn't last long—. *(Wraps her shawl around her.)* Goodbye, Torvald. I don't want to see the children. I know I leave them in better hands than mine. The way I am now I can't be anything to them.

Helmer.   But some day, Nora—some day—?

Nora.   How can I tell? I have no idea what's going to become of me.

Helmer.   But you're still my wife, both as you are now and as you will be.

Nora.   Listen, Torvald—when a wife leaves her husband's house, the way I am doing now, I have heard he has no more legal responsibilities for her. At any rate, I now release you from all responsibility. You are not to feel yourself obliged to me for anything, and I have no obligations to you. There has to be full freedom on both sides. Here is your ring back. Now give me mine.

Helmer.   Even this?

Nora.   Even this.

Helmer.   Here it is.

Nora.   There. So now it's over. I'm putting the keys here. The maids know everything about the house—better than I. Tomorrow, after I'm gone, Kristine will come over and pack my things from home. I want them sent after me.

Helmer.   Over! It's all over! Nora, will you never think of me?

Nora.   I'm sure I'll often think of you and the children and this house.

Helmer.   May I write to you, Nora?

Nora.   No—never. I won't have that.

Helmer. But send you things—? You must let me

Nora. Nothing, nothing.

Helmer. —help you, when you need help—

Nora. I told you, no; I won't have it. I'll accept nothing from strangers.

Helmer. Nora—can I never again be more to you than a stranger?

Nora *(picks up her bag).* Oh Torvald—then the most wonderful of all would have to happen—

Helmer. Tell me what that would be—!

Nora. For that to happen, both you and I would have to change so that—Oh Torvald, I no longer believe in the wonderful.

Helmer. But I *will* believe. Tell me! Change, so that—?

Nora. So that our living together would become a true marriage. Goodbye. *(She goes out through the hall.)*

Helmer *(sinks down on a chair near the door and covers his face with his hands).* Nora! Nora! *(Looks around him and gets up.)* All empty. She's gone. *(With sudden hope.)* The most wonderful—?!

From downstairs comes the sound of a heavy door slamming shut.

QUESTIONS

1. What evidence does the play provide that *A Doll's House* is about not only Nora's marriage but the institution of marriage itself? **2.** On a number of occasions Nora recalls her father. What relevance do these recollections have to the development of the theme? **3.** Is Krogstad presented as a stock villain, or are we meant to sympathize with him? **4.** What function does Dr. Rank serve in the play?

WRITING TOPICS

1. Does the fact that Nora abandons her children undermine her otherwise heroic decision to walk out on a hollow marriage? For an 1880 German production of the play, Ibsen—in response to public demand—provided an alternate ending in which Nora, after struggling with her conscience, decides that she cannot abandon her children. Is this ending better than the original ending? Explain. **2.** How does the subplot involving Mrs. Linde and Krogstad add force to the main plot of *A Doll's House?*

CONFORMITY
AND
REBELLION

The Accused, 1886 by Odilon Redon

ESSAYS

A Modest Proposal   1729

JONATHAN SWIFT [1667–1745]

It is a melancholy object to those who walk through this great town[1] or travel   1
in the country, when they see the streets, the roads, and cabin doors, crowded
with beggars of the female sex, followed by three, four, or six children, all in
rags and importuning every passenger for an alms. These mothers, instead of
being able to work for their honest livelihood, are forced to employ all their
time in strolling to beg sustenance for their helpless infants, who, as they grow
up, either turn thieves for want of work, or leave their dear native country to
fight for the Pretender in Spain, or sell themselves to the Barbados.[2]

    I think it is agreed by all parties that this prodigious number of children in   2
the arms, or on the backs, or at the heels of their mothers, and frequently of
their fathers, is in the present deplorable state of the kingdom a very great
additional grievance; and therefore whoever could find out a fair, cheap, and
easy method of making these children sound, useful members of the common-
wealth would deserve so well of the public as to have his statue set up for a
preserver of the nation.

    But my intention is very far from being confined to provide only for the   3
children of professed beggars; it is of a much greater extent, and shall take in
the whole number of infants at a certain age who are born of parents in effect
as little able to support them as those who demand our charity in the streets.

    As to my own part, having turned my thoughts for many years upon this   4
important subject, and maturely weighed the several schemes of other projec-
tors,[3] I have always found them grossly mistaken in their computation. It is
true, a child just dropped from its dam may be supported by her milk for a
solar year, with little other nourishment; at most not above the value of two
shillings,[4] which the mother may certainly get, or the value in scraps, by her

---

[1] Dublin.
[2] Many Irishmen joined the army of the exiled James Stuart (1688–1766), who laid claim to the
British throne. Other Irishmen exchanged their labor for passage to the British colony of Barbados,
in the Caribbean.
[3] People with projects.
[4] A shilling was worth about twenty-five cents.

lawful occupation of begging; and it is exactly at one year that I propose to provide for them in such a manner as instead of being a charge upon their parents or the parish, or wanting food and raiment for the rest of their lives, they shall on the contrary contribute to the feeding, and partly to the clothing, of many thousands.

There is likewise another great advantage in my scheme, that it will prevent those voluntary abortions, and that horrid practice of women murdering their bastard children, alas, too frequent among us, sacrificing the poor innocent babes, I doubt, more to avoid the expense than the shame, which would move tears and pity in the most savage and inhuman breast.   5

The number of souls in this kingdom being usually reckoned one million and a half, of these I calculate there may be about two hundred thousand couples whose wives are breeders; from which number I subtract thirty thousand couples who are able to maintain their own children, although I apprehend there cannot be so many under the present distress of the kingdom; but this being granted, there will remain an hundred and seventy thousand breeders. I again subtract fifty thousand for those women who miscarry, or whose children die by accident or disease within the year. There only remain an hundred and twenty thousand children of poor parents annually born. The question therefore is, how this number shall be reared and provided for, which, as I have already said, under the present situation of affairs, is utterly impossible by all the methods hitherto proposed. For we can neither employ them in handicraft or agriculture; we neither build houses (I mean in the country) nor cultivate land. They can very seldom pick up a livelihood by stealing till they arrive at six years old except where they are of towardly parts[5]; although I confess they learn the rudiments much earlier, during which time they can however be looked upon only as probationers, as I have been informed by a principal gentleman in the country of Cavan, who protested to me that he never knew above one or two instances under the age of six, even in a part of the kingdom so renowned for the quickest proficiency in that art.   6

I am assured by our merchants that a boy or a girl before twelve years old is no salable commodity; and even when they come to this age they will not yield above three pounds, or three pounds and half a crown at most on the Exchange[6]; which cannot turn to account either to the parents or the kingdom, the charge of nutriment and rags having been at least four times that value.   7

I shall now therefore humbly propose my own thoughts, which I hope will not be liable to the least objection.   8

I have been assured by a very knowing American of my acquaintance in London, that a young healthy child well nursed is at a year old a most delicious, nourishing, and wholesome food, whether stewed, roasted, baked, or boiled; and I make no doubt that it will equally serve in a fricassee or a ragout.   9

I do therefore humbly offer it to public consideration that of the hundred   10

---

[5] Able and eager to learn.
[6] A pound was twenty shillings, a crown, five shillings.

and twenty thousand children, already computed, twenty thousand may be reserved for breed, whereof only one fourth part to be males, which is more than we allow to sheep, black cattle, or swine; and my reason is that these children are seldom the fruits of marriage, a circumstance not much regarded by our savages, therefore one male will be sufficient to serve four females. That the remaining hundred thousand may at a year old be offered in sale to the persons of quality and fortune through the kingdom, always advising the mother to let them suck plentifully in the last month, so as to render them plump and fat for a good table. A child will make two dishes at an entertainment for friends; and when the family dines alone, the fore or hind quarter will make a reasonable dish, and seasoned with a little pepper or salt will be very good boiled on the fourth day, especially in winter.

11   I have reckoned upon a medium that a child just born will weigh twelve pounds, and in a solar year if tolerably nursed increaseth to twenty-eight pounds.

12   I grant this food will be somewhat dear, and therefore very proper for landlords, who, as they have already devoured most of the parents, seem to have the best title to the children.

13   Infant's flesh will be in season throughout the year, but more plentiful in March, and a little before and after. For we are told by a grave author, an eminent French physician,[7] that fish being a prolific diet, there are more children born in Roman Catholic countries about nine months after Lent than at any other season; therefore, reckoning a year after Lent, the markets will be more glutted than usual, because the number of popish infants is at least three to one in this kingdom; and therefore it will have one other collateral advantage, by lessening the number of Papists among us.

14   I have already computed the charge of nursing a beggar's child (in which list I reckon all cottagers, laborers, and four-fifths of the farmers) to be about two shillings per annum, rags included; and I believe no gentleman would repine to give ten shillings for the carcass of a good fat child, which, as I have said, will make four dishes of excellent nutritive meat, when he hath only some particular friend or his own family to dine with him. Thus the squire will learn to be a good landlord, and grow popular among the tenants; the mother will have eight shillings net profit, and be fit for work till she produces another child.

15   Those who are more thrifty (as I must confess the times require) may flay the carcass; the skin of which artificially[8] dressed will make admirable gloves for ladies, and summer boots for fine gentlemen.

16   As to our city of Dublin, shambles[9] may be appointed for this purpose in the most convenient parts of it, and butchers we may be assured will not be wanting; although I rather recommend buying the children alive, and dressing them hot from the knife as we do roasting pigs.

---

[7] François Rabelais, sixteenth-century French comic writer.
[8] Skillfully.
[9] Slaughterhouses.

A very worthy person, a true lover of his country, and whose virtues I highly   17
esteem, was lately pleased in discoursing on this matter to offer a refinement
upon my scheme. He said that many gentlemen of his kingdom, having of late
destroyed their deer, he conceived that the want of venison might be well
supplied by the bodies of young lads and maidens, not exceeding fourteen years
of age nor under twelve, so great a number of both sexes in every country
being now ready to starve for want of work and service; and these to be disposed
of by their parents, if alive, or otherwise by their nearest relations. But with
due deference to so excellent a friend and so deserving a patriot, I cannot be
altogether in his sentiments; for as to the males, my American acquaintance
assured me from frequent experience that their flesh was generally tough and
lean, like that of our schoolboys, by continual exercise, and their taste disagreeable; and to fatten them would not answer the charge. Then as to the females;
it would, I think with humble submission, be a loss to the public, because they
soon would become breeders themselves; and besides, it is not improbable that
some scrupulous people might be apt to censure such a practice (although
indeed very unjustly) as a little bordering upon cruelty; which, I confess, hath
always been with me the strongest objection against any project, how well soever
intended.

But in order to justify my friend, he confessed that this expedient was put   18
into his head by the famous Psalmanazar,[10] a native of the island Formosa,
who came from thence to London above twenty years ago, and in conversation
told my friend that in his country when any young person happened to be put
to death, the executioner sold the carcass to persons of quality as a prime
dainty; and that in his time the body of a plump girl of fifteen, who was crucified for an attempt to poison the emperor, was sold to his Imperial Majesty's
prime minister of state, and other great mandarins of the court, in joints from
the gibbet, at four hundred crowns. Neither indeed can I deny that if the same
use were made of several plump young girls in this town, who without one
single groat[11] to their fortunes cannot stir abroad without a chair,[12] and appear
at the playhouse and assemblies in foreign fineries which they never will pay
for, the kingdom would not be the worse.

Some persons of a desponding spirit are in great concern about the vast   19
number of poor people who are aged, diseased, or maimed, and I have been
desired to employ my thoughts what course may be taken to ease the nation of
so grievous an encumbrance. But I am not in the least pain upon the matter,
because it is very well known that they are every day dying and rotting by cold
and famine, and filth and vermin, as fast as can be reasonably expected. And
as to the younger laborers, they are now in almost as hopeful a condition.
They cannot get work, and consequently pine away for want of nourishment
to a degree that if any time they are accidentally hired to common labor, they

---

[10] George Psalmanazar was a Frenchman who passed himself off as a native of Formosa.
[11] A coin worth about four cents.
[12] A sedan chair, an enclosed chair carried by poles on the front and back.

have not strength to perform it; and thus the country and themselves are happily delivered from the evils to come.

I have too long digressed, and therefore shall return to my subject. I think 20
the advantages by the proposal which I have made are obvious and many, as
well as of the highest importance.

For first, as I have already observed, it would greatly lessen the number of 21
Papists, with whom we are yearly overrun, being the principal breeders of the
nation as well as our most dangerous enemies; and who stay at home on purpose to deliver the kingdom to the Pretender, hoping to take their advantage
by the absence of so many good Protestants, who have chosen rather to leave
their country than to stay at home and pay tithes against their conscience to
an Episcopal curate.

Secondly, the poorer tenants will have something valuable of their own, 22
which by law may be made liable to distress,[13] and help to pay their landlord's
rent, their corn and cattle being already seized and money a thing unknown.

Thirdly, whereas the maintenance of an hundred thousand children, from 23
two years old and upwards, cannot be computed at less than ten shillings a
piece per annum, the nation's stock will be thereby increased fifty thousand
pounds per annum, besides the profit of a new dish introduced to the tables of
all gentlemen of fortune in the kingdom who have any refinement in taste.
And the money will circulate among ourselves, the goods being entirely of our
own growth and manufacture.

Fourthly, the constant breeders, besides the gain of eight shillings sterling 24
per annum by the sale of their children, will be rid of the charge of maintaining them after the first year.

Fifthly, this food would likewise bring great custom to taverns, where the 25
vintners will certainly be so prudent as to procure the best receipts[14] for dressing it to perfection, and consequently have their houses frequented by all the
fine gentlemen, who justly value themselves upon their knowledge in good
eating; and a skillful cook, who understands how to oblige his guests, will
contrive to make it as expensive as they please.

Sixthly, this would be a great inducement to marriage, which all wise nations have either encouraged by rewards or enforced by laws and penalties. It 26
would increase the care and tenderness of mothers toward their children, when
they were sure of a settlement for life to the poor babes, provided in some sort
by the public, to their annual profit instead of expense. We should see an
honest emulation among the married women, which of them could bring the
fattest child to the market. Men would become as fond of their wives during
the time of their pregnancy as they are now of their mares in foal, their cows
in calf, or sows when they are ready to farrow; nor offer to beat or kick them
(as is too frequent a practice) for fear of a miscarriage.

---

[13] Seizure for payment of debts.
[14] Recipes.

Many other advantages might be enumerated. For instance, the addition of   27
some thousand carcasses in our exportation of barreled beef, the propagation
of swine's flesh, and improvements in the art of making good bacon, so much
wanted among us by the great destruction of pigs, too frequent at our tables,
which are no way comparable in taste or magnificence to a well-grown, fat,
yearling child, which roasted whole will make a considerable figure at a lord
mayor's feast or any other public entertainment. But this and many others I
omit, being studious of brevity.

Supposing that one thousand families in this city would be constant custom-   28
ers for infants' flesh, besides others who might have it at merry meetings, particularly weddings and christenings, I compute that Dublin would take off annually about twenty thousand carcasses, and the rest of the kingdom (where
probably they will be sold somewhat cheaper) the remaining eighty thousand.

I can think of no one objection that will possibly be raised against this pro-   29
posal, unless it should be urged that the number of people will be thereby
much lessened in the kingdom. This I freely own, and it was indeed one principal design in offering it to the world. I desire the reader will observe, that I
calculate my remedy for this one individual kingdom of Ireland and for no
other that ever was, is, or I think ever can be upon earth. Therefore let no
man talk to me of other expedients: of taxing our absentees at five shillings a
pound: of using neither clothes nor household furniture except what is of our
own growth and manufacture: of utterly rejecting the materials and instruments
that promote foreign luxury: of curing the expensiveness of pride, vanity, idleness, and gaming in our women: of introducing a vein of parsimony, prudence,
and temperance: of learning to love our country, in the want of which we differ
even from Laplanders and the inhabitants of Topinamboo[15]: of quitting our
animosities and factions, nor acting any longer like the Jews, who were murdering one another at the very moment their city was taken[16]: of being a little
cautious not to sell our country and conscience for nothing: of teaching landlords to have at least one degree of mercy toward their tenants: lastly, of putting
a spirit of honesty, industry, and skill into our shopkeepers; who, if a resolution
could now be taken to buy only our native goods, would immediately unite to
cheat and exact upon us in the price, the measure, and the goodness, nor
could ever yet be brought to make one fair proposal of just dealing, though
often and earnestly invited to it.

Therefore I repeat, let no man talk to me of these and the like expedients,   30
till he hath at least some glimpse of hope that there will be some hearty and
sincere attempt to put them in practice.

But as to myself, having been wearied out for many years with offering vain,   31
idle, visionary thoughts, and at length utterly despairing of success, I fortunately fell upon this proposal, which, as it is wholly new, so it hath something

---

[15] A district in Brazil, inhabited in Swift's day by primitive tribes.
[16] While the Roman emperor Titus laid siege to Jerusalem in 70 A.D., bloody fighting erupted
among factions within the city.

solid and real, of no expense and little trouble, full in our own power, and whereby we can incur no danger in disobliging England. For this kind of commodity will not bear exportation, the flesh being of too tender a consistence to admit a long continuance in salt, although perhaps I could name a country[17] which would be glad to eat up our whole nation without it.

After all, I am not so violently bent upon my own opinion as to reject any   32 offer proposed by wise men, which shall be found equally innocent, cheap, easy, and effectual. But before something of that kind shall be advanced in contradiction to my scheme, and offering a better, I desire the author or authors will be pleased maturely to consider two points. First, as things now stand, how they will be able to find food and raiment for an hundred thousand useless mouths and backs. And secondly, there being a round million of creatures in human figure throughout this kingdom, whose sole subsistence put into a common stock would leave them in debt two millions of pounds sterling, adding those who are beggars by profession to the bulk of farmers, cottagers, and laborers, with their wives and children who are beggars in effect; I desire those politicians who dislike my overture, and may perhaps be so bold to attempt an answer, that they will first ask the parents of these mortals whether they would not at this day think it a great happiness to have been sold for food at a year old in this manner I prescribe, and thereby have avoided such a perpetual scene of misfortunes as they have since gone through by the oppression of landlords, the impossibility of paying rent without money or trade, the want of common sustenance, with neither house nor clothes to cover them from the inclemencies of the weather, and the most inevitable prospect of entailing the like or greater miseries upon their breed forever.

I profess, in the sincerity of my heart, that I have not the least personal   33 interest in endeavoring to promote this necessary work, having no other motive than the public good of my country, by advancing our trade, providing for infants, relieving the poor, and giving some pleasure to the rich. I have no children by which I can propose to get a single penny; the youngest being nine years old, and my wife past childbearing.

QUESTIONS

1. In what sense is Swift's proposal "modest"?   **2.** What are the major divisions of the essay? What function does each serve?   **3.** What function does paragraph 29 serve?   **4.** Explain what Swift means when he says in paragraph 20 that "I have too long digressed. . . ."   **5.** Characterize the tone of the essay, paying particular attention to the speaker's use of diction.

WRITING TOPIC

Some knowledge of Swift's life and other works would make it clear that in this essay he is being satiric. Without that knowledge, that is, on the basis of the essay alone, how would you demonstrate that Swift is writing satire?

---

[17]England.

My Wood   1936

E. M. FORSTER   [1879–1970]

A few years ago I wrote a book which dealt in part with the difficulties of the   1
English in India.[1] Feeling that they would have had no difficulties in India
themselves, the Americans read the book freely. The more they read it the
better it made them feel, and a cheque to the author was the result. I bought
a wood with the cheque. It is not a large wood—it contains scarcely any trees,
and it is intersected, blast it, by a public footpath. Still, it is the first property
that I have owned, so it is right that other people should participate in my
shame, and should ask themselves, in accents that will vary in horror, this very
important question: What is the effect of property upon the character? Don't
let's touch economics; the effect of private ownership upon the community as
a whole is another question—a more important question, perhaps, but another
one. Let's keep to psychology. If you own things, what's their effect on you?
What's the effect on me of my wood?

In the first place, it makes me feel heavy. Property does have this effect.   2
Property produces men of weight, and it was a man of weight who failed to get
into the Kingdom of Heaven. He was not wicked, that unfortunate millionaire
in the parable, he was only stout; he stuck out in front, not to mention behind,
and as he wedged himself this way and that in the crystalline entrance and
bruised his well-fed flanks, he saw beneath him a comparatively slim camel
passing through the eye of a needle and being woven into the robe of God.[2]
The Gospels all through couple stoutness and slowness. They point out what
is perfectly obvious, yet seldom realized: that if you have a lot of things you
cannot move about a lot, that furniture requires dusting, dusters require servants, servants require insurance stamps, and the whole tangle of them makes
you think twice before you accept an invitation to dinner or go for a bathe in
the Jordan. Sometimes the Gospels proceed further and say with Tolstoy[3] that
property is sinful; they approach the difficult ground of asceticism here, where
I cannot follow them. But as to the immediate effects of property on people,
they just show straightforward logic. It produces men of weight. Men of weight
cannot, by definition, move like the lightning from the East unto the West,
and the ascent of a fourteen-stone[4] bishop into a pulpit is thus the exact an-
tithesis of the coming of the Son of Man. My wood makes me feel heavy.

In the second place, it makes me feel it ought to be larger.   3

The other day I heard a twig snap in it. I was annoyed at first, for I thought   4
that someone was blackberrying, and depreciating the value of the under-

---

[1] *A Passage to India* (1924).
[2] See Matthew 19:23–24; Mark 10:23–25; Luke 16:19–31 and 18:24–25.
[3] Leo Tolstoy (1828–1910), Russian novelist. See his story "The Death of Iván Ilých" (p. 595).
[4] 196-pound.

growth. On coming nearer, I saw it was not a man who had trodden on the twig and snapped it, but a bird, and I felt pleased. My bird. The bird was not equally pleased. Ignoring the relation between us, it took fright as soon as it saw the shape of my face, and flew straight over the boundary hedge into a field, the property of Mrs. Henessy, where it sat down with a loud squawk. It had become Mrs. Henessy's bird. Something seemed grossly amiss here, something that would not have occurred had the wood been larger. I could not afford to buy Mrs. Henessy out, I dared not murder her, and limitations of this sort beset me on every side. Ahab did not want that vineyard—he only needed it to round off his property, preparatory to plotting a new curve—and all the land around my wood has become necessary to me in order to round off the wood. A boundary protects. But—poor little thing—the boundary ought in its turn to be protected. Noises on the edge of it. Children throw stones. A little more, and then a little more, until we reach the sea. Happy Canute! Happier Alexander! And after all, why should even the world be the limit of possession? A rocket containing a Union Jack, will, it is hoped, be shortly fired at the moon. Mars. Sirius. Beyond which . . . But these immensities ended by saddening me. I could not suppose that my wood was the destined nucleus of universal dominion—it is so very small and contains no mineral wealth beyond the blackberries. Nor was I comforted when Mrs. Henessy's bird took alarm for the second time and flew clean away from us all, under the belief that it belonged to itself.

In the third place, property makes its owner feel that he ought to do something to it. Yet he isn't sure what. A restlessness comes over him, a vague sense that he has a personality to express—the same sense which, without any vagueness, leads the artist to an act of creation. Sometimes I think I will cut down such trees as remain in the wood, at other times I want to fill up the gaps between them with new trees. Both impulses are pretentious and empty. They are not honest movements towards money-making or beauty. They spring from a foolish desire to express myself and from an inability to enjoy what I have got. Creation, property, enjoyment form a sinister trinity in the human mind. Creation and enjoyment are both very, very good, yet they are often unattainable without a material basis, and at such moments property pushes itself in as a substitute, saying, "Accept me instead—I'm good enough for all three." It is not enough. It is, as Shakespeare said of lust, "The expense of spirit in a waste of shame"; it is "Before, a joy proposed; behind, a dream." [5] Yet we don't know how to shun it. It is forced on us by our economic system as the alternative to starvation. It is also forced on us by an internal defect in the soul, by the feeling that in property may lie the germs of self-development and of exquisite or heroic deeds. Our life on earth is, and ought to be, material and carnal. But we have not yet learned to manage our materialism and carnality properly; they are still entangled with the desire for ownership, where (in the words of Dante) "Possession is one with loss."

5

[5]This sonnet is reprinted on p. 451.

And this brings us to our fourth and final point: the blackberries.   6

Blackberries are not plentiful in this meagre grove, but they are easily seen   7
from the public footpath which traverses it, and all too easily gathered. Foxgloves, too—people will pull up the foxgloves, and ladies of an educational
tendency even grub for toadstools to show them on the Monday in class. Other
ladies, less educated, roll down the bracken in the arms of their gentlemen
friends. There is paper, there are tins. Pray, does my wood belong to me or
doesn't it? And, if it does, should I not own it best by allowing no one else to
walk there? There is a wood near Lyme Regis, also cursed by a public footpath,
where the owner has not hesitated on this point. He has built high stone walls
each side of the path, and has spanned it by bridges, so that the public circulate
like termites while he gorges on the blackberries unseen. He really does own
his wood, this able chap. Dives in Hell did pretty well, but the gulf dividing
him from Lazarus could be traversed by vision, and nothing traverses it here.[6]
And perhaps I shall come to this in time. I shall wall in and fence out until I
really taste the sweets of property. Enormously stout, endlessly avaricious,
pseudocreative, intensely selfish, I shall weave upon my forehead the quadru-
ple crown of possession until those nasty Bolshies[7] come and take it off again
and thrust me aside into the outer darkness.

QUESTIONS
1. What is the significance of the first three sentences of the essay? **2.** Does
Forster consider his purchase good fortune, bad fortune, or both? **3.** What does
Forster mean when he concludes paragraph 4 with the comment that the bird flew
off "under the impression that it belonged to itself"? **4.** Characterize the tone of
the essay.

WRITING TOPIC
Paraphrase paragraph 5, and then discuss Forster's assertion that "Creation, property, enjoyment form a sinister trinity in the human mind."

---

[6] In the New Testament (Luke 16:19–31), Dives was a rich man from whom the pauper Lazarus
begged. Upon his death, Dives was sent to Hades, and from there he was able to see Lazarus in
Heaven.
[7] Bolsheviks, i.e., Communists.

What if Shakespeare Had Had A Sister?[1]

1928

VIRGINIA WOOLF [1882–1941]

It was disappointing not to have brought back in the evening some important statement, some authentic fact. Women are poorer than men because—this or that. Perhaps now it would be better to give up seeking for the truth, and receiving on one's head an avalanche of opinion hot as lava, discoloured as dish-water. It would be better to draw the curtains; to shut out distractions; to light the lamp; to narrow the enquiry and to ask the historian, who records not opinions but facts, to describe under what conditions women lived, not throughout the ages, but in England, say in the time of Elizabeth.

For it is a perennial puzzle why no woman wrote a word of that extraordinary literature when every other man, it seemed, was capable of song or sonnet. What were the conditions in which women lived, I asked myself; for fiction, imaginative work that is, is not dropped like a pebble upon the ground, as science may be; fiction is like a spider's web, attached ever so lightly perhaps, but still attached to life at all four corners. Often the attachment is scarcely perceptible; Shakespeare's plays, for instance, seem to hang there complete by themselves. But when the web is pulled askew, hooked up at the edge, torn in the middle, one remembers that these webs are not spun in midair by incorporeal creatures, but are the work of suffering human beings, and are attached to grossly material things, like health and money and the houses we live in.

I went, therefore, to the shelf where the histories stand and took down one of the latest, Professor Trevelyan's *History of England*. Once more I looked up Women, found "position of," and turned to the pages indicated. "Wife-beating," I read, "was a recognised right of man, and was practised without shame by high as well as low. . . . Similarly," the historian goes on, "the daughter who refused to marry the gentleman of her parents' choice was liable to be locked up, beaten and flung about the room, without any shock being inflicted on public opinion. Marriage was not an affair of personal affection, but of family avarice, particularly in the 'chivalrous' upper classes. . . . Betrothal often took place while one or both of the parties was in the cradle, and marriage when they were scarcely out of the nurses' charge." That was about 1470, soon after Chaucer's time. The next reference to the position of women is some two

---

[1] *A Room of One's Own*, from which this essay is taken, is based on two lectures Woolf delivered on women and literature at Newnham College and Girton College, Cambridge University. In the opening chapter, Woolf declares that without "money and a room of her own" a woman cannot write. In the following chapter, she recounts her unsuccessful attempt to turn up information at the British Library on the lives of women. This essay is from Chapter 3, from which a few passages are omitted. It ends with the concluding paragraph of the book.

hundred years later, in the time of the Stuarts. "It was still the exception for women of the upper and middle class to choose their own husbands, and when the husband had been assigned, he was lord and master, so far at least as law and custom could make him. Yet even so," Professor Trevelyan concludes, "neither Shakespeare's women nor those of authentic seventeenth-century memoirs, like the Verneys and the Hutchinsons, seem wanting in personality and character." Certainly, if we consider it, Cleopatra must have had a way with her; Lady Macbeth, one would suppose, had a will of her own; Rosalind, one might conclude, was an attractive girl. Professor Trevelyan is speaking no more than the truth when he remarks that Shakespeare's women do not seem wanting in personality and character. Not being a historian, one might go even further and say that women have burnt like beacons in all the works of all the poets from the beginning of time—Clytemnestra, Antigone, Cleopatra, Lady Macbeth, Phèdre, Cressida, Rosalind, Desdemona, the Duchess of Malfi, among the dramatists; then among the prose writers: Millamant, Clarissa, Becky Sharp, Anna Karenine, Emma Bovary, Madame de Guermantes[2]—the names flock to mind, nor do they recall women "lacking in personality and character." Indeed, if woman had no existence save in the fiction written by men, one would imagine her a person of the utmost importance; very various; heroic and mean; splendid and sordid; infinitely beautiful and hideous in the extreme; as great as a man, some think even greater. But this is woman in fiction. In fact, as Professor Trevelyan points out, she was locked up, beaten and flung about the room.

A very queer, composite being thus emerges. Imaginatively she is of the highest importance; practically she is completely insignificant. She pervades poetry from cover to cover; she is all but absent from history. She dominates the lives of kings and conquerors in fiction; in fact she was the slave of any boy whose parents forced a ring upon her finger. Some of the most inspired words, some of the most profound thoughts in literature fall from her lips; in real life she could hardly read, could scarcely spell, and was the property of her husband.   4

It was certainly an odd monster that one made up by reading the historians first and the poets afterwards—a worm winged like an eagle; the spirit of life and beauty in a kitchen chopping up suet. But these monsters, however amusing to the imagination, have no existence in fact. What one must do to bring her to life was to think poetically and prosaically at one and the same moment, thus keeping in touch with fact—that she is Mrs. Martin, aged thirty-six, dressed in blue, wearing a black hat and brown shoes; but not losing sight of fiction either—that she is a vessel in which all sorts of spirits and forces are coursing and flashing perpetually. The moment, however, that one tries this method with the Elizabethan woman, one branch of illumination fails; one is held up by the scarcity of facts. One knows nothing detailed, nothing perfectly true and substantial about her. History scarcely mentions her. And I turned to Professor   5

---

[2] All women characters from great works of literature.

Trevelyan again to see what history meant to him. I found by looking at his chapter headings that it meant—

"The Manor Court and the Methods of Open-field Agriculture . . . The   6
Cistercians and Sheep-farming . . . The Crusades . . . The University . . . The House of Commons . . . The Hundred Years' War . . . The Wars of the Roses . . . The Renaissance Scholars . . . The Dissolution of the Monasteries . . . Agrarian and Religious Strife . . . The Origin of English Sea-power . . . The Armada . . ." and so on. Occasionally an individual woman is mentioned, an Elizabeth, or a Mary; a queen or a great lady. But by no possible means could middle-class women with nothing but brains and character at their command have taken part in any one of the great movements which, brought together, constitute the historian's view of the past. Nor shall we find her in any collection of anecdotes. Aubrey hardly mentions her.[3] She never writes her own life and scarcely keeps a diary; there are only a handful of her letters in existence. She left no plays or poems by which we can judge her. . . . Here am I asking why women did not write poetry in the Elizabethan age, and I am not sure how they were educated; whether they were taught to write; whether they had sitting-rooms to themselves; how many women had children before they were twenty-one; what, in short, they did from eight in the morning till eight at night. They had no money evidently; according to Professor Trevelyan they were married whether they liked it or not before they were out of the nursery, at fifteen or sixteen very likely. It would have been extremely odd, even upon this showing, had one of them suddenly written the plays of Shakespeare, I concluded, and I thought of that old gentleman, who is dead now, but was a bishop, I think, who declared that it was impossible for any woman, past, present, or to come, to have the genius of Shakespeare. He wrote to the papers about it. He also told a lady who applied to him for information that cats do not as a matter of fact go to heaven, though they have, he added, souls of a sort. How much thinking those old gentlemen used to save one! How the borders of ignorance shrank back at their approach! Cats do not go to heaven. Women cannot write the plays of Shakespeare.

Be that as it may, I could not help thinking, as I looked at the works of   7
Shakespeare on the shelf, that the bishop was right at least in this; it would have been impossible, completely and entirely, for any woman to have written the plays of Shakespeare in the age of Shakespeare. Let me imagine, since facts are so hard to come by, what would have happened had Shakespeare had a wonderfully gifted sister, called Judith, let us say. Shakespeare himself went, very probably—his mother was an heiress—to the grammar school, where he may have learnt Latin—Ovid, Virgil and Horace—and the elements of grammar and logic. He was, it is well known, a wild boy who poached rabbits, perhaps shot a deer, and had, rather sooner than he should have done, to marry a woman in the neighbourhood, who bore him a child rather quicker than was right. That escapade sent him to seek his fortune in London. He had,

---

[3] John Aubrey (1626–1697), author of *Brief Lives*, a biographical work.

it seemed, a taste for the theatre; he began by holding horses at the stage door. Very soon he got work in the theatre, became a successful actor, and lived at the hub of the universe, meeting everybody, knowing everybody, practising his art on the boards, exercising his wits in the streets, and even getting access to the palace of the queen. Meanwhile his extraordinarily gifted sister, let us suppose, remained at home. She was as adventurous, as imaginative, as agog to see the world as he was. But she was not sent to school. She had no chance of learning grammar and logic, let alone of reading Horace and Virgil. She picked up a book now and then, one of her brother's perhaps, and read a few pages. But then her parents came in and told her to mend the stockings or mind the stew and not moon about with books and papers. They would have spoken sharply but kindly, for they were substantial people who knew the conditions of life for a woman and loved their daughter—indeed, more likely than not she was the apple of her father's eye. Perhaps she scribbled some pages up in an apple loft on the sly, but was careful to hide them or set fire to them. Soon, however, before she was out of her teens, she was to be betrothed to the son of a neighbouring wool-stapler. She cried out that marriage was hateful to her, and for that she was severely beaten by her father. Then he ceased to scold her. He begged her instead not to hurt him, not to shame him in this matter of her marriage. He would give her a chain of beads or a fine petticoat, he said; and there were tears in his eyes. How could she disobey him? How could she break his heart? The force of her own gift alone drove her to it. She made up a small parcel of her belongings, let herself down by a rope one summer's night and took the road to London. She was not seventeen. The birds that sang in the hedge were not more musical than she was. She had the quickest fancy, a gift like her brother's, for the tune of words. Like him, she had a taste for the theatre. She stood at the stage door; she wanted to act, she said. Men laughed in her face. The manager—a fat, loose-lipped man—guffawed. He bellowed something about poodles dancing and women acting—no woman, he said, could possibly be an actress.[4] He hinted—you can imagine what. She could get no training in her craft. Could she even seek her dinner in a tavern or roam the streets at midnight? Yet her genius was for fiction and lusted to feed abundantly upon the lives of men and women and the study of their ways. At last—for she was very young, oddly like Shakespeare the poet in her face, with the same grey eyes and rounded brows—at last Nick Greene the actor-manager took pity on her; she found herself with child by that gentleman and so—who shall measure the heat and violence of the poet's heart when caught and tangled in a woman's body?—killed herself one winter's night and lies buried at some cross-roads where the omnibuses now stop outside the Elephant and Castle.[5]

That, more or less, is how the story would run, I think, if a woman in Shakespeare's day had had Shakespeare's genius. But for my part, I agree with

8

---

[4] In Shakespeare's day, women's roles were played by boys.
[5] A London neighborhood.

the deceased bishop, if such he was—it is unthinkable that any woman in Shakespeare's day should have had Shakespeare's genius. For genius like Shakespeare's is not born among labouring, uneducated, servile people. It was not born in England among the Saxons and the Britons. It is not born today among the working classes. How, then, could it have been born among women whose work began, according to Professor Trevelyan, almost before they were out of the nursery, who were forced to it by their parents and held to it by all the power of law and custom? Yet genius of a sort must have existed among women as it must have existed among the working classes. Now and again an Emily Brontë or a Robert Burns blazes out and proves its presence.[6] But certainly it never got itself on to paper. When, however, one reads of a witch being ducked, of a woman possessed by devils, of a wise woman selling herbs, or even of a very remarkable man who had a mother, then I think we are on the track of a lost novelist, a suppressed poet, of some mute and inglorious[7] Jane Austen, some Emily Brontë who dashed her brains out on the moor or mopped and mowed about the highways crazed with the torture that her gift had put her to. Indeed, I would venture to guess that Anon, who wrote so many poems without signing them, was often a woman. It was a woman Edward Fitzgerald,[8] I think, suggested who made the ballads and the folk-songs, crooning them to her children, beguiling her spinning with them, or the length of the winter's night.

This may be true or it may be false—who can say?—but what is true in it, so it seemed to me, reviewing the story of Shakespeare's sister as I had made it, is that any woman born with a great gift in the sixteenth century would certainly have gone crazed, shot herself, or ended her days in some lonely cottage outside the village, half witch, half wizard, feared and mocked at. For it needs little skill in psychology to be sure that a highly gifted girl who had tried to use her gift for poetry would have been so thwarted and hindered by other people, so tortured and pulled asunder by her own contrary instincts, that she must have lost her health and sanity to a certainty. No girl could have walked to London and stood at a stage door and forced her way into the presence of actor-managers without doing herself a violence and suffering an anguish which may have been irrational—for chastity may be a fetish invented by certain societies for unknown reasons—but were none the less inevitable. Chastity had then, it has even now, a religious importance in a woman's life, and has so wrapped itself round with nerves and instincts that to cut it free and bring it to the light of day demands courage of the rarest. To have lived a free life in London in the sixteenth century would have meant for a woman who was poet and playwright a nervous stress and dilemma which might well have killed her. Had she survived, whatever she had written would have been twisted and deformed, issuing from a strained and morbid imagination. And undoubt-

9

---

[6] Emily Brontë (1818–1848), English novelist, and Robert Burns (1759–1796), Scottish poet.
[7] See Thomas Gray's "Elegy Written in a Country Churchyard," p. 670, 1.59.
[8] Edward Fitzgerald (1809–1883), translator and poet.

edly, I thought, looking at the shelf where there are no plays by women, her work would have gone unsigned. That refuge she would have sought certainly. It was the relic of the sense of chastity that dictated anonymity to women even so late as the nineteenth century. Currer Bell, George Eliot, George Sand,[9] all the victims of inner strife as their writings prove, sought ineffectively to veil themselves by using the name of a man. Thus they did homage to the convention, which if not implanted by the other sex was liberally encouraged by them (the chief glory of a woman is not to be talked of, said Pericles,[10] himself a much-talked-of man), that publicity in women is detestable. . . .

That woman, then, · who was born with a gift of poetry in the sixteenth   10
century, was an unhappy woman, a woman at strife against herself. All the conditions of her life, all her own instincts, were hostile to the state of mind which is needed to set free whatever is in the brain. But what is the state of mind that is most propitious to the act of creation, I asked? Can one come by any notion of the state that furthers and makes possible that strange activity? Here I opened the volume containing the Tragedies of Shakespeare. What was Shakespeare's state of mind, for instance, when he wrote *Lear* and *Antony and Cleopatra?* It was certainly the state of mind most favourable to poetry that there has ever existed. But Shakespeare himself said nothing about it. We only know casually and by chance that he "never blotted a line."[11] Nothing indeed was ever said by the artist himself about his state of mind until the eighteenth century perhaps. Rousseau[12] perhaps began it. At any rate, by the nineteenth century self-consciousness had developed so far that it was the habit for men of letters to describe their minds in confessions and autobiographies. Their lives also were written, and their letters were printed after their deaths. Thus, though we do not know what Shakespeare went through when he wrote *Lear,* we do know what Carlyle went through when he wrote the *French Revolution;* what Flaubert went through when he wrote *Madame Bovary;* what Keats was going through when he tried to write poetry against the coming of death and the indifference of the world.

And one gathers from this enormous modern literature of confession and   11
self-analysis that to write a work of genius is almost always a feat of prodigious difficulty. Everything is against the likelihood that it will come from the writer's mind whole and entire. Generally material circumstances are against it. Dogs will bark; people will interrupt; money must be made; health will break down. Further, accentuating all these difficulties and making them harder to bear is the world's notorious indifference. It does not ask people to write poems and novels and histories; it does not need them. It does not care whether Flaubert finds the right word or whether Carlyle scrupulously verifies this or that fact.

---

[9] The pseudonyms of Charlotte Brontë (1816–1855) and Mary Ann Evans (1819–1880), English novelists, and Amandine Aurore Lucie Dupin (1804–1876), French novelist.

[10] Pericles (d. 429 B.C.), Athenian statesman and general.

[11] According to Ben Jonson, Shakespeare's contemporary.

[12] Jean-Jacques Rousseau (1712–1778), French philosopher, author of *The Confessions of Jean-Jacques Rousseau.*

Naturally, it will not pay for what it does not want. And so the writer, Keats, Flaubert, Carlyle, suffers, especially in the creative years of youth, every form of distraction and discouragement. A curse, a cry of agony, rises from those books of analysis and confession. "Mighty poets in their misery dead"[13]—that is the burden of their song. If anything comes through in spite of all this, it is a miracle, and probably no book is born entire and uncrippled as it was conceived.

But for women, I thought, looking at the empty shelves, these difficulties   12 were infinitely more formidable. In the first place, to have a room of her own, let alone a quiet room or a sound-proof room, was out of the question, unless her parents were exceptionally rich or very noble, even up to the beginning of the nineteenth century. Since her pin money, which depended on the good will of her father, was only enough to keep her clothed, she was debarred from such alleviations as came even to Keats or Tennyson or Carlyle, all poor men, from a walking tour, a little journey to France, from the separate lodging which, even if it were miserable enough, sheltered them from the claims and tyrannies of their families. Such material difficulties were formidable; but much worse were the immaterial. The indifference of the world which Keats and Flaubert and other men of genius have found so hard to bear was in her case not indifference but hostility. The world did not say to her as it said to them, Write if you choose; it makes no difference to me. The world said with a guffaw, Write? What's the good of your writing? . . .

I told you in the course of this paper that Shakespeare had a sister; but do   13 not look for her in Sir Sidney Lee's life of the poet. She died young—alas, she never wrote a word. She lies buried where the omnibuses now stop, opposite the Elephant and Castle. Now my belief is that this poet who never wrote a word and was buried at the cross-roads still lives. She lives in you and in me, and in many other women who are not here tonight, for they are washing up the dishes and putting the children to bed. But she lives; for great poets do not die; they are continuing presences; they need only the opportunity to walk among us in the flesh. This opportunity, as I think, it is now coming within your power to give her. For my belief is that if we live another century or so— I am talking of the common life which is the real life and not of the little separate lives which we live as individuals—and have five hundred a year each of us and rooms of our own; if we have the habit of freedom and the courage to write exactly what we think; if we escape a little from the common sitting-room and see human beings not always in their relation to each other but in relation to reality; and the sky, too, and the trees or whatever it may be in themselves; if we look past Milton's bogey, for no human being should shut out the view; if we face the fact, for it is a fact, that there is no arm to cling

---

[13] From William Wordsworth's poem "Resolution and Independence."

to, but that we go alone and that our relation is to the world of reality and not only to the world of men and women, then the opportunity will come and the dead poet who was Shakespeare's sister will put on the body which she has so often laid down. Drawing her life from the lives of the unknown who were her forerunners, as her brother did before her, she will be born. As for her coming without that preparation, without that effort on our part, without that determination that when she is born again she shall find it possible to live and write her poetry, that we cannot expect, for that would be impossible. But I maintain that she would come if we worked for her, and that so to work, even in poverty and obscurity, is worth while.

QUESTIONS

1. How does Woolf explain the contrast between the women of fact and the women of fiction? **2.** Analyze the effect of Woolf's concluding remarks about the bishop (paragraph 6): "Cats do not go to heaven. Women cannot write the plays of Shakespeare." In this connection, consider her later comment (paragraph 8) that "I agree with the deceased bishop, if such he was—it is unthinkable that any woman in Shakespeare's day should have had Shakespeare's genius." Does this contradict what she has been saying? **3.** Explain the link Woolf makes (paragraph 9) between chastity and the problem of the gifted woman writer.

WRITING TOPIC

Speculate on why it was the case that, while women were little more than men's servants throughout history, they were portrayed in fiction "as great as a man, some think even greater" (paragraph 3)?

Letter From Birmingham Jail[1]   1963

MARTIN LUTHER KING, JR. [1929–1968]

MY DEAR FELLOW CLERGYMEN:

   While confined here in the Birmingham city jail, I came across your recent   1
statement calling my present activities "unwise and untimely." Seldom do I
pause to answer criticism of my work and ideas. If I sought to answer all the
criticisms that cross my desk, my secretaries would have little time for anything
other than such correspondence in the course of the day, and I would have no
time for constructive work. But since I feel that you are men of genuine good
will and that your criticisms are sincerely set forth, I want to try to answer your
statement in what I hope will be patient and reasonable terms.

   I think I should indicate why I am here in Birmingham, since you have   2
been influenced by the view which argues against "outsiders coming in." I have
the honor of serving as president of the Southern Christian Leadership Conference, an organization operating in every southern state, with headquarters in
Atlanta, Georgia. We have some eighty-five affiliated organizations across the
South, and one of them is the Alabama Christian Movement for Human Rights.
Frequently we share staff, educational, and financial resources with our affili-
ates. Several months ago the affiliate here in Birmingham asked us to be on
call to engage in a nonviolent direct-action program if such were deemed necessary. We readily consented, and when the hour came we lived up to our
promise. So I, along with several members of my staff, am here because I was
invited here. I am here because I have organizational ties here.

   But more basically, I am in Birmingham because injustice is here. Just as   3
the prophets of the eighth century B.C. left their villages and carried their "thus
saith the Lord" far beyond the boundaries of their home towns, and just as the
Apostle Paul left his village of Tarsus[2] and carried the gospel of Jesus Christ to
the far corners of the Greco-Roman world, so am I compelled to carry the
gospel of freedom beyond my own home town. Like Paul, I must constantly
respond to the Macedonian call for aid.[3]

   Moreover, I am cognizant of the interrelatedness of all communities and   4
states. I cannot sit idly by in Atlanta and not be concerned about what happens

---

   [1]This response to a published statement by eight fellow clergymen from Alabama (Bishop
C. C. J. Carpenter, Bishop Joseph A. Durick, Rabbi Hilton L. Grafman, Bishop Paul Hardin,
Bishop Holan B. Harmon, the Reverend George M. Murray, the Reverend Edward V. Ramage
and the Reverend Earl Stallings) was composed under somewhat constricting circumstances. Begun
on the margins of the newspaper in which the statement appeared while I was in jail, the letter
was continued on scraps of writing paper supplied by a friendly Negro trusty, and concluded on a
pad my attorneys were eventually permitted to leave me. Although the text remains in substance
unaltered, I have indulged in the author's prerogative of polishing it for publication [King's note].
   [2]Birthplace of St. Paul in present-day Turkey.
   [3]St. Paul was frequently called upon to aid the Christian community in Macedonia.

in Birmingham. Injustice anywhere is a threat to justice everywhere. We are caught in an inescapable network of mutuality, tied in a single garment of destiny. Whatever affects one directly, affects all indirectly. Never again can we afford to live with the narrow, provincial "outside agitator" idea. Anyone who lives inside the United States can never be considered an outsider anywhere within its bounds.

You deplore the demonstrations taking place in Birmingham. But your state-   5
ment, I am sorry to say, fails to express a similar concern for the conditions that brought about the demonstrations. I am sure that none of you would want to rest content with the superficial kind of social analysis that deals merely with effects and does not grapple with underlying causes. It is unfortunate that demonstrations are taking place in Birmingham, but it is even more unfortunate that the city's white power structure left the Negro community with no alternative.

In any nonviolent campaign there are four basic steps: collection of the facts   6
to determine whether injustices exist; negotiation; self-purification; and direct action. We have gone through all these steps in Birmingham. There can be no gainsaying the fact that racial injustice engulfs this community. Birmingham is probably the most thoroughly segregated city in the United States. Its ugly record of brutality is widely known. Negroes have experienced grossly unjust treatment in the courts. There have been more unsolved bombings of Negro homes and churches in Birmingham than in any other city in the nation. These are the hard, brutal facts of the case. On the basis of these conditions, Negro leaders sought to negotiate with the city fathers. But the latter consistently refused to engage in good-faith negotiation.

Then, last September, came the opportunity to talk with leaders of Birming-   7
ham's economic community. In the course of the negotiations, certain promises were made by the merchants—for example, to remove the stores' humiliating racial signs. On the basis of these promises, the Reverend Fred Shuttlesworth and the leaders of the Alabama Christian Movement for Human Rights agreed to a moratorium on all demonstrations. As the weeks and months went by, we realized that we were the victims of a broken promise. A few signs, briefly removed, returned; the others remained.

As in so many past experiences, our hopes had been blasted, and the shadow   8
of deep disappointment settled upon us. We had no alternative except to prepare for direct action, whereby we would present our very bodies as a means of laying our case before the conscience of the local and the national community. Mindful of the difficulties involved, we decided to undertake a process of self-purification. We began a series of workshops on nonviolence, and we repeatedly asked ourselves: "Are you able to accept blows without retaliating?" "Are you able to endure the ordeal of jail?" We decided to schedule our direct-action program for the Easter season, realizing that except for Christmas, this is the main shopping period of the year. Knowing that a strong economic-withdrawal program would be the by-product of direct action, we felt that this would be the best time to bring pressure to bear on the merchants for the needed change.

Then it occurred to us that Birmingham's mayoral election was coming up   9
in March, and we speedily decided to postpone action until after election-day.
When we discovered that the Commissioner of Public Safety, Eugene "Bull"
Connor, had piled up enough votes to be in the run-off, we decided again to
postpone action until the day after the run-off so that the demonstrations could
not be used to cloud the issues. Like many others, we waited to see Mr. Connor defeated, and to this end we endured postponement after postponement.
Having aided in this community need, we felt that our direct-action program
could be delayed no longer.

You may well ask, "Why direct action? Why sit-ins, marches, and so forth?   10
Isn't negotiation a better path?" You are quite right in calling for negotiation.
Indeed, this is the very purpose of direct action. Nonviolent direct action seeks
to create such a crisis and foster such a tension that a community which has
constantly refused to negotiate is forced to confront the issue. It seeks so to
dramatize the issue that it can no longer be ignored. My citing the creation of
tension as part of the work of the nonviolent-resister may sound rather shocking. But I must confess that I am not afraid of the word "tension." I have
earnestly opposed violent tension, but there is a type of constructive, nonviolent tension which is necessary for growth. Just as Socrates[4] felt that it was
necessary to create a tension in the mind so that individuals could rise from
the bondage of myths and half-truths to the unfettered realm of creative analysis and objective appraisal, so must we see the need for nonviolent gadflies to
create the kind of tension in society that will help men rise from the dark
depths of prejudice and racism to the majestic heights of understanding and
brotherhood.

The purpose of our direct-action program is to create a situation so crisis-   11
packed that it will inevitably open the door to negotiation. I therefore concur
with you in your call for negotiation. Too long has our beloved Southland
been bogged down in a tragic effort to live in monologue rather than dialogue.

One of the basic points in your statement is that the action that I and my   12
associates have taken in Birmingham is untimely. Some have asked: "Why
didn't you give the new city administration time to act?" The only answer that
I can give to this query is that the new Birmingham administration must be
prodded about as much as the outgoing one, before it will act. We are sadly
mistaken if we feel that the election of Albert Boutwell as mayor will bring the
millennium to Birmingham. While Mr. Boutwell is a much more gentle person than Mr. Connor, they are both segregationists, dedicated to maintenance
of the status quo. I have hoped that Mr. Boutwell will be reasonable enough
to see the futility of massive resistance to desegregation. But he will not see this
without pressure from devotees of civil rights. My friends, I must say to you
that we have not made a single gain in civil rights without determined legal
and nonviolent pressure. Lamentably, it is an historical fact that privileged
groups seldom give up their privileges voluntarily. Individuals may see the moral

---

[4]Socrates (469–399 B.C.), a Greek philosopher who often pretended ignorance in arguments in
order to expose the errors in his opponent's reasoning.

light and voluntarily give up their unjust posture; but, as Reinhold Niebuhr[5] has reminded us, groups tend to be more immoral than individuals.

We know through painful experience that freedom is never voluntarily given   13
by the oppressor; it must be demanded by the oppressed. Frankly, I have yet to engage in a direct-action campaign that was "well timed" in the view of those who have not suffered unduly from the disease of segregation. For years now I have heard the word "Wait!" It rings in the ear of every Negro with piercing familiarity. This "Wait" has almost always meant "Never." We must come to see, with one of our distinguished jurists, that "justice too long delayed is justice denied."

We have waited for more than 340 years for our constitutional and God-   14
given rights. The nations of Asia and Africa are moving with jetlike speed toward gaining political independence, but we still creep at horse-and-buggy pace toward gaining a cup of coffee at a lunch counter. Perhaps it is easy for those who have never felt the stinging darts of segregation to say, "Wait." But when you have seen vicious mobs lynch your mothers and fathers at will and drown your sisters and brothers at whim; when you have seen hate-filled policemen curse, kick, and even kill your black brothers and sisters; when you see the vast majority of your twenty million Negro brothers smothering in an airtight cage of poverty in the midst of an affluent society; when you suddenly find your tongue twisted and your speech stammering as you seek to explain to your six-year-old daughter why she can't go to the public amusement park that has just been advertised on television, and see tears welling up in her eyes when she is told that Funtown is closed to colored children, and see ominous clouds of inferiority beginning to form in her little mental sky, and see her beginning to distort her personality by developing an unconscious bitterness toward white people; when you have to concoct an answer for a five-year-old son who is asking, "Daddy, why do white people treat colored people so mean?"; when you take a cross-country drive and find it necessary to sleep night after night in the uncomfortable corners of your automobile because no motel will accept you; when you are humiliated day in and day out by nagging signs reading "white" and "colored"; when your first name becomes "nigger," your middle name becomes "boy" (however old you are) and your last name becomes "John," and your wife and mother are never given the respected title "Mrs."; when you are harried by day and haunted by night by the fact that you are a Negro, living constantly at tiptoe stance, never quite knowing what to expect next, and are plagued with inner fears and outer resentments; when you are forever fighting a degenerating sense of "nobodiness"—then you will understand why we find it difficult to wait. There comes a time when the cup of endurance runs over, and men are no longer willing to be plunged into the abyss of despair. I hope, sirs, you can understand our legitimate and unavoidable impatience.

You express a great deal of anxiety over our willingness to break laws. This   15

---

[5] Reinhold Niebuhr (1892–1971), American philosopher and theologian.

is certainly a legitimate concern. Since we so diligently urge people to obey the Supreme Court's decision of 1954 outlawing segregation in the public schools, at first glance it may seem rather paradoxical for us consciously to break laws. One may well ask: "How can you advocate breaking some laws and obeying others?" The answer lies in the fact that there are two types of laws: just and unjust. I would be the first to advocate obeying just laws. One has not only a legal but a moral responsibility to obey just laws. Conversely, one has a moral responsibility to disobey unjust laws. I would agree with St. Augustine that "an unjust law is no law at all."

Now, what is the difference between the two? How does one determine whether   16
a law is just or unjust? A just law is a man-made code that squares with the moral law or the law of God. An unjust law is a code that is out of harmony with the moral law. To put it in the terms of St. Thomas Aquinas: An unjust law is a human law that is not rooted in eternal law and natural law. Any law that uplifts human personality is just. Any law that degrades human personality is unjust. All segregation statutes are unjust because segregation distorts the soul and damages the personality. It gives the segregator a false sense of superiority and the segregated a false sense of inferiority. Segregation, to use the terminology of the Jewish philosopher Martin Buber, substitutes an "I–it" relationship for an "I–thou" relationship and ends up relegating persons to the status of things. Hence segregation is not only politicially, economically, and sociologically unsound, it is morally wrong and sinful. Paul Tillich has said that sin is separation. Is not segregation an existential expression of man's tragic separation, his awful estrangement, his terrible sinfulness? Thus it is that I can urge men to obey the 1954 decision of the Supreme Court, for it is morally right; and I can urge them to disobey segregation ordinances, for they are morally wrong.

Let us consider a more concrete example of just and unjust laws. An unjust   17
law is a code that a numerical or power majority group compels a minority group to obey but does not make binding on itself. This is *difference* made legal. By the same token, a just law is a code that a majority compels a minority to follow and that it is willing to follow itself. This is *sameness* made legal.

Let me give another explanation. A law is unjust if it is inflicted on a mi-   18
nority that, as a result of being denied the right to vote, had no part in enacting or devising the law. Who can say that the legislature of Alabama which set up that state's segregation laws was democratically elected? Throughout Alabama all sorts of devious methods are used to prevent Negroes from becoming registered voters, and there are some counties in which, even though Negroes constitute a majority of the population, not a single Negro is registered. Can any law enacted under such circumstances be considered democratically structured?

Sometimes a law is just on its face and unjust in its application. For in-   19
stance, I have been arrested on a charge of parading without a permit. Now, there is nothing wrong in having an ordinance which requires a permit for a parade. But such an ordinance becomes unjust when it is used to maintain segregation and to deny citizens the First-Amendment privilege of peaceful assembly and protest.

I hope you are able to see the distinction I am trying to point out. In no 20
sense do I advocate evading or defying the law, as would the rabid segregation-
ist. That would lead to anarchy. One who breaks an unjust law must do so
openly, lovingly, and with a willingness to accept the penalty. I submit that an
individual who breaks a law that conscience tells him is unjust, and who willingly accepts the penalty of imprisonment in order to arouse the conscience of
the community over its injustice, is in reality expressing the highest respect for
law.

Of course, there is nothing new about this kind of civil disobedience. It was 21
evidenced sublimely in the refusal of Shadrach, Meshach, and Abednego to
obey the laws of Nebuchadnezzar, on the ground that a higher moral law was
at stake.[6] It was practiced superbly by the early Christians, who were willing to
face hungry lions and the excruciating pain of chopping blocks rather than
submit to certain unjust laws of the Roman Empire. To a degree, academic
freedom is a reality today because Socrates practiced civil disobedience. In our
own nation, the Boston Tea Party represented a massive act of civil disobedience.

We should never forget that everything Adolf Hitler did in Germany was 22
"legal" and everything the Hungarian freedom fighters did in Hungary was
"illegal." It was "illegal" to aid and comfort a Jew in Hitler's Germany. Even
so, I am sure that, had I lived in Germany at the time, I would have aided
and comforted my Jewish brothers. If today I lived in a Communist country
where certain principles dear to the Christian faith are suppressed, I would
openly advocate disobeying that country's anti-religious laws.

I must make two honest confessions to you, my Christian and Jewish broth- 23
ers. First, I must confess that over the past few years I have been gravely disappointed with the white moderate. I have almost reached the regrettable conclusion that the Negro's great stumbling block in his stride toward freedom is
not the white Citizen's Counciler[7] or the Ku Klux Klanner, but the white
moderate, who is more devoted to "order" than to justice; who prefers a negative peace which is the absence of tension to a positive peace which is the
presence of justice; who constantly says, "I agree with you in the goal you seek,
but I cannot agree with your methods of direct action"; who paternalistically
believes he can set the timetable for another man's freedom; who lives by a
mythical concept of time and who constantly advises the Negro to wait for a
"more convenient season." Shallow understanding from people of good will is
more frustrating than absolute misunderstanding from people of ill will. Luke-
warm acceptance is much more bewildering than outright rejection.

I had hoped that the white moderate would understand that law and order 24
exist for the purpose of establishing justice and that when they fail in this
purpose they become the dangerously structured dams that block the flow of
social progress. I had hoped that the white moderate would understand that the

---

[6] See Daniel 1:7–3:30.
[7] White Citizen's Councils sprang up in the South after 1954 (the year the Supreme Court
declared segregated education unconstitutional) to fight against desegregation.

present tension in the South is a necessary phase of the transition from an obnoxious negative peace, in which the Negro passively accepted his unjust plight, to a substantive and positive peace, in which all men will respect the dignity and worth of human personality. Actually, we who engage in nonviolent direct action are not the creators of tension. We merely bring to the surface the hidden tension that is already alive. We bring it out in the open, where it can be seen and dealt with. Like a boil that can never be cured so long as it is covered up but must be opened with all its ugliness to the natural medicines of air and light, injustice must be exposed, with all the tension its exposure creates, to the light of human conscience and the air of national opinion, before it can be cured.

In your statement you assert that our actions, even though peaceful, must   25
be condemned because they precipitate violence. But is this a logical assertion? Isn't this like condemning a robbed man because his possession of money precipitated the evil act of robbery? Isn't this like condemning Socrates because his unswerving commitment to truth and his philosophical inquiries precipitated the act by the misguided populace in which they made him drink hemlock? Isn't this like condemning Jesus because his unique God-consciousness and never-ceasing devotion to God's will precipitated the evil act of crucifixion? We must come to see that, as the federal courts have consistently affirmed, it is wrong to urge an individual to cease his efforts to gain his basic constitutional rights because the quest may precipitate violence. Society must protect the robbed and punish the robber.

I had also hoped that the white moderate would reject the myth concerning   26
time in relation to the struggle for freedom. I have just received a letter from a white brother in Texas. He writes: "All Christians know that the colored people will receive equal rights eventually, but it is possible that you are in too great a religious hurry. It has taken Christianity almost two thousand years to accomplish what it has. The teachings of Christ take time to come to earth." Such an attitude stems from a tragic misconception of time, from the strangely irrational notion that there is something in the very flow of time that will inevitably cure all ills. Actually, time itself is neutral; it can be used either destructively or constructively. More and more I feel that the people of ill will have used time much more effectively than have the people of good will. We will have to repent in this generation not merely for the hateful words and actions of the bad people, but for the appalling silence of the good people. Human progress never rolls in on wheels of inevitability; it comes through the tireless efforts of men willing to be co-workers with God, and without this hard work, time itself becomes an ally of the forces of social stagnation. We must use time creatively, in the knowledge that the time is always ripe to do right. Now is the time to make real the promise of democracy and transform our pending national elegy into a creative psalm of brotherhood. Now is the time to lift our national policy from the quicksand of racial injustice to the solid rock of human dignity.

You speak of our activity in Birmingham as extreme. At first I was rather   27
disappointed that fellow clergymen would see my nonviolent efforts as those of

an extremist. I began thinking about the fact that I stand in the middle of two opposing forces in the Negro community. One is a force of complacency, made up in part of Negroes who, as a result of long years of oppression, are so drained of self-respect and a sense of "somebodiness" that they have adjusted to segregation; and in part of a few middle-class Negroes who, because of a degree of academic and economic security and because in some ways they profit by segregation, have become insensitive to the problems of the masses. The other force is one of bitterness and hatred, and it comes perilously close to advocating violence. It is expressed in the various black nationalist groups that are springing up across the nation, the largest and best-known being Elijah Muhammad's Muslim movement.[8] Nourished by the Negro's frustration over the continued existence of racial discrimination, this movement is made up of people who have lost faith in America, who have absolutely repudiated Christianity, and who have concluded that the white man is an incorrigible "devil."

I have tried to stand between these two forces, saying that we need emulate   28
neither the "do-nothingism" of the complacent nor the hatred and despair of the black nationalist. For there is the more excellent way of love and nonviolent protest. I am grateful to God that, through the influence of the Negro church, the way of nonviolence became an integral part of our struggle.

If this philosophy had not emerged, by now many streets of the South would,   29
I am convinced, be flowing with blood. And I am further convinced that if our white brothers dismiss as "rabble-rousers" and "outside agitators" those of us who employ nonviolent direct action, and if they refuse to support our nonviolent efforts, millions of Negroes will, out of frustration and despair, seek solace and security in black-nationalist ideologies—a development that would inevitably lead to a frightening racial nightmare.

Oppressed people cannot remain oppressed forever. The yearning for free-   30
dom eventually manifests itself, and that is what has happened to the American Negro. Something within has reminded him of his birthright of freedom, and something without has reminded him that it can be gained. Consciously or unconsciously, he has been caught up by the *Zeitgeist*,[9] and with his black brothers of Africa and his brown and yellow brothers of Asia, South America, and the Caribbean, the United States Negro is moving with a sense of great urgency toward the promised land of racial justice. If one recognizes this vital urge that has engulfed the Negro community, one should readily understand why public demonstrations are taking place. The Negro has many pent-up resentments and latent frustrations, and he must release them. So let him march; let him make prayer pilgrimages to the city hall; let him go on freedom rides[10]— and try to understand why he must do so. If his repressed emotions are not released in nonviolent ways, they will seek expression through violence; this is

---

[8] Elijah Muhammad (1897–1975), leader of a black Muslim religious group that rejected integration and called upon blacks to fight to establish their own nation.

[9] The spirit of the time.

[10] In 1961, hundreds of blacks and whites, under the direction of the Congress of Racial Equality (CORE), deliberately violated laws in Southern states that required segregation in buses and bus terminals.

not a threat but a fact of history. So I have not said to my people, "Get rid of your discontent." Rather, I have tried to say that this normal and healthy discontent can be channeled into the creative outlet of nonviolent direct action. And now this approach is being termed extremist.

But though I was initially disappointed at being categorized as an extremist, 31
as I continued to think about the matter I gradually gained a measure of satisfaction from the label. Was not Jesus an extremist for love: "Love your enemies, bless them that curse you, do good to them that hate you, and pray for them which despitefully use you, and persecute you." Was not Amos an extremist for justice: "Let justice roll down like waters and righteousness like an ever-flowing stream." Was not Paul an extremist for the Christian gospel: "I bear in my body the marks of the Lord Jesus." Was not Martin Luther an extremist: "Here I stand; I cannot do otherwise, so help me God." And John Bunyan: "I will stay in jail to the end of my days before I make a butchery of my conscience." And Abraham Lincoln: "This nation cannot survive half slave and half free." And Thomas Jefferson: "We hold these truths to be self-evident, that all men are created equal. . . ." So the question is not whether we will be extremists, but what kind of extremists we will be. Will we be extremists for hate or for love? Will we be extremists for the preservation of injustice or for the extension of justice? In that dramatic scene on Calvary's hill three men were crucified. We must never forget that all three were crucified for the same crime—the crime of extremism. Two were extremists for immorality, and thus fell below their environment. The other, Jesus Christ, was an extremist for love, truth, and goodness, and thereby rose above his environment. Perhaps the South, the nation, and the world are in dire need of creative extemists.

I had hoped that the white moderate would see this need. Perhaps I was too 32
optimistic; perhaps I expected too much. I suppose I should have realized that few members of the oppressor race can understand the deep groans and passionate yearnings of the oppressed race, and still fewer have the vision to see that injustice must be rooted out by strong, persistent, and determined action. I am thankful, however, that some of our white brothers in the South have grasped the meaning of this social revolution and committed themselves to it. They are still all too few in quantity, but they are big in quality. Some—such as Ralph McGill, Lillian Smith, Harry Golden, James McBride Dabbs, Ann Braden, and Sarah Patton Boyle—have written about our struggle in eloquent and prophetic terms. Others have marched with us down nameless streets of the South. They have languished in filthy, roach-infested jails, suffering the abuse and brutality of policemen who view them as "dirty nigger-lovers." Unlike so many of their moderate brothers and sisters, they have recognized the urgency of the moment and sensed the need for powerful "action" antidotes to combat the disease of segregation.

Let me take note of my other major disappointment. I have been so greatly 33
disappointed with the white church and its leadership. Of course, there are some notable exceptions. I am not unmindful of the fact that each of you has taken some significant stands on this issue. I commend you, Reverend Stallings, for your Christian stand on this past Sunday, in welcoming Negroes to

your worship service on a nonsegregated basis. I commend the Catholic leaders of this state for integrating Spring Hill College several years ago.

But despite these notable exceptions, I must honestly reiterate that I have   34
been disappointed with the church. I do not say this as one of those negative critics who can always find something wrong with the church. I say this as a minister of the gospel, who loves the church; who was nurtured in its bosom; who has been sustained by its spiritual blessings and who will remain true to it as long as the cord of life shall lengthen.

When I was suddenly catapulted into the leadership of the bus protest in   35
Montgomery, Alabama, a few years ago, I felt we would be supported by the white church. I felt that the white ministers, priests, and rabbis of the South would be among our strongest allies. Instead, some have been outright opponents, refusing to understand the freedom movement and misrepresenting its leaders; all too many others have been more cautious than courageous and have remained silent behind the anesthetizing security of stained-glass windows.

In spite of my shattered dreams. I came to Birmingham with the hope that   36
the white religious leadership of this community would see the justice of our cause and, with deep moral concern, would serve as the channel through which our just grievances could reach the power structure. I had hoped that each of you would understand. But again I have been disappointed.

I have heard numerous southern religious leaders admonish their worshipers   37
to comply with a desegregation decision because it is the law, but I have longed to hear white ministers declare: "Follow this decree because integration is morally right and because the Negro is your brother." In the midst of blatant injustices inflicted upon the Negro, I have watched white churchmen stand on the sideline and mouth pious irrelevancies and sanctimonious trivialities. In the midst of a mighty struggle to rid our nation of racial and economic injustice, I have heard many ministers say: "Those are social issues, with which the gospel has no real concern." And I have watched many churches commit themselves to a completely otherworldly religion which makes a strange, un-Biblical distinction between body and soul, between the sacred and the secular.

I have traveled the length and breadth of Alabama, Mississippi, and all the   38
other southern states. On sweltering summer days and crisp autumn mornings I have looked at the South's beautiful churches with their lofty spires pointing heavenward. I have beheld the impressive outlines of her massive religious-education buildings. Over and over I have found myself asking: "What kind of people worship here? Who is their God? Where were their voices when the lips of Governor Barnett dripped with words of interposition and nullification? Where were they when Governor Wallace gave a clarion call for defiance and hatred? Where were their voices of support when bruised and weary Negro men and women decided to rise from the dark dungeons of complacency to the bright hills of creative protest?"

Yes, these questions are still in mind. In deep disappointment I have wept   39
over the laxity of the church. But be assured that my tears have been tears of

love. There can be no deep disappointment where there is not deep love. Yes, I love the church. How could I do otherwise? I am in the rather unique position of being the son, the grandson, and the great-grandson of preachers. Yes, I see the church as the body of Christ. But, oh! How we have blemished and scarred that body through social neglect and through fear of being nonconformists.

There was a time when the church was very powerful—in the time when   40
the early Christians rejoiced at being deemed worthy to suffer for what they believed. In those days the church was not merely a thermometer that recorded the ideas and principles of popular opinion; it was a thermostat that transformed the mores of society. Whenever the early Christians entered a town, the people in power became disturbed and immediately sought to convict the Christians for being "disturbers of the peace" and "outside agitators." But the Christians pressed on, in the conviction that they were "a colony of heaven," called to obey God rather than man. Small in number, they were big in commitment. They were too God-intoxicated to be "astronomically intimidated." By their effort and example they brought an end to such ancient evils as infanticide and gladiatorial contests.

Things are different now. So often the contemporary church is a weak, in-   41
effectual voice with an uncertain sound. So often it is an archdefender of the status quo. Far from being disturbed by the presence of the church, the power structure of the average community is consoled by the church's silent—and often even vocal—sanction of things as they are.

But the judgment of God is upon the church as never before. If today's   42
church does not recapture the sacrificial spirit of the early church, it will lose its authenticity, forfeit the loyalty of millions, and be dismissed as an irrelevant social club with no meaning for the twentieth century. Every day I meet young people whose disappointment with the church has turned into outright disgust.

Perhaps I have once again been too optimistic. Is organized religion too   43
inextricably bound to the status quo to save our nation and the world? Perhaps I must turn my faith to the inner spiritual church, the church within the church, as the true *ekklesia*[11] and the hope of the world. But again I am thankful to God that some noble souls from the ranks of organized religion have broken loose from the paralyzing chains of conformity and joined us as active partners in the struggle for freedom. They have left their secure congregations and walked the streets of Albany, Georgia, with us. They have gone down the highways of the South on tortuous rides for freedom. Yes, they have gone to jail with us. Some have been dismissed from their churches, have lost the support of their bishops and fellow ministers. But they have acted in the faith that right defeated is stronger than evil triumphant. Their witness has been the spiritual salt that has preserved the true meaning of the gospel in these troubled times. They have carved a tunnel of hope through the dark mountain of disappointment.

---

[11] The Greek *New Testament* word for the early Christian church.

I hope the church as a whole will meet the challenge of this decisive hour.   44
But even if the church does not come to the aid of justice, I have no despair
about the future. I have no fear about the outcome of our struggle in Birmingham, even if our motives are at present misunderstood. We will reach the goal
of freedom in Birmingham and all over the nation, because the goal of America is freedom. Abused and scorned though we may be, our destiny is tied up
with America's destiny. Before the pilgrims landed at Plymouth, we were here.
Before the pen of Jefferson etched the majestic words of the Declaration of
Independence across the pages of history, we were here. For more than two
centuries our forebears labored in this country without wages; they made cotton
king; they built the homes of their masters while suffering gross injustice and
shameful humiliation—and yet out of a bottomless vitality they continued to
thrive and develop. If the inexpressible cruelties of slavery could not stop us,
the opposition we now face will surely fail. We will win our freedom because
the sacred heritage of our nation and the eternal will of God are embodied in
our echoing demands.

Before closing I feel impelled to mention one other point in your statement   45
that has troubled me profoundly. You warmly commended the Birmingham
police force for keeping "order" and "preventing violence." I doubt that you
would have so warmly commended the police force if you had seen its dogs
sinking their teeth into unarmed, nonviolent Negroes. I doubt that you would
so quickly commend the policemen if you were to observe their ugly and inhumane treatment of Negroes here in the city jail; if you were to watch them
push and curse old Negro women and young Negro girls; if you were to see
them slap and kick old Negro men and young boys; if you were to observe
them, as they did on two occasions, refuse to give us food because we wanted
to sing our grace together. I cannot join you in your praise of the Birmingham
police department.

It is true that the police have exercised a degree of discipline in handling the   46
demonstrators. In this sense they have conducted themselves rather "nonviolently" in public. But for what purpose? To preserve the evil system of segregation. Over the past few years I have consistently preached that nonviolence
demands that the means we use must be as pure as the ends we seek. I have
tried to make clear that it is wrong to use immoral means to attain moral ends.
But now I must affirm that it is just as wrong, or perhaps even more so, to use
moral means to preserve immoral ends. Perhaps Mr. Connor and his policemen have been rather nonviolent in public, as was Chief Pritchett in Albany,
Georgia, but they have used the moral means of nonviolence to maintain the
immoral end of racial injustice. As T. S. Eliot[12] has said, "The last temptation
is the greatest treason: To do the right deed for the wrong reason."

I wish you had commended the Negro sit-inners and demonstrators of Bir-   47
mingham for their sublime courage, their willingness to suffer, and their amazing discipline in the midst of great provocation. One day the South will rec-

---

[12]Thomas Stearns Eliot (1888–1965), American-born poet.

ognize its real heroes. They will be the James Merediths,[13] with the noble sense of purpose that enables them to face jeering and hostile mobs, and with the agonizing loneliness that characterizes the life of the pioneer. They will be old, oppressed, battered Negro women, symbolized in a seventy-two-year-old woman in Montgomery, Alabama, who rose up with a sense of dignity and with her people decided not to ride segregated buses, and who responded with ungrammatical profundity to one who inquired about her weariness: "My feets is tired, but my soul is at rest." They will be the young high school and college students, the young ministers of the gospel and a host of their elders, courageously and nonviolently sitting in at lunch counters and willingly going to jail for conscience' sake. One day the South will know that when these disinherited children of God sat down at lunch counters, they were in reality standing up for what is best in the American dream and for the most sacred values in our Judaeo-Christian heritage, thereby bringing our nation back to those great wells of democracy which were dug deep by the founding fathers in their formulation of the Constitution and the Declaration of Independence.

Never before have I written so long a letter. I'm afraid it is much too long   48
to take your precious time. I can assure you that it would have been much shorter if I had been writing from a comfortable desk, but what else can one do when he is alone in a narrow jail cell, other than write long letters, think long thoughts, and pray long prayers?

If I have said anything in this letter that overstates the truth and indicates an   49
unreasonable impatience, I beg you to forgive me. If I have said anything that understates the truth and indicates my having a patience that allows me to settle for anything less than brotherhood, I beg God to forgive me.

I hope this letter finds you strong in the faith. I hope that circumstances will   50
soon make it possible for me to meet each of you, not as an integrationist or a civil-rights leader but as a fellow clergyman and a Christian brother. Let us all hope that the dark clouds of a racial prejudice will soon pass away and the deep fog of misunderstanding will be lifted from our fear-drenched communities, and in some not too distant tomorrow the radiant stars of love and brotherhood will shine over our great nation with all their scintillating beauty.

Yours for the cause of Peace and Brotherhood,
MARTIN LUTHER KING, JR.

QUESTIONS
1. Identify some of King's figures of speech and discuss their effectiveness. **2.** Does your own experience bear out King's distinction (paragraph 10) between "violent" and "nonviolent" tension? Explain. **3.** Summarize and explain the argument King makes in paragraph 46 about "means" and "ends."

WRITING TOPIC
Central to King's argument is his distinction between just and unjust laws. Defend or take issue with that distinction.

---

[13]James Meredith was the first black to be admitted as a student at the University of Mississippi.

The Right Stuff

1979

TOM WOLFE [b. 1931]

A young man might go into military flight training believing that he was entering some sort of technical school in which he was simply going to acquire a
certain set of skills. Instead, he found himself all at once enclosed in a fraternity. And in this fraternity, even though it was military, men were not rated
by their outward rank as ensigns, lieutenants, commanders, or whatever. No,
herein the world was divided into those who had it and those who did not.
This quality, this *it*, was never named, however, nor was it talked about in any
way.

As to just what this ineffable quality was . . . well, it obviously involved
bravery. But it was not bravery in the simple sense of being willing to risk your
life. The idea seemed to be that any fool could do that, if that was all that was
required, just as any fool could throw away his life in the process. No, the idea
here (in the all-enclosing fraternity) seemed to be that a man should have the
ability to go up in a hurtling piece of machinery and put his hide on the line
and then have the moxie, the reflexes, the experience, the coolness, to pull it
back in the last yawning moment—and then to go up again *the next day*, and
the next day, and every next day, even if the series should prove infinite—and,
ultimately, in its best expression, do so in a cause that means something to
thousands, to a people, a nation, to humanity, to God. Nor was there *a test*
to show whether or not a pilot had this righteous quality. There was, instead,
a seemingly infinite series of tests. A career in flying was like climbing one of
those ancient Babylonian pyramids made up of a dizzy progression of steps and
ledges, a ziggurat, a pyramid extraordinarily high and steep; and the idea was
to prove at every foot of the way up that pyramid that you were one of the
elected and anointed ones who had *the right stuff* and could move higher and
higher and even—ultimately, God willing, one day—that you might be able
to join that special few at the very top, that elite who had the capacity to bring
tears to men's eyes, the very Brotherhood of the Right Stuff itself.

None of this was to be mentioned, and yet it was acted out in a way that a
young man could not fail to understand. When a new flight (i.e., a class) of
trainees arrived at Pensacola, they were brought into an auditorium for a little
lecture. An officer would tell him: "Take a look at the man on either side of
you." Quite a few actually swiveled their heads this way and that, in the interest of appearing diligent. Then the officer would say: "One of the three of you
is not going to make it!"—meaning, not get his wings. That was the opening
theme, the *motif* of primary training. We already know that one-third of you
do not have the right stuff—it only remains to find out who.

Furthermore, that was the way it turned out. At every level in one's progress
up that staggeringly high pyramid, the world was once more divided into those

men who had the right stuff to continue the climb and those who had to be *left behind* in the most obvious way. Some were eliminated in the course of the opening classroom work, as either not smart enough or not hardworking enough, and were left behind. Then came the basic flight instruction, in single-engine, propeller-driven trainers, and a few more—even though the military tried to make this stage easy—were washed out and left behind. Then came more demanding levels, one after the other, formation flying, instrument flying, jet training, all-weather flying, gunnery, and at each level more were washed out and left behind. By this point easily a third of the original candidates had been, indeed, eliminated . . . from the ranks of those who might prove to have the right stuff.

In the Navy, in addition to the stages that Air Force trainees went through, the neophyte always had waiting for him, out in the ocean, a certain grim gray slab; namely, the deck of an aircraft carrier; and with it perhaps the most difficult routine in military flying, carrier landings. He was shown films about it, he heard lectures about it, and he knew that carrier landings were hazardous. He first practiced touching down on the shape of a flight deck painted on an airfield. He was instructed to touch down and gun right off. This was safe enough—the shape didn't move, at least—but it could do terrible things to, let us say, the gyroscope of the soul. *That shape!—it's so damned small!* And more candidates were washed out and left behind. Then came the day, without warning, when those who remained were sent out over the ocean for the first of many days of reckoning with the slab. The first day was always a clear day with little wind and a calm sea. The carrier was so steady that it seemed, from up there in the air, to be resting on pilings, and the candidate usually made his first carrier landing successfully, with relief and even *élan*. Many young candidates looked like terrific aviators up to that very point—and it was not until they were actually standing on the carrier deck that they first began to wonder if they had the proper stuff, after all. In the training film the flight deck was a grand piece of gray geometry, perilous, to be sure, but an amazing abstract shape as one looks down upon it on the screen. And yet once the newcomer's two feet were on it . . . *Geometry*—my God, man, this is a . . . skillet! It *heaved*, it moved up and down underneath his feet, it pitched up, it pitched down, it rolled to port (this great beast *rolled!*) and it rolled to starboard, as the ship moved into the wind and, therefore, into the waves, and the wind kept sweeping across, sixty feet up in the air out in the open sea, and there were no railings whatsoever. This was a *skillet!*—a frying pan!—a short-order grill!—not gray but black, smeared with skid marks from one end to the other and glistening with pools of hydraulic fluid and the occasional jet-fuel slick, all of it still hot, sticky, greasy, runny, virulent from God knows what traumas—still ablaze!—consumed in detonations, explosions, flames, combustion, roars, shrieks, whines, blasts, horrible shudders, fracturing impacts, as little men in screaming red and yellow and purple and green shirts with black Mickey Mouse helmets over their ears skittered about on the surface as if for their very lives (you've said it now!), hooking fighter planes onto the catapult shuttles so that

5

they can explode their afterburners and be slung off the deck in a red-mad fury with a *kaboom!* that pounds through the entire deck—a procedure that seems absolutely controlled, orderly, sublime, however, compared to what he is about to watch as aircraft return to the ship for what is known in the engineering stoicisms of the military as "recovery and arrest." To say that an F–4 was coming back onto this heaving barbecue from out of the sky at a speed of 135 knots . . . that might have been the truth in the training lecture, but it did not begin to get across the idea of what the newcomer saw from the deck itself, because it created the notion that perhaps the plane was gliding in. On the deck one knew differently! As the aircraft came closer and the carrier heaved on into the waves and the plane's speed did not diminish and the deck did not grow steady—indeed, it pitched up and down five or ten feet per greasy heave—one experienced a neural alarm that no lecture could have prepared him for: This is not an *airplane* coming toward me, it is a brick with some poor sonof-abitch riding it *(someone much like myself!)*, and it is not *gliding*, it is *falling*, a fifty-thousand-pound brick, headed not for a stripe on the deck but for *me*—and with a horrible *smash!* it hits the skillet, and with a blur of momentum as big as a freight train's it hurtles toward the far end of the deck—another blind-ing storm—another roar as the pilot pushes the throttle up to full military power and another smear of rubber screams out over the skillet—and this is nominal!—quite okay!—for a wire stretched across the deck has grabbed the hook on the end of the plane as it hit the deck tail down, and the smash was the rest of the fifteen-ton brute slamming onto the deck, as it tripped up, so that it is now straining against the wire at full throttle, in case it hadn't held and the plane had "boltered" off the end of the deck and had to struggle up into the air again. And already the Mickey Mouse helmets are running toward the fiery monster . . .

And the candidate, looking on, begins to *feel* that great heaving sun-blazing   6
deathboard of a deck wallowing in his own vestibular system—and suddenly he finds himself backed up against his own limits. He ends up going to the flight surgeon with so-called conversion symptoms. Overnight he develops blurred vision or numbness in his hands and feet or sinusitis so severe that he cannot tolerate changes in altitude. On one level the symptom is real. He really can-not see too well or use his fingers or stand the pain. But somewhere in his subconscious he knows it is a plea and a beg-off; he shows not the slightest concern (the flight surgeon notes) that the condition might be permanent and affect him in whatever life awaits him outside the arena of the right stuff.

Those who remained, those who qualified for carrier duty—and even more   7
so those who later on qualified for *night* carrier duty—began to feel a bit like Gideon's warriors. *So many have been left behind!* The young warriors were now treated to a deathly sweet and quite unmentionable sight. They could gaze at length upon the crushed and wilted pariahs who had washed out. They could inspect those who did not have the righteous stuff.

The military did not have very merciful instincts. Rather than packing up   8
these poor souls and sending them home, the Navy, like the Air Force and the Marines, would try to make use of them in some other role, such as flight

controller. So the washout has to keep taking classes with the rest of his group, even though he can no longer touch an airplane. He sits there in the classes staring at sheets of paper with cataracts of sheer human mortification over his eyes while the rest steal looks at him . . . this man reduced to an ant, this untouchable, this poor sonofabitch. And in what test had he been found wanting? Why, it seemed to be nothing less than *manhood* itself. Naturally, this was never mentioned, either. Yet there it was. *Manliness, manhood, manly courage.* . . there was something ancient, primordial, irresistible about the challenge of this stuff, no matter what a sophisticated and rational age one might think he lived in.

Perhaps because it could not be talked about, the subject began to take on superstitious and even mystical outlines. A man either had it or he didn't! There was no such thing as having *most* of it. Moreover, it could blow at any seam. One day a man would be ascending the pyramid at a terrific clip, and the next—bingo—he would reach his own limits in the most unexpected way. Conrad and Schirra met an Air Force pilot who had had a great pal at Tyndall Air Force Base in Florida. This man had been the budding ace of the training class; he had flown the hottest fighter-style trainer, the T–38, like a dream; and then he began the routine step of being checked out in the T–33. The T–33 was not nearly as hot an aircraft as the T–38; it was essentially the old P–80 jet fighter. It had an exceedingly small cockpit. The pilot could barely move his shoulders. It was the sort of airplane of which everybody said, "You don't get into it, you *wear* it." Once inside a T–33 cockpit this man, this budding ace, developed claustrophobia of the most paralyzing sort. He tried everything to overcome it. He even went to a psychiatrist, which was a serious mistake for a military officer if his superiors learned of it. But nothing worked. He was shifted over to flying jet transports, such as the C–135. Very demanding and necessary aircraft they were, too, and he was still spoken of as an excellent pilot. But as everyone knew—and, again, it was never explained in so many words—only those who were assigned to fighter squadrons, the "fighter jocks," as they called each other with a self-satisfied irony, remained in the true fraternity. Those assigned to transports were not humiliated like washouts—*somebody* had to fly those planes—nevertheless, they, too, had been *left behind* for lack of the right stuff.

Or a man could go for a routine physical one fine day, feeling like a million dollars, and be grounded for *fallen arches*. It happened!—just like that! (And try raising them.) Or for breaking his wrist and losing only *part* of its mobility. Or for a minor deterioration of eyesight, or for any of hundreds of reasons that would make no difference to a man in an ordinary occupation. As a result all fighter jocks began looking upon doctors as their natural enemies. Going to see a flight surgeon was a no-gain proposition; a pilot could only hold his own or lose in the doctor's office. To be grounded for a medical reason was no humiliation, looked at objectively. But it was a humiliation, nonetheless—for it meant you no longer had that indefinable, unutterable, integral stuff. (It could blow at *any* seam.)

All the hot young fighter jocks began trying to test the limits themselves in a superstitious way. They were like believing Presbyterians of a century before who used to probe their own experience to see if they were truly among *the elect*. When a fighter pilot was in training, whether in the Navy or the Air Force, his superiors were continually spelling out strict rules for him, about the use of the aircraft and conduct in the sky. They repeatedly forbade so-called hot-dog stunts, such as outside loops, buzzing, flat-hatting, hedgehopping and flying under bridges. But somehow one got the message that the man who truly *had* it could ignore those rules—not that he should make a point of it, but that he *could*—and that after all there was only one way to find out—and that in some strange unofficial way, peeking through his fingers, his instructor halfway expected him to challenge all the limits. They would give a lecture about how a pilot should never fly without a good solid breakfast—eggs, bacon, toast, and so forth—because if he tried to fly with his blood-sugar level too low, it could impair his alertness. Naturally, the next day every hot dog in the unit would get up and have a breakfast consisting of one cup of black coffee and take off and go up into a vertical climb until the weight of the ship exactly canceled out the upward pull of the engine and his air speed was zero, and he would hang there for one thick adrenal instant—and then fall like a rock, until one of three things happened: he keeled over nose first and regained his aerodynamics and all was well, he went into a spin and fought his way out of it, or he went into a spin and had to eject or crunch it, which was always supremely possible.

Likewise, "hassling"—mock dogfighting—was strictly forbidden, and so naturally young fighter jocks could hardly wait to go up in, say, a pair of F–100s and start the duel by making a pass at each other at 800 miles an hour, the winner being the pilot who could slip in behind the other one and get locked in on his tail ("wax his tail"), and it was not uncommon for some eager jock to try too tight an outside turn and have his engine flame out, whereupon, unable to restart it, he has to eject . . . and he shakes his fist at the victor as he floats down by parachute and his half-a-million-dollar aircraft goes *kaboom!* on the palmetto grass or the desert floor, and he starts thinking about how he can get together with the other guy back at the base in time for the two of them to get their stories straight before the investigation: "I don't know what happened, sir. I was pulling up after a target run, and it just flamed out on me." Hassling was forbidden, and hassling that led to the destruction of an aircraft was a serious court-martial offense, and the man's superiors knew that the engine hadn't *just flamed out*, but every unofficial impulse on the base seemed to be saying: "Hell, we wouldn't give you a nickel for a pilot who hasn't done some crazy rat-racing like that. It's all part of the right stuff."

The other side of this impulse showed up in the reluctance of the young jocks to admit it when they had maneuvered themselves into a bad corner they couldn't get out of. There were two reasons why a fighter pilot hated to declare an emergency. First, it triggered a complex and very public chain of events at the field: all other incoming fights were held up, including many of one's comrades who were probably low on fuel; the fire trucks came trundling out to the runway like yellow toys (as seen from way up there), the better to illustrate one's hapless state; and the bureaucracy began to crank up the paper monster for the investigation that always followed. And second, to declare an emergency, one first had to reach that conclusion in his own mind, which to the young pilot was the same as saying: "A minute ago I *had* it—now I need your help!" To have a bunch of young fighter pilots up in the air thinking this way used to drive flight controllers crazy. They would see a ship beginning to drift off the radar, and they couldn't rouse the pilot on the microphone for anything other than a few meaningless mumbles, and they would know he was probably out there with engine failure at a low altitude, trying to reignite by lowering his auxiliary generator rig, which had a little propeller that was supposed to spin in the slipstream like a child's pinwheel.

"Whiskey Kilo Two Eight, do you want to declare an emergency?"   14

This would rouse him!—to say: "Negative, negative, Whiskey Kilo Two Eight   15
is not declaring an emergency."

Kaboom. Believers in the right stuff would rather crash and burn.   16

One fine day, after he had joined a fighter squadron, it would dawn on the   17
young pilot exactly how the losers in the great fraternal competition were now being left behind. Which is to say, not by instructors or other superiors or by failures at prescribed levels of competence, but by death. At this point the essence of the enterprise would begin to dawn on him. Slowly, step by step, the ante had been raised until he was now involved in what was surely the grimmest and grandest gamble of manhood. Being a fighter pilot—for that matter, simply taking off in a single-engine jet fighter of the Century series, such as an F–102, or any of the military's other marvelous bricks with fins on them—presented a man, on a perfectly sunny day, with more ways to get himself killed than his wife and children could imagine in their wildest fears. If he was barreling down the runway at two hundred miles an hour, completing the takeoff run, and the board started lighting up red, should he (a) abort the takeoff (and try to wrestle with the monster, which was gorged with jet fuel, out in the sand beyond the end of the runway) or (b) eject (and hope that the goddamned human cannonball trick works at zero altitude and he doesn't shatter an elbow or a kneecap on the way out) or (c) continue the takeoff and deal with the problem aloft (knowing full well that the ship may be on fire and therefore seconds away from exploding)? He would have one second to sort out the options and act, and this kind of little workaday decision came up all the time. Occasionally a man would look coldly at the binary problem he was now confronting every day—Right Stuff/Death—and decide it wasn't worth it and voluntarily shift over to transports or reconnaissance or whatever. And his comrades would wonder, for a day or so, what evil virus had invaded his soul . . . . as they left him behind. More often, however, the reverse would happen. Some college graduate would enter Navy aviation through the Reserves, simply as an alternative to the Army draft, fully intending to return to civilian life, to some waiting profession or family business; would become involved in the ob-

sessive business of ascending the ziggurat pyramid of flying; and, at the end of his enlistment, would astound everyone back home and very likely himself as well by signing up for another one. What on earth got into him? He couldn't explain it. After all, the very words for it had been amputated. A Navy study showed that two-thirds of the fighter pilots who were rated in the top rungs of their groups—i.e., the hottest young pilots—reenlisted when the time came, and practically all were college graduates. By this point, a young fighter jock was like the preacher in *Moby Dick* who climbs up into the pulpit on a rope ladder and then pulls the ladder up behind him; except the pilot could not use the words necessary to express the vital lessons. Civilian life, and even home and hearth, now seemed not only far away but far *below*, back down many levels of the pyramid of the right stuff.

A fighter pilot soon found he wanted to associate only with other fighter pilots. Who else could understand the nature of the little proposition (right stuff/death) they were all dealing with? And what other subject could compare with it? It was riveting! To talk about it in so many words was forbidden, of course. The very words *death, danger, bravery, fear* were not to be uttered except in the occasional specific instance or for ironic effect. Nevertheless, the subject could be adumbrated in *code* or *by example.* Hence the endless evenings of pilots huddled together talking about flying. On these long and drunken evenings (the bane of their family life) certain theorems would be propounded and demonstrated—and all by *code* and *example.* One theorem was: There are no *accidents* and no fatal flaws in the machines; there are only pilots with the wrong stuff. (I.e., blind Fate can't kill me.) When Bud Jennings crashed and burned in the swamps at Jacksonville, the other pilots in Pete Conrad's squadron said: *How could he have been so stupid?* It turned out that Jennings had gone up in the SNJ with his cockpit canopy opened in a way that was expressly forbidden in the manual, and carbon monoxide had been sucked in from the exhaust, and he passed out and crashed. All agreed that Bud Jennings was a good guy and a good pilot, but his epitaph on the ziggurat was: *How could he have been so stupid?* This seemed shocking at first, but by the time Conrad had reached the end of that bad string at Pax River, he was capable of his own corollary to the theorem: viz., no single factor ever killed a pilot; there was always a chain of mistakes. But what about Ted Whelan, who fell like a rock from 8,100 feet when his parachute failed? Well, the parachute was merely part of the chain: first, someone should have caught the structural defect that resulted in the hydraulic leak that triggered the emergency; second, Whelan did not check out his seat-parachute rig, and the drogue failed to separate the main parachute from the seat; but even after those two mistakes, Whelan had fifteen or twenty seconds, as he fell, to disengage himself from the seat and open the parachute manually. Why just stare at the scenery coming up to smack you in the face! And everyone nodded. (He failed—but I wouldn't have!) Once the theorem and the corollary were understood, the Navy's statistics about one in every four Navy aviators dying meant nothing. The figures were averages, and averages applied to those with average stuff.

18

A riveting subject, especially if it were one's own hide that was on the line. 19
Every evening at bases all over America, there were military pilots huddled in
officers clubs eagerly cutting the right stuff up in coded slices so they could talk
about it. What more compelling topic of conversation was there in the world?
In the Air Force there were even pilots who would ask the tower for priority
landing clearance so that they could make the beer call on time, at 4 p.m.
sharp, at the Officers Club. They would come right out and state the reason.
The drunken rambles began at four and sometimes went on for ten or twelve
hours. Such conversations! They diced that righteous stuff up into little bits,
bowed ironically to it, stumbled blindfolded around it, groped, lurched, belched,
staggered, bawled, sang, roared, and feinted at it with self-deprecating humor.
Nevertheless!—they never mentioned it by name. No, they used the approved
codes, such as: "Like a jerk I got myself into a hell of a corner today." They
told of how they "lucked out of it." To get across the extreme peril of his
exploit, one would use certain oblique cues. He would say, "I looked over at
Robinson"—who would be known to the listeners as a non-com who sometimes rode backseat to read radar—"and he wasn't talking any more, he was
just staring at the radar, like this, giving it that *zombie* look. Then I *knew* I was
in trouble!" Beautiful! Just right! For it would also be known to the listeners
that the non-coms advised one another: "*Never* fly with a lieutenant. *Avoid*
captains and majors. Hell, man, do yourself a favor: don't fly with anybody
below colonel." Which in turn said: "Those young bucks shoot dice with death!"
And yet once in the air the non-com had his own standards. He was determined to remain as outwardly cool as the pilot, so that when the pilot did
something that truly petrified him, he would say nothing; instead, he would
turn silent, catatonic, like a zombie. Perfect! *Zombie.* There you had it, compressed into a single word all of the foregoing. I'm a hell of a pilot! I shoot
dice with death! And now all you fellows know it! And I haven't spoken of that
unspoken stuff even once!

QUESTIONS

1. In paragraph 18, Wolfe says that the pilots operated on the theorem that "There
are no accidents or fatal flaws in the machines; there are only pilots with the wrong
stuff." Does Wolfe agree or disagree with this theorem?   **2.** Occasionally (e.g.,
in paragraphs 2, 7, and 19) Wolfe uses the term "righteous stuff" rather than "right
stuff." What different connotations do these two phrases have?

WRITING TOPICS

1. What is Wolfe's attitude toward the men with the right stuff?
2. Compare and contrast Wolfe's view of heroes and "the right stuff" with James
Thurber's in his story "The Greatest Man in the World" (p. 220).

Conformity and Rebellion

QUESTIONS AND WRITING TOPICS

1. What answers do the works in this section provide to the question posed by Albert Camus in the following passage:

> The present interest of the problem of rebellion only springs from the fact that nowadays whole societies have wanted to discard the sacred. We live in an unsacrosanct moment in history. Insurrection is certainly not the sum total of human experience. But history today, with all its storm and strife, compels us to say that rebellion is one of the essential dimensions of man. It is our historic reality. Unless we choose to ignore reality, we must find our values in it. Is it possible to find a rule of conduct outside the realm of religion and its absolute values? That is the question raised by rebellion.

Writing Topic: Use this observation as the basis for an analysis of the central characters in Mann's "Gladius Dei" and Ellison's " 'Repent, Harlequin!' Said the Ticktockman."

2. What support do the works in this section offer for Emily Dickinson's assertion that "Much Madness is divinest Sense"? **Writing Topic:** The central characters in Mann's "Gladius Dei" and Ellison's " 'Repent Harlequin!' Said the Ticktockman" are viewed by society as mad. How might it be argued that they exhibit "divinest sense"?

3. Which works in this section can be criticized on the grounds that while they attack the established order, they fail to provide any alternatives? **Writing Topic:** Discuss the validity of this objection for two of the following works: Wordsworth's "The World Is Too Much with Us," Lowell's "Patterns," Frost's "Departmental," Reed's "Naming of Parts," Forster's "My Wood."

4. In a number of these works, a single individual rebels against society and suffers defeat or death. Are these works therefore pessimistic and despairing? If not, then what is the purpose of the rebellions, and why do the authors choose to bring their characters to such ends? **Writing Topic:** Compare two works from this section that offer support for the idea that a single individual can have a decisive effect on the larger society.

5. Examine some of the representatives of order—Mister Blüthenzweig in "Gladius Dei," the lawyer in "Bartleby the Scrivener," Torvald Helmer, Old Man Warner in "The Lottery," the Ticktockman—and discuss what attitudes they share and how effectively they function as representatives of law and order. **Writing Topic:** Compare and contrast the kinds of order that each represents.

6. Amy Lowell's "Patterns," Karl Shapiro's "The Conscientious Objector," Lawrence Ferlinghetti's "In Goya's Greatest Scenes," and Henry Reed's "Naming of Parts" are, in different ways, antiwar poems. Which of these poems do you find the most articulate and convincing antiwar statement? **Writing Topic:** Discuss the argument that, while condemning war, none of these poems examines the specific reasons that a nation may be obliged to fight—self-defense and national self-interest, for example—and that consequently they are irresponsible.

7. Most of us live out our lives in the ordinary and humdrum world that is rejected in such poems as Wordsworth's "The World Is Too Much with Us" and Auden's "The Unknown Citizen." Can it be said that these poems are counsels to social irresponsibility? **Writing**

Topic: Consider whether "we" in Wordsworth's poem and the unknown citizen are simply objects of scorn or whether they deserve sympathy and perhaps even respect.

8. Many works in this section deal explicitly with the relationship between the individual and the state. What similarities of outlook do you find among them? **Writing Topic:** Compare and contrast the way that relationship is perceived in Ellison's " 'Repent, Harlequin!' Said the Ticktockman" and King's "Letter from Birmingham Jail."

Love
and
Hate

Separation II, 1896 by Edvard Munch

Love and death, it is often noted, are the two great themes of literature. Much of the literary art we have placed in the sections "Innocence and Experience" and "Conformity and Rebellion" speaks of love and death as well. But in those works other thematic interests dominate. In this section we gather a number of works in which love and hate are thematically central.

The rosy conception of love presented in many popular and sentimental stories ill prepares us for the complicated reality we will face. We know, and Ellen Goodman's essay "Being Loved Anyway" shows, that the course of true love never runs smooth, but in those popular stories the obstacles that hindered the lovers are simple and external. If the young lover can land the high-paying job or convince the beloved's parents that he or she is worthy despite social differences, all will be well. But love in life is rarely that simple. The external obstacles may be insuperable, or the obstacles may lie deep within the personality. The major obstacle may very well be an individual's difficult and painful effort to understand that he or she has been deceived by an immature and sentimental conception of love, a problem examined by Katherine Anne Porter in "The Necessary Enemy."

In this age of psychoanalytic awareness, the claims of the flesh are well recognized. But psychoanalytic theory teaches us, as well, to recognize the aggressive aspect of the human condition. The omnipresent selfishness that civilization attempts to check may be aggressively violent as well as lustful. Remarkably, many literary treatments of love envision the lovers sometimes as victims of the chaos that seems to surround them and sometimes as serene and safe in the midst of violence. D. H. Lawrence's "The Horse Dealer's Daughter" is embroidered on a fabric of violence and chaos. William Faulkner in "Dry September" recognizes the erotic sources of certain kinds of violence in stories ostensibly about hate. And Matthew Arnold in "Dover Beach" finds love the only refuge from a chaotic world in which "ignorant armies clash by night."

The cliché has it that love and hate are closely related, and much evidence supports this proposition. But why should love and hate, seeming opposites, lie so close together in the emotional lives of men and women? We are all egos, separate from each other. And as separate individuals, we develop elaborate behavior mechanisms which defend us from each other. Self-esteem is terribly important, and threats to self-esteem must somehow be neutralized. But the erotic love relationship differs from other relationships in that it may be defined as a rejection of separateness. The common metaphor speaks of two lovers as joining, as merging into one. That surrender of the "me" to join in an "us" leaves the lovers uniquely vulnerable to psychic injury. In short, the defenses are down, and the self-esteem of each of the lovers depends importantly on the behavior of the other. If the lover is betrayed by the beloved, the emotional consequences are uniquely disastrous—hence the peculiarly close relationship of passionate hatred with erotic love.

Words like *love* and *hate* are so general that poets rarely use them except as one term in a metaphor designed to project sharply some aspect of emotional life. The simple sexuality in such poems as Marvell's "To His Coy Mistress" and Marlowe's "The Passionate Shepherd to His Love" may be juxtaposed with the hatred and violence generated in Othello by sexual jealousy or with the quick reprisal of the slighted Barbara Allan. And Shakespeare's description of lust in "Th' Expense of Spirit in a Waste of Shame" notes an aspect of love quite overlooked by Edmund Waller and Robert Burns in their songs.

Perhaps more than anything, the works in this section celebrate the elemental impulses of men or women that run counter to those rational formulations by which we govern our lives. We pursue Othello's love for Desdemona and Iago's hate for Othello and arrive at an irreducible mystery, for neither Othello's love nor Iago's hate yields satisfactorily to rational explanation. Reason does not tell us why Othello and Desdemona love one another or why Iago hates rather than honors Othello.

Love is an act of faith springing from our deep-seated need to join with another human being not only in physical nakedness but in emotional and spiritual nakedness as well. While hate is a denial of that faith and, therefore, a retreat into spiritual isolation, love is an attempt to break out of the isolation. And as Erich Fromm writes in *The Art of Loving*:

> The basic need to fuse with another person so as to transcend the prison of one's separateness is closely related to another specifically human desire, that to know the "secret of man." While life in its merely biological aspects is a miracle and a secret, man in his human aspects is an unfathomable secret to himself—and to his fellow man. We know ourselves, and yet even with all the efforts we may make, we do not know ourselves. We know our fellow man, and yet we do not know him, because we are not a thing, and our fellow man is not a thing. The further we search into the depths of our being, or someone else's being, the more the goal of knowledge eludes us. Yet we cannot help desiring to penetrate into the secret of man's soul, into the innermost nucleus which is "he."
>
> There is one way, a desperate one, to know the secret: it is that of complete power over another person; the power which makes him do what we want, feel what we want, think what we want; which transforms him into a thing, our thing, our possession. The ultimate degree of this attempt to know lies in the extremes of sadism, the desire and ability to make a human being suffer; to torture him, to force him to betray his secret in his suffering. In this craving for penetrating man's secret, his and hence our own, lies an essential motivation for the depth and intensity of cruelty and destructiveness. . . .
>
> The other path to knowing "the secret" is love. Love is active penetration of the other person, in which my desire to know is stilled by union. In the act of fusion I know you, I know myself, I know everybody—and I "know" nothing. I know in the only way knowledge of that which is alive is possible for man—by experience of union—not by any knowledge our thought can give. Sadism is motivated by the wish to know the secret, yet I remain as ignorant as I was before. I have torn the other being apart limb from limb, yet all I have done is to destroy him. Love is the only way of knowledge, which in the act of union answers my quest. In the act of loving, of giving myself, in the act of penetrating the other person, I find myself, I discover myself, I discover us both, I discover man.

LOVE
AND
HATE

A Husband Parting from His Wife and Child, 1799 by William Blake

FICTION

The Storm   (1898)

KATE CHOPIN [1851–1904]

I

The leaves were so still that even Bibi thought it was going to rain. Bobinôt, who was accustomed to converse on terms of perfect equality with his little son, called the child's attention to certain sombre clouds that were rolling with sinister intention from the west, accompanied by a sullen, threatening roar. They were at Friedheimer's store and decided to remain there till the storm had passed. They sat within the door on two empty kegs. Bibi was four years old and looked very wise.

"Mama'll be 'fraid, yes," he suggested with blinking eyes.

"She'll shut the house. Maybe she got Sylvie helpin' her this evenin'," Bobinôt responded reassuringly.

"No; she ent got Sylvie. Sylvie was helpin' her yistiday," piped Bibi.

Bobinôt arose and going across to the counter purchased a can of shrimps, of which Calixta was very fond. Then he returned to his perch on the keg and sat stolidly holding the can of shrimps while the storm burst. It shook the wooden store and seemed to be ripping great furrows in the distant field. Bibi laid his little hand on his father's knee and was not afraid.

II

Calixta, at home, felt no uneasiness for their safety. She sat at a side window sewing furiously on a sewing machine. She was greatly occupied and did not notice the approaching storm. But she felt very warm and often stopped to mop her face on which the perspiration gathered in beads. She unfastened her white sacque at the throat. It began to grow dark, and suddenly realizing the situation she got up hurriedly and went about closing windows and doors.

Out on the small front gallery she had hung Bobinôt's Sunday clothes to air and she hastened out to gather them before the rain fell. As she stepped outside, Alcée Laballière rode in at the gate. She had not seen him very often since her marriage, and never alone. She stood there with Bobinôt's coat in her hands, and the big rain drops began to fall. Alcée rode his horse under the shelter of a side projection where the chickens had huddled and there were plows and a harrow piled up in the corner.

"May I come and wait on your gallery till the storm is over, Calixta?" he asked.

"Come 'long in, M'sieur Alcée."

His voice and her own startled her as if from a trance, and she seized Bobinôt's vest. Alcée, mounting to the porch, grabbed the trousers and snatched Bibi's braided jacket that was about to be carried away by a sudden gust of wind. He expressed an intention to remain outside, but it was soon apparent that he might as well have been out in the open: the water beat in upon the boards in driving sheets, and he went inside, closing the door after him. It was even necessary to put something beneath the door to keep the water out.

"My! what a rain! It's good two years since it rain' like that," exclaimed Calixta as she rolled up a piece of bagging and Alcée helped her to thrust it beneath the crack.

She was a little fuller of figure than five years before when she married; but she had lost nothing of her vivacity. Her blue eyes still retained their melting quality; and her yellow hair, dishevelled by the wind and rain, kinked more stubbornly than ever about her ears and temples.

The rain beat upon the low, shingled roof with a force and clatter that threatened to break an entrance and deluge them there. They were in the dining room—the sitting room—the general utility room. Adjoining was her bed room, with Bibi's couch along side her own. The door stood open, and the room with its white, monumental bed, its closed shutters, looked dim and mysterious.

Alcée flung himself into a rocker and Calixta nervously began to gather up from the floor the lengths of a cotton sheet which she had been sewing.

"If this keeps up, *Dieu sait*[1] if the levees goin' to stan' it!" she exclaimed.

"What have you got to do with the levees?"

"I got enough to do! An' there's Bobinôt with Bibi out in that storm—if he only didn' left Friedheimer's!"

"Let us hope, Calixta, that Bobinôt's got sense enough to come in out of a cyclone."

She went and stood at the window with a greatly disturbed look on her face. She wiped the frame that was clouded with moisture. It was stiflingly hot. Alcée got up and joined her at the window, looking over her shoulder. The rain was coming down in sheets obscuring the view of far-off cabins and enveloping the distant wood in a gray mist. The playing of the lightning was incessant. A bolt struck a tall chinaberry tree at the edge of the field. It filled all visible space with a blinding glare and the crash seemed to invade the very boards they stood upon.

Calixta put her hands to her eyes, and with a cry, staggered backward. Alcée's

---

[1] God knows.

arm encircled her, and for an instant he drew her close and spasmodically to him.

"*Bonte!*"[2] she cried, releasing herself from his encircling arm and retreating from the window, "the house'll go next! If I only knew w'ere Bibi was!" She would not compose herself; she would not be seated. Alcée clasped her shoulders and looked into her face. The contact of her warm, palpitating body when he had unthinkingly drawn her into his arms, had aroused all the old-time infatuation and desire for her flesh.

"Calixta," he said, "don't be frightened. Nothing can happen. The house is too low to be struck, with so many tall trees standing about. There! aren't you going to be quiet? say, aren't you?" He pushed her hair back from her face that was warm and steaming. Her lips were as red and moist as pomegranate seed. Her white neck and a glimpse of her full, firm bosom disturbed him powerfully. As she glanced up at him the fear in her liquid blue eyes had given place to a drowsy gleam that unconsciously betrayed a sensuous desire. He looked down into her eyes and there was nothing for him to do but to gather her lips in a kiss. It reminded him of Assumption.[3]

"Do you remember—in Assumption. Calixta?" he asked in a low voice broken by passion. Oh! she remembered; for in Assumption he had kissed her and kissed and kissed her; until his senses would well nigh fail, and to save her he would resort to a desperate flight. If she was not an immaculate dove in those days, she was still inviolate; a passionate creature whose very defenselessness had made her defense, against which his honor forbade him to prevail. Now— well, now—her lips seemed in a manner free to be tasted, as well as her round, white throat and her whiter breasts.

They did not heed the crashing torrents, and the roar of the elements made her laugh as she lay in his arms. She was a revelation in that dim, mysterious chamber; as white as the couch she lay upon. Her firm, elastic flesh that was knowing for the first time its birthright, was like a creamy lily that the sun invites to contribute its breath and perfume to the undying life of the world.

The generous abundance of her passion, without guile or trickery, was like a white flame which penetrated and found response in depths of his own sensuous nature that had never yet been reached.

When he touched her breasts they gave themselves up in quivering ecstasy, inviting his lips. Her mouth was a fountain of delight. And when he possessed her, they seemed to swoon together at the very borderland of life's mystery.

He stayed cushioned upon her, breathless, dazed, enervated, with his heart beating like a hammer upon her. With one hand she clasped his head, her lips lightly touching his forehead. The other hand stroked with a soothing rhythm his muscular shoulders.

---

[2] An exclamation: Goodness!

[3] A holiday commemorating the ascent of the Virgin Mary to heaven. Assumption is also the name of a Louisiana parish (county) where Calixta and Alcée had had a rendezvous in an earlier story.

The growl of the thunder was distant and passing away. The rain beat softly upon the shingles, inviting them to drowsiness and sleep. But they dared not yield.

The rain was over; and the sun was turning the glistening green world into a palace of gems. Calixta, on the gallery, watched Alcée ride away. He turned and smiled at her with a beaming face; and she lifted her pretty chin in the air and laughed aloud.

III

Bobinôt and Bibi, trudging home, stopped without at the cistern to make themselves presentable.

"My! Bibi, w'at will yo' mama say! You ought to be ashame'. You oughtn' put on those good pants. Look at 'em! An' that mud on yo' collar! How you got that mud on yo' collar, Bibi? I never saw such a boy!" Bibi was the picture of pathetic resignation. Bobinôt was the embodiment of serious solicitude as he strove to remove from his own person and his son's the signs of their tramp over heavy roads and through wet fields. He scraped the mud off Bibi's bare legs and feet with a stick and carefully removed all traces from his heavy brogans. Then, prepared for the worst—the meeting with an over-scrupulous housewife, they entered cautiously at the back door.

Calixta was preparing supper. She had set the table and was dripping coffee at the hearth. She sprang up as they came in.

"Oh, Bobinôt! You back! My! but I was uneasy. W'ere you been during the rain? An' Bibi? he ain't wet? he ain't hurt?" She had clasped Bibi and was kissing him effusively. Bobinôt's explanations and apologies which he had been composing all along the way, died on his lips as Calixta felt him to see if he were dry, and seemed to express nothing but satisfaction at their safe return.

"I brought you some shrimps, Calixta," offered Bobinôt, hauling the can from his ample side pocket and laying it on the table.

"Shrimps! Oh, Bobinôt! you too good fo' anything!" and she gave him a smacking kiss on the cheek that resounded. "*J'vous reponds,*[4] we'll have a feas' to night! umph-umph!"

Bobinôt and Bibi began to relax and enjoy themselves, and when the three seated themselves at table they laughed much and so loud that anyone might have heard them as far away as Laballière's.

IV

Alcée Laballière wrote to his wife, Clarisse, that night. It was a loving letter, full of tender solicitude. He told her not to hurry back, but if she and the babies liked it at Biloxi, to stay a month longer. He was getting on nicely; and though

---

[4] I'm telling you.

he missed them, he was willing to bear the separation a while longer—realizing that their health and pleasure were the first things to be considered.

V

As for Clarisse, she was charmed upon receiving her husband's letter. She and the babies were doing well. The society was agreeable; many of her old friends and acquaintances were at the bay. And the first free breath since her marriage seemed to restore the pleasant liberty of her maiden days. Devoted as she was to her husband, their intimate conjugal life was something which she was more than willing to forego for a while.

So the storm passed and everyone was happy.

The Horse Dealer's Daughter   1922

D. H. LAWRENCE   [1885–1930]

"Well, Mabel, and what are you going to do with yourself?" asked Joe, with foolish flippancy. He felt quite safe himself. Without listening for an answer, he turned aside, worked a grain of tobacco to the tip of his tongue, and spat it out. He did not care about anything, since he felt safe himself.

The three brothers and the sister sat round the desolate breakfast table, attempting some sort of desultory consultation. The morning's post had given the final tap to the family fortune, and all was over. The dreary dining-room itself, with its heavy mahogany furniture, looked as if it were waiting to be done away with.

But the consultation amounted to nothing. There was a strange air of ineffectuality about the three men, as they sprawled at table, smoking and reflecting vaguely on their own condition. The girl was alone, a rather short, sullen-looking young woman of twenty-seven. She did not share the same life as her brothers. She would have been good-looking, save for the impassive fixity of her face, "bull-dog," as her brothers called it.

There was a confused tramping of horses' feet outside. The three men all sprawled round in their chairs to watch. Beyond the dark hollybushes that separated the strip of lawn from the high-road, they could see a cavalcade of shire horses swinging out of their own yard, being taken for exercise. This was the last time. These were the last horses that would go through their hands. The young men watched with critical, callous look. They were all frightened at the collapse of their lives, and the sense of disaster in which they were involved left them no inner freedom.

Yet they were three fine, well-set fellows enough. Joe, the eldest, was a man of thirty-three, broad and handsome in a hot, flushed way. His face was red, he twisted his black moustache over a thick finger, his eyes were shallow and restless. He had a sensual way of uncovering his teeth when he laughed, and his bearing was stupid. Now he watched the horses with a glazed look of helplessness in his eyes, a certain stupor of downfall.

The great draught-horses swung past. They were tied head to tail, four of them, and they heaved along to where a lane branched off from the highroad, planting their great hoofs floutingly in the fine black mud, swinging their great rounded haunches sumptuously, and trotting a few sudden steps as they were led into the lane, round the corner. Every movement showed a massive, slumbrous strength, and a stupidity which held them in subjection. The groom at the head looked back, jerking the leading rope. And the cavalcade moved out of sight up the lane, the tail of the last horse bobbed up tight and stiff, held out taut from the swinging great haunches as they rocked behind the hedges in a motion like sleep.

Joe watched with glazed hopeless eyes. The horses were almost like his own body to him. He felt he was done for now. Luckily he was engaged to a woman as old as himself, and therefore her father, who was steward of a neighbouring estate, would provide him with a job. He would marry and go into harness. His life was over, he would be a subject animal now.

He turned uneasily aside, the retreating steps of the horses echoing in his ears. Then, with foolish restlessness, he reached for the scraps of bacon-rind from the plates, and making a faint whistling sound, flung them to the terrier that lay against the fender. He watched the dog swallow them, and waited till the creature looked into his eyes. Then a faint grin came on his face, and in a high, foolish voice he said:

"You won't get much more bacon, shall you, you little bitch?"

The dog faintly and dismally wagged its tail, then lowered its haunches, circled round, and lay down again.

There was another helpless silence at the table. Joe sprawled uneasily in his seat, not willing to go till the family conclave was dissolved. Fred Henry, the second brother, was erect, clean-limbed, alert. He had watched the passing of the horses with more sangfroid. If he was an animal, like Joe, he was an animal which controls, not one which is controlled. He was master of any horse, and he carried himself with a well-tempered air of mastery. But he was not master of the situations of life. He pushed his coarse brown moustache upwards, off his lip, and glanced irritably at his sister, who sat impassive and inscrutable.

"You'll go and stop with Lucy for a bit, shan't you?" he asked. The girl did not answer.

"I don't see what else you can do," persisted Fred Henry.

"Go as a skivvy," Joe interpolated laconically.

The girl did not move a muscle.

"If I was her, I should go in for training for a nurse," said Malcolm, the youngest of them all. He was the baby of the family, a young man of twenty-two, with a fresh, jaunty *museau*. [1]

But Mabel did not take any notice of him. They had talked at her and round her for so many years, that she hardly heard them at all.

The marble clock on the mantelpiece softly chimed the half-hour, the dog rose uneasily from the hearthrug and looked at the party at the breakfast table. But still they sat on in ineffectual conclave.

"Oh, all right," said Joe suddenly, apropos of nothing. "I'll get a move on."

He pushed back his chair, straddled his knees with a downward jerk, to get them free, in horsey fashion, and went to the fire. Still he did not go out of the room; he was curious to know what the others would do or say. He began to charge his pipe, looking down at the dog and saying, in a high, affected voice:

"Going wi' me? Going wi' me are ter? Tha'rt goin' further than tha counts on just now, dost hear?"

The dog faintly wagged its tail, the man stuck out his jaw and covered his

---

[1] Face.

pipe with his hands, and puffed intently, losing himself in the tobacco, looking down all the while at the dog with an absent brown eye. The dog looked up at him in mournful distrust. Joe stood with his knees stuck out, in real horsey fashion.

"Have you had a letter from Lucy?" Fred Henry asked of his sister.

"Last week," came the neutral reply.

"And what does she say?"

There was no answer.

"Does she *ask* you to go and stop there?" persisted Fred Henry.

"She says I can if I like."

"Well, then, you'd better. Tell her you'll come on Monday."

This was received in silence.

"That's what you'll do then, is it?" said Fred Henry, in some exasperation.

But she made no answer. There was a silence of futility and irritation in the room. Malcolm grinned fatuously.

"You'll have to make up your mind between now and next Wednesday," said Joe loudly, "or else find yourself lodgings on the kerbstone."

The face of the young woman darkened, but she sat on immutable.

"Here's Jack Fergusson!" exclaimed Malcolm, who was looking aimlessly out of the window.

"Where?" exclaimed Joe, loudly.

"Just gone past."

"Coming in?"

Malcolm craned his neck to see the gate.

"Yes," he said.

There was a silence. Mabel sat on like one condemned, at the head of the table. Then a whistle was heard from the kitchen. The dog got up and barked sharply. Joe opened the door and shouted:

"Come on."

After a moment a young man entered. He was muffled up in overcoat and a purple woollen scarf, and his tweed cap, which he did not remove, was pulled down on his head. He was of medium height, his face was rather long and pale, his eyes looked tired.

"Hello, Jack! Well, Jack!" exclaimed Malcolm and Joe. Fred Henry merely said, "Jack."

"What's doing?" asked the newcomer, evidently addressing Fred Henry.

"Same. We've got to be out by Wednesday. Got a cold?"

"I have—got it bad, too."

"Why don't you stop in?"

"*Me* stop in? When I can't stand on my legs, perhaps I shall have a chance." The young man spoke huskily. He had a slight Scotch accent.

"It's a knock-out, isn't it?" said Joe, boisterously, "if a doctor goes round croaking with a cold. Looks bad for the patients, doesn't it?"

The young doctor looked at him slowly.

"Anything the matter with *you*, then?" he asked sarcastically.

"Not as I know of. Damn your eyes, I hope not. Why?"

"I thought you were very concerned about the patients, wondered if you might be one yourself."

"Damn it, no, I've never been patient to no flaming doctor, and hope I never shall be," returned Joe.

At this point Mabel rose from the table, and they all seemed to become aware of her existence. She began putting the dishes together. The young doctor looked at her, but did not address her. He had not greeted her. She went out of the room with the tray, her face impassive and unchanged.

"When are you off then, all of you?" asked the doctor.

"I'm catching the eleven-forty," replied Malcolm. "Are you goin' down wi' th' trap, Joe?"

"Yes, I've told you I am going down wi' th' trap, haven't I?"

"We'd better be getting her in then. So long, Jack, if I don't see you before I go," said Malcolm, shaking hands.

He went out, followed by Joe, who seemed to have his tail between his legs.

"Well, this is the devil's own," exclaimed the doctor, when he was left alone with Fred Henry. "Going before Wednesday, are you."

"That's the orders," replied the other.

"Where, to Northampton?"

"That's it."

"The devil!" exclaimed Fergusson, with quiet chagrin.

And there was silence between the two.

"All settled up, are you?" asked Fergusson.

"About."

There was another pause.

"Well, I shall miss yer, Freddy, boy," said the young doctor.

"And I shall miss thee, Jack," returned the other.

"Miss you like hell," mused the doctor.

Fred Henry turned aside. There was nothing to say. Mabel came in again, to finish clearing the table.

"What are *you* going to do, then, Miss Pervin?" asked Fergusson. "Going to your sister's, are you?"

Mabel looked at him with her steady, dangerous eyes, that always made him uncomfortable, unsettling his superficial ease.

"No," she said.

"Well, what in the name of fortune are *you* going to do? Say what you mean to do," cried Fred Henry, with futile intensity.

But she only averted her head, and continued her work. She folded the white table-cloth, and put on the chenille cloth.

"The sulkiest bitch that ever trod!" muttered her brother.

But she finished her task with perfectly impassive face, the young doctor watching her interestedly all the while. Then she went out.

Fred Henry stared after her, clenching his lips, his blue eyes fixing in sharp antagonism, as he made a grimace of sour exasperation.

"You could bray her into bits, and that's all you'd get out of her," he said in a small, narrowed tone.

The doctor smiled faintly.

"What's she *going* to do, then?" he asked.

"Strike me if I know!" returned the other.

There was a pause. Then the doctor stirred.

"I'll be seeing you to-night, shall I?" he said to his friend.

"Ay—where's it to be? Are we going over to Jessdale?"

"I don't know. I've got such a cold on me. I'll come round to the Moon and Stars, anyway."

"Let Lizzie and May miss their night for once, eh?"

"That's it—if I feel as I do now."

"All's one—"

The two young men went through the passage and down to the back door together. The house was large, but it was servantless now, and desolate. At the back was a small bricked house-yard, and beyond that a big square, gravelled fine and red, and having stables on two sides. Sloping, dank, winter-dark fields stretched away on the open sides.

But the stables were empty. Joseph Pervin, the father of the family, had been a man of no education, who had become a fairly large horse dealer. The stables had been full of horses, there was a great turmoil and come-and-go of horses and of dealers and grooms. Then the kitchen was full of servants. But of late things had declined. The old man had married a second time, to retrieve his fortunes. Now he was dead and everything was gone to the dogs, there was nothing but debt and threatening.

For months, Mabel had been servantless in the big house, keeping the home together in penury for her ineffectual brothers. She had kept house for ten years. But previously it was with unstinted means. Then, however brutal and coarse everything was, the sense of money had kept her proud, confident. The men might be foul-mouthed, the women in the kitchen might have bad reputations, her brothers might have illegitimate children. But so long as there was money, the girl felt herself established and brutally proud, reserved.

No company came to the house, save dealers and coarse men. Mabel had no associates of her own sex, after her sister went away. But she did not mind. She went regularly to church, she attended to her father. And she lived in the memory of her mother, who had died when she was fourteen, and whom she had loved. She had loved her father, too, in a different way, depending upon him, and feeling secure in him, until at the age of fifty-four he married again. And then she had set hard against him. Now he had died and left them all hopelessly in debt.

She had suffered badly during the period of poverty. Nothing, however, could shake the curious sullen, animal pride that dominated each member of the family. Now, for Mabel, the end had come. Still she would not cast about her. She would follow her own way just the same. She would always hold the keys of her own situation. Mindless and persistent, she endured from day to day.

What should she think? Why should she answer anybody? It was enough that this was the end and there was no way out. She need not pass any more darkly along the main street of the small town, avoiding every eye. She need not demean herself any more, going into the shops and buying the cheapest food. This was at an end. She thought of nobody, not even of herself. Mindless and persistent, she seemed in a sort of ecstasy to be coming nearer to her fulfilment, her own glorification, approaching her dead mother, who was glorified.

In the afternoon she took a little bag, with shears and sponge and a small scrubbing brush, and went out. It was a grey, wintry day, with saddened, dark green fields and an atmosphere blackened by the smoke of foundries not far off. She went quickly, darkly along the causeway, heeding nobody, through the town to the churchyard.

There she always felt secure, as if no one could see her, although as a matter of fact she was exposed to the stare of every one who passed along under the churchyard wall. Nevertheless, once under the shadow of the great looming church, among the graves, she felt immune from the world, reserved within the thick churchyard wall as in another country.

Carefully she clipped the grass from the grave, and arranged the pinky white, small chrysanthemums in the tin cross. When this was done, she took an empty jar from a neighbouring grave, brought water, and carefully, most scrupulously sponged the marble head-stone and the coping-stone.

It gave her sincere satisfaction to do this. She felt in immediate contact with the world of her mother. She took minute pains, went through the park in a state bordering on pure happiness, as if in performing this task she came into a subtle, intimate connection with her mother. For the life she followed here in the world was far less real than the world of death she inherited from her mother.

The doctor's house was just by the church. Fergusson, being a mere hired assistant, was slave to the country-side. As he hurried now to attend to the out-patients in the surgery, glancing across the graveyard with his quick eye, he saw the girl at her task at the grave. She seemed so intent and remote, it was like looking into another world. Some mystical element was touched in him. He slowed down as he walked, watching her as if spell-bound.

She lifted her eyes, feeling him looking. Their eyes met. And each looked away again at once, each feeling, in some way, found out by the other. He lifted his cap and passed on down the road. There remained distinct in his consciousness, like a vision, the memory of her face, lifted from the tombstone in the churchyard, and looking at him with slow, large, portentous eyes. It *was* portentous, her face. It seemed to mesmerize him. There was a heavy power in her eyes which laid hold of his whole being, as if he had drunk some powerful drug. He had been feeling weak and done before. Now the life came back into him, he felt delivered from his own fretted, daily self.

He finished his duties at the surgery as quickly as might be, hastily filling up the bottle of the waiting people with cheap drugs. Then, in perpetual haste, he set off again to visit several cases in another part of his round, before tea-time.

At all times he preferred to walk if he could, but particularly when he was not well. He fancied the motion restored him.

The afternoon was falling. It was grey, deadened, and wintry, with a slow, moist, heavy coldness sinking in and deadening all the faculties. But why should he think or notice? He hastily climbed the hill and turned across the dark green fields, following the black cinder-track. In the distance, across a shallow dip in the country, the small town was clustered like smouldering ash, a tower, a spire, a heap of low, raw, extinct houses. And on the nearest fringe of the town, sloping into the dip, was Oldmeadow, the Pervins' house. He could see the stables and the outbuildings distinctly, as they lay towards him on the slope. Well, he would not go there many more times! Another resource would be lost to him, another place gone: the only company he cared for in the alien, ugly little town he was losing. Nothing but work, drudgery, constant hastening from dwelling to dwelling among the colliers and the ironworkers. It wore him out, but at the same time he had a craving for it. It was a stimulant to him to be in the homes of the working people, moving as it were through the innermost body of their life. His nerves were excited and gratified. He could come so near, into the very lives of the rough, inarticulate, powerfully emotional men and women. He grumbled, he said he hated the hellish hole. But as a matter of fact it excited him, the contact with the rough, strongly-feeling people was a stimulant applied direct to his nerves.

Below Oldmeadow, in the green, shallow, soddened hollow of fields lay a square, deep pond. Roving across the landscape, the doctor's quick eye detected a figure in black passing through the gate of the field, down towards the pond. He looked again. It would be Mabel Pervin. His mind suddenly became alive and attentive.

Why was she going down there? He pulled up on the path on the slope above, and stood staring. He could just make sure of the small black figure moving in the hollow of the failing day. He seemed to see her in the midst of such obscurity, that he was like a clairvoyant, seeing rather with the mind's eye than with ordinary sight. Yet he could see her positively enough, whilst he kept his eye attentive. He felt, if he looked away from her, in the thick, ugly falling dusk, he would lose her altogether.

He followed her minutely as she moved, direct and intent, like something transmitted rather than stirring in voluntary activity, straight down the field towards the pond. There she stood on the bank for a moment. She never raised her head. Then she waded slowly into the water.

He stood motionless as the small black figure walked slowly and deliberately towards the centre of the pond, very slowly, gradually moving deeper into the motionless water, and still moving forward as the water got up to her breast. Then he could see her no more in the dusk of the dead afternoon.

"There!" he exclaimed. "Would you believe it?"

And he hastened straight down, running over the wet, soddened fields, pushing through the hedges, down into the depression of callous wintry obscurity.

It took him several minutes to come to the pond. He stood on the bank, breathing heavily. He could see nothing. His eyes seemed to penetrate the dead water. Yes, perhaps that was the dark shadow of her black clothing beneath the surface of the water.

He slowly ventured into the pond. The bottom was deep, soft clay, he sank in, and the water clasped dead cold round his legs. As he stirred he could smell the cold, rotten clay that fouled up into the water. It was objectionable in his lungs. Still, repelled and yet not heeding, he moved deeper into the pond. The cold water rose over his thighs, over his loins, upon his abdomen. The lower part of his body was all sunk in the hideous cold element. And the bottom was so deeply soft and uncertain, he was afraid of pitching with his mouth underneath. He could not swim, and was afraid.

He crouched a little, spreading his hands under the water and moving them round, trying to feel for her. The dead cold pond swayed upon his chest. He moved again, a little deeper, and again, with his hands underneath, he felt all around the water. And he touched her clothing. But it evaded his fingers. He made a desperate effort to grasp it.

And so doing he lost his balance and went under, horribly, suffocating in the foul earthy water, struggling madly for a few moments. At last, after what seemed an eternity, he got his footing, rose again into the air and looked around. He gasped, and knew he was in the world. Then he looked at the water. She had risen near him. He grasped her clothing, and drawing her nearer, turned to take his way to land again.

He went very slowly, carefully, absorbed in the slow progress. He rose higher, climbing out of the pond. The water was now only about his legs; he was thankful, full of relief to be out of the clutches of the pond. He lifted her and staggered on to the bank, out of the horror of wet, grey clay.

He laid her down on the bank. She was quite unconscious and running with water. He made the water come from her mouth, he worked to restore her. He did not have to work very long before he could feel the breathing begin again in her; she was breathing naturally. He worked a little longer. He could feel her live beneath his hands; she was coming back. He wiped her face, wrapped her in his overcoat, looked round into the dim, dark grey world, then lifted her and staggered down the bank and across the fields.

It seemed an unthinkably long way, and his burden so heavy he felt he would never get to the house. But at last he was in the stable-yard, and then in the house-yard. He opened the door and went into the house. In the kitchen he laid her down on the hearth-rug, and called. The house was empty. But the fire was burning in the grate.

Then again he kneeled to attend to her. She was breathing regularly, her eyes were wide open and as if conscious, but there seemed something missing in her look. She was conscious in herself, but unconscious of her surroundings.

He ran upstairs, took blankets from a bed, and put them before the fire to warm. Then he removed her saturated, earthy-smelling clothing, rubbed her dry with a towel, and wrapped her naked in the blankets. Then he went into the dining-room, to look for spirits. There was a little whisky. He drank a gulp himself, and put some into her mouth.

The effect was instantaneous. She looked full into his face, as if she had been seeing him for some time, and yet had only just become conscious of him.

"Dr. Fergusson?" she said.

"What?" he answered.

He was divesting himself of his coat, intending to find some dry clothing upstairs. He could not bear the smell of the dead, clayey water, and he was mortally afraid for his own health.

"What did I do?" she asked.

"Walked into the pond," he replied. He had begun to shudder like one sick, and could hardly attend to her. Her eyes remained full on him, he seemed to be going dark in his mind, looking back at her helplessly. The shuddering became quieter in him, his life came back in him, dark and unknowing, but strong again.

"Was I out of my mind?" she asked, while her eyes were fixed on him all the time.

"Maybe, for the moment," he replied. He felt quiet, because his strength had come back. The strange fretful strain had left him.

"Am I out of my mind now?" she asked.

"Are you?" he reflected a moment. "No," he answered truthfully. "I don't see that you are." He turned his face aside. He was afraid now, because he felt dazed, and felt dimly that her power was stronger than his, in this issue. And she continued to look at him fixedly all the time. "Can you tell me where I shall find some dry things to put on?" he asked.

"Did you dive into the pond for me?" she asked.

"No," he answered. "I walked in. But I went in overhead as well."

There was silence for a moment. He hesitated. He very much wanted to go upstairs to get into dry clothing. But there was another desire in him. And she seemed to hold him. His will seemed to have gone to sleep, and left him, standing there slack before her. But he felt warm inside himself. He did not shudder at all, though his clothes were sodden on him.

"Why did you?" she asked.

"Because I didn't want you to do such a foolish thing," he said.

"It wasn't foolish," she said, still gazing at him as she lay on the floor, with a sofa cushion under her head. "It was the right thing to do. I knew best, then."

"I'll go and shift these wet things," he said. But still he had not the power to move out of her presence, until she sent him. It was as if she had the life of his body in her hands, and he could not extricate himself. Or perhaps he did not want to.

Suddenly she sat up. Then she became aware of her own immediate condition. She felt the blankets about her, she knew her own limbs. For a moment it seemed as if her reason were going. She looked round, with wild eye, as if seeking something. He stood still with fear. She saw her clothing lying scattered.

"Who undressed me?" she asked, her eyes resting full and inevitable on his face.

"I did," he replied, "to bring you round."

For some moments she sat and gazed at him awfully, her lips parted.

"Do you love me, then?" she asked.

He only stood and stared at her, fascinated. His soul seemed to melt.

She shuffled forward on her knees, and put her arms around him, round his legs, as he stood there, pressing her breasts against his knees and thighs, clutching him with strange, convulsive certainty, pressing his thighs against her, drawing him to her face, her throat, as she looked up at him with flaring, humble eyes of transfiguration, triumphant in first possession.

"You love me," she murmured, in strange transport, yearning and triumphant and confident. "You love me. I know you love me, I know."

And she was passionately kissing his knees, through the wet clothing, passionately and indiscriminately kissing his knees, his legs, as if unaware of everything.

He looked down at the tangled wet hair, the wild, bare, animal shoulders. He was amazed, bewildered, and afraid. He had never thought of loving her. He had never wanted to love her. When he rescued her and restored her, he was a doctor, and she was a patient. He had had no single personal thought of her. Nay, this introduction of the personal element was very distasteful to him, a violation of his professional honour. It was horrible to have her there embracing his knees. It was horrible. He revolted from it, violently. And yet—and yet—he had not the power to break away.

She looked at him again, with the same supplication of powerful love, and that same transcendent, frightening light of triumph. In view of the delicate flame which seemed to come from her face like a light, he was powerless. And yet he had never intended to love her. He had never intended. And something stubborn in him could not give way.

"You love me," she repeated, in a murmur of deep rhapsodic assurance. "You love me."

Her hands were drawing him, drawing him down to her. He was afraid, even a little horrified. For he had, really, no intention of loving her. Yet her hands were drawing him towards her. He put out his hand quickly to steady himself, and grasped her bare shoulder. A flame seemed to burn the hand that grasped her soft shoulder. He had no intention of loving her: his whole will was against his yielding. It was horrible. And yet wonderful was the touch of her shoulders, beautiful the shining of her face. Was she perhaps mad? He had a horror of yielding to her. Yet something in him ached also.

He had been staring away at the door, away from her. But his hand remained on her shoulder. She had gone suddenly very still. He looked down at her. Her eyes were now wide with fear, with doubt, the light was dying from her face, a shadow of terrible greyness was returning. He could not bear the touch of her eyes' question upon him, and the look of death behind the question.

With an inward groan he gave way, and let his heart yield towards her. A sudden gentle smile came on his face. And her eyes, which never left his face, slowly, slowly filled with tears. He watched the strange water rise in her eyes, like some slow fountain coming up. And his heart seemed to burn and melt away in his breast.

He could not bear to look at her any more. He dropped on his knees and caught her head with his arms and pressed her face against his throat. She was very still. His heart, which seemed to have broken, was burning with a kind of agony in his breast. And he felt her slow, hot tears wetting his throat. But he could not move.

He felt the hot tears wet his neck and the hollows of his neck, and he remained motionless, suspended through one of man's eternities. Only now it had become indispensable to him to have her face pressed close to him; he could never let her go again. He could never let her head go away from the close clutch of his arm. He wanted to remain like that for ever, with his heart hurting him in a pain that was also life to him. Without knowing, he was looking down on her damp, soft brown hair.

Then, as it were suddenly, he smelt the horrid stagnant smell of that water. And at the same moment she drew away from him and looked at him. Her eyes were wistful and unfathomable. He was afraid of them, and he fell to kissing her, not knowing what he was doing. He wanted her eyes not to have that terrible, wistful, unfathomable look.

When she turned her face to him again, a faint delicate flush was glowing, and there was again dawning that terrible shining of joy in her eyes, which really terrified him, and yet which he now wanted to see, because he feared the look of doubt still more.

"You love me?" she said, rather faltering.

"Yes." The word cost him a painful effort. Not because it wasn't true. But because it was too newly true, the *saying* seemed to tear open again his newly-torn heart. And he hardly wanted it to be true, even now.

She lifted her face to him, and he bent forward and kissed her on the mouth, gently, with the one kiss that is an eternal pledge. And as he kissed her his heart strained again in his breast. He never intended to love her. But now it was over. He had crossed over the gulf to her, and all that he had left behind had shrivelled and become void.

After the kiss, her eyes again slowly filled with tears. She sat still, away from him, with her face drooped aside, and her hands folded in her lap. The tears fell very slowly. There was complete silence. He too sat there motionless and silent on the hearthrug. The strange pain of his heart that was broken seemed to consume him. That he should love her? That this was love! That he should be ripped open in this way! Him, a doctor! How they would all jeer if they knew! It was agony to him to think they might know.

In the curious naked pain of the thought he looked again to her. She was sitting there drooped into a muse. He saw a tear fall, and his heart flared hot. He saw for the first time that one of her shoulders was quite uncovered, one arm bare, he could see one of her small breasts; dimly, because it had become almost dark in the room.

"Why are you crying?" he asked, in an altered voice.

She looked up at him, and behind her tears the consciousness of her situation for the first time brought a dark look of shame to her eyes.

"I'm not crying, really," she said, watching him half frightened.

He reached his hand, and softly closed it on her bare arm.

"I love you! I love you!" he said in a soft, low vibrating voice, unlike himself.

She shrank, and dropped her head. The soft, penetrating grip of his hand on her arm distressed her. She looked up at him.

"I want to go," she said. "I want to go and get you some dry things."

"Why?" he said. "I'm all right."

"But I want to go," she said. "And I want you to change your things."

He released her arm, and she wrapped herself in the blanket, looking at him rather frightened. And still she did not rise.

"Kiss me," she said wistfully.

He kissed her, but briefly, half in anger.

Then, after a second, she rose nervously, all mixed up in the blanket. He watched her in her confusion, as she tried to extricate herself and wrap herself up so that she could walk. He watched her relentlessly, as she knew. And as she went, the blanket trailing, and as he saw a glimpse of her feet and her white leg, he tried to remember her as she was when he had wrapped her in the blanket. But then he didn't want to remember, because she had been nothing to him then, and his nature revolted from remembering her as she was when she was nothing to him.

A tumbling, muffled noise from within the dark house startled him. Then he heard her voice:—"There are clothes." He rose and went to the foot of the stairs, and gathered up the garments she had thrown down. Then he came back to the fire, to rub himself down and dress. He grinned at his own appearance when he had finished.

The fire was sinking, so he put on coal. The house was now quite dark, save for the light of a street-lamp that shone in faintly from beyond the holly trees. He lit the gas with matches he found on the mantelpiece. Then he emptied the pockets of his own clothes, and threw all his wet things in a heap into the scullery. After which he gathered up her sodden clothes, gently, and put them in a separate heap on the copper-top in the scullery.

It was six o'clock on the clock. His own watch had stopped. He ought to go back to the surgery. He waited, and still she did not come down. So he went to the foot of the stairs and called:

"I shall have to go."

Almost immediately he heard her coming down. She had on her best dress of black voile, and her hair was tidy, but still damp. She looked at him—and in spite of herself, smiled.

"I don't like you in those clothes," she said.

"Do I look a sight?" he answered.

They were shy of one another.

"I'll make you some tea," she said.

"No, I must go."

"Must you?" And she looked at him again with the wide, strained, doubtful eyes. And again, from the pain of his breast, he knew how he loved her. He went and bent to kiss her, gently, passionately, with his heart's painful kiss.

"And my hair smells so horrible," she murmured in distraction. "And I'm so awful, I'm so awful! Oh, no, I'm too awful." And she broke into bitter, heart-broken sobbing. "You can't want to love me, I'm horrible."

"Don't be silly, don't be silly," he said, trying to comfort her, kissing her, holding her in his arms. "I want you, I want to marry you, we're going to be married, quickly, quickly—tomorrow if I can."

But she only sobbed terribly, and cried:

"I feel awful. I feel awful. I feel I'm horrible to you."

"No, I want you, I want you," was all he answered, blindly, with that terrible intonation which frightened her almost more than her horror lest he should *not* want her.

QUESTIONS

1. In what way does Mabel's character change? In what way does Jack Fergusson's? **2.** Why does Fergusson resist the attraction he feels toward Mabel? Why does he finally yield? **3.** What function is served by the presence of Mabel's brothers in the first third of the story?

WRITING TOPICS

1. The central episode in the story is Mabel's attempted suicide. What symbolic qualities do the events at the pond have? **2.** Looking back at her attempted suicide, Mabel says, "It was the right thing to do." Does Lawrence's description of the event support her view?

Dry September

1931

WILLIAM FAULKNER [1897–1962]

I

Through the bloody September twilight, aftermath of sixty-two rainless days, it had gone like a fire in a dry grass—the rumor, the story, whatever it was. Something about Miss Minnie Cooper and a Negro. Attacked, insulted, frightened: none of them, gathered in the barber shop on that Saturday evening where the ceiling fan stirred, without freshening it, the vitiated air, sending back upon them in recurrent surges of stale pomade and lotion, their own stale breath and odors, knew exactly what had happened.

"Except it wasn't Will Mayes," a barber said. He was a man of middle age; a thin, sand-colored man with a mild face, who was shaving a client. "I know Will Mayes. He's a good nigger. And I know Miss Minnie Cooper, too."

"What do you know about her?" a second barber said.

"Who is she?" the client said. "A young girl?"

"No," the barber said. "She's about forty, I reckon. She aint married. That's why I dont believe—"

"Believe, hell!" a hulking youth in a sweat-stained silk shirt said. "Wont you take a white woman's word before a nigger's?"

"I don't believe Will Mayes did it," the barber said. "I know Will Mayes."

"Maybe you know who did it, then. Maybe you already got him out of town, you damn niggerlover."

"I don't believe anybody did anything. I dont believe anything happened. I leave it to you fellows if them ladies that get old without getting married dont have notions that a man cant—"

"Then you are a hell of a white man," the client said. He moved under the cloth. The youth had sprung to his feet.

"You dont?" he said. "Do you accuse a white woman of lying?"

The barber held the razor poised above the half-risen client. He did not look around.

"It's this durn weather," another said. "It's enough to make a man do anything. Even to her."

Nobody laughed. The barber said in his mild, stubborn tone: "I aint accusing nobody of nothing. I just know and you fellows know how a woman that never—"

"You damn niggerlover!" the youth said.

"Shut up, Butch," another said. "We'll get the facts in plenty of time to act."

"Who is? Who's getting them?" the youth said. "Facts, hell! I—"

"You're a fine white man," the client said. "Aint you?" In his frothy beard he looked like a desert rat in the moving pictures. "You tell them, Jack," he said to the youth. "If there aint any white men in this town, you can count on me, even if I aint only a drummer and a stranger."

"That's right, boys," the barber said. "Find out the truth first. I know Will Mayes."

"Well, by God!" the youth shouted. "To think that a white man in this town—"

"Shut up, Butch," the second speaker said. "We got plenty of time."

The client sat up. He looked at the speaker. "Do you claim that anything excuses a nigger attacking a white woman? Do you mean to tell me you are a white man and you'll stand for it? You better go back North where you came from. The South dont want your kind here."

"North what?" the second said. "I was born and raised in this town."

"Well, by God!" the youth said. He looked about with a strained, baffled gaze, as if he was trying to remember what it was he wanted to say or to do. He drew his sleeve across his sweating face. "Damn if I'm going to let a white woman—"

"You tell them, Jack," the drummer said. "By God, if they—"

The screen door crashed open. A man stood in the door, his feet apart and his heavy-set body poised easily. His white shirt was open at the throat; he wore a felt hat. His hot, bold glance swept the group. His name was McLendon. He had commanded troops at the front in France and had been decorated for valor.

"Well," he said, "are you going to sit there and let a black son rape a white woman on the streets of Jefferson?"

Butch sprang up again. The silk of his shirt clung flat to his heavy shoulders. At each armpit was a dark halfmoon. "That's what I been telling them! That's what I—"

"Did it really happen?" a third said. "This aint the first man scare she ever had, like Hawkshaw says. Wasn't there something about a man on the kitchen roof, watching her undress, about a year ago?"

"What?" the client said. "What's that?" The barber had been slowly forcing him back into the chair; he arrested himself reclining, his head lifted, the barber still pressing him down.

McLendon whirled on the third speaker. "Happen? What the hell difference does it make? Are you going to let the black sons get away with it until one really does it?"

"That's what I'm telling them!" Butch shouted. He cursed, long and steady, pointless.

"Here, here," a fourth said. "Not so loud. Dont talk so loud."

"Sure," McLendon said; "no talking necessary at all. I've done my talking. Who's with me?" He poised on the balls of his feet, roving his gaze.

The barber held the drummer's face down, the razor poised. "Find out the facts first, boys. I know Willy Mayes. It wasn't him. Let's get the sheriff and do this thing right."

McLendon whirled upon him his furious, rigid face. The barber did not look away. They looked like men of different races. The other barbers had ceased also above their prone clients. "You mean to tell me," McLendon said, "that you'd take a nigger's word before a white woman's? Why, you damn niggerloving—"

The third speaker rose and grasped McLendon's arm; he too had been a soldier, "Now, now. Let's figure this thing out. Who knows anything about what really happened?"

"Figure out hell!" McLendon jerked his arm free. "All that're with me get up from there. The ones that aint—" He roved his gaze, dragging his sleeve across his face.

Three men rose. The drummer in the chair sat up. "Here," he said, jerking at the cloth about his neck; "get this rag off me. I'm with him. I dont live here, but by God, if our mothers and wives and sisters—" He smeared the cloth over his face and flung it to the floor. McLendon stood in the floor and cursed the others. Another rose and moved toward him. The remainder sat uncomfortable, not looking at one another, then one by one they rose and joined him.

The barber picked the cloth from the floor. He began to fold it neatly. "Boys, dont do that. Will Mayes never done it. I know."

"Come on," McLendon said. He whirled. From his hip pocket protruded the butt of a heavy automatic pistol. They went out. The screen door crashed behind them reverberant in the dead air.

The barber wiped the razor carefully and swiftly, and put it away, and ran to the rear, and took his hat from the wall. "I'll be back as soon as I can," he said to the other barbers. "I cant let—" He went out, running. The two other barbers followed him to the door and caught it on the rebound, leaning out and looking up the street after him. The air was flat and dead. It had a metallic taste at the base of the tongue.

"What can he do?" the first said. The second one was saying "Jees Christ, Jees Christ" under his breath. "I'd just as lief be Will Mayes as Hawk, if he gets McLendon riled."

"Jees Christ, Jees Christ," the second whispered.

"You reckon he really done it to her?" the first said.

II

She was thirty-eight or thirty-nine. She lived in a small frame house with her invalid mother and a thin, sallow, unflagging aunt, where each morning between ten and eleven she would appear on the porch in a lace-trimmed boudoir cap, to sit swinging in the porch swing until noon. After dinner she lay down for a while, until the afternoon began to cool. Then, in one of the three or four new voile dresses which she had each summer, she would go downtown to spend the afternoon in the stores with the other ladies, where they would handle the goods and haggle over the prices in cold, immediate voices, without any intention of buying.

She was of comfortable people—not the best in Jefferson, but good people enough—and she was still on the slender side of ordinary looking, with a bright, faintly haggard manner and dress. When she was young she had had a slender, nervous body and a sort of hard vivacity which had enabled her for a time to ride upon the crest of the town's social life as exemplified by the high school party and church social period of her contemporaries while still children enough to be unclassconscious.

She was the last to realize that she was losing ground; that those among whom she had been a little brighter and louder flame than any other were beginning to learn the pleasure of snobbery—male—and retaliation—female. That was when her face began to wear that bright, haggard look. She still carried it to parties on shadowy porticoes and summer lawns, like a mask or a flag, with that bafflement of furious repudiation of truth in her eyes. One evening at a party she heard a boy and two girls, all schoolmates, talking. She never accepted another invitation.

She watched the girls with whom she had grown up as they married and got homes and children, but no man ever called on her steadily until the children of the other girls had been calling her "aunty" for several years, the while their mothers told them in bright voices about how popular Aunt Minnie had been as a girl. Then the town began to see her driving on Sunday afternoons with the cashier in the bank. He was a widower of about forty—a high-colored man, smelling always faintly of the barber shop or of whisky. He owned the first automobile in town, a red runabout; Minnie had the first motoring bonnet and veil the town ever saw. Then the town began to say: "Poor Minnie." "But she is old enough to take care of herself," others said. That was when she began to ask her old schoolmates that their children call her "cousin" instead of "aunty."

It was twelve years now since she had been relegated into adultery by public opinion, and eight years since the cashier had gone to a Memphis bank, returning for one day each Christmas, which he spent at an annual bachelors' party at a hunting club on the river. From behind their curtains the neighbors would see the party pass, and during the over-the-way Christmas day visiting they would tell her about him, about how well he looked, and how they heard that he was prospering in the city, watching with bright, secret eyes her haggard, bright face. Usually by that hour there would be the scent of whisky on her breath. It was supplied her by a youth, a clerk at the soda fountain: "Sure; I buy it for the old gal. I reckon she's entitled to a little fun."

Her mother kept to her room altogether now; the gaunt aunt ran the house. Against that background Minnie's bright dresses, her idle and empty days, had a quality of furious unreality. She went out in the evenings only with women now, neighbors, to the moving pictures. Each afternoon she dressed in one of the new dresses and went downtown alone, where her young "cousins" were already strolling in the late afternoons with their delicate, silken heads and thin, awkward arms and conscious hips, clinging to one another or shrieking and giggling with paired boys in the soda fountain when she passed and went on along the serried store fronts, in the doors of which the sitting and lounging men did not even follow her with their eyes any more.

III

The barber went swiftly up the street where the sparse lights, insect-swirled, glared in rigid and violent suspension in the lifeless air. The day had died in a pall of dust; above the darkened square, shrouded by the spent dust, the sky was as clear as the inside of a brass bell. Below the east was a rumor of the twice-waxed moon.

When he overtook them McLendon and three others were getting into a car parked in an alley. McLendon stooped his thick head, peering out beneath the top. "Changed your mind, did you?" he said. "Damn good thing; by God, tomorrow when this town hears about how you talked tonight—"

"Now, now," the other ex-soldier said. "Hawkshaw's all right. Come on, Hawk; jump in."

"Will Mayes never done it, boys," the barber said. "If anybody done it. Why, you all know well as I do there aint any town where they got better niggers than us. And you know how a lady will kind of think things about men when there aint any reason to, and Miss Minnie anyway—"

"Sure, sure," the soldier said. "We're just going to talk to him a little; that's all."

"Talk hell!" Butch said. "When we're through with the—"

"Shut up, for God's sake!" the soldier said. "Do you want everybody in town—"

"Tell them, by God!" McLendon said. "Tell every one of the sons that'll let a white woman—"

"Let's go; let's go: here's the other car." The second car slid squealing out of a cloud of dust at the alley mouth. McLendon started his car and took the lead. Dust lay like fog in the street. The street lights hung nimbused as in water. They drove on out of town.

A rutted lane turned at right angles. Dust hung above it too, and above all the land. The dark bulk of the ice plant, where the Negro Mayes was night watchman, rose against the sky. "Better stop here, hadn't we?" the soldier said. McLendon did not reply. He hurled the car up and slammed to a stop, the headlights glaring on the blank wall.

"Listen here, boys," the barber said; "if he's here, dont that prove he never done it? Dont it? If it was him, he would run. Dont you see he would?" The second car came up and stopped. McLendon got down; Butch sprang down beside him. "Listen, boys," the barber said.

"Cut the lights off!" McLendon said. The breathless dark rushed down. There was no sound in it save their lungs as they sought air in the parched dust in which for two months they had lived; then the diminishing crunch of Mc-Lendon's and Butch's feet, and a moment later McLendon's voice:

"Will! . . . Will!"

Below the east the wan hemorrhage of the moon increased. It heaved above the ridge, silvering the air, the dust, so that they seemed to breathe, live, in a bowl of molten lead. There was no sound of nightbird nor insect, no sound save their breathing and a faint ticking of contracting metal about the cars. Where their bodies touched one another they seemed to sweat dryly, for no more moisture came. "Christ!" a voice said; "let's get out of here."

But they didn't move until vague noises began to grow out of the darkness ahead; then they got out and waited tensely in the breathless dark. There was another sound: a blow, a hissing expulsion of breath and McLendon cursing in undertone. They stood a moment longer, then they ran forward. They ran in a stumbling clump, as though they were fleeing something. "Kill him, kill the son," a voice whispered. McLendon flung them back.

"Not here," he said. "Get him into the car." "Kill him, kill the black son!" the voice murmured. They dragged the Negro to the car. The barber had waited beside the car. He could feel himself sweating and he knew he was going to be sick at the stomach.

"What is it, captains?" the Negro said. "I aint done nothing. 'Fore God, Mr John." Someone produced handcuffs. They worked busily about the Negro as though he were a post, quiet, intent, getting in one another's way. He submitted to the handcuffs, looking swiftly and constantly from dim face to dim face. "Who's here, captains?" he said, leaning to peer into the faces until they could feel his breath and smell his sweaty reek. He spoke a name or two. "What you all say I done, Mr John?"

McLendon jerked the car door open. "Get in!" he said.

The Negro did not move. "What you all going to do with me, Mr John? I aint done nothing. White folks, captains, I aint done nothing: I swear 'fore God." He called another name.

"Get in!" McLendon said. He struck the Negro. The others expelled their breath in a dry hissing and struck him with random blows and he whirled and cursed them, and swept his manacled hands across their faces and slashed the barber upon the mouth, and the barber struck him also. "Get him in there," McLendon said. They pushed at him. He ceased struggling and got in and sat quietly as the others took their places. He sat between the barber and the soldier, drawing his limbs in so as not to touch them, his eyes going swiftly and constantly from face to face. Butch clung to the running board. The car moved on. The barber nursed his mouth with his handkerchief.

"What's the matter, Hawk?" the soldier said.

"Nothing," the barber said. They regained the highroad and turned away from town. The second car dropped back out of the dust. They went on, gaining speed; the final fringe of houses dropped behind.

"Goddamn, he stinks!" the soldier said.

"We'll fix that," the drummer in front beside McLendon said. On the running board Butch cursed into the hot rush of air. The barber leaned suddenly forward and touched McLendon's arm.

"Let me out, John," he said.

"Jump out, niggerlover," McLendon said without turning his head. He drove swiftly. Behind them the sourceless lights of the second car glared in the dust. Presently McLendon turned into a narrow road. It was rutted with disuse. It led back to an abandoned brick kiln—a series of reddish mounds and weed- and vine-choked vats without bottom. It had been used for pasture once, until one day the owner missed one of his mules. Although he prodded carefully in the vats with a long pole, he could not even find the bottom of them.

"John," the barber said.

"Jump out, then," McLendon said, hurling the car along the ruts. Beside the barber the Negro spoke:

"Mr. Henry."

The barber sat forward. The narrow tunnel of the road rushed up and past. Their motion was like an extinct furnace blast: cooler, but utterly dead. The car bounded from rut to rut.

"Mr. Henry," the Negro said.

The barber began to tug furiously at the door. "Look out, there!" the soldier said, but the barber had already kicked the door open and swung onto the running board. The soldier leaned across the Negro and grasped at him, but he had already jumped. The car went on without checking speed.

The impetus hurled him crashing through dust-sheathed weeds, into the ditch. Dust puffed about him, and in a thin, vicious crackling of sapless stems he lay choking and retching until the second car passed and died away. Then he rose and limped on until he reached the highroad and turned toward town, brushing at his clothes with his hands. The moon was higher, riding high and clear of the dust at last, and after a while the town began to glare beneath the dust. He went on, limping. Presently he heard cars and the glow of them grew in the dust behind him and he left the road and crouched again in the weeds until they passed. McLendon's car came last now. There were four people in it and Butch was not on the running board.

They went on; the dust swallowed them; the glare and the sound died away. The dust of them hung for a while, but soon the eternal dust absorbed it again. The barber climbed back onto the road and limped on toward town.

IV

As she dressed for supper on that Saturday evening, her own flesh felt like fever. Her hands trembled among the hooks and eyes, and her eyes had a feverish look, and her hair swirled crisp and crackling under the comb. While she was still dressing the friends called for her and sat while she donned her sheerest underthings and stockings and a new voile dress. "Do you feel strong enough to go out?" they said, their eyes bright too, with a dark glitter. "When you have had time to get over the shock, you must tell us what happened. What he said and did; everything."

In the leafed darkness, as they walked toward the square, she began to breathe deeply, something like a swimmer preparing to dive, until she ceased trembling, the four of them walking slowly because of the terrible heat and out of solicitude for her. But as they neared the square she began to tremble again, walking with her head up, her hands clenched at her sides, their voices about her murmurous, also with that feverish, glittering quality of their eyes.

They entered the square, she in the center of the group, fragile in her fresh dress. She was trembling worse. She walked slower and slower, as children eat ice cream, her head up and her eyes bright in the haggard banner of her face, passing the hotel and the coatless drummers in chairs along the curb looking around at her: "That's the one: see? The one in pink in the middle." "Is that her? What did they do with the nigger? Did they—?" "Sure.. He's all right." "All right, is he?" "Sure. He went on a little trip." Then the drug store, where even the young men lounging in the doorway tipped their hats and followed with their eyes the motion of her hips and legs when she passed.

They went on, passing the lifted hats of the gentlemen, the suddenly ceased voices, deferent, protective. "Do you see?" the friends said. Their voices sounded like long, hovering sighs of hissing exultation. "There's not a Negro on the square. Not one."

They reached the picture show. It was like a miniature fairyland with its lighted lobby and colored lithographs of life caught in its terrible and beautiful mutations. Her lips began to tingle. In the dark, when the picture began, it would be all right; she could hold back the laughing so it would not waste away so fast and so soon. So she hurried on before the turning faces, the undertones of low astonishment, and they took their accustomed places where she could see the aisle against the silver glare and the young men and girls coming in two and two against it.

The lights flicked away; the screen glowed silver, and soon life began to unfold, beautiful and passionate and sad, while still the young men and girls entered, scented and sibilant in the half dark, their paired backs in silhouette delicate and sleek, their slim, quick bodies awkward, divinely young, while beyond them the silver dream accumulated, inevitably on and on. She began to laugh. In trying to suppress it, it made more noise than ever; heads began to turn. Still laughing, her friends raised her and led her out, and she stood at the curb, laughing on a high, sustained note, until the taxi came up and they helped her in.

They removed the pink voile and the sheer underthings and the stockings, and put her to bed, and cracked ice for her temples, and sent for the doctor. He was hard to locate, so they ministered to her with hushed ejaculations, renewing the ice and fanning her. While the ice was fresh and cold she stopped laughing and lay still for a time, moaning only a little. But soon the laughing welled again and her voice rose screaming.

"Shhhhhhhhhhh! Shhhhhhhhhhhhhhh!" they said, freshening the ice-pack, smoothing her hair, examining it for gray; "poor girl!" Then to one another: "Do you suppose anything really happened?" their eyes darkly aglitter, secret and passionate. "Shhhhhhhhhhh! Poor girl! Poor Minnie!"

V

It was midnight when McLendon drove up to his neat new house. It was trim and fresh as a birdcage and almost as small, with its clean, green-and-white paint. He locked the car and mounted the porch and entered. His wife rose from a chair beside the reading lamp. McLendon stopped in the floor and stared at her until she looked down.

"Look at that clock," he said, lifting his arm, pointing. She stood before him, her face lowered, a magazine in her hands. Her face was pale, strained, and weary-looking. "Haven't I told you about sitting up like this, waiting to see when I come in?"

"John," she said. She laid the magazine down. Poised on the balls of his feet, he glared at her with his hot eyes, his sweating face.

"Didn't I tell you?" He went toward her. She looked up then. He caught her shoulder. She stood passive, looking at him.

"Don't, John. I couldn't sleep . . . The heat; something. Please, John. You're hurting me."

"Didn't I tell you?" He released her and half struck, half flung her across the chair, and she lay there and watched him quietly as he left the room.

He went on through the house, ripping off his shirt, and on the dark, screened porch at the rear he stood and mopped his head and shoulders with the shirt and flung it away. He took the pistol from his hip and laid it on the table beside the bed, and sat on the bed and removed his shoes, and rose and slipped his trousers off. He was sweating again already, and he stooped and hunted furiously for the shirt. At last he found it and wiped his body again, and, with his body pressed against the dusty screen, he stood panting. There was no movement, no sound, not even an insect. The dark world seemed to lie stricken beneath the cold moon and the lidless stars.

The Chase*

1967

ALBERTO MORAVIA   [b. 1907]

I have never been a sportsman—or, rather, I have been a sportsman only once, and that was the first and last time. I was a child, and one day, for some reason or other, I found myself together with my father, who was holding a gun in his hand, behind a bush, watching a bird that had perched on a branch not very far away. It was a large, gray bird—or perhaps it was brown—with a long—or perhaps a short—beak; I don't remember. I only remember what I felt at that moment as I looked at it. It was like watching an animal whose vitality was rendered more intense by the very fact of my watching it and of the animal's not knowing that I was watching it.

At that moment, I say, the notion of wildness entered my mind, never again to leave it: everything is wild which is autonomous and unpredictable and does not depend upon us. Then all of a sudden there was an explosion; I could no longer see the bird and I thought it had flown away. But my father was leading the way, walking in front of me through the undergrowth. Finally he stooped down, picked up something and put it in my hand. I was aware of something warm and soft and I lowered my eyes: there was a bird in the palm of my hand, its dangling, shattered head crowned with a plume of already-thickening blood. I burst into tears and dropped the corpse on the ground, and that was the end of my shooting experience.

I thought again of this remote episode in my life this very day after watching my wife, for the first and also the last time, as she was walking through the streets of the city. But let us take things in order.

What had my wife been like; what was she like now? She once had been, to put it briefly, "wild"—that is, entirely autonomous and unpredictable; latterly she had become "tame"—that is, predictable and dependent. For a long time she had been like the bird that, on that far-off morning in my childhood, I had seen perching on the bough; latterly, I am sorry to say, she had become like a hen about which one knows everything in advance—how it moves, how it eats, how it lays eggs, how it sleeps, and so on.

Nevertheless I would not wish anyone to think that my wife's wildness consisted of an uncouth, rough, rebellious character. Apart from being extremely beautiful, she is the gentlest, politest, most discreet person in the world. Rather her wildness consisted of the air of charming unpredictability, of independence in her way of living, with which during the first years of our marriage she acted in my presence, both at home and abroad. Wildness signified intimacy, privacy, secrecy. Yes, my wife as she sat in front of her dressing table, her eyes fixed on the looking glass, passing the hairbrush with a repeated motion over her long,

---

* Translated by Angus Davidson.

loose hair, was just as wild as the solitary quail hopping forward along a sun-filled furrow or the furtive fox coming out into a clearing and stopping to look around before running on. She was wild because I, as I looked at her, could never manage to foresee when she would give a last stroke with the hairbrush and rise and come toward me; wild to such a degree that sometimes when I went into our bedroom the smell of her, floating in the air, would have something of the acrid quality of a wild beast's lair.

Gradually she became less wild, tamer. I had had a fox, a quail, in the house, as I have said; then one day I realized that I had a hen. What effect does a hen have on someone who watches it? It has the effect of being, so to speak, an automaton in the form of a bird; automatic are the brief, rapid steps with which it moves about; automatic its hard, terse pecking; automatic the glance of the round eyes in its head that nods and turns; automatic its ready crouching down under the cock; automatic the dropping of the egg wherever it may be and the cry with which it announces that the egg has been laid. Good-by to the fox; good-by to the quail. And her smell—this no longer brought to my mind, in any way, the innocent odor of a wild animal; rather I detected in it the chemical suavity of some ordinary French perfume.

Our flat is on the first floor of a big building in a modern quarter of the town; our windows look out on a square in which there is a small public garden, the haunt of nurses and children and dogs. One day I was standing at the window, looking in a melancholy way at the garden. My wife, shortly before, had dressed to go out; and once again, watching her, I had noticed the irrevocable and, so to speak, invisible character of her gestures and personality: something which gave one the feeling of a thing already seen and already done and which therefore evaded even the most determined observation. And now, as I stood looking at the garden and at the same time wondering why the adorable wildness of former times had so completely disappeared, suddenly my wife came into my range of vision as she walked quickly across the garden in the direction of the bus stop. I watched her and then I almost jumped for joy; in a movement she was making to pull down a fold of her narrow skirt and smooth it over her thigh with the tips of her long, sharp nails, in this movement I recognized the wildness that in the past had made me love her. It was only an instant, but in that instant I said to myself: She's become wild again because she's convinced that I am not there and am not watching her. Then I left the window and rushed out.

But I did not join her at the bus stop; I felt that I must not allow myself to be seen. Instead I hurried to my car, which was standing nearby, got in and waited. A bus came and she got in together with some other people; the bus started off again and I began following it. Then there came back to me the memory of that one shooting expedition in which I had taken part as a child, and I saw that the bus was the undergrowth with its bushes and trees, my wife the bird perching on the bough while I, unseen, watched it living before my eyes. And the whole town, during this pursuit, became, as though by magic, a fact of nature like the countryside: the houses were hills, the streets valleys, the vehicles hedges and woods, and even the passers-by on the pavements had something unpredictable and autonomous—that is, wild—about them. And in my mouth, behind my clenched teeth, there was the acrid, metallic taste of gunfire; and my eyes, usually listless and wandering, had become sharp, watchful, attentive.

These eyes were fixed intently upon the exit door when the bus came to the end of its run. A number of people got out, and then I saw my wife getting out. Once again I recognized, in the manner in which she broke free of the crowd and started off toward a neighboring street, the wildness that pleased me so much. I jumped out of the car and started following her.

She was walking in front of me, ignorant of my presence, a tall woman with an elegant figure, long-legged, narrow-hipped, broad-backed, her brown hair falling on her shoulders.

Men turned around as she went past; perhaps they were aware of what I myself was now sensing with an intensity that quickened the beating of my heart and took my breath away: the unrestricted, steadily increasing, irresistible character of her mysterious wildness.

She walked hurriedly, having evidently some purpose in view, and even the fact that she had a purpose of which I was ignorant added to her wildness; I did not know where she was going, just as on that far-off morning I had not known what the bird perching on the bough was about to do. Moreover I thought the gradual, steady increase in this quality of wildness came partly from the fact that as she drew nearer to the object of this mysterious walk there was an increase in her—how shall I express it?—of biological tension, of existential excitement, of vital effervescence. Then, unexpectedly, with the suddenness of a film, her purpose was revealed.

A fair-haired young man in a leather jacket and a pair of corduroy trousers was leaning against the wall of a house in that ancient, narrow street. He was idly smoking as he looked in front of him. But as my wife passed close to him, he threw away his cigarette with a decisive gesture, took a step forward and seized her arm. I was expecting her to rebuff him, to move away from him, but nothing happened: evidently obeying the rules of some kind of erotic ritual, she went on walking beside the young man. Then after a few steps, with a movement that confirmed her own complicity, she put her arm around her companion's waist and he put his around her.

I understood then that this unknown man who took such liberties with my wife was also attracted by wildness. And so, instead of making a conventional appointment with her, instead of meeting in a café with a handshake, a falsely friendly and respectful welcome, he had preferred, by agreement with her, to take her by surprise—or, rather, to pretend to do so—while she was apparently taking a walk on her own account. All this I perceived by intuition, noticing that at the very moment when he stepped forward and took her arm her wildness had, so to speak, given an upward bound. It was years since I had seen my wife so alive, but alas, the source of this life could not be traced to me.

They walked on thus entwined and then, without any preliminaries, just like two wild animals, they did an unexpected thing: they went into one of the dark doorways in order to kiss. I stopped and watched them from a distance, peering into the darkness of the entrance. My wife was turned away from me and was bending back with the pressure of his body, her hair hanging free. I looked at that long, thick mane of brown hair, which as she leaned back fell free of her shoulders, and I felt at that moment her vitality reached its diapason, just as happens with wild animals when they couple and their customary wildness is redoubled by the violence of love. I watched for a long time and then, since this kiss went on and on and in fact seemed to be prolonged beyond the limits of my power of endurance, I saw that I would have to intervene.

I would have to go forward, seize my wife by the arm—or actually by that hair, which hung down and conveyed so well the feeling of feminine passivity—then hurl myself with clenched fists upon the blond young man. After this encounter I would carry off my wife, weeping, mortified, ashamed, while I was raging and broken-hearted, upbraiding her and pouring scorn upon her.

But what else would this intervention amount to but the shot my father fired at that free, unknowing bird as it perched on the bough? The disorder and confusion, the mortification, the shame, that would follow would irreparably destroy the rare and precious moment of wildness that I was witnessing inside the dark doorway. It was true that this wildness was directed against me; but I had to remember that wildness, always and everywhere, is directed against everything and everybody. After the scene of my intervention it might be possible for me to regain control of my wife, but I should find her shattered and lifeless in my arms like the bird that my father placed in my hand so that I might throw it into the shooting bag.

The kiss went on and on: well, it was a kiss of passion—that could not be denied. I waited until they finished, until they came out of the doorway, until they walked on again still linked together. Then I turned back.

The Girls in Their Summer Dresses

1939

IRWIN SHAW [1913–1984]

Fifth Avenue was shining in the sun when they left the Brevoort.[1] The sun was warm, even though it was February, and everything looked like Sunday morning—the buses and the well-dressed people walking slowly in couples and the quiet buildings with the windows closed.

Michael held Frances' arm tightly as they walked toward Washington Square[2] in the sunlight. They walked lightly, almost smiling, because they had slept late and had a good breakfast and it was Sunday. Michael unbuttoned his coat and let it flap around him in the mild wind.

"Look out," Frances said as they crossed Eighth Street. "You'll break your neck." Michael laughed and Frances laughed with him.

"She's not so pretty," Frances said. "Anyway, not pretty enough to take a chance of breaking your neck."

Michael laughed again. "How did you know I was looking at her?"

Frances cocked her head to one side and smiled at her husband under the brim of her hat. "Mike, darling," she said.

"O.K.," he said. "Excuse me."

Frances patted his arm lightly and pulled him along a little faster toward Washington Square. "Let's not see anybody all day," she said. "Let's just hang around with each other. You and me. We're always up to our neck in people, drinking their Scotch or drinking our Scotch; we only see each other in bed. I want to go out with my husband all day long. I want him to talk only to me and listen only to me."

"What's to stop us?" Michael asked.

"The Stevensons. They want us to drop by around one o'clock and they'll drive us into the country."

"The cunning Stevensons," Mike said. "Transparent. They can whistle. They can go driving in the country by themselves."

"Is it a date?"

"It's a date."

Frances leaned over and kissed him on the tip of the ear.

"Darling," Michael said, "this is Fifth Avenue."

"Let me arrange a program," Frances said. "A planned Sunday in New York for a young couple with money to throw away."

---

[1] The Brevoort was a New York hotel on lower Fifth Avenue. At the time that this story was written, the Brevoort's bar was famous as a gathering place for literary people.

[2] A park at the south end of Fifth Avenue.

"Go easy."

"First let's go to the Metropolitan Museum of Art," Frances suggested, because Michael had said during the week he wanted to go. "I haven't been there in three years and there're at least ten pictures I want to see again. Then we can take the bus down to Radio City and watch them skate. And later we'll go down to Cavanagh's and get a steak as big as a blacksmith's apron, with a bottle of wine, and after that there's a French picture at the Filmarte that everybody says—say, are you listening to me?"

"Sure," he said. He took his eyes off the hatless girl with the dark hair, cut dancer-style like a helmet, who was walking past him.

"That's the program for the day," Frances said flatly. "Or maybe you'd just rather walk up and down Fifth Avenue."

"No," Michael said. "Not at all."

"You always look at other women," Frances said. "Everywhere. Every damned place we go."

"No, darling," Michael said, "I look at everything. God gave me eyes and I look at women and men in subway excavations and moving pictures and the little flowers of the field. I casually inspect the universe."

"You ought to see the look in your eye," Frances said, "as you casually inspect the universe on Fifth Avenue."

"I'm a happily married man." Michael pressed her elbow tenderly. "Example for the whole twentieth century—Mr. and Mrs. Mike Loomis. Hey, let's have a drink," he said, stopping.

"We just had breakfast."

"Now listen, darling," Mike said, choosing his words with care, "it's a nice day and we both felt good and there's no reason why we have to break it up. Let's have a nice Sunday."

"All right. I don't know why I started this. Let's drop it. Let's have a good time."

They joined hands consciously and walked without talking among the baby carriages and the old Italian men in their Sunday clothes and the young women with Scotties in Washington Square Park.

"At least once a year everyone should go to the Metropolitan Museum of Art," Frances said after a while, her tone a good imitation of the tone she had used at breakfast and at the beginning of their walk. "And it's nice on Sunday. There're a lot of people looking at the pictures and you get the feeling maybe Art isn't on the decline in New York City, after all—"

"I want to tell you something," Michael said very seriously. "I have not touched another woman. Not once. In all the five years."

"All right," Frances said.

"You believe that, don't you?"

"All right."

They walked between the crowded benches, under the scrubby city-park trees.

"I try not to notice it," Frances said, "but I feel rotten inside, in my stomach, when we pass a woman and you look at her and I see that look in your eye and that's the way you looked at me the first time. In Alice Maxwell's house. Standing there in the living room, next to the radio, with a green hat on and all those people."

"I remember the hat," Michael said.

"The same look," Frances said. "And it makes me feel bad. It makes me feel terrible."

"Sh-h-h, please, darling, sh-h-h."

"I think I would like a drink now," Frances said.

They walked over to a bar on Eighth Street, not saying anything, Michael automatically helping her over curbstones and guiding her past automobiles. They sat near a window in the bar and the sun streamed in and there was a small, cheerful fire in the fireplace. A little Japanese waiter came over and put down some pretzels and smiled happily at them.

"What do you order after breakfast?" Michael asked.

"Brandy, I suppose," Frances said.

"Courvoisier," Michael told the waiter. "Two Courvoisiers."

The waiter came with the glasses and they sat drinking the brandy in the sunlight. Michael finished half his and drank a little water.

"I look at women," he said. "Correct. I don't say it's wrong or right. I look at them. If I pass them on the street and I don't look at them, I'm fooling you, I'm fooling myself."

"You look at them as though you want them," Frances said, playing with her brandy glass. "Every one of them."

"In a way," Michael said, speaking softly and not to his wife, "in a way that's true. I don't do anything about it, but it's true."

"I know it. That's why I feel bad."

"Another brandy," Michael called. "Waiter, two more brandies."

He sighed and closed his eyes and rubbed them gently with his fingertips. "I love the way women look. One of the things I like best about New York is the battalions of women. When I first came to New York from Ohio that was the first thing I noticed, the million wonderful women, all over the city. I walked around with my heart in my throat."

"A kid," Frances said. "That's a kid's feeling."

"Guess again," Michael said. "Guess again. I'm older now. I'm a man getting near middle age, putting on a little fat, and I still love to walk along Fifth Avenue at three o'clock on the east side of the street between Fiftieth and Fifty-seventh Streets. They're all out then, shopping, in their furs and their crazy hats, everything all concentrated from all over the world into seven blocks—the best furs, the best clothes, the handsomest women, out to spend money and feeling good about it."

The Japanese waiter put the two drinks down, smiling with great happiness.

"Everything is all right?" he asked.

"Everything is wonderful," Michael said.

"If it's just a couple of fur coats," Frances said, "and forty-five dollar hats—"

"It's not the fur coats. Or the hats. That's just the scenery for that particular kind of woman. Understand," he said, "you don't have to listen to this."

"I want to listen."

"I like the girls in the offices. Neat with their eyeglasses, smart, chipper, knowing what everything is about. I like the girls on Forty-fourth Street at lunchtime, the actresses, all dressed up on nothing a week. I like the salesgirls in the stores, paying attention to you first because you're a man, leaving the lady customers waiting. I got all this stuff accumulated in me because I've been thinking about it for ten years and now you've asked for it and here it is."

"Go ahead," Frances said.

"When I think of New York City, I think of all the girls on parade in the city. I don't know whether it's something special with me or whether every man in the city walks around with the same feeling inside him, but I feel as though I'm at a picnic in this city. I like to sit near the women in the theatres, the famous beauties who've taken six hours to get ready and look it. And the young girls at the football games, with the red cheeks, and when the warm weather comes, the girls in their summer dresses." He finished his drink. "That's the story."

Frances finished her drink and swallowed two or three times extra. "You say you love me?"

"I love you."

"I'm pretty, too," Frances said. "As pretty as any of them."

"You're beautiful," Michael said.

"I'm good for you," Frances said, pleading. "I've made a good wife, a good housekeeper, a good friend. I'd do any damn thing for you."

"I know," Michael said. He put his hand out and grasped hers.

"You'd like to be free to—" Frances said.

"Sh-h-h."

"Tell the truth." She took her hand away from under his.

Michael flicked the edge of his glass with his finger. "O.K.," he said gently. "Sometimes I feel I would like to be free."

"Well," Frances said, "any time you say."

"Don't be foolish." Michael swung his chair around to her side of the table and patted her thigh.

She began to cry silently into her handkerchief, bent over just enough so that nobody else in the bar would notice. "Someday," she said, crying, "you're going to make a move."

Michael didn't say anything. He sat watching the bartender slowly peel a lemon.

"Aren't you?" Frances asked harshly. "Come on, tell me. Talk. Aren't you?"

"Maybe," Michael said. He moved his chair back again. "How the hell do I know?"

"You know," Frances persisted. "Don't you know?"

"Yes," Michael said after a while, "I know."

Frances stopped crying then. Two or three snuffles into the handkerchief and she put it away and her face didn't tell anything to anybody. "At least do me one favor," she said.

"Sure."

"Stop talking about how pretty this woman is or that one. Nice eyes, nice breasts, a pretty figure, good voice." She mimicked his voice. "Keep it to yourself. I'm not interested."

Michael waved to the waiter. "I'll keep it to myself," he said.

Frances flicked the corners of her eyes. "Another brandy," she told the waiter.

"Two," Michael said.

"Yes, ma'am, yes, sir," said the waiter, backing away.

Frances regarded Michael coolly across the table. "Do you want me to call the Stevensons?" she asked. "It'll be nice in the country."

"Sure," Michael said. "Call them."

She got up from the table and walked across the room toward the telephone. Michael watched her walk, thinking what a pretty girl, what nice legs.

QUESTIONS

1. Is Frances's anger justified? Explain.   **2.** What is the effect of the final sentence of the story?

Shiloh[1]

1982

BOBBIE ANN MASON [b. 1940]

Leroy Moffitt's wife, Norma Jean, is working on her pectorals. She lifts three-pound dumbbells to warm up, then progresses to a twenty-pound barbell. Standing with her legs apart, she reminds Leroy of Wonder Woman.

"I'd give anything if I could just get these muscles to where they're real hard," says Norma Jean. "Feel this arm. It's not as hard as the other one."

"That's 'cause you're right-handed," says Leroy, dodging as she swings the barbell in an arc.

"Do you think so?"

"Sure."

Leroy is a truckdriver. He injured his leg in a highway accident four months ago, and his physical therapy, which involves weights and a pulley, prompted Norma Jean to try building herself up. Now she is attending a body-building class. Leroy has been collecting temporary disability since his tractor-trailer jackknifed in Missouri, badly twisting his left leg in its socket. He has a steel pin in his hip. He will probably not be able to drive his rig again. It sits in the backyard, like a gigantic bird that has flown home to roost. Leroy has been home in Kentucky for three months, and his leg is almost healed, but the accident frightened him and he does not want to drive any more long hauls. He is not sure what to do next. In the meantime, he makes things from craft kits. He started by building a miniature log cabin from notched Popsicle sticks. He varnished it and placed it on the TV set, where it remains. It reminds him of a rustic Nativity scene. Then he tried string art (sailing ships on black velvet), a macramé owl kit, a snap-together B-17 Flying Fortress, and a lamp made out of a model truck, with a light fixture screwed in the top of the cab. At first the kits were diversions, something to kill time, but now he is thinking about building a full-scale log house from a kit. It would be considerably cheaper than building a regular house, and besides, Leroy has grown to appreciate how things are put together. He has begun to realize that in all the years he was on the road he never took time to examine anything. He was always flying past scenery.

"They won't let you build a log cabin in any of the new subdivisions," Norma Jean tells him.

"They will if I tell them it's for you," he says, teasing her. Ever since they were married, he has promised Norma Jean he would build her a new home one day. They have always rented, and the house they live in is small and nondescript. It does not even feel like a home, Leroy realizes now.

Norma Jean works at the Rexall drugstore, and she has acquired an amazing

---

[1] Scene in southwest Tennessee of a Union victory during the Civil War; now a national military park. Shiloh, which means "tranquillity" or "rest," is also the name of a sacred place in the Old Testament.

amount of information about cosmetics. When she explains to Leroy the three stages of complexion care, involving creams, toners, and moisturizers, he thinks happily of other petroleum products—axle grease, diesel fuel. This is a connection between him and Norma Jean. Since he has been home, he has felt unusually tender about his wife and guilty over his long absences. But he can't tell what she feels about him. Norma Jean has never complained about his traveling; she has never made hurt remarks, like calling his truck a "widow-maker." He is reasonably certain she has been faithful to him, but he wishes she would celebrate his permanent homecoming more happily. Norma Jean is often startled to find Leroy at home, and he thinks she seems a little disappointed about it. Perhaps he reminds her too much of the early days of their marriage, before he went on the road. They had a child who died as an infant, years ago. They never speak about their memories of Randy, which have almost faded, but now that Leroy is home all the time, they sometimes feel awkward around each other, and Leroy wonders if one of them should mention the child. He has the feeling that they are waking up out of a dream together—that they must create a new marriage, start afresh. They are lucky they are still married. Leroy has read that for most people losing a child destroys the marriage—or else he heard this on *Donahue*. He can't always remember where he learns things anymore.

At Christmas, Leroy bought an electric organ for Norma Jean. She used to play the piano when she was in high school. "It don't leave you," she told him once. "It's like riding a bicycle."

The new instrument had so many keys and buttons that she was bewildered by it at first. She touched the keys tentatively, pushed some buttons, then pecked out "Chopsticks." It came out in an amplified fox-trot rhythm, with marimba sounds.

"It's an orchestra!" she cried.

The organ had a pecan-look finish and eighteen preset chords, with optional flute, violin, trumpet, clarinet, and banjo accompaniments. Norma Jean mastered the organ almost immediately. At first she played Christmas songs. Then she bought *The Sixties Songbook* and learned every tune in it, adding variations to each with the rows of brightly colored buttons.

"I didn't like these old songs back then," she said. "But I have this crazy feeling I missed something."

"You didn't miss a thing," said Leroy.

Leroy likes to lie on the couch and smoke a joint and listen to Norma Jean play "Can't Take My Eyes Off You" and "I'll Be Back." He is back again. After fifteen years on the road, he is finally settling down with the woman he loves. She is still pretty. Her skin is flawless. Her frosted curls resemble pencil trimmings.

Now that Leroy has come home to stay, he notices how much the town has changed. Subdivisions are spreading across western Kentucky like an oil slick. The sign at the edge of town says "Pop: 11,500"—only seven hundred more than it said twenty years before. Leroy can't figure out who is living in all the new houses. The farmers who used to gather around the courthouse square on Saturday afternoons to play checkers and spit tobacco juice have gone. It has been years since Leroy has thought about the farmers, and they have disappeared without his noticing.

Leroy meets a kid named Stevie Hamilton in the parking lot at the new shopping center. While they pretend to be strangers meeting over a stalled car, Stevie tosses an ounce of marijuana under the front seat of Leroy's car. Stevie is wearing orange jogging shoes and a T-shirt that says CHATTAHOOCHEE SUPER-RAT. His father is a prominent doctor who lives in one of the expensive subdivisions in a new white-columned brick house that looks like a funeral parlor. In the phone book under his name there is a separate number, with the listing "Teenagers."

"Where do you get this stuff?" asks Leroy. "From your pappy?"

"That's for me to know and you to find out," Stevie says. He is slit-eyed and skinny.

"What else you got?"

"What you interested in?"

"Nothing special. Just wondered."

Leroy used to take speed on the road. Now he has to go slowly. He needs to be mellow. He leans back against the car and says, "I'm aiming to build me a log house, soon as I get time. My wife, though, I don't think she likes the idea."

"Well, let me know when you want me again," Stevie says. He has a cigarette in his cupped palm, as though sheltering it from the wind. He takes a long drag, then stomps it on the asphalt and slouches away.

Stevie's father was two years ahead of Leroy in high school. Leroy is thirty-four. He married Norma Jean when they were both eighteen, and their child Randy was born a few months later, but he died at the age of four months and three days. He would be about Stevie's age now. Norma Jean and Leroy were at the drive-in, watching a double feature (*Dr. Strangelove* and *Lover Come Back*), and the baby was sleeping in the back seat. When the first movie ended, the baby was dead. It was the sudden infant death syndrome. Leroy remembers handing Randy to a nurse at the emergency room, as though he were offering her a large doll as a present. A dead baby feels like a sack of flour. "It just happens sometimes," said the doctor, in what Leroy always recalls as a nonchalant tone. Leroy can hardly remember the child anymore, but he still sees vividly a scene from *Dr. Strangelove* in which the President of the United States was talking in a folksy voice on the hot line to the Soviet premier about the bomber accidentally headed toward Russia. He was in the War Room, and the world map was lit up. Leroy remembers Norma Jean standing catatonically beside him in the hospital and himself thinking: Who is this strange girl? He had forgotten who she was. Now scientists are saying that crib death is caused by a virus. Nobody knows anything, Leroy thinks. The answers are always changing.

When Leroy gets home from the shopping center, Norma Jean's mother, Mabel Beasley, is there. Until this year, Leroy has not realized how much time

she spends with Norma Jean. When she visits, she inspects the closets and then
the plants, informing Norma Jean when a plant is droopy or yellow. Mabel
calls the plants "flowers," although there are never any blooms. She always notices if Norma Jean's laundry is piling up. Mabel is a short, overweight woman
whose tight, brown-dyed curls look more like a wig than the actual wig she
sometimes wears. Today she has brought Norma Jean an off-white dust ruffle
she made for the bed; Mabel works in a custom-upholstery shop.

"This is the tenth one I made this year," Mabel says. "I got started and couldn't
stop."

"It's real pretty," says Norma Jean.

"Now we can hide things under the bed," says Leroy, who gets along with
his mother-in-law primarily by joking with her. Mabel has never really forgiven
him for disgracing her by getting Norma Jean pregnant. When the baby died,
she said that fate was mocking her.

"What's that thing?" Mabel says to Leroy in a loud voice, pointing to a tangle of yarn on a piece of canvas.

Leroy holds it up for Mabel to see. "It's my needlepoint," he explains. "This
is a *Star Trek* pillow cover."

"That's what a woman would do," says Mabel. "Great day in the morning!"

"All the big football players on TV do it," he says.

"Why, Leroy, you're always trying to fool me. I don't believe you for one
minute. You don't know what to do with yourself—that's the whole trouble.
Sewing!"

"I'm aiming to build us a log house," says Leroy. "Soon as my plans come."

"Like *heck* you are," says Norma Jean. She takes Leroy's needlepoint and
shoves it into a drawer. "You have to find a job first. Nobody can afford to
build now anyway."

Mabel straightens her girdle and says, "I still think before you get tied down
y'all ought to take a little run to Shiloh."

"One of these days, Mama," Norma Jean says impatiently.

Mabel is talking about Shiloh, Tennessee. For the past few years, she has
been urging Leroy and Norma Jean to visit the Civil War battleground there.
Mabel went there on her honeymoon—the only real trip she ever took. Her
husband died of a perforated ulcer when Norma Jean was ten, but Mabel, who
was accepted into the United Daughters of the Confederacy in 1975, is still
preoccupied with going back to Shiloh.

"I've been to kingdom come and back in that truck out yonder," Leroy says
to Mabel, "but we never yet set foot in that battleground. Ain't that something?
How did I miss it?"

"It's not even that far," Mabel says.

After Mabel leaves, Norma Jean reads to Leroy from a list she has made.
"Things you could do," she announces. "You could get a job as a guard at
Union Carbide, where they'd let you set on a stool. You could get on at the
lumberyard. You could do a little carpenter work, if you want to build so bad.
You could—"

"I can't do something where I'd have to stand up all day."

"You ought to try standing up all day behind a cosmetics counter. It's amazing that I have strong feet, coming from two parents that never had strong feet at all." At the moment Norma Jean is holding on to the kitchen counter, raising her knees one at a time as she talks. She is wearing two-pound ankle weights.

"Don't worry," says Leroy. "I'll do something."

"You could truck calves to slaughter for somebody. You wouldn't have to drive any big old truck for that."

"I'm going to build you this house," says Leroy. "I want to make you a real home."

"I don't want to live in any log cabin."

"It's not a cabin. It's a house."

"I don't care. It looks like a cabin."

"You and me together could lift those logs. It's just like lifting weights."

Norma Jean doesn't answer. Under her breath, she is counting. Now she is marching through the kitchen. She is doing goose steps.

Before his accident, when Leroy came home he used to stay in the house with Norma Jean, watching TV in bed and playing cards. She would cook fried chicken, picnic ham, chocolate pie—all his favorites. Now he is home alone much of the time. In the mornings, Norma Jean disappears, leaving a cooling place in the bed. She eats a cereal called Body Buddies, and she leaves the bowl on the table, with the soggy tan balls floating in a milk puddle. He sees things about Norma Jean that he never realized before. When she chops onions, she stares off into a corner, as if she can't bear to look. She puts on her house slippers almost precisely at nine o'clock every evening and nudges her jogging shoes under the couch. She saves bread heels for the birds. Leroy watches the birds at the feeder. He notices the peculiar way goldfinches fly past the window. They close their wings, then fall, then spread their wings to catch and lift themselves. He wonders if they close their eyes when they fall. Norma Jean closes her eyes when they are in bed. She wants the lights turned out. Even then, he is sure she closes her eyes.

He goes for long drives around town. He tends to drive a car rather carelessly. Power steering and an automatic shift make a car feel so small and inconsequential that his body is hardly involved in the driving process. His injured leg stretches out comfortably. Once or twice he has almost hit something, but even the prospect of an accident seems minor in a car. He cruises the new subdivisions, feeling like a criminal rehearsing for a robbery. Norma Jean is probably right about a log house being inappropriate here in the new subdivisions. All the houses look grand and complicated. They depress him.

One day when Leroy comes home from a drive he finds Norma Jean in tears. She is in the kitchen making a potato and mushroom-soup casserole, with grated-cheese topping. She is crying because her mother caught her smoking.

"I didn't hear her coming. I was standing here puffing away pretty as you please," Norma Jean says, wiping her eyes.

"I knew it would happen sooner or later," says Leroy, putting his arm around her.

"She don't know the meaning of the word 'knock,' " says Norma Jean. "It's a wonder she hadn't caught me years ago."

"Think of it this way," Leroy says. "What if she caught me with a joint?"

"You better not let her!" Norma Jean shrieks. "I'm warning you, Leroy Moffitt!"

"I'm just kidding. Here, play me a tune. That'll help you relax."

Norma Jean puts the casserole in the oven and sets the timer. Then she plays a ragtime tune, with horns and banjo, as Leroy lights up a joint and lies on the couch, laughing to himself about Mabel's catching him at it. He thinks of Stevie Hamilton—a doctor's son pushing grass. Everything is funny. The whole town seems crazy and small. He is reminded of Virgil Mathis, a boastful policeman Leroy used to shoot pool with. Virgil recently led a drug bust in a back room at a bowling alley, where he seized ten thousand dollars' worth of marijuana. The newspaper had a picture of him holding up the bags of grass and grinning widely. Right now, Leroy can imagine Virgil breaking down the door and arresting him with a lungful of smoke. Virgil would probably have been alerted to the scene because of all the racket Norma Jean is making. Now she sounds like a hard-rock band. Norma Jean is terrific. When she switches to a Latin-rhythm version of "Sunshine Superman," Leroy hums along. Norma Jean's foot goes up and down, up and down.

"Well, what do you think?" Leroy says, when Norma Jean pauses to search through her music.

"What do I think about what?"

His mind has gone blank. Then he says, "I'll sell my rig and build us a house." That wasn't what he wanted to say. He wanted to know what she thought—what she *really* thought—about them.

"Don't start in on that again," says Norma Jean. She begins playing "Who'll Be the Next in Line?"

Leroy used to tell hitchhikers his whole life story—about his travels, his hometown, the baby. He would end with a question: "Well, what do you think?" It was just a rhetorical question. In time, he had the feeling that he'd been telling the same story over and over to the same hitchhikers. He quit talking to hitchhikers when he realized how his voice sounded—whining and self-pitying, like some teenage-tragedy song. Now Leroy has the sudden impulse to tell Norma Jean about himself, as if he had just met her. They have known each other so long they have forgotten a lot about each other. They could become reacquainted. But when the oven timer goes off and she runs to the kitchen, he forgets why he wants to do this.

The next day, Mabel drops by. It is Saturday and Norma Jean is cleaning. Leroy is studying the plans of his log house, which have finally come in the mail. He has them spread out on the table—big sheets of stiff blue paper, with diagrams and numbers printed in white. While Norma Jean runs the vacuum, Mabel drinks coffee. She sets her coffee cup on a blueprint.

"I'm just waiting for time to pass," she says to Leroy, drumming her fingers on the table.

As soon as Norma Jean switches off the vacuum, Mabel says in a loud voice, "Did you hear about the datsun dog that killed the baby?"

Norma Jean says, "The word is 'dachshund.' "

"They put the dog on trial. It chewed the baby's legs off. The mother was in the next room all the time." She raises her voice. "They thought it was neglect."

Norma Jean is holding her ears. Leroy manages to open the refrigerator and get some Diet Pepsi to offer Mabel. Mabel still has some coffee and she waves away the Pepsi.

"Datsuns are like that," Mabel says. "They're jealous dogs. They'll tear a place to pieces if you don't keep an eye on them."

"You better watch out what you're saying, Mabel," says Leroy.

"Well, facts is facts."

Leroy looks out the window at his rig. It is like a huge piece of furniture gathering dust in the backyard. Pretty soon it will be an antique. He hears the vacuum cleaner. Norma Jean seems to be cleaning the living room rug again.

Later, she says to Leroy, "She just said that about the baby because she caught me smoking. She's trying to pay me back."

"What are you talking about?" Leroy says, nervously shuffling blueprints.

"You know good and well," Norma Jean says. She is sitting in a kitchen chair with her feet up and her arms wrapped around her knees. She looks small and helpless. She says, "The very idea, her bringing up a subject like that! Saying it was neglect."

"She didn't mean that," Leroy says.

"She might not have *thought* she meant it. She always says things like that. You don't know how she goes on."

"But she didn't really mean it. She was just talking."

Leroy opens a king-sized bottle of beer and pours it into two glasses, dividing it carefully. He hands a glass to Norma Jean and she takes it from him mechanically. For a long time, they sit by the kitchen window watching the birds at the feeder.

Something is happening. Norma Jean is going to night school. She has graduated from her six-week body-building course and now she is taking an adult-education course in composition at Paducah Community College. She spends her evenings outlining paragraphs.

"First you have a topic sentence," she explains to Leroy. "Then you divide it up. Your secondary topic has to be connected to your primary topic."

To Leroy, this sounds intimidating. "I never was any good in English," he says.

"It makes a lot of sense."

"What are you doing this for, anyhow?"

She shrugs. "It's something to do." She stands up and lifts her dumbbells a few times.

"Driving a rig, nobody cared about my English."

"I'm not criticizing your English."

Norma Jean used to say, "If I lose ten minutes' sleep, I just drag all day."

Now she stays up late, writing compositions. She got a B on her first paper—a how-to theme on soup-based casseroles. Recently Norma Jean has been cooking unusual foods—tacos, lasagna, Bombay chicken. She doesn't play the organ anymore, though her second paper was called "Why Music Is Important to Me." She sits at the kitchen table, concentrating on her outlines, while Leroy plays with his log house plans, practicing with a set of Lincoln Logs. The thought of getting a truckload of notched, numbered logs scares him, and he wants to be prepared. As he and Norma Jean work together at the kitchen table, Leroy has the hopeful thought that they are sharing something, but he knows he is a fool to think this. Norma Jean is miles away. He knows he is going to lose her. Like Mabel, he is just waiting for time to pass.

One day, Mabel is there before Norma Jean gets home from work, and Leroy finds himself confiding in her. Mabel, he realizes, must know Norma Jean better than he does.

"I don't know what's got into that girl," Mabel says. "She used to go to bed with the chickens. Now you say she's up all hours. Plus her a-smoking. I like to died."

"I want to make her this beautiful home," Leroy says, indicating the Lincoln Logs. "I don't think she even wants it. Maybe she was happier with me gone."

"She don't know what to make of you, coming home like this."

"Is that it?"

Mabel takes the roof off his Lincoln Log cabin. "You couldn't get *me* in a log cabin," she says. "I was raised in one. It's no picnic, let me tell you."

"They're different now," says Leroy.

"I tell you what," Mabel says, smiling oddly at Leroy.

"What?"

"Take her on down to Shiloh. Y'all need to get out together, stir a little. Her brain's all balled up over them books."

Leroy can see traces of Norma Jean's features in her mother's face. Mabel's worn face has the texture of crinkled cotton, but suddenly she looks pretty. It occurs to Leroy that Mabel has been hinting all along that she wants them to take her with them to Shiloh.

"Let's all go to Shiloh," he says. "You and me and her. Come Sunday."

Mabel throws up her hands in protest. "Oh, no, not me. Young folks want to be by theirselves."

When Norma Jean comes in with groceries, Leroy says excitedly, "Your mama here's been dying to go to Shiloh for thirty-five years. It's about time we went, don't you think?"

"I'm not going to butt in on anybody's second honeymoon," Mabel says.

"Who's going on a honeymoon, for Christ's sake?" Norma Jean says loudly.

"I never raised no daughter of mine to talk that-a-way," Mabel says.

"You ain't seen nothing yet," says Norma Jean. She starts putting away boxes and cans, slamming cabinet doors.

"There's a log cabin at Shiloh," Mabel says. "It was there during the battle. There's bullet holes in it."

"When are you going to *shut up* about Shiloh, Mama?" asks Norma Jean.

"I always thought Shiloh was the prettiest place, so full of history," Mabel goes on. "I just hoped y'all could see it once before I die, so you could tell me about it." Later, she whispers to Leroy, "You do what I said. A little change is what she needs."

"Your name means 'the king,' " Norma Jean says to Leroy that evening. He is trying to get her to go to Shiloh, and she is reading a book about another century.

"Well, I reckon I ought to be right proud."

"I guess so."

"Am I still king around here?"

Norma Jean flexes her biceps and feels them for hardness. "I'm not fooling around with anybody, if that's what you mean," she says.

"Would you tell me if you were?"

"I don't know."

"What does *your* name mean?"

"It was Marilyn Monroe's real name."

"No kidding!"

"Norma comes from the Normans. They were invaders," she says. She closes her book and looks hard at Leroy. "I'll go to Shiloh with you if you'll stop staring at me."

On Sunday, Norma Jean packs a picnic and they go to Shiloh. To Leroy's relief, Mabel says she does not want to come with them. Norma Jean drives, and Leroy, sitting beside her, feels like some boring hitchhiker she has picked up. He tries some conversation, but she answers him in monosyllables. At Shiloh, she drives aimlessly through the park, past bluffs and trails and steep ravines. Shiloh is an immense place, and Leroy cannot see it as a battleground. It is not what he expected. He thought it would look like a golf course. Monuments are everywhere, showing through the thick clusters of trees. Norma Jean passes the log cabin Mabel mentioned. It is surrounded by tourists looking for bullet holes.

"That's not the kind of log house I've got in mind," says Leroy apologetically.

"I know *that*."

"This is a pretty place. Your mama was right."

"It's O.K.," says Norma Jean. "Well, we've seen it. I hope she's satisfied."

They burst out laughing together.

At the park museum, a movie on Shiloh is shown every half hour, but they decide that they don't want to see it. They buy a souvenir Confederate flag for Mabel, and then they find a picnic spot near the cemetery. Norma Jean has brought a picnic cooler, with pimiento sandwiches, soft drinks, and Yodels. Leroy eats a sandwich and then smokes a joint, hiding it behind the picnic cooler. Norma Jean has quit smoking altogether. She is picking cake crumbs from the cellophane wrapper, like a fussy bird.

Leroy says, "So the boys in gray ended up in Corinth. The Union soldiers zapped 'em finally. April 7, 1862."

They both know that he doesn't know any history. He is just talking about some of the historical plaques they have read. He feels awkward, like a boy on a date with an older girl. They are still just making conversation.

"Corinth is where Mama eloped to," says Norma Jean.

They sit in silence and stare at the cemetery for the Union dead and, beyond, at a tall cluster of trees. Campers are parked nearby, bumper to bumper, and small children in bright clothing are cavorting and squealing. Norma Jean wads up the cake wrapper and squeezes it tightly in her hand. Without looking at Leroy, she says, "I want to leave you."

Leroy takes a bottle of Coke out of the cooler and flips off the cap. He holds the bottle poised near his mouth but cannot remember to take a drink. Finally he says, "No, you don't."

"Yes, I do."

"I won't let you."

"You can't stop me."

"Don't do me that way."

Leroy knows Norma Jean will have her own way. "Didn't I promise to be home from now on?" he says.

"In some ways, a woman prefers a man who wanders," says Norma Jean. "That sounds crazy, I know."

"You're not crazy."

Leroy remembers to drink from his Coke. Then he says, "Yes, you *are* crazy. You and me could start all over again. Right back at the beginning."

"We *have* started all over again," says Norma Jean. "And this is how it turned out."

"What did I do wrong?"

"Nothing."

"Is this one of those women's lib things?" Leroy asks.

"Don't be funny."

The cemetery, a green slope dotted with white markers, looks like a subdivision site. Leroy is trying to comprehend that his marriage is breaking up, but for some reason he is wondering about white slabs in a graveyard.

"Everything was fine till Mama caught me smoking," says Norma Jean, standing up. "That set something off."

"What are you talking about?"

"She won't leave me alone—*you* won't leave me alone." Norma Jean seems to be crying, but she is looking away from him. "I feel eighteen again. I can't face that all over again." She starts walking away. "No, it *wasn't* fine. I don't know what I'm saying. Forget it."

Leroy takes a lungful of smoke and closes his eyes as Norma Jean's words sink in. He tries to focus on the fact that thirty-five hundred soldiers died on the grounds around him. He can only think of that war as a board game with plastic soldiers. Leroy almost smiles, as he compares the Confederates' daring attack on the Union camps and Virgil Mathis's raid on the bowling alley. General Grant, drunk and furious, shoved the Southerners back to Corinth, where Mabel and Jet Beasley were married years later, when Mabel was still thin and good-looking. The next day, Mabel and Jet visited the battleground, and then Norma Jean was born, and then she married Leroy and they had a baby, which they lost, and now Leroy and Norma Jean are here at the same battleground. Leroy knows he is leaving out a lot. He is leaving out the insides of history. History was always just names and dates to him. It occurs to him that building a house out of logs is similarly empty—too simple. And the real inner workings of a marriage, like most of history, have escaped him. Now he sees that building a log house is the dumbest idea he could have had. It was clumsy of him to think Norma Jean would want a log house. It was a crazy idea. He'll have to think of something else, quickly. He will wad the blueprints into tight balls and fling them into the lake. Then he'll get moving again. He opens his eyes. Norma Jean has moved away and is walking through the cemetery, following a serpentine brick path.

Leroy gets up to follow his wife, but his good leg is asleep and his bad leg still hurts him. Norma Jean is far away, walking rapidly toward the bluff by the river, and he tries to hobble toward her. Some children run past him, screaming noisily. Norma Jean has reached the bluff, and she is looking out over the Tennessee River. Now she turns toward Leroy and waves her arms. Is she beckoning to him? She seems to be doing an exercise for her chest muscles. The sky is unusually pale—the color of the dust ruffle Mabel made for their bed.

QUESTIONS

1. Why does Norma Jean decide to leave Leroy?   **2.** Why does Norma Jean hide her smoking from her mother?   **3.** What is the significance of Shiloh?

WRITING TOPIC

Do you believe that Norma Jean is justified in leaving her husband? Explain.

LOVE
AND
HATE

RAINBOW

HEART

MOON

Midsummer Wall, 1966 by Jim Dine

POETRY .

Bonny Barbara Allan

ANONYMOUS

It was in and about the Martinmas[1] time,
   When the green leaves were a falling,
That Sir John Graeme, in the West Country,
   Fell in love with Barbara Allan.

He sent his man down through the town,
   To the place where she was dwelling:
"O haste and come to my master dear,
   Gin° ye be Barbara Allan."   *if*

O hooly,° hooly rose she up,   *slowly*
   To the place where he was lying,   10
And when she drew the curtain by:
   "Young man, I think you're dying."

"O it's I'm sick, and very, very sick,
   And 'tis a' for Barbara Allan."
"O the better for me ye s'° never be,   *ye shall*
   Though your heart's blood were a-spilling.

"O dinna° ye mind,° young man," said she,   *don't/remember*
   "When ye was in the tavern a drinking,
That ye made the healths gae° round and round,   *go*
   And slighted Barbara Allan?"   20

He turned his face unto the wall,
   And death was with him dealing:
"Adieu, adieu, my dear friends all,
   And be kind to Barbara Allan."

And slowly, slowly raise she up,
   And slowly, slowly left him,

Bonny Barbara Allan
  [1] November 11.

And sighing said, she could not stay,
   Since death of life had reft him.

She had not gane a mile but twa,   *
   When she heard the dead-bell ringing,   30
And every jow° that the dead-bell geid,°   stroke/gave
   It cried, "Woe to Barbara Allan!"

"O mother, mother, make my bed!
   O make it saft and narrow!
Since my love died for me to-day,
   I'll die for him to-morrow."

Since There's No Help, Come Let Us Kiss and Part   1619

MICHAEL DRAYTON   [1563–1631]

Since there's no help, come let us kiss and part;
Nay, I have done, you get no more of me,
And I am glad, yea glad with all my heart
That thus so cleanly I myself can free;
Shake hands forever, cancel all our vows,
And when we meet at any time again,
Be it not seen in either of our brows
That we one jot of former love retain.
Now at the last gasp of love's latest breath,
When, his pulse failing, passion speechless lies,   10
When faith is kneeling by his bed of death,
And innocence is closing up his eyes,
     Now if thou wouldst, when all have given him over,
     From death to life thou mightst him yet recover.

QUESTIONS
1. Describe the scene in lines 9–12. Why is "innocence" described as closing "love's" eyes?   **2.** How might the lady save love from death?

The Passionate Shepherd to His Love[1]   1600

CHRISTOPHER MARLOWE   [1564–1593]

Come live with me and be my love,
And we will all the pleasures prove
That valleys, groves, hills, and fields,
Woods, or steepy mountain yields.

And we will sit upon the rocks,
Seeing the shepherds feed their flocks,
By shallow rivers to whose falls
Melodious birds sing madrigals.

And I will make thee beds of roses
And a thousand fragrant posies,   10
A cap of flowers, and a kirtle°   skirt
Embroidered all with leaves of myrtle;

A gown made of the finest wool
Which from our pretty lambs we pull;
Fair lined slippers for the cold,
With buckles of the purest gold;

A belt of straw and ivy buds,
With coral clasps and amber studs:
And if these pleasures may thee move,
Come live with me, and be my love.   20

The shepherds' swains shall dance and sing
For thy delight each May morning:
If these delights thy mind may move,
Then live with me and be my love.

The Passionate Shepherd . . .
   [1]This poem has elicited many responses over the centuries. Sir Walter Ralegh's early answer
follows. C. Day Lewis's twentieth-century response appears on p. 467.

The Nymph's Reply
to the Shepherd

1600

SIR WALTER RALEGH [1552?–1618][1]

If all the world and love were young,
And truth in every shepherd's tongue,
These pretty pleasures might me move
To live with thee and be thy love.

Time drives the flocks from field to fold
When rivers rage and rocks grow cold,
And Philomel° becometh dumb;   the nightingale
The rest complains of cares to come.

The flowers do fade, and wanton fields
To wayward winter reckoning yields;   10
A honey tongue, a heart of gall,
Is fancy's spring, but sorrow's fall.

Thy gowns, thy shoes, thy beds of roses,
Thy cap, thy kirtle, and thy posies
Soon break, soon wither, soon forgotten—
In folly ripe, in reason rotten.

Thy belt of straw and ivy buds,
Thy coral clasps and amber studs,
All these in me no means can move
To come to thee and be thy love.   20

But could youth last and love still breed,
Had joys no date° nor age no need,   end
Then these delights my mind might move
To live with thee and be thy love.

---

[1] Chronology has been dispensed with here to facilitate comparison with Marlowe's "Passionate Shepherd."

Sonnets   1609

WILLIAM SHAKESPEARE   [1564–1616]

18

Shall I compare thee to a summer's day?
Thou art more lovely and more temperate:
Rough winds do shake the darling buds of May,
And summer's lease hath all too short a date:
Sometime too hot the eye of heaven shines,
And often is his gold complexion dimmed;
And every fair from fair sometimes declines,
By chance or nature's changing course untrimmed;
But thy eternal summer shall not fade,
Nor lose possession of that fair thou ow'st,°   ownest
Nor shall death brag thou wander'st in his shade,   11
When in eternal lines to time thou grow'st:
    So long as men can breathe, or eyes can see,
    So long lives this, and this gives life to thee.

QUESTIONS
1. Why does the poet argue that "a summer's day" is an inappropriate metaphor
for his beloved?   **2.** What is "this" in line 14?

129

Th' expense of spirit in a waste of shame
Is lust in action; and till action, lust
Is perjured, murderous, bloody, full of blame,
Savage, extreme, rude, cruel, not to trust;
Enjoyed no sooner but despiséd straight;
Past reason hunted; and no sooner had,
Past reason hated, as a swallowed bait,
On purpose laid to make the taker mad:
Mad in pursuit, and in possession so;
Had, having, and in quest to have, extreme;   10
A bliss in proof,° and proved, a very woe;   experience
Before, a joy proposed; behind, a dream.
    All this the world well knows; yet none knows well
    To shun the heaven that leads men to this hell.

QUESTIONS

1. Paraphrase "Th' expense of spirit in a waste of shame/Is lust in action." **2.** Describe the sound patterns and metrical variations in lines 3 and 4. What do they contribute to the "sense" of the lines?

WRITING TOPIC

How do the sound patterns, the metrical variations, and the paradox in the final couplet contribute to the sense of this sonnet?

130

My mistress' eyes are nothing like the sun;
Coral is far more red than her lips' red;
If snow be white, why then her breasts are dun;
If hairs be wires, black wires grow on her head.
I have seen roses damasked,° red and white,   variegated
But no such roses see I in her cheeks;
And in some perfumes is there more delight
Than in the breath that from my mistress reeks.
I love to hear her speak, yet well I know
That music hath a far more pleasing sound;   10
I grant I never saw a goddess go;
My mistress, when she walks, treads on the ground.
    And yet, by heaven, I think my love as rare
    As any she belied with false compare.[1]

A Valediction: Forbidding Mourning

1633

JOHN DONNE [1572–1631]

As virtuous men pass mildly away,
    And whisper to their souls to go,
Whilst some of their sad friends do say
    The breath goes now, and some say, No;

Sonnet 130
[1] I.e., as any woman misrepresented with false comparisons.

So let us melt, and make no noise,
    No tear-floods, nor sigh-tempests move,
'Twere profanation of our joys
    To tell the laity our love.

Moving of th' earth° brings harms and fears,   earthquake
    Men reckon what it did and meant;   10
But trepidation of the spheres,
    Though greater far, is innocent.[1]

Dull sublunary° lovers' love   under the moon
    (Whose soul is sense) cannot admit
Absence, because it doth remove
    Those things which elemented it.

But we by a love so much refined
    That our selves know not what it is,
Inter-assuréd of the mind,
    Care less, eyes, lips, and hands to miss.   20

Our two souls therefore, which are one,
    Though I must go, endure not yet
A breach, but an expansion,
    Like gold to airy thinness beat.

If they be two, they are two so
    As stiff twin compasses are two;
Thy soul, the fixed foot, makes no show
    To move, but doth, if th' other do.

And though it in the center sit,
    Yet when the other far doth roam,   30
It leans and harkens after it,
    And grows erect, as that comes home.

Such wilt thou be to me, who must
    Like th' other foot, obliquely run;
Thy firmness makes my circle just,
    And makes me end where I begun.

A *Valediction: Forbidding Mourning*
    [1] The movement of the heavenly spheres is harmless.

QUESTIONS
1. Two kinds of love are described in this poem—spiritual and physical. How does the simile drawn in the first two stanzas help define the differences between them? **2.** How does the contrast between earthquakes and the movement of the spheres in stanza three further develop the contrast between the two types of lovers? **3.** Explain the comparison between a drawing compass and the lovers in the last three stanzas.

Go, Lovely Rose!   1645

EDMUND WALLER   [1606–1687]

Go, lovely rose!
Tell her that wastes her time and me
    That now she knows,
When I resemble° her to thee,   compare
How sweet and fair she seems to be.

Tell her that's young,
And shuns to have her graces spied,
    That hadst thou sprung
In deserts, where no men abide,
Thou must have uncommended died.   10

Small is the worth
Of beauty from the light retired;
    Bid her come forth,
Suffer herself to be desired,
And not blush so to be admired.

Then die! that she
The common fate of all things rare
    May read in thee;
How small a part of time they share
That are so wondrous sweet and fair!   20

To His Coy Mistress   1681

ANDREW MARVELL   [1621–1678]

Had we but world enough, and time,
This coyness, lady, were no crime.

We would sit down, and think which way
To walk, and pass our long love's day.
Thou by the Indian Ganges' side
Shouldst rubies find; I by the tide
Of Humber would complain. I would
Love you ten years before the flood,
And you should, if you please, refuse
Till the conversion of the Jews.   10
My vegetable love should grow
Vaster than empires and more slow;
An hundred years should go to praise
Thine eyes, and on thy forehead gaze;
Two hundred to adore each breast,
But thirty thousand to the rest;
An age at least to every part,
And the last age should show your heart.
For, lady, you deserve this state,
Nor would I love at lower rate.   20
    But at my back I always hear
Time's wingéd chariot hurrying near;
And yonder all before us lie
Deserts of vast eternity.
Thy beauty shall no more be found,
Nor, in thy marble vault, shall sound
My echoing song; then worms shall try
That long-preserved virginity,
And your quaint honor turn to dust,
And into ashes all my lust: 30
The grave's a fine and private place,
But none, I think, do there embrace.
    Now therefore, while the youthful hue
Sits on thy skin like morning dew,
And while thy willing soul transpires
At every pore with instant fires,
Now let us sport us while we may,
And now, like amorous birds of prey,
Rather at once our time devour   39
Than languish in his slow-chapped° power.   slow-jawed
Let us roll our strength and all
Our sweetness up into one ball,
And tear our pleasures with rough strife
Thorough the iron gates of life:
Thus, though we cannot make our sun
Stand still, yet we will make him run.

QUESTIONS

1. State the argument of the poem (see ll. 1–2, 21–22, 33–34). **2.** Compare the figures of speech in the first verse paragraph with those in the last. How do they differ? **3.** Characterize the attitude toward life recommended by the poet.

WRITING TOPIC

In what ways does the conception of love in this poem differ from that in Donne's "A Valediction: Forbidding Mourning"? In your discussion consider the imagery in both poems.

A Poison Tree   1794

WILLIAM BLAKE   [1757–1827]

I was angry with my friend:
I told my wrath, my wrath did end.
I was angry with my foe:
I told it not, my wrath did grow.

And I watered it in fears,
Night & morning with my tears;
And I sunnéd it with smiles,
And with soft deceitful wiles.

And it grew both day and night,
Till it bore an apple bright.
And my foe beheld it shine,
And he knew that it was mine,

And into my garden stole,
When the night had veil'd the pole;
In the morning glad I see
My foe outstretched beneath the tree.

QUESTIONS

1. Is anything gained from the parallel readers might draw between this tree and the tree in the Garden of Eden? Explain. **2.** Can you articulate what the "poison" is? **3.** Does your own experience verify the first stanza of the poem?

A Red, Red Rose   1796

ROBERT BURNS   [1759–1796]

O My Luve's like a red, red rose,
   That's newly sprung in June;

O My Luve's like a melodie
   That's sweetly played in tune.

As fair art thou, my bonnie lass,
   So deep in luve am I;
And I will luve thee still, my dear,
   Till a' the seas gang dry.

Till a' the seas gang dry, my dear,
   And the rocks melt wi' the sun: 10
O I will love thee still, my dear,
   While the sands o' life shall run.

And fare thee weel, my only luve,
   And fare thee weel awhile!
And I will come again, my luve,
   Though it were ten thousand mile.

from

Song of Myself   1855

WALT WHITMAN [1819–1892]

11

Twenty-eight young men bathe by the shore,
Twenty-eight young men and all so friendly;
Twenty-eight years of womanly life and all so lonesome.

She owns the fine house by the rise of the bank,
She hides handsome and richly drest aft the blinds of the window.

Which of the young men does she like the best?
Ah the homeliest of them is beautiful to her.

Where are you off to, lady? for I see you,
You splash in the water there, yet stay stock still in your room.

Dancing and laughing along the beach came the twenty-ninth bather,   10
The rest did not see her, but she saw them and loved them.

The beards of the young men glisten'd with wet, it ran from their long
    hair,
Little streams pass'd all over their bodies.

An unseen hand also pass'd over their bodies,
It descended tremblingly from their temples and ribs.

The young men float on their backs, their white bellies bulge to the sun,
    they do not ask who seizes fast to them,
They do not know who puffs and declines with pendant and bending
    arch,
They do not think whom they souse with spray.

Dover Beach*   1867

MATTHEW ARNOLD   [1822–1888]

The sea is calm tonight.
The tide is full, the moon lies fair
Upon the straits; on the French coast the light
Gleams and is gone; the cliffs of England stand,
Glimmering and vast, out in the tranquil bay.
Come to the window, sweet is the night-air!
Only, from the long line of spray
Where the sea meets the moon-blanched land,
Listen! you hear the grating roar
Of pebbles which the waves draw back, and fling,   10
At their return, up the high strand,
Begin, and cease, and then again begin,
With tremulous cadence slow, and bring
The eternal note of sadness in.

Sophocles long ago
Heard it on the Aegean, and it brought
Into his mind the turbid ebb and flow
Of human misery; we
Find also in the sound a thought,
Hearing it by this distant northern sea.   20

---

*This poem is considered in detail in the appendix "Three Critical Approaches: Formalist, Sociological, Psychoanalytic" at the end of the book.

The Sea of Faith
Was once, too, at the full, and round earth's shore
Lay like the folds of a bright girdle furled.
But now I only hear
Its melancholy, long, withdrawing roar,
Retreating, to the breath
Of the night-wind, down the vast edges drear
And naked shingles° of the world.   pebble beaches

Ah, love, let us be true
To one another! for the world, which seems   30
To lie before us like a land of dreams,
So various, so beautiful, so new,
Hath really neither joy, nor love, nor light,
Nor certitude, nor peace, nor help for pain;
And we are here as on a darkling plain
Swept with confused alarms of struggle and flight,
Where ignorant armies clash by night.

Mine Enemy Is
Growing Old   (ca. 1881)

EMILY DICKINSON   [1830–1886]

Mine Enemy is growing old—
I have at last Revenge—
The Palate of the Hate departs—
If any would avenge

Let him be quick—the Viand flits—
It is a faded Meat—
Anger as soon as fed is dead—
'Tis starving makes it fat—

QUESTION
1. Explain the paradox contained in the last two lines.

WRITING TOPIC
Compare this poem with Blake's "A Poison Tree."

Pied Beauty   1877

GERARD MANLEY HOPKINS   [1844–1889]

Glory be to God for dappled things—
    For skies of couple-colour as a brinded° cow;   brindled
        For rose-moles all in stipple upon trout that swim;
Fresh-firecoal chestnut-falls,[1] finches' wings;
    Landscape plotted and pieced[2]—fold, fallow, and plough;
        And all trades, their gear and tackle, and trim.°   equipment
All things counter,° original, spare, strange;   contrasted
    Whatever is fickle, freckled (who knows how?)
        With swift, slow; sweet, sour; adazzle, dim;
He fathers-forth whose beauty is past change: 10
            Praise him.

Fire and Ice   1923

ROBERT FROST   [1874–1963]

Some say the world will end in fire,
Some say in ice,
From what I've tasted of desire
I hold with those who favor fire.
But if it had to perish twice,
I think I know enough of hate
To say that for destruction ice
Is also great
And would suffice.

The Love Song
of J. Alfred Prufrock   1917

T. S. ELIOT   [1888–1965]

    S'io credessi che mia risposta fosse
    a persona che mai tornasse al mondo,

Pied Beauty
  [1] Fallen chestnuts, with the outer husks removed, colored like fresh fire coal.
  [2] Reference to the variegated pattern of land put to different uses.

questa fiamma staria senza più scosse.
Ma per ciò che giammai di questo fondo
non tornò vivo alcun, s'i'odo il vero,
senza tema d'infamia ti rispondo. [1]

Let us go then, you and I,
When the evening is spread out against the sky
Like a patient etherized upon a table;
Let us go, through certain half-deserted streets,
The muttering retreats
Of restless nights in one-night cheap hotels
And sawdust restaurants with oyster shells:
Streets that follow like a tedious argument
Of insidious intent
To lead you to an overwhelming question . . .   10
Oh, do not ask, "What is it?"
Let us go and make our visit.

In the room the women come and go
Talking of Michelangelo.

The yellow fog that rubs its back upon the windowpanes,
The yellow smoke that rubs its muzzle on the windowpanes,
Licked its tongue into the corners of the evening,
Lingered upon the pools that stand in drains,
Let fall upon its back the soot that falls from chimneys,
Slipped by the terrace, made a sudden leap,   20
And seeing that it was a soft October night,
Curled once about the house, and fell asleep.

And indeed there will be time
For the yellow smoke that slides along the street,
Rubbing its back upon the windowpanes;
There will be time, there will be time
To prepare a face to meet the faces that you meet;
There will be time to murder and create,
And time for all the works and days of hands
That lift and drop a question on your plate;   30
Time for you and time for me,

. . . Prufrock
[1] From Dante, *Inferno*, XXVII, 61–66. The speaker is Guido da Montefeltro, who is imprisoned in a flame in the level of Hell reserved for false counselors. He tells Dante and Virgil, "If I thought my answer were given to one who might return to the world, this flame would stay without further movement. But since from this depth none has ever returned alive, if what I hear is true, I answer you without fear of infamy."

And time yet for a hundred indecisions,
And for a hundred visions and revisions,
Before the taking of a toast and tea.

In the room the women come and go
Talking of Michelangelo.

And indeed there will be time
To wonder, "Do I dare?" and, "Do I dare?"
Time to turn back and descend the stair,
With a bald spot in the middle of my hair—   40
(They will say: "How his hair is growing thin!")
My morning coat, my collar mounting firmly to the chin,
My necktie rich and modest, but asserted by a simple pin—
(They will say: "But how his arms and legs are thin!")
Do I dare
Disturb the universe?
In a minute there is time
For decisions and revisions which a minute will reverse.

For I have known them all already, known them all—
Have known the evenings, mornings, afternoons,   50
I have measured out my life with coffee spoons;
I know the voices dying with a dying fall
Beneath the music from a farther room.
   So how should I presume?

And I have known the eyes already, known them all—
The eyes that fix you in a formulated phrase,
And when I am formulated, sprawling on a pin,
When I am pinned and wriggling on the wall,
Then how should I begin
To spit out all the butt-ends of my days and ways?   60
   And how should I presume?

And I have known the arms already, known them all—
Arms that are braceleted and white and bare
(But in the lamplight, downed with light brown hair!)
Is it perfume from a dress
That makes me so digress?
Arms that lie along a table, or wrap about a shawl.
   And should I then presume?
   And how should I begin?

                    .   .   .   .   .

Shall I say, I have gone at dusk through narrow streets   70
And watched the smoke that rises from the pipes
Of lonely men in shirt-sleeves, leaning out of windows? . . .

I should have been a pair of ragged claws
Scuttling across the floors of silent seas.

        · · · · ·

And the afternoon, the evening, sleeps so peacefully!
Smoothed by long fingers,
Asleep . . . tired . . . or it malingers,
Stretched on the floor, here beside you and me.
Should I, after tea and cakes and ices,
Have the strength to force the moment to its crisis?   80
But though I have wept and fasted, wept and prayed,
Though I have seen my head (grown slightly bald) brought in
    upon a platter,[2]
I am no prophet—and here's no great matter;
I have seen the moment of my greatness flicker,
And I have seen the eternal Footman hold my coat, and snicker,
And in short, I was afraid.

And would it have been worth it, after all,
After the cups, the marmalade, the tea,
Among the porcelain, among some talk of you and me,
Would it have been worth while,   90
To have bitten off the matter with a smile,
To have squeezed the universe into a ball
To roll it toward some overwhelming question,
To say: "I am Lazarus,[3] come from the dead,
Come back to tell you all, I shall tell you all"—
If one, settling a pillow by her head,
    Should say: "That is not what I meant at all.
    That is not it, at all."

And would it have been worth it, after all,
Would it have been worth while,   100
After the sunsets and the dooryards and the sprinkled streets,
After the novels, after the teacups, after the skirts that trail along the floor—
And this, and so much more?—
It is impossible to say just what I mean!
But as if a magic lantern threw the nerves in patterns on a screen:

---

[2] Like the head of John the Baptist. See Matthew 14:3–12.
[3] See John 11:1–14 and Luke 16:19–26.

Would it have been worth while
If one, settling a pillow or throwing off a shawl,
And turning toward the window, should say:
  "That is not it at all,
  That is not what I meant, at all."   110

    . . . . .

No! I am not Prince Hamlet, nor was meant to be;
Am an attendant lord, one that will do
To swell a progress,° start a scene or two,   state journey
Advise the prince; no doubt, an easy tool,
Deferential, glad to be of use,
Politic, cautious, and meticulous;
Full of high sentence,° but a bit obtuse;   sententiousness
At times, indeed, almost ridiculous—
Almost, at times, the Fool.

I grow old . . . I grow old . . .   120
I shall wear the bottoms of my trousers rolled.°   cuffed

Shall I part my hair behind? Do I dare to eat a peach?
I shall wear white flannel trousers, and walk upon the beach.
I have heard the mermaids singing, each to each.

I do not think that they will sing to me.

I have seen them riding seaward on the waves
Combing the white hair of the waves blown back
When the wind blows the water white and black.

We have lingered in the chambers of the sea
By sea-girls wreathed with seaweed red and brown   130
Till human voices wake us, and we drown.

QUESTIONS

1. This poem may be understood as a stream of consciousness passing through the mind of Prufrock. The "you and I" of line 1 may be different aspects of his personality. Or perhaps the "you and I" is parallel to Guido who speaks the epigraph and Dante to whom he tells the story that resulted in his damnation—hence, "you" is the reader and "I" is Prufrock. Apparently, Prufrock is on his way to a tea and is pondering his relationship with a certain woman. The poem is disjointed because it proceeds by psychological rather than logical stages. To what social class does Prufrock belong? How does Prufrock respond to the attitudes and values of his class? Does he change in the course of the poem? **2.** Line 92 provides a good example of literary allusion (see the last stanza of Marvell, "To His Coy Mistress," especially ll. 41–42). How does an awareness of the allusion contribute to the reader's response to the stanza here?   **3.**   What might the song of the mermaids (l. 124) signify, and why does Prufrock think they will not sing to him (l. 125)?   **4.**   T. S. Eliot once said that some poetry "can communicate without being understood." Is this such a poem?

WRITING TOPIC
What sort of man is J. Alfred Prufrock? How does the poet establish his characteristics?

Love Is Not All   1931

EDNA ST. VINCENT MILLAY   [1892–1950]

Love is not all: it is not meat nor drink
Nor slumber nor a roof against the rain;
Nor yet a floating spar to men that sink
And rise and sink and rise and sink again;
Love can not fill the thickened lung with breath,
Nor clean the blood, nor set the fractured bone;
Yet many a man is making friends with death
Even as I speak, for lack of love alone.
It well may be that in a difficult hour,
Pinned down by pain and moaning for release,   10
Or nagged by want past resolution's power,
I might be driven to sell your love for peace,
Or trade the memory of this night for food.
It well may be. I do not think I would.

if everything happens
that can't be done   1944

E. E. CUMMINGS   [1894–1962]

if everything happens that can't be done
(and anything's righter
than books
could plan)
the stupidest teacher will almost guess
(with a run
skip
around we go yes)
there's nothing as something as one

one hasn't a why or because or although   10
(and buds know better
than books
don't grow)
one's anything old being everything new
(with a what
which
around we come who)
one's everyanything so

so world is a leaf so tree is a bough
(and birds sing sweeter   20
than books
tell how)
so here is away and so your is a my
(with a down
up
around again fly)
forever was never till now

now i love you and you love me
(and books are shuter
than books   30
can be)
and deep in the high that does nothing but fall
(with a shout
each
around we go all)
there's somebody calling who's we

we're anything brighter than even the sun
(we're everything greater
than books
might mean)   40
we're everyanything more than believe
(with a spin
leap
alive we're alive)
we're wonderful one times one

QUESTIONS
1. What fundamental contrast is stated by the poem?   **2.**   Lines 2–4 and 6–8 of each stanza could be printed as single lines. Why do you think Cummings decided to print them as he does?   **3.**   What common attitude toward lovers is expressed by the last lines of the stanzas?   **4.**   Is the poem free verse or formal verse?

WRITING TOPIC
What relation do the parenthetical lines in each stanza bear to the poem as a whole?

Song[1]   1935

C. DAY LEWIS [1904–1972]

Come, live with me and be my love,
And we will all the pleasures prove
Of peace and plenty, bed and board,
That chance employment may afford.

I'll handle dainties on the docks
And thou shalt read of summer frocks:
At evening by the sour canals
We'll hope to hear some madrigals.

Care on thy maiden brow shall put
A wreath of wrinkles, and thy foot   10
Be shod with pain: not silken dress
But toil shall tire thy loveliness.

Hunger shall make thy modest zone
And cheat fond death of all but bone—
If these delights thy mind may move,
Then live with me and be my love.

from

Five Songs   (1937)

W. H. AUDEN [1907–1973]

That night when joy began
Our narrowest veins to flush,
We waited for the flash
Of morning's levelled gun.

Song
[1] See Christopher Marlowe's "The Passionate Shepherd to His Love," p. 449.

But morning let us pass,
And day by day relief
Outgrew his nervous laugh,
Grows credulous of peace.

As mile by mile is seen
No trespasser's reproach,   10
And love's best glasses reach
No fields but are his own.

QUESTIONS

1. Describe the sound relationships among the last words in the lines of each stanza. **2.** What is the controlling metaphor in the poem? Is it appropriate for a love poem? **3.** If it were suggested that the poem describes a homosexual relationship, would your response to the poem's figurative language change?

I Knew a Woman   1958

THEODORE ROETHKE   [1908–1963]

I knew a woman, lovely in her bones,
When small birds sighed, she would sigh back at them;
Ah, when she moved, she moved more ways than one:
The shapes a bright container can contain!
Of her choice virtues only gods should speak,
Or English poets who grew up on Greek
(I'd have them sing in chorus, cheek to cheek).

How well her wishes went! She stroked my chin,
She taught me Turn, and Counter-turn, and Stand;
She taught me Touch, that undulant white skin;   10
I nibbled meekly from her proffered hand;
She was the sickle; I, poor I, the rake,
Coming behind her for her pretty sake
(But what prodigious mowing we did make).

Love likes a gander, and adores a goose:
Her full lips pursed, the errant note to seize;
She played it quick, she played it light and loose;
My eyes, they dazzled at her flowing knees;
Her several parts could keep a pure repose,
Or one hip quiver with a mobile nose   20
(She moved in circles, and those circles moved).

Let seed be grass, and grass turn into hay:
I'm martyr to a motion not my own;
What's freedom for? To know eternity.
I swear she cast a shadow white as stone.
But who would count eternity in days?
These old bones live to learn her wanton ways:
(I measure time by how a body sways).

One Art   1976

ELIZABETH BISHOP   [1911–1979]

The art of losing isn't hard to master;
so many things seem filled with the intent
to be lost that their loss is no disaster.

Lose something every day. Accept the fluster
of lost door keys, the hour badly spent.
The art of losing isn't hard to master.

Then practice losing farther, losing faster:
places, and names, and where it was you meant
to travel. None of these will bring disaster.

I lost my mother's watch. And look! my last, or   10
next-to-last, of three loved houses went.
The art of losing isn't hard to master.

I lost two cities, lovely ones. And, vaster,
some realms I owned, two rivers, a continent.
I miss them, but it wasn't a disaster.

—Even losing you (the joking voice, a gesture
I love) I shan't have lied. It's evident
the art of losing's not too hard to master
though it may look like (*Write* it!) like disaster.

Those Winter Sundays   1975

ROBERT HAYDEN   [1913–1980]

Sundays too my father got up early
and put his clothes on in the blueblack cold,

then with cracked hands that ached
from labor in the weekday weather made
banked fires blaze. No one ever thanked him.

I'd wake and hear the cold splintering, breaking.
When the rooms were warm, he'd call,
and slowly I would rise and dress,
fearing the chronic angers of that house,

Speaking indifferently to him,   10
who had driven out the cold
and polished my good shoes as well.
What did I know, what did I know
of love's austere and lonely offices?

The Dover Bitch   1968

A CRITICISM OF LIFE

ANTHONY HECHT   [b. 1922]

So there stood Matthew Arnold and this girl
With the cliffs of England crumbling away behind them,
And he said to her, "Try to be true to me,
And I'll do the same for you, for things are bad
All over, etc., etc."
Well now, I knew this girl. It's true she had read
Sophocles in a fairly good translation
And caught that bitter allusion to the sea,
But all the time he was talking she had in mind
The notion of what his whiskers would feel like   10
On the back of her neck. She told me later on
That after a while she got to looking out
At the lights across the channel, and really felt sad,
Thinking of all the wine and enormous beds
And blandishments in French and the perfumes.
And then she got really angry. To have been brought
All the way down from London, and then be addressed
As sort of a mournful cosmic last resort
Is really tough on a girl, and she was pretty.
Anyway, she watched him pace the room   20
And finger his watch-chain and seem to sweat a bit,
And then she said one or two unprintable things.

But you mustn't judge her by that. What I mean to say is,
She's really all right. I still see her once in a while
And she always treats me right. We have a drink
And I give her a good time, and perhaps it's a year
Before I see her again, but there she is,
Running to fat, but dependable as they come,
And sometimes I bring her a bottle of *Nuit d'Amour.*

QUESTIONS

1. This poem is a response to Matthew Arnold's "Dover Beach," which appears earlier in this section. Arnold's poem is often read as a pained response to the breakdown of religious tradition and social and political order in the mid-nineteenth century. Is this poem, in contrast, optimistic? Is the relationship between the speaker and the girl at the end of the poem admirable? Explain.   **2.**   Do you suppose Hecht was moved to write this poem out of admiration for "Dover Beach"? Explain.

WRITING TOPIC

What is the fundamental difference between the speaker's conception of love in Arnold's poem and the "girl's" conception of love as reported in this poem?

The Ache of Marriage   1964

DENISE LEVERTOV   [b. 1923]

The ache of marriage:

thigh and tongue, beloved,
are heavy with it,
it throbs in the teeth

We look for communion
and are turned away, beloved,
each and each

It is leviathan and we
in its belly
looking for joy, some joy   10
not to be known outside it

two by two in the ark of
the ache of it.

The Mutes   1967

DENISE LEVERTOV   [b. 1923]

Those groans men use
passing a woman on the street
or on the steps of the subway

to tell her she is a female
and their flesh knows it,

are they a sort of tune,
an ugly enough song, sung
by a bird with a slit tongue

but meant for music?

Or are they the muffled roaring   10
of deafmutes trapped in a building that is
slowly filling with smoke?

Perhaps both.

Such men most often
look as if groan were all they could do,
yet a woman, in spite of herself,

knows it's a tribute:
if she were lacking all grace
they'd pass her in silence:

so it's not only to say she's   20
a warm hole. It's a word

in grief-language, nothing to do with
primitive, not an ur-language[1];
language stricken, sickened, cast down

in decrepitude. She wants to
throw the tribute away, disgusted, and can't,

The Mutes
   [1] Primordial language.

it goes on buzzing in her ear,
it changes the pace of her walk,
the torn posters in echoing corridors   30

spell it out, it
quakes and gnashes as the train comes in.
Her pulse sullenly

had picked up speed,
but the cars slow down and
jar to a stop while her understanding

keeps on translating:
'Life after life after life goes by

without poetry,
without seemliness,   40
without love.'

QUESTIONS
1. Explain the title. **2.** Why does the tribute go on "buzzing in her ear" (l. 28)? **3.** Is this poem an attack on men? Explain.

The Farmer's Wife   1960

ANNE SEXTON [1928–1974]

From the hodge porridge
of their country lust,
their local life in Illinois,
where all their acres look
like a sprouting broom factory,
they name just ten years now
that she has been his habit;
as again tonight he'll say
honey bunch let's go
and she will not say how there   10
must be more to living
than this brief bright bridge
of the raucous bed or even
the slow braille touch of him
like a heavy god grown light,

that old pantomime of love
that she wants although
it leaves her still alone,
built back again at last,
mind's apart from him, living   20
her own self in her own words
and hating the sweat of the house
they keep when they finally lie
each in separate dreams
and then how she watches him,
still strong in the blowzy bag
of his usual sleep while
her young years bungle past
their same marriage bed
and she wishes him cripple, or poet,   30
or even lonely, or sometimes,
better, my lover, dead.

Living in Sin   1955

ADRIENNE RICH   [b. 1929]

She had thought the studio would keep itself;
no dust upon the furniture of love.
Half heresy, to wish the taps less vocal,
the panes relieved of grime. A plate of pears,
a piano with a Persian shawl, a cat
stalking the picturesque amusing mouse
had risen at his urging.
Not that at five each separate stair would writhe
under the milkman's tramp; that morning light
so coldly would delineate the scraps   10
of last night's cheese and three sepulchral bottles;
that on the kitchen shelf among the saucers
a pair of beetle-eyes would fix her own—
Envoy from some village in the moldings . . .
Meanwhile, he, with a yawn,
sounded a dozen notes upon the keyboard,
declared it out of tune, shrugged at the mirror,
rubbed at his beard, went out for cigarettes;
while she, jeered by the minor demons,
pulled back the sheets and made the bed and found   20
a towel to dust the table-top,
and let the coffee-pot boil over on the stove.

By evening she was back in love again,
though not so wholly but throughout the night
she woke sometimes to feel the daylight coming
like a relentless milkman up the stairs.

Crow's First Lesson[1]   1970

TED HUGHES [b. 1930]

God tried to teach Crow how to talk.
"Love," said God. "Say, Love."
Crow gaped, and the white shark crashed into the sea
And went rolling downwards, discovering its own depth.

"No, no," said God, "Say Love, Now try it. LOVE."
Crow gaped, and a bluefly, a tsetse, a mosquito
Zoomed out and down
To their sundry flesh-pots.

"A final try," said God. "Now, LOVE."
Crow convulsed, gaped, retched and   10
Man's bodiless prodigious head
Bulbed out onto the earth, with swivelling eyes,
Jabbering protest—

And Crow retched again, before God could stop him.
And woman's vulva dropped over man's neck and tightened.
The two struggled together on the grass.
God struggled to part them, cursed, wept—

Crow flew guiltily off.

Daddy   1965

SYLVIA PLATH [1932–1963]

You do not do, you do not do
Any more, black shoe

Crow's First Lesson
    [1] In Hughes's collection of poems about him, Crow seems to be a supernatural demigod, combining human and animal traits. His exploits form a kind of creation myth.

In which I have lived like a foot
For thirty years, poor and white,
Barely daring to breathe or Achoo.

Daddy, I have had to kill you,
You died before I had time—
Marble-heavy, a bag full of God,
Ghastly statue with one grey toe
Big as a Frisco seal   10

And a head in the freakish Atlantic
Where it pours bean green over blue
In the waters off beautiful Nauset.
I used to pray to recover you.
Ach, du.[1]

In the German tongue, in the Polish town
Scraped flat by the roller
Of wars, wars, wars.
But the name of the town is common.
My Polack friend   20

Says there are a dozen or two.
So I never could tell where you
Put your foot, your root,
I never could talk to you.
The tongue stuck in my jaw.

It stuck in a barb wire snare.
Ich, ich, ich, ich,[2]
I could hardly speak.
I thought every German was you.
And the language obscene   30

An engine, an engine
Chuffing me off like a Jew.
A Jew to Dachau, Auschwitz, Belsen.
I began to talk like a Jew.
I think I may well be a Jew.

Daddy
   [1] German for "Ah, you."
   [2] German for "I, I, I, I."

The snows of the Tyrol, the clear beer of Vienna
Are not very pure or true.
With my gypsy ancestress and my weird luck
And my Taroc pack and my Taroc pack
I may be a bit of a Jew.   40

I have always been scared of *you*,
With your Luftwaffe,[3] your gobbledygoo.
And your neat moustache
And your Aryan eye, bright blue.
Panzer-man,[4] panzer-man, O You—

Not God but a swastika
So black no sky could squeak through.
Every woman adores a Fascist,
The boot in the face, the brute
Brute heart of a brute like you.   50

You stand at the blackboard, daddy,
In the picture I have of you,
A cleft in your chin instead of your foot
But no less a devil for that, no not
Any less the black man who

Bit my pretty red heart in two.
I was ten when they buried you.
At twenty I tried to die
And get back, back, back to you.   60
I thought even the bones would do.

But they pulled me out of the sack,
And they stuck me together with glue.
And then I knew what to do.
I made a model of you,
A man in black with a Meinkampf[5] look

And a love of the rack and the screw.
And I said I do, I do.
So daddy, I'm finally through.
The black telephone's off at the root,
The voices just can't worm through.   70

---

[3] Name of the German air force during World War II.
[4] Panzer refers to German armored divisions during World War II.
[5] *My Battle*, the title of Adolf Hitler's political autobiography.

If I've killed one man, I've killed two—
The vampire who said he was you
And drank my blood for a year,
Seven years, if you want to know.
Daddy, you can lie back now.

There's a stake in your fat black heart
And the villagers never liked you.
They are dancing and stamping on you.
They always *knew* it was you.
Daddy, daddy, you bastard, I'm through.   80

QUESTIONS
1. How do the allusions to Nazism function in the poem? **2.** Does the poem exhibit the speaker's love for her father or her hatred for him? Explain. **3.** What sort of man does the speaker marry (see stanzas 13 and 14)? **4.** How does the speaker characterize her husband and her father in the last two stanzas? Might the "Daddy" of the last line of the poem refer to something more than the speaker's father? Explain.

WRITING TOPIC
What is the effect of the peculiar structure, idiosyncratic rhyme, unusual words (such as *achoo, gobbledygoo*), and repetitions in the poem? What emotional associations does the title "Daddy" possess? Are those associations reinforced or contradicted by the poem?

Brothers and Sisters   1982

KATHLEEN CUSHMAN   [b. 1950]

As if in some badly made home movie, their faces shift
and come into abrupt focus, each one
bringing its little shock of quick memories—six
faces, surrounding mine like some canny,
protective device in times of civil strife, and spliced
from *fat cheeks* to *school* to *now* in odd sequence.

Their names jumble together in the fast chant
we all knew to count after the bad day
one of us was left standing at the gas pumps, crying,
while the packed Pontiac rolled on for miles, rocking   10
in motion-sick, false assurance that it had us all:

a litter, displacing mother-and-father conflicts
by its sheer size; and, locked tight in the web of the overlapping arms

at the supper table, it's true I didn't have much
to do with the mother in the charcoal-gray maternity dress,
or with the father piling bags of groceries out of the trunk.

More my business was keeping straight the gang I led
in uniform with lunchboxes and the right coats
to the parish school, or the secrets elaborately
concealed from the oldest sister, who studied French   20
for hours before the bathroom mirror, pursing her lips
and making sounds we despised in the back of her throat,

or somehow breaking the tyranny of the stubborn
younger sister already bigger than me at nine
and passing down clothes, humiliating
me, thwarting the given order,
or squashing the one closest to me into a hiding place—
damp, electric, bursting with what we had that they didn't
and never would—being thrown on each other from the start,
mother to one another, sister, self with no boundaries guarded.   30

Big and Little, we were two camps under the same command,
jealous of privilege, rations, uniforms, but marked
by the brands we all shared: a last name, bones,
freckles, our mother's voice, the same books
dog-eared in the passages she had marked: "*Children—
skip this.*" And, suddenly,

we are all the same age—all grown:
bearing the marks of each other's teeth, stretched out
into crazy patterns still branding us, our alliances
shifting, old enmities subdued and new ones born   40
to burn fiercely into the family flesh—

                              no one else
is to know all this but us; even love
will not initiate the outsiders; it is a closed club,
speaks its secret language,
the password less than a flicker of the eyelid,
knowing, impenetrable, beyond influence.

QUESTIONS

1. What is "the given order" (l. 26)? **2.** Explain "And, suddenly, / we are all the same age" (ll. 37–38). **3.** What does the speaker mean when she says, "even love / will not initiate the outsiders" (ll. 43–44)? **4.** In what sense is this a poem about love? About hate? **5.** Does the family described in this poem strike you as unique and special? Explain.

LOVE
AND
HATE

The Return of the Prodigal Son, c. 1642 by Rembrandt van Rijn

DRAMA

Othello

ca. 1604

WILLIAM SHAKESPEARE   [1564–1616]

CHARACTERS

Duke of Venice
Brabantio,   a Senator
Senators
Gratiano,   Brother to Brabantio
Lodovico,   Kinsman to Brabantio
Othello,   a noble Moor; in the service of the Venetian State
Cassio,   his Lieutenant
Iago,   his Ancient
Roderigo,   a Venetian Gentleman
Montano,   Othello's predecessor in the Government of Cyprus
Clown,   Servant to Othello
Desdemona,   Daughter to Brabantio, and Wife to Othello
Emilia,   Wife to Iago
Bianca,   Mistress to Cassio
Sailor, Officers, Gentlemen, Messengers, Musicians, Heralds, Attendants

SCENE

For the first Act, in Venice; during the rest of the Play, at a Sea-port in Cyprus

Act I

SCENE 1.   Venice. A Street.

(Enter Roderigo and Iago.)

Roderigo.   Tush! Never tell me; I take it much unkindly
  That thou, Iago, who hast had my purse
  As if the strings were thine, shouldst know of this.[1]

---

[1] I.e., Othello's successful courtship of Desdemona.

Iago.   'Sblood,[2] but you will not hear me:
    If ever I did dream of such a matter,
    Abhor me.
Roderigo.   Thou told'st me thou didst hold him[3] in thy hate.
Iago.   Despise me if I do not. Three great ones of the city,
    In personal suit to make me his lieutenant,
    Off-capp'd[4] to him; and, by the faith of man,   10
    I know my price, I am worth no worse a place;
    But he, as loving his own pride and purposes,
    Evades them, with a bombast circumstance[5]
    Horribly stuff'd with epithets of war;
    And, in conclusion,
    Nonsuits[6] my mediators;[7] for, 'Certes,'[8] says he,
    'I have already chosen my officer.'
    And what was he?
    Forsooth, a great arithmetician,
    One Michael Cassio, A Florentine,   20
    A fellow almost damn'd in a fair wife;[9]
    That never set a squadron in the field,
    Nor the division of a battle knows
    More than a spinster; unless[10] the bookish theoric,[11]
    Wherein the toged consuls can propose
    As masterly as he: mere prattle, without practice,
    Is all his soldiership. But he, sir, had the election;
    And I—of whom his eyes had seen the proof
    At Rhodes, at Cyprus, and on other grounds
    Christian and heathen—must be be-lee'd[12] and calm'd   30
    By debitor and creditor; this counter-caster,[13]
    He, in good time, must his lieutenant be,
    And I—God bless the mark!—his Moorship's ancient.[14]
Roderigo.   By heaven, I rather would have been his hangman.
Iago.   Why, there's no remedy: 'tis the curse of service,
    Preferment goes by letter and affection,
    Not by the old gradation,[15] where each second
    Stood heir to the first. Now, sir, be judge yourself,
    Whe'r[16] I in any just term am affin'd[17]
    To love the Moor.

---

[2] By God's blood.   [3] I.e., Othello.   [4] Took off their caps.   [5] Pompous wordiness, circumlocution.   [6] Turns down.   [7] Spokesmen.   [8] In truth.   [9] A much debated phrase. In the Italian source the Captain (i.e., Cassio) was married, and it may be that Shakespeare originally intended Bianca to be Cassio's wife but later changed his mind and failed to alter the phrase here accordingly. Or perhaps Iago simply sneers at Cassio as a notorious ladies' man.   [10] Except.   [11] Theory.   [12] Left without wind for my sails.   [13] Bookkeeper (*cf.* "arithmetician" above).   [14] Ensign (but Iago's position in the play seems to be that of Othello's aide-de-camp).   [15] Seniority.   [16] Whether.   [17] Obliged.

Roderigo.   I would not follow him then.   40
Iago.   O! sir, content you;
    I follow him to serve my turn upon him;
    We cannot all be masters, nor all masters
    Cannot be truly follow'd. You shall mark
    Many a duteous and knee-crooking knave,
    That, doting on his own obsequious bondage,
    Wears out his time, much like his master's ass,
    For nought but provender, and when he's old, cashier'd;
    Whip me such honest knaves. Others there are
    Who, trimm'd in forms and visages of duty,   50
    Keep yet their hearts attending on themselves,
    And, throwing but shows of service on their lords,
    Do well thrive by them, and when they have lin'd their coats
    Do themselves homage: these fellows have some soul;
    And such a one do I profess myself. For, sir,
    It is as sure as you are Roderigo,
    Were I the Moor, I would not be Iago:
    In following him, I follow but myself;
    Heaven is my judge, not I for love and duty,
    But seeming so, for my peculiar end: 60
    For when my outward action doth demonstrate
    The native act and figure of my heart
    In compliment extern,[18] 'tis not long after
    But I will wear my heart upon my sleeve
    For daws to peck at: I am not what I am.
Roderigo.   What a full fortune does the thick-lips owe,[19]
    If he can carry 't thus!
Iago.   Call up her father;
    Rouse him, make after him, poison his delight,
    Proclaim him in the streets, incense her kinsmen,
    And, though he in a fertile climate dwell,[20]   70
    Plague him with flies; though that his joy be joy,
    Yet throw such changes of vexation on 't
    As it may lose some colour.
Roderigo.   Here is her father's house; I'll call aloud.
Iago.   Do; with like timorous[21] accent and dire yell
    As when, by night and negligence, the fire
    Is spied in populous cities.
Roderigo.   What, ho! Brabantio: Signior Brabantio, ho!
Iago.   Awake! what, ho! Brabantio! thieves! thieves! thieves!
    Look to your house, your daughter, and your bags!   80
    Thieves! thieves!

---

[18] External show.   [19] Own.   [20] I.e., is fortunate.   [21] Frightening.

(Enter Brabantio, above, at a window.)

Brabantio.   What is the reason of this terrible summons?
  What is the matter there?
Roderigo.   Signior, is all your family within?
Iago.   Are your doors lock'd?
Brabantio.   Why? wherefore ask you this?
Iago.   'Zounds![22] sir, you're robb'd; for shame, put on your gown;
  Your heart is burst, you have lost half your soul;
  Even now, now, very now, an old black ram
  Is tupping[23] your white ewe. Arise, arise!
  Awake the snorting[24] citizens with the bell,   90
  Or else the devil will make a grandsire of you.
  Arise, I say.
Brabantio.   What! have you lost your wits?
Roderigo.   Most reverend signior, do you know my voice?
Brabantio.   Not I, what are you?
Roderigo.   My name is Roderigo.
Brabantio.   The worser welcome:
  I have charg'd thee not to haunt about my doors:
  In honest plainness thou hast heard me say
  My daughter is not for thee; and now, in madness,
  Being full of supper and distempering draughts,
  Upon malicious knavery dost thou come   100
  To start my quiet.
Roderigo.   Sir, sir, sir!
Brabantio.   But thou must needs be sure
  My spirit and my place[25] have in them power
  To make this bitter to thee.
Roderigo.   Patience, good sir.
Brabantio.   What tell'st thou me of robbing? this is Venice;
  My house is not a grange.[26]
Roderigo.   Most grave Brabantio,
  In simple and pure soul I come to you.
Iago.   'Zounds! sir, you are one of those that will not serve God if the devil
  bid you. Because we come to do you service and you think we are ruffians,
  you'll have your daughter covered with a Barbary horse; you'll have your
  nephews neigh to you; you'll have coursers for cousins and gennets[27] for
  germans.[28]
Brabantio.   What profane wretch art thou?
Iago.   I am one, sir, that comes to tell you, your daughter and the Moor are
  now making the beast with two backs.

---

[22] By God's wounds.   [23] Copulating.   [24] Snoring.   [25] Position.
[26] Isolated farm house.   [27] Spanish horses.   [28] Blood relations.

Brabantio.   Thou art a villain.

Iago.   You are—a senator.

Brabantio.   This thou shalt answer; I know thee, Roderigo.

Roderigo.   Sir, I will answer any thing. But, I beseech you,   120
   If 't be your pleasure and most wise consent,—
   As partly, I find, it is,—that your fair daughter,
   At this odd-even[29] and dull watch o' the night,
   Transported with no worse nor better guard
   But with a knave of common hire, a gondolier,
   To the gross clasps of a lascivious Moor,—
   If this be known to you, and your allowance,[30]
   We then have done you bold and saucy wrongs;
   But if you know not this, my manners tell me
   We have your wrong rebuke. Do not believe   130
   That, from[31] the sense of all civility,
   I thus would play and trifle with your reverence:
   Your daughter, if you have not given her leave,
   I say again, hath made a gross revolt;
   Tying her duty, beauty, wit and fortunes
   In[32] an extravagant[33] and wheeling stranger
   Of here and every where. Straight satisfy yourself:
   If she be in her chamber or your house,
   Let loose on me the justice of the state
   For thus deluding you.

Brabantio.   Strike on the tinder, ho!   140
   Give me a taper! call up all my people!
   This accident[34] is not unlike my dream;
   Belief of it oppresses me already.
   Light, I say! light!   *(Exit, from above.)*

Iago.   Farewell, for I must leave you:
   It seems not meet nor wholesome to my place
   To be produc'd,[35] as, if I stay, I shall,
   Against the Moor; for I do know the state,
   However this may gall him with some check,[36]
   Cannot with safety cast him; for he's embark'd
   With such loud reason to the Cyprus wars,—   150
   Which even now stand in act,—that, for their souls,
   Another of his fathom[37] they have none,
   To lead their business; in which regard,
   Though I do hate him as I do hell-pains,
   Yet, for necessity of present life,

---

[29] Between night and morning.   [30] By your approval.   [31] Away from.   [32] To.
[33] Expatriate.   [34] Happening.   [35] I.e., as a witness.   [36] Restraining adversity.
[37] Caliber, ability.

I must show out a flag and sign of love,
Which is indeed but sign. That you shall surely find him,
Lead to the Sagittary[38] the raised search;
And there will I be with him. So, farewell.   *(Exit.)*

(Enter below, Brabantio, and servants with torches.)

Brabantio.   It is too true an evil: gone she is,   160
And what's to come of my despised time
Is nought but bitterness. Now, Roderigo,
Where didst thou see her? O, unhappy girl!
With the Moor, sayst thou? Who would be a father!
How didst thou know 'twas she? O, she deceives me
Past thought. What said she to you? Get more tapers!
Raise all my kindred! Are they married, think you?
Roderigo.   Truly, I think they are.
Brabantio.   O heaven! How got she out? O treason of the blood:
Fathers, from hence trust not your daughters' minds   170
By what you see them act. Are there not charms
By which the property of youth and maidhood
May be abus'd? Have you not read, Roderigo,
Of some such thing?
Roderigo.   Yes, sir, I have indeed.
Brabantio.   Call up my brother. O! that you had had her.
Some one way, some another! Do you know
Where we may apprehend her and the Moor?
Roderigo.   I think I can discover him, if you please
To get good guard and go along with me.   180
Brabantio.   Pray you, lead on. At every house I'll call;
I may command at most. Get weapons, ho!
And raise some special officers of night.
On, good Roderigo; I'll deserve[39] your pains.   *(Exeunt.)*

SCENE 2.   Another street.

(Enter Othello, Iago, and Attendants, with torches.)

Iago.   Though in the trade of war I have slain men,
Yet do I hold it very stuff o' the conscience
To do no contriv'd murder: I lack iniquity
Sometimes to do me service. Nine or ten times
I had thought to have yerk'd[40] him here under the ribs.
Othello.   'Tis better as it is.

---

[38] The name of an inn(?).   [39] I.e., reward.   [40] Stabbed.

Iago.   Nay, but he prated,
And spoke such scurvy and provoking terms
Against your honour
That, with the little godliness I have,
I did full hard forbear him. But, I pray, sir,   10
Are you fast married? Be assur'd of this,
That the magnifico[41] is much belov'd,
And hath in his effect a voice potential
As double[42] as the duke's; he will divorce you,
Or put upon you what restraint and grievance
The law—with all his might to enforce it on—
Will give him cable.[43]
Othello.   Let him do his spite:
My services which I have done the signiory[44]
Shall out-tongue his complaints. 'Tis yet to know,[45]
Which when I know that boasting is an honour   20
I shall promulgate, I fetch my life and being
From men of royal siege, and my demerits[46]
May speak unbonneted[47] to as proud a fortune
As this[48] that I have reach'd; for know, Iago,
But that I love the gentle Desdemona,
I would not my unhoused[49] free condition
Put into circumscription and confine
For the sea's worth. But, look! what lights come yond?
Iago.   Those are the raised[50] father and his friends:
You were best[51] go in.
Othello.   Not I; I must be found: 30
My parts, my title, and my perfect[52] soul
Shall manifest me rightly. Is it they?
Iago.   By Janus,[53] I think no.

(Enter Cassio and certain Officers, with torches.)

Othello.   The servants of the duke, and my lieutenant.
The goodness of the night upon you, friends!
What is the news?
Cassio.   The duke does greet you, general,
And he requires your haste-post-haste appearance,
Even on the instant.

---

[41] One of the grandees, or rulers, of Venice; here, Brabantio. [42] Iago means that Brabantio's influence equals that of the Doge's with his double vote. [43] I.e., scope. [44] The Venetian government. [45] I.e., the signiory does not as yet know. [46] Merits. [47] I.e., as equals. [48] I.e., that of Desdemona's family. [49] Unconfined. [50] Aroused. [51] Had better. [52] Untroubled by a bad conscience. [53] The two-faced Roman god of portals and doors and (hence) of beginnings and ends.

Othello.   What is the matter, think you?
Cassio.   Something from Cyprus, as I may divine.
  It is a business of some heat;[54] the galleys   40
  Have sent a dozen sequent[55] messengers
  This very night at one another's heels,
  And many of the consuls,[56] rais'd and met,
  Are at the duke's already. You have been hotly call'd for;
  When, being not at your lodging to be found,
  The senate hath sent about three several[57] quests
  To search you out.
Othello.   'Tis well I am found by you.
  I will but spend a word here in the house,
  And go with you.   *(Exit.)*
Cassio.   Ancient, what makes he here?
Iago.   Faith, he to-night hath boarded a land carrack;[58]   50
  If it prove lawful prize, he's made for ever.
Cassio.   I do not understand.
Iago.   He's married.
Cassio.   To who?

(Re-enter Othello.)

Iago.   Marry,[59] to—Come, captain; will you go?
Othello.   Have with you.
Cassio.   Here comes another troop to seek for you.
Iago.   It is Brabantio. General, be advis'd;
  He comes to bad intent.

(Enter Brabantio, Roderigo, and Officers, with torches and weapons.)

Othello.   Holla! stand there!
Roderigo.   Signior, it is the Moor.
Brabantio.   Down with him, thief!

(They draw on both sides.)

Iago.   You, Roderigo! Come, sir, I am for you.[60]
Othello.   Keep up your bright swords, for the dew will rust them.
  Good signior, you shall more command with years   60
  Than with your weapons.
Brabantio.   O thou foul thief! where hast thou stow'd my daughter?
  Damn'd as thou art, thou hast enchanted her;

---

[54] Urgency.   [55] Following one another.   [56] I.e., senators.   [57] Separate.
[58] Treasure ship.   [59] By the Virgin Mary.   [60] Let you and me fight.

For I'll refer me to all things of sense,
If she in chains of magic were not bound,
Whether a maid so tender, fair, and happy,
So opposite to marriage that she shunn'd
The wealthy curled darlings of our nation,
Would ever have, to incur a general mock,
Run from her guardage to the sooty bosom   70
Of such a thing as thou; to fear, not to delight.
Judge me the world, if 'tis not gross in sense[61]
That thou hast practis'd on her with foul charms,
Abus'd her delicate youth with drugs or minerals
That weaken motion:[62] I'll have 't disputed on;
'Tis probable, and palpable to thinking.
I therefore apprehend and do attach[63] thee
For an abuser of the world, a practiser
Of arts inhibited and out of warrant.[64]
Lay hold upon him: if he do resist,   80
Subdue him at his peril.
Othello.   Hold your hands,
Both you of my inclining,[65] and the rest:
Were it my cue to fight, I should have known it
Without a prompter. Where will you that I go
To answer this your charge?
Brabantio.   To prison; till fit time
Of law and course of direct session[66]
Call thee to answer.
Othello.   What if I do obey?
How may the duke be therewith satisfied,
Whose messengers are here about my side,
Upon some present[67] business of the state   90
To bring me to him?
Officer.   'Tis true, most worthy signior;
The duke's in council, and your noble self,
I am sure, is sent for.
Brabantio.   How! the duke in council!
In this time of the night! Bring him away.
Mine's not an idle cause: the duke himself,
Or any of my brothers of the state,[68]
Cannot but feel this wrong as 'twere their own;
For if such actions may have passage free,
Bond-slaves and pagans shall our statesmen be.   *(Exeunt.)*

---

[61] Obvious.   [62] Normal reactions.   [63] Arrest.   [64] Prohibited and illegal.   [65] Party.
[66] Normal process of law.   [67] Immediate, pressing.   [68] Fellow senators.

SCENE 3.   A Council Chamber.

(The Duke and Senators sitting at a table. Officers attending.)

Duke.   There is no composition[69] in these news
    That gives them credit.
First Senator.   Indeed, they are disproportion'd;
    My letters say a hundred and seven galleys.
Duke.   And mine, a hundred and forty.
Second Senator.   And mine, two hundred:
    But though they jump[70] not on a just[71] account,—
    As in these cases, where the aim[72] reports,
    'Tis oft with difference,—yet do they all confirm
    A Turkish fleet, and bearing up to Cyprus.
Duke.   Nay, it is possible enough to judgment:
    I do not so secure me in[73] the error,   10
    But the main article[74] I do approve[75]
    In fearful sense.
Sailor *(within)*.   What, ho! what, ho! what, ho!
Officer.   A messenger from the galleys.

(Enter a Sailor.)

Duke.   Now, what's the business?
Sailor.   The Turkish preparation makes for Rhodes;
    So was I bid report here to the state
    By Signior Angelo.
Duke.   How say you by this change?
First Senator.   This cannot be
    By no[76] assay[77] of reason; 'tis a pageant[78]
    To keep us in false gaze.[79] When we consider
    The importancy of Cyprus to the Turk,   20
    And let ourselves again but understand,
    That as it more concerns the Turk than Rhodes,
    So may he with more facile question bear[80] it,
    For that it stands not in such warlike brace,[81]
    But altogether lacks the abilities
    That Rhodes is dress'd in: if we make thought of this,
    We must not think the Turk is so unskilful
    To leave that latest which concerns him first,

---

[69] Consistency, agreement.   [70] Coincide.   [71] Exact.   [72] Conjecture.   [73] Draw comfort from.   [74] Substance.   [75] Believe.   [76] Any.   [77] Test.   [78] (Deceptive) show.   [79] Looking in the wrong direction.   [80] More easily capture.   [81] State of defense.

Neglecting an attempt of ease and gain,
To wake and wage a danger profitless.   30
Duke.   Nay, in all confidence, he's not for Rhodes.
Officer.   Here is more news.

(Enter a Messenger.)

Messenger.   The Ottomites,[82] reverend and gracious,
Steering with due course toward the isle of Rhodes,
Have there injointed[83] them with an after fleet.[84]
First Senator.   Ay, so I thought. How many, as you guess?
Messenger.   Of thirty sail; and now they do re-stem[85]
Their backward course, bearing with frank appearance
Their purposes toward Cyprus. Signior Montano,
Your trusty and most valiant servitor,   40
With his free duty[86] recommends[87] you thus,
And prays you to believe him.
Duke.   'Tis certain then, for Cyprus.
Marcus Luccicos, is not he in town?
First Senator.   He's now in Florence.
Duke.   Write from us to him; post-post-haste dispatch.
First Senator.   Here comes Brabantio and the valiant Moor.

(Enter Brabantio, Othello, Iago, Roderigo, and Officers.)

Duke.   Valiant Othello, we must straight employ you
Against the general enemy Ottoman.
(*To Brabantio*) I did not see you; welcome, gentle signior;   50
We lack'd your counsel and your help to-night.
Brabantio.   So did I yours. Good your Grace, pardon me;
Neither my place nor aught I heard of business
Hath rais'd me from my bed, nor doth the general care
Take hold of me, for my particular grief
Is of so flood-gate[88] and o'erbearing nature
That it engluts and swallows other sorrows
And it is still itself.
Duke.   Why, what's the matter?
Brabantio.   My daughter! O! my daughter.
Duke. }
Senators. }   Dead?
Brabantio.   Ay, to me;
She is abus'd, stol'n from me, and corrupted   60

---

[82] Turks.   [83] Joined.   [84] Fleet that followed after.   [85] Steer again.   [86] Unqualified
expressions of respect.   [87] Informs.   [88] Torrential.

By spells and medicines bought of mountebanks;
For nature so preposterously to err,
Being not deficient, blind, or lame of sense,
Sans[89] witchcraft could not.

Duke.   Whoe'er he be that in this foul proceeding
Hath thus beguil'd your daughter of herself
And you of her, the bloody book of law
You shall yourself read in the bitter letter
After your own sense; yea, though our proper[90] son
Stood[91] in your action.[92]

Brabantio.   Humbly I thank your Grace.   70
Here is the man, this Moor; whom now, it seems,
Your special mandate for the state affairs
Hath hither brought.

Duke. }
Senators. }   We are very sorry for it.

Duke (to Othello).   What, in your own part, can you say to this?

Brabantio.   Nothing, but this is so.

Othello.   Most potent, grave, and reverend signiors,
My very noble and approv'd[93] good masters,
That I have ta'en away this old man's daughter,
It is most true; true, I have married her:
The very head and front of my offending   80
Hath this extent, no more. Rude am I in my speech,
And little bless'd with the soft phrase of peace;
For since these arms of mine had seven years' pith,[94]
Till now some nine moons wasted,[95] they have us'd
Their dearest action in the tented field;
And little of this great world can I speak,
More than pertains to feats of broil and battle;
And therefore little shall I grace my cause
In speaking for myself. Yet, by your gracious patience,
I will a round[96] unvarnish'd tale deliver   90
Of my whole course of love; what drugs, what charms,
What conjuration, and what mighty magic,
For such proceeding I am charg'd withal,
I won his daughter.

Brabantio.   A maiden never bold;
Of spirit so still and quiet, that her motion
Blush'd at herself;[97] and she, in spite of nature,
Of years, of country, credit, every thing,

---

[89] Without.   [90] Own.   [91] Were accused.   [92] Suit.   [93] Tested (by past experience).   [94] Strength.   [95] Past.   [96] Blunt.   [97] I.e., (her modesty was such
that) she blushed at her own emotions; or: could not move without blushing.

To fall in love with what she fear'd to look on!
It is a judgment maim'd and most imperfect
That will confess[98] perfection so could err   100
Against all rules of nature, and must be driven
To find out practices of cunning hell,
Why this should be. I therefore vouch again
That with some mixtures powerful o'er the blood,
Or with some dram conjur'd to this effect,
He wrought upon her.

Duke.   To vouch this, is no proof,
Without more certain and more overt test
Than these thin habits[99] and poor likelihoods
Of modern[100] seeming do prefer against him.

First Senator.   But, Othello, speak: 110
Did you by indirect and forced courses
Subdue and poison this young maid's affections;
Or came it by request and such fair question[101]
As soul to soul affordeth?

Othello.   I do beseech you;
Send for the lady to the Sagittary,
And let her speak of me before her father:
If you do find me foul in her report,
The trust, the office I do hold of you,
Not only take away, but let your sentence
Even fall upon my life.

Duke.   Fetch Desdemona hither.   120

Othello.   Ancient, conduct them; you best know the place.

(Exeunt Iago and Attendants.)

And, till she come, as truly as to heaven
I do confess the vices of my blood,
So justly to your grave ears I'll present
How I did thrive in this fair lady's love,
And she in mine.

Duke.   Say it, Othello.

Othello.   Her father lov'd me; oft invited me;
Still[102] question'd me the story of my life
From year to year, the battles, sieges, fortunes   130
That I have pass'd.
I ran it through, even from my boyish days
To the very moment that he bade me tell it;

---

[98] Assert.   [99] Weak appearances.   [100] Commonplace.   [101] Conversation.
[102] Always, regularly.

Wherein I spake of most disastrous chances,
Of moving accidents by flood and field,
Of hair-breadth 'scapes i' the imminent deadly breach,
Of being taken by the insolent foe
And sold to slavery, of my redemption thence
And portance[103] in my travel's history;
Wherein of antres[104] vast and deserts idle,[105]   140
Rough quarries, rocks, and hills whose heads touch heaven,
It was my hint[106] to speak, such was the process;
And of the Cannibals that each other eat,
The Anthropophagi,[107] and men whose heads
Do grow beneath their shoulders. This to hear
Would Desdemona seriously incline;
But still the house-affairs would draw her thence;
Which ever as she could with haste dispatch,
She'd come again, and with a greedy ear
Devour up my discourse. Which I observing,   150
Took once a pliant[108] hour, and found good means
To draw from her a prayer of earnest heart
That I would all my pilgrimage dilate,[109]
Whereof by parcels[110] she had something heard,
But not intentively:[111] I did consent;
And often did beguile her of her tears,
When I did speak of some distressful stroke
That my youth suffer'd. My story being done,
She gave me for my pains a world of sighs:
She swore, in faith, 'twas strange, 'twas passing[112] strange;   160
'Twas pitiful, 'twas wondrous pitiful:
She wish'd she had not heard it, yet she wish'd
That heaven had made her[113] such a man; she thank'd me,
And bade me, if I had a friend that lov'd her,
I should but teach him how to tell my story,
And that would woo her. Upon this hint I spake.
She lov'd me for the dangers I had pass'd,
And I lov'd her that she did pity them.
This only is the witchcraft I have us'd:
Here comes the lady; let her witness it.   170

(*Enter Desdemona, Iago, and Attendants.*)

Duke.   I think this tale would win my daughter too.
Good Brabantio,

---

[103] Behavior.   [104] Caves.   [105] Empty, sterile.   [106] Opportunity.   [107] Man-
eaters.   [108] Suitable.   [109] Relate in full.   [110] Piecemeal.   [111] In
sequence.   [112] Surpassing.   [113] Direct object; not "for her."

Take up this mangled matter at the best;
Men do their broken weapons rather use
Than their bare hands.
Brabantio.   I pray you, hear her speak:
If she confess that she was half the wooer,
Destruction on my head, if my bad blame
Light on the man! Come hither, gentle mistress:
Do you perceive in all this noble company
Where most you owe obedience?
Desdemona.   My noble father,   180
I do perceive here a divided duty:
To you I am bound for life and education;
My life and education both do learn[114] me
How to respect you; you are the lord of duty,
I am hitherto your daughter: but here's my husband;
And so much duty as my mother show'd
To you, preferring you before her father,
So much I challenge[115] that I may profess
Due to the Moor my lord.
Brabantio.   God be with you! I have done.
Please it your Grace, on to the state affairs;   190
I had rather to adopt a child than get it.
Come hither, Moor:
I here do give thee that with all my heart
Which, but thou hast[116] already, with all my heart
I would keep from thee. For your sake,[117] jewel,
I am glad at soul I have no other child;
For thy escape would teach me tyranny,
To hang clogs on them. I have done, my lord.
Duke.   Let me speak like yourself and lay a sentence,[118]
Which as a grize[119] or step, may help these lovers   200
Into your favour.
When remedies are past, the griefs are ended
By seeing the worst, which[120] late on hopes depended.
To mourn a mischief that is past and gone
Is the next way to draw new mischief on.
What cannot be preserv'd when Fortune takes,
Patience her injury a mockery makes.[121]
The robb'd that smiles steals something from the thief;
He robs himself that spends a bootless grief.
Brabantio.   So let the Turk of Cyprus us beguile;   210
We lose it not so long as we can smile.

---

[114] Teach.   [115] Claim as right.   [116] Didn't you have it.   [117] Because of you.
[118] Provide a maxim.   [119] Step.   [120] The antecedent is "griefs."   [121] To suffer an
irreparable loss patiently is to make light of injury (i.e., to triumph over adversity).

He bears the sentence[122] well that nothing bears
But the free comfort which from thence he hears;
But he bears both the sentence and the sorrow
That, to pay grief, must of poor patience borrow.
These sentences, to sugar, or to gall,
Being strong on both sides, are equivocal:[123]
But words are words: I never yet did hear
That the bruis'd heart was pierced[124] through the ear.
I humbly beseech you, proceed to the affairs of state.   220

Duke.   The Turk with a most mighty preparation makes for Cyprus. Othello,
the fortitude[125] of the place is best known to you; and though we have there
a substitute of most allowed sufficiency,[126] yet opinion, a sovereign mistress
of effects, throws a more safer voice on you:[127] you must therefore be content
to slubber[128] the gloss of your new fortunes with this more stubborn[129] and
boisterous expedition.

Othello.   The tyrant custom, most grave senators,
Hath made the flinty and steel couch of war
My thrice-driven[130] bed of down: I do agnize[131]
A natural and prompt alacrity   230
I find in hardness, and do undertake
These present wars against the Ottomites.
Most humbly therefore bending to your state,[132]
I crave fit disposition[133] for my wife,
Due reference of place and exhibition,[134]
With such accommodation and besort[135]
As levels with[136] her breeding.

Duke.   If you please,
Be 't at her father's.

Brabantio.   I'll not have it so.

Othello.   Nor I.

Desdemona.   Nor I; I would not there reside,
To put my father in impatient thoughts   240
By being in his eye. Most gracious duke,
To my unfolding[137] lend your gracious ear;
And let me find a charter[138] in your voice
To assist my simpleness.

Duke.   What would you, Desdemona?

Desdemona.   That I did love the Moor to live with him,
My downright violence and storm of fortunes

---

[122] (1) Verdict, (2) Maxim.   [123] Sententious comfort (like the Duke's trite maxims) can hurt
as well as soothe.   [124] (1) Lanced (i.e., cured), (2) Wounded.   [125] Strength.
[126] Admitted competence.   [127] General opinion, which mainly determines action, thinks
Cyprus safer with you in command.   [128] Besmear.   [129] Rough.   [130] Made as soft
as possible.   [131] Recognize.   [132] Submitting to your authority.   [133] Disposal.
[134] Provision.   [135] Fitness.   [136] Is proper to.   [137] Explanation.   [138] Permission.

May trumpet to the world; my heart's subdu'd
Even to the very quality of my lord;[139]
I saw Othello's visage in his mind,   250
And to his honours and his valiant parts
Did I my soul and fortunes consecrate.
So that, dear lords, if I be left behind,
A moth of peace, and he go to the war,
The rites[140] for which I love him are bereft me,
And I a heavy interim shall support[141]
By his dear[142] absence. Let me go with him.
Othello.   Let her have your voices.
Vouch with me, heaven, I therefore beg it not
To please the palate of my appetite,   260
Nor to comply with heat,—the young affects[143]
In me defunct,—and proper satisfaction,
But to be free and bounteous to her mind;
And heaven defend[144] your good souls that you think
I will your serious and great business scant
For[145] she is with me. No, when light-wing'd toys
Of feather'd Cupid seel[146] with wanton dulness
My speculative and offic'd instruments,[147]
That[148] my disports corrupt and taint my business,
Let housewives make a skillet of my helm,   270
And all indign[149] and base adversities
Make head against my estimation![150]
Duke.   Be it as you shall privately determine,
Either for her stay or going. The affair cries haste,
And speed must answer it.
First Senator.   You must away to-night.
Othello.   With all my heart.
Duke.   At nine i' the morning here we'll meet again.
Othello, leave some officer behind,
And he shall our commission bring to you;
With such things else of quality and respect   280
As doth import you.[151]
Othello.   So please your Grace, my ancient;
A man he is of honesty and trust:
To his conveyance I assign my wife,
With what else needful your good grace shall think
To be sent after me.

---

[139] I.e., I have become a soldier, like Othello.   [140] I.e., of marriage, or of war, or of
both.   [141] Endure.   [142] Closely concerning (i.e., Desdemona).   [143] The passions
of youth (hence, here, *immoderate* sexual passion).   [144] Forbid.   [145] Because.
[146] Blind (v.) by sewing up the eyelids (a term from falconry).   [147] Reflective and executive
faculties and organs.   [148] So that.   [149] Shameful.   [150] Reputation.   [151] Concern.

Duke.   Let it be so.
Good-night to every one. (*To Brabantio*) And, noble signior,
If virtue no delighted[152] beauty lack,
Your son-in-law is far more fair than black.
First Senator.   Adieu, brave Moor! use Desdemona well.
Brabantio.   Look to her, Moor, if thou hast eyes to see: 290
She has deceiv'd her father, and may thee.

(Exeunt Duke, Senators, Officers, &c.)

Othello.   My life upon her faith! Honest Iago,
My Desdemona must I leave to thee:
I prithee, let thy wife attend on her;
And bring them after in the best advantage.[153]
Come, Desdemona; I have but an hour
Of love, of worldly matters and direction,
To spend with thee: we must obey the time.

(Exeunt Othello and Desdemona.)

Roderigo.   Iago!
Iago.   What sayst thou, noble heart?   300
Roderigo.   What will I do, think'st thou?
Iago.   Why, go to bed, and sleep.
Roderigo.   I will incontinently[154] drown myself.
Iago.   Well, if thou dost, I shall never love thee after.
Why, thou silly gentleman!
Roderigo.   It is silliness to live when to live is torment; and then have we a
prescription to die when death is our physician.
Iago.   O! villanous; I have looked upon the world for four times seven years,
and since I could distinguish betwixt a benefit and an injury, I never found
man that knew how to love himself. Ere I would say, I would drown myself
for the love of a guinea-hen, I would change my humanity with a baboon.
Roderigo.   What should I do? I confess it is my shame to be so fond;[155] but
it is not in my virtue[156] to amend it.
Iago.   Virtue! a fig! 'tis in ourselves that we are thus, or thus. Our bodies are
our gardens, to the which our wills are gardeners; so that if we will plant
nettles or sow lettuce, set hyssop and weed up thyme, supply it with one
gender[157] of herbs or distract it with many, either to have it sterile with
idleness or manured with industry, why, the power and corrigible[158] authority
of this lies in our wills. If the balance of our lives had not one scale of reason

---

152 Delightful.   153 Opportunity.   154 Forthwith.   155 Infatuated.
156 Strength.   157 Kind.   158 Corrective.

to poise another of sensuality, the blood and baseness of our natures would conduct us to most preposterous conclusions; but we have reason to cool our raging motions, our carnal stings, our unbitted[159] lusts, whereof I take this that you call love to be a sect or scion.[160]

Roderigo. It cannot be.

Iago. It is merely a lust of the blood and a permisson of the will. Come, be a man. Drown thyself! drown cats and blind puppies. I have professed me thy friend, and I confess me knit to thy deserving with cables of perdurable toughness; I could never better stead thee than now. Put money in thy purse; follow these wars; defeat thy favour[161] with a usurped[162] beard; I say, put money in thy purse. It cannot be that Desdemona should long continue her love to the Moor,—put money in thy purse,—nor he his to her. It was a violent commencement in her, and thou shalt see an answerable sequestration;[163] put but money in thy purse. These Moors are changeable in their wills;—fill thy purse with money:—the food that to him now is as luscious as locusts,[164] shall be to him shortly as bitter as coloquintida.[165] She must change for youth: when she is sated with his body, she will find the error of her choice. She must have change, she must: therefore put money in thy purse. If thou wilt needs damn thyself, do it a more delicate way than drowning. Make all the money thou canst. If sanctimony and a frail vow betwixt an erring[166] barbarian and a supersubtle[167] Venetian be not too hard for my wits and all the tribe of hell, thou shalt enjoy her; therefore make money. A pox of drowning thyself! it is clean out of the way: seek thou rather to be hanged in compassing thy joy than to be drowned and go without her.

Roderigo. Wilt thou be fast to my hopes, if I depend on the issue?[168]

Iago. Thou art sure of me: go, make money. I have told thee often, and I retell thee again and again, I hate the Moor; my cause is hearted; thine hath no less reason. Let us be conjunctive[169] in our revenge against him; if thou canst cuckold him, thou dost thyself a pleasure, me a sport. There are many events in the womb of time which will be delivered. Traverse;[170] go: provide thy money. We will have more of this to-morrow. Adieu.

Roderigo. Where shall we meet i' the morning?

Iago. At my lodging.

Roderigo. I'll be with thee betimes.

Iago. Go to: farewell. Do you hear, Roderigo?

Roderigo. What say you?

Iago. No more of drowning, do you hear?

Roderigo. I am changed. I'll sell all my land.

Iago. Go to; farewell! put money enough in your purse.   (*Exit Roderigo.*)

Thus do I ever make my fool my purse;

---

[159] I.e., uncontrolled.   [160] Offshoot.   [161] Change thy appearance (for the worse?). [162] Assumed.   [163] Estrangement.   [164] Sweet-tasting fruits (perhaps the carob, the edible seed-pod of an evergreen tree in the Mediterranean area).   [165] Purgative derived from a bitter apple.   [166] Vagabond.   [167] Exceedingly refined.   [168] Rely on the outcome. [169] Allied.   [170] March.

For I mine own gain'd knowledge should profane,   360
If I would time expend with such a snipe[171]
But for my sport and profit. I hate the Moor,
And it is thought abroad[172] that 'twixt my sheets
He has done my office: I know not if 't be true,
But I, for mere suspicion in that kind,
Will do as if for surety.[173] He holds me well;[174]
The better shall my purpose work on him.
Cassio's a proper[175] man; let me see now:
To get his place; and to plume up[176] my will
In double knavery; how, how? Let's see: 370
After some time to abuse Othello's ear
That he[177] is too familiar with his wife:
He hath a person and a smooth dispose[178]
To be suspected; framed[179] to make women false,
The Moor is of a free and open nature,
That thinks men honest that but seem to be so,
And will as tenderly be led by the nose
As asses are.
I have 't; it is engender'd: hell and night
Must bring this monstrous birth to the world's light.   (*Exit.*)

Act II

SCENE 1.   A Sea-port Town in Cyprus. An open place near the Quay.

(*Enter Montano and two Gentlemen.*)

Montano.   What from the cape can you discern at sea?
First Gentleman.   Nothing at all: it is a high-wrought flood;
   I cannot 'twixt the heaven and the main[180]
   Descry a sail.
Montano.   Methinks the wind hath spoke aloud at land;
   A fuller blast ne'er shook our battlements;
   If it hath ruffian'd so upon the sea,
   What ribs of oak, when mountains melt on them,
   Can hold the mortise?[181] What shall we hear of this?
Second Gentleman.   A segregation[182] of the Turkish fleet;   10
   For do but stand upon the foaming shore,

---

[171] Dupe.   [172] People think.   [173] As if it were certain.   [174] In high regard.
[175] Handsome.   [176] Make ready.   [177] I.e., Cassio.   [178] Bearing.   [179] Designed,
apt.   [180] Ocean.   [181] Hold the joints together.   [182] Scattering.

The chidden billow seems to pelt the clouds;
The wind-shak'd surge, with high and monstrous mane,
Seems to cast water on the burning bear[183]
And quench the guards of the ever-fixed pole:[184]
I never did like[185] molestation view
On the enchafed[186] flood.

Montano.   If that[187] the Turkish fleet
Be not enshelter'd and embay'd, they are drown'd;
It is impossible they bear it out.

(Enter a Third Gentleman.)

Third Gentleman.   News, lad! our wars are done.   20
The desperate tempest hath so bang'd the Turks
That their designment halts;[188] a noble ship of Venice
Hath seen a grievous wrack and suffrance[189]
On most part of their fleet.

Montano.   How! is this true?

Third Gentleman.   The ship is here put in,
A Veronesa;[190] Michael Cassio,
Lieutenant to the warlike Moor Othello,
Is come on shore: the Moor himself's at sea,
And is in full commission here for Cyprus.

Montano.   I am glad on 't; 'tis a worthy governor.   30

Third Gentleman.   But this same Cassio, though he speak of comfort
Touching the Turkish loss, yet he looks sadly
And prays the Moor be safe; for they were parted
With foul and violent tempest.

Montano.   Pray heaven he be;
For I have serv'd him, and the man commands
Like a full soldier. Let's to the sea-side, ho!
As well to see the vessel that's come in
As to throw out our eyes for brave Othello,
Even till we make the main and the aerial blue
An indistinct regard.[191]

Third Gentleman.   Come, let's do so;   40
For every minute is expectancy
Of more arrivance.

---

[183] Ursa Minor (the Little Dipper).   [184] Polaris, the North Star, almost directly above the Earth's axis, is part of the constellation of the Little Bear, or Dipper.   [185] Similar.   [186] Agitated.   [187] If.   [188] Plan is stopped.   [189] Damage.   [190] Probably a *type* of ship, rather than a ship from Verona—not only because Verona is an inland city but also because of "a noble ship of Venice" above.   [191] Till our (straining) eyes can no longer distinguish sea and sky.

(Enter Cassio.)

Cassio.   Thanks, you the valiant of this warlike isle,
That so approve the Moor. O! let the heavens
Give him defence against the elements,
For I have lost him on a dangerous sea.
Montano.   Is he well shipp'd?
Cassio.   His bark is stoutly timber'd, and his pilot
Of very expert and approv'd allowance;[192]
Therefore my hopes, not surfeited to death,[193]   50
Stand in bold cure.[194]

(Within, 'A sail!—a sail!—a sail!' Enter a Messenger.)

Cassio.   What noise?
Messenger.   The town is empty; on the brow o' the sea
Stand ranks of people, and they cry 'A sail!'
Cassio.   My hopes do shape him for the governor.

(Guns heard.)

Second Gentleman.   They do discharge their shot of courtesy;
Our friends at least.
Cassio.   I pray you, sir, go forth.
And give us truth who 'tis that is arriv'd.
Second Gentleman.   I shall.   *(Exit)*
Montano.   But, good lieutenant, is your general wiv'd?   60
Cassio.   Most fortunately: he hath achiev'd a maid
That paragons[195] description and wild fame;
One that excels the quirks[196] of blazoning pens,
And in th' essential vesture of creation[197]
Does tire the ingener.[198]

(Re-enter Second Gentleman.)

How now! who has put in?
Second Gentleman.   'Tis one Iago, ancient to the general.
Cassio.   He has had most favourable and happy speed:
Tempests themselves, high seas, and howling winds,
The gutter'd[199] rocks, and congregated sands,

---

[192] Admitted and proven to be expert. [193] Overindulged. [194] With good chance of being fulfilled.
[195] Exceeds, surpasses.   [196] Ingenuities.   [197] I.e., just as God made her; or: (even in)
the (mere) essence of human nature.   [198] Inventor (i.e., of her praises?).
[199] Jagged; or: submerged.

Traitors ensteep'd[200] to clog the guiltless keel,   70
As having sense of beauty, do omit
Their mortal[201] natures, letting go safely by
The divine Desdemona.
Montano.   What is she?
Cassio.   She that I spake of, our great captain's captain,
Left in the conduct of the bold Iago,
Whose footing[202] here anticipates our thoughts
A se'nnight's[203] speed. Great Jove, Othello guard,
And swell his sail with thine own powerful breath,
That he may bless this bay with his tall[204] ship,
Make love's quick pants in Desdemona's arms,   80
Give renew'd fire to our extincted spirits,
And bring all Cyprus comfort!

(Enter Desdemona, Emilia, Iago, Roderigo, and Attendants.)

                              O! behold,
The riches of the ship is come on shore.
Ye men of Cyprus, let her have your knees.
Hail to thee, lady! and the grace of heaven,
Before, behind thee, and on every hand,
Enwheel thee round!
Desdemona.   I thank you, valiant Cassio.
What tidings can you tell me of my lord?
Cassio.   He is not yet arriv'd; nor know I aught
But that he's well, and will be shortly here.   90
Desdemona.   O! but I fear—How lost you company?
Cassio.   The great contention of the sea and skies
Parted our fellowship. But hark! a sail.

(Cry within, 'A sail—a sail!' *Guns heard.)*

Second Gentleman.   They give their greeting to the citadel:
This likewise is a friend.
Cassio.   See for the news!   *(Exit Gentleman.)*
Good ancient, you are welcome:—*(To Emilia)* welcome, mistress.
Let it not gall your patience, good Iago,
That I extend my manners; 'tis my breeding
That gives me this bold show of courtesy.   *(Kissing her.)*
Iago.   Sir, would she give you so much of her lips   100
As of her tongue she oft bestows on me,
You'd have enough.

---

[200] Submerged.   [201] Deadly.   [202] Landing.   [203] Week's.   [204] Brave.

Desdemona.   Alas! she has no speech.

Iago.   In faith, too much;
  I find it still when I have list[205] to sleep:
  Marry, before your ladyship, I grant,
  She puts her tongue a little in her heart,
  And chides with thinking.[206]

Emilia.   You have little cause to say so.

Iago.   Come on, come on; you are pictures[207] out of doors,
  Bells[208] in your parlours, wild cats in your kitchens,   110
  Saints in your injuries, devils being offended,
  Players[209] in your housewifery,[210] and housewives[211] in your beds.

Desdemona.   O! fie upon thee, slanderer.

Iago.   Nay, it is true, or else I am a Turk:
  You rise to play and go to bed to work.

Emilia.   You shall not write my praise.

Iago.   No, let me not.

Desdemona.   What wouldst thou write of me, if thou shouldst praise me?

Iago.   O gentle lady, do not put me to 't,
  For I am nothing if not critical.

Desdemona.   Come on; assay. There's one gone to the harbour?   120

Iago.   Ay, madam.

Desdemona *(aside)*.   I am not merry, but I do beguile
  The thing I am by seeming otherwise.
  (To Iago.) Come, how wouldst thou praise me?

Iago.   I am about it; but indeed my invention
  Comes from my pate[212] as birdlime does from frize;[213]
  It plucks out brains and all: but my muse labours
  And thus she is deliver'd.
  If she be fair and wise, fairness and wit,
  The one's for use, the other useth it.   130

Desdemona.   Well prais'd! How if she be black and witty?

Iago.   If she be black,[214] and thereto have a wit,
  She'll find a white that shall her blackness fit.

Desdemona.   Worse and worse.

Emilia.   How if fair and foolish?

Iago.   She never yet was foolish that was fair,
  For even her folly[215] help'd to an heir.

Desdemona.   These are old fond[216] paradoxes to make fools laugh i' the ale-
  house. What miserable praise has thou for her that's foul and foolish?

---

[205] Wish.   [206] I.e., without words.   [207] I.e., made up, "painted."   [208] I.e.,
jangly.   [209] Triflers, wastrels.   [210] Housekeeping.   [211] (1) Hussies, (2) (unduly)
frugal with their sexual favors, (3) businesslike, serious.   [212] Head.   [213] Coarse
cloth.   [214] Brunette, dark haired.   [215] Here also, wantonness.   [216] Foolish.

Iago.   There's none so foul and foolish thereunto,   140
  But does foul pranks which fair and wise ones do.
Desdemona.   O heavy ignorance! thou praisest the worst best. But what praise
  couldst thou bestow on a deserving woman indeed, one that, in the authority
  of her merit, did justly put on the vouch[217] of very malice itself?
Iago.   She that was ever fair and never proud,
  Had tongue at will and yet was never loud,
  Never lack'd gold and yet went never gay,
  Fled from her wish and yet said 'Now I may,
  She that being anger'd, her revenge being nigh,
  Bade her wrong stay and her displeasure fly,   150
  She that in wisdom never was so frail
  To change the cod's head for the salmon's tail,[218]
  She that could think and ne'er disclose her mind,
  See suitors following and not look behind,
  She was a wight, if ever such wight were,—
Desdemona.   To do what?
Iago.   To suckle fools and chronicle small beer.[219]
Desdemona.   O most lame and impotent conclusion! Do not learn of him,
  Emilia, though he be thy husband. How say you, Cassio? Is he not a most
  profane and liberal[220] counsellor?
Cassio.   He speaks home,[221] madam; you may relish him more in the   160
  soldier than in[222] the scholar.
Iago (aside).   He takes her by the palm: ay, well said, whisper; with as little a
  web as this will I ensnare as great a fly as Cassio. Ay, smile upon her, do; I
  will gyve[223] thee in thine own courtship. You say true, 'tis so, indeed. If such
  tricks as these strip you out of your lieutenantry, it had been better you had
  not kissed your three fingers so oft, which now again you are most apt to play
  the sir[224] in. Very good; well kissed! an excellent courtesy! 'tis so, indeed.
  Yet again your fingers to your lips? would they were clyster-pipes[225] for your
  sake! (A trumpet heard.) The Moor! I know his trumpet.[226]
Cassio.   'Tis truly so.   170
Desdemona.   Let's meet him and receive him.
Cassio.   Lo! where he comes.

(Enter Othello and Attendants.)

Othello.   O my fair warrior!
Desdemona.   My dear Othello!

---

[217] Compel the approval.   [218] To make a foolish exchange (a bawdy secondary meaning is
probable).   [219] I.e., keep petty household accounts.   [220] Free-spoken, licentious.
[221] To the mark, aptly.   [222] As . . . as.   [223] Entangle.   [224] Gentleman.
[225] Syringes, enema pipes.   [226] I.e., Othello's distinctive trumpet call.

Othello.   It gives me wonder great as my content
To see you here before me. O my soul's joy!
If after every tempest come such calms,
May the winds blow till they have waken'd death!
And let the labouring bark climb hills of seas
Olympus-high, and duck again as low
As hell's from heaven! If it were now to die,
'Twere now to be most happy, for I fear   180
My soul hath her content so absolute
That not another comfort like to this
Succeeds in unknown fate.
Desdemona.   The heavens forbid
But that our loves and comforts should increase
Even as our days do grow!
Othello.   Amen to that, sweet powers!
I cannot speak enough of this content;
It stops me here; it is too much of joy:
And this, and this, the greatest discords be   *(Kissing her.)*
That e'er our hearts shall make!
Iago *(aside).*   O! you are well tun'd now,   190
But I'll set down [227] the pegs that make this music,
As honest as I am.
Othello.   Come, let us to the castle.
News, friends; our wars are done, the Turks are drown'd.
How does my old acquaintance of this isle?
Honey, you shall be well desir'd[228] in Cyprus;
I have found great love amongst them. O my sweet,
I prattle out of fashion, and I dote
In mine own comforts. I prithee, good Iago,
Go to the bay and disembark my coffers.
Bring thou the master to the citadel;   200
He is a good one, and his worthiness
Does challenge much respect. Come, Desdemona,
Once more well met at Cyprus.

(Exeunt all except Iago and Roderigo.)

Iago.   Do thou meet me presently at the harbour. Come hither. If thou be'st
valiant, as they say base men being in love have then a nobility in their
natures more than is native to them, list[229] me. The lieutenant to-night
watches on the court of guard:[230] first, I must tell thee this, Desdemona is
directly in love with him.
Roderigo.   With him! Why, 'tis not possible.

---

[227] Loosen.   [228] Welcomed.   [229] Listen to.   [230] Guardhouse.

Iago.   Lay thy finger thus, and let thy soul be instructed. Mark me with what violence she first loved the Moor but for bragging and telling her fantastical lies; and will she love him still for prating? let not thy discreet heart think it. Her eye must be fed; and what delight shall she have to look on the devil? When the blood is made dull with the act of sport, there should be, again to inflame it, and to give satiety a fresh appetite, loveliness in favour, sympathy in years, manners, and beauties; all which the Moor is defective in. Now, for want of these required conveniences, her delicate tenderness will find itself abused, begin to heave the gorge,[231] disrelish and abhor the Moor; very nature will instruct her in it, and compel her to some second choice. Now, sir, this granted, as it is a most pregnant[232] and unforced position, who stands so eminently in the degree of this fortune as Cassio does? a knave very voluble, no further conscionable[233] than in putting on the mere form of civil and humane seeming, for the better compassing of his salt[234] and most hidden loose affection? why, none; why, none: a slipper[235] and subtle knave, a finder-out of occasions, that has an eye can stamp and counterfeit advantages, though true advantage never present itself; a devilish knave! Besides, the knave is handsome, young, and hath all those requisites in him that folly and green minds look after; a pestilent complete knave! and the woman hath found him already.

Roderigo.   I cannot believe that in her; she is full of most blessed condition.

Iago.   Blessed fig's end! the wine she drinks is made of grapes;[236] if she had been blessed she would never have loved the Moor; blessed pudding! Didst thou not see her paddle with the palm of his hand? didst not mark that?

Roderigo.   Yes, that I did; but that was but courtesy.

Iago.   Lechery, by this hand! an index[237] and obscure prologue to the history of lust and foul thoughts. They met so near with their lips, that their breaths embraced together. Villanous thoughts, Roderigo! when these mutualities so marshal the way, hard at hand comes the master and main exercise, the incorporate[238] conclusion. Pish![239] But, sir, be you ruled by me: I have brought you from Venice. Watch you to-night; for the command, I'll lay 't upon you: Cassio knows you not. I'll not be far from you: do you find some occasion to anger Cassio, either by speaking too loud, or tainting[240] his discipline; or from what other course you please, which the time shall more favourably minister.

Roderigo.   Well.

Iago.   Sir, he is rash and very sudden in choler, and haply may strike at you: provoke him, that he may; for even out of that will I cause these of Cyprus to mutiny, whose qualification[241] shall come into no true taste again but by the displanting of Cassio. So shall you have a shorter journey to your desires by the means I shall then have to prefer[242] them; and the impediment most

---

[231] Vomit.   [232] Obvious.   [233] Conscientious.   [234] Lecherous.   [235] Slippery.
[236] I.e., she is only flesh and blood.   [237] Pointer.   [238] Carnal. [239] Exclamation of disgust.   [240] Disparaging.   [241] Appeasement.   [242] Advance.

profitably removed, without the which there were no expectation of our prosperity.

Roderigo.   I will do this, if I can bring it to any opportunity.

Iago.   I warrant thee. Meet me by and by at the citadel: I must fetch his necessaries ashore. Farewell.

Roderigo.   Adieu.   (*Exit.*)

Iago.   That Cassio loves her, I do well believe it;
That she loves him, 'tis apt,[243] and of great credit:[244]
The Moor, howbeit that I endure him not,
Is of a constant, loving, noble nature;
And I dare think he'll prove to Desdemona
A most dear[245] husband. Now, I do love her too;
Not out of absolute lust,—though peradventure[246]
I stand accountant[247] for as great a sin,—
But partly led to diet my revenge,
For that I do suspect the lusty Moor
Hath leap'd into my seat; the thought whereof
Doth like a poisonous mineral gnaw my inwards;
And nothing can or shall content my soul
Till I am even'd with him, wife for wife;
Or failing so, yet that I put the Moor
At least into a jealousy so strong
That judgment cannot cure. Which thing to do,
If this poor trash[248] of Venice, whom I trash[249]
For his quick hunting, stand the putting-on,[250]
I'll have our Michael Cassio on the hip;
Abuse him to the Moor in the rank garb,[251]
For I fear Cassio with my night-cap too,
Make the Moor thank me, love me, and reward me
For making him egregiously an ass
And practising upon his peace and quiet
Even to madness. 'Tis here, but yet confus'd:
Knavery's plain face is never seen till us'd.   (*Exit.*)

SCENE 2.   A Street.

(*Enter a Herald with a proclamation; people following.*)

Herald.   It is Othello's pleasure, our noble and valiant general, that, upon certain tidings now arrived, importing the mere[252] perdition of the Turkish

---

[243] Natural, probable.   [244] Easily believable.   [245] A pun on the word in the sense of expensive.   [246] Perchance, perhaps.   [247] Accountable.   [248] I.e., Roderigo.
[249] Check, control.   [250] Inciting.   [251] Gross manner.   [252] Utter.

fleet, every man put himself into triumph; some to dance, some to make bonfires, each man to what sport and revels his addiction leads him; for, besides these beneficial news, it is the celebration of his nuptial. So much was his pleasure should be proclaimed. All offices[253] are open, and there is full liberty of feasting from this present hour of five till the bell have told eleven. Heaven bless the isle of Cyprus and our noble general Othello!

(Exeunt.)

SCENE 3.   A Hall in the Castle.

(Enter Othello, Desdemona, Cassio, and Attendants.)

Othello.   Good Michael, look you to the guard to-night:
    Let's teach ourselves that honourable stop,[254]
    Not to outsport discretion.
Cassio.   Iago hath direction what to do:
    But, notwithstanding, with my personal[255] eye
    Will I look to 't.
Othello.   Iago is most honest.
    Michael, good-night; to-morrow with your earliest
    Let me have speech with you. *(To Desdemona.)* Come, my dear love,
    The purchase made, the fruits are to ensue;
    That profit's yet to come 'twixt me and you.   10
    Good-night.

(Exeunt Othello, Desdemona, and Attendants.)

(Enter Iago.)

Cassio.   Welcome, Iago; we must to the watch.
Iago.   Not this hour, lieutenant; 'tis not yet ten o' the clock. Our general casts us thus early for the love of his Desdemona, who let us not therefore blame; he hath not yet made wanton the night with her, and she is sport for Jove.
Cassio.   She's a most exquisite lady.
Iago.   And, I'll warrant her, full of game.
Cassio.   Indeed, she is a most fresh and delicate creature.
Iago.   What an eye she has! methinks it sounds a parley[256] of provocation.
Cassio.   An inviting eye: and yet methinks right modest.   20
Iago.   And when she speaks, is it not an alarum[257] to love?
Cassio.   She is indeed perfection.
Iago.   Well, happiness to their sheets! Come, lieutenant, I have a stoup of

---

[253] Kitchens and storehouses.   [254] Discipline.   [255] Own.   [256] Conference
[257] Call-to-arms.

wine, and here without are a brace[258] of Cyprus gallants that would fain have a measure to the health of black Othello.

Cassio.   Not to-night, good Iago: I have very poor and unhappy brains for drinking: I could well wish courtesy would invent some other custom of entertainment.

Iago.   O! they are our friends; but one cup: I'll drink for you.

Cassio.   I have drunk but one cup to-night, and that was craftily qualified[259] too, and, behold, what innovation[260] it makes here: I am unfortunate in the infirmity, and dare not task my weakness with any more.

Iago.   What, man! 'tis a night of revels; the gallants desire it.

Cassio.   Where are they?

Iago.   Here at the door; I pray you, call them in.

Cassio.   I'll do 't; but it dislikes me.   (*Exit.*)

Iago.   If I can fasten but one cup upon him,
With that which he hath drunk to-night already,
He'll be as full of quarrel and offence
As my young mistress' dog. Now, my sick fool Roderigo,   40
Whom love has turn'd almost the wrong side out,
To Desdemona hath to-night carous'd
Potations pottle-deep;[261] and he's to watch.
Three lads of Cyprus, noble swelling spirits,
That hold their honours in a wary distance,[262]
The very elements[263] of this warlike isle,
Have I to-night fluster'd with flowing cups,
And they watch too. Now, 'mongst this flock of drunkards,
Am I to put our Cassio in some action
That may offend the isle. But here they come.   50
If consequence[264] do but approve my dream,
My boat sails freely, both with wind and stream.

(*Re-enter Cassio, with him Montano, and Gentlemen. Servant following with wine.*)

Cassio.   'Fore God, they have given me a rouse[265] already.

Montano.   Good faith, a little one; not past a pint, as I am a soldier.

Iago.   Some wine, ho!
   (*Sings.*)   And let me the canakin[266] clink, clink;
                     And let me the canakin clink:
                     A soldier's a man;
                     A life's but a span;
                     Why then let a soldier drink.   60
     Some wine, boys!

---

[258] Pair.   [259] Diluted.   [260] Change, revolution.   [261] Bottoms-up.   [262] Take
offense easily.   [263] Types.   [264] Succeeding events.   [265] Drink.   [266] Small
cup.

Cassio.   'Fore God, an excellent song.

Iago.   I learned it in England, where indeed they are most potent in potting; your Dane, your German, and your swag-bellied[267] Hollander,—drink ho!— are nothing to your English.

Cassio.   Is your Englishman so expert in his drinking?

Iago.   Why, he drinks you[268] with facility your Dane dead drunk; he sweats not to overthrow your Almain;[269] he gives your Hollander a vomit ere the next pottle can be filled.

Cassio.   To the health of our general!   70

Montano.   I am for it, lieutenant; and I'll do you justice.

Iago.   O sweet England!

(*Sings.*)   King Stephen was a worthy peer,
                    His breeches cost him but a crown;
                He held them sixpence all too dear,
                    With that he call'd the tailor lown.[270]
                He was a wight of high renown,
                    And thou art but of low degree:
                'Tis pride that pulls the country down,
                    Then take thine auld cloak about thee.   80

Some wine, ho!

Cassio.   Why, this is a more exquisite song than the other.

Iago.   Will you hear 't again?

Cassio.   No; for I hold him to be unworthy of his place that does those things. Well, God's above all; and there be souls must be saved, and there be souls must not be saved.

Iago.   It's true, good lieutenant.

Cassio.   For mine own part,—no offence to the general, nor any man of quality,—I hope to be saved.

Iago.   And so do I too, lieutenant.   90

Cassio.   Ay; but, by your leave, not before me; the lieutenant is to be saved before the ancient. Let's have no more of this; let's to our affairs. God forgive us our sins! Gentlemen, let's look to our business. Do not think, gentlemen, I am drunk: this is my ancient; this is my right hand, and this is my left hand. I am not drunk now; I can stand well enough, and speak well enough.

All.   Excellent well.

Cassio.   Why, very well, then; you must not think then that I am drunk.

(*Exit.*)

Montano.   To the platform, masters; come, let's set the watch.

Iago.   You see this fellow that is gone before;
He is a soldier fit to stand by Caesar   100
And give direction; and do but see his vice;
'Tis to his virtue a just equinox,[271]

---

[267] With a pendulous belly.   [268] The "ethical" dative, i.e., you'll see that he drinks.
[269] German.   [270] Lout, rascal.   [271] Equivalent.

The one as long as the other; 'tis pity of him.
I fear the trust Othello puts him in,
On some odd time of his infirmity,
Will shake this island.
Montano.   But is he often thus?
Iago.   'Tis evermore the prologue to his sleep;
   He'll watch the horologe a double set,[272]
   If drink rock not his cradle.
Montano.   It were well   110
   The general were put in mind of it.
   Perhaps he sees it not; or his good nature
   Prizes the virtue that appears in Cassio,
   And looks not on his evils. Is not this true?

(Enter Roderigo.)

Iago *(aside to him).*   How now, Roderigo!
   I pray you, after the lieutenant; go.   *(Exit Roderigo.)*
Montano.   And 'tis great pity that the noble Moor
   Should hazard such a place as his own second
   With one of an ingraft[273] infirmity;
   It were an honest action to say   120
   So to the Moor.
Iago.   Not I, for this fair island:
   I do love Cassio well, and would do much
   To cure him of this evil. But hark! what noise?

(Cry within, 'Help! Help!' Re-enter Cassio, driving in Roderigo.)

Cassio.   You rogue! you rascal!
Montano.   What's the matter, lieutenant?
Cassio.   A knave teach me my duty!
   I'll beat the knave into a twiggen[274] bottle.
Roderigo.   Beat me!
Cassio.   Dost thou prate, rogue?

(Striking Roderigo.)

Montano *(staying him).*   Nay, good lieutenant;
   I pray you, sir, hold your hand.
Cassio.   Let me go, sir,
   Or I'll knock you o'er the mazzard.[275]

---

[272] Stand watch twice twelve hours.   [273] Ingrained.   [274] Wicker.   [275] Head.

Montano.   Come, come; you're drunk.   130
Cassio.   Drunk!

(They fight.)

Iago *(aside to Roderigo).*   Away, I say! go out, and cry a mutiny.
(Exit Roderigo.)

   Nay, good lieutenant! God's will, gentlemen!
   Help, ho! Lieutenant! sir! Montano! sir!
   Help, masters! Here's a goodly watch indeed!

(Bell rings.)

   Who's that that rings the bell? Diablo, ho!
   The town will rise: God's will! lieutenant, hold!
   You will be sham'd for ever.

(Re-enter Othello and Attendants.)

Othello.   What is the matter here?
Montano.   'Zounds! I bleed still; I am hurt to the death.

(He faints.)

Othello.   Hold, for your lives!
Iago.   Hold, ho, lieutenant! Sir! Montano! gentlemen!   140
   Have you forgot all sense of place and duty?
   Hold! the general speaks to you; hold for shame!
Othello.   Why, how now, ho! from whence ariseth this?
   Are we turn'd Turks, and to ourselves do that
   Which heaven hath forbid the Ottomites?
   For Christian shame put by this barbarous brawl;
   He that stirs next to carve for his own rage
   Holds his soul light; he dies upon his motion.
   Silence that dreadful bell! it frights the isle
   From her propriety. What is the matter, masters?   150
   Honest Iago, that look'st dead with grieving,
   Speak, who began this? On thy love, I charge thee.
Iago.   I do not know; friends all but now, even now,
   In quarter[276] and in terms like bride and groom
   Devesting[277] them for bed; and then, but now,—
   As if some planet had unwitted men,—
   Swords out, and tilting one at other's breast,

---

[276] On duty.   [277] Undressing.

In opposition bloody. I cannot speak
Any beginning to this peevish odds,[278]
And would in action glorious I had lost   160
Those legs that brought me to a part of it!
Othello.   How comes it, Michael, you are thus forgot?
Cassio.   I pray you, pardon me; I cannot speak.
Othello.   Worthy Montano, you were wont be civil;
The gravity and stillness of your youth
The world hath noted, and your name is great
In mouths of wisest censure:[279] what's the matter,
That you unlace[280] your reputation thus
And spend your rich opinion[281] for the name
Of a night-brawler? give me answer to it.   170
Montano.   Worthy Othello, I am hurt to danger;
Your officer, Iago, can inform you,
While I spare speech, which something now offends[282] me,
Of all that I do know; nor know I aught
By me that 's said or done amiss this night,
Unless self-charity be sometimes a vice,
And to defend ourselves it be a sin
When violence assails us.
Othello.   Now, by heaven,
My blood begins my safer guides to rule,
And passion, having my best judgment collied,[283]   180
Assays to lead the way. If I once stir,
Or do but lift this arm, the best of you
Shall sink in my rebuke. Give me to know
How this foul rout began, who set it on;
And he that is approv'd[284] in this offence,
Though he had twinn'd with me—both at a birth—
Shall lose me. What! in a town of war,
Yet wild, the people's hearts brimful of fear,
To manage private and domestic quarrel,
In night, and on the court and guard of safety!   190
'Tis monstrous. Iago, who began 't?
Montano.   If partially affin'd,[285] or leagu'd in office,
Thou dost deliver more or less than truth,
Thou art not soldier.
Iago.   Touch me not so near;
I had rather[286] have this tongue cut from my mouth
Than it should do offence to Michael Cassio;

---

[278] Silly quarrel.   [279] Judgment.   [280] Undo.   [281] High reputation.   [282] Pains, harms.   [283] Clouded.   [284] Proved (i.e., guilty).   [285] Favorably biased (by ties of friendship, or as Cassio's fellow officer).   [286] More quickly.

Yet, I persuade myself, to speak the truth
Shall nothing wrong him. Thus it is, general.
Montano and myself being in speech,
There comes a fellow crying out for help,   200
And Cassio following with determin'd sword
To execute upon him. Sir, this gentleman
Steps in to Cassio, and entreats his pause;
Myself the crying fellow did pursue,
Lest by his clamour, as it so fell out,
The town might fall in fright; he, swift of foot,
Outran my purpose, and I return'd the rather
For that I heard the clink and fall of swords,
And Cassio high in oath, which till to-night
I ne'er might say before. When I came back,—   210
For this was brief,—I found them close together,
At blow and thrust, even as again they were
When you yourself did part them.
More of this matter can I not report:
But men are men; the best sometimes forget:
Though Cassio did some little wrong to him,
As men in rage strike those that wish them best,
Yet, surely Cassio, I believe, receiv'd
From him that fled some strange indignity,
Which patience could not pass.
Othello.   I know, Iago.   220
Thy honesty and love doth mince[287] this matter,
Making it light to Cassio. Cassio, I love thee;
But never more be officer of mine.

(Enter Desdemona, attended.)

Look! if my gentle love be not rais'd up;
(To Cassio.) I'll make thee an example.
Desdemona.   What's the matter?
Othello.   All's well now, sweeting; come away to bed.
Sir, for your hurts, myself will be your surgeon.
Lead him off.   *(Montano is led off.)*
Iago, look with care about the town,
And silence those whom this vile brawl distracted.   230
Come, Desdemona; 'tis the soldier's life,
To have their balmy slumbers wak'd with strife.

(Exeunt all but Iago and Cassio.)

---

[287] Tone down.

Iago.   What! are you hurt, lieutenant?

Cassio.   Ay; past all surgery.

Iago.   Marry, heaven forbid!

Cassio.   Reputation, reputation, reputation! O! I have lost my reputation. I have lost the immortal part of myself, and what remains is bestial. My reputation, Iago, my reputation!

Iago.   As I am an honest man, I thought you had received some bodily wound; there is more offence in that than in reputation. Reputation is an idle and most false imposition;[288] oft got without merit, and lost without deserving: you have lost no reputation at all, unless you repute yourself such a loser. What! man; there are ways to recover the general again; you are but now cast in his mood,[289] a punishment more in policy[290] than in malice; even so as one would beat his offenceless dog to affright an imperious lion. Sue to him again, and he is yours.

Cassio.   I will rather sue to be despised than to deceive so good a commander with so slight, so drunken and so indiscreet an officer. Drunk! and speak parrot![291] and squabble, swagger, swear, and discourse fustian[292] with one's own shadow! O thou invisible spirit of wine! if thou hast no name to be known by, let us call thee devil!

Iago.   What was he that you followed with your sword? What hath he done to you?

Cassio.   I know not.

Iago.   Is 't possible?

Cassio.   I remember a mass of things, but nothing distinctly; a quarrel, but nothing wherefore. O God! that men should put an enemy in their mouths to steal away their brains; that we should, with joy, pleasance,[293] revel, and applause, transform ourselves into beasts.

Iago.   Why, but you are now well enough; how came you thus recovered?

Cassio.   It hath pleased the devil drunkenness to give place to the devil wrath; one unperfectness shows me another, to make me frankly despise myself.

Iago.   Come, you are too severe a moraler. As the time, the place, and the condition of this country stands, I could heartily wish this had not befallen, but since it is as it is, mend it for your own good.

Cassio.   I will ask him for my place again; he shall tell me I am a drunkard! Had I as many mouths as Hydra,[294] such an answer would stop them all. To be now a sensible man, by and by a fool, and presently a beast! O strange! Every inordinate cup is unblessed and the ingredient[295] is a devil.

Iago.   Come, come; good wine is a good familiar creature if it be well used; exclaim no more against it. And, good lieutenant, I think you think I love you.

---

[288] Something external.   [289] Dismissed because he is angry.   [290] I.e., more for the sake of the example, or to show his fairness.   [291] I.e., without thinking.   [292] I.e., nonsense.   [293] Pleasure.   [294] Many-headed snake in Greek mythology.   [295] Contents.

Cassio.   I have well approved it, sir. I drunk!

Iago.   You or any man living may be drunk at some time, man. I'll tell you
what you shall do. Our general's wife is now the general; I may say so in this
respect, for that he hath devoted and given up himself to the contemplation,
mark, and denotement of her parts and graces: confess yourself freely to her;
importune her; she'll help to put you in your place again. She is of so free,
so kind, so apt, so blessed a disposition, that she holds it a vice in her goodness
not to do more than she is requested. This broken joint between you and her
husband entreat her to splinter;[296] and, my fortunes against any lay[297] worth
naming, this crack of your love shall grow stronger than it was before.

Cassio.   You advise me well.

Iago.   I protest, in the sincerity of love and honest kindness.

Cassio.   I think it freely; and betimes in the morning I will beseech the virtuous
Desdemona to undertake for me. I am desperate of my fortunes if they check
me here.

Iago.   You are in the right. Good-night, lieutenant; I must to the watch.

Cassio.   Good-night, honest Iago!   *(Exit.)*

Iago.   And what's he then that says I play the villain?   290
When this advice is free I give and honest,
Probal[298] to thinking and indeed the course
To win the Moor again? For 'tis most easy
The inclining Desdemona to subdue
In any honest suit; she's fram'd as fruitful[299]
As the free elements. And then for her
To win the Moor, were 't to renounce his baptism,
All seals and symbols of redeemed sin,
His soul is so enfetter'd to her love,
That she may make, unmake, do what she list,   300
Even as her appetite shall play the god
With his weak function.[300] How am I then a villain
To counsel Cassio to this parallel[301] course,
Directly to his good? Divinity of hell!
When devils will the blackest sins put on,
They do suggest at first with heavenly shows,
As I do now; for while this honest fool
Plies Desdemona to repair his fortunes,
And she for him pleads strongly to the Moor,
I'll pour this pestilence into his ear   310
That she repeals[302] him for her body's lust;
And, by how much she strives to do him good,
She shall undo her credit with the Moor.

---

[296] Bind up with splints.   [297] Wager.   [298] Provable.   [299] Generous.   [300] Faculties.
[301] Purposeful.   [302] I.e., seeks to recall.

So will I turn her virtue into pitch,
And out of her own goodness make the net
That shall enmesh them all.

(Re-enter Roderigo.)

                    How now, Roderigo!

Roderigo.   I do follow here in the chase, not like a hound that hunts, but one
that fills up the cry.[303] My money is almost spent; I have been to-night
exceedingly well cudgelled; and I think the issue will be, I shall have so much
experience for my pains; and so, with no money at all and a little more wit,
return again to Venice.

Iago.   How poor are they that have not patience!
What wound did ever heal but by degrees?
Thou know'st we work by wit and not by witchcraft,
And wit depends on dilatory time.
Does 't not go well? Cassio hath beaten thee,
And thou by that small hurt hast cashiered Cassio.
Though other things grow fair against the sun,
Yet fruits that blossom first will first be ripe:
Content thyself awhile. By the mass, 'tis morning;   330
Pleasure and action make the hours seem short.
Retire thee; go where thou art billeted:
Away, I say; thou shalt know more hereafter:
Nay, get thee gone. *(Exit Roderigo.)* Two things are to be done,
My wife must move for Cassio to her mistress;
I'll set her on;
Myself the while to draw the Moor apart,
And bring him jump[304] when he may Cassio find
Soliciting his wife: ay, that's the way:
Dull not device by coldness and delay.   *(Exit.)*

Act III

SCENE 1.   Cyprus. Before the Castle.

(Enter Cassio, and some Musicians.)

Cassio.   Masters, play here, I will content your pains;[305]
Something that's brief; and bid 'Good-morrow, general.'   *(Music.)*

(Enter Clown.)

---

[303] Pack (hunting term).   [304] At the exact moment.   [305] Reward your efforts.

Clown.   Why, masters, have your instruments been in Naples, that they speak i' the nose[306] thus?

First Musician.   How, sir, how?

Clown.   Are these, I pray you, wind-instruments?

First Musician.   Ay, marry, are they, sir.

Clown.   O! thereby hangs a tale.

First Musician.   Whereby hangs a tale, sir?

Clown.   Marry, sir, by many a wind-instrument that I know. But, masters, here's money for you; and the general so likes your music, that he desires you, for love's sake, to make no more noise with it.

First Musician.   Well, sir, we will not.

Clown.   If you have any music that may not be heard, to 't again; but, as they say, to hear music the general does not greatly care.

First Musician.   We have none such, sir.

Clown.   Then put up your pipes in your bag, for I'll away. Go; vanish into air; away!   *(Exeunt Musicians.)*

Cassio.   Dost thou hear, mine honest friend?

Clown.   No, I hear not your honest friend; I hear you.

Cassio.   Prithee, keep up thy quillets.[307] There's a poor piece of gold for thee. If the gentlewoman that attends the general's wife be stirring, tell her there's one Cassio entreats her a little favour of speech: wilt thou do this?

Clown.   She is stirring, sir: if she will stir hither, I shall seem to notify unto her.

Cassio.   Do, good my friend.   *(Exit Clown.)*

(Enter Iago.)

In happy time, Iago.

Iago.   You have not been a-bed, then?

Cassio.   Why, no; the day had broke
Before we parted. I have made bold, Iago,
To send in to your wife; my suit to her
Is, that she will to virtuous Desdemona   30
Procure me some access.

Iago.   I'll send her to you presently;
And I'll devise a mean to draw the Moor
Out of the way, that your converse and business
May be more free.

Cassio.   I humbly thank you for 't.   *(Exit Iago.)*
I never knew
A Florentine more kind and honest.[308]

---

[306] Naples was notorious for venereal disease, and syphilis was believed to affect the nose.
[307] Quibbles.   [308] Cassio means that not even a fellow Florentine could behave to him in a friendlier fashion than does Iago.

(Enter Emilia.)

Emilia.   Good-morrow, good lieutenant: I am sorry
For your displeasure,[309] but all will soon be well.
The general and his wife are talking of it,
And she speaks for you stoutly: the Moor replies   40
That he you hurt is of great fame in Cyprus
And great affinity,[310] and that in wholesome wisdom
He might not but refuse you; but he protests he loves you,
And needs no other suitor but his likings
To take the safest occasion by the front[311]
To bring you in again.[312]
Cassio.   Yet, I beseech you,
If you think fit, or that it may be done,
Give me advantage of some brief discourse
With Desdemona alone.
Emilia.   Pray you, come in:
I will bestow you where you shall have time   50
To speak your bosom[313] freely.
Cassio.   I am much bound to you.   *(Exeunt.)*

SCENE 2.   A Room in the Castle.

(Enter Othello, Iago, and Gentlemen.)

Othello.   These letters give, Iago, to the pilot,
And by him do my duties to the senate;
That done, I will be walking on the works;
Repair there to me.
Iago.   Well, my good lord, I'll do 't.
Othello.   This fortification, gentlemen, shall we see 't?
Gentlemen.   We'll wait upon your lordship.   *(Exeunt.)*

SCENE 3.   Before the Castle.

(Enter Desdemona, Cassio, and Emilia.)

Desdemona.   Be thou assur'd, good Cassio, I will do
All my abilities in thy behalf.
Emilia.   Good madam, do: I warrant it grieves my husband,
As if the case were his.

---

[309] Disgrace.   [310] Family connection.   [311] Forelock.   [312] Restore you (to Othello's favor).   [313] Heart, inmost thoughts.

Desdemona.   O! that's an honest fellow. Do not doubt, Cassio,
But I will have my lord and you again
As friendly as you were.

Cassio.   Bounteous madam,
Whatever shall become of Michael Cassio,
He's never any thing but your true servant.

Desdemona.   I know 't; I thank you. You do love my lord;   10
You have known him long; and be you well assur'd
He shall in strangeness[314] stand no further off
Than in a politic[315] distance.

Cassio.   Ay, but, lady,
That policy may either last so long,
Or feed upon such nice[316] and waterish diet,
Or breed itself so out of circumstance,
That, I being absent and my place supplied,
My general will forget my love and service.

Desdemona.   Do not doubt[317] that; before Emilia here
I give thee warrant of thy place. Assure thee,   20
If I do vow a friendship, I'll perform it
To the last article; my lord shall never rest;
I'll watch him tame,[318] and talk him out of patience;
His bed shall seem a school, his board a shrift;[319]
I'll intermingle every thing he does
With Cassio's suit. Therefore be merry, Cassio;
For thy solicitor shall rather die
Than give thy cause away.[320]

(Enter Othello, and Iago at a distance.)

Emilia.   Madam, here comes my lord.

Cassio.   Madam, I'll take my leave.   30

Desdemona.   Why, stay, and hear me speak.

Cassio.   Madam, not now; I am very ill at ease,
Unfit for mine own purposes.

Desdemona.   Well, do your discretion.   *(Exit Cassio.)*

Iago.   Ha! I like not that.

Othello.   What dost thou say?

Iago.   Nothing, my lord: or if—I know not what.

Othello.   Was not that Cassio parted from my wife?

Iago.   Cassio, my lord? No, sure, I cannot think it,
That he would steal away so guilty-like,
Seeing you coming.

---

[314] Aloofness.   [315] I.e., dictated by policy.   [316] Slight, trivial.   [317] Fear.
[318] Outwatch him (i.e., keep him awake) till he submits.   [319] Confessional.   [320] Abandon
your cause.

Othello.   I do believe 'twas he.   40
Desdemona.   How now, my lord!
  I have been talking with a suitor here,
  A man that languishes in your displeasure.
Othello.   Who is 't you mean?
Desdemona.   Why, your lieutenant, Cassio. Good my lord,
  If I have any grace or power to move you,
  His present[321] reconciliation take;
  For if he be not one that truly loves you,
  That errs in ignorance and not in cunning,
  I have no judgment in an honest face.   50
  I prithee[322] call him back.
Othello.   Went he hence now?
Desdemona.   Ay, sooth; so humbled,
  That he hath left part of his grief with me,
  To suffer with him. Good love, call him back.
Othello.   Not now, sweet Desdemona; some other time.
Desdemona.   But shall 't be shortly?
Othello.   The sooner, sweet, for you.
Desdemona.   Shall 't be to-night at supper?
Othello.   No, not to-night.
Desdemona.   To-morrow dinner, then?
Othello.   I shall not dine at home;
  I meet the captains at the citadel.
Desdemona.   Why, then, to-morrow night; or Tuesday morn;
  Or Tuesday noon, or night; or Wednesday morn: 60
  I prithee name the time, but let it not
  Exceed three days: in faith, he's penitent;
  And yet his trespass, in our common reason,—
  Save that they say, the wars must make examples
  Out of their best,—is not almost[323] a fault
  To incur a private check.[324] When shall he come?
  Tell me, Othello: I wonder in my soul,
  What you could ask me, that I should deny,
  Or stand so mammering[325] on. What! Michael Cassio,   70
  That came a wooing with you, and so many a time,
  When I have spoke of you dispraisingly,
  Hath ta'en your part; to have so much to do
  To bring him in! Trust me, I could do much,—
Othello.   Prithee, no more; let him come when he will;
  I deny thee nothing.
Desdemona.   Why, this is not a boon;

---

[321] Immediate.   [322] Pray thee.   [323] Hardly.   [324] (Even) a private reprimand.
[325] Shilly-shallying.

'Tis as I should entreat you wear your gloves,
Or feed on nourishing dishes, or keep you warm,
Or sue to you to do a peculiar profit
To your own person: nay, when I have a suit   80
Wherein I mean to touch your love indeed,
It shall be full of poise[326] and difficult weight,
And fearful to be granted.
Othello.   I will deny thee nothing:
Whereon, I do beseech thee, grant me this,
To leave me but a little to myself.
Desdemona.   Shall I deny you? no: farewell, my lord.
Othello.   Farewell, my Desdemona: I'll come to thee straight.
Desdemona.   Emilia, come. Be as your fancies teach you;
Whate'er you be, I am obedient.   (*Exit, with Emilia.*)
Othello.   Excellent wretch![327] Perdition catch my soul,   90
But I do love thee! and when I love thee not,
Chaos is[328] come again.
Iago.   My noble lord,—
Othello.   What dost thou say, Iago?
Iago.   Did Michael Cassio, when you woo'd my lady,
Know of your love?
Othello.   He did, from first to last: why dost thou ask?
Iago.   But for a satisfaction of my thought;
No further harm.
Othello.   Why of thy thought, Iago?
Iago.   I did not think he had been acquainted with her.
Othello.   O! yes; and went between us very oft.   100
Iago.   Indeed!
Othello.   Indeed! ay, indeed; discern'st thou aught in that?
Is he not honest?
Iago.   Honest, my lord?
Othello.   Honest! ay, honest.
Iago.   My lord, for aught I know.
Othello.   What dost thou think?
Iago.   Think, my lord!
Othello.   Think, my lord!
By heaven, he echoes me,
As if there were some monster in his thought
Too hideous to be shown. Thou dost mean something:
I heard thee say but now, thou lik'dst not that,
When Cassio left my wife; what didst not like?   110
And when I told thee he was of my counsel
In my whole course of wooing, thou criedst, 'Indeed!'

---

[326] Weight.   [327] Here, a term of endearment.   [328] Will have.

And didst contract and purse thy brow together,
As if thou then hadst shut up in thy brain
Some horrible conceit.[329] If thou dost love me,
Show me thy thought.

Iago.   My lord, you know I love you.

Othello.   I think thou dost;
And, for[330] I know thou art full of love and honesty,
And weigh'st thy words before thou givest them breath,
Therefore these stops[331] of thine fright me the more;   120
For such things in a false disloyal knave
Are tricks of custom, but in a man that's just
They are close dilations,[332] working from the heart
That passion cannot rule.

Iago.   For Michael Cassio,
I dare be sworn I think that he is honest.

Othello.   I think so too.

Iago.   Men should be what they seem;
Or those that be not, would they might seem none!

Othello.   Certain men should be what they seem.

Iago.   Why then, I think Cassio's an honest man.

Othello.   Nay, yet there's more in this.   130
I pray thee, speak to me as to thy thinkings,
As thou dost ruminate, and give thy worst of thoughts
The worst of words.

Iago.   Good my lord, pardon me;
Though I am bound to every act of duty,
I am not bound to[333] that all slaves are free to.
Utter my thoughts? Why, say they are vile and false;
As where's that palace whereinto foul things
Sometimes intrude not? who has a breast so pure
But some uncleanly apprehensions[334]
Keep leets and law-days,[335] and in session sit   140
With meditations lawful?

Othello.   Thou dost conspire against thy friend, Iago,
If thou but think'st him wrong'd, and mak'st his ear
A stranger to thy thoughts.

Iago.   I do beseech you,
Though I perchance am vicious in my guess,—
As, I confess, it is my nature's plague
To spy into abuses, and oft my jealousy[336]
Shapes faults that are not,—that your wisdom yet,

---

[329] Fancy.   [330] Because.   [331] Interruptions, hesitations.   [332] Secret (i.e., involuntary, unconscious) revelations.   [333] Bound with regard to.   [334] Conceptions.
[335] Sittings of the local courts.   [336] Suspicion.

From one that so imperfectly conceits,
Would take no notice, nor build yourself a trouble   150
Out of his scattering and unsure observance.
It were not for your quiet nor your good,
Nor for my manhood, honesty, or wisdom,
To let you know my thoughts.
Othello.   What dost thou mean?
Iago.   Good name in man and woman, dear my lord,
Is the immediate jewel of[337] their souls:
Who steals my purse steals trash; 'tis something, nothing;
'Twas mine, 'tis his, and has been slave to thousands;
But he that filches from me my good name
Robs me of that which not enriches him,   160
And makes me poor indeed.
Othello.   By heaven, I'll know thy thoughts.
Iago.   You cannot, if my heart were in your hand;
Nor shall not, whilst 'tis in my custody.
Othello.   Ha!
Iago.   O! beware, my lord, of jealousy;
It is the green-ey'd monster which doth mock
The meat it feeds on: that cuckold[338] lives in bliss
Who, certain of his fate, loves not his wronger;
But, O! what damned minutes tells[339] he o'er
Who dotes, yet doubts; suspects, yet soundly loves!   170
Othello.   O misery!
Iago.   Poor and content is rich, and rich enough,
But riches fineless[340] is as poor as winter
To him that ever fears he shall be poor.
Good heaven, the souls of all my tribe defend
From jealousy!
Othello.   Why, why is this?
Think'st thou I'd make a life of jealousy,
To follow still the changes of the moon
With fresh suspicions? No; to be once in doubt
Is once to be resolved. Exchange me for a goat   180
When I shall turn the business of my soul
To such exsufflicate[341] and blown[342] surmises,
Matching thy inference. 'Tis not to make me jealous
To say my wife is fair, feeds well, loves company,
Is free of speech, sings, plays, and dances well;
Where virtue is, these are more virtuous:
Nor from mine own weak merits will I draw

---

[337] Jewel closest to.   [338] Husband of an adulterous woman.   [339] Counts.   [340] Boundless.
[341] Spat out (?).   [342] Fly-blown.

The smallest fear, or doubt of her revolt;
For she had eyes, and chose me. No, Iago;
I'll see before I doubt; when I doubt, prove;   190
And, on the proof, there is no more but this,
Away at once with love or jealousy!
Iago.   I am glad of it; for now I shall have reason
To show the love and duty that I bear you
With franker spirit; therefore, as I am bound,
Receive it from me; I speak not yet of proof.
Look to your wife; observe her well with Cassio;
Wear your eye thus, not jealous nor secure:
I would not have your free and noble nature
Out of self-bounty[343] be abus'd; look to 't: 200
I know our country disposition[344] well;
In Venice they do let heaven see the pranks
They dare not show their husbands; their best conscience
Is not to leave 't undone, but keep 't unknown.
Othello.   Dost thou say so?
Iago.   She did deceive her father, marrying you;
And when she seem'd to shake and fear your looks,
She lov'd them most.
Othello.   And so she did.
Iago.   Why, go to,[345] then;
She that so young could give out such a seeming,
To seel her father's eyes up close as oak,   210
He thought 'twas witchcraft; but I am much to blame;
I humbly do beseech you of your pardon
For too much loving you.
Othello.   I am bound to thee for ever.
Iago.   I see, this hath a little dash'd your spirits.
Othello.   Not a jot, not a jot.
Iago.   I' faith, I fear it has.
I hope you will consider what is spoke
Comes from my love. But I do see you're mov'd;
I am to pray you not to strain my speech
To grosser issues nor to larger reach
Than to suspicion.   220
Othello.   I will not.
Iago.   Should you do so, my lord,
My speech should fall into such vile success
As my thoughts aim not at. Cassio's my worthy friend—
My lord, I see you're mov'd.

---

[343] Innate generosity.   [344] I.e., that of Venice.   [345] Colloquialism; here, something like "all right."

Othello.   No, not much mov'd:
   I do not think but Desdemona's honest.[346]
Iago.   Long live she so! and long live you to think so!
Othello.   And yet, how nature erring from itself,—
Iago.   Ay, there's the point: as, to be bold with you,
   Not to affect many proposed matches
   Of her own clime,[347] complexion, and degree,[348]   230
   Whereto, we see, in all things nature tends;
   Foh! one may smell in such, a will most rank,
   Foul disproportion, thoughts unnatural.
   But pardon me; I do not in position[349]
   Distinctly[350] speak of her, though I may fear
   Her will, recoiling[351] to her better judgment,
   May fall to match you with her country forms
   And happily[352] repent.
Othello.   Farewell, farewell:
   If more thou dost perceive, let me know more;
   Set on thy wife to observe. Leave me, Iago.   240
Iago.   My lord, I take my leave.   *(Going.)*
Othello.   Why did I marry? This honest creature, doubtless,
   Sees and knows more, much more, than he unfolds.
Iago *(returning)*.   My lord, I would I might entreat your honour
   To scan this thing no further; leave it to time.
   Although 'tis fit that Cassio have his place,
   For, sure he fills it up with great ability,
   Yet, if you please to hold him off awhile,
   You shall by that perceive him and his means:
   Note if your lady strain his entertainment[353]   250
   With any strong or vehement importunity;
   Much will be seen in that. In the mean time,
   Let me be thought too busy[354] in my fears,
   As worthy cause I have to fear I am,
   And hold her free, I do beseech your honour.
Othello.   Fear not my government.
Iago.   I once more take my leave.   *(Exit.)*
Othello.   This fellow's of exceeding honesty,
   And knows all qualities, with a learned spirit,
   Of human dealings; if I do prove her haggard,[355]   260
   Though that her jesses[356] were my dear heart-strings,
   I'd whistle her off and let her down the wind,[357]

---

[346] Chaste.   [347] Country.   [348] Social rank.   [349] In definite assertion.
[350] Specifically.   [351] Reverting.   [352] Perhaps.   [353] Urge his re-welcome (i.e., to
Othello's trust and favor).   [354] Meddlesome.   [355] Wild hawk.   [356] Leather thongs
by which the hawk's legs were strapped to the trainer's wrist.   [357] I'd let her go and take care
of herself.

To prey at fortune. Haply, for I am black,
And have not those soft parts of conversation
That chamberers[358] have, or, for I am declin'd
Into the vale of years—yet that's not much—
She's gone, I am abus'd;[359] and my relief
Must be to loathe her. O curse of marriage!
That we can call these delicate creatures ours,
And not their appetites. I had rather be a toad,   270
And live upon the vapour of a dungeon,
Than keep a corner in the thing I love
For others' uses. Yet, 'tis the plague of great ones;
Prerogativ'd[360] are they less than the base;
'Tis destiny unshunnable, like death:
Even then this forked plague[361] is fated to us
When we do quicken.[362]
                              Look! where she comes.
If she be false, O! then heaven mocks itself.
I'll not believe it.

(Re-enter Desdemona and Emilia.)

Desdemona.   How now, my dear Othello!
Your dinner and the generous[363] islanders   280
By you invited, do attend your presence.
Othello.   I am to blame.
Desdemona.   Why do you speak so faintly?
Are you not well?
Othello.   I have a pain upon my forehead here.[364]
Desdemona.   Faith, that's with watching; 'twill away again:
Let me but bind it hard, within this hour
It will be well.
Othello.   Your napkin[365] is too little:

(She drops her handkerchief.)

Let it alone. Come, I'll go in with you.
Desdemona.   I am very sorry that you are not well.

                              (Exeunt Othello and Desdemona.)

Emilia.   I am glad I have found this napkin;   290
This was her first remembrance from the Moor;

---

[358] Courtiers; or (more specifically): gallants, frequenters of bed chambers.   [359] Deceived.
[360] Privileged.   [361] I.e., the cuckold's proverbial horns.   [362] Are conceived, come
alive.   [363] Noble.   [364] Othello again refers to his cuckoldom.   [365] Handkerchief.

My wayward husband hath a hundred times
Woo'd me to steal it, but she so loves the token,
For he conjur'd her she should ever keep it,
That she reserves it evermore about her
To kiss and talk to. I'll have the work ta'en out,[366]
And giv 't Iago:
What he will do with it heaven knows, not I;
I nothing but[367] to please his fantasy.[368]

(Enter Iago.)

Iago.   How now! what do you here alone?   300
Emilia.   Do not you chide; I have a thing for you.
Iago.   A thing for me? It is a common thing—
Emilia.   Ha!
Iago.   To have a foolish wife.
Emilia.   O! is that all? What will you give me now
   For that same handkerchief?
Iago.   What handkerchief?
Emilia.   What handkerchief!
   Why, that the Moor first gave to Desdemona:
   That which so often you did bid me steal.
Iago.   Hath stol'n it from her?   310
Emilia.   No, faith; she let it drop by negligence,
   And, to the advantage, I, being there, took 't up.
   Look, here it is.
Iago.   A good wench; give it me.
Emilia.   What will you do with 't, that you have been so earnest
   To have me filch it?
Iago.   Why, what's that to you?   *(Snatches it.)*
Emilia.   If it be not for some purpose of import
   Give 't me again; poor lady! she'll run mad
   When she shall lack it.
Iago.   Be not acknown on 't;[369] I have use for it.
   Go, leave me.   *(Exit Emilia.)*
   I will in Cassio's lodging lose this napkin,   321
   And let him find it; trifles light as air
   Are to the jealous confirmations strong
   As proofs of holy writ; this may do something.
   The Moor already changes with my poison:
   Dangerous conceits are in their natures poisons,
   Which at the first are scarce found to distaste,[370]

---

[366] Pattern copied.   [367] I.e., only want.   [368] Whim.   [369] You know nothing about it.   [370] Scarce can be tasted.

But with a little act upon the blood,
Burn like the mines of sulphur. I did say so:
Look! where he comes!

(Enter Othello.)

                     Not poppy,[371] nor mandragora,[372]   330
Nor all the drowsy syrups[373] of the world,
Shall ever medicine thee to that sweet sleep
Which thou ow'dst yesterday.

Othello.   Ha! ha! false to me?

Iago.   Why, how now, general! no more of that.

Othello.   Avaunt! be gone! thou hast set me on the rack;
  I swear 'tis better to be much abus'd
  Than but to know 't a little.

Iago.   How now, my lord!

Othello.   What sense had I of her stol'n hours of lust?
  I saw 't not, thought it not, it harm'd not me;
  I slept the next night well, was free and merry;   340
  I found not Cassio's kisses on her lips;
  He that is robb'd, not wanting what is stol'n,
  Let him not know 't, and he's not robb'd at all.

Iago.   I am sorry to hear this.

Othello.   I had been happy, if the general camp,[374]
  Pioners[375] and all, had tasted her sweet body,
  So[376] I had nothing known. O! now, for ever
  Farewell the tranquil mind; farewell content!
  Farewell the plumed troop and the big wars
  That make ambition virtue! O, farewell!   350
  Farewell the neighing steed, and the shrill trump,
  The spirit-stirring drum, the ear-piercing fife,
  The royal banner, and all quality,
  Pride, pomp, and circumstance[377] of glorious war!
  And, O you mortal engines,[378] whose rude throats
  The immortal Jove's dread clamours counterfeit,
  Farewell! Othello's occupation's gone!

Iago.   Is it possible, my lord?

Othello.   Villain, be sure thou prove my love a whore,
  Be sure of it; give me the ocular proof;   360
  Or, by the worth of mine eternal soul,
  Thou hadst been better have been born a dog
  Than answer my wak'd wrath.

Iago.   Is 't come to this?

---

[371] Opium.   [372] A soporific.   [373] I.e., soporifics.   [374] Whole army.   [375] Lowest
rank of manual laborers in the army.   [376] As long as.   [377] Pageantry.   [378] Deadly
artillery.

Othello.   Make me to see 't; or, at the least, so prove it,
  That the probation[379] bear no hinge nor loop
  To hang a doubt on; or woe upon thy life!
Iago.   My noble lord—
Othello.   If thou dost slander her and torture me,
  Never pray more; abandon all remorse;
  On horror's head horrors accumulate;   370
  Do deeds to make heaven weep, all earth amaz'd;
  For nothing canst thou to damnation add
  Greater than that.
Iago.   O grace! O heaven forgive me!
  Are you a man! have you a soul or sense?
  God be wi' you; take mine office. O wretched fool!
  That liv'st to make thine honesty a vice.
  O monstrous world! Take note, take note, O world!
  To be direct and honest is not safe.
  I thank you for this profit,[380] and, from hence
  I'll love no friend, sith[381] love breeds such offence.   380
Othello.   Nay, stay; thou shouldst be honest.
Iago.   I should be wise; for honesty's a fool,
  And loses that it works for.
Othello.   By the world,
  I think my wife be honest and think she is not;
  I think that thou art just and think thou art not.
  I'll have some proof. Her name, that was as fresh
  As Dian's[382] visage, is now begrim'd and black
  As mine own face. If there be cords or knives,
  Poison or fire or suffocating streams,
  I'll not endure it. Would I were satisfied!   390
Iago.   I see, sir, you are eaten up with passion.
  I do repent me that I put it to you.
  You would be satisfied?
Othello.   Would! nay, I will.
Iago.   And may; but how? how satisfied, my lord?
  Would you, the supervisor,[383] grossly gape on;
  Behold her tupp'd?
Othello.   Death and damnation! O!
Iago.   It were a tedious[384] difficulty, I think,
  To bring them to that prospect; damn them then,
  If ever mortal eyes do see them bolster[385]
  More[386] than their own! What then? how then?   400
  What shall I say? Where's satisfaction?
  It is impossible you should see this,

---

[379] Proof.   [380] Lesson.   [381] Since.   [382] Diana's, the goddess of the moon.
[383] Observer. [384] Laborious.   [385] Lie together.   [386] Other.

Were they as prime[387] as goats, as hot as monkeys,
As salt as wolves in pride,[388] and fools as gross
As ignorance made drunk; but yet, I say,
If imputation, and strong circumstances,
Which lead directly to the door of truth,
Will give you satisfaction, you may have it.

Othello.   Give me a living reason she's disloyal.

Iago.   I do not like the office;   410
But, sith I am enter'd in this cause so far,
Prick'd to 't by foolish honesty and love,
I will go on. I lay with Cassio lately;
And, being troubled with a raging tooth,
I could not sleep.
There are a kind of men so loose of soul
That in their sleeps will mutter their affairs;
One of this kind is Cassio.
In sleep I heard him say, 'Sweet Desdemona,
Let us be wary, let us hide our loves!'   420
And then, sir, would he gripe[389] and wring my hand,
Cry, 'O, sweet creature!' and then kiss me hard,
As if he pluck'd up kisses by the roots,
That grew upon my lips; then laid his leg
Over my thigh, and sigh'd, and kiss'd; and then
Cried, 'Cursed fate, that gave thee to the Moor!'

Othello.   O monstrous! monstrous!

Iago.   Nay, this was but his dream.

Othello.   But this denoted a foregone conclusion:[390]
'Tis a shrewd doubt,[391] though it be but a dream.

Iago.   And this may help to thicken other proofs   430
That do demonstrate thinly.

Othello.   I'll tear her all to pieces.

Iago.   Nay, but be wise; yet we see nothing done;
She may be honest yet. Tell me but this:
Have you not sometimes seen a handkerchief
Spotted with strawberries in your wife's hand?

Othello.   I gave her such a one; 'twas my first gift.

Iago.   I know not that; but such a handkerchief—
I am sure it was your wife's—did I to-day
See Cassio wipe his beard with.

Othello.   If it be that,—

Iago.   If it be that, or any that was hers,   440
It speaks against her with the other proofs.

Othello.   O! that the slave had forty thousand lives;

---

[387] Lustful.   [388] Heat.   [389] Seize.   [390] Previous consummation.   [391] (1) Cursed,
(2) Acute, suspicion.

One is too poor, too weak for my revenge.
Now do I see 'tis true. Look here, Iago;
All my fond love thus do I blow to heaven:
'Tis gone.
Arise, black vengeance, from the hollow hell!
Yield up, O love! thy crown and hearted throne
To tyrannous hate. Swell, bosom, with thy fraught,[392]
For 'tis of aspics'[393] tongues!

Iago.   Yet be content.[394]   450

Othello.   O! blood, blood, blood!

Iago.   Patience, I say; your mind, perhaps, may change.

Othello.   Never, Iago. Like to the Pontic sea,[395]
Whose icy current and compulsive course
Ne'er feels retiring ebb, but keeps due on
To the Propontic and the Hellespont,[396]
Even so my bloody thoughts, with violent pace,
Shall ne'er look back, ne'er ebb to humble love,
Till that a capable[397] and wide revenge
Swallow them up.   (*Kneels.*)
                  Now, by yond marble heaven,   460
In the due reverence of a sacred vow
I here engage my words.

Iago.   Do not rise yet.   (*Kneels.*)
Witness, you ever-burning lights above!
You elements that clip[398] us round about!
Witness, that here Iago doth give up
The execution of his wit, hands, heart,
To wrong'd Othello's service! Let him command,
And to obey shall be in me remorse,[399]
What bloody business ever.[400]   (*They rise.*)

Othello.   I greet thy love,
Not with vain thanks, but with acceptance bounteous,   470
And will upon the instant put thee to 't:
Within these three days let me hear thee say
That Cassio 's not alive.

Iago.   My friend is dead; 'tis done at your request:
But let her live.

Othello.   Damn her, lewd minx! O, damn her!
Come, go with me apart; I will withdraw.
To furnish me with some swift means of death
For the fair devil. Now art thou my lieutenant.

Iago.   I am your own for ever.   (*Exeunt.*)

---

[392] Burden.   [393] Poisonous snakes.   [394] Patient.   [395] The Black Sea.   [396] The
Sea of Marmara, The Dardanelles.   [397] Comprehensive.   [398] Encompass.   [399] Probably
a corrupt line; the meaning appears to be: "to obey shall be my solemn obligation."   [400] Soever.

SCENE 4.   Before the Castle.

(Enter Desdemona, Emilia, and Clown.)

Desdemona.   Do you know, sirrah,[401] where Lieutenant Cassio lies?[402]
Clown.   I dare not say he lies any where.
Desdemona.   Why, man?
Clown.   He is a soldier; and for one to say a soldier lies, is stabbing.[403]
Desdemona.   Go to;[404] where lodges he?
Clown.   To tell you where he lodges is to tell you where I lie.
Desdemona.   Can anything be made of this?
Clown.   I know not where he lodges, and for me to devise[405] a lodging, and say he lies here or he lies there, were to lie in mine own throat.
Desdemona.   Can you inquire him out, and be edified by report?
Clown.   I will catechize the world for him; that is, make questions, and by them answer.
Desdemona.   Seek him, bid him come hither; tell him I have moved my lord in his behalf, and hope all will be well.
Clown.   To do this is within the compass of man's wit, and therefore I will attempt the doing it.   *(Exit.)*
Desdemona.   Where should I lose that handkerchief, Emilia?
Emilia.   I know not, madam.
Desdemona.   Believe me, I had rather have lost my purse
Full of cruzadoes;[406] and, but my noble Moor   20
Is true of mind, and made of no such baseness
As jealous creatures are, it were enough
To put him to ill thinking.
Emilia.   Is he not jealous?
Desdemona.   Who! he? I think the sun where he was born
Drew all such humours from him.
Emilia.   Look! where he comes.
Desdemona.   I will not leave him now till Cassio
Be call'd to him.

(Enter Othello.)

                    How is 't with you, my lord?
Othello.   Well, my good lady. *(Aside)* O! hardness to dissemble.
How do you, Desdemona?
Desdemona.   Well, my good lord.
Othello.   Give me your hand. This hand is moist,[407] my lady.   30

---

[401] Common form of address to inferiors.   [402] Lives.   [403] I.e., is cause for stabbing.
[404] Here apparently: "Come on!"   [405] Invent.   [406] Portuguese gold coins.   [407] A supposed symptom of a lustful nature.

Desdemona.   It yet has felt no age nor known no sorrow.
Othello.   This argues fruitfulness and liberal[408] heart;
Hot, hot, and moist; this hand of yours requires
A sequester[409] from liberty, fasting and prayer,
Much castigation, exercise devout;
For here 's a young and sweating devil here,
That commonly rebels. 'Tis a good hand,
A frank one.
Desdemona.   You may, indeed, say so;
For 'twas that hand that gave away my heart.
Othello.   A liberal hand; the hearts of old gave hands,   40
But our new heraldry[410] is hands not hearts.
Desdemona.   I cannot speak of this. Come now, your promise.
Othello.   What promise, chuck?[411]
Desdemona.   I have sent to bid Cassio come speak with you.
Othello.   I have a salt and sorry rheum offends me.
Lend me thy handkerchief.
Desdemona.   Here, my lord.
Othello.   That which I gave you.
Desdemona.   I have it not about me.
Othello.   Not?
Desdemona.   No, indeed, my lord.
Othello.   That is a fault.
That handkerchief
Did an Egyptian[412] to my mother give;   50
She was a charmer,[413] and could almost read
The thoughts of people; she told her, while she kept it,
'Twould make her amiable[414] and subdue my father
Entirely to her love, but if she lost it
Or made a gift of it, my father's eye
Should hold her loathed, and his spirits should hunt
After new fancies.[415] She dying gave it me;
And bid me, when my fate would have me wive,
To give it her. I did so; and take heed on 't;
Make it a darling like your precious eye;   60
To lose 't or give 't away, were such perdition
As nothing else could match.
Desdemona.   Is 't possible?
Othello.   'Tis true; there 's magic in the web of it;
A sibyl,[416] that had number'd in the world

---

[408]With overtones of: too free, loose.   [409]Separation.   [410]I.e., new heraldic symbolism
(Othello means that the new way is not to give the heart together with the hand).   [411]Common
term of endearment.   [412]Gypsy.   [413]Sorceress.   [414]Lovable, desirable.   [415]Loves.
[416]Prophetess.

The sun to course two hundred compasses,
In her prophetic fury sew'd the work;
The worms were hallow'd that did breed the silk,
And it was dy'd in mummy[417] which the skilful
Conserv'd of maidens' hearts.
Desdemona. Indeed! is 't true?
Othello. Most veritable; therefore look to 't well. 70
Desdemona. Then would to heaven that I had never seen it!
Othello. Ha! wherefore?
Desdemona. Why do you speak so startingly and rash?
Othello. Is 't lost? is 't gone? speak, is it out o' the way?
Desdemona. Heaven bless us!
Othello. Say you?
Desdemona. It is not lost; but what an if[418] it were?
Othello. How!
Desdemona. I say, it is not lost.
Othello. Fetch 't, let me see 't!
Desdemona. Why, so I can, sir, but I will not now.
This is a trick to put me from my suit: 80
Pray you let Cassio be receiv'd again.
Othello. Fetch me the handkerchief; my mind misgives.
Desdemona. Come, come;
You'll never meet a more sufficient[419] man.
Othello. The handkerchief!
Desdemona. I pray, talk[420] me of Cassio.
Othello. The handkerchief!
Desdemona. A man that all his time
Hath founded his good fortunes on your love,
Shar'd dangers with you,—
Othello. The handkerchief!
Desdemona. In sooth, you are to blame. 90
Othello. Away! (*Exit.*)
Emilia. Is not this man jealous?
Desdemona. I ne'er saw this before.
Sure, there's some wonder in this handkerchief;
I am most unhappy in the loss of it.
Emilia. 'Tis not a year or two shows us a man;
They are all but[421] stomachs, and we all but[421] food;
They eat us hungerly, and when they are full
They belch us. Look you! Cassio and my husband.

(*Enter Iago and Cassio.*)

---

[417] Drug (medicinal or magic) derived from embalmed bodies. [418] If.
[419] Adequate. [420] Talk to. [421] Only . . . only.

Iago.   There is no other way; 'tis she must do 't:
    And, lo! the happiness;[422] go and importune her.   100
Desdemona.   How now, good Cassio! what 's the news with you?
Cassio.   Madam, my former suit: I do beseech you
    That by your virtuous means I may again
    Exist, and be a member of his love
    Whom I with all the office[423] of my heart
    Entirely honour; I would not be delay'd.
    If my offence be of such mortal kind
    That nor my service past, nor present sorrows,
    Nor purpos'd merit in futurity,
    Can ransom me into his love again,   110
    But to know so must be my benefit;
    So shall I clothe me in a forc'd content,
    And shut myself up in some other course
    To fortune's alms.
Desdemona.   Alas! thrice-gentle Cassio!
    My advocation is not now in tune;
    My lord is not my lord, nor should I know him,
    Were he in favour[424] as in humour alter'd.
    So help me every spirit sanctified,
    As I have spoken for you all my best
    And stood within the blank of[425] his displeasure   120
    For my free speech. You must awhile be patient;
    What I can do I will, and more I will
    Than for myself I dare: let that suffice you.
Iago.   Is my lord angry?
Emilia.   He went hence but now,
    And certainly in strange unquietness.
Iago.   Can he be angry? I have seen the cannon,
    When it hath blown his ranks[426] into the air,
    And, like the devil, from his very arm
    Puff'd his own brother; and can he be angry?
    Something of moment[427] then; I will go meet him;   130
    There's matter in 't indeed, if he be angry.
Desdemona.   I prithee, do so. *(Exit Iago.)* Something, sure, of state,[428]
    Either from Venice, or some unhatch'd[429] practice
    Made demonstrable here in Cyprus to him,
    Hath puddled[430] his clear spirit; and, in such cases
    Men's natures wrangle with inferior things,
    Though great ones are their object. 'Tis even so;

---

[422] "What luck!"   [423] Duty.   [424] Appearance.   [425] As the target for.   [426] I.e.,
his soldiers.   [427] Important.   [428] Public affairs.   [429] Abortive or budding plot.
[430] Muddied.

For let our finger ache, and it indues[431]
Our other healthful members even to that sense
Of pain. Nay, we must think men are not gods,   140
Nor of them look for such observancy[432]
As fits the bridal.[433] Beshrew me much, Emilia,
I was—unhandsome warrior as I am—
Arraigning his unkindness with[434] my soul;
But now I find I had suborn'd the witness,[435]
And he 's indicted falsely.
Emilia.   Pray heaven it be state matters, as you think,
And no conception,[436] nor no jealous toy[437]
Concerning you.
Desdemona.   Alas the day! I never gave him cause.   150
Emilia.   But jealous souls will not be answer'd so;
They are not ever jealous for the cause,
But jealous for they are jealous; 'tis a monster
Begot upon itself, born on itself.
Desdemona.   Heaven keep that monster from Othello's mind!
Emilia.   Lady, amen.
Desdemona.   I will go seek him. Cassio, walk hereabout;
If I do find him fit, I'll move your suit
And seek to effect it to my uttermost.
Cassio.   I humbly thank your ladyship.   160

(*Exeunt Desdemona and Emilia.*)

(*Enter Bianca.*)

Bianca.   Save you, friend Cassio!
Cassio.   What make you from home?
How is it with you, my most fair Bianca?
I' faith, sweet love, I was coming to your house.
Bianca.   And I was going to your lodging, Cassio.
What! keep a week away? seven days and nights?
Eight score eight hours? and lovers' absent hours,
More tedious than the dial eight score times?
O weary reckoning!
Cassio.   Pardon me, Bianca,
I have this while with leaden thoughts been press'd;
But I shall, in a more continuate[438] time,   170
Strike off[439] this score of absence. Sweet Bianca,

(*Giving her Desdemona's handkerchief.*)

Take me this work out.

---

[431] Brings, leads.   [432] Attention.   [433] Wedding.   [434] To.   [435] I.e., caused my soul to bring in wrong charges.   [436] Fancy, supposition.   [437] Fancy.   [438] Uninterrupted.   [439] Cancel (i.e., make up for).

Bianca.   O Cassio! whence came this?
  This is some token from a newer friend;
  To the felt absence now I feel a cause;
  Is 't come to this? Well, well.
Cassio.   Go to, woman!
  Throw your vile guesses in the devil's teeth,
  From whence you have them. You are jealous now
  That this is from some mistress, some remembrance:
  No, in good troth, Bianca.
Bianca.   Why, whose is it?   180
Cassio.   I know not, sweet; I found it in my chamber.
  I like the work well; ere it be demanded,——[440]
  As like enough it will,—I'd have it copied;
  Take it and do 't; and leave me for this time.
Bianca.   Leave you! wherefore?
Cassio.   I do attend here on[441] the general,
  And think it no addition,[442] nor my wish,
  To have him see me woman'd.
Bianca.   Why, I pray you?
Cassio.   Not that I love you not.
Bianca.   But that you do not love me.
  I pray you, bring me on the way a little   190
  And say if I shall see you soon at night.
Cassio.   'Tis but a little way that I can bring you,
  For I attend here; but I'll see you soon.
Bianca.   'Tis very good; I must be circumstanc'd.[443]   (*Exeunt.*)

Act IV

SCENE 1.   Cyprus. Before the Castle.

(*Enter Othello and Iago.*)

Iago.   Will you think so?
Othello.   Think so, Iago!
Iago.   What!
  To kiss in private?
Othello.   An unauthoriz'd kiss.
Iago.   Or to be naked with her friend a-bed
  An hour or more, not meaning any harm?
Othello.   Naked a-bed, Iago, and not mean harm?

---

[440] Asked for.   [441] Wait for.   [442] Advantage, credit.   [443] Governed by circumstances.

It is hypocrisy against the devil:[444]
They that mean virtuously, and yet do so,
The devil their virtue tempts, and they tempt heaven.

Iago.   If they do nothing, 'tis a venial slip;
But if I give my wife a handkerchief,—   10

Othello.   What then?

Iago.   Why, then, 'tis hers, my lord; and, being hers,
She may, I think, bestow 't on any man.

Othello.   She is protectress of her honour too;
May she give that?

Iago.   Her honour is an essence that 's not seen;
They have it very oft that have it not:[445]
But for the handkerchief,—

Othello.   By heaven, I would most gladly have forgot it:—
Thou said'st,—O! it comes o'er my memory,   20
As doth the raven[446] o'er the infected house,
Boding to all,—he had my handkerchief.

Iago.   Ay, what of that?

Othello.   That's not so good now.

Iago.   What,
If I had said I had seen him do you wrong?
Or heard him say, as knaves be such abroad,[447]
Who having, by their own importunate suit,
Or voluntary dotage[448] of some mistress,
Convinced or supplied them,[449] cannot choose
But they must blab.

Othello.   Hath he said any thing?

Iago.   He hath, my lord; but be you well assur'd,   30
No more than he'll unswear.

Othello.   What hath he said?

Iago.   Faith, that he did— I know not what he did.

Othello.   What? what?

Iago.   Lie—

Othello.   With her?

Iago.   With her, on her; what you will.

Othello.   Lie with her; lie on her! We say, lie on her, when they belie her.
Lie with her! that's fulsome. Handkerchief,—confessions,—handkerchief! To
confess, and be hanged for his labour. First, to be hanged, and then to
confess: I tremble at it. Nature would not invest herself in such shadowing
passion without some instruction.[450] It is not words that shake me thus. Pish!
Noses, ears, and lips. It is possible?—Confess!—Handkerchief!—O devil!

---

[444] I.e., by not committing the sin which the situation invites.   [445] I.e., some unchaste
women are thought chaste.   [446] (1) A bad omen, (2) A carrier of the plague.   [447] As
there are some such in the world.   [448] Foolish affection.   [449] Overcome (their reluctance) or satisfied (their desires).   [450] I would not fall into such passion unless there were some
real grounds for it.

(Falls in a trance.)

Iago.   Work on,
My medicine, work! Thus credulous fools are caught;
And many worthy and chaste dames even thus,
All guiltless, meet reproach. What, ho! my lord!
My lord, I say! Othello!

(Enter Cassio.)

                        How now, Cassio!
Cassio.   What's the matter?
Iago.   My lord is fallen into an epilepsy;[451]
This is his second fit; he had one yesterday.
Cassio.   Rub him about the temples.
Iago.   No, forbear;
The lethargy[452] must have his quiet course,   50
If not, he foams at mouth, and by and by
Breaks out to savage madness. Look! he stirs;
Do you withdraw yourself a little while,
He will recover straight; when he is gone,
I would on great occasion[453] speak with you.   *(Exit Cassio.)*
How is it, general? have you not hurt your head?
Othello.   Dost thou mock me?[454]
Iago.   I mock you! no, by heaven.
Would you would bear your fortune like a man!
Othello.   A horned man's a monster and a beast.
Iago.   There's many a beast then, in a populous city,   60
And many a civil[455] monster.
Othello.   Did he confess it?
Iago.   Good sir, be a man;
Think every bearded fellow that's but yok'd
May draw[456] with you; there's millions now alive
That nightly lie in those unproper[457] beds
Which they dare swear peculiar;[458] your case is better.
O! 'tis the spite of hell, the fiend's arch-mock,
To lip[459] a wanton in a secure[460] couch,
And to suppose her chaste. No, let me know;
And knowing what I am, I know what she shall be.   70
Othello.   O! thou art wise; 'tis certain.

---

[451] Seizure, fit.   [452] Coma.   [453] Important matter.   [454] Another allusion to the cuckold's horns.   [455] Citizen.   [456] I.e., pull the burden of cuckoldom.   [457] Not exclusively their own.   [458] Exclusively their own.   [459] Kiss.   [460] I.e., without suspicion of having a rival.

Iago.   Stand you awhile apart;
   Confine yourself but in a patient list.[461]
   Whilst you were here o'erwhelmed with your grief,—
   A passion most unsuiting such a man,—
   Cassio came hither; I shifted him away,
   And laid good 'scuse upon your ecstasy;[462]
   Bade him anon return and here speak with me;
   The which he promis'd. Do but encave yourself,
   And mark the fleers, the gibes, and notable scorns,
   That dwell in every region of his face;   80
   For I will make him tell the tale anew,
   Where, how, how oft, how long ago, and when
   He hath, and is again to cope[463] your wife:
   I say, but mark his gesture. Marry, patience;
   Or I shall say you are all in all in spleen,[464]
   And nothing of a man.
Othello.   Dost thou hear, Iago?
   I will be found most cunning in my patience;
   But—dost thou hear?—most bloody.
Iago.   That's not amiss:
   But yet keep time[465] in all. Will you withdraw?   *(Othello goes apart.)*
   Now will I question Cassio of Bianca,   90
   A housewife[466] that by selling her desires
   Buys herself bread and clothes; it is a creature
   That dotes on Cassio; as 'tis the strumpet's plague
   To beguile many and be beguil'd by one.
   He, when he hears of her, cannot refrain
   From the excess of laughter. Here he comes:

(Re-enter Cassio.)

   As he shall smile, Othello shall go mad;
   And his unbookish[467] jealousy must construe
   Poor Cassio's smiles, gestures, and light behaviour
   Quite in the wrong. How do you now, lieutenant?   100
Cassio.   The worser that you give me the addition[468]
   Whose want[469] even kills me.
Iago.   Ply Desdemona well, and you are sure on 't.
   (Speaking lower.) Now, if this suit lay in Bianca's power,
   How quickly should you speed!
Cassio.   Alas! poor caitiff![470]
Othello.   Look! how he laughs already!

---

461 Bounds of patience.   462 Derangement, trance.   463 Close with.   464 Completely
overcome by passion.   465 Maintain control.   466 Hussy.   467 Unpracticed,
naive.   468 Title.   469 The want of which.   470 Wretch.

Iago.   I never knew woman love man so.

Cassio.   Alas! poor rogue, I think i' faith, she loves me.

Othello.   Now he denies it faintly, and laughs it out.

Iago.   Do you hear, Cassio?

Othello.   Now he importunes him   110
To tell it o'er: go to; well said, well said.

Iago.   She gives it out that you shall marry her;
Do you intend it?

Cassio.   Ha, ha, ha!

Othello.   Do you triumph, Roman?[471] do you triumph?

Cassio.   I marry her! what? a customer?[472] I prithee, bear some charity to my
wit;[473] do not think it so unwholesome. Ha, ha, ha!

Othello.   So, so, so, so. They laugh that win.[474]

Iago.   Faith, the cry goes that you shall marry her.

Cassio.   Prithee, say true.   120

Iago.   I am a very villain else.

Othello.   Have you scored me?[475] Well.

Cassio.   This is the monkey's own giving out: she is persuaded I will marry
her, out of her own love and flattery, not out of my promise.

Othello.   Iago beckons me;[476] now he begins the story.

Cassio.   She was here even now; she haunts me in every place. I was the other
day talking on the sea-bank with certain Venetians, and thither comes this
bauble,[477] and, by this hand, she falls me thus about my neck;—

Othello.   Crying, 'O dear Cassio!' as it were; his gesture imports it.

Cassio.   So hangs and lolls and weeps upon me; so hales[478] and pulls me; ha,
ha, ha!

Othello.   Now he tells how she plucked him to my chamber. O! I see that
nose of yours, but not the dog I shall throw it to.

Cassio.   Well, I must leave her company.

Iago.   Before me![479] look, where she comes.

Cassio.   'Tis such another fitchew![480] marry, a perfumed one.

(Enter Bianca.)

What do you mean by this haunting of me?

Bianca.   Let the devil and his dam haunt you! What did you mean by that
same handkerchief you gave me even now? I was a fine fool to take it. I must
take out the work! A likely piece of work, that you should find it in your
chamber, and not know who left it there! This is some minx's token, and I
must take out the work! There, give it your hobby-horse;[481] wheresoever you
had it I'll take out no work on 't.

---

[471] I.e., one who triumphs(?).   [472] Courtesan, prostitute.   [473] Give me credit for some
sense.   [474] "He who laughs last laughs longest"(?).   [475] Wounded, defaced(?); or: settled
my account(?).   [476] Signals.   [477] Plaything.   [478] Hauls.   [479] An exclamation
of surprise.   [480] Polecat, noted both for its strong smell and for its lechery.   [481] Harlot.

Cassio.   How now, my sweet Bianca! how now, how now!

Othello.   By heaven, that should be[482] my handkerchief!

Bianca.   An you'll come to supper to-night, you may; an you will not, come when you are next prepared[483] for.   *(Exit.)*

Iago.   After her, after her.

Cassio.   Faith, I must; she'll rail in the street else.

Iago.   Will you sup there?

Cassio.   Faith, I intend so.

Iago.   Well, I may chance to see you, for I would very fain[484] speak with you.

Cassio.   Prithee come; will you?

Iago.   Go to; say no more.   *(Exit Cassio.)*

Othello *(advancing)*.   How shall I murder him, Iago?

Iago.   Did you perceive how he laughed at his vice?

Othello.   O! Iago!

Iago.   And did you see the handkerchief?

Othello.   Was that mine?

Iago.   Yours, by this hand; and to see how he prizes the foolish woman your wife! she gave it him, and he hath given it his whore.

Othello.   I would have him nine years a-killing. A fine woman! a fair woman! a sweet woman!

Iago.   Nay, you must forget that.

Othello.   Ay, let her rot, and perish, and be damned to-night; for she shall not live. No, my heart is turned to stone; I strike it, and it hurts my hand. O! the world hath not a sweeter creature; she might lie by an emperor's side and command him tasks.

Iago.   Nay, that's not your way.[485]

Othello.   Hang her! I do but say what she is. So delicate with her needle! An admirable musician! O, she will sing the savageness out of a bear. Of so high and plenteous wit and invention!

Iago.   She's the worse for all this.

Othello.   O! a thousand, a thousand times. And then, of so gentle a condition![486]

Iago.   Ay, too gentle.[487]

Othello.   Nay, that's certain;—but yet the pity of it, Iago!
O! Iago, the pity of it, Iago!

Iago.   If you are so fond over her iniquity, give her patent to offend; for, if it touch not you, it comes near nobody.

Othello.   I will chop her into messes.[488] Cuckold me!

Iago.   O! 'tis foul in her.

Othello.   With mine officer!

Iago.   That's fouler.

---

[482] I.e., I think that is.   [483] Expected (Bianca means that if he does not come that night, she will never want to see him again).   [484] Gladly.   [485] Proper course.   [486] So much the high-born lady.   [487] I.c., yielding.   [488] Bits.

Othello.   Get me some poison, Iago; this night: I'll not expostulate with her, lest her body and beauty unprovide my mind again.[489] This night, Iago.

Iago.   Do it not with poison, strangle her in her bed, even the bed she hath contaminated.

Othello.   Good, good; the justice of it pleases; very good.

Iago.   And for Cassio, let me be his undertaker;[490] you shall hear more by midnight.

Othello.   Excellent good. *(A trumpet within.)* What trumpet is that same?

Iago.   Something from Venice, sure. 'Tis Lodovico,
Come from the duke; and see, your wife is with him.

(Enter Lodovico, Desdemona, and Attendants.)

Lodovico.   God save you, worthy general!

Othello.   With all my heart, sir.

Lodovico.   The duke and senators of Venice greet you.

(Gives him a packet.)

Othello.   I kiss the instrument of their pleasures.

(Opens the packet, and reads.)

Desdemona.   And what's the news, good cousin Lodovico?

Iago.   I am very glad to see you, signior;
Welcome to Cyprus.

Lodovico.   I thank you. How does Lieutenant Cassio?

Iago.   Lives, sir.   200

Desdemona.   Cousin, there's fall'n between him and my lord
An unkind[491] breach; but you shall make all well.

Othello.   Are you sure of that?

Desdemona.   My lord?

Othello *(reads).*   'This fail you not to do, as you will'—

Lodovico.   He did not call; he's busy in the paper.
Is there division[492] twixt my lord and Cassio?

Desdemona.   A most unhappy one; I would do much
To atone[493] them, for the love I bear to Cassio.

Othello.   Fire and brimstone!

Desdemona.   My lord?

Othello.   Are you wise?   210

Desdemona.   What! is he angry?

Lodovico.   May be the letter mov'd him;

---

[489] Unsettle my intention.   [490] Dispatcher.   [491] Unnatural.   [492] Estrangement.
[493] Reconcile.

For, as I think, they do command him home,
Deputing Cassio in his government.
Desdemona.　　Trust me, I am glad on 't.
Othello.　　　　　　　　　　Indeed!
Desdemona.　　　　　　　　　　　　My lord?
Othello.　　I am glad to see you mad.
Desdemona.　　　　　　　　　Why, sweet Othello?
Othello.　Devil!　　　　　　　　　　　　　*(Strikes her.)*
Desdemona.　　I have not deserved this.
Lodovico.　My lord, this would not be believ'd in Venice,
　　Though I should swear I saw 't; 'tis very much;
　　Make her amends, she weeps.
Othello.　　　　　　　　O devil, devil!
　　If that the earth could teem with woman's tears,　　　　　　220
　　Each drop she falls[494] would prove a crocodile.[495]
　　Out of my sight!
Desdemona.　　I will not stay to offend you.　　　　　*(Going.)*
Lodovico.　Truly, an obedient lady;
　　I do beseech your lordship, call her back.
Othello.　Mistress!
Desdemona.　　My lord?
Othello.　　　　　　　　What would you with her, sir?
Lodovico.　Why, I, my lord?
Othello.　Ay; you did wish that I would make her turn:
　　Sir, she can turn, and turn, and yet go on,
　　And turn again; and she can weep, sir, weep;
　　And she's obedient, as you say, obedient,　　　　　　　　230
　　Very obedient. Proceed you in your tears.
　　Concerning this, sir—O well-painted passion!—
　　I am commanded home. Get you away;
　　I'll send for you anon. Sir, I obey the mandate,
　　And will return to Venice. Hence! avaunt![496]　　*(Exit Desdemona.)*
　　Cassio shall have my place. And, sir, to-night,
　　I do entreat that we may sup together;
　　You are welcome, sir, to Cyprus. Goats and monkeys!　　*(Exit.)*
Lodovico.　Is this the noble Moor whom our full senate
　　Call all-in-all sufficient? is this the noble nature　　　　240
　　Whom passion could not shake? whose solid virtue
　　The shot of accident nor dart of chance
　　Could neither graze nor pierce?
Iago.　　　　　　　　　He is much chang'd.
Lodovico.　Are his wits safe? is he not light of brain?
Iago.　He's that he is; I may not breathe my censure.

---

[494] Lets fall.　　[495] The crocodile's tears were supposed to be hypocritical.　　[496] Begone!

What he might be, if, what he might, he is not,
I would to heaven he were![497]
Lodovico.   What! strike his wife!
Iago.   Faith, that was not so well; yet would I knew
That stroke would prove the worst!
Lodovico.   Is it his use?
Or did the letters work upon his blood,   250
And new-create this fault?
Iago.   Alas, alas!
It is not honesty in me to speak
What I have seen and known. You shall observe him,
And his own courses[498] will denote him so
That I may save my speech. Do but go after
And mark how he continues.
Lodovico.   I am sorry that I am deceiv'd in him.   *(Exeunt.)*

SCENE 2.   A Room in the Castle.

(Enter Othello and Emilia.)

Othello.   You have seen nothing, then?
Emilia.   Nor ever heard, nor ever did suspect.
Othello.   Yes, you have seen Cassio and her together.
Emilia.   But then I saw no harm, and then I heard
Each syllable that breath made up between them.
Othello.   What! did they never whisper?
Emilia.   Never, my lord.
Othello.   Nor send you out o' the way?
Emilia.   Never.
Othello.   To fetch her fan, her gloves, her mask, nor nothing?[499]
Emilia.   Never, my lord.   10
Othello.   That's strange.
Emilia.   I durst, my lord, to wager she is honest,
Lay down my soul at stake: if you think other,
Remove your thought; it doth abuse your bosom.
If any wretch have put this in your head,
Let heaven requite it with the serpent's curse!
For, if she be not honest, chaste, and true,
There's no man happy; the purest of their wives
Is foul as slander.

---

[497] Another of Iago's gnomic speeches; perhaps approximately: "If now he is not himself, I wish he would be what he could be!"   [498] Actions.   [499] Anything.

Othello.   Bid her come hither; go.   *(Exit Emilia.)*   20
  She says enough; yet she 's a simple[500] bawd
  That cannot say as much. This is a subtle whore,
  A closet lock and key of villanous secrets;
  And yet she 'll kneel and pray; I have seen her do 't.

(Re-enter Emilia with Desdemona.)

Desdemona.   My lord, what is your will?
Othello.   Pray, chuck, come hither.
Desdemona.   What is your pleasure?
Othello.   Let me see your eyes;
  Look in my face.
Desdemona.   What horrible fancy 's this?
Othello *(to Emilia).*   Some of your function,[501] mistress;
  Leave procreants alone and shut the door;
  Cough or cry 'hem' if any body come;
  Your mystery,[502] your mystery; nay, dispatch.   *(Exit Emilia.)*
Desdemona.   Upon my knees, what doth your speech import?   31
  I understand a fury in your words.
  But not the words.
Othello.   Why, what art thou?
Desdemona.   Your wife, my lord; your true
  And loyal wife.
Othello.   Come, swear it, damn thyself;
  Lest, being like one of heaven, the devils themselves
  Should fear to seize thee; therefore be double-damn'd;
  Swear thou art honest.
Desdemona.   Heaven doth truly know it.
Othello.   Heaven truly knows that thou art false as hell.
Desdemona.   To whom, my lord? with whom? how am I false?   40
Othello.   Ah! Desdemona; away, away, away!
Desdemona.   Alas, the heavy day!—Why do you weep?
  Am I the motive of these tears, my lord?
  If haply you my father do suspect
  An instrument of this your calling back,
  Lay not your blame on me; if you have lost him,
  Why, I have lost him too.
Othello.   Had it pleas'd heaven
  To try me with affliction, had he rain'd
  All kinds of sores and shames on my bare head,
  Steep'd me in poverty to the very lips,   50

---

[500] Simpleminded.   [501] To your duty, business.   [502] Trade.

Given to captivity me and my utmost hopes,
I should have found in some part of my soul
A drop of patience; but, alas! to make me
The fixed figure for the time of scorn[503]
To point his slow and moving finger at;
Yet could I bear that too; well, very well:
But there, where I have garner'd[504] up my heart,
Where either I must live or bear no life,
The fountain from the which my current runs
Or else dries up; to be discarded thence!   60
Or keep it as a cistern for foul toads
To knot and gender in![505] Turn thy complexion there,[506]
Patience, thou young and rose-lipp'd cherubin;
Ay, there, look grim as hell!

Desdemona.   I hope my noble lord esteems me honest.
Othello.   O! ay; as summer flies are in the shambles,[507]
That quicken even with blowing. O thou weed!
Who art so lovely fair and smell'st so sweet
That the sense aches at thee, would thou hadst ne'er been born.

Desdemona.   Alas! what ignorant sin have I commited?   70
Othello.   Was this fair paper, this most goodly book,
Made to write 'whore' upon? What committed!
Committed! O thou public commoner![508]
I should make very forges of my cheeks,
That would to cinders burn up modesty,
Did I but speak thy deeds. What committed!
Heaven stops the nose at it and the moon winks,[509]
The bawdy wind that kisses all it meets
Is hush'd within the hollow mine of earth,
And will not hear it. What committed!   80
Impudent strumpet!

Desdemona.   By heaven, you do me wrong.
Othello.   Are not you a strumpet?
Desdemona.   No, as I am a Christian.
If to preserve this vessel for my lord
From any other foul unlawful touch
Be not to be a strumpet, I am none.
Othello.   What! not a whore?
Desdemona.   No, as I shall be sav'd.
Othello.   Is it possible?
Desdemona.   O! heaven forgive us.

---

[503] I.e., the scornful world.   [504] Stored.   [505] Bunch up and procreate.   [506] I.e.,
change your color to suit the "cistern for foul toads."   [507] Slaughterhouse.   [508] Harlot.
[509] Closes her eyes.

Othello.   I cry you mercy,[510] then;
 I took you for that cunning whore of Venice
 That married with Othello. You, mistress,   90
 That have the office opposite to Saint Peter,
 And keep the gate of hell!

(Re-enter Emilia.)

                              You, you, ay, you!
 We have done our course; there's money for your pains.
 I pray you, turn the key and keep our counsel.   *(Exit.)*
Emilia.   Alas! what does this gentleman conceive?[511]
 How do you, madam? how do you, my good lady?
Desdemona.   Faith, half asleep.
Emilia.   Good madam, what's the matter with my lord?
Desdemona.   With who?
Emilia.   Why, with my lord, madam.   100
Desdemona.   Who is thy lord?
Emilia.   He that is yours, sweet lady.
Desdemona.   I have none; do not talk to me, Emilia;
 I cannot weep, nor answer have I none,
 But what should go by water.[512] Prithee, to-night
 Lay on my bed my wedding sheets: remember:
 And call thy husband hither.
Emilia.   Here is a change indeed!   *(Exit.)*
Desdemona.   'Tis meet I should be us'd so, very meet.
 How have I been behav'd, that he might stick
 The small'st opinion on my least misuse?[513]

(Re-enter Emilia, with Iago.)

Iago.   What is your pleasure, madam? How is it with you?   110
Desdemona.   I cannot tell. Those that do teach young babes
 Do it with gentle means and easy tasks;
 He might have chid me so; for, in good faith,
 I am a child to chiding.
Iago.   What's the matter, lady?
Emilia.   Alas, Iago, my lord hath so bewhor'd her,
 Thrown such despite[514] and heavy terms upon her,
 As true hearts cannot bear.
Desdemona.   Am I that name, Iago?
Iago.   What name, fair lady?
Desdemona.   Such as she says my lord did say I was.

---

[510] Beg your pardon.   [511] Imagine.   [512] Be conveyed by means of tears.   [513] The least suspicion on my slightest misconduct.   [514] Abuse.

Emilia.   He call'd her whore; a beggar in his drink   120
    Could not have laid such terms upon his callat.[515]
Iago.   Why did he so?
Desdemona.   I do not know; I am sure I am none such.
Iago.   Do not weep, do not weep. Alas the day!
Emilia.   Has she forsook so many noble matches,
    Her father and her country and her friends,
    To be call'd whore? would it not make one weep?
Desdemona.   It is my wretched fortune.
Iago.   Beshrew[516] him for it!
    How comes this trick upon him?
Desdemona.   Nay, heaven doth know.
Emilia.   I will be hang'd, if some eternal villain,   130
    Some busy and insinuating rogue,
    Some cogging[517] cozening slave, to get some office,
    Have not devis'd this slander; I 'll be hang'd else.
Iago.   Fie! there is no such man; it is impossible.
Desdemona.   If any such there be, heaven pardon him!
Emilia.   A halter pardon him, and hell gnaw his bones!
    Why should he call her whore? who keeps her company?
    What place? what time? what form? what likelihood?
    The Moor 's abus'd by some most villanous knave,
    Some base notorious knave, some scurvy fellow.   140
    O heaven! that such companions[518] thou'dst unfold,
    And put in every honest hand a whip
    To lash the rascals naked through the world,
    Even from the east to west!
Iago.   Speak within door.
Emilia.   O! fie upon them. Some such squire he was
    That turn'd your wit the seamy side without,[519]
    And made you to suspect me with the Moor.
Iago.   You are a fool; go to.
Desdemona.   O good Iago,
    What shall I do to win my lord again?
    Good friend, go to him; for, by this light of heaven,   150
    I know not how I lost him. Here I kneel:
    If e'er my will did trespass 'gainst his love,
    Either in discourse of thought or actual deed,
    Or that mine eyes, mine ears, or any sense,
    Delighted them[520] in any other form;
    Or that I do not yet,[521] and ever did,
    And ever will, though he do shake me off
    To beggarly divorcement, love him dearly,

---

[515] Slut.   [516] Curse.   [517] Cheating.   [518] Fellows   (derogatory).
[519] Outward.   [520] Found delight.   [521] Still.

Comfort forswear me! Unkindness may do much;
And his unkindness may defeat[522] my life,   160
But never taint my love. I cannot say 'whore':
It does abhor me now I speak the word;
To do the act that might the addition earn
Not the world's mass of vanity could make me.

Iago.   I pray you be content, 'tis but his humour;
The business of the state does him offence,
And he does chide with you.

Desdemona.   If 'twere no other,—

Iago.   'Tis but so, I warrant.   *(Trumpets.)*
Hark! how these instruments summon to supper;
The messengers of Venice stay the meat: 170
Go in, and weep not; all things shall be well.

(Exeunt Desdemona and Emilia.)

(Enter Roderigo.)

How now, Roderigo!

Roderigo.   I do not find that thou dealest justly with me.

Iago.   What in the contrary?[523]

Roderigo.   Every day thou daffest me[524] with some device, Iago; and rather,
as it seems to me now, keepest from me all conveniency,[525] than suppliest
me with the least advantage of hope. I will indeed no longer endure it, nor
am I yet persuaded to put up[526] in peace what already I have foolishly suffered.

Iago.   Will you hear me, Roderigo?

Roderigo.   Faith, I have heard too much, for your words and performances are
no kin together.

Iago.   You charge me most unjustly.

Roderigo.   With nought but truth. I have wasted myself out of my means. The
jewels you have had from me to deliver to Desdemona would half have
corrupted a votarist;[527] you have told me she has received them, and returned
me expectations and comforts of sudden respect[528] and acquaintance, but I
find none.

Iago.   Well; go to; very well.

Roderigo.   Very well! go to! I cannot go to, man; nor 'tis not very well: by this
hand, I say, it is very scurvy, and begin to find myself fobbed[529] in it.

Iago.   Very well.

Roderigo.   I tell you 'tis not very well. I will make myself known to Desdemona;
if she will return me my jewels, I will give over my suit and repent my
unlawful solicitation; if not, assure yourself I will seek satisfaction of you.

Iago.   You have said now.[530]

---

[522] Destroy.   [523] I.e., what reason do you have for saying that.   [524] You put me
off.   [525] Favorable circumstances.   [526] Put up with.   [527] Nun.   [528] Immediate
consideration.   [529] Cheated.   [530] I.e., "I suppose you're through?" (?); or: "Now you're
talking" (?).

Roderigo.   Ay, and said nothing, but what I protest intendment of doing.

Iago.   Why, now I see there's mettle in thee, and even from this instant do build on thee a better opinion than ever before. Give me thy hand, Roderigo; thou hast taken against me a most just exception; but yet, I protest, I have dealt most directly in thy affair.

Roderigo.   It hath not appeared.

Iago.   I grant indeed it hath not appeared, and your suspicion is not without wit and judgment. But, Roderigo, if thou hast that in thee indeed, which I have greater reason to believe now than ever, I mean purpose, courage, and valour, this night show it: if thou the next night following enjoy not Desdemona, take me from this world with treachery and devise engines for[531] my life.

Roderigo.   Well, what is it? is it within reason and compass?

Iago.   Sir, there is especial commission come from Venice to depute Cassio in Othello's place.

Roderigo.   Is that true? why, then Othello and Desdemona return again to Venice.

Iago.   O, no! he goes into Mauritania, and takes away with him the fair Desdemona, unless his abode be lingered here by some accident; wherein none can be so determinate[532] as the removing of Cassio.

Roderigo.   How do you mean, removing of him?

Iago.   Why, by making him uncapable of Othello's place; knocking out his brains.

Roderigo.   And that you would have me do?

Iago.   Ay; if you dare do yourself a profit and a right. He sups to-night with a harlotry,[533] and thither will I go to him; he knows not yet of his honourable fortune. If you will watch his going thence,—which I will fashion to fall out between twelve and one,—you may take him at your pleasure; I will be near to second your attempt, and he shall fall between us. Come, stand not amazed at it, but go along with me; I will show you such a necessity in his death that you shall think yourself bound to put it on him. It is now high supper-time, and the night grows to waste; about it.

Roderigo.   I will hear further reason for this.

Iago.   And you shall be satisfied.   *(Exeunt.)*

SCENE 3.   Another Room in the Castle.

(Enter Othello, Lodovico, Desdemona, Emilia, and Attendants.)

Lodovico.   I do beseech you, sir, trouble yourself no further.

Othello.   O! pardon me; 'twill do me good to walk.

Lodovico.   Madam, good-night; I humbly thank your ladyship.

---

[531] Devices against.   [532] Effective.   [533] Harlot.

Desdemona.   Your honour is most welcome.

Othello.   Will you walk, sir?
O! Desdemona,—

Desdemona.   My lord?

Othello.   Get you to bed on the instant; I will be returned forthwith; dismiss
your attendant there; look it be done.

Desdemona.   I will, my lord.   *(Exeunt Othello, Lodovico, and Attendants.)*

Emilia.   How goes it now? He looks gentler than he did.   240

Desdemona.   He says he will return incontinent;[534]
He hath commanded me to go to bed,
And bade me to dismiss you.

Emilia.   Dismiss me!

Desdemona.   It was his bidding; therefore, good Emilia,
Give me my nightly wearing, and adieu:
We must not now displease him.

Emilia.   I would you had never seen him.

Desdemona.   So would not I; my love doth so approve him,
That even his stubbornness,[535] his checks[536] and frowns,—
Prithee, unpin me,—have grace and favour in them.   250

Emilia.   I have laid those sheets you bade me on the bed.

Desdemona.   All's one.[537] Good faith! how foolish are our minds!
If I do die before thee, prithee, shroud me
In one of those same sheets.

Emilia.   Come, come, you talk.

Desdemona.   My mother had a maid call'd Barbara;
She was in love, and he she lov'd prov'd mad[538]
And did forsake her; she had a song of 'willow';
An old thing 'twas, but it express'd her fortune,
And she died singing it; that song to-night
Will not go from my mind; I have much to do   260
But to go hang my head all at one side,
And sing it like poor Barbara. Prithee, dispatch.

Emilia.   Shall I go fetch your night-gown?

Desdemona.   No, unpin me here.
This Lodovico is a proper man.

Emilia.   A very handsome man.

Desdemona.   He speaks well.

Emilia.   I know a lady in Venice would have walked barefoot to Palestine for
a touch of his nether lip.

Desdemona *(sings)*.
The poor soul sat sighing by a sycamore tree,
Sing all a green willow;   270

---

[534] At once.   [535] Roughness.   [536] Rebukes.   [537] I.e., it doesn't matter.
[538] Wild.

Her hand on her bosom, her head on her knee,
   Sing willow, willow, willow:
The fresh streams ran by her, and murmur'd her moans;
   Sing willow, willow, willow:
Her salt tears fell from her and soften'd the stones;—

Lay by these:—
   Sing willow, willow, willow:

Prithee, hie thee;[539] he 'll come anon.—

  Sing all a green willow must be my garland.
    Let nobody blame him, his scorn I approve,—   280
Nay, that's not next. Hark! who is it that knocks?
Emilia.   It is the wind.
Desdemona.
  I call'd my love false love; but what said he then?
    Sing willow, willow, willow:
  If I court moe[540] women, you 'll couch with moe men.

So, get thee gone; good-night. Mine eyes do itch;
Doth that bode weeping?
Emilia.   'Tis neither here nor there.
Desdemona.   I have heard it said so. O! these men, these men!
Dost thou in conscience think, tell me, Emilia,
That there be women do abuse their husbands   290
In such gross kind?
Emilia.   There be some such, no question.
Desdemona.   Wouldst thou do such a deed for all the world?
Emilia.   Why, would not you?
Desdemona.   No, by this heavenly light!
Emilia.   Nor I neither by this heavenly light;
I might do 't as well i' the dark.
Desdemona.   Wouldst thou do such a deed for all the world?
Emilia.   The world is a huge thing; 'tis a great price
For a small vice.
Desdemona.   In troth, I think thou wouldst not.
Emilia.   In troth, I think I should, and undo 't when I had done. Marry, I
would not do such a thing for a joint-ring,[541] nor measures of lawn,[542] nor
for gowns, petticoats, nor caps, nor any petty exhibition;[543] but for the whole
world, who would not make her husband a cuckold to make him a monarch?
I should venture purgatory for 't.

---

[539] Hurry.   [540] More.   [541] Ring made in separable halves.   [542] Fine linen.
[543] Offer, gift.

Desdemona. Beshrew me, if I would do such a wrong
For the whole world.
Emilia. Why, the wrong is but a wrong i' the world; and having the world for
your labour, 'tis a wrong in your own world, and you might quickly make it
right.
Desdemona. I do not think there is any such woman.
Emilia. Yes, a dozen; and as many to the vantage,[544] as   310
Would store[545] the world they played for.
But I do think it is their husbands' faults
If wives do fall. Say that they slack their duties,
And pour our treasures into foreign laps,
Or else break out in peevish jealousies,
Throwing restraint upon us; or say they strike us,
Or scant[546] our former having[547] in despite;
Why, we have galls;[548] and though we have some grace,
Yet have we some revenge. Let husbands know
Their wives have sense like them; they see and smell,   320
And have their palates both for sweet and sour,
As husbands have. What is it that they do
When they change us for others? Is it sport?[549]
I think it is; and doth affection breed it?
I think it doth; is 't frailty that thus errs?
It is so too; and have not we affections,
Desires for sport, and frailty, as men have?
Then, let them use us well; else let them know,
The ills we do, their ills instruct us so.
Desdemona. Good-night, good night; heaven me such usage[550] send,   330
Not to pick bad from bad, but by bad mend!   (*Exeunt.*)

Act V

SCENE 1. Cyprus. A Street.

(*Enter Iago and Roderigo.*)

Iago. Here, stand behind this bulk;[551] straight will he come:
Wear thy good rapier bare, and put it home.
Quick, quick; fear nothing; I 'll be at thy elbow.
It makes us, or it mars us; think on that,
And fix most firm thy resolution.

---

[544] Over and above.   [545] Populate.   [546] Reduce.   [547] Allowance.   [548] Spirits,
temper.   [549] Lust, sexual enjoyment.   [550] Habits (?), treatment (?).   [551] Jutting part
of a wall.

Roderigo. Be near at hand; I may miscarry in 't.

Iago. Here, at thy hand: be bold, and take thy stand. *(Retires.)*

Roderigo. I have no great devotion to the deed;
And yet he has given me satisfying reasons:
'Tis but a man gone: forth, my sword; he dies. 10

Iago. I have rubb'd this young quat[552] almost to the sense,[553]
And he grows angry. Now, whether he kill Cassio,
Or Cassio him, or each do kill the other,
Every way makes my gain: live Roderigo,
He calls me to a restitution large
Of gold and jewels that I bobb'd[554] from him,
As gifts to Desdemona;
It must not be: if Cassio do remain,
He hath a daily beauty in his life
That makes me ugly: and, besides, the Moor 20
May unfold me to him; there stand I in much peril.
No, he must die. But so;[555] I hear him coming.

(Enter Cassio.)

Roderigo. I know his gait; 'tis he. Villain, thou diest!

(Makes a pass at Cassio.)

Cassio. That thrust had been mine enemy indeed
But that my coat is better than thou know'st;
I will make proof of thine.

(Draws, and wounds Roderigo.)

Roderigo.   O! I am slain.

(Iago from behind wounds Cassio in the leg, and exit.)

Cassio. I am maim'd for ever. Help, ho! murder! murder! *(Falls.)*

(Enter Othello, at a distance.)

Othello. The voice of Cassio: Iago keeps his word.

Roderigo. O! villain that I am!

Othello.   It is e'en so.

Cassio. O, help, ho! light! a surgeon! 30

---

[552] Pimple.   [553] To the quick.   [554] Swindled.   [555] I.e., that's the only way.

Othello.   'Tis he: O brave Iago, honest and just!
   That hast such noble sense of thy friend's wrong;
   Thou teachest me. Minion,[556] your dear lies dead,
   And your unblest fate hies; strumpet, I come!
   Forth of my heart those charms, thine eyes, are blotted;
   Thy bed lust-stain'd shall with lust's blood be spotted.   *(Exit.)*

(Enter Lodovico and Gratiano, at a distance.)

Cassio.   What ho! no watch? no passage?[557] murder! murder!
Gratiano.   'Tis some mischance; the cry is very direful.
Cassio.   O, help!
Lodovico.   Hark!   40
Roderigo.   O wretched villain!
Lodovico.   Two or three groans: it is a heavy[558] night;
   These may be counterfeits; let 's think 't unsafe
   To come in to the cry[559] without more help.
Roderigo.   Nobody come? then shall I bleed to death.
Lodovico.   Hark!

(Re-enter Iago, with a light.)

Gratiano.   Here 's one comes in his shirt, with light and weapons.
Iago.   Who 's there? whose noise is this that cries on murder?
Lodovico.   We do not know.
Iago.   Did not you hear a cry?
Cassio.   Here, here! for heaven's sake, help me.
Iago.   What's the matter?   50
Gratiano.   This is Othello's ancient, as I take it.
Lodovico.   The same indeed; a very valiant fellow.
Iago.   What are you here that cry so grievously?
Cassio.   Iago? O! I am spoil'd, undone by villains!
   Give me some help.
Iago.   O me, lieutenant! what villains have done this?
Cassio.   I think that one of them is hereabout,
   And cannot make away.
Iago.   O treacherous villains!
   (To Lodovico and Gratiano.) What are you there? come in, and
   give some help.
Roderigo.   O! help me here.   60

---

[556] (Cassio's) darling, i.e., Desdemona.   [557] Passer-by.   [558] Dark.   [559] Where the cry comes from.

Cassio. That's one of them.
Iago. O murderous slave! O villain!

(Stabs Roderigo.)

Roderigo. O damn'd Iago! O inhuman dog!
Iago. Kill men i' the dark! Where be these bloody thieves?
   How silent is this town! Ho! murder! murder!
   What may you be? are you of good or evil?
Lodovico. As you shall prove us, praise us.
Iago. Signior Lodovico?
Lodovico. He, sir.
Iago. I cry you mercy. Here 's Cassio hurt by villains.
Gratiano. Cassio!   70
Iago. How is it, brother?
Cassio. My leg is cut in two.
Iago. Marry, heaven forbid.
   Light, gentlemen; I 'll bind it with my shirt.

(Enter Bianca.)

Bianca. What is the matter, ho? who is 't that cried?
Iago. Who is 't that cried!
Bianca. O my dear Cassio! my sweet Cassio!
   O Cassio, Cassio, Cassio!
Iago. O notable strumpet! Cassio, may you suspect
   Who they should be that have thus mangled you?
Cassio. No.   80
Gratiano. I am sorry to find you thus; I have been to seek you.
Iago. Lend me a garter. So. O! for a chair,
   To bear him easily hence!
Bianca. Alas; he faints! O Cassio, Cassio, Cassio!
Iago. Gentlemen all, I do suspect this trash[560]
   To be a party in this injury.
   Patience awhile, good Cassio. Come, come.
   Lend me a light. Know we this face, or no?
   Alas! my friend and my dear countryman,
   Roderigo? no: yes, sure, O heaven! Roderigo.   90
Gratiano. What! of Venice?
Iago. Even he, sir, did you know him?
Gratiano. Know him! ay.

---

[560] I.e., Bianca.

Iago.   Signior Gratiano? I cry you gentle pardon;
　　These bloody accidents must excuse my manners,
　　That so neglected you.
Gratiano.　　　　　　I am glad to see you.
Iago.   How do you, Cassio? O! a chair, a chair!
Gratiano.   Roderigo!

(*A chair brought in.*)

Iago.   He, he, 'tis he,—O! that 's well said; the chair:
　　Some good men bear him carefully from hence;
　　I 'll fetch the general's surgeon. (*To Bianca.*) For you, mistress,   100
　　Save you your labour. He that lies slain here, Cassio,
　　Was my dear friend. What malice was between you?
Cassio.   None in the world; nor do I know that man.
Iago (*to Bianca*).   What! look you pale? O! bear him out o' the air—

(*Cassio and Roderigo are borne off.*)

　　Stay you, good gentlemen. Look you pale, mistress?—
　　Do you perceive the gastness[561] of her eye?
　　Nay, if you stare, we shall hear more anon.
　　Behold her well; I pray you, look upon her.
　　Do you see, gentlemen? nay, guiltiness will speak
　　Though tongues were out of use.   110

(*Enter Emilia.*)

Emilia.   'Las! what 's the matter? what 's the matter, husband?
Iago.   Cassio hath here been set on in the dark
　　By Roderigo and fellows that are 'scaped:
　　He 's almost slain, and Roderigo dead.
Emilia.   Alas! good gentleman; alas! good Cassio!
Iago.   This is the fruit of whoring. Prithee, Emilia,
　　Go know of Cassio where he supp'd to-night.
　　(*To Bianca.*) What! do you shake at that?
Bianca.   He supp'd at my house; but I therefore shake not.
Iago.   O! did he so? I charge you, go with me.   120
Emilia.   Fie, fie, upon thee, strumpet!
Bianca.   I am no strumpet, but of life as honest
　　As you that thus abuse me.
Emilia.　　　　　　As I! foh! fie upon thee!

---

[561] Terror.

Iago.   Kind gentlemen, let 's go see poor Cassio dress'd.[562]
Come, mistress, you must tell 's another tale.
Emilia, run you to the citadel,
And tell my lord and lady what hath happ'd.
Will you go on afore? *(Aside.)* This is the night
That either makes me or fordoes[563] me quite.   *(Exeunt.)*

SCENE 2.   A Bedchamber in the Castle. Desdemona in bed asleep. A light burning.

(Enter Othello.)

Othello.   It is the cause,[564] it is the cause, my soul;
Let me not name it to you, you chaste stars!
It is the cause. Yet I 'll not shed her blood,
Nor scar that whiter skin of hers than snow,
And smooth as monumental alabaster.
Yet she must die, else she 'll betray more men.
Put out the light, and then put out the light:
If I quench thee, thou flaming minister,[565]
I can again thy former light restore,
Should I repent me; but once put out thy light,   10
Thou cunning'st[566] pattern of excelling nature,
I know not where is that Promethean[567] heat
That can thy light relume.[568] When I have pluck'd the rose,
I cannot give it vital growth again,
It needs must wither: I 'll smell it on the tree. *(Kisses her.)*
O balmy breath, that dost almost persuade
Justice to break her sword! One more, one more.
Be thus when thou art dead, and I will kill thee,
And love thee after. One more, and this the last:
So sweet was ne'er so fatal. I must weep,   20
But they are cruel tears; this sorrow 's heavenly,
It strikes where it doth love. She wakes.
Desdemona.   Who 's there? Othello?
Othello.   Ay, Desdemona.
Desdemona.   Will you come to bed, my lord?
Othello.   Have you pray'd to-night, Desdemona?
Desdemona.   Ay, my lord.

---

[562] Bandaged.   [563] Ruins.   [564] I.e., Desdemona's unchastity (Othello means that the severity of the punishment is required by the nature of her sin).   [565] I.e, the candle.
[566] Most intricately wrought.   [567] In Greek mythology the demi-god Prometheus stole fire from the gods and gave it to man.   [568] Relight.

Othello.   If you bethink yourself of any crime
Unreconcil'd as yet to heaven and grace,
Solicit for it straight.

Desdemona.   Alas! my lord, what may you mean by that?

Othello.   Well, do it, and be brief; I will walk by:[569]   30
I would not kill thy unprepared spirit;
No; heaven forfend![570] I would not kill thy soul.

Desdemona.   Talk you of killing?

Othello.   Ay, I do.

Desdemona.   Then heaven
Have mercy on me!

Othello.   Amen! with all my heart.

Desdemona.   If you say so, I hope you will not kill me.

Othello.   Hum!

Desdemona.   And yet I fear you; for you are fatal then
When your eyes roll so. Why I should fear I know not,
Since guiltiness I know not; but yet I feel I fear.

Othello.   Think on thy sins.

Desdemona.   They are loves I bear to you.   40

Othello.   Ay, and for that thou diest.

Desdemona.   That death's unnatural that kills for loving.
Alas! why gnaw you so your nether lip?
Some bloody passion shakes your very frame;
These are portents,[571] but yet, I hope, I hope
They do not point on me.

Othello.   Peace, and be still!

Desdemona.   I will so. What 's the matter?

Othello.   That handkerchief which I so lov'd and gave thee
Thou gav'st to Cassio.

Desdemona.   No, by my life and soul!
Send for the man and ask him.

Othello.   Sweet soul, take heed,   50
Take heed of perjury; thou 'rt on thy death-bed.

Desdemona.   Ay, but not yet to die.

Othello.   Yes, presently;[572]
Therefore confess thee freely of thy sin;
For to deny each article with oath
Cannot remove nor choke the strong conception[573]
That I do groan withal. Thou art to die.

Desdemona.   Then Lord have mercy on me!

Othello.   I say, amen.

Desdemona.   And have you mercy too! I never did
Offend you in my life; never lov'd Cassio

---

[569] Nearby.   [570] Forbid.   [571] Omens.   [572] At once.   [573] Belief.

But with such general warranty[574] of heaven   60
As I might love; I never gave him token.

Othello.   By heaven, I saw my handkerchief in 's hand.
O perjur'd woman! thou dost stone[575] my heart,
And mak'st me call what I intend to do
A murder, which I thought a sacrifice:
I saw the handkerchief.

Desdemona.   He found it then;
I never gave it him. Send for him hither;
Let him confess a truth.

Othello.   He had confessed.

Desdemona.   What, my lord?

Othello.   That he hath us'd thee.

Desdemona.   How? Unlawfully?

Othello.   Ay.   70

Desdemona.   He will not say so.

Othello.   No; his mouth is stopp'd:
Honest Iago hath ta'en order for 't.[576]

Desdemona.   O! my fear interprets. What! is he dead?

Othello.   Had all his hairs been lives, my great revenge
Had stomach[577] for them all.

Desdemona.   Alas! he is betray'd and I undone.

Othello.   Out, strumpet! Weep'st thou for him to my face?

Desdemona.   O! banish me, my lord, but kill me not!

Othello.   Down, strumpet!

Desdemona.   Kill me to-morrow; let me live to-night!   80

Othello.   Nay, if you strive,—

Desdemona.   But half an hour!

Othello.   Being done, there is no pause.

Desdemona.   But while I say one prayer!

Othello.   It is too late.   *(He smothers her.)*

Emilia *(within).*   My lord, my lord! what, ho! my lord, my lord!

Othello.   What noise is this? Not dead? Not yet quite dead?
I that am cruel am yet merciful;
I would have thee linger in thy pain.
So, so.

Emilia *(within).*   What, ho! my lord, my lord!

Othello.   Who's there?

Emilia *(within).*   O! good my lord, I would speak a word with you!   90

Othello.   Yes; 'tis Emilia: by and by.[578] She's dead.
'Tis like[579] she comes to speak of Cassio's death;
The noise was high. Ha! no more moving?

---

[574] Permission.   [575] Turn to stone.   [576] Taken steps.   [577] Appetite.   [578] I.e.,
"just a moment."   [579] Likely.

Still as the grave. Shall she come in? were 't good?[580]
I think she stirs again: no. What 's best to do?
If she come in she'll sure speak to my wife:
My wife! my wife! what wife? I have no wife;
O, insupportable! O heavy hour!
Methinks it should be now a huge eclipse
Of sun and moon, and that the affrighted globe   100
Should yawn[581] at alteration.

Emilia (*within.*)   I do beseech you
That I may speak with you, O! good my lord.

Othello.   I had forgot thee: O! come in, Emilia:
Soft, by and by: let me the curtains draw.
Where art thou?   (*Unlocks the door.*)

(*Enter Emilia*).

                        What 's the matter with thee now?

Emilia.   O! my good lord, yonder 's foul murder done.

Othello.   What! now?

Emilia.   But now, my lord.

Othello.   It is the very error[582] of the moon;
She comes more near the earth than she was wont,   110
And makes men mad.

Emilia.   Cassio, my lord, has kill'd a young Venetian
Call'd Roderigo.

Othello.   Roderigo kill'd!
And Cassio kill'd?

Emilia.   No, Cassio is not kill'd.

Othello.   Not Cassio kill'd! then murder 's out of tune,
And sweet revenge grows harsh.

Desdemona.   O! falsely, falsely murder'd.

Emilia.   Alas! what cry is that?

Othello.   That! what?

Emilia.   Out, and alas! that was my lady's voice:
Help! Help, ho! help! O lady, speak again!   120
Sweet Desdemona! O! sweet mistress, speak.

Desdemona.   A guiltless death I die.

Emilia.   O! who hath done this deed?

Desdemona.   Nobody; I myself; farewell:
Commend me to my kind lord. O! farewell!   (*Dies.*)

Othello.   Why, how should she be murder'd?

Emilia.   Alas! who knows?

Othello.   You heard her say herself it was not I.

---

[580] Would that be wise.   [581] Open up (as in an earthquake).   [582] Straying.

Emilia.   She said so; I must needs report the truth.

Othello.   She 's like a liar gone to burning hell;
  'Twas I that kill'd her.

Emilia.   O! the more angel she,   130
  And you the blacker devil.

Othello.   She turn'd to folly, and she was a whore.

Emilia.   Thou dost belie her, and thou art a devil.

Othello.   She was false as water.

Emilia.   Thou art rash as fire to say
  That she was false! O! she was heavenly true.

Othello.   Cassio did tup her; ask thy husband else.
  O! I were damn'd beneath all depth in hell
  But that I did proceed[583] upon just grounds
  To this extremity. Thy husband knew it all.

Emilia.   My husband!   140

Othello.   Thy husband.

Emilia.   That she was false to wedlock?

Othello.   Ay, with Cassio. Nay, had she been true,
  If heaven would make me such another world
  Of one entire and perfect chrysolite,[584]
  I'd not have sold her for it.

Emilia.   My husband!

Othello.   Ay, 'twas he that told me first:
  An honest man he is, and hates the slime
  That sticks on filthy deeds.

Emilia.   My husband!

Othello.   What needs this iterance,[585] woman? I say thy husband.   150

Emilia.   O mistress! villany hath made mocks with love.
  My husband say that she was false!

Othello.   He, woman;
  I say, thy husband: dost understand the word?
  My friend, thy husband, honest, honest Iago.

Emilia.   If he say so, may his pernicious soul
  Rot half a grain a day! he lies to the heart:
  She was too fond of her most filthy bargain.[586]

Othello.   Ha!

Emilia.   Do thy worst:
  This deed of thine is no more worthy heaven   160
  Than thou wast worthy her.

Othello.   Peace! you were best.[587]

Emilia.   Thou hast not half the power to do me harm
  As I have to be hurt. O gull! O dolt!

---

[583] Had I not proceeded.   [584] Topaz.   [585] Repetition.   [586] I.e., Othello.
[587] You'd better be quiet.

As ignorant as dirt! thou hast done a deed,—
I care not for thy sword; I'll make thee known,
Though I lost twenty lives. Help! help, ho! help!
The Moor has kill'd my mistress! murder! murder!

(Enter Montano, Gratiano, Iago, and others.)

Montano.   What is the matter? How now, general!
Emilia.   O! are you come, Iago? you have done well,
That men must lay their murders on your neck.   170
Gratiano.   What is the matter?
Emilia.   Disprove this villain if thou be'st a man:
He says thou told'st him that his wife was false.
I know thou didst not, thou 'rt not such a villain.
Speak, for my heart is full.
Iago.   I told him what I thought, and told no more
Than what he found himself was apt and true.
Emilia.   But did you ever tell him she was false?
Iago.   I did.
Emilia.   You told a lie, an odious damned lie;   180
Upon my soul, a lie, a wicked lie;
She false with Cassio! Did you say with Cassio?
Iago.   With Cassio, mistress. Go to, charm[588] your tongue.
Emilia.   I will not charm my tongue; I am bound to speak.
My mistress here lies murder'd in her bed.
All.   O heavens forfend!
Emilia.   And your reports have set the murder on.
Othello.   Nay, stare not, masters; it is true, indeed.
Gratiano.   'Tis a strange truth.
Montano.   O monstrous act!
Emilia.   Villany! villany! villany!   190
I think upon 't, I think, I smell 't; O villany!
I thought so then;[589] I'll kill myself for grief.
O! villany, villany!
Iago.   What! are you mad? I charge you, get you home.
Emilia.   Good gentlemen, let me have leave to speak:
'Tis proper I obey him, but not now.
Perchance, Iago, I will ne'er go home.
Othello.   O! O! O!   *(Falls on the bed.)*
Emilia.   Nay, lay thee down and roar,
For thou hast kill'd the sweetest innocent
That e'er did lift up eye.

---

[588] I.e., into silence.   [589] *Cf.* "I will be hang'd, if some eternal villain, /Some busy and insinuating rogue, /Some cogging cozening slave, to get some office, /Have not devis'd this slander . . ." (IV, ii, 130 ff.). Emilia means, not that she guessed Iago's guilt, but that she rightly guessed the slanderer's motive.

Othello.   O! she was foul.   *(Rises.)*

    I scarce did know you, uncle. There lies your niece,   201

    Whose breath, indeed, these hands have newly stopp'd:

    I know this act shows terrible and grim.

Gratiano.   Poor Desdemona! I am glad thy father's dead.

    Thy match was mortal to him, and pure grief

    Shore[590] his old thread in twain: did he live now,

    This sight would make him do a desperate turn,

    Yea, curse his better angel from his side,

    And fall to reprobation.[591]

Othello.   'Tis pitiful; but yet Iago knows   210

    That she with Cassio hath the act of shame

    A thousand times committed; Cassio confess'd it:

    And she did gratify[592] his amorous works

    With that recognizance and pledge of love

    Which I first gave her. I saw it in his hand:

    It was a handkerchief, an antique token

    My father gave my mother.

Emilia.   O heaven! O heavenly powers!

Iago.   Come, hold your peace.

Emilia.   'Twill out, 'twill out; I hold my peace, sir? no;

    No, I will speak as liberal as the north;[593]   220

    Let heaven and men and devils, let them all,

    All, all, cry shame against me, yet I'll speak.

Iago.   Be wise, and get you home.

Emilia.   I will not.

(Iago threatens to stab Emilia.)

Gratiano.   Fie!

    Your sword upon a woman!

Emilia.   O thou dull Moor! that handkerchief thou speak'st of

    I found by fortune and did give my husband;

    For often, with a solemn earnestness,

    More than, indeed, belong'd to such a trifle,

    He begg'd of me to steal it.

Iago.   Villainous whore!

Emilia.   She give it Cassio! no, alas! I found it,   230

    And I did give 't my husband.

Iago.   Filth, thou liest!

Emilia.   By heaven, I do not, I do not, gentlemen.

    O murderous coxcomb![594] what should such a fool

    Do with so good a wife?

---

[590] Cut.   [591] Damnation.   [592] Reward.   [593] I.e, the north wind (?), the supposedly free-spoken people of north England (?).   [594] Idiot.

Othello.   Are there no stones[595] in heaven
    But what serve for the thunder? Precious villain!

(He runs at Iago. Iago stabs Emilia.)

Gratiano.   The woman falls; sure, he has kill'd his wife.   *(Exit Iago.)*
Emilia.   Ay, ay; O! lay me by my mistress' side.
Gratiano.   He 's gone; but his wife 's kill'd.
Montano.   'Tis a notorious[596] villain. Take you this weapon,
    Which I have here recover'd from the Moor.   240
    Come, guard the door without; let him not pass,
    But kill him rather. I'll after that same villain,
    For 'tis a damned slave.   *(Exeunt Montano and Gratiano.)*
Othello.   I am not valiant neither,
    But every puny whipster[597] gets my sword.
    But why should honour outlive honesty?
    Let it go all.
Emilia.   What did thy song bode, lady?
    Hark, canst thou hear me? I will play the swan,
    And die in music:—
    (Sings.)   Willow, willow, willow.
    Moor, she was chaste; she lov'd thee, cruel Moor;
    So come my soul to bliss as I speak true;   250
    So speaking as I think, I die, I die.   *(Dies.)*
Othello.   I have another weapon in this chamber;
    It is a sword of Spain, the ice-brook's temper.[598]
    O! here it is. Uncle, I must come forth.
Gratiano *(within)*.   If thou attempt it, it will cost thee dear:
    Thou hast no weapon, and perforce must suffer.
Othello.   Look in upon me then, and speak with me,
    Or, naked[599] as I am, I will assault thee.

(Re-enter Gratiano.)

Gratiano.   What is the matter?
Othello.   Behold! I have a weapon;
    A better never did itself sustain   260
    Upon a soldier's thigh: I have seen the day,
    That with this little arm, and this good sword,
    I have made my way through more impediments
    Than twenty times your stop: but, O vain boast!

---

[595] I.e., thunderbolts (to strike Iago down).   [596] Notable.   [597] I.e., a small boy whipping a top.   [598] Tempered in icy water (or the reference may be to Innsbruck, famed for the quality of its steel, but this hardly fits "a sword of Spain").   [599] Unarmed.

Who can control his fate? 'tis not so now.
Be not afraid, though you do see me weapon'd;
Here is my journey's end, here is my butt,[600]
And very sea-mark of my utmost sail.[601]
Do you go back dismay'd? 'tis a lost fear;
Man but a rush[602] against Othello's breast,   270
And he retires. Where should Othello go?
Now how dost thou look now? O ill-starr'd wench!
Pale as thy smock! when we shall meet at compt,[603]
This look of thine will hurl my soul from heaven,
And fiends will snatch at it. Cold, cold, my girl!
Even like thy chastity.
O! cursed, cursed slave. Whip me, ye devils,
From the possession of this heavenly sight!
Blow me about in winds! roast me in sulphur!
Wash me in steep-down gulfs of liquid fire!   280
O Desdemona! Desdemona! dead!
Oh! Oh! Oh!

(Enter Lodovico, Montano, Cassio carried in a chair, and Officers with Iago, prisoner.)

Lodovico.   Where is this rash and most unfortunate man?
Othello.   That's he that was Othello; here I am.
Lodovico.   Where is that viper? bring the villain forth.
Othello.   I look down towards his feet;[604] but that 's a fable.
   If that thou be'st a devil, I cannot kill thee.   *(Wounds Iago.)*
Lodovico.   Wrench his sword from him.   *(Othello is disarmed.)*
Iago.   I bleed, sir; but not kill'd.
Othello.   I am not sorry neither; I'd have thee live;
   For, in my sense,[605] 'tis happiness to die.   290
Lodovico.   O thou Othello! that wert once so good,
   Fall'n in the practice[606] of a damned slave,[607]
   What shall be said to thee?
Othello.   Why, any thing:
   An honourable murderer, if you will;
   For nought did I in hate, but all in honour.
Lodovico.   This wretch hath part confess'd his villany:
   Did you and he consent in Cassio's death?
Othello.   Ay.
Cassio.   Dear general, I never gave you cause.

---

[600] Goal, end, limit.   [601] Destination of my farthest journey.   [602] Wield but a reed.
[603] On the day of judgment.   [604] I.e, for the Devil's cloven hoof.   [605] The way I
feel.   [606] Plot, machination.   [607] I.e., Iago.

Othello.   I do believe it, and I ask your pardon.   300
   Will you, I pray, demand that demi-devil
   Why he hath thus ensnar'd my soul and body?
Iago.   Demand me nothing: what you know, you know:
   From this time forth I never will speak word.
Lodoviro.   What! not to pray?
Gratiano.   Torments will ope[608] your lips.
Othello.   Well, thou dost best.
Lodovico.   Sir, you shall understand what hath befall'n,
   Which, as I think, you know not. Here is a letter
   Found in the pocket of the slain Roderigo,
   And here another; the one of them imports   310
   The death of Cassio to be undertook
   By Roderigo.
Othello.   O villain!
Cassio.   Most heathenish and most gross!
Lodovico.   Now here's another discontented paper,
   Found in his pocket too; and this, it seems,
   Roderigo meant to have sent this damned villain,
   But that, belike,[609] Iago in the interim[610]
   Came in and satisfied him.
Othello.   O the pernicious caitiff!
   How came you, Cassio, by that handkerchief
   That was my wife's?
Cassio.   I found it in my chamber;   320
   And he himself confess'd but even now
   That there he dropp'd it for a special purpose
   Which wrought to his desire.
Othello.   O fool! fool! fool!
Cassio.   There is besides in Roderigo's letter
   How he upbraids Iago that he made him
   Brave me upon the watch; whereon it came
   That I was cast:[611] and even but now he spake,
   After long seeming dead, Iago hurt him,
   Iago set him on.
Lodovico.   You must forsake this room and go with us;   330
   Your power and your command is taken off,
   And Cassio rules in Cyprus. For this slave,
   If there be any cunning cruelty
   That can torment him much and hold him long,
   It shall be his. You shall close prisoner rest,

---

[608] Open.   [609] Most likely.   [610] In the meantime.   [611] Dismissed.

Till that the nature of your fault be known
To the Venetian state. Come, bring him away.
Othello.   Soft you; a word or two before you go.
I have done the state some service, and they know 't;
No more of that. I pray you, in your letters,   340
When you shall these unlucky deeds relate,
Speak of me as I am; nothing extenuate,
Nor set down aught[612] in malice: then, must you speak
Of one that lov'd not wisely but too well;
Of one not easily jealous, but, being wrought,
Perplex'd[613] in the extreme; of one whose hand
Like the base Indian,[614] threw a pearl away
Richer. than all his tribe; of one whose subdu'd[615] eyes
Albeit unused to the melting mood,
Drop tears as fast as the Arabian trees   350
Their med'cinable gum. Set you down this;
And say besides, that in Aleppo once,
Where a malignant and a turban'd Turk
Beat a Venetian and traduc'd the state,
I took by the throat the circumcised dog,
And smote him, thus.   *(Stabs himself.)*
Lodovico.   O bloody period![616]
Gratiano.   All that's spoke is marr'd.
Othello.   I kiss'd thee ere I killed thee; no way but this.
                                        (Falling upon Desdemona.)
Killing myself to die upon a kiss.   *(Dies.)*
Cassio.   This did I fear, but thought he had no weapon;
For he was great of heart.
Lodovico *(to Iago).*   O Spartan dog!
More fell[617] than anguish, hunger, or the sea.
Look on the tragic loading of this bed;
This is thy work; the object poisons sight;
Let it be hid. Gratiano, keep the house,
And seize upon the fortunes of the Moor,
For they succeed on you. To you, lord governor,
Remains the censure of this hellish villain,
The time, the place, the torture; O! enforce it.
Myself will straight aboard, and to the state   370
This heavy act with heavy heart relate.   *(Exeunt.)*

---

[612] Anything.   [613] Distracted.   [614] The Folio reads "Iudean." Both readings denote the
foolish infidel who fails to appreciate the treasure he possesses.   [615] Overcome (by grief).
[616] Ending.   [617] Grim, cruel.

QUESTIONS

1. In what sense might it be said that Othello is responsible for his own down-fall?   **2.** Compare the speeches of Cassio and Iago in Act II, Scene 1. What does the difference in language and style reveal about their characters?   **3.** Carefully determine how much time elapses between the arrival at Cyprus and the end of the action. Can you find narrated events that could not possibly have occurred within that time? Do the chronological inconsistencies disturb you? Explain.   **4.** The first part of Act IV, Scene 2 (until Othello exits), is sometimes called the "brothel" scene. What features of Othello's language and behavior justify that designation?   **5.** Discuss the relationship between love and hate in this play.

WRITING TOPICS

1. Examine the reasons Iago gives for his actions. Do you find them consistent and convincing? Explain.   **2.** Discuss the functions of the minor characters, such as Roderigo, Bianca, and Emilia, in the play.   **3.** Othello crumbles in Act III, Scene 3, as Iago creates the jealousy that destroys Othello's self-confidence and peace of mind. Is the rapidity of Othello's emotional collapse justified? Does his being black have anything to do with his emotional turmoil?

LOVE
AND
HATE

Grosse Heidelberger Liederhandschrift "Codex Manesse" fol. 249ᵛ.

ESSAYS

The Necessary Enemy   1948

KATHERINE ANNE PORTER [1890–1980]

She is a frank, charming, fresh-hearted young woman who married for love.   1
She and her husband are one of those gay, good-looking young pairs who
ornament this modern scene rather more in profusion perhaps than ever before
in our history. They are handsome, with a talent for finding their way in their
world, they work at things that interest them, their tastes agree and their hopes.
They intend in all good faith to spend their lives together, to have children
and do well by them and each other—to be happy, in fact, which for them is
the whole point of their marriage. And all in stride, keeping their wits about
them. Nothing romantic, mind you; their feet are on the ground.

Unless they were this sort of person, there would be not much point to what   2
I wish to say; for they would seem to be an example of the high-spirited, right-
minded young whom the critics are always invoking to come forth and do their
duty and practice all those sterling old-fashioned virtues which in every generation seem to be falling into disrepair. As for virtues, these young people are
more or less on their own, like most of their kind; they get very little moral or
other aid from their society; but after three years of marriage this very contemporary young woman finds herself facing the oldest and ugliest dilemma of
marriage.

She is dismayed, horrified, full of guilt and forebodings because she is find-   3
ing out little by little that she is capable of hating her husband, whom she
loves faithfully. She can hate him at times as fiercely and mysteriously, indeed
in terribly much the same way, as often she hated her parents, her brothers
and sisters, whom she loves, when she was a child. Even then it had seemed
to her a kind of black treacherousness in her, her private wickedness that, just
the same, gave her her only private life. That was one thing her parents never
knew about her, never seemed to suspect. For it was never given a name. They
did and said hateful things to her and to each other as if by right, as if in them
it was a kind of virtue. But when they said to her, "Control your feelings," it
was never when she was amiable and obedient, only in the black times of her
hate. So it was her secret, a shameful one. When they punished her, sometimes for the strangest reasons, it was, they said, only because they loved her—

575

it was for her good. She did not believe this, but she thought herself guilty of something worse than ever they had punished her for. None of this really frightened her: the real fright came when she discovered that at times her father and mother hated each other; this was like standing on the doorsill of a familiar room and seeing in a lightning flash that the floor was gone, you were on the edge of a bottomless pit. Sometimes she felt that both of them hated her, but that passed, it was simply not a thing to be thought of, much less believed. She thought she had outgrown all this, but here it was again, an element in her own nature she could not control, or feared she could not. She would have to hide from her husband, if she could, the same spot in her feelings she had hidden from her parents, and for the same no doubt disreputable, selfish reason: she wants to keep his love.

Above all, she wants him to be absolutely confident that she loves him, for   4
that is the real truth, no matter how unreasonable it sounds, and no matter how her own feelings betray them both at times. She depends recklessly on his love; yet while she is hating him, he might very well be hating her as much or even more, and it would serve her right. But she does not want to be served right, she wants to be loved and forgiven—that is, to be sure he would forgive her anything, if he had any notion of what she had done. But best of all she would like not to have anything in her love that should ask for forgiveness. She doesn't mean about their quarrels—they are not so bad. Her feelings are out of proportion, perhaps. She knows it is perfectly natural for people to disagree, have fits of temper, fight it out; they learn quite a lot about each other that way, and not all of it disappointing either. When it passes, her hatred seems quite unreal. It always did.

Love. We are early taught to say it. I love you. We are trained to the thought   5
of it as if there were nothing else, or nothing else worth having without it, or nothing worth having which it could not bring with it. Love is taught, always by precept, sometimes by example. Then hate, which no one meant to teach us, comes of itself. It is true that if we say I love you, it may be received without doubt, for there are times when it is hard to believe. Say I hate you, and the one spoken to believes it instantly, once for all.

Say I love you a thousand times to that person afterward and mean it every   6
time, and still it does not change the fact that once we said I hate you, and meant that too. It leaves a mark on that surface love had worn so smooth with its eternal caresses. Love must be learned, and learned again and again; there is no end to it. Hate needs no instruction, but waits only to be provoked . . . hate, the unspoken word, the unacknowledged presence in the house, that faint smell of brimstone among the roses, that invisible tongue-tripper, that unkempt finger in every pie, that sudden oh-so-curiously *chilling* look—could it be boredom?—on your dear one's features, making them quite ugly. Be careful: love, perfect love, is in danger.

If it is not perfect, it is not love, and if it is not love, it is bound to be hate   7
sooner or later. This is perhaps a not too exaggerated statement of the extreme

position of Romantic Love, more especially in America, where we are all brought up on it, whether we know it or not. Romantic Love is changeless, faithful, passionate, and its sole end is to render the two lovers happy. It has no obstacles save those provided by the hazards of fate (that is to say, society), and such sufferings as the lovers may cause each other are only another word for delight: exciting jealousies, thrilling uncertainties, the ritual dance of courtship within the charmed closed circle of their secret alliance; all *real* troubles come from without, they face them unitedly in perfect confidence. Marriage is not the end but only the beginning of true happiness, cloudless, changeless to the end. That the candidates for this blissful condition have never seen an example of it, nor ever knew anyone who had, makes no difference. That is the ideal and they will achieve it.

How did Romantic Love manage to get into marriage at last, where it was most certainly never intended to be? At its highest it was tragic; the love of Héloise and Abélard.[1] At its most graceful, it was the homage of the trouvère for his lady. In its most popular form, the adulterous strayings of solidly married couples who meant to stray for their own good reasons, but at the same time do nothing to upset the property settlements or the line of legitimacy; at its most trivial, the pretty trifling of shepherd and shepherdess. | 8

This was generally condemned by church and state and a word of fear to honest wives whose mortal enemy it was. Love within the sober, sacred realities of marriage was a matter of personal luck, but in any case, private feelings were strictly a private affair having, at least in theory, no bearing whatever on the fixed practice of the rules of an institution never intended as a recreation ground for either sex. If the couple discharged their religious and social obligations, furnished forth a copious progeny, kept their troubles to themselves, maintained public civility and died under the same roof, even if not always on speaking terms, it was rightly regarded as a successful marriage. Apparently this testing ground was too severe for all but the stoutest spirits; it too was based on an ideal, as impossible in its way as the ideal Romantic Love. One good thing to be said for it is that society took responsiblity for the conditions of marriage, and the sufferers within its bonds could always blame the system, not themselves. But Romantic Love crept into the marriage bed, very stealthily, by centuries, bringing its absurd notions about love as eternal springtime and marriage as a personal adventure meant to provide personal happiness. To a Western romantic such as I, though my views have been much modified by painful experience, it still seems to me a charming work of the human imagination, and it is a pity its central notion has been taken too literally and has hardened into a convention as cramping and enslaving as the older one. The refusal to acknowledge the evils in ourselves which therefore are implicit in any human situation is as extreme and unworkable a proposition as the doctrine of total | 9

---

[1] Pierre Abélard (1079–1142), philosopher and theologian, fell in love with his student Héloise (1101?–1164?), who became his mistress and later, after a secret marriage, his wife. When Héloise's powerful uncle had Abelard emasculated as punishment, he became a monk. Héloise then became a nun.

depravity; but somewhere between them, or maybe beyond them, there does exist a possibility for reconciliation between our desires for impossible satisfactions and the simple unalterable fact that we also desire to be unhappy and that we create our own sufferings; and out of these sufferings we salvage our fragments of happiness.

Our young woman who has been taught that an important part of her human nature is not real because it makes trouble and interferes with her peace of mind and shakes her self-love, has been very badly taught; but she has arrived at a most important stage of her re-education. She is afraid her marriage is going to fail because she has not love enough to face its difficulties; and this because at times she feels a painful hostility toward her husband, and cannot admit its reality because such an admission would damage in her own eyes her view of what love should be, an absurd view, based on her vanity of power. Her hatred is real as her love is real, but her hatred has the advantage at present because it works on a blind instinctual level, it is lawless; and her love is subjected to a code of ideal conditions, impossible by their very nature of fulfillment, which prevents its free growth and deprives it of its right to recognize its human limitations and come to grips with them. Hatred is natural in a sense that love, as she conceives it, a young person brought up in the tradition of Romantic Love, is not natural at all. Yet it did not come by hazard, it is the very imperfect expression of the need of the human imagination to create beauty and harmony out of chaos, no matter how mistaken its notion of these things may be, nor how clumsy its methods. It has conjured love out of the air, and seeks to preserve it by incantations; when she spoke a vow to love and honor her husband until death, she did a very reckless thing, for it is not possible by an act of the will to fulfill such an engagement. But it was the necessary act of faith performed in defense of a mode of feeling, the statement of honorable intention to practice as well as she is able the noble, acquired faculty of love, that very mysterious overtone to sex which is the best thing in it. Her hatred is part of it, the necessary enemy and ally.

QUESTIONS

1. What is love? Examine your definition and, as best you can, discover its sources. **2.** How is it possible to hate a person you love? **3.** Explain what Porter means when she says that it is not possible by an act of will to "love and honor" a mate "until death."

WRITING TOPIC

Compare this essay with Ellen Goodman's "Being Loved Anyway" (p. 586). How do they differ? How are they similar in their essential argument?

Courtship Through the Ages   1939

JAMES THURBER   [1894–1961]

Surely nothing in the astonishing scheme of life can have nonplussed Nature   1
so much as the fact that none of the females of any of the species she created
really cared very much for the male, as such. For the past ten million years
Nature has been busily inventing ways to make the male attractive to the female, but the whole business of courtship, from the marine annelids up to
man, still lumbers heavily along, like a complicated musical comedy. I have
been reading the sad and absorbing story in Volume 6 (Cole to Dama) of the
Encyclopaedia Britannica. In this volume you can learn all about cricket, cotton, costume designing, crocodiles, crown jewels, and Coleridge, but none of
these subjects is so interesting as the Courtship of Animals, which recounts the
sorrowful lengths to which all males must go to arouse the interest of a lady.

We all know, I think, that Nature gave man whiskers and a mustache with   2
the quaint idea in mind that these would prove attractive to the female. We
all know that, far from attracting her, whiskers and mustaches only made her
nervous and gloomy, so that man had to go in for somersaults, tilting with
lances, and performing feats of parlor magic to win her attention; he also had
to bring her candy, flowers, and the furs of animals. It is common knowledge
that in spite of all these "love displays" the male is constantly being turned
down, insulted, or thrown out of the house. It is råther comforting, then, to
discover that the peacock, for all his gorgeous plumage, does not have a particularly easy time in courtship; none of the males in the world do. The first
peahen, it turned out, was only faintly stirred by her suitor's beautiful train.
She would often go quietly to sleep while he was whisking it around. The
Britannica tells us that the peacock actually had to learn a certain little trick to
wake her up and revive her interest: he had to learn to vibrate his quills so as
to make a rustling sound. In ancient times man himself, observing the ways of
the peacock, probably tried vibrating his whiskers to make a rustling sound; if
so, it didn't get him anywhere. He had to go in for something else; so, among
other things, he went in for gifts. It is not unlikely that he got this idea from
certain flies and birds who were making no headway at all with rustling sounds.

One of the flies of the family Empidae, who had tried everything, finally hit   3
on something pretty special. He contrived to make a glistening transparent balloon which was even larger than himself. Into this he would put sweetmeats
and tidbits and he would carry the whole elaborate envelope through the air to
the lady of his choice. This amused her for a time, but she finally got bored
with it. She demanded silly little colorful presents, something that you couldn't
eat but that would look nice around the house. So the male Empis had to go
around gathering flower petals and pieces of bright paper to put into his balloon. On a courtship flight a male Empis cuts quite a figure now, but he can

hardly be said to be happy. He never knows how soon the female will demand heavier presents, such as Roman coins and gold collar buttons. It seems probable that one day the courtship of the Empidae will fall down, as man's occasionally does, of its own weight.

The bowerbird is another creature that spends so much time courting the female that he never gets any work done. If all the male bowerbirds became nervous wrecks within the next ten or fifteen years, it would not surprise me. The female bowerbird insists that a playground be built for her with a specially constructed bower at the entrance. This bower is much more elaborate than an ordinary nest and is harder to build; it costs a lot more, too. The female will not come to the playground until the male has filled it up with a great many gifts: silvery leaves, red leaves, rose petals, shells, beads, berries, bones, dice, buttons, cigar bands, Christmas seals, and the Lord knows what else. When the female finally condescends to visit the playground, she is in a coy and silly mood and has to be chased in and out of the bower and up and down the playground before she will quit giggling and stand still long enough even to shake hands. The male bird is, of course, pretty well done in before the chase starts, because he has worn himself out hunting for eyeglass lenses and begonia blossoms. I imagine that many a bowerbird, after chasing a female for two or three hours, says the hell with it and goes home to bed. Next day, of course, he telephones someone else and the same trying ritual is gone through with again. A male bowerbird is as exhausted as a night-club habitué before he is out of his twenties.

The male fiddler crab has a somewhat easier time, but it can hardly be said that he is sitting pretty. He has one enormously large and powerful claw, usually brilliantly colored, and you might suppose that all he had to do was reach out and grab some passing cutie. The very earliest fiddler crabs may have tried this, but, if so, they got slapped for their pains. A female fiddler crab will not tolerate any caveman stuff; she never has and she doesn't intend to start now. To attract a female, a fiddler crab has to stand on tiptoe and brandish his claw in the air. If any female in the neighborhood is interested—and you'd be surprised how many are not—she comes over and engages him in light badinage, for which he is not in the mood. As many as a hundred females may pass the time of day with him and go on about their business. By nightfall of an average courting day, a fiddler crab who has been standing on tiptoe for eight or ten hours waving a heavy claw in the air is in pretty sad shape. As in the case of the male of all species, however, he gets out of bed next morning, dashes some water on his face, and tries again.

The next time you encounter a male web-spinning spider, stop and reflect that he is too busy worrying about his love life to have any desire to bite you. Male web-spinning spiders have a tougher life than any other males in the animal kingdom. This is because the female web-spinning spiders have very poor eyesight. If a male lands on a female's web, she kills him before he has time to lay down his cane and gloves, mistaking him for a fly or a bumblebee who has tumbled into her trap. Before the species figured out what to do about this, millions of males were murdered by ladies they called on. It is the nature of spiders to perform a little dance in front of the female, but before a male spinner could get near enough for the female to see who he was and what he was up to, she would lash out at him with a flat-iron or a pair of garden shears. One night, nobody knows when, a very bright male spinner lay awake worrying about calling on a lady who had been killing suitors right and left. It came to him that this business of dancing as a love display wasn't getting anybody anywhere except the grave. He decided to go in for web-twitching, or strand-vibrating. The next day he tried it on one of the nearsighted girls. Instead of dropping in on her suddenly, he stayed outside the web and began monkeying with one of its strands. He twitched it up and down and in and out with such a lilting rhythm that the female was charmed. The serenade worked beautifully; the female let him live. The *Britannica's* spider-watchers, however, report that this system is not always successful. Once in a while, even now, a female will fire three bullets into a suitor or run him through with a kitchen knife. She keeps threatening him from the moment he strikes the first low notes on the outside strings, but usually by the time he has got up to the high notes played around the center of the web, he is going to town and she spares his life.

Even the butterfly, as handsome a fellow as he is, can't always win a mate   7
merely by fluttering around and showing off. Many butterflies have to have scent scales on their wings. Hepialus carries a powder puff in a perfumed pouch. He throws perfume at the ladies when they pass. The male tree cricket, Oecanthus, goes Hepialus one better by carrying a tiny bottle of wine with him and giving drinks to such doxies as he has designs on. One of the male snails throws darts to entertain the girls. So it goes, through the long list of animals, from the bristle worm and his rudimentary dance steps to man and his gift of diamonds and sapphires. The golden-eye drake raises a jet of water with his feet as he flies over a lake; Hepialus has his powder puff, Oecanthus his wine bottle, man his etchings. It is a bright and melancholy story, the age-old desire of the male for the female, the age-old desire of the female to be amused and entertained. Of all the creatures on earth, the only males who could be figured as putting an irony into their courtship are the grebes and certain other diving birds. Every now and then a courting grebe slips quietly down to the bottom of a lake and then, with a mighty "Whoosh!" pops out suddenly a few feet from his girl friend, splashing water all over. She seems to be persuaded that this is a purely loving display, but I like to think that the grebe always has a faint hope of drowning her or scaring her to death.

I will close this investigation into the mournful burdens of the male with   8
Britannica's story about a certain Argus pheasant. It appears that the Argus displays himself in front of a female who stands perfectly still without moving a feather. . . . The male Argus the *Britannica* tells about was confined in a cage with a female of another species, a female who kept moving around, emptying ashtrays and fussing with lampshades all the time the male was showing off his talents. Finally, in disgust, he stalked away and began displaying in front of his water trough. He reminds me of a certain male *(Homo sapiens)* of

my acquaintance who one night after dinner asked his wife to put down her detective magazine so that he could read a poem of which he was very fond. She sat quietly enough until he was well into the middle of the thing, intoning with great ardor and intensity. Then suddenly there came a sharp, disconcerting *slap!* It turned out that all during the male's display, the female had been intent on a circling mosquito and had finally trapped it between the palms of her hands. The male in this case did not stalk away and display in front of a water trough; he went over to Tim's and had a flock of drinks and recited the poem to the fellas. I am sure they all told bitter stories of their own about how their displays had been interrupted by females. I am also sure that they all ended up singing "Honey, Honey, Bless Your Heart."

QUESTIONS

1. Here is a direct quote from the *Encyclopaedia Britannica* on the courtship of bowerbirds: "These birds clear playgrounds, in which special bowers (quite unlike nests) are constructed by some species. In the playground (if a bower is made opposite its entrance) is deposited a collection of bright objects. The objects differ with the species; they may include silvery leaves, flowers, shells, berries, bones, etc. When the female visits the playground, the male pursues her amorously round it (through the bower, when present). Here it appears that the bright objects collected serve instead of the brilliant plumage of the male birds to stimulate the female." Compare Thurber's account in the fourth paragraph. In what way does it differ from the description in the encyclopaedia?   **2.**   What devices does Thurber use to remind his readers that he is speaking of humans as well as animals and insects?   **3.**   What assumptions about the nature of the relationship between men and women is this essay based on? Explain.

WRITING TOPIC
What makes this essay funny?

The Iks

LEWIS THOMAS [b. 1913]

The small tribe of Iks, formerly nomadic hunters and gatherers in the mountain valleys of northern Uganda, have become celebrities, literary symbols of the ultimate fate of disheartened, heartless mankind at large. Two disastrously conclusive things happened to them: the government decided to have a national park, so they were compelled by law to give up hunting in the valleys and become farmers on poor hillside soil, and then they were visited for two years by an anthropologist who detested them and wrote a book about them.

The message of the book is that the Iks have transformed themselves into an irreversibly disagreeable collection of unattached, brutish creatures, totally selfish and loveless, in response to the dismantling of their traditional culture. Moreover, this is what the rest of us are like in our inner selves, and we will all turn into Iks when the structure of our society comes all unhinged.

The argument rests, of course, on certain assumptions about the core of human beings, and is necessarily speculative. You have to agree in advance that man is fundamentally a bad lot, out for himself alone, displaying such graces as affection and compassion only as learned habits. If you take this view, the story of the Iks can be used to confirm it. These people seem to be living together, clustered in small, dense villages, but they are really solitary, unrelated individuals with no evident use for each other. They talk, but only to make ill-tempered demands and cold refusals. They share nothing. They never sing. They turn the children out to forage as soon as they can walk, and desert the elders to starve whenever they can, and the foraging children snatch food from the mouths of the helpless elders. It is a mean society.

They breed without love or even casual regard. They defecate on each other's doorsteps. They watch their neighbors for signs of misfortune, and only then do they laugh. In the book they do a lot of laughing, having so much bad luck. Several times they even laughed at the anthropologist, who found this especially repellent (one senses, between the lines, that the scholar is not himself the world's luckiest man). Worse, they took him into the family, snatched his food, defecated on his doorstep, and hooted dislike at him. They gave him two bad years.

It is a depressing book. If, as he suggests, there is only Ikness at the center of each of us, our sole hope for hanging onto the name of humanity will be in endlessly mending the structure of our society, and it is changing so quickly and completely that we may never find the threads in time. Meanwhile, left to ourselves alone, solitary, we will become the same joyless, zestless, untouching lone animals.

But this may be too narrow a view. For one thing, the Iks are extraordinary. They are absolutely astonishing, in fact. The anthropologist has never seen people like them anywhere, nor have I. You'd think, if they were simply examples of the common essence of mankind, they'd seem more recognizable. Instead, they are bizarre, anomalous. I have known my share of peculiar, difficult, nervous, grabby people, but I've never encountered any genuinely, consistently detestable human beings in all my life. The Iks sound more like abnormalities, maladies.

I cannot accept it. I do not believe that the Iks are representative of isolated, revealed man, unobscured by social habits. I believe their behavior is something extra, something laid on. This unremitting, compulsive repellence is a kind of complicated ritual. They must have learned to act this way; they copied it, somehow.   7

I have a theory, then. The Iks have gone crazy.   8

The solitary Ik, isolated in the ruins of an exploded culture, has built a new   9
defense for himself. If you live in an unworkable society you can make up one of your own, and this is what the Iks have done. Each Ik has become a group, a one-man tribe on its own, a constituency.

Now everything falls into place. This is why they do seem, after all, vaguely   10
familiar to all of us. We've seen them before. This is precisely the way groups of one size or another, ranging from committees to nations, behave. It is, of course, this aspect of humanity that has lagged behind the rest of evolution, and this is why the Ik seems so primitive. In his absolute selfishness, his incapacity to give anything away, no matter what, he is a successful committee. When he stands at the door of his hut, shouting insults at his neighbors in a loud harangue, he is a city addressing another city.

Cities have all the Ik characteristics. They defecate on doorsteps, in rivers   11
and lakes, their own or anyone else's. They leave rubbish. They detest all neighboring cities, give nothing away. They even build institutions for deserting elders out of sight.

Nations are the most Iklike of all. No wonder the Iks seem familiar. For   12
total greed, rapacity, heartlessness, and irresponsibility there is nothing to match a nation. Nations, by law, are solitary, self-centered, withdrawn into themselves. There is no such thing as affection between nations, and certainly no nation ever loved another. They bawl insults from their doorsteps, defecate into whole oceans, snatch all the food, survive by detestation, take joy in the bad luck of others, celebrate the death of others, live for the death of others.

That's it, and I shall stop worrying about the book. It does not signify that   13
man is a sparse, inhuman thing at his center. He's all right. It only says what we've always known and never had enough time to worry about, that we haven't yet learned how to stay human when assembled in masses. The Ik, in his despair, is acting out this failure, and perhaps we should pay closer attention. Nations have themselves become too frightening to think about, but we might learn some things by watching these people.

QUESTIONS

1. To what, in the "civilized" world, do the Iks correspond? Is this essay about the Iks or about us? Explain.   **2.**   What is Thomas's view of human nature in this essay? How does it differ from the anthropologist's?

WRITING TOPIC

Analyze the sentence structure of the next to last paragraph. The paragraph defines *nation* with sentences of disparate length and forcefulness. Describe the relationship between the paragraph's rhetorical structure (i.e., sentence length, rhythm, balance, sequence of assertions) and the message it conveys.

Being Loved Anyway 1980

ELLEN GOODMAN [b. 1941]

From time to time, my Uncle Mike likes to pass on the wisdom of one gener- 1
ation to another. In his own fashion.

On the subject of enduring love, for example, he and my aunt are role 2
models of believability. They like each other. They have a good time together.
And they have managed it for roughly forty-one years.

So, when someone asks him the secret, he is more than willing to share the 3
fact that he modeled his own success on his father's.

"My father would get up in the morning, look in the mirror and say, 'You're 4
no bargain.' "

This, I think, would make a hell of a Valentine. 5

Maybe I'm just tired of people who pick at each other's imperfections like 6
pimples. Maybe I know too many people trying to figure out if their mate is
living up to expectations. Maybe I've met too many "6"s who think they are
slumming with anything less than a "10." But I think he is on to something.

If you start your day looking your own flaws in the face, you might work up 7
a pretty good appetite of gratitude before breakfast. If you know you're no bargain in the morning, by evening you could be atwitter with appreciation for
someone who actually loves you anyway.

From my own, not particularly vast, experience and my uncle's advice, it 8
seems that this is the glue of any long-term attachment: Being Loved Anyway.

There are at least two ingredients to the sticky stuff: (1) you have to know 9
your own worst, and (2) you have to find someone who also knows it, but
doesn't think it's all that awful. Being Loved Anyway, you see, is not being
regarded as perfect but being accepted as imperfect.

I don't suppose that sounds very romantic. Other people may want sonnets 10
to their perfection and flowers for their pedestal. They may want doilies of
adoration.

But frankly, adoration would make me nervous. I'd keep waiting to be dis- 11
covered.

I have a friend who got involved with a man who was in awe of her. It was 12
outrageously flattering—for about three months. The problem was, she said,
she couldn't yell at her children in front of him. The problem was, she had to
keep washing her hair. She simply couldn't live up to it.

To this day, she refuses to trust the durability of any relationship in which 13
she is still regularly shaving her legs.

I have another friend who, as they say in the shrink trade, has difficulty 14
getting close. He is sure that someone will find out that his heart of darkness
is made of mud, rather than chocolate.

But because he never lets anyone in, he never trusts anyone in love with 15 him, since, by definition, she doesn't know him, because if she did know him, she would reject him. You get the picture.

If there is a constant in life, it must be the human fear of being unlovable. In a recent interview, Phil Donahue was asked for the fourth time what he wanted from love and sighed, finally, "Sometimes I think I invented insecurity." Baloney.

Insecurity was invented by the first kid who was caught being bad and asked his mother, "Do you love me anyway?"

The kid lives in all of us. The kid who is sure she won't be loved if she is bad. This kid is the one making the decision every day between the safety of hiding and the risk of discovery and the security of Being Loved Anyway.

I suppose it cuts both ways. We can't trust our own feelings for someone else until we've been "dis-illusioned," embarrassed, hurt a time or two—and have come out caring.

Now I don't want to make this negative. We shouldn't send all our Valentines to those who love us at our worst. Or those whose worst we love. I know people who have been loved for their weaknesses and hated for their strengths, and it was perfectly dreadful.

We are told that people stay in love because of chemistry, or because they remain intrigued with each other, because of many kindnesses, because of luck. I also suspect that laughing together is vastly underrated.

But part of it has got to be forgiveness and gratefulness. The understanding that, so, you're no bargain, but you love and you are loved. Anyway.

QUESTIONS
1. This brief essay focuses on the differences between the mask we hide behind in public and our self-awareness. What are those differences? **2.** Examine the concrete details Goodman uses to support her abstract assertions about love and relationships. How do those details function in the essay? **3.** In paragraph 19, Goodman uses the word "dis-illusioned." Why does she insert the hyphen?

WRITING TOPIC
Describe your own conception of love. Does Goodman's view alter that conception? If so, how? If not, why not?

Love and Hate

QUESTIONS AND WRITING TOPICS

1. Every story in this section incorporates some sexual element. Distinguish among the functions served by the sexual aspects of the stories. **Writing Topic:** Contrast the function of sexuality in Lawrence's "The Horse Dealer's Daughter" and Faulkner's "Dry September."

2. Examine the works in this section in terms of the support they provide for the contention that love and hate are closely related emotions. **Writing Topic:** Discuss the relationship among race, love, and hate in Shakespeare's *Othello* and Faulkner's "Dry September."

3. What images are characteristically associated with love in the prose and poetry of this section? What images are associated with hate? What insight, if any, does this use of figurative language provide into our cultural evaluations of nature? **Writing Topic:** Compare the image patterns in Shakespeare's sonnets 18 and 130 with the image patterns in Donne's "A Valediction: Forbidding Mourning."

4. The Greeks have three words that can be translated by the English word *love: eros, agape,* and *philia.* Discover the differences among these three manifestations of love. **Writing Topic:** For each of these three types of human love, find a story or poem that you think is representative. In analyzing each work, discuss the extent to which the primary notion of love being addressed or celebrated is tempered by the other two types.

5. Blake's "A Poison Tree," Dickinson's "Mine Enemy Is Growing Old," Plath's "Daddy," and Thomas's "The Iks" all deal with hatred. Distinguish among the sources of the hatred expressed in these works. **Writing Topic:** Compare and contrast the source of the hatred in two of these works.

6. Chopin's "The Storm" and Moravia's "The Chase" deal with infidelity. Distinguish between the attitudes toward infidelity developed by these stories. **Writing Topic:** Describe the effects of marital infidelity on the life of the major character in each story.

7. Mason's "Shiloh" and Sexton's poem "The Farmer's Wife" deal with failed marriages. Why do they fail? **Writing Topic:** Compare and contrast the sources of the marital conflict in these pieces.

8. Moravia's "The Chase" and Shaw's "The Girls in Their Summer Dresses" deal with jealousy. Contrast both the sources of the jealousy and the resolution of the problems caused by jealousy in the stories. **Writing Topic:** Who in your opinion has the better reason for being jealous, the husband in "The Chase" or the wife in "The Girls in Their Summer Dresses"? Explain.

9. Define and discuss the differences in the description of love in such essays as Porter's "The Necessary Enemy" and Goodman's "Being Loved Anyway" and such stories as Lawrence's "The Horse Dealer's Daughter" and Chopin's "The Storm." **Writing Topic:** Compare and contrast the attitudes toward love that emerge from one of these essays and one of these stories.

10. Which works in this section treat love or hate in a way that corresponds with your own experience or conception of those emotional states? Which contradict your experience? **Writing Topic:** Isolate, in each case, the elements in the work that provoke your response and discuss them in terms of their "truth' or "falsity."

The Presence of Death

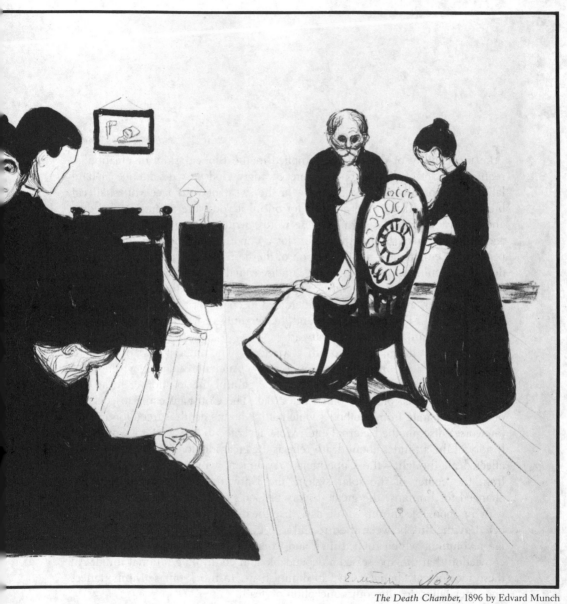

The Death Chamber, 1896 by Edvard Munch

The inevitability of death is not implied in the Biblical story of creation; it required an act of disobedience before an angry God passed sentence of hard labor and mortality on humankind: "In the sweat of your face you shall eat bread till you return to the ground, for out of it you were taken; you are dust and to dust you shall return." These words, written down some 2,800 years ago, preserve an ancient explanation for a condition of life that yet remains persistently enigmatic—the dissolution of the flesh and the personality as accident or age culminates in death, the "undiscovered country, from whose bourn / No traveller returns." Though we cannot know what death is like, from earliest times men and women have attempted to characterize death, to cultivate beliefs about it. The mystery of it and the certainty of it make death, in every age, an important theme for literary art.

Beliefs about the nature of death vary widely. The ancient Jews of the Pentateuch reveal no conception of immortality. Ancient Buddhist writings describe death as a mere translation from one painful life to another in an ongoing expiation that only the purest can avoid. The Christians came to conceive of a soul, separate from the body, which at the body's death is freed for a better (or worse) disembodied eternal life. More recently in the western world, the history of the attitudes about death reflects the great ideological revolutions that affected all thought—the Copernician revolution, which displaced the earth from the center of the solar system; the Darwinian revolution, which exchanged for humans, the greatest glory of God's creation, an upright primate with an opposable thumb whose days, like the dinosaur's, are likely to be numbered by the flux between the fire and ice of geological history; and the Freudian revolution, which robbed men and women of their proudest certainty, the conviction that they possessed a dependable and controlling rational mind. All these ideological changes serve to diminish us, to mock our self-importance, and, inevitably, to alter our conception of death.

But despite the impact of intellectual history, death remains invested with a special awe—perhaps because it infallibly mediates between all human differences. For the churchly, death, like birth and marriage, is the occasion for solemn ritual that reaffirms for the congregation its own communal life and the promise of a better life hereafter—though the belief in immortality does not eliminate sadness and regret. For those for whom there is no immortality, death is nonetheless a ceremonial affair, full of awe, for nothing human is so purely defined, so utterly important, as life ended. Furthermore, both the religious and the secular see death in moral terms. For both, the killer is hateful. For both, there are some deaths that are deserved, some deaths that human weakness makes inevitable, some deaths that are outrageously unfair. For both, there are courageous deaths, which exalt the community, and cowardly deaths too embarrassing to recognize.

Death sometimes comes, one feels, as a release from a dark and menacing world. And this conception of *release* from the prison of life animates much of the essentially optimistic religious poetry of death—John Donne's sonnet "Death, Be Not Proud" is an outstanding example. Another view that establishes death as the great leveler, bringing kings and emperors to that selfsame dust, reassures the impoverished when they contrast their misery with the wealth of the mighty.

That leveling aspect of death, apparent in Shelley's "Ozymandias," leads easily and logically to the tradition wherein life itself is made absurd by the fact of death. You may remember that Macbeth finally declares that life is "a tale / Told by an idiot, full of sound and fury, / Signifying nothing." And the contemplation of suicide, which the pain and absurdity of life would seem to commend, provokes such diverse responses as Arna Bontemp's "A Summer Tragedy" and Edward Arlington Robinson's ironic "Richard Cory." Some rage against death—Dylan Thomas in "Do Not Go Gentle into That Good Night"; others caution a quiet resignation—Frost in "After Apple-Picking" and Catherine Davis in her answer to Thomas, "After a Time." Much writing about death is elegiac; it speaks the melancholy response of the living to the fact of death as in Donne's "Meditation 17" and such poems as Gray's "Elegy Written in a Country Churchyard," Housman's "To an Athlete Dying Young," Ransom's "Bells for John Whiteside's Daughter," and Roethke's "Elegy for Jane."

In short, literary treatments of death display immense diversity. Selzer's essay reveals the rage of a dying patient, while in Tolstoy's "The Death of Iván Ilých," dying leads to a redemptive awareness. In Malamud's tragicomic "Idiots First," the protagonist insists upon and wins fair treatment from death, and in Cummings's "nobody loses all the time," the comic lightens the weight of death. The inevitability of death and the way one confronts it, paradoxically, lend to life its meaning and its value.

THE
PRESENCE
OF DEATH

Sacred to Washington, 1822 by Margarett Smith

FICTION

The Death of Iván Ilých*   1886

LEO TOLSTOY [1828–1910]

CHAPTER I

During an interval in the Melvínski trial in the large building of the Law Courts the members and public prosecutor met in Iván Egorovich Shébek's private room, where the conversation turned on the celebrated Krasóvski case. Fëdor Vasílievich warmly maintained that it was not subject to their jurisdiction, Iván Egórovich maintained the contrary, while Peter Ivánovich, not having entered into the discussion at the start, took no part in it but looked through the *Gazette* which had just been handed in.

"Gentlemen," he said, "Iván Ilých has died!"

"You don't say so!"

"Here, read it yourself," replied Peter Ivánovich, handing Fëdor Vasílievich the paper still damp from the press. Surrounded by a black border were the words: "Praskóvya Fëdorovna Goloviná, with profound sorrow, informs relatives and friends of the demise of her beloved husband Iván Ilých Golovín, Member of the Court of Justice, which occurred on February the 4th of this year 1882. The funeral will take place on Friday at one o'clock in the afternoon."

Iván Ilých had been a colleague of the gentlemen present and was liked by them all. He had been ill for some weeks with an illness said to be incurable. His post had been kept open for him, but there had been conjectures that in case of his death Alexéev might receive his appointment, and that either Vínnikov or Shtábel would succeed Alexéev. So on receiving the news of Iván Ilých's death the first thought of each of the gentlemen in that private room was of the changes and promotions it might occasion among themselves or their acquaintances.

"I shall be sure to get Shtábel's place or Vínnikov's," thought Fëdor Vasílievich. "I was promised that long ago, and the promotion means an extra eight hundred rubles a year for me besides the allowance."

"Now I must apply for my brother-in-law's transfer from Kalúga," thought

---

* Translated by Aylmer Maude.

Peter Ivánovich. "My wife will be very glad, and then she won't be able to say that I never do anything for her relations."

"I thought he would never leave his bed again," said Peter Ivánovich aloud. "It's very sad."

"But what really was the matter with him?"

"The doctors couldn't say—at least they could, but each of them said something different. When last I saw him I thought he was getting better."

"And I haven't been to see him since the holidays. I always meant to go."

"Had he any property?"

"I think his wife had a little—but something quite trifling."

"We shall have to go to see her, but they live so terribly far away."

"Far away from you, you mean. Everything's far away from your place."

"You see, he never can forgive my living on the other side of the river," said Peter Ivánovich, smiling at Shébek. Then, still talking of the distances between different parts of the city, they returned to the Court.

Besides considerations as to the possible transfers and promotions likely to result from Iván Ilých's death, the mere fact of the death of a near acquaintance aroused, as usual, in all who heard of it the complacent feeling that "it is he who is dead and not I."

Each one thought or felt, "Well, he's dead but I'm alive!" But the more intimate of Iván Ilých's acquaintances, his so-called friends, could not help thinking also that they would now have to fulfill the very tiresome demands of propriety by attending the funeral service and paying a visit of condolence to the widow.

Fëdor Vasílievich and Peter Ivánovich had been his nearest acquaintances. Peter Ivánovich had studied law with Iván Ilých and had considered himself to be under obligations to him.

Having told his wife at dinner-time of Iván Ilých's death, and of his conjecture that it might be possible to get her brother transferred to their circuit, Peter Ivánovich sacrificed his usual nap, put on his evening clothes, and drove to Iván Ilých's house.

At the entrance stood a carriage and two cabs. Leaning against the wall in the hall downstairs near the cloak-stand was a coffin-lid covered with cloth of gold, ornamented with gold cord and tassels, that had been polished up with metal powder. Two ladies in black were taking off their fur cloaks. Peter Ivánovich recognized one of them as Iván Ilých's sister, but the other was a stranger to him. His colleague Schwartz was just coming downstairs, but on seeing Peter Ivánovich enter he stopped and winked at him, as if to say: "Iván Ilých has made a mess of things—not like you and me."

Schwartz's face with his Piccadilly whiskers, and his slim figure in evening dress, had as usual an air of elegant solemnity which contrasted with the playfulness of his character and had a special piquancy here, or so it seemed to Peter Ivánovich.

Peter Ivánovich allowed the ladies to precede him and slowly followed them upstairs. Schwartz did not come down but remained where he was, and Peter

Ivánovich understood that he wanted to arrange where they should play bridge that evening. The ladies went upstairs to the widow's room, and Schwartz with seriously compressed lips but a playful look in his eyes, indicated by a twist of his eye-brows the room to the right where the body lay.

Peter Ivánovich, like everyone else on such occasions, entered feeling uncertain what he would have to do. All he knew was that at such times it is always safe to cross oneself. But he was not quite sure whether one should make obeisances while doing so. He therefore adopted a middle course. On entering the room he began crossing himself and made a slight movement resembling a bow. At the same time, as far as the motion of his head and arm allowed, he surveyed the room. Two young men—apparently nephews, one of whom was a high school pupil—were leaving the room, crossing themselves as they did so. An old woman was standing motionless, and a lady with strangely arched eyebrows was saying something to her in a whisper. A vigorous, resolute Church Reader, in a frock-coat, was reading something in a loud voice with an expression that precluded any contradiction. The butler's assistant, Gerásim, stepping lightly in front of Peter Ivánovich, was strewing something on the floor. Noticing this, Peter Ivánovich was immediately aware of a faint odour of a decomposing body.

The last time he had called on Iván Ilých, Peter Ivánovich had seen Gerásim in the study. Iván Ilých had been particularly fond of him and he was performing the duty of a sick nurse.

Peter Ivánovich continued to make the sign of the cross slightly inclining his head in an intermediate direction between the coffin, the Reader, and the icons on the table in a corner of the room. Afterwards, when it seemed to him that this movement of his arm in crossing himself had gone on too long, he stopped and began to look at the corpse.

The dead man lay, as dead men always lie, in a specially heavy way, his rigid limbs sunk in the soft cushions of the coffin, with the head forever bowed on the pillow. His yellow waxen brow with bald patches over his sunken temples was thrust up in the way peculiar to the dead, the protruding nose seeming to press on the upper lip. He was much changed and had grown even thinner since Peter Ivánovich had last seen him, but, as is always the case with the dead, his face was handsomer and above all more dignified than when he was alive. The expression on the face said that what was necessary had been accomplished, and accomplished rightly. Besides this there was in that expression a reproach and a warning to the living. This warning seemed to Peter Ivánovich out of place, or at least not applicable to him. He felt a certain discomfort and so he hurriedly crossed himself once more and turned and went out of the door—too hurriedly and too regardless of propriety, as he himself was aware.

Schwartz was waiting for him in the adjoining room with legs spread wide apart and both hands toying with his top-hat behind his back. The mere sight of that playful, well-groomed, and elegant figure refreshed Peter Ivánovich. He felt that Schwartz was above all these happenings and would not surrender to any depressing influences. His very look said that this incident of a church service for Iván Ilých could not be a sufficient reason for infringing the order of the session—in other words, that it would certainly not prevent his unwrapping a new pack of cards and shuffling them that evening while a footman placed four fresh candles on the table: in fact, there was no reason for supposing that this incident would hinder their spending the evening agreeably. Indeed he said this in a whisper as Peter Ivánovich passed him, proposing that they should meet for a game at Fëdor Vasílievich's. But apparently Peter Ivánovich was not destined to play bridge that evening. Praskóvya Fëdorovna (a short, fat woman who despite all efforts to the contrary had continued to broaden steadily from her shoulders downwards and who had the same extraordinarily arched eyebrows as the lady who had been standing by the coffin), dressed all in black, her head covered with lace, came out of her own room with some other ladies, conducted them to the room where the dead body lay, and said: "The service will begin immediately. Please go in."

Schwartz, making an indefinite bow, stood still, evidently neither accepting nor declining this invitation. Praskóvya Fëdorovna recognizing Peter Ivánovich, sighed, went close up to him, took his hand, and said: "I know you were a true friend to Iván Ilých . . . " and looked at him awaiting some suitable response. And Peter Ivánovich knew that, just as it had been the right thing to cross himself in that room, so what he had to do here was to press her hand, sigh, and say, "Believe me . . . " So he did all this and as he did it felt that the desired result had been achieved: that both he and she were touched.

"Come with me. I want to speak to you before it begins," said the widow. "Give me your arm."

Peter Ivánovich gave her his arm and they went to the inner rooms, passing Schwartz who winked at Peter Ivánovich compassionately.

"That does for our bridge! Don't object if we find another player. Perhaps you can cut in when you do escape," said his playful look.

Peter Ivánovich sighed still more deeply and despondently, and Praskóvya Fëdorovna pressed his arm gratefully. When they reached the drawing-room, upholstered in pink cretonne and lighted by a dim lamp, they sat down at the table—she on a sofa and Peter Ivánovich on a low pouffe, the springs of which yielded spasmodically under his weight. Praskóvya Fëdorovna had been on the point of warning him to take another seat, but felt that such a warning was out of keeping with her present condition and so changed her mind. As he sat down on the pouffe Peter Ivánovich recalled how Iván Ilých had arranged this room and had consulted him regarding this pink cretonne with green leaves. The whole room was full of furniture and knick-knacks, and on her way to the sofa the lace of the widow's black shawl caught on the carved edge of the table. Peter Ivánovich rose to detach it, and the springs of the pouffe, relieved of his weight, rose also and gave him a push. The widow began detaching her shawl herself, and Peter Ivánovich again sat down, suppressing the rebellious springs of the pouffe under him. But the widow had not quite freed herself and Peter Ivánovich got up again, and again the pouffe rebelled and even creaked. When this was all over she took out a clean cambric handkerchief and began to weep. The episode with the shawl and the struggle with the pouffe had cooled Peter Iván-ovich's emotions and he sat there with a sullen look on his face. This awkward situation was interrupted by Sokolóv, Iván Ilých's butler, who came to report that the plot in the cemetery that Praskóvya Fëdorovna had chosen would cost two hundred rubles. She stopped weeping and, looking at Peter Ivánovich with the air of a victim, remarked in French that it was very hard for her. Peter Ivánovich made a silent gesture signifying his full conviction that it must indeed be so.

"Please smoke," she said in a magnanimous yet crushed voice, and turned to discuss with Sokolóv the price of the plot for the grave.

Peter Ivánovich while lighting his cigarette heard her inquiring very circum-stantially into the price of different plots in the cemetery and finally decide which she would take. When that was done she gave instructions about engaging the choir. Sokólov then left the room.

"I look after everything myself," she told Peter Ivánovich, shifting the albums that lay on the table; and noticing that the table was endangered by his cigarette-ash, she immediately passed him an ashtray, saying as she did so: "I consider it an affectation to say that my grief prevents my attending to practical affairs. On the contrary, if anything can—I won't say console me, but—distract me, it is seeing to everything concerning him." She again took out her handkerchief as if preparing to cry, but suddenly, as if mastering her feeling, she shook herself and began to speak calmly. "But there is something I want to talk to you about."

Peter Ivánovich bowed, keeping control of the springs of the pouffe, which immediately began quivering under him.

"He suffered terribly the last few days."

"Did he?" said Peter Ivánovich.

"Oh, terribly! He screamed unceasingly, not for minutes but for hours. For the last three days he screamed incessantly. It was unendurable. I cannot un-derstand how I bore it; you could hear him three rooms off. Oh, what I have suffered!"

"Is it possible that he was conscious all that time?" asked Peter Ivánovich.

"Yes," she whispered. "To the last moment. He took leave of us a quarter of an hour before he died, and asked us to take Volódya away."

The thought of the sufferings of this man he had known so intimately, first as a merry little boy, then as a school-mate, and later as a grown-up colleague, suddenly struck Peter Ivánovich with horror, despite an unpleasant conscious-ness of his own and this woman's dissimulation. He again saw that brow, and that nose pressing down on the lip, and felt afraid for himself.

"Three days of frightful suffering and then death! Why, that might suddenly, at any time, happen to me," he thought, and for a moment felt terrified. But—he did not himself know how—the customary reflection at once occurred to him that this had happened to Iván Ilých and not to him, and that it should not and could not happen to him, and that to think that it could would be yielding to depression which he ought not to do, as Schwartz's expression plainly showed. After which reflection Peter Ivánovich felt reassured, and began to ask with interest about the details of Iván Ilých's death, as though death was an accident natural to Iván Ilých but certainly not to himself.

After many details of the really dreadful physical sufferings Iván Ilých had endured (which details he learnt only from the effect those sufferings had produced on Praskóvya Fëdorovna's nerves) the widow apparently found it necessary to get to business.

"Oh, Peter Ivánovich, how hard it is! How terribly, terribly hard!" and she again began to weep.

Peter Ivánovich sighed and waited for her to finish blowing her nose. When she had done so he said, "Believe me . . ." and she again began talking and brought out what was evidently her chief concern with him—namely, to question him as to how she could obtain a grant of money from the government on the occasion of her husband's death. She made it appear that she was asking Peter Ivánovich's advice about her pension, but he soon saw that she already knew about that to the minutest detail, more even than he did himself. She knew how much could be got out of the government in consequence of her husband's death, but wanted to find out whether she could not possibly extract something more. Peter Ivánovich tried to think of some means of doing so, but after reflecting for a while and, out of propriety, condemning the government for its niggardliness, he said he thought that nothing more could be got. Then she sighed and evidently began to devise means of getting rid of her visitor. Noticing this, he put out his cigarette, rose, pressed her hand, and went out into the anteroom.

In the dining-room where the clock stood that Iván Ilých had liked so much and had bought at an antique shop, Peter Ivánovich met a priest and a few acquaintances who had come to attend the service, and he recognized Iván Ilých's daughter, a handsome young woman. She was in black and her slim figure appeared slimmer than ever. She had a gloomy, determined, almost angry expression, and bowed to Peter Ivánovich as though he were in some way to blame. Behind her, with the same offended look, stood a wealthy young man, an examining magistrate, whom Peter Ivánovich also knew and who was her fiancé, as he had heard. He bowed mournfully to them and was about to pass into the death-chamber, when from under the stairs appeared the figure of Iván Ilých's schoolboy son, who was extremely like his father. He seemed a little Iván Ilých, such as Peter Ivánovich remembered when they studied law together. His tear-stained eyes had in them the look that is seen in the eyes of boys of thirteen or fourteen who are not pure-minded. When he saw Peter Ivánovich he scowled morosely and shame-facedly. Peter Ivánovich nodded to him and entered the death-chamber. The service began: candles, groans, incense, tears, and sobs. Peter Ivánovich stood looking gloomily down at his feet. He did not look once at the dead man, did not yield to any depressing influence, and was one of the first to leave the room. There was no one in the anteroom, but Gerásim darted out of the dead man's room, rummaged with his strong hands among the fur coats to find Peter Ivánovich's and helped him on with it.

"Well, friend Gerásim," said Peter Ivánovich, so as to say something. "It's a sad affair, isn't it?"

"It's God's will. We shall all come to it some day," said Gerásim, displaying his teeth—the even, white teeth of a healthy peasant—and, like a man in the thick of urgent work, he briskly opened the front door, called the coachman, helped Peter Ivánovich into the sledge, and sprang back to the porch as if in readiness for what he had to do next.

Peter Ivánovich found the fresh air particularly pleasant after the smell of incense, the dead body, and carbolic acid.

"Where to, sir?" asked the coachman.

"It's not too late even now. . . . I'll call around on Fëdor Vasílievich."

He accordingly drove there and found them just finishing the first rubber, so that it was quite convenient for him to cut in.

CHAPTER II

Iván Ilých's life had been most simple and most ordinary and therefore most terrible.

He had been a member of the Court of Justice, and died at the age of forty-five. His father had been an official who after serving in various ministries and departments of Petersburg had made the sort of career which brings men to positions from which by reason of their long service they cannot be dismissed, though they are obviously unfit to hold any responsible position, and for whom therefore posts are specially created, which though fictitious carry salaries of from six to ten thousand rubles that are not fictitious, and in receipt of which they live on to a great age.

Such was the Privy Councillor and superfluous member of various superfluous institutions, Ilyá Epímovich Golovín.

He had three sons, of whom Iván Ilých was the second. The eldest son was following in his father's footsteps only in another department, and was already approaching that stage in the service at which a similar sinecure would be reached. The third son was a failure. He had ruined his prospects in a number of positions and was now serving in the railway department. His father and brothers, and still more their wives, not merely disliked meeting him, but avoided remembering his existence unless compelled to do so. His sister had married Baron Greff, a Petersburg official of her father's type. Iván Ilých was *le phénix de la famille*[1] as people said. He was neither as cold and formal as his elder brother nor as wild as the younger, but was a happy mean between them—an intelligent, polished, lively and agreeable man. He had studied with his younger brother at the School of Law, but the latter had failed to complete the course and was expelled when he was in the fifth class. Iván Ilých finished the course well. Even when he was at the School of Law he was just what he remained for the rest of his life: a capable, cheerful, good-natured, and sociable man, though strict in the fulfilment of what he considered to be his duty: and

---

[1] The phoenix of the family, here meaning "rare bird" or "prodigy."

he considered his duty to be what was so considered by those in authority. Neither as a boy nor as a man was he a toady, but from early youth was by nature attracted to people of high station as a fly is drawn to the light, assimilating their ways and views of life and establishing friendly relations with them. All the enthusiasms of childhood and youth passed without leaving much trace on him; he succumbed to sensuality, to vanity, and latterly among the highest classes to liberalism, but always within limits which his instinct unfailingly indicated to him as correct.

At school he had done things which had formerly seemed to him very horrid and made him feel disgusted with himself when he did them; but when later on he saw that such actions were done by people of good position and that they did not regard them as wrong, he was able not exactly to regard them as right, but to forget about them entirely or not be at all troubled at remembering them.

Having graduated from the School of Law and qualified for the tenth rank of the civil service, and having received money from his father for his equipment, Iván Ilých ordered himself clothes at Scharmer's, the fashionable tailor, hung a medallion inscribed *respice finen*[2] on his watch-chain, took leave of his professor and the prince who was patron of the school, had a farewell dinner with his comrades at Donon's first-class restaurant, and with his new and fashionable portmanteau, linen, clothes, shaving and other toilet appliances, and a travelling rug, all purchased at the best shops, he set off for one of the provinces where, through his father's influence, he had been attached to the Governor as an official for special service.

In the province Iván Ilých soon arranged as easy and agreeable a position for himself as he had had at the School of Law. He performed his official tasks, made his career, and at the same time amused himself pleasantly and decorously. Occasionally he paid official visits to country districts, where he behaved with dignity both to his superiors and inferiors, and performed the duties entrusted to him, which related chiefly to the sectarians,[3] with an exactness and incorruptible honesty of which he could not but feel proud.

In official matters, despite his youth and taste for frivolous gaiety, he was exceedingly reserved, punctilious, and even severe; but in society he was often amusing and witty, and always good-natured, correct in his manner, and *bon enfant*, as the governor and his wife—with whom he was like one of the family—used to say of him.

In the provinces he had an affair with a lady who made advances to the elegant young lawyer, and there was also a milliner; and there were carousals with aides-de-camp who visited the district, and after-supper visits to a certain outlying street of doubtful reputation; and there was too some obsequiousness to his chief and even to his chief's wife, but all this was done with such a tone of good breeding that no hard names could be applied to it. It all came under

---

[2] Regard the end.
[3] A large sect, whose members were placed under many legal restrictions, which broke away from the Orthodox Church in the seventeenth century.

the heading of the French saying: "Il faut que jeunesse se passe."[4] It was all done with clean hands, in clean linen, with French phrases, and above all among people of the best society and consequently with the approval of people of rank.

So Iván Ilých served for five years and then came a change in his official life. The new and reformed judicial institutions were introduced, and new men were needed. Iván Ilých became such a new man. He was offered 'the post of Examining Magistrate, and he accepted it though the post was in another province and obliged him to give up the connexions he had formed and to make new ones. His friends met to give him a send-off; they had a group-photograph taken and presented him with a silver cigarette-case, and he set off to his new post.

As examining magistrate Iván Ilých was just as *comme il faut*[5] and decorous a man, inspiring general respect and capable of separating his official duties from his private life, as he had been when acting as an official on special service. His duties now as examining magistrate were far more interesting and attractive than before. In his former position it had been pleasant to wear an undress uniform made by Scharmer, and to pass through the crowd of petitioners and officials who were timorously awaiting an audience with the governor, and who envied him as with free and easy gait he went straight into his chief's private room to have a cup of tea and a cigarette with him. But not many people had then been directly dependent on him—only police officials and the sectarians when he went on special missions—and he liked to treat them politely, almost as comrades, as if he were letting them feel that he who had the power to crush them was treating them in this simple, friendly way. There were then but few such people. But now, as an examining magistrate, Iván Ilých felt that everyone without exception, even the most important and self-satisfied, was in his power, and that he need only write a few words on a sheet of paper with a certain heading, and this or that important, self-satisfied person would be brought before him in the role of an accused person or a witness, and if he did not choose to allow him to sit down, would have to stand before him and answer his questions. Iván Ilých never abused his power; he tried on the contrary to soften its expression, but the consciousness of it and of the possibility of softening its effect, supplied the chief interest and attraction of his office. In his work itself, especially in his examinations, he very soon acquired a method of eliminating all considerations irrelevant to the legal aspect of the case, and reducing even the most complicated case to a form in which it would be presented on paper only in its externals, completely excluding his personal opinion of the matter, while above all observing every prescribed formality. The work was new and Iván Ilých was one of the first men to apply the new Code of 1864.[6]

On taking up the post of examining magistrate in a new town, he made new acquaintances and connexions, placed himself on a new footing, and assumed

---

[4] Youth must have its fling.
[5] Proper.
[6] Judicial procedures were thoroughly reformed after the emancipation of the serfs in 1861.

a somewhat different tone. He took up an attitude of rather dignified aloofness towards the provincial authorities, but picked out the best circle of legal gentlemen and wealthy gentry living in the town and assumed a tone of slight dissatisfaction with the government, of moderate liberalism, and of enlightened citizenship. At the same time, without at all altering the elegance of his toilet, he ceased shaving his chin and allowed his beard to grow as it pleased.

Iván Ilých settled down very pleasantly in this new town. The society there, which inclined towards opposition to the Governor, was friendly, his salary was larger, and he began to play *vint*,[7] which he found added not a little to the pleasure of life, for he had a capacity for cards, played good-humouredly, and calculated rapidly and astutely, so that he usually won.

After living there for two years he met his future wife, Praskóvya Fëdorovna Míkhel, who was the most attractive, clever, and brilliant girl of the set in which he moved, and among other amusements and relaxations from his labours as examining magistrate, Iván Ilých established light and playful relations with her.

While he had been an official on special service he had been accustomed to dance, but now as an examining magistrate it was exceptional for him to do so. If he danced now, he did it as if to show that though he served under the reformed order of things, and had reached the fifth official rank, yet when it came to dancing he could do it better than most people. So at the end of an evening he sometimes danced with Praskóvya Fëdorovna, and it was chiefly during these dances that he captivated her. She fell in love with him. Iván Ilých had at first no definite intention of marrying, but when the girl fell in love with him he said to himself: "Really, why shouldn't I marry?"

Praskóvya Fëdorovna came of a good family, was not bad looking and had some little property. Iván Ilých might have aspired to a more brilliant match, but even this was good. He had his salary, and she, he hoped, would have an equal income. She was well connected, and was a sweet, pretty, and thoroughly correct young woman. To say that Iván Ilých married because he fell in love with Praskóvya Fëdorovna and found that she sympathized with his views of life would be as incorrect as to say that he married because his social circle approved of the match. He was swayed by both these considerations: the marriage gave him personal satisfaction, and at the same time it was considered the right thing by the most highly placed of his associates.

So Iván Ilých got married.

The preparations for marriage and the beginning of married life, with its conjugal caresses, the new furniture, new crockery, and new linen, were very pleasant until his wife became pregnant—so that Iván Ilých had begun to think that marriage would not impair the easy, agreeable, gay and always decorous character of his life, approved of by society and regarded by himself as natural, but would even improve it. But from the first months of his wife's pregnancy, something new, unpleasant, depressing, and unseemly, and from which there was no way of escape, unexpectedly showed itself.

---

[7] A card game similar to bridge.

His wife, without any reason—*de gaieté de coeur* as Iván Ilých expressed it to himself—began to disturb the pleasure and propriety of their life. She began to be jealous without any cause, expected him to devote his whole attention to her, found fault with everything, and made coarse and ill-mannered scenes.

At first Iván Ilých hoped to escape from the unpleasantness of this state of affairs by the same easy and decorous relation to life that had served him heretofore: he tried to ignore his wife's disagreeable moods, continued to live in his usual easy and pleasant way, invited friends to his house for a game of cards, and also tried going out to his club or spending his evenings with friends. But one day his wife began upbraiding him so vigorously, using such coarse words, and continued to abuse him every time he did not fulfil her demands, so resolutely and with such evident determination not to give way till he submitted—that is, till he stayed at home and was bored just as she was—that he became alarmed. He now realized that matrimony—at any rate with Praskóvya Fëdorovna—was not always conducive to the pleasures and amenities of life but on the contrary often infringed both comfort and propriety, and that he must therefore entrench himself against such infringement. And Iván Ilých began to seek for means of doing so. His official duties were the one thing that imposed upon Praskóvya Fëdorovna, and by means of his official work and the duties attached to it he began struggling with his wife to secure his own independence.

With the birth of their child, the attempts to feed it and the various failures in doing so, and with the real and imaginary illnesses of mother and child, in which Iván Ilých's sympathy was demanded but about which he understood nothing, the need of securing for himself an existence outside his family life became still more imperative.

As his wife grew more irritable and exacting and Iván Ilých transferred the centre of gravity of his life more and more to his official work, so did he grow to like his work better and became more ambitious than before.

Very soon, within a year of his wedding, Iván Ilých had realized that marriage, though it may add some comforts to life, is in fact a very intricate and difficult affair towards which in order to perform one's duty, that is, to lead a decorous life approved of by society, one must adopt a definite attitude just as towards one's official duties.

And Iván Ilých evolved such an attitude towards married life. He only required of it those conveniences—dinner at home, housewife, and bed—which it could give him, and above all that propriety of external forms required by public opinion. For the rest he looked for light-hearted pleasure and propriety, and was very thankful when he found them, but if he met with antagonism and querulousness he at once retired into his separate fenced-off world of official duties, where he found satisfaction.

Iván Ilých was esteemed a good official, and after three years was made Assistant Public Prosecutor. His new duties, their importance, the possibility of indicting and imprisoning anyone he chose, the publicity his speeches received, and the success he had in all these things, made his work still more attractive.

More children came. His wife became more and more querulous and ill-tempered, but the attitude Iván Ilých had adopted towards his home life rendered him almost impervious to her grumbling.

After seven years' service in that town he was transferred to another province as Public Prosecutor. They moved, but were short of money and his wife did not like the place they moved to. Though the salary was higher the cost of living was greater, besides which two of their children died and family life became still more unpleasant for him.

Praskóvya Fëdorovna blamed her husband for every inconvenience they encountered in their new home. Most of the conversations between husband and wife, especially as to the children's education, led to topics which recalled former disputes, and those disputes were apt to flare up again at any moment. There remained only those rare periods of amorousness which still came to them at times but did not last long. These were islets at which they anchored for a while and then again set out upon that ocean of veiled hostility which showed itself in their aloofness from one another. This aloofness might have grieved Iván Ilých had he considered that it ought not to exist, but he now regarded the position as normal, and even made it the goal at which he aimed in family life. His aim was to free himself more and more from those unpleasantnesses and to give them a semblance of harmlessness and propriety. He attained this by spending less and less time with his family, and when obliged to be at home he tried to safeguard his position by the presence of outsiders. The chief thing however was that he had his official duties. The whole interest of his life now centered in the official world and that interest absorbed him. The consciousness of his power, being able to ruin anybody he wished to ruin, the importance, even the external dignity of his entry into court, or meetings with his subordinates, his success with superiors and inferiors, and above all his masterly handling of cases, of which he was conscious—all this gave him pleasure and filled his life, together with chats with his colleagues, dinners, and bridge. So that on the whole Iván Ilých's life continued to flow as he considered it should do—pleasantly and properly.

So things continued for another seven years. His eldest daughter was already sixteen, another child had died, and only one son was left, a schoolboy and a subject of dissension. Iván Ilých wanted to put him in the School of Law, but to spite him Praskóvya Fëdorovna entered him at the High School. The daughter had been educated at home and had turned out well: the boy did not learn badly either.

CHAPTER III

So Iván Ilých lived for seventeen years after his marriage. He was already a Public Prosecutor of long standing, and had declined several proposed transfers while awaiting a more desirable post, when an unanticipated and unpleasant occurrence quite upset the peaceful course of his life. He was expecting to be offered the post of presiding judge in a University town, but Happe somehow came to the front and obtained the appointment instead. Iván Ilých became

irritable, reproached Happe, and quarrelled both with him and with his immediate superiors—who became colder to him and again passed him over when
other appointments were made.

This was in 1880, the hardest year of Iván Ilých's life. It was then that it
became evident on the one hand that his salary was insufficient for them to live
on, and on the other that he had been forgotten, and not only this, but that
what was for him the greatest and most cruel injustice appeared to others a quite
ordinary occurrence. Even his father did not consider it his duty to help him.
Iván Ilých felt himself abandoned by everyone, and that they regarded his position with a salary of 3,500 rubles as quite normal and even fortunate. He alone
knew that with the consciousness of the injustices done him, with his wife's
incessant nagging, and with the debts he had contracted by living beyond his
means, his position was far from normal.

In order to save money that summer he obtained leave of absence and went
with his wife to live in the country at her brother's place.

In the country, without his work, he experienced *ennui* for the first time in
his life, and not only *ennui* but intolerable depression, and he decided that it
was impossible to go on living like that, and that it was necessary to take energetic
measures.

Having passed a sleepless night pacing up and down the veranda, he decided
to go to Petersburg and bestir himself, in order to punish those who had failed
to appreciate him and to get transferred to another ministry.

Next day, despite many protests from his wife and her brother, he started for
Petersburg with the sole object of obtaining a post with a salary of five thousand
rubles a year. He was no longer bent on any particular department, or tendency,
or kind of activity. All he now wanted was an appointment to another post with
a salary of five thousand rubles, either in the administration, in the banks, with
the railways, in one of the Empress Márya's Institutions,[8] or even in the customs—but it had to carry with it a salary of five thousand rubles and be in a
ministry other than that in which they had failed to appreciate him.

And this quest of Iván Ilých's was crowned with remarkable and unexpected
success. At Kursk an acquaintance of his, F. I. Ilyín, got into the first-class
carriage, sat down beside Iván Ilých, and told him of a telegram just received
by the Governor of Kursk announcing that a change was about to take place in
the ministry: Peter Ivánovich was to be superseded by Iván Semënovich.

The proposed change, apart from its significance for Russia, had a special
significance for Iván Ilých, because by bringing forward a new man, Peter
Petróvich, and consequently his friend Zachár Ivánovich, it was highly favourable for Iván Ilých, since Zachár Ivánovich was a friend and colleague of his.

In Moscow this news was confirmed, and on reaching Petersburg Iván Ilých
found Zachár Ivánovich and received a definite promise of an appointment in
his former Department of Justice.

---

[8] A charitable organization founded in the late eighteenth century by the Empress Márya.

A week later he telegraphed to his wife: "Zachár in Miller's place. I shall receive appointment on presentation of report."

Thanks to this change of personnel, Iván Ilých had unexpectedly obtained an appointment in his former ministry which placed him two stages above his former colleagues besides giving him five thousand rubles salary and three thousand five hundred rubles for expenses connected with his removal. All his ill humour towards his former enemies and the whole department vanished, and Iván Ilých was completely happy.

He returned to the country more cheerful and contented than he had been for a long time. Praskóvya Fëdorovna also cheered up and a truce was arranged between them. Iván Ilých told of how he had been fêted by everybody in Petersburg, how all those who had been his enemies were put to shame and now fawned on him, how envious they were of his appointment, and how much everybody in Petersburg had liked him.

Praskóvya Fëdorovna listened to all this and appeared to believe it. She did not contradict anything, but only made plans for their life in the town to which they were going. Iván Ilých saw with delight that these plans were his plans, that he and his wife agreed, and that, after a stumble, his life was regaining its due and natural character of pleasant lightheartedness and decorum.

Iván Ilých had come back for a short time only, for he had to take up his new duties on the 10th of September. Moreover, he needed time to settle into the new place, to move all his belongings from the province, and to buy and order many additional things: in a word, to make such arrangements as he had resolved on, which were almost exactly what Praskóvya Fëdorovna too had decided on.

Now that everything had happened so fortunately, and that he and his wife were at one in their aims and moreover saw so little of one another, they got on together better than they had done since the first years of marriage. Iván Ilých had thought of taking his family away with him at once, but the insistence of his wife's brother and her sister-in-law, who had suddenly become particularly amiable and friendly to him and his family, induced him to depart alone.

So he departed, and the cheerful state of mind induced by his success and by the harmony between his wife and himself, the one intensifying the other, did not leave him. He found a delightful house, just the thing both he and his wife had dreamt of. Spacious, lofty reception rooms in the old style, a convenient and dignified study, rooms for his wife and daughter, a study for his son— it might have been specially built for them. Iván Ilých himself superintended the arrangements, chose the wall-papers, supplemented the furniture (preferably with antiques which he considered particularly *comme il faut*), and supervised the upholstering. Everything progressed and progressed and approached the ideal he had set himself: even when things were only half completed they exceeded his expectations. He saw what a refined and elegant character, free from vulgarity, it would all have when it was ready. On falling asleep he pictured to himself how the reception-room would look. Looking at the yet unfinished drawing-room he could see the fireplace, the screen, the what-not, the little chairs dotted here and there, the dishes and plates on the walls, and the bronzes, as they would be when everything was in place. He was pleased by the thought of how his wife and daughter, who shared his taste in this matter, would be impressed by it. They were certainly not expecting as much. He had been particularly successful in finding, and buying cheaply, antiques which gave a particularly aristocratic character to the whole place. But in his letters he intentionally understated everything in order to be able to surprise them. All this so absorbed him that his new duties—though he liked his official work—interested him less than he had expected. Sometimes he even had moments of absentmindedness during the Court Sessions, and would consider whether he should have straight or curved cornices for his curtains. He was so interested in it all that he often did things himself, rearranging the furniture, or rehanging the curtains. Once when mounting a step-ladder to show the upholsterer, who did not understand, how he wanted the hangings draped, he made a false step and slipped, but being a strong and agile man he clung on and only knocked his side against the knob of the window frame. The bruised place was painful but the pain soon passed, and he felt particularly bright and well just then. He wrote: "I feel fifteen years younger." He thought he would have everything ready by September, but it dragged on till mid-October. But the result was charming not only in his eyes but to everyone who saw it.

In reality it was just what is usually seen in the houses of people of moderate means who want to appear rich, and therefore succeed only in resembling others like themselves: there were damasks, dark wood, plants, rugs, and dull and polished bronzes—all the things people of a certain class have in order to resemble other people of that class. His house was so like the others that it would never have been noticed, but to him it all seemed to be quite exceptional. He was very happy when he met his family at the station and brought them to the newly furnished house all lit up, where a footman in a white tie opened the door into the hall decorated with plants, and when they went on into the drawing-room and the study uttering exclamations of delight. He conducted them everywhere, drank in their praises eagerly, and beamed with pleasure. At tea that evening, when Praskóvya Fëdorovna among other things asked him about his fall, he laughed, and showed them how he had gone flying and had frightened the upholsterer.

"It's a good thing I'm a bit of an athlete. Another man might have been killed, but I merely knocked myself, just here; it hurts when it's touched, but it's passing off already—it's only a bruise."

So they began living in their new home—in which, as always happens, when they got thoroughly settled in they found they were just one room short—and with the increased income, which as always was just a little (some five hundred rubles) too little, but it was all very nice.

Things went particularly well at first, before everything was finally arranged and while something had still to be done: this thing bought, that thing ordered, another thing moved, and something else adjusted. Though there were some disputes between husband and wife, they were both so well satisfied and had so much to do that it all passed off without any serious quarrels. When nothing was left to arrange it became rather dull and something seemed to be lacking, but they were then making acquaintances, forming habits, and life was growing fuller.

Iván Ilých spent his mornings at the law court and came home to dinner, and at first he was generally in a good humour, though he occasionally became irritable just on account of his house. (Every spot on the tablecloth or the upholstery, and every broken window-blind string, irritated him. He had devoted so much trouble to arranging it all that every disturbance of it distressed him.) But on the whole his life ran its course as he believed life should do: easily, pleasantly, and decorously.

He got up at nine, drank his coffee, read the paper, and then put on his undress uniform and went to the law courts. There the harness in which he worked had already been stretched to fit him and he donned it without a hitch: petitioners, inquiries at the chancery, the chancery itself, and the sittings public and administrative. In all this the thing was to exclude everything fresh and vital, which always disturbs the regular course of official business, and to admit only official relations with people, and then only on official grounds. A man would come, for instance, wanting some information. Iván Ilých, as one in whose sphere the matter did not lie, would have nothing to do with him: but if the man had some business with him in his official capacity, something that could be expressed on officially stamped paper, he would do everything, positively everything he could within the limits of such relations, and in doing so would maintain the semblance of friendly human relations, that is, would observe the courtesies of life. As soon as the official relations ended, so did everything else. Iván Ilých possessed this capacity to separate his real life from the official side of affairs and not mix the two, in the highest degree, and by long practice and natural aptitude had brought it to such a pitch that sometimes, in the manner of a virtuoso, he would even allow himself to let the human and official relations mingle. He let himself do this just because he felt that he could at any time he chose resume the strictly official attitude again and drop the human relation. And he did it all easily, pleasantly, correctly, and even artistically. In the intervals between the sessions he smoked, drank tea, chatted a little about politics, a little about general topics, a little about cards, but most of all about official appointments. Tired, but with the feelings of a virtuoso— one of the first violins who has played his part in an orchestra with precision— he would return home to find that his wife and daughter had been out paying calls, or had a visitor, and that his son had been to school, had done his homework with his tutor, and was duly learning what is taught at High Schools. Everything was as it should be. After dinner, if they had no visitors, Iván Ilých sometimes read a book that was being much discussed at the time, and in the evening settled down to work, that is, read official papers, compared the depositions of witnesses, and noted paragraphs of the Code applying to them. This was neither dull nor amusing. It was dull when he might have been playing bridge, but if no bridge was available it was at any rate better than doing nothing or sitting with his wife. Iván Ilých's chief pleasure was giving little dinners to which he invited men and women of good social position, and just as his drawing-room resembled all other drawing-rooms so did his enjoyable little parties resemble all other such parties.

Once they even gave a dance. Iván Ilých enjoyed it and everything went off well, except that it led to a violent quarrel with his wife about the cakes and sweets. Praskóvya Fëdorovna had made her own plans, but Iván Ilých insisted on getting everything from an expensive confectioner and ordered too many cakes, and the quarrel occurred because some of those cakes were left over and the confectioner's bill came to forty-five rubles. It was a great and disagreeable quarrel. Praskóvya Fëdorovna called him "a fool and an imbecile," and he clutched at his head and made angry allusions to divorce.

But the dance itself had been enjoyable. The best people were there, and Iván Ilých had danced with Princess Trúfonova, a sister of the distinguished founder of the Society "Bear my Burden."

The pleasures connected with his work were pleasures of ambition; his social pleasures were those of vanity; but Iván Ilých's greatest pleasure was playing bridge. He acknowledged that whatever disagreeable incident happened in his life, the pleasure that beamed like a ray of light above everything else was to sit down to bridge with good players, not noisy partners, and of course to four-handed bridge (with five players it was annoying to have to stand out, though one pretended not to mind), to play a clever and serious game (when the cards allowed it) and then to have supper and drink a glass of wine. After a game of bridge, especially if he had won a little (to win a large sum was unpleasant), Iván Ilých went to bed in specially good humour.

So they lived. They formed a circle of acquaintances among the best people and were visited by people of importance and by young folk. In their views as to their acquaintances, husband, wife and daughter were entirely agreed, and tacitly and unanimously kept at arm's length and shook off the various shabby friends and relations who, with much show of affection, gushed into the drawing-room with its Japanese plates on the walls. Soon these shabby friends ceased to obtrude themselves and only the best people remained in the Golovíns' set.

Young men made up to Lisa, and Petríshchev, an examining magistrate and Dmítri Ivanovich Petríshchev's son and sole heir, began to be so attentive to her that Iván Ilých had already spoken to Praskóvya Fëdorovna about it, and considered whether they should not arrange a party for them or get up some private theatricals.

So they lived, and all went well, without change, and life flowed pleasantly.

CHAPTER IV

They were all in good health. It could not be called ill health if Iván Ilých sometimes said that he had a queer taste in his mouth and felt some discomfort in his left side.

But this discomfort increased and, though not exactly painful, grew into a sense of pressure in his side accompanied by ill humour. And his irritability became worse and worse and began to mar the agreeable, easy, and correct life that had established itself in the Golovín family. Quarrels between husband and wife became more and more frequent, and soon the ease and amenity disappeared and even the decorum was barely maintained. Scenes again became frequent, and very few of those islets remained on which husband and wife could meet without an explosion. Praskóvya Fëdorovna now had good reason to say that her husband's temper was trying. With characteristic exaggeration she said he had always had a dreadful temper, and that it had needed all her good nature to put up with it for twenty years. It was true that now the quarrels were started by him. His bursts of temper always came just before dinner, often just as he began to eat his soup. Sometimes he noticed that a plate or dish was chipped, or the food was not right, or his son put his elbow on the table, or his daughter's hair was not done as he liked it, and for all this he blamed Praskóvya Fëdorovna. At first she retorted and said disagreeable things to him, but once or twice he fell into such a rage at the beginning of dinner that she realized it was due to some physical derangement brought on by taking food, and so she restrained herself and did not answer, but only hurried to get the dinner over. She regarded this self-restraint as highly praiseworthy. Having come to the conclusion that her husband had a dreadful temper and made her life miserable, she began to feel sorry for herself, and the more she pitied herself the more she hated her husband. She began to wish he would die; yet she did not want him to die because then his salary would cease. And this irritated her against him still more. She considered herself dreadfully unhappy just because not even his death could save her, and though she concealed her exasperation, that hidden exasperation of hers increased his irritation also.

After one scene in which Iván Ilých had been particularly unfair and after which he had said in explanation that he certainly was irritable but that it was due to his not being well, she said that if he was ill it should be attended to, and insisted on his going to see a celebrated doctor.

He went. Everything took place as he had expected and as it always does. There was the usual waiting and the important air assumed by the doctor, with which he was so familiar (resembling that which he himself assumed in court), and the sounding and listening, and the questions which called for answers that were forgone conclusions and were evidently unnecessary, and the look of importance which implied that "if only you put yourself in our hands we will arrange everything—we know indubitably how it has to be done, always in the same way for everybody alike." It was all just as it was in the law courts. The doctor put on just the same air towards him as he himself put on towards an accused person.

The doctor said that so-and-so indicated that there was so-and-so inside the patient, but if the investigation of so-and-so did not confirm this, then he must assume that and that. If he assumed that and that, then . . . and so on. To Iván Ilých only one question was important: was his case serious or not? But the doctor ignored that inappropriate question. From his point of view it was not the one under consideration, the real question was to decide between a floating kidney, chronic catarrh, or appendicitis. It was not a question of Iván Ilých's life or death, but one between a floating kidney and appendicitis. And that question the doctor solved brilliantly, as it seemed to Iván Ilých, in favour of the appendix, with the reservation that should an examination of the urine give fresh indications the matter would be reconsidered. All this was just what Iván Ilých had himself brilliantly accomplished a thousand times in dealing with men on trial. The doctor summed up just as brilliantly, looking over his spectacles triumphantly and even gaily at the accused. From the doctor's summing up Iván Ilých concluded that things were bad, but that for the doctor, and perhaps for everybody else, it was a matter of indifference, though for him it was bad. And this conclusion struck him painfully, arousing in him a great feeling of pity for himself and of bitterness towards the doctor's indifference to a matter of such importance.

He said nothing of this, but rose, placed the doctor's fee on the table, and remarked with a sigh: "We sick people probably often put inappropriate questions. But tell me, in general, is this complaint dangerous, or not? . . ."

The doctor looked at him sternly over his spectacles with one eye, as if to say: "Prisoner, if you will not keep to the questions put to you, I shall be obliged to have you removed from the court."

"I have already told you what I consider necessary and proper. The analysis may show something more." And the doctor bowed.

Iván Ilých went out slowly, seated himself disconsolately in his sledge, and drove home. All the way home he was going over what the doctor had said, trying to translate those complicated, obscure, scientific phrases into plain language and find in them an answer to the question: "Is my condition bad? Is it very bad? Or is there as yet nothing much wrong?" And it seemed to him that the meaning of what the doctor had said was that it was very bad. Everything in the streets seemed depressing. The cabmen, the houses, the passers-by, and the shops, were dismal. His ache, this dull gnawing ache that never ceased for a moment, seemed to have acquired a new and more serious significance from the doctor's dubious remarks. Iván Ilých now watched it with a new and oppressive feeling.

He reached home and began to tell his wife about it. She listened, but in the middle of his account his daughter came in with her hat on, ready to go out with her mother. She sat down reluctantly to listen to this tedious story, but could not stand it long, and her mother too did not hear him to the end.

"Well, I am very glad," she said. "Mind now to take your medicine regularly. Give me the prescription and I'll send Gerásim to the chemist's." And she went to get ready to go out.

While she was in the room Iván Ilých had hardly taken time to breathe, but he sighed deeply when she left it.

"Well," he thought, "perhaps it isn't so bad after all."

He began taking his medicine and following the doctor's directions, which had been altered after the examination of the urine. But then it happened that there was a contradiction between the indications drawn from the examination of the urine and the symptoms that showed themselves. It turned out that what was happening differed from what the doctor had told him, and that he had either forgotten, or blundered, or hidden something from him. He could not, however, be blamed for that, and Iván Ilých still obeyed his orders implicitly and at first derived some comfort from doing so.

From the time of his visit to the doctor, Iván Ilých's chief occupation was the exact fulfilment of the doctor's instructions regarding hygiene and the taking of medicine, and the observation of his pain and his excretions. His chief interests came to be people's ailments and people's health. When sickness, deaths, or recoveries, were mentioned in his presence, especially when the illness resembled his own, he listened with agitation which he tried to hide, asked questions, and applied what he heard to his own case.

The pain did not grow less, but Iván Ilých made efforts to force himself to think that he was better. And he could do this so long as nothing agitated him. But as soon as he had any unpleasantness with his wife, any lack of success in his official work, or held bad cards at bridge, he was at once acutely sensible of his disease. He had formerly borne such mischances, hoping soon to adjust what was wrong, to master it and attain success, or make a grand slam. But now every mischance upset him and plunged him into despair. He would say to himself: "There now, just as I was beginning to get better and the medicine had begun to take effect, comes this accursed misfortune, or unpleasantness . . . " And he was furious with the mishap, or with the people who were causing the unpleasantness and killing him, for he felt that this fury was killing him but could not restrain it. One would have thought that it should have been clear to him that this exasperation with circumstances and people aggravated his illness, and that he ought therefore to ignore unpleasant occurrences. But he drew the very opposite conclusion: he said that he needed peace, and he watched for everything that might disturb it and became irritable at the slightest infringement of it. His condition was rendered worse by the fact that he read medical books and consulted doctors. The progress of his disease was so gradual that he could deceive himself when comparing one day with another—the difference was so slight. But when he consulted the doctors it seemed to him that he was getting worse, and even very rapidly. Yet despite this he was continually consulting them.

That month he went to see another celebrity, who told him almost the same as the first had done but put his questions rather differently, and the interview with this celebrity only increased Iván Ilých's doubts and fears. A friend of a friend of his, a very good doctor, diagnosed his illness again quite differently from the others, and though he predicted recovery, his questions and suppositions bewildered Iván Ilých still more and increased his doubts. A homoeopathist diagnosed the disease in yet another way, and prescribed medicine which Iván Ilých took secretly for a week. But after a week, not feeling any improvement and having lost confidence both in the former doctor's treatment and in this one's, he became still more despondent. One day a lady acquaintance mentioned a cure effected by a wonder-working icon. Iván Ilých caught himself listening attentively and beginning to believe that it had occurred. This incident alarmed him. "Has my mind really weakened to such an extent?" he asked himself. "Nonsense! It's all rubbish. I mustn't give way to nervous fears but having chosen a doctor must keep strictly to his treatment. That is what I will do. Now it's all settled. I won't think about it, but will follow the treatment seriously till summer, and then we shall see. From now there must be no more of this wavering!" This was easy to say but impossible to carry out. The pain in his side oppressed him and seemed to grow worse and more incessant, while the taste in his mouth grew stranger and stranger. It seemed to him that his breath had a disgusting smell, and he was conscious of a loss of appetite and strength. There was no deceiving himself: something terrible, new, and more important than anything before in his life, was taking place within him of which he alone was aware. Those about him did not understand or would not understand it, but thought everything in the world was going on as usual. That tormented Iván Ilých more than anything. He saw that his household, especially his wife and daughter who were in a perfect whirl of visiting, did not understand anything of it and were annoyed that he was so depressed and so exacting, as if he were to blame for it. Though they tried to disguise it he saw that he was an obstacle in their path, and that his wife had adopted a definite line in regard to his illness and kept to it regardless of anything he said or did. Her attitude was this: "You know," she would say to her friends, "Iván Ilých can't do as other people do, and keep to the treatment prescribed for him. One day he'll take his drops and keep strictly to his diet and go to bed in good time, but the next day unless I watch him he'll suddenly forget his medicine, eat sturgeon— which is forbidden—and sit up playing cards till one o'clock in the morning."

"Oh, come, when was that?" Iván Ilých would ask in vexation. "Only once at Peter Ivánovich's."

"And yesterday with Shébek."

"Well, even if I hadn't stayed up, this pain would have kept me awake."

"Be that as it may you'll never get well like that, but will always make us wretched."

Praskóvya Fëdorovna's attitude to Iván Ilých's illness, as she expressed it both to others and to him, was that it was his own fault and was another of the annoyances he caused her. Iván Ilých felt that this opinion escaped her involuntarily—but that did not make it easier for him.

At the law courts too, Iván Ilých noticed, or thought he noticed, a strange attitude towards himself. It sometimes seemed to him that people were watching him inquisitively as a man whose place might soon be vacant. Then again, his friends would suddenly begin to chaff him in a friendly way about his low spirits, as if the awful, horrible, and unheard-of thing that was going on within him, incessantly gnawing at him and irresistibly drawing him away, was a very agreeable subject for jests. Schwartz in particular irritated him by his jocularity, vivacity, and *savoir-faire*, which reminded him of what he himself had been ten years ago.

Friends came to make up a set and they sat down to cards. They dealt, bending the new cards to soften them, and he sorted the diamonds in his hand and found he had seven. His partner said "No trumps" and supported him with two diamonds. What more could be wished for? It ought to be jolly and lively. They would make a grand slam. But suddenly Iván Ilých was conscious of that gnawing pain, that taste in his mouth, and it seemed ridiculous that in such circumstances he should be pleased to make a grand slam.

He looked at his partner Mikháil Mikháylovich, who rapped the table with his strong hand and instead of snatching up the tricks pushed the cards courteously and indulgently towards Iván Ilých that he might have the pleasure of gathering them up without the trouble of stretching out his hand for them. "Does he think I am too weak to stretch out my arm?" thought Iván Ilých, and forgetting what he was doing he over-trumped his partner, missing the grand slam by three tricks. And what was most awful of all was that he saw how upset Mikháil Mikháylovich was about it but did not himself care. And it was dreadful to realize why he did not care.

They all saw that he was suffering, and said: "We can stop if you are tired. Take a rest." Lie down? No, he was not at all tired, and he finished the rubber. All were gloomy and silent. Iván Ilých felt that he diffused this gloom over them and could not dispel it. They had supper and went away, and Iván Ilých was left alone with the consciousness that his life was poisoned and was poisoning the lives of others, and that this poison did not weaken but penetrated more and more deeply into his whole being.

With this consciousness, and with physical pain besides the terror, he must go to bed, often to lie awake the greater part of the night. Next morning he had to get up again, dress, go to the law courts, speak, and write; or if he did not go out, spend at home those twenty-four hours a day each of which was a torture. And he had to live thus all alone on the brink of an abyss, with no one who understood or pitied him.

CHAPTER V

So one month passed and then another. Just before the New Year his brother-in-law came to town and stayed at their house. Iván Ilých was at the law courts and Praskóvya Fëdorovna had gone shopping. When Iván Ilých came home and entered his study he found his brother-in-law there—a healthy, florid man—unpacking his portmanteau himself. He raised his head on hearing Iván Ilých's footsteps and looked up at him for a moment without a word. That stare told Iván Ilých everything. His brother-in-law opened his mouth to utter an exclamation of surprise but checked himself, and that action confirmed it all.

"I have changed, eh?"

"Yes, there is a change."

And after that, try as he would to get his brother-in-law to return to the subject of his looks, the latter would say nothing about it. Praskóvya Fëdorovna came home and her brother went out to her. Iván Ilých locked the door and began to examine himself in the glass, first full face, then in profile. He took up a portrait of himself taken with his wife, and compared it with what he saw in the glass. The change in him was immense. Then he bared his arms to the elbow, looked at them, drew the sleeves down again, sat down on an ottoman, and grew blacker than night.

"No, no, this won't do!" he said to himself, and jumped up, went to the table, took up some law papers and began to read them, but could not continue. He unlocked the door and went into the reception-room. The door leading to the drawing-room was shut. He approached it on tiptoe and listened.

"No, you are exaggerating!" Praskóvya Fëdorovna was saying.

"Exaggerating! Don't you see it? Why, he's a dead man! Look at his eyes—there's no light in them. But what is it that is wrong with him?"

"No one knows. Nikoláevich (that was another doctor) said something, but I don't know what. And Leshchetítsky (this was the celebrated specialist) said quite the contrary . . . ."

Iván Ilých walked away, went to his own room, lay down, and began musing: "The kidney, a floating kidney." He recalled all the doctors had told him of how it detached itself and swayed about. And by an effort of imagination he tried to catch that kidney and arrest it and support it. So little was needed for this, it seemed to him. "No, I'll go to see Peter Ivánovich again." (That was the friend whose friend was a doctor.) He rang, ordered the carriage, and got ready to go.

"Where are you going, Jean?" asked his wife, with a specially sad and exceptionally kind look.

This exceptionally kind look irritated him. He looked morosely at her.

"I must go to see Peter Ivánovich."

He went to see Peter Ivánovich, and together they went to see his friend, the doctor. He was in, and Iván Ilých had a long talk with him.

Reviewing the anatomical and physiological details of what in the doctor's opinion was going on inside him, he understood it all.

There was something, a small thing, in the vermiform appendix. It might all come right. Only stimulate the energy of one organ and check the activity of another, then absorption would take place and everything would come right. He got home rather late for dinner, ate his dinner, and conversed cheerfully, but could not for a long time bring himself to go back to work in his room. At last, however, he went to his study and did what was necessary, but the consciousness that he had put something aside—an important, intimate matter which he would revert to when his work was done—never left him. When he had finished his work he remembered that this intimate matter was the thought of his vermiform appendix. But he did not give himself up to it, and went to the drawing-room for tea. There were callers there, including the examining magistrate who was a desirable match for his daughter, and they were conversing, playing the piano and singing. Iván Ilých, as Praskóvya Fëdorovna remarked, spent that evening more cheerfully than usual, but he never for a moment forgot that he had postponed the important matter of the appendix. At eleven o'clock he said good-night and went to his bedroom. Since his illness he had slept alone in a small room next to his study. He undressed and took up a novel by Zola, but instead of reading it he fell into thought, and in his imagination that desired improvement in the vermiform appendix occurred. There was the absorption and evacuation and the reestablishment of normal activity. "Yes, that's it!" he said to himself. "One need only assist nature, that's all." He remembered his medicine, rose, took it, and lay down on his back watching for the beneficent action of the medicine and for it to lessen the pain. "I need only take it regularly and avoid all injurious influences. I am already feeling better, much better." He began touching his side: it was not painful to the touch. "There, I really don't feel it. It's much better already." He put out the light and turned on his side . . . "The appendix is getting better, absorption is occurring." Suddenly he felt the old, familiar, dull, gnawing pain, stubborn and serious. There was the same familiar loathsome taste in his mouth. His heart sank and he felt dazed. "My God! My God!" he muttered. "Again, again! And it will never cease." And suddenly the matter presented itself in a quite different aspect. "Vermiform appendix! Kidney!" he said to himself. "It's not a question of appendix or kidney, but of life and . . . death. Yes, life was there and now it is going, going and I cannot stop it. Yes. Why deceive myself? Isn't it obvious to everyone but me that I'm dying, and that it's only a question of weeks, days . . . it may happen this moment. There was light and now there is darkness. I was here and now I'm going there! Where?" A chill came over him, his breathing ceased, and he felt only the throbbing of his heart.

"When I am not, what will there be? There will be nothing. Then where shall I be when I am no more? Can this be dying? No, I don't want to!" He jumped up and tried to light the candle, felt for it with trembling hands, dropped candle and candlestick on the floor, and fell back on his pillow.

"What's the use? It makes no difference," he said to himself, staring with wide-open eyes into the darkness. "Death. Yes, death. And none of them know or wish to know it, and they have no pity for me. Now they are playing." (He heard through the door the distant sound of a song and its accompaniment.) "It's all the same to them, but they will die too! Fools! I first, and they later, but it will be the same for them. And now they are merry . . . the beasts!"

Anger choked him and he was agonizingly, unbearably miserable. "It is impossible that all men have been doomed to suffer this awful horror!" He raised himself.

"Something must be wrong. I must calm myself—must think it all over from the beginning." And he again began thinking. "Yes, the beginning of my illness: I knocked my side, but I was still quite well that day and the next. It hurt a little, then rather more. I saw the doctors, then followed despondency and anguish, more doctors, and I drew nearer to the abyss. My strength grew less and I kept coming nearer and nearer, and now I have wasted away and there is no light in my eyes. I think of the appendix—but this is death! I think of mending the appendix, and all the while here is death! Can it really be death?" Again terror seized him and he gasped for breath. He leant down and began feeling for the matches, pressing with his elbow on the stand beside the bed. It was in his way and hurt him, he grew furious with it, pressed on it still harder, and upset it. Breathless and in despair he fell on his back, expecting death to come immediately.

Meanwhile the visitors were leaving. Praskóvya Fëdorovna was seeing them off. She heard something fall and came in.

"What has happened?"

"Nothing. I knocked it over accidentally."

She went out and returned with a candle. He lay there panting heavily, like a man who has run a thousand yards, and stared upwards at her with a fixed look.

"What is it, Jean?"

"No . . . o . . . thing. I upset it." ("Why speak of it? She won't understand," he thought.)

And in truth she did not understand. She picked up the stand, lit his candle, and hurried away to see another visitor off. When she came back he still lay on his back, looking upwards.

"What is it? Do you feel worse?"

"Yes."

She shook her head and sat down.

"Do you know, Jean, I think we must ask Leshchetítsky to come and see you here."

This meant calling in the famous specialist, regardless of expense. He smiled malignantly and said "No." She remained a little longer and then went up to him and kissed his forehead.

While she was kissing him he hated her from the bottom of his soul and with difficulty refrained from pushing her away.

"Good-night. Please God you'll sleep."

"Yes."

CHAPTER VI

Iván Ilých saw that he was dying, and he was in continual despair.

In the depth of his heart he knew he was dying, but not only was he not accustomed to the thought, he simply did not and could not grasp it.

The syllogism he had learnt from Kiezewetter's Logic:[9] "Caius is a man, men are mortal, therefore Caius is mortal," had always seemed to him correct as applied to Caius, but certainly not as applied to himself. That Caius—man in the abstract—was mortal, was perfectly correct, but he was not Caius, not an abstract man, but a creature quite, quite separate from all others. He had been little Ványa, with a mamma and a papa; with Mítya and Volódya, and the toys, a coachman and a nurse, afterwards with Kátenka and with all the joys, griefs, and delights of childhood, boyhood, and youth. What did Caius know of the

---

[9] Karl Kiezewetter (1766–1819), author of an outline of logic widely used in Russian schools at the time.

smell of that striped leather ball Ványa had been so fond of? Had Caius kissed his mother's hand like that, and did the silk of her dress rustle so for Caius? Had he rioted like that at school when the pastry was bad? Had Caius been in love like that? Could Caius preside at a session as he did? "Caius really was mortal, and it was right for him to die; but for me, little Ványa, Iván Ilých, with all my thoughts and emotions, it's altogether a different matter. It cannot be that I ought to die. That would be too terrible."

Such was his feeling.

"If I had to die like Caius I should have known it was so. An inner voice would have told me so, but there was nothing of the sort in me and I and all my friends felt that our case was quite different from that of Caius. And now here it is!" he said to himself. "It can't be. It's impossible! But here it is. How is this? How is one to understand it?"

He could not understand it, and tried to drive this false, incorrect, morbid thought away and to replace it by other proper and healthy thoughts. But that thought and not the thought only but the reality itself, seemed to come and confront him.

And to replace that thought he called up a succession of others, hoping to find in them some support. He tried to get back into the former current of thoughts that had once screened the thought of death from him. But strange to say, all that had formerly shut off, hidden, and destroyed, his consciousness of death, no longer had that effect. Iván Ilých now spent most of his time in attempting to re-establish that old current. He would say to himself: "I will take up my duties again—after all I used to live by them." And banishing all doubts he would go to the law courts, enter into conversation with his colleagues, and sit carelessly as was his wont, scanning the crowd with a thoughtful look and leaning both his emaciated arms on the arms of his oak chair; bending over as usual to a colleague and drawing his papers nearer he would interchange whispers with him, and then suddenly raising his eyes and sitting erect would pronounce certain words and open the proceedings. But suddenly in the midst of those proceedings the pain in his side, regardless of the stage the proceedings had reached, would begin its own gnawing work. Iván Ilých would turn his attention to it and try to drive the thought of it away, but without success. *It* would come and stand before him and look at him, and he would be petrified and the light would die out of his eyes, and he would again begin asking himself whether *It* alone was true. And his colleagues and subordinates would see with surprise and distress that he, the brilliant and subtle judge, was becoming confused and making mistakes. He would shake himself, try to pull himself together, manage somehow to bring the sitting to a close, and return home with the sorrowful consciousness that his judicial labours could not as formerly hide from him what he wanted them to hide, and could not deliver him from *It*. And what was worst of all was that *It* drew his attention to itself not in order to make him take some action but only that he should look at *It*, look it straight in the face: look at it and without doing anything, suffer inexpressibly.

And to save himself from this condition Iván Ilých looked for consolations—new screens—and new screens were found and for a while seemed to save him, but then they immediately fell to pieces or rather became transparent, as if *It* penetrated them and nothing could veil *It*.

In these latter days he would go into the drawing-room he had arranged—that drawing-room where he had fallen and for the sake of which (how bitterly ridiculous it seemed) he had sacrificed his life—for he knew that his illness originated with that knock. He would enter and see that something had scratched the polished table. He would look for the cause of this and find that it was the bronze ornamentation of an album, that had got bent. He would take up the expensive album which he had lovingly arranged, and feel vexed with his daughter and her friends for their untidiness—for the album was torn here and there and some of the photographs turned upside down. He would put it carefully in order and bend the ornamentation back into position. Then it would occur to him to place all those things in another corner of the room, near the plants. He could call the footman, but his daughter or wife would come to help him. They would not agree, and his wife would contradict him, and he would dispute and grow angry. But that was all right, for then he did not think about *It*. *It* was invisible.

But then, when he was moving something himself, his wife would say: "Let the servants do it. You will hurt yourself again." And suddenly *It* would flash through the screen and he would see it. It was just a flash, and he hoped it would disappear, but he would involuntarily pay attention to his side. "It sits there as before, gnawing just the same!" And he could no longer forget *It*, but could distinctly see it looking at him from behind the flowers. "What is it all for?"

"It really is so! I lost my life over that curtain as I might have done when storming a fort. Is that possible? How terrible and how stupid. It can't be true! It can't, but it is!"

He would go to his study, lie down, and again be alone with *It*: face to face with *It*. And nothing could be done with *It* except to look at it and shudder.

CHAPTER VII

How it happened it is impossible to say because it came about step by step, unnoticed, but in the third month of Iván Ilých's illness, his wife, his daughter, his son, his acquaintances, the doctors, the servants, and above all he himself, were aware that the whole interest he had for other people was whether he would soon vacate his place, and at last release the living from the discomfort caused by his presence and be himself released from his sufferings.

He slept less and less. He was given opium and hypodermic injections of morphine, but this did not relieve him. The dull depression he experienced in a somnolent condition at first gave him a little relief, but only as something new, afterwards it became as distressing as the pain itself or even more so.

Special foods were prepared for him by the doctors' orders, but all those foods became increasingly distasteful and disgusting to him.

For his excretions also special arrangements had to be made, and this was a torment to him every time—a torment from the uncleanliness, the unseemliness, and the smell, and from knowing that another person had to take part in it.

But just through this most unpleasant matter Iván Ilých obtained comfort. Gerásim, the butler's young assistant, always came in to carry the things out. Gerásim was a clean, fresh peasant lad, grown stout on town food and always cheerful and bright. At first the sight of him, in his clean Russian peasant costume, engaged on that disgusting task embarrassed Iván Ilých.

Once when he got up from the commode too weak to draw up his trousers, he dropped into a soft armchair and looked with horror at his bare, enfeebled thighs with the muscles so sharply marked on them.

Gerásim with a firm light tread, his heavy boots emitting a pleasant smell of tar and fresh winter air, came in wearing a clean Hessian apron, the sleeves of his print shirt tucked up over his strong bare young arms; and refraining from looking at his sick master out of consideration for his feelings, and restraining the joy of life that beamed from his face, went up to the commode.

"Gerásim!" said Iván Ilých in a weak voice.

Gerásim started, evidently afraid he might have committed some blunder, and with a rapid movement turned his fresh, kind, simple young face which just showed the first downy signs of a beard.

"Yes, sir?"

"That must be very unpleasant for you. You must forgive me. I am helpless."

"Oh, why, sir," and Gerásim's eyes beamed and he showed his glistening white teeth, "what's a little trouble? It's a case of illness with you, sir."

And his deft strong hands did their accustomed task, and he went out of the room stepping lightly. Five minutes later he as lightly returned.

Iván Ilých was still sitting in the same position in the armchair.

"Gerásim," he said when the latter had replaced the freshly-washed utensil. "Please come here and help me." Gerásim went up to him. "Lift me up. It is hard for me to get up, and I have sent Dmítri away."

Gerásim went up to him, grasped his master with his strong arms deftly but gently, in the same way that he stepped—lifted him, supported him with one hand, and with the other drew up his trousers and would have set him down again, but Iván Ilých asked to be led to the sofa. Gerásim, without an effort and without apparent pressure, led him, almost lifting him, to the sofa and placed him on it.

"Thank you. How easily and well you do it all!"

Gerásim smiled again and turned to leave the room. But Iván Ilých felt his presence such a comfort that he did not want to let him go.

"One thing more, please move up that chair. No, the other one—under my feet. It is easier for me when my feet are raised."

Gerásim brought the chair, set it down gently in place, and raised Iván Ilých's legs on to it. It seemed to Iván Ilých that he felt better while Gerasim was holding up his legs.

"It's better when my legs are higher," he said. "Place that cushion under them."

Gerásim did so. He again lifted the legs and placed them, and again Iván Ilých felt better while Gerásim held his legs. When he set them down Iván Ilých fancied he felt worse.

"Gerásim," he said. "Are you busy now?"

"Not at all, sir," said Gerásim, who had learnt from the townsfolk how to speak to gentlefolk.

"What have you still to do?"

"What have I to do? I've done everything except chopping the logs for to-morrow."

"Then hold my legs up a bit higher, can you?"

"Of course I can. Why not?" And Gerásim raised his master's legs higher and Iván Ilých thought that in that position he did not feel any pain at all.

"And how about the logs?"

"Don't trouble about that, sir. There's plenty of time."

Iván Ilých told Gerásim to sit down and hold his legs, and began to talk to him. And strange to say it seemed to him that he felt better while Gerásim held his legs up.

After that Iván Ilých would sometimes call Gerásim and get him to hold his legs on his shoulders, and he liked talking to him. Gerásim did it all easily, willingly, simply, and with a good nature that touched Iván Ilých. Health, strength, and vitality in other people were offensive to him, but Gerásim's strength and vitality did not mortify but soothed him.

What tormented Iván Ilých most was the deception, the lie, which for some reason they all accepted, that he was not dying but was simply ill, and that he only need keep quiet and undergo a treatment and then something very good would result. He however knew that do what they would nothing would come of it, only still more agonizing suffering and death. This deception tortured him—their not wishing to admit what they all knew and what he knew, but wanting to lie to him concerning his terrible condition, and wishing and forcing him to participate in that lie. Those lies—lies enacted over him on the eve of his death and destined to degrade this awful, solemn act to the level of their visitings, their curtains, their sturgeon for dinner—were a terrible agony for Iván Ilých. And strangely enough, many times when they were going through their antics over him he had been within a hairbreadth of calling out to them: "Stop lying! You know and I know that I am dying. Then at least stop lying about it!" But he had never had the spirit to do it. The awful, terrible act of his dying was, he could see, reduced by those about him to the level of a casual, un-pleasant, and almost indecorous incident (as if someone entered a drawing-room diffusing an unpleasant odour) and this was done by that very decorum which he had served all his life long. He saw that no one felt for him, because no one even wished to grasp his position. Only Gerásim recognized it and pitied him.

And so Iván Ilých felt at ease only with him. He felt comforted when Gerásim supported his legs (sometimes all night long) and refused to go to bed, saying: "Don't you worry, Iván Ilých. I'll get sleep enough later on," or when he suddenly became familiar and exclaimed: "If you weren't sick it would be another matter, but as it is, why should I grudge a little trouble?" Gerásim alone did not lie; everything showed that he alone understood the facts of the case and did not consider it necessary to disguise them, but simply felt sorry for his emaciated and enfeebled master. Once when Iván Ilých was sending him away he even said straight out: "We shall all of us die, so why should I grudge a little trouble?"—expressing the fact that he did not think his work burdensome, because he was doing it for a dying man and hoped someone would do the same for him when his time came.

Apart from this lying, or because of it, what most tormented Iván Ilých was that no one pitied him as he wished to be pitied. At certain moments after prolonged suffering he wished most of all (though he would have been ashamed to confess it) for someone to pity him as a sick child is pitied. He longed to be petted and comforted. He knew he was an important functionary, that he had a beard turning grey, and that therefore what he longed for was impossible, but still he longed for it. And in Gerásim's attitude towards him there was something akin to what he wished for, and so that attitude comforted him. Iván Ilých wanted to weep, wanted to be petted and cried over, and then his colleague Shébek would come, and instead of weeping and being petted, Iván Ilých would assume a serious, severe, and profound air, and by force of habit would express his opinion on a decision of the Court of Cassation and would stubbornly insist on that view. This falsity around him and within him did more than anything else to poison his last days.

CHAPTER VIII

It was morning. He knew it was morning because Gerásim had gone, and Peter the footman had come and put out the candles, drawn back one of the curtains, and begun quietly to tidy up. Whether it was morning or evening, Friday or Sunday, made no difference, it was all just the same: the gnawing, unmitigated, agonizing pain, never ceasing for an instant, the consciousness of life inexorably waning but not yet extinguished, that approach of that ever dreaded and hateful Death which was the only reality, and always the same falsity. What were days, weeks, hours, in such a case?

"Will you have some tea, sir?"

"He wants things to be regular, and wishes the gentlefolk to drink tea in the morning," thought Iván Ilých, and only said "No."

"Wouldn't you like to move onto the sofa, sir?"

"He wants to tidy up the room, and I'm in the way. I am uncleanliness and disorder," he thought, and said only:

"No, leave me alone."

The man went on bustling about. Iván Ilých stretched out his hand. Peter came up, ready to help.

"What is it, sir?"

"My watch."

Peter took the watch which was close at hand and gave it to his master.

"Half-past eight. Are they up?"

"No sir, except Vladímir Ivánich" (the son) "who has gone to school. Praskóvya Fëdorovna ordered me to wake her if you asked for her. Shall I do so?"

"No, there's no need to." "Perhaps I'd better have some tea," he thought, and added aloud: "Yes, bring me some tea."

Peter went to the door but Iván Ilých dreaded being left alone. "How can I keep him here? Oh yes, my medicine." "Peter, give me my medicine." "Why not? Perhaps it may still do me some good." He took a spoonful and swallowed it. "No, it won't help. It's all tomfoolery, all deception," he decided as soon as he became aware of the familiar, sickly, hopeless taste. "No, I can't believe in it any longer. But the pain, why this pain? If it would only cease just for a moment!" And he moaned. Peter turned towards him. "It's all right. Go and fetch me some tea."

Peter went out. Left alone Iván Ilých groaned not so much with pain, terrible though that was, as from mental anguish. Always and for ever the same, always these endless days and nights. If only it would come quicker! If only *what* would come quicker? Death, darkness? . . . No, no! Anything rather than death!

When Peter returned with the tea on a tray, Iván Ilých stared at him for a time in perplexity, not realizing who and what he was. Peter was disconcerted by that look and his embarrassment brought Iván Ilých to himself.

"Oh, tea! All right, put it down. Only help me to wash and put on a clean shirt."

And Iván Ilých began to wash. With pauses for rest, he washed his hands and then his face, cleaned his teeth, brushed his hair, and looked in the glass. He was terrified by what he saw, especially by the limp way in which his hair clung to his pallid forehead.

While his shirt was being changed he knew that he would be still more frightened at the sight of his body, so he avoided looking at it. Finally he was ready. He drew on a dressing-gown, wrapped himself in a plaid, and sat down in the armchair to take his tea. For a moment he felt refreshed, but as soon as he began to drink the tea he was again aware of the same taste, and the pain also returned. He finished it with an effort, and then lay down stretching out his legs, and dismissed Peter.

Always the same. Now a spark of hope flashes up, then a sea of despair rages, and always pain; always pain, always despair, and always the same. When alone he had a dreadful and distressing desire to call someone, but he knew beforehand that with others present it would be still worse. "Another dose of morphine—to lose consciousness. I will tell him, the doctor, that he must think of something else. It's impossible, impossible, to go on like this."

An hour and another pass like that. But now there is a ring at the door bell. Perhaps it's the doctor? It is. He comes in fresh, hearty, plump, and cheerful, with that look on his face that seems to say: "There now, you're in a panic about something, but we'll arrange it all for you directly!" The doctor knows this expression is out of place here, but he has put it on once for all and can't take it off—like a man who has put on a frock-coat in the morning to pay a round of calls.

The doctor rubs his hands vigorously and reassuringly.

"Brr! How cold it is! There's such a sharp frost; just let me warm myself!" he says, as if it were only a matter of waiting till he was warm, and then he would put everything right.

"Well now, how are you?"

Iván Ilých feels that the doctor would like to say: "Well, how are our affairs?" but that even he feels that this would not do, and says instead: "What sort of a night have you had?"

Iván Ilých looks at him as much as to say: "Are you really never ashamed of lying?" But the doctor does not wish to understand this question, and Iván Ilých says: "Just as terrible as ever. The pain never leaves me and never subsides. If only something . . . "

"Yes, you sick people are always like that. . . . There, now I think I am warm enough. Even Praskóvya Fëdorovna, who is so particular, could find no fault with my temperature. Well, now I can say good-morning," and the doctor presses his patient's hand.

Then, dropping his former playfulness, he begins with a most serious face to examine the patient, feeling his pulse and taking his temperature, and then begins the sounding and auscultation.

Ivan Ilých knows quite well and definitely that all this is nonsense and pure deception, but when the doctor, getting down on his knee, leans over him, putting his ear first higher then lower, and performs various gymnastic movements over him with a significant expression on his face, Iván Ilých submits to it all as he used to submit to the speeches of the lawyers, though he knew very well that they were all lying and why they were lying.

The doctor, kneeling on the sofa, is still sounding him when Praskóvya Fëdorovna's silk dress rustles at the door and she is heard scolding Peter for not having let her know of the doctor's arrival.

She comes in, kisses her husband, and at once proceeds to prove that she has been up a long time already, and only owing to a misunderstanding failed to be there when the doctor arrived.

Iván Ilých looks at her, scans her all over, sets against her the whiteness and plumpness and cleanness of her hands and neck, the gloss of her hair, and the sparkle of her vivacious eyes. He hates her with his whole soul. And the thrill of hatred he feels for her makes him suffer from her touch.

Her attitude towards him and his disease is still the same. Just as the doctor had adopted a certain relation to his patient which he could not abandon, so had she formed one towards him—that he was not doing something he ought

to do and was himself to blame, and that she reproached him lovingly for this—
and she could not now change that attitude.

"You see he doesn't listen to me and doesn't take his medicine at the proper
time. And above all he lies in a position that is no doubt bad for him—with his
legs up."

She described how he made Gerásim hold his legs up.

The doctor smiled with a contemptuous affability that said: "What's to be
done? These sick people do have foolish fancies of that kind, but we must forgive
them."

When the examination was over the doctor looked at his watch, and then
Praskóvya Fëdorovna announced to Iván Ilých that it was of course as he pleased,
but she had sent to-day for a celebrated specialist who would examine him and
have a consultation with Michael Danílovich (their regular doctor).

"Please don't raise any objections. I am doing this for my own sake," she said
ironically, letting it be felt that she was doing it all for his sake and only said
that to leave him no right to refuse. He remained silent, knitting his brows. He
felt that he was so surrounded and involved in a mesh of falsity that it was hard
to unravel anything.

Everything she did for him was entirely for her own sake, and she told him
she was doing for herself what she actually was doing for herself, as if that was
so incredible that he must understand the opposite.

At half-past eleven the celebrated specialist arrived. Again the sounding began
and the significant conversations in his presence and in another room, about
the kidneys and the appendix, and the questions and answers, with such an air
of importance that again, instead of the real question of life and death which
now alone confronted him, the question arose of the kidney and appendix which
were not behaving as they ought to and would now be attacked by Michael
Danílovich and the specialist and forced to amend their ways.

The celebrated specialist took leave of him with a serious though not hopeless
look, and in reply to the timid question Iván Ilých, with eyes glistening with
fear and hope, put to him as to whether there was a chance of recovery, said
that he could not vouch for it but there was a possibility. The look of hope with
which Iván Ilých watched the doctor out was so pathetic that Praskóvya Fëdorovna, seeing it, even wept as she left the room to hand the doctor his fee.

The gleam of hope kindled by the doctor's encouragement did not last long.
The same room, the same pictures, curtains, wall-paper, medicine bottles, were
all there, and the same aching suffering body, and Iván Ilých began to moan.
They gave him a subcutaneous injection and he sank into oblivion.

It was twilight when he came to. They brought him his dinner and he swallowed some beef tea with difficulty, and then everything was the same again
and night was coming on.

After dinner, at seven o'clock, Praskóvya Fëdorovna came into the room in
evening dress, her full bosom pushed up by her corset, and with traces of powder
on her face. She had reminded him in the morning that they were going to the
theatre. Sarah Bernhardt was visiting the town and they had a box, which he

had insisted on their taking. Now he had forgotten about it and her toilet offended him, but he concealed his vexation when he remembered that he had himself insisted on their securing a box and going because it would be an instructive and aesthetic pleasure for the children.

Praskóvya Fëdorovna came in, self-satisfied but yet with a rather guilty air. She sat down and asked how he was but, as he saw, only for the sake of asking and not in order to learn about it, knowing that there was nothing to learn— and then went on to what she really wanted to say: that she would not on any account have gone but that the box had been taken and Helen and their daughter were going, as well as Petríshchev (the examining magistrate, their daughter's fiancé) and that it was out of the question to let them go alone; but that she would have much preferred to sit with him for a while; and he must be sure to follow the doctor's orders while she was away.

"Oh, and Fëdor Petróvich" (the fiancé) "would like to come in. May he? And Lisa?"

"All right."

Their daughter came in in full evening dress, her fresh young flesh exposed (making a show of that very flesh which in his own case caused so much suffering), strong, healthy, evidently in love, and impatient with illness, suffering, and death, because they interfered with her happiness.

Fëdor Petróvich came in too, in evening dress, his hair curled *á la Capoul*, a tight stiff collar round his long sinewy neck, an enormous white shirt-front and narrow black trousers tightly stretched over his strong thighs. He had one white glove tightly drawn on, and was holding his opera hat in his hand.

Following him the schoolboy crept in unnoticed, in a new uniform, poor little fellow, and wearing gloves. Terribly dark shadows showed under his eyes, the meaning of which Iván Ilých knew well.

His son had always seemed pathetic to him, and now it was dreadful to see the boy's frightened look of pity. It seemed to Iván Ilých that Vásya was the only one besides Gerásim who understood and pitied him.

They all sat down and again asked how he was. A silence followed. Lisa asked her mother about the opera-glasses, and there was an altercation between mother and daughter as to who had taken them and where they had been put. This occasioned some unpleasantness.

Fëdor Petróvich inquired of Iván Ilých whether he had ever seen Sarah Bernhardt. Iván Ilých did not at first catch the question, but then replied: "No, have you seen her before?"

"Yes, In *Adrienne Lecouvreur*." [10]

Praskóvya Fëdorovna mentioned some roles in which Sarah Bernhardt was particularly good. Her daughter disagreed. Conversation sprang up as to the elegance and realism of her acting—the sort of conversation that is always repeated and is always the same.

---

[10] A play by the French dramatist Eugène Scribe (1791–1861).

In the midst of the conversation Fëdor Petróvich glanced at Iván Ilých and became silent. The others also looked at him and grew silent. Iván Ilých was staring with glittering eyes straight before him, evidently indignant with them. This had to be rectified, but it was impossible to do so. The silence had to be broken, but for a time no one dared to break it and they all became afraid that the conventional deception would suddenly become obvious and the truth become plain to all. Lisa was the first to pluck up courage and break that silence, but by trying to hide what everybody was feeling, she betrayed it.

"Well, if we are going it's time to start," she said, looking at her watch, a present from her father, and with a faint and significant smile at Fëdor Petróvich relating to something known only to them. She got up with a rustle of her dress.

They all rose, said good-night, and went away.

When they had gone it seemed to Iván Ilých that he felt better; the falsity had gone with them. But the pain remained—that same pain and that same fear that made everything monotonously alike, nothing harder and nothing easier. Everything was worse.

Again minute followed minute and hour followed hour. Everything remained the same and there was no cessation. And the inevitable end of it all became more and more terrible.

"Yes, send Gerásim here," he replied to a question Peter asked.

CHAPTER IX

His wife returned late at night. She came in on tiptoe, but he heard her, opened his eyes, and made haste to close them again. She wished to send Gerásim away and to sit with him herself, but he opened his eyes and said: "No, go away."

"Are you in great pain?"

"Always the same."

"Take some opium."

He agreed and took some. She went away.

Till about three in the morning he was in a state of stupefied misery. It seemed to him that he and his pain were being thrust into a narrow, deep black sack, but though they were pushed further and further in they could not be pushed to the bottom. And this, terrible enough in itself, was accompanied by suffering. He was frightened yet wanted to fall through the sack, he struggled but yet co-operated. And suddenly he broke through, fell, and regained consciousness. Gerásim was sitting at the foot of the bed dozing quietly and patiently, while he himself lay with his emaciated stockinged legs resting on Gerásim's shoulders; the same shaded candle was there and the same unceasing pain.

"Go away, Gerásim," he whispered.

"It's all right, sir. I'll stay a while."

"No. Go away."

He removed his legs from Gerásim's shoulders, turned sideways onto his arm, and felt sorry for himself. He only waited till Gerásim had gone into the next room and then restrained himself no longer but wept like a child. He wept on account of his helplessness, his terrible loneliness, the cruelty of man, the cruelty of God, and the absence of God.

"Why hast Thou done all this? Why hast Thou brought me here? Why, why dost Thou torment me so terribly?"

He did not expect an answer and yet wept because there was no answer and could be none. The pain again grew more acute, but he did not stir and did not call. He said to himself: "Go on! Strike me! But what is it for? What have I done to Thee? What is it for?"

Then he grew quiet and not only ceased weeping but even held his breath and became all attention. It was as though he were listening not to an audible voice but to the voice of his soul, to the current of thoughts arising within him.

"What is it you want?" was the first clear conception capable of expression in words, that he heard.

"What do you want? What do you want?" he repeated to himself.

"What do I want? To live and not to suffer," he answered.

And again he listened with such concentrated attention that even his pain did not distract him.

"To live? How?" asked his inner voice.

"Why, to live as I used to—well and pleasantly."

"As you lived before, well and pleasantly?" the voice repeated.

And in imagination he began to recall the best moments of his pleasant life. But strange to say none of these best moments of his pleasant life now seemed at all what they had then seemed—none of them except the first recollections of childhood. There, in childhood, there had been something really pleasant with which it would be possible to live if it could return. But the child who had experienced that happiness existed no longer, it was like a reminiscence of somebody else.

As soon as the period began which had produced the present Iván Ilých, all that had then seemed joys now melted before his sight and turned into something trivial and often nasty.

And the further he departed from childhood and the nearer he came to the present the more worthless and doubtful were the joys. This began with the School of Law. A little that was really good was still found there—there was light-heartedness, friendship, and hope. But in the upper classes there had already been fewer of such good moments. Then during the first years of his official career, when he was in the service of the Governor, some pleasant moments again occurred: they were the memories of love for a woman. Then all became confused and there was still less of what was good; later on again there was still less that was good, and the further he went the less there was. His marriage, a mere accident, then the disenchantment that followed it, his wife's bad breath and the sensuality and hypocrisy: then that deadly official life and those preoccupations about money, a year of it, and two, and ten, and twenty, and always the same thing. And the longer it lasted the more deadly it became. "It is as if I had been going downhill while I imagined I was going up.

And that is really what it was. I was going up in public opinion, but to the same extent life was ebbing away from me. And now it is all done and there is only death."

"Then what does it mean? Why? It can't be that life is so senseless and horrible. But if it really has been so horrible and senseless, why must I die and die in agony? There is something wrong!"

"Maybe I did not live as I ought to have done," it suddenly occurred to him. "But how could that be, when I did everything properly?" he replied, and immediately dismissed from his mind this, the sole solution of all the riddles of life and death, as something quite impossible.

"Then what do you want now? To live? Live how? Live as you lived in the law courts when the usher proclaimed 'The judge is coming!' " "The judge is coming, the judge!" he repeated to himself. "Here he is, the judge. But I am not guilty!" he exclaimed angrily. "What is it for?" And he ceased crying, but turning his face to the wall continued to ponder on the same question: Why, and for what purpose, is there all this horror? But however much he pondered he found no answer. And whenever the thought occurred to him, as it often did, that it all resulted from his not having lived as he ought to have done, he at once recalled the correctness of his whole life and dismissed so strange an idea.

CHAPTER X

Another fortnight passed. Iván Ilých now no longer left his sofa. He would not lie in bed but lay on the sofa, facing the wall nearly all the time. He suffered ever the same unceasing agonies and in his loneliness pondered always on the same insoluble question: "What is this? Can it be that it is Death?" And the inner voice answered: "Yes, it is Death."

"Why these sufferings?" And the voice answered, "For no reason—they just are so." Beyond and besides this there was nothing.

From the very beginning of his illness, ever since he had first been to see the doctor, Iván Ilých's life had been divided between two contrary and alternating moods: now it was despair and the expectation of this uncomprehended and terrible death, and now hope and an intently interested observation of the functioning of his organs. Now before his eyes there was only a kidney or an intestine that temporarily evaded its duty, and now only that incomprehensible and dreadful death from which it was impossible to escape.

These two states of mind had alternated from the very beginning of his illness, but the further it progressed the more doubtful and fantastic became the conception of the kidney, and the more real the sense of impending death.

He had but to call to mind what he had been three months before and what he was now, to call to mind with what regularity he had been going downhill, for every possibility of hope to be shattered.

Latterly during that loneliness in which he found himself as he lay facing the back of the sofa, a loneliness in the midst of a populous town and surrounded by numerous acquaintances and relations but that yet could not have been more complete anywhere—either at the bottom of the sea or under the earth—during that terrible loneliness Iván Ilých had lived only in memories of the past. Pictures of his past rose before him one after another. They always began with what was nearest in time and then went back to what was most remote—to his childhood—and rested there. If he thought of the stewed prunes that had been offered him that day, his mind went back to the raw shrivelled French plums of his childhood, their peculiar flavour and the flow of saliva when he sucked their stones, and along with the memory of that taste came a whole series of memories of those days: his nurse, his brother, and their toys. "No, I mustn't think of that. . . . It is too painful," Iván Ilých said to himself, and brought himself back to the present—to the button on the back of the sofa and the creases in its morocco. "Morocco is expensive, but it does not wear well: There had been a quarrel about it. It was a different kind of quarrel and a different kind of morocco that time when we tore father's portfolio and were punished, and mamma brought us some tarts. . . ." And again his thoughts dwelt on his childhood, and again it was painful and he tried to banish them and fix his mind on something else.

Then again together with that chain of memories another series passed through his mind—of how his illness had progressed and grown worse. There also the further back he looked the more life there had been. There had been more of what was good in life and more of life itself. The two merged together. "Just as the pain went on getting worse and worse so my life grew worse and worse," he thought. "There is one bright spot there at the back, at the beginning of life, and afterwards all becomes blacker and blacker and proceeds more and more rapidly—in inverse ratio to the square of the distance from death," thought Iván Ilých. And the example of a stone falling downwards with increasing velocity entered his mind. Life, a series of increasing sufferings, flies, further and further towards its end—the most terrible suffering. "I am flying. . . ." He shuddered, shifted himself, and tried to resist, but was already aware that resistance was impossible, and again with eyes weary of gazing but unable to cease seeing what was before them, he stared at the back of the sofa and waited—awaiting that dreadful fall and shock and destruction.

"Resistance is impossible!" he said to himself. "If I could only understand what it is all for! But that too is impossible. An explanation would be possible if it could be said that I have not lived as I ought to. But it is impossible to say that," and he remembered all the legality, correctitude, and propriety of his life. "That at any rate can certainly not be admitted," he thought, and his lips smiled ironically as if someone could see that smile and be taken in by it. "There is no explanation! Agony, death. . . . What for?"

CHAPTER XI

Another two weeks went by in this way and during that fortnight an event occurred that Iván Ilých and his wife had desired. Petríshchev formally proposed. It happened in the evening. The next day Praskóvya Fëdorovna came into her husband's room considering how best to inform him of it, but that very night there had been a fresh change for the worse in his condition. She found him still lying on the sofa but in a different position. He lay on his back, groaning and staring fixedly straight in front of him.

She began to remind him of his medicines, but he turned his eyes towards her with such a look that she did not finish what she was saying; so great an animosity, to her in particular, did that look express.

"For Christ's sake, let me die in peace!" he said.

She would have gone away, but just then their daughter came in and went up to say good morning. He looked at her as he had done at his wife, and in reply to her inquiry about his health said dryly that he would soon free them all of himself. They were both silent and after sitting with him for a while went away.

"Is it our fault?" Lisa said to her mother. "It's as if we were to blame! I am sorry for papa, but why should we be tortured?"

The doctor came at his usual time. Iván Ilých answered "Yes" and "No," never taking his angry eyes from him, and at last said: "You know you can do nothing for me, so leave me alone."

"We can ease your sufferings."

"You can't even do that. Let me be."

The doctor went into the drawing-room and told Praskóvya Fëdorovna that the case was very serious and that the only resource left was opium to allay her husband's sufferings, which must be terrible.

It was true, as the doctor said, that Iván Ilých's physical sufferings were terrible, but worse than the physical sufferings were his mental sufferings which were his chief torture.

His mental sufferings were due to the fact that that night, as he looked at Gerásim's sleepy, good-natured face with its prominent cheek-bones, the question suddenly occurred to him: "What if my whole life has really been wrong?"

It occurred to him that what had appeared perfectly impossible before, namely that he had not spent his life as he should have done, might after all be true. It occurred to him that his scarcely perceptible attempts to struggle against what was considered good by the most highly placed people, those scarcely noticeable impulses which he had immediately suppressed, might have been the real thing, and all the rest false. And his professional duties and the whole arrangement of his life and of his family, and all his social and official interests, might all have been false. He tried to defend all those things to himself and suddenly felt the weakness of what he was defending. There was nothing to defend.

"But if that is so," he said to himself, "and I am leaving this life with the consciousness that I have lost all that was given me and it is impossible to rectify it—what then?"

He lay on his back and began to pass his life in review in quite a new way. In the morning when he saw first his footman, then his wife, then his daughter, and then the doctor, their every word and movement confirmed to him the awful truth that had been revealed to him during the night. In them he saw himself—all that for which he had lived—and saw clearly that it was not real at all, but a terrible and huge deception which had hidden both life and death. This consciousness intensified his physical suffering tenfold. He groaned and tossed about, and pulled at his clothing which choked and stifled him. And he hated them on that account.

He was given a large dose of opium and became unconscious, but at noon his sufferings began again. He drove everybody away and tossed from side to side.

His wife came to him and said:

"Jean my dear, do this for me. It can't do any harm and often helps. Healthy people often do it."

He opened his eyes wide.

"What? Take communion? Why? It's unnecessary! However. . . ."

She began to cry.

"Yes, do, my dear. I'll send for our priest. He is such a nice man."

"All right. Very well," he muttered.

When the priest came and heard his confession, Iván Ilých was softened and seemed to feel a relief from his doubts and consequently from his sufferings, and for a moment there came a ray of hope. He again began to think of the vermiform appendix and the possibility of correcting it. He received the sacrament with tears in his eyes.

When they laid him down again afterwards he felt a moment's ease, and the hope that he might live awoke in him again. He began to think of the operation that had been suggested to him. "To live! I want to live!" he said to himself.

His wife came in to congratulate him after his communion, and when uttering the usual conventional words she added:

"You feel better, don't you?"

Without looking at her he said "Yes."

Her dress, her figure, the expression of her face, the tone of her voice, all revealed the same thing. "This is wrong, it is not as it should be. All you have lived for and still live for is falsehood and deception, hiding life and death from you." And as soon as he admitted that thought, his hatred and his agonizing physical suffering again sprang up, and with that suffering a consciousness of the unavoidable, approaching end. And to this was added a new sensation of grinding shooting pain and a feeling of suffocation.

The expression of his face when he uttered that "yes" was dreadful. Having uttered it, he looked her straight in the eyes, turned on his face with a rapidity extraordinary in his weak state and shouted:

"Go away! Go away and leave me alone!"

CHAPTER XII

From that moment the screaming began that continued for three days, and was so terrible that one could not hear it through two closed doors without horror. At the moment he answered his wife he realized that he was lost, that there was no return, that the end had come, the very end, and his doubts were still unsolved and remained doubts.

"Oh! Oh! Oh!" he cried in various intonations. He had begun by screaming "I won't!" and continued screaming on the letter "o."

For three whole days, during which time did not exist for him, he struggled in that black sack into which he was being thrust by an invisible, resistless force. He struggled as a man condemned to death struggles in the hands of the executioner, knowing that he cannot save himself. And every moment he felt that despite all his efforts he was drawing nearer and nearer to what terrified him. He felt that his agony was due to his being thrust into that black hole and still more to his not being able to get right into it. He was hindered from getting into it by his conviction that his life had been a good one. That very justification of his life held him fast and prevented his moving forward, and it caused him most torment of all.

Suddenly some force struck him in the chest and side, making it still harder to breathe, and he fell through the hole and there at the bottom was a light. What had happened to him was like the sensation one sometimes experiences in a railway carriage when one thinks one is going backwards while one is really going forwards and suddenly becomes aware of the real direction.

"Yes, it was all not the right thing," he said to himself, "but that's no matter. It can be done. But what *is* the right thing?" he asked himself, and suddenly grew quiet.

This occurred at the end of the third day, two hours before his death. Just then his schoolboy son had crept softly in and gone up to the bedside. The dying man was still screaming desperately and waving his arms. His hand fell on the boy's head, and the boy caught it, pressed it to his lips, and began to cry.

At that very moment Iván Ilých fell through and caught sight of the light, and it was revealed to him that though his life had not been what it should have been, this could still be rectified. He asked himself, "What *is* the right thing?" and grew still, listening. Then he felt that someone was kissing his hand. He opened his eyes, looked at his son, and felt sorry for him. His wife came up to him and he glanced at her. She was gazing at him open-mouthed, with undried tears on her nose and cheek and a despairing look on her face. He felt sorry for her too.

"Yes, I am making them wretched," he thought. "They are sorry, but it will be better for them when I die." He wished to say this but had not the strength to utter it. "Besides, why speak? I must act," he thought. With a look at his wife he indicated his son and said: "Take him away . . . sorry for him . . . sorry for you too. . . ." He tried to add, "forgive me," but said "forego" and waved his hand, knowing that He whose understanding mattered would understand.

And suddenly it grew clear to him that what had been oppressing him and would not leave him was all dropping away at once from two sides, from ten sides, and from all sides. He was sorry for them, he must act so as not to hurt them: release them and free himself from these sufferings. "How good and how simple!" he thought. "And the pain?" he asked himself. "What has become of it? Where are you, pain?"

He turned his attention to it.

"Yes, here it is. Well, what of it? Let the pain be."

"And death . . . where is it?"

He sought his former accustomed fear of death and did not find it. "Where is it? What death?" There was no fear because there was no death.

In place of death there was light.

"So that's what it is!" he suddenly exclaimed aloud. "What joy!"

To him all this happened in a single instant, and the meaning of that instant did not change. For those present his agony continued for another two hours. Something rattled in his throat, his emaciated body twitched, then the gasping and rattle became less and less frequent.

"It is finished!" said someone near him.

He heard these words and repeated them in his soul.

"Death is finished," he said to himself. "It is no more!"

He drew in a breath, stopped in the midst of a sigh, stretched out, and died.

QUESTIONS

1. Why does Tolstoy begin the story immediately after Ilých's death and then move back to recount his life? **2.** Is there any evidence that Ilých's death is a moral judgment—that is, a punishment for his life? Explain. **3.** Why is Gerásim, Ilých's peasant servant, most sympathetic to his plight?

WRITING TOPIC

At the very end, Ilých achieves peace and understanding, and the questions that have been torturing him are resolved. He realizes that "though his life had not been what it should have been, this could still be rectified." What does this mean?

An Occurrence at Owl Creek Bridge (1891)

AMBROSE BIERCE [1842–1914?]

I

A man stood upon a railroad bridge in northern Alabama, looking down into the swift water twenty feet below. The man's hands were behind his back, the wrists bound with a cord. A rope closely encircled his neck. It was attached to a stout cross-timber above his head and the slack fell to the level of his knees. Some loose boards laid upon the sleepers supporting the metals of the railway supplied a footing for him and his executioners—two private soldiers of the Federal army, directed by a sergeant who in civil life may have been a deputy sheriff. At a short remove upon the same temporary platform was an officer in the uniform of his rank, armed. He was a captain. A sentinel at each end of the bridge stood with his rifle in the position known as "support," that is to say, vertical in front of the left shoulder, the hammer resting on the forearm thrown straight across the chest—a formal and unnatural position, enforcing an erect carriage of the body. It did not appear to be the duty of these two men to know what was occurring at the centre of the bridge; they merely blockaded the two ends of the foot planking that traversed it.

Beyond one of the sentinels nobody was in sight; the railroad ran straight away into a forest for a hundred yards, then, curving, was lost to view. Doubtless there was an outpost farther along. The other bank of the stream was open ground—a gentle acclivity topped with a stockade of vertical tree trunks, loopholed for rifles, with a single embrasure through which protruded the muzzle of a brass cannon commanding the bridge. Midway of the slope between bridge and fort were the spectators—a single company of infantry in line, at "parade rest," the butts of the rifles on the ground, the barrels inclining slightly backward against the right shoulder, the hands crossed upon the stock. A lieutenant stood at the right of the line, the point of his sword upon the ground, his left hand resting upon his right. Excepting the group of four at the centre of the bridge, not a man moved. The company faced the bridge, staring stonily, motionless. The sentinels, facing the banks of the stream, might have been statues to adorn the bridge. The captain stood with folded arms, silent, observing the work of his subordinates, but making no sign. Death is a dignitary who when he comes announced is to be received with formal manifestations of respect, even by those most familiar with him. In the code of military etiquette silence and fixity are forms of deference.

The man who was engaged in being hanged was apparently about thirty-five years of age. He was a civilian, if one might judge from his habit, which was that of a planter. His features were good—a straight nose, firm mouth, broad forehead, from which his long, dark hair was combed straight back, falling behind his ears to the collar of his well-fitting frock-coat. He wore a mustache and pointed beard, but no whiskers; his eyes were large and dark gray, and had a kindly expression which one would hardly have expected in one whose neck was in the hemp. Evidently this was no vulgar assassin. The liberal military code makes provision for hanging many kinds of persons, and gentlemen are not excluded.

The preparations being complete, the two private soldiers stepped aside and each drew away the plank upon which he had been standing. The sergeant turned to the captain, saluted and placed himself immediately behind that officer, who in turn moved apart one pace. These movements left the condemned man and the sergeant standing on the two ends of the same plank, which spanned three of the cross-ties of the bridge. The end upon which the civilian stood almost, but not quite, reached a fourth. This plank had been held in place by the weight of the captain; it was now held by that of the sergeant. At a signal from the former the latter would step aside, the plank would tilt and the condemned man go down between two ties. The arrangement commended itself to his judgment as simple and effective. His face had not been covered nor his eyes bandaged. He looked a moment at his "unsteadfast footing," then let his gaze wander to the swirling water of the stream racing madly beneath his feet. A piece of dancing driftwood caught his attention and his eyes followed it down the current. How slowly it appeared to move! What a sluggish stream!

He closed his eyes in order to fix his last thoughts upon his wife and children. The water, touched to gold by the early sun, the brooding mists under the banks at some distance down the stream, the fort, the soldiers, the piece of drift—all had distracted him. And now he became conscious of a new disturbance. Striking through the thought of his dear ones was a sound which he could neither ignore nor understand, a sharp, distinct, metallic percussion like the stroke of a blacksmith's hammer upon the anvil; it had the same ringing quality. He wondered what it was, and whether immeasurably distant or near by—it seemed both. Its recurrence was regular, but as slow as the tolling of a death knell. He awaited each stroke with impatience and—he knew not why—apprehension. The intervals of silence grew progressively longer; the delays became maddening. With their greater infrequency the sounds increased in strength and sharpness. They hurt his ear like the thrust of a knife; he feared he would shriek. What he heard was the ticking of his watch.

He unclosed his eyes and saw again the water below him. "If I could free my hands," he thought, "I might throw off the noose and spring into the stream. By diving I could evade the bullets and, swimming vigorously, reach the bank, take to the woods and get away home. My home, thank God, is as yet outside their lines; my wife and little ones are still beyond the invader's farthest advance."

As these thoughts, which have here to be set down in words, were flashed into the doomed man's brain rather than evolved from it the captain nodded to the sergeant. The sergeant stepped aside.

II

Peyton Farquhar was a well-to-do planter, of an old and highly respected Alabama family. Being a slave owner and like other slave owners a politician he was naturally an original secessionist and ardently devoted to the Southern cause. Circumstances of an imperious nature, which it is unnecessary to relate here, had prevented him from taking service with the gallant army that had fought the disastrous campaigns ending with the fall of Corinth, and he chafed under the inglorious restraint, longing for the release of his energies, the larger life of the soldier, the opportunity for distinction. That opportunity, he felt, would come, as it comes to all in war time. Meanwhile he did what he could. No service was too humble for him to perform in aid of the South, no adventure too perilous for him to undertake if consistent with the character of a civilian who was at heart a soldier, and who in good faith and without too much qualification assented to at least a part of the frankly villainous dictum that all is fair in love and war.

One evening while Farquhar and his wife were sitting on a rustic bench near the entrance to his grounds, a gray-clad soldier rode up to the gate and asked for a drink of water. Mrs. Farquhar was only too happy to serve him with her own white hands. While she was fetching the water her husband approached the dusty horseman and inquired eagerly for news from the front.

"The Yanks are repairing the railroads," said the man, "and are getting ready for another advance. They have reached the Owl Creek bridge, put it in order and built a stockade on the north bank. The commandant has issued an order, which is posted everywhere, declaring that any civilian caught interfering with the railroad, its bridges, tunnels or trains will be summarily hanged. I saw the order."

"How far is it to the Owl Creek bridge?" Farquhar asked.

"About thirty miles."

"Is there no force on this side of the creek?"

"Only a picket post half a mile out, on the railroad, and a single sentinel at this end of the bridge."

"Suppose a man—a civilian and student of hanging—should elude the picket post and perhaps get the better of the sentinel," said Farquhar, smiling, "what could he accomplish?"

The soldier reflected. "I was there a month ago," he replied. "I observed that the flood of last winter had lodged a great quantity of driftwood against the wooden pier at this end of the bridge. It is now dry and would burn like tow."

The lady had now brought the water, which the soldier drank. He thanked her ceremoniously, bowed to her husband and rode away. An hour later, after nightfall, he repassed the plantation, going northward in the direction from which he had come. He was a Federal scout.

III

As Peyton Farquhar fell straight downward through the bridge he lost consciousness and was as one already dead. From this state he was awakened—ages later, it seemed to him—by the pain of a sharp pressure upon his throat, followed by a sense of suffocation. Keen, poignant agonies seemed to shoot from his neck downward through every fibre of his body and limbs. These pains appeared to flash along well-defined lines of ramification and to beat with an inconceivably rapid periodicity. They seemed like streams of pulsating fire heating him to an intolerable temperature. As to his head, he was conscious of nothing but a feeling of fulness—of congestion. These sensations were unaccompanied by thought. The intellectual part of his nature was already effaced; he had power only to feel, and feeling was torment. He was conscious of motion. Encompassed in a luminous cloud, of which he was now merely the fiery heart, without material substance, he swung through unthinkable arcs of oscillation, like a vast pendulum. Then all at once, with terrible suddenness, the light about him shot upward with the noise of a loud plash; a frighful roaring was in his ears, and all was cold and dark. The power of thought was restored; he knew that the rope had broken and he had fallen into the stream. There was no additional strangulation; the noose about his neck was already suffocating him and kept the water from his lungs. To die of hanging at the bottom of a river!—the idea seemed to him ludicrous. He opened his eyes in the darkness and saw above him a gleam of light, but how distant, how inaccessible! He was still sinking, for the light became fainter and fainter until it was a mere glimmer. Then it began to grow and brighten, and he knew that he was rising toward the surface—knew it with reluctance, for he was now very comfortable. "To be hanged and drowned," he thought, "that is not so bad; but I do not wish to be shot. No; I will not be shot; that is not fair."

He was not conscious of an effort, but a sharp pain in his wrist apprised him that he was trying to free his hands. He gave the struggle his attention, as an idler might observe the feat of a juggler, without interest in the outcome. What splendid effort!—what magnificent, what superhuman strength! Ah, that was a fine endeavor! Bravo! The cord fell away; his arms parted and floated upward, the hands dimly seen on each side in the growing light. He watched them with a new interest as first one and then the other pounced upon the noose at his neck. They tore it away and thrust it fiercely aside, its undulations resembling those of a water-snake. "Put it back, put it back!" He thought he shouted these words to his hands, for the undoing of the noose had been succeeded by the direst pang that he had yet experienced. His neck ached horribly, his brain was on fire; his heart, which had been fluttering faintly, gave a great leap, trying to force itself out at his mouth. His whole body was racked and wrenched with an insupportable anguish! But his disobedient hands gave no need to the command. They beat the water vigorously with quick, downward strokes, forcing him to the surface. He felt his head emerge; his eyes were blinded by the sunlight; his chest expanded convulsively, and with a supreme and crowning agony his lungs engulfed a great draught of air, which instantly he expelled in a shriek!

He was now in full possession of his physical senses. They were, indeed, preternaturally keen and alert. Something in the awful disturbance of his organic system had so exalted and refined them that they made record of things never before perceived. He felt the ripples upon his face and heard their separate sounds as they struck. He looked at the forest on the bank of the stream, saw the individual trees, the leaves and the veining of each leaf—saw the very insects upon them: the locusts, the brilliant-bodied flies, the gray spiders stretching their webs from twig to twig. He noted the prismatic colors in all the dewdrops upon a million blades of grass. The humming of the gnats that danced above the eddies of the stream, the beating of the dragon-flies' wings, the strokes of the water-spiders' legs, like oars which had lifted their boat—all these made audible music. A fish slid along beneath his eyes and he heard the rush of its body parting the water.

He had come to the surface facing down the stream; in a moment the visible world seemed to wheel slowly round, himself the pivotal point, and he saw the bridge, the fort, the soldiers upon the bridge, the captain, the sergeant, the two privates, his executioners. They were in silhouette against the blue sky. They shouted and gesticulated, pointing at him. The captain had drawn his pistol, but did not fire; the others were unarmed. Their movements were grotesque and horrible, their forms gigantic.

Suddenly he heard a sharp report and something struck the water smartly within a few inches of his head, spattering his face with spray. He heard a second report, and saw one of the sentinels with his rifle at his shoulder, a light cloud of blue smoke rising from the muzzle. The man in the water saw the eye of the man on the bridge gazing into his own through the sights of the rifle. He observed that it was a gray eye and remembered having read that gray eyes were keenest, and that all famous marksmen had them. Nevertheless, this one had missed.

A counter-swirl had caught Farquhar and turned him half round; he was again looking into the forest on the bank opposite the fort. The sound of a clear, high voice in a monotonous singsong now rang out behind him and came across the water with a distinctness that pierced and subdued all other sounds, even the beating of the ripples in his ears. Although no soldier, he had frequented camps enough to know the dread significance of that deliberate, drawling, as-pirated chant; the lieutenant on shore was taking a part in the morning's work. How coldly and pitilessly—with what an even, calm intonation, presaging, and enforcing tranquility in the men—with what accurately measured intervals fell those cruel words:

"Attention, company! . . . Shoulder arms! . . . Ready! . . . Aim! . . . Fire!"

Farquhar dived—dived as deeply as he could. The water roared in his ears like the voice of Niagara, yet he heard the dulled thunder of the volley and, rising again toward the surface, met shining bits of metal, singularly flattened, oscillating slowly downward. Some of them touched him on the face and hands, then fell away, continuing their descent. One lodged between his collar and neck; it was uncomfortably warm and he snatched it out.

As he rose to the surface, gasping for breath, he saw that he had been a long time under water; he was perceptibly farther down stream—nearer to safety. The soldiers had almost finished reloading; the metal ramrods flashed all at once in the sunshine as they were drawn from the barrels, turned in the air, and thrust into their sockets. The two sentinels fired again, independently and ineffectually.

The hunted man saw all this over his shoulder; he was now swimming vigorously with the current. His brain was as energetic as his arms and legs; he thought with the rapidity of lightning.

"The officer," he reasoned, "will not make that martinet's error a second time. It is as easy to dodge a volley as a single shot. He has probably already given the command to fire at will. God help me, I cannot dodge them all!"

An appalling plash within two yards of him was followed by a loud, rushing sound, *diminuendo*, which seemed to travel back through the air to the fort and died in an explosion which stirred the very river to its deeps! A rising sheet of water curved over him, fell down upon him, blinded him, strangled him! The cannon had taken a hand in the game. As he shook his head free from the commotion of the smitten water he heard the deflected shot humming through the air ahead, and in an instant it was cracking and smashing the branches in the forest beyond.

"They will not do that again," he thought; "the next time they will use a charge of grape. I must keep my eye upon the gun; the smoke will apprise me— the report arrives too late; it lags behind the missile. That is a good gun."

Suddenly he felt himself whirled round and round—spinning like a top. The water, the banks, the forests, the now distant bridge, fort and men—all were commingled and blurred. Objects were represented by their colors only; circular horizontal streaks of color—that was all he saw. He had been caught in a vortex and was being whirled on with a velocity of advance and gyration that made him giddy and sick. In a few moments he was flung upon the gravel at the foot of the left bank of the stream—the southern bank—and behind a projecting point which concealed him from his enemies. The sudden arrest of his motion, the abrasion of one of his hands on the gravel, restored him, and he wept with delight. He dug his fingers into the sand, threw it over himself in handfuls and audibly blessed it. It looked like diamonds, rubies, emeralds; he could think of nothing beautiful which it did not resemble. The trees upon the bank were giant garden plants; he noted a definite order in their arrangement, inhaled the fragrance of their blooms. A strange, roseate light shone through the spaces among their trunks and the wind made in their branches the music of aeolian harps. He had no wish to perfect his escape—was content to remain in that enchanting spot until retaken.

A whiz and rattle of grapeshot among the branches high above his head roused him from his dream. The baffled cannoneer had fired him a random farewell. He sprang to his feet, rushed up the sloping bank, and plunged into the forest.

All that day he traveled, laying his course by the rounding sun. The forest seemed interminable; nowhere did he discover a break in it, not even a wood-man's road. He had not known that he lived in so wild a region. There was something uncanny in the revelation.

By night fall he was fatigued, footsore, famishing. The thought of his wife and children urged him on. At last he found a road which led him in what he knew to be the right direction. It was as wide and straight as a city street, yet it seemed untraveled. No fields bordered it, no dwelling anywhere. Not so much as the barking of a dog suggested human habitation. The black bodies of the trees formed a straight wall on both sides, terminating on the horizon in a point, like a diagram in a lesson in perspective. Overhead, as he looked up through this rift in the wood, shone great golden stars looking unfamiliar and grouped in strange constellations. He was sure they were arranged in some order which had a secret and malign significance. The wood on either side was full of singular noises, among which—once, twice, and again, he distinctly heard whispers in an unknown tongue.

His neck was in pain and lifting his hand to it he found it horribly swollen. He knew that it had a circle of black where the rope had bruised it. His eyes felt congested; he could no longer close them. His tongue was swollen with thirst; he relieved its fever by thrusting it forward from between his teeth into the cold air. How softly the turf had carpeted the untraveled avenue—he could no longer feel the roadway beneath his feet!

Doubtless, despite his suffering, he had fallen asleep while walking, for now he sees another scene—perhaps he has merely recovered from a delirium. He stands at the gate of his own home. All is as he left it, and all bright and beautiful in the morning sunshine. He must have traveled the entire night. As he pushes open the gate and passes up the wide white walk, he sees a flutter of female garments; his wife, looking fresh and cool and sweet, steps down from the veranda to meet him. At the bottom of the steps she stands waiting, with a smile of ineffable joy, an attitude of matchless grace and dignity. Ah, how beautiful she is! He springs forward with extended arms. As he is about to clasp her he feels a stunning blow upon the back of the neck; a blinding white light blazes all about him with a sound like the shock of a cannon—then all is darkness and silence!

Peyton Farquhar was dead; his body, with a broken neck, swung gently from side to side beneath the timbers of the Owl Creek bridge.

The Jilting
of Granny Weatherall   1930

KATHERINE ANNE PORTER   [1890–1980]

She flicked her wrist neatly out of Doctor Harry's pudgy careful fingers and pulled the sheet up to her chin. The brat ought to be in knee breeches. Doctoring around the country with spectacles on his nose! "Get along now, take your schoolbooks and go. There's nothing wrong with me."

Doctor Harry spread a warm paw like a cushion on her forehead where the forked green vein danced and made her eyelids twitch. "Now, now, be a good girl, and we'll have you up in no time."

"That's no way to speak to a woman nearly eighty years old just because she's down. I'd have you respect your elders, young man."

"Well, Missy, excuse me." Doctor Harry patted her cheek. "But I've got to warn you, haven't I? You're a marvel, but you must be careful or you're going to be good and sorry."

"Don't tell me what I'm going to be. I'm on my feet now, morally speaking. It's Cornelia. I had to go to bed to get rid of her."

Her bones felt loose, and floated around in her skin, and Doctor Harry floated like a balloon around the foot of the bed. He floated and pulled down his waistcoat and swung his glasses on a cord. "Well, stay where you are, it certainly can't hurt you."

"Get along and doctor your sick," said Granny Weatherall. "Leave a well woman alone. I'll call for you when I want you. . . . Where were you forty years ago when I pulled through milk-leg and double pneumonia? You weren't even born. Don't let Cornelia lead you on," she shouted, because Doctor Harry appeared to float up to the ceiling and out. "I pay my own bills, and I don't throw my money away on nonsense!"

She meant to wave good-by, but it was too much trouble. Her eyes closed of themselves, it was like a dark curtain drawn around the bed. The pillow rose and floated under her, pleasant as a hammock in a light wind. She listened to the leaves rustling outside the window. No, somebody was swishing newspapers: no, Cornelia and Doctor Harry were whispering together. She leaped broad awake, thinking they whispered in her ear.

"She was never like this, *never* like this!" "Well, what can we expect?" "Yes, eighty years old. . . ."

Well, and what if she was? She still had ears. It was like Cornelia to whisper around doors. She always kept things secret in such a public way. She was always being tactful and kind. Cornelia was dutiful; that was the trouble with her. Dutiful and good: "So good and dutiful," said Granny, "that I'd like to spank her." She saw herself spanking Cornelia and making a fine job of it.

"What'd you say, Mother?"

Granny felt her face tying up in hard knots.

"Can't a body think, I'd like to know?"

"I thought you might want something."

"I do. I want a lot of things. First off, go away and don't whisper."

She lay and drowsed, hoping in her sleep that the children would keep out and let her rest a minute. It had been a long day. Not that she was tired. It was always pleasant to snatch a minute now and then. There was always so much to be done, let me see: tomorrow.

Tomorrow was far away and there was nothing to trouble about. Things were finished somehow when the time came; thank God there was always a little margin over for peace: then a person could spread out the plan of life and tuck in the edges orderly. It was good to have everything clean and folded away, with the hair brushes and tonic bottles sitting straight on the white embroidered linen: the day started without fuss and the pantry shelves laid out with rows of jelly glasses and brown jugs and white stone-china jars with blue whirligigs and words painted on them: coffee, tea, sugar, ginger, cinnamon, allspice: and the bronze clock with the lion on top nicely dusted off. The dust that lion could collect in twenty-four hours! The box in the attic with all those letters tied up, well she'd have to go through that tomorrow. All those letters—George's letters and John's letters and her letters to them both—lying around for the children to find afterwards made her uneasy. Yes, that would be tomorrow's business. No use to let them know how silly she had been once.

While she was rummaging around she found death in her mind and it felt clammy and unfamiliar. She had spent so much time preparing for death there was no need for bringing it up again. Let it take care of itself now. When she was sixty she had felt very old, finished, and went around making farewell trips to see her children and grandchildren, with a secret in her mind: This is the very last of your mother, children! Then she made her will and came down with a long fever. That was all just a notion like a lot of other things, but it was lucky too, for she had once for all got over the idea of dying for a long time. Now she couldn't be worried. She hoped she had better sense now. Her father had lived to be one hundred and two years old and had drunk a noggin of strong hot toddy on his last birthday. He told the reporters it was his daily habit, and he owed his long life to that. He had made quite a scandal and was very pleased about it. She believed she'd just plague Cornelia a little.

"Cornelia! Cornelia!" No footsteps, but a sudden hand on her cheek. "Bless you, where have you been?"

"Here, mother."

"Well, Cornelia, I want a noggin of hot toddy."

"Are you cold, darling?"

"I'm chilly, Cornelia. Lying in bed stops the circulation. I must have told you that a thousand times."

Well, she could just hear Cornelia telling her husband that Mother was getting childish and they'd have to humor her. The thing that most annoyed her was that Cornelia thought she was deaf, dumb, and blind. Little hasty glances and tiny gestures tossed around her and over her head saying, "Don't cross her, let her have her way, she's eighty years old," and she sitting there as if she lived in a thin glass cage. Sometimes Granny almost made up her mind to pack up and move back to her own house where nobody could remind her every minute that she was old. Wait, wait, Cornelia, till your own children whisper behind your back!

In her day she had kept a better house and had got more work done. She wasn't too old yet for Lydia to be driving eighty miles for advice when one of the children jumped the track, and Jimmy still dropped in and talked things over: "Now, Mammy, you've a good business head, I want to know what you think of this? . . ." Old Cornelia couldn't change the furniture around without asking. Little things, little things! They had been so sweet when they were little. Granny wished the old days were back again with the children young and everything to be done over. It had been a hard pull, but not too much for her. When she thought of all the food she had cooked, and all the clothes she had cut and sewed, and all the gardens she had made—well, the children showed it. There they were, made out of her, and they couldn't get away from that. Sometimes she wanted to see John again and point to them and say, Well, I didn't do so badly, did I? But that would have to wait. That was for tomorrow. She used to think of him as a man, but now all the children were older than their father, and he would be a child beside her if she saw him now. It seemed strange and there was something wrong in the idea. Why, he couldn't possibly recognize her. She had fenced in a hundred acres once, digging the post holes herself and clamping the wires with just a negro boy to help. That changed a woman. John would be looking for a young woman with the peaked Spanish comb in her hair and the painted fan. Digging post holes changed a woman. Riding country roads in the winter when women had their babies was another thing: sitting up nights with sick horses and sick negroes and sick children and hardly ever losing one. John, I hardly ever lost one of them! John would see that in a minute, that would be something he could understand, she wouldn't have to explain anything!

It made her feel like rolling up her sleeves and putting the whole place to rights again. No matter if Cornelia was determined to be everywhere at once, there were a great many things left undone on this place. She would start tomorrow and do them. It was good to be strong enough for everything, even if all you made melted and changed and slipped under your hands, so that by the time you finished you almost forgot what you were working for. What was it I set out to do? she asked herself intently, but she could not remember. A fog rose over the valley, she saw it marching across the creek swallowing the trees and moving up the hill like an army of ghosts. Soon it would be at the near edge of the orchard, and then it was time to go in and light the lamps. Come in, children, don't stay out in the night air.

Lighting the lamps had been beautiful. The children huddled up to her and breathed like little calves waiting at the bars in the twilight. Their eyes followed the match and watched the flame rise and settle in a blue curve, then they moved away from her. The lamp was lit, they didn't have to be scared and hang on to mother any more. Never, never, never more. God, for all my life I thank Thee. Without Thee, my God, I could never have done it. Hail, Mary, full of grace.

I want you to pick all the fruit this year and see that nothing is wasted. There's always someone who can use it. Don't let good things rot for want of using. You waste life when you waste good food. Don't let things get lost. It's bitter to lose things. Now, don't let me get to thinking, not when I am tired and taking a little nap before supper. . . .

The pillow rose about her shoulders and pressed against her heart and the memory was being squeezed out of it: oh, push down the pillow, somebody: it would smother her if she tried to hold it. Such a fresh breeze blowing and such a green day with no threats in it. But he had not come, just the same. What does a woman do when she has put on the white veil and set out the white cake for a man and he doesn't come? She tried to remember. No, I swear he never harmed me but in that. He never harmed me but in that . . . and what if he did? There was the day, the day, but a whirl of dark smoke rose and covered it, crept up and over into the bright field where everything was planted so carefully in orderly rows. That was hell, she knew hell when she saw it. For sixty years she had prayed against remembering him and against losing her soul in the deep pit of hell, and now the two things were mingled in one and the thought of him was a smoky cloud from hell that moved and crept in her head when she had just got rid of Doctor Harry and was trying to rest a minute. Wounded vanity, Ellen, said a sharp voice in the top of her mind. Don't let your wounded vanity get the upper hand of you. Plenty of girls get jilted. You were jilted, weren't you? Then stand up to it. Her eyelids wavered and let in streamers of blue-gray light like tissue paper over her eyes. She must get up and pull the shades down or she'd never sleep. She was in bed again and the shades were not down. How could that happen? Better turn over, hide from the light, sleeping in the light gave you nightmares. "Mother, how do you feel now?" and a stinging wetness on her forehead. But I don't like having my face washed in cold water!

Hapsy? George? Lydia? Jimmy? No, Cornelia, and her features were swollen and full of little puddles. "They're coming, darling, they'll all be here soon." Go wash your face, child, you look funny.

Instead of obeying, Cornelia knelt down and put her head on the pillow. She seemed to be talking but there was no sound. "Well, are you tongue-tied? Whose birthday is it? Are you going to give a party?"

Cornelia's mouth moved urgently in strange shapes. "Don't do that, you bother me, daughter."

"Oh, no, Mother, Oh, no. . . ."

Nonsense. It was strange about children. They disputed your every word. "No what, Cornelia?"

"Here's Doctor Harry."

"I won't see that boy again. He just left five minutes ago."

"That was this morning, Mother. It's night now. Here's the nurse."

"This is Doctor Harry, Mrs. Weatherall. I never saw you look so young and happy!"

"Ah, I'll never be young again—but I'd be happy if they'd let me lie in peace and get rested."

She thought she spoke up loudly, but no one answered. A warm weight on her forehead, a warm bracelet on her wrist, and a breeze went on whispering, trying to tell her something. A shuffle of leaves in the everlasting hand of God. He blew on them and they danced and rattled. "Mother, don't mind, we're going to give you a little hypodermic." "Look here, daughter, how do ants get in this bed? I saw sugar ants yesterday." Did you send for Hapsy too?

It was Hapsy she really wanted. She had to go a long way back through a great many rooms to find Hapsy standing with a baby on her arm. She seemed to herself to be Hapsy also, and the baby on Hapsy's arm was Hapsy and himself and herself, all at once, and there was no surprise in the meeting. Then Hapsy melted from within and turned flimsy as gray gauze and the baby was a gauzy shadow, and Hapsy came up close and said, "I thought you'd never come," and looked at her very searchingly and said, "You haven't changed a bit!" They leaned forward to kiss, when Cornelia began whispering from a long way off, "Oh, is there anything you want to tell me? Is there anything I can do for you?"

Yes, she had changed her mind after sixty years and she would like to see George. I want you to find George. Find him and be sure to tell him I forgot him. I want him to know I had my husband just the same and my children and my house like any other woman. A good house too and a good husband that I loved and fine children out of him. Better than I hoped for even. Tell him I was given back everything he took away and more. Oh, no, oh, God, no, there was something else besides the house and the man and the children. Oh, surely they were not all? What was it? Something not given back. . . . Her breath crowded down under her ribs and grew into a monstrous frightening shape with cutting edges; it bored up into her head, and the agony was unbelievable: Yes, John, get the doctor now, no more talk, my time has come.

When this one was born it should be the last. The last. It should have been born first, for it was the one she had truly wanted. Everything came in good time. Nothing left out, left over. She was strong, in three days she would be as well as ever. Better. A woman needed milk in her to have her full health.

"Mother, do you hear me?"

"I've been telling you—"

"Mother, Father Connolly's here."

"I went to Holy Communion only last week. Tell him I'm not so sinful as all that."

"Father just wants to speak to you."

He could speak as much as he pleased. It was like him to drop in and inquire about her soul as if it were a teething baby, and then stay on for a cup of tea and a round of cards and gossip. He always had a funny story of some sort, usually about an Irishman who made his little mistakes and confessed them, and the point lay in some absurd thing he would blurt out in the confessional showing his struggles between native piety and original sin. Granny felt easy about her soul. Cornelia, where are your manners? Give Father Connolly a chair. She had her secret comfortable understanding with a few favorite saints who cleared a straight road to God for her. All as surely signed and sealed as the papers for the new Forty Acres. Forever . . . heirs and assigns forever. Since the day the wedding cake was not cut, but thrown out and wasted. The whole bottom dropped out of the world, and there she was blind and sweating with nothing under her feet and the walls falling away. His hand had caught her under the breast, she had not fallen, there was the freshly polished floor with the green rug on it, just as before. He had cursed like a sailor's parrot and said, "I'll kill him for you." Don't lay a hand on him, for my sake leave something to God. "Now, Ellen, you must believe what I tell you. . . ."

So there was nothing, nothing to worry about any more, except sometimes in the night one of the children screamed in a nightmare, and they both hustled out shaking and hunting for the matches and calling, "There, wait a minute, here we are!" John, get the doctor now, Hapsy's time has come. But there was Hapsy standing by the bed in a white cap. "Cornelia, tell Hapsy to take off her cap. I can't see her plain."

Her eyes opened very wide and the room stood out like a picture she had seen somewhere. Dark colors with the shadows rising towards the ceiling in long angles. The tall black dresser gleamed with nothing on it but John's picture, enlarged from a little one, with John's eyes very black when they should have been blue. You never saw him, so how do you know how he looked? But the man insisted the copy was perfect, it was very rich and handsome. For a picture, yes, but it's not my husband. The table by the bed had a linen cover and a candle and a crucifix. The light was blue from Cornelia's silk lampshades. No sort of light at all, just frippery. You had to live forty years with kerosene lamps to appreciate honest electricity. She felt very strong and she saw Doctor Harry with a rosy nimbus around him.

"You look like a saint, Doctor Harry, and I vow that's as near as you'll ever come to it."

"She's saying something."

"I heard you, Cornelia. What's all this carrying-on?"

"Father Connolly's saying—"

Cornelia's voice staggered and bumped like a cart in a bad road. It rounded corners and turned back again and arrived nowhere. Granny stepped up in the cart very lightly and reached for the reins, but a man sat beside her and she knew him by his hands, driving the cart. She did not look in his face, for she knew without seeing, but looked instead down the road where the trees leaned over and bowed to each other and a thousand birds were singing a Mass. She felt like singing too, but she put her hand in the bosom of her dress and pulled out a rosary, and Father Connolly murmured Latin in a very solemn voice and tickled her feet. My God, will you stop that nonsense? I'm a married woman. What if he did run away and leave me to face the priest by myself? I found another a whole world better. I wouldn't have exchanged my husband for anybody except St. Michael himself, and you may tell him that for me with a thank you in the bargain.

Light flashed on her closed eyelids, and a deep roaring shook her. Cornelia, is that lightning? I hear thunder. There's going to be a storm. Close all the windows. Call the children in. . . . "Mother, here we are, all of us." "Is that you, Hapsy?" "Oh, no, I'm Lydia. We drove as fast as we could." Their faces drifted above her, drifted away. The rosary fell out of her hands and Lydia put it back. Jimmy tried to help, their hands fumbled together, and Granny closed two fingers around Jimmy's thumb. Beads wouldn't do, it must be something alive. She was so amazed her thoughts ran round and round. So, my dear Lord, this is my death and I wasn't even thinking about it. My children have come to see me die. But I can't, it's not time. Oh, I always hated surprises. I wanted to give Cornelia the amethyst set—Cornelia, you're to have the amethyst set, but Hapsy's to wear it when she wants, and, Doctor Harry, do shut up. Nobody sent for you. Oh, my dear Lord, do wait a minute. I meant to do something about the Forty Acres, Jimmy doesn't need it and Lydia will later on, with that worthless husband of hers. I meant to finish the altar cloth and send six bottles of wine to Sister Borgia for her dyspepsia. I want to send six bottles of wine to Sister Borgia, Father Connolly, now don't let me forget.

Cornelia's voice made short turns and tilted over and crashed. "Oh, Mother, oh, Mother, oh, Mother. . . ."

"I'm not going, Cornelia. I'm taken by surprise. I can't go."

You'll see Hapsy again. What about her? "I thought you'd never come." Granny made a long journey outward, looking for Hapsy. What if I don't find her? What then? Her heart sank down and down, there was no bottom to death, she couldn't come to the end of it. The blue light from Cornelia's lampshade drew into a tiny point in the center of her brain, it flickered and winked like an eye, quietly it fluttered and dwindled. Granny lay curled down within herself, amazed and watchful, staring at the point of light that was herself; her body was now only a deeper mass of shadow in an endless darkness and this darkness would curl around the light and swallow it up. God, give a sign!

For the second time there was no sign. Again no bridegroom and the priest in the house. She could not remember any other sorrow because this grief wiped them all away. Oh, no, there's nothing more cruel than this—I'll never forgive it. She stretched herself with a deep breath and blew out the light.

QUESTIONS

1. Characterize Granny. What facts do we know about her life? 2. Why, after sixty full years, does the jilting by George loom so large in Granny's mind? Are we to accept her own strong statements that the pain of the jilting was more than

compensated for by the happiness she ultimately found with her husband John, her children, and her grandchildren? Explain.   **3.**   Why does the author not present us with Granny's final thoughts in an orderly and sequential pattern? **4.**   Granny is revealed to us not only through her direct thoughts but also through the many images that float through her mind—the fog, the blowing breeze, "a whirl of dark smoke," and others. What do these images reveal about Granny?

WRITING TOPIC

The final paragraph echoes Christ's parable of the bridegroom (Matthew 25:1– 13). Why does Granny connect this final, deep religious grief with the grief she felt when George jilted her?

A Summer Tragedy   1973

ARNA BONTEMPS   [1902–1973]

Old Jeff Patton, the black share farmer, fumbled with his bow tie. His fingers trembled and the high, stiff collar pinched his throat. A fellow loses his hand for such vanities after thirty or forty years of simple life. Once a year, or maybe twice if there's a wedding among his kinfolks, he may spruce up, but generally fancy clothes do nothing but adorn the wall of the big room and feed the moths. That had been Jeff Patton's experience. He had not worn his stiff-bosomed shirt more than a dozen times in all his married life. His swallow-tailed coat lay on the bed beside him, freshly brushed and pressed, but it was as full of holes as the overalls in which he worked on weekdays. The moths had used it badly. Jeff twisted his mouth into a hideous toothless grimace as he contended with the obstinate bow. He stamped his good foot and decided to give up the struggle.

"Jennie," he called.

"What's that, Jeff?" His wife's shrunken voice came out of the adjoining room like an echo. It was hardly bigger than a whisper.

"I reckon you'll have to he'p me wid this heah bow tie, baby," he said meekly. "Dog if I can hitch it up."

Her answer was not strong enough to reach him, but presently the old woman came to the door, feeling her way with a stick. She had a wasted, dead-leaf appearance. Her body, as scrawny and gnarled as a string bean, seemed less than nothing in the ocean of frayed and faded petticoats that surrounded her. These hung an inch or two above the tops of her heavy unlaced shoes and showed little grotesque piles where the stockings had fallen down from her negligible legs.

"You oughta could do a heap mo' wid a thing like that'n me—beingst as you got yo' good sight."

"Looks like I oughta could," he admitted. "But my fingers is gone democrat on me. I get all mixed up in the looking glass an' can't tell wicha way to twist the devilish thing."

Jennie sat on the side of the bed, and old Jeff Patton got down on one knee while she tied the bow knot. It was a slow and painful ordeal for each of them in this position. Jeff's bones cracked, his knee ached, and it was only after a half dozen attempts that Jennie worked a semblance of a bow into the tie.

"I got to dress maself now," the old woman whispered. "These is ma old shoes an' stockings, and I ain't so much as unwrapped ma dress."

"Well, don't worry 'bout me no mo', baby," Jeff said. "That 'bout finishes me. All I gotta do now is slip on that old coat 'n ves' an' I'll be fixed to leave."

Jennie disappeared again through the dim passage into the shed room. Being blind was no handicap to her in that black hole. Jeff heard the cane placed against the wall beside the door and knew that his wife was on easy ground. He

652

put on his coat, took a battered top hat from the bed post, and hobbled to the front door. He was ready to travel. As soon as Jennie could get on her Sunday shoes and her old black silk dress, they would start.

Outside the tiny log house, the day was warm and mellow with sunshine. A host of wasps were humming with busy excitement in the trunk of a dead sycamore. Gray squirrels were searching through the grass for hickory nuts, and blue jays were in the trees, hopping from branch to branch. Pine woods stretched away to the left like a black sea. Among them were scattered scores of log houses like Jeff's, houses of black share farmers. Cows and pigs wandered freely among the trees. There was no danger of loss. Each farmer knew his own stock and knew his neighbor's as well as he knew his neighbor's children.

Down the slope to the right were the cultivated acres on which the colored folks worked. They extended to the river, more than two miles away, and they were today green with the unmade cotton crop. A tiny thread of a road, which passed directly in front of Jeff's place, ran through these green fields like a pencil mark.

Jeff, standing outside the door, with his absurd hat in his left hand, surveyed the wide scene tenderly. He had been forty-five years on these acres. He loved them with the unexplained affection that others have for the countries to which they belong.

The sun was hot on his head, his collar still pinched his throat, and the Sunday clothes were intolerably hot. Jeff transferred the hat to his right hand and began fanning with it. Suddenly the whisper that was Jennie's voice came out of the shed room.

"You can bring the car round front whilst you's waitin'," it said feebly. There was a tired pause; then it added, "I'll soon be fixed to go."

"A'right, baby," Jeff answered. "I'll get it in a minute."

But he didn't move. A thought struck him that made his mouth fall open. The mention of the car brought to his mind with new intensity, the trip he and Jennie were to take. Fear came into his eyes; excitement took his breath. Lord, Jesus!

"Jeff. . . . O Jeff," the old woman's whisper called.

He awakened with a jolt. "Hunh, baby?"

"What you doin'?"

"Nuthin. Jes studyin'. I jes been turnin' things round 'n round in ma mind."

"You could be gettin' the car," she said.

"Oh yes, right away, baby."

He started round to the shed, limping heavily on his bad leg. There were three frizzly chickens in the yard. All his other chickens had been killed or stolen recently. But the frizzly chickens had been saved somehow. That was fortunate indeed, for these curious creatures had a way of devouring "poison" from the yard and in that way protecting against conjure and black luck and spells. But even the frizzly chickens seemed now to be in a stupor. Jeff thought they had some ailment; he expected all three of them to die shortly.

The shed in which the old T-model Ford stood was only a grass roof held up by four corner poles. It had been built by tremulous hands at a time when the little rattletrap car had been regarded as a peculiar treasure. And, miraculously, despite wind and downpour, it still stood.

Jeff adjusted the crank and put his weight upon it. The engine came to life with a sputter and bang that rattled the old car from radiator to tail light. Jeff hopped into the seat and put his foot on the accelerator. The sputtering and banging increased. The rattling became more violent. That was good. It was good banging, good sputtering and rattling, and it meant that the aged car was still in running condition. She could be depended on for this trip.

Again Jeff's thought halted as if paralyzed. The suggestion of the trip fell into the machinery of his mind like a wrench. He felt dazed and weak. He swung the car out into the yard, made a half turn, and drove around to the front door. When he took his hands off the wheel, he noticed that he was trembling violently. He cut off the motor and climbed to the ground to wait for Jennie.

A few minutes later she was at the window, her voice rattling against the pane like a broken shutter.

"I'm ready, Jeff."

He did not answer, but limped into the house and took her by the arm. He led her slowly through the big room, down the step, and across the yard.

"You reckon I'd oughta lock the do'?" he asked softly.

They stopped and Jennie weighed the question. Finally she shook her head. "Ne' mind the door," she said. "I don't see no cause to lock up things."

"You right," Jeff agreed. "No cause to lock up."

Jeff opened the door and helped his wife into the car. A quick shudder passed over him. Jesus! Again he trembled.

"How come you shaking so?" Jennie whispered.

"I don't know," he said.

"You mus' be scairt, Jeff."

"No, baby, I ain't scairt."

He slammed the door after her and went around to crank up again. The motor started easily. Jeff wished that it had not been so responsive. He would have liked a few more minutes in which to turn things around in his head. As it was, with Jennie chiding him about being afraid, he had to keep going. He swung the car into the little pencil-mark road and started off toward the river, driving very slowly, very cautiously.

Chugging across the green countryside, the small battered Ford seemed tiny indeed. Jeff felt a familiar excitement, a thrill, as they came down the first slope to the immense levels on which the cotton was growing. He could not help reflecting that the crops were good. He knew what that meant, too; he had made forty-five of them with his own hands. It was true that he had worn out nearly a dozen mules, but that was the fault of old man Stevenson, the owner of the land. Major Stevenson had the old notion that one mule was all a share farmer needed to work a thirty-acre plot. It was an expensive notion, the way it killed mules from overwork but the old man held to it. Jeff thought it killed a good many share farmers as well as mules, but he had no sympathy for them. He had always been strong, and he had been taught to have no patience with weakness in men. Women or children might be tolerated if they were puny, but a weak man was a curse. Of course, his own children—

Jeff's thought halted there. He and Jennie never mentioned their dead children any more. And naturally, he did not wish to dwell upon them in his mind. Before he knew it, some remark would slip out of his mouth and that would make Jennie feel blue. Perhaps she would cry. A woman like Jennie could not easily throw off the grief that comes from losing five grown children within two years. Even Jeff was still staggered by the blow. His memory had not been much good recently. He frequently talked to himself. And, although he had kept it a secret, he knew that his courage had left him. He was terrified by the least unfamiliar sound at night. He was reluctant to venture far from home in the daytime. Sometimes he became afraid and trembled without knowing what had frightened him. The feeling would just come over him like a chill.

The car rattled slowly over the dusty road. Jennie sat erect and silent with a little absurd hat pinned to her hair. Her useless eyes seemed very large, very white in their deep sockets. Suddenly Jeff heard her voice, and he inclined his head to catch the words.

"Is we passed Delia Moore's house yet?" she asked.

"Not yet," he said.

"You must be drivin' mighty slow, Jeff."

"We just as well take our time, baby."

There was a pause. A little puff of steam was coming out of the radiator of the car. Heat wavered above the hood. Delia Moore's house was nearly half a mile away. After a moment Jennie spoke again.

"You ain't really scairt, is you, Jeff?"

"Nah, baby, I ain't scairt."

"You know how we agreed—we gotta keep on goin'."

Jewels of perspiration appeared on Jeff's forehead. His eyes rounded, blinked, became fixed on the road.

"I don't know," he said with a shiver, "I reckon it's the only thing to do."

"Hm."

A flock of guinea fowls, pecking in the road, were scattered by the passing car. Some of them took to their wings; others hid under bushes. A blue jay, swaying on a leafy twig, was annoying a roadside squirrel. Jeff held an even speed till he came near Delia's place. Then he slowed down noticeably.

Delia's house was really no house at all, but an abandoned stone building converted into a dwelling. It sat near a crossroads, beneath a single black cedar tree. There Delia, a cattish old creature of Jennie's age, lived alone. She had been there more years than anybody could remember, and long ago had won the disfavor of such women as Jennie. For in her young days Delia had been gayer, yellower, and saucier than seemed proper in those parts. Her ways with menfolks had been dark and suspicious. And the fact that she had had as many husbands as children did not help her reputation.

"Yonder's old Delia," Jeff said as they passed.

"What she doin'?"

"Jes sittin' in the do'," he said.

"She see us?"

"Hm," Jeff said. "Musta did."

That relieved Jennie. It strengthened her to know that her old enemy had seen her pass in her best clothes. That would give the old she-devil something to chew her gums and fret about, Jennie thought. Wouldn't she have a fit if she didn't find out? Old evil Delia! This would be just the thing for her. It would pay her back for being so evil. It would also pay her, Jennie thought, for the way she used to grin at Jeff—long ago, when her teeth were good.

The road became smooth and red, and Jeff could tell by the smell of the air that they were nearing the river. He could see the rise where the road turned and ran along parallel to the stream. The car chugged on monotonously. After a long silent spell, Jennie leaned against Jeff and spoke.

"How many bale o' cotton you think we got standin'?" she said.

Jeff wrinkled his forehead as he calculated.

"'Bout twenty-five, I reckon."

"How many you make las' year?"

"Twenty-eight," he said. "How come you ask that?"

"I's jes thinkin'," Jennie said quietly.

"It don't make a speck o' difference though," Jeff reflected. "If we get much or if we get little, we still gonna be in debt to old man Stevenson when he gets through counting up agin us. It's took us a long time to learn that."

Jennie was not listening to these words. She had fallen into a trancelike meditation. Her lips twitched. She chewed her gums and rubbed her gnarled hands nervously. Suddenly, she leaned forward, buried her face in the nervous hands, and burst into tears. She cried aloud in a dry, cracked voice that suggested the rattle of fodder on dead stalks. She cried aloud like a child, for she had never learned to suppress a genuine sob. Her slight old frame shook heavily and seemed hardly able to sustain such violent grief.

"What's the matter, baby?" Jeff asked awkwardly. "Why you cryin' like all that?"

"I's jes thinkin'," she said.

"So you the one what's scairt now, hunh?"

"I ain't scairt, Jeff. I's jes thinkin' 'bout leavin' eve'thing like this—eve'thing we been used to. It's right sad-like."

Jeff did not answer, and presently Jennie buried her face again and cried.

The sun was almost overhead. It beat down furiously on the dusty wagon-path road, on the parched roadside grass and the tiny battered car. Jeff's hands, gripping the wheel, became wet with perspiration; his forehead sparkled. Jeff's lips parted. His mouth shaped a hideous grimace. His face suggested the face of a man being burned. But the torture passed and his expression softened again.

"You mustn't cry, baby," he said to his wife. "We gotta be strong. We can't break down."

Jennie waited a few seconds, then said, "You reckon we oughta do it, Jeff? You reckon we oughta go 'head an' do it, really?"

Jeff's voice choked; his eyes blurred. He was terrified to hear Jennie say the thing that had been in his mind all morning. She had egged him on when he had wanted more than anything in the world to wait, to reconsider, to think things over a little longer. Now she was getting cold feet. Actually, there was no need of thinking the question through again. It would only end in making the same painful decision once more. Jeff knew that. There was no need of fooling around longer.

"We jes as well to do like we planned," he said. "They ain't nothin' else for us now—it's the bes' thing."

Jeff thought of the handicaps, the near impossibility, of making another crop with his leg bothering him more and more each week. Then there was always the chance that he would have another stroke, like the one that had made him lame. Another one might kill him. The least it could do would be to leave him helpless. Jeff gasped—Lord Jesus! He could not bear to think of being helpless, like a baby, on Jennie's hands. Frail, blind Jennie.

The little pounding motor of the car worked harder and harder. The puff of steam from the cracked radiator became larger. Jeff realized that they were climbing a little rise. A moment later the road turned abruptly, and he looked upon the face of the river.

"Jeff."

"Hunh?"

"Is that the water I hear?"

"Hm. Tha's it."

"Well, which way you goin' now?"

"Down this-a way," he said. "The road runs 'long 'side o' the water a lil piece."

She waited a while calmly. Then she said, "Drive faster."

"A'right, baby," Jeff said.

The water roared in the bed of the river. It was fifty or sixty feet below the level of the road. Between the road and the water there was a long smooth slope, sharply inclined. The slope was dry, the clay hardened by prolonged summer heat. The water below, roaring in a narrow channel, was noisy and wild.

"Jeff."

"Hunh?"

"How far you goin'?"

"Jes a lil piece down the road."

"You ain't scairt, is you, Jeff?"

"Nah, baby," he said trembling. "I ain't scairt."

"Remember how we planned it, Jeff. We gotta do it like we said. Brave-like."

"Hm."

Jeff's brain darkened. Things suddenly seemed unreal, like figures in a dream. Thoughts swam in his mind foolishly, hysterically, like little blind fish in a pool within a dense cave. They rushed again. Jeff soon became dizzy. He shuddered violently and turned to his wife.

"Jennie, I can't do it. I can't." His voice broke pitifully.

She did not appear to be listening. All the grief had gone from her face. She sat erect, her unseeing eyes wide open, strained and frightful. Her glossy black skin had become dull. She seemed as thin, as sharp and bony, as a starved bird. Now, having suffered and endured the sadness of tearing herself away from beloved things, she showed no anguish. She was absorbed with her own thoughts, and she didn't even hear Jeff's voice shouting in her ear.

Jeff said nothing more. For an instant there was light in his cavernous brain. The great chamber was, for less than a second, peopled by characters he knew and loved. They were simple, healthy creatures, and they behaved in a manner that he could understand. They had quality. But since he had already taken leave of them long ago, the remembrance did not break his heart again. Young Jeff Patton was among them, the Jeff Patton of fifty years ago who went down to New Orleans with a crowd of country boys to the Mardi Gras doings. The gay young crowd, boys with candy-striped shirts and rouged brown girls in noisy silks, was like a picture in his head. Yet it did not make him sad. On that very trip Slim Burns had killed Joe Beasley—the crowd had been broken up. Since then Jeff Patton's world had been the Greenbriar Plantation. If there had been other Mardi Gras carnivals, he had not heard of them. Since then there had been no time; the years had fallen on him like waves. Now he was old, worn out. Another paralytic stroke (like the one he had already suffered) would put him on his back for keeps. In that condition, with a frail blind woman to look after him, he would be worse off than if he were dead.

Suddenly Jeff's hands became steady. He actually felt brave. He slowed down the motor of the car and carefully pulled off the road. Below, the water of the stream boomed, a soft thunder in the deep channel. Jeff ran the car onto the clay slope, pointed it directly toward the stream, and put his foot heavily on the accelerator. The little car leaped furiously down the steep incline toward the water. The movement was nearly as swift and direct as a fall. The two old black folks, sitting quietly side by side, showed no excitement. In another instant the car hit the water and dropped immediately out of sight.

A little later it lodged in the mud of a shallow place. One wheel of the crushed and upturned little Ford became visible above the rushing water.

Idiots First   1963

BERNARD MALAMUD   [b. 1914]

The thick ticking of the tin clock stopped. Mendel, dozing in the dark, awoke in fright. The pain returned as he listened. He drew on his cold embittered clothing, and wasted minutes sitting at the edge of the bed.

"Isaac," he ultimately sighed.

In the kitchen, Isaac, his astonished mouth open, held six peanuts in his palm. He placed each on the table. "One . . . two . . . nine."

He gathered each peanut and appeared in the doorway. Mendel, in loose hat and long overcoat, still sat on the bed. Isaac watched with small eyes and ears, thick hair graying the sides of his head.

"Schlaf," he nasally said.

"No," muttered Mendel. As if stifling he rose. "Come, Isaac."

He wound his old watch though the sight of the stopped clock nauseated him. Isaac wanted to hold it to his ear.

"No, it's late." Mendel put the watch carefully away. In the drawer he found the little paper bag of crumpled ones and fives and slipped it into his overcoat pocket. He helped Isaac on with his coat.

Isaac looked at one dark window, then at the other. Mendel stared at both blank windows.

They went slowly down the darkly lit stairs, Mendel first, Isaac watching the moving shadows on the wall. To one long shadow he offered a peanut.

"Hungrig."

In the vestibule the old man gazed through the thin glass. The November night was cold and bleak. Opening the door he cautiously thrust his head out. Though he saw nothing he quickly shut the door.

"Ginzburg, that he came to see me yesterday," he whispered in Isaac's ear.

Isaac sucked air.

"You know who I mean?"

Isaac combed his chin with his fingers.

"That's the one, with the black whiskers. Don't talk to him or go with him if he asks you."

Isaac moaned.

"Young people he don't bother so much," Mendel said in afterthought.

It was suppertime and the street was empty but the store windows dimly lit their way to the corner. They crossed the deserted street and went on. Isaac, with a happy cry, pointed to the three golden balls. Mendel smiled but was exhausted when they got to the pawnshop.

The pawnbroker, a red-bearded man with black horn-rimmed glasses, was eating a whitefish at the rear of the store. He craned his head, saw them, and settled back to sip his tea.

In five minutes he came forward, patting his shapeless lips with a large white handkerchief.

Mendel, breathing heavily, handed him the worn gold watch. The pawn-broker, raising his glasses, screwed in his eyepiece. He turned the watch over once. "Eight dollars."

The dying man wet his cracked lips. "I must have thirty-five."

"So go to Rothschild."

"Cost me myself sixty."

"In 1905." The pawnbroker handed back the watch. It had stopped ticking. Mendel wound it slowly. It ticked hollowly.

"Isaac must go to my uncle that he lives in California."

"It's a free country," said the pawnbroker.

Isaac, watching a banjo, snickered.

"What's the matter with him?" the pawnbroker asked.

"So let be eight dollars," muttered Mendel, "but where will I get the rest till tonight?"

"How much for my hat and coat?" he asked.

"No sale." The pawnbroker went behind the cage and wrote out a ticket. He locked the watch in a small drawer but Mendel still heard it ticking.

In the street he slipped the eight dollars into the paper bag, then searched in his pockets for a scrap of writing. Finding it, he strained to read the address by the light of the street lamp.

As they trudged to the subway, Mendel pointed to the sprinkled sky.

"Isaac, look how many stars are tonight."

"Eggs," said Isaac.

"First we will go to Mr. Fishbein, after we will eat."

They got off the train in upper Manhattan and had to walk several blocks before they located Fishbein's house.

"A regular palace," Mendel murmured, looking forward to a moment's warmth.

Isaac stared uneasily at the heavy door of the house.

Mendel rang. The servant, a man with long sideburns, came to the door and said Mr. and Mrs. Fishbein were dining and could see no one.

"He should eat in peace but we will wait till he finishes."

"Come back tomorrow morning. Tomorrow morning Mr. Fishbein will talk to you. He don't do business or charity at this time of the night."

"Charity I am not interested—"

"Come back tomorrow."

"Tell him it's life or death—"

"Whose life or death?"

"So if not his, then mine."

"Don't be such a big smart aleck."

"Look me in my face," said Mendel, "and tell me if I got time till tomorrow morning?"

The servant stared at him, then at Isaac, and reluctantly let them in.

The foyer was a vast high-ceilinged room with many oil paintings on the walls, voluminous silken draperies, a thick flowered rug at foot, and a marble staircase.

Mr. Fishbein, a paunchy bald-headed man with hairy nostrils and small patent leather feet, ran lightly down the stairs, a large napkin tucked under a tuxedo coat button. He stopped on the fifth step from the bottom and examined his visitors.

"Who comes on Friday night to a man that he has guests, to spoil him his supper?"

"Excuse me that I bother you, Mr. Fishbein," Mendel said. "If I didn't come now I couldn't come tomorrow."

"Without more preliminaries, please state your business. I'm a hungry man."

"Hungrig," wailed Isaac.

Fishbein adjusted his pince-nez. "What's the matter with him?"

"This is my son Isaac. He is like this all his life."

Isaac mewled.

"I am sending him to California."

"Mr. Fishbein don't contribute to personal pleasure trips."

"I am a sick man and he must go tonight on the train to my Uncle Leo."

"I never give to unorganized charity," Fishbein said, "but if you are hungry I will invite you downstairs in my kitchen. We having tonight chicken with stuffed derma."

"All I ask is thirty-five dollars for the train ticket to my uncle in California. I have already the rest."

"Who is your uncle? How old a man?"

"Eighty-one years, a long life to him."

Fishbein burst into laughter. "Eighty-one years and you are sending him this halfwit."

Mendel, flailing both arms, cried, "Please, without names."

Fishbein politely conceded.

"Where is open the door there we go in the house," the sick man said. "If you will kindly give me thirty-five dollars, God will bless you. What is thirty-five dollars to Mr. Fishbein? Nothing. To me, for my boy, is everything."

Fishbein drew himself up to his tallest height.

"Private contributions I don't make—only to institutions. This is my fixed policy."

Mendel sank to his creaking knees on the rug.

"Please, Mr. Fishbein, if not thirty-five, give maybe twenty."

"Levinson!" Fishbein angrily called.

The servant with the long sideburns appeared at the top of the stairs.

"Show this party where is the door—unless he wishes to partake food before leaving the premises."

"For what I got chicken won't cure it," Mendel said.

"This way if you please," said Levinson, descending.

Isaac assisted his father up.

"Take him to an institution," Fishbein advised over the marble balustrade. He ran quickly up the stairs and they were at once outside, buffeted by winds.

The walk to the subway was tedious. The wind blew mournfully. Mendel, breathless, glanced furtively at shadows. Isaac, clutching his peanuts in his frozen fist, clung to his father's side. They entered a small park to rest for a minute on a stone bench under a leafless two-branched tree. The thick right branch was raised, the thin left one hung down. A very pale moon rose slowly. So did a stranger as they approached the bench.

"Gut yuntif" [Happy holiday], he said hoarsely.

Mendel, drained of blood, waved his wasted arms. Isaac yowled sickly. Then a bell chimed and it was only ten. Mendel let out a piercing anguished cry as the bearded stranger disappeared into the bushes. A policeman came running, and though he beat the bushes with his nightstick, could turn up nothing. Mendel and Isaac hurried out of the little park. When Mendel glanced back the dead tree had its thin arm raised, the thick one down. He moaned.

They boarded a trolley, stopping at the home of a former friend, but he had died years ago. On the same block they went into a cafeteria and ordered two fried eggs for Isaac. The tables were crowded except where a heavy-set man sat eating soup with kasha. After one look at him they left in haste, although Isaac wept.

Mendel had another address on a slip of paper but the house was too far away, in Queens, so they stood in a doorway shivering.

What can I do, he frantically thought, in one short hour?

He remembered the furniture in the house. It was junk but might bring a few dollars. "Come, Isaac." They went once more to the pawnbroker's to talk to him, but the shop was dark and an iron gate—rings and gold watches glinting through it—was drawn tight across his place of business.

They huddled behind a telephone pole, both freezing. Isaac whimpered.

"See the big moon, Isaac. The whole sky is white."

He pointed but Isaac wouldn't look.

Mendel dreamed for a minute of the sky lit up, long sheets of light in all directions. Under the sky, in California, sat Uncle Leo drinking tea with lemon. Mendel felt warm but woke up cold.

Across the street stood an ancient brick synagogue.

He pounded on the huge door but no one appeared. He waited till he had breath and desperately knocked again. At last there were footsteps within, and the synagogue door creaked open on its massive brass hinges.

A darkly dressed sexton, holding a dripping candle, glared at them.

"Who knocks this time of night with so much noise on the synagogue door?"

Mendel told the sexton his troubles. "Please, I would like to speak to the rabbi."

"The rabbi is an old man. He sleeps now. His wife won't let you see him. Go home and come back tomorrow."

"To tomorrow I said goodbye already. I am a dying man."

Though the sexton seemed doubtful he pointed to an old wooden house next door. "In there he lives." He disappeared into the synagogue with his lit candle casting shadows around him.

Mendel, with Isaac clutching his sleeve, went up the wooden steps and rang the bell. After five minutes a big-faced, gray-haired bulky woman came out on the porch with a torn robe thrown over her nightdress. She emphatically said the rabbi was sleeping and could not be waked.

But as she was insisting, the rabbi himself tottered to the door. He listened a minute and said, "Who wants to see me let them come in."

They entered a cluttered room. The rabbi was an old skinny man with bent shoulders and a wisp of white beard. He wore a flannel nightgown and black skullcap; his feet were bare.

"Vey is mir" [Woe is me], his wife muttered. "Put on shoes or tomorrow comes sure pneumonia." She was a woman with a big belly, years younger than her husband. Staring at Isaac, she turned away.

Mendel apologetically related his errand. "All I need more is thirty-five dollars."

"Thirty-five?" said the rabbi's wife. "Why not thirty-five thousand? Who has so much money? My husband is a poor rabbi. The doctors take away every penny."

"Dear friend," said the rabbi, "if I had I would give you."

"I got already seventy," Mendel said, heavy-hearted. "All I need more is thirty-five."

"God will give you," said the rabbi.

"In the grave," said Mendel. "I need tonight. Come, Isaac."

"Wait," called the rabbi.

He hurried inside, came out with a fur-lined caftan, and handed it to Mendel.

"Yascha," shrieked his wife, "not your new coat!"

"I got my old one. Who needs two coats for one body?"

"Yascha, I am screaming—"

"Who can go among poor people, tell me, in a new coat?"

"Yascha," she cried, "what can this man do with your coat? He needs tonight the money. The pawnbrokers are asleep."

"So let him wake them up."

"No." She grabbed the coat from Mendel.

He held on to a sleeve, wrestling her for the coat. Her I know, Mendel thought. "Shylock," he muttered. Her eyes glittered.

The rabbi groaned and tottered dizzily. His wife cried out as Mendel yanked the coat from her hands.

"Run," cried the rabbi.

"Run, Isaac."

They ran out of the house and down the steps.

"Stop, you thief," called the rabbi's wife.

The rabbi pressed both hands to his temples and fell to the floor.

"Help!" his wife wept. "Heart attack! Help!"

But Mendel and Isaac ran through the streets with the rabbi's new fur-lined caftan. After them noiselessly ran Ginzburg.

It was very late when Mendel bought the train ticket in the only booth open.

There was no time to stop for a sandwich so Isaac ate his peanuts and they hurried to the train in the vast deserted station.

"So in the morning," Mendel gasped as they ran, "there comes a man that he sells sandwiches and coffee. Eat but get change. When reaches California the train, will be waiting for you on the station Uncle Leo. If you don't recognize him he will recognize you. Tell him I send best regards."

But when they arrived at the gate to the platform it was shut, the light out.

Mendel, groaning, beat on the gate with his fists.

"Too late," said the uniformed ticket collector, a bulky, bearded man with hairy nostrils and a fishy smell.

He pointed to the station clock. "Already past twelve."

"But I see standing there still the train," Mendel said, hopping in his grief.

"It just left—in one more minute."

"A minute is enough. Just open the gate."

"Too late I told you."

Mendel socked his bony chest with both hands. "With my whole heart I beg you this little favor."

"Favors you had enough already. For you the train is gone. You shoulda been dead already at midnight. I told you that yesterday. This is the best I can do."

"Ginzburg!" Mendel shrank from him.

"Who else?" The voice was metallic, eyes glittered, the expression amused.

"For myself," the old man begged, "I don't ask a thing. But what will happen to my boy?"

Ginzburg shrugged slightly. "What will happen happens. This isn't my responsibility. I got enough to think about without worrying about somebody on one cylinder."

"What then is your responsibility?"

"To create conditions. To make happen what happens. I ain't in the anthropomorphic business."

"Whatever business you in, where is your pity?"

"This ain't my commodity. The law is the law."

"Which law is this?"

"The cosmic universal law, goddamit, the one I got to follow myself."

"What kind of a law is it?" cried Mendel. "For God's sake, don't you understand what I went through in my life with this poor boy? Look at him. For thirty-nine years, since the day he was born, I wait for him to grow up, but he don't. Do you understand what this means in a father's heart? Why don't you let him go to his uncle?" His voice had risen and he was shouting.

Isaac mewled loudly.

"Better calm down or you'll hurt somebody's feelings," Ginzburg said with a wink toward Isaac.

"All my life," Mendel cried, his body trembling, "what did I have? I was poor. I suffered from my health. When I worked I worked too hard. When I didn't work was worse. My wife died a young woman. But I didn't ask from anybody nothing. Now I ask a small favor. Be so kind, Mr. Ginzburg."

The ticket collector was picking his teeth with a match stick.

"You ain't the only one, my friend, some got it worse than you. That's how it goes in this country."

"You dog you." Mendel lunged at Ginzburg's throat and began to choke. "You bastard, don't you understand what it means human?"

They struggled nose to nose, Ginzburg, though his astonished eyes bulged, began to laugh. "You pipsqueak nothing. I'll freeze you to pieces."

His eyes lit in rage and Mendel felt an unbearable cold like an icy dagger invading his body, all of his parts shriveling.

Now I die without helping Isaac.

A crowd gathered. Isaac yelped in fright.

Clinging to Ginzburg in his last agony, Mendel saw reflected in the ticket collector's eyes the depth of his terror. But he saw that Ginzburg, staring at himself in Mendel's eyes, saw mirrored in them the extent of his own awful wrath. He beheld a shimmering, starry, blinding light that produced darkness.

Ginzburg looked astounded. "Who me?"

His grip on the squirming old man slowly loosened, and Mendel, his heart barely beating, slumped to the ground.

"Go." Ginzburg muttered, "take him to the train."

"Let pass," he commanded a guard.

The crowd parted. Isaac helped his father up and they tottered down the steps to the platform where the train waited, lit and ready to go.

Mendel found Isaac a coach seat and hastily embraced him. "Help Uncle Leo, Isaakil. Also remember your father and mother."

"Be nice to him," he said to the conductor. "Show him where everything is."

He waited on the platform until the train began slowly to move. Isaac sat at the edge of his seat, his face strained in the direction of his journey. When the train was gone, Mendel ascended the stairs to see what had become of Ginzburg.

QUESTIONS

1. Can this story be read as a religious drama? In this connection, consider the rabbi, the only person who helps Mendel. His compassion and his indifference to material things reveal him as a man of God. What does the supernatural Ginzburg represent? **2.** What is the significance of the fact that Isaac, for whom Mendel is determined to provide before death claims him, is an idiot? **3.** Mendel wins his battle with Ginzburg. What does that victory signify?

WRITING TOPIC

How do the various episodes in this story establish Mendel's character and prepare the reader for the final, climactic confrontation between Mendel and Ginzburg?

THE
PRESENCE
OF DEATH

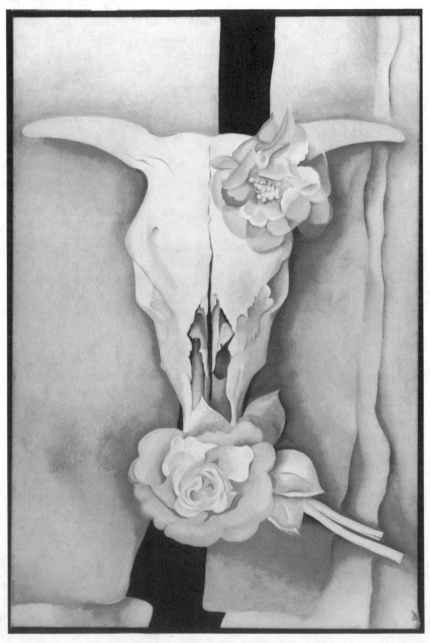

Cow's Skull with Calico Roses, 1931 by Georgia O'Keeffe.

POETRY

Edward

ANONYMOUS

1

"Why does your brand° sae° drap wi' bluid,   sword/so
      Edward, Edward,
Why does your brand sae drap wi' bluid,
  And why sae sad gang° ye, O?"   go
"O I ha'e killed my hawk sae guid,
      Mither, mither,
O I ha'e killed my hawk sae guid,
  And I had nae mair but he, O."

2

"Your hawke's bluid was never sae reid,°   red
      Edward, Edward,   10
Your hawke's bluid was never sae reid,
  My dear son I tell thee, O."
"O I ha'e killed my reid-roan steed,
      Mither, mither,
O I ha'e killed my reid-roan steed,
  That erst was sae fair and free, O."

3

"Your steed was auld, and ye ha'e gat mair,
      Edward, Edward,
Your steed was auld, and ye ha'e gat mair,
  Some other dule° ye drie,° O."   grief/suffer
"O I ha'e killed my fader dear,   21
      Mither, mither,
O I ha'e killed my fader dear,
  Alas, and wae° is me, O!"   woe

4

"And whatten penance wul ye drie for that,
          Edward, Edward?
And whatten penance wul ye drie for that,
     My dear son, now tell me O?"
"I'll set my feet in yonder boat,
          Mither, mither,   30
I'll set my feet in yonder boat,
     And I'll fare over the sea, O."

5

"And what wul ye do wi' your towers and your ha',
          Edward, Edward?
And what wul ye do wi' your towers and your ha',
     That were sae fair to see, O?"
"I'll let them stand tul they down fa',
          Mither, mither,
I'll let them stand tul they down fa',   39
     For here never mair maun° I be, O."   must

6

"And what wul ye leave to your bairns° and your wife,   children
          Edward, Edward?
And what wul ye leave to your bairns and your wife,
     Whan ye gang over the sea, O?"
"The warlde's° room, let them beg thrae° life,   world's/through
          Mither, mither,
The warlde's room, let them beg thrae life,
     For them never mair wul I see, O."

7

"And what wul ye leave to your ain mither dear,
          Edward, Edward?   50
And what wul ye leave to your ain mither dear,
     My dear son, now tell me, O?"
"The curse of hell frae° me sall° ye bear,   from/shall
          Mither, mither,
The curse of hell frae me sall ye bear,
     Sic° counsels ye gave to me, O."   such

QUESTIONS
1. Why does the mother reject Edward's answers to her first two questions?   **2.** Does the poem provide any clues as to the motive of the murder?   **3.** Edward has murdered his father and then bitterly turns away from his mother, wife, and children. What basis is there in the poem for nevertheless sympathizing with Edward?

WRITING TOPIC
What effects are achieved through the question-and-answer technique and the repetition of lines?

Sonnet   1609

WILLIAM SHAKESPEARE   [1564–1616]

73

That time of year thou mayst in me behold
When yellow leaves, or none, or few, do hang
Upon those boughs which shake against the cold,
Bare ruined choirs, where late the sweet birds sang.
In me thou see'st the twilight of such day
As after sunset fadeth in the west;
Which by and by black night doth take away,
Death's second self, that seals up all in rest.
In me thou see'st the glowing of such fire,
That on the ashes of his youth doth lie,   10
As the deathbed whereon it must expire,
Consumed with that which it was nourished by.
This thou perceiv'st, which makes thy love more strong,
To love that well which thou must leave ere long.

Death, Be Not Proud   1633

JOHN DONNE   [1572–1631]

Death, be not proud, though some have calléd thee
Mighty and dreadful, for thou art not so;
For those whom thou think'st thou dost overthrow
Die not, poor Death, nor yet canst thou kill me.
From rest and sleep, which but thy pictures be,
Much pleasure; then from thee much more must flow,

And soonest our best men with thee do go,
Rest of their bones, and soul's delivery.
Thou art slave to fate, chance, kings, and desperate men,
And dost with poison, war, and sickness dwell,   10
And poppy or charms can make us sleep as well
And better than thy stroke; why swell'st thou then?
One short sleep past, we wake eternally
And death shall be no more; Death, thou shalt die.

Elegy Written in a
Country Churchyard   1753

THOMAS GRAY   [1716–1771]

The curfew tolls the knell of parting day,
    The lowing herd wind slowly o'er the lea,
The plowman homeward plods his weary way,
    And leaves the world to darkness and to me.

Now fades the glimmering landscape on the sight,
    And all the air a solemn stillness holds,
Save where the beetle wheels his droning flight,
    And drowsy tinklings lull the distant folds;

Save that from yonder ivy-mantled tower
    The moping owl does to the moon complain   10
Of such, as wandering near her secret bower,
    Molest her ancient solitary reign.

Beneath those rugged elms, that yew tree's shade,
    Where heaves the turf in many a moldering heap,
Each in his narrow cell forever laid,
    The rude° forefathers of the hamlet sleep.   untaught

The breezy call of incense-breathing Morn,
    The swallow twittering from the straw-built shed,
The cock's shrill clarion, or the echoing horn,°   hunter's horn
    No more shall rouse them from their lowly bed.   20

For them no more the blazing hearth shall burn,
    Or busy housewife ply her evening care;
No children run to lisp their sire's return,
    Or climb his knees the envied kiss to share.

Oft did the harvest to their sickle yield,
    Their furrow oft the stubborn glebe° has broke;   field
How jocund did they drive their team afield!
    How bowed the woods beneath their sturdy stroke!

Let not Ambition mock their useful toil,
    Their homely joys, and destiny obscure;   30
Nor Grandeur hear with a disdainful smile
    The short and simple annals of the poor.

The boast of heraldry,° the pomp of power,   noble birth
    And all that beauty, all that wealth e'er gave,
Awaits alike the inevitable hour.
    The paths of glory lead but to the grave.

Nor you, ye proud, impute to these the fault,
    If Memory o'er their tomb no trophies° raise,   memorial
Where through the long-drawn aisle and fretted° vault   decorated
    The pealing anthem swells the note of praise.   40

Can storied° urn or animated bust   inscribed
    Back to its mansion call the fleeting breath?
Can Honor's voice provoke the silent dust,
    Or Flattery soothe the full cold ear of Death?

Perhaps in this neglected spot is laid
    Some heart once pregnant with celestial fire;
Hands that the rod of empire might have swayed,
    Or waked to ecstasy the living lyre.

But Knowledge to their eyes her ample page
    Rich with the spoils of time did ne'er unroll;   50
Chill Penury repressed their noble rage,
    And froze the genial current of the soul.

Full many a gem of purest ray serene,
    The dark unfathomed caves of ocean bear:
Full many a flower is born to blush unseen,
    And waste its sweetness on the desert air.

Some village Hampden,[1] that with dauntless breast
   The little tyrant of his fields withstood;
Some mute inglorious Milton here may rest,
   Some Cromwell guiltless of his country's blood.   60

The applause of listening senates to command,
   The threats of pain and ruin to despise,
To scatter plenty o'er a smiling land,
   And read their history in a nation's eyes,

Their lot forbade: nor circumscribed alone
   Their growing virtues, but their crimes confined;
Forbade to wade through slaughter to a throne,
   And shut the gates of mercy on mankind,

The struggling pangs of conscious truth to hide,
   To quench the blushes of ingenuous shame,   70
Or heap the shrine of Luxury and Pride
   With incense kindled at the Muse's flame.

Far from the madding crowd's ignoble strife,
   Their sober wishes never learned to stray;
Along the cool sequestered vale of life
   They kept the noiseless tenor of their way.

Yet even these bones from insult to protect
   Some frail memorial still erected nigh,
With uncouth rhymes and shapeless sculpture decked,
   Implores the passing tribute of a sigh.   80

Their name, their years, spelt by the unlettered Muse,
   The place of fame and elegy supply:
And many a holy text around she strews,
   That teach the rustic moralist to die.

For who to dumb Forgetfulness a prey,
   This pleasing anxious being e'er resigned,
Left the warm precincts of the cheerful day,
   Nor cast one longing lingering look behind?

On some fond breast the parting soul relies,
   Some pious drops the closing eye requires;   90

Elegy Written in a Country Churchyard
   [1] John Hampden (1594–1643) championed the people against the autocratic policies of Charles I.

Even from the tomb the voice of Nature cries,
    Even in our ashes live their wonted fires.

For thee, who mindful of the unhonored dead
    Dost in these lines their artless tale relate;
If chance, by lonely contemplation led,
    Some kindred spirit shall inquire thy fate,

Haply some hoary-headed swain may say,
    "Oft have we seen him at the peep of dawn
Brushing with hasty steps the dews away
    To meet the sun upon the upland lawn.   100

"There at the foot of yonder nodding beech
    That wreathes its old fantastic roots so high,
His listless length at noontide would he stretch,
    And pore upon the brook that babbles by.

"Hard by yon wood, now smiling as in scorn,
    Muttering his wayward fancies he would rove,
Now drooping, woeful wan, like one forlorn,
    Or crazed with care, or crossed in hopeless love.

"One morn I missed him on the customed hill,
    Along the heath and near his favorite tree;   110
Another came; nor yet beside the rill,
    Nor up the lawn, nor at the wood was he;

"The next with dirges due in sad array
    Slow through the churchway path we saw him borne.
Approach and read (for thou canst read) the lay,
    Graved on the stone beneath yon aged thorn."

THE EPITAPH

Here rests his head upon the lap of Earth
    A youth to Fortune and to Fame unknown
Fair Science° frowned not on his humble birth,   learning
    And Melancholy marked him for her own.   120

Large was his bounty, and his soul sincere,
    Heaven did a recompense as largely send:
He gave to Misery all he had, a tear,
    He gained from Heaven ('twas all he wished) a friend.

No farther seek his merits to disclose,
*   Or draw his frailties from their dread abode*
(There they alike in trembling hope repose),
*   The bosom of his Father and his God.*

QUESTIONS
1. Why have the people Gray honors in this poem lived and died in obscurity? Does the poet offer any suggestions for change? Explain. **2.** Why would "Ambition mock their useful toil" (l. 29)?

WRITING TOPIC
Does this poem celebrate the advantages of obscurity and ignorance over fame, wealth, and knowledge?

The Destruction
of Sennacherib[1]   1815

GEORGE GORDON, LORD BYRON   [1788–1824]

The Assyrian came down like the wolf on the fold,
And his cohorts were gleaming in purple and gold;
And the sheen of their spears was like stars on the sea,
When the blue wave rolls nightly on deep Galilee.

Like the leaves of the forest when summer is green,
That host with their banners at sunset were seen:
Like the leaves of the forest when autumn hath blown,
That host on the morrow lay withered and strown.

For the Angel of Death spread his wings on the blast,
And breathed in the face of the foe as he passed;   10
And the eyes of the sleepers waxed deadly and chill,
And their hearts but once heaved—and for ever grew still!

And there lay the steed with his nostril all wide,
But through it there rolled not the breath of his pride;
And the foam of his gasping lay white on the turf,
And cold as the spray of the rock-beating surf.

And there lay the rider distorted and pale,
With the dew on his brow, and the rust on his mail;

The Destruction of Sennacherib
   [1] Byron retells the account of the Assyrian siege of Jerusalem, found in II Kings 19, which culminates in the death of 185,000 Assyrian troops at the hand of the angel of the Lord.

And the tents were all silent, the banners alone,
The lances unlifted, the trumpet unblown.   20

And the widows of Ashur[2] are loud in their wail,
And the idols are broke in the temple of Baal;[3]
And the might of the Gentile,[4] unsmote by the sword,
Hath melted like snow in the glance of the Lord!

Ozymandias[1]   1818

PERCY BYSSHE SHELLEY   [1792–1822]

I met a traveller from an antique land
Who said: Two vast and trunkless legs of stone
Stand in the desert . . . Near them, on the sand,
Half sunk, a shattered visage lies, whose frown,
And wrinkled lip, and sneer of cold command,
Tell that its sculptor well those passions read
Which yet survive, stamped on these lifeless things,
The hand that mocked them, and the heart that fed:
And on the pedestal these words appear:
"My name is Ozymandias, king of kings: 10
Look on my works, ye Mighty, and despair!"
Nothing beside remains. Round the decay
Of that colossal wreck, boundless and bare
The lone and level sands stretch far away.

Ode on a Grecian Urn   1820

JOHN KEATS   [1795–1821]

I

Thou still unravished bride of quietness,
    Thou foster child of silence and slow time,
Sylvan historian, who canst thus express
    A flowery tale more sweetly than our rhyme:

---

[2] Another name for Assyria.
[3] A Canaanite deity.
[4] A non-Hebrew, in this case Sennacherib, the King of Assyria.

Ozymandias
[1] Egyptian monarch of the thirteenth century B.C., said to have erected a huge statue of himself.

What leaf-fringed legend haunts about thy shape
  Of deities or mortals, or of both,
    In Tempe or the dales of Arcady?[1]
  What men or gods are these? What maidens loath?
What mad pursuit? What struggle to escape?
    What pipes and timbrels? What wild ecstasy?   10

II

Heard melodies are sweet, but those unheard
  Are sweeter; therefore, ye soft pipes, play on;
Not to the sensual ear, but, more endeared,
  Pipe to the spirit ditties of no tone:
Fair youth, beneath the trees, thou canst not leave
  Thy song, nor ever can those trees be bare;
    Bold Lover, never, never canst thou kiss,
Though winning near the goal—yet, do not grieve;
    She cannot fade, though thou hast not thy bliss,
Forever wilt thou love, and she be fair!   20

III

Ah, happy, happy boughs! that cannot shed
  Your leaves, nor ever bid the Spring adieu;
And, happy melodist, unweariéd,
  Forever piping songs forever new;
More happy love! more happy, happy love!
  Forever warm and still to be enjoyed,
    Forever panting, and forever young;
All breathing human passion far above,[2]
    That leaves a heart high-sorrowful and cloyed,
    A burning forehead, and a parching tongue.   30

IV

Who are these coming to the sacrifice?
  To what green altar, O mysterious priest,
Lead'st thou that heifer lowing at the skies,
  And all her silken flanks with garlands dressed?

Ode on a Grecian Urn
  [1] Tempe and Arcady are valleys in Greece famous for their beauty. In ancient times, Tempe was regarded as sacred to Apollo.

  [2] I.e., far above all breathing human passion.

What little town by river or sea shore,
  Or mountain-built with peaceful citadel,
    Is emptied of this folk, this pious morn?
And, little town, thy streets forevermore
  Will silent be; and not a soul to tell
    Why thou art desolate, can e'er return.   40

        V

O Attic³ shape! Fair attitude! with brede
  Of marble men and maidens overwrought,
With forest branches and the trodden weed;
  Thou, silent form, dost tease us out of thought
As doth eternity: Cold Pastoral!
  When old age shall this generation waste,
    Thou shalt remain, in midst of other woe
  Than ours, a friend to man, to whom thou say'st,
"Beauty is truth, truth beauty,—that is all
  Ye know on earth, and all ye need to know."   50

QUESTIONS
1. Describe the scene the poet sees depicted on the urn. Describe the scene the poet imagines as a consequence of the scene on the urn. **2.** Why are the boughs, the piper, and the lovers happy in stanza 3? **3.** Explain the assertion of stanza 2 that "Heard melodies are sweet, but those unheard/Are sweeter." **4.** Does the poem support the assertion of the last two lines? What does that assertion mean?

WRITING TOPIC
In what sense might it be argued that this poem is about mortality and immortality? In this connection, consider the meaning of the phrase "Cold Pastoral!" (l. 45).

When I Have Fears   1848

JOHN KEATS [1795–1821]

When I have fears that I may cease to be
  Before my pen has gleaned my teeming brain,
Before high-piléd books, in charact'ry,°   written symbols

---

³ Athenian, thus simple and graceful.

Hold like rich garners the full-ripened grain;
When I behold, upon the night's starred face,
    Huge cloudy symbols of a high romance,
And think that I may never live to trace
    Their shadows, with the magic hand of chance;
And when I feel, fair creature of an hour,
    That I shall never look upon thee more,   10
Never have relish in the faery° power   magical
    Of unreflecting love!—then on the shore
Of the wide world I stand alone, and think
Till Love and Fame to nothingness do sink.

QUESTIONS
1. What consequences of death does the poet fear in each of the three quatrains? **2.** What value have "Love and Fame" in the face of death?

After Great Pain, a Formal Feeling Comes   (ca. 1862)

EMILY DICKINSON   [1830–1886]

After great pain, a formal feeling comes—
The Nerves sit ceremonious, like Tombs—
The stiff Heart questions was it He, that bore,
And Yesterday, or Centuries before?

The Feet, mechanical, go round—
Of Ground, or Air, or Ought—
A Wooden way
Regardless grown,
A Quartz contentment, like a stone—

This is the Hour of Lead—   10
Remembered, if outlived,
As Freezing persons, recollect the Snow—
First—Chill—then Stupor—then the letting go—

QUESTION
1. Is this poem about physical or psychic pain? Explain.

WRITING TOPIC
What is the meaning of "stiff Heart" (l. 3) and "Quartz contentment" (l. 9)? What part do they play in the larger pattern of images?

I Heard a Fly Buzz— When I Died   (ca. 1862)

EMILY DICKINSON   [1830–1886]

I heard a Fly buzz—when I died—
The Stillness in the Room
Was like the Stillness in the Air—
Between the Heaves of Storm—

The Eyes around—had wrung them dry—
And Breaths were gathering firm
For that last Onset—when the King
Be witnessed—in the Room—

I willed my Keepsakes—Signed away
What portion of me be   10
Assignable—and then it was
There interposed a Fly—

With Blue—uncertain stumbling Buzz—
Between the light—and me—
And then the Windows failed—and then
I could not see to see—

Apparently with No Surprise (ca. 1884)

EMILY DICKINSON   [1830–1886]

Apparently with no surprise
To any happy flower,
The frost beheads it at its play
In accidental power.
The blond assassin passes on,
The sun proceeds unmoved
To measure off another day
For an approving God.

To an Athlete Dying Young   1896

A. E. HOUSMAN   [1859–1936]

The time you won your town the race
We chaired you through the market place;
Man and boy stood cheering by,
And home we brought you shoulder-high.

Today, the road all runners come,
Shoulder-high we bring you home,
And set you at your threshold down,
Townsman of a stiller town.

Smart lad, to slip betimes away
From fields where glory does not stay   10
And early though the laurel grows
It withers quicker than the rose.

Eyes the shady night has shut
Cannot see the record cut,
And silence sounds no worse than cheers
After earth has stopped the ears:

Now you will not swell the rout
Of lads that wore their honors out,
Runners whom renown outran
And the name died before the man.   20

So set, before its echoes fade,
The fleet foot on the sill of shade,
And hold to the low lintel up
The still defended challenge cup.

And round that early laureled head
Will flock to gaze the strengthless dead
And find unwithered on its curls
The garland briefer than a girl's.

Sailing to Byzantium[1]

1927

WILLIAM BUTLER YEATS   [1865–1939]

1

That is no country for old men. The young
In one another's arms, birds in the trees
—Those dying generations—at their song,
The salmon-falls, the mackerel-crowded seas,
Fish, flesh, or fowl, commend all summer long
Whatever is begotten, born, and dies.
Caught in that sensual music all neglect
Monuments of unaging intellect.

2

An aged man is but a paltry thing,
A tattered coat upon a stick, unless   10
Soul clap its hands and sing, and louder sing
For every tatter in its mortal dress,
Nor is there singing school but studying
Monuments of its own magnificence;
And therefore I have sailed the seas and come
To the holy city of Byzantium.

3

O sages standing in God's holy fire
As in the gold mosaic of a wall,
Come from the holy fire, perne in a gyre,[2]
And be the singing-masters of my soul.   20
Consume my heart away; sick with desire
And fastened to a dying animal
It knows not what it is; and gather me
Into the artifice of eternity.

Sailing to Byzantium
   [1] Capital of the ancient Eastern Roman Empire, Byzantium (modern Istanbul) is celebrated for its great art, including mosaics (in ll. 17–18, Yeats addresses the figures in one of these mosaics). In *A Vision*, Yeats cites Byzantium as possibly the only civilization which had achieved what he called "Unity of Being," a state where "religious, aesthetic and practical life were one. . . ."
   [2] I.e., whirl in a spiral motion. Yeats associated this motion with the cycles of history and the fate of the individual. Here he entreats the sages represented in the mosaic to take him out of the natural world described in the first stanza and into the eternal world of art.

4

Once out of nature I shall never take
My bodily form from any natural thing,
But such a form as Grecian goldsmiths make
Of hammered gold and gold enameling
To keep a drowsy Emperor awake;[3]
Or set upon a golden bough to sing   30
To lords and ladies of Byzantium
Of what is past, or passing, or to come.

QUESTIONS
1. This poem incorporates a series of contrasts, among them "That" country and Byzantium, the real birds of the first stanza and the artificial bird of the final stanza. What others do you find? **2.** What are the meanings of "generations" (l. 3)? **3.** For what is the poet "sick with desire" (l. 21): **4.** In what sense is eternity an "artifice" (l. 24)?

WRITING TOPIC
In what ways are the images of bird and song used throughout this poem?

Richard Cory   1897

EDWIN ARLINGTON ROBINSON [1869–1935]

Whenever Richard Cory went down town,
We people on the pavement looked at him:
He was a gentleman from sole to crown,
Clean favored, and imperially slim.

And he was always quietly arrayed,
And he was always human when he talked;
But still he fluttered pulses when he said,
"Good-morning," and he glittered when he walked.

And he was rich—yes, richer than a king—
And admirably schooled in every grace: 10
In fine, we thought that he was everything
To make us wish that we were in his place.

---

[3] "I have read somewhere," Yeats wrote, "that in the Emperor's palace at Byzantium was a tree made of gold and silver, and artificial birds that sang." The poet wishes to become an artificial bird (a work of art) in contrast to the real birds of the first stanza.

So on we worked, and waited for the light,
And went without the meat, and cursed the bread;
And Richard Cory, one calm summer night,
Went home and put a bullet through his head.

Mr. Flood's Party   1921

EDWIN ARLINGTON ROBINSON   [1869–1935]

Old Eben Flood, climbing alone one night
Over the hill between the town below
And the forsaken upland hermitage
That held as much as he should ever know
On earth again of home, paused warily.
The road was his with not a native near;
And Eben, having leisure, said aloud,
For no man else in Tilbury Town to hear:

"Well, Mr. Flood, we have the harvest moon
Again, and we may not have many more;   10
The bird is on the wing, the poet says,
And you and I have said it here before.
Drink to the bird." He raised up to the light
The jug that he had gone so far to fill,
And answered huskily: "Well, Mr. Flood,
Since you propose it, I believe I will."

Alone, as if enduring to the end
A valiant armor of scarred hopes outworn,
He stood there in the middle of the road
Like Roland's ghost winding a silent horn.   20
Below him, in the town among the trees,
Where friends of other days had honored him,
A phantom salutation of the dead
Rang thinly till old Eben's eyes were dim.

Then, as a mother lays her sleeping child
Down tenderly, fearing it may awake,
He set the jug down slowly at his feet
With trembling care, knowing that most things break;
And only when assured that on firm earth
It stood, as the uncertain lives of men   30
Assuredly did not, he paced away,
And with his hand extended paused again:

"Well, Mr. Flood, we have not met like this
In a long time; and many a change has come
To both of us, I fear, since last it was
We had a drop together. Welcome home!"
Convivially returning with himself,
Again he raised the jug up to the light;
And with an acquiescent quaver said:
"Well, Mr. Flood, if you insist, I might.   40

"Only a very little, Mr. Flood—
For auld lang syne. No more, sir; that will do."
So, for the time, apparently it did,
And Eben evidently thought so too;
For soon amid the silver loneliness
Of night he lifted up his voice and sang,
Secure, with only two moons listening,
Until the whole harmonious landscape rang—

"For auld lang syne." The weary throat gave out,
The last word wavered; and the song being done,   50
He raised again the jug regretfully
And shook his head, and was again alone.
There was not much that was ahead of him,
And there was nothing in the town below—
Where strangers would have shut the many doors
That many friends had opened long ago.

After Apple-Picking   1914

ROBERT FROST   [1874–1963]

My long two-pointed ladder's sticking through a tree
Toward heaven still,
And there's a barrel that I didn't fill
Beside it, and there may be two or three
Apples I didn't pick upon some bough.
But I am done with apple-picking now.
Essence of winter sleep is on the night,
The scent of apples: I am drowsing off.
I cannot rub the strangeness from my sight
I got from looking through a pane of glass   10
I skimmed this morning from the drinking trough
And held against the world of hoary grass.

It melted, and I let it fall and break.
But I was well
Upon my way to sleep before it fell,
And I could tell
What form my dreaming was about to take.
Magnified apples appear and disappear,
Stem end and blossom end,
And every fleck of russet showing clear.   20
My instep arch not only keeps the ache,
It keeps the pressure of a ladder-round.
I feel the ladder sway as the boughs bend.
And I keep hearing from the cellar bin
The rumbling sound
Of load on load of apples coming in.
For I have had too much
Of apple-picking: I am overtired
Of the great harvest I myself desired.
There were ten thousand thousand fruit to touch,   30
Cherish in hand, lift down, and not let fall.
For all
That struck the earth,
No matter if not bruised or spiked with stubble,
Went surely to the cider-apple heap
As of no worth.
One can see what will trouble
This sleep of mine, whatever sleep it is.
Were he not gone,
The woodchuck could say whether it's like his   40
Long sleep, as I describe its coming on,
Or just some human sleep.

QUESTIONS
1. What does apple-picking symbolize?   **2.** At the end of the poem, why is the speaker uncertain about what kind of sleep is coming on him?

Nothing Gold Can Stay   1923

ROBERT FROST   [1874-1963]

Nature's first green is gold,
Her hardest hue to hold.
Her early leaf's a flower;
But only so an hour.

Then leaf subsides to leaf.
So Eden sank to grief,
So dawn goes down to day.
Nothing gold can stay.

QUESTIONS
1. Does this poem protest or accept the transitoriness of things? **2.** Why does Frost use the word "subsides" in line 5 rather than a word like "expands" or "grows"? **3.** How are "Nature's first green" (l. 1), "Eden" (l. 6), and "dawn" (l. 7) linked together?

'Out, Out—'[1]   1916

ROBERT FROST [1874–1963]

The buzz-saw snarled and rattled in the yard
And made dust and dropped stove-length sticks of wood,
Sweet-scented stuff when the breeze drew across it.
And from there those that lifted eyes could count
Five mountain ranges one behind the other
Under the sunset far into Vermont.
And the saw snarled and rattled, snarled and rattled,
As it ran light, or had to bear a load.
And nothing happened: day was all but done.
Call it a day, I wish they might have said   10
To please the boy by giving him the half hour
That a boy counts so much when saved from work.
His sister stood beside them in her apron
To tell them 'Supper.' At the word, the saw,
As if to prove saws knew what supper meant,
Leaped out at the boy's hand, or seemed to leap—
He must have given the hand. However it was,
Neither refused the meeting. But the hand!
The boy's first outcry was a rueful laugh,
As he swung toward them holding up the hand   20
Half in appeal, but half as if to keep
The life from spilling. Then the boy saw all—
Since he was old enough to know, big boy
Doing a man's work, though a child at heart—

'Out, Out'
[1] The title is taken from the famous speech of Macbeth upon hearing that his wife has died (*Macbeth*, Act V, Scene 5).

He saw all spoiled. 'Don't let him cut my hand off—
The doctor, when he comes. Don't let him, sister!'
So. But the hand was gone already.
The doctor put him in the dark of ether.
He lay and puffed his lips out with his breath.
And then—the watcher at his pulse took fright.   30
No one believed. They listened at his heart.
Little—less—nothing!—and that ended it.
No more to build on there. And they, since they
Were not the one dead, turned to their affairs.

WRITING TOPIC
Compare this poem with Emily Dickinson's "Apparently with No Surprise."

Design   1936

ROBERT FROST   [1874–1963]

I found a dimpled spider, fat and white,
On a white heal-all, holding up a moth
Like a white piece of rigid satin cloth—
Assorted characters of death and blight
Mixed ready to begin the morning right,
Like the ingredients of a witches' broth—
A snow-drop spider, a flower like a froth,
And dead wings carried like a paper kite.

What had that flower to do with being white,
The wayside blue and innocent heal-all?   10
What brought the kindred spider to that height,
Then steered the white moth thither in the night?
What but design of darkness to appall?—
If design govern in a thing so small.

Tract   1917

WILLIAM CARLOS WILLIAMS   [1883–1963]

I will teach you my townspeople
how to perform a funeral—
for you have it over a troop
of artists—

unless one should scour the world—
you have the ground sense necessary.

See! the hearse leads.
I begin with a design for a hearse.
For Christ's sake not black—
nor white either—and not polished!   10
Let it be weathered—like a farm wagon—
with gilt wheels (this could be
applied fresh at small expense)
or no wheels at all:
a rough dray to drag over the ground.

Knock the glass out!
My God—glass, my townspeople!
For what purpose? Is it for the dead
to look out or for us to see
how well he is housed or to see   20
the flowers or the lack of them—
or what?
To keep the rain and snow from him?
He will have a heavier rain soon:
pebbles and dirt and what not.
Let there be no glass—
and no upholstery! phew!
and no little brass rollers
and small easy wheels on the bottom—
my townspeople what are you thinking of!   30

A rough plain hearse then
with gilt wheels and no top at all.
On this the coffin lies
by its own weight.
                      No wreaths please—
especially no hot-house flowers.
Some common memento is better,
something he prized and is known by:
his old clothes—a few books perhaps—
God knows what! You realize   40
how we are about these things,
my townspeople—
something will be found—anything—
even flowers if he had come to that.
So much for the hearse.

For heaven's sake though see to the driver!
Take off the silk hat! In fact
that's no place at all for him
up there unceremoniously
dragging our friend out of his own dignity!   50
Bring him down—bring him down!
Low and inconspicuous! I'd not have him ride
on the wagon at all—damn him—
the undertaker's understrapper!
Let him hold the reins
and walk at the side
and inconspicuously too!

Then briefly as to yourselves:
Walk behind—as they do in France,
seventh class, or if you ride   60
Hell take curtains! Go with some show
of inconvenience; sit openly—
to the weather as to grief.
Or do you think you can shut grief in?
What—from us? We who have perhaps
nothing to lose? Share with us
share with us—it will be money
in your pockets.
              Go now
I think you are ready.   70

Bells for John Whiteside's Daughter

1924

JOHN CROWE RANSOM   [1888–1974]

There was such speed in her little body,
And such lightness in her footfall,
It is no wonder that her brown study°   reverie
Astonishes us all.

Her wars were bruited in our high window.
We looked among orchard trees and beyond,
Where she took arms against her shadow,
Or harried unto the pond

The lazy geese, like a snow cloud
Dripping their snow on the green grass,   10
Tricking and stopping, sleepy and proud,
Who cried in goose, Alas,

For the .tireless heart within the little
Lady with rod that made them rise
From their noon apple-dreams, and scuttle
Goose-fashion under the skies!

But now go the bells, and we are ready;
In one house we are sternly stopped
To say we are vexed at her brown study,
Lying so primly propped.   20

Dulce et Decorum Est   1920

WILFRED OWEN   [1893–1918]

Bent double, like old beggars under sacks,
Knock-kneed, coughing like hags, we cursed through sludge,
Till on the haunting flares we turned our backs,
And towards our distant rest began to trudge.
Men marched asleep. Many had lost their boots,
But limped on, blood-shod. All went lame, all blind;
Drunk with fatigue; deaf even to the hoots
Of gas-shells dropping softly behind.

Gas! GAS! Quick, boys!—An ecstasy of fumbling,
Fitting the clumsy .helmets just in time,   10
But someone still was yelling out and stumbling
And flound'ring like a man in fire or lime.—
Dim through the misty panes and thick green light,
As under a green sea, I saw him drowning.
In all my dreams before my helpless sight
He plunges at me, guttering, choking, drowning.

If in some smothering dreams, you too could pace
Behind the wagon that we flung him in,
And watch the white eyes writhing in his face,
His hanging face, like a devil's sick of sin,   20
If you could hear, at every jolt, the blood
Come gargling from the froth-corrupted lungs

Bitter as the cud
Of vile, incurable sores on innocent tongues,—
My friend, you would not tell with such high zest
To children ardent for some desperate glory,
The old lie: *Dulce et decorum est*
Pro patria mori. [1]

nobody loses all the time   1926

E. E. CUMMINGS   [1894–1962]

nobody loses all the time

i had an uncle named
Sol who was a born failure and
nearly everybody said he should have gone
into vaudeville perhaps because my Uncle Sol could
sing McCann He Was A Diver on Xmas Eve like Hell Itself which
may or may not account for the fact that my Uncle

Sol indulged in that possibly most inexcusable
of all to use a highfalootin phrase
luxuries that is or to   10
wit farming and be
it needlessly
added

my Uncle Sol's farm
failed because the chickens
ate the vegetables so
my Uncle Sol had a
chicken farm till the
skunks ate the chickens when

my Uncle Sol   20
had a skunk farm but
the skunks caught cold and
died and so
my Uncle Sol imitated the
skunks in a subtle manner

or by drowning himself in the watertank
but somebody who'd given my Uncle Sol a Victor

Dulce et Decorum Est
 [1] A quotation from the Latin poet Horace, "It is sweet and fitting to die for one's country."

Victrola and records while he lived presented to
him upon the auspicious occasion of his decease a
scrumptious not to mention splendiferous funeral with   30
tall boys in black gloves and flowers and everything and

i remember we all cried like the Missouri
when my Uncle Sol's coffin lurched because
somebody pressed a button
(and down went
my Uncle
Sol

and started a worm farm)

QUESTIONS
1. Explain the title. **2.** What is the speaker's attitude toward Uncle Sol?

In Memory of W. B. Yeats.   1940
(D. JAN. 1939)

W. H. AUDEN   [1907–1973]

1

He disappeared in the dead of winter:
The brooks were frozen, the airports almost deserted,
And snow disfigured the public statues;
The mercury sank in the mouth of the dying day.
O all the instruments agree
The day of his death was a dark cold day.

Far from his illness
The wolves ran on through the evergreen forests,
The peasant river was untempted by the fashionable quays;
By mourning tongues   10
The death of the poet was kept from his poems.

But for him it was his last afternoon as himself,
An afternoon of nurses and rumors;
The provinces of his body revolted,
The squares of his mind were empty,
Silence invaded the suburbs,
The current of his feeling failed: he became his admirers.

Now he is scattered among a hundred cities
And wholly given over to unfamiliar affections;
To find his happiness in another kind of wood   20
And be punished under a foreign code of conscience.
The words of a dead man
Are modified in the guts of the living.

But in the importance and noise of tomorrow
When the brokers are roaring like beasts on the floor of the Bourse,[1]
And the poor have the sufferings to which they are fairly accustomed,
And each in the cell of himself is almost convinced of his freedom;
A few thousand will think of this day
As one thinks of a day when one did something slightly unusual.
O all the instruments agree   30
The day of his death was a dark cold day.

2

You were silly like us: your gift survived it all;
The parish of rich women, physical decay,
Yourself; mad Ireland hurt you into poetry.
Now Ireland has her madness and her weather still,
For poetry makes nothing happen: it survives
In the valley of its saying where executives
Would never want to tamper; it flows south
From ranches of isolation and the busy griefs,
Raw towns that we believe and die in; it survives,   40
A way of happening, a mouth.

3

Earth, receive an honored guest;
William Yeats is laid to rest:
Let the Irish vessel lie
Emptied of its poetry.

In the nightmare of the dark
All the dogs of Europe bark,
And the living nations wait,
Each sequestered in its hate;

In Memory of W. B. Yeats
  [1] A European stock exchange, especially that in Paris.

Intellectual disgrace   50
Stares from every human face,
And the seas of pity lie
Locked and frozen in each eye.

Follow, poet, follow right
To the bottom of the night,
With your unconstraining voice
Still persuade us to rejoice;

With the farming of a verse
Make a vineyard of the curse,
Sing of human unsuccess   60
In a rapture of distress;

In the deserts of the heart
Let the healing fountain start,
In the prison of his days
Teach the free man how to praise.

QUESTIONS
1. In what sense does a dead poet become "his admirers" (l. 17)? **2.** Is Auden's statement that "poetry makes nothing happen" (l. 36) consistent with the attitudes expressed in the final three stanzas?

WRITING TOPIC
Why does Auden view the death of Yeats as a significant event?

Musée des Beaux Arts   1940

W. H. AUDEN [1907–1973]

About suffering they were never wrong,
The Old Masters: how well they understood
Its human position; how it takes place
While someone else is eating or opening a window or just walking dully
    along;
How, when the aged are reverently, passionately waiting
For the miraculous birth, there always must be

Landscape with the Fall of Icarus, c. 1560 by Pieter Brueghel the Elder

Children who did not specially want it to happen, skating
On a pond at the edge of the wood:
They never forgot
That even the dreadful martyrdom must run its course   10
Anyhow in a corner, some untidy spot
Where the dogs go on with their doggy life and the torturer's horse
Scratches its innocent behind on a tree.
In Brueghel's *Icarus*,[1] for instance: how everything turns away
Quite leisurely from the disaster; the ploughman may
Have heard the splash, the forsaken cry,
But for him it was not an important failure; the sun shone
As it had to on the white legs disappearing into the green
Water; and the expensive delicate ship that must have seen
Something amazing, a boy falling out of the sky,   20
Had somewhere to get to and sailed calmly on.

Musée des Beaux Arts
  [1]This poem describes and comments on Pieter Breughel's painting *Landscape with the Fall of Icarus*. (See above.) According to myth, Daedalus and his son Icarus made wings, whose feathers they attached with wax, to escape Crete. Icarus flew so near the sun that the wax melted and he fell.

Elegy for Jane   1958
MY STUDENT, THROWN BY A HORSE

THEODORE ROETHKE   [1908–1963]

I remember the neckcurls, limp and damp as tendrils;
And her quick look, a sidelong pickerel smile;
And how, once startled into talk, the light syllables leaped for her,
And she balanced in the delight of her thought,
A wren, happy, tail into the wind,
Her song trembling the twigs and small branches.
The shade sang with her;
The leaves, their whispers turned to kissing;
And the mold sang in the bleached valleys under the rose.

Oh, when she was sad, she cast herself down into such a pure depth,   10
Even a father could not find her:
Scraping her cheek against straw;
Stirring the clearest water.

My sparrow, you are not here,
Waiting like a fern, making a spiny shadow.
The sides of wet stones cannot console me,
Nor the moss, wound with the last light.

If only I could nudge you from this sleep,
My maimed darling, my skittery pigeon.
Over this damp grave I speak the words of my love: 20
I, with no rights in this matter,
Neither father nor lover.

Between the World and Me   1935

RICHARD WRIGHT   [1908–1960]

And one morning while in the woods I stumbled suddenly upon the
    thing,
Stumbled upon it in a grassy clearing guarded by scaly oaks and elms.
And the sooty details of the scene rose, thrusting themselves between the
    world and me. . . .

There was a design of white bones slumbering forgottenly upon a cushion
  of ashes.
There was a charred stump of a sapling pointing a blunt finger accusingly
  at the sky.
There were torn tree limbs, tiny veins of burnt leaves, and a scorched coil
  of greasy hemp;
A vacant shoe, an empty tie, a ripped shirt, a lonely hat, and a pair of
  trousers stiff with black blood.
And upon the trampled grass were buttons, dead matches, butt-ends of
  cigars and cigarettes, peanut shells, a drained gin-flask, and a whore's
  lipstick;
Scattered traces of tar, restless arrays of feathers, and the lingering smell of
  gasoline.
And through the morning air the sun poured yellow surprise into the eye
  sockets of a stony skull. . . .   10
And while I stood my mind was frozen with a cold pity for the life that
  was gone.
The ground gripped my feet and my heart was circled by icy walls of
  fear—
The sun died in the sky; a night wind muttered in the grass and fumbled
  the leaves in the trees; the woods poured forth the hungry yelping of
  hounds; the darkness screamed with thirsty voices; and the witnesses
  rose and lived: The dry bones stirred, rattled, lifted, melting themselves
  into my bones.
The grey ashes formed flesh firm and black, entering into my flesh.
The gin-flask passed from mouth to mouth; cigars and cigarettes glowed,
  the whore smeared the lipstick red upon her lips,
And a thousand faces swirled around me, clamoring that my life be
  burned. . . .

And then they had me, stripped me, battering my teeth into my throat till
  I swallowed my own blood.
My voice was drowned in the roar of their voices, and my black wet body
  slipped and rolled in their hands as they bound me to the sapling.
And my skin clung to the bubbling hot tar, falling from me in limp
  patches.   20
And the down and quills of the white feathers sank into my raw flesh, and
  I moaned in my agony.
Then my blood was cooled mercifully, cooled by a baptism of gasoline.
And in a blaze of red I leaped to the sky as pain rose like water, boiling
  my limbs.
Panting, begging I clutched childlike, clutched to the hot sides of death.
Now I am dry bones and my face a stony skull staring in my yellow
  surprise at the sun. . . .

Do Not Go Gentle into That Good Night   1952

DYLAN THOMAS   [1914–1953]

Do not go gentle into that good night,
Old age should burn and rave at close of day;
Rage, rage against the dying of the light.

Though wise men at their end know dark is right,
Because their words had forked no lightning they
Do not go gentle into that good night.

Good men, the last wave by, crying how bright
Their frail deeds might have danced in a green bay,
Rage, rage against the dying of the light.

Wild men who caught and sang the sun in flight,   10
And learn, too late, they grieved it on its way,
Do not go gentle into that good night.

Grave men, near death, who see with blinding sight
Blind eyes could blaze like meteors and be gay,
Rage, rage against the dying of the light.

And you, my father, there on the sad height,
Curse, bless, me now with your fierce tears, I pray.
Do not go gentle into that good night.
Rage, rage against the dying of the light.

QUESTIONS
1.   What do wise, good, wild, and grave men have in common?   **2.**   Why does the poet use the adjective "gentle" rather than the adverb "gently"?   **3.**   What is the "sad height" (l.16)?

The Death of the Ball Turret Gunner   1945

RANDALL JARRELL   [1914–1965]

From my mother's sleep I fell into the State,
And I hunched in its belly till my wet fur froze.

Six miles from earth, loosed from its dream of life,
I woke to black flak and the nightmare fighters.
When I died they washed me out of the turret with a hose.

QUESTIONS
1. To what do "its" (ll. 2 and 3) and "they" (l. 5) refer?   **2.**   Why is the mother described as asleep?

Aubade ¹   1977

PHILIP LARKIN   [1922–1985]

I work all day, and get half drunk at night.
Waking at four to soundless dark, I stare.
In time the curtain-edges will grow light.
Till then I see what's really always there:
Unresting death, a whole day nearer now,
Making all thought impossible but how
And where and when I shall myself die.
Arid interrogation: yet the dread
Of dying, and being dead,
Flashes afresh to hold and horrify.   10

The mind blanks at the glare. Not in remorse
—The good not done, the love not given, time
Torn off unused—nor wretchedly because
An only life can take so long to climb
Clear of its wrong beginnings, and may never;
But at the total emptiness for ever,
The sure extinction that we travel to
And shall be lost in always. Not to be here,
Not to be anywhere,
And soon; nothing more terrible, nothing more true.   20

This is a special way of being afraid
No trick dispels. Religion used to try,
That vast moth-eaten musical brocade
Created to pretend we never die,
And specious stuff that says *No rational being*
Can fear a thing it will not feel, not seeing
That this is what we fear—no sight, no sound.

Aubade.
¹ Morning song.

No touch or taste to smell, nothing to think with.
Nothing to love or link with,
The anaesthetic from which none come round.   30

And so it stays just on the edge of vision,
A small unfocused blur, a standing chill
That slows each impulse down to indecision.
Most things may never happen: this one will.
And realisation of it rages out
In furnace-fear when we are caught without
People or drink. Courage is no good:
It means not scaring others. Being brave
Lets no one off the grave.
Death is no different whined at than withstood.   40

Slowly light strengthens, and the room takes shape.
It stands plain as a wardrobe, what we know,
Have always known, know that we can't escape,
Yet can't accept. One side will have to go.
Meanwhile telephones crouch, getting ready to ring
In locked-up offices, and all the uncaring
Intricate rented world begins to rouse.
The sky is white as clay, with no sun.
Work has to be done.
Postmen like doctors go from house to house.   50

After a Time   (1961?)

CATHERINE DAVIS   [b. 1924]

After a time, all losses are the same.
One more thing lost is one thing less to lose;
And we go stripped at last the way we came.

Though we shall probe, time and again, our shame,
Who lack the wit to keep or to refuse,
After a time, all losses are the same.

No wit, no luck can beat a losing game;
Good fortune is a reassuring ruse:
And we go stripped at last the way we came.

Rage as we will for what we think to claim,   10
Nothing so much as this bare thought subdues:
After a time, all losses are the same.

The sense of treachery—the want, the blame—
Goes in the end, whether or not we choose,
And we go stripped at last the way we came.

So we, who would go raging, will go tame
When what we have we can no longer use:
After a time, all losses are the same;
And we go stripped at last the way we came.

QUESTIONS

1. What difference in effect would occur if the refrain "After a time" were changed to "When life is done"? **2.** What are the various meanings of "stripped" in line 3 and line 19? **3.** Explain the meaning of "The sense of treachery" (l. 13). **4.** Does this poem say that life is meaningless? Explain.

WRITING TOPIC

Compare this poem with Dylan Thomas's "Do Not Go Gentle into That Good Night."

Woodchucks   1972

MAXINE KUMIN [b. 1925]

Gassing the woodchucks didn't turn out right.
The knockout bomb from the Feed and Grain Exchange
was featured as merciful, quick at the bone
and the case we had against them was airtight
both exits shoehorned shut with puddingstone,
but they had a sub-sub-basement out of range.

Next morning they turned up again, no worse
for the cyanide than we for our cigarettes
and state-store Scotch, all of us up to scratch.
They brought down the marigolds as a matter of course   10
and then took over the vegetable patch
nipping the broccoli shoots, beheading the carrots.

The food from our mouths, I said, righteously thrilling
to the feel of the .22, the bullets' neat noses.
I, a lapsed pacifist fallen from grace
puffed with Darwinian pieties for killing,
now drew a bead on the littlest woodchuck's face.
He died down in the everbearing roses.

Ten minutes later I dropped the mother. She
flipflopped in the air and fell, her needle teeth   20

still hooked in a leaf of early Swiss chard.
Another baby next. O one-two-three
the murderer inside me rose up hard,
the hawkeye killer came on stage forthwith.

There's one chuck left. Old wily fellow, he keeps
me cocked and ready day after day after day.
All night I hunt his humped-up form. I dream
I sight along the barrel in my sleep.
If only they'd all consented to die unseen
gassed underground the quiet Nazi way.   30

To Aunt Rose   1961

ALLEN GINSBERG   [b. 1926]

Aunt Rose—now—might I see you
with your thin face and buck tooth smile and pain
                of rheumatism—and a long black heavy shoe
                        for your bony left leg
limping down the long hall in Newark on the running carpet
                past the black grand piano
                        in the day room
                                where the parties were
                and I sang Spanish loyalist songs[1]
                        in a high squeaky voice   10
                                (hysterical) the committee listening
                while you limped around the room
                        collected the money—
Aunt Honey, Uncle Sam, a stranger with a cloth arm
                in his pocket
                        and huge young bald head
                                of Abraham Lincoln Brigade

To Aunt Rose
    [1] Between 1936 and 1939, a civil war occurred in Spain in which rebel forces under General Francisco Franco defeated the Loyalist forces supporting the politically liberal monarchy. In some ways a foreshadowing of World War II, the Spanish Civil War attracted the attention of the great powers, with Russia supporting the Loyalist forces and Germany and Italy supporting the rebel forces. Many American writers and intellectuals saw the war as a struggle between fascism and democracy and supported the Loyalist cause energetically; the Abraham Lincoln Brigade (line 17) was a volunteer unit of Americans that went to Spain to fight on the Loyalist side.

—your long sad face
      your tears of sexual frustration
         (what smothered sobs and bony hips   20
            under the pillows of Osborne Terrace)
—the time I stood on the toilet seat naked
      and you powdered my thighs with Calomine
         against the poison ivy—my tender
           and shamed first black curled hairs
what were you thinking in secret heart then
         knowing me a man already—
and I an ignorant girl of family silence on the thin pedestal
         of my legs in the bathroom—Museum of Newark.

              Aunt Rose   30
Hitler is dead, Hitler is in Eternity; Hitler is with
         Tamburlane and Emily Brontë[2]

Though I see you walking still, a ghost on Osborne Terrace
         down the long dark hall to the front door
         limping a little with a pinched smile
         in what must have been a silken
            flower dress
welcoming my father, the Poet, on his visit to Newark
        —see you arriving in the living room
         dancing on your crippled leg   40
         and clapping hands his book
           had been accepted by Liveright[3]

Hitler is dead and Liveright's gone out of business
The Attic of the Past and *Everlasting Minute* are out of print
         Uncle Harry sold his last silk stocking
         Claire quit interpretive dancing school
         Buba sits a wrinkled monument in Old
           Ladies Home blinking at new babies

last time I saw you was the hospital
         pale skull protruding under ashen skin   50
           blue veined unconscious girl
            in an oxygen tent
         the war in Spain has ended long ago
           Aunt Rose

---

[2] Tamburlane (1336?–1405) Mongol conqueror; Emily Brontë (1818–1848) English novelist.
[3] A publishing firm.

Five Ways to Kill a Man   1963

EDWIN BROCK   [b. 1927]

There are many cumbersome ways to kill a man:
you can make him carry a plank of wood
to the top of a hill and nail him to it. To do this
properly you require a crowd of people
wearing sandals, a cock that crows, a cloak
to dissect, a sponge, some vinegar and one
man to hammer the nails home.

Or you can take a length of steel,
shaped and chased° in a traditional way,   ornamented
and attempt to pierce the metal cage he wears.   10
But for this you need white horses,
English trees, men with bows and arrows,
at least two flags, a prince and a
castle to hold your banquet in.

Dispensing with nobility, you may, if the wind
allows, blow gas at him. But then you need
a mile of mud sliced through with ditches,
not to mention black boots, bomb craters,
more mud, a plague of rats, a dozen songs
and some round hats made of steel.   20

In an age of aeroplanes, you may fly
miles above your victim and dispose of him by
pressing one small switch. All you then
require is an ocean to separate you, two
systems of government, a nation's scientists,
several factories, a psychopath and
land that no one needs for several years.

These are, as I began, cumbersome ways
to kill a man. Simpler, direct, and much more neat
is to see that he is living somewhere in the middle   30
of the twentieth century, and leave him there.

Seaman, 1941   1971

MOLLY HOLDEN   [1927–1981]

This was not to be expected.

Waves, wind, and tide brought him again
to Barra.[1] Clinging to driftwood many hours
the night before, he had not recognized
the current far offshore his own nor
known he drifted home. He gave up, anyway,
some time before the smell of land reached out
or dawn outlined the morning gulls.

                     They found him
on the white sand southward of the ness,[2]   10
not long enough in the sea to be
disfigured, cheek sideways as in sleep;
old men who had fished with his father
and grandfather knew him at once,
before they even turned him on his back, by the set
of the dead shoulders, and were shocked.

This was not to be expected.

His mother, with hot eyes, preparing the parlor
for his corpse, would have preferred, she thought,
to have been told by telegram rather
than so to know that convoy, ship, and son
had only been a hundred miles northwest
of home when the torpedoes struck.
She could have gone on thinking that
he'd had no chance; but to die offshore,
in Hebridean tides, as if he'd stayed
a fisherman for life and never gone to war
was not to be expected.

For the Anniversary
of My Death

1967

W. S. MERWIN [b. 1927]

Every year without knowing it I have passed the day
When the last fires will wave to me
And the silence will set out

Seaman, 1941
   [1] An island in the Hebrides off the western coast of Scotland.
   [2] Promontory.

Tireless traveller
Like the beam of a lightless star

Then I will no longer
Find myself in life as in a strange garment
Surprised at the earth
And the love of a woman
And the shamelessness of men   10
As today writing after three days of rain
Hearing the wren sing and the falling cease
And bowing not knowing to what

People*   (trans. 1962)

YEVGENY YEVTUSHENKO [b. 1933]

No people are uninteresting.
Their fate is like the chronicle of planets.

Nothing in them is not particular,
and planet is dissimilar from planet.

And if a man lived in obscurity
making his friends in that obscurity
obscurity is not uninteresting.

To each his world is private,
and in that world one excellent minute.

And in that world one tragic minute.   10
These are private.

In any man who dies there dies with him
his first snow and kiss and fight.
It goes with him.

They are left books and bridges
and painted canvas and machinery.

Whose fate is to survive.
But what has gone is also not nothing:

People
   * Translated by Robin Milner-Gulland and Peter Levi.

by the rule of the game something has gone.
Not people die but worlds die in them.   20

Whom we knew as faulty, the earth's creatures.
Of whom, essentially, what did we know?

Brother of a brother? Friend of friends?
Lover of lover?

We who knew our fathers
in everything, in nothing.

They perish. They cannot be brought back.
The secret worlds are not regenerated.

And every time again and again
I make my lament against destruction.   30

The Dead Ladies   1973

FOR MAUREEN SUGDEN

MARY GORDON   [b. 1949]

> We can sit down and weep;
> we can go shopping
> *Elizabeth Bishop*

What's to be done with death,
My friend?
                We sit
Cross legged, hating men.

Virginia[1] filled her English skirt
With stones.
Always well bred she left behind

The Dead Ladies
[1]Virginia Woolf (1882-1941), British novelist, committed suicide by weighting herself with stones
and walking into the Ouse River.

Her sensible shoes, her stick,
Her hat, her last note
(An apology)   10
And walked in water
'Til it didn't matter.

We speak of Sylvia[2]
Who could not live
For babies or for poetry.

You switch on Joplin's[3] blues
The room looms black
With what we know
But are afraid to think.

Too scared to say: "and us?"   20
We leave for work.
Hearts in our mouths.
In love with the wrong men.

QUESTIONS

1. What is the implied difference between the three women mentioned in the poem "and us" (l. 20)? **2.** What do you suppose the poet means by the assertion in line 4 that she and her friend hate men? How can that assertion be reconciled with the last line of the poem? **3.** What is the point of mentioning three famous women, all of whom died what might be called tragic and untimely deaths?

---

[2] Sylvia Plath (1932–1963), American poet, committed suicide by asphyxiating herself with cooking gas.
[3] Janice Joplin (1943–1970), popular American singer, apparently died of an overdose of drugs.

THE
PRESENCE
OF DEATH

Orderly Retreat, 1943 by Philip Evergood

DRAMA

End of the World *   1984

ARTHUR KOPIT   [b. 1937]

Act One: The Commission

Music: *lazy, bluesy music for a hard-boiled detective. It is "Trent's Theme."*
Curtain up.

Spotlight *up on* **Michael Trent,** *downstage, in a trench coat. Stage dark around*
him. He puffs on a cigarette. The music continues under.

Trent.   I have now, at most, two hours left—two hours to solve a mystery which
 so far seems to yield no solution. If I fail, it is highly possible that I and all
 of you will die sooner than we'd hoped. Do I exaggerate? Of course. That is
 my method. I am a playwright. My name is Trent, Michael Trent. I work
 out of Stamford, Connecticut—that's where my office is, that's where this
 case began, when Philip Stone came to see me with a notion for a play.
 Generally I don't take commissions. This time I did.

Lights up on **Philip Stone,** *a man in his sixties, large, elegant, powerful.*

---

*Author's Note: This play derives from real events. In the spring of 1981 I was approached by
Leonard Davis, who wished to commission me to write a play about nuclear proliferation, based
on a scenario he had written. Between that day and August 1983 I worked on the project—although
not on his scenario—which turned out to be very different from his scenario. The events that unfold in my play mirror, almost exactly, the experiences I had when I embarked on the commission.

   Much of the play—in particular the section entitled "The Investigation"—is based on personal
interviews. Though some of those interviewed asked that they not be named, those who can be
named include Walter Slocum, Fritz Ermath, Joel Resnick, Douglas Olin, Ambassador Edward
Rowny, and Kurt Guthe. I would like to thank all of them for their patience, time, and generosity.

   Those whose written work proved especially valuable in the creation of this play and in my understanding of the issues involved include Herman Kahn, Freeman Dyson, Colin Gray, Keith Payne,
Jack Geiger, Jonathan Schell, George Kennan, Richard Pipes, and Edward Teller.

   In particular I wish to thank Roger Molander for his extraordinary help and encouragement during the writing of this play, and Robert Scheer for allowing me to use an extensive section of his

Stone.   I can only tell you it is a matter of great urgency, and I would be most appreciative if I could see you tonight!

Blackout on **Stone.**

Trent.   I'd never met the man, though I knew of course who he was—who didn't? He told me what he wanted, which was a play, but gave no details. He assured me he'd pay well—a man as rich as Stone ought to pay well; I told him to come right out. To put it mildly, I was in great need of money at the time. Most playwrights need money *all* the time. It's not one of your top-paying professions. Besides, I had a wife, a kid, and two golden retrievers to support. As things now stand, you won't see any one of them. I want to keep them out of this!

Lights up on Trent's office in Stamford, Connecticut. It looks like the sort of office Philip Marlowe[1] might use. On the glass door, reversed, are the following words:

MICHAEL TRENT, PLAYWRIGHT
—No Domestic Comedies—

This is my office. At least, as it looked ten months ago, on the night Stone came by and changed my life irrevocably. Actually, in *real* life, where these events occurred, it doesn't look like this at all. Neither do the characters who were, and still are, involved. I have altered these details, not so much to protect the innocent, as to heighten interest. That's how playwrights work. We've got limited time. You don't want to stay here all night any more than I do. *(A buzzer sounds on Trent's cluttered desk)* Yah!

Stella *(Voice only).*   Mike, there's a guy out here says his name is, get this— Philip Stone! *(Sound of Stella giggling)*

Trent.   Hey, dollface, this guy *is* Philip Stone. Tell him I'll be with him in a minute. *(To audience)* It was important that Stone think I was in the middle

---

book *With Enough Shovels,* published by Random House, as the basis for Philip Stone's final speech. I would also like to thank Physicians for Social Responsibility for their continued support.

A word about Audrey Wood. Audrey Wood was my agent from 1960, when my play *Oh Dad, Poor Dad, Mamma's Hung You in the Closet and I'm Feelin' So Sad* was produced at Harvard, until 1981, when she suffered a devastating massive stroke. She was a crucial, integral, and loving part of my life. When I came to the writing of this play and found I needed to write in an agent for Michael Trent, my playwright/detective, I instinctively used Audrey's name, never intending to keep her name in the play. But I have done so.

I kept it in while writing it in the belief that her presence, as I went along, would force me to delve into the material and into myself as deeply as I could—for to do any less would be to belittle her.

And I kept it in in the hope that what I wrote might, in some small way, measure up to the measure of her—A. K.

[1] Hard-boiled private eye in a number of Raymond Chandler (1888–1959) novels.

of a project. If he didn't, he might figure he could get me cheap. My pulse was going wild; I'd been hoping to sell out for years. This could be it. *(Into the intercom)* Send Stone in. *(Back to audience)* Actually, I didn't even have a secretary. And that's all I'm going to tell you. From here on, you're going to have to figure out what I'm making up, and what I'm not, on your own. Be warned: the roads are very slippery, the ones we're going on tonight.

Trent starts typing. The office door opens and Philip Stone walks in. Black greatcoat. Sense of mystery and menace.

Stone.   Trent?

Trent *(Typing wildly).*   Just a second, be right with you, finishing touches here. Yes . . . Yes-yes, good, hah-hah, amazing, what a scene, never *seen* a scene like this!

Stone.   Perhaps the moment is inopportune.

Trent.   NO! No-no, almost finished! Last few lines. Real bitch, this play; been working on it for a year—commission from the RSC.[2] There! Yes! Got it! Beginning to think I'd *never* get it right! *(Rips the page from the typewriter, rises, and goes over to Stone, hand extended)* Mr. Stone, Michael Trent. Great honor to meet you. *(Into the intercom)* Stella, hold my calls. *(To Stone)* Can I offer you a drink?

Stone.   Thank you. Yes. A Scotch would be welcome, most welcome indeed.

Trent.   All I've got is beer.

Stone.   I'll stay like this . . . Mr. Trent, I am not a man who wastes words or time; words take time to say, time is precious. I have conceived an outline for a play. I wish to see this play produced, and quickly. I will provide the capital, you will write it. How much do you want, when can you begin?

Stunned pause. Then Trent rushes to the door.

Trent.   Stella!

Enter Stella, a real dish.

Stella.   Yes, boss!

Trent.   Be an angel. Run down to B.J.'s and get a bottle of Scotch.

Stella.   Right, boss!

Exit Stella.

Trent *(To audience).*   If you're going to invent a secretary, might as well go with it all the way! *(To Stone, trying to control his euphoria)* Well, this is

---

[2] The RSC (Royal Shakespeare Company) is an outstanding repertory theater company based in Stratford-on-Avon in Great Britain.

just very . . . very flattering. Let me check my appointment book here, see what sort of commissions I've got lined up. *(Rummages through the mess on his desk; he finds the appointment book)* Here it is. Let's see now . . . *(Flips the pages)* And you say you want this play written . . . ?

Stone.   Right away!

Trent.   Right away, I see . . . Well, I could shuffle this, I guess. Delay this commission here . . . Might have to give up some work over here, that's something I really wanted too, *damn!* What, uh, kind of dollars exactly are we, uh, talking about?

Stone.   As I said before, sir, tell me what you want.

Trent.   (So I *did* hear him right!) *What I WANT!* Well, that's not so . . . easy to say. It depends very much on how long this will take to *write.* Then to *rewrite!* . . . Then to rewrite *that* revision! I do very careful work, I'm sure you've heard. Then of course we have to factor in the research. If this project, I don't know it yet, takes research of some sort—

Stone.   It will.

Trent.   There you are! So *that* must be factored in. Plus of course transportation, limousine, mind you now I don't absolutely *need* a limousine—

Stone.   I use a limousine. No reason you should not.

Trent.   My God, the theater needs men like you!

Stone.   Don't you want to hear the idea?

Trent.   No. No-no, I'll just begin. Obviously, if it matters all this much to you, it's got to be worth *something!* I'll need a day or two to figure out the terms, of course. Where can you be reached? You seem to have appeared a bit out of thin air.

Stone *(Handing him a card).*   My business card.

Trent.   Good. Thank you. Well! I don't see that we need to discuss this any further—you've got yourself a playwright! I've got myself a producer! *(Stone holds out a manila envelope)* This the idea?

Stone.   Yes.

Trent.   Well, I can't wait to read it!

Stone.   Why not read it now?

Trent.   Well, because right now I just can't give it my complete attention. We'll talk tomorrow. Sir, a great, *great* pleasure meeting you! *(Trent ushers him out)* Till tomorrow.

Stone.   Till tomorrow.

Exit Stone.

Trent *(To audience).*   I didn't want to look at his idea while he was here in case I hated it.

The door opens. Stone pops back in.

Stone.   Sir. Forgive me. But in my excitement I forgot to give you this . . .
(*Hands Trent an envelope*) . . . *retainer*. As a token of good faith. (*Leaves*)

Trent tears open the envelope. He pulls out five bills.

Trent.   *Five thousand dollars!* (*Opens the door*) SIR, YOU ARE TOO GEN-
EROUS!
Stone (*Offstage*).   What?
Trent.   *That* was the wrong thing to say. I meant to say, MAYBE WE CAN
DO SOME *MORE* PLAYS! YOU KNOW—AFTER THIS! (*To the audi-
ence*) Five thousand dollars! . . . Well, it may not seem like a lot to you.
But to a playwright, as an advance, it's enough to save his life. It really is.

Enter Stone, somber-faced.

Stone.   Sir, you do not understand. I have no interest in producing plays. I
am interested in producing one play only. *This is it!*

Exit Stone.

*Trent clearly taken aback by this. Nervously, he opens the manila envelope and
peeks inside. Cautiously, he slides the pages out. He stares down at the title
page. Then he stares out with a look of alarm.*

Blackout.

*Lights up on Audrey Wood, Trent's agent. She is a woman in her sixties. Very
short. She wears a tiny pillbox hat. She is hardly visible above her desk. At the
moment, she is talking on the phone with Trent.*

Audrey.   Dear, I checked him out. He's legitimate, he has the money. So I'd
say you've got a deal.
Trent.   Audrey, his idea is terrible!
Audrey.   Then don't take it.
Trent.   How can I not take a deal like this? This is a definitional sweetheart
deal, this is the deal of a lifetime!
Audrey.   Dear, what do you want me to do?
Trent.   ADVISE me!
Audrey.   Take the deal.
Trent.   Audrey, you don't understand. You haven't read this man's scenario.
There is no way anyone, ANYONE! can write a play based on this. Do you
know why? Because the characters are completely cardboard, and the plot
preposterous.

Audrey.   Dear, listen, calm down, brush your hair, make yourself presentable, come in and show me this notorious scenario. I'm sure it's not half as
bad as you think. Really, dear, you're still young, you've got a lovely wife, a
lovely child, this is no time to panic.

Trent.   I've used up the advance.

Pause.

Audrey.   *What?*

Trent.   *I've used up the advance.*

Audrey.   Darling, I'm sorry, I must have misunderstood. I thought you got
this advance last night.

Trent.   I did.

She checks her watch.

Audrey.   Dear, it is ten-thirty in the morning. What do you *do* up there in
Connecticut?

Trent.   Audrey, I used it to pay our mortgage. We owed three months—I'm
sorry, that's the way it is—we're going through a rough time here.

Audrey.   Maybe you should go out to the Coast.

Trent.   I DON'T WANT TO GO TO THE COAST! I'LL START TAKING
MORE DRUGS THAN I'M TAKING NOW!

Audrey.   Darling, you mustn't take drugs. It's bad for your health.

Trent.   I'll see you this afternoon.

Audrey.   Dear, I'm afraid you may have to take this deal.

Trent.   I'll see you this after— *(But Audrey has already clicked off)*—noon.
(Lights off on Audrey. Trent turns to audience) Okay, I know exactly what
you're thinking: Where is the problem? You take the money, you write what
you can, the play's no good, no one does the play, you've got your money,
basta!³ end of deal. If I could actually count on that, you're right, no problem. Here's the hitch: this guy is so rich he's liable to produce this play no
matter *how* bad it is! Why should this matter?

Audrey's Assistant *(Voice only).*   Miss Wood will see you now!

Trent.   One second! I'll be right with her. *(To audience)* People who write
plays are a little crazy, okay? For one thing, no one writes plays to make
money. I mean you *do*, of course. But you don't go into it, as a profession,
because that's where you figure the big bucks lie. You do it . . . and you
spend your life doing it, because it *matters*. And you have a kind of pact with
yourself. And it says you don't screw around with what matters or else it's
gone.

---

³ *Basta* is Italian for "enough."

Audrey's Assistant *(Voice only).*   Miss Wood will see you now!
Trent.   Yes, yes. Coming!

Lights back up on Audrey. Trent walks over, manila envelope in hand.

Audrey.   Dear, if you want to get out of this, I'll loan you the money.
Trent.   No, I can't do that.
Audrey.   Of course you can, don't be a fool.
Trent.   Look, here's his scenario. Four pages. Actually, only three. The first
    page is taken by the title.
Audrey.   What's the title?
Trent.   *The End of the World.*
Audrey.   Ohhhh, dear.
Trent.   You know what it deals with?
Audrey.   I was afraid to ask.
Trent.   Nuclear proliferation.
Audrey.   Oh dear, oh dear, oh dear.
Trent.   I mean, is that an exciting subject or isn't it?
Audrey.   Why does he want to *do* this play?
Trent.   No idea.
Audrey.   Well, let's call him up! *(Buzzing her intercom)* Get me Philip Stone.
    Bob Montgomery has his number. *(Back to Trent)* Montgomery's his lawyer.
    He called after you did. Stone will agree to whatever terms you want.
Trent.   The man is mad!
Audrey.   That's no reason not to work with him. *(The intercom buzzes)* Yes?
Audrey's Assistant *(Voice only).*   Philip Stone on the line.
Audrey *(Into phone).*   Philip Stone? Audrey Wood—I am Michael Trent's agent.
    I gather you met with my client last night. Mr. Trent is sitting here with me
    in my office now. *(To Trent)* Say hello, dear.
Trent *(Picking up a second phone).*   Hello!

Lights up on Stone, on the phone.

Stone.   Hello!
Audrey *(Into phone).*   Dear, we would like to know why you're so anxious to
    produce this particular play.
Stone.   I want to produce it because I believe the earth is doomed.
Audrey.   I'm sorry . . . *What?*
Stone.   Doomed! I believe the earth is doomed!

Audrey stares at Trent.

Audrey.   He *is* mad! *(Into phone)* Mr. Stone, I'm sorry, are you suggesting
    that a production of your play could prevent this doom?

Stone.   Yes, I think perhaps it could.
Trent *(Sotto voce).*   Ask him if he's planning on road companies.

She waves him off.

Audrey.   Well, dear, I must say this is certainly one of the *worthiest* projects I've come across in a very long time.
Stone.   Possibly ever.
Audrey.   . . . Yes. Possibly ever. *(To Trent, sotto voce) You've got to get out of this! (Back to Stone)* Darling, you still there?
Stone.   Still here!
Audrey.   How long would you say we have till doom strikes?
Stone.   My statistics suggest it could be almost any time.
Audrey.   So then you'll be anxious to get it on this season.
Stone.   I was hoping for this spring.
Audrey *(To Trent).*   I've never heard of anything like this. *(Back into phone)* I take it you've never produced before.
Stone.   No.
Audrey.   Well, you have to be prepared for this play closing. Rapidly.
Stone.   Why?
Audrey.   Well, I think there's a good chance audiences may not like it. Just by definition. Frankly, unless I'm missing some essential elements, it sounds rather *downbeat* to me.
Stone.   I'm sorry, I don't understand. If audiences don't like it, do I *have* to close the play?
Audrey *(Stunned).*   Well . . . no, of course not.
Stone.   Then I won't.
Audrey.   But what if no one comes?
Stone.   No one at *all?*
Audrey.   Dear, it's been known to happen!
Stone.   I find it hard to believe someone would not come in *eventually. (Audrey and Trent stare at each other in astonishment)* In the winter, for example. It's *warm* inside a theater. People are bound to come in . . . No, I'm going to keep this thing running. The earth's future is at stake! One doesn't close a play when the earth's future is at stake.
Audrey *(To Trent, sotto voce).   We've got to keep this man to ourselves! (Back to Stone)* Dear, I think this is one of the most unusual and worthwhile projects I've ever come across. Hold on a sec. *(Cups her hand over the mouthpiece)* What if he really *knows* something here?
Trent.   What do you mean?
Audrey.   About the earth! About its doom!
Trent.   Oh, my God.
Audrey.   Dear, listen, why take a chance? *Talk* with the man. If a play of yours could in some way help prevent global doom, well!
Trent.   Oh, my God!

Audrey *(Into the phone).*   If you like, my client will meet with you this afternoon.

Blackout on Audrey and Stone.

Trent. *(To audience).*   I was, of course, an innocent . . . As I soon found out.

Lights up on Stone.

Stone.   To put it mildly, sir, I am thrilled by your stopping by. Already I feel hope rising in my breast. Charles! Some drinks! Scotch, if you like; we have it.
Trent *(To audience).*   I told him I wanted nothing.
Stone.   Good. All business. For me, then, nothing either.
Trent *(To audience).*   Stone had requested that the meeting be at his place. Now I was in his apartment. *(Stone's sumptuous Fifth Avenue apartment glides into view)* If I'd ever wanted booze this was it, but something warned me. I sensed a need for clearheadedness: the height had already made me dizzy enough. As a rule, I dislike elevators. For some reason, I cannot rid my mind of the image of what lies underneath as I ascend. Because of this, whenever possible, I walk upstairs. Stone lived in a penthouse forty floors up. There is a limit to any neurosis; forty floors was mine. Now the world was reeling. Looking down through the half-opened window of Stone's library, which I desperately did not *want* to do but felt myself *compelled* to do, I saw the people on the streets below wobbling like rubber. Like dolls made of rubber. The buildings were also like rubber. And, in the hot summer sun, seemed to be *melting*!
Stone *(Coming up behind him).*   Extraordinary perspective from up here.
Trent.   . . . Yes.
Stone.   Why don't you sit down?
Trent.   Thank you. *(Stone leads him to a seat. To audience)* And I missed the seat!

Trent, *in sitting, indeed misses the seat. He lands on the floor like a clown. Stunned expression. Beat.*

Blackout.

Lights up on Audrey.

Audrey *(To audience).*   *What does an agent do?* *(Pause)* This is a question I am asked all the time . . . In *theory*, an agent is supposed to find her client *work* . . . Now, while this has certainly been *known* to happen, fortunately,

for all concerned, we do much, much more. Take this instance here. Michael Trent had been my client now for nearly fifteen years, and, relatively
speaking, we'd done well together; though he wasn't rich, neither was he
starving. Comfortable, I would say, is what he was—till recently . . . Now,
all writers go through down periods; this was something more. What worried
me about Michael was his growing eccentricity. He imagined himself as a
kind of *detective!* Even on the hottest, brightest summer day he would wear
a trench coat, collar up; slouch hat, brim down! Frankly, he looked ridiculous. Well, I'm very fond of him. And consider it my job to protect him
from harm . . . Anyway, when this Stone project came along, though financially the deal was incredible, unprecedented, something just said to me,
Audrey, watch out! I decided I needed help . . . So I called a meeting: Merv
Rosenblatt—he's the president of our agency, and Paul Cowan, Agent to the
Stars! Paul refused to come downstairs to *my* office, I refused to go up to *his*,
so we agreed to meet for lunch at the Russian Tea Room. (*A booth from the
Russian Tea Room glides on*) Paul was the first to arrive— (*Enter* **Paul Cowan,**
in sweat suit)—dressed in his normal dapper style.

Paul (*Sullenly*).   Hi, Audrey. (*Slides in next to her and starts chewing on a
napkin.*)

Audrey.   Merv Rosenblatt came next. (*Enter* **Merv Rosenblatt,** *in sharp, pin-
striped suit with carnation in lapel. He is suntanned*) He'd canceled a lunch
with Frank Perdue,[4] that's how important this meeting was!

Merv.   Okay, what's this about global doom?

Paul.   I'm sure it's an exaggeration.

Merv.   Hi, Paul. Hope that's not a contract you're chewing on.

Paul.   No-no. Napkin. Listen, why don't we get started. I've got a screening
in twenty minutes. (*To someone unseen by us*) Hey! I'll be in till seven, gimme
a call! (*To someone else*) Hi! (*Back to Audrey*) Sorry, Audrey. Go ahead.

Audrey.   Gentlemen. At this very instant, not ten blocks from here, my client
is meeting with Philip Stone.

Paul.   Who's he?

Audrey.   Paul, I sent you a memo on *all* of this!

Paul.   Well, I can't remember! What are we, playing games?

Audrey.   Philip Stone is the man who's vowed to keep my client's play running no matter what.

Paul.   Right. Now I remember! This is the kind of producer our theater
NEEDS! Mervin, what would you like?

Merv.   Campari and soda.

Paul.   CAMPARI AND SODA AND A BLOODY MARY! Now, when can
I meet this guy?

Audrey.   Well—

---

[4] Frank Perdue is an entrepreneur in the poultry business who performs in his company's com-
mercials.

Headwaiter. PHONE CALL FOR MR. COWAN!

Paul. Bring it here!

Merv. Isn't Stone the guy who says we're doomed?

Audrey. He's the one.

Merv. Well, that's *not* the kind of producer our theater needs! What the hell's Paul talking about?

Headwaiter *(Arriving with plug-in phone).* Here you are, Mr. Cowan.

Paul. You think I'm gonna plug it in? Plug it in.

The Waiter climbs over Merv.

Merv *(From beneath the Waiter).* Paul, is this really necessary?

Paul. How do I know? *(The Waiter climbs back out. Paul picks up the phone. To the others)* Keep talking; I can listen. *(Starts scribbling on the tablecloth)*

Audrey. Stone says he's willing to pay anything my client wants.

Paul *(Still on phone).* Maybe it's a project Paramount would like.

Audrey. I've read Stone's scenario and it's terrible.

Paul. Why don't we let Paramount decide.

Audrey. It's about nuclear war.

Paul *(Into phone).* Hold on. *(To Audrey)* Paramount will only consider projects about nuclear war if there's an upbeat ending.

Audrey. This has no ending whatsoever.

Paul. Well, that, I would say, is a problem. *(Back into phone)* Yeah. Go ahead. *(Continues scribbling on the tablecloth)*

Audrey. My instinct is to turn the project down.

Paul. Are you mad?

Audrey. Paul, I will not stand for rudeness! I am seeking advice, all right? *Seeking.* And I've brought you in on this as a courtesy.

Paul. Mervin, talk to her.

Merv. Audrey, if your client turns this project down, how will we find out if the earth is doomed?

Paul. Right! At least have him stay with this till we find out *that.* I've got deals pending here.

Audrey. My client feels it is unethical to—

Merv. *What?*

Audrey. *Unethical*—

Paul *(Into phone).* Hold on. *(To Audrey)* WHAT?

Audrey. My client feels it is unethical to accept a deal knowing from the outset that there's no way it can be done.

Paul *(Into phone).* Did you hear that? Can you believe what you're hearing here? *(To Audrey)* So you're advising him to turn this *down?*

Audrey. I'm not advising him to do *anything.*

Paul. WELL, WHAT KIND OF GODDAMN ADVICE IS *THAT?*

Merv. Paul!

Paul. Where the hell are our drinks? WOULD YOU PLEASE BRING OUR

GODDAMN DRINKS! *(Into phone)* I better call you back. *(Hangs up. To Audrey)* Audrey, look, far be it from me to butt into your affairs, but how much did your client earn last year?

Audrey.   Not a lot.

Paul.   I will personally guarantee him twice what he made just to keep this project alive. Mervin, are you in on this?

Merv.   Well—

Paul.   Mervin's in. Audrey, all your client has to do is string this guy along. Meanwhile, we interest him in *other* worthy projects—I've got I'd say ten— and, simultaneously, find out if the earth is doomed. If it is, we make plans.

Audrey.   What sort of plans?

Paul.   How do I know? You just gave me this today!

Merv.   When he says doomed, does he mean the West Coast, too?

Audrey.   I believe that's included, yes.

Paul.   You know I have to tell you, from the little I am gleaning here, this doesn't sound like what I'd call a box-office smash.

Merv.   Well now, *Earthquake* did quite well.

Paul.   As a FILM? Hey, this could be sensational. But I understand he's talk-ing drama, right?

Audrey.   Drama.

Paul *(To Merv).*   We could take the Winter Garden after *Cats*[5] is gone, blow the whole place up. I mean, it's halfway there already, right? *(To Audrey)* What about this as a musical?

Merv.   Paul!

Paul.   Don't reject things out of hand. *(To Audrey)* Who are the main char-acters?

Audrey.   Well, the main one I would say is the President.

Paul *(To Merv).*   Who could we get?

Merv ponders. Paul ponders. The same inspired casting idea hits them simul-taneously.

Audrey.   Gentlemen, Ron is President, right now!

Paul.   Well, when he LEAVES!

Audrey.   The man wants to do the play this spring.

Merv.   Name the other characters, we can always cast the President.

Audrey.   There's only one other major character: the Soviet premier.

Merv ponders. Paul ponders.

Paul.   Ann-Margret's looking for something.

Audrey.   Paul, the premier is a *man!*

---

[5] The Winter Garden is a Broadway theatre. *Cats*, a successful, long-running musical, opened at the Winter Garden in October 1982.

Paul.   It's written that it cannot be a woman? Where? In what Russian document? I don't speak Russian; do you speak Russian? The British have a woman; why can't the Russians?

Merv.   Audrey, Ann-Margret's a good idea.

Paul.   No, great idea, *great* idea! Look, the important thing is this: cast it right, I don't care what the thing's about, it runs! You want my advice? Your client *doesn't* take this deal. He *grabs* this deal! GRABS this deal!

Merv.   And, meanwhile, finds out if the earth is doomed.

Paul.   Right. CHECK!

Blackout.

Lights up on Trent, still on the floor. Charles *helps him to a chair.*

Trent *(To Stone).*   I don't know why . . . I suddenly felt quite dizzy.

Stone *(Warm and helpful).*   Perhaps it was the open window . . . Many people—perfectly *normal* people, people of a *sunny disposition*—confronted suddenly by an open window, all at once find themselves wondering if they shouldn't jump. The notion takes their breath away. And they faint. Charles, bring our guest some water. *(Exit Charles)* Now obviously I'm not saying this was you.

Trent.   It certainly sounds that way.

Stone.   Well, I'm only speculating. Anyway, I don't think you were literally about to jump. I think you were just *thinking* about jumping!

Trent.   I'm the most self-protective person you have ever *met!*

Stone.   That's why you fainted. Trent, look, why shilly-shally? You're a man of imagination. How can you *look* at a window and NOT think about jumping?

Trent.   I didn't realize that's what imagination led to.

Stone.   For God's sake, man, the window was *open!* What do you want, a written invitation?

Trent.   I think I'd like something stronger than water.

Stone.   CHARLES!

Charles *(Reentering instantly).*   You shouted?

Stone.   Our guest would like something stronger than water.

Charles.   I'm not surprised.

Exit Charles.

Stone.   Now listen, Trent. If you're not going to be honest with me, *or* yourself, what's the point of our going on? In front of you is an open window; beyond, forty exhilarating floors below, *oblivion!* Now. How can you, as a normal human being, not at least *contemplate* jumping out?

Trent.   I don't contemplate jumping out because I'm not in *despair!*

Stone.   What's despair got to do with this?

Trent.   I'd have thought everything.

Stone.   I'm beginning to think you're some kind of ninny. Trent, listen to me. We are on the verge of beating a dead horse. I did *not* expect you to jump out the window, all right? In fact, to be perfectly fair, I'd have been astounded had you even stood on the LEDGE! The point is this. *(Enter Charles, rolling a cart filled with booze)* Ah, thank you, Charles. The point is this. *(Trent hurries toward the cart)* Trent, are you listening?

Trent *(Grabbing a bottle).*   Avidly.

Stone.   THE POINT IS THIS! *(Trent starts to open it)* The urge to leap out of windows does not derive from despair. It derives from *curiosity*.

Trent.   . . . Curiosity?

Stone.   Yes sir, curiosity, rampant curiosity! I myself feel the urge *all the time*. Fortunately, I resist . . . Fortunate for me. Fortunate for those down below. *(Grins)* Enough! On to business. Your agent informs me you have certain reservations about my scenario. If you'd be so kind, I'd like to hear what these reservations are; please speak freely, our relationship will founder if it isn't based on absolute, unwavering trust.

Trent.   Right. Uhhh, thank you. Well! I would say, offhand, that the single biggest problem with your scenario is that it's basically *implausible*.

Stone.   It's *supposed* to be implausible.

Trent.   I see . . . Well, I didn't catch that.

Stone.   Do you honestly think the next world war is going to start in some *plausible* way?

Trent.   No, I see what you mean.

Stone.   In fact, *I* think this basic implausibility is the most plausible thing *in* my scenario . . . And I worked very hard to achieve it.

Trent.   Yes, well, you've succeeded.

Stone.   So when can I expect a script? *(Trent looks about as if for a way to escape)* You understand, I don't mean to rush you now, but time is clearly of the essence here, I'm sure you can see why.

Trent.   Doom, you mean.

Stone.   Yes, sir, doom. Could be any moment now.

Trent.   Look, Stone, I've got to tell you something. The truth is, I just don't see doom in your scenario. I mean, I see *theatrical* doom. That's written all over the place. But historic doom? global doom? Can't seem to catch sight of it.

Stone.   That's because it's not in.

Trent.   Not *in*?

Stone.   My scenario.

Trent.   The global doom you are so concerned about is not IN your scenario?

Stone.   That's correct.

Trent.   Well, don't you want to *put* it in?

Stone.   No, sir!

Trent.   Why?

Stone.   Because if I put in everything I know, no one will BELIEVE me, sir!

Trent. But NO ONE WILL BELIEVE WHAT YOU'VE GOT!

Stone. By gad, we're at an impasse here!

Trent. Maybe what we need is a new approach.

Stone. Good idea! What do you suggest?

Trent. That you tell me what you know. And let *me* figure out how to dramatize it—how's that sound?

Stone. No, sir, I cannot.

Trent. I thought our relationship was based on TRUST!

Stone. And so it is. And you're just going to have to trust me when I tell you doom approaches.

Trent. Stone, listen. Let me explain something about basic dramatic construction: I cannot go out on the stage during my play and say to my audience, "Hey! Trust me! Doom approaches!" I have got to *convince* them that doom approaches. And how'm I going to do that if you can't convince ME?

Stone. It's a stickler.

Trent. It's a stickler, absolutely right. Now, what I'm going to do—*(Downs his drink)*—is go home. *(Puts down his glass)* And let you think this whole thing over. It's been a fascinating afternoon. No need to show me to the door.

Stone. Trent! For God's sake, don't you understand? If I could just TELL you how I *know* doom is approaching, why, what's to stop me from telling *everyone?* You see? And then why would I need a play? I wouldn't!

Trent. Stone. As I see it, there are only two possibilities here. Either you are certifiable. Or you're certifiable. In the first instance, you are certifiable because you've made all this up; in the second, you are certifiable because you *haven't* made it up but won't TALK! To this, I have but two possible responses. Out the door. And out the door. Farewell. Farewell.

Stone. No! Please, sir, you mustn't! Look, sir, I am on my knees! Future generations are on their knees!

Trent. All I see is you.

Stone. That's because you are shortsighted, sir. You see only the immediate!

Trent. No. I see a door, that's what I see. And I'm going through it!

Stone. Trent! *(Grabs Trent's legs)* The fate of the world lies in your hands.

Trent. Really? You know what? Fuck it! Let it blow!

Stone. It's attitudes like this, sir, that will do us in, attitudes like this!

Trent. Hey! Hold on . . . I've just figured out the problem. You know the problem? I'm the wrong writer for this project! With the right writer, this project could just go ZOOM! What you must do, right away, is call my agent: she will send you another writer!

Stone. But you, sir, are the writer that I want.

Trent. Wonderful! Why?

Stone. I can't tell you that.

Trent. Stone, listen to me: if you don't let me out this door this instant, I am going to create, before your eyes, in his room, a doom such as you have never dreamed! *(Stone takes out a gun)* Oh, my God.

Stone.   Now I suggest you sit down over there.

Trent.   HELP!

Stone.   I am the only tenant on this floor.

Trent.   CHARLES!

Stone.   Charles works for me; he's used to my behavior. Sir, please sit down. This is no frivolous enterprise! My life is in jeopardy. And, like it or not, so is yours. *(Trent decides to sit)* Now. When I am done, if you still wish to leave my employ, you may do so. Furthermore, you may keep the money I have paid so far. How does that strike you, sir? Is that fairness or not?

Trent.   That . . . seems quite fair. Yes.

Stone.   Good. So, with your permission, then, I will put this morbid instrument away.

Trent.   Oh. Yes. Please.

Stone.   I find guns tend to have a will of their own! Fascinating creatures. I call this particular gun Fred.

Trent.   Fred! That's a *nice* name for a gun.

Stone.   Yes, it is. It's strong. Guns *need* good strong names. You can get into all *kinds* of trouble if your gun doesn't have a good strong name. Donald, for example. That's a dreadful name for a gun!

Trent.   Yes. Yes, I can see that. Gun wouldn't *respect* you if you called it Donald.

Stone.   Exactly! Gun like that could turn on you and *kill* you! Any moment! Have *you* ever had a gun?

Trent.   No. *(Pause)* Well. Actually, I once had a BB gun.

Stone.   And what did you call it?

Trent.   Uhhhhhhh, Jim.

Stone.   Jim! Yes, that's a *good* name for a gun.

Trent *(Heading for the phone).*   You know, I wonder, would you mind very much if I asked my agent to come over here?

Stone.   No need, sir! We'll be through in a trice!

Trent.   Good.

Stone.   Next time, though. Now, on to doom.

Trent.   Global doom!

Stone.   Clear this whole thing up!

Trent.   Good.

Stone.   Tell me, sir, what these ten countries have in common: India, Egypt, Iraq, Argentina, Israel, Japan, Korea, South Africa, Libya, Brazil.

Trent.   No idea.

Stone.   Within ten years, sir, each of these countries will possess the bomb.

Trent.   Really!

Stone.   Yes, sir.

Trent.   And to you this means we're doomed.

Stone.   No, sir! No, not in and of itself. This is but the *clay* from which our doom will be shaped! Sculpted! Formed!

Trent.   You see doom as a work of *art?*

Stone.   Yes sir. Exactly! And, to me, this is part of its *horror . . .* and *allure.*
(*Stone smiles at Trent. Trent leans back and studies Stone with a new intensity. Sotto voce*) Now, the reason I believe doom approaches rapidly has to do with certain . . . *information* I stumbled upon quite by accident about a year ago, I shan't tell you how, not now at least . . . This information is at first blush so incredible that were I to simply tell you what it is, you would be bound not to believe it, just as I at first did not and in some ways still do not, *cannot!* though I know full well all of it is true. You see my dilemma here. If I tell you what I know, you will say Stone is mad, and leave. End of project, end of hope. On the other hand, if somehow you believe what I reveal, then I can only conclude that you are the one who's mad. So what am I to do? The answer's obvious. What I have come to know, on my own, you must somehow come to know on your own, as well . . . How? . . . By proceeding systematically . . . and *following your nose.*

Trent.   My nose tells me to get out of here.

Stone.   Of course! To save yourself from a terror such as you have never known! Why do your eyes dart toward the window, sir? That's no way out.

Trent.   *Why a play?*

Stone.   Why, indeed! . . . Because the theater, sir, alone among the arts, engages, in equal measure, the emotion and the intellect. And both must be touched here, if we are to survive.

Silence.

Trent.   Why me?

Stone.   As I said, sir: I cannot tell you that.

Trent.   *Why?*

Stone.   Because at this moment, sir, your greatest strength is your innocence.

Pause.

Trent.   Well, I can't work like that, I'm sorry. (*Stone turns away*) All right. Look. I *will* work on this, okay? . . . BUT *only* if you tell me what it is about *my* plays that makes you think I am right for this job.

Stone.   Well, sir, the truth is, and I hope you take this in the proper spirit—I've never actually *seen* a play of yours.

Trent.   WHAT?

Stone.   But I've been assured they're very good.

Trent.   Stone, you are out of your goddamn mind!

Stone.   No sir. Would that I were.

Trent.   Well, something's cuckoo here. And I think I'll leave before it's me! (*Starts out*)

Stone (*Drawing his gun*). Sorry, sir, I object. (*Trent sees the gun and stops*) Sir, I am a desperate man! . . . But I am also a *gambling* man. I will gamble. I will tell you this: . . . *we have met before.*

Trent *(Amazed)*.   *Where?*

Stone.   I cannot tell you that.

Trent.   STONE, I CANNOT TAKE THESE GAMES ANYMORE! NOW, IF YOU WANT TO SHOOT ME, SHOOT ME, BUT THAT'S IT, GOODBYE!

Stone.   SIR!

Trent.   *I don't recall meeting you, all right?*

Stone.   I am aware.

Trent.   So how important could this meeting have been?

Stone.   To me, crucial.

Trent.   When did this meeting take place?

Stone.   I can't tell you that.

Trent.   How many were there?

Stone.   I can't tell you that, either!

Trent.   I see! And yet, at this meeting, something happened which has convinced you I could save the world from doom!

Stone.   Yes, sir. Absolutely!

Trent.   Aren't you a bit surprised I don't remember?

Stone.   No, sir. I *thought* you might blot it out.

Trent.   BLOT IT OUT?

Stone.   Yes, sir.

Trent.   If the incident was anything like this, of COURSE I've blotted it out! People must be blotting you from their lives all the time! I AM LEAVING!

Stone.   All right, sir! All right! *(Trent stops and turns back)* I will tell you this . . . but *only* this . . . More than this and my cause is lost. *(Pause)* This . . . particular incident . . . *convinced* me . . . that you, sir, had a thorough understanding of *evil*.

Trent.   . . . *I?*

Stone.   Yes, sir. You. *(Trent stares at him in astonishment)* And now, sir, it is *my* turn to leave. I hope you take this job. *(Warm smile)* Good day.

Trent turns to the audience. As he does, the light in the room fades almost to black. However, the sky beyond the open window does not dim at all. In this darkened room, Stone, unmoving, is a shadowy presence.

Trent.   I had, of course, no idea what he meant. *(Pause)* I would say I took the job . . . because of *two* factors . . . *(Music: "Trent's Theme")* One, of course, was the money. How could I turn down a deal like that? *(Takes out a cigarette)* And the other, of course, was curiosity.

Lights the cigarette. Puffs.

The light through the window has been growing brighter. Now, blazing white, it seems to beckon.

Act Two: The Investigation

Music: "Trent's Theme." It continues as lights come up on a seedy hotel room. It is night. Through the one window in this room, a red neon hotel sign is visible across the street; the sign says "Sunset Motel." Except for this light, the only other light in the room comes from a lamp. Trent, in his trench coat, looks out at the audience.

Trent.   To be precise, ten months, five days, twelve hours, and . . . *(Checks his watch)* . . . twenty-three minutes have passed now since Philip Stone came into my life wielding a four-page scenario of dubious merit. Frankly, I've still no idea what he meant when he said I understood evil. As far as I know, I'm a pussycat, a sweetheart, aces—what the hell was he talking about? *(Puffs on a cigarette)* Not that I haven't uncovered some rather peculiar goings-on, you understand! No-no, quite the contrary, this case has been a real eye-opener! There's funny business going on out there, and I had no idea of it. Can't remember when I've been so depressed by a case. *(Pours a shot of bourbon)* And I've never made so much money, either. Tells you something about money, doesn't it. You know what it tells you? Tells you, without all this money I'd be even *more* depressed. By the way, this is Washington. The Pentagon's back that way. I was there early this morning. *(There is a soft rap on the door. He tenses)* I know it isn't Stella; Stella has a key. *(Sets his glass down quietly)* She came down on the six o'clock shuttle. About an hour ago, I sent her across the street to case the lobby of a two-bit fleabag called the Sunset Motel—*(Starts moving cautiously toward the window)*—where I'm supposed to meet with a man who claims he can clear up everything. A man who calls himself The Shadow—really, I'm not kidding, that's what the message said. Is Stone behind all this? If so, I've been set up. Why? *(Another rap. Trent peers out through the half-opened slats of the Venetian blinds)* I can see the lobby from here. No sign of Stella.
Muffled Voice *(Softly, from other side of door)*.   Mr. Trent? *(Trent turns off the lamp. The room is now dark except for the flickering neon sign of the Sunset Motel. Another knock)* Mr. Trent?
Trent.   The door's open.

*The door opens. A **Man** stands silhouetted in the bright hallway.*

Man In Hallway.   Mr. Trent?
Trent.   Stay where you are.
Man in Hallway.   Mr. Trent! Apparently, you have not understood the conditions of this meeting . . . The man you are about to see is not supposed to talk to outsiders. By agreeing to do just this for *you*, he places into jeopardy not only his job but his life. For this reason, you were specifically in-

structed to come alone. Instead, you sent an emissary to check out our hotel. Naturally, the meeting place must now be changed. One more violation and the meeting will be off. We will come for you when we're ready. Your friend has been sent back to New York. *(Leaves)*

Trent visible only in the eerie red glow of the neon light.

Trent.   Poor Stella. And she hates flying, too! *(Music: "Trent's Theme")* I'll tell you, this whole thing, it's not been easy on her . . . Right from the start.

Lights up on Stella. The hotel room disappears.

Stella *(To audience)*.   Mike's instructions were simple. He said, "Dollface, I want you to get me every book and article published last year that deals with nuclear weapons." Wow, I thought! Within a week, his desktop looked like the Adirondacks.
Trent.   That's when the trouble began.

Lights up on Audrey.

Audrey *(To audience)*.   About a month after he'd started his research, Stella gave me a call at home. She asked if she could come by. She said it was urgent. I told her to come right over. *(To Stella)* And he's been working?
Stella.   'Round the clock!
Audrey.   So what's the problem, dear?
Stella.   Well, it's his . . . moaning.
Audrey.   . . . *Moaning?*

Stella nods. She holds out a small cassette player. She pushes the Play button. A terrible loud moan is heard. Audrey is aghast.

Trent *(To audience)*.   Actually, I was not aware I was *making* this dreadful noise. I thought I was just reading quietly to myself. I did *hear* the noise, and thought it came from next door. I was in fact about to complain to the landlord, telling him it was hurting my concentration.
Audrey.   Well, this is not right, dear, not right at all. I'll call him in the morning.
Trent *(To audience)*.   Which she did. Gave me a real chewing out!
Audrey.   I told him that, in my book, professionals, real professionals, do not sit around moaning. They knuckle down and DO THEIR JOB! No one had *asked* him to be a writer. He agreed.
Trent.   I told her not to worry, I'd figure out the problem. I asked her to arrange a meeting with Stone, and asked if she could be there, too. Frankly, I didn't want to be alone with this guy when I gave him the bad news.

Lights up on Stone in Audrey's office. He is staring at Trent in cold fury.

Stone.   Well, sir, all I can say is, obviously I've misjudged you! A grave mistake, indeed.

Audrey *(To Stone)*.   Now, let's not panic. I'm sure we can work this out. *(To Trent)* Dear, Mr. Stone has been very generous to you. Don't you think you owe him a little more *time?*

Trent.   I cannot write a play from this material. NO one can write a play from this material! This stuff is INDESCRIBABLE!

Audrey.   Dear, we know the project's difficult. *(To Stone)* I think the research may be getting him down. *(Taking her client aside)* Dear, if you don't deliver a draft to this nice gentleman—doesn't have to be a *good* draft, you understand, just a *draft*—I think this man may not only destroy you financially but possibly have you killed, that's just a feeling I have. Now, what exactly is the problem, please spell it out; perhaps in the *talking*, things will seem easier. *(To Stone)* We're getting there!

Trent *(With obvious pain)*.   I have been finding things . . . I did not *expect!*

Audrey.   Dear, that's what research is *about!*

Stone.   This is a waste of time. Clearly, Mr. Trent does not have the temperament for serious material.

Trent.   Look, there are certain things playwrights *know!* One of those is what makes a play. This material does not!

Audrey.   Dear, that is the silliest thing you've ever said—*anything* can make a play. You just have to figure out how to *handle* it! I've never seen you like this, really! *(To Stone)* And yet something tells me we're not that far apart.

Stone.   If this is not far apart, I am a rabbit!

Trent *(To Stone)*.   Look! In every play there is a central character and this central character does not just *want* something; he NEEDS something, needs it so badly if he doesn't *get this thing* he will die . . . not necessarily physically, could be emotionally, spiritually, all right? In fact, dramatically, the worse his potential fate, the better. But! BUT! only up to a point. And that's the problem in this instance. Here, the consequences of failure are so far beyond our imagination, so far beyond anything we have ever experienced, or even DREAMED, an audience could not believe, fully believe, what it was watching . . . It will all seem like a lie.

Audrey.   Dear, maybe if you just gave it more *time.*

Trent.   I cannot READ this stuff anymore! I DON'T WANT TO *READ* ABOUT THIS STUFF ANYMORE! "The Prompt and Delayed Effects of Thermonuclear Explosions" is not what I wish to read at night! I am scaring the shit out of my family! My son runs from me in HORROR when he sees me coming. You know why? Because I have become a sentimental goddamn dishrag! I see him walking toward me and I start to weep. I see him playing on the lawn with his dogs and I start to weep. I DON'T WANT TO HAVE TO THINK ABOUT THIS STUFF EVERY DAY! WHAT SORT OF

PEOPLE CAN *THINK ABOUT THIS STUFF EVERY DAY? (A sudden look of amazement comes over Trent's face)* . . . I'll work on it.

Audrey.   *What?*

Trent.   I know what to do . . . I'll work on it, I can work on it! I KNOW WHAT TO DO! *(Audrey stares at him in astonishment, then looks at Stone triumphantly. Lights to black on everyone but Trent. To audience)* Through Stone, I arranged to meet with some of the people who think about this stuff every day . . . The ones I asked to meet held opinions that seemed to me to go against all common sense. Anyhow, it was a way in. When there's a mystery, there's at least the possibility of a play. Whatever—it was all I had to go on. Stone said he thought I was doing the right thing. *(Pause)* The first man I talked to, I will call . . . General Wilmer. *(The library of **General Wilmer**'s sumptuous Virginia estate starts to glide in)* He was one of the President's chief advisers on nuclear policy. He had a Ph.D. in physics. *(The General is seated behind an elegant Empire desk. There is an intercom on the desk. He wears casual country-squire clothes)* His house was in Virginia, about an hour's drive from Washington. Usually, he worked at the Pentagon. But this was a Saturday afternoon . . . *(The General lights a pipe)* A lovely autumn day.

General Wilmer.   So you want to make a play out of this.

Trent.   Well, that's what I'm hoping.

General Wilmer.   Some kind of Strangelove thing?

Trent.   No, I wouldn't think so.

General Wilmer.   Good. Because the Strangelove scenario only works if you postulate a Doomsday weapon, and no one contemplates that. To save ourselves by threatening to annihilate ourselves is surely the height of preposterousness!

Trent.   I would think so, yes.

Silence.

General Wilmer.   So have you got a plot?

Trent.   Well, no, I'm afraid I don't.

General Wilmer.   Don't plays *need* plots?

Trent.   Well, I'm hoping to find one. That's one of the reasons I've come down to Washington.

General Wilmer *(Merrily).*   Not plot in the sense of conspiracy, I trust!

Trent *(Laughing).*   No-no! Plot in the sense of narrative thrust. The thing that makes you ask what happens next. That kind of thing. *(The General smiles and tamps down the tobacco)* So how long have you known Philip Stone?

General Wilmer.   I've never met the man. *(Relights the pipe)*

Trent.   Well, then how did he arrange this meeting?

General Wilmer.   Someone else set it up. *(Puffs as an **Aide-de-Camp** in military uniform enters. He carries a folder. The General gestures to his desk. The*

Aide puts the folder on the desk and leaves) So. You don't understand why we need more nuclear weapons.

Trent. Right. It's probably 'cause I'm new at this.

Pause.

General Wilmer. I gave a talk last month at Princeton, and it was on this very issue. And a number of the students started shouting, "Why don't we just *stop* this madness?" And I said, "You know, it's easy to avoid a nuclear war. All you have to do is surrender." *(Grins)* The problem is to find a way to *avoid* nuclear war while preserving the values that we cherish . . . Okay. Don't we have enough to accomplish this right now? Of course we do. Right *now*. But we don't need to deter the Russians now; why would they attack? They'd gain nothing . . . Deterrence comes into play during *crisis*. During crisis, people tend to think in peculiar ways. A successful deterrent says to the Russians, "No matter what, your best case scenario is just no good."

Trent. But that's where we are right now.

General Wilmer. Of course! But what makes you think we're going to stay where we are? . . . And things may turn better for us, or for them. Either way, it's dangerous. That's because any imbalance at all is dangerous, even if the imbalance is only *imagined*. In this business, it's how you're *perceived* that counts! *(The Aide enters with a note, which he gives to the General, then leaves. The General glances at the note. Crumples it. Puts it in a pocket)* For example, the weaker side starts thinking: Maybe we'd better hit these guys before they get even *stronger*. The stronger side, knowing what the weaker side's thinking, says: Maybe we'd better do what they *think* we're gonna do, even though we don't want to, 'cause otherwise they *might*. In which case, we're done for. So they do. You see? And all this comes about because of one simple, fundamental truth, and it governs everything we do: the guy who goes first goes best.

Trent. You want more so you can go *first*?

General Wilmer. In a crisis? Absolutely.

Trent. Well, that is a piece of encouraging news!

General Wilmer. Well, what's the alternative? We say we'd never, under any conditions, go first. And the Russians actually believe us. So *they* go first.

Trent. Why would they go first if they believe us? I thought you just said they'd go first because they're afraid *we'd* go first!

General Wilmer. Either way.

Trent. EITHER WAY?

General Wilmer. Well, you certainly can't expect them to believe us *completely*.

Trent. . . . So it doesn't matter *what* we say.

General Wilmer. In a way, that's true.

Trent.   Maybe we should back up a bit. I think I may have started at too high a level! Why do we need nuclear weapons in the first place?

General Wilmer.   To prevent their use.

Trent.   Good. Just what I thought. YET if we suddenly realize we *can't* prevent their use, we'd better hurry up and use them.

General Wilmer.   Right.

Trent.   Isn't there some kind of basic contradiction here?

General Wilmer.   Absolutely! It's what makes the problem so difficult to solve.

Trent.   Do you enjoy this job?

General Wilmer.   Someone's got to do it. *(The intercom buzzes)* Yes?

Man's Voice.   The turtle is in Zurich.

General Wilmer *(Stunned)*.   . . . Zurich? What's it doing in Zurich?

Man's Voice.   No one knows. *Should we feed it?*

General Wilmer.   . . . Not till we find out what it's doing there. *(Clicks off)*

Trent.   So the turtle is in Zurich! *(Wilmer relights his pipe)* Well, I'm GLAD the turtle is in Zurich.

Wilmer smiles at him.

General Wilmer.   No, you're not. *(Pause)* Look. The sole purpose of possessing nuclear weapons . . .

Trent.   . . . is not to win wars but to *prevent* them. I've *got* that. Solid.

General Wilmer.   Good. Now. In order to *prevent* a nuclear war, you have to be able to *fight* a nuclear war at *all levels*, even though they're probably unwinnable and unfightable. You understand, this doesn't mean you want to. Doesn't even mean you *will*. That's because, for the purpose of deterrence, a bluff taken seriously is far more helpful than a serious threat taken as a bluff. What we're talking about now is credibility. Okay? . . . To this end, what your opponent *thinks* you'll do is much more important than what you *actually* will do. *(Buzzer sounds. He flicks the intercom)* I'm sorry, not now. *(Clicks off)* For example, for the purpose of deterrence, it's a good idea to tell the Russians that if they move into Western Europe—*(Buzzer sounds. He flicks the intercom)* What?

Little Boy's Voice.   Dad?

General Wilmer.   Dear. Not now. All right? *(Clicks off)*—that if they move into Western Europe we will use nuclear weapons to stop their advance. No ambiguity there: you make *this* move, we make *this* move. However! Should deterrence fail, it would seem wiser not to use our nuclear weapons at all, the reason being that once we've gone nuclear, the likelihood of Soviet nuclear retaliation is overwhelming. *(Enter Aide with note. He hands it to Wilmer. Wilmer keeps talking)* What's more, the probability is that it would escalate. What this means is that instead of Western Europe being overrun by the Soviets—*(He glances at the note)*—a thing we certainly don't want! *(To the Aide)* Have his mother take care of it. *(Exit the Aide)*—Western Europe, *and* the United States, AND the Soviet Union would quickly and effectively cease to exist. In fact, according to our latest figures, so probably would the entire world. *(Buzzer sounds. He flicks it. With annoyance)* Yes?

Woman's Voice.   This is for *you* to handle, dear.

General Wilmer.   I'll take care of it later. *(Clicks off)* Okay, so here we are, then, with two policies, one overt—you move here and we will strike; the second, *covert*—we may choose not to do any such thing. The Soviets, who know it makes no *sense* for us to strike with nuclear weapons if they move in, nonetheless are deterred from moving in because it's *just possible* we might be *crazy* enough to do it. *Now.* What this means is that, for every level of engagement, we must possess a credible response, even if this response is quite incredible on its surface. This is one of the reasons it's important for our President, whoever he is, to every so often say something that sounds a bit insane. *(Pause)* Fear, you see. That's the great deterrent . . . Don't want to do too much to reduce the fear. By the way, that's the problem with a nuclear freeze: to the extent that it makes people feel safer, it raises the chances of war. You look shocked. I'll tell you something shocking—I think things are going just fine. And you should relax. We really *do* know what we're doing. Take a look. In the past forty years, have we had a nuclear war? No. Why? . . . Nuclear weapons. The fact is, nuclear weapons not only prevent *nuclear* war, they prevent *all* war . . . And I think they just may be the best damned thing that's ever happened to us. Really do!

Beat. Blackout on everything but Trent.

Music.   "Trent's Theme." Trent walks downstage to the audience.

Trent *(To audience).*   My conversation with General Wilmer had left me in a quandary: I didn't know whether to laugh or cry. I was on the verge of doing both when the general gave me a call.

Lights up on Wilmer.

General Wilmer.   I've been thinking. Maybe you should meet a man named Stanley Berent. If you like, I can set it up.

Lights off on Wilmer.

Trent *(To audience).*   I'd come across Berent's name in my research. He was a Russian scholar, connected to Georgetown University, and a real hard-liner, particularly where the Soviet Union was concerned. *(Japanese koto music heard)* We met at a small Japanese restaurant I assume he frequented out of war guilt. We sat on tatami mats, cross-legged, which made the experience even more excruciating. An inescapable feeling of unreality began to hang over all of this.

The restaurant has slid into view during the above.

Berent *(Eastern European accent).*   No, I agree with you completely—our present nuclear policy does not make sense, not at all!

Trent *(To audience).*   Why had the general sent me to *this* man?

Berent.   What we must do—very simple: we must stop regarding nuclear war as some kind of goddamn inevitable holocaust . . . and start looking at it as a goddamn WAR!

Trent.   . . . What?

Berent.   We have to learn how to wage nuclear war *rationally.*

Trent.   *What?*

Berent.   Rationally. We have got to learn how to wage nuclear war *rationally.* I'm sorry—*sake?*

Trent.   Uhhhhh, thank you.

Berent.   You see, even though a strong case can be made for the fact that nuclear war is essentially an act of insane desperation, and therefore fundamentally irrational, this doesn't mean that once you're in the thing you shouldn't do it *right!*

Trent.   I see. *(Pause)* Of course, this would seem to suggest you think it's possible to *win* a nuclear war.

Berent.   No-no! *Limited* nuclear war. No one can win an all-out nuclear war. Unless, of course, the other side decides not to hit back, and one could never count on that, ALTHOUGH, I must say—*(Gives a brief, sharp command to a Waitress in fluent Japanese)*—although, I must say, in all the scenarios I've seen, the side that hits first definitely comes out best. So if push comes to shove, you do go first, no question of it, particularly if you employ what we call a controlled counterforce strike with restraint. In effect, you hit everything but your opponent's cities.

Trent.   That's the restraint part.

Berent.   Right. His cities are held hostage. And what you—I'm sorry! Chopsticks?

Trent.   Yes, chopsticks.

Berent.   And what you do is, you tell him you'll demolish them if he doesn't capitulate. Now, this is actually quite reasonable *if*, big if, *big* if, IF you have an adequate civil-defense system. That way, even if the Russians strike back, you should be able to absorb the blow and still have enough left to strike back at *them.* And this time just wipe them out. This is what I mean when I talk about credibility. What I have just described to you is a CREDIBLE offensive and defensive nuclear strategy. What we have now, forgive my French, is diddly-shit. *(To the Waitress, a short command in Japanese, at which she nods and leaves. To Trent)* You don't speak Japanese, I take it.

Trent.   No. Why? Are you passing secrets?

Berent *(Laughing).*   Secrets? I'm not privy to any secrets. Ah, thank you. *(A Waiter delivers a noodle dish)* Now. Do I *really* know how to fight a limited nuclear war? Not at all. No one does. No one's *fought* one. And yet if we're not prepared, we're in the soup. Okay. What do I propose?

Trent.   You're not eating.

Berent.   I'm not hungry. What do I propose. I propose we send a clear signal to the Russians, and this signal says: You fuck around with us, we're gonna fuck around with you! This is the sort of talk the Russians understand. How do we do this? First, we build the MX, the Trident 2, the Pershing II, and the Cruise. Why do I want these things? Because they have the ability to take out hardened targets. If we get into a major crisis with these people, I want the ability to disarm them to the greatest extent possible.

Trent.   *Disarm?*

Berent.   Remove. Surgically remove. As much of their military capability as is possible.

Trent.   That's called a first strike, I believe.

Berent.   Oh, no.

Trent.   It's *not?*

Berent.   No.

Pause.

Trent.   Why?

Berent.   Because the connotation is *aggressive*. This is a *defensive* act.

Trent.   I see . . . Out of curiosity, what do you call it?

Berent.   Anticipatory retaliation.

Trent.   Ah!

Berent.   Some prefer "preemptive strike," but that can get cumbersome. Because, if you sense they're about to preempt *you*, then what you have to do is *pre*-preempt them.

Trent (*Getting into the spirit now*).   And of course if they should somehow become *aware* that you've discovered their *plans* to preempt, and are about to *pre*-preempt, they'll have to start discussing a *pre*-pre-preemptive strike. And one can obviously just get lost in this kind of talk.

Berent.   That's right. Anticipatory retaliation simply covers everything! Unfortunately, we can't even begin to consider this if we don't have the proper weapons.

Trent.   And we don't have them now?

Berent.   No, sir, we do not.

Trent.   I realize you're going to lose all respect for me. But isn't it possible we'd be better off *not* getting these things?

Berent.   Of course! . . . If the Russians didn't have them.

Trent.   They *have* them?

Berent.   They're *getting* them.

Trent.   WHERE DOES THIS ALL END?

Berent.   When each of us is secure.

Trent.   Well, that's fair enough.

Berent.   Unfortunately, we're not even close . . . To be secure, the United States must possess a credible nuclear-war fighting policy. Now, what might such a policy be?

Trent.   Got me.

Berent.   In a war, what do you think the Russian command would least like to lose?

Trent.   I would say, offhand, Russia.

Berent.   Short of that.

Trent.   Half of Russia?

Berent.   Short of *that*.

Trent.   A third of Russia.

Berent.   Wrong approach. The point is to avoid killing civilians needlessly. Now, come on, think. In a war, outside of its population, what can the Soviet leaders least afford to lose?

Trent.   . . . I don't know.

Berent.   Oh, come on!

Trent.   No, really, I don't know.

Berent.   ThemSELVES!

Trent.   Themselves?

Berent.   Of course! Without a Kremlin, without leadership—you know what Russia's got? It's got shit, that's what it's got!

Trent.   So how do we get rid of their leaders?

Berent.   Well, we know where they are. And we bomb them.

Trent.   . . . Surely they're not just going to sit there and *wait*!

Berent.   No-no! They're going to hide. That's expected.

Trent.   I would think Russia has a lot of hiding places.

Berent.   Of course. And we know where they are. And we target them.

Trent.   Sounds to me like you're about to wipe out all of Russia.

Berent.   Well, that's certainly not what we *intend*.

Trent.   It's just a side effect, you mean.

Berent.   Correct.

Trent.   And this wouldn't piss them off?

Berent.   Piss *who* off?

Trent.   The Russians who are left. I see! They're all *gone*.

Berent.   That's right.

Trent.   Listen. Question. Let's say we've successfully wiped out their leaders, somehow some of their population still exist, and we decide we want to stop this thing. With *whom* do we negotiate?

Berent.   Well, that is a genuine problem.

Trent.   Listen, this is just off the top of my head. Don't you think it might be a good idea to try really very seriously to *negotiate* something with these fellas *now*?

Berent.   Of course! That would be *wonderful*! And yet, if history shows anything, it shows that the Soviet Union cannot be trusted to keep the terms of a treaty!

Trent.   Hold it! Hold it, hold it! Are you trying to tell me we shouldn't enter into treaties with these guys till we're convinced they can be TRUSTED?

Berent.   That's correct.

Trent.   If we knew they could be trusted, why would we need TREATIES? SAYONARA! *(Berent stares at him in astonishment. To audience)* I could barely contain my excitement! *(Rises as Berent and the restaurant fade from view)* I called Stone at the first pay phone I could find. *(Lights up on Stone. He is in a room next to a wing chair, its back to us)* Okay, I've got it!

Stone *(Trace of nervousness in his voice)*.   Got what, sir?

Trent.   The answer. The mystery is solved. I've discovered why we're doomed.

Stone.   Really. And why is that?

Trent.   We're in the hands of assholes! *(Silence)* . . . Hello?

Stone *(Sotto voce)*.   I'm afraid I cannot speak right now.

Trent.   Why?

The lights have come up enough to reveal that there is a man sitting in the wing chair—we see only his legs. The man appears to be smoking, for smoke curls upward from the chair.

Stone.   Sir, I can only tell you, if you persist in believing these men you've met are not smart, or not . . . *(In a whisper)* dangerous . . . *(Back to his normal voice)* . . . you are gravely mistaken. I can say no more, not now.

Stone hangs up. Turns back to his mysterious companion. Lights to black on them both.

Trent *(To audience)*.   There are times you want to chuck it all. This wasn't one. I was on to something here, no question. I decided to check out the guys they call war-gamers, the guys who *play* with these war scenarios. I called General Wilmer and asked if he could arrange it—things had gone so well with the last meeting he'd set up! He said he would. Gladly. And he did. *(Lights up on Jim and Pete)* I will call them Jim and Pete. *(We are in Jim's kitchen)* Both were connected with the Harley Corporation, a government think tank in nearby Virginia. *(Pete and Jim are preparing a meal—tiny birds stuffed, seasoned, wrapped in gauze, to be cooked in a microwave)* But the place was off-limits to plain ol' folk like me, so they very graciously invited me to Jim's house, though perhaps it was Pete's, I was never altogether sure— one of theirs. For a meal in my honor. Why had they gone to all this trouble for me? Something was very odd.

Jim *(While working at the meal)*.   So you talked with Stanley Berent!

Pete *(Also while working at the meal)*.   Bet *that* was fun!

Trent.   He poked a lot of holes in our deterrence strategy.

Jim.   I'm sure he was right, it's not hard to do.

They work in tandem on the meal; lots of coordinated teamwork.

Pete. There's a curious paradox built into deterrence strategy, and no one has a *clue* how to get around it. The paradox is this: Deterrence is dependent upon strength—well, that's obvious; the stronger your nuclear arsenal, the more the other side's deterred. *However*, should deterrence *fail* for any reason, your strength *instantly* becomes your greatest liability, *inviting* attack *instead* of preventing it.

Jim. HOIST on your own petard!

Pete. And *that* is where all these crazy scenarios come in in which war breaks out PRECISELY because *no one* WANTS it to! Really! I'm not kidding. This business is *filled* with paradox! Here, I'll run one by you.

Jim. I think, before you do, we should point out it isn't *easy* starting a nuclear war.

Pete. Right! Sorry. Getting carried away.

Jim. In fact, we can run scenario after scenario—the Persian Gulf is the most popular.

Pete. That's the hot spot!

Jim. People just will not go nuclear.

Pete. Right! And at first it absolutely drove us up the wall! Here we had all these tests designed to see what happens when people go nuclear?

Jim. And no one would do it!

Pete. To the man, they just refused to believe there wasn't some other way to resolve the crisis!

Jim. Well, the military started freaking out. They figured all those guys down in the silos?—maybe they won't push the button when they're told.

Pete. Real freak-out scene.

Jim. The whole Pentagon—

Pete. They just went bananas! *Total* banana scene.

Jim. Some general called me up. He said, "You incompetent jackass, what the hell kind of scenario are you *giving* these guys?" I said, "We're giving 'em every scenario we can think of, SIR! No one'll push the button, SIR!" You know what he said?

Pete. Get this!—"Don't tell 'em it's the button!"

Jim. "Really!" we said. "Then what good's the test?"

Pete. Anyway, happy ending.

Jim. Finally we solved it.

Pete. *You* solved it.

Jim. *I* solved it, *you* solved it, what's it matter? We *solved* the thing!

Pete. What a bitch!

Jim. People think it's *easy* starting a nuclear war?

Pete. Hey! Let 'em try!

Trent. Okay, I'll bite: how *do* you start a nuclear war?

Jim. Well, *first* you have to assume that a nuclear war is the *last* thing either side wants.

Pete. Right! That's the key! Who would've thought it! Jim?

Jim.   Okay. Let's say we're in a confrontation situation where we and the Soviets are facing down in the Middle East: let's say, Iran. Big Soviet pourdown. Let's further say we're losing conventionally on the ground—

Pete.   Not hard to believe—

Jim.   —and the President decides he wants the option of using nuclear weapons in the area, so he moves them in.

Pete.   Mind you, he doesn't want to *use* them now.

Jim.   Right! Absolutely not! Last thing he wants!

Pete.   He's just hoping, by showing strength, the Soviets will rethink their position and pull back.

Jim.   In other works, it's a *bluff.*

Pete.   Right, good ol' poker bluff!

Jim.   And, by the way, probably the proper move to make.

Pete.   Now, at the *same* time we ask our NATO allies to join us in raising the military alert level in Europe. Why? We want to tie the Soviet forces down that are in Eastern Europe.

Jim.   Again, absolutely the right move.

Pete.   So far, the President's batting a thousand. No appeasement here. Yet not too strong, nothing precipitous.

Jim.   Okay. The Soviets now go to a higher level of readiness themselves. Why? They want to tie *our* forces down so *we* don't shift 'em to the Middle East.

Pete.   Now we start to move nuclear weapons out of storage! *(Mimics the sound of a trumpet)*

Jim.   Okay, now let's suppose the Soviets, in the heat of this crisis, *misinterpret* the moves we've made, and believe that in fact we're about to *launch* these weapons! Not a farfetched supposition!

Pete.   Particularly, given their tendency to paranoia!

Jim.   Right!

Pete.   Okay. Now, at *this* point the issue for them is *not* do they want to be *in* a war.

Jim.   They're already *in* a war in the Middle East!

Pete.   Right. The issue isn't even do they want to launch a nuclear attack against the West.

Jim.   That's because they know they'll HAVE to if the West attacks *them!*

Pete.   You see?

Jim.   *The only issue*—

Pete.   Absolutely ONLY issue—

Jim.   —is do they want to go *first* and *preempt* this attack?

Pete.   Or wait it out—

Jim.   —and go second.

Pete.   Now, they recognize, just as much as we . . .

Jim.   . . . that going *first*—

Pete.   —is going *best.*

Jim.   Right!

Pete.   And by a shocking margin, too. No scenario *ever* shows ANYTHING else! I mean, these notions of our riding out a nuclear attack and then launching again, without substantial loss of capability—well, it's nonsense.

Jim.   By the way, you have to posit here that events are moving rapidly. A short time frame is crucial to this scenario. No time to sit back and say, "Hey! wait, why would he want to shoot at me? I know he's in trouble, but he isn't crazy!" No. He doesn't have *time* to think things out. He's got to make a move! Okay, What's he do? *(Pete makes the gesture and sound of a missile taking off).* He shoots. Now, are we saying it's a likely thing? No. But, from the Soviet perspective, they HAVE to shoot. Under these conditions, holding back is clearly wrong, politically and militarily.

Pete.   And *that*—

Jim.   —is how a nuclear war begins.

Pete.   Not out of anger.

Jim.   Or greed.

Pete.   But *fear!*

Jim.   With neither side *wanting* to.

Pete.   Yet each side *having* to.

Jim.   'Cause the other guy thinks they're *going* to.

Pete.   So they'd better.

Pete and Jim *(Together, à la W. C. Fields).*   HOIST ON OUR OWN PETARD!

Jim.   By the way, where *is* the petard?

Pete *(Tossing a jar of mustard).*   Petard!

Jim   *(Catching it).* Petard!

Pete and Jim *(Together, à la W. C. Fields).*   Ahhhh, yes!

Trent.   You guys are a scream.

Jim.   Actually—should we tell him?

Pete.   Sure.

Jim.   Actually, over at the center, we all try to scream at least once a day.

Pete.   Usually it happens in the cafeteria.

Jim.   Someone on the staff will stand up and shout "SCREAMIN' TIME!" And everyone just, you know . . . *(Gives a choked comic scream)*

Pete.   It's a ritual we only do when no one from the Pentagon's around.

Jim.   We did it once when some honcho military brass were there.

Pete.   *Freaked them out!*

Jim.   Within minutes we had lost I don't know *how* many grants! *(Laughs)*

Pete.   So, anyway, now we're pretty choosy 'bout who we scream in front of.

Jim.   I'll tell you . . . I sometimes think, if it really happens, and we all, you know . . . *(Makes the sound and gesture of a giant explosion)* . . . and by the way, the whole thing *could* be over! No matter what anybody says, no one knows *what* happens to the ozone layer in a nuclear war. Really! No idea! *(Laughs)* Okay, so I sometimes think, now it's all over, and we're all up there in the big debriefing space in the sky, and the Good Lord decides to hold a symposium 'cause he's curious: how did this thing happen? And everybody says, "Hey, don't look at me, I didn't wanna do it!" The end result being that everyone realizes *no* one wanted to do it! But there was suddenly no choice. Or no choice they could *see*. And the symposium gets nowhere.

Trent.   How do we get out of this?

Pete.   Well, you try like hell to not get *into* these kinds of conflicts!

Jim.   Obviously, sometimes it can't be helped.

Trent.   This is not pleasant news.

Pete (*Putting the birds into the microwave*).   On the other hand, let's not exaggerate. Things are not that bad, maybe we *shouldn't* get out of it. (*With a laugh, to Jim*) Would you not love to have a snapshot of this man's expression?

Jim mimes taking a snapshot of Trent.

Trent.   So you mean we're just supposed to sit around, twiddle our thumbs, and WAIT?

Pete.   Well . . .

Jim.   Sometimes . . . there's really not an awful lot you *can* do.

Pete.   Except *hold on*.

Jim.   And hope for some kind of discontinuity.

Pete.   Right.

Trent.   Ah! Discontinuity! What the hell is that?

Pete.   It's an event . . . by definition unpredictable, which causes a sudden and radical shift in the general mode of thinking.

Jim.   Sadat's going to Jerusalem is the prime example.

Pete.   Sadat looked down the road and saw nuclear weapons in Cairo and Alexandria in maybe five, ten years, and he just didn't like what he saw.

Jim.   So he decided he was gonna do something about it.

Pete.   And what he decided to do no one, I mean *no* one, anticipated.

Jim.   And it changed the whole ball game.

Pete.   *Just like that!*

Jim.   And THAT—

Pete.   —is a discontinuity.

Trent.   Okay! all right! . . . any candidates?

Pete.   Well, I'd say the best we've come up with so *far* is . . . (*Looks to Jim for help*)

Jim (*To Pete*).   Extraterrestrial?

Pete.   Yah. (*To Trent*) Extraterrestrial.

Trent (*Stunned*).   You mean, like E.T. comes down?

Pete.   You got it!

Trent.   Jesus Christ!

Jim.   That's another!

Trent.   You guys are a riot!

Jim.   Hey! In this business? Important to keep smiling.

Trent.   No, I can see that. Listen, have you guys given any real thought to, you know, touring the country? Nightclubs, things like that?

Pete.   Oh, sure, it's occurred to us.

Trent.   I'm sure it has.

Jim.   People are very interested in this nuclear issue.

Pete.   And we're right there at the dirty heart of it!

Trent.   Good. Listen, while we're on the subject of humor, what's your attitude toward doom?

Pete.   . . . Doom?

Pete looks at Jim. Jim looks at Pete.

Jim.   It's just no solution.

Pete.   No. No solution.

Trent.   I'm being serious!

Pete and Jim *(Together)*.   So are we! *(They smile at Trent)*

Blackout on Jim and Pete. Trent turns to the audience. Music: "Trent's Theme."

Trent.   Okay. Even with *my* lousy sinuses, I could tell something wasn't smelling right. I figured it was *my* fault. What've I missed? I decided to retrace my steps. *(Trent's office has begun to reappear)* The next day I was back in my office in Stamford, going through all my notes, when Stella came in with a rather large package.

Enter Stella pushing a huge flat object wrapped in plain brown paper.

Stella.   Boy, is this big!

On the wrapper, crayoned in enormous black letters, are these words:

MICHAEL TRENT—PLAYWRIGHT
and
DETECTIVE

Trent.   Hey, dollface, what gives?

Stella.   I dunno. I found it in the hallway. Someone left it outside your door. I had t' bring it in, 'cause otherwise I couldn't get out. *(Starts to unwrap it)*

Trent.   *(To audience)*.   It had no return address.

Inside the package is an oversized, framed photograph. This is the photograph:

Crazy Crate, photograph by Dr. Cochran

Trent and Stella stare at it in silence.

Stella.   Hey, Mike, how do ya *build* a box like that?
Trent.   I dunno.
Stella.   Hey! Maybe there's instructions in the back. *(Checks in back)* Mikey! Look! . . . A card.

Stella hands the small white card to Trent. Trent, not needing to read, moves toward the audience. As he does, Stella, the box, and the office disappear into the dark.

Trent *(To audience).*   The card said, "If you want help with your quest, be in Washington tomorrow night, ten o'clock." And it was signed "The Shadow." *(There is the sound of a knock from the darkness behind him. Trent turns toward the sound)* It's open!

The door of his hotel room has appeared. It opens. The Man who appeared earlier is seen, silhouetted against a dazzlingly bright white hallway light.

Man in Hallway.   We're ready, Mr. Trent.

Trent.   Right! *(Blackout except for a pin-spot of light on Trent)* I am led down the backstairs to a car—an old Ford wagon. In the rear seat are two men. I get in. No one says a word to me. And the car pulls out . . . Fog moves in off the Potomac . . . We are heading toward the center of the capital, that much I can tell. We move at a crawl. Even the road is scarcely visible. *(Pause)* And then . . . the sky begins to *glow*. A dazzling milky phosphorescence! I have never seen anything like this in my life! And then I hear *music. (Music dimly heard)* . . . *Band* music. *(So it is)* And then I see the *source* of this strange light! *(Music louder)* We approach the Jefferson Memorial. On the grounds surrounding it are rows upon rows of giant klieg lights! The lawn— what I can see of it—is packed. Obviously, it's a concert of some sort. We pass near a clearing in the fog, and I see that in the crowd are many men in military uniforms! . . . The car stops. I can see a sign but can't make out what it says. The people who have brought me here tell me to get out. "But how will I recognize The Shadow?" I say. "Don't worry," they say. "But where should I walk?" "Wherever you wish." So I get out and the car drives off. *(Pause)* I head for the sign. The sign says: U.S. Marine Corps Band. *(Music louder)* Well, I don't like crowds in the best of times, and this is terrible! So I decide to go toward the Memorial, which looms through the fog like a spectral white mushroom. *(The interior of the Jefferson Memorial begins to form around him)* The rotunda is empty. I look down through the fog and can see . . . almost no one. *(Jefferson's statue can be discerned only in shape. The same for the surrounding columns)* And then I hear . . .

Footsteps suddenly moving toward him. Then they stop on the far side of a shimmering shaft of light caused by the klieg lights' piercing the fog. All we can see of this Man are the bottoms of his legs.

Man's Voice.   Mr. Trent?

Trent.   And I recognize the voice!

The Man walks toward Trent, through the eerie light. The first feature we see is that he is in uniform. But we can't yet make out his face. And then he moves forward, into a better light. It is General Wilmer. He smiles.

General Wilmer *(Warmly).*   Shall we talk?

Beat. Blackout.

Act Three: The Discovery

Lights up on Trent in his trench coat.

Trent.   Okay. I have proceeded systematically, I have followed my nose and have found the piece of the puzzle I was looking for. Unfortunately, instead of the puzzle being solved, the puzzle has expanded . . . I am a man who knows too much . . . and not enough. *Why me? Why has Stone picked me?* *(The cozy living room of Trent's house in Connecticut slides into view. Through rear windows, open, with curtains fluttering in a gentle spring breeze, we can see trees and a meadow)* By the way, this is my house in Connecticut—my beloved retreat to which I have retreated. Fat chance! About an hour ago, Stone called to say he was coming out to see how I'm doing. *How I'm doing!* . . . All right, the truth: I have told him the meeting with The Shadow was canceled. Actually, I didn't have the nerve to tell him this directly, I left a message. I've told the same thing to my agent and my wife. I need time to think things through! It's not an easy racket, writing plays; stay out of it!

Alex *(Offstage).*   DAD!

Trent.   That's my son. He's eleven.

Boy's Voice.   I think your producer's here!

Trent.   Great. Here it goes.

Boy's Voice.   Should I tell Mom to let him in?

Trent.   No-no! Let him find his own way in! *(To audience)* My wife is on the patio, in a chaise, reading Yeats. That's what life's like here in the country. Now, if things go well today—and at this point I've no idea just how that's possible—you won't be meeting either my wife *or* my son; as I said earlier, I don't want them involved in this!

Stone.   TRENT!

Trent.   The Call of the Wild! *(To Stone)* I'M IN THE LIVING ROOM, PHIL! *(To audience)* What you are about to see is scrambling of the highest order! *(Trent removes his trench coat. Enter Stone)* Phil! *(Stone stops and turns his gaze on Trent. He stares at Trent closely. Then, after a moment, Stone grins)* Well, I'm glad to see you're happy!

Stone walks slowly over to Trent and rests his hands on Trent's shoulders. Trent stares back, terrified. Stone continues to grin.

Stone.   I haven't seen you in such a long time!

Trent.   That's right! About . . . a month, I guess—maybe . . . more.

Stone.   Why was the meeting canceled?

Trent.   Oh! With, uhh, The Shadow? I don't know, they didn't say. Security, I suspect. I'm waiting now to see when it will be rescheduled.

Stone.   What makes you think it will be rescheduled?

Trent.   Well, that's what they said.

Stone.   And yet, for some reason, they neglected to tell you why it was canceled.

Trent.   No-no, uh, *security!* . . . I mean they, you know, *said* that. Said it. "Too risky for him to meet with you tonight"—that's what they said.

Enter Ann, Trent's wife. She is in her sixth month of pregnancy.

Ann.   Dear, Audrey has arrived.

Trent.   What?

Ann *(Going toward Stone)*.   Hi! I'm Ann Trent.

Trent.   Ann! Out! Get out!

Ann.   *What?*

He rushes toward her.

Trent *(Sotto voce)*.   Get out of here! Go! I'll tell you about it later. I don't want you involved in this! Out, get out! *(Leads/pushes/coaxes her out of the room as Audrey enters)* Audrey!

Stone.   I was not aware you were joining us today!

Audrey.   No. Nor was my client. Dear, I need to speak to you alone.

Trent *(Startled)*.   Of course.

Audrey.   Mr. Stone, would you mind very much if my client and I went into—

Stone.   No, please, dear lady, you stay here, I can use the time to look around the house. I *love* country houses! And this is such a charming one. *(Exits)*

Trent stares after him, perplexed.

Trent.   Well, he's the weirdest man I've ever met!

Audrey.   Dear, I'm afraid I have some extremely bad news for you.

Trent.   Oh!

Audrey.   Could I have a drink?

Trent.   Uhhhh, right. Ummmm—

Audrey.   *Martini.*

Trent.   With an *olive!*

Audrey.   No, dear. Lemon twist.

Trent.   Right, of course. *(Heading for the bar)* So what's the, uh, bad news?

Audrey.   Well. It seems, dear, that your producer has instituted legal action against you.

Trent.   *What?*

Audrey.   He is bringing suit against you, dear. For fraud and breach of contract.

Trent.   WHAT?

Audrey.   Sssh. Dear. Please.

Trent.   *Why?*

Audrey.   I'm not sure.

Trent.   Well, how much is he suing me for? I mean, is it the retainer, the advance?

Audrey.   I'm afraid it's a bit more than that.

Trent.   How can it be for more, that's all I made!

Audrey.   The suit is for fifteen million dollars.

Trent.   Fifteen million DOLLARS?

Audrey.   Yes, dear, dollars.

Trent.   But that makes no SENSE!

Audrey.   I know.

Trent.   Maybe it's not dollars! Maybe it's zlotys!

Audrey.   No, dear, dollars, Yankee dollars.

Trent.   WHAT'S HE THINK I'VE GOT?

Audrey.   Well . . . it's not worth a *great* deal . . . but you've got this house.

Trent *(Staring in direction that Stone went).*   Oh, my God!

Audrey.   Perhaps if you turned in your *script!*

Trent.   Oh, come on, Audrey! No one sues a playwright for fifteen million dollars because he's a few weeks late delivering a script! I mean, what's he hope to gain? A house? He doesn't need another house!

Stone *(Who has entered, unnoticed).*   It's not the house that interests me . . . It's your *ruination. (They turn to him, astonished)* And I expect your legal fees alone should accomplish that. You look surprised; that surprises me. Did you really think I'd allow your treachery to go unchallenged?

Trent.   What are you talking about?

Stone.   Sir, please, the time for innocence is past.

Audrey.   *What* treachery?

Stone.   Evidence suggests, madam, that your client has in fact found what he set *out* to find.

Trent.   That's not TRUE!

Stone.   And I believe otherwise.

Audrey.   Michael, have you lied to Mr. Stone?

Trent.   Not at all.

Audrey.   You owe my client an apology.

Stone.   Tell this lady what you've done.

Trent.   *I don't know WHAT you are TALKING about.*

Stone.   Does the name "The Shadow" ring a bell?

Trent.   The meeting was called OFF!

Stone.   AND THAT, SIR, IS A LIE!

Audrey.   Mr. Stone, forgive me. If my client says the meeting was called off, the meeting was called off.

Stone.   I disagree.

Audrey. Michael?

Trent. It was called off.

Audrey. The matter's closed.

Stone. THIS MAN HAS VIOLATED THE TERMS OF OUR AGREE-MENT!

Audrey. Mr. Stone!

Trent. Audrey.

Audrey. Dear, let me handle this! *(To Stone)* I believe the time has come, sir, for you to leave.

Stone *(To Trent)*. Tell her what you've done.

Audrey. Is there something wrong, sir, with your ears?

Trent. Audrey.

Audrey. I SAID STAY OUT OF THIS! I CAN HANDLE THIS! *(To Stone)* Mr. Stone, if my client says the meeting was called off, it was called off. My clients do not lie to me.

Trent *(Weakly)*. Audrey, please.

Audrey. DEAR, STAY OUT OF THIS! *(To Stone)* The matter's therefore closed. Except, sir, for your appalling lack of manners. Where, may I ask, were you brought up?

Trent. I LIED!!!! *(She turns to him as if struck)* I lied, I lied! I'm sorry! *(He holds his head in his hands and fights tears. She does not know what to do, where to turn. She turns to Stone)*

Audrey *(To Stone)*. Would you . . . be so kind . . .

Stone. A drink?

Audrey. Yes, please, some . . . water would be nice, I think. *(To Trent)* Why? Don't you trust me?

Trent. Of course I trust you! This has nothing to do with trust! I just had no idea what to say. I haven't even told Ann! I've told no one!

Audrey *(Taking the glass from Stone)*. I owe you an apology.

Stone. Not at all.

Audrey *(To Trent)*. I don't understand what's happening.

Trent *(To Stone, angrily)*. Did you set the meeting up? *(Stone shakes his head no)* Then how do you know it happened?

Stone. I've had you followed, sir. Ever since you accepted this job.

Trent. Great!

Stone. I should add, in all this time my emissaries have never actually seen you *writing*.

Trent. What do you think, I write in the *street?* I write in my OFFICE!

Stone. Good! Then you can show me some pages.

Trent. *Pages?*

Stone. Sir, doom approaches, I need pages.

Trent. ANYONE CAN WRITE PAGES!

Stone. I ask only to see yours.

Trent. Well, I never show pages till I'm done. Audrey can confirm this. Audrey, are you all right? *(She nods)* Anyhow, the important thing isn't pages, the important thing is *concept!* CONCEPT is what we should be talking about! Without a concept, a play is nothing.

Stone. Sir, a play may be nothing without a concept—without pages, it is even less.

Trent. Who said that? Aristotle, I believe.

Audrey *(Sotto voce).* Dear, this man is *suing* you!

Trent. Okay, fine, you want pages? I'll give you pages! I've got pages *here—* *(Runs to a drawer, opens it)*—and in here—*(Opens another drawer)*—pages everywhere! You want pages? Here! Pages! *(Starts flinging the pages into the air. Stone looks down at them)*

Stone. These are not pages from a play!

Trent. Right! For that, you need a CONCEPT!

Audrey. *Michael.*

Trent *(To Audrey, sotto voce).* I'm okay, I know what I'm doing. Really. *(To Stone)* Now, do you want to hear what my concept is? Because I will tell you. Gladly. Because this is a concept I am wild about! And it took a long time finding. In fact, I only found it today. But well worth the waiting, because this concept means this play will be *fun.*

Stone. *What?*

Trent. Fun! Fun to write, fun to look at.

Audrey. Dear, are we talking about the same play?

Trent. Of course! The play that deals with doom! Going to be fun! So you want to hear what this concept is? Okay, here it is . . . *(Very long pause, during which time he takes out a cigarette and hopes that a concept will come. The lighting of the cigarette, in a kind of Philip Marlowe way, seems to do the trick. A look of astonishment comes over his face, which he masks from the others)* The playwright . . . is conceived . . . as being very much like a *detective.* (To Audrey) Wha'd'ya think?

Stone. *What* playwright?

Trent. The playwright who's at the CENTER of this play!

Stone. What's a playwright doing in this play?

Trent. He's in this play because he is the only reality I can hang on to here! And this playwright is sent on a *strannnnge* mission by a man, I would say quite like *you,* a kindly man, a man who would surely never, for example, sue anyone. And this playwright *respects* this man because this playwright is without doubt the very salt of the earth! Though possibly with some knowledge of evil—I still haven't figured that one out, I may have to come back to you for that, I'm nowhere on that so far, that's the truth, I just can't remember where we met. *(Silence)* Okay, so this playwright, down he goes to Washington, figuring if this mystery can be solved anywhere, there's the spot.

Audrey. Dear, what happened down in Washington?

Trent. The case took a turn for the worse, all right? I didn't think it possible.

Audrey. Michael, *please!*

Trent.   I DO NOT BELIEVE WHAT THE SHADOW TOLD ME, OKAY?
And there you are. Now, what am I to do with that?

Enter Ann Trent, carrying a tea tray.

Ann.   Tea time!

Trent (*Angry, sotto voce*).   Ann, I asked you specifically—

Ann.   Dear, I am not coming to sit in on your meeting, this is *your* meeting,
not mine. *(To Audrey and Stone)* I just thought you might all like some iced
tea. The mint is from the garden. *(To Trent, sotto voce)* I was being *nice.* You
might try the same. *(She sets the tray down and leaves. Silence)*

Stone.   When is your wife due?

Trent.   Uh, due where? . . . Oh! Uhhh, she's, let's see, in her sixth month,
so in four, I mean three. Unless doom strikes first, of course. I'm sorry, I'm
just very edgy today.

*Ann comes back in, holding the sugar bowl. She comes face to face with a glow-
ering Trent. She puts the bowl down on the floor.*

Ann.   The sugar.

She tiptoes back out.

Stone.   She's very graceful, your wife.

Trent.   Yes. *(Silence)* Look, you want to know what happened down in Washington? You show me what to do with it, I'll tell you what happened. Is that
fair? Fair enough? Terrific. This guy, The Shadow, he says, "Okay, tell me
what you *think* you know." So I started in. I told him I thought the notion
of using nuclear weapons to prevent the use of nuclear weapons—*(To Audrey)*—which is the system we depend upon—*(To them both)*—simply doesn't
work, not in the *long* run, too many places where the system just plain breaks
down! Breakdown, in fact, I said, seems built in. What we've got, I said, is
a fail-safe built-in breakdown machine. He said: "So how can I help you?"
I said I want to know where I've gone wrong. He said: "You're not wrong.
You've *got* it!"*(Audrey stares at him, stunned. To Stone, with a gesture toward Audrey)* I would think my expression probably looked a bit like that!
(To them both) I said, "Wait, hold on, you're telling me the system doesn't
work?" He said: "Why are you surprised? That's what you told me." I said:
"But I didn't think I was right!" He said: "Well, you are." I said: "Well then,
how come you and I are the only two who seem to know it?" You know what
he said? Hold on to your seats, folks. He said actually *everybody* knew. It was
common knowledge.

Audrey.   . . . Dear, that makes no sense.

Trent *(Excitedly).*   That's right! Of COURSE it makes no sense! But WHY does it make no sense?

Audrey.   Well . . . *(Pause)* Well, because if everyone knows . . . that what they're working on doesn't *work* . . .

Trent.   . . . Yes?

Audrey   . . . Why would they keep working?

Trent.   EXACTLY!

Audrey.   I assume these are people who can find other jobs.

Alex *(Offstage).*   DAD, CAN I ASK YOU A QUESTION?

Trent.   No! And stay out of here. Go to your room. *(Back to Audrey and Stone)* All right. So I asked what you asked: If they know it doesn't work, why do they keep working? . . . *"Because they don't believe what they know!"* *(Audrey stares at him blankly)* Look, look, they know it doesn't work, okay? I mean, they've run the charts, the projections, intellectually they are fine, they understand, *but* they just can't BELIEVE it! Why? Because it SEEEEEEMS as if it should work. It's worked so far, right? So why not forever? You see? Logic! Worst thing that's ever *happened* to man! Oh, my God!

Audrey.   What?

Trent.   Down in Washington? Where I went to interview all these guys? There was something on their walls. I mean, each one had it. And I remember thinking: I wonder if these guys belong to some kind of club. Anyway, I didn't give it too much thought . . . Other guys, they put up posters of Bo Derek. These guys—they had Escher prints! *(Pause)* The Shadow! Let me show you how he got in touch with me! *(Looks up)* DOWN!

The photograph of the "crazy crate" descends on wires.

Audrey *(To audience).*   Aren't playwrights' houses *wonderful!*

Trent.   Look. You see? It doesn't work! And yet it *does.* It's not possible! And yet it *is.*

Audrey.   How does one *construct* an object like this?

Trent.   Not quite sure.

Audrey.   I'd love one in my office.

Trent.   So would I. Here's the Escher print they all had. DOWN!

Another hugely oversized print descends on wires, this one larger even than the first. Audrey stares up, puzzled.

Audrey.   Dear, what's happened to your second floor? *(Now she sees the picture)* . . . Well, there's something very wrong with this.

They stare at the picture.

This is the picture that descends:

Waterfall, 1961 by M. C. Escher

Audrey. I'm afraid I'm quite confused. How does one get the water to flow both up and down?

Trent. It's a puzzler. (*Snaps his fingers, and the Escher print disappears*)

Audrey. Thank you, dear.

Trent. Okay, what he said so far, that the system doesn't work, that I can accept. But I said, "Surely, not *everyone* is like this. *Some* must believe what they know. You, for instance." "Absolutely," he said. "So, then, why are *you* working on it?" And he grinned . . . and said, *"Guess." (Silence)* Well, I was stumped. So I went back to the very first question I'd asked him, weeks before: "If the system doesn't work, why do we need more weapons?" His answer remained the same: we need more so we can strike first.

Audrey.   What!

Trent.   It's a defensive act.

Audrey.   Hitting someone first is a *defensive* act?

Trent.   If you know he's planning to hit you.

Audrey.   Why would he be planning to hit you?

Trent.   Because he thinks you're planning to hit him.

Audrey.   Well . . . he's *right*.

Trent.   There you are.

Audrey.   Dear, by this scheme, nobody does anything *offensive*.

Trent.   Exactly. Every act of aggression is defensive here. It's a completely moral system!

Audrey.   Well, something's wrong with it!

Trent.   I know.

Audrey.   Not quite sure what.

Trent.   It's a puzzler! *(To Stone)* So I said to him, "This is crazy, this is suicidal! If we strike first, they'll just retaliate, and wipe us out in return!"

Audrey.   THAT'S what's wrong with it!

Trent.   That's just one of them.

Audrey.   With one like that, you don't *need* any more.

Trent.   Exactly! And he agreed! *"That's why we've abandoned deterrence." (Looks to Audrey for her response)*

Audrey.   . . . What?

Trent.   Exactly! WHAT? I mean, even if deterrence *doesn't* work, it works a *bit*. You don't just chuck it out, not without a substitute! Not a substitute, he said. An *improvement*! . . . And he grinned and said: "It seems, at least in theory, that a better mousetrap has been designed!" . . . Look, he said, an attack by us right now is suicidal because the enemy can always retaliate and wipe us out. However—what if we could *prevent* retaliation? "Well, in the future," he said, "which is what we're working toward, we think it may be possible, technologically, to do just this. And if we *can*, even if for the briefest time, a week, a month, create some kind of invulnerable window shade allowing our missiles out but nothing in, a kind of 'ion curtain'—incoming missiles hit it, bam! they disintegrate; then, in that brief moment of invulnerability, we can just . . . *take care of things*."

Audrey.   That's barbaric!

Trent.   Ahhhh! Watch! No! Not at all! It's *defensive*! It's defensive because the Russians are working on the very same plan!

Audrey.   How do we know?

Trent.   Well, if *we* are, they *have* to be. Just in case *we* are. Which means *they* are—you see? Defensive! Again, a completely moral system. *(To Stone)*

I *told* you this was fun! *(To Audrey)* BUT! *(To Stone)* Here's the best part. *(To Audrey)* Here's the *twist!* Even *this* doesn't work. *(To them both)* Watch! Let's say this ion curtain has been built and Sears has it, we call up and order one. Two weeks for delivery, they say. Well, that's not so bad, so we say send it on. PROBLEM: Surely the Soviets know somebody who works for Sears. "Psst! Guess what the Americans have just ordered!" Well! The Soviets know what's in store for them if we get this thing. Which means they have got to preempt. Whch means we must PRE—preempt! We're right back where we started! You cannot beat the system, not from within; it simply doesn't work, *cannot* work, not in ANY permutation! It's that goddamn Escher print. "Right!" he said. And I could see his eyes—they were on FIRE! I mean, this man was *excited!* I thought, Am I dreaming this? This makes no sense! *(Pause)* And a moment later he was gone, in the fog, by the bandstand.

Long silence.

Audrey.   Dear, there's something very *wrong* here, something . . . you have *missed*, I think, I couldn't . . . say, of course, just *what*, I'm not an expert, dear, but clearly somewhere in your research you've gone wrong, that's just obvious, because this just makes no sense, as you yourself have even pointed out. *(Pause)* I mean, the world you are describing, dear, this is not a world I know. Furthermore, it's not a world I *care* to know, that's the truth, dear, I don't want to know any more. I think I need some air . . . Perhaps a stroll across the field! It's such a lovely day. Not the sort of day one wants to spend inside! *(She smiles and goes to get her purse. She stops near Stone. Pause)* Mr. Stone, if you would be so kind as to help him. Show him where he's wrong. I don't think I can be much more help to him on this . . . Not right now. I need to think this through. *(She stares at Trent. Pause)* Keep with it, dear. *(She walks out. Long pause)*
Trent.   Is this what you mean by doom? That no one will believe?
Stone.   Not quite. *(He smiles ever so faintly. Then he rises and pours himself a glass of iced tea)*
Trent.   Look, Stone, I am stumped, all right? I am at the end! What the hell was The Shadow up to? And why have you picked me for this?

Stone stares at him. Pause.

Stone.   Have you ever been to the South Pacific?
Trent *(Puzzled)*.   No.
Stone.   Remarkable place! Beautiful beyond imagining! The imagination belittles its beauty. *(Pause)* Anyway, I was there in the early fifties. A close friend of mine was involved in our nuclear tests and asked if I'd like to go along on the viewing ship. It was not inappropriate for me to be there, for among my many financial interests at that time was a laboratory and development center. It was in Utah.

Trent.   . . . You make weapons?

Stone *(Slight smile)*.   I used to. *(Pause)* In any event, there we were on this ship, this battleship, not too far from where the detonation was to take place, which was near an island known, interestingly enough, as Christmas Island. *(Smiles. Pause)* We'd been told the bomb was to be a small one, and so none of us was particularly worried. Even though I'd never seen one go off, I figured, well, these people must know what they are doing! *(Pause)* Actually, the truth is I was in a kind of funk! That's because I hadn't come all this way just to see a *little* bomb! This one was ten kilotons, smaller even than the bomb at Hiroshima! These bombs were classified as *tactical* weapons. These are weapons you would use in combat. And, quite frankly, I was disappointed. I wanted some BIG-time stuff, and I'm not ashamed to say it, either. There's a glitter to nuclear weapons. I had sensed it in others and *felt it in myself.* If you come to these things as a scientist, it is irresistible, to feel it's there in your hands, so to speak, the ability to release this energy that fuels the stars! . . . to make it do your bidding! to make it perform these miracles! to lift a million tons of rock into the sky. And all from a thimbleful of stuff. *Irresistible! (Pause)* Well, we were standing by the railing when the countdown came on, we could hear it over the P-A. We'd all been adequately briefed, and we were in suits, some kind of lead, tinted visors on our helmets. And then I saw these . . . *birds.* Albatrosses! Phenomenal creatures, truly! They'd been flying beside the ship for days, accompanying us to the site, so to speak. Watching them was a wonder! *(Pause. Then in a tone of great amazement)* And suddenly I could see that they were smoking. Their feathers were on fire! And they were doing cartwheels . . . The light persisted for some time. It was instantaneously bright, and lingered, long enough for me to see the birds crash into the water. *(Alex has come in unobserved by the others, and stands to the side, listening)* They were sizzling. Smoking! They were not vaporized, it's just that they were absorbing such intense radiation that they were being consumed by the heat! And so far there'd been no shock, none of the blast damage we talk about when we discuss the effects of these bombs. Instead, there were just these smoking, twisting, fantastically contorted birds crashing into things . . . And I could see vapor rising from the inner lagoon as the surface of the water was heated by the intense flash. *(Pause)* Well, I'd never seen anything like this in my life! . . . And I thought: *This is what it will be like at the end of time. (Pause)* And we all felt . . . the *thrill* of that idea. *(Long pause. Stone stares at Trent, who stares back at him in horror)* This is your son, I believe. *(Trent turns toward his son in horror. Alex looks frightened)* I've never met the lad, though of course I heard you speak of him many years ago. I guess he must be . . . eleven now. *(Trent turns toward Stone. Trent seems stunned by this last remark. To Alex)* I met your father shortly after you were born.

Trent is reeling now. He stares from one to the other.

Alex.   Was that a movie you saw?

Stone.   Just now? Describing? *(Alex nods)* Yes. A movie. *(Alex nods and leaves. Trent stares out, stunned. The lights start to fade on everything but Trent)* I think I'm going to have some more iced tea! *(He crosses to the pitcher and pours himself a glass of tea. Soon Stone is but a shape in the dark)*

Light on Trent.

Trent.   Now I know where we met! . . . It was at *our* place, our apartment! We were living in the city then, and some friends came by to see our child, he'd just been born; obviously, one of them brought Stone—who? doesn't matter, Stone was there, I can see him, in a corner, *listening*, as I . . . tell. *(Pause)* But *evil*? *(Long pause)* Our son had just been born. We'd brought him home. He was what, five days old, I guess. *(Pause)* And then one day my wife went out . . . And I was left alone with him. And I was very excited. Because it was the first time I was alone with him. And I picked him up, this tiny thing, and started walking around the living room. We lived on a high floor, overlooking the river, the Hudson. Light was streaming in; it was a lovely, lilting autumn day, cool, beautiful. And I looked down at this tiny creature, this tiny thing, and I realized . . . *(Pause)* I realized I had never had anyone completely in my power before! . . . And I'd never known what that *meant!* Never felt anything remotely like that before! And I saw I was standing near a window. And it was open. It was but a few feet away. And I thought: I could . . . *drop him out!* And I went *toward* the window, because I couldn't believe this thought had come into my head—*where had it come from?* Not one part of me felt anything for this boy but love, not one part! My wife and I had planned, we were both in love, there was no anger, no resentment, nothing dark in me toward him at all, no one could ever have been more in love with his child than I, as much yes, but not more, not more, and I was thinking: I can throw him out of here! . . . and then he will be falling ten, twelve, fifteen, twenty stories down, and as he's falling, I will be *unable to get him back!* . . . And I felt a *thrill!* I FELT A THRILL! IT WAS THERE! . . . And, of course, I resisted this. It wasn't hard to do, resisting wasn't hard . . . BUT I DIDN'T STAY BY THE WINDOW! . . . AND I CLOSED IT! I resisted by moving away; back into the room . . . And I sat down with him. *(Pause)* Well, there's not a chance I would have done it, not a chance! *(Pause)* But I couldn't *take* a chance, it was very, very . . . seductive. *(Pause. He looks at Stone. The lights come back a bit. Stone is sipping his tea, his eyes on Trent)* If doom comes . . . it will come in *that* way.

Stone.   I would think.

Pause.

Trent.   You want it to come, don't you!
Stone.   What?
Trent.   Doom. You'd like to see it come!

Stone.   No-no, of course not, that's ridiculous. *(He sips)* I just know that if it did, it would not be altogether without interest. I mean, it has its appeal, that's all I mean. It arouses my *curiosity*. *(Smiles)* But then, many things arouse my curiosity. Mustn't make too much of it. This is really good iced tea! My compliments to your wife. I think the secret is fresh mint, nothing like fresh mint; if you don't mind, I shall pick some from your garden when I leave. *(Pause)* I'm glad you've taken this job.

Trent.   Don't you understand, I can't write this play! Really, that's the truth, it is totally beyond me!

Stone puts his hands on Trent's shoulders.

Stone *(Warmly).*   Work on it.

He turns and starts out. At the rear of the room, by the window, he stops and looks out. Then he looks back at Trent.

The lights go nearly to black on everything but Trent and the field outside the house. In this darkened room, Stone is but a shadowy presence. The curtains on the rear window flutter. Trent stares out, lost in thought. Through the rear window, Ann can be seen strolling out across the bright field, hand in hand with Alex.

QUESTIONS

1. Presenting the playwright Michael Trent as a private eye adds a comic dimension to the play. But can you think of any serious reasons for this style of characterization? Why do you suppose Kopit made his central character a playwright? **2.** Toward the end of Act One, Trent and Stone discuss the fascinating temptation provided by the open window forty stories above the street. What is the relationship of that exchange to the play as a whole? **3.** What causes Trent to moan loudly as he pursues his research? Why does he not wish to read such stuff as "The Prompt and Delayed Effects of Thermonuclear Explosions"? How would you answer Trent's thematically central question: "WHAT SORT OF PEOPLE CAN *THINK ABOUT THAT STUFF EVERY DAY?*" Why does Trent differ from such people? **4.** What is the significance of the photograph of the Crazy Crate and the Escher print that appear in Act Two and Act Three, respectively?

WRITING TOPICS

1. How does Stone's description in Act Three of an atomic bomb explosion relate to Trent's subsequent account of the temptation to drop his infant son from a high window? How does the word *thrill* figure in these speeches? What conclusion about the "end of the world" can one draw from them? Explain. **2.** Characters in the play, particularly Trent, frequently speak directly to the audience, sometimes even interrupting conversations with other characters. Is this violation of dramatic illusion distracting? Can it be justified? Analyze the cumulative effect of such interruptions and the play's insistence on including the audience.

THE
PRESENCE
OF DEATH

The Revenant, 1949 by Andrew Wyeth

ESSAYS

Meditation XVII, from *Devotions upon Emergent Occasions*   1623

JOHN DONNE   [1572–1631]

Nunc lento sonitu dicunt morieris.
Now this bell tolling softly for another says to me, Thou must die.

Perchance he for whom this bell tolls may be so ill as that he knows not it tolls   1
for him; and perchance I may think myself so much better than I am, as that
they who are about me and see my state may have caused it to toll for me, and
I know not that. The church is catholic, universal, so are all her actions; all
that she does belongs to all. When she baptizes a child, that action concerns
me; for that child is thereby connected to that head which is my head too, and
ingrafted into that body whereof I am a member. And when she buries a man,
that action concerns me: all mankind is of one author and is one volume; when
one man dies, one chapter is not torn out of the book, but translated into a
better language; and every chapter must be so translated. God employs several
translators; some pieces are translated by age, some by sickness, some by war,
some by justice; but God's hand is in every translation, and his hand shall bind
up all our scattered leaves again for that library where every book shall lie open
to one another. As therefore the bell that rings to a sermon calls not upon the
preacher only, but upon the congregation to come, so this bell calls us all; but
how much more me, who am brought so near the door by this sickness. There
was a contention as far as a suit[1] (in which piety and dignity, religion and
estimation, were mingled) which of the religious orders should ring to prayers
first in the morning; and it was determined that they should ring first that rose
earliest. If we understand aright the dignity of this bell that tolls for our evening
prayer, we would be glad to make it ours by rising early, in that application,
that it might be ours as well as his whose indeed it is. The bell doth toll for

---

[1]An argument settled by a lawsuit.

him that thinks it doth, and though it intermit again, yet from that minute that that occasion wrought upon him, he is united to God. Who casts not up his eye to the sun when it rises? but who takes off his eye from a comet when that breaks out? Who bends not his ear to any bell which upon any occasion rings? but who can remove it from that bell which is passing a piece of himself out of this world? No man is an island, entire of itself; every man is a piece of the continent, a part of the main. If a clod be washed away by the sea, Europe is the less, as well as if a promontory were, as well as if a manor of thy friend's or of thine own were. Any man's death diminishes me, because I am involved in mankind; and therefore never send to know for whom the bell tolls; it tolls for thee. Neither can we call this a begging of misery or a borrowing of misery, as though we were not miserable enough of ourselves but must fetch in more from the next house, in taking upon us the misery of our neighbors. Truly it were an excusable convetousness if we did; for affliction is a treasure, and scarce any man hath enough of it. No man hath affliction enough that is not matured and ripened by it, and made fit for God by that affliction. If a man carry treasure in bullion, or in a wedge of gold, and have none coined into current moneys, his treasure will not defray him as he travels. Tribulation is treasure in the nature of it, but it is not current money in the use of it, except we get nearer and nearer our home, heaven, by it. Another man may be sick too, and sick to death, and this affliction may lie in his bowels as gold in a mine and be of no use to him; but this bell that tells me of his affliction digs out and applies that gold to me, if by this consideration of another's danger I take mine own into contemplation and so secure myself by making my recourse to my God, who is our only security.

QUESTIONS

1.   John Donne is justly admired for his use of figurative language. What extended metaphors does he use to characterize mankind and death?   **2.**   What does Donne mean when he asserts that the death bell "tolls for thee"?   **3.**   Toward the end of his meditation, Donne states that "tribulation is treasure." What does he mean? What will that treasure purchase?

WRITING TOPIC

In what sense is "No man is an island, entire of itself" an accurate description of the human condition? In what sense is it inaccurate?

Once More to the Lake   1941

E. B. WHITE   [1899–1985]

August 1941

One summer, along about 1904, my father rented a camp on a lake in Maine   1
and took us all there for the month of August. We all got ringworm from some
kittens and had to rub Pond's Extract on our arms and legs night and morning,
and my father rolled over in a canoe with all his clothes on; but outside of that
the vacation was a success and from then on none of us ever thought there was
any place in the world like that lake in Maine. We returned summer after
summer—always on August 1 for one month. I have since become a salt-water
man, but sometimes in summer there are days when the restlessness of the
tides and the fearful cold of the sea water and the incessant wind that blows
across the afternoon and into the evening make me wish for the placidity of a
lake in the woods. A few weeks ago this feeling got so strong I bought myself a
couple of bass hooks and a spinner and returned to the lake where we used to
go, for a week's fishing and to revisit old haunts.

I took along my son, who had never had any fresh water up his nose and   2
who had seen lily pads only from train windows. On the journey over to the
lake I began to wonder what it would be like. I wondered how time would have
marred this unique, this holy spot—the coves and streams, the hills that the
sun set behind, the camps and the paths behind the camps. I was sure that the
tarred road would have found it out, and I wondered in what other ways it
would be desolated. It is strange how much you can remember about places
like that once you allow your mind to return into the grooves that lead back.
You remember one thing, and that suddenly reminds you of another thing. I
guess I remembered clearest of all the early mornings, when the lake was cool
and motionless, remembered how the bedroom smelled of the lumber it was
made of and of the wet woods whose scent entered through the screen. The
partitions in the camp were thin and did not extend clear to the top of the
rooms, and as I was always the first up I would dress softly so as not to wake
the others, and sneak out into the sweet outdoors and start out in the canoe,
keeping close along the shore in the long shadows of the pines. I remembered
being very careful never to rub my paddle against the gunwale for fear of disturbing the stillness of the cathedral.

The lake had never been what you would call a wild lake. There were cot-   3
tages sprinkled around the shores, and it was in farming country although the
shores of the lake were quite heavily wooded. Some of the cottages were owned
by nearby farmers, and you would live at the shore and eat your meals at the
farmhouse. That's what our family did. But although it wasn't wild, it was a
fairly large and undisturbed lake and there were places in it that, to a child at
least, seemed infinitely remote and primeval.

I was right about the tar: it led to within half a mile of the shore. But when   4
I got back there, with my boy, and we settled into a camp near a farmhouse
and into the kind of summertime I had known, I could tell that it was going
to be pretty much the same as it had been before—I knew it, lying in bed the
first morning, smelling the bedroom and hearing the boy sneak quietly out and
go off along the shore in a boat. I began to sustain the illusion that he was I,
and therefore, by simple transposition, that I was my father. This sensation
persisted, kept cropping up all the time we were there. It was not an entirely
new feeling, but in this setting it grew much stronger. I seemed to be living a
dual existence. I would be in the middle of some simple act, I would be picking up a bait box or laying down a table fork, or I would be saying something,
and suddenly it would be not I but my father who was saying the words or
making the gesture. It gave me a creepy sensation.

We went fishing the first morning. I felt the same damp moss covering the   5
worms in the bait can, and saw the dragonfly alight on the tip of my rod as it
hovered a few inches from the surface of the water. It was the arrival of this fly
that convinced me beyond any doubt that everything was as it always had been,
that the years were a mirage and that there had been no years. The small waves
were the same, chucking the rowboat under the chin as we fished at anchor,
and the boat was the same boat, the same color green and the ribs broken in
the same places, and under the floorboards the same fresh-water leavings and
débris—the dead helgramite, the wisps of moss, the rusty discarded fishhook,
the dried blood from yesterday's catch. We stared silently at the tips of our
rods, at the dragonflies that came and went. I lowered the tip of mine into the
water, tentatively, pensively dislodging the fly, which darted two feet away,
poised, darted two feet back, and came to rest again a little farther up the rod.
There had been no years between the ducking of this dragonfly and the other
one—the one that was part of memory. I looked at the boy, who was silently
watching his fly, and it was my hands that held his rod, my eyes watching. I
felt dizzy and didn't know which rod I was at the end of.

We caught two bass, hauling them in briskly as though they were mackerel,   6
pulling them over the side of the boat in a businesslike manner without any
landing net, and stunning them with a blow on the back of the head. When
we got back for a swim before lunch, the lake was exactly where we had left it,
the same number of inches from the dock, and there was only the merest
suggestion of a breeze. This seemed an utterly enchanted sea, this lake you
could leave to its own devices for a few hours and come back to, and find that
it had not stirred, this constant and trustworthy body of water. In the shallows,
the dark, water-soaked sticks and twigs, smooth and old, were undulating in
clusters on the bottom against the clean ribbed sand, and the track of the
mussel was plain. A school of minnows swam by, each minnow with its small
individual shadow, doubling the attendance, so clear and sharp in the sunlight.
Some of the other campers were in swimming, along the shore, one of them
with a cake of soap, and the water felt thin and clear and unsubstantial. Over
the years there had been this person with the cake of soap, this cultist, and
here he was. There had been no years.

Up to the farmhouse to dinner through the teeming, dusty field, the road 7
under our sneakers was only a two-track road. The middle track was missing,
the one with the marks of the hooves and the splotches of dried, flaky manure.
There had always been three tracks to choose from in choosing which track to
walk in; now the choice was narrowed down to two. For a moment I missed
terribly the middle alternative. But the way led past the tennis court, and something about the way it lay there in the sun reassured me; the tape had loosened
along the backline, the alleys were green with plantains and other weeds, and
the net (installed in June and removed in September) sagged in the dry noon,
and the whole place steamed with midday heat and hunger and emptiness.
There was a choice of pie for dessert, and one was blueberry and one was
apple, and the waitresses were the same country girls, there having been no
passage of time, only the illusion of it as in a dropped curtain—the waitresses
were still fifteen; their hair had been washed, that was the only difference—
they had been to the movies and seen the pretty girls with the clean hair.

Summertime, oh, summertime, pattern of life indelible, the fade-proof lake, 8
the woods unshatterable, the pasture with the sweetfern and the juniper forever
and ever, summer without end; this was the background, and the life along the
shore was the design, the cottages with their innocent and tranquil design, their
tiny docks with the flagpole and the American flag floating against the white
clouds in the blue sky, the little paths over the roots of the trees leading from
camp to camp and the paths leading back to the outhouses and the can of lime
for sprinkling, and at the souvenir counters at the store the miniature birch-
bark canoes and the postcards that showed things looking a little better than
they looked. This was the American family at play, escaping the city heat,
wondering whether the newcomers in the camp at the head of the cove were
"common" or "nice," wondering whether it was true that the people who drove
up for Sunday dinner at the farmhouse were turned away because there wasn't
enough chicken.

It seemed to me, as I kept remembering all this, that those times and those 9
summers had been infinitely precious and worth saving. There had been jollity
and peace and goodness. The arriving (at the beginning of August) had been
so big a business in itself, at the railway station the farm wagon drawn up, the
first smell of the pine-laden air, the first glimpse of the smiling farmer, and the
great importance of the trunks and your father's enormous authority in such
matters, and the feel of the wagon under you for the long ten-mile haul, and
at the top of the last long hill catching the first view of the lake after eleven
months of not seeing this cherished body of water. The shouts and cries of the
other campers when they saw you, and the trunks to be unpacked, to give up
their rich burden. (Arriving was less exciting nowadays, when you sneaked up
in your car and parked it under a tree near the camp and took out the bags
and in five minutes it was all over, no fuss, no loud wonderful fuss about
trunks.)

Peace and goodness and jollity. The only thing that was wrong now, really, 10
was the sound of the place, an unfamiliar nervous sound of the outboard motors. This was the note that jarred, the one thing that would sometimes break

the illusion and set the years moving. In those other summertimes all motors were inboard; and when they were at a little distance, the noise they made was a sedative, an ingredient of summer sleep. They were one-cylinder and two-cylinder engines, and some were make-and-break and some were jump-spark, but they all made a sleepy sound across the lake. The one-lungers throbbed and fluttered, and the twin-cylinder ones purred and purred, and that was a quiet sound, too. But now the campers all had outboards. In the daytime, in the hot mornings, these motors made a petulant, irritable sound; at night, in the still evening when the afterglow lit the water, they whined about one's ears like mosquitoes. My boy loved our rented outboard, and his great desire was to achieve single-handed mastery over it, and authority, and he soon learned the trick of choking it a little (but not too much), and the adjustment of the needle valve. Watching him I would remember the things you could do with the old one-cylinder engine with the heavy flywheel, how you could have it eating out of your hand if you got really close to it spiritually. Motorboats in those days didn't have clutches, and you would make a landing by shutting off the motor at the proper time and coasting in with a dead rudder. But there was a way of reversing them, if you learned the trick, by cutting the switch and putting it on again exactly on the final dying revolution of the flywheel, so that it would kick back against compression and begin reversing. Approaching a dock in a strong following breeze, it was difficult to slow up sufficiently by the ordinary coasting method, and if a boy felt he had complete mastery over his motor, he was tempted to keep it running beyond its time and then reverse it a few feet from the dock. It took a cool nerve, because if you threw the switch a twentieth of a second too soon you would catch the flywheel when it still had speed enough to go up past center, and the boat would leap ahead, charging bull-fashion at the dock.

We had a good week at the camp. The bass were biting well and the sun shone endlessly, day after day. We would be tired at night and lie down in the accumulated heat of the little bedrooms after the long hot day and the breeze would stir almost imperceptibly outside and the smell of the swamp drift in through the rusty screens. Sleep would come easily and in the morning the red squirrel would be on the roof, tapping out his gay routine. I kept remembering everything, lying in bed in the mornings—the small steamboat that had a long rounded stern like the lip of a Ubangi, and how quietly she ran on the moonlight sails, when the older boys played their mandolins and the girls sang and we ate doughnuts dipped in sugar, and how sweet the music was on the water in the shining night, and what it had felt like to think about girls then. After breakfast we would go up to the store and the things were in the same place—the minnows in a bottle, the plugs and spinners disarranged and pawed over by the youngsters from the boys' camp, the Fig Newtons and the Beeman's gum. Outside, the road was tarred and cars stood in front of the store. Inside, all was just as it had always been, except there was more Coca-Cola and not so much Moxie and root beer and birch beer and sarsaparilla. We would walk out with the bottle of pop apiece and sometimes the pop would backfire up our

11

noses and hurt. We explored the streams, quietly, where the turtles slid off the sunny logs and dug their way into the soft bottom; and we lay on the town wharf and fed worms to the tame bass. Everywhere we went I had trouble making out which was I, the one walking at my side, the one walking in my pants.

One afternoon while we were there at the lake a thunderstorm came up. It   12
was like the revival of an old melodrama that I had seen long ago with childish awe. The second-act climax of the drama of the electrical disturbance over a lake in America had not changed in any important respect. This was the big scene, still the big scene. The whole thing was so familiar, the first feeling of oppression and heat and a general air around camp of not wanting to go very far away. In midafternoon (it was all the same) a curious darkening of the sky, and a lull in everything that had made life tick; and then the way the boats suddenly swung the other way at their moorings with the coming of a breeze out of the new quarter, and the premonitory rumble. Then the kettle drum, then the snare, then the bass drum and cymbals, then crackling light against the dark, and the gods grinning and licking their chops in the hills. Afterward the calm, the rain steadily rustling in the calm lake, the return of light and hope and spirits, and the campers running out in joy and relief to go swimming in the rain, their bright cries perpetuating the deathless joke about how they were getting simply drenched, and the children screaming with delight at the new sensation of bathing in the rain, and the joke about getting drenched linking the generations in a strong indestructible chain. And the comedian who waded in carrying an umbrella.

When the others went swimming, my son said he was going in, too. He   13
pulled his dripping trunks from the line where they had hung all through the shower and wrung them out. Languidly, and with no thought of going in, I watched him, his hard little body, skinny and bare, saw him wince slightly as he pulled up around his vitals the small, soggy, icy garment. As he buckled the swollen belt, suddenly my groin felt the chill of death.

QUESTIONS
1. White perceives himself as three different people in this essay. How does the author create that confusion of identity?   **2.**   The descriptive passages here create a sense of place. What other function do they serve?

WRITING TOPIC
In what sense is this essay as much about mortality as about a summer vacation?

The American Way of Death   1963

JESSICA MITFORD   [b. 1917]

O Death, where is thy sting? O grave, where is thy victory?[1] Where, indeed.   1
Many a badly stung survivor, faced with the aftermath of some relative's funeral, has ruefully concluded that the victory has been won hands down by a
funeral establishment—in disastrously unequal battle.

Much has been written of late about the affluent society in which we live,   2
and much fun poked at some of the irrational "status symbols" set out like
golden snares to trap the unwary consumer at every turn. Until recently, little
has been said about the most irrational and wierdest of the lot, lying in ambush
for all of us at the end of the road—the modern American funeral.

If the Dismal Traders (as an eighteenth-century English writer calls them)   3
have traditionally been cast in a comic role in literature, a universally recognized symbol of humor from Shakespeare to Dickens to Evelyn Waugh, they
have successfully turned the tables in recent years to perpetrate a huge, macabre and expensive practical joke on the American public. It is not consciously conceived of as a joke, of course; on the contrary, it is hedged with
admirably contrived rationalizations.

Gradually, almost imperceptibly, over the years the funeral men have con-   4
structed their own grotesque cloud-cuckooland where the trappings of Gracious
Living are transformed, as in a nightmare, into the trappings of Gracious Dying.
The same familiar Madison Avenue language, with its peculiar adjectival range
designed to anesthetize sales resistance to all sorts of products, has seeped into
the funeral industry in a new and bizarre guise. The emphasis is on the same
desirable qualities that we have all been schooled to look for in our daily search
for excellence: comfort, durability, beauty, craftsmanship. The attuned ear will
recognize too the convincing quasi-scientific language, so reassuring even if
unintelligible.

So that this too, too solid flesh might not melt, we are offered "solid cop-   5
per—a quality casket which offers superb value to the client seeking long-last-
ing protection," or "the Colonial Classic Beauty—18 gauge lead coated steel,
seamless top, lap-jointed welded body construction." Some are equipped with
foam rubber, some with innerspring mattresses. Elgin offers "the revolutionary
'Perfect-Posture' bed." Not every casket need have a silver lining, for one may
choose between "more than 60 color matched shades, magnificent and unique
masterpieces" by the Cheney casket-lining people. Shrouds no longer exist.
Instead, you may patronize a grave-wear couturière who promises "handmade
original fashions—styles from the best in life for the last memory—dresses,
men's suits, negligees, accessories." For the final, perfect grooming: "Nature-

---

[1] See First Corinthians 15:55.

768

Glo—the ultimate in cosmetic embalming." And, where have we heard the phrase "peace of mind protection" before? No matter. In funeral advertising, it is applied to the Wilbert Burial Vault, with its 3/8-inch precast asphalt inner liner plus extra-thick, reinforced concrete—all this "guaranteed by Good Housekeeping." Here again the Cadillac, status symbol par excellence, appears in all its gleaming glory, this time transformed into a pastel-colored funeral hearse.

You, the potential customer for all this luxury, are unlikely to read the lyri-   6
cal descriptions quoted above, for they are culled from *Mortuary Management* and *Casket and Sunnyside*, two of the industry's eleven trade magazines. For you there are ads in your daily newspaper, generally found on the obituary page, stressing dignity, refinement, high-caliber professional service and that intangible quality, *sincerity*. The trade advertisements are, however, instructive, because they furnish an important clue to the frame of mind into which the funeral industry has hypnotized itself.

A new mythology, essential to the twentieth-century American funeral rite,   7
has grown up—or rather has been built up step by step—to justify the peculiar customs surrounding the disposal of our dead. And, just as the witch doctor must be convinced of his own infallibility in order to maintain a hold over his clientele, so the funeral industry has had to "sell itself" on its articles of faith in the course of passing them along to the public.

The first of these is the tenet that today's funeral procedures are founded in   8
"American tradition." The story comes to mind of a sign on the freshly sown lawn of a brand-new Midwest college: "There is a tradition on this campus that students never walk on this strip of grass. This tradition goes into effect next Tuesday." The most cursory look at American funerals of past times will establish the parallel. Simplicity to the point of starkness, the plain pine box, the laying out of the dead by friends and family who also bore the coffin to the grave—these were the hallmarks of the traditional funeral until the end of the nineteenth century.

Secondly, there is the myth that the American public is only being given   9
what it wants—an opportunity to keep up with the Joneses to the end. "In keeping with our high standard of living, there should be an equally high standard of dying," says the past president of the Funeral Directors of San Francisco. "The cost of a funeral varies according to individual taste and the niceties of living the family has been accustomed to." Actually, choice doesn't enter the picture for the average individual, faced, generally for the first time, with the necessity of buying a product of which he is totally ignorant, at a moment when he is least in a position to quibble. In point of fact the cost of a funeral almost always varies, not "according to individual taste" but according to what the traffic will bear.

Thirdly, there is an assortment of myths based on half-digested psychiatric   10
theories. The importance of the "memory picture" is stressed—meaning the last glimpse of the deceased in open casket, done up with the latest in embalming techniques and finished off with a dusting of makeup. A newer one, im-

pressively authentic-sounding, is the need for "grief therapy," which is beginning to go over big in mortuary circles. A historian of American funeral directing hints at the grief-therapist idea when speaking of the new role of the undertaker—"the dramaturgic role, in which the undertaker becomes a stage manager to create an appropriate atmosphere and to move the funeral party through a drama in which social relationships are stressed and an emotional catharsis or release is provided through ceremony."

Lastly, a whole new terminology, as ornately shoddy as the satin rayon casket liner, has been invented by the funeral industry to replace the direct and serviceable vocabulary of former times. Undertaker has been supplanted by "funeral director" or "mortician." (Even the classified section of the telephone directory gives recognition to this; in its pages you will find "Undertakers—see Funeral Directors.") Coffins are "caskets"; hearses are "coaches," or "professional cars"; flowers are "floral tributes"; corpses generally are "loved ones," but mortuary etiquette dictates that a specific corpse be referred to by name only— as, "Mr. Jones"; cremated ashes are "cremains." Euphemisms such as "slumber room," "reposing room," and "calcination—the *kindlier* heat" abound in the funeral business.   11

If the undertaker is the stage manager of the fabulous production that is the modern American funeral, the stellar role is reserved for the occupant of the open casket. The decor, the stagehands, the supporting cast are all arranged for the most advantageous display of the deceased, without which the rest of the paraphernalia would lose its point—*Hamlet* without the Prince of Denmark. It is to this end that a fantastic array of costly merchandise and services is pyramided to dazzle the mourners and facilitate the plunder of the next of kin.   12

Grief therapy, anyone? But it's going to come high. According to the funeral industry's own figures, the *average* undertaker's bill in 1961 was $708 for casket and "services," to which must be added the cost of a burial vault, flowers, clothing, clergy and musician's honorarium, and cemetery charges. When these costs are added to the undertaker's bill, the total average cost for an adult's funeral is, as we shall see, closer to $1,450.   13

The question naturally arises, *is* this what most people want for themselves and their families? For several reasons, this has been a hard one to answer until recently. It is a subject seldom discussed. Those who have never had to arrange for a funeral frequently shy away from its implications, preferring to take comfort in the thought that sufficient unto the day is the evil thereof. Those who have acquired personal and painful knowledge of the subject would often rather forget about it. Pioneering "Funeral Societies" or "Memorial Associations," dedicated to the principle of dignified funerals at reasonable cost, have existed in a number of communities throughout the country, but their membership has been limited for the most part to the more sophisticated element in the population—university people, liberal intellectuals—and those who, like doctors and lawyers, come up against problems in arranging funerals for their clients.   14

Some indication of the pent-up resentment felt by vast numbers of people 15 against the funeral interests was furnished by the astonishing response to an article by Roul Tunley, titled "Can You Afford to Die?" in *The Saturday Evening Post* of June 17, 1961. As though a dike had burst, letters poured in from every part of the country to the *Post*, to the funeral societies, to local newspapers. They came from clergymen, professional people, old-age pensioners, trade unionists. Three months after the article appeared, an estimated six thousand had taken pen in hand to comment on some phase of the high cost of dying. Many recounted their own bitter experiences at the hands of funeral directors; hundreds asked for advice on how to establish a consumer organization in communities where none exists; others sought information about pre-need plans. The membership of the funeral societies skyrocketed. The funeral industry, finding itself in the glare of public spotlight, has begun to engage in serious debate about its own future course—as well it might.

Is the funeral inflation bubble ripe for bursting? A few years ago, the United 16 States public suddenly rebelled against the trend in the auto industry towards ever more showy cars, with their ostentatious and nonfunctional fins, and a demand was created for compact cars patterned after European models. The all-powerful auto industry, accustomed to *telling* the customer what sort of car he wanted, was suddenly forced to *listen* for a change. Overnight, the little cars became for millions a new kind of status symbol. Could it be that the same cycle is working itself out in the attitude towards the final return of dust to dust, that the American public is becoming sickened by ever more ornate and costly funerals, and that a status symbol of the future may indeed be the simplest kind of "funeral without fins"?

QUESTIONS

1. What four "articles of faith" does Mitford attribute to the funeral industry? **2.** In the final three paragraphs, Mitford speculates about what most people want. What assumptions does she put forward? Do you agree with her? Explain.

WRITING TOPIC

What other "costly and ornate" cultural customs would you consider open to ridicule? Imitating Mitford's approach and style, write an essay critical of "The American Way of ___." (Examples might include high school proms, weddings, football half-time shows, etc.)

The Discus Thrower

1977

RICHARD SELZER [b.1928]

I spy on my patients. Ought not a doctor to observe his patients by any means
and from any stance, that he might the more fully assemble evidence? So I
stand in the doorways of hospital rooms and gaze. Oh, it is not all that furtive
an act. Those in bed need only look up to discover me. But they never do.

From the doorway of Room 542 the man in the bed seems deeply tanned.
Blue eyes and close-cropped white hair give him the appearance of vigor and
good health. But I know that his skin is not brown from the sun. It is rusted,
rather, in the last stage of containing the vile repose within. And the blue eyes
are frosted, looking inward like the windows of a snowbound cottage. This man
is blind. This man is also legless—the right leg missing from midthigh down,
the left from just below the knee. It gives him the look of a bonsai, roots and
branches pruned into the dwarfed facsimile of a great tree.

Propped on pillows, he cups his right thigh in both hands. Now and then
he shakes his head as though acknowledging the intensity of his suffering. In
all of this he makes no sound. Is he mute as well as blind?

The room in which he dwells is empty of all possessions—no get-well cards,
small, private caches of food, day-old flowers, slippers, all the usual kickshaws
of the sickroom. There is only the bed, a chair, a nightstand, and a tray on
wheels that can be swung across his lap for meals.

"What time is it?" he asks.
"Three o'clock."
"Morning or afternoon?"
"Afternoon."
He is silent. There is nothing else he wants to know.
"How are you?" I say.
"Who is it?" he asks.
"It's the doctor. How do you feel?"
He does not answer right away.
"Feel?" he says.
"I hope you feel better," I say.
I press the button at the side of the bed.
"Down you go," I say.
"Yes, down," he says.
He falls back upon the bed awkwardly. His stumps, unweighted by legs and
feet, rise in the air, presenting themselves. I unwrap the bandages from the
stumps, and begin to cut away the black scabs and the dead, glazed fat with
scissors and forceps. A shard of white bone comes loose. I pick it away. I wash
the wounds with disinfectant and redress the stumps. All this while, he does

not speak. What is he thinking behind those lids that do not blink? Is he remembering a time when he was whole? Does he dream of feet? Of when his body was not a rotting log?

He lies solid and inert. In spite of everything, he remains impressive, as though he were a sailor standing athwart a slanting deck.   20

"Anything more I can do for you?" I ask.

For a long moment he is silent.

"Yes," he says at last and without the least irony. "You can bring me a pair of shoes."

In the corridor, the head nurse is waiting for me.

"We have to do something about him," she says. "Every morning he orders   25
scrambled eggs for breakfast, and, instead of eating them, he picks up the plate and throws it against the wall."

"Throws his plate?"

"Nasty. That's what he is. No wonder his family doesn't come to visit. They probably can't stand him any more than we can."

She is waiting for me to do something.

"Well?"

"We'll see," I say.   30

The next morning I am waiting in the corridor when the kitchen delivers his breakfast. I watch the aide place the tray on the stand and swing it across his lap. She presses the button to raise the head of the bed. Then she leaves.

In time the man reaches to find the rim of the tray, then on to find the dome of the covered dish. He lifts off the cover and places it on the stand. He fingers across the plate until he probes the eggs. He lifts the plate in both hands, sets it on the palm of his right hand, centers it, balances it. He hefts it up and down slightly, getting the feel of it. Abruptly, he draws back his right arm as far as he can.

There is the crack of the plate breaking against the wall at the foot of his bed and the small wet sound of the scrambled eggs dropping to the floor.

And then he laughs. It is a sound you have never heard. It is something new under the sun. It could cure cancer.

Out in the corridor, the eyes of the head nurse narrow.   35

"Laughed, did he?"

She writes something down on her clipboard.

A second aide arrives, brings a second breakfast tray, puts it on the night-stand, out of his reach. She looks over at me shaking her head and making her mouth go. I see that we are to be accomplices.

"I've got to feed you," she says to the man.

"Oh, no you don't," the man says.   40

"Oh, yes I do," the aide says, "after the way you just did. Nurse says so."

"Get me my shoes," the man says.

"Here's oatmeal," the aide says. "Open." And she touches the spoon to his lower lip.

"I ordered scrambled eggs," says the man.
"That's right," the aide says.   45
I step forward.
"Is there anything I can do?" I say.
"Who are you?" the man asks.

In the evening I go once more to that ward to make my rounds. The head nurse reports to me that Room 542 is deceased. She has discovered this quite by accident, she says. No, there had been no sound. Nothing. It's a blessing, she says.

I go into his room, a spy looking for secrets. He is still there in his bed. His   50
face is relaxed, grave, dignified. After a while, I turn to leave. My gaze sweeps the wall at the foot of the bed, and I see the place where it has been repeatedly washed, where the wall looks very clean and very white.

QUESTIONS
1. Why does the patient in Room 542 hurl his scrambled eggs against the wall?   **2.**   What unstated assumptions govern the nurse's attitude towards the dying man?

WRITING TOPICS
1.   Compare the characterization of this dying man with the characterization of Iván Ilých in Tolstoy's story.   **2.**   Analyze the essay's rhetorical devices with special attention to sentence structure, images, and understatement. How does Selzer's rhetoric contribute to this account of a patient's death?

To Hell with Dying   1967

ALICE WALKER   [b.1944]

"To hell with dying," my father would say. "These children want Mr. Sweet!"   1

Mr. Sweet was a diabetic and an alcoholic and a guitar player and lived   2
down the road from us on a neglected cotton farm. My older brothers and
sisters got the most benefit from Mr. Sweet, for when they were growing up he
had quite a few years ahead of him and so was capable of being called back
from the brink of death any number of times—whenever the voice of my father
reached him as he lay expiring. "To hell with dying, man," my father would
say, pushing the wife away from the bedside (in tears although she knew the
death was not necessarily the last one unless Mr. Sweet really wanted it to be).
"These children want Mr. Sweet!" And they did want him, for at a signal from
Father they would come crowding around the bed and throw themselves on
the covers, and whoever was the smallest at the time would kiss him all over
his wrinkled brown face and tickle him so that he would laugh all down in his
stomach, and his mustache, which was long and sort of straggly, would shake
like Spanish moss and was also that color.

Mr. Sweet had been ambitious as a boy, wanted to be a doctor or lawyer or   3
sailor, only to find that black men fare better if they are not. Since he could
become none of these things he turned to fishing as his only earnest career and
playing the guitar as his only claim to doing anything extraordinarily well. His
son, the only one that he and his wife, Miss Mary, had, was shiftless as the
day is long and spent money as if he were trying to see the bottom of the mint,
which Mr. Sweet would tell him was the clean brown palm of his hand. Miss
Mary loved her "baby," however, and worked hard to get him the "li'l necessaries" of life, which turned out mostly to be women.

Mr. Sweet was a tall, thinnish man with thick kinky hair going dead white.   4
He was dark brown, his eyes were squinty and sort of bluish, and he chewed
Brown Mule tobacco. He was constantly on the verge of being blind drunk,
for he brewed his own liquor and was not in the least a stingy sort of man, and
was always very melancholy and sad, though frequently when he was "feelin'
good" he'd dance around the yard with us, usually keeling over just as my
mother came to see what the commotion was.

Toward all of us children he was very kind, and had the grace to be shy with   5
us, which is unusual in grown-ups. He had great respect for my mother for
she never held his drunkenness against him and would let us play with him
even when he was about to fall in the fireplace from drink. Although Mr.
Sweet would sometimes lose complete or nearly complete control of his head
and neck so that he would loll in his chair, his mind remained strangely acute
and his speech not too affected. His ability to be drunk and sober at the same
time made him an ideal playmate, for he was as weak as we were and we could

usually best him in wrestling, all the while keeping a fairly coherent conversation going.

We never felt anything of Mr. Sweet's age when we played with him. We loved his wrinkles and would draw some on our brows to be like him, and his white hair was my special treasure and he knew it and would never come to visit us just after he had had his hair cut off at the barbershop. Once he came to our house for something, probably to see my father about fertilizer for his crops because, although he never paid the slightest attention to his crops, he liked to know what things would be best to use on them if he ever did. Anyhow, he had not come with his hair since he had just had it shaved off at the barbershop. He wore a huge straw hat to keep off the sun and also to keep his head away from me. But as soon as I saw him I ran up and demanded that he take me up and kiss me with his funny beard which smelled so strongly of tobacco. Looking forward to burying my small fingers into his woolly hair I threw away his hat only to find he had done something to his hair, that it was no longer there! I let out a squall which made my mother think that Mr. Sweet had finally dropped me in the well or something and from that day I've been wary of men in hats. However, not long after, Mr. Sweet showed up with his hair grown out and just as white and kinky and impenetrable as it ever was.

Mr. Sweet used to call me his princess, and I believed it. He made me feel pretty at five and six, and simply outrageously devastating at the blazing age of eight and a half. When he came to our house with his guitar the whole family would stop whatever they were doing to sit around him and listen to him play. He liked to play "Sweet Georgia Brown," that was what he called me sometimes, and also he liked to play "Caldonia" and all sorts of sweet, sad, wonderful songs which he sometimes made up. It was from one of these songs that I heard that he had had to marry Miss Mary when he had in fact loved somebody else (now living in Chi-ca-go, or De-stroy, Michigan). He was not sure that Joe Lee, her "baby," was also his baby. Sometimes he would cry and that was an indication that he was about to die again. And so we would all get prepared, for we were sure to be called upon.

I was seven the first time I remember actually participating in one of Mr. Sweet's "revivals"—my parents told me I had participated before, I had been the one chosen to kiss him and tickle him long before I knew the rite of Mr. Sweet's rehabilitation. He had come to our house, it was a few years after his wife's death, and was very sad, and also, typically, very drunk. He sat on the floor next to me and my older brother, the rest of the children were grown up and lived elsewhere, and began to play his guitar and cry. I held his woolly head in my arms and wished I could have been old enough to have been the woman he loved so much and that I had not been lost years and years ago.

When he was leaving, my mother said to us that we'd better sleep light that night for we'd probably have to go over to Mr. Sweet's before daylight. And we did. For soon after we had gone to bed one of the neighbors knocked on our door and called my father and said that Mr. Sweet was sinking fast and if he wanted to get in a word before the crossover he'd better shake a leg and get over to Mr. Sweet's house. All the neighbors knew to come to our house if something was wrong with Mr. Sweet, but they did not know how we always managed to make him well, or at least stop him from dying, when he was so often near death. As soon as we heard the cry we got up, my brother and I and my mother and father, and put on our clothes. We hurried out of the house and down the road for we were always afraid that we might someday be too late and Mr. Sweet would get tired of dallying.

When we got to the house, a very poor shack really, we found the front 10 room full of neighbors and relatives and someone met us at the door and said it was all very sad that old Mr. Sweet Little (for Little was his family name, although we mostly ignored it) was about to kick the bucket. My parents were advised not to take my brother and me into the "death room," seeing we were so young and all, but we were so much more accustomed to the death room than he that we ignored him and dashed in without giving his warning a second thought. I was almost in tears, for these deaths upset me fearfully, and the thought of how much depended on me and my brother (who was such a ham most of the time) made me very nervous.

The doctor was bending over the bed and turned back to tell us for at least 11 the tenth time in the history of my family that, alas, old Mr. Sweet Little was dying and that the children had best not see the face of implacable death (I didn't know what "implacable" was, but whatever it was, Mr. Sweet was not!). My father pushed him rather abruptly out of the way saying, as he always did and very loudly for he was saying it to Mr. Sweet, "To hell with dying, man, these children want Mr. Sweet"—which was my cue to throw myself upon the bed and kiss Mr. Sweet all around the whiskers and under the eyes and around the collar of his nightshirt where he smelled so strongly of all sorts of things, mostly liniment.

I was very good at bringing him around, for as soon as I saw that he was 12 struggling to open his eyes I knew he was going to be all right, and so could finish my revival sure of success. As soon as his eyes were open he would begin to smile and that way I knew that I had surely won. Once, though, I got a tremendous scare, for he could not open his eyes and later I learned that he had had a stroke and that one side of his face was stiff and hard to get into motion. When he began to smile I could tickle him in earnest because I was sure that nothing would get in the way of his laughter, although once he began to cough so hard that he almost threw me off his stomach, but that was when I was very small, little more than a baby, and my bushy hair had gotten in his nose.

When we were sure he would listen to us we would ask him why he was in 13 bed and when he was coming to see us again and could we play his guitar, which more than likely would be leaning against the bed. His eyes would get all misty and he would sometimes cry out loud, but we never let it embarrass us, for he knew that we loved him and that we sometimes cried too for no reason. My parents would leave the room to just the three of us; Mr. Sweet, by that time, would be propped up in bed with a number of pillows behind his head and with me sitting and lying on his shoulder and along his chest. Even when he had trouble breathing he would not ask me to get down. Looking into my eyes he would shake his white head and run a scratchy old finger all around my hairline, which was rather low down, nearly to my eyebrows, and made some people say I looked like a baby monkey.

My brother was very generous in all this, he let me do all the revivaling—   14
he had done it for years before I was born and so was glad to be able to pass it on to someone new. What he would do while I talked to Mr. Sweet was pretend to play the guitar, in fact pretend that he was a young version of Mr. Sweet, and it always made Mr. Sweet glad to think that someone wanted to be like him—of course, we did not know this then, we played the thing by ear, and whatever he seemed to like, we did. We were desperately afraid that he was just going to take off one day and leave us.

It did not occur to us that we were doing anything special; we had not   15
learned that death was final when it did come. We thought nothing of triumphing over it so many times, and in fact became a trifle contemptuous of people who let themselves be carried away. It did not occur to us that if our father had been dying we could not have stopped it, that Mr. Sweet was the only person over whom we had power.

When Mr. Sweet was in his eighties I was studying in the university many   16
miles from home. I saw him whenever I went home, but he was never on the verge of dying that I could tell and I began to feel that my anxiety for his health and psychological well-being was unnecessary. By this time he not only had a mustache but a long flowing snow-white beard, which I loved and combed and braided for hours. He was very peaceful, fragile, gentle, and the only jarring note about him was his old steel guitar, which he still played in the old sad, sweet, down-home blues way.

On Mr. Sweet's ninetieth birthday I was finishing my doctorate in Massa-   17
chusetts and had been making arrangements to go home for several weeks' rest. That morning I got a telegram telling me that Mr. Sweet was dying again and could I please drop everything and come home. Of course I could. My dissertation could wait and my teachers would understand when I explained to them when I got back. I ran to the phone, called the airport, and within four hours I was speeding along the dusty road to Mr. Sweet's.

The house was more dilapidated than when I was last there, barely a shack,   18
but it was overgrown with yellow roses which my family had planted many years ago. The air was heavy and sweet and very peaceful. I felt strange walking through the gate and up the old rickety steps. But the strangeness left me as I caught sight of the long white beard I loved so well flowing down the thin body over the familiar quilt coverlet. Mr. Sweet!

His eyes were closed tight and his hands, crossed over his stomach, were   19
thin and delicate, no longer scratchy. I remembered how always before I had run and jumped up on him just anywhere; now I knew he would not be able to support my weight. I looked around at my parents, and was surprised to see that my father and mother also looked old and frail. My father, his own hair

very gray, leaned over the quietly sleeping old man, who, incidentally, smelled still of wine and tobacco, and said, as he'd done so many times, "To hell with dying, man! My daughter is home to see Mr. Sweet!" My brother had not been able to come as he was in the war in Asia. I bent down and gently stroked the closed eyes and gradually they began to open. The closed, wine-stained lips twitched a little, then parted in a warm, slightly embarrassed smile. Mr. Sweet could see me and he recognized me and his eyes looked very spry and twinkly for a moment. I put my head down on the pillow next to his and we just looked at each other for a long time. Then he began to trace my peculiar hairline with a thin, smooth finger. I closed my eyes when his finger halted above my ear (he used to rejoice at the dirt in my ears when I was little), his hand stayed cupped around my cheek. When I opened my eyes, sure that I had reached him in time, his were closed.

Even at twenty-four how could I believe that I had failed? that Mr. Sweet   20
was really gone? He had never gone before. But when I looked at my parents I saw that they were holding back tears. They had loved him dearly. He was like a piece of rare and delicate china which was always being saved from breaking and which finally fell. I looked long at the old face, the wrinkled forehead, the red lips, the hands that still reached out to me. Soon I felt my father pushing something cool into my hands. It was Mr. Sweet's guitar. He had asked them months before to give it to me; he had known that even if I came next time he would not be able to respond in the old way. He did not want me to feel that my trip had been for nothing.

The old guitar! I plucked the strings, hummed "Sweet Georgia Brown." The   21
magic of Mr. Sweet lingered still in the cool steel box. Through the window I could catch the fragrant delicate scent of tender yellow roses. The man on the high old-fashioned bed with the quilt coverlet and the flowing white beard had been my first love.

QUESTIONS
1. How would you characterize Mr. Sweet? According to the author, what prevented him from being a more successful man?   **2.** This piece was published in a collection of short stories and is usually placed in the fiction section of books such as this. Does it seem to you a fictional account or an essay? Defend your answer.

WRITING TOPIC
Write a persuasive essay arguing that this piece is about love, not death.

The Presence of Death

QUESTIONS AND WRITING TOPICS

1. Although Gray's "Elegy Written in a Country Churchyard," Housman's "To an Athlete Dying Young," Ransom's "Bells for John Whiteside's Daughter," Auden's "In Memory of W. B. Yeats," and Roethke's "Elegy for Jane" employ different poetic forms, they all embody a poetic mode called *elegy*. Define *elegy* in terms of the characteristic tone of these poems. Compare the elegiac tone of these poems. **Writing Topic:** Compare the elagiac tone of one of these poems with the tone of Owen's "Dulce et Decorum Est" or Thomas's "Do Not Go Gentle into That Good Night."

2. What figurative language in the prose and poetry of this section is commonly associated with death itself? With dying? Contrast the characteristic imagery of this section with the characteristic imagery of love poetry. **Writing Topic:** Compare the imagery in Shakespeare's sonnet 18 (p.451) with the imagery in sonnet 73 (p.669).

3. In Tolstoy's "The Death of Iván Illých" and Donne's "Meditation XVII," death and dying are considered from a religious viewpoint. **Writing Topic:** Discuss whether these works develop a similar attitude toward death, or whether the attitudes they develop differ crucially.

4. State the argument against resignation to death made in Thomas's "Do Not Go Gentle into That Good Night." State the argument of Catherine Davis's reply, "After a Time." **Writing Topic:** Using these positions as the basis of your discussion, select for analysis two works that support Thomas's argument and two works that support Davis's.

5. Yevtushenko, in his poem "People," writes, "Not people die but worlds die in them." **Writing Topic:** Illustrate the meaning of this line with a discussion of Bierce's "An Occurrence at Owl Creek Bridge" or Katherine Anne Porter's "The Jilting of Granny Weatherall" or Arna Bontemps's "A Summer Tragedy" or E. B. White's "Once More to the Lake."

6. Discuss the attitude toward death developed in Larkin's poem "Aubade." **Writing Topic:** Contrast the treatment of death in "Aubade" with the treatment of death developed in any other work in this section.

7. Although Kopit's *End of the World* presents a grim picture of the human condition, it is often funny. What function does humor serve in the play? **Writing Topic:** Does the play embody a hopeful vision of the human condition? Discuss.

8. Contrast the attitudes toward death revealed in Donne's "Meditation XVII" and Selzer's "The Discus Thrower." **Writing Topic:** Analyze the figurative language and other stylistic elements in each essay. How does style account for the contrasting attitudes toward death expressed in these essays?

9. Which works in this section treat death and dying in a way that corresponds most closely with your own attitudes toward mortality? Which contradict your attitudes? **Writing Topic:** Isolate, in each case, the elements in the work responsible for your response and discuss them in terms of their "truth" or "falsity."

APPENDICES

The Vanity of the Artist's Dream, 1830 by Charles Bird King

APPENDICES

Poems About Poetry

Most of us would probably define poetry as a form of writing that employs rhyme and metrical regularity and deals with serious and "heavy" subjects (unless, of course, it's light verse). But you don't have to go further than the poems in this anthology to see that many poems do not use rhyme, have no metrical regularity, and deal with ordinary subjects in prosaic language. Maybe we can best define poetry (someone once did) as the kind of writing where the lines don't end at the same place on the right-hand side of the page. Here are a few poems about poetry, in which poets attempt to describe what it is, how it works, what it does, and why it does it.

Poetry   1921

MARIANNE MOORE   [1887–1972]

I, too, dislike it: there are things that are important beyond all
          this fiddle.
     Reading it, however, with a perfect contempt for it, one
          discovers in
     it after all, a place for the genuine.
          Hands that can grasp, eyes
          that can dilate, hair that can rise
               if it must, these things are important not because a

high-sounding interpretation can be put upon them but because
          they are   10
     useful. When they become so derivative as to become
          unintelligible,
     the same thing may be said for all of us, that we
          do not admire what
          we cannot understand: the bat
               holding on upside down or in quest of something to

eat, elephants pushing, a wild horse taking a roll, a tireless wolf
          under
     a tree, the immovable critic twitching his skin like a horse
          that feels a flea, the base-   20
     ball fan, the statistician—

> nor is it valid
>> to discriminate against 'business documents and
>
> school-books';[1] all these phenomena are important. One must
>> make a distinction
>> however: when dragged into prominence by half poets, the
>>> result is not poetry,
>> nor till the poets among us can be
>>> 'literalists of
>>> the imagination'—[2] above   30
>>>> insolence and triviality and can present
>
> for inspection, imaginary gardens with real toads in them, shall
>> we have
>> it. In the meantime, if you demand on the one hand,
>> the raw material of poetry in
>>> all its rawness and
>>> that which is on the other hand
>>>> genuine, then you are interested in poetry.

Pitcher   1960

ROBERT FRANCIS   [b. 1901]

His art is eccentricity, his aim
How not to hit the mark he seems to aim at,

His passion how to avoid the obvious,
His technique how to vary the avoidance.

The others throw to be comprehended. He
Throws to be a moment misunderstood.

Yet not too much. Not errant, arrant, wild,
But every seeming aberration willed.

Poetry
  [1] "Diary of Tolstoy (Dutton), p. 84. 'Where the boundary between prose and poetry lies, I shall never be able to understand. The question is raised in manuals of style, yet the answer to it lies beyond me. Poetry is verse; prose is not verse. Or else poetry is everything with the exception of business documents and school books' " [Moore's note].
  [2] "Yeats: *Ideas of Good and Evil* (A. H. Bullen), p. 182: 'The limitation of his view was from the very intensity of his vision; he was a too literal realist of imagination, as others are of nature; and because he believed that the figures seen by the mind's eye, when exalted by inspiration, were "eternal existences," symbols of divine essences, he hated every grace of style that might obscure their lineaments' " [Moore's note].

Not to, yet still, still to communicate
Making the batter understand too late.   10

QUESTIONS

1. The poem describes the art of the baseball pitcher. But the description is an extended metaphor for the art of the poet. Is the pitcher described accurately? **2.** Is the analogy between pitcher and poet apt? Explain.

Very Like a Whale   1945

OGDEN NASH [1902–1971]

One thing that literature would be greatly the better for
Would be a more restricted employment by authors of simile and metaphor.
Authors of all races, be they Greeks, Romans, Teutons or Celts,
Can't seem just to say that anything is the thing it is but have to go out of
    their way to say that it is like something else.
What does it mean when we are told
That the Assyrian came down like a wolf on the fold?[1]
In the first place, George Gordon Byron had had enough experience
To know that it probably wasn't just one Assyrian, it was a lot of Assyr-
    ians.
However, as too many arguments are apt to induce apoplexy and thus
    hinder longevity,
We'll let it pass as one Assyrian for the sake of brevity.   10
Now then, this particular Assyrian, the one whose cohorts were gleam-
    ing in purple and gold,
Just what does the poet mean when he says he came down like a wolf on
    the fold?
In heaven and earth more than is dreamed of in our philosophy there are
    a great many things,
But I don't imagine that among them there is a wolf with purple and gold
    cohorts or purple and gold anythings.
No, no, Lord Byron, before I'll believe that this Assyrian was actually
    like a wolf I must have some kind of proof;
Did he run on all fours and did he have a hairy tail and a big red mouth
    and big white teeth and did he say Woof woof?
Frankly I think it very unlikely, and all you were entitled to say, at the
    very most,

Very Like a Whale
    [1]Nash is responding to Lord Byron's "The Destruction of Sennacherib," a poetic account of the events in 2 Kings 19. Byron's poem appears on p. 1123.

Was that the Assyrian cohorts came down like a lot of Assyrian cohorts
    about to destroy the Hebrew host.
But that wasn't fancy enough for Lord Byron, oh dear me no, he had to
    invent a lot of figures of speech and then interpolate them,
With the result that whenever you mention Old Testament soldiers to
    people they say Oh yes, they're the ones that a lot of wolves dressed
    up in gold and purple ate them.   20
That's the kind of thing that's being done all the time by poets, from
    Homer to Tennyson;
They're always comparing ladies to lilies and veal to venison,
And they always say things like that the snow is a white blanket after a
    winter storm.
Oh it is, is it, all right then, you sleep under a six-inch blanket of snow
    and I'll sleep under a half-inch blanket of unpoetical blanket material
    and we'll see which one keeps warm,
And after that maybe you'll begin to comprehend dimly
What I mean by too much metaphor and simile.

A Poem about a Poem about a Poem

1961

ROBERT CONQUEST   [b. 1917]

". . . *often writes not about life but poetry*"—[a critic]

To gallop horses (or eat buns)
    Is Life, and may be Song,
(To sink drains or interpret dreams
Or listen to a Baby's screams)
But not to write a poem, it seems.
    That isn't Life, it's wrong.

And yet—at least I thought so once
    The time I wrote those lines—
To ride a verse is quite a thing,
(Sinking a rhyme, interpreting   10
The wordless cry, the concept's ring.
    The field of sensuous signs.)

But let the bays, the greys, the duns
    Go pounding round the course.
Stallions may sometimes turn vicious.

But art gets so damned meretricious.
Yes, horses are better than wishes:
>   I wish I had a horse.

Constantly Risking Absurdity   1958

LAWRENCE FERLINGHETTI [b. 1919]

>   Constantly risking absurdity
>   and death
>   whenever he performs
>   above the heads
>   of his audience
>   the poet like an acrobat
>   climbs on rime
>   to a high wire of his own making
> and balancing on eyebeams
>   above a sea of faces   10
>   paces his way
>   to the other side of day
>   performing entrechats
>   and sleight-of-foot tricks
> and other high theatrics
>   and all without mistaking
>   any thing
>   for what it may not be
>
>   For he's the super realist
>   who must perforce perceive   20
>   taut truth
>   before the taking of each stance or step
>   in his supposed advance
>   toward that still higher perch
> where Beauty stands and waits
>   with gravity
>   to start her death-defying leap
>
>   And he
>   a little charleychaplin man
>   who may or may not catch   30
>   her fair eternal form
>   spreadeagled in the empty air
>   of existence

The Writer   1976

RICHARD WILBUR   [b. 1921]

In her room at the prow of the house
Where light breaks, and the windows are tossed with linden,
My daughter is writing a story.

I pause in the stairwell, hearing
From her shut door a commotion of typewriter-keys
Like a chain hauled over a gunwale.

Young as she is, the stuff
Of her life is a great cargo, and some of it heavy:
I wish her a lucky passage.

But now it is she who pauses,   10
As if to reject my thought and its easy figure.
A stillness greatens, in which

The whole house seems to be thinking.
And then she is at it again with a bunched clamor
Of strokes, and again is silent.

I remember the dazed starling
Which was trapped in that very room, two years ago;
How we stole in, lifted a sash

And retreated, not to affright it;
And how for a helpless hour, through the crack of the door,   20
We watched the sleek, wild, dark

And iridescent creature
Batter against the brilliance, drop like a glove
To the hard floor, or the desk-top,

And wait then, humped and bloody,
For the wits to try it again; and how our spirits
Rose when, suddenly sure,

It lifted off from a chair-back,
Beating a smooth course for the right window
And clearing the sill of the world.   30

It is always a matter, my darling,
Of life or death, as I had forgotten. I wish
What I wished you before, but harder.

QUESTIONS
1. What is the relationship between the "dazed starling" and the young
writer?   **2.** What is the significance of the alternate clamor of the typewriter and
silence?   **3.** What does the speaker wish for his daughter?

WRITING TOPIC
How do the central metaphors of the poem, the ship (stanzas 1–3) and the bird (6–
10), convey the theme?

A Poet's Progress   1950

MICHAEL HAMBURGER   [b. 1924]

Like snooker balls thrown on the table's faded green,
Rare ivory and weighted with his best ambitions,
At first his words are launched: not certain what they mean,
He loves to see them roll, rebound, assume positions
Which—since not he—some power beyond him has assigned.

But now the game begins: dead players, living critics
Are watching him—and suddenly one eye goes blind,
The hand that holds the cue shakes like a paralytic's,
Till every thudding, every clinking sound portends
New failure, new defeat. Amazed, he finds that still   10
It is not he who guides his missiles to their ends
But an unkind geometry that mocks his will.

If he persists, for years he'll practise patiently,
Lock all the doors, learn all the tricks, keep noises out,
Though he may pick a ghost or two for company
Or pierce the room's inhuman silence with a shout.
More often silence wins; then soon the green felt seems
An evil playground, lawless, lost to time, forsaken,
And he a fool caught in the water weeds of dreams
Whom only death or frantic effort can awaken.   20

At last, a master player, he can face applause,
Looks for a fit opponent, former friends, emerges;
But no one knows him now. He questions his own cause,

And has forgotten why he yielded to those urges,
Took up a wooden cue to strike a coloured ball.
Wise now, he goes on playing; both his house and heart
Unguarded solitudes, hospitable to all
Who can endure the cold intensity of art.

For Saundra   1968

NIKKI GIOVANNI   [b. 1943]

i wanted to write
a poem
that rhymes
but revolution doesn't lend
itself to be-bopping

then my neighbor
who thinks i hate
asked—do you ever write
tree poems—i like trees
so i thought   10

i'll write a beautiful green tree poem
peeked from my window
to check the image
noticed the school yard was covered
with asphalt
no green—no trees grow
in manhattan

then, well, i thought the sky
i'll do a big blue sky poem

but all the clouds have winged   20
low since no-Dick[1] was elected

so i thought again
and it occurred to me
maybe i shouldn't write
at all

For Saundra
  [1] A derogatory reference to Richard Nixon.

but clean my gun
and check my kerosene supply

perhaps these are not poetic
times
at all   30

Today Is a Day of Great Joy   1968

VICTOR HERNANDEZ CRUZ   [b. 1949]

when they stop poems
in the mail & clap
their hands & dance to
them
when women become pregnant
by the side of poems
the strongest sounds making
the river go along

it is a great day

as poems fall down to   10
movie crowds in restaurants
in bars

when poems start to
knock down walls to
choke politicians
when poems scream &
begin to break the air

that is the time of
true poets that is
the time of greatness   20

a true poet aiming
poems & watching things
fall to the ground

it is a great day.

Reading Fiction

An author is a god, creator of the world he or she describes. That world has a limited and very special landscape. It is peopled with men and women of a particular complexion, of particular gifts and failings. Its history, almost always, is determined by the tight interaction of its people within its narrow geography. Everything that occurs in a work of fiction—every figure, every tree, every furnished room and crescent moon and dreary fog—has been *purposely* put there by its creator. When a story pleases, when it moves its reader, he has responded to that carefully created world. The pleasure, the emotional commitment, the human response are not results of analysis. The reader has not registered in some mental adding machine the several details that establish character, the particular appropriateness of the weather to the events in the story, the marvelous rightness of the furnishings, the manipulation of the point of view, the plot, the theme, the style. He or she has recognized and accepted the world of the author and has been delighted (or saddened or made angry) by what happens in it.

But how does it come about that readers recognize the artificial worlds, often quite different from their own, that authors create? And why is it that readers who recognize some fictional worlds effortlessly are bewildered and lost in other fictional worlds? Is it possible to extend the boundaries of readers' recognition? Can more and more of the landscapes and societies of fiction be made available to that onlooking audience?

The answer to the first of these questions is easy. Readers are comfortable in literary worlds that, however exotic the landscapes and the personalities that people them, incorporate moral imperatives which reflect the value system in the readers' world. Put another way, much fiction ends with its virtuous characters rewarded and its villains punished. This we speak of as poetic justice. Comedies, and most motion pictures of the recent past, end this way. But such endings are illustrations of poetic justice, and *poetic* seems to suggest that somehow such endings are ideal rather than "real." Not much experience of life is required to recognize that injustice, pain, frustration, and downright villainy often prevail, that the beautiful young girl and the strong, handsome hero do not always overcome all obstacles, marry, and live happily ever after, that not every man is strong and handsome nor every woman beautiful. But readers, knowing that, respond to tragic fiction as well—where virtue is defeated, where obstacles prove too much for the men and women, where ponderous forces result in defeat, even death. Unhappy outcomes are painful to contemplate, but it is not difficult to recognize the world in which they occur. That world is much like our own. And unhappy outcomes serve to emphasize the very ideals which we have established in this world as the aims and goals of human activity. Consequently, both the "romantic" comedies that gladden with justice and success and the "realistic" stories that end in defeat provide readers with recognizable and available emotional worlds, however exotic the settings and the characters in those stories might be.

If we look at fiction this way, the answer to the question "Why is it that some readers are bewildered and lost in some fictional worlds?" is clearly implied. Some fictional worlds *seem* to incorporate a strange set of moral imperatives. Readers are not altogether certain who are the virtuous characters and who are the villains or even what constitutes virtue and evil. Sometimes tragic oppositions in a fictional world that brooks no compromise puzzle readers who live in a world where compromise has become almost a virtue. Sometimes, particularly in more recent fiction that reflects the ever-widening influence of psychoanalytic theory, the landscape and the behavior of characters is designed to represent deep interiors, the less-than-rational hearts and minds of characters. Those weird interiors are not part of the common awareness of readers; the moral questions raised there are not the same moral questions that occupy most of our waking hours. Such fictional worlds are difficult to map, and bewildered readers may well reject these underworlds for the sunshine of the surfaces they know more immediately.

Studying Literature

It might be useful to distinguish here between overlapping kinds of discussion that seek to explain the effectiveness of a piece of writing. *Literary history* deals with literature as the product of a particular time and place. Certain genres that were popular and universally accessible in medieval times—religious allegory, for instance—are remote today unless they are read in historical perspective. Also, many authors have been influenced measurably by their predecessors, and an understanding of a derivative work's literary antecedents can contribute to a reader's appreciation of it. Features of Elizabethan culture and theatrical conventions established by early Renaissance drama, for example, illuminate many obscure passages in Shakespeare's plays. (Most of the glosses and footnotes in this book provide readers with historical information—the meaning of an archaic word, the attributes of a mythological character, or the significance of an allusion to an earlier literary work.) For modern readers, such information can often revive a "dead" work. Nonetheless, interpreting obscure clues, however important they may be for textual explication, is not *literary criticism*.

Although he or she may rely on the work of the literary historian (and may well be a literary historian), the critic's role is to evaluate literature. Criticism divides into two major branches—theory and practice. The basic question that *theoretical criticism* asks is "What constitutes literary merit?," and the theoretical critic attempts to define a set of *criteria* by which any literary work may be judged.

Practical criticism, on the other hand, asks of specific works "Are they saying well what they wish to say?" The practical critic adopts the criteria of a theoretical position and measures particular pieces of literature against these standards to determine, primarily, whether the works in question are good or bad, major or minor. In the section "Three Critical Approaches" that follows, we illustrate the application of three critical theories to a story and a poem.

Theories, of course, change, and the history of criticism reflects shifting tastes and cultural values. These changes may themselves influence the direction of creative art. Nonetheless, regardless of practical critics' theoretical criteria, to determine the quality of a literary work they must examine the *craft* that an author has brought to it; they must determine how an author manipulates language and theme to create something that affects the reader. Both literary history and criticism make particular use of this technical vocabulary in discussing form and the features that shape it.

Literary criticism frequently trespasses into nonliterary disciplines—notably psychology and sociology—for theory and subsequent practice. Although any reader, however unconsciously, responds to the effect of an author's craft, for the critic to assert that certain combinations of ideas will invariably generate the same response in the sensitive reader is a dangerous business. What are we to make of the spectacle of two critics, or two teachers, testifying that the same story affects them quite differently? Is one of them wrong? Are both of them wrong? Perhaps, but we do the best we can, and we use all the varieties of human experience that authors and critics and theoreticians share in an attempt to respond significantly to significant literature.

Fiction and Reality

Why do people read fiction (or go to movies)? The question is not so easy to answer as one might suppose. The first response is likely to have something to do with "amusement" or "entertainment." But you have doubtless read stories and novels (or seen movies) that end tragically. Is it accurate to say that they were amusing or entertaining? Is it entertaining to be sad or to be made angry by the defeat of "good" people? Or does the emotional impact of such stories somehow enlarge our own humanity? Fiction teaches its readers by providing them a vast range of experience that they could not acquire otherwise. Especially for the relatively young, conceptions of love, of success in life, of war, of malignant evil and cleansing virtue are learned from fiction—not from life. And herein lies a great danger, for literary artists are notorious liars, and their lies frequently become the source of people's convictions about human nature and human society.

To illustrate, a huge number of television series based on the exploits of the FBI, or the Miami police force, or the dedicated surgeons at the general hospital, or the young lawyers always end with a capture, with a successful (though dangerous) operation, with justice triumphant. But, in the real world, police are able to resolve only about 10 percent of reported crime, disease ravages, and economic and political power often extends into the courtroom. The very existence of such television drama bespeaks a yearning that things should be different; their heroes are heroic in that they regularly overcome those obstacles that we all experience but that, alas, we do not overcome.

Some writers, beginning about the middle of the nineteenth century, were particularly incensed at the real damage which a lying literature promotes, and they devoted their energies to exposing and counteracting the lies of the novelists, particularly those lies that formed attitudes about what constituted human success and happiness. Yet that popular fiction, loosely called *escapist*, is still most widely read for reasons that would probably fill several studies in social psychology. It needs no advocate. The fiction in this book, on the other hand, has been chosen largely because it does not lie about life—at least it does not lie about life in the ordinary way. And the various authors employ a large variety of literary methods and modes in an effort to illuminate the deepest wells of human experience. Consequently, many of these stories do not retail high adventure (though some do), since an adventurous inner life does not depend on an incident-filled outer life. Some stories, like Porter's "The Jilting of Granny Weatherall," might almost be said to be about what does *not* happen rather than what does—not-happening being as much incident, after all, as happening.

All fiction attempts to be interesting, to involve the reader in situations, to force some aesthetic response from him—most simply put and, in the widest sense of the word, to entertain. Some fiction aspires to nothing more. Other fiction seeks, as well, to establish some truth about the nature of man—Tolstoy's "The Death of Iván Ilých" and Hemingway's "A Clean, Well-Lighted Place" ask the reader to perceive the inner life of central figures. Some fiction seeks to explore the relationships among people—Faulkner's "Dry September" and Lawrence's "The Horse Dealer's Daughter" depend for their force on the powerful interaction of one character with another. Still other fiction seeks to explore the connection between people and society—Ellison's " 'Repent, Harlequin!' Said the Ticktockman" acquires its force from the implied struggle between people seeking a free and rich emotional life and the tyrannically ordering society that would sacrifice their humanity to some ideal of social efficiency.

We have been talking about that aspect of fiction which literary theorists identify as *theme*. Theorists also talk about plot, characterization, setting, point of view, and conflict—all terms naming aspects of fiction that generally have to do with the author's technique. Let us here deal with one story—James Joyce's "Araby." Read it. Then compare your private responses to the story with what we hope will be helpful and suggestive remarks about the methods of fiction.

The Methods of Fiction

One can perceive only a few things simultaneously and can hardly respond to everything contained in a well-wrought story all at once. Upon finishing the story, the reader likely thinks back, makes adjustments, and reflects on the significance of things before reaching that set of emotional and intellectual experiences that we have been calling *response*. Most readers of short stories respond first to what may be called the *tone* of the opening lines. Now tone is an aspect of literature about which it is particularly difficult to talk, because it is an aura—a shimmering and shifting atmosphere that depends for its substance on rather delicate emotional responses to language and situation. Surely, before learning anything at all about the plot of "Araby," the reader has experienced a tone.

> North Richmond Street, being blind, was a quiet street except at the hour when
> the Christian Brothers' School set the boys free. An uninhabited house of two

storeys stood at the blind end, detached from its neighbors in a square ground. The other houses of the street, conscious of decent lives within them, gazed at one another with brown imperturbable faces.

Is the scene gay? Vital and active? Is this opening appropriate for a story that goes on to celebrate joyous affirmations about life and living? You should answer these questions negatively. Why? Because the dead end street is described as "blind," because the Christian Brothers' School sounds much like a prison (it sets the boys free), because a vacant house fronts the dead end, because the other houses, personified, are conscious of decent lives within (a mildly ironic description—*decent* suggesting ordinary, thin-lipped respectability rather than passion or heroism), because those houses gaze at one another with "brown imperturbable faces"—*brown* being nondescript, as opposed, say, to scarlet, gold, bright blue, and *imperturbable faces* reinforcing the priggish decency within.

Compare this opening from Faulkner's "Dry September":

> Through the bloody September twilight, aftermath of sixty-two rainless days, it had gone like fire in a dry grass—the rumor, the story, whatever it was. Something about Miss Minnie Cooper and a Negro.

The tone generated by "bloody twilight," "rainless days," "fire in a dry grass" is quite different from the blind, brown apathy of "Araby." And unsurprisingly, Faulkner's story involves movement to a horrifying violence. "Araby," on the other hand, is a story about the dawning of awareness in the mind and heart of the child of one of those decent families in brown and blind North Richmond Street. Tone, of course, permeates all fiction, and it may change as the narrative develops. Since short stories generally reveal change, the manipulation of tone is just one more tool used in the working of design.

Short stories, of course, are short, but this fact implies some serious considerations. In some ways, a large class of good short fiction deals with events that may be compared to the tip of the proverbial iceberg. The events animating the story represent only a tiny fraction of the characters' lives and experiences; yet, that fraction is terribly important and provides the basis for wide understanding both to the characters within the story and to its readers. In "Araby," the plot, the connected sequence of events, may be simply stated. A young boy who lives in a rather drab, respectable neighborhood develops a crush on the sister of one of his playmates. She asks him if he intends to go to a charity fair that she cannot attend. He resolves to go and purchase a gift for her. He is tormented by the late and drunken arrival of his uncle who has promised him the money he needs. When the boy finally arrives at the bazaar, he is disappointed by the difference between his expectation and the actuality of the almost deserted fair. He perceives some minor events, overhears some minor conversation, and finally sees himself "as a creature driven and derided by vanity." Yet this tiny stretch of experience out of the life of the boy introduces him to an awareness about the differences between imagination and reality, between his romantic infatuation and the vulgar reality all about him. We are talking now about what is called the *theme* of the story. Emerging from the workaday events that constitute its plot is a general statement about intensely idealized childish "love," the shattering recognition of the false sentimentality that occasions it, and the enveloping vulgarity of adult life. The few pages of the story, by detailing a few events out of a short period of the protagonist's life, illuminate one aspect of the loss of innocence that we all endure and that is always painful. In much of the literature in the section on innocence and experience, the protagonists learn painfully the moral complexities of a world that had once seemed uncomplicated and predictable. That education does not always occur, as in "Araby," at an early age, either in literature or life.

Certainly theme is a centrally important aspect of prose fiction, but "good" themes do not necessarily ensure good stories. One may write a wretched story with the same theme as "Araby." What, then, independent of theme, is the difference between good stories and bad stories? Instinctively you know how to answer this question. Good stories, to begin with, are interesting; they present characters you care about; however fantastic, they are yet somehow plausible; they project a moral world you recognize. One of the obvious differences between short stories and novels requires that story writers develop character rapidly and limit the number of developed characters. Many stories have only one fleshed character; the other characters are frequently two-dimensional projections or even stereotypes. We see their surface only, not their souls. Rarely does a short story have more than three developed characters. Again, unlike novels, short stories usually work themselves out in restricted geographical setting, in a single place, and within a rather short period of time.

We often speak of character, setting, plot, theme, and style as separate aspects of a story in order to break down a complex narrative into more manageable parts. But it is important to understand that this analytic process of separating various elements is something we have done to the story—the story (if it is a good one) is an integrated whole. The closer we examine the separate elements, the clearer it becomes that each is integrally related to the others.

It is part of the boy's character that he lives in a brown imperturbable house in North Richmond Street, that he does the things he does (which is, after all, the plot), that he learns what he does (which is the theme), and that all of this characterization emerges from Joyce's rich and suggestive style. Consider this paragraph:

> Her image accompanied me even in places the most hostile to romance. On Saturday evenings when my aunt went marketing I had to go to carry some of the parcels. We walked through the flaring streets, jostled by drunken men and bargaining women, amid the curses of labourers, the shrill litanies of shop-boys who stood on guard by the barrels of pigs' cheeks, the nasal chanting of street-singers, who sang a *come-all-you* about O'Donovan Rossa, or a ballad about the troubles in our native land. These noises converged in a single sensation of life for me: I imagined that I bore my chalice safely through a throng of foes. Her name sprang to my lips at moments in strange prayers and praises which I myself did not understand. My eyes were often full of tears (I could not tell why) and at times a flood from my heart seemed to pour itself out into my bosom. I thought little of the future. I did not know whether I would ever speak to her or not or, if I spoke to her, how I could tell her of my confused adoration. But my body was like a harp and her words and gestures were like fingers running upon the wires.

This paragraph furthers the plot. But it suggests much more. The boy thinks of his friend's sister even when he carries parcels for his aunt during the shopping trips through a crowded and coarse part of town. In those coarse market streets the shop-boys cry shrill "litanies," the girl's name springs to his lips in strange "prayers and praises," and the boy confesses a confused "adoration." Further, he bears "his chalice safely through a throng of foes." Now the words *litanies, prayers, praises, adoration* all come from a special vocabulary that is easy to identify. It is the vocabulary of the church. The *chalice* and the *throng of foes* come from the vocabulary of chivalric romance, which is alluded to in the first line of the quoted paragraph. Joyce's diction evokes a sort of holy chivalry that characterizes the boy on this otherwise altogether ordinary shopping trip. This paragraph suggests to the careful reader that the boy has cast his awakening sexuality in a mold that mixes the disparate shapes of the heroic knight, winning his lady by force of arms, and the ascetic penitent, adoring the holy virgin, mother of god.

Playing the word game, of course, can be dangerous. But from the beginning of this story to its end, a certain religious quality shimmers. That now-dead priest of the story's second paragraph had three books (at least). One is a romantic chivalric novel by Sir Walter Scott; one is a sensational account of the adventures of a famous criminal-turned-detective; one is what a priest might be expected to have at hand—an Easter week devotional guide. That priest who read Scott novels might have understood the boy's response—that mixture of religious devotion and romance. Shortly after the shopping trip, the boy finally speaks to the girl, and it is instructive to see her as he does. He stands at the *railings* and looks up (presumably) at her, she bowing her head towards him. "The light from the lamp opposite our door caught the white curve of her neck, lit up her hair that rested there and, falling, lit up the hand upon the railing. It fell over one side of her dress and caught the white border of a petticoat, just visible as she stood at ease." Skip the petticoat, for a moment. Might the description of Mangan's sister remind the careful reader of quite common sculptured representations of the Virgin Mary? But the petticoat! And the white curve of her neck! This erotic overlay characterizes the boy's response. The sexuality is his own; the chivalry, the religious adoration, comes from the culture in which he is immersed—comes from Scott, the ballads sung in the market place, the "Arab's Farewell to his Steed" that the boy's uncle threatens to recite. And it is the culture that so romanticizes and elevates the boy's yearning.

He finally gets to Araby—"the syllables of the word . . . were called to [him] through the silence in which [his] soul luxuriated and cast an Eastern enchantment over [him]." His purpose is to serve his lady—to bring her something from that exotic place. What he finds is a weary-looking man guarding a turnstile, the silence that pervades a church after a service, and two men counting money on a salver (that tray is called a *salver* by design). And in this setting he overhears a young lady flirting with two gentlemen:

"O, I never said such a thing!"
"O, but you did!"

"O, but I didn't!"
"Didn't she say that?"
"Yes, I heard her."
"O, there's a . . . fib!"

This is Araby, this is love in a darkened hall where money is counted. Is it any wonder that the boy, in the moment of personal illumination that Joyce calls an epiphany, sees himself as a creature driven and derided by vanity?

"Araby" is a careful, even a delicate story. Nothing much happens—what does occurs largely in the boy's perception and imagination. The story focuses on the boy's confusion of sexual attraction with the lofty sentiments of chivalry and religion. The climax occurs when he confronts the darkened, money-grubbing fair and the banal expression of the sexual attraction between the gentlemen and the young lady. The result is a sudden deflation of the boy's ego, his sense of self, as he recognizes his own delusions about the nature of love and the relationship between men, women, heroism, God, and money.

We would like to conclude with a discussion of one feature of fiction that sometimes proves troublesome to developing readers. Often the events of a story, upon which much depends, puzzle or annoy readers. Why does that fool do that? Why doesn't X simply tell Y the way he feels and then the tragedy would be averted? In a sense, such responses reflect the intrusion of a reader into the world of the story. The reader, a sensible and sensitive person, understands some things about life after all and is oppressed by the characters' inability to understand at least as much. Characters choose to die when they might with a slight adjustment live. They risk danger when with a slight adjustment they might proceed safely. They suffer the pain of an unfortunate marriage when with a little trouble they might be free to live joyously. If the "whys" issuing from the reader are too insistent, too sensible, then the story must fail, at least for that reader. But many "whys" are not legitimate. Many are intrusions of the reader's hindsight, the reader's altogether different cultural and emotional fix. Henry James urged that authors must be allowed their *donnée*, their "given." They create the societies and the rules by which they operate within their own fictional worlds. Sometimes this creation is so close to the reader's own world that it is hardly possible to object. Those who have grown up in a small southern town will recognize the atmosphere of Faulkner's "Dry September." But few readers of this book know 1895 Dublin and Irish middle-class society, which plays a brooding role in "Araby" (as it does in almost all of Joyce's work). None know the futuristic world of Harlan Ellison's Harlequin. In every case, we must finally imagine those worlds, even where setting is familiar. If we cannot, the events that take place in them will be of no consequence. If those worlds are unimaginable, then the stories must fail. If they strain belief or remain foreign to the reader's heart, they must likewise fail. But all response to fiction depends on the reader's acquiescence to the world of the author and his or her perceptions of the moral consequences of acts and attitudes in that world. At best, that acquiescence will provide much pleasure as well as emotional insight into the reader's own existence.

Reading Poetry

For many people, the question "What is poetry?" is irrelevant if not irreverent. The attempt to answer such a question leads to abstract intellectual analysis, the very opposite of the emotional pleasure one seeks in a good poem. Why does it matter what poetry is so long as readers enjoy poems? Doesn't the attempt to define the nature of poetry lead to technical analysis of poetic devices so that study, finally, destroys pleasure?

These are valid issues that touch on very real dangers. If the study of poetry bogs down in theoretical or historical issues and the study of a poem becomes a mere exercise in the identification and discussion of poetic devices, the reader may well find that reading a poem is more effort than pleasure. He or she may begin to feel like the many nineteenth-century poets who complained that science, in laying bare the laws of nature, robbed the universe of its ancient awe and mystery. Walt Whitman, for example, describes such a feeling in his poem "When I Heard the Learn'd Astronomer."

> When I heard the learn'd astronomer,
> When the proofs, the figures, were ranged in columns before me,
> When I was shown the charts and diagrams, to add, divide, and measure them,
> When I sitting heard the astronomer where he lectured with much applause in
>   the lecture-room,
> How soon unaccountable I became tired and sick,
> Till rising and gliding out I wander'd off by myself,
> In the mystical moist night-air, and from time to time,
> Look'd up in perfect silence at the stars.

The distinction implicit in Whitman's poem between the mind (intellectual knowledge) and the heart (emotion and feelings) is very old, but still a useful one. All of us have no doubt felt at some time that the overexercise of the mind interfered with our capacity to feel. Compelled to analyze, dissect, categorize, and classify, we finally yearn for the simple and "mindless" pleasure of unanalytical enjoyment, the pleasure of sensuous experience. But we derive pleasure in a variety of ways, and while we needn't assert a *necessary* connection between understanding and pleasure, understanding can enhance pleasure. The distinction between the mind and the heart is, after all, a fiction or metaphor that cannot be pushed too far before it breaks down. Readers may very well enjoy Dylan Thomas's "Fern Hill" without understanding Thomas's use of symbolism of color or religious imagery. But understanding that symbolism and imagery will certainly deepen the pleasure derived from the poem.

We don't mean to suggest by all this that every poem needs to be studied in detail or that it is possible to say in the abstract what kind and amount of study will be rewarding. Some poems are straightforward, requiring little by way of analysis; others, dense and complex, seem to yield little without some study. But study of even the simplest poems can be rewarding. (Consider the effect of the special vocabulary implied by such words as "arrayed," "imperially," "crown," and "glittered" in Edwin Arlington Robinson's "Richard Cory.") On the other hand, it is possible to be moved on first reading by the tone and quality of such complex poems as Wallace Stevens's "Sunday Morning" and T. S. Eliot's "The Love Song of J. Alfred Prufrock" even though they are difficult to understand immediately.

As to our original question—What is poetry?—we cannot offer anything like a definitive and comprehensive answer. Poetry is a form of writing that often employs rhyme, a regular rhythm, unusual word order, and an intense or heightened language. This formal definition will serve about as well as any although it is by no means comprehensive, as any collection of poems will readily demonstrate. Up to about a century ago, poetry was governed by rather precise and often elaborate rules and conventions; if a poem did not use rhyme, it certainly was characterized by rhythmic regularity, or meter. Further, there existed a long tradition of poetic types (epic, elegiac, odic, etc.), each with quite specific rules and characteristics. While these traditions still retain some force, the old notion that these forms are part of the natural scheme of things has been largely abandoned. No one insists that the form of writing we call poetry must exhibit a combination of fixed characteristics.

Consider poetry from a different angle and ask not what poetry is but rather what functions it serves. Poetry fulfills some deep and abiding need of ours, for no culture we know of has been without it. We know also that in ancient societies, before the advent of science and technology in the modern sense, the arts were not divided by types or differentiated from science. In ancient tribal societies, poetry, dance, sculpture, and painting might all be parts of a tribal ceremony designed to propitiate the gods and thereby ensure a full harvest or a successful hunt. Poetry, then, was part of a primitive (we would now label it "superstitious") science that defined and helped control the external world. Though one can only guess in these matters, it is probably safe to assume that in such a primitive society the inner emotional world of the individual was not sharply distinguished from the outer world of nature. Nature and the gods who controlled it might be harsh and unpredictable, and the function of ritual was to control and appease these gods (to ensure rain, for example). But ritual also nurtured and strengthened the individual's communal spirit and conditioned his feelings about the arduous work that the life of the tribe required.

The conditions of our lives are, of course, vastly different. We operate within an enormous industrialized society that developed over centuries as people abandoned primitive explanations of the universe and sought others. One result of that development was a continuing differentiation and specialization of human endeavors, as science broke away from art and both divided into separate if related disciplines. Science became astronomy, biology, physics, and the like, while art branched into various types of aesthetic creation. And it was modern science, not poetry or the other arts, that produced profound and measurable changes in human life. Poetry might movingly and memorably remind us of the sorrow of unrequited love or the ravages of growing old, but science created a technology that produced undreamed of material wealth and power.

Is the very persistence of poetry evidence that it serves some important function, however obscure? On the other hand, maybe poetry is merely a vestigial organ of evolution that, like the appendix, continues to exist even though it has outlived its usefulness. Certainly, the historical process we have sketched here seems to involve a gradual diminution in the importance we attach to poetry.

It would be misleading, of course, to suggest that the scientist and the poet exist in separate worlds. But the differences between them are important. The truth that science seeks is the truth of physical reality. Social sciences such as psychology, sociology, and economics have attempted to demonstrate that human behavior can be understood in terms of a set of definite and quantifiable mechanisms. And, though no one would assert that science has achieved final answers, it is clear that the spectacular discoveries of science have left many, Walt Whitman among them, with the feeling that our importance in the universe has diminished. Further, modern physical science has uncovered a disturbing indeterminateness and asymmetry in the universe that have far-reaching philosophical implications not only for science but for society as a whole. As the old scientific verities crumble, so, too, do the old social verities.

Science may describe and educate us about the outer world and its inexorable laws with as rigorous an objectivity and neutrality as it can achieve. It may explain to us that in a naturalistic world death comes to all living creatures or that sunsets result from certain physical phenomena; but it is silent on the terror of death and its human or emotional meaning or on the beauty of a sunset. To understand those emotions, to give them form and meaning, we turn to poetry—we read it and, perhaps, even write it. For poetry, so to speak, educates our emotions and our feelings, allows us to learn who we are and to articulate what we feel.

We might wonder whether such an assertion makes sense. What we feel, we feel. We don't need a poem to tell us that. Not so. Often we don't know what we feel except in a vague and inarticulate way. A powerful poem articulates and thereby clarifies. Further, a poem may even deepen feelings. Although the literary historian might correctly observe that it is an academic exercise in wit, Andrew Marvell's poem "To His Coy Mistress" may well help the reader understand his own feelings about physical love and mortality. The outrageous absurdity of death cutting down a person whose life has barely begun is articulated in Robert Frost's " 'Out, Out—' " and John Crowe Ransom's "Bells for John Whiteside's Daughter." The confusion that often attends the powerful emotions generated by love and death is arrested by the poet who provides order.

Poetry at its highest and most general level is a form of communication, a means of defining, affirming, and deepening its reader's humanity. This is not to say that one should approach poetry solemnly, expecting always to be loftily enlightened. Poetry is a complex form of communication that provides pleasure in various ways. One may, for instance, look upon a poem as a kind of game in which the poet skillfully works within a set of self-imposed rules—rhyme, meter, and stanzaic pattern—and delights in clever rhymes, as when Lord Byron rhymes "intellectual" with "henpecked you all" or "maxim" with "tax 'em." Anyone familiar with Plato's theory that everything in our world is an imperfect replica of an ideal heavenly form will appreciate the beauty and condensed brilliance of William Butler Yeats's lines from "Among School Children":

> Plato thought nature but a spume that plays
> Upon a ghostly paradigm of things.

Some will discover in poetry, as children often do in nursery rhymes, the pleasure of rhythm, meter, and sound—the musical aspects of poetry. The pleasures of poetry range from the loftiest insights and discoveries to memorable lines and clever rhymes.

A discussion of the major techniques and devices of poetry will provide some suggestions about how to approach poems and also furnish tools and a vocabulary for analyzing and discussing them. Keep in mind that a tool is not an end in itself but the means to an end. The end is fuller understanding and, thereby, deeper enjoyment of poetry.

The Words of Poetry

It is not unusual to hear some great and original philosopher, sociologist or economist referred to as a mediocre writer. Yet, even while judging the writing poor, one may at the same time recognize and honor the originality and significance of the idea conveyed. Such a distinction cannot be made in poetry. If a poem is written poorly, it is a poor poem. "In reading prose," Ralph Waldo Emerson said, "I am sensitive as soon as a sentence drags; but in poetry, as soon as one word drags." *Where* a poem arrives is inseparable from *how* it arrives. Everything must be right in a poem, every word. "The correction of prose," said Yeats, "is endless; a poem comes right with a click like a closing box."

"Poetry is heightened language" means, among other things, that the poet strives for precision and richness in the words he or she uses, and "precision" and "richness" are not contradictory for the poet. Words have dictionary or denotative meanings as well as associative or connotative meanings; they also have histories and relationships with other words. The English language is rich in synonyms, groups of words whose denotative meanings are roughly the same but whose connotations vary widely (portly, stout, fat; horse, steed, courser; official, statesman, politician). Many words are identical in sound and often in spelling but different in meaning (forepaws, four paws; lie [recline] lie [fib]).

The meanings of words have changed in the course of time, and the poet may consciously select a word whose older meaning adds a dimension to the poem. There are, of course, no rules that can be given to a reader for judging a poet's effectiveness and skill in the handling of words (or anything else, for that matter). All we can do is look at particular works for examples of how a good poet manipulates words.

In a moving and passionate poem on his dying father, "Do Not Go Gentle into That Good Night," Dylan Thomas pleads with his father not to accept death passively but rather to "Rage, rage against the dying of the light." He then declares in the following stanzas that neither "wise men" nor "good men" nor "wild men" accept death quietly. And neither, Thomas says, do "grave men," punning on *grave* in its meaning of both "serious" and "burial place." William Blake's poem about the inhumane jobs children were forced into in eighteenth-century England, "The Chimney Sweeper" begins:

> When my mother died I was very young,
> And my Father sold me while yet my tongue
> Could scarcely cry " 'weep! 'weep! 'weep! 'weep!"
> So your chimneys I sweep, and in soot I sleep.

" 'Weep," a clipped form of "sweep," is what the boy cries as he walks a street looking for work, but *weep* clearly evokes the tears and sorrow of the mother's death and the sadness of the small boy's cruel life. And this is only part of Blake's skillful handling of words. "Cry" is also an effective pun, the precise word to describe how the boy seeks work while simultaneously reinforcing the emotional meaning of *weep*.

Henry Reed's "Naming of Parts" develops a contrast between the instructions a group of soldiers are receiving on how to operate a rifle (in order to cause death) and the lovely world of nature (which represents life and beauty). In the fourth stanza, bees are described as "assaulting and fumbling the flowers." "Fumbling," with its meaning of awkwardness and nervous uncertainty, may strike us as an arresting and perhaps puzzling word at first. Yet anyone who has watched a bee pollinating a flower will find the word extremely effective. In addition, of course, *fumbling* is a word often used to describe the actions of human beings caught up in sexual passion—a connotation precisely appropriate to the poet's purposes, since pollination is, in a sense, a sexual process. Furthermore, these various interpretations of *fumbling* contrast powerfully with the cold, mechanical precision of the death-dealing instruments the recruits are learning to use. The next line of Reed's poem exhibits yet another resource of words: "They call it easing the Spring." The line is an exact repetition of a phrase used two lines earlier except *Spring* is now capitalized. While *Spring* retains its first meaning as part of the bolt action of the rifle, the capitalization makes it the season of the year when flowers are pollinated and the world of nature is reborn. With a mere typographical device, Reed had charged a single word with the theme of his poem. These few illustrations will suggest how sensitive the poet is to words and how much more pleasure the reader will find in poems if he or she develops the same sensitivity.

Sometimes meanings are not inherent in the isolated words but created in the poet's use of the word. A tree is a tree and a rose is a rose. A tree is also the apple tree in Frost's "After Apple-Picking" and something quite different in William Blake's "A Poison Tree"; a rose is specially defined in Robert Burns's "A Red, Red Rose" and Edmund Waller's "Go, Lovely Rose!" In these poems, because *tree* and *rose* are given such rich and varied meaning and are so central to the poems' development and meaning, they exceed mere connotation and become images that, finally, are symbolic.

Imagery

The world is revealed to us through our senses—sight, sound, taste, touch, and smell. And while some philosophers and psychologists might challenge the statement, it seems pretty clear that much, if not all, of our knowledge is linked to sensory experience. *Imagery* is the representation in poetry of sensory experience, one of the means by which the poet creates a world that we all know and share. Or, put another way, imagery allows the poet to create a recognizable world by drawing upon a fund of common experiences. Bad poetry is often bad because the imagery is stale ("golden sunset," "the smiling sun," "the rolling sea") or so skimpy that the poem dissolves into vague and shadowy and meaningless abstractions.

A good poet never loses touch with the sensory world. The invisible, the intangible, the abstract, are anchored to the visible, the tangible, the concrete. Andrew Marvell begins his poem "To His Coy Mistress" with an elaborate statement of how he would court his beloved if their lives were measured in centuries rather than years. In the second stanza, he describes the reality:

>   But at my back I always hear
> Time's wingéd chariot hurrying near;
> And yonder all before us lie
> Deserts of vast eternity.
> Thy beauty shall no more be found,
> Nor, in thy marble vault, shall sound
> My echoing song; then worms shall try
> That long-preserved virginity,
> And your quaint honor turn to dust,
> And into ashes all my lust:
> The grave's a fine and private place,
> But none, I think, do there embrace.

Time, eternity, honor, and *lust* are all abstractions, but Marvell joins each to a sensuous image that gives to the abstraction an extraordinary sharpness and power. Time is a winged *chariot*, eternity a sequence of *deserts*, honor turns to *dust* and lust to *ashes*. Time has long been associated with the chariot of Apollo and eternity, for the damned, with a desert. "Ashes" and "dust" echo the funeral service. Nonetheless, Marvell gives life to these stock images by renewing their appeal to the senses.

Any analysis of the imagery of a poem will soon reveal that our definition of imagery as the representation of sensory experience needs to be qualified. One of the primary functions of language is to bring meaning and order into our lives, and poetry is the most intense use of language. We will find, therefore, that the images in poetry tend to be charged with meanings. A rose may be only a rose, but it becomes much more in Burns's and Waller's poems. Imagery, then, is closely related to, perhaps inseparable from, *figurative* language, the language which *says* one thing and *means* another.

The difference between good and bad poetry often turns on the skill with which imagery (or figurative language) is used. When Robert Frost in his poem "Birches" compares life to "a pathless wood," the image strikes us as natural and appropriate (the comparison of life to a path or road is a common one, as is a wood or forest to a state of moral bewilderment). We are accustomed to the imagery of birds, flowers, and sunsets in love poems, but when John Donne in "A Valediction: Forbidding Mourning" describes the relationship between himself and his beloved in terms of a drawing compass, the image may seem jarring or even ludicrous. Such a bold and daring comparison is a kind of challenge. The poet intends not only to surmount the reader's feeling that the image is strange but to develop it with such skill that the reader will accept it as natural and appropriate. And as Donne elaborates the comparison through various stages and concludes it (and the poem) with the brilliantly appropriate image of the completed circle, we recognize that he has successfully met the challenge.

Figurative Language

Figurative language is the general phrase we use to describe the many devices of language that allow us to speak nonliterally, to say one thing and mean another. Any attempt to communicate an emotion will very quickly utilize figurative language. When Robert Burns compares his love to a red rose, he does so not because he is unable to find the literal language he needs but because what he wants to say can only be expressed in figurative language. (Literal language might be used by a scientist to describe the physiological state of someone in love, but that is not what interests Burns.) The world of emotions, feelings, attitudes remains shadowy and insubstantial until figurative language gives it form and substance.

Consider, for example, these familiar old sayings: "The grass is always greener on the other side of the fence"; "A rolling stone gathers no moss"; "A bird in the hand is worth two in the bush"; "The early bird catches the worm." While these sayings unquestionably make sense in literal terms (the grass you see from a distance looks greener than the grass under your feet), the meaning of these phrases to a native speaker of English is clearly nonliteral. When we use them we are not speaking about grass or rolling stones or birds; we are making general and highly abstract observations about human attitudes and behavior. Yet strangely these generalizations and abstractions are embodied in concrete and sensuous imagery. Try to explain what any one of these expressions means and you will quickly discover that you are using many more words and much vaguer language than the expression itself. Indeed, this is precisely what happens when you attempt to paraphrase—that is, put into your own words—the meaning of a poem. Like poetry, these sayings rely on the figurative use of language.

Since poetry is an intense and heightened use of language that explores the world of feeling, it uses more varied figurative devices than does ordinary language. One of the most common figurative devices, *metaphor*, where one thing is called something else, occurs frequently in ordinary speech. "School is a rat race," we say, or "She's a bundle of nerves," and the meaning is perfectly clear—too clear, perhaps, because these metaphors are by now so common and unoriginal they have lost whatever vividness they may once have had. But when Thomas Nashe declares that "Beauty is but a flower / Which wrinkles will devour" or W. H. Auden, commenting on the death of William Butler Yeats, says, "Let the Irish vessel lie / Emptied of its poetry," we have metaphors that compel readers to confront certain painful aspects of life.

Simile is closely related to metaphor. But where metaphor says that one thing *is* another, simile says that one things is *like* another, as in Burns's "O My Luve's like a red, red rose" and Frost's "life is too much like a pathless wood." The distinction between simile and metaphor, while easy enough to make technically, is often difficult to distinguish in terms of effects. Frost establishes a comparison between life and a pathless wood and keeps the two even more fully separated by adding the qualifiers, "too much." Burns's simile maintains the same separation and, in addition, because it occurs in the opening line of the poem, eliminates any possible confusion the reader might momentarily experience about the subject of the poem if the line read, "O My Love is a red, red rose." The reader can test the difference in effect between simile and metaphor by changing a metaphor into a simile or a simile into a metaphor to see if the meaning of the poem is thereby altered.

The critical vocabulary useful in discussions of poetry includes several additional terms, all of which name particular figures of speech: *metonymy, synecdoche, personification, hyperbole, understatement, paradox.* These terms are defined and illustrated in the Glossary of Literary Terms. But, though there may be a certain academic pleasure in recognizing the figures a poet uses, naming a figure of speech will never explain its effectiveness. The reader must, finally, perceive the usefulness of figures and respond emotionally to the construction of language that the poet creates in order to touch the reader's nerves.

Symbol

A *symbol* is anything that stands for or suggests something else. In this sense, most words are symbolic: the word *tree* stands for an object in the real world. When we speak of a symbol in poetry, however, we usually mean something more precise. In poetry, a symbol is an object or event that suggests more than itself. It is one of the most common and most powerful devices available to the poet, for it allows him or her to convey economically and simply a wide range of meanings.

It is useful to distinguish between two kinds of symbols, *public symbols* and *contextual symbols*. Public symbols are those objects or events that history has invested with rich meanings and associations. In a sense, then, a public symbol is a ready-made symbol. Yeats utilizes such a symbol in his poem "Leda and the Swan," assuming that his readers will be familiar with the myths that tell of the erotic affairs of Zeus and the consequences of those affairs—in this case, the birth of Clytemnestra, the wife of Agamemnon, and Helen, the most beautiful woman of antiquity, whose abduction precipitated the Trojan War. In "The Conscientious Objector," Karl Shapiro uses Noah's Ark and the Mayflower as symbols of a political prison whose inmates refuse to conform.

When poets use a public symbol, they are drawing from what they assume is a common and shared fund of knowledge and tradition. If Yeats's readers are unaware of the symbolic meaning with which history has invested the Trojan War, it is doubtful that the poem will have much meaning for them. Nor will Shapiro's poem be clear unless we understand that Noah's Ark and the Mayflower evoke unique virtue and daring and heroic nonconformity.

In contrast to public symbols, contextual symbols are objects or events that are symbolic by virtue of the poet's handling of them in a particular poem—that is, by virtue of the context. Consider, for example, the opening lines of Robert Frost's "After Apple-Picking":

> My long two-pointed ladder's sticking through a tree
> Toward heaven still,
> And there's a barrel that I didn't fill
> Beside it, and there may be two or three
> Apples I didn't pick upon some bough.

The apple tree is a literal tree, but as one reads through the poem, it becomes clear that the apple tree also symbolizes the speaker's life with a wide range of possible meanings (do the few apples he hasn't picked symbolize the hopes, dreams, aspirations that even the fullest life cannot satisfy?).

Amy Lowell's "Patterns" is rich in symbols. The speaker is an aristocratic lady whose life and most vital emotions are kept in rigid control by a series of patterns that the society she lives in has imposed on her. She describes herself as walking in her elegant gown down the garden paths laid out in precise patterns. Her gown is real; the path is a real path. But it very quickly becomes apparent that the patterned paths and her elegant gown are symbolic of the narrowly restricted and oppressive life her deepest feelings are at war with. They are the visible manifestation, the symbols, of the trap in which she is caught. She weeps when she notices "The daffodils and squills / Flutter in the breeze / As they please" because the flowers symbolize a freedom she knows she will never have.

The paths and flowers in Amy Lowell's poem are clear and easily recognizable examples of contextual symbols. However, contextual symbols by their very nature tend to present more difficulties than public symbols, because recognizing them depends on a sensitivity to everything else in the poem. In T. S. Eliot's dense and difficult poem "The Love Song of J. Alfred Prufrock," the speaker twice says, "In the room the women come and go / Talking of Michelangelo," a couplet that is baffling at first because it seems to have no clear relationship to what precedes and follows it. But as one reads through the poem, he begins to see that Prufrock is a man, like the young woman in Amy Lowell's poem, trapped in a life of upper-class superficialities and meaninglessness. The women discussing Michelangelo symbolize this dilettantish and arid life from which Prufrock desperately wishes to escape. Prufrock reminds himself that he will have time "To prepare a face to meet the faces that you meet." In the poem, that face is a symbol of a lonely existence in a society where people play elaborate games in order to conceal from others their real emotions and feelings.

A final word on symbols. The reader who fails to recognize a symbol has missed an important part of the poem's meaning. On the other hand, one of the pitfalls of reading poetry is that some readers become so intent on finding symbols they tend to forget that an object must first have a literal meaning before it can function as a symbol. Or, put in terms of our earlier definition, an object or event is itself before it is something else.

The setting of "After Apple-Picking" is an orchard, and the setting of "Patterns" the paths of a manorial garden. As we begin to understand the theme of each poem, we come to recognize the symbolic meanings these objects gradually take on. But there are rules that will allow a reader to identify symbols. If you do not know what Troy symbolizes and have never heard of Helen of Troy, you will not discover the meanings of these public symbols by repeated and intensive readings of the poem; like unfamiliar words, you must look up (or be told of) their significance. On the other hand, the recognition of contextual symbols often depends on careful and sensitive reading. Readers may very well disagree on whether or not something should be taken as a symbol. When this occurs, one can only consider whether the symbolic reading adds meanings that are consistent with other elements in the poem. Is the fly in Emily Dickinson's "I Heard a Fly Buzz—When I Died" a symbol or merely an insect? Your answer will depend on what you see as the theme of the poem.

Archibald MacLeish renders the modern critical attitude toward symbolism in poetry and, at the same time, argues for the view that poems do not "mean" in the ordinary sense of that word. The various elements of a poem—imagery, figurative language, symbol—coalesce to form an *object*, something characterized not by its truth but by its objective correlation to some human experience. And most remarkably, MacLeish renders these rather complex critical positions in a poem rich in contextual symbols:

ARS POETICA

A poem should be palpable and mute
As a globed fruit,

Dumb
As old medallions to the thumb,

Silent as the sleeve-worn stone
Of casement ledges where the moss has grown—

A poem should be wordless
As the flight of birds.

A poem should be motionless in time
As the moon climbs,

Leaving, as the moon releases
Twig by twig the night-entangled trees,

Leaving, as the moon behind the winter leaves,
Memory by memory the mind—

A poem should be motionless in time
As the moon climbs.

A poem should be equal to:
Not true.

For all the history of grief
An empty doorway and a maple leaf.

For love
The leaning grasses and two lights above the sea—

A poem should not mean
But be.

Music

The *music* of poetry, by which we mean the poetic use of all the devices of sound and rhythm inherent in language, is at once central to the poetic effect and yet the most difficult to account for. We can discuss the way in which figurative language works with some clarity because we are using words to explain words. Any listener who has ever tried to explain the effect of a piece of music (or who has read music criticism) will be familiar with the problem of describing a nonverbal medium with words.

The possible musical effects of language are complex. The terms we have to describe various musical devices deal only with the most obvious and easily recognizable patterns. *Alliteration, assonance, consonance, caesura, meter, onomatopoeia, rhythm,* and *rhyme* (all of them defined in the Glossary) are the key traditional terms for discussing the music of poetry. Along with the other terms already introduced, they are an indispensable part of the vocabulary one needs to discuss poetry. But the relationship between sound and sense can be perceived nicely in a celebrated passage from Alexander Pope's poem "An Essay on Criticism," in which the meaning of each line, first a condemnation of mechanical bad verse, then an illustration of well-managed verse, is ingeniously supported by the musical devices:

> These[1] equal syllables alone require,
> Though oft the ear the open vowels tire;
> While expletives their feeble aid do join;
> And ten low words oft creep in one dull line:
> While they ring round the same unvaried chimes,
> With sure returns of still expected rhymes;
> Where 'er you find "the cooling western breeze,"
> In the next line, it "whispers through the trees";
> If crystal streams "with pleasing murmurs creep,"
> The reader's threatened (not in vain) with "sleep";
> Then, at the last and only couplet fraught
> With some unmeaning thing they call a thought,
> A needless Alexandrine[2] ends the song
> That, like a wounded snake, drags its slow length along.
>
>   . . . . . .
>
> True ease in writing comes from art, not chance,
> As those move easiest who have learned to dance.
> 'Tis not enough no harshness gives offense,
> The sound must seem an echo to the sense:
> Soft is the strain when Zephyr gently blows,
> And the smooth stream in smoother numbers flows;
> But when loud surges lash the sounding shore,
> The hoarse, rough verse should like the torrent roar:
> When Ajax[3] strives some rock's vast weight to throw,
> The line too labors, and the words move slow;
> Not so, when swift Camilla[4] scours the plain,
> Flies o'er the unbending corn, and skims along the main.

When Pope speaks of open vowels, the line is loaded with open vowels. When Pope condemns the use of ten monosyllables, the line contains ten monosyllables. When Pope urges that the sound should echo the sense and speaks of the wind, the line is rich in sibilants that hiss, like the wind. When he speaks of Ajax striving, the combination of final consonants and initial sounds slow the line; when he speaks of Camilla's swiftness, the final consonants and initial sounds form liaisons that are swiftly pronounceable.

Or, consider the opening lines of Wilfred Owen's poem "Dulce et Decorum

---

[1] Bad poets.
[2] Twelve-syllable line.
[3] A Greek warrior celebrated for his strength.
[4] A swift-footed queen in Virgil's *Aeneid*.

Est," describing a company of battle-weary soldiers trudging toward their camp and rest:

> Bent double, like old beggars under sacks,
> Knock-kneed, coughing like hags, we cursed through sludge.

These lines are dominated by a series of harsh, explosive consonant sounds (*b*, *d*, *k*, *g*) that reinforce the meaning of the lines (a description of tired World War I soldiers). More specifically, the first two syllables of each line are heavily stressed, which serves to slow the reading. And, finally, while the poem ultimately develops a prevailing meter, the meter is only faintly suggested in these opening lines, through the irregular rhythms used to describe a weary stumbling march.

Let us remember, then, that analysis of musical (or for that matter any other) devices can illuminate and enrich our understanding of poetry. But let us also remember that analysis has its limitations. Dylan Thomas once remarked:

> You can tear a poem apart to see what makes it technically tick and say to yourself when the works are laid out before you—the vowels, the consonants, the rhymes, and rhythms—"Yes, this is it. This is why the poem moves me so. It is because of the craftsmanship." But you're back where you began. The best craftsmanship always leaves holes and gaps in the works of the poem so that something that is not in the poem can creep, crawl, flash, or thunder in.

Another writer, X. J. Kennedy, doubtless with MacLeish's poetic critical observations in mind, puts the same idea with less reverence:

ARS POETICA

> The goose that laid the golden egg
> Died looking up its crotch
> To find out how its sphincter worked.
> Would you lay well? Don't watch.

Reading Drama

Plays are fundamentally different from other literary forms. Unlike stories and poems, almost all plays are designed to be performed, not to be read. Consequently, the aural and the visual aspects of the drama, which should be at least as important as its dialogue, are left altogether to the imagination of the reader (with the aid of some meager stage directions). Great effort is invested in such matters as costuming, set design, lighting effects, and stage movement by the director and his staff; all of that effort is lost to the reader who must somehow contrive to supply imaginatively some of those dramatic features not contained on the printed page.

As much as possible, the way to read a play is to imagine that you are its director. Hence you will concern yourself with creating the set and the lighting. You will see people dressed so that their clothes give support to their words. You will think about timing—how long between events and speeches—and blocking—how the characters move as they interact on stage. Perhaps the best way to confront the literature of the stage, to respond most fully to what is there, is to attempt to produce some scenes in class or after class. If possible, attend the rehearsals of plays in production on the campus. Nothing will provide better insight into the complexities of the theater than attending a rehearsal where the problems are encountered and solved.

As an exercise, read the opening speeches of any of the plays here and make decisions. How should the lines be spoken (quietly, angrily, haltingly)? What should the characters do as they speak (remain stationary, look in some direction, traverse the stage)? How should the stage be lit (partially, brightly, in some color that contributes to the mood of the dialogue and action)? What should the characters who are not speaking do? What possibilities exist for conveying appropriate signals solely through gesture and facial expression—signals not contained in the words you read?

Staging

Since plays are written to be staged, the particular kind of theater available to the dramatist is often crucial to the structure of the play. The Greek theater of Dionysius in Athens, for which Sophocles wrote, was an open-air amphitheater seating about 14,000 people. The skene, or stage house, from which actors entered, was fixed, though it might have had painted panels to suggest the scene. Consequently, there is no scene shifting in *Oedipus Rex*. All the dialogue and action take place in the same location before the skene building, which represents the Palace of Oedipus. Important things happen elsewhere, but the audience is informed of these events by messenger. A death occurs, but not in sight of the audience, partly as a matter of taste and partly because the conditions of the Greek stage prevented the playwright from moving the action inside the palace. Later dramatists, writing for a more flexible stage and a more intimate theater, were able to profit from the intensely dramatic nature of murder and suicide, but the Greeks, almost invariably, chose to tell, rather than show, the most gripping physical events in their stories.

Further, an outdoor theater of vast dimensions implies obvious restrictions on acting style. Facial expression can play no important role in such a theater, and, in fact, the actors of Sophoclean tragedy wore masks, larger than life and probably equipped with some sort of megaphone device to aid in voice projection. Those voices were denied the possibility of subtle variety in tone and expression, and the speeches were probably delivered in rather formal declamatory style. The characters wore special built-up footwear which made them larger than life. In addition to these limitations. Sophocles had as well to write within the formal limitations imposed by the Athenian government, which made available only three principal actors, all male, as the cast (exclusive of the chorus) for each play. Consequently, there are never more than three players on stage at once, and the roles are designed so that each actor takes several parts—signified by different masks. Yet, despite the austerity of production values, the unavoidable clumsiness of fortuitous messengers appearing at all the right moments, and the sharply restricted dramatis personae, among the few Greek plays that have survived are some still universally regarded as superlatively fine dramatic representations of tragic humanity.

Until recently we thought we had a clear conception of what Shakespeare's stage looked like. Scholarship has raised some doubts about this conception, but though we no longer accept the accuracy of the reconstruction shown here, we still have a good enough understanding of the shape of the playing area to recreate roughly the staging of a Shakespearean play. That staging was altogether different from the Greek. Though both theaters were open air, the enclosure around the Elizabethan stage was much smaller and the audience capacity limited to something between 2,000 and 3,000. As in classical drama, men played all the roles, but they no longer wore masks, and a stage that protruded into the audience made for great intimacy. Hence the actors' art expanded to matters of facial expression, and the style of speech and movement was certainly closer than was Greek style to what we might loosely call realism. Shakespeare has Hamlet caution the actors: "Suit the action to the word, the word to the action, with this special observance, that you o'erstep not the modesty of nature: for anything so overdone is from the purpose of playing, whose end, both at first and now, was and is, to hold as 't were, the mirror up to nature. . . ." But the characteristic matter of Shakespearean tragedy certainly did not lend itself to a modern realistic style. Those great speeches are written

Interior of the Swan Theatre, London, 1596

The Globe Theatre

Hypothetical reconstruction of the interior of the Globe Theatre in the days of Shakespeare

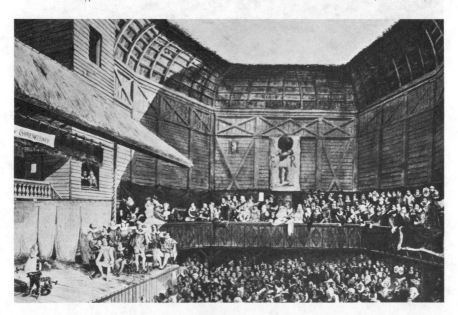

A seventeenth-century French box stage

The ancient theater at Epidaurus, Greece

in verse; they frequently are meant to augment the rather meager set design by providing verbal pictures to set the stage; they are much denser in texture, image, and import than is ordinary speech. These characteristics all serve to distinguish the Shakespearean stage from the familiar realism of most recent theater and film.

The Elizabethan stage made possible a tremendous versatility for the dramatist and the acting company. Most of the important action was played out on the uncurtained main platform, jutting into the audience and surrounded on three sides by spectators. The swiftly moving scenes followed each other without interruption, doubtless using different areas of the stage to signify different locations. There was some sort of terrace or balcony one story above the main stage, and there was an area at the back of the main protruding stage that could be curtained off when not in use. Although Shakespeare's plays are usually divided into five separate acts in printed versions, they were played straight through, without intermission, much like a modern motion picture.

Though more versatile and intimate than the Greek stage, the Elizabethan stage had limitations which clearly influenced the playwright. Those critical imperatives of time, place, and action (i.e., the time represented should not exceed one day, the location should be fixed in one place, and the action should be limited to one cohesive story line—one plot), the so-called unities that Aristotle discovered in the drama of Sophocles, may well reflect the physical conditions of the Greek theater. Elizabethan dramatists largely ignored them, and in *Othello* we move from Venice to Cyprus, from the fortifications of the island to the city streets to Desdemona's bedchamber. Certainly some props were used to suggest these locations, but nothing comparable to the furniture of Ibsen's stage. Instead, the playwright often wove a sort of literary scenery into the speeches of the characters. For example, in *Othello*, Roderigo has occasion to say to Iago, "Here is her father's house; I'll call aloud." The second act of *Othello* opens with some gentlemen at "an open place near the Quay." Notice the dialogue:

> **Montano.** What from the cape can you discern at sea?
> **First Gentleman.** Nothing at all: it is a high-wrought flood;
>   I cannot 'twixt the heaven and the main
>   Descry a sail.
> **Montano.** Methinks the wind hath spoke aloud at land;
>   A fuller blast ne'er shook our battlements;
>   If it hath ruffian'd so upon the sea,
>   What ribs of oak, when mountains melt on them,
>   Can hold the mortise?

There is no sea, of course, and Elizabethan technology was not up to a wind machine. The men are, doubtless, looking off stage and creating the stormy setting through language. An open-air theater which played in daylight had few techniques for controlling lighting, and speeches had to be written to supply the effect:

> But look, the morn, in russet mantle clad,
> Walks o'er the dew of yon high eastern hill.

Further, the company had not the resources to place armies on the stage; hence, a speaker in *King Henry* V boldly invites the audience to profit from imagination:

> Piece out our imperfections with your thoughts;
> Into a thousand parts divide one man,
> And make imaginary puissance;
> Think, when we talk of horses, that you see them
> Printing their proud hoofs i' the receiving earth.
> For 'tis your thoughts that now must deck our kings.

The theater in the Petit-Bourbon Palace, built about twenty-five years after Shakespeare's death, was a forerunner of the common "box stage" on which so much recent drama is acted. Essentially, this stage is a box with one wall removed so that the audience can see into the playing area. Such a stage lends itself to realistic settings. Since the stage is essentially a room, it can easily be furnished to look like one. If street scenes are required, painted backdrops provide perspective and an accompanying sense of distance. Sets at an angle to the edge of the stage might be constructed. The possibilities for scenic design allowed by such a stage soon produced great set designers, and the structure of such a stage led to the development of increasingly sophisticated stage machinery, which in turn freed the dramatist from the physical limitations imposed by earlier stages. By Ibsen's time the versatility of the box stage enabled him to write elaborately detailed stage settings for the various locations in which the drama unfolds. Further, the furnishing of the stage in Ibsen's plays sometimes functions symbolically to convey visually the choking quality of certain bourgeois life-styles.

None of the historical stages has passed into mere history. The modern theater still uses Greek amphitheaters such as that at Epidaurus, constructs approximations of the Elizabethan stage for Shakespeare festivals, and employs the box stage with ever-increasing inventiveness. Early in the twentieth century, some plays were produced in the "round," the action taking place on a stage in the center of the theater with the audience on all sides. A number of theaters were built that incorporated a permanent in-the-round arrangement. But versatility has become so important to the modern production designer that some feel the very best theater is simply a large empty room (with provisions for technical flexibility in the matter of lighting) that can be rearranged to suit the requirements of specific productions. This ideal of a "theater space" that can be freely manipulated has become increasingly attractive—some have been constructed—since it frees the dramatist and the performance from limitations built into permanent stage design.

Drama and Society

The history of dramatic literature (like the history of literature in general) provides evidence for another kind of history as well—the history of changing attitudes, changing values, and even changing taste. In ancient Greece, in Elizabethan England when Shakespeare wrote his enduring tragedies, right up to the end of the eighteenth century, certain expectations controlled the nature of tragedy. Those expectations were discussed by Aristotle as early as 335 B.C.; they involved the fall of a noble figure from a high place. Such tragedy reflects important cultural attitudes. It flourished in conjunction with a certain sort of politics and certain notions about human nature. The largest part of an audience of several thousand Athenians in the fifth century B.C. was certainly not itself noble. Neither was Shakespeare's audience at the Globe Theatre in London. That audience, much as a modern audience, was composed of tradesmen, artisans, and petty officials. In Greece, even slaves attended the tragedy festivals. Why then were there no tragedies in which the central figure was a storekeeper, a baker, or a butcher?

There have been many attempts to answer this difficult question, and those answers tend to make assumptions about the way individuals see themselves and their society. If the butcher down the street dies, well, that is sad, but after all rather unimportant to society. If the king falls, however, society itself is touched, and a general grief prevails that makes possible sweeping observations about the chancy conditions of life. A culture always elevates some of its members to the status of heroes—often by virtue of the office they hold. Even now, societies are collectively moved, and moved profoundly, by the death of a president, a prime minister—a Kennedy, a de Gaulle, a Churchill—when they are not nearly so moved by immense disasters such as killing storms or earthquakes or civil wars. But things have changed, and most rapidly within the last 150 years or so.

Simply stated, new cultural values—new attitudes about human nature—have developed, especially since the advent of industrialism and since Freud began publishing his systematic observations about the way men's minds interact with their bodies. The result has been an increasing humanization of those who used to be heroes and an increasing realization of the capacity for heroism in those who are merely bakers and butchers. Thus Henrik Ibsen, frequently referred to as "the father of modern drama," can compel a serious emotional response from his audience over the tribulations of a middle-class lawyer's wife in A *Doll's House*. Realistic plays succeed in spite of their commonplace heroes because, as a society, we can now accept the experiences of ordinary people as emblems of our own. Perhaps we can because political institutions in the modern republics and in the socialist countries have, theoretically, exalted common men and women and rejected political aristocracy. Certainly the reasons for the change are complex. But it remains true that neither Sophocles nor Shakespeare could have written A *Doll's House*.

Dramatic Irony

Dramatic irony allows the audience to know more than the characters do about their own circumstances. Consequently, that audience *hears more* (the ironic component) than do the characters who speak. Shakespeare's *Othello* provides an excellent illustration of the uses of dramatic irony. At the end of Act II, Cassio, who has lost his position as Othello's lieutenant, asks Iago for advice on how to regain favor. Iago, who, unknown to Cassio, had engineered Cassio's disgrace, advises him to ask Desdemona, Othello's adored wife, to intervene. Actually this is good advice; ordinarily the tactic would succeed, so much does Othello love his wife and wish to please her. But Iago explains, in a soliloquy to the audience, that he is laying groundwork for the ruin of all the objects of his envy and hatred—Cassio, Desdemona, and Othello:

> . . . for while this honest fool
> Plies Desdemona to repair his fortunes,
> And she for him pleads strongly to the Moor,
> I'll pour this pestilence into his ear
> That she repeals him for her body's lust;
> And, by how much she strives to do him good,
> She shall undo her credit with the Moor.
> So will I turn her virtue into pitch,
> And out of her own goodness make the net
> That shall enmesh them all.

Of course Desdemona, Cassio, and Othello are ignorant of Iago's enmity. Worse, all of them consider Iago a loyal friend. But the audience knows Iago's design, and that knowledge provides the chilling dramatic irony of Act III, scene 3.

When Cassio asks for Desdemona's help, she immediately consents, declaring, "I'll intermingle every thing he does / With Cassio's suit." At this, the audience, knowing what it does, grows a little uneasy—that audience, after all, rather likes Desdemona and doesn't want her injured. As Iago and Othello come on stage, Cassio, understandably ill as ease, leaves at the approach of the commander who has stripped him of his rank, thus providing Iago with a magnificent tactical advantage. And as Cassio leaves, Iago utters an exclamation and four simple words that may rank among the most electrifying in all of English drama:

> Ha! I like not that.

They are certainly not very poetic words; they do not conjure up any telling images; they do not mean much either to Othello or Desdemona. But they are for the audience the intensely anticipated first drop of poison. Othello hasn't heard clearly:

> What dost thou say?

Maybe it all will pass, and Iago's clever design will fail. But what a hiss of held breath the audience expels when Iago replies:

> Nothing, my lord: or if—I know not what.

And Othello is hooked:

> Was not that Cassio parted from my wife?

The bait taken, Iago begins to play his line:

> Cassio, my lord? No, sure, I cannot think it,
> That he would steal away so guilty-like,
> Seeing you coming.

And from this point on in the scene, Iago cleverly and cautiously leads Othello. He assumes the role of Cassio's great friend—reluctant to say anything that might cast suspicion on him. But he is also the "friend" of Othello and cannot keep silent his suspicions. So honest Iago (he is often called "honest" by the others in the play), apparently full of sympathy and kindness, skillfully brings the trusting Othello to emotional chaos. And every word they exchange is doubly meaningful to the audience, which perceives Othello led on the descent into a horrible jealousy by his "friend." The scene ends with Othello visibly shaken and convinced of Desdemona's faithlessness and Cassio's perfidy:

> Damn her, lewd minx! O, damn her!
> Come, go with me apart; I will withdraw,
> To furnish me with some swift means of death
> For the fair devil. Now art thou my lieutenant.

To which Iago replies:

> I am your own for ever.

Now, all of Iago's speeches in this scene operate on the audience through dramatic irony. The tension, the horror, the urge to cry out, to save Cassio, Desdemona, and Othello from the devilish Iago—all the emotional tautness in the audience results from irony, from knowing what the victims do not know. The play would have much less force if the audience did not know Iago's intentions from the outset and did not anticipate as he bends so many innocent events to his own increasingly evil ends. Note that dramatic irony is not limited to the drama; poetry, sometimes (as in Robert Browning's "My Last Duchess"), and fiction, often (as in Frank O'Connor's "My Oedipus Complex"), make use of this technique. But dramatic irony is the special tool of the dramatist, well suited to produce an electric tension in a live audience that overhears the interaction of people on stage.

Drama and Its Audience

Scholarly ordering that identifies the parts of drama and discusses the perceptive distinctions made by Aristotle among its parts can help you confront a play and understand how your responses were triggered by the playwright, the designers of the play, and the performers. But such analysis cannot substitute for the emotional experience produced by successful drama—your deepest responses have to do with states of mind, not with the three dramatic unities. Plays, perhaps more than other art forms, address themselves to the complex melange of belief, attitude, intellect and awareness that constitutes a human psyche. A lyric poem may simply meditate on the transience of life or express the pain of love unrequited. Plays, however, set characters within demanding social and cultural settings. Those cultural imperatives create dissatisfaction and conflict that may lead to a heightened awareness of or a tragic insight into one's own limitations. For example, many of the plays in this anthology embody beliefs and assumptions about fundamental issues. What happens when the viewer's (or reader's) assumptions and beliefs conflict with those embodied in the play? If we do not believe that the world is ruled by the gods or a God, can we appreciate *Oedipus Rex?* If we believe that a woman's place is in the home and that, above all, nothing can justify a mother's abandoning her children, can we get anything out of *A Doll's House?* If we believe as a matter of principle that only a strong deterrent force can prevent an enemy nation from attacking us, will *End of the World* therefore fail in its attempt to demonstrate the absurdity of deterrence theory? These are questions that can not be answered easily. We can say, however, that one of the functions of art is to force us to reexamine our most cherished abstract beliefs in the revealing light of the artist's work. Thus, despite our abstract beliefs about motherhood, Ibsen's skill in creating character and social structure in *A Doll's House* may compel our sympathy for Nora and force us to re-think our position.

Reading Essays

Essays differ from fiction in that they generally do not create imaginary worlds inhabited by fictional characters. We know, for example, through media accounts and the testimony of his friends, that Martin Luther King, Jr. was indeed jailed in Birmingham, Alabama, where he wrote his famous argument for social justice, "Letter from Birmingham Jail." And, although we cannot independently verify that George Orwell actually shot an elephant, or that Richard Selzer is describing a real patient, their works exhibit the formal non-fictional qualities of the essay rather than the imagined world of the short story.

Writers turn to the essay form when they wish to confront their readers directly with an idea, a problem (often with a proposed solution), an illuminating experience, an important definition, some flaw (or virtue) in the social system. Usually, the essay is relatively short, and almost always it embodies the writer's personal viewpoint. And although the essay may share many elements with other literary forms, it generally speaks with the voice of a real person about the real world. The term *essay* derives from the French verb *essayer*, "to try," "to attempt." That verb, in turn, was derived from the Latin verb *exigere*, "to weigh out," "to examine."

While the French term calls attention to the personal perspective that characterizes the essay, the Latin verb suggests another dimension. The essay not only examines personal experiences but also explores and clarifies ideas, argues for or against a position. Thus, "My First Encounter with Death" is obviously the title of an essay. So is "The American Way of Death." The titles, however, suggest that the first essay will be intensely personal and the second will be less personal and more analytical, perhaps even argumentative.

As you read an essay, you need to ask yourself, "What is the central argument or idea?" Sometimes the answer is obvious and immediate. One essay attacks extravagant funerals fostered by the undertaker industry, another justifies feminism by revealing the miserable position of women in Elizabethan society. In either case, these essays, if successful, will change—or, perhaps, reinforce—the reader's attitudes toward death rituals and the status of women.

Some essays address the inner lives of their readers. E. B. White's "Once More to the Lake" and John Donne's "Meditation XVII," for example, do not attack or justify anything. Rather, they insist that we be aware of our mortality; that awareness might well alter our behavior, our interaction with or perception of the people around us. Such essays often investigate the nature of love, of courage, of what it means to be human.

Types of Essays

In Freshman Composition you probably read and were required to write narrative, descriptive, expository, and argumentative essays. Let us recall the characteristics of each of these types, while keeping in mind that in the real world, essays, more interested in effectiveness than in purity of form, frequently combine features of different formal types.

Narrative Essays

Narrative essays are often autobiographical and recount a sequence of related events. But those events are chosen because they suggest or illustrate some truth or insight. In "Shooting an Elephant," for example, George Orwell narrates an episode from his life that led him to an important insight about imperialism. In "Confessions of a Blue-Chip Black," Roger Wilkins narrates a number of disparate episodes in his life that painfully taught him what it meant to be Black in a racist society. And E. B. White, in "Once More to the Lake," narrates an episode in his life that chilled him by revealing the inevitability of his own death. In these narrative essays, the writers discover in their own experiences the evidence for generalizations about themselves and their societies.

Descriptive Essays

Descriptive essays depict in words sensory observations—they evoke in the reader's imagination the sights and sounds, perhaps even the smells that transport him or her to such places as Joan Didion's Las Vegas or E. M. Forster's little patch of woodland. Sometimes the writer is satisfied simply to create a lifelike evocation of some engaging object or landscape; but Didion and Forster use their descriptions as vehicles for expressing ideas about the debasement of marriage and the corrupting power of property ownership. The descriptive essay, like the narrative essay, often addresses complex issues that trouble our lives— but it does so by appealing primarily to sensory awareness—sight, sound, touch, taste, smell—rather than to intellect. The power of description is so great that often narrative and expository essays use lengthy descriptive passages to communicate forcefully.

Expository Essays

Expository essays attempt to explain and elucidate, to organize and provide information. Often they will embody an extended definition of a complex conception such as love or patriotism. Or expository essays may describe a process—how to do something. This essay, for example, is clearly not narrative, since it doesn't depend for its form on a chronological sequence of meaningful events. It is not descriptive in the pure sense of that type, since it does not depend on conveying sensory impressions of anything. It is, in fact, expository. It acquaints its readers with the techniques and types of essays and provides some tips to help students read essays both analytically and pleasurably. To that end, we have made use of a number of rhetorical strategies that you will remember from your freshman writing course. We *classify* essays by type; we *compare and contrast* them; we use *definition*; we give *examples* to make a point; we imply that there is a *cause and effect* relationship between what readers bring to an essay and the pleasure they derive from it. Similarly the essay authors represented in this book use a variety of such rhetorical strategies to achieve their aims.

Argumentative Essays

Although we described Orwell's "Shooting an Elephant" as a narrative essay, we might reasonably assert that it is also argumentative, since it is designed to convince readers that imperialism is as destructive to the oppressors as to the oppressed. The argumentative essay wishes to persuade its readers. Thus, it usually deals with controversial ideas; it marshals arguments and evidence to support a view; it anticipates and answers opposing arguments. Martin Luther King, Jr. accomplishes all these ends in his "Letter from Birmingham Jail." So does Jonathan Swift in "A Modest Proposal," although his approach is more complicated in that he relies on irony and satire.

Analyzing the Essay

The Thesis

The best way to begin analyzing an essay is to ask, "What is the point of this piece of writing; what is the author trying to show, attack, defend or prove?" If you can answer that question satisfactorily and succinctly, then the analysis of the essay's elements (that is, its rhetorical strategies, its structure, its style, tone, and language) becomes easier. Ellen Goodman's "Being Loved Anyway" is a very short and relatively simple essay, and the author clearly states the thesis when she says "Being Loved Anyway . . . . is not being regarded as perfect but being accepted as imperfect." On the other hand, a much more complex and ambitious essay such as Virginia Woolf's "If Shakespeare Had Had a Sister" does not yield up its thesis quite so easily. We might say that Woolf's examination of the historical record leads her to argue that women did not write during the Elizabethan period because literary talent could not flourish in a social system that made women the ill-educated property of men. This defensible formulation of the essay's thesis, as you will see when you read the essay, leaves a good deal out—notably the exhortation to action with which Woolf concludes the piece.

Structure and Detail

Read carefully the first and last paragraphs of a number of essays. Attend to the writers' strategy for engaging you at the outset with an irresistible proposition.

> In Moulmein, in Lower Burma, I was hated by large numbers of people—the only time in my life that I have been important enough for this to happen to me.

> Surely nothing in the astonishing scheme of life can have nonplussed Nature so much as the fact that none of the females of any of the species she created really cared very much for the male, as such.

> I spy on my patients.

These randomly chosen opening sentences are startling, and most readers will eagerly read on to find out what it was that made the writer so hated in Burma, why females naturally do not care for males, why the doctor spies on his or her patients. You will find that the opening lines of all well-wrought essays instantly capture your attention.

Endings, too, are critical. And if you examine the concluding lines of any of the essays in this collection, you will find forceful assertions that focus the matter that precedes them to sharp intensity. Essayists, unsurprisingly, systematically use gripping beginnings and forceful endings.

Let us turn to what comes between those beginnings and endings.

Essays often deal with abstract issues—the nature of love, the inevitability of death, the evils of imperialism. Though such abstractions do significantly influence our lives, they tend to remain impersonal and distant. Reading about great ideas becomes a sort of academic task—we may record the ideas in notebooks, but we tend to relegate them to some intellectual sphere, separate from the pain and passion of our own humanity. The accomplished essay writer, however, forces us to confront such issues by converting abstract ideas into concrete and illustrative detail.

For example, George Orwell points out early in "Shooting an Elephant" that the "anti-European feeling was very bitter" in British-controlled Burma. But he immediately moves from the abstraction of "anti-European feeling" to "if a European woman went through the bazaars alone somebody would probably spit betel juice over her dress" and "when a nimble Burman tripped me up on the football field and the referee (another Burman) looked the other way, the crowd yelled with hideous laughter." The tiny bits of hateful experience, because they are physical and concrete, powerfully reinforce the abstract assertion about "anti-European feeling" that lies at the center of Orwell's essay, and the narrative account of the speaker's behavior in front of the mob culminates in a specific statement—"I perceived in this moment that when the white man turns tyrant it is his own freedom that he destroys." The large generality emerges from deeply felt personal experience.

And, in another essay, Dr. Richard Selzer spies on the terminally ill patient who has become a "discus thrower." How, after all, can a writer, trying to deal with the inevitability of death, convey the intense pain and emotional agony of a dying man? Selzer's patient concretizes that pain and agony in a simple repetitive act:

> In time the man reaches to find the rim of the tray, then on to find the dome of the covered dish. He lifts off the cover and places it on the stand. He fingers across the plate until he probes the eggs. He lifts the plate in both hands, sets it on the palm of his right hand, centers it, balances it. He hefts it up and down slightly, getting the feel of it. Abruptly, he draws back his right arm as far as he can.
>
> There is the crack of the plate breaking against the wall at the foot of his bed and the small wet sound of the scrambled eggs dropping to the floor.
>
> And then he laughs. It is a sound you have never heard.

Can you imagine any objective and clinical description of the anguish and rage of a dying man that would convey the feeling more effectively than the concrete details of this understated narrative anecdote?

Style and Tone

The word *style* refers to all the writing skills that contribute to the effect of any piece of literature. And *tone*—the attitude conveyed by the language a writer chooses—is a particularly significant aspect of writing style. As an illustration of the effect of tone, consider these opening lines of two essays (Katherine Anne Porter's "The Necessary Enemy" and Ellen Goodman's "Being Loved Anyway") that probe the nature of enduring love.

> She is a frank, charming, fresh-hearted young woman who married for love. She and her husband are one of those gay, good-looking young pairs who ornament this modern scene rather more in profusion perhaps than ever before in our history. They are handsome, with a talent for finding their way in their world, they work at things that interest them, their tastes agree and their hopes. They intend in all good faith to spend their lives together, to have children and do well by them and each other—to be happy, in fact, which for them is the whole point of their marriage.

> From time to time, my Uncle Mike likes to pass on the wisdom of one generation to another. In his own fashion.
>
> On the subject of enduring love, for example, he and my aunt are role models of believability. They like each other. They have a good time together. And they have managed it for roughly forty-one years.
>
> So, when someone asks him the secret, he is more than willing to share the fact that he modeled his own success on his father's.
>
> "My father would get up in the morning, look in the mirror and say, 'You're no bargain.'"
>
> This, I think, would make a hell of a Valentine.

The tonal differences between these excerpts produce differing voices. The first has a formal tone—the speaker is setting up a problem for analysis; her third-person voice speaks from some distance as she describes the young couple. The second voice is personal and informal; she speaks in the first-person and invites the reader to participate in an intimate exchange of ideas.

The writers' diction reinforces the distinctive tone of voice each creates. The first speaks of a "young woman who married for love" and of a couple whose "tastes agree and their hopes." Contrast the tone created by these rather abstract statements with that of the second writer, who characterizes her uncle and aunt tersely: "They like each other. They have a good time together." The first generally uses long, complex sentences; the second uses short, less complex sentences. And the sentence "This, I think, would make a hell of a Valentine" is simply unimaginable in the tone of voice created by the first writer.

The tone a writer creates contributes substantially to the message he or she conveys. Jonathan Swift might have written a sound, academic essay about the economic diseases of Ireland and how to cure them—but his invention of the speaker of "A Modest Proposal," who ironically and sardonically proposes the establishment of a baby meat exporting industry, jars the reader in ways no scholarly essay could. The sometimes flamboyant tone of Tom Wolfe in "The Right Stuff" exactly matches the flamboyant peculiarity of the jet fighter pilot. The high seriousness of Donne's tone in "Meditation XVII" perfectly suits his contemplation of the relationship among the living, the dying, and the dead.

Style is a more difficult quality to define than tone. Dictionaries will tell you that style is both "a manner of expression in language" and "excellence in expression." Certainly it is easier to distinguish between various *manners* of expression than it is to describe just what constitutes *excellence* in expression. For example, the manners of expression of John Donne in "Meditation XVII," of Richard Selzer in "The Discus Thrower," of Jessica Mitford in "The American Way of Death" clearly differ. The first muses about death in a style characterized by formality and complex extended images. The second achieves informality with a style characterized by short direct sentences and understatement. The essay's figurative language describes the dying patient rather than the nature of death. The third uses the breezy style of a muckraking journalist, replete with contemptuous asides and sardonic exclamations.

Nonetheless, we can describe the excellence of each style. Donne, an Anglican priest, meditates on the brotherhood of all men while living, and the promise of eternal life in the face of physical death. He creates a remarkable image when he argues that "all mankind is of one author." Not so remarkable, you might argue; God is often called the "author of mankind." But Donne insists on the figurative quality of God as author and the intimate relationship among all people when he adds that all humankind "is one volume." Then he extends this metaphor by arguing that "when one man dies, one chapter is not torn out of the book, but translated into a better language." The daring image is further extended. "God," Donne tells us, "employs several translators; some pieces are translated by age, some by sickness, some by war, some by justice." By alluding to the actual making of a book by the bookbinder, Donne elaborates on the central image and reestablishes the idea of brotherhood—"God's hand is in every translation, and his hand shall bind up all our scattered leaves again for that library where every book shall lie open to one another." Surely, this magnificent figurative characterization of death (regardless of your personal beliefs) exhibits stylistic excellence.

Richard Selzer deals with death also.

> From the doorway of Room 542 the man in the bed seems deeply tanned. Blue eyes and close-cropped white hair give him the appearance of vigor and good health. But I know that his skin is not brown from the sun. It is rusted, rather, in the last stage of containing the vile repose within. And the blue eyes are frosted, looking inward like the windows of a snowbound cottage. This man is blind.

Here you see a very different style. Whereas Donne's sentences are long and move with the rolling cadence of oratory, Selzer's are terse and direct. Selzer's metaphors and similes characterize the ugliness of dying. The man's skin is not tanned by the sun; it is "rusted." His sightless eyes are frosted "like the windows of a snowbound cottage." These images, together with the artful simplicity of Selzer's short, halting sentences, powerfully convey the degradation and the impotence of the dying. Here again, style plays a significant role.

Jessica Mitford's attack on the American funeral industry begins:

> O Death, where is thy sting? O grave, where is thy victory? Where indeed? Many a badly stung survivor, faced with the aftermath of some relative's funeral, has ruefully concluded that the victory has been won hands down by a funeral establishment—in disastrously unequal battle.

This essay opens with a quote from St. Paul's Epistle to the Corinthians— certainly a sober and exalted allusion. But immediately, the tone turns sardonic with the question "Where indeed?" And the writer compounds the sarcasm by extending the Biblical metaphor that compares death with a painful bee-sting to the equally painful experience of the "stung" survivor who has been conned into enormous expenditure by a funeral establishment. Her breezy style juxtaposes the ancient Biblical promise of a spiritual victory over death with the crass modern reality—the only victor, nowadays, is the greedy funeral director. The perception is "rueful," and the victory "has been won hands down" in an encounter characterized as a "disastrously unequal battle." Mitford's language, playing off the high seriousness of the Biblical quotation, stylistically advances her purpose by introducing a note of mockery. Certainly her argument gains force from the pervasive sardonic tone that characterizes her style.

Three different writers, all discussing some aspect of death, exhibit three distinctive manners of expression and three distinctive varieties of excellence— in short, three distinctive styles.

Your principal concern, when reading an essay, must always be to discover the essay's central thesis. What does the writer wish you to understand about his or her experience, the world, or yourself? Once you have understood the essay's thesis, you can increase your pleasure by examining the means the author used to convey it, and, perhaps, recognize techniques that will enhance the quality of your own writing. To that end, you ought to examine the essay's structure and the rhetorical strategies that shape it. How does it begin and end? What type is it—narrative, descriptive, expository, argumentative? How do rhetorical strategies—definition, cause and effect, classification, exemplification, comparison and contrast—function to serve the author's purposes? Then, discover the sources of reading pleasure by closely analyzing the language of the essay. Watch writers energize abstract ideas with detailed and moving experience; consider the uses of figurative language—the metaphors and similes that create both physical and emotional landscapes in the prose; respond to the tone of voice and the stylistic choices that create it. When you have done all this successfully, when you have discovered not only *what* the author has said, but also *how* the author moved you to his or her point of view—then you will have understood the essay.

Three Critical Approaches: Formalist, Sociological, Psychoanalytic

Literary criticism has to do with the *value* of literature, its goodness or badness, not with the history of literature. Because value judgments tend to be highly subjective, lively, and sometimes even acrimonious, debates among literary critics accompany their diverse responses to and judgments of the same work. The judgments literary critics make about a story or poem are bound to reflect their own cherished values. The truth of a work of art is, obviously, very different from the truth of a mathematical formula. Certainly one's attitudes toward war, religion, sex, and politics are irrelevant to the truth of a formula but quite relevant to one's judgment of a literary work.

Yet, any examination of the broad range of literary criticism reveals that groups of critics (and all readers, ultimately, are critics) share certain assumptions about literature. These shared assumptions govern the way that critics approach a work, the elements they tend to look for and emphasize, the details they find significant or insignificant, and, finally, their overall judgment of the value of the work. In order to illustrate diverse critical methodologies, we have examined two of the works in this anthology—Matthew Arnold's poem, "Dover Beach" (p. 458), and Nathaniel Hawthorne's short story, "My Kinsman, Major Molineux" (p.7)—from three different critical positions: the formalist, the sociological, and the psychoanalytic. We have selected these three critical positions not because they are the only ones (there are others), but because they represent three major and distinctive approaches of literary criticism that may help readers formulate their own responses to a work of literature.

We do not suggest that one approach is more valid than the others or that the lines dividing the approaches are always clear and distinct. Readers will, perhaps, discover one approach more congenial to their temperament, more "true" to their sense of the world, than another. Again, they may find that some works seem to lend themselves to one approach, other works to a different approach. More likely, they will find themselves utilizing more than one approach in dealing with a single work. What the reader will discover in reading the three analyses of the Arnold poem and the Hawthorne story is not that they contradict one another, but that, taken together, they complement and enrich one's understanding and enjoyment of these works.

Formalist Criticism

While the formalist critic would not deny the relevance of sociological, biographical, and historical information to a work of art, he or she insists that the function of criticism is to focus on the work itself as a verbal structure and to discover the ways in which the work achieves (or does not achieve) unity. The job of criticism is to show how the various parts of the work are wedded together into an organic whole. That is to say, we must examine the *form* of the work, for it is the form that is its meaning. Put somewhat oversimply, the formalist critic views a work as a timeless aesthetic object; we may find whatever we wish in the work as long as what we find is demonstrably in the work itself.

DOVER BEACH

From the perspective of the formalist critic, the fact that Matthew Arnold was deeply concerned with how man could live a civilized and enjoyable life under the pressures of modern industrialization or that Arnold appears to have suffered in his youth an intense conflict between sexual and spiritual love may be interesting but ought not to be the focal point in an analysis of his poetry. After all, the historian is best equipped to reconstruct and illuminate Matthew Arnold's Victorian England, and it is the biographer's and psychologist's job to tell us about his personal life. A critic of "Dover Beach" who speculates on these matters is doing many things, perhaps quite interesting things, but is not giving us a description of the work itself.

"Dover Beach" is a dramatic monologue, a poem in which a speaker addresses another person at a particular time and place. In the opening lines, Arnold skillfully sets the scene, introduces the image of the sea that is to dominate the poem, and establishes a moment of tranquility and moon-bathed loveliness appropriate to a poem in which a man addresses his beloved. The beauty of the scene is established through visual images that give way, beginning with line 9, to a series of auditory images that undermine or bring into serious question the atmosphere established by the opening eight lines. In this contrast between visual and auditory imagery, a contrast that is developed through the entire poem, Arnold embodies one of the poem's major themes: appearance differs from reality.

In the second stanza, the "eternal note of sadness" struck in the final line of the first stanza is given an historical dimension and universalized by the allusion to Sophocles, the great Greek tragedian of fifth-century B.C. Athens. We become aware that the sadness and misery the speaker refers to are not the consequences of some momentary despair or particular historical event but are rather perennial, universal conditions of man's mortal life. Indeed, the allusion to Sophocles and the Aegean extends the feeling not only over centuries of time but over an immense geographical area, from the Aegean to the English Channel.

The third stanza develops further the dominant sea imagery. But the real, literal seas of the earlier stanzas now become a metaphor for faith, perhaps religious faith, which once gave unity and meaning to human life but now has ebbed away and left us stranded, helpless, bereft of virtually any defenses against sadness and misery. The "bright girdle furled," suggesting a happy and universal state, turns into a "roar" down the "naked shingles [i.e., pebble beaches] of the world."

The poet, therefore, turns, in the final stanza, to his beloved, to their love for each other as the only possible hope, meaning, and happiness in such a world. And his words to her echo the imagery of the opening lines with the important difference that the controlling verb *is* of the opening lines, denoting the actual and the real, is now replaced by the verb *seems*. The beautiful world is an illusion that conceals the bleak truth that the world provides no relief for our misery. This grim realization leads to the powerful final image which compares life to a battle of armies at night. We have moved from the calm, serene, moon-bathed loveliness of the opening scene to an image of violence in a dark world where it is impossible to distinguish friend from foe or indeed even to understand what is happening.

"Dover Beach," then, is a meditation upon the irremediable pain and anguish of human existence, in the face of which the only possibility for joy and love and beauty is to be found in an intimate relationship between two human beings. The depth of the speaker's sadness is emphasized by his powerful evocation in the opening lines of the beauty of the scene. The first eight lines move with a quiet ease and flow with liquids and nasals, a movement enhanced by the balancing effect of the caesuras. In lines 9 to 14, the sounds also echo the sense, for now the sounds are much harsher as the plosive *b*s intrude and most of the lines are broken irregularly by more than one caesura.

We have already noted that the dominant image of the poem, the key to the poem's structure, is the sea. It is the real sea the speaker describes in the opening stanza, but when it sounds the "eternal note of sadness," the sea becomes symbolic. In the second stanza, the speaker is reminded of another real sea, the Aegean, which he associates with Sophocles, and the developing unity is achieved, not only at the literal level (Sophocles listening to the Aegean parallels the speaker's listening to the northern sea) but at the symbolic level (Sophocles perceived the ebb and flow of human misery as the speaker perceives the eternal note of sadness). The third stanza further develops the sea image but presents something of a problem, for it is not altogether clear what the speaker means by "Faith." If Arnold means religious faith, and that seems most likely, we face the problem of determining what period of history he is alluding to. "Dover Beach" establishes two reference points in time—the present and fifth-century B.C. Athens—that are related to each other by negative auditory images. Since the function of the lines about the Sea of Faith is to provide a sharp contrast between the present and fifth-century Athens (the visual image of "a bright girdle furled" associates the Sea of Faith with the opening eight lines), the time when the Sea of Faith was full must lie somewhere between these two points or earlier than the fifth century. Since a formalist critic deals only with the work *itself* and since there appears to be nothing elsewhere in the poem that will allow us to make a choice, we might conclude that these lines weaken the poem.

For the formalist critic, however, the final stanza presents the most serious problem. Most critics of whatever persuasion agree that they are moving and memorable lines, poignant in the speaker's desperate turning to his beloved in the face of a world whose beauty is a deception, and powerful in their description of that world, especially in the final image of ignorant armies clashing by night. But what, the formalist critic will ask, has become of the sea image? Is it not strange that the image which had dominated the poem throughout, has given it its unity, is in the climactic stanza simply dropped? On the face of it, at least, we, as formalist critics, would have to conclude that the abandonment of the unifying image in the concluding stanza is a serious structural weakness, lessened perhaps by the power of the images that replace it, but a structural weakness nonetheless. On the other hand, a formalist critic might commend the poet for his effective alternation of visual and auditory imagery throughout the poem. The first four lines of the final stanza return to visual images of an illusory "good" world (controlled by *seems*, as we have already noted) and concludes with a simile that fuses a sombre vision of darkness and night, with the harsh auditory images of *alarms* and *clashes*.

MY KINSMAN, MAJOR MOLINEUX

This rather strange story by Hawthorne may be summarized easily. After an opening paragraph in which Hawthorne comments on the harsh treatment of colonial governors appointed by the British crown at the hands of the people of the Massachusetts Bay Colony, we meet an eighteen-year-old boy named Robin who crosses the ferry one night into an unnamed town. He is the second son of a country minister and has been sent to town to seek out his powerful kinsman, Major Molineux, who, presumably, will use his influence to help the boy make his way in the world. Strangely, the boy is unsuccessful in locating the residence of his kinsman. Worse, he is mocked and threatened by the several people he accosts and is almost seduced by a pretty harlot. Finally, he is told to wait in a certain spot, and shortly a boisterous procession, led by a man with a face painted half red and half black, passes. The procession conducts an open cart in which his kinsman, Major Molineux, tarred and feathered, is being led out of the town and into exile. The boy joins in the laughter at the plight of his once powerful relative but soon decides (his prospects blasted) to return home. A kindly bystander urges him to stay and make his way in the world without the help of his kinsman.

The formalist critic would note that the story is about a young man's initiation into the rude adult world where he must make his own way unprotected by a sheltering family. The world is at best morally ambiguous and at worst menacingly hostile. The transformation in Robin from self-confident but ignorant grown child to a self-doubting but aware young adult is conveyed through a series of events culminating in a violent climax. Those events, and the atmosphere surrounding them, make for a story that creates, through irony, a

mounting suspense released for Robin and the reader with explosive suddenness. Hawthorne's considerable skill in creating that suspense and his method
for releasing it are fundamental to the successful embodiment of the *theme*.
Naive Robin, a "good child," becomes experienced Robin, more sober and
more aware of the evil aspect of the human condition.

The story opens with an apparently superfluous preface in which Hawthorne
tells his readers that royal governors in Massachusetts Bay (that is, governors
appointed by the English crown rather than elected by the people) were treated
roughly, even if they were fair and lenient. The discussion is to serve as "a
preface to the following adventures, which chanced upon a summer night, not
far from a hundred years ago [approximately 1732]." Hawthorne concludes that
opening paragraph: "The reader, in order to avoid a long and dry detail of
colonial affairs, is requested to dispense with an account of the train of circumstances that had caused much temporary inflammation of the popular mind."
Now it is an article of faith for the formalist critic that no part of a literary
work is superfluous. Art is *organic*. All its parts are essential to the whole. The
reader may remain ignorant of some particular events that caused some particular social inflammation, but he or she cannot go on to the adventures of that
summer night without some expectation that they will have something to do
with the politics of colonial Massachusetts. If this prefatory paragraph is really
superfluous, then it constitutes a flaw in the work. If it is not, we shall have,
finally, to understand its function in the story.

The narrative begins with an account of the arrival of an eighteen-year-old
country-bred youth on his first visit to town, at nine o'clock of a moonlit evening. All of the details provided in this second paragraph are significant and
repay close reading. The young man from the country, on his first visit to
town, dressed humbly but serviceably, with brown curly hair, well-shaped features, and bright cheerful eyes, presents an agreeable character. His physical
description is pleasing. He is doubtless rather innocent (being country-bred and
on his first visit to town). But he arrives at night and remains hidden in darkness until illuminated by some light-giving source. The moonlight alone doesn't
suffice, and we require the help of the boatman's lantern to see him.

The manipulation of the light and the darkness in the story is crucial. As
Robin walks about the town looking for the lodging of his kinsman, Major
Molineux, he encounters six different people. The first, a rather dignified old
man, is stopped by Robin "just when the light from the open door and windows of a barber's shop fell upon both their features." The second encounter
is within the inn, where there is light. The third encounter is with the harlot
who is discerned by Robin as "a strip of scarlet petticoat, and the occasional
sparkle of an eye, as if the moonbeams were trembling on some bright thing."
We will see those moonbeams trembling on something altogether different later
on. The fourth encounter, like the first two, ends with a threat from the sleepy
watchman who carried a lantern. The fifth encounter is with the demonic man
with the parti-colored face who "stepped back into the moonlight" when he
unmuffled to Robin.

Now for all the local illumination that surrounds the threats, the temptation, and the final promise to Robin that his kinsman would soon be by, Robin remains in the dark. He does not understand why his questions generate such fierce threats from the elderly gentleman, the innkeeper, the watchman, and the demonic man. He sees the harlot in her parlor but doubts (quite rightly) her words and, finally, frightened a bit by the watchman, resists her seduction. The sixth encounter differs from the rest. The kindly stranger dimly sees Robin in the darkness—a literal and metaphorical darkness—and joins him. What of all this?

When the climactic moment occurs, when the procession arrives, it is lit by a dense multitude of torches "concealing, by their glare, whatever object they illuminated." This is rather a strange statement. When there is at last adequate light, the very glare conceals—and conceals what Robin must discover. Yet again, when the demonic leader of the procession fixes his eyes on Robin, "the unsteady brightness of the [torches] formed a veil which he could not penetrate." Finally, as the cart stops before Robin, "the torches blazed the brightest, there the moon shone out like day, and there, in tar-and-feathery dignity, sat his kinsman, Major Molineux!"

The orchestration of the light and darkness in the story becomes a metaphor for Robin's condition. Throughout, he is blind, despite the light. Rebuffs and laughter repeatedly greet his reiterated simple question, and in every case Robin—being, as he says, a "shrewd" youth—rationalizes the responses so that he can accept them without loss of self-esteem. The old man who threatens him is a "country representative" who simply doesn't know how powerful his kinsman is. The innkeeper who expels him is responding to Robin's poverty. The grinning demonic man with face painted half red, half black generates the ejaculation "Strange things we travellers see!" And Robin engages in some philosophical speculations upon the weird sight, which "settled this point shrewdly, rationally, and satisfactorily." In every case, however, Robin's rationalizations are wrong. As "shrewd" as he is, he constantly misunderstands because he is optimistic and self-confident. The reality would shatter both his optimism and his confidence. Despite the lighted places in the darkness, the places where the fate of his kinsman is hinted, he remains in the dark. At the climax, as the light becomes brighter and brighter, it does not illuminate but rather conceals by glare, forming an impenetrable veil through which he cannot see. Finally, when the torches blaze the brightest and the moon shines out like day, Robin sees! Presumably, now, he understands correctly the events of that long night.

But what is it that Robin understands? The question might be put another way. What is it that from the outset Robin doesn't understand? A good-looking, "shrewd" lad with a powerful relative, he expects the people he meets to behave with kindness and civility. A country youth, a minister's son, his experience of the world is limited. As the night wears on, the reader perceives Robin doggedly refusing to recognize that some sinister, evil action is afoot. Robin doesn't accept the existence of evil—everything can be explained in some rational way. With the temptation by the lovely harlot, Robin discovers within himself a sinfulness he might indignantly deny—and he does, after all, resist the temptation. But his weakness might be the beginning of wisdom, because Robin must discover that the human condition is not simple—it is complex. As he waits by the church, he peers into the window and notices the "awful radiance" within; he notices that a solitary ray of moonlight dares to rest upon the open page of the Bible. He wonders whether "that heavenly light" was "visible because no earthly and impure feet were within the walls?" And the thought makes him shiver with a strong loneliness. The implication that humans are inevitably impure grows strong.

This notion is driven home by the cryptic exchange between Robin and the kindly stranger when a great shout comes up from the still distant crowd. Robin is astonished by the numerous voices which constitute that one shout, and the stranger replies, "May not a man have several voices, Robin, as well as two complexions?" The notion that a man may have several voices has never occurred to Robin. In his attempt to deal with the strange sight of the man with two complexions, Robin rationalizes. But he does not learn from the evidence of his senses that man is complex, has different, even conflicting aspects. The stranger tries to teach him this truth—a man has many voices. Robin responds rather fatuously, thinking of the pretty harlot, "Perhaps a man may; but Heaven forbid that a woman should!" What does he mean? Doubtless he wishes to believe that the harlot was indeed the major's housekeeper, that she told the truth, spoke with one voice, and was not the embodiment of a sort of satanic evil attempting to entrap him. All in all, Robin's view of the world from the outset is simplistic. And that view encourages him in his optimistic confidence. The stranger tells him that the world is not simple—that each man speaks with many voices, that the human condition comprises many aspects. The heavenly radiance enters only into an empty church, unsoiled by impure human feet. But Robin still does not understand.

The procession approaches. Grotesque sounds—"tuneless bray," the "antipodes of music," "din"—announce the rout. Laughter dominates, and the light grows brighter and brighter. But still Robin does not understand. There sits his kinsman in tar-and feathery dignity. Their eyes meet in an anguished and humiliating recognition. And Robin laughs.

That laughter is the outward symbol of his understanding. He has learned of human complexity. He has learned that he too contains a satanic aspect. His innocent optimism, based on an unrealistic conception of man, is altered to experienced doubt by his new understanding of the complexity and universality of that evil aspect of humanity that is symbolized by the behavior of the mob and the wild abiding laughter that infects even Robin.

The story is based on colonial history. The opening paragraph serves to remind us of the literal level on which the story operates. Mobs did roam the streets of Boston, did disguise themselves as Indians, did tar and feather and expel crown officers. But our attention is directed to a young, inexperienced boy. Finally, we must ask what has happened. How is Robin changed by his experiences? The images of darkness and light, the temptation scene, the moonlit church, the mob, and Robin's response to it all weave together into a single cord, the strands of which guide him to a new awareness both of himself and of his world.

Sociological Criticism

In contrast to the formalistic critic, who maintains that the proper job of criticism is to approach each work of art as a self-contained aesthetic object and to attempt to illuminate its inherent structure and unity, the sociological critic asserts that since all men are the products of a particular time and place, we can never fully understand a work without some understanding of the social forces that molded the author and all that he did and thought. The sociological critic feels that the formalistic critic's attempt to view a work as timeless denies the fundamental and self-evident fact that authors do not (and cannot) divest themselves of all the shaping forces of their history and environment. Consequently, critics must look to those forces if they are to understand an author's works.

DOVER BEACH

To understand "Dover Beach," we must, according to the sociological critic, know something about the major intellectual and social currents of Victorian England and the way in which Arnold responded to them. By the time Arnold was born in 1822, the rapid advances in technology that had begun with the Industrial Revolution of the eighteenth century were producing severe strains on the social and intellectual fabric. An agrarian economy was giving way to an industrial economy, and the transition was long and painful. The new economy was creating a new merchant middle class whose growing wealth and power made it increasingly difficult for the upper classes to maintain exclusive political power. The passage of the celebrated Reform Bill of 1832, extending suffrage to any man who owned property worth at least ten pounds in annual rent, shifted political power to the middle class and gave cities a greater political voice. It was not until 1867 that the franchise was extended to the lower classes. The intervening years were marked by severe social crises: depression, unemployment, rioting. Indeed, during these critical years when England was attempting to cope with the new problems of urban industrialism, the agitation and rioting of the lower classes created genuine fears of revolution (Englishmen remembered very clearly the French Revolution of 1789).

The ferment was no less intense and disruptive in the more rarefied world of intellectual and theoretical debate. While it would be erroneous to assume that pre-industrial England was a world of idyllic stability, there can be little doubt that the pace of change was much slower than during the nineteenth century. Despite sectarian strife, perhaps the greatest stabilizing force in pre-industrial England was religion. It offered answers to the ultimate questions of human existence and, on the basis of those answers, justification and authority for the temporal order—kingship (or political control by a small aristocracy), sharp class distinctions, and the like. The technology that made industrialism possible grew out of the scientific discoveries and methodologies that challenged some of our fundamental assumptions and faith. Specific scientific discoveries seemed to undermine the old religious faith (for example, Darwin's *Origin of Species*, published in 1859); the scientific approach of skepticism and empirical investigation, in addition to critical scholarship, led to numerous studies of the Bible not as a sacred text of infallible truth but as a historical text that arose out of a particular time and place in human history. Close examination of the Bible itself resulted in discoveries of inconsistencies and contradictions as well as demonstrable evidence of its temporal rather than supernatural origin.

Matthew Arnold, born into a substantial middle-class family and educated at England's finest schools, established himself early as an important poet and as one of the leading social critics of the period. In much of his poetry and his voluminous prose writings, Arnold addressed critical questions of his time. The old values, particularly religious, were crumbling under the onslaught of new ideas; Arnold recognized that a simple reactionary defense of the old values was not possible (even if one still believed in them). Unless some new system of values could be formulated, society was likely to, at worst, fall into anarchy or, at best, offer the prospect of an arid and narrow life to individuals. And since the destiny of the nation was clearly devolving into the hands of the middle class, Arnold spent much of his career attempting to show the middle class the way to a richer and fuller life.

For an understanding of "Dover Beach," however, Arnold's attempt to define and advance cultural values is less important than his confrontation with the pain and dilemma of his age. Caught in what he called in one of his poems "this strange disease of modern life," Arnold found that modern discoveries made religious faith impossible, and yet he yearned for the security and certainty of his childhood faith. In his darker and more despairing moments, it seemed to him that with the destruction of old values the world was dissolving into chaos and meaninglessness. In these moments, he saw himself as "wandering between two worlds, one dead, / The other powerless to be born."

"Dover Beach" expresses one of those dark moments in Arnold's life—a moment shared by many of Arnold's contemporaries and modern readers as well, who, in many ways, instinctively understand the mood and meaning of the poem because the realities to which it responds are still very much with us. Simply stated, it is a poem in which the speaker declares that even in a setting of the utmost loveliness and tranquility (a sociological critic might very well here discuss the opening lines in much the same way a formalistic critic does) the uncertainty and chaos of modern life cannot for long be forgotten or ignored. For uncertainty and chaos so permeate the life and consciousness of the speaker that everything he sees, everything he meditates upon, is infected. The scene of silent loveliness described in the opening lines turns into a grating roar that sounds the eternal note of sadness.

In the second stanza, the speaker turns to ancient Greece and its greatest tragic playwright in an effort to generalize and thereby lessen and defend against the overwhelming despair he feels. If the confusion and chaos of modern life are part of the eternal human condition, then perhaps it can be borne with resignation. Yet the third stanza seems to deny this possibility, for it suggests that at some other time in history Christian faith gave meaning and direction to life but now that faith is no longer available.

Trapped in a world where faith is no longer possible, the speaker turns in the final stanza—turns with a kind of desperation because no other possibilities seem to exist—to the beloved and their relationship as the only chance of securing from a meaningless and grim life some fragment of meaning and joy. Everything else, he tells her, everything positive in which we might place our faith, is a mere "seeming." The real world, he concludes, in a powerful and strikingly modern image, is like two armies battling in darkness. Whether or not the final image is an allusion to a particular historical battle (as many critics have suggested), it is a graphic image to describe what modern life seemed to a sensitive Victorian who could see no way out of the dilemma.

For sociological critics, then, an understanding of "Dover Beach" requires some knowledge of the major stresses and intellectual issues of Victorian England, because the poem is a response to and comment upon those issues by one of the great Victorian poets and social critics. Our description of those issues and Arnold's ideas is extremely sketchy and selective; it merely illustrates the approach a sociological critic might take in dealing with the poem. Nevertheless, the sketchiness of the presentation raises important questions about sociological criticism: Where does the sociological critic stop? How deep and detailed an understanding of the times and the writer's relationship to the period is necessary to understand the work? The formalistic critic might charge that sociological critics are in constant danger of becoming so immersed in sociological matters (and even biography) that they lose sight of the works they set out to investigate. The danger, of course, is a real one, and sociological critics must be mindful, always, that their primary focus is art, not sociology, history, or biography; the extent of their sociological investigations will be controlled and limited by the work they are attempting to illuminate. To this charge, the sociological critic might very well respond (perhaps in pique) that formalistic critics become so preoccupied with matters of structure and unity that their criticism becomes arid and apparently divorced from all the human concerns that make people want to read poems in the first place. The sociological critic would agree with the comment made by Leon Trotsky, the Russian Marxist revolutionary, in his book *Literature and Revolution*:

> The methods of formal analysis are necessary, but insufficient. You may count up the alliterations in popular proverbs, classify metaphors, count up the number of vowels and consonants in a wedding song. It will undoubtedly enrich our knowledge of folk art, in one way or another; but if you don't know the peasant system of sowing, and the life that is based on it, if you don't know the part the scythe plays, and if you have not mastered the meaning of the church calendar to the peasant of the time when the peasant marries, or when the peasant women give birth, you will have only understood the outer shell of folk art, but the kernel will not have been reached.

As a final note, a few remarks need to be made on a special form of sociological criticism, namely, ideological (i.e., Marxist, Christian, etc.) criticism.

While sociological critics differ from formalistic critics in their approach to literature, they tend to share with formalistic critics the view that works of art are important in their own right and do not need to be justified in terms of any other human activity or interest. The Marxist critic, on the other hand, while sharing many of the assumptions and the approaches of the sociological critic, carries the approach an important step further. Marxist critics see literature as one activity among many that are to be studied and judged in terms of a larger and all-encompassing ideology. They hold that one cannot understand the literature of the past unless one understands how it reflects the relationships between economic production and social class. And since the Marxist sees his or her duty—indeed, the duty of all responsible and humane people—as not merely to describe the world but to change it in such a way as to free the oppressed masses of the world, she or he will not be content merely to illuminate a work, as does the sociological critic, or to demonstrate its aesthetic unity and beauty, as does the formalist critic. The Marxist critic will judge contemporary literature by the contribution it makes to bringing about revolution or in some way making the masses of workers (the proletariat) more conscious of their oppression and, therefore, more equipped to struggle against the oppressors.

The Marxist critic might describe "Dover Beach" very much as the sociological critic, but would go on to point out that the emotion Arnold expresses in the poem is predictable, the inevitable end product of a dehumanizing, capitalistic economy in which a small class of oligarchs is willing, at whatever cost, to protect and increase its wealth and power. Moreover, the Marxist critic, as a materialist who believes that humanity makes its own history, would find Arnold's reference to "the eternal note of sadness" a mystic evasion of the real sources of human alienation and pain; Arnold's misery can be clearly and unmystically explained by the socioeconomic conditions of his time. It is Arnold's refusal to face this fact which leads him to the conclusion typical of a bourgeois artist-intellectual who refuses to face the truth; the cure for Arnold's pain cannot be found in a love relationship, because relationships between people, like everything else, are determined by socioeconomic conditions. The cure for the pain which he describes so well will be found in the world of action, in the struggle to create a socioeconomic system that is just and humane. "Dover Beach," then, is both a brilliant evocation of the alienation and misery caused by a capitalistic economy and a testimony to the inability of bourgeois intellectuals to understand what is responsible for their feelings.

MY KINSMAN, MAJOR MOLINEUX

"My Kinsman, Major Molineux" presents a nocturnal world, viewed largely from the point of view of its young hero, where nothing makes sense to him. It appears to be an allegoric or symbolic world, a dreamlike world where everything seems to mean something else. Robin searches for the meaning to the strange behavior of townspeople he accosts, for some key which will unlock the mystery. The sociological critic also searches for the key, and finds it in the opening paragraph of the story, the paragraph that in any short story is crucial in setting the stage for the action about to unfold.

That paragraph, the sociological critic would note, is not a part of the narrative itself but is rather a straightforward summary of the historical situation in the American colonies prior to the Revolutionary War. We are given this summary, Hawthorne tells us, "as a preface to the following adventures." No critic, of whatever persuasion, can ignore that paragraph. In contrast to the actual story, the opening paragraph is clear and straightforward: On the eve of the Revolution, the bitterness and hostility of the colonists toward the mother country had become so intense that no colonial administrators, even those who were kindest in exercising their power, were safe from the wrath of the people. It is in the context of this moment of American history, when there occurred a "temporary inflammation of the popular mind," that the story of Robin's search for his kinsman must be read and interpreted. For "My Kinsman, Major Molineux" is an examination of and comment upon the American colonies as they prepared to achieve, by violence if necessary, independence from the increasingly intolerable domination of England.

We are introduced to Robin as he arrives in town, an energetic, likable, and innocent young man who has left the secure comfort of his rural family to commence a career. He is on the verge of manhood and independence, filled with anticipation and promise, as well as apprehension, as he confronts an uncertain future. But Robin, unlike most young men in his position, has the advantage of a wealthy cousin who has offered to help the young man establish himself. The story narrates Robin's polite and reasonable inquiries as to where Major Molineux resides and the bafflingly rude and hostile responses of the townspeople.

The mystery is Major Molineux, or, rather, the hostility his name evokes. For the reader, at least, the mystery begins to dispel when he learns that the major, an aristocratic and commanding figure, represents inherited wealth and civil and military rank—in short, the authority and values of the mother country. To Robin, fresh from the simple and nonpolitical world of his pastoral home, Major Molineux is a real person, his cousin, whose aid he seeks. To the townspeople, on the other hand, Molineux is a symbol of the hated mother country in a political struggle that is turning increasingly ugly.

This difference between what Major Molineux means to Robin and what he means to the townspeople is prepared for at the very outset of the narrative. Robin has left the morally simplistic and nonpolitical world of his country home and come to a town that is seething with revolutionary fervor. The country is the past, America's past; the town is the present, the place where America's future will be decided. As Robin winds his way through the metropolis vainly searching for his kinsman, Hawthorne skillfully weaves into the narrative details suggestive of the political theme. Robin, we are told, enters the town "with as eager an eye as if he were entering London city." Before entering the tavern, "he beheld the broad countenance of a British hero swinging before the door." Once in the tavern, he observes a group of men who look like sailors drinking punch, which, Hawthorne tells us, "the West India trade had long since made a familiar drink in the colony." More significantly, this episode ends when the innkeeper, in response to Robin's inquiry about his cousin, merely points to a poster offering a reward for a runaway "bounden servant" and ominously advises Robin to leave. The suggestion is clear—anyone seeking Major Molineux must be a willing bond servant (bond servitude being a form of limited slavery used by England to help populate the American colonies) and, therefore, an enemy of the revolutionaries.

Robin continues his wanderings, his confusion deepening, until a stranger he accosts tells him that Major Molineux will soon pass by the very spot where they are standing. As Robin waits, his thoughts drift to his country home and family. In a dreamlike state, he dwells upon the warmth and security of the life he has left, the sturdy simplicity of a happy family bound together by a gentle and loving clergyman father. The dream ends abruptly, however, when Robin, attempting to follow his family into their home, finds the door locked. After an evening of "ambiguity and weariness," it is natural that Robin's thoughts should turn back to his home. It is just as natural that his dream should end as it does, for Robin has begun the journey to manhood and independence from which there is no turning back. Although he is not fully aware of the fact, he shares a good deal with the townspeople who have so baffled and angered him. The world of manhood and independence is the complex and ambiguous world where political battles are fought out, and Robin, like America itself, is set upon a course of action from which there is no turning back. The simplicities of an older, rural America, where authority is vested in a gentle father and the Scriptures or figures of authority like Major Molineux, must inevitably yield to the ambiguities of the metropolis, where the future will be decided.

That future, Robin's and the nation's, is dramatically embodied in the climactic episode, when Robin finally finds his kinsman. Tarred and feathered, Major Molineux sits in the midst of a garish and riotous procession, led by a man whose face is half red and half black. This man, Hawthorne tells us, is the personification of war and its consequences:

> The single horseman, clad in a military dress, and bearing a drawn sword, rode onward as the leader, and, by his fierce and variegated countenance, appeared like war personified; the red of one cheek an emblem of fire and sword; the blackness of the other betokened the mourning that attends them.

The strange Indian masquerade of those in the procession is a clear allusion to the disguise of the rebellious participants in the Boston tea party. The incomprehensible words addressed to Robin earlier by various townspeople are clearly passwords arranged to identify the conspirators against established authority.

The meaning of the night's events begins to dawn on Robin as he joins in the laughter of the throng as it wildly celebrates the demise of Major Molineux, whom Hawthorne compares to "some dead potentate, mighty no more, but majestic still in his agony." The entire scene, the entire story which this scene brings to a climax, gives Robin's laughter a crucial meaning. In joining in the laughter of the throng, Robin identifies himself with the political goals of the revolutionaries. But more than that, in so doing he begins, finally, to see that his personal relationship, to both his home and his cousin, is parallel with and inseparable from the relationship of the colonies to its past and the mother country. Robin's joy in seeing his dignified and powerful cousin a scorned captive of the townspeople is intensely personal, the joy a young man feels, ambivalent though it may be, when he is released from the bonds of an authority figure. But the meaning of that authority figure, as the story makes clear, cannot be separated from the political theme, as Robin himself now recognizes.

Such a reading is not meant to imply that "My Kinsman, Major Molineux" is a simple story, a kind of allegory, which embodies in dramatic action a straightforward set of abstract ideas. It is, rather, a story revealing how complex a particular historical event is. That Hawthorne himself had equivocal feelings about the event is made clear by his description of the major, whose dignity and majestic bearing the utmost humiliation cannot altogether extinguish. This fact, together with the unflattering way the townspeople are presented throughout, suggests that Hawthorne viewed the event itself, as least in part, as the victory of mob rule over dignified and settled authority.

At any rate, the procession past, the tension released, Robin turns to the friendly citizen and asks directions back to the ferry. Defeated in his purpose, shaken by and perhaps not yet fully comprehending the extraordinary events of the evening, he decides to return to his family. But the kindly stranger urges Robin to stay. "Perhaps," he says, "as you are a shrewd youth, you may rise in the world without the help of your kinsman, Major Molineux." The stranger's comment is an appropriate conclusion to the story, for it appeals to Robin as a man, as an American man who must achieve independence through his own efforts, however difficult and ambiguous the struggle. Robin must make his way without the aid of his wealthy and powerful kinsman, just as America must make its way without the aid of the mother country. However problematical that freedom is, however dangerous and frightening, it is the inescapable price that real independence exacts.

Psychoanalytic Criticism

Psychoanalytic criticism always proceeds from a set of principles which describe the inner life of *all* men and women. Though there is now a great diversity of conviction about the nature of inner life and how to deal with it, certainly all analysts, and all psychoanalytic critics, assume that the development of the psyche in humans is analogous to the development of physique. Doctors can provide charts indicating physical growth stages, and analysts can supply similar charts, based on generations of case histories, indicating stages in the growth of the psyche. Obviously the best psychoanalytic critic is a trained analyst, but few analysts engage in literary criticism. Most of that criticism is performed by more or less knowledgeable amateurs, and much of that criticism is based on a relatively few universal principles set down by Sigmund Freud which describe the dominating human drives and the confusions they produce. We, must examine those principles.

First among them is the universality of the Oedipus complex. Freud contends that everyone moves through a psychic history which at one point, in early childhood, involves an erotic attachment to the parent of the opposite sex and an accompanying hostility and aggression against the parent of the same sex, who is seen as a rival in the jealous struggle. Such feelings, part of the natural biography of the psyche, pass or are effectively controlled in most cases. But sometimes, the child grown to adulthood is still strongly gripped by that Oedipal mode, which then may result in neurotic or even psychotic behavior. A famous lengthy analysis of Shakespeare's *Hamlet* argues that Hamlet is best understood as gripped by Oedipal feelings which account for his difficulties and his inability to act decisively, and the Laurence Olivier film of *Hamlet* presents such an interpretation. But how could Shakespeare create an Oedipal Hamlet when Freud was not to be born for some two and a half centuries? Freud did not invent the Oedipus complex—he simply described it. It was always there, especially noticeable in the work of great literary artists who in every era demonstrate a special insight into the human condition. At one point in Sophocles's *Oedipus Rex*, written about 429 B.C., Iocastê the queen says to her son-husband, "Have no more fear of sleeping with your mother: / How many men, in dreams, have lain with their mothers / No reasonable man is troubled by such things." And the situation of Oedipus, and the awareness of Iocastê, provide for Freud the very name for the psychic phase he detects.

Paralleling the Oedipal phase in the natural history of the psyche is the aggressive phase. This psychic feature urges physical and destructive attacks on those who exercise authority, that is, those in a position to control and to deny the primal desires of each of us. For the young, the authority figure is frequently the father. For the more mature, that authority figure may be the police officer, the government official, the office manager. As far back as the Hebrew Bible story of the Tower of Babel and the old Greek myths in which the giant Titans, led by Cronus, overthrow their father Uranus, and Zeus and the Olympians subsequently overthrow Cronus, there appears evidence of the rebellion against the father-authority figure. Freud views that aggressive hostility as another ever present component of the developing psyche. But, in the interest of civilization and the advantages which organized society provides, that aggressiveness must be controlled. The mechanisms of control are various. Early on comes the command to honor one's father and mother. The culture demands of its members that they love and revere their parents. What, then, of the frequent hostility which children feel toward those parents who punish them and deny them the freedom they seek? That hostility often results in guilt—one is supposed to love not hate one's parents—and the guilt can be severe as children (or adults) detect the variance between their desires and their "duty." Such guilt feelings sometimes generate behavior that effectively punishes. The punishment may be internal—may take the form of psychotic withdrawal or psychosomatic illness. Or the guilt may generate external behavior that requires punishment at the hands of society. In any case, the psychoanalytic critic is constantly aware that the author and/or the characters suffer and resuffer a primal tension that results from the conflict between psychic aggressions and social obligations.

DOVER BEACH

"Dover Beach" is richly suggestive of the fundamental psychic dilemma of the human in civilization. And since men and women in civilization are, by definition, discontent because their social duties require them to repress their primal urges, it is not surprising that the opening visual images of the poem which create a lovely and tranquil scene—calm sea, glimmering cliffs, a tranquil bay, sweet night air—are quickly modified by the ominous "only" that begins the seventh line of the poem. That *only*, in the sense of "in contrast," is addressed to a lady who has been called to the window to see the quiet and reassuring scene. No reassurance, finally, remains, as the images shift to an auditory mode:

> Listen! you hear the grating roar
> Of pebbles which the waves draw back, and fling

The tone is strangely changed, the emotional impact of "roar" suggesting something quite different from the serenity of the opening image, and the second stanza closes with the sounds of the surf bringing "the eternal note of sadness in."

Why should sadness be an *eternal* note? And why is the visual imagery largely pleasing while the auditory imagery is largely ominous? The answers to these two questions provide the focus for a psychoanalytic reading of the poem.

The "eternal note of sadness" (an auditory image) represents Arnold's recognition that, however sweet the night air and calm the sea, the central human experience is sadness. At the point in the poem where that sadness is recognized, the poet recalls the great Greek tragedian Sophocles who heard that same note of sadness over 2,000 years ago. (It is, after all, an eternal sadness.) For Sophocles, the sadness brings to mind the "turbid ebb and flow of human misery." Now Sophocles's greatest and best known tragedy, *Oedipus Rex*, ends with the chorus pointing out that no man should count himself happy until at the moment of his death he can look back over a life without pain. Fate, as it afflicted Oedipus, afflicts us all. And the fate of Oedipus provided Freud with the name of that psychic mode through which we all pass. We would all be guilty of parental murder and incest were it not for the necessity to repress those urges in order to construct a viable society. The unacceptable passions are controlled by guilt. We may not commit murder or incest on pain of punishment. We may not even desire to commit murder or incest on pain of possible psychic punishment. The dilemma, the guarantee of guilt or the guarantee of discontent, defines that eternal note of sadness which the poet hears.

We might go further. There is agreement that in infancy and very early childhood the tactile and the visual senses are most important. Somewhat later the auditory sense increases in importance. Consequently, children recognize security—certitude, peace, help for pain—tactilely and visually, in the warmth and the form of the omnipresent and succoring mother. Later, through their ears comes the angry "no!" When discipline and painful interaction with others begin, they experience the auditory admonition which frustrates their desires. It is immensely interesting to the psychoanalytic critic that in "Dover Beach" the tranquilities are visual but the ominous sadness is auditory—the "roar" which brings in the "note" of sadness, the "roar" of the sea of faith retreating to the breath of the night-wind, the "alarms," and the "clash" of ignorant armies by night.

We need to look at the opening lines of the final stanza. Certainly the principal agency developed by society to enforce the morality it required was religion. Ancient religious teaching recognized those very primal urges that Freud systematically described and made them offenses against God. Faith, then, became the condition that made society possible; religious injunction and religious duty served as a sort of cultural superego, a mass conscience, that not only controlled human aggression but substituted for it a set of ideal behavior patterns that could guarantee a set of gratifying rewards for humanity. Hence the poet recalls:

> The Sea of Faith
> Was once, too, at the full, and round earth's shore
> Lay like the folds of a bright girdle furled.

This is a strange image. Surely the emotional tone of "the folds of a bright girdle furled" is positive—that bright girdle is a "good" thing, not an ominous thing. Yet, that girdle (i.e., a sash or belt worn round the waist) is restrictive. It is furled (i.e., rolled up, bound) around the land. In short, the Sea of Faith contains, limits, strictly controls the land. In the context of the poem, that containment is a good thing, for without the restricting Sea of Faith the world, despite appearances,

> Hath really neither joy, nor love, nor light,
> Nor certitude, nor peace, nor help for pain.

Without strong religious faith, acting as a cultural superego, the primal aspects of men and women are released—aggression comes to dominate human activity:

> And we are here as on a darkling plain
> Swept with confused alarms of struggle and flight,
> Where ignorant armies clash by night.

A certain confusion persists. On the one hand, the Sea of Faith serves a useful function as an emblem of the superego (loosely, the conscience), the name Freud gives to the guilt-inducing mechanism that incessantly "watches" the ego to punish it for certain kinds of behavior. When it is at the full, ignorant armies, presumably, do not clash by night. On the other hand, the superego as associated with auditory imagery is ominous. It reverberates with the painful experience of frustration. Finally, however, the usefulness of the Sea of Faith is illusory. The note of sadness is eternal. Sophocles, long before the foundation of Christianity, heard it. What emerges from the poem's images, understood psychoanalytically, is a progression from a mild note of sadness (frustrated desires) to alarms and clashes (threatening uncontrolled aggressive desires). The calm sea and the fair moon suggest a land of dreams—illusory and without substance. Sadness, struggle, and flight are real.

We need to deal with the girl to whom the poet speaks; we need to understand his relationship to her. The quest for that understanding involves another psychoanalytic principle, another set of images, and a reconsideration of the image of the Sea of Faith.

In earliest infancy, the ego, the sense of self, is not yet formed. The infant child considers the mother, particularly the mother's breast, as part of itself. A gradual and a painful recognition must occur in which the child is dissociated from the mother. The process begins with the birth trauma. In the womb, the child is utterly safe, never hungry, never cold. After birth, there are discomforts. But for a time the mother and her nourishing breast are so much present that the infant does not distinguish where he or she ends and the other, the mother, begins. But this state of affairs does not continue, and the infant becomes increasingly dissociated. Slowly it learns what is "self" and what is not, what it can control by will (moving its arm, say) and what it cannot (its mother's availability). In short, it learns the borders of its being, the edges of its existence.

Images of borders and edges constantly recur in the poem. Such images may be taken as emblems of dissociation—that is, symbols of the separation between the warm, nourishing mother and the child. Consequently, they are symbols of painful dissatisfaction. The Sea of Faith that

> . . . round earth's shore
> Lay like the folds of a bright girdle furled

seems, on the other hand, much like that warm, encompassing mother who, to the infant, was a part of itself. But dissociation occurs, and the distressed poet perceives that comforting entity withdrawing, retreating "down the vast edges drear / And naked shingles of the world." The poet has an edge and can no longer reside safely in close association with the source of comfort and security.

Instantly the poet turns to the girl and says

> Ah, love, let us be true
> To one another!

He perceives his companion not erotically but as the source of security, as a replacement for the withdrawing emblematic mother. He offers his "love" a mutual fidelity not to reassure her of his commitment but to assure himself of hers. He wishes to dissolve the edges of his ego and associate, as in infancy, with his "mother." Such an association will protect him from a world in which "ignorant armies clash by night."

MY KINSMAN, MAJOR MOLINEUX

The story opens with Robin crossing a river to an unnamed town after dark. If one takes a psychoanalytic stance, the mysterious opening nicely symbolizes a sort of spiritual journey into mysterious realms. More specifically, the opening suggests an inward journey into the dark recesses of the human spirit. Robin has to confront the psychic confusion resulting from the conflict between the civilized and the psychological response to paternal authority. Robin takes his journey to discover and deal with the paternal figure that is identified in his mind with safety and security, his powerful kinsman, Major Molineux. From a psychoanalytic point of view, it is reasonable to point out that Robin has at least two fathers, since his kinsman, if Robin ever finds him, will serve a paternal function. Some critics suggest that every male Robin encounters serves as a surrogate father. Note that the men Robin meets, with one exception, all act threateningly, all offer to punish him, all assume a position of authority, and, hence, all in some respect are paternalistic. The one exception, the kindly stranger who joins Robin in his watch and who urges him to make his own way without the aid of a paternalistic power is in some ways himself a kind of unreal, idealized father figure, who, though kindly and helpful, requires no price for his help.

From the psychoanalytic point of view, the story is precisely about the price required of young men by their fathers. The price, of course, is not coin. It is behavior. Robin must behave as authority wishes, not as Robin wishes. In return, he will be secure—but almost certainly discontent. Perhaps, deeper than consciousness, Robin feels the pinch of such an economy and unwittingly seeks to avoid payment. After all, the story runs its course as Robin seeks directions to the house of his kinsman. But a kind of haunting inefficiency constantly disrupts his search. Early he realizes that he should have asked the ferryman to take him to Major Molineux. But he didn't. He stops an old gentleman by seizing hold of his coat—rather curious behavior to an elderly stranger. And the stranger's response to the youth's behavior is an angry threat. That threat provokes the first round of recurrent laughter from the loungers in the barber shop. And the threat frightens Robin. Next he becomes "entangled in a succession of crooked and narrow streets," a set of literal streets near the waterfront (but also a lovely metaphor for the human psyche), where he is attracted to an inn. There he receives his second rebuff from the innkeeper, another threat, and is followed out into the street by more laughter.

Robin responds to this rebuff with considerable anger, thinks violent thoughts, but continues to pursue his quest in a most curious way. He walks up and down the main street of the town hoping to run into his kinsman. Actually he is thrilled by the rich and exotic shopwindows and strollers. It is reasonable to assert that at this point, regardless of his rationalization, Robin is not at all seeking his kinsman. He is, for once, doing what he wishes to do. He is enjoying himself, free from any paternal interference. Remarkably, as he gawks along the exotic street, he hears the distinctive cough of the old gentleman he first encountered, the gentleman who threatened him with the stocks, the gentleman who proclaimed, "I have—hem, hem—authority." Robin responds by declaring "Mercy on us!" and ducking around a corner to avoid meeting him and therefore escape authority. Strange as this evasion of authority might seem, stranger still is the half-opened door through which around that corner Robin discerns "a strip of scarlet petticoat, and the occasional sparkle of an eye."

This encounter is quite different from the others which occur both before and after. That red petticoat and sparkling eye belong to a vivacious and devastatingly attractive lady. A harlot, to be sure, but awfully attractive. She tells Robin, in response to his standard question, that Major Molineux is asleep within (an outrageous lie which Robin can't help but doubt), and she takes him by the hand "and the touch was light, and the force was gentleness, and though Robin read in her eyes what he did not hear in her words, yet the slender-waisted woman in the scarlet petticoat proved stronger than the athletic country youth. She had drawn his half-willing footsteps nearly to the threshold" when the watchman appeared. The girl hastily withdraws, and Robin is once again warned by authority of punishment for bad behavior.

The frightened youth does not realize until the watchman has turned the corner that *he* would certainly know the whereabouts of his kinsman, Major Molineux, but his tardy shouted request to the vanished watchman is answered only by more vague laughter. Why didn't Robin ask for directions immediately? Well, he was about to sin against the paternal authority which generally represses and most particularly represses the sexual instincts of sons. The psychoanalytic critic might go even further here in explaining the sources of Robin's guilty demeanor before the watchman whose appearance is fantastically coincidental. (Is he the ever present psychic "watchman" who cries "guilty" at even our ego-gratifying *thoughts* when they violate the "law"?) The desirable girl in the scarlet petticoat says that Major Molineux cohabits with her. Her eyes and her behavior invite Robin to a sexual encounter which he, however nervously, welcomes. If Major Molineux is a surrogate father for Robin, is not the lovely scarlet lady a surrogate mother? And is not an Oedipal situation developed? For students not familiar with principles of psychoanalytic criticism, this will seem a rather wild reading. But reserve judgment. Consider how the story ends. Then, perhaps, the Oedipal feature will not seem bizarre.

Now events move rapidly. Robin, brought to his "senses" by the intrusion of the watchman, remembers that he is a "good" boy and rejects the lovely beckoning arm. But he is upset and feeling violent. He intends to succeed in his quest, even if it means clubbing someone with his stout oak cudgel. The next man he meets, mysteriously muffled, is forced to answer—and answer he does. The muffling, dropped, reveals a hideous, satanic face painted half red and half black. Certainly that painting is a disguise. But this man, we later discover, is the leader of the mob which destroys Major Molineux's power and dignity and, as such, represents a certain aspect first of the community but also of each man in it, particularly of Robin. An old-fashioned Freudian would have no trouble identifying him as Robin's embodied *id*, the name given by Freud to the insistent selfish, lustful, and aggressive aspect of man's psyche, just as he would have no trouble earlier identifying the intrusive watchman as Robin's *superego*. Our awful demonic parti-colored citizen tells Robin to wait where he is and within an hour he will surely meet his kinsman, Major Molineux.

Robin waits and experiences some dreams which are almost hallucinations. He is standing by a church and notices the graves. Perhaps the major is already dead and will appear to haunt him. Wouldn't it be nice to be at home, safe in his family circle? And he is there, but when he seeks to follow his family into the house, the door is closed and locked in his face. It is a normal dream for a frightened young man the first time away from home. But in the context of the story, this dream acts as a metaphor for Robin's expulsion from the safety of home. Even if he would submit again to the "father" in return for security, the opportunity is denied. One father only remains for him—his kinsman, Major Molineux (who may be dead). It is his home that Robin must seek for shelter from all the perils of independence. But the price is the same—submission and repression. The rioters draw near, the tumult grows loud, the torches cast a great light into the darkness—some revelation is at hand. And the light reveals the demonic man on horseback with a drawn sword leading a riotous procession around a cart in which the powerful, gray, dignified, upright, fatherly Major Molineux sits trembling and humiliated. All the figures Robin encountered during the story return—old "hem-hem," the laughing innkeeper, the saucy harlot. And all laugh. But Robin's laugh is louder than all the rest! For the psychoanalytic critic, that laugh cannot be interpreted other than as the laugh of exultant release from the tyranny of the father, of established authority, and the prospect of independent activity free of stifling inner guilt.

The psychoanalytic critic might go further. He or she might call attention to the drawn sword held by the embodied id and remark on the relationship between that phallic symbol and the thwarted desire of Robin in the encounter with the harlot. Certain figures which recur throughout the history of literature (and in dreams and psychiatric case histories) are accepted by Freudian critics as symbols of the sexual and aggressive aspects of the human condition. Such deep reading, like all deep reading, is perilous. Yet to the reader well versed in the premises of psychoanalysis and the universal symbols behind which the mind conceals its primal nature, the bold analysis enriches the literary art.

Did Hawthorne deliberately design the psychoanalytic structure of "My Kinsman, Major Molineux"? A difficult question. He certainly did not incorporate an embodied superego and id. He never heard of those psychic abstractions. He certainly did not incorporate by design a phallic sword suggesting that Robin's sexual freedom is obtained through Major Molineux's exile. But, the psychoanalytic critic responds, Hawthorne, as a sensitive artist, perceives the deep struggle between desire and duty, between primal urge and social restraint. And that struggle he incorporates. As for the drawn sword, he had no idea of its psychic significance. He would be appalled by the modern psychoanalytic response. But, for the analyst, that does not in the least contradict the modern conviction that universal symbols, however unconscious, struggle to the surface in all art. That psychoanalytic critic would admire Hawthorne's "My Kinsman, Major Molineux" for effectively and accurately portraying the rite of passage of young Robin from innocence to experience, from repressed childhood to independent manhood.

Writing About Literature *

Writing compels the student to discover and come to terms with his or her own often complex response to an author's work. Every element in a literary work has been deliberately incorporated by the author—the description of the setting, the events that constitute the plot, the particular speeches of characters, the imagery. A rather mysterious intellectual and emotional event occurs within the reader as a result of the writer's purposeful manipulation of language. An essay about literature inevitably attempts some description of the author's purposes and techniques and some discussion of the reader's response.

As an illustration of the relationship between author's purpose and reader's response, consider these opening lines of a poem by W. H. Auden (the poem appears on p. 467):

> That night when joy began
> Our narrowest veins to flush,
> We waited for the flash
> Of morning's levelled gun.

The stanza tells of a new joy, probably erotic, that the speaker and his companion experience one night. But the reader must see that the speaker is apprehensive about that joy. The writer has created that mood of apprehension by using a violent image—the flash of morning's gun—to characterize the speaker's fears about the consequences of possible discovery. The images in the subsequent stanzas of the poem suggest that the lovers are trespassers and that the leveled gun they fear belongs to the keeper of the forbidden fields they enjoyed. Thus the reader responds to the poem with an awareness that the lovers have risked danger for the sake of joy.

Though the correspondence between "writer's purpose" and "reader's response" is by no means exact, any attempt to write about literature is, in one way or another, an attempt to discover and describe that correspondence. In other words, whatever the assignment, your fundamental task is to provide the answers to two questions: How do I respond to this piece? How has the author brought about my response?

While the line between imaginative literature and the essay is, like that between prose and poetry, sometimes difficult to draw, the essay tends to rely on direct statement and logical discourse rather than on the indirection and fig-

---

* See, as well, the appendices "Reading Fiction," "Reading Poetry," "Reading Drama" "Reading Essays," and "Three Critical Approaches." Those discussions may well suggest useful approaches to writing assignments.

urative language of poetry, fiction, and drama. Although an essay can be exceedingly complex and dense, essays mostly stake out a limited area to explore and treat it directly and lucidly. Thus, Roger Wilkins's "Confessions of a Blue-Chip Black," focusses on early traumatic experiences of rejection by whites. In "What If Shakespeare Had Had a Sister?" Virginia Woolf explores a mystery: why women were not poets in an age "when every man, it seemed, was capable of song or sonnet."

Despite their directness, much can be said about these essays. An analysis of Wilkins's piece might examine and evaluate his skill in choosing and recounting the childhood experiences that effectively convey his sense of trauma and alienation. Woolf's essay raises many possibilities: is she, in fact, examining only the question of why women did not write poetry in Shakespeare's age? What attitudes toward men does the essay express? Does her answer to the question she poses seem convincing?

The Journal

Many instructors will require you to keep a journal, a day-by-day account of your reactions to and reflections about what you've been reading. Even if a journal is not required, you might want to keep one for a variety of reasons. From a purely practical perspective, a journal provides valuable mental exercise: forcing yourself to write in a journal regularly is an excellent way to limber up your writing abilities and overcome the fear of facing a blank page. Because journals are like diaries in the sense that they are not meant to be seen by anyone else, you need not worry about whether you are constructing grammatical sentences, whether you are writing cohesive paragraphs and developing your ideas, or even whether you are always making sense. You are free to comment on some aspect of a work or set down a highly personal recollection that something in the work triggered. What is important is that you are recording your reactions, ideas, feelings, questions. If you are conscientious about keeping your journal, you may come to find the act of writing a challenging and—who knows?—even a pleasant activity.

A journal's usefulness extends beyond personal pleasure. When the time comes to write a formal essay for your class, the journal can provide you with a large range of possible topics. Suppose while you were reading Alastair Reid's poem "Curiosity" you confided to your journal your own curiosity about the reasons the poet selected cats and dogs to carry the theme. You might write an interesting essay on this topic, based on the thesis that, although both are domestic animals, the cat is a far wilder creature than the more docile and domestic dog. Perhaps you noted E. M. Forster's feelings about property ownership in "My Wood" as something to reflect further on in order to sharpen your understanding of the author's basic assumptions or to examine your own reasons for agreeing or disagreeing with him. Either would make a good topic for an essay.

You can also use a journal to record unfamiliar words that you encounter in your reading and plan to look up later. In reading Stevie Smith's "To Carry the Child," for example, you might wonder what *carapace* means. You enter the word in your journal, and, when you look it up, you find that *carapace* means a bony shell, such as a turtle's. With this knowledge you can return to the poem and appreciate the image, which might suggest the topic for an essay.

Some of your journal entries will probably be confessions of bafflement and confusion. Why does Tolstoy begin "The Death of Iván Ilých" at the end? Why does Crane in "The Bride Comes to Yellow Sky" open part III with a reference to a character's shirt and the place where it was made as well as the ethnic origin of the people who made it? Does Richard Rodriguez, in "Going Home Again: The New American Scholarship Boy," finally regret that he has lost touch with his ethnic heritage? What is Richard Selzer's "The Discus Thrower" about? Working out an answer to any of these questions could lead to an interesting essay.

Anything you want to enter in your journal is relevant, including the most personal feelings and recollections triggered by a work. Tom Wolfe's "The Right Stuff" might provide the opportunity for an essay on cliques that draw upon your own experiences as a member of an exclusive group or as one who was excluded. Elizabeth Bishop's "One Art" might remind you of a personal loss you experienced. Or you might jot down, after reading Kate Chopin's "The Storm," your moral disapproval of the story's central event—marital infidelity. You might then reread the story to discover whether it seems to disapprove of infidelity or whether you have imposed on it your own personal moral values. Sorting out such feelings could result in an essay on the interaction between the moral values of a reader and those embodied in a particular work.

Finally, remember that (unless your instructor has specific guidelines for your journal keeping) your journal will be the one place where you can write as much or as little as you please, as often or infrequently as you wish, with care and deliberation or careless speed. Its only purpose is to serve your needs. But if you write fairly regularly, you will probably be surprised not only at how much easier the act of writing becomes but also at how many ideas suddenly pop into your head in the act of writing. Henry Adams was surely right when he observed, "The habit of expression leads to the search for something to express."

The Summary Report

Another form of writing, more structured than the journal, is the summary report. In a summary report, you answer, in order, a series of basic questions about a literary work. Your instructor may assign such a report, but even if he or she does not, you might want to try one occasionally as a way of coming to terms with the essential elements of a work. Instructors usually ask that a summary report be limited to a page (or at most two pages) of looseleaf notebook paper or to both sides of a five-by-eight-inch note card. If you are doing one for your own satisfaction only, you might want to allow yourself a little more space than these limits specify. Summary reports not only are good exercise but also give you a valuable resource when, at the end of the semester, you sit down to review the term's reading assignments.

The general format for a summary report is similar for all genres, but the details in each genre, of course, vary. For example, the essential elements of both a play and a story will include plot, whereas plot will be irrelevant for the essay and most (though not all) poems. Listed below are the essential elements for summary reports in each of the four genres. Following the lists are three sample summary reports. If the listed elements do not apply to the particular work you are trying to cover in a summary report, make appropriate deletions and changes in the elements.

Short Story

1. Author and title; date of publication
2. Name (if any) of central character and character's important traits
3. Point of view
4. Setting of action; significance, if any, of setting
5. Summary of plot
6. Nature of conflict
7. Tone
8. Style
9. Central event(s)
10. Theme
11. Evaluation

Poem

1. Author and title; date of publication
2. Speaker
3. Occasion of the poem
4. Setting
5. Formal Structure
6. Image patterns
7. Symbols
8. Theme
9. Other noteworthy elements
10. Evaluation

Play

1. Author and title; date of publication
2. Name of central character and character's important traits
3. Other important characters
4. Setting, place and time

   5. Summary of plot
   6. Nature of conflict
   7. Style
   8. Central event(s)
   9. Theme
  10. Evaluation

Essay

   1. Author and title; date of publication
   2. Thesis (unifying idea or argument)
   3. Tone/Voice
   4. Style
   5. Noteworthy uses of rhetorical strategies (e.g., classification, comparison and contrast, analogy, cause and effect, definition, etc.)
   6. Other noteworthy elements
   7. Evaluation

(Student's name)

Frank O'Connor, "My Oedipus Complex," 1950

Central character: Larry, an adult male

Point of view: First-person narration of events that occurred during Larry's early childhood.

Setting: Larry's childhood home.

Summary of plot: Until Larry was five, his father, Mick, was away in the army most of the time. Larry's comfortable life with his mother abruptly ends when the war ends and his father returns home. Larry no longer has his mother to himself, and he begins to see his father as an enemy. Larry's constant struggle to regain the dominant place in his mother's affections ends when his brother is born. The new baby absorbs all the mother's time, so now the father, too, is excluded from the mother's attention. One night, Larry awakens to find his father in bed with him. He had been driven from his own bed by the mother's attention to the crying infant. Now the child and his father become friends, bound together by the experience of rejection.

Nature of conflict: The competition between the narrator and his father for the mother's attention.

Tone: Humorous and ironic because we understand the reason for Larry's puzzlement and pain, though he didn't at the time.

Style: The language, except when dialogue is reproduced, is ironic, civilized, and precise, but nonetheless relaxed. One hears an educated adult, not a small boy.

<u>Central events</u>: The first is the permanent return of the fa-
ther when Larry realizes that things are going to be different (and worse) for him. The second occurs when Larry discovers his father in bed with him, and they, both rejected,
become friends.

<u>Theme</u>: Depends on Freud's theory that young male children
love their mothers possessively and see their fathers as ri-
vals for their mothers' love. The idea of sibling rivalry is
also important to the story. Tension and antagonism are replaced by friendship when the authority figure, the father,
suffers the same rejection as the child.

<u>Evaluation</u>: A clever story because it depends for much of its
effect on what the reader knows and the young boy doesn't.
The poetic justice of the ending delighted me, as did the
ironic line that set the tone for the story: "The war was
the most peaceful period of my life."

(Student's name)
William Shakespeare, Sonnet 73, 1609
<u>Speaker</u>: Lyric voice.
<u>Occasion of the poem</u>: Speaker's realization that he is grow-
ing old and will soon die.
<u>Setting</u>: None.
<u>Formal structure</u>: A sonnet in iambic pentameter rhyming
ababcdcdefefgg.
<u>Image patterns</u>: As the rhyme scheme shows, the sonnet divides
into three quatrains and a concluding couplet. The image in
the first quatrain evokes autumn, in the second, twilight,
and in the third, a dying fire. Together, they make up a pattern of endings.
<u>Symbols</u>: Because the speaker associates himself with the ap-
proaching end of a year, of a day, and of a fire, it is clear
that these images symbolize the speaker's keen sense of his
(everyone's?) mortality.
<u>Theme</u>: The poet calls upon his friend to cherish him (the
poet) and life, because our stay on earth is brief and death
inevitable.
<u>Other noteworthy elements</u>: The ordering of the symbols is
very effective. They go from wide (year) to narrow (day) to
specific and concrete (fire). The progression is also effective because the first image describes the bare boughs of
winter, the second refers to sleep ("Death's second self"),

and the third refers to "ashes" and "the deathbed," each one making the reality of death more immediate and vivid.

Evaluation: I found this a very hard poem to understand. I was confused by line 4 until I recognized that "choirs" were "choir stalls" and not "birds." The image in the third quatrain was also hard, but once I realized that "his" in line 10 meant "its," the image became clear. In fact, I was, finally, impressed with how much meaning Shakespeare packed into 14 lines.

(student's name)

Tom Wolfe, "The Right Stuff," 1979

Thesis: The "ineffable quality" that separates the successful military pilot from those who don't make the grade is based on the ability to confront death over and over again with coolness and intelligence and confidence.

Tone/Voice: Serious and lively. Occasionally, Wolfe seems to qualify his admiration for the pilots with irony, as in the last lines of the second paragraph.

Style: Energetic with many long, complex sentences. Often elevated formal language is combined with colorful slang.

Noteworthy uses of rhetorical strategies: The author uses analogy very effectively, especially at the end of the second paragraph, where he compares the tests the pilots have to pass to climbing an ancient pyramid. He also uses many examples that make what he is saying interesting and understandable (my favorite one is when he tells about the non-coms' advice not to ride with anyone below colonel).

Other noteworthy elements: Even though Wolfe's style is pretty formal (his sentences are often very long and he uses a lot of words I didn't know), I found the essay pleasurable to read and easy to understand. I think this was true for two main reasons: (1) the long sentences are not complicated because usually Wolfe just strings out clauses and phrases, and (2) Wolfe alternates between his own formal and elevated voice and the imagined voices of the pilots. Also, Wolfe made me understand what makes military pilots (and all those who choose to brave death) tick.

Evaluation: As I already mentioned, I found the essay easy to read. The subject matter was interesting and applicable beyond the specific profession the author was describing; many professions and occupations have a small group of superstars.

Formal Writing

Your journal will allow you to struggle with your reading privately. It may produce wonders of understanding; it should, as well, reveal to you lapses in understanding. The summary report, although a useful tool for identifying the substance of a work, remains, after all, a set of notes. It asks little of your wits. Most instructors will demand some demonstration of those wits—they will ask you to write formal essays that provide evidence of your talent for critical response. Formal essays about imaginative literature characteristically fall into one of three modes: explication, analysis, and comparison and contrast. Essays about essays usually involve analysis, though, of course, you may effectively compare and contrast the essays you have analyzed. You may also be asked to write a *personal response* to a poem, story, play, or essay. Such writing reveals your subjective response to a work, based on your own experience and values. But that response must, in turn, be based on thoughtful and objective consideration of the work you discuss.

Explication

In explication, you examine a work in as much detail as possible, line by line, stanza by stanza, scene by scene, explaining each part as fully as you can and showing how the author's techniques produce the reader's response. An explication is essentially a demonstration of your thorough understanding of the poem, the story, or the play.

Here is a sample essay that explicates a relatively difficult poem, Dylan Thomas's "Do Not Go Gentle into That Good Night." (The poem appears on p. 698.)

```
        Dylan Thomas's villanelle "Do Not Go Gentle into That
   Good Night" is addressed to his aged father. The poem is re-
   markable in a number of ways, most notably in that contrary
   to the most common poetic treatments of the inevitability of
   death which argue for serenity or celebrate the peace that
   death provides, this poem urges resistance and rage in the
   face of death. It justifies that unusual attitude by describ-
   ing the rage and resistance to death of four kinds of men,
   all of whom can summon up the image of a complete and satis-
   fying life that is denied to them by death.
        The first tercet of the intricately rhymed villanelle
   opens with an arresting line. The adjective "gentle" appears
   where we would expect the adverb "gently." The strange dic-
   tion suggests that "gentle" may describe both the going
   (i.e., gently dying) and the person (i.e., gentleman) who
```

confronts death. Further, the speaker characterizes "night," here clearly a figure for death, as "good." Yet in the next line, the speaker urges that the aged should violently resist death, characterized as the "close of day" and "the dying of the light." In effect, the first three lines argue that however good death may be, the aged should refuse to die gently, should passionately rave and rage against death.

In the second tercet, the speaker turns to a description of the way the first of four types of men confronts inevitable death (which is figuratively defined throughout the poem as "that good night" and "the dying of the light"). These are the "wise men," the scholars, the philosophers, those who understand the nature and even the necessity of death, men who "know dark is right." But they do not acquiesce in death "because their words had forked no lightning," because their published wisdom failed to bring them to that sense of completeness and fulfillment that can accept death. Therefore, wise as they are, they reject the theoretical rightness" of death and refuse to "go gentle."

The second sort of men--"good men," the moralists, the social reformers, those who attempt to better the world through action as the wise men attempt to better it through "words"--also rage against death. Their deeds are, after all, "frail." With sea imagery, the speaker suggests that these men might have accomplished fine and fertile things-- their deeds "might have danced in a green bay." But, with the "last wave" gone, they see only the frailty, the impermanence of their acts, and so they, too, rage against the death that deprives them of the opportunity to leave a meaningful legacy.

So, too, the "wild men," the poets who "sang" the loveliness and vitality of nature, learn, as they approach death, that the sensuous joys of human existence wane. As the life-giving sun moves toward dusk, as death approaches, their singing turns to grieving, and they refuse to surrender gently, to leave willingly the warmth and pleasure and beauty that life may entail.

And finally, with a pun suggestive of death, the "grave men," those who go through life with such high seriousness as never to experience gaiety and pleasure, see, as death approaches, all the joyous possibilities that they were blind

to in life. And they, too, rage against the dying of a light
that they had never properly seen before.

The speaker then calls upon his aged father to join
these men raging against death. It is only in this final
stanza that we discover that the entire poem is addressed to
the speaker's father and that, despite the generalized statements about old age and the focus upon types of men, the poem
is a personal lyric. The edge of death becomes a "sad
height," that summit of wisdom and experience old age at-
tains that includes the sad knowledge of life's failure to
satisfy the vision we all pursue. The depth and complexity of
the speaker's sadness is startlingly given in the second line
when he calls upon his father to both curse and bless him.
These opposites richly suggest several related possibilities.
Curse me for not living up to your expectations. Curse me for
remaining alive as you die. Bless me with forgiveness for my
failings. Bless me for teaching you to rage against death.
And the curses and blessings are contained in the "fierce
tears"--fierce because you will burn and rave and rage
against death. As the poem closes by bringing together the
two powerful refrains, we may reasonably feel that the
speaker himself, while not facing imminent death, rages because his father's death will cut off a relationship that is
incomplete.

The explication, as you can see, deals with the entire poem by coming to grips with each element in it. This same mode can be used to write about the drama as well, but the length of plays will probably require that you focus on a single segment—a scene, for example—rather than the entire play.

You can learn a great deal about the technique of drama by selecting a short self-contained scene and writing a careful description of it. This method, a variety of explication, will force you to confront every speech and stage direction and to come to some conclusion regarding its function. Why is the set furnished as it is? Why do the characters speak the words they do or hold their peace? What do we learn of characters from the interchanges among them? Assume that everything that occurs in the play, whether on the printed page or on the stage, is put there for a purpose. Seek to discover the purpose, and you will, at the same time, discover the peculiar nature of dramatic art.

Fiction, too, can be treated effectively in a formal explication. As with drama, it will be necessary to limit the text—you will not be able to explicate a 10-page story in a 1,000-word essay. Choose a key passage—a half page that re-flects the form and content of the overall story, if possible. Often the first half page of a story, where the author, like the playwright, must supply information to the reader, will make a fine text for an explication. Although the explication will deal principally with only an excerpt, feel free to range across the story and show how the introductory material foreshadows what is to come. Or, perhaps, you can explicate the climax of the story—the half page that most pointedly establishes the story's theme—and subject it to a close line-by-line reading that illuminates the whole story.

Analysis

Analyzing literature is not the same kind of exercise as analyzing a chemical compound: breaking a literary work down into its elements is only the first step in literary analysis. When you are assigned an analysis essay, you are expected to focus on one of the elements that contribute to the complex compound that is the substance of any work of literary merit. This process requires that you extricate the element you plan to explore from the other elements that you can identify, study this element—not only in isolation but also in relation to the other elements and the work as a whole—and, using the insights you have gained from your special perspective, make an informed statement about it.

This process may sound complicated, but if you approach it methodically, each stage follows naturally from the stage that precedes it. If, for example, an instructor assigns an analysis essay on some aspect of characterization in *Othello*, you would begin by thinking about each character in the play. You might decide to deal with Othello himself because he is a major character and because you found yourself wondering how Othello was deceived so easily by Iago's lies. After more thought, you formulate a statement: "From a realistic perspective, it is hard to believe that a man of Othello's position could be so gullible; however, Shakespeare develops the character with such craft that we accept the Moor as flesh and blood." At this point, you have moved from the broad *subject* of characterization in *Othello* to a *thesis*, a statement that you must prove.

The process is no different in analyzing an essay. A writing assignment might ask you to focus on some aspect of the style or structure of any essay you have read. For example, you might want to analyze the structure of Martin Luther King's "Letter from Birmingham Jail" from the point of view of the order in which the author takes up and answers his critics' charges. Or, you might wish to take issue with his distinction between a just and an unjust law.

You may be one among the many students who find it difficult to find a starting point. For example, you have been assigned an analysis essay on a very broad subject, such as "imagery in love poetry." A few poems come to mind, but you don't know where to begin. You read these poems and underline all the images that you can find. You look at these images over and over, finding no relation among them. You read some more poems, again underlining the images, but you still do not have even the germ of a thesis.

The technique of free writing might help to overcome your block. You have read and reread the works you intend to write about. Now, put the assignment temporarily out of your mind and start writing about one or two of the poems without organizing your ideas, without trying to reach a point. Write down what you like about a poem, what you dislike about it, what sort of person the speaker is, which images seemed striking to you—write anything at all about the work. If you do this for some minutes, you will probably discover that you are voicing opinions. Pick one that interests you or seems the most promising to explore. Now go back over the poems and seek to discover how specific images might have elicited your responses.

There are a few variations on the basic form of the analysis assignment. Occasionally, an instructor will narrow the subject to a specific assignment: "Analyze the development of Othello's character in Act I," or analyze the opening paragraph of Orwell's "Shooting an Elephant." While this sort of assignment makes it easier to focus and limits the amount of text you will have to study, the process from this point on is no different from the process that you would employ addressing a broader subject. Sometimes instructors will supply you with a thesis, and you will have to work backward from the thesis to find supporting material. Again, careful analysis of the text is required.

The problem you will have to deal with when writing an analytical essay remains the same regardless of the literary genre you are asked to discuss. You still must find an arguable thesis that deals with the literary sources of your response to the work. For instance, an analysis of a poem might show how a particular pattern of imagery contributes to the meaning of the poem. Or it might argue, from clues within the poem, that the speaker of the poem is a certain kind of character. Or it might demonstrate how the connotations of certain words the poet has chosen to use help to create a particular mood. An analysis may also go outside the poem to throw light on it (see the discussion of sociological criticism in the previous appendix). For instance, a poem might be analyzed as an embodiment of (or departure from) a particular religious, social, political, or scientific doctrine; as an example of traditional poetic form such as the ballad or the pastoral elegy; or as a new expression of an ancient myth. These are but a few examples; the possibilities are almost endless.

Though plays can be analyzed, like stories and poems, in terms of theme, image patterns, and the like, the playwright must solve problems that are unique to drama as a literary form meant to be acted on a stage before an audience. For example, the mechanics of staging a play limit the extent to which the playwright can shift the locations and times of the action, whereas the writer of fiction can make such shifts very readily with a few words of narration. Similarly, the writer of fiction can, if he or she wishes, tell the story through a narrator who not only can comment on the meaning of events but can describe the thoughts and motives of some or even all of the characters. In a play, on the other hand, the curtain rises and the characters must convey information through their own words or behavior. The audience does not know what the characters think unless they speak their thoughts aloud. As *readers* of a play we may read the stage directions and any other information the author has provided for the director and actors (and perhaps for readers). We must bear in mind that the audience viewing the play can only know such things as the time of year, the location of the setting, the relationships among characters, or the events that have led up to the action with which the play begins if they are stated in the program or if someone or something on the stage conveys that information.

Playwrights have developed many techniques for solving their special problems, and you may wish to focus on one of these in your analysis of some aspect of a play. For example, you might explain the role of the Chorus or the dramatic function of the messenger in Sophocles's *Oedipus Rex*. Or you might argue that the passage of time is distorted for dramatic purposes in Shakespeare's *Othello*. All of these subjects would involve the consideration of problems that are peculiar to the drama as a literary form that is meant to be acted on a stage.

When you confront the assignment to write about a play, ask yourself some fundamental questions. For instance, what sort of person is the protagonist? Is he or she admirable? If so, in what respects? Generous? Wise? Courageous? Fairminded? What evidence do you find to support your judgment? Does it come from his or her own speeches and behavior or from what other characters say? If the latter, are we meant to take the opinions of those characters as the truth? Is the tragic conclusion of the play brought about by some flaw or weakness in the character or merely by the malice of others?

Of course, these questions represent only a very few of those you might ask as you think about a play and search for a thesis. If you do choose to deal with some aspect of characterization, you may find that a minor character interests you more as a subject than a major one. And, as we have suggested, you can also ask questions about imagery, about theme, or about various formal or structural aspects of a play. If you ask yourself enough questions, you will discover some thesis you can argue for.

Let's turn now to the analysis of a story. Suppose that your instructor has made the following assignment: Write an analysis of Harlan Ellison's story, " 'Repent Harlequin!' Said the Ticktockman," in which you discuss the theme of the story in terms of the characters and the setting. Now consider the following opening (taken from a student paper):

```
    " 'Repent, Harlequin!' Said the Ticktockman" is a story
depicting a society in which time governs one's life. The
setting is America, the time approximately A.D. 2400 some-
where in the heart of the country. Business deals, work
shifts, and school lessons are started and finished with ex-
acting precision. Tardiness is intolerable as this would
hinder the system. In a society of order, precision, and
punctuality, there is no room for likes, dislikes, scruples,
```

or morals. Thus, personalities in people no longer exist. As
these "personless" people know no good or bad, they very
happily follow in the course of activities which their society has dictated.

At the outset, can you locate a thesis statement? The only sentences that would
seem to qualify are the last three in the paragraph. But notice that, although
those sentences are not unreasonable responses to the story, they do not establish a thesis that is *responsive to the assignment*. Because the assignment calls
for a discussion of theme in terms of character and setting, there should be a
thesis statement about the way in which character and setting embody the theme.
Here is another opening paragraph on the same assignment (also taken from a
student paper):

> Harlan Ellison's "'Repent, Harlequin!' Said the
> Ticktockman" opens with a quotation from Thoreau's essay
> "Civil Disobedience," which establishes the story's theme.
> Thoreau's observations about three varieties of men, those
> who serve the state as machines, those who serve it with
> their heads, and those who serve it with their consciences,
> are dramatized in Ellison's story, which takes place about
> 400 years in the future in a setting characterized by ma-
> chinelike order. The interaction among the three characters,
> each of whom represents one of Thoreau's types, results in a
> telling restatement of his observation that "heroes, pa-
> triots, martyrs, reformers in the great sense, and men . . .
> necessarily resist [the state] and . . . are commonly treated
> as enemies by it."

Compare the two opening paragraphs sentence by sentence for their respon-
siveness to the assignment. The first sentence of the first opening does not refer
to the theme of the story (or to its setting or characterization). In the second
sentence, the discussion of the setting ignores the most important aspect—that
the story is set in a machine- and time-dominated future. The last three sentences deal rather obliquely with character, but they are imprecise and do not
establish a thesis. The second opening, on the other hand, immediately alludes
to the theme of the story. It goes on to emphasize the relevant aspects of the
futuristic setting and then moves to a discussion of the three characters that
animate the story in terms of their reactions to the setting. The last sentence
addresses the assignment directly and also serves as a thesis statement for the
paper. It states the proposition or argument that will be supported by the information and evidence in the rest of the paper. The reader of the second opening
will expect the next paragraph of the paper to discuss the setting of the story

and subsequent paragraphs to discuss the response to the setting of the three principal characters.

The middles of essays are largely determined by their opening paragraphs. However long the middle of any essay may be, each of its paragraphs ought to be responsive to some explicit statement made at the beginning of the essay. Note that it is practically impossible to predict what the paragraph following the first opening will deal with. Here is the first half of that next paragraph as the student wrote it:

> The Harlequin is a man in the society with no sense of time. His having a personality enables him to have a sense of moral values and a mind of his own. The Harlequin thinks that it is obscene and wrong to let time totally govern the lives of people. So he sets out to disrupt the time schedule with ridiculous antics such as showering people with jelly beans in order to try to break up the military fashion in which they are used to doing things.

The paragraph then goes on to discuss the Ticktockman, the capture and brainwashing of the Harlequin, and the resulting lateness of the Ticktockman.

Note that nothing in the opening of this student's paper prepared for the introduction of the Harlequin. In fact, the opening concluded rather inaccurately that the people within the story "happily follow in the course of activities which their society has dictated." Hence, the introduction of the Harlequin in the second paragraph represents a wholly new and unanticipated element of the story. Further, because the student has not dealt with the theme of the story (remember the assignment explicitly asked for a discussion of *theme* in terms of character and setting), the student's comments about the Harlequin's antics remain disconnected from any clear purpose. They are essentially devoted to what teachers constantly warn against: a mere plot summary. The student has obviously begun to write before he or she has analyzed the story sufficiently to understand its theme. With further thought, the student would have perceived that the central thematic issue is resistance to an oppressive state—the issue stated in the epigraph from Thoreau. The second opening, on the other hand, makes that thematic point clearly and ought to be followed by a discussion of the environment (that is, the setting) in which the action occurs. Here is such a paragraph taken from the second student's paper.

> Ellison creates a society that reflects one possible future development of the modern American passion for productivity and efficiency. The setting is in perfect keeping with the time-conscious people who inhabit the city. It is pictured as a neat, colorless, and mechanized city. No mention is made of nature: grass, flowers, trees, and birds do not

```
appear. The buildings are in a "Mondrian arrangement," stark
and geometrical. The cold steel slidewalks, slowstrips, and
expresstrips move with precision. Like a chorus line, people
move in unison to board the movers without a wasted motion.
Doors close silently and lock themselves automatically. An
ideal efficiency so dominates the social system that any
"wasted time" is deducted from the life of an inefficient
citizen.
```

Once the setting has been established, as in the paragraph just quoted, writers attentive to the assignment will turn to the characters. But they will insistently link those characters to thematic considerations. It might be well to proceed with a short transitional paragraph that shapes the remainder of the middle of the essay:

```
      Into this smoothly functioning but coldly mechanized so-
ciety, Ellison introduces three characters: pretty Alice, one
of Thoreau's machinelike creatures; the Ticktockman, one of
those who "serve the state chiefly with their heads, and, as
they rarely make any moral distinctions, they are as likely
to serve the Devil without intending it, as God"; and Ever-
ett C. Marm, the Harlequin, whose conscience forces him to
resist the oppressive state.
```

The reader will now expect a paragraph devoted to each of the three characters:

```
      Pretty Alice is, probably, very pretty. (Everett didn't
fall in love with her brains.) In the brief section in which
we meet her, we find her hopelessly ordinary in her atti-
tudes. She is upset that Marm finds it necessary to go about
"annoying people." She finds him ridiculous and wishes only
that he would stay home, as other people do. Clearly, she has
no understanding of what Everett is struggling against.
Though her anger finally leads her to betray him, Everett
himself can't believe that she has done so. His own loyal and
understanding nature colors his view of her so thoroughly
that he cannot imagine the treachery that must have been so
simple and satisfying for Alice, whose only desire is to be
like everybody else.
      The Ticktockman is more complex. He sees himself as a
servant of the state, and he performs his duties with resolu-
tion and competence. He skillfully supports a system he has
never questioned. The system exists; it must be good. His
```

conscience is simply not involved in the performance of his duty. He is one of those who follow orders and expect others to follow orders. As a result, the behavior of the Harlequin is more than just an irritant or a rebellion against authority. It is unnerving. The Ticktockman wishes to understand that behavior, and with Everett's time-card in his hand, he muses that he has the name of "what he is . . . not who he is. . . . Before I can exercise proper revocation, I have to know who this what is." And when he confronts Everett, he does not just liquidate him. He insists that Everett repent. He tries to convince Everett that the system is sound, and when he cannot win the argument, he dutifully reconditions Everett, since he is, after all, more interested in justifying the system than in destroying its enemies. It is easy to see this man as a competent servant of the Devil who thinks he is serving God.

But only Everett C. Marm truly serves the state because his conscience requires him to resist. He is certainly not physically heroic. His very name suggests weak conformity. Though he loves his Pretty Alice, he cannot resign from the rebellious campaign his conscience insists upon. So, without violence, and mainly with the weapon of laughter, he attacks the mechanical precision of the system and succeeds in breaking it down simply by making people late. He is himself, as Alice points out, always late, and the delays that his antics produce seriously threaten the well-being of the smooth but mindless system he hates. He is, of course, captured. He refuses, even then, to submit and has his personality destroyed by the authorities that fear him. The Ticktockman is too strong for him.

An appropriate ending emerges naturally from this student's treatment of the assignment. Having established that the story presents characters who deal in different ways with the oppressive quality of life in a time- and machine-obsessed society, the student concludes with a view of the author's explicit and implicit criticisms of such a society:

Harlequin is defeated, but Ellison, finally, leaves us with an optimistic note. The idea of rebellion against the system will linger in the minds of others. There will be more Harlequins and more disruption of this system. Many rebels will be defeated, but any system that suppresses individual-

ism will give birth to resistance. And Harlequin's defeat is
by no means total. The story ends with the Ticktockman him—
self arriving three minutes late for work.

Comparison and Contrast

An essay in comparison and contrast, showing how two works are similar to
and different from one another, almost always starts with a recognition of similarities, most likely similarities of subject matter. While it is possible to compare *any* two works, the best comparison and contrast essays emerge from the
analysis of two works similar enough to illuminate each other (most comparison and contrast assignments will involve two works of the same genre). Two
works about love, or death, or conformity, or innocence, or discovery give you
something to begin with. But these are very large categories; two random poems
about the same subject may be so dissimilar that a comparison and contrast
essay about them would be very difficult. Both Shelley's "Ozymandias" and
Randall Jarrell's "The Death of the Ball Turret Gunner" are about death, but
they deal with the subject so differently that they would probably not yield a
very interesting essay. On the other hand, not only are Dickinson's "Apparently
with No Surprise" and Frost's "Design" both about death, but they both use
remarkably similar events as the occasion for the poem. And starting with these
similarities, you would soon find yourself noting the contrast (in tone, for example, and theme) between nineteenth-century and twentieth-century views of
the nature of God.

Before you begin writing your paper, you ought to have clearly in mind the
points of comparison and contrast you wish to discuss and the order in which
you can most effectively discuss them. You will need to give careful thought
to the best way to organize your paper. As a general rule, it is best to avoid
dividing the paper into separate discussions of each work. That method tends
to produce two separate, loosely joined analysis essays. The successful comparison and contrast essay treats some point of similarity or contrast between the
two works, then moves on to succeeding points, and ends with an evaluation
of the comparative merits of the works.

Like analysis essays—indeed like any essay that goes beyond simple explication—comparison and contrast essays require theses. However, a comparison
and contrast thesis is generally not difficult to formulate: you must identify the
works under consideration and summarize briefly your reasons for making the
comparison.

Here is a student paper that compares and contrasts a Dylan Thomas poem
("Do Not Go Gentle into That Good Night," explicated earlier in this discussion) with the poetic response it triggered from a poet with different views.

Dylan Thomas's "Do Not Go Gentle into That Good Night"
and Catherine Davis's "After a Time" demand comparison: Dav—

is's poem was written in deliberate response to Thomas's.
Davis assumes the reader's familiarity with "Do Not Go
Gentle," which she uses to articulate her contrasting ideas.
"After a Time," although it is a literary work in its own
right, might even be thought of as serious parody—perhaps the
greatest compliment one writer can pay another.

"Do Not Go Gentle into That Good Night" was written by
a young man of thirty-eight who addresses it to his old and
ailing father. It's interesting to note that the author himself had very little of his own self-destructive life left as
he was composing this piece. Perhaps that's why he seems to
have more insight into the subject of death than most men of
his age. He advocates raging and fighting against it, not
giving in and accepting it.

"After a Time" was written by a woman of about the same
age and is addressed to no one in particular. Davis has a
different philosophy about death. She "answers" Thomas's
poem and presents her differing views, using the same poetic
form—a villanelle. Evidently, she felt it necessary to present a contrasting point of view eight years after Thomas's
death.

While "Do Not Go Gentle" protests and rages against
death, Davis's poem suggests a quiet resignation and acquiescence. She seems to feel that raging against death is useless
and profitless. She argues that we'll eventually become tame,
anyway, after the raging is done. At the risk of sounding
sexist, I think it interesting that the man rages and the
woman submits, as if the traditionally perceived differences
between the behavior of men and women are reflected in the
poems.

Thomas talks about different types of men and why they
rage against death. "Wise men" desire immortality. They rage
against death occurring before they've made their mark on
history. "Good men" lament the frailty of their deeds. Given
more time, they might have accomplished great things. "Wild
men" regret their constant hedonistic pursuits. With more
time they could prove their worth. "Grave men" are quite the
opposite and regret they never took time for the pleasures in
life. Now it's too late. They rage against death because
they're not ready for it.

His father's death is painful to Thomas because he sees

himself lying in that bed; his dying father reminds him of
his own inevitable death. The passion of the last stanza, in
which the poet asks his father to bless and curse him, suggests that he has doubts about his relationship with his father. He may feel that he has not been enough of a son. He
put off doing things with and for his father because he always felt there would be time later. Now time has run out and
he feels cheated. He's raging for his father now. He'll rage
for himself later.

Catherine Davis advocates a calm submission, a peaceful
acquiescence. She feels raging is useless and says that those
of us who rage will finally "go tame / When what we have we
can no longer use." When she says "One more thing lost is
one thing less to lose," the reader can understand and come
to terms with the loss of different aspects of the mind and
body, such as strength, eyesight, hearing, and intellect.
Once we've lost one of these, it's one thing less to worry
about losing. After a time, everything will be lost, and
we'll accept that, too, because we'll be ready for it.

In a contest of imagery. Thomas would certainly win the
day. His various men not only rage and rave, they burn. Their
words "forked no lightning," their deeds might have "danced
in a green bay," they "sang the sun in flight," and they see
that "blind eyes could blaze like meteors." Davis's images
are quiet--generally abstract and without much sensory
suggestiveness. She gives us "things lost," a "reassuring
ruse," and "all losses are the same." Her most powerful im-
age--"And we go stripped at last the way we came"--makes its
point with none of the excitement of Thomas's rage. And yet,
I prefer the quiet intelligence of Davis to the high energy
of Thomas.

"And we go stripped at last the way we came" can give
strange comfort and solace to those of us who always envied
those in high places. Death is a great leveler. Men are not
all created equal at birth, not by a long shot. But we will
bloody well all be equal when we make our final exit. Kings,
popes, and heads of state will go just as "stripped" as the
rest of us. They won't get to take anything with them. All
wealth, power, and trappings will be left behind. We will all
finally and ultimately be equal. So why rage? It won't do us
any good.

The Personal Response

The examples and suggestions for writing we have made focus upon some formal aspect of the work such as characterization, image patterns, and diction. Your instructor may, however, make an assignment that asks you to use a particular work as the springboard for a more personal essay. Instead of "characterization in *Othello*," you may be asked to analyze the nature of jealousy in the play and then apply it to your own life and experiences; instead of analyzing the uses of irony in Robert Browning's "My Last Duchess," your instructor might ask you to use the poem as the basis for a discussion of your personal views on the relationship between art and life. This sort of assignment requires analysis as a springboard for an impressionistic or autobiographical essay, perhaps an essay in which you oppose your ideas to those of the author. Or, to put it another way, what we have said about the essays you will be reading will be true about those you write: none is likely to be a pure example of one type or another.

Suppose, for example, that you have been asked to write an essay on the topic, "Is Swift's 'A Modest Proposal' Relevant to Our World?" Your instructor has explained the assignment by describing some of the conditions of eighteenth-century Ireland that aroused Swift's indignation and has also given you some useful biographical information about Swift's life and other writings (he was Irish himself and one of the greatest satirists in an age of great satire). Since Swift and the problem of starvation and absentee land ownership passed from the Irish scene some 200 years ago, can Swift's essay, your instructor inquires, be of more than historical interest? Here is one student's response to that assignment:

> It is probably accurate to say that a visitor to Dublin today could find a lot of poverty and beggars asking for handouts—what country does not have both? But it is doubtful that she would find the conditions as terrible and pervasive as Swift describes them in the opening paragraph of his essay "A Modest Proposal." Ireland now is independent and has social welfare programs that offer the very poorest relief from abject poverty. But this doesn't mean that Swift's essay is irrelevant to our own time. On the contrary, I believe that what Swift has to say is every bit as meaningful and powerful today as it was when he wrote it more than two centuries ago. The specific conditions in Ireland may have changed, but the poverty and exploitation Swift protested can be found everywhere in the modern world. And Swift is such a good writer that despite the old-fashioned words ("hath") and references that need footnoting ("the Pretender"), the speaker sounds eerily modern.

A few years ago, a group of the biggest stars in the musical world made a hit recording, "We Are the World," with proceeds going to help the starving people of Ethiopia. More recently, I and millions of other Americans joined "Hands Across America" as a way of calling attention to how many Americans go to bed hungry every night. And the United States is the richest country in the world. In fact, all over the modern world, starvation is a threat. Right now, according to news reports, thousands of Americans are homeless, and people are still threatened with starvation in Ethiopia and the Sudan. So today is not very different from Swift's day.

As in Swift's day, people suffer malnutrition and die of starvation while thousands of others have much, much more than they need. And often, just as Swift says in his essay, there is a direct connection between the luxurious lifestyle of the rich and the misery of the poor. He points out that most of the productive land of eighteenth-century Ireland was owned by absentee English landlords who were interested only in how much wealth they could bleed out of the country. They had no interest in reinvesting money in the country and no concern about the welfare of its citizens. Modern society is much more complicated than eighteenth-century life, so the connection between the misery of the poor and the luxury of others is often more difficult to see. Does my standard of living depend on the exploitation of laborers in other countries? I have a hunch it does.

But there are places where the connection is direct and clear. In the United States (I use the United States because I know it best and because it is the richest country in the world), one of the most obvious examples of exploitation is the treatment of poor people by slumlords. These slumlords buy run-down buildings in the poorest sections of cities for the sole purpose of charging the highest possible rent without using any of their profits for improvements to the buildings. One might say that every tenement owner of this type is an absentee landlord who has bought an Ireland to exploit.

So the subject matter of Swift's essay is still relevant. But even so, it's a safe guess that a lot of essays protesting poverty and injustice, written before and after Swift's, have been forgotten. I think we continue to read "A Modest Proposal" because it is so brilliantly written.

Swift obviously could have written a powerful essay directly attacking absentee landlords' cruel exploitation of the Irish poor. But such a direct approach would not have allowed him to make his case with such devastating force. In a straightforward essay, he could have included all the information and statistics, but almost everything else would have been different. A direct essay would have had to preach, attack, denounce. How much more effective the ironic approach is.

Irony works more effectively because instead of directly attacking the absentee landlords, Swift invents a concerned but objective observer who has given a lot of thought to what everyone agrees is a serious problem. Beginning with the ironic title, the speaker remains low-keyed and detached. He lays out the problem, shows the flaws of previous attempts to solve it, gives the reader the necessary data, and then moves into the heart of his essay with the paragraph: "I shall now therefore humbly propose my own thoughts, which I hope will not be liable to the least objection."

Although he maintains the same calm tone (and maybe because of that tone), the next sentence hits the reader like a sledgehammer. Swift's solution to the problem is so ghastly, so outrageous that we now realize he is being ironic. Or is he? Maybe he is one of those deadly calm madmen, an ancestor of Adolph Hitler or Idi Amin. But if there is any doubt about Swift's intention, it is resolved very quickly when the speaker says: "I grant this food will be somewhat dear, and therefore very proper for landlords, who, as they have already devoured most of the parents, seem to have the best title to the children."

Swift continues in the same calm, methodical way to present the arguments for his solution (one thinks of the Nazis' "Final Solution" when he suggests that the carcasses of the children be flayed and the skin used to make gloves and boots), and the irony makes his attack more powerful. For if we accept his basic idea—there is no reason why children shouldn't be slaughtered for food—everything else he has to say is convincing. In fact, the speaker points out that the absentee landlords do accept his basic idea because they are the ones directly responsible for the misery and starvation of the Irish poor.

In addition to the quiet tone, Swift's use of words contributes to the power of the essay. Once readers understand
that Swift is being ironic, they can appreciate the way he
describes certain things. He does not talk about mothers and
childbirth; he refers to "dams" and "breeders" as if people
were cattle. He does not say they need food and clothing, but
rather "nutriment and rags" as if they were products rather
than human beings. It is the kind of dehumanizing language
one can imagine the absentee landlords used when they talked
about the poor people of Ireland.

This kind of ugliness is what I had in mind at the beginning when I said that Swift sounds eerily modern. The
speaker's detached and calm tone makes him sound like some
modern bureaucrat or cost-efficiency expert who deals with
the problems of human misery as if he were dealing with cans
of tomatoes that have to be manufactured, stored, and mar-
keted so as to make the biggest profit possible. The difference is that the bureaucrat's detachment is real whereas
Swift's is a device to give his passionate outrage enough
power to bring about a change for the better.

The writer of this essay has done an interesting and creditable job. At the
outset, she has rightly recognized that while the essay topic calls for an historical comparison between our own day and Swift's, it does not require formal
research on Ireland in the eighteenth century. The only historical information
the student has drawn upon is supplied by Swift's essay itself, the instructor,
and the student's own general knowledge. The writer has also understood that,
having answered "yes" to the question posed by the topic, she must work out
and marshal her arguments in the most persuasive way possible, taking care
that the essay has an interesting beginning, a coherent and detailed body, and
an end that concludes rather than merely stops.

The opening paragraph, for many writers the most difficult, gets the essay
off to an effective start. The writer begins with some comparisons between
modern and eighteenth-century societies that require no specialized historical
knowledge, announces her position on the relevance of Swift's essay to the
modern world, and concludes with the two specific arguments that have led
her to her position: (1) that the conditions that Swift protested are still with us,
and (2) that Swift's writing is so good that the essay has a vitality and power
that transcend the specific historical conditions that prompted it.

In the next three paragraphs, the writer supports the first argument. She
effectively draws upon her own experiences and knowledge to demonstrate that
the misery of eighteenth-century Dublin is to be found throughout the modern
world. Her larger generalization—that there is probably a connection between

the luxury of some and the misery of many—is stated modestly and supported by an observation about slumlords based on common knowledge and requiring no formal documentation.

In any case, the writer has by now made a convincing case for the argument that the problem Swift dealt with in his essay continues to plague the modern world. She now turns to her second argument, the power of Swift's writing. She signals this change with a transitional paragraph, the fifth one, that harkens back to what has been said previously—"So the subject matter of Swift's essay is still relevant"—and then restates the second argument—"I think we continue to read 'A Modest Proposal' because it is so brilliantly written." (Note that the paragraph you have just read is likewise a transition passage in our analysis of the student's essay).

The writer, unsurprisingly, devotes more space to the second argument than to the first, since anaylzing Swift's prose style is a more difficult task than showing that the subject matter of his essay remains relevant today. The writer has obviously worked hard at sorting out elements of Swift's style and ordering her analysis. She begins by announcing that the primary, pervasive stylistic element is irony. But rather than immediately launching into her analysis of Swift's irony, she first deals with the more general question of why a writer attacking social injustice might choose the indirect approach of irony rather than direct statement. As she makes her argument for the greater effectiveness of irony, she also analyzes the elements of that irony in terms of tone and persona—that is, the narrative voice created by Swift.

A particularly interesting part of the writer's analysis, showing that she has thought seriously about Swift's essay and irony, occurs when she momentarily calls into question her own earlier assertion that the prevailing tone of Swift's essay is irony. She resolves the matter immediately with an appropriate quotation from Swift's essay, but the very fact that she raises the issue shows her awareness of how much irony depends upon the reader's acceptance of the writer's underlying assumptions about what is reasonable.

Having dealt with tone and narrative voice, the writer concludes the analysis, in the next-to-last paragraph, with a brief consideration of Swift's diction. Even without this final support, the essay would be a good one. With it, we have the extra supporting detail that makes the essay superior. In addition, this paragraph leads naturally to the final paragraph of the essay.

The final paragraph shows once again how carefully the writer has thought out the structure of the essay. Rather than stopping abruptly (as would have been the case had the essay ended with the next-to-last paragraph) or giving a perfunctory summary of her main points (unnecessary in a short essay), the writer brings the essay nicely to rest by returning to her remark in the opening paragraph that "the speaker sounds eerily modern." The detailed analysis of "A Modest Proposal" allows her to explain succinctly what she meant by that remark as well as to remind us that her two major arguments—that Swift's subject is still relevant and that Swift's writing is brilliant—are really intertwined and inseparable.

The Writing Process

If you have thought about an assignment sufficiently and reread the work you intend to write about with enough care to formulate a thesis, then you have already accomplished a major part of the task. You have, however loosely, constructed an argument and marshaled some of the evidence to support it. Now you must begin to be rigorous. Take notes. The most efficient method is to use three-by-five-inch cards. Take one note per card, and use some key words at the top to identify the subject of the note. This procedure allows you to arrange your note cards in the most workable order when you are drafting your paper.

As you take your notes and then arrange the cards, you will begin to get some sense of the number of paragraphs you will need to support the thesis you have announced in the opening paragraph. Generally, each paragraph will focus on one major point (perhaps with its own mini-thesis), and bring together the evidence necessary to support that point.

As you write and rewrite, you should make sure that the progression of ideas from paragraph to paragraph is clear. To accomplish this, link each paragraph to the preceding one with a transitional word or phrase. Even the most carefully organized essay may seem abrupt or disjointed to the reader if you neglect to provide bridges between the paragraphs. A simple "However," "Nevertheless," "Furthermore," or "On the other hand" will often be adequate. Sometimes the entire opening sentence of a paragraph may provide the transition (and avoid the monotony of the standard words and phrases). Let us assume, for example, that you are writing an essay in which you argue that in Dylan Thomas's poem "Fern Hill" the mature speaker, now keenly aware of mortality, perceives the innocence of his childhood as a state of religious grace. In one or more paragraphs, you have analyzed the religious imagery of the poem, and you now begin a new paragraph with the sentence, "While the religious imagery dominates the poem, it is supported by a well-developed pattern of color imagery." Such a transitional sentence signals the reader that you will now consider another pattern of imagery that provides further evidence to support the thesis, since, as you will show, the color imagery is in fact a subpattern of the religious imagery.

Simply stated, in a tightly organized essay there ought to be a reason why one paragraph follows rather than precedes another. In fact, you may test the organization of your essay by asking yourself whether the paragraphs can be rearranged without significant effect. If they can be, chances are that your organization is weak, your ideas unclarified.

Having worked out an opening paragraph with a thesis and worked through the body of your essay to support the thesis, you now must confront the problem of how to conclude. Your conclusion should be brief, rarely more than three or four sentences. Ideally, it should leave the reader with a sense of both completeness and significance. For a short paper, it is unnecessary to restate or summarize your main points, because your reader will not have trouble remembering them. If your essay has been primarily appreciative and impression-istic, a general statement about the value of the work to you might bring the essay nicely to rest. Or you might conclude with a statement about the relevance of the work to the world we live in. When you have said all you have to say, you have finished. Avoid the common error of turning the conclusion into a beginning by taking up new evidence or ideas in the final paragraph.

Exploring Fiction, Poetry, Drama, and the Essay

Here are a number of questions you might ask yourself when you are faced with a writing assignment. To a large extent, they are elaborations of the questions that you answer for a summary report. Your answers to these questions can help you overcome the awful whiteness of the empty page.

Fiction

1. From what point of view is the story told? Can you speculate on the appropriateness of that point of view? If a story is told from the point of view of a first-person narrator who participates in the action, what significant changes would occur if it were told from the point of view of an omniscient author? And, of course, *vice versa*. Note that first-person narrators do not know what other characters think. On the other hand, omniscient narrators know everything about the lives of the characters. How would the story you are writing about be changed if the viewpoint were changed?

2. What is the tone of the story? The first several paragraphs will establish that tone. Does the tone change with events, or remain fixed? How does the tone contribute to the effect of the story?

3. Who are the principal characters in the story (there will rarely be more than two in a short story—the other characters will often be portrayed sketchily; sometimes they are even stereotypes)? What functions do the minor characters serve? Do any of the characters change during the course of the story? How, and why?

4. What is the plot of the story? Do the events that constitute the plot emerge logically from the nature of the characters and circumstances, or are the plot elements coincidental and arbitrary?

5. What is the setting of the story? Does the setting play an important role in the story, or is it simply the place where things happen? You might ask yourself what the consequences of some other setting might be for the effectiveness of the story.

6. What is the theme of the story? This, finally, is the most significant question to answer. All of the elements of fiction—point of view, tone, character, plot, setting—have been marshaled to project a theme—the moral proposition the author wishes to advance. Although themeless stories exist, they are rare. When you write about fiction, or any literary form, you must resist the tendency to do the easiest thing—retell the plot, incident by incident. You must, instead, come to understand the artful devices the author uses to convey the theme, and, in your paper, reveal that understanding.

Poetry

1. Who is the speaker? What does the poem reveal about the speaker's character? In some poems the speaker may be nothing more than a voice meditating on a theme, while in others the speaker takes on a specific personality. For example, the speaker in Shelley's "Ozymandias" is a voice meditating on the transitoriness of all things; except for the views he expresses in the poem, we know nothing about his character. The same might be said of the speaker in Hopkins's "Spring and Fall" but with this important exception: we know that he is older than Margaret and therefore has a wisdom she does not.

2. Is the speaker addressing a particular person? If so, who is that person, and why is the speaker interested in him or her? Many poems, like "Ozymandias," are addressed to no one in particular and therefore to anyone, any reader. Others, such as Donne's "A Valediction: Forbidding Mourning," while addressed to specific person, reveal nothing about that person because the focus of the poem is on the speaker's feelings and attitudes. In a dramatic monologue (see "Glossary of Literary Terms"), the speaker usually addresses a silent auditor. The identity of the auditor will be important to the poem.

3. Does the poem have a setting? Is the poem occasioned by a particular event? The answer to these questions will often be "no" for lyric poems, such as Frost's "Fire and Ice." It will always be "yes" if the poem is a dramatic monologue or a poem that tells or implies a story, such as Tennyson's "Ulysses" and Lowell's "Patterns."

4. Is the theme of the poem stated directly or indirectly? Some poems, such as Owen's "Dulce et Decorum Est" and Dunbar's "We Wear the Mask," use language in a fairly straightforward and literal way and state the theme, often in the final lines. Others, relying more heavily on figurative language and symbolism, may conclude with a statement of the theme that is more difficult to apprehend because it is made with figurative language and symbols. This difference will be readily apparent if you compare the final lines of the Owen and Dunbar poems mentioned above with, say, the final stanza of Stevens's "Sunday Morning."

5. If the speaker is describing specific events, from what perspective (roughly similar to point of view in fiction) is he or she doing so? Is the speaker recounting events of the past or events that are occurring in the present? If past events are being recalled, what present meaning do they have for the speaker? These questions are particularly appropriate to the works in the section "Innocence and Experience," many of which contrast an early innocence with adult experience.

6. Does a close examination of the figurative language (see "Glossary of Literary Terms") of the poem reveal any patterns? Yeats's "Sailing to Byzantium" may begin to open up to you once you recognize the pattern of bird imagery. Likewise, Thomas's attitude toward his childhood in "Fern Hill" will be clearer if you detect the pattern of Biblical imagery that associates childhood with Adam and Eve before the fall.

7. What is the structure of the poem? Since narrative poems, those that tell stories, reveal a high degree of selectivity, it is useful to ask why the poet has focused on particular details and left out others. Analyzing the structure of a nonnarrative or lyric poem can be more difficult because it does not contain an obvious series of chronologically related events. The structure of Thomas's "Fern Hill," for example, is based in part on a description of perhaps a day and a half in the speaker's life as a child. But more significant in terms of its structure is the speaker's present

realization that the immortality he felt as a child was merely a stage in the inexorable movement of life toward death. The structure of the poem, therefore, will be revealed through an analysis of patterns of images (Biblical, color, day and night, dark and light) that embody the theme. To take another example, Marvell's "To His Coy Mistress" is divided into three verse paragraphs, the opening words of each ("Had we . . . ," "But . . . ," "Now therefore . . . ,") suggesting a logically constructed argument.

8. What do sound and meter (see "Glossary of Literary Terms") contribute to the poem? Alexander Pope said that in good poetry "the sound must seem an echo to the sense," a statement that is sometimes easier to agree with than to demonstrate. For sample analyses of the music of poetry, see the section on music in the appendix "Reading Poetry" and the discussion of "Dover Beach" under formalist criticism in "Three Critical Approaches."

9. What was your response to the poem on first reading? Did your response change after rereadings and study of the poem?

Drama

1. How does the play begin? Is the exposition presented dramatically through the interaction among characters, or novelistically through long, unrealistic, and unwieldy speeches that convey a lot of information, or through some trickery such as the reading of long letters or lengthy reports delivered by a messenger?

2. How does the information conveyed in exposition (which may occur at various moments throughout the play) establish the basis for dramatic irony—that is, the ironic response generated in an audience when it knows more than do the characters? For example, because we know that Iago is a villain in Shakespeare's *Othello*, we hear an ironic dimension in his speeches that the characters do not hear, and that irony is the source of much tension in the audience. An assessment of dramatic irony in a play makes an interesting and instructive writing assignment.

3. Who are the principal characters, and how are the distinctive qualities of each dramatically conveyed? Inevitably, there will be minor characters in a play. What function do they serve? A paper that thoughtfully assesses the role of minor characters can often succeed better than the attempt to analyze the major figures who may embody too much complexity to deal with in 1,000 words.

4. Where is the play set? Does it matter that it is set there? Why? Does the setting play some significant role in the drama, or is it merely a place, anyplace?

5. What is the central conflict in the play? How is it resolved? Do you need to know something of the historical circumstances out of which the play emerged, or something of the life of the author in order fully to appreciate the play? If so, how does that information enhance your understanding?

6. Since plays are usually written to be performed rather than read, what visual and auditory elements of the play are significant to your response? Obviously, if you are writing from a reading text, you will have to place yourself in the position of the director and the actors in order to respond to this aspect of drama.

7. What is the play's theme? How does the dramatic action embody that theme?

Note that any one of these questions might provoke an effective paper—one could do a thousand words on the settings of *Othello*, or the minor characters of *A Doll's House*, or the methods of exposition in *Oedipus Rex*. But each of those papers, to be successful, needs to relate the issues it deals with to the thematic force of the play. Plot summaries (except as a variety of note-taking) are unsatisfactory.

Essays

1. What is the author's thesis (or unifying idea)? What evidence or arguments does the author advance to support the thesis? Is the thesis convincing? If not, why not? Does the author rely on any basic but unstated assumptions?
2. What is the author's tone? Select for analysis a passage you consider illustrative of the author's tone. Does the author maintain that tone consistently throughout the essay?
3. How would you characterize the author's style? For example, are the syntax, length of sentences, and diction elevated and formal or familiar and informal?
4. What rhetorical strategies does the author use? For example, can you identify the effective use of classification, comparison and contrast, analogy, cause and effect, or definition? Note that one of these rhetorical strategies may constitute the unifying idea of the essay and the means of structuring it. Tom Wolfe's "The Right Stuff" is an essay in definition that effectively uses examples, some of which are anecdotal narratives.
5. If the essay is narrative/autobiographical, does the author adhere strictly to chronology or does he or she alter the sequence? If so, why? For example, compare and contrast the way in which Richard Rodriguez in "Going Home Again: The New American Scholarship Boy" and Roger Wilkins in "Confessions of a Blue-Chip Black" use narration and autobiography to illuminate and support the generalizations they wish to make about being Chicano and Black in America.
6. What are the major divisions in the essay and how are they set off? Are the transitions between the divisions effective and easy to follow?
7. Analyze the author's opening paragraph. Is it effective in gaining the reader's attention? Does it clearly state the essay's thesis? If it does not, at what point does the author's thesis and purpose become clear?

A Final Word

Many questions may be asked about literature. Your assignment may require you to compare and contrast literary works, to analyze the language of a work, to discuss the interaction of parts of work, to discuss the theme of a work. Sometimes the instructor may give you free choice and ask simply that you write an essay on one of the pieces you read. This liberty will require that you create your own feasible boundaries—you will have to find a specific focus that suits the piece you choose and is manageable within a paper of the assigned length. But be sure that you do create boundaries—that, as we urged at the outset, you have a clear thesis.

   Give yourself time. If you attempt to write your paper the night before it is due, you are unlikely to write a paper that is worth reading. Even professional writers rarely accomplish serious and thoughtful writing overnight. You must give yourself time to think before you write a draft. Let the draft age a bit before rewriting a final draft. If you do not allow yourself a reasonable time period, you will convert an assignment that has the potential to enlarge your understanding and to produce real pleasure into an obstacle that you will surely trip over.

Consider also that finally you have to feel something, know something, bring something of yourself to the assignment. We can discuss formal methods for dealing with the problem of writing essays—but if you bring neither awareness, nor information, nor genuine interest to the task, the essay will remain an empty form.

Suggestions For Writing

Fiction

1. Explicate the opening paragraph or page of a story in order to demonstrate how it sets the tone and anticipates what is to follow.

2. Select a story that uses a central symbol or symbolic event and analyze its function. Some suggestions:
   A. The pond episode in Lawrence's "The Horse Dealer's Daughter."
   B. Iván's fall from the ladder in Tolstoy's "The Death of Iván Ilých."
   C. The quilt in Walker's "Everyday Use."

3. Select a story in which the narrative does not unfold chronologically and explain why.

4. Here are some suggestions for essays in comparison and contrast:
   A. Compare and contrast the function of art as revealed in Mann's *"Gladius Dei"* and Barthelme's "The Sandman."
   B. Compare and contrast the idea of "the hero" in Crane's "The Bride Comes to Yellow Sky" and Thurber's "The Greatest Man In the World."
   C. Compare and contrast the significance of the religious experience of the central characters in the final paragraphs of Tolstoy's "The Death of Iván Ilých" and Porter's "The Jilting of Granny Weatherall."
   D. Compare and contrast the attitude toward sexuality in Chopin's "The Storm" and Shaw's "The Girls in Their Summer Dresses."
   E. Compare and contrast the marriages in Shaw's "The Girls in Their Summer Dresses" and Mason's "Shiloh."

5. Write an essay on an especially interesting story title.

6. Did the ending of any story you read violate your expectations? What led you to those expectations? Do you find the author's ending more satisfactory than the one you had anticipated?

7. Select a story you feel is weak, and explain why you feel so. You might consider the credibility of the plot or of a character's behavior.

Poetry

1. Select a short lyric poem you found difficult, and explicate it line by line. Conclude with a paragraph or two describing how the process of explication helped you to clarify the meaning of the poem.

2. Here is a list of poems about poets and poetry. Select two and compare and contrast their treatment of the subject.
   Auden, "In Memory of W. B. Yeats"
   Conquest, "A Poem about a Poem about a Poem"
   Housman, "Terence, This Is Stupid Stuff"
   Moore, "Poetry"
   MacLeish, "Ars Poetica"
   Kennedy, "Ars Poetica"
   Francis, "Pitcher"
   Hamburger, "A Poet's Progress"
   Wallace, "In a Spring Still Not Written Of"
   Giovanni, "For Saundra"
   Cruz, "Today Is a Day of Great Joy"

3. The poems listed below tell or imply a story. Select one, and write out the story in your own words. Use your imagination to fill in details.
   Anonymous, "Bonny Barbara Allen"
   Anonymous, "Edward"
   Tennyson, "Ulysses"
   Browning, "My Last Duchess"
   Hardy, "The Ruined Maid"
   Lowell, "Patterns"
   Eliot, "The Love Song of J. Alfred Prufrock"
   Owen, "Dulce et Decorum Est"
   Wright, "Between the World and Me"

4. Analyze a poem in which the author uses a particular kind of diction. Identify the pattern, and explain how it functions in the poem. Some suggestions:
   A. The language of bureaucracy in Auden's "The Unknown Citizen" or Frost's "Departmental."
   B. Contrasting patterns of diction in Reed's "Naming of Parts."
   C. Colloquial and formal diction in Hughes's "Same in Blues."
   D. Colloquial diction in Jordan's "A Poem About Intelligence for My Brothers and Sisters."
   E. Prosaic diction in Forchè's "The Colonel" or Kirby's "The Last Song on the Jukebox."

5. As an exercise to illuminate the importance of connotation, select a poem that you like, identify some of its key words, and then consult a dictionary or thesaurus for synonyms of those key words. Reread the poem, substituting the synonyms for the words the poet used (for purposes of this exercise, ignore the fact that the synonyms may have more or fewer syllables and thus alter the rhythm). Write an essay analyzing the effects of your substitutions. Provide a sample of the rewritten poem.

6. Select one of the following titles for an essay in comparison and contrast.
    A. The Cost of Conformity: Dickinson's "What Soft—Cherubic Creatures" and Cummings's "the Cambridge ladies who live in furnished souls."
    B. The Psychology of Hate: Blake's "A Poison Tree" and Dickinson's "Mine Enemy Is Growing Old."
    C. The Meaning of Love: Marvell's "To His Coy Mistress" and Donne's "A Valediction: Forbidding Mourning."
    D. The Images of Love: Shakespeare's Sonnet 130 and Millay's "Love Is Not All."
    E. In Praise of a Beloved: Shakespeare's Sonnet 130 and Roethke's "I Knew a Woman."
    F. Remembering Childhood: Frost's "Birches" and Thomas's "Fern Hill."
    G. What the Young Can Never Understand: Snodgrass's "April Inventory," and Wallace's "In a Spring Still Not Written Of."
    H. The Woman's Role: Swenson's "Women" and Sexton's "Cinderella."
    I. The Meaning of Nature: Dickinson's "Apparently with No Surprise" and Frost's "Design."
    J. Untimely Death: Frost's " 'Out, Out—' " and Housman's "To an Athlete Dying Young" or Ransom's "Bells for John Whiteside's Daughter" and Roethke's "Elegy for Jane."
    K. The Meaning of Old Age: Yeats's "Sailing to Byzantium" and Housman's "To an Athlete Dying Young."

7. Analyze the allusions in a poem. Include in your discussion an explanation of the allusion and what it contributes to the poem. Some suggestions:
   Eliot's "The Love Song of J. Alfred Prufrock."
   Auden's "The Unknown Citizen" or "Musée des Beaux Arts."
   Reid's "Curiosity."
   Milton's Sonnet XVII.
   Wordsworth's "The World Is Too Much with Us."
   Cummings's "the Cambridge ladies who live in furnished souls."
   Arnold's "Dover Beach."
   Plath's "Daddy."
   Yeats's "Sailing to Byzantium."
   Frost's " 'Out, Out—'."

8. Analyze the use of irony in a poem. Some suggestions:
   Browning's "My Last Duchess."
   Hardy's "The Ruined Maid."
   Robinson's "Richard Cory."
   Frost's " 'Out, Out—'."
   Swenson's "Women."
   Bishop's "One Art."
   Holden's "Seaman, 1941."

9. Analyze the use of one form of figurative language in a poem. Some suggestions:
    A. Hyperbole in Burns's "A Red, Red Rose" or Marvell's "To His Coy Mistress."
    B. Simile and metaphor in Donne's "A Valedition: Forbidding Mourning," Marvell's "To His Coy Mistress," Burns's "A Red, Red Rose," Keats's "On

First Looking into Chapman's Homer," Shakespeare's sonnets 18 and 130, or MacLeish's "Ars Poetica."

C. Symbols in Waller's "Go Lovely Rose!" Blake's "The Tyger," Yeats's "The Second Coming," Frost's "Fire and Ice," Lowell's "Patterns," Reid's "Curiosity," or Meinke's "Advice to My Son."

D. Paradox in Wallace's "In a Spring Still Not Written Of," Meinke's "Advice to My Son," Yeats's "Easter 1916," Blake's "The Tyger," Stevens's "Sunday Morning," or Donne's "Death, Be Not Proud."

10. Look carefully at the reproduction of Breughel's painting *The Fall of Icarus* (p. 695), and jot down your impressions of it. Include a sentence or two on the "statement" you think Breughel is making. Now read Auden's poem "Musée des Beaux Arts." In an essay, compare your impressions of the painting with those of the poet. If the poem taught you something about the painting, include that in your essay.

Drama

1. Explicate the opening scene of a play in order to demonstrate how the dramatist lays the groundwork for what is to follow. Some questions you might consider: What information necessary to understanding the action are we given? What do we learn about the characters and their relationships? Do settings and costumes contribute to the exposition?

2. Analyze a play in order to show how nonverbal elements, such as costumes and stage sets, contribute to the theme.

3. Select a minor character in a play, and analyze that character's function. Some possibilities: Roderigo in *Othello*; Dr. Rank in *A Doll's House*; Jim and Pete in *End of the World*.

4. Analyze the language of a play for patterns of imagery that contribute to the development of character, mood, or the theme. Some suggestions: images of bestial sexuality in Shakespeare's *Othello*; images of blindness and seeing in Sophocles's *Oedipus Rex*; images used by Helmer to express his affection for Nora in Ibsen's *A Doll's House*.

5. Assume you are the director of one of the plays in this anthology. For one of the major characters, write a set of director's notes intended for the actor playing the role, in which you describe your conception of how the role should be played.

6. In an essay, describe the playwright's method for achieving dramatic irony in one of the plays you have read.

7. When you attend a performance of a play, you are usually given a program indicating, among other things, the number of acts, the elapsed time between acts, the time and place of the action. It will not include the stage directions of the printed version of the play. Examine the stage directions of a play, and suggest how a director might convey in a performance what the dramatist describes in the stage directions.

8. If you have the opportunity to see the film version of any of the works in this anthology, write an essay evaluating the success or failure of the film adaptation. Some suggestions:

   A. What did the film adaptation omit? Can you suggest why?
   B. What did the film adaptation add? Can you suggest why?
   C. Melville's "Bartleby the Scrivener" is a first-person narration. How does the film director deal with the problem of the narrative voice?
   D. Write an essay on the general problems of transposing a story into a film.

Essays

1. Carefully analyze the first paragraph or two of an essay in order to demonstrate how it sets the tone and attracts the reader's attention. Look for unusual language, imagery, prose rhythm, and notable sentence structure as evidence to support your assertions.

2. Select an essay that uses a central symbol or symbolic event and analyze its function. Some suggestions:

   A. Shooting the elephant in Orwell's essay.
   B. The Iks in Thomas's essay.
   C. The lake in White's "Once More to the Lake."
   D. The tolling bell in Donne's "Meditation XVII."
   E. Las Vagas wedding chapels in Didion's "Marrying Absurd."
   F. The guitar in Walker's "To Hell with Dying."
   G. The plate in Selzer's "The Discus Thrower."

3. Here are some suggestions for studies in comparison and contrast:

   A. Compare and contrast the attitudes toward romantic love in Porter's "The Necessary Enemy" and Goodman's "Being Loved Anyway."
   B. Compare and contrast the treatment of death in Selzer's "The Discus Thrower" and Walker's "To Hell with Dying."
   C. Compare and contrast the experience of minorities as revealed in Wilkins's "Confessions of a Blue-Chip Black" and Rodriguez's "Going Home Again: The New American Scholarship Boy."
   D. Compare and contrast the satirical methods of Swift in "A Modest Proposal" and Thomas in "The Iks."
   E. Compare and contrast the prose style of Wolfe's "The Right Stuff" and Woolf's "What If Shakespeare Had Had a Sister?"

4. Select an essay you particularly like and create a set of notes in which you systematically convert the original to brief study aids. After a few days, try to recreate the essay, or a portion of it, from your notes. Compare your effort with the original and write an analysis of the differences.

5. Discover, describe, and analyze the unspoken assumptions that an author depends upon. Some suggestions:

   A. The sacredness of life in Swift's "A Modest Proposal."
   B. The solemnity of marriage in Didion's "Marrying Absurd."
   C. The survival of the soul in Donne's "Meditation XVII."
   D. The nature of power in Orwell's "Shooting an Elephant."

> E. The right to equal justice in King's "Letter from Birmingham Jail."
> F. The elements of superiority in Wolfe's "The Right Stuff."
> G. Sex tension in Thurber's "Courtship Among the Animals."
> H. The proper response to death in Mitford's "The American Way of Death."
> I. The nature of love in Porter's "The Necessary Enemy" or Goodman's "Being Loved Anyway."

And one final general question: One of the commonly accepted notions of art is that it helps us to clarify our own feelings, to give us in vivid and memorable form what we had perhaps felt or thought only vaguely. Select a work (one that you found especially relevant to your own life), and describe how it clarified your own feelings.

Some Matters of Form

Titles

The first word and all main words of titles have their first letters capitalized. Ordinarily (unless, of course, they are the first or last word), articles (*a, an,* and *the*), prepositions (*in, on, of, with, about,* etc.), and conjuctions (*and, but, or,* etc.) do not have their first letters capitalized.

The titles of parts of larger collections, short stories, poems, articles, essays, and songs are enclosed in quotation marks.

The titles of plays, books, movies, periodicals, operas, paintings, and newspapers are italicized. In typed and handwritten manuscripts, italics are represented by underlining.

The title you give your own essay is neither placed in quotation marks nor underlined. However, a quotation used as a part of your title would be enclosed in quotation marks (see the following section on quotations). Similarly, the title of a literary work used as a part of your title would be either placed in quotation marks or underlined depending on the type of work it is.

Quotations

Quotation marks indicate you are transcribing someone else's words; those words must, therefore, be *exactly* as they appear in your source.

As a general rule, quotations of not more than four lines of prose or two lines of poetry are placed between quotation marks and incorporated in your own text:

```
At the climactic moment, Robin observes "an uncovered cart.
There the torches blazed the brightest, there the moon shone
out like day, and there, in tar-and-feathery dignity, sat his
kinsman, Major Molineux!"
```

If you are quoting two lines of verse in your text, indicate the division between lines with a slash:

```
Prufrock hears the dilletantish talk in a room where "the
women come and go/Talking of Michelangelo."
```

Longer quotations are indented five typewriter spaces and can be single-spaced. They are not enclosed in quotation marks, since the indentation signals a quotation.

As noted above, anything quoted, whether enclosed in quotation marks or indented, must be reproduced exactly. If you insert anything—even a word—the inserted material must be placed within brackets. If you wish to omit some material from a passage in quotation marks, the omission (ellipsis) must be indicated by three spaced periods: . . . (an ellipsis mark). When an ellipsis occurs between complete sentences or at the end of a sentence, a fourth period, indicating the end of the sentence, should be inserted.

Full quotation from original:

```
"Richard Wright, like Dostoevsky before him, sends his hero
underground to discover the truth about the upper world, a
world that has forced him to confess to a crime he has not
committed."
```

With insertion and omissions:

```
"Richard Wright . . . sends his hero [Fred Daniels] under-
ground to discover the truth about the upper world. . . ."
```

Use a full line of spaced periods to indicate the omission of a line or more of poetry (or of a whole paragraph or more of prose):

```
For I have known them all already, known them all--
Have known the evenings, mornings, afternoons,
I have measured out my life with coffee spoons;
. . . . . . . . . . . . . . . . . . . . . . . . . . . . . . . . . . . .
And I have known the eyes already, known them all--
The eyes that fix you in a formulated phrase.
```

Periods and commas are placed *inside* quotation marks:

```
In "My Oedipus Complex," the narrator says, "The war was the
most peaceful period of my life."
```

Other punctuation marks go outside the quotation marks unless they are part of the material being quoted.

For poetry quotations, provide the line number or numbers in parentheses immediately following the quotation:

> With ironic detachment, Prufrock declares that he is "no
> prophet" (line 83).

Documentation

You must acknowledge the source of ideas you paraphrase and material you quote. Such acknowledgments are extremely important, for even an unintentional failure to give formal credit to others for their words or ideas can leave you open to an accusation of plagiarism—that is, the presentation of someone else's ideas as your own.

If you use published works as you prepare your paper, you should list those sources as the last page of your essay. Then, in the body of your essay, you will use parenthetical citations that refer to the works you quote or paraphrase. Here is a sample bibliography that illustrates the mechanical form for a list of citations. These samples will probably satisfy your needs, but if you use different kinds of source material, you should consult Joseph Gibaldi and Walter S. Achtert, *MLA Handbook for Writers of Research Papers*, 2nd ed. (New York: The Modern Language Association of America, 1984). That *Handbook* provides sample entries for every imaginable source.

Works Cited

Abcarian, Richard, and Marvin Klotz, eds. Literature: The Hu-
    man Experience. 4th ed. New York: St. Martin's, 1986.
Cooper, Wendy. Hair, Sex, Society, Symbolism. New York:
    Stein, 1971.
Fiedler, Leslie. "Come Back to the Raft Ag'in, Huck Honey."
    Partisan Review 15 (1948): 664–671.
Joyce, James. "Araby." Literature: The Human Experience. 4th
    ed. Eds. Richard Abcarian and Marvin Klotz. New York:
    St. Martin's, 1986. 67–71.
---Dubliners. Eds. Robert Scholes and A. Walton Litz. New
    York: Penguin, 1976.

The first of these citations is this book. You would use it if you used materials from the editors' introduction or critical appendices. The entry illustrates the form for citing a book with two editors. Note that the first editor's name is presented surname first, but the second is presented with the surname last.

The second entry illustrates the form for citing a book with one author. The third gives the form for an article published in a periodical (note that the title of the article is in quotes and the title of the journal is underlined). The fourth entry shows how to cite a work included in an anthology. The fifth citation, because it is by the same author as the fourth, begins with three hyphens in place of the author's name.

The following paragraph demonstrates the use of parenthetical citations.

> Leslie Fiedler's controversial view of the relationship between Jim and Huck (669–670) uses a method often discussed by other critics (Abcarian and Klotz 1297–1298). Cooper's 1971 study (180) raises similar issues, but such methods are not useful when one deals with such a line as "North Richmond Street, being blind, was a quiet street except at the hour when the Christian Brothers' School set the boys free" (Joyce, "Araby" 67). But when Joyce refers to the weather (Dubliners 224), the issue becomes clouded.

This rather whimiscal paragraph illustrates the form your parenthetical citations should take. The first citation gives only the page reference, which is all that is necessary, because the author's name is given in the text and only one work by that author appears in the list of works cited.

The second citation gives the editors' names and thus identifies the work being cited. It then indicates the appropriate pages.

The third citation, because the author's name is mentioned in the text, gives only a page reference.

The fourth citation must provide the author's name *and* the work cited, because two works by the same author appear in the bibliography.

The last citation, because it refers to an author with two works in the list of works cited, gives the name of the work and the page where the reference can be found.

In short, your parenthetical acknowledgement should contain (1) the *minimum* information required to lead the reader to the appropriate work in the list of works cited and (2) the location within the work to which you refer.

Rather than parenthetical references, some instructors may prefer footnotes (or endnotes). Here is the same paragraph documented with footnotes.

> Leslie Fiedler's controversial view of the relationship between Jim and Huck[1] uses a method often discussed by other critics.[2] Cooper's 1971 study[3] raises similar issues, but such methods are not useful when one deals with such a line as "North Richmond Street, being blind, was a quiet street except at the hour when the Christian Brothers' School set

the boys free."[4] But when Joyce refers to the weather,[5] the issue becomes clouded.

    [1]"Come back to the Raft Ag'in, Huck Honey," <u>Partisan Review</u> 15 (1948): 664–671.

    [2]Richard Abcarian and Marvin Klotz, eds., <u>Literature: The Human Experience</u> (New York: St. Martin's, 1986) 1297–1298.

    [3]<u>Hair, Sex, Society, Symbolism</u> (New York: Stein, 1971) 180.

    [4]James Joyce, "Araby," <u>Literature: The Human Experience,</u> eds. Richard Abcarian and Marvin Klotz (New York: St. Martin's, 1986) 67.

    [5]<u>Dubliners,</u> eds. Robert Scholes and A. Walton Litz (New York: Penguin, 1976) 224.

Note that when the author's name is given in the text, you do not have to repeat it in the footnote. Subsequent references to a work generally require only the surname of the author (or authors, editor, or editors) and the page number; thus:

    [4]Cooper 175.

If you need to find a model for a different kind of source, don't despair. Simply refer to the MLA Handbook (1984).

The main thing to remember about footnoting, and about citations in general, is that the object is to give credit to others wherever it is due and to enable your reader to go directly to your sources, if he or she wishes to do so, as quickly and easily as possible.

Summing Up: A Checklist

1. Start early. You're going to need time for thinking, time for reading and taking notes, time for writing, and (very important) time for breaks between steps.

2. Read the work carefully, and more than once.

3. If you are allowed to choose a topic, choose one that interests you and that you can explore in some depth in a paper of the assigned length. If you have trouble finding a topic, ask yourself as many questions as you can about the work: *What* is it about? *Who* is it about? *Why* do I respond to it as I do? And so forth. Many kinds of questions have been suggested in the preceding pages, and there are numerous questions following the selections and at the ends of the four main sections in this anthology.

4. Convert your topic into a clearly defined thesis: a proposition you intend to argue for and support with evidence from the work. If you have trouble shaping a

thesis, try the technique of free writing—forget about form and just scribble down all your thoughts and opinions: what you like, what you don't like, anything at all. Then ask yourself what made you think or feel as you do.

5. Once you have a thesis, reread the work and take careful notes on three-by-five-inch cards, one note to a card, with a page (or, for poetry, line) reference and a short descriptive heading to remind you of the note's significance. Then arrange the cards in the order that seems appropriate to follow in your essay.

6. Start writing, and keep going. This is a rough draft—essentially a blueprint—and is for your eyes only, so don't worry about formalities and polishing. The point is to get your ideas down on paper in approximately the right order. If making a rough outline first will help you, do it. If spontaneous writing works better, do that. But do get a clear statement of your thesis into your first paragraph; it will guide you as you write, since everything you write will (or should) be related to it.

7. Take a break. Let the rough draft cool for at least a few hours, preferably overnight. When you come back to it, you'll be refreshed and you'll think more clearly. You may find that you want to do some reorganizing or add or delete material. You may also want to go back and reread or at least take another look at the work you're writing about.

8. Now, more carefully, working from your rough draft, write a second draft. This will be fuller, clearer, more polished. You'll have a chance to revise (assuming you followed step 1, above), so don't get unnecessarily bogged down; but write this version as *if* it were the version your reader will see. This version, when finished, should be logically and clearly organized. The point of each paragraph should be clear—well expressed and well supported by details or examples—and its relationship to the thesis should be apparent. Transitions between paragraphs should be supplied wherever necessary to make the argument progress smoothly. Quotations should be in place and accurately transcribed.

9. Take a break. This time allow the draft to age for two or three days. At the moment, you're too close to the draft to read it objectively.

10. Pick up the draft as if you were the reader and had never seen it before. Now you will make your final revisions. More than polishing is involved here. This is the time to cut out, mercilessly, things that are not pertinent to your discussion, no matter how interesting or well written they may be. Putting yourself in your reader's place, clarify anything that is vague or ambiguous. Make sure each word is the most precise one you could have chosen for your purpose. Watch, too, for overkill—points that are driven into the ground by too much discussion or detail. Finally, no matter how careful you think you have been, check all your quotations and citations for accuracy. Instructors—rightly—take these things seriously.

11. Type or neatly write out in ink the final copy for submission to your instructor, taking care to follow any special instructions about format that you have been given. Don't rush; be meticulous. When you have finished, proofread the final copy very carefully, keeping an eye out for errors in spelling or punctuation, omitted words, disagreement between subjects and verbs or between pronouns and antecedents, and other flaws (such as typographical errors) that will detract from what you have worked so hard to write.

Glossary of Literary Terms

Alexandrine See Meter.

Allegory A form of symbolism in which ideas or abstract qualities are represented as characters in a narrative and dramatic situation, resulting in a moral or philosophic statement.

Alliteration The repetition within a line or phrase of the same initial consonant sound.

Death, thou shalt die.—John Donne, "Death, Be Not Proud," l. 14, p. 669

And mouth with myriad subtleties—Paul Laurence Dunbar, "We Wear the Mask," l. 5, p. 267

Allusion A reference, explicit or indirect, to something outside the work itself. The reference is usually to some famous person, event, or other literary work.

No! I am not Prince Hamlet, nor was meant to be—T. S. Eliot, "The Love Song of J. Alfred Prufrock," l. 111, p. 460

W. H. Auden, title of "The Unknown Citizen," p. 278

Ambiguity A phrase, statement, or situation that may be understood in two or more ways. As a literary device, it is used to enrich meaning or achieve irony.

my Uncle Sol imitated the
skunks in a subtle manner

or by drowning himself in the watertank—E. E. Cummings, "nobody loses all the time." ll. 24–26, p. 691

Anapest See Meter.

Antistrophe See Strophe.

Apostrophe A direct address to a person who is absent or to an abstract or inanimate entity.

John Donne, "Death, Be Not Proud," p. 669

Archetype Themes, images, and narrative patterns that are universal and thus embody some enduring aspects of man's experience. Some of these themes are the death and rebirth of the hero, the underground journey, and the search for the father.

Assonance The repetition of vowel sounds in a line, stanza, or sentence.

W. H. Auden, *from* "Five Songs," p. 467

Ballad A narrative poem, originally of folk origin, usually focusing upon a climactic episode and told without comment. The most common form is a quatrain of alternating four- and three-stress iambic lines, with the second and fourth lines rhyming. Often the ballad will employ a *refrain*—that is, the last line of each stanza will be identical or similar.

"Edward," p. 667

"Bonny Barbara Allan," p. 447

Blank Verse Lines of unrhymed iambic pentameter.

William Shakespeare, *Othello*, p. 481

Cacophony Harsh and discordant language. *Compare* Euphony.

Is perjured, murderous, bloody, full of blame,
Savage, extreme, rude, cruel, not to trust—William Shakespeare, Sonnet 129, ll. 3–4, p. 451

Caesura A strong phrasal pause within a line of verse.

There is a loveliness exists.
Preserves us.//Not for specialists.—W. D. Snodgrass, "April Inventory," ll. 59–60, p. 89

Carpe Diem   Latin, meaning "seize the day." A work, generally a lyric poem, in which the speaker calls the attention of his auditor (often a young girl) to the shortness of life and youth and then urges her to enjoy life while there is time.
    Andrew Marvell, "To His Coy Mistress," p. 454

Catharsis   One of the key concepts in *The Poetics* of Aristotle by which he attempts to account for the fact that representations of suffering and death in drama paradoxically leave the audience feeling relieved rather than depressed. According to Aristotle, a tragic hero arouses in the viewer feelings of "pity and fear," pity because the hero is a person of great moral worth, and fear because the viewer identifies with the hero.

Central Intelligence   *See* Point of View.

Comedy   In drama, situations that are designed to delight and amuse rather than concern or sadden. Comedy usually is concerned with social values and ends happily. *Compare* Tragedy.

Conceit   A figure of speech that establishes an elaborate parallel between unlike things.
    John Donne, "A Valediction: Forbidding Mourning," ll. 25–36, p. 452

Conflict   The struggle of a protagonist, or main character, with forces that threaten to destroy him. The struggle creates suspense and is usually resolved at the end of the story. The force opposing the main character may be either another person—the antagonist—(as in O'Connor's "My Oedipus Complex"), or society (as in Ellison's " 'Repent, Harlequin!' Said the Ticktockman"), or natural forces (as in Malamud's "Idiots First"), or an internal conflict within the main character (as in Joyce's "Araby").

Connotation   The associative and suggestive meanings of a word in contrast to its literal meaning. *Compare* Denotation.

Consonance   Repetition of the final consonant sounds in stressed syllables.
    That night when joy began
    Our narrowest veins to flush,
    We waited for the flash.
    Of morning's levelled gun—W. H. Auden, *from* "Five Songs," ll. 1–4, p. 467

Couplet   A pair of rhymed lines.
    The grave's a fine and private place,
    But none, I think, do there embrace.—Andrew Marvell, "To His Coy Mistress,"
        p. 454

Dactyl   *See* Meter.

Denotation   The literal, dictionary definition of a word. *Compare* Connotation.

Denouement   The final outcome or unraveling of the main conflict; literally, the "untying" of the plot following the climax.

Diction   The choice of words in a work of literature, generally applied to indicate such distinctions as abstract or concrete, formal or colloquial, literal or figurative.

Didactic   A term applied to works whose primary and avowed purpose is to teach or to persuade the reader of the truth of some philosophical, religious, or moral statement or doctrine.

Dimeter   *See* Meter.

Dramatic Distance   In fiction, the point of view which enables the reader to know more than the narrator of the story.

Dramatic Irony   *See* Irony.

Dramatic Monologue   A type of poem in which the speaker, who is not the poet, addresses another person (or persons) whose presence is known only from the speaker's words. Such poems are dramatic because the speaker interacts with another character at a specific time and place; they are monologues because the entire poem is uttered by the speaker.

   Robert Browning, "My Last Duchess," p. 73
   Matthew Arnold, "Dover Beach," p. 458
   T. S. Eliot, "The Love Song of J. Alfred Prufrock," p. 460

Elegy   Usually a poem lamenting the death of a particular person, but often used to describe meditative poems on the subject of mortality.

   W. H. Auden, "In Memory of W. B. Yeats," p. 692
   Thomas Gray, "Elegy Written in a Country Churchyard," p. 670

End-rhyme   *See* Rhyme.

End-stopped Line   A line of verse that constitutes a complete logical and grammatical unit. A line of verse that does not constitute a complete syntactic unit is designated *run-on*. Thus in the opening lines of Browning's "My Last Duchess"

   That's my last Duchess painted on the wall,
   Looking as if she were alive. I call
   That piece a wonder, now: . . . .

The opening line is end-stopped, while the second line is run-on, because the direct object of *call* "runs on" to the third line.

English Sonnet   *See* Sonnet.

Epode   *See* Strophe.

Euphony   Sounds that are pleasing to the ear. *Compare* Cacophony.

Farce   A type of comedy, usually satiric, that relies on exaggerated character types, ridiculous situations, and, often, horseplay.

Figurative Language   A general term covering the many ways in which language is used nonliterally. *See* Hyperbole, Irony, Metaphor, Metonymy, Paradox, Simile, Symbol, Synecdoche, Understatement.

First-person Narrator   *See* Point of View.

Foot   *See* Meter.

Free Verse   Poetry, usually unrhymed, that does not adhere to the metric regularity of traditional verse.

   Lawrence Ferlinghetti, "Constantly Risking Absurdity," p. 787

Hexameter   *See* Meter.

Hubris   In Greek tragedy, overweening pride usually exhibited in a character's defiance of the gods. Oedipus, in Sophocles's *Oedipus Rex*, is guilty of hubris.

Hyperbole   Exaggeration; overstatement. *Compare* Understatement.

   Robert Burns, "A Red, Red Rose," p. 456

Iamb   *See* Meter.

Imagery   Narrowly, language that embodies an appeal to the senses, particularly sight.

   William Shakespeare, Sonnet 18, p. 451
   William Shakespeare, Sonnet 130, p. 452
   Robert Frost, "Birches," p. 81

The term is often applied to all figurative language.

Internal Rhyme   *See* Rhyme.

Irony   Language in which the intended meaning is different from or opposite to the literal meaning. Verbal irony includes overstatement (hyperbole), understatement, and opposite statement.

   The grave's a fine and private place,
   But none, I think, do there embrace.—Andrew Marvell, "To His Coy Mistress,"
      ll. 31–32, p. 454

> Was he free? Was he happy? The question is absurd:
> Had anything been wrong, we should certainly have heard.—W. H. Auden,
>   "The Unknown Citizen," ll. 28–29, p. 278

Dramatic irony occurs when a reader knows things a character is ignorant of or when the speech and action of characters reveal them to be different from what they believe themselves to be.

> Robert Browning, "My Last Duchess," pp. 73
> William Shakespeare, *Othello*, Act III, Scene 3, pp. 520–533

Italian Sonnet   *See* Sonnet.

Lyric   Originally, a song accompanied by lyre music. Now, a relatively short poem expressing the thought or feeling of a single speaker. Almost all of the nondramatic poetry in this anthology is lyric poetry.

Metaphor   A figurative expression consisting of two elements in which one element is provided with special attributes by being equated with a second unlike element.

> If only I could nudge you from this sleep,
> My maimed darling, my skittery pigeon—Theodore Roethke, "Elegy for Jane,"
>   ll. 18–19, p. 696

Meter   Refers to recurrent patterns of accented and unaccented syllables in verse. A metrical unit is called a *foot*, and there are four basic accented patterns. An *iamb*, or *iambic foot*, consists of an inaccented syllable followed by an accented syllable (bĕfóre, tŏdáy.) A *trochee*, or *trochaic foot*, consists of an accented syllable followed by an unaccented syllable (fúnñy, phántŏm). An *anapest*, or *anapestic foot*, consists of two unaccented syllables followed by an accented syllable (in the line "If eṽ | ĕrŷthing háp | pĕns thăt cán't | bĕ dóne," the second and third metrical feet are anapests). A *dactyl*, or *dactyllic foot*, consists of a stressed syllable followed by two unstressed syllables (sýllăblĕ, métrĭcăl). One common variant, consisting of two stressed syllables, is called a *spondee*, or *spondaic foot* (dáybřeak, moónshíne).

Lines are classified according to the number of metrical feet they contain.

one foot	monometer
two feet	dimeter
three feet	trimeter
four feet	tetrameter
five feet	pentameter
six feet	hexameter (An iambic hexameter line is an *Alexandrine*.)

Here are some examples of various metrical patterns:

> Tŏ eách | hĭs súff | erĭngs: áll | aře mén,   *iambic tetrameter*
>   Cŏndemńed | ălĭké | tŏ groán;   *iambic trimeter*

> Ońce ŭp | oń ă mídnĭght | dréarŷ, | whíle Ĭ | póndeřed |
>   wéak ănd | wéarŷ   *trochaic octameter*

> Ĭs thís | thĕ rég | ĭon, thís | thĕ soíl, | thĕ clíme,   *iambic pentameter*
> Fóllŏw ĭt | úttĕrlŷ,   *dactyllic dimeter*
> Hópe bĕ | yońd hópe: *dimeter line—trochee and spondee*

Metonymy   A figure of speech in which a word stands for a closely related idea. In the expression "The pen is mightier than the sword," *pen* and *sword* are metonyms for written ideas and military force respectively.

> Free hearts, free foreheads—you and I are old.—Alfred, Lord Tennyson, "Ulysses,"
>   l. 49, p. 261

Monometer   *See* Meter.

Near Rhyme   *See* Rhyme.

Octave   *See* Sonnet.

Ode   Usually a long, serious poem on exalted subjects, often in the form of an address.
John Keats, "Ode on a Grecian Urn," p. 675

Off Rhyme   *See* Rhyme.

Omniscient Narrator   *See* Point of View.

Onomatopoeia   Language that sounds like what it means. Words like *buzz, bark,* and
hiss are onomatopoetic. Also, sound patterns that reinforce the meaning over one or
more lines may be designated onomatopoetic.

> Is lust in action; and till action, lust
> Is perjured, murderous, bloody, full of blame—William Shakespeare, Sonnet
> 129, ll. 2–4, p. 451

Opposite Statement   *See* Irony.

Overstatement   *See* Hyperbole.

Paradox   A statement that seems self-contradictory or absurd but is, somehow, valid.

> And death shall be no more; Death, thou shalt die—John Donne, "Death, Be
> Not Proud," l. 14, p. 669

Pentameter   *See* Meter.

Persona   Literally "mask." The term is applied to a narrator in fiction (James Joyce's
"Araby") or the speaker in a poem (Robert Browning's "My Last Duchess"). The
persona's views may be different from the author's views.

Personification   The attribution of human qualities to nature, animals, or things.
Edmund Waller, "Go, Lovely Rose!" p. 454
John Donne, "Death, Be Not Proud," p. 669

Petrarchan Sonnet   *See* Sonnet.

Plot   A series of actions in a story or drama which bear a significant relationship to
each other. E. M. Forster illuminates the definition: " 'The King died, and then the
Queen died,' is a story. 'The King died and then the Queen died of grief,' is a plot."

Point of View   The person or intelligence a writer of fiction creates to tell the story to
the reader. The major techniques are:

> *First person,* where the story is told by someone, often, though not necessarily,
> the principal character, who identifies himself as "I."
> Toni Cade Bambara, "The Lesson," p. 64
> *Third person,* where the story is told by someone (not defined as "I") who is not a
> participant in the action and who refers to the characters by name or as "he,"
> "she," and "they."
> Harlan Ellison, " 'Repent, Harlequin!' Said the Ticktockman," p. 242
> *Omniscient,* a variation on the third person, where the narrator knows everything
> about the characters and events, can move about in time and place as well as
> from character to character at will, and can, whenever he wishes, enter the
> mind of any character.
> Leo Tolstoy, "The Death of Iván Ilých," p. 595
> *Central intelligence,* another variation on the third person, where narrative ele-
> ments are limited to what a single character sees, thinks, and hears.

Quatrain   A four-line stanza that may incorporate various metrical patterns.
"Bonny Barbara Allan," p. 447
Thomas Gray, "Elegy Written in a Country Churchyard," p. 670

Refrain   *See* Ballad.

Rhyme   The repetition of the final stressed vowel sound and any sounds following (debate, relate; pelican, belly can) produces perfect rhyme. When rhyming words appear at the end of lines, the poem is *end-rhymed*. When rhyming words appear within one line, the line contains *internal rhyme*. When the correspondence in sounds is imperfect (heaven, given; began, gun), *off rhyme*, or *near rhyme*, is produced.

Off rhyme: W. H. Auden, *from* "Five Songs," p. 467

Rhythm   The alternation of accented and unaccented syllables in language. A regular pattern of alternation produces *meter*. Irregular alternation of stressed and unstressed syllables produces *free verse*.

Run-on Line   *See* End-stopped Line.

Satire   Writing in a comic mode that holds a subject up to scorn and ridicule, often with the purpose of correcting human vice and folly.

E. E. Cummings, "the Cambridge ladies who live in furnished souls," p. 276

W. H. Auden, "The Unknown Citizen," p. 278

Robert Frost, "Departmental," p. 271

Harlan Ellison, " 'Repent, Harlequin!' Said the Ticktockman," p. 242

Scansion   The analysis of the metrical or rhythmical pattern of a poem. *See* Meter.

Sestet   *See* Sonnet.

Setting   The place where the story occurs. Often the setting contributes significantly to the story; for example, the radiance of Munich in "Gladius Dei" highlights the gloom of the religious zealot Hieronymus.

Shakespearean Sonnet   *See* Sonnet.

Simile   A figurative expression in which an element is provided with special attributes through a comparison with something quite different. The words *like* or *as* create the comparison, e.g. "O My Luve's like a red, red rose."

Robert Burns, "A Red, Red Rose," p. 456

Soliloquy   A dramatic convention in which an actor, alone on the stage, speaks his thoughts aloud.

William Shakespeare, *Othello*, Iago's speech, Act I, Scene 3, pp. 499–500

Sonnet   A lyric poem of fourteen lines, usually of iambic pentameter. The two major types are the Petrarchan (or Italian) and Shakespearean (or English). The *Petrarchan sonnet* is divided into an octave (the first eight lines, rhymed abbaabba) and a sestet (the final six lines, usually rhymed cdecde or cdcdcd). The *Shakespearean sonnet* consists of three quatrains and a concluding couplet, rhymed abab cdcd efef gg.

William Shakespeare, Sonnets, pp. 451, 452, 669

Spondee   *See* Meter.

Stanza   The grouping of the lines of a poem in a recurring pattern of meter, rhyme, and number of lines. Among the most common are the *couplet* and the *quatrain*.

Stream of Consciousness   The narrative technique of some modern fiction which attempts to reproduce the full and uninterrupted flow of a character's mental process, in which ideas, memories, and sense impressions may intermingle without logical transitions. A characteristic of this technique is the abandonment of conventional rules of syntax and punctuation.

Katherine Anne Porter, "The Jilting of Granny Weatherall," p. 644

Strophe   In Greek tragedy, the unit of verse the chorus chanted as it moved to the left in a dance rhythm. The chorus sang the *antistrophe* as it moved to the right and the *epode* while standing still.

Symbol   A thing or an action that embodies more than its literal, concrete meaning.

Alastair Reid, "Curiosity," p. 88

Peter Meinke, "Advice to My Son," p. 95

Synecdoche A figure of speech in which a part is used to signify the whole.

> Perhaps in this neglected spot is laid
> > Some heart once pregnant with celestial fire;
> Hands that the rod of empire might have swayed,
> > Or waked to ecstasy the living lyre.—Thomas Gray, "Elegy Written in a
> > Country Churchyard," ll. 45–48, p. 670

Synesthesia In literature, the description of one kind of sensory experience in terms of another. Taste might be described as a color or a song.

Tetrameter *See* Meter.

Theme The moral proposition that a literary work is designed to advance. The theme of Kate Chopin's "The Storm" might be briefly stated: Adultery can be a positive rather than a destructive experience.

Third-person Narrator *See* Point of View.

Tone The attitude embodied in the language a writer chooses. The tone of a work might be sad, joyful, ironic, solemn, playful.

> Compare: Matthew Arnold, "Dover Beach," p. 458, with Anthony Hecht, "The
> > Dover Bitch," p. 470

Tragedy The dramatic representation of serious and important actions which bring misfortune to the chief character. Aristotle saw tragedy as the fall of a noble figure from a high position as the result of a flaw in his character. *Compare* Comedy.

Trimeter *See* Meter.

Trochee *See* Meter.

Understatement A figure of speech that represents something as less important than it really is. *Compare* Hyperbole.

> . . . This grew; I gave commands;
> Then all smiles stopped together. . . .—Robert Browning, "My Last Duchess,"
> > ll. 45–46, p. 73

Villanelle A French verse form of nineteen lines (of any length) divided into six stanzas—five triplets and a final quatrain—employing two rhymes and two refrains. The refrains consist of lines one (repeated as lines six, twelve, and eighteen) and three (repeated as lines nine, fifteen, and nineteen).

> Dylan Thomas "Do Not Go Gentle into That Good Night," p. 698
> Catherine Davis, "After a Time," p. 700

Alberto Moravia, "The Chase" from *Command and I Will Obey You* by Alberto Moravia, translated by Angus Davidson. Translation copyright © 1969 by Martin Secker & Warburg, Limited. Reprinted by permission of Farrar, Straus & Giroux, Inc.

Randall Jarrell, "The Death of the Ball Turret Gunner" from *The Complete Poems* by Randall Jarrell. Copyright © 1945, 1948, 1969 by Mrs. Randall Jarrell. Copyright renewed © 1972, 1975 by Mrs. Randall Jarrell. Reprinted by permission of Farrar, Straus & Giroux, Inc.

Elizabeth Bishop, "One Art" from *The Complete Poems 1927–1979* by Elizabeth Bishop. Copyright © 1983 by Alice Helen Methfessel. Copyright © 1976 by Elizabeth Bishop. Originally appeared in *The New Yorker*. Reprinted by permission of Farrar, Straus & Giroux, Inc.

Joan Didion, "Marrying Absurd" from *Slouching Toward Bethlehem* by Joan Didion. Copyright © 1961, 1964, 1965, 1967, 1968 by Joan Didion. Reprinted by permission of Farrar, Straus & Giroux, Inc.

Tom Wolfe, excerpts from *The Right Stuff* by Tom Wolfe. Copyright © 1979 by Tom Wolfe. Reprinted by permission of Farrar, Straus & Giroux, Inc.

Arthur Kopit, *End of the World.* Copyright © 1984 by Arthur Kopit. All rights reserved. Reprinted by permission of Hill and Wang, a division of Farrar, Straus & Giroux, Inc.

THE UNIVERSITY OF GEORGIA PRESS: X. J. Kennedy, "First Confession" and "Ars Poetica" reprinted from *Cross Ties* © 1985 X. J. Kennedy. Reprinted by permission of the University of Georgia Press.

G. K. HALL & COMPANY: Claude McKay, "If We Must Die" from *The Selected Poems of Claude McKay.* Copyright 1981 and reprinted with the permission of G. K. Hall & Co., Boston.

MICHAEL HAMBURGER, "A Poet's Progress" from *Collected Poems* by Michael Hamburger. Reprinted with permission of the author.

HARCOURT BRACE JOVANOVICH: E. M. Forster, "My Wood" from *Abinger Harvest*, copyright 1936, 1964 by Edward Morgan Foster. Reprinted by permission of Harcourt Brace Jovanovich, Inc.

Flannery O'Connor, "Good Country People," from *A Good Man Is Hard to Find and Other Stories*, copyright © 1955 by Flannery O'Connor; renewed 1983 by Regina O'Connor. Reprinted by permission of Harcourt Brace Jovanovich, Inc.

E. E. Cummings, "if everything happens that can't be done," copyright 1944 by E. E. Cummings; renewed 1972 by Nancy T. Andrews. Reprinted from *Complete Poems 1913–1962* by E. E. Cummings by permission of Harcourt Brace Jovanovich, Inc.

George Orwell, "Shooting an Elephant," from *Shooting an Elephant and Other Essays* by George Orwell, copyright 1950 by Sonia Brownell Orwell; renewed 1978 by Sonia Pitt-Rivers. Reprinted by permission of Harcourt Brace Jovanovich, Inc.

Katherine Anne Porter, "The Jilting of Granny Weatherall," from *Flowering Judas and Other Stories*, copyright 1930, 1958 by Katherine Anne Porter. Reprinted by permission of Harcourt Brace Jovanovich, Inc.

Sophocles, "Oedipus Rex" from *The Oedipus Rex of Sophocles: An English Version* by Dudley Fitts, copyright 1949 by Harcourt Brace Jovanovich, Inc.; renewed 1977 by Cornelia Fitts and Robert Fitzgerald. CAUTION: All rights, including professional, amateur, motion picture, recitation, lecturing, public reading, radio broadcasting, and television are strictly reserved. Inquiries on all rights should be addressed to the Copyrights and Permissions Department, Harcourt Brace Jovanovich, Inc., Orlando, FL 32887.

Alice Walker, "To Hell with Dying" copyright © 1967 by Alice Walker. "Everyday Use," copyright © 1973 by Alice Walker. Reprinted from her volume *In Love & Trouble* by permission of Harcourt Brace Jovanovich, Inc.

Richard Wilbur, "The Writer" from *The Mind Reader*, copyright © 1971 by Richard Wilbur. Reprinted by permission of Harcourt Brace Jovanovich, Inc.

Virginia Woolf, "What If Shakespeare Had Had a Sister?" from *A Room of One's Own* by Virginia Woolf, copyright 1929 by Harcourt Brace Jovanovich, Inc.; renewed 1957 by Leonard Woolf. Reprinted by permission of the publisher.

T. S. Eliot, "The Love Song of J. Alfred Prufrock" from *Collected Poems 1909–1962* by T. S. Eliot, copyright 1936 by Harcourt Brace Jovanovich, Inc.; copyright © 1963, 1964 by T. S. Eliot. Reprinted by permission of the publisher.

HARPER & ROW: Countee Cullen, "Incident" from *On These I Stand: An Anthology of the Best Poems of Countee Cullen.* Copyright 1925 by Harper & Row, Publishers, Inc. Renewed 1953 by Ida M. Cullen. Reprinted by permission of Harper & Row, Publishers, Inc.

Carolyn Forché, "The Colonel" from *The Country Between Us* by Carolyn Forché. Copyright © 1980 by Carolyn Forché. Reprinted by permission of Harper & Row, Publishers, Inc.

Allen Ginsberg, "To Aunt Rose" from *Collected Poems 1947–1980* by Allen Ginsberg. Copyright © 1958 by Allen Ginsberg. Reprinted by permission of Harper & Row, Publishers, Inc.

Ted Hughes, "Crow's First Lesson" from *New Selected Poems* by Ted Hughes. Copyright © 1971 by Ted Hughes. Reprinted by permission of Harper & Row, Publishers, Inc.

Martin Luther King, Jr., "Letter from Birmingham Jail, April 16, 1963" from *Why We Can't Wait* by Martin Luther King, Jr. Copyright © 1963 by Martin Luther King, Jr. Reprinted by permission of Harper & Row, Publishers, Inc.

E. B. White, "Once More to the Lake" from *Essays of E. B. White.* Copyright © 1941 by E. B. White. Reprinted by permission of Harper & Row, Publishers, Inc.

Bobbie Ann Mason, "Shiloh" (originally appeared in *The New Yorker*) from *Shiloh and Other Stories* by Bobbie Ann Mason. Copyright © 1982 by Bobbie Ann Mason. Reprinted by permission of Harper & Row, Publishers, Inc.

Sylvia Plath, "Daddy" from *The Collected Poems of Sylvia Plath* edited by Ted Hughes. Copyright © 1963 by Ted Hughes. Reprinted by permission of Harper & Row, Publishers, Inc.

HARVARD UNIVERSITY PRESS: Poems #465, "I Heard a Fly Buzz"; #1509, "Mine Enemy Is Growing Old"; #341, "After Great Pain"; #435, "Much Madness"; #401, "What Soft—Cherubic Creatures"; #162, "Apparently with No Surprise," by Emily Dickinson. Reprinted by permission of the publishers and the Trustees of Amherst College from *The Poems of Emily Dickinson*, edited by Thomas H. Johnson, Cambridge, Mass.: The Belknap Press of Harvard University Press, Copyright 1951, © 1955, 1979, 1983 by the President and Fellows of Harvard College.

JOHN HAWKINS AND ASSOCIATES, INC.: Richard Wright, "Between the World and Me" copyright © 1935 by Partisan Review. Reprinted by permission of John Hawkins and Associates, Inc.

A. M. HEATH: George Orwell, "Shooting an Elephant" from *Shooting an Elephant and Other Stories* by George Orwell reprinted by permission of the Estate of the late Sonia Brownell Orwell and Secker and Warburg Limited.

THE HOGARTH PRESS: Virginia Woolf, Chapter 3 and an excerpt from *A Room of One's Own* by Virginia Woolf reprinted by permission of the author's estate and the Hogarth Press.

ALAN HOLDEN: "Seaman, 1941" by Molly Holden. Sole copyright, Alan Holden.

HENRY HOLT AND COMPANY, INC.: Robert Frost, "After Apple-Picking," "Design," "Nothing Gold Can Stay," "Birches," "'Out, Out—'," "Fire and Ice," "Departmental" from *The Poetry of Robert Frost* edited by Edward Connery Lathem. Copyright © 1969 by Holt, Rinehart and Winston, Inc. Copyright © 1958 by Robert Frost. Copyright © 1970 by Lesley Frost Ballantine. Reprinted by permission of Henry Holt and Company, Inc.

A. E. Housman, "Terence, This Is Stupid Stuff," "To An Athlete Dying Young" from "A Shropshire Lad"— Authorised Edition—from *The Collected Poems of A. E. Housman*. Copyright 1939, 1940, © 1965 by Holt, Rinehart and Winston, Inc. Copyright © 1967, 1968 by Robert E. Symons. Reprinted by permission of Henry Holt and Company, Inc.

HOUGHTON MIFFLIN COMPANY: Archibald MacLeish, "Ars Poetica" from *New and Collected Poems 1917–1976* by Archibald MacLeish. Copyright © 1976 by Archibald MacLeish. Reprinted by permission of Houghton Mifflin Company.

Anne Sexton, "Cinderella" from *Transformations* by Anne Sexton. Copyright © 1971 by Anne Sexton. "The Farmer's Wife" from *To Bedlam and Part Way Back* by Anne Sexton. Copyright © 1960 by Anne Sexton. Reprinted by permission of Houghton Mifflin Company.

OLWYN HUGHES, LITERARY AGENCY: Sylvia Plath, "Daddy" from *Collected Poems* by Sylvia Plath, copyright by Ted Hughes 1965, 1981, published by Faber and Faber, London.

INTERNATIONAL CREATIVE MANAGEMENT, INC.: "Myth" from *Breaking Open* by Muriel Rukeyser. Reprinted by permission of International Creative Management. Copyright © 1973.

VIRGINIA KIDD: Ursula K. Le Guin, "The Ones Who Walk Away from Omelas" copyright © 1973, 1975 by Ursula K. Le Guin; reprinted by permission of the author and the author's agent, Virginia Kidd.

THE KILIMANJARO CORPORATION: Harlan Ellison, " 'Repent, Harlequin!' Said the Ticktockman" copyright © 1965 by Harlan Ellison. Reprinted by arrangement with, and permission of, the Author and the Author's agent, Richard Curtis Associates, Inc., New York. All rights reserved.

DAVID KIRBY, "The Last Song on the Jukebox" by David Kirby from *Sarah Bernhardt's Leg* © David Kirby 1983.

ETHERIDGE KNIGHT, "Hard Rock Returns to Prison from the Hospital for the Criminal Insane" from *Poems from Prison* by Etheridge Knight. Reprinted by permission of the author.

PHILIP LARKIN: "Aubade" by Philip Larkin, © Philip Larkin 1977.

THE ADELE LEONE AGENCY, INC.: "The Dead Ladies" by Mary Gordon, from *New American Poetry*, ed. Richard Monaco (1973).

LITTLE, BROWN AND COMPANY: Ogden Nash, "Very Like a Whale" from *Verses from 1929 On* by Ogden Nash. Copyright 1934 by Ogden Nash. First appeared in *The Saturday Evening Post*.

A Doll's House by Henrik Ibsen, translated by Otto Reinert. Copyright © 1977 by Otto Reinert. Reprinted from *Twenty-Three Plays: An Introductory Anthology*, edited by Otto Reinert and Peter Arnott, by permission of Little, Brown and Company (Inc.).

LIVERIGHT PUBLISHING CORPORATION: E. E. Cummings, "the Cambridge ladies who live in furnished souls" reprinted from *Tulips and Chimneys* by E. E. Cummings by permission of Liveright Publishing Corporation. Copyright 1923, 1925, and renewed 1951, 1953 by E. E. Cummings. Copyright © 1973, 1976 by the Trustees for the E. E. Cummings Trust. Copyright © 1973, 1976 by George James Firmage. "nobody loses all the time" is reprinted from *IS 5* by E. E. Cummings by permission of Liveright Publishing Corporation. Copyright 1926 by Horace Liveright. Copyright renewed 1953 by E. E. Cummings. Copyright © by the E. E. Cummings Trust. Copyright © 1985 by George James Firmage.

Robert Hayden, "Those Winter Sundays" is reprinted from *Angle of Ascent, New and Selected Poems* by Robert Hayden, by permission of Liveright Publishing Corporation. Copyright © 1975, 1972, 1970, 1966 by Robert Hayden.

MACMILLAN PUBLISHING COMPANY: Marianne Moore, "Poetry" reprinted with permission of Macmillan Publishing Company from *Collected Poems* by Marianne Moore. Copyright 1935 by Marianne Moore, renewed 1963 by Marianne Moore and T. S. Eliot.

William Butler Yeats, "Leda and the Swan," "Sailing to Byzantium" reprinted with permission of Macmillan Publishing Company from *Collected Poems* by William Butler Yeats. Copyright 1928 by Macmillan Publishing Company, renewed 1956 by Georgie Yeats. "Easter 1916," reprinted with permission of Macmillan Publishing

Company from *Collected Poems* by William Butler Yeats. Copyright 1924 by Macmillan Publishing Company, renewed 1952 by Bertha Georgie Yeats. "Adam's Curse" from *Collected Poems* by William Butler Yeats (New York: Macmillan, 1956).

Edwin Arlington Robinson, "Mr. Flood's Party". Reprinted with permission of Macmillan Publishing Company from *Collected Poems* by Edwin Arlington Robinson. Copyright 1921 by Edwin Arlington Robinson, renewed 1949 by Ruth Nivison.

THE MARVELL PRESS: "Poetry of Departures" by Philip Larkin is reprinted from *The Less Deceived* by permission of The Marvell Press, England.

PETER MEINKE, "Advice to My Son" by Peter Meinke from *Trying to Surprise God*, University of Pittsburgh Press, 1981, © Peter Meinke. Reprinted by permission of the author.

ROBERT MEZEY: "My Mother" by Robert Mezey. From *The Door Standing Open* published by Houghton Mifflin Company and *White Blossoms* published by Cummington Press. Reprinted by permission of the author.

EDNA ST. VINCENT MILLAY, "Sonnet xcix" from *Collected Poems*, by Edna St. Vincent Millay (Harper & Row). Copyright © 1931, 1958 by Edna St. Vincent Millay and Norma Millay Ellis. Reprinted by permission.

WILLIAM MORROW & COMPANY, INC.: Nikki Giovanni, "Revolutionary Dreams" from *The Women and the Men* by Nikki Giovanni. Copyright © 1970, 1974, 1975 by Nikki Giovanni. By permission of William Morrow & Company, Inc. "For Saundra" from *Black Feeling, Black Talk, Black Judgement* by Nikki Giovanni. Copyright © 1968, 1970 by Nikki Giovanni. By permission of William Morrow & Company.

Richard Selzer, "The Discus Thrower" from *Confessions of A Knife* by Richard Selzer. Copyright © 1979 by David Goldman and Janet Selzer. Reprinted by permission of William Morrow & Company.

NEW DIRECTIONS: Lawrence Ferlinghetti, "Constantly Risking Absurdity" and "In Goya's Greatest Scenes" from *A Coney Island of the Mind* by Lawrence Ferlinghetti. Copyright © by Lawrence Ferlinghetti. Reprinted by permission of New Directions Publishing Corporation.

Denise Levertov, "The Ache of Marriage," "The Mutes" from *Poems 1960–1967* by Denise Levertov. Copyright © 1964 & 1966 by Denise Levertov Goodman. Reprinted by permission of New Directions Publishing Corporation.

Wilfred Owen, "Dulce et Decorum Est" from *Collected Poems* by Wilfred Owen. Copyright © 1963 by Chatto & Windus. Reprinted by permission of New Directions Publishing Corporation.

Stevie Smith, "To Carry the Child" from *Collected Poems* by Stevie Smith. Copyright © 1972 by Stevie Smith. Reprinted by permission of New Directions Publishing Corporation.

Dylan Thomas, "Fern Hill," "Do Not Go Gentle into That Good Night" from *The Poems of Dylan Thomas*. Copyright 1946 by New Directions Publishing Corporation: 1952 by Dylan Thomas. Reprinted by permission of New Directions Publishing Corporation.

William Carlos Williams, "Tract" from *Collected Earlier Poems* by William Carlos Williams. Copyright 1938 by New Directions Publishing Corporation. Reprinted by permission of New Directions Publishing Corporation.

THE NEW YORKER: Kathleen Cushman, "Brothers and Sisters" reprinted by permission; © 1982 Kathleen Cushman. Originally in *The New Yorker*.

Alastair Reid, "Curiosity" from *Weathering* (E. P. Dutton). © 1959, 1987 Alastair Reid. Originally in *The New Yorker*.

W. W. NORTON & COMPANY, INC.: Adrienne Rich, "Living in Sin" is reprinted from *The Fact of a Doorframe, Poems Selected and New, 1950–1984* by Adrienne Rich, by permission of W. W. Norton & Company, Inc. Copyright © 1984 by Adrienne Rich. Copyright © 1975, 1978 by W. W. Norton & Company, Inc. Copyright © 1981 by Adrienne Rich.

HAROLD OBER ASSOCIATES: Langston Hughes, "Same in Blues" reprinted by permission of Harold Ober Associates Incorporated. Copyright 1951 by Langston Hughes. Copyright renewed 1979 by George Houston Bass.

OXFORD UNIVERSITY PRESS: Leo Tolstoy, "The Death of Ivan Ilych" from *The Death of Ivan Ilych, and Other Stories* by Leo Tolstoy, translated by Louise and Aylmer Maude and published by Oxford University Press.

PENGUIN BOOKS LTD.: Yevgeny Yevtushenko, "People" from *Selected Poems* by Yevgeny Yevtushenko, translated with an introduction by Robin Milner-Gulland and Peter Levi, S. J. (Penguin Modern European Poets, 1962), copyright © Robin Milner-Gulland and Peter Levi, 1962, p. 85.

A. D. PETERS & COMPANY LTD.: C. Day Lewis, "Song" reprinted by permission of A. D. Peters & Company Ltd.

RANDOM HOUSE, INC.: Frank O'Connor, "My Oedipus Complex" copyright 1950 by Frank O'Connor. Reprinted from *Collected Stories*, by Frank O'Connor, by permission of Alfred A. Knopf, Inc.

W. H. Auden, "The Unknown Citizen," Stanza II from "Five Songs," "Musée des Beaux Arts" Copyright 1940 and renewed 1968 by W. H. Auden. Reprinted from *W. H. Auden: Collected Poems*, edited by Edward Mendelson, by permission of Random House, Inc.

W. D. Snodgrass, "April Inventory" copyright 1957 by W. D. Snodgrass. Reprinted from *Heart's Needle* by W. D. Snodgrass, by permission of Alfred A. Knopf, Inc.

John Crowe Ransom, "Bells for John Whiteside's Daughter" copyright 1924 by Alfred A. Knopf, Inc., and renewed 1952 by John Crowe Ransom. Reprinted from *Selected Poems, Third Edition, Revised and Enlarged*, by John Crowe Ransom, by permission of Alfred A. Knopf, Inc.

Wallace Stevens, "Sunday Morning" copyright 1923 and renewed 1951 by Wallace Stevens. Reprinted from *The Collected Poems of Wallace Stevens*, by permission of Alfred A. Knopf, Inc.

William Faulkner, "Dry September" copyright 1930 and renewed 1958 by William Faulkner. Reprinted from *The Collected Stories of William Faulkner*, by permission of Random House, Inc.

Langston Hughes, "Harlem" copyright 1951 by Langston Hughes. Reprinted from *Selected Poems of Langston Hughes*, by permission of Alfred A. Knopf, Inc.

Karl Shapiro, "The Conscientious Objector" copyright 1947 and renewed 1975 by Karl Shapiro. Reprinted from *Collected Poems, 1940–1978* by Karl Shapiro, by permission of Random House, Inc.

Thomas Mann, "Gladius Dei" copyright 1936 and renewed 1964 by Alfred A. Knopf, Inc. Reprinted from *Stories of Three Decades*, by Thomas Mann, by permission of Alfred A. Knopf, Inc.

Victor Hernandez Cruz, "Today Is a Day of Great Joy" from *Snaps*, by Victor Hernandez Cruz. Copyright © 1969 by Victor Hernandez Cruz. Reprinted by permission of Random House, Inc.

Toni Cade Bambara, "The Lesson" from *Gorilla, My Love*, by Toni Cade Bambara. Copyright © 1972 by Toni Cade Bambara. Reprinted by permission of Random House, Inc.

Rosmarie Waldrop, "Confession to Settle a Curse" from *The Aggressive Ways of The Casual Stranger*, by Rosmarie Waldrop. Copyright © 1972 by Rosmarie Waldrop. Reprinted by permission of Random House, Inc.

OTTO REINHART, notes to *Othello* by Otto Reinhart. Copyright 1964. Reprinted by permission of the author.

IRWIN SHAW: "The Girls in Their Summer Dresses" by Irwin Shaw. Reprinted by permission of the author.

SIMON & SCHUSTER, INC.: Ellen Goodman, "Being Loved Anyway" from *At Large*. Copyright © 1981 by The Washington Post Company. Reprinted with permission of Summit Books, a Division of Simon & Schuster, Inc.

Jessica Mitford, "The American Way of Death" copyright © 1963, 1978 by Jessica Mitford. Reprinted by permission of Simon & Schuster, Inc.

Roger Wilkins, "Confessions of a Blue-Chip Black" from *A Man's Life*. Copyright © 1982 by Roger Wilkins. Reprinted by permission of Simon & Schuster, Inc.

MAY SWENSON, "Women" by May Swenson is reprinted by permission of the author, Copyright © 1968 by May Swenson.

MRS. JAMES THURBER: James Thurber "The Greatest Man in the World." Copyright © 1935 James Thurber. Copyright © 1963 Helen W. Thurber and Rosemary A. Thurber. From *The Middle Aged Man on the Flying Trapeze*, published by Harper & Row. "Courtship Through the Ages" copyright © 1942 by James Thurber. Copyright © 1970 by Helen W. Thurber and Rosemary A. Thurber. From *My World—and Welcome to It*, published by Harcourt Brace Jovanovich.

UNIVERSITY OF PENNSYLVANIA PRESS: Josephine Jacobsen, "Tears" from *The Chinese Insomniacs* (University of Pennsylvania Press, 1981). First appeared in *The Nation*.

VANDERBILT UNIVERSITY PRESS: Helen Sorrells, "From a Correct Address in a Suburb of a Major City," from *Seeds as They Fall* by Helen Sorrells. Copyright © 1971 by Helen Sorrells. Published by Vanderbilt University Press, Nashville, Tennessee.

VIKING PENGUIN INC.: James Joyce, "Araby" from *Dubliners* by James Joyce. Copyright 1916 by B. W. Huebsch. Definitive text copyright © 1967 by the estate of James Joyce. Reprinted by permission of Viking Penguin Inc.

Maxine Kumin, "Woodchucks" from *Our Ground Time Here Will Be Brief* by Maxine Kumin. Copyright © 1972 by Maxine Kumin. Reprinted by permission of Viking Penguin Inc.

D. H. Lawrence, "Piano" from *The Complete Poems of D. H. Lawrence*, edited by Vivian de Sola Pinto and F. Warren Roberts. Copyright © 1964, 1972 by Angelo Ravagli and C. M. Weekley, Executors of the Estate of Frieda Lawrence Ravagli. Reprinted by permission of Viking Penguin Inc. "The Horse Dealer's Daughter," from *The Complete Short Stories of D. H. Lawrence, Vol. II*. Copyright 1922 by Thomas Seltzer, Inc. Copyright renewed 1950 by Frieda Lawrence. Reprinted by permission of Viking Penguin Inc.

Phyllis McGinley, "Country Club Sunday" from *Times Three* by Phyllis McGinley. Copyright 1946, renewed © 1973 by Phyllis McGinley. Originally published in *The New Yorker*. Reprinted by permission of Viking Penguin Inc.

Lewis Thomas, "The Iks" from *The Lives of a Cell* by Lewis Thomas. Copyright © 1973 by the Massachusetts Medical Society. Reprinted by permission of Viking Penguin Inc.

ROBERT WALLACE, "In a Spring Still Not Written Of" by Robert Wallace © 1965 by Robert Wallace. Reprinted with permission of the author.

WESLEYAN UNIVERSITY PRESS: Robert Francis, "Pitcher." Copyright © 1953 by Robert Francis. Reprinted from THE ORB WEAVER by permission of Wesleyan University Press.

PICTURE CREDITS

INNOCENCE AND EXPERIENCE *Part Opener, p. 2: The Peaceable Kingdom*, c. 1840–1845 by Edward Hicks. Oil on canvas, 18 x 24-⅛". The Brooklyn Museum, Dick S. Ramsay Fund. *Fiction, p. 6: The Mistletoe Merchant*, 1904 by Pablo Picasso. Photograph, The Bettmann Archive. *Poetry, p. 70: The Mysterious Rose Garden*, c. 1894–1895 by Aubrey Beardsley. Black ink over graphite on white paper, 224 x 125 mm. Courtesy of the Fogg Art Museum, Harvard University, Bequest of Grenville L. Winthrop. *Drama, p. 102: Fauteuil Rouge (The Red Armchair)*, 1931 by Pablo Picasso. Oil on cradled panel, 51-½ x 39". Gift of Mr. and Mrs. Daniel Saidenberg, © The Art Institute of Chicago. All rights reserved. *Essays, p. 146: The Merry-go-round*, 1916 by Mark Gertler. The Tate Gallery, London.

CONFORMITY AND REBELLION *Part Opener, p. 176: The Uprising*, c. 1860 by Honoré Daumier. Oil on canvas, 34-½ x 44-½". The Phillips Collection, Washington. *Fiction, p. 180: Epoch*, 1950 by Ben Shahn. Tempera on board, 52 x 31". '51-31-5, Philadelphia Museum of Art: Purchased: Bloomfield Moore Fund.

Poetry, p. 258: Au Moulin Rouge, Le Depart du Quadrille, 1892, after a painting by Henri de Toulouse-Lautrec. Photograph, The Bettmann Archive. *Drama, p. 292: Self Portrait*, c. 1900–1905 by Gwen John. National Portrait Gallery, London. *Essays, p. 350: The Accused*, 1886 by Odilon Redon. Charcoal, sheet: 21 x 14-⅜". Collection, The Museum of Modern Art, New York. Acquired through the Lillie P. Bliss Bequest.

LOVE AND HATE   *Part Opener, p. 392: Separation II*, 1896 by Edvard Munch. Lithograph, 41 x 62.5 cm. Copyright Oslo Kommunes Kunstsamlinger. Munch Museet (OKK G/i 210–12). *Fiction, p. 398: A Husband Parting From His Wife and Child*, 1799 by William Blake. Pen and watercolor on paper, 11-⅞ x 8-⅞". '64-110-3, Philadelphia Museum of Art: Given by Mrs. William T. Tonner. *Poetry, p. 446: Midsummer Wall*, 1966 by Jim Dine. Color lithograph on paper, 41-½ x 29-¹¹⁄₁₆" (sheet). Collection of Whitney Museum of American Art. Gift of Mr. and Mrs. Herbert C. Lee. Acq. No. 66.103. *Drama, p. 480: The Return of the Prodigal Son*, c. 1642 by Rembrandt van Rijn. Pen and wash in bistre with white gouache. Teylers Museum, Haarlem, Holland. *Essays, p. 574: Grosse Heidelberger Liederhandschrift "Codex Manesse" fol 249ᵛ*. Universitätsbibliothek, Heidelberg.

THE PRESENCE OF DEATH   *Part Opener, p. 590: The Death Chamber*, 1896 by Edvard Munch. Lithograph, printed in black, 15-¼ x 21-⅝". Collection, The Museum of Modern Art, New York. Gift of Abby Aldrich Rockefeller. *Fiction, p. 594: Sacred to Washington*, 1822 by Margarett Smith. Watercolor, 20-¼ x 16-½". The Baltimore Museum of Art. Gift of Edgar William and Bernice Chrysler Garbisch, New York. BMA 1967.76.6. *Poetry, 666: Cow's Skull with Calico Roses*, 1931 by Georgia O'Keeffe. Oil on canvas, 91.2 x 61 cm. Gift of Georgia O'Keeffe. 1947.712. © copyright 1987 The Art Institute of Chicago. All rights reserved. *p. 695: Landscape with the Fall of Icarus*, c. 1560 by Pieter Brueghel the Elder. Museum of Fine Arts, Brussels. Photograph, Art Resource, New York. *Drama, p. 710: Orderly Retreat*, 1943 by Philip Evergood. Oil, 40 x 25". From the Carleton College Collection. Gift of the Encyclopedia Britannica. *p. 744: Crazy Crate*, photograph by Dr. Cochran. *p. 753: Waterfall*, 1961 by M. C. Escher. Lithograph, 38 x 30 cm. Haags Gemeentemuseum, 's Gravenhage, Holland. © M. C. Escher Heirs, c/o Cordon Art, Baarn, Holland. *Essays, p. 760: The Revenant*, 1949 by Andrew Wyeth. From the collection of The New Britain Museum of American Art, Harriet Russell Stanley Memorial Fund. Photograph E. Irving Blomstrann.

APPENDICES   *Opener, p. 782: The Vanity of the Artist's Dream*, 1830 by Charles Bird King. Oil on canvas, 36 x 30". Courtesy of the Fogg Art Museum, Harvard University. Gift of Grenville Winthrop. *pp. 814–815: The Globe Theatre; Interior of the Globe Theatre in the days of Shakespeare; and a French theater during Moliere's management:* Courtesy of the Bettmann Archive, Inc. *Interior of the Swan Theatre*, London: Courtesy of Culver Pictures. *The Greek theater at Epidaurus:* Courtesy of the Greek National Tourist Office.

INDEX OF AUTHORS AND TITLES